CONTEXTS OF THE CONSTITUTION

A Documentary Collection on Principles of American Constitutional Law

By

NEIL H. COGAN
Dean and Professor of Law
Quinnipiac College School of Law

New York, New York
FOUNDATION PRESS
1999

Cover Design: Keith Stout, Manhattan, New York
Photograph: Magna Carta, June 15, 1215
United States Constitution, ratified June 25, 1788
Declaration of Independence, July 4, 1776

 TEXT IS PRINTED ON 10% POST CONSUMER RECYCLED PAPER

This book is dedicated to my son,
Jacob Katz Cogan,
Great-grandson of Jacob Katz and Jacob Katz, of blessed memories

When He finished speaking with him on Mt. Sinai, He gave Moses the two tablets of the Testimony, stone tablets inscribed with the finger of God.

The Sages commented:

But did Moses learn the entire Torah? It is written in Scripture: "Its measure is longer than the earth and broader than the sea." Job 11:19. Did Moses really learn something so vast in just forty days? The answer is, God taught Moses the general principles . . . .

Exodus Rabbah, Ki Tissa 41:6

*

PREFACE

This collection of texts provides contexts to formative principles of the American Constitution. It is to those principles, as understood and developed in two centuries of constitutional self-government, that we look in resolving disputes about text, meaning and understanding.

In addition to a chapter of primary texts, the collection divides the texts by principles of constitutionalism, republicanism and democracy, structure, federalism, equality and rights. The collection is intended both to stand on its own in courses and seminars on constitutional theory and to supplement courses in constitutional law. Each text is either complete or only lightly edited, so that the reader will have the speaker's full statement of the principle about which he or she was concerned.

There may be, indeed hopefully there will be, differences of opinion about which text belongs under what principle. It is the author's hope that this collection will provide a resource for a critical analysis of constitutional discourse by present and future judges and lawyers, political theorists and politicians, historians, essayists and editorial writers, and citizens, residents, and interested observers.

NEIL H. COGAN

August 1999
New Haven, Connecticut

*

CONTEXTS OF THE CONSTITUTION: A DOCUMENTARY COLLECTION ON PRINCIPLES OF AMERICAN CONSTITUTIONAL LAW

Chapter I.   Primary Texts

Chapter II.   Principles of Constitutionalism

Chapter VI. Principles of Equality

*

CONTEXTS OF THE CONSTITUTION

A Documentary Collection
on Principles of American
Constitutional Law

*

CHAPTER I

PRIMARY TEXTS

A. COMPACT MADE ON BOARD
THE MAY FLOWER

November 11, 1620

In the name of God, amen. We whose names are under written, the loyal subjects of our dread sovereign Lord, King James, by the grace of God, of Great Britain, France and Ireland, King, Defender of the Faith, &c. Having undertaken for the glory of God, and advancement of the christian faith, and the honour of our King and country, a voyage to plant the first colony in the northern parts of Virginia; do by these presents solemnly and mutually, in the presence of God and one another, covenant and combine ourselves together into a civil body politick, for our better ordering and preservation, and furtherance of the ends aforesaid: And by virtue hereof, do enact, constitute and frame such just and equal laws, ordinances, acts, constitutions and officers, from time to time, as shall be thought most meet and covenient for the general good of the colony; into which we promise all due submission and obedience. In witness whereof, we have hereunto subscribed our names, at Cape Cod, the eleventh of November, in the reign of our sovereign Lord, King James, of England, France and Ireland, the eighteenth, and of Scotland the fifty-fourth, Anno. Dom. 1620.

John Carver,	John Howland,
William Bradford,	Stephen Hopkins,
Edward Winslow,	Edward Tilly,
William Brewster,	John Tilly,
Isaac Allerton,	Frances Cooke,
Miles Standish,	Thomas Rogers,
John Alden,	Thomas Tinker,
Samuel Fuller,	John Ridgdale,
Christopher Martin,	Edward Fuller,
William Mullins,	John Turner,
William White,	Francis Eaton,
Richard Warren,	James Chilton,
John Craxton,	Richard Bilteridge,
John Billington,	George Soule,
Joses Fletcher,	Richard Clark,
John Goodman,	Richard Gardiner,
Digery Priest,	John Allerton,
Thomas Williams,	Thomas English,
Gilbert Winslow,	Edward Doten,
Edmund Margeson,	Edward Leister,
	Peter Brown.

B. THE FUNDAMENTAL ORDERS OF CONNECTICUT

January 14, 1639

FOREASMUCH as it hath pleased the Almighty God by the wise disposition of his divine providence so to order and dispose of things that we the inhabitants and residents of Windsor, Harteford, and Wethersfield are now cohabiting and dwelling in and upon the River of Conectecotte and the lands thereunto adjoining; and well knowing where a people are gathered together the word of God requires that to maintain the peace and union of such a people there should be an orderly and decent Government established according to God, to order and dispose of the affairs of the people at all seasons as occasion shall require; do therefore associate and conjoin ourselves to be as one Public State or Commonwealth; and do, for ourselves and our Successors, and such as shall be adjoined to us at any time hereafter, enter into combination and confederation together, to maintain and preserve the liberty and purity of the gospel of our Lord Jesus which we now profess, as also the discipline of the Churches, which according to the truth of the said gospel is now practiced amongst us; as also in our Civil Affairs to be guided and governed according to such laws, rules, orders, and decrees, as shall be made ordered and decreed, as followeth:—

1. It is Ordered, sentenced, and decreed, that there shall be yearly two General Assemblies or Courts, the one the second Thursday in April, the other the second Thursday in September following; the first shall be called the Court of Election, wherein shall be yearly chosen from time to time so many magistrates and other public officers as shall be found requisite: whereof one to be chosen Governor for the year ensuing and until another be chosen, and no other magistrate to be chosen for more than one year; provided always there be six chosen besides the Governor; which being chosen and sworn according to an oath recorded for that purpose, shall have power to administer justice according to the laws here established, and for want thereof according to the rule of the word of God; which choice shall be made by all that are admitted freemen and have taken the Oath of Fidelity, and do cohabit within this jurisdiction, (having been admitted inhabitants by the major part of the town wherein they live,) or the major part of such as shall be then present.

2. It is Ordered, sentenced, and decreed, that the election of the aforesaid magistrate shall be on this manner: every person present and qualified for choice shall bring in (to the persons deputed to receive them) one single paper, with the name of him written in it whom he desires to have Governor, and he that hath the greatest number of papers shall be Governor for that year. And the rest of the magistrates

or public officers to be chosen in this manner: The secretary for the time being shall first read the names of all that are to be put to choice and then shall severally nominated them distinctly, and every one that would have the person nominated to be chosen shall bring in one single paper written upon, and he that would not have him chosen shall bring in a blank; and every one that hath more written papers than blanks shall be a magistrate for that year; which papers shall be received and told by one or more that shall be then chosen by the court and sworn to be faithful therein; but in case there should not be six chosen as aforesaid, besides the Governor, out of those which are nominated, then he or they which have the most written papers shall be a magistrate or magistrates for the ensuing year, to make up the foresaid number.

3. It is Ordered, sentenced, and decreed, that the secretary shall not nominate any person, nor shall any person be chosen newly into the magistracy, which was not propounded in some General Court before, to be nominated the next election; and to that end it shall be lawful for each of the towns aforesaid by their deputies to nominate any two whom they conceive fit to be put to election; and the court may add so many more as they judge requisite.

4. It is Ordered, sentenced, and decreed, that no person be chosen Governor above once in two years, and that the Governor be always a member of some approved congregation, and formerly of the magistracy within this jurisdiction; and all the magistrates, freemen of this commonwealth; and that no magistrate or other public officer shall execute any part of his or their office before they are severally sworn, which shall be done in the face of the court if they be present, and in case of absence by some deputed for that purpose.

5. It is Ordered, sentenced, and decreed, that to the aforesaid Court of election the several towns shall send their deputies, and when the elections are ended they may proceed in any public service as at other courts. Also the other General Court in September shall be for making of laws, and any other public occasion which concerns the good of the commonwealth.

6. It is Ordered, sentenced, and decreed, that the Governor shall, either by himself or by the secretary, send out summons to the constables of every town for the calling of these two standing courts, one month at least before their several times: And also if the Governor and the greatest part of the magistrates see cause upon any special occasion to call a General Court, they may give order to the secretary so to do within fourteen days warning: and if urgent necessity so require, upon a shorter notice, giving sufficient grounds for it to the deputies when they meet, or else be questioned for the same; And if the Governor and major part of magistrates shall either neglect or refuse to call the two general standing courts or either of them, as also at other times when the occasions of the commonwealth require, the freemen thereof, or the major part of them, shall petition to them so to do: if then it be either

denied or neglected, the said freemen or the major part of them shall have power to give order to the constables of the several towns to do the same, and so may meet together, and choose to themselves a moderator, and may proceed to do any act of power which any other General Court may.

7. It is Ordered, sentenced, and decreed, that after there are warrants given out for any of the said General Courts, the constable or constables of each town shall forthwith give notice distinctly to the inhabitants of the same, in some public assembly or by going or sending from house to house, that at a place and time by him or them limited and set, they meet and assemble themselves together to elect and choose certain deputies to be at the General Court then following, to agitate the affairs of the commonwealth; which said deputies shall be chosen by all that are admitted inhabitants in the several towns and have taken the oath of fidelity; provided that none be chosen a deputy for any General Court which is not a freeman of this commonwealth.

The foresaid deputies shall be chosen in manner following: every person that is present and qualified as before expressed, shall bring the names of such, written in several papers, as they desire to have chosen for that employment, and these three or four, more or less, being the number agreed on to be chosen for that time, that have the greatest number of papers written for them, shall be deputies for that court; whose names shall be endorsed on the back side of the warrant and returned into the court, with the constable or constables' hand unto the same.

8. It is Ordered, sentenced, and decreed, that Windsor, Hartford, and Wethersfield shall have power, each town, to send four of their freedmen as their deputies to every General Court; and whatsoever other towns shall be hereafter added to this jurisdiction, they shall send so many deputies as the court shall judge meet, a reasonable proportion to the number of freemen that are in the said towns being to be attended therein; which deputies shall have the power of the whole town to give their votes and allowance to all such laws and orders as may be for the public good, and unto which the said towns are to be bound.

9. It is Ordered and decreed, that the deputies thus chosen shall have power and liberty to appoint a time and a place of meeting together before any General Court, to advise and consult of all such things as may concern the good of the public, as also to examine their own elections, whether according to the order, and if they or the greatest part of them find any election to be illegal they may seclude such for present from their meeting, and return the same and their reasons to the court; and if it prove true, the court may fine the party or parties so intruding and the town, if they see cause, and give out a warrant to go to a new election in a legal way, either in part or in whole. Also the said deputies shall have power to fine any that shall be disorderly at their meetings, or for not coming in due time or place according to appointment; and they

may return the said fines into the court if it be refused to be paid, and the treasurer to take notice of it, and to estreat or levy the same as he doth other fines.

10. It is Ordered, sentenced, and decreed, that every General Court, except such as through neglect of the Governor and the greatest part of magistrates the freemen themselves do call, shall consist of the Governor, or some one chosen to moderate the court, and four other magistrates at least, with the major part of the deputies of the several towns legally chosen; and in case the freemen or major part of them, through neglect or refusal of the Governor and major part of the magistrates, shall call a court, it shall consist of the major part of freemen that are present or their deputies, with a moderator chosen by them: In which said General Courts shall consist the supreme power of the Commonwealth, and they only shall have power to make laws or repeal them, to grant levies, to admit of freemen, dispose of lands undisposed of, to several towns or persons, and also shall have power to call either court or magistrate or any other person whatsoever into question for any misdemeanor, and many for just causes displace, or deal otherwise, according to the nature of the offence; and also may deal in any other matter that concerns the good of this commonwealth, except election of magistrates, which shall be done by the whole body of freemen.

In which Court the Governor or Moderator shall have power to order the court, to give liberty of speech, and silence unseasonable and disorderly speakings, to put all things to vote, and in case the vote be equal to have the casting voice. But none of these courts shall be adjourned or dissolved without the consent of the major part of the court.

11. It is ordered, sentenced, and decreed, that when any General Court upon the occasions of the commonwealth have agreed upon any sum or sums of money to be levied upon the several towns within this Jurisdiction, that a committee be chosen to set out and appoint what shall be the proportion of every town to pay of the said levy; provided the committees be made up of an equal number out of each town.

14th January, 1638–39, the 11 Orders above said are voted.

THE OATH OF THE GOVERNOR, FOR THE PRESENT.

I, N. W. being now chosen to be Governor within this Jurisdiction for the year ensuing, and until a new be chosen, do swear by the great and dreadful name of the everliving God, to promote the public good and peace of the same, according to the best of my skill; as also will maintain all lawful privileges of this commonwealth; as also that all wholesome laws that are or shall be made by lawful authority here established, by duly executed; and will further the execution of justice according to the rule of God's word; so help me God, in the name of the Lord Jesus Christ.

THE OATH OF A MAGISTRATE, FOR THE PRESENT.

I, N. W. being chosen a Magistrate within this Jurisdiction for the year ensuing, do swear by the great and dreadful name of the everliving God, to promote the public good and peace of the same, according to the best of my skill, and that I will maintain all the lawful privileges thereof according to my understanding, as also assist in the execution of all such wholesome laws as are made or shall be made by lawful authority here established, and will further the execution of Justice for the time aforesaid, according to the righteous rule of God's word; so help me God, etc.

THE OATH OF A CONSTABLE.

I, A. B., of W, do swear by the great and dreadful name of the everliving God, that for the year ensuing, and until a new be chosen, I will faithfully execute the office and place of a Constable, for and within the said plantation of W. and the limits thereof, and that I will endeavour to preserve the public peace of the said place, and Commonwealth, and will do my best endeavour to see all watches and wards executed, and to obey and execute all lawful commands or warrants that come from any Magistrate or Magistrates or Court; so help me God, in the Lord Jesus Christ.

C. THE FRAME OF THE GOVERNMENT [OF PENNSYLVANIA], AND THE LAWS AGREED UPON IN ENGLAND

April 25, 1682

Of the Province of Pennsylvania, in America: together with certain laws in England, by the Governor and divers freemen of the aforesaid Province. To be further explained and confirmed there by the first Provincial Council that shall be held, if they see meet.

THE PREFACE.

When the great and wise God had made the world, of all his creatures it pleased him to choose man his deputy to rule it; and to fit him for so great a charge and trust, he did not only qualify him with skill and power, but with integrity to use them justly. This native goodness was equally his honour and his happiness; and whilst he stood here, all went well; there was no need of coercive or compulsive means; the precept of divine love and truth in his bosom was the guide and keeper of his innocency. But lust prevailing against duty, made a lamentable breach upon it; and the law, that before had no power over him, took place upon him and his disobedient posterity, that such as would not live

6

conformable to the holy law within, should fall under the reproof and correction, of the just law without, in a judicial administration.

This the apostle teaches us in divers of his epistles. The law (says he) was added because of transgression: In another place, knowing that the law was not made for the righteous man; but for the disobedient and ungodly, for sinners, for unholy and prophane, for murderers, for whore-mongers, for them that defile themselves with mankind, and for men-stealers, for liars, for perjured persons, &c. But this is not all, he opens and carries the matter of government a little further: Let every soul be subject to the higher powers, for there is no power but of God. The powers that be are ordained of God: whosoever therefore resisteth the power, resisteth the ordinance of God. For rulers are not a terror to good works, but to Evil: wilt thou then not be afraid of the power? Do that which is good, and thou shalt have praise of the same.—He is the minister of God to thee for good.—Wherefore ye must needs be subject, not only for wrath, but for conscience sake.

This settles the divine right of government beyond exception, and that for two ends; first, to terrify evil-doers; secondly, to cherish those that do well; which gives government a life beyond corruption, and makes it as durable in the world, as good men shall be. So that government seems to me a part of religion itself, a thing sacred in its institution and end. For if it does not directly remove the cause, it crushes the effects of evil, and is as such (tho' a lower yet) an emanation of the same Divine Power, that is both author and object of pure religion; the difference lying here, that the one is more free and mental, the other more corporal and compulsive in its operations: but that is only to evil-doers; government itself being otherwise as capable of kindness, goodness and charity, as a more private society. They weekly err, that think there is no other use of government than correction, which is the coarsest part of it: daily experience tells us, that the care and regulation of many other affairs more soft and daily necessary, make up much the greatest part of government; and which must have fol-lowed the peopling of the world, had Adam never fell, and will continue among men on earth under the highest attainments they may arrive at, by the coming of the blessed second Adam, the Lord from Heaven. Thus much of government in general, as to its rise and end.

For particular frames and models, it will become me to say little; and comparatively I will say nothing. My reasons are: first, that the age is too nice and difficult for it; there being nothing the wits of men are more busy and divided upon. 'Tis true, they seem to agree in the end, to wit, happiness; but in the means they differ, as to divine, so to this human felicity; and the cause is much the same, not always want of light and knowledge, but want of using them rightly. Men side with their passions against their reason, and their sinister interests have so strong a bias upon their minds, that they lean to them against the good of the things they know.

Secondly, I do not find a model in the world, that time, place, and some singular emergences have not necessarily altered; nor is it easy to frame a civil government, that shall serve all places alike.

Thirdly, I know what is said by the several admirers of monarchy, aristocracy and democracy, which are the rule of one, a few, and many, and are the three common ideas of government, when men discourse on that subject. But I choose to solve the controversy with this small distinction, and it belongs to all three; any government is free to the people under it (whatever be the frame) where the laws rule, and the people are a party to those laws, and more than this is tyranny, oligarchy, and confusion.

But lastly, when all is said, there is hardly one frame of government in the world so ill designed by its first founders, that in good hands would not do well enough; and story tells us, the best in ill ones can do nothing that is great or good; witness the Jewish and Roman states. Governments, like clocks, go from the motion men give them, and as governments are made and moved by men, so by them they are ruined too. Wherefore governments rather depend upon men, than men upon governments. Let men be good, and the government cannot be bad; if it be ill, they will cure it. But if men be bad, let the government be never so good, they will endeavour to warp and spoil to their turn.

I know some say, let us have good laws, and no matter for the men that execute them: but let them consider, that though good laws do well, good men do better; for good laws may want good men, and be abolished or invaded by ill men; but good men will never want good laws, nor suffer ill ones. 'Tis true, good laws have some awe upon ill ministers, but that is where they have not power to escape or abolish them, and the people are generally wise and good: but a loose and depraved people (which is to the question) love laws and an administration like themselves. That therefore, which makes a good constitution, must keep it, viz: men of wisdom and virtue, qualities that because they descend not with worldly inheritances, must be carefully propagated by a virtuous education of youth, for which after ages will owe more to the care and prudence of founders, and the successive magistracy, than to their parents for their private patrimonies.

These considerations of the weight of government, and the nice and various opinions about it, made it uneasy to me to think of publishing the ensuing frame and conditional laws, foreseeing both the censures they will meet with from men of differing humours and engagements, and the occasion they may give of discourse beyond my design.

But next to the power of necessity (which is a solicitor that will take no denial) this induced me to a compliance, that we have (with reverence to God, and good conscience to men) to the best of our skill, contrived and composed the FRAME and LAWS of this government, to the great end of all government, viz: to support power in reverence with the people, and to secure the people from the abuse of power; that they may be free by their just obedience, and the magistrates honourable for their just administration: for liberty without obedience is confusion, and obedience without liberty is slavery. To carry this evenness is partly owing to the constitution, and partly to the magistracy; where either of these fail, government will be subject to convulsions; but where both are wanting, it must be totally subverted: then where both meet, the government is like to endure. Which I humbly pray and hope God will please to make the lot of this of Pennsylvania. Amen.

WILLIAM PENN.

THE FRAME.

TO ALL PEOPLE, to whom these presents shall come. WHEREAS king Charles the second, by his letters patent, under the great seal of England; for the consideration therein mentioned, hath been graciously pleased to give and grant unto me William Penn (by the name of William Penn, Esq. son and heir of Sir William Penn, deceased) and to my heirs and assigns forever, all that tract of land or province, called Pennsylvania, in America, with divers great powers, preheminences, royalties, jurisdictions, and authorities, necessary for the well-being and government thereof: NOW KNOW YE, that for the well-being and government of the said province, and for the encouragement of all the freemen and planters that may be therein concerned, in pursuance of the powers aforementioned, I the said William Penn have declared, granted, and confirmed, and by these presents, for me, my heirs and assigns, do declare, grant and confirm unto all the freemen, planters and adventurers, of, in and to the said province, these liberties, franchises, and properties, to be held, enjoyed and kept by the freemen, planters and inhabitants of the said province of Pennsylvania for ever.

Imprimis. That the government of this province shall, according to the powers of the patent, consist of the Governor and freemen of the said province, in form of a Provincial Council and General Assembly, by whom all laws shall be made, officers chosen, and publick affairs transacted, as is hereafter respectively declared. That is to say,

Second. That the freemen of the said province shall, on the twentieth day of the twelfth month, which shall be in this present year, one thousand six hundred eighty and two, meet and assemble in some fit place, of which timely notice shall be before hand given, by the governor or his deputy, and then and there shall choose out of themselves seventy-two persons of most note for their wisdom, virtue and ability, who shall meet on the tenth day of the first month next ensuing, and always be called and act as the Provincial Council of the said province.

Third. That at the first choice of such Provincial Council, one third part of the said Provincial Council shall be chosen to serve for three years next ensuing; one-third part for two years then next ensuing, and one-third part for one year then next following such election, and no longer; and that the said third part shall go out accordingly. And on the twentieth day of the twelfth month as aforesaid, yearly for ever afterward, the freemen of the said province shall in like manner meet and assemble together, and then chuse twenty four persons, being one third of the said number, to serve in Provincial Council for three years. It being intended, that one third part of the whole Provincial Council (always consisting and to consist of seventy two persons, as aforesaid) falling off yearly, it shall be yearly supplied by such new yearly elections, as aforesaid; and that no one person shall continue therein longer than three years: and in case any member shall decease before the last election during his time, that then at the next election ensuing his decease, another shall be chosen to supply his place for the remaining time he was to have served, and no longer.

Fourth. That after the first seven years, every one of the said third parts that goeth yearly off, shall be uncapable of being chosen again for one whole year following: that so all may be fitted for government, and have experience of the care and burden of it.

Fifth. That the Provincial Council in all cases of matters of moment, as their arguing upon bills to be passed into laws, erecting courts of justice, giving judgment upon criminals impeached, and choice of officers, in such manner as is herein after mentioned; not less than two thirds of the whole Provincial Council shall make a quorum; and that the consent and approbation of two thirds of such quorum shall be had in all such cases and matters of moment. And moreover, that in all cases and matters of lesser moment, twenty-four members of the said Provincial Council shall make a quorum, the majority of which twenty four shall and may always determine in such cases and causes of lesser moment.

Sixth. That in this Provincial Council, the governor or his deputy shall or may always preside, and have a treble voice; and the said Provincial Council shall always continue, and sit upon its own adjournments and committees.

Seventh. That the governor and Provincial Council shall prepare and propose to the General Assembly hereafter mentioned, all bills, which they shall at any time think fit to be passed into laws within the said province; which bills shall be published and affixed to the most noted places in the inhabited parts thereof thirty days before the meeting of the General Assembly, in order to the passing them into laws or rejecting of them, as the General Assembly shall see meet.

Eighth. That the governor and Provincial Council shall take care that all laws, statutes and ordinances, which shall at any time be made within the said province, be duly and diligently executed.

Ninth.   That the governor and Provincial Council shall at all times have the care of the peace and safety of the province, and that nothing be by any person attempted to the subversion of this frame of government.

Tenth.   That the governor and Provincial Council shall at all times settle and order the situation of all cities, ports and market towns in every county, modelling therein all public buildings, streets, and market places, and shall appoint all necessary roads and high-ways in the province.

Eleventh.   That the governor and Provincial Council shall at all times have power to inspect the management of the publick treasury, and punish those who shall convert any part thereof to any other use, than what hath been agreed upon by the governor, Provincial Council and General Assembly.

Twelfth.   That the governor and Provincial Council shall erect and order all publick schools, and encourage and reward the authors of useful sciences and laudable inventions in the said province.

Thirteenth.   That for the better management of the powers and trust aforesaid, the Provincial Council shall from time to time divide itself into four distinct and proper committees, for the more easy administration of the affairs of the province, which divides the seventy-two into four eighteens, every one of which eighteens shall consist of six out of each of the three orders or yearly elections, each of which shall have a distinct portion of business, as followeth: first, a committee of plantations, to situate and settle cities, ports, market-towns and high-ways, and to hear and decide all suits and controversies relating to plantations. Secondly, a committee of justice and safety, to secure the peace of the province, and punish the male-administration of those who subvert justice to the prejudice of the publick or private interest. Thirdly, a committee of trade and treasury, who shall regulate all trade and commerce according to law, encourage manufacture and country growth, and defray the publick charge of the province. And fourthly, a committee of manners, education, and arts, that all wicked and scandalous living may be prevented, and that youth may be successively trained up in virtue and useful knowledge and arts: the quorum of each of which committees being six, that is, two out of each of the three orders or yearly elections as aforesaid, making a constant and standing council of twenty-four, which will have the power of the Provincial Council, being the quorum of it, in all cases not excepted in the fifth article; and in the said committees and standing Council of the province, the governor or his deputy shall or may preside as aforesaid; and in the absence of the governor or his deputy, if no one is by either of them appointed, the said committees or Council, shall appoint a president for that time, and not otherwise; and what shall be resolved at such committees, shall be reported to the said Council of the province, and shall be by them resolved and confirmed before the same shall be put in execution; and that these respective committees shall not sit at one and the same time, except in cases of necessity.

Fourteenth. And to the end that all laws prepared by the governor and provincial Council aforesaid, may yet have the more full concurrence of the freemen of the province, it is declared, granted, and confirmed, that at the time and place or places for the choice of a Provincial Council as aforesaid, the said freemen shall yearly choose members to serve in General Assembly as their representatives, not exceeding two hundred persons, who shall yearly meet on the twentieth day of the second month, which shall be in the year one thousand six hundred eighty and three following, in the capital, town, or city of the said province, where during eight days the several members may freely confer with one another; and, if any of them see meet, with a committee of the Provincial Council (consisting of Three out of each of the four committees aforesaid, being twelve in all) which shall be at that time purposely appointed to receive from any of them proposals for the alteration or amendment of any of the said proposed and promulgated bills; and on the ninth day from their so meeting, the said General Assembly, after reading over the proposed bills by the clerk of the Provincial Council, and the occasion and motives for them being opened by the governor or his deputy, shall give their affirmative or negative, which to them seemeth best, in such manner as hereinafter is expressed. But not less than two thirds shall make a quorum in the passing of laws, and choice of such officers as are by them to be chosen.

Fifteenth. That the laws so prepared and proposed as aforesaid, that are assented to by the General Assembly, shall be enrolled as laws of the province, with this stile: *By the Governor, with the assent and approbation of the freemen in Provincial Council and General Assembly.*

Sixteenth. That for the better establishment of the Government and laws of this province, and to the end there may be an universal satisfaction in the laying of the fundamentals thereof; the General Assembly shall or may for the first year consist of all the freemen of and in said province, and ever after it shall be yearly chosen, as aforesaid; which number of two hundred shall be enlarged as the country shall increase in people, so as it do not exceed five hundred at any time: the appointment and proportioning of which, as also the laying and methodizing of the choice of the Provincial Council and General Assembly in future times, most equally to the divisions of the hundreds and counties, which the country shall hereafter be divided into; shall be in the power of the Provincial Council to propose, and the General Assembly to resolve.

Seventeenth. That the governor and the Provincial Council shall erect, from time to time, standing courts of justice in such places and number as they shall judge convenient for the good government of the said province. And that the Provincial Council shall, on the thirteenth day of the first month yearly, elect and present to the governor or his deputy, a double number of persons to serve for judges, treasurers, master of rolls, within the said province for the year next ensuing; and the freemen of the said province in the county courts, when they shall be erected, and till then in the General Assembly shall, on the three and twentieth day of the second month yearly, elect and present to the governor or his deputy, a double number of persons to serve for sheriffs, justices of the peace, and coroners, for the year next ensuing; out of which respective elections and presentments, the governor or his deputy shall nominate and commissionate the proper number for each office the third day after the said presentments; or else the first named in such presentment for each office, shall stand and serve for that office the year ensuing.

Eighteenth. But forasmuch as the present condition of the province requires some immediate settlement, and admits not of so quick a revolution of officers; and to the end the said province may, with all convenient speed, be well ordered and settled, I, William Penn, do therefore think fit, to nominate and appoint such persons for judges, treasurers, masters of the rolls, sheriffs, justices of the peace, and coroners, as are most fitly qualified for those employments; to whom I shall make and grant commissions for the said offices respectively, to hold to them to whom the same shall be granted, for so long time as every such person shall well behave himself in the office or place to him respectively granted, and no longer. And upon the decease or displacing of any of the said officers, the succeeding officer or officers shall be chosen as aforesaid.

Nineteenth. That the General Assembly shall continue so long as may be needful to impeach criminals fit to be there impeached; to pass bills into laws, that they shall think fit to pass into laws, and till such time as the governor and Provincial Council shall declare, that they have nothing further to propose unto them for their assent and approbation; and that declaration shall be a dismiss to the General Assembly for that time, which General Assembly shall be notwithstanding capable of assembling together, upon the summons of the Provincial Council, at any time during that year, if the said Provincial Council shall see occasion for their so assembling.

Twentieth. That all the elections of members or representatives of the people, to serve in Provincial Council and General Assembly, and all questions to be determined by both or either of them, that relate to passing of bills into laws, to the choice of officers, to impeachments made by the General Assembly, and judgment of criminals upon such impeachments by the Provincial Council, and to all other cases by them respectively judged of importance, shall be resolved and determined by the ballot; and, unless on sudden and indispensible occasions, no business in Provincial Council, or its respective committees, shall be finaly determined the same day that it is moved.

Twenty-first. That at all times, when and so often as it shall happen, that the Governor shall or may be an infant, under the age of one and twenty years, and no guardians or commissioners are appointed in writing by the father of the said infant, or that such guardians or commissioners shall be deceased; that during such minority, the Provincial Council shall, from time to time, as they shall see meet, constitute and appoint guardians or commissioners, not exceeding three; one of which three shall preside as deputy and chief guardian, during such minority, and shall have and execute, with the consent of the other two, all the power of a governor, in all the public affairs and concerns of the said province.

Twenty-second. That as often as any day of the month, mentioned in any article of this charter, shall fall upon the first day of the week, commonly called the Lord's day, the business appointed for that day, shall be deferred till next day, unless in case of emergency.

Twenty-third. That no act, law or ordinance whatsoever, shall at any time hereafter be made or done, by the governor of this province, his heirs or assigns, or by the freemen in the Provincial Council or the General Assembly, to alter, change or diminish the form or effect of this charter, or any part or clause thereof, without the consent of the governor, his heirs or assigns, and six parts of seven of the said freemen in Provincial Council, and General Assembly.

And lastly. That I the said William Penn, for myself, my heirs, and assigns, have solemnly declared, granted and confirmed, and do hereby solemnly declare, grant and confirm, that neither I, my heirs nor assigns, shall procure or do any thing or things, whereby the liberties in this charter contained and expressed, shall be infringed or broken; and if any thing be procured by any person or persons contrary to these premises, it shall be held of no force or effect. In Witness whereof, I the said William Penn have unto this present charter of liberties, set my hand and broad seal, this five and twentieth day of the second month, vulgarly called April, in the year of our Lord, one thousand six hundred and eighty-two.

WILLIAM PENN.

LAWS AGREED UPON IN ENGLAND.

First. That the charter of liberties, declared, granted and confirmed, the five and twentieth day of the second month, called April, 1682, before divers witnesses by William Penn, governor and chief proprietary of Pennsylvania, to all the freemen and planters of the said province, is hereby declared and approved, and shall be for ever held for fundamental, in the government thereof, according to the limitations mentioned in the said charter.

Second.   That every Inhabitant in the said province, that is or shall be a purchaser of one hundred acres of land or upwards, his heirs and assigns, and every person who shall have paid his passage, and taken up one hundred acres of land, at one penny an acre, and have cultivated ten acres thereof, and every person that hath been a servant or bondsman, and is free by his service, that shall have taken up his fifty acres of land, and cultivated twenty thereof, and every inhabitant, artificer, or other resident in the said province, that pays scot and lot to the government, shall be deemed and accounted a freeman of the said province; and every such person shall and may be capable of electing or being elected representatives of the people in Provincial Council or General Assembly in the said province.

Third.   That all elections of members or representatives of the people and freemen of the province of Pennsylvania, to serve in Provincial Council or General Assembly, to be held within the said province, shall be free and voluntary; and that the elector that shall receive any reward or gift, in meat, drink, monies or otherwise, shall forfeit his right to elect; and such person as shall, directly or indirectly, give, promise, or bestow any such reward as aforesaid, to be elected, shall forfeit his election, and be thereby incapable to serve as aforesaid.   And the Provincial Council and General Assembly shall be the sole judges of the regularity or irregularity of the elections of their own respective members.

Fourth.   That no money or goods shall be raised upon, or paid by any of the people of this province, by way of a publick tax, custom or contribution, but by a law for that purpose made; and whosoever shall levy, collect or pay any money or goods contrary thereunto, shall be held a publick enemy to the province, and a betrayer of the liberties of the people thereof.

Fifth.   That all courts shall be open, and justice shall neither be sold, denied or delayed.

Sixth.   That in all courts all persons of all persuasions may freely appear in their own way, and according to their own manner, and there personally plead their own cause themselves, or if unable, by their friends.   And the first process shall be the exhibition of the complaint in court, fourteen days before the trial; and that the party complained against may be fitted for the same, he or she shall be summoned no less than ten days before, and a copy of the complaint delivered him or her, at his or her dwelling house.   But before the complaint of any person be received, he shall solemnly declare in court, that he believes in his conscience his cause is just.

Seventh.   That all pleadings, processes, and records in courts, shall be short, and in english, and in an ordinary and plain character, that they may be understood, and justice speedily administered.

Eighth.   That all trials shall be by twelve men, and as near as may be, peers or equals, and of the neighborhood, and men without just exception.   In cases of life, there shall be first twenty-four returned by the sheriff for a grand inquest, of whom twelve at least shall find the complaint to be true; and then the twelve men, or peers, to be likewise returned by the sheriff, shall have the final judgment.   But reasonable challenges shall be always admitted against the said twelve men or any of them.

Ninth.   That all fees in all cases shall be moderate, and settled by the Provincial Council and General Assembly, and be hung up in a table in every respective court; and whosoever shall be convicted of taking more, shall pay two-fold, and be dismissed his employment, one moiety of which shall go to the party wronged.

Tenth.   That all prisons shall be workhouses for felons, vagrants, and loose and idle persons; whereof one shall be in every county.

Eleventh.   That all prisoners shall be bailable by sufficient sureties, unless for capital offences, where the proof is evident, or the presumption great.

Twelfth.   That all persons wrongfully imprisoned or prosecuted at law, shall have double damages against the informer or prosecutor.

Thirteenth.   That all prisons shall be free, as to fees, food, and lodging.

Fourteenth.   That all lands and goods shall be liable to pay debts, except where there is legal issue, and then all the goods, and one third of the land only.

Fifteenth.   That all wills and writing attested by two witnesses, shall be of the same force, as to lands as other conveyances, being legally proved within forty days, either within or without the said province.

Sixteenth.   That seven years quiet possession shall give an unquestionable right, except in cases of infants, lunaticks, married women, or persons beyond the seas.

Seventeenth.   That all briberies and extortions whatsoever, shall be severely punished.

Eighteenth.   That all fines shall be moderate, and saving mens contenements, merchandize or wainage.

Nineteenth.   That all marriages (not forbidden by the law of God, as to nearness of blood and affinity by marriage) shall be encouraged; but the parents or guardians shall be first consulted, and the marriage shall be published before it be solemnized, and it shall be solemnized by taking one another as husband and wife, before credible witnesses, and a certificate of the whole, under the hands of parties and witnesses, shall be brought to the proper register of that county, and shall be registered in his office.

Twentieth. And to prevent frauds and vexatious suits within the said province, that all charters, gifts, grants and conveyances of land, (except leases for a year or under) and all bills, bonds, and specialties have five pounds, and not under three months, made in the said province, shall be enrolled or registered in the public enrolment office of the said province within the space of two months next after the making thereof, else to be void in law. And all deeds, grants, and conveyances of land (except as aforesaid) within the said province, and made out of the said province, shall be inrolled or registered as aforesaid, within six months next after the making thereof, and settling and constituting an enrolment office or registry within the said province, else to be void in law against all persons whatsoever.

Twenty-first. That all defacers or corruptors of charters, gifts, grants, bonds, bills, wills, contracts and conveyances, or that shall deface or falsify any enrolment, registry or record within this province, shall make double satisfaction for the same; half whereof shall go to the party wronged, and they shall be dismissed of all places of trust, and be publickly disgraced as false men.

Twenty-second. That there shall be a register for births, marriages, burials, wills, and letters of administration, distinct from the other registry.

Twenty-third. That there shall be a register for all servants, where their names, time, wages, and days of payment, shall be registered.

Twenty-fourth. That all lands and goods of felons shall be liable to make satisfaction to the party wronged twice the value; and for want of lands or goods, the felons shall be bond-men to work in the common prison or work-house, or otherwise, till the party injured be satisfied.

Twenty-fifth. That the estates of capital offenders, as traitors and murderers, shall go one third to the next of kin to the sufferer, and the remainder to the next of kin to the criminal.

Twenty-sixth. That all witnesses, coming or called to testify their knowledge in or to any matter or thing in any court, or before any lawful authority within the said province, shall there give or deliver in their evidence or testimony, by solemnly promising to speak the truth, the whole truth, and nothing but the truth, to the matter or thing in question. And in case any person so called to evidence, shall be convicted of wilful falsehood, such person shall suffer and undergo such damage or penalty, as the person or persons against whom he or she bore false witness, did or should undergo; and shall also make satisfaction to the party wronged, and be publicly exposed as a false witness, never to be credited in any court, or before any magistrate, in the said province.

Twenty-seventh. And to the end that all officers chosen to serve within this province, may with more care and diligence answer the trust reposed in them, it is agreed, that no such person shall enjoy more than one publick office at one time.

Twenty-eighth. That all children within this province of the age of twelve years, shall be taught some useful trade or skill, to the end none may be idle, but the poor may work to live, and the rich, if they become poor, may not want.

Twenty-ninth. That servants be not kept longer than their time, and such as are careful, be both justly and kindly used in their service, and put in fitting equipage at the expiration thereof, according to custom.

Thirtieth. That all scandalous and malicious reporters, backbiters, defamers and spreaders of false news, whether against magistrates or private persons, shall be accordingly severely punished, as enemies to the peace and concord of this province.

Thirty-first. That for the encouragement of the planters and traders in this province, who are incorporated into a society, the patent granted to them by William Penn, Governor of the said province, is hereby ratified and confirmed.

Thirty-second. * * *

Thirty-third. That all factors or correspondents in the said province wronging their employers, shall make satisfaction, and one third over, to their said employers: and in case of the death of any such factor or correspondent, the committee of trade shall take care to secure so much of the deceased party's estate, as belongs to his said respective employers.

Thirty-fourth. That all treasurers, judges, masters of the rolls, sheriffs, justices of the peace, and other officers and persons whatsoever, relating to courts or trials of causes, or any other service in the government; and all members elected to serve in Provincial Council and General Assembly, and all that have right to elect such members, shall be such as profess faith in Jesus Christ, and that are not convicted of ill fame, or unsober and dishonest conversation, and that are of one and twenty years of age at least; and that all such so qualified, shall be capable of the said several employments and privileges as aforesaid.

Thirty-fifth. That all persons living in this province, who confess and acknowledge the one almighty and eternal God, to be the creator, upholder and ruler of the world, and that hold themselves obliged in concience to live peaceably and justly in civil society, shall in no ways be molested or prejudiced for their religious persuasion or practice in matters of faith and worship, nor shall they be compelled at any time to frequent or maintain any religious worship, place or ministry whatever.

Thirty-sixth. That according to the good example of the primitive christians, and for the ease of the creation, every first day of the week, called the Lord's day, people shall abstain from their common daily labour, that they may the better dispose themselves to worship God according to their understandings.

Thirty-seventh. That as careless and corrupt administration of justice draws the wrath of God upon magistrates, so the wildness and looseness of the people provoke the indignation of God against a country; therefore, that all such offences against God, as swearing, cursing, lying, prophane talking, drunkenness, drinking of healths, obscene words, incest, sodomy, rapes, whoredom, fornication, and other uncleanness (not to be repeated.) All treasons, misprisons, murders, duels, felonies, seditions, maims, forcible entries, and other violences, to the persons and estates of the inhabitants within this province: all prizes, stage plays, cards, dice, may-games, masques, revels, bull-baitings, cock-fightings, bearbaitings and the like, which excite the people to rudeness, cruelty, looseness and irreligion, shall be respectively discouraged, and severely punished, according to the appointment of the governor and freemen in Provincial Council and General Assembly, as also all proceedings contrary to these laws, that are not here made expressly penal.

Thirty-eight. That a copy of these laws shall be hung up in the Provincial Council, and in public courts of justice, and that they shall be read yearly, at the opening of every Provincial Council and General Assembly, and courts of justice, and their assent shall be testified by their standing up, after the reading thereof.

Thirty-ninth. That there shall be at no time any alteration of any of these laws, without the consent of the governor, his heirs or assigns, and six parts of seven of the freemen, met in Provincial Council and General Assembly.

Fortieth. That all other matters and things not herein provided for, which shall and may concern the publick justice, peace or safety of the said province; and the raising and imposing taxes, customs, duties, or other charges whatsoever, shall be, and are hereby referred to the order, prudence and determination of the governor and freemen in Provincial Council and General Assembly, to be held from time to time in the said province.

D. THE CHARTER OF PRIVILEGES TO THE PROVINCE AND COUNTIES [OF PENNSYLVANIA]

October 8, 1701

WILLIAM PENN, Proprietary & Governr of the Province of Pennsylvania & Territories thereunto belonging.

To all to whom these presents shall come, sendeth Greeting:

WHEREAS, KING CHARLES THE SECOND, by his Letters Patents under the Great Seal of England, bearing date the fourth day of

March, in the year One Thousand Six hundred & Eighty, was Graciously pleased to Give and Grant unto me, my heirs & Assigns, forever, this Province of Pennsylvania, with Divers Great Powers and Jurisdictions for the Well Government thereof; and whereas the King's Dearest Brother, James, Duke of York and Albany, &c., by his Deeds of feoffment under his hand & Seal, duly perfecting, bearing Date the Twenty-fourth Day of August, One thousand Six hundred Eighty & two, Did grant unto me, my heirs and Assigns, all that Tract of Land now Called the Territories of Pennsylvi'a, together with Powers and Jurisdictions for the good Government thereof; AND WHEREAS, for the Encouragement of all the freemen and Planters that might be Concerned in ye said Province and Territories, and for the good Government thereof, I, the said Willm. Penn, in the year One Thousand Six hundred Eighty & three, for me, my heirs and assigns, Did grant and Confirm unto all the freemen, Planters and adventurers therein, Divers Liberties, ffranchises & Propertys, as by the said Grant Entituled the FRAME of ye GOVERNMENT of the PROVINCE of PENNSYLVANIA & TERRITORIES thereunto belonging, in AMERICA, may appear; which Charter or fframe, being found in some parts of it not so suitable to ye Present Circumstances of the Inhabitants, was in the third month, in the year One thousand seven hundred, Delivered up to me by six parts of seven of freemen of this Province and Territories, in General Assembly mett, provision being made in the said Charter for that end and Purpose; AND WHEREAS, I was then pleased to promise that I would restore the said Charter to them again with necessary alterations, or in Liew thereof, Give them another better adapted to answer the Present Circumstances & condition of the said Inhabitants, which they have now, by their Representatives in General Assembly mett at Philadelphia, Requested me to grant; know ye therefore, that I, for the further well being and good Govrmt of the said Province and Territories, and in pursuance of the Rights and Powers before mentioned, I, the said WILLIAM PENN, do Declare, grant and Confirm unto all the freemen, Planters and adventurers, and other inhabitants in this Province and Territories, these following Liberties, ffranchises and Privileges, so far as in me lyeth, to be held, enjoyed and kept by the freemen, planters & adventurers, & other Inhabitants of and in the said Province and Territories thereunto Annexed, forever;

FIRST: Because no people can be truly happy, though under the greatest Enjoyment of Civil Liberties, if abridg'd of the freedom of their Consciences as to their Religious profession & Worship; and Almighty God being the only Lord of Conscience, ffather of Lights & Spirits, and the author as well as object of all Divine Knowledge, ffaith and Worship, who only doth Enlighten the Mind & perswade and Convince the Understandings of People, I do hereby Grant and Declare that no person or persons, inhabiting in this Province or Territories, who shall Confess and acknowledge one Almighty God, the Creator, Upholder and Ruler of the World, and Profess him or themselves obliged to Live Quietly under the Civil Government, shall be in any Case molested or prejudiced in his or their person or Estate because of his or their Consciencious perswasion or Practice, nor be Compelled to frequent or maintain any Religious Worship, place or ministry contrary to his or their mind, or to do or suffer any other act or thing Contrary to their Religious perswasion. And that all persons who also profess to believe in JESUS CHRIST the SAVIOUR of the World, shall be Capable (notwithstanding their other perswasions and Practices in Point of Conscience and Religion) to serve this Governmt in any Capacity, both Legislatively and Exexcutively, he or they Solemnly promising, when Lawfully required, allegiance to the King as Sovereign, and fidelity to the Proprietor and Governour, and Taking yᵉ attests as now Established, by the Law made at New Castle, in the Year One Thousand seven hundred, Intitled at act Directing the attests of several offices and ministers, as now amended and Confirmed by this present Assembly.

SECONDLY: for the well governing of this Province and Territories, there shall be an Assembly Yearly Chosen by the freemen thereof, to Consist of four persons out of each County of most note for Virtue, Wisdom & Ability, (or of a greater number at any time as the Governour and Assembly shall agree,) upon the first day of October, forever; and shall sitt on the fourteenth day of the said month, at Philadelphia, unless the Governour and Council for the time being shall see Cause to appoint another place within the said Province or Territories, which assembly shall have power to Choose a Speaker and other their officers, and shall be Judges of the Qualifications and Elections of their own members, sitt upon their own adjournments, appoint Committees, prepare bills in or to pass into Laws, Impeach Criminals and Redress Grievances; and shall have all other powers and Privileges of an Assembly, according to the Rights of the free born subjects of England, and as is usual in any of the King's Plantacons in America. And if any County or Counties shall refuse or neglect to Choose their Respective Representatives, as aforesaid, or if Chosen do not meet to serve in Assembly, those who are so Chosen & mett shall have the full power of an Assembly, in as Ample manner as if all the Representatives had been Chosen and mett; Provided they are not less than two thirds of the whole number thot ought to mett; And that the Qualifications of Electors & Elected, and all other matters and things Relating to Elections of Representatives to serve in Assemblys, though not herein particularly Exprest, shall be and Remain as by a Law of this Govermt, made at New Castle in the year One thousd seven hundred, Intitled an Act to ascertain the number of members of Assembly, and to Regulate the Elections.

THIRDLY: that the freemen in each Respective County, at the time and place of meeting for Electing their Representatives to serve in Assembly, may, as often as there shall be occasion, Choose a Double number of persons to present to the Govr for Sherifs and Coroners, to serve for three years, if they so long behave themselves well, out of which respective Elections & Presentments The Gor shall nominate and Commissionate One for each of the said officers, The Third Day after such presentment, or else the first named in such presentment for Each office, as aforesaid, shall stand and serve in that office for the time before Respectively Limited; and in case of death or Default, such vacancies shall be supplied by ye Governour to serve to the End of the said Term: PROVIDED always, that if the said freemen shall at any time neglect or Decline to Choose a person or persons for Either or both the aforesaid offices, then and in such Case the persons that are or shall be in the Respective offices of Sherif or Coroner at the time of Election, shall remain therein untill they shall be Removed by another Election, as aforesaid. And that ye Justices of the Respective Counties shall or may nominate & present to the Govr, three persons to serve for Clerk of the Peace for the said County when there is a vacancy, One of which the Governour shall Commissionate within Ten Days after such present-ment, or else the first nominated shall serve in the said office During good behaviour.

FOURTHLY: that the Laws of this Govrmt shall be in this stile, vizt: [By the Governour with the Consent and approbation of the freemen in General Assembly mett,] and shall be, after Confirmation by the Governour, forthwith Recorded in the Rolls office, and kept at Philadia, unless the Govr and Assembly shall agree to appoint another place.

FIFTHLY; That all Criminals shall have the same Privileges of Witnesses and Council as their Prosecutors.

SIXTHLY: That no person or persons shall or may, at any time hereafter, be obliged to answer any Complaint, matter or thing Whatso-ever Relating to Property before the Governr and Council, or in any other place but in the ordinary Courts of Justice, unless appeals thereun-to shall be hereafter by Law appointed.

SEVENTHLY: That no person within this Governmt shall be Li-censed by the Governor to keep Ordinary, Tavern, or House of Publick Entertainment, but such who are first Recommended to him under the hand of the Justice of the Respective Counties, signed in open Court, wch Justices are and shall be hereby Impowered to suppress & forbid any person keeping such Publick House, as aforesaid, upon their misbe-haviour, on such Penalties as the Law doth or shall direct. and to Recommend others from time to time as they shall see occasion.

EIGHTHLY: If any person, through Temptation or melancholly, shall Destroy himself, his Estate, Real & Personal, shall, notwithstand-ing, Descend to his wife and Children or Relations as if he had Died a natural Death; and if any person shall be Destroyed or kill'd by Casualty or accident, there shall be no forfeiture to the Governour by Reason thereof; And no act, Law or Ordinance, whatsoever, shall at any Time hereafter be made or done to alter, Change or Diminish the form or effect of this Charter, or of any part or Clause therein, Contrary to the true Intent and meaning thereof, without the Consent of the Govr for the time being, and Six parts of Seven of the Assembly mett. But because the happiness of mankind depends so much upon the Enjoying of Liberty of their Consciences, as aforesaid, I do hereby Solemnly Declare, promise and Grant for me, my heirs and assigns, that the first article of this Charter, Relating to Liberty of Conscience, and Every part and Clause therein, according to the true Intent and meaning thereof, shall be kept and remain without any alteration, Inviobly forever.

And LASTLY, I, the said William Penn, Proprietor & Govr of th Province of Pennsylvania and Territories thereunto belonging, for my self, my heirs and Assigns, have solemnly Declared, Granted and Confirmed, and do hereby Solemnly Declare, Grant and Confirm, that neither I, my heirs or Assigns, shall procure or do any thing or things whereby the Liberties in this Charter Contained and Exprest, nor any part thereof, shall be infringed or Broken; and if any thing shall be procured or done by any person or persons, Contrary to these presents, it shall be held of no force or effect.

IN WITNESS whereof, I, the said William Penn, att Philadia, in Pennsylvania, have unto this present Charter of Liberties sett my hand and Broad Seal, this Twenty Eight Day of October, In the Year of our Lord One thousand Seven hundred and one, being the thirteenth year of the Reign of King WILLIAM the Third, over England, Scotland, ffrance and Ireland, &c., and in the Twenty first year of my Govrmt. And Notwithstanding the Closure and test of this present Charter, as aforesaid, I think fitt to add this following proviso thereunto as part of the same, that is to say: that notwithstanding any Clause or Clauses in the above menconed Charter, obliged the Province and Territories to Join together in Legislation, I am Content and do hereby Declare that If the Representatives of the Province and Territories shall not hereafter agree to Joyn together in Legislation, and if the same shall be signified to me or my Deputy, in open Assembly or otherwise, from under the hands and Seals of the Representatives (for the time being) of the province or Territories, or the major part of Either of them, any time within three years from the date hereof; That in such Case the Inhabitants of Each of the three Counties of this Province shall not have Less than Eight persons to Represent them in Assembly for the Province, and the Inhabitants of the Town of Philadia (when the said Town is incorporated) Two persons to Represent them in Assembly; and the Inhabitants of Each County in the Territories shall have as many persons to Represent them in a Distinct Assembly for yᵉ Territories as shall be by them Requested, as aforesaid, Notwithstanding which seperation of the Province and Territories in Respect of Legislation, I Do hereby promise, Grant and Declare that the Inhabitants of both Province & Territories shall separately Enjoy all other Liberties, Privileges and benefitts Granted Jointly to them in this Charter; any Law usage or Custom of this Govrmt heretofore made & practised, or any Law made and passed by this General Assembly to the Contrary hereof, Notwithstanding.

Copia Vera.

WILLIAM PENN.

p. Jos. ANTROBUS,

Clerk of the Assembly.

This Charter of Privileges being Distinctly Read in Assembly, and the whole & every part thereof being approved of and agreed to by us, we do thankfully Receive the same from our Proprietor & Govr, at Philadelphia, This Twenty Eight Day of October, 1701.

Signed on behalf and by order, of the Assembly

p. JOS. GROWDON, Speaker.

Edwd. Shippen,	)	
Phineas Pemberton,	)	
Samll. Carpenter,	)	Propry. & Gov'rs Council.
Griffith Owen,	)	
Caleb Pusey,	)	
Thos. Story.	)	

E. RESOLUTIONS OF THE STAMP ACT CONGRESS

October 19, 1765

DECLARATION OF RIGHTS.

The members of this congress, sincerely devoted, with the warmest sentiments of affection and duty to his majesty's person and government, inviolably attached to the present happy establishment of the protestant succession, and with minds deeply impressed by a sense of the present and impending misfortunes of the British colonies on this continent; having considered as maturely as time would permit, the circumstances of said colonies, esteem it our indispensable duty to make the following declarations, of our humble opinions, respecting the most essential rights and liberties of the colonists, and of the grievances under which they labor, by reason of several late acts of parliament.

1st. That his majesty's subjects in these colonies, owe the same allegiance to the crown of Great Britain, that is owing from his subjects born within the realm, and all due subordination to that august body, the parliament of Great Britain.

2d. That his majesty's liege subjects in these colonies are entitled to all the inherent rights and privileges of his natural born subjects within the kingdom of Great Britain,

3d.   That it is inseparably essential to the freedom of a people, and the undoubted rights of Englishmen, that no taxes should be imposed on them, but with their own consent, given personally, or by their representatives.

4th.   That the people of these colonies are not, and from their local circumstances, cannot be represented in the house of commons in Great Britain.

5th.   That the only representatives of the people of these colonies, are persons chosen therein by themselves; and that no taxes ever have been, or can be constitutionally imposed on them, but by their respective legislatures.

6th.   That all supplies to the crown, being free gifts of the people, it is unreasonable and inconsistent with the principles and spirit of the British constitution, for the people of Great Britain to grant to his majesty the property of the colonists.

7th.   That trial by jury is the inherent and invaluable right of every British subject in these colonies.

8th.   That the late act of parliament entitled, an act for granting and applying certain stamp duties, and other duties in the British colonies and plantations in America, &c., by imposing taxes on the inhabitants of these colonies, and the said act, and several other acts, by extending the jurisdiction of the courts of admiralty beyond its ancient limits, have a manifest tendency to subvert the rights and liberties of the colonists.

9th.   That the duties imposed by several late acts of parliament, from the peculiar circumstances of these colonies, will be extremely buthensome and grievous, and from the scarcity of specie, the payment of them absolutely impracticable.

10th.   That as the profits of the trade of these colonies ultimately centre in Great Britain, to pay for the manufactures which they are obliged to take from thence, they eventually contribute very largely to all supplies granted there to the crown.

11th.   That the restrictions imposed by several late acts of parliament, on the trade of these colonies, will render them unable to purchase the manufactures of Great Britain.

12th.   That the increase, prosperity, and happiness of these colonies, depend on the full and free enjoyment of their rights and liberties, and an intercourse, with Great Britain, mutually affectionate and advantageous.

13th.   That it is the right of the British subjects in these colonies, to petition the king or either house of parliament.

Lastly, That it is the indispensable duty of these colonies to the best of sovereigns, to the mother country, and to themselves, to endeavor, by a loyal and dutiful address to his majesty, and humble application to both houses of parliament, to procure the repeal of the act for granting and applying certain stamp duties, of all clauses of any other acts of parliament, whereby the jurisdiction of the admiralty is extended as aforesaid, and of the other late acts for the restriction of the American commerce.

F. DECLARATION AND RESOLVES [OF THE FIRST CONTINENTAL CONGRESS]

October 14, 1774

Whereas, since the close of the last war, the British parliament, claiming a power, of right, to bind the people of America by statutes in all cases whatsoever, hath, in some acts, expressly imposed taxes on them, and in others, under various pretences, but in fact for the purpose of raising a revenue, hath imposed rates and duties payable in these colonies, established a board of commissioners, with unconstitutional powers, and extended the jurisdiction of courts of admiralty, not only for collecting the said duties, but for the trial of causes merely arising within the body of a county.

And whereas, in consequence of other statutes, judges, who before held only estates at will in their offices, have been made dependant on the crown alone for their salaries, and standing armies kept in times of peace: And whereas it has lately been resolved in parliament, that by force of a statute, made in the thirty-fifth year of the reign of King Henry the Eighth, colonists may be transported to England, and tried there upon accusations for treasons and misprisions, or concealments of treasons committed in the colonies, and by a late statute, such trials have been directed in cases therein mentioned:

And whereas, in the last session of parliament, three statutes were made; one entitled, "An act to discontinue, in such manner and for such time as are therein mentioned, the landing and discharging, lading, or shipping of goods, wares and merchandise, at the town, and within the harbour of Boston, in the province of Massachusetts-Bay in North-America;" another entitled, "An act for the better regulating the government of the province of Massachusetts-Bay in New England;" and another entitled, "An act for the impartial administration of justice, in the cases of persons questioned for any act done by them in the execution of the law, or for the suppression of riots and tumults, in the province of the Massachusetts-Bay in New England;" and another statute was then made, "for making more effectual provision for the government of the province of Quebec, etc." All which statutes are impolitic, unjust, and cruel, as well as unconstitutional, and most dangerous and destructive of American rights:

And whereas, assemblies have been frequently dissolved, contrary to the rights of the people, when they attempted to deliberate on grievances; and their dutiful, humble, loyal, and reasonable petitions to the crown for redress, have been repeatedly treated with contempt, by his Majesty's ministers of state:

The good people of the several colonies of New-Hampshire, Massachusetts-Bay, Rhode-Island and Providence Plantations, Connecticut, New-York, New-Jersey, Pennsylvania, Newcastle, Kent, and Sussex on Delaware, Maryland, Virginia, North-Carolina, and South-Carolina, justly alarmed at these arbitrary proceedings of parliament and administration, have severally elected, constituted, and appointed deputies to meet, and sit in general Congress, in the city of Philadelphia, in order to obtain such establishment, as that their religion, laws, and liberties, may not be subverted: Whereupon the deputies so appointed being now assembled, in a full and free representation of these colonies, taking into their most serious consideration, the best means of attaining the ends aforesaid, do, in the first place, as Englishmen, their ancestors in like cases have usually done, for asserting and vindicating their rights and liberties, DECLARE,

That the inhabitants of the English colonies in North-America, by the immutable laws of nature, the principles of the English constitution, and the several charters or compacts, have the following RIGHTS:

Resolved, N. C. D. 1.   That they are entitled to life, liberty and property: and they have never ceded to any foreign power whatever, a right to dispose of either without their consent.

Resolved, N. C. D. 2.   That our ancestors, who first settled these colonies, were at the time of their emigration from the mother country, entitled to all the rights, liberties, and immunities of free and natural-born subjects, within the realm of England.

Resolved, N. C. D. 3.   That by such emigration they by no means forfeited, surrendered, or lost any of those rights, but that they were, and their descendants now are, entitled to the exercise and enjoyment of all such of them, as their local and other circumstances enable them to exercise and enjoy.

Resolved, 4.   That the foundation of English liberty, and of all free government, is a right in the people to participate in their legislative council: and as the English colonists are not represented, and from their local and other circumstances, cannot properly be represented in the British parliament, they are entitled to a free and exclusive power of legislation in their several provincial legislatures, where their right of representation can alone be preserved, in all cases of taxation and internal polity, subject only to the negative of their sovereign, in such manner as has been heretofore used and accustomed: But, from the necessity of the case, and a regard to the mutual interest of both countries, we cheerfully consent to the operation of such acts of the

British parliament, as are bona fide, restrained to the regulation of our external commerce, for the purpose of securing the commercial advantages of the whole empire to the mother country, and the commercial benefits of its respective members; excluding every idea of taxation internal or external, for raising a revenue on the subjects, in America, without their consent.

Resolved, *N. C. D.* 5.   That the respective colonies are entitled to the common law of England, and more especially to the great and inestimable privilege of being tried by their peers of the vicinage, according to the course of that law.

Resolved, 6.   That they are entitled to the benefit of such of the English statutes, as existed at the time of their colonization; and which they have, by experience, respectively found to be applicable to their several local and other circumstances.

Resolved, *N. C. D.* 7.   That these, his majesty's colonies, are likewise entitled to all the immunities and privileges granted and confirmed to them by royal charters, or secured by their several codes of provincial laws.

Resolved, *N. C. D.* 8.   That they have a right peaceably to assemble, consider of their grievances, and petition the king; and that all prosecutions, prohibitory proclamations, and commitments for the same, are illegal.

Resolved, *N. C. D.* 9.   That the keeping a standing army in these colonies, in times of peace, without the consent of the legislature of that colony, in which such army is kept, is against law.

Resolved, *N. C. D.* 10.   It is indispensably necessary to good government, and rendered essential by the English constitution, that the constituent branches of the legislature be independent of each other; that, therefore, the exercise of legislative power in several colonies, by a council appointed, during pleasure, by the crown, is unconstitutional, dangerous and destructive to the freedom of American legislation.

All and each of which the aforesaid deputies, in behalf of themselves, and their constituents, do claim, demand, and insist on, as their indubitable rights and liberties; which cannot be legally taken from them, altered or abridged by any power whatever, without their own consent, by their representatives in their several provincial legislatures.

In the course of our inquiry, we find many infringements and violations of the foregoing rights, which, from an ardent desire, that harmony and mutual intercourse of affection and interest may be restored, we pass over for the present, and proceed to state such acts and measures as have been adopted since the last war, which demonstrate a system formed to enslave America.

Resolved, *N. C. D.*   That the following acts of parliament are infringements and violations of the rights of the colonists; and that the repeal of them is essentially necessary, in order to restore harmony between Great-Britain and the American colonies, viz.

The several acts of 4 Geo. III. ch. 15, and ch. 34.—5 Geo. III. ch. 25.—6 Geo. III. ch. 52.—7 Geo. III. ch. 41. and ch. 46.—8 Geo. III. ch. 22. which impose duties for the purpose of raising a revenue in America, extend the power of the admiralty courts beyond their ancient limits, deprive the American subject of trial by jury, authorise the judges certificate to indemnify the prosecutor from damages, that he might otherwise be liable to, requiring oppressive security from a claimant of ships and goods seized, before he shall be allowed to defend his property, and are subversive of American rights.

Also 12 Geo. III. ch. 24. intituled, "An act for the better securing his majesty's dockyards, magazines, ships, ammunition, and stores," which declares a new offence in America, and deprives the American subject of a constitutional trial by jury of the vicinage, by authorising the trial of any person, charged with the committing any offence described in the said act, out of the realm, to be indicted and tried for the same in any shire or county within the realm.

Also the three acts passed in the last session of parliament, for stopping the port and blocking up the harbour of Boston, for altering the charter and government of Massachusetts-Bay, and that which is enti-tled, "An act for the better administration of justice, etc."

Also the act passed in the same session for establishing the Roman Catholic religion, in the province of Quebec, abolishing the equitable system of English laws, and erecting a tyranny there, to the great danger (from so total a dissimilarity of religion, law and government) of the neighbouring British colonies, by the assistance of whose blood and treasure the said country was conquered from France.

Also the act passed in the same session, for the better providing suitable quarters for officers and soldiers in his majesty's service, in North-America.

Also, that the keeping a standing army in several of these colonies, in time of peace, without the consent of the legislature of that colony, in which such army is kept, is against law.

To these grievous acts and measures, Americans cannot submit, but in hopes their fellow subjects in Great-Britain will, on a revision of them, restore us to that state, in which both countries found happiness and prosperity, we have for the present, only resolved to pursue the following peaceable measures: 1. To enter into a non-importation, non-consump-tion, and non-exportation agreement or association. 2. To prepare an address to the people of Great-Britain, and a memorial to the inhabitants of British America: and 3. To prepare a loyal address to his majesty, agreeable to resolutions already entered into.

G. A DECLARATION OF RIGHTS AND THE CONSTITUTION OR FORM OF GOVERNMENT [OF VIRGINIA]

May 6, 1776

At a GENERAL CONVENTION of Delegates and Representatives, from the several Counties and Corporations of *Virginia*, held at the Capitol in the City of *Williamsburg*, on *Monday* the 6th of *May* 1776.

CHAPTER I.

A Declaration of Rights made by the representatives of the good people of Virginia, *assembled in full and free Convention; which rights do pertain to them, and their posterity, as the basis and foundation of government.*

I. THAT all men are by nature equally free and independent, and have certain inherent rights, of which, when they enter into a state of society, they cannot, by any compact, deprive or devest their posterity; namely, the enjoyment of life and liberty, with the means of acquiring and possessing property, and pursuing and obtaining happiness and safety.

II. THAT all power is vested in, and consequently derived from, the people; that Magistrates are their trustees and servants, and at all times amenable to them.

III. THAT government is, or ought to be, instituted for the common benefit, protection and security, of the people, nation, or community; of all the various modes and forms of government, that is best, which is capable of producing the greatest degree of happiness and safety, and is most effectually secured against the danger of mal-administration; and that when any government shall be found inadequate or contrary to these purposes, a majority of the community hath an indubitable, unalienable, and indeseasible right, to reform, alter, or abolish it, in such manner as shall be judged most conducive to the public weal.

IV. THAT no man, or set of men, are entitled to exclusive or separate emoluments or privileges from the community, but in consideration of public services; which not being descendible, neither ought the offices of Magistrate, Legislator, or Judge, to be hereditary.

V. THAT the Legislative, and Executive powers of the state should be separate and distinct from the Judiciary; and that the members of the two first may be restrained from oppression, by feeling and participating the burthens of the people, they should, at fixed periods, be reduced to a private station, return into that body from which they were originally taken, and the vacancies be supplied by frequent certain, and regular elections, in which all, or any part of the former members, to be again eligible, or ineligible, as the laws shall direct.

VI. THAT elections of members to serve as representatives of the people, in Assembly, ought to be free; and that all men, having sufficient evidence of permanent common interest with, and attachment to, the community, have the right of suffrage, and cannot be taxed or deprived of their property for public uses without their own consent, or that of their representatives so elected, nor bound by any law to which they have not, in like manner, assented, for the public good.

VII. THAT all power of suspending laws, or the execution of laws, by any authority without consent of the representatives of the people, is injurious to their rights and ought not to be exercised.

VIII. THAT in all capital or criminal prosecutions a man hath a right to demand the cause and nature of his accusation, to be confronted with the accusers and witnesses, to call for evidence in his favour, and to a speedy trial by an impartial jury of his vicinage, without whose unanimous consent he cannot be found guilty, nor can he be compelled to give evidence against himself; that no man be deprived of his liberty except by the law of the land, or the judgment of his peers.

IX. THAT excessive bail ought not to be required, nor excessive fines imposed, nor cruel and unusual punishments inflicted.

X. THAT general warrants, whereby an officer or messenger may be commanded to search suspected places without evidence of a fact committed, or to seize any person or persons not named, or whose offence is not particularly described and supported by evidence, are grievous and oppressive, and ought not to be granted.

XI. THAT in controversies respecting property, and in suits between man and man, the ancient trial by jury is preferable to any other, and ought to be held sacred.

XII. THAT the freedom of the press is one of the great bulwarks of liberty, and can never be restrained but by despotick governments.

XIII. THAT a well regulated militia, composed of the body of the people, trained to arms, is the proper, natural and safe defence of a free state; that standing armies, in time of peace, should be avoided, as dangerous to liberty; and that in all cases, the military should be under strict subordination to, and governed by, the civil power.

XIV. THAT the people have a right, to uniform government; and therefore, that no government separate from, or independent of, the government of *Virginia*, ought to be erected or established within the limits thereof.

XV. THAT no free government, or the blessing of liberty, can be preserved to any people but by a firm adherence to justice, moderation, temperance, frugality, and virtue, and by frequent recurrence to fundamental principles.

XVI. THAT religion, or the duty which we owe to our Creator, and the manner of discharging it, can be directed only by reason and conviction, not by force or violence, and therefore all men are equally entitled to the free exercise of religion, according to the dictates of conscience; and that it is the mutual duty of all to practise Christian forbearance, love, and charity, towards each other.

CHAPTER II.

The Constitution or Form of Government, agreed to and resolved upon by the Delegates and Representatives of the several Counties and Corporations of Virginia.

I. WHEREAS *George* the third, King of *Great Britain* and *Ireland*, and elector of *Hanover*, heretofore entrusted with the exercise of the kingly office in this government, hath endeavoured to pervert the same into a detestable and insupportable tyranny, by putting his negative on laws the most wholesome and necessary for the public good: By denying his Governors permission to pass laws of immediate and pressing importance, unless suspended in their operation for his assent, and, when so suspended, neglecting to attend to them for many years: By refusing to pass certain other laws, unless the persons to be benefited by them would relinquish the inestimable right-of representation in the Legislature: By dissolving Legislative Assemblies repeatedly and continually, for opposing with manly firmness his invasions of the rights of the people: When dissolved, by refusing to call others for a long space of time, thereby leaving the political system without any Legislative head: By endeavouring to prevent the population of our country, and, for that purpose, obstructing the laws for the naturalization of foreigners: By keeping among us, in time of peace, standing armies and ships of war: By affecting to render the military independent of, and superiour to, the civil power: By combining with others to subject us to a foreign jurisdiction, giving his assent to their pretended acts of Legislation: For quartering large bodies of armed troops among us: For cutting off our trade with all parts of the world: For imposing taxes on us without our consent: For depriving us of the benefits of trial by jury: For transporting us beyond seas, to be tried for pretended offences: For suspending our own Legislatures, and declaring themselves invested with power to legislate for us in all cases whatsoever: By plundering our seas, ravaging our coasts, burning our towns, and destroying the lives of our people: By inciting insurrections of our fellow subjects, with the allurements of forfeiture and confiscation: By prompting our negroes to rise in arms among us, those very negroes whom, by an inhuman use of his negative, he hath refused us permission to exclude by law: By endeavouring to bring on the inhabitants of our frontiers, the merciless *Indian* savages, whose known rule of warfare is an undistinguished destruction of all ages, sexes, and conditions of existence: By transporting, at this time, a large army of foreign mercenaries, to complete the works of death, desolation, and tyranny, already begun with circumstances of cruelty and perfidy unworthy the head of a civilized nation: By answering our repeated petitions for redress with a repetition of injuries: And finally, by abandoning the helm of government, and declaring us out of his allegiance and protection. By which several acts of misrule, the government of this country, as formerly exercised under the crown of *Great Britain*, is totally dissolved.

II. WE therefore, the Delegates and Representatives of the good people of *Virginia*, having maturely considered the premises, and viewing with great concern the deplorable condition to which this once happy country must be reduced, unless some regular adequate mode of civil polity is speedily adopted, and in compliance with a recommendation of the General Congress, do ordain and declare the future form of government of *Virginia* to be as followeth:

III. THE Legislative, Executive, and Judiciary departments, shall be separate and distinct, so that neither exercise the powers properly belonging to the other; nor shall any person exercise the powers of more than one of them at the same time, except that the Justices of the county courts shall be eligible to either House of Assembly.

IV. THE Legislative shall be formed of two distinct branches, who, together, shall be a complete Legislature. They shall meet once or oftener, every year, and shall be called the General Assembly of *Virginia*.

V. ONE of these shall be called the House of Delegates, and consist of two Representatives to be chosen for each county, and for the district of *West Augusta*, annually, of such men as actually reside in and are freeholders of the same, or duly qualified according to law, and also one Delegate or Representative to be chosen annually for the city of *Williamsburg*, and one for the borough of *Norfolk*, and a Representative for each of such other cities and boroughs as may hereafter be allowed particular representation by the Legislature; but when any city or borough shall so decrease as that the number of persons having right of suffrage therein shall have been for the space of seven years successively less than half the number of voters in some one county in *Virginia*, such city or borough thenceforward shall cease to send a Delegate or Representative to the Assembly.

VI. THE other shall be called the Senate, and consist of twenty four members, of whom thirteen shall constitute a House to proceed on business, for whose election the different counties shall be divided into twenty four districts, and each county of the respective district, at the time of the election of its Delegates, shall vote for one Senator, who is actually a resident and freeholder within the district, or duly qualified according to law, and is upwards of twenty five years of age; and the sheriffs of each county, within five days at farthest after the last county election in the district, shall meet at some convenient place, and from the poll so taken in their respective counties return as a Senator the man who shall have the greatest number of votes in the whole district. To keep up this Assembly by rotation, the districts shall be equally divided into four classes, and numbered by lot. At the end of one year after the general election, the six members elected by the first division shall be displaced, and the vacancies thereby occasioned supplied from such class or division, by new election, in the manner aforesaid. This rotation shall be applied to each division, according to its number, and continued in due order annually.

VII. THAT the right of suffrage in the election of members of both Houses shall remain as exercised at present, and each House shall choose its own Speaker, appoint its own officers, settle its own rules of proceeding, and direct writs of election for supplying intermediate vacancies.

VIII. ALL laws shall originate in the House of Delegates, to be approved or rejected by the Senate, or to be amended with the consent of the House of Delegates; except money bills, which in no instance shall be altered by the Senate, but wholly approved or rejected.

IX. A Governor, or Chief Magistrate, shall be chosen annually, by joint ballot of both Houses, to be taken in each House respectively, deposited in the conference room, the boxes examined jointly by a Committee of each House, and the numbers severally reported to them, that the appointments may be entered (which shall be the mode of taking the joint ballot of both Houses in all cases) who shall not continue in that office longer than three years successively, nor be eligible until the expiration of four years after he shall have been out of that office. An adequate, but moderate salary, shall be settled on him during his continuance in office; and he shall, with the advice of a Council of State, exercise the executive powers of government according to the laws of this commonwealth; and shall not, under any pretence, exercise any power or prerogative by virtue of any law, statute, or custom, of *England:* But be shall, with the advice of the Council of State, have the power of granting reprieves or pardons, except where the prosecution shall have been carried on by the House of Delegates, or the law shall otherwise particularly direct; in which cases, no reprieve or pardon shall be granted, but by resolve of the House of Delegates.

X. EITHER House of the General Assembly may adjourn themselves respectively. The Governor shall not prorogue or adjourn the Assembly during their sitting, nor dissolve them at any time; but he shall, if necessary, either by advice of the Council of State, or on application of a majority of the House of Delegates, call them before the time to which they shall stand prorogued or adjourned.

XI. A Privy Council or Council of State, consisting of eight members, shall be chosen by joint ballot of both Houses of Assembly, either from their own members or the people at large, to assist in the administration of government. They shall annually choose out of their own members a President, who, in case of the death, inability, or necessary absence of the Governor from the government, shall act as Lieutenant Governor. Four members shall be sufficient to act, and their advice and proceedings shall be entered of record, and signed by the members present (to any part whereof any member may enter his dissent) to be laid before the General Assembly, when called for by them. This Council may appoint their own clerk, who shall have a salary settled by law, and take an oath of secrecy in such matters as he shall be directed by the Board to conceal. A sum of money appropriated to that purpose shall be divided annually among the members, in proportion to their attendance; and they shall be incapable during their continuance in office, of sitting in either House of Assembly. Two members shall be removed by joint ballot of both Houses of Assembly at the end of every three years, and be ineligible for the three next years. These vacancies, as well as those occasioned by death or incapacity, shall be supplied by new elections, in the same manner.

XII. THE Delegates for *Virginia* to the Continental Congress shall be chosen annually, or superseded in the mean time by joint ballot of both Houses of Assembly.

XIII. THE present militia officers shall be continued, and vacancies supplied by appointment of the Governor, with the advice of the Privy Council, or recommendations from the respective county courts; but the Governor and Council shall have a power of suspending any officer, and ordering a court-martial on complaint of misbehaviour or inability, or to supply vacancies of officers happening when in actual service. The Governor may embody the militia, with the advice of the Privy Council, and when embodied, shall alone have the direction of the militia under the laws of the country.

XIV. THE two Houses of Assembly shall, by joint ballot, appoint Judges of the Supreme Court of Appeals, and General Count, Judges in Chancery, Judges of Admiralty, Secretary, and the Attorney General, to be commissioned by the Governor, and continue in office during good behaviour. In case of death, incapacity, or resignation, the Governor, with the advice of the Privy Council, shall appoint persons to succeed in office, to be approved or displaced by both Houses. These officers shall have fixed and adequate salaries, and, together with all others holding lucrative offices, and all Ministers of the Gospel of every denomination, be incapable of being elected members of either House of Assembly, or the Privy Council.

XV. THE Governor, with the advice of the Privy Council, shall appoint Justices of the Peace for the counties; and in case of vacancies, or a necessity of increasing the number hereafter, such appointments to be made upon the recommendation of the respective county courts. The present acting Secretary in *Virginia*, and clerks of all the county courts, shall continue in office. In case of vacancies, either by death, incapacity, or resignation, a Secretary shall be appointed as before directed, and the clerks by the respective courts. The present and future clerks shall hold their offices during good behaviour, to be judged of and determined in the General Court. The Sheriffs and Coroners shall be nominated by the respective courts, approved by the Governor, with the advice of the Privy Council, and commissioned by the Governor. The Justices shall appoint constables, and all fees of the aforesaid officers be regulated by law.

XVI. THE Governor, when he is out of office, and others offending against the state, either by mal-administration, corruption, or other means by which the safety of the state may be endangered, shall be impeachable by the House of Delegates. Such impeachment to be prosecuted by the Attorney General, or such other person or persons as the House may appoint in the General Court, according to the laws of the land. If found guilty, he or they shall be either for ever disabled to hold any office under government, or removed from such office *pro tempore*, or subjected to such pains or penalties as the law shall direct.

XVII. IF all, or any of the Judges of the General Court, shall, on good grounds (to be judged of by the House of Delegates) be accused of any of the crimes or offences before-mentioned, such House of Delegates may, in like manner, impeach the Judge or Judges so accused, to be prosecuted in the Court of Appeals; and he or they, if found guilty, shall be punished in the same manner as is prescribed in the preceding clause.

XVIII. COMMISSIONS and grants shall run *In the name of the* COMMONWEALTH *of* VIRGINIA, and bear test by the Governor with the seal of the commonwealth annexed. Writs shall run in the same manner, and bear test by the clerks of the several courts. Indictments shall conclude, *Against the peace and dignity of the commonwealth.*

XIX. A Treasurer shall be appointed annually, by joint ballot of both Houses.

XX. ALL escheats, penalties, and forfeitures, heretofore going to the King, shall go to the commonwealth, save only such as the Legislature may abolish, or otherwise provide for.

XXI. THE territories contained within the charters erecting the colonies of *Maryland, Pennsylvania, North* and *South Carolina*, are hereby ceded, released, and for ever confirmed to the people of those colonies respectively, with all the rights of property, jurisdiction, and government, and all other rights whatsoever which might at any time heretofore have been claimed by *Virginia*, except the free navigation and use of the rivers *Potowmack* and *Pobomoke*, with the property of the *Virginia* shores or strands bordering on either of the said rivers, and all improvements which have been or shall be made thereon. The western and northern extent of *Virginia* shall in all other respects stand as fixed by the charter of King *James* the first, in the year one thousand six hundred and nine, and by the public treaty of peace between the Courta of *Great Britain* and *France* in the year one thousand seven hundred and sixty three; unless, by act of Legislature, one or more territories shall hereafter be laid off, and governments established westward of the *Allegheny* mountains. And no purchase of lands shall be made of the *Indian* natives but on behalf the public, by authority of the General Assembly.

XXII. In order to introduce this government, the representatives of the people met in Convention shall choose a Governor and Privy Council, also such other officers directed to be chosen by both Houses as may be judged necessary to be immediately appointed. The Senate to be first chosen by the people, to continue until the last day of *March* next, and the other officers until the end of the succeeding section of Assembly. In case of vacancies, the Speaker of either House shall issue writs for new elections.

H.   THE DECLARATION OF INDEPENDENCE

July 4, 1776

In CONGRESS.

The unanimous Declaration of the thirteen united States of America,

When in the Course of human events, it becomes necessary for one people to dissolve the political bands which have connected them with another, and to assume among the powers of the earth, the separate and equal station to which the Laws of Nature and of Nature's God entitle them, a decent respect to the opinions of mankind requires that they should declare the causes which impel them to the separation.—We hold these truths to be self-evident, that all men are created equal, that they are endowed by their Creator with certain unalienable Rights, that among these are Life, Liberty and the pursuit of Happiness.—That to secure these rights, Governments are instituted among Men, deriving their just powers from the consent of the governed,—That whenever any Form of Government becomes destructive of these ends, it is the Right of the People to alter or to abolish it; and to institute new Government, laying its foundation on such principles and organizing its powers in such form, as to them shall seem most likely to effect their Safety and Happiness. Prudence, indeed, will dictate that Governments long established should not be changed for light and transient causes; and accordingly all experience hath shewn, that mankind are more disposed to suffer, while evils are sufferable, than to right themselves by abolishing the forms to which they are accustomed. But when a long train of abuses and usurpations, pursuing invariably the same Object evinces a design to reduce them under absolute Despotism, it is their right, it is their duty, to throw off such Government, and to provide new Guards for their future security.—Such has been the patient sufferance of these Colonies; and such is now the necessity which constrains them to alter their former Systems of Government. The history of the present King of

Great Britain is a history of repeated injuries and usurpations, all having in direct object the establishment of an absolute Tyranny over these States. To prove this, let Facts be submitted to a candid world.—He has refused his Assent to Laws, the most wholesome and necessary for the public good.—He has forbidden his Governors to pass Laws of immediate and pressing importance, unless suspended in their operation till his Assent should be obtained; and when so suspended, he has utterly neglected to attend to them.—He has refused to pass other Laws for the accommodation of large districts of people, unless those people would relinquish the right of Representation in the Legislature, a right inestimable to them and formidable to tyrants only.—He has called together legislative bodies at places unusual, uncomfortable, and distant from the depository of their public Records, for the sole purpose of fatiguing them into compliance with his measures.—He has dissolved Representative Houses repeatedly, for opposing with manly firmness his invasions on the rights of the people.—He has refused for a long time, after such dissolutions, to cause others to be elected; whereby the Legislative powers, incapable of Annihilation, have returned to the People at large for their exercise; the State remaining in the mean time exposed to all the dangers of invasion from without, and convulsions within.—He has endeavoured to prevent the population of these States; for that purpose obstructing the Laws for Naturalization of Foreigners; refusing to pass others to encourage their migrations hither, and raising the conditions of new Appropriations of Lands.—He has obstructed the Administration of Justice, by refusing his Assent to Laws for establishing Judiciary powers—He has made Judges dependent on his Will alone, for the tenure of their offices, and the amount and payment of their salaries.—He has erected a multitude of New Offices, and sent hither swarms of Officers to harrass our people, and eat out their substance.—He has kept among us, in times of peace, Standing Armies without the Consent of our legislatures.—He has affected to render the Military independent of and superior to the Civil power.—He has combined with others to subject us to a jurisdiction foreign to our constitution, and unacknowledged by our laws; giving his Assent to their Acts of pretended Legislation:—For Quartering large bodies of armed troops among us:—For protecting them, by a mock Trial, from punishment for any Murders which they should commit on the Inhabitants of these States:—For calling off our Trade with all parts of the world:—For imposing Taxes on us without our Consent:—For depriving us in many cases, of the benefits of Trial by Jury:—For transporting us beyond Seas to be tried for pretended offences—For abolishing the free System of English Laws in a neighbouring Province, establishing therein an Arbitrary government, and enlarging its Boundaries so as to render it at once an example and fit instrument for introducing the same absolute rule into these Colonies:—For taking away our Charters, abolishing our most valuable Laws and altering fundamentally the Forms of our Governments:—For suspending our own Legislatures, and declaring themselves invested with power to legislate for us in all cases whatsoever.—He has abdicated Government here, by declaring us out of his Protection and waging War against us.— He has plundered our seas, ravaged our Coasts, burnt our towns, and destroyed the Lives of our people.—He is at this time transporting large Armies of foreign Mercenaries to compleat the works of death, desolation and tyranny, already begun with circumstances of Cruelty & perfidy scarcely paralleled in the most barbarous ages, and totally unworthy the Head of a civilized nation.—He has constrained our fellow Citizens taken Captive on the high Seas to bear Arms against their Country, to become the executioners of their friends and Brethren, or to fall themselves by their Hands.—He has excited domestic insurrections amongst us, and has endeavoured to bring on the inhabitants of our frontiers, the merciless Indian Savages, whose known rule of warfare, is an undistinguished destruction of all ages, sexes and conditions. In every stage of these Oppressions We have Petitioned for Redress in the most humble terms: Our repeated Petitions have been answered only by repeated injury. A Prince, whose character is thus marked by every act which may define a Tyrant, is unfit to be the ruler of a free people. Nor have We been wanting in attentions to our Brittish brethren. We have warned them from time to time of attempts by their legislature to extend an unwarrantable jurisdiction over us. We have reminded them of the circumstances of our emigration and settlement here. We have appealed to their native justice and magnanimity, and we have conjured them by the ties of our common kindred to disavow these usurpations, which, would inevitably interrupt our connections and correspondence They too have been deaf to the voice of justice and of consanguinity. We must, therefore, acquiesce in the necessity, which denounces our Separation, and hold them, as we hold the rest of mankind, Enemies in War, in Peace Friends.—

We, therefore, the Representatives of the united States of America, in General Congress, Assembled, appealing to the Supreme Judge of the world for the rectitude of our intentions, do, in the Name, and by Authority of the good People of these Colonies, solemnly publish and declare, That these United Colonies are, and of Right ought to be Free and Independent States; that they are Absolved from all Allegiance to the British Crown, and that all political connection between them and the State of Great Britain, is and ought to be totally dissolved; and that as Free and Independent States, they have full Power to levy War, conclude Peace, contract Alliances, establish Commerce, and to do all other Acts and Things which Independent States may of right do.—And for the support of this Declaration, with a firm reliance on the protection of divine Providence, we mutually pledge to each other our Lives, our Fortunes and our sacred Honor.

I. ACT OF CONFEDERATION OF THE UNITED STATES OF AMERICA

November 15, 1777

To all to whom these Presents shall come, we the under signed Delegates of the States affixed to our Names send greeting. Whereas the Delegates of the United States of America in Congress assembled did on the fifteenth day of November in the Year of our Lord One Thousand Seven Hundred and Seventy seven, and in the Second Year of the Independence of America agree to certain articles of Confederation and perpetual Union between the States of Newhampshire, Massachusetts-bay, Rhodeisland and Providence Plantations, Connecticut, New York, New Jersey, Pennsylvania, Delaware, Maryland, Virginia, North-Carolina, South-Carolina and Georgia in the Words following, viz, "Articles of Confederation and perpetual Union between the States of Newhampshire, Massachusetts-bay, Rhodeisland and Providence Plantations, Connecticut, New-York, New-Jersey, Pennsylvania, Delaware, Maryland, Virginia, North-Carolina, South-Carolina and Georgia.

Article I.   The Stile of this confederacy shall be "The United States of America."

Article II.   Each state retains its sovereignty, freedom and independence, and every Power, Jurisdiction and right, which is not by this confederation expressly delegated to the United States, in Congress assembled.

Article III.   The said states hereby severally enter into a firm league of friendship with each other, for their common defence, the security of their Liberties, and their mutual and general welfare, binding themselves to assist each other, against all force offered to, or attacks made upon them, or any of them, on account of religion, sovereignty, trade, or any other pretence whatever.

Article IV.   The better to secure and perpetuate mutual friendship and intercourse among the people of the different states in this union, the free inhabitants of each of these states, paupers, vagabonds and fugitives from Justice excepted, shall be entitled to all privileges and immunities of free citizens in the several states; and the people of each state shall have free ingress and regress to and from any other state, and shall enjoy therein all the privileges of trade and commerce, subject to the same duties, impositions and restrictions as the inhabitants thereof respectively, provided that such restriction shall not extend so far as to prevent the removal of property imported into any state, to any other state of which the Owner is an inhabitant; provided also that no imposition, duties or restriction shall be laid by any state, on the property of the united states, or either of them.

If any Person guilty of, or charged with treason, felony, or other high misdemeanor in any state, shall flee from Justice, and be found in any of the united states, he shall upon demand of the Governor or executive power, of the state from which he fled, be delivered up and removed to the state having jurisdiction of his offence.

Full faith and credit shall be given in each of these states to the records, acts and judicial proceedings of the courts and magistrates of every other state.

Article V. For the more convenient management of the general interests of the united states, delegates shall be annually appointed in such manner as the legislature of each state shall direct, to meet in Congress on the first Monday in November, in every year, with a power reserved to each state, to recal its delegates, or any of them, at any time within the year, and to send others in their stead, for the remainder of the Year.

No state shall be represented in Congress by less than two, nor by more than seven Members; and no person shall be capable of being a delegate for more than three years in any term of six years; nor shall any person, being a delegate, be capable of holding any office under the united states, for which he, or another for his benefit receives any salary, fees or emolument of any kind.

Each state shall maintain its own delegates in a meeting of the states, and while they act as members of the committee of the states.

In determining questions in the united states, in Congress assembled, each state shall have one vote.

Freedom of speech and debate in Congress shall not be impeached or questioned in any Court, or place out of Congress, and the members of congress shall be protected in their persons from arrests and imprisonments, during the time of their going to and from, and attendance on congress, except for treason, felony, or breach of the peace.

Article VI. No state without the Consent of the united states in congress assembled, shall send any embassy to, or receive any embassy from, or enter into any conference, agreement, alliance or treaty with any King prince or state; nor shall any person holding any office of profit or trust under the united states, or any of them, accept of any present, emolument, office or title of any kind whatever from any king, prince or foreign state; nor shall the united states in congress assembled, or any of them, grant any title of nobility.

No two or more states shall enter into any treaty, confederation or alliance whatever between them, without the consent of the united states in congress assembled, specifying accurately the purposes for which the same is to be entered into, and how long it shall continue.

No state shall lay any imposts or duties, which may interfere with any stipulations in treaties, entered into by the united states in congress assembled, with any king, prince or state, in pursuance of any treaties already proposed by congress, to the courts of France and Spain.

No vessels of war shall be kept up in time of peace by any state, except such number only, as shall be deemed necessary by the united states in congress assembled, for the defence of such state, or its trade; nor shall any body of forces be kept up by any state, in time of peace, except such number only, as in the judgment of the united states, in congress assembled, shall be deemed requisite to garrison the forts necessary for the defence of such state; but every state shall always keep up a well regulated and disciplined militia, sufficiently armed and accoutred, and shall provide and constantly have ready for use, in public stores, a due number of field pieces and tents, and a proper quantity of arms, ammunition and camp equipage.

No state shall engage in any war without the consent of the united states in congress assembled, unless such state be actually invaded by enemies, or shall have received certain advice of a resolution being formed by some nation of Indians to invade such state, and the danger is so imminent as not to admit of a delay, till the united states in congress assembled can be consulted: nor shall any state grant commissions to any ships or vessels of war, nor letters of marque or reprisal, except it be after a declaration of war by the united states in congress assembled, and then only against the kingdom or state and the subjects thereof, against which war has been so declared, and under such regulations as shall be established by the united states in congress assembled, unless such state be infested by pirates, in which case vessels of war may be fitted out for that occasion, and kept so long as the danger shall continue, or until the united states in congress assembled shall determine otherwise.

Article VII. When land-forces are raised by any state for the common defence, all officers of or under the rank of colonel, shall be appointed by the legislature of each state respectively by whom such forces shall be raised, or in such manner as such state shall direct, and all vacancies shall be filled up by the state which first made the appointment.

Article VIII. All charges of war, and all other expences that shall be incurred for the common defence or general welfare, and allowed by the united states in congress assembled, shall be defrayed out of a common treasury, which shall be supplied by the several states, in proportion to the value of all land within each state, granted to or surveyed for any Person, as such land and the buildings and improvements thereon shall be estimated according to such mode as the united states in congress assembled, shall from time to time direct and appoint. The taxes for paying that proportion shall be laid and levied by the authority and direction of the legislatures of the several states within the time agreed upon by the united states in congress assembled.

Article IX.   The united states in congress assembled, shall have the sole and exclusive right and power of determining on peace and war, except in the cases mentioned in the sixth article—of sending and receiving ambassadors—entering into treaties and alliances, provided that no treaty of commerce shall be made whereby the legislative power of the respective states shall be restrained from imposing such imposts and duties on foreigners, as their own people are subjected to, or from prohibiting the exportation or importation of any species of goods or commodities whatsoever—of establishing rules for deciding in all cases, what captures on land or water shall be legal, and in what manner prizes taken by land or naval forces in the service of the united states shall be divided or appropriated—of granting letters of marque and reprisal in times of peace—appointing courts for the trial of piracies and felonies committed on the high seas and establishing courts for receiving and determining finally appeals in all cases of captures, provided that no member of congress shall be appointed a judge of any of the said courts.

The united states in congress assembled shall also be the last resort on appeal in all disputes and differences now subsisting or that hereafter may arise between two or more states concerning boundary, jurisdiction or any other cause whatever; which authority shall always be exercised in the manner following. Whenever the legislative or executive authority or lawful agent of any state in controversy with another shall present a petition to congress stating the matter in question and praying for a hearing, notice thereof shall be given by order of congress to the legislative or executive authority of the other state in controversy, and a day assigned for the appearance of the parties by their lawful agents, who shall then be directed to appoint by joint consent, commissioners or judges to constitute a court for hearing and determining the matter in question: but if they cannot agree, congress shall name three persons out of each of the united states, and from the list of such persons each party shall alternately strike out one, the petitioners beginning, until the number shall be reduced to thirteen; and from that number not less than seven, nor more than nine names as congress shall direct, shall in the presence of congress be drawn out by lot, and the persons whose names shall be so drawn or any five of them, shall be commissioners or judges, to hear and finally determine the controversy, so always as a major part of the judges who shall hear the cause shall agree in the determination: and if either party shall neglect to attend at the day appointed, without shewing reasons, which congress shall judge suffi-cient, or being present shall refuse to strike, the congress shall proceed to nominate three persons out of each state, and the secretary of congress shall strike in behalf of such party absent or refusing; and the judgment and sentence of the court to be appointed, in the manner before prescribed, shall be final and conclusive; and if any of the parties shall refuse to submit to the authority of such court, or to appear or defend their claim or cause, the court shall nevertheless proceed to pronounce sentence, or judgment, which shall in like manner be final and decisive, the judgment or sentence and other proceedings being in either case transmitted to congress, and lodged among the acts of congress for the security of the parties concerned: provided that every commissioner, before he sits in judgment, shall take an oath to be administered by one of the judges of the supreme or superior court of the state, where the cause shall be tried, "well and truly to hear and determine the matter in question, according to the best of his judgment, without favour, affection or hope ofreward:" provided also that no state shall be deprived of territory for the benefit of the united states.

All controversies concerning the private right of soil claimed under different grants of two or more states, whose jurisdictions as they may respect such lands, and the states which passed such grants are adjusted, the said grants or either of them being at the same time claimed to have originated antecedent to such settlement of jurisdiction, shall on the petition of either party to the congress of the united states, be finally determined as near as maybe in the same manner as is before prescribed for deciding disputes respecting territorial jurisdiction between different states.

The united states in congress assembled shall also have the sole and exclusive right and power of regulating the alloy and value of coin struck by their own authority, or by that of the respective states—fixing the standard of weights and measures throughout the united states—regulating the trade and managing all affairs with the Indians, not members of any of the states, provided that the legislative right of any state within its own limits be not infringed or violated—establishing and regulating post-offices from one state to another, throughout all the united states, and exacting such postage on the papers passing thro' the same as may be requisite to defray the expences of the said office—appointing all officers of the land forces, in the service of the united states, excepting regimental officers—appointing all the officers of the naval forces, and commissioning all officers whatever in the service of the united states—making rules for the government and regulation of the said land and naval forces, and directing their operations.

The united states in congress assembled shall have authority to appoint a committee, to sit in the recess of congress, to be denominated "A Committee of the States," and to consist of one delegate from each state; and to appoint such other committees and civil officers as may be necessary for managing the general affairs of the united states under their direction—to appoint one of their number to preside, provided that no person be allowed to serve in the office of president more than one year in any term of three years; to ascertain the necessary sums of Money to be raised for the service of the united states, and to appropriate and apply the same for defraying the public expences—to borrow money, or emit bills on the credit of the united states, transmitting every half year to the respective states an account of the sums of money so borrowed or emitted,—to build and equip a navy—to agree upon the number of land forces, and to make requisitions from each state for its quota, in proportion to the number of white inhabitants in such state; which requisition shall be binding, and thereupon the legislature of each state shall appoint the regimental officers, raise the men and cloath, arm and equip them in a soldier like manner, at the expence of the united states, and the officers and men so cloathed, armed and equipped shall march to the place appointed, and within the time agreed on by the united states in congress assembled: But if the united states in congress assembled shall, on consideration of circumstances judge proper that any state should not raise men, or should raise a smaller number than its quota, and that any other state should raise a greater number of men than the quota thereof, such extra number shall be raised, officered, cloathed, armed and equipped in the same manner as the quota of such state, unless the legislature of such state shall judge that such extra number cannot be safely spared out of the same, in which case they shall raise officer, cloath, arm and equip as many of such extra number as they judge can be safely spared. And the officers and men so cloathed, armed and equipped, shall march to the place appointed, and within the time agreed on by the united states in congress assembled.

The united states in congress assembled shall never engage in a war, nor grant letters of marque and reprisal in time of peace, nor enter into any treaties or alliances, nor coin money, nor regulate the value thereof, nor ascertain the sums and expences necessary for the defence and welfare of the united states, or any of them, nor emit bills, nor borrow money on the credit of the united states, nor appropriate money, nor agree upon the number of vessels of war, to be built or purchased, or the number of land or sea forces to be raised, nor appoint a commander in chief of the army or navy, unless nine states assent to the same: nor shall a question on any other point, except for adjourning from day to day be determined, unless by the votes of a majority of the united states in congress assembled.

The congress of the united states shall have power to adjourn to any time within the year, and to any place within the united states, so that no period of adjournment be for a longer duration than the space of six Months, and shall publish the Journal of their proceedings monthly, except such parts thereof relating to treaties, alliances or military operations, as in their judgment require secresy; and the yeas and nays of the delegates of each state on any question shall be entered on the Journal, when it is desired by any delegate; and the delegates of a state, or any of them, at his or their request shall be furnished with a transcript of the said Journal, except such parts as are above excepted, to lay before the legislatures of the several states.

Article X. The committee of the states, or any nine of them, shall be authorized to execute, in the recess of congress, such of the powers of congress as the united states in congress assembled, by the consent of nine states, shall from time to time think expedient to vest them with; provided that no power be delegated to the said committee, for the exercise of which, by the articles of confederation, the voice of nine states in the congress of the united states assembled is requisite.

Article XI. Canada acceding to this confederation, and joining in the measures of the united states, shall be admitted into, and entitled to all the advantages of this union: but no other colony shall be admitted into the same, unless such admission be agreed to by nine states.

Article XII. All bills of credit emitted, monies borrowed and debts contracted by, or under the authority of congress, before the assembling of the united states, in pursuance of the present confederation, shall be deemed and considered as a charge against the united states, for payment and satisfaction whereof the said united states, and the public faith are hereby solemnly pledged.

Article XIII. Every state shall abide by the determinations of the united states in congress assembled, on all questions which by this confederation are submitted to them. And the Articles of this confederation shall be inviolably observed by every state, and the union shall be perpetual; nor shall any alteration at any time hereafter be made in any of them; unless such alteration be agreed to in a congress of the united states, and be afterwards confirmed by the legislatures of every state.

And Whereas it hath pleased the Great Governor of the World to incline the hearts of the legislatures we respectively represent in congress, to approve of, and to authorize us to ratify the said articles of confederation and perpetual union. Know Ye that we the undersigned delegates, by virtue of the power and authority to us given for that purpose, do by these presents, in the name and in behalf of our respective constituents, fully and entirely ratify and confirm each and every of the said articles of confederation and perpetual union, and all and singular the matters and things therein contained: And we do further solemnly plight and engage the faith of our respective constituents, that they shall abide by the determinations of the united states in congress assembled, on all questions, which by the said confederation are submitted to them. And that the articles thereof shall be inviolably observed by the states we respectively represent, and that the union shall be perpetual. In Witness whereof we have hereunto set our hands in Congress. Done at Philadelphia in the state of Pennsylvania the ninth Day of July in the Year of our Lord one Thousand seven Hundred and Seventy-eight, and in the third year of the independence of America.

J. THE CONSTITUTION, OR FRAME OF GOVERNMENT, FOR THE COMMONWEALTH OF MASSACHUSETTS

1780

Preamble.

THE end of the institution, maintenance and administration of government, is to secure the existence of the body politick; to protect it; and to furnish the individuals who compose it, with the power of enjoying, in safety and tranquillity, their natural rights, and the blessings of life: And whenever these great objects are not obtained, the people have a right to alter the government, and to take measures necessary for their safety, prosperity and happiness.

The body politick is formed by a voluntary association of individuals: It is a social compact, by which the whole people covenants with each citizen, and each citizen with the whole people, that all shall be governed by certain laws, for the common good. It is the duty of the people, therefore, in framing a Constitution of Government, to provide for an equitable mode of making laws, as well as for an impartial interpretation, and a faithful execution of them; that every man may, at all times, find his security in them.

WE, therefore, the People of *Massachusetts*, acknowledging with grateful hearts, the goodness of the Great Legislature of the Universe, in affording us, in the course of His Providence, an opportunity, deliberately and peaceably, without fraud, violence or surprize, of entering into an original, explicit, and solemn compact with each other; and of forming a new Constitution of Civil Government, for ourselves and posterity; and devoutly imploring His direction in so interesting a design, DO agree upon, ordain and establish, the following *Declaration of Rights, and Frame of Government*, as the CONSTITUTION of the COMMONWEALTH of MASSACHUSETTS.

PART I.

A Declaration of the Rights of the Inhabitants of the Commonwealth of Massachusetts.

ARTICLE

I. ALL men are born free and equal, and have certain natural, essential and unalienable rights; among which may be reckoned the right of enjoying and defending their lives and liberties; that of acquiring, possessing, and protecting property; in fine, that of seeking and obtaining their safety and happiness.

II. It is the right as well as the duty of all men in society, publickly, and at stated seasons, to worship the SUPREME BEING, the Great

Creator and Preserver of the Universe. And no subject shall be hurt, molested, or restrained, in his person, liberty, or estate, for worshipping GOD in the manner and season most agreeable to the dictates of his own conscience; or for his religious profession or sentiments; provided he doth not disturb the publick peace, or obstruct others in their religious worship.

III. As the happiness of a people, and the good order and preservation of civil government, essentially depend upon piety, religion and morality, and as these cannot be generally dissused through a community, but by the institution of the publick worship of GOD, and of publick instructions in piety, religion and morality. Therefore, to promote their happiness, and to secure the good order and preservation of their government, the people of this Commonwealth, have a right to invest their legislature with power to authorize and require, and the legislature shall, from time to time, authorize and require, the several towns, parishes, precincts, and other bodies politick, or religious societies, to make suitable provision, at their own expence, for the institution of the publick worship of GOD, and for the support and maintenance of publick protestant teachers of piety, religion and morality, in all cases where such provision shall not be made voluntarily.

And the people of this commonwealth have also a right to, and do, invest their legislature with authority to enjoin upon all the subjects, an attendance upon the instructions of the publick teachers aforesaid, at stated times and seasons, if there be any on whose instructions they can conscientiously and conveniently attend.

Provided notwithstanding, that the several towns, parishes, precincts, and other bodies politick, or religious societies, shall, at all times, have the exclusive right of electing their publick teachers, and of contracting with them for their support and maintenance.

And all monies paid by the subject to the support of the publick worship, and of the publick teachers aforesaid, shall, if he require it, be uniformly applied to the support of the publick teacher or teachers of his own religious sect or denomination, provided there be any on whose instructions he attends; otherwise it may be paid towards the support of the teacher or teachers of the parish or precinct in which the said monies are raised.

And every denomination of christians, demeaning themselves peaceably, and as good subjects of the Commonwealth, shall be equally under the protection of the law: And no subordination of any one sect or denomination to another shall ever be established by law.

IV. The people of this Commonwealth, have the sole and exclusive right of governing themselves, as a free, sovereign, and independent state; and do, and forever hereafter shall, exercise and enjoy every power, jurisdiction and right, which is not, or may not hereafter, be by them expressly delegated to the United States of America, in Congress assembled.

V. All power residing originally in the people, and being derived from them, the several magistrates and officers of government, vested with authority, whether legislative, executive, or judicial, are their substitutes and agents, and are at all times accountable to them.

VI. No man, nor corporation, or association of men have any other title to obtain advantages, or particular and exclusive privileges, distinct from those of the community, than what arises from the consideration of services rendered to the publick; and this title being in nature neither hereditary, nor transmissible to children, or descendants, or relations by blood, the idea of a man born a magistrate, lawgiver, or judge, is absurd and unnatural.

VII. Government is instituted for the common good; for the protection, sasety, prosperity and happiness of the people; and not for the profit, honour, or private interest of any one man, family, or class of men: Therefore the people alone have an incontestible, unalienable, and indefeasible right to institute government; and to reform, alter, or totally change the same, when their protection, safety, prosperity and happiness require it.

VIII. In order to prevent those who are vested with authority, from becoming oppressors, the people have a right, at such periods, and in such manner as they shall establish by their frame of government, to cause their publick officers to return to private life; and to fill up vacant places by certain and regular elections and appointments.

IX. All elections ought to be free, and all the inhabitants of this Commonwealth, having such qualifications as they shall establish by their frame of government, have an equal right to elect officers, and to be elected, for publick employments.

X. Each individual of the society, has a right to be protected by it, in the enjoyment of his life, liberty and property, according to standing laws. He is obliged consequently, to contribute his share to the expence of this protection; to give his personal service, or an equivalent, when necessary: But no part of the property of any individual, can, with justice, be taken from him, or applied to publick uses, without his own consent, or that of the representative body of the people: In fine, the people of this Commonwealth, are not controulable by any other laws, than those to which their constitutional representative body have given their consent. And whenever the publick exigences require, that the property of any individual should be appropriated to publick uses, he shall receive a reasonable compensation therefor.

XI. Every subject of the Commonwealth, ought to find a certain remedy, by having recourse to the laws for all injuries or wrongs which he may receive in his person, property, or character. He ought to obtain right and justice freely, and without being obliged to purchase it;

completely, and without any denial; promptly and without delay; conformably to the laws.

XII. No subject shall be held to answer for any crime or offence until the same is fully and plainly, substantially and formally, described to him; or be compelled to accuse, or furnish evidence against himself. And every subject shall have a right to produce all proofs, that may be favourable to him; to meet the witnesses against him, face to face, and to be fully heard in his defence by himself, or his counsel, at his election. And no subject shall be arrested, imprisoned, despoiled, or deprived of his property, immunities, or privileges, put out of the protection of the law, exiled, or deprived of his life, liberty, or estate, but by the judgment of his peers, or the law of the land.

And the legislature shall not make any law, that shall subject any person to a capital or infamous punishment, excepting for the government of the army and navy, without trial by jury.

XIII. In criminal prosecutions, the verification of facts in the vicinity where they happen, is one of the greatest securities of the life, liberty and property of the citizen.

XIV. Every subject has a right to be secure from all unreasonable searches and seizures, of his person, his houses, his papers, and all his possessions. All warrants, therefore, are contrary to this right, if the cause or foundation of them be not previously supported by oath or affirmation; and if the order in the warrant to a civil officer, to make search in suspected places, or to arrest one or more suspected persons, or to seize their property, be not accompanied with a special designation of the persons or objects of search, arrest, or seizure: And no warrant ought to be issued, but in cases, and with the formalities, prescribed by the laws.

XV. In all controversies concerning property, and in all suits between two or more persons, except in cases in which it has heretofore been otherways used and practised, the parties have a right to a trial by a jury; and this method of procedure shall be held sacred, unless in causes arising on the high seas, and such as relate to mariner's wages, the legislature shall hereafter find it necessary to alter it.

XVI. The Liberty of the Press is essential to the security of freedom in a State, it ought not, therefore, to be restrained in this Commonwealth.

XVII. The people have a right to keep and to bear arms for the common defence. And as in time of peace armies are dangerous to liberty, they ought not to be maintained without the consent of the legislature; and the military power shall always be held in an exact subordination to the civil authority, and be governed by it.

XVIII. A frequent recurrence to the fundamental principles of the constitution, and a constant adherence to those of piety, justice, moderation, temperance, industry, and frugality, are absolutely necessary to preserve the advantages of liberty, and to maintain a free government. The people ought consequently, to have a particular attention to all those principles, in the choice of their officers and representatives: And they have a right to require of their lawgivers and magistrates, an exact and constant observance of them, in the formation and execution of the laws necessary for the good administration of the Commonwealth.

XIX.   The people have a right, in an orderly and peaceable manner, to assemble to consult upon the common good: Give instructions to their representatives; and to request of the legislative body, by the way of addresses, petitions, or remonstrances, redress of the wrongs done them, and of the grievances they suffer.

XX.   The power of suspending the laws, or the execution of the laws, ought never to be exercised but by the legislature, or by authority derived from it, to be exercised in such particular cases only as the legislature shall expressly provide for.

XXI.   The freedom of deliberation, speech and debate, in either house of the legislature, is so essential to the rights of the people, that it cannot be the foundation of any accusation or prosecution, action, or complaint, in any other court or place whatsoever.

XXII.   The legislature ought frequently to assemble for the redress of grievances, for correcting, strengthening, and confirming the laws, and for making new laws, as the common good may require.

XXIII.   No subsidy, charge, tax, impost, or duties, ought to be established, taxed, laid, or levied, under any pretext whatsoever, without the consent of the people or their representatives in the legislature.

XXIV.   Laws made to punish for actions done before the existence of such laws, and which have not been declared crimes by preceding laws, are unjust, oppressive and inconsistent with the fundamental principles of a free government.

XXV.   No subject ought, in any case, or in any time to be declared guilty of treason or felony by the legislature.

XXVI.   No magistrate or court of law, shall demand excessive bail or sureties, impose excessive fines, or inflict cruel or unusual punishments.

XXVII.   In time of peace no soldier ought to be quartered in any house without the consent of the owner; and in time of war such quarters ought not to be made but by the civil magistrate, in a manner ordained by the legislature.

XXVIII.   No person can in any case be subjected to law martial, or to any penalties or pains, by virtue of that law, except those employed in the army or navy, and except the militia in actual service, but by authority of the legislature.

XXIX. It is essential to the preservation of the rights of every individual, his life, property and character, that there be an impartial interpretation of the laws, and administration of justice. It is the right of every citizen to be tried by judges, as free impartial and independent as the lot of humanity will admit. It is therefore not only the best policy, but for the security of the rights of the people, and of every citizen, that the Judges or the Supreme Judicial Court should hold their office as long as they behave themselves well; and that they should have honourable salaries ascertained and established by standing laws.

XXX. In the government of this Commonwealth, the legislative department shall never exercise the executive and judicial powers, or either of them: The executive shall never exercise the legislative and judicial powers, or either of them: The judicial shall never exercise the legislative and executive powers, or either of them: To the end it may be a government of laws and not of men.

PART II.

Frame of Government.

THE people inhabiting the territory formerly called the Province of *Massachusetts. Bay*, do hereby solemnly and mutually agree with each other, to form themselves into a free, sovereign, and independent body politick, by the name of THE COMMONWEALTH of MASSACHUSETTS.

CHAPTER I.

The LEGISLATIVE POWER.

SECT. I. The General Court.

ARTICLE

I. THE department of legislation shall be formed by two branches, *a Senate, and House of Representatives*: Each of which shall have a negative on the other.

The legislative body shall assemble every year on the last Wednesday in May, and at such other times as they shall judge necessary; and shall dissolve and be dissolved on the day next preceding the said last Wednesday in May; and shall be stiled, THE GENERAL COURT *of* MASSACHUSETTS.

II. No bill or resolve of the Senate or House of Representatives shall become a law, and have force as such, until it shall have been laid before the Governour for his revisal: And if he upon such revision, approve thereof, he shall signify his approbation by signing the same: But if he have any objection to the passing of such bill or resolve, he shall return the same, together with his objections thereto, in writing, to the Senate or House of Representatives, in which soever the same shall have originated; who shall enter the objections sent down by the Governour, at large, on their records, and proceed to reconsider the said bill or resolve: But if after such reconsideration, two thirds of the said Senate or House of Representatives, shall notwithstanding the said objections, agree to pass the same, it shall, together with the objections, be sent to the other branch of the legislature, where it shall also be reconsidered, and if approved by two thirds of the members present, it shall have the force of a law: But in all such cases, the votes of both houses shall be determined by yeas and nays; and the names of the persons voting for, or against, the said bill or resolve, shall be entered upon the publick records of the Commonwealth.

And in order to prevent unnecessary delays, if any bill or resolve shall not be returned by the Governour within five days after it shall have been presented, the same shall have the force of a law.

III.   The General Court shall forever have full power and authority to erect and constitute judicatories and courts of record, or other courts, to be held in the name of the Commonwealth, for the hearing, trying, and determining of all manner of crimes, offences, pleas, processes, plaints, actions, matters, causes and things, whatsoever, arising or happening within the Commonwealth, or between or concerning persons inhabiting, or residing, or brought within the same; whether the same be criminal or civil, or whether the said crimes be capital or not capital, and whether the said pleas be real, personal, or mixt; and for the awarding and making out of execution thereupon: To which courts and judicatories are hereby given and granted full power and authority, from time to time to administer oaths or affirmations, for the better discovery of truth in any matter in controversy or depending before them.

IV.   And further, full power and authority are hereby given and granted to the said, General Court from time to time, to make, ordain, and establish, all manner of wholesome and reasonable orders, laws, statutes, and ordinances, directions and instructions, either with penalties or without, so as the same be not repugnant or contrary to this Constitution, as they shall judge to be for the good and welfare of this Commonwealth, and for the government and ordering thereof, and of the subjects of the same, and for the necessary support and defence of the government thereof; and to name and settle annually, or provide by fixed laws, for the naming and settling all civil officers within the said Commonwealth; the election and constitution of whom are not hereafter in this Form of Government otherwise provided for; and to set forth the several duties, powers, and limits, of the several civil and military officers of this Commonwealth, and the forms of such oaths or affirmations as shall be respectively administered unto them for the execution of their several offices and places, so as the same be not repugnant or contrary to this Constitution; and to impose and levy proportional and reasonable assessments, rates and taxes, upon all the inhabitants of, and persons resident, and estates lying, within the said Commonwealth; and also to impose and levy, reasonable duties and excises, upon any produce, goods, wares, merchandize, and commodities whatsoever, brought into, produced, manufactured, or being within the same; to be issued and disposed of by warrant, under the hand of the Governour of this Commonwealth for the time being, with the advice and consent of the Council, for the publick service, in the necessary defence and support of the government of the said Commonwealth, and the protection and preservation of the subjects thereof, according to such acts as are or shall be in force within the same.

And while the publick charges of government, or any part thereof, shall be assessed on polls and estates, in the manner that has hitherto been practised; in order that such assessments may be made with equality, there shall be a valuation of estates within the Commonwealth taken anew once in every ten years at the least, and as much oftener as the General Court shall order.

SECT. II. Senate.

ARTICLE

I. THERE shall be annually elected by the freeholders and other inhabitants of this Commonwealth, qualified as in this Constitution is provided, Forty persons to be Counsellors and Senators for the year ensuing their election; to be chosen by the inhabitants of the districts, into which the commonwealth may from time to time be divided by the General Court for that purpose: And the General Court assigning the numbers to be elected by the respective districts, shall govern themselves by the proportion of the publick taxes paid by the said districts; and timely make known to the inhabitants of the Commonwealth, the limits of each district, and the number of Counsellors and Senators to be chosen therein; provided that the number of such districts shall be never less than thirteen; and that no district be so large as to entitle the same to choose more than six Senators.

And the several counties in this Commonwealth shall, until the General Court shall determine it necessary to alter the said districts, be districts for the choice of Counsellors and Senators (except that the counties of Duke's County and Nantucket shall form one district for that purpose) and shall elect the following number for Counsellors and Senators, viz. *Suffolk* Six, *Essex* Six, *Middlesex* Five, *Hampshire* Four, *Plymouth* Three, *Barnstable* One, *Bristol* Three, *York* Two, *Duke's County* and *Nantucket* One, *Worcester* Five, *Cumberland* One, *Lincoln* One, *Berkshire* Two.

II. The Senate shall be the first branch of the legislature; and the Senators shall be chosen in the following manner, viz. There shall be a meeting on the first Monday in April annually, forever, of the inhabitants of each town in the federal counties of this Commonwealth; to be called by the Selectmen, and warned in due course of law, at least seven days before the first Monday in April, for the purpose of electing persons to be Senators and Counsellors: And at such meetings every male inhabitant of twenty one years of age and upwards, having a freehold estate within the Commonwealth, of the annual income of three pounds, or any estate of the value of sixty pounds, shall have a right to give in his vote for Senators for the district of which he is an inhabitant. And to remove all doubts concerning the meaning of the word "Inhabitant" in this Constitution, every person shall be considered as an inhabitant, for the purpose of electing and being elected into any office, or place within this State, in that town, district or plantation, where he dwelleth, or hath his home.

The Selectman of the several towns shall preside at such meetings impartially; and shall receive the votes of all the inhabitants of such towns present and qualified to vote for Senators, and shall sort and count them in open town meeting, and in presence of the Town Clerk, who shall make a fair record, in presence of the Selectmen, and in open town meeting, of the name of every person voted for, and of the number of votes against his name; and a fair copy of this record shall be attested by the Selectmen and the Town Clerk, and shall be sealed up, directed to the Secretary of the Commonwealth for the time being, with a super-scription, expressing the purport of the contents thereof, and delivered by the Town Clerk of such town, to the Sheriff of the county in which such town lies, thirty days at least before the last Wednesday in *May* annually; or it shall be delivered into the Secretary's office seventeen days at least before the said last Wednesday in *May*; and the Sheriff of each county shall deliver all such certificates by him received into the Secretary's office seventeen days before the said last Wednesday in *May*.

And the inhabitants of plantations unincorporated, qualified as this Constitution provides, who are, or shall be, empowered and required to assess taxes upon themselves toward the support of government, shall have the same privilege of voting for Counsellors and Senators in the plantations where they reside, as town inhabitants have in their respective towns; and the plantation meetings for that purpose shall be held annually on the same first Monday in *April*, at such place in the plantations respectively, as the Assessors thereof shall direct; which Assessors shall have like authority for notifying the electors, collecting and returning the votes, as the Selectmen and Town Clerks have in their several towns, by this Constitution. And all other persons living in places unincorporated (qualified as aforesaid) who shall be assessed to the support of government by the Assessors of an adjacent town, shall have the privilege of giving in their votes for Counsellors and Senators, in the town where they shall be assessed, and be notified of the place of meeting by the Selectmen of the town where they shall be assessed, for that purpose accordingly.

III. And that there may be a due convention of Senators on the last Wednesday in *May* annually, the Governour with five of the Council, for the time being, shall, as soon as may be, examine the returned copies of such records; and fourteen days before the said day he shall issue his summons to such persons as shall appear to be chosen by a majority of voters, to attend on that day, and take their seats accordingly: Provided nevertheless, that for the first year the said returned copies shall be examined by the President and five of the Council of the former Constitution of Government; and the said President shall, in like manner, issue his summons to the person so elected, that they may take their seats as aforesaid.

IV. The Senate shall be the final judge of the elections, returns and qualifications of their own members, as pointed out in the Constitution; and shall on the said last Wednesday in *May* annually, determine and declare who are elected by each district, to be Senators by a majority of votes: And in case there shall not appear to be the full number of Senators returned, elected by a majority of votes, for any district, the deficiency shall be supplied in the following manner, viz. The members of the House of Representatives, and such Senators as shall be declared elected, shall take the names of such persons as shall be found to have the highest number of votes in such district, and not elected, amounting to twice the number of Senators wanting, if there be so many voted for; and out of these, shall elect by ballot a number of Senators sufficient to fill up the vacancies in such district; and in this manner all such vacancies shall be filled up in every district of the Commonwealth; and in like manner all vacancies in the Senate, arising by death, removal out of the State, or otherwise, shall be supplied as soon as may be, after such vacancies shall happen.

V. Provided nevertheless, that no person shall be capable of being elected as a Senator, who is not seized in his own right of a freehold within this Commonwealth, of the value of three hundred pounds at least, or possessed of personal estate to the value of six hundred pounds at least, or of both to the amount of the same sum, and who has not been an inhabitant of this Commonwealth for the space of five years immediately preceding his election, and at the time of his election, he shall be an inhabitant in the district for which he shall be chosen.

VI. The Senate shall have power to adjourn themselves, provided such adjournments do not exceed two days at a time.

VII. The Senate shall choose its own President, appoint its own officers and determine its own rules of proceedings.

VIII. The Senate shall be a court with full authority to hear and determine all impeachments made by the House of Representatives, against any officer or officers of the Commonwealth, for misconduct and maladministration in their offices, but previous to the trial of every impeachment, the members of the Senate shall respectively be sworn, truly and impartially to try and determine the charge in question, according to evidence. Their judgment, however, shall not extend further than to removal from office, and disqualification to hold or enjoy any place of honour, trust or profit, under this Commonwealth: But the party so convicted, shall be nevertheless, liable to indictment, trial, judgment, and punishment, according to the laws of the land.

IX.   Not less than sixteen members of the Senate shall constitute a quorum for doing business.

SECT. III. House of Representatives.
ARTICLE

I.   THERE shall be in the Legislature of this Commonwealth, a representation of the people, annually elected, and founded upon the principle of equality.

II.   And in order to provide for a representation of the citizens of this Commonwealth, founded upon the principle of equality, every corporate town containing one hundred and fifty rateable polls, may elect one Representative: Every corporate town, containing three hundred and seventy five rateable polls, may elect two Representatives: Every corporate town, containing six hundred rateable polls, may elect three Representatives; and proceeding in that manner, making two hundred and twenty five rateable polls the mean increasing number for every additional Representative.

Provided nevertheless, that each town now incorporated, not having one hundred and fifty rateable polls, may elect one Representative: But no place shall hereafter be incorporated with the privilege of electing a Representative, unless there are within the same one hundred and fifty rateable polls.

And the House of Representatives shall have power, from time to time, to impose fines upon such towns as shall neglect to choose and return members to the same agree to this Constitution.

The expences of travelling to the General Assembly, and returning home, on every session and no more, shall be paid by the government, out of the publick treasury, to every member who shall attend as seasonably as he can, in the judgment of the House, and does not depart without leave.

III.   Every member of the House of Representatives shall be chosen by written votes; and for one year at least next preceding his election, shall have been an inhabitant of, and have been seized in his own right of a freehold of the value of one hundred pounds within the town he shall be chosen to represent, or any rateable estate to the value of two hundred pounds; and he shall cease to represent the said town immediately on his ceasing to be qualified as aforesaid.

IV.   Every male person, being twenty one years of age, and resident in any particular town in this Commonwealth for the space of one year next preceding, having a freehold estate within the same town, of the annual income of three pounds, or any estate of the value of sixty pounds, shall have a right to vote in the choice of a Representative, or Representatives for the said town.

V. The members of the House of Representatives shall be chosen annually in the month of *May*, ten days at least before the last Wednesday of that month.

VI. The House of Representatives shall be the Grand Inquest of this Commonwealth; and all impeachments made by them, shall be heard and tried by the Senate.

VII. All money bills shall originate in the House of Representatives; but the Senate may propose or concur with amendments, as on other bills.

VIII. The House of Representatives shall have power to adjourn themselves, provided such adjournment shall not exceed two days at a time.

IX. Not less than sixty members of the House of Representatives, shall constitute a quorum for doing business.

X. The House of Representatives shall be the judge of the returns, elections and qualifications of its own members as pointed out in the Constitution; shall chuse their own Speaker, appoint their own officers, and settle the rules and orders of proceeding in their own House: They shall have authority to punish by imprisonment, every person, not a member, who shall be guilty of disrespect to the House, by any disorderly or contemptuous behaviour in its presence; or who, in the town where the General Court is sitting, and during the time of it sitting, shall threaten harm to the body or estate of any of its members, for any thing said or done in the House; or who shall assault any of them therefor; or who shall assault, or arrest any witness, or other person, ordered to attend the House, in his way in going, or returning; or who shall rescue any person arrested by the order of the House.

And no member of the House of Representatives shall be arrested or held to bail on mean process, during his going unto, returning from, or his attending the General Assembly.

XI. The Senate shall have the same powers in the like cases; and the Governour and Council shall have the same authority to punish in like cases. Provided that no imprisonment on the warrant or order of the Governour, Council, Senate, or House of Representatives, for either of the above described offences, be for a term exceeding thirty days.

And the Senate and House of Representatives may try, and determine, all cases where their rights and privileges are concerned, and which, by the Constitution, they have authority to try and determine, by committees of their own members, or in such, other way as they may respectively think best.

CHAPTER II.
EXECUTIVE POWER.
SECT. I. Governour.
ARTICLE

I. THERE shall be a supreme executive Magistrate, who shall be stiled, THE GOVERNOUR OF THE COMMONWEALTH OF MASSACHUSETTS; and whose title shall be—HIS EXCELLENCY.

II. The Governour shall be chosen annually: And no person shall be eligible to this office, unless at the time of his election, he shall have been an inhabitant of this Commonwealth for seven years next preceding; and unless he shall, at the same time, be seized in his own right, of a freehold within the Commonwealth, of the value of one thousand pounds; and unless he shall declare himself to be of the christian religion.

III. Those persons who shall be qualified to vote for Senators and Representatives, within the several towns of this Commonwealth, shall, at a meeting to be called for that purpose, on the first Monday of *April* annually, give in their votes for a Governour, to the Selectmen, who shall preside at such meetings; and the Town Clerk, in the presence, and with the assistance of the Selectmen, shall, in open town meeting, sort and count the votes, and form a list of the persons voted for, with the number of votes for each person against his name; and shall make a fair record of the same in the town books, and a publick declaration thereof in the said meeting; and shall, in the presence of the inhabitants, seal up copies of the said list, attested by him and the Selectmen, and transmit the same to the Sheriff of the county, thirty days at least before the last Wednesday in *May*; and the Sheriff shall transmit the same to the Secretary's office, seventeen days at least before the said last Wednesday in *May*; or the Selectmen may cause returns of the same to be made to the office of the Secretary of the Commonwealth, seventeen days at least before the said day; and the Secretary shall lay the same before the Senate and House of Representatives, on the last Wednesday in *May*, to be by them examined: And in case of an election by a majority of all the votes returned, the choice shall be by them declared and published: But if no person shall have a majority of votes, the House of Representatives shall, by ballot, elect two out of four persons who had the highest numbers of votes, if so many shall have been voted for; but, if otherwise, out of the number voted for; and make return to the Senate of the two persons so elected; on which, the Senate shall proceed, by ballot, to elect one, who shall be declared Governour.

IV. The Governour shall have authority from time to time, at his discretion, to assemble and call together the Counsellors of this Commonwealth for the time being; and the Governour, with the said Counsellors, or five of them at least, shall, and may, from time to time, hold and keep a Council, for the ordering and directing the affairs of the Commonwealth, agreeably to the Constitution and the laws of the land.

V. The Governour with the advice of Council, shall have full power and authority, during the session of the General Court, to adjourn or prorogue the same to any time the two Houses shall desire; and to dissolve the same on the day next preceding the last Wednesday in *May*; and, in the recess of the said Court, to prorogue the same from time to time, not exceeding ninety days in any one recess; and to call it together sooner than the time to which it may be adjourned or prorogued, if the welfare of the Commonwealth shall require the same: And in case of any infectious distemper prevailing in the place where the said Court is next at any time to convene, or any other cause happening whereby danger may arise to the health or lives of the members from their attendance, he may direct the session to be held at some other the most convenient place within the State.

And the Governour shall dissolve the said General Court on the day next preceding the last Wednesday in *May*.

VI. In cases of disagreement between the two Houses, with regard to the necessity, expediency or time of adjournment, or prorogation, the Governour, with advice of the, Council, shall have a right to adjourn or prorogue the General Court, not exceeding ninety days, as he shall determine the publick good shall require.

VII. The Governour of this Commonwealth for the time being, shall be the commander in chief of the army and navy, and of all the military forces of the State, by sea and land; and shall have full power by himself, or by any commander, or other officer or officers, from time to time, to train, instruct, exercise and govern the militia and navy; and, for the special defence and safety of the Commonwealth, to assemble in martial array, and put in warlike posture, the inhabitants thereof, and to lead and conduct them, and with them, to encounter, repel, resist, expel and pursue, by force of arms, as well by sea as by land, within or without the limits of this Commonwealth, and also to kill, slay and destroy, if necessary, and conquer, by all sitting ways, enterprizes and means whatsoever, all and every such person and persons as shall, at any time hereafter, in a hostile manner attempt or enterprize the destruction, invasion, detriment, or annoyance of this Commonwealth; and to use and exercise, over the army and navy, and over the militia in actual service, the law martial in time of war, or invasion, and also in time of rebellion, declared by the legislature to exist, as occasion shall necessarily require; and to take and surprize, by all ways and means whatsoever, all and every such person or persons, with their ships, arms, ammunition and other goods, as shall, in a hostile manner, invade, or attempt the invading, conquering, or annoying this Commonwealth; and that the Governour be intrusted with all these and other powers, incident to the offices of Captain General and Commander in Chief, and Admiral, to be exercised agreeably to the rules and regulations of the Constitution, and the laws of the land, and not otherwise.

Provided, that the said Governour shall not, at any time hereafter, by virtue of any power by this Constitution granted, or hereafter to be granted to him by the legislature, transport any of the inhabitants of this Commonwealth, or oblige them to march out of the limits of the same, without their free and voluntary consent, or the consent of the General Court; except so far as may be necessary to march or transport them by land or water, for the defence of such part of the State, to which they cannot otherwise conveniently have access.

VIII.   The power of pardoning offences, except such as persons may be convicted of before the Senate by an impeachment of the House, shall be in the Governour, by and with the advice of Council: But no charter of pardon, granted by the Governour, with advice of the Council, before conviction, shall avail the party pleading the same, notwithstanding any general or particular expressions contained therein, descriptive of the offence, or offences intended to be pardoned.

IX.   All judicial officers, the Attorney General, the Solicitor General, all Sheriffs, Coroners, and Registers of Probate, shall be nominated and appointed by the Governour, by and with the advice and consent of the Council; and every suchnomination shall be made by the Governour, and made at least seven days prior to such appointment.

X.   The Captains and Subalterns of the militia, shall be elected by the written votes of the trainband and alarm list of their respective companies, of twenty one years of age and upwards: The field officers of regiments, shall be elected by the written votes of the Captains and Subalterns of their respective regiments: The Brigadiers shall be elected in like manner, by the field officers of their respective brigades: And such officers, so elected, shall be commissioned by the Governour, who shall determine their rank.

The legislature shall, by standing laws, direct the time and manner of convening the electors, and of collecting votes, and of certifying to the Governour the officers elected.

The Major Generals shall be appointed by the Senate and House of Representatives, each having a negative upon the other; and be commissioned by the Governour.

And if the electors of Brigadiers, Field Officers, Captains or Subalterns, shall neglect or refuse to make such elections, after being duly notified, according to the laws for the time being, then the Governour, with advice of Council, shall appoint suitable persons to fill such offices.

And no officer duly commissioned to command in the militia, shall be removed from his office, but by the address of both Houses to the Governour, or by fair trial in court-martial, pursuant to the laws of the Commonwealth for the time being.

The commanding officers of regiments shall appoint their Adjutants, and Quartermasters; the Brigadiers their Brigade Majors; and the Major Generals their Aids; and the Governour shall appoint the Adjutant General.

The Governour with advice of Council, shall appoint all officers of the continental army, whom by the confederation of the United States it is provided that this Commonwealth shall appoint—as also all officers of forts and garrisons. The divisions of the militia into brigades, regiments and companies, made in pursuance of the militia laws now in force, shall be considered as the proper divisions of the militia of this Commonwealth, until the same shall be altered in pursuance of some future law.

XI. No monies shall be issued out of the treasury of this Commonwealth, and disposed of (except such sums as may be appropriated for the redemption of bills of credit, or Treasurer's notes, or for the payment of interest arising thereon) but by warrant under the hand of the Governour for the time being, with the advice and consent of the Council, for the necessary defence and support of the Commonwealth; and for the protection and preservation of the inhabitants thereof, agreeably to the acts and resolves of the General Court.

XII. All publick boards, the Commissary General, all superintending officers of publick magazines and stores, belonging to this Commonwealth, and all commanding officers of forts and garrisons within the same, shall once in every three months, officially, and without requisition, and at other times, when required by the Governour, deliver to him an account of all goods, stores, provisions, ammunition, cannon with their appendages, and small arms with their accoutrements, and of all other publick property whatever under their care respectively; distinguishing the quantity, number, quality and kind of each, as particularly as may be; together with the condition of such forts and garrisons: And the said commanding officer shall exhibit to the Governour, when required by him, true and exact plans of such forts, and of the land and sea, or harbour or harbours adjacent.

And the said boards, and all publick officers, shall communicate to the Governour, as soon as may be after receiving the same, all letters, dispatches, and intelligences of a publick nature, which shall be directed to them respectively.

XIII. As the publick good requires that the Governour should not be under the undue influence of any of the members of the General Court, by a dependance on them for his support—that he should in all cases, act with freedom for the benefit of the publick—that he should not have his attention necessarily diverted from that object to his private concerns—and that he should maintain the dignity of the Commonwealth in the character of its chief magistrate—it is necessary that he should have an honourable stated salary, of a fixed and permanent value, amply sufficient for those purposes, and established by standing laws:

And it shall be among the first acts of the General Court, after the commencement of this Constitution, to establish such salary by law accordingly.

Permanent and honourable salaries shall also be establifhed by law for the Justices of the supreme judicial court.

And if it shall be found that any of the salaries aforesaid, so established, are insufficient, they shall, from time to time, be enlarged as the General Court shall judge proper.

SECT. II.　Lieutenant Governour.

ARTICLE

I.　THERE shall be annually elected a LIEUTENANT GOVERNOUR of the Commonwealth of *Massachusetts,* whose title shall be—HIS HONOUR—and who shall be qualified, in point of religion, property, and residence in the Commonwealth, in the same manner with the Governour: And the day and manner of his election, and the qualifications of the electors, shall be the same as are required in the election of a Governour. The return of the votes for this officer, and the declaration of his election, shall be in the same manner: And if no one person shall be found to have a majority of all the votes returned, the vacancy shall be filled by the Senate and House of Representatives, in the same manner as the Governour is to be elected, in case no one person shall have a majority of the votes of the people to be Governour.

II.　The Governour, and in his absence, the Lieutenant Governour, shall be President of the Council, but shall have no vote in Council: And the Lieutenant Governour shall always be a member of the Council, except when the chair of the Governour shall be vacant.

III.　Whenever the chair of the Governour shall be vacant, by reason of his death, or absence from the Commonwealth, or otherwise, the Lieutenant Governour, for the time being, shall during such vacancy, perform all the duties incumbent upon the Governour, and shall have and exercise all the powers and authorities, which by this Constitution the Governour is vested with, when personally present.

SECT. III.　Council, and the Manner of Settling Elections by the Legislature.

ARTICLE

I.　THERE shall be a COUNCIL for advising the Governour in the executive part of government, to consist of nine persons besides the Lieutenant Governour, whom the Governour for the time being, shall have full power and authority, from time to time, at his discretion, to assemble and call together. And the Governour, with the said Counsellors, or five of them at least, shall and may, from time to time, hold and keep, a Council, for the ordering and directing the affairs of the Commonwealth, according to the laws of the land.

II. Nine Counsellors shall be annually chosen from among the persons returned for Counsellors and Senators, on the last Wednesday in *May*, by the joint ballot of the Senators and Representatives assembled in one room: And in case there shall not be found upon the first choice, the whole number of nine persons, who will accept a seat in the Council, the deficiency shall be made up by the electors aforesaid, from among the people at large; and the number of Senators left, shall constitute the Senate for the year. The seats of the persons thus elected from the Senate, and accepting the trust, shall be vacated in the Senate.

III. The Counsellors, in the civil arrangements of the Commonwealth, shall have rank next after the Lieutenant Governour.

IV. Not more than two Counsellors shall be chosen out of any one district of this Commonwealth.

V. The resolutions and advice of the Council, shall be recorded in a register, and signed by the members present; and this record may be called for, at any time, by either House of the Legislature; and any member of the Council, may insert his opinion contrary to the resolution of the majority.

VI. Whenever the offices of the Governour and Lieutenant Governour shall be vacant, by reason of death, absence, or otherwise, then the Council or the major part of them, shall, during such vacancy, have full power and authority, to do, and execute, all and every such acts, matters and things, as the Governour, or the Lieutenant Governour, might or could, by virtue of this Constitution, do or execute, if they, or either of them, were personally present.

VII. And whereas the elections appointed to be made by this Constitution, on the last Wednesday in *May* annually, by the two Houses of the Legislature, may not be completed on that day, the said elections may be adjourned from day to day, until the same shall be completed. And the order of elections shall be as follows: The vacancies in the Senate, if any, shall first be filled up; the Governour and Lieutenant Governour, shall then be elected, provided there shall be no choice of them by the people: And afterwards the two Houses shall proceed to the election of the Council.

Sect. IV. Secretary, Treasurer, Commissary, &c.

ARTICLE

I. THE Secretary, Treasurer, and Receiver General, and the Commissary General, Notaries Publick, and Naval Officers, shall be chosen annually, by joint ballot of the Senato: and Representatives in one room. And that the citizens of this Commonwealth, may be assured, from time to time, that the monies remaining in the publick treasury, upon the settlement and liquidation of the publick accounts, are their property, no man shall be eligible as Treasurer and Receiver General, more than five years successively.

II. The records of the Commonwealth, shall be kept in the office of the Secretary, who may appoint his Deputies, for whose conduct he shall be accountable, and he shall attend the Governour and Council, the Senate and House of Representatives, in person, or by his Deputies, as they shall respectively require.

CHAPTER III.
JUDICIARY POWER.
ARTICLE

I. THE tenure that all commission officers shall by law have in their offices, shall be expressed in their respective commissions. All judicial officers, duly appointed, commissioned and sworn, shall hold their offices during good behaviour, excepting such concerning whom there is different provision made in this Constitution: Provided nevertheless, the Governour, with consent of the Council, may remove them upon the address of both houses of the Legislature.

II. Each branch of the Legislature, as well as the Governour and Council, shall have authority to require the opinions of the Justices of the Supreme Judicial Court, upon important questions of law, and upon solemn occasions.

III. In order that the people may not suffer from the long continuance in place of any Justice of the Peace, who shall fail of discharging the important duties of his office, with ability or fidelity, all commissions of Justices of the Peace, shall expire and become void, in the term of seven years from their respective dates; and upon the expiration of any commission, the same may, if necessary, be renewed, or another person appointed, as shall most conduce to the well being of the Commonwealth.

IV. The Judges of Probate of Wills, and for granting letters of administration, shall hold their courts at such place or places, on fixed days as the convenience of the people shall require. And the Legislature shall, from time to time, hereafter appoint such times and places; until which appointments, the said courts shall be holden at the times and places, which the respective Judges shall direct.

V. All causes of marriage, divorce and alimony, and all appeals from the Judges of Probate, shall be heard and determined by the Governour and Council, until the Legislature shall, by law, make other provision.

CHAPTER IV.
DELEGATES to CONGRESS.

THE Delegates of the Commonwealth, to the Congress of the United States, shall, sometime in the month of *June* annually, be elected by the joint ballot of the Senate and House of Representatives, assembled together in one room; to serve in Congress for one year, to commence on the first Monday in *November* then next ensuing. They shall have commissions under the hand of the Governour, and the great seal of the Commonwealth; but may be recalled at any time within the year, and others chosen and commissioned, in the same manner, in their stead.

CHAPTER V.

The UNIVERSITY at CAMBRIDGE, and ENCOURAGEMENT of LITERATURE: &c.

Sect. I. The University.

ARTICLE

I. WHEREAS our wise and pious ancestors, so early as the year one thousand six hundred and thirty six, laid the foundation of Harvard College, in which University, many persons of great eminence have, by the blessing of GOD, been initiated in those arts and sciences, which qualified them for publick employments both in church and state: And whereas the encouragement of arts and sciences, and all good literature, tends to the honour of GOD, the advantage of the christian religion, and the great benefit of this and the other United States of *America*—it is declared, That the PRESIDENT and FELLOWS of HARVARD COLLEGE, in their corporate capacity, and their successours in that capacity, their officers and servants, shall have, hold, use, exercise and enjoy, all the powers, authorities, rights, liberties, privileges, immunities and franchises, which they now have, or are entitled to have, hold, use, exercise and enjoy: And the same are hereby ratified and confirmed unto them, the said President and Fellows of Harvard College, and to their successours, and to their officers and servants, respectively, forever.

II. And whereas there have been at sundry times, by divers persons, gifts, grants, devises of houses, lands, tenements, goods, chattels, legacies and conveyances, heretofore made, either to Harvard College, in *Cambridge*, in *Newengland,* or to the President and Fellows of Harvard College, or to the said College, by some other description, under several charters successively: It is declared, That all the said gifts, grants, devises, legacies and conveyances, are hereby forever confirmed unto the President and Fellows of Harvard College, and to their successours, in the capacity aforesaid, according to the true intent and meaning of the donor or donors, grantor or grantors, devisor or devisors.

III. And whereas by an act of the General Court of the Colony of *Massachusetts Bay,* passed in the year one thousand six hundred and forty two, the Governour and Deputy Governour, for the time being, and all the magistrates of that jurisdiction, were, with the President, and a number of the clergy in the said act described, constituted the Overseers of Harvard College: And it being necessary, in this new Constitution of Government, to ascertain who shall be deemed successours to the said

Governour, Deputy Governour, and Magistrates: IT IS DECLARED, That the Governour, Lieutenant Governour, Council and Senate of this Commonwealth, are, and shall be deemed, their successours; who, with the President of Harvard College, for the time being, together with the Ministers of the congregational churches in the towns of *Cambridge, Watertown, Charlestown, Boston, Roxbury*, and *Dorchester*, mentioned in the said act, shall be, and hereby are, vested with all the powers and authority, belonging, or in any way appertaining, to the Overseers of Harvard College: *Provided*, That nothing herein shall be construed to prevent the Legislature of this Commonwealth, from making such alterations in the government of the said University, as shall be conducive to its advantage, and the interest of the republick of letters, in as full a manner as might have been done by the Legislature of the late Province of *Massachusetts Bay*.

SECT. II.   The Encouragement of Literature, &c.

WISDOM and knowledge, as well as virtue, diffused generally among the body of the people, being necessary for the preservation of their rights and liberties; and as these depend on spreading the opportunities and advantages of education in the various parts of the country, and among the different orders of the people, it shall be the duty of legislatures and magistrates, in all future periods of this Commonwealth, to cherish the interests of literature and the sciences, and all seminaries of them; especially the university at *Cambridge*, publick schools, and grammar schools in the towns; to encourage private societies, and publick institutions, rewards and immunities, for the promotion of agriculture, arts, sciences, commerce, trades, manufactures, and a natural history of the country; to countenance and inculcate the principles of humanity and general benevolence, publick and private charity, industry and frugality, honesty and punctuality in their dealings; sincerity, good humour, and all social affections, and generous sentiments among the people.

CHAPTER VI.

OATHS AND SUBSCRIPTIONS; INCOMPATIBILITY OF, AND EXCLUSION FROM, OFFICES; PECUNIARY QUALIFICATIONS; COMMISSIONS; WRITS; CONFIRMATION OF LAWS; HABEAS CORPUS; THE ENACTING STILE; CONTINUANCE OF OFFICERS; PROVISION FOR A FUTURE REVISAL OF THE CONSTITUTION

ARTICLE

I.   ANY person chosen Governour, Lieutenant Governour, Counsellor, Senator, or Representative, and accepting the trust, shall, before he proceed to execute the duties of his place or office, make and subscribe the following declaration, viz.

"I, A. B. do declare, that I believe the christian religion, and have a firm persuasion of its truth; and that I am seized and possessed, in my

own right, of the property required by the Constitution, as one qualifica-
tion for the office or place to which I am elected."

And the Governour, Lieutenant Governour, and Counsellors, shall make and subscribe the said declaration, in the presence of the two Houses of Assembly; and the Senators and Representatives first elected under this Constitution, before the President and five of the Council of the former Constitution, and forever afterwards before the Governour and Council for the time being.

And every person chosen to either of the places or offices aforesaid, as also any person appointed or commissioned to any judicial, executive, military, or other office under the government, shall, before he enters on the discharge of the business of his place or office, take and subscribe the following declaration, and oaths or affirmations, viz.

"I, A. B. do truly and sincerely acknowledge, profess, testify and declare, that the Commonwealth of Massachusetts, *is, and of right ought to be, a free, sovereign and independent State; and I do swear, that I will bear true faith and allegiance to the said Commonwealth, and that I will defend the same against traiterous conspiracies, and all bestile attempts whatsoever: And that I do renounce and abjure all allegiance, subjection and obedience, to the King, Queen, or Government of* Greatbritain [as the case may be] *and every other foreign power whatsoever: And that no foreign Prince, Person, Prelate, State or Potentate, hath, or ought to have, any jurisdiction, superiority, preeminence, authority, dispensing, or other power, in any matter, civil, ecclesiastical or spiritual, within this Com- monwealth; except the authority and power which is or may be, vested by their Constituents in the Congress of the United States: And I do further testify and declare, that no man, or body of men, bath, or can have, any right to absolve or discharge me from the obligation of this oath, declaration or affirmation; and that I do make this acknowledgment, profession, testimony, declaration, denial, renunciation and abjuration, heartily and truly, according to the common meaning and acceptation of the foregoing words, without any equivocation, mental evasion, or secret reservation whatsoever. So help me GOD."*

"I, A. B. do solemnly swear and affirm, that I will faithfully and impartially discharge and perform all the duties incumbent on me as _____; according to the best of my abilities and understanding, agree- ably to the rules and regulations of the Constitution, and the laws of this Commonwealth. So help me GOD."

Provided always, that when any person chosen or appointed as aforesaid, shall be of the denomination of the people called Quakers, and shall decline taking the said oaths, he shall make his affirmation in the foregoing form, and subscribe the same, omitting the words, *"I do swear," "and abjure," "oath or," "and abjuration,"* in the first oath; and in the second oath, the words *"swear and;"* and in each of them the words *"So help me GOD;"* subjoining instead thereof, *"This I do under the pains and penalties of perjury."*

And the said oaths or affirmations shall be taken and subscribed by the Governour, Lieutenant Governour, and Counsellors, before the President of the Senate, in the presence of the two Houses of Assembly; and by the Senators and Representatives first elected under this Constitution, before the President and five of the Council of the former Constitution; and forever afterwards before the Governour and Council for the time being: And by the residue of the officers aforesaid, before such persons, and in such manner, as from time to time, shall be prescribed by the Legislature.

II.   No Governour, Lieutenant Governour, or Judge of the supreme judicial court, shall hold any other office or place, under the authority of this Commonwealth, except such as by this Constitution they are admitted to hold, saving that the Judges of the said court may hold the offices of Justices of the Peace through the State; nor shall they hold any other place or office, or receive any pension or salary from any other State, or Government, or power whatever.

No person shall be capable of holding or exercising at the same time, more than one of the following offices within this State, viz. Judge of Probate—Sheriff—Register of Probate—or Register of Deeds—and never more than any two offices which are to be held by appointment of the Governour, or the Governour and Council, or the Senate, or the House of Representatives, or by the election of the people of the State at large, or of the people of any county, military offices and the offices of Justices of the Peace excepted, shall be held by one person.

No person holding the office of Judge of the supreme judicial court—Secretary—Attorney General—Solicitor General—Treasurer or Receiver General—Judge of Probate—Commissary General—President, Professor, or Instructor of Harvard College—Sheriff—Clerk of the House of Representatives—Register of Probate—Register of Deeds—Clerk of the Supreme Judicial Court—Clerk of the Inferiour Court of Common Pleas—or Officer of the Customs, including in this description Naval Officers—shall at the same time, have a seat in the Senate or House of Representatives; but their being chosen or appointed to, and accepting the same, shall operate as a resignation of their seat in the Senate or House of Representatives; and the place so vacated, shall be filled up.

And the same rule shall take place in case any Judge of the said Supreme Judicial Court, or Judge of Probate, shall accept a seat in Council; or any Counsellor shall accept of either of those offices or places.

And no person shall ever be admitted to hold a seat in the Legislature, or any office of trust or importance under the government of this Commonwealth, who shall, in the due course of law, have been convicted of bribery or corruption, in obtaining an election or appointment.

III. In all cases where sums of money are mentioned in this Constitution, the value thereof shall be computed in silver, at six shillings and eight pence per ounce: And it shall be in the power of the Legislature from time to time, to increase such qualifications, as to property, of the persons to be elected to offices, as the circumstances of the Commonwealth shall require.

IV. All commissions shall be in the name of the Commonwealth of *Massachusetts,* signed by the Governour, and attested by the Secretary or his Deputy, and have the great seal of the Commonwealth affixed thereto.

V. All writs issuing out of the clerk's office in any of the courts of law, shall be in the name of the Commonwealth of *Massachusetts*: They shall be under the seal of the court from whence they issue: They shall bear test of the first Justice of the Court to which they shall be returnable, who is not a party, and be signed by the clerk of such court.

VI. All the laws which have heretofore been adopted, used and approved, in the Province, Colony, or State of *Massachusetts Bay*, and usually practiced on in the courts of law, shall still remain and be in full force, until altered or repealed by the Legislature; such parts only excepted as are repugnant to the rights and liberties contained in this Constitution.

VII. The privilege and benefit of the writ of Habeas Corpus, shall be enjoyed in this Commonwealth, in the most free, easy, cheap, expeditious and ample manner; and shall not be suspended by the Legislature, except upon the most urgent and pressing occasions, and for a limited time not exceeding twelve months.

VIII. The enacting Stile, in making and passing all acts, statutes and laws, shall be—"Be it enacted by the Senate and House of Representatives, in General Court assembled, and by the authority of the same."

IX. To the end there may be no failure of Justice, or danger arise to the Commonwealth from a change of the Form of Government—all officers, civil and military, holding commissions under the government and people of *Massachusetts Bay*, in *Newengland*, and all other officers of the said government and people, at the time this Constitution shall take effect, shall have, hold, use, exercise and enjoy, all the powers and authority to them granted or committed, until other persons shall be appointed in their stead: And all courts of law shall proceed in the execution of the business of their respective departments; and all the executive and legislative officers, bodies and powers shall continue in full force, in the enjoyment and exercise of all their trusts, employments and authority; until the General Court, and the supreme and executive officers under this Constitution, are designated and invested with their respective trusts, powers and authority.

X. In order the more effectually to adhere to the principles of the Constitution, and to correct those violations which by any means may be made therein, as well as to form such alterations, as from experience shall be found necessary—the General Court, which shall be in the year of our Lord one thousand seven hundred and ninety five, shall issue precepts to the Selectmen of the several towns, and to the Assessors of the unincorporated plantations, directing them to convene the qualified voters of their respective towns and plantations for the purpose of collecting their sentiments on the necessity or expediency of revising the Constitution, in order to amendments.

And if it shall appear by the returns made, that two thirds of the qualified voters throughout the State, who shall assemble and vote in consequence of the said precepts, are in favour of such revision or amendments, the General Court shall issue precepts, or direct them to be issued from the Secretary's office to the several towns, to elect delegates to meet in convention for the purpose aforesaid.

The said delegates to be chosen in the same manner and proportion, as their Representatives in the second branch of the Legislature are, by this Constitution, to be chosen.

XI.   This form of government shall be enrolled on parchment, and deposited in the Secretary's office, and be a part of the laws of the land; and printed copies thereof shall be prefixed to the book containing the laws of this Commonwealth, in all future editions of the said laws.

JAMES BOWDOIN, *President.*

Attest.—SAMUEL BARRETT, *Secretary.*

K. ORDINANCE FOR THE GOVERNMENT OF THE TERRITORY OF THE UNITED STATES NORTH–WEST OF THE RIVER OHIO

July 13, 1787

An Ordinance for the Government of the Territory of the United States, North-West of the River Ohio.

Be it Ordained by the United States in Congress assembled, That the said territory, for the purposes of temporary government, be one district; subject, however, to be divided into two districts, as future circumstances may, in the opinion of Congress, make it expedient.

Be it ordained by the authority aforesaid, That the estates both of resident and non-resident proprietors in the said territory, dying intestate, shall descend to, and be distributed among their children, and the descendants of a deceased child in equal parts; the descendants of a deceased child or grandchild to take the share of their deceased parent in equal parts among them: And where there shall be no children or descendants, then in equal parts to the next of kin, in equal degree; and among collaterals the children of a deceased brother or sister of the intestate, shall have in equal parts among them their deceased parents share; and there shall in no case be a distinction between kindred of the whole, and half blood; saving in all cases to the widow of the intestate her third part of the real estate for life, and one third part of the personal estate; and this law relative to descents and dower, shall remain in full force until altered by the Legislature of the district. And until the governor and judges shall adopt laws as herein after mentioned, estates in the said territory may be devised or bequeathed by wills in writing, signed and Sealed by him or her, in whom the estate may be, (being of full age) and attested by three witnesses;—and real estates may be conveyed by lease and release, or bargain and sale, signed sealed, and delivered by the person, being of full age, in whom the estate may be, and attested by two witnesses, provided such wills be duly proved, and such conveyances be acknowledged or the execution thereof duly proved, and be recorded, within one year after proper magistrates, courts, and registers shall be appointed for that purpose; and personal property may be transferred by delivery, saving however, to the French and Canadian inhabitants and other settlers of the Kaskaskies, Saint Vincents and the Neighbouring Villages who have heretofore professed themselves Citizens of Virginia, their laws and customs now in force among them, relative to the descent and conveyance of property.

Be it ordained by the authority aforesaid, That there shall be appointed from time to time, by Congress, a governor, whose Commission shall continue in force for the term of three years, unless sooner revoked by Congress; he shall reside in the district, and have a freehold estate therein, in one thousand acres of land, while in the exercise of his Office.

There shall be appointed from time to time, by Congress, a secretary, whose Commission shall continue in force for four years, unless sooner revoked, he shall reside in the district, and have a freehold estate therein, in five hundred Acres of land, while in the exercise of his Office; it shall be his duty to keep and preserve the acts and laws passed by the Legislature, and the public records of the district, and the proceedings of the governor in his executive department; and transmit authentic copies of such acts and proceedings every six months, to the Secretary of Congress: There shall also be appointed a court to consist of three judges, any two of whom to form a Court, who shall have a common law jurisdiction, and reside in the district, and have each therein a freehold estate in five hundred acres of land while in the exercise of their Offices; and their Commissions shall continue in force during good behaviour.

The governor and judges or a majority of them shall adopt and publish in the district, such laws of the original States, criminal and civil, as may be necessary, and best suited to the circumstances of the district, and report them to Congress, from time to time, which laws shall be in force in the district until the organization of the general Assembly therein, unless disapproved of by Congress; but afterwards the legislature shall have authority to alter them as they shall think fit.

The governor for the time being, shall be commander in chief of the militia, appoint and Commission all Officers in the same, below the rank of general Officers; all general Officers shall be appointed and Commissioned by Congress.

Previous to the organization of the general assembly the governor shall appoint such Magistrates and other civil officers, in each County or Township as he shall find Necessary for the preservation of the peace and good order in the same: After the general Assembly shall be organized, the powers and duties of Magistrates and other Civil Officers shall be regulated and defined by the said assembly, but all magistrates and other civil Officers, not herein otherwise directed, shall during the continuance of this temporary government be appointed by the governor.

For the prevention of crimes and injuries, the laws to be adopted or made shall have force in all parts of the district, and for the execution of process, criminal and Civil, the governor shall make proper divisions thereof—and he shall proceed from time to time as circumstances may require to lay out the parts of the district in which the Indian titles shall have been extinguished, into Counties and townships, subject however, to such alterations, as may thereafter be made by the Legislature.

So soon as there shall be five thousand free male inhabitants, of full age, in the district, upon giving proof thereof to the governor, they shall receive authority, with time and place to elect representatives from their Counties or Townships, to represent them in the general assembly; provided that for every five hundred free male inhabitants there shall be one representative, and so on progressively with the number of free male inhabitants, shall the right of representation increase, until the number of representatives shall amount to twenty five, after which the number and proportion of representatives shall be regulated by the legislature; provided that no person be eligible or qualified to act as a representative, unless he shall have been a Citizen of one of the United States three years and be a resident in the district, or unless he shall have resided in the district three years, and in either case shall likewise hold in his own right, in fee simple two hundred acres of land within the same: Provided also, that a freehold in fifty acres of land in the district, having been a Citizen of one of the states, and being resident in the district; or the like freehold and two years residence in the district shall be necessary to qualify a man as an elector of a representative.

The representatives thus elected, shall serve for the term of two years, and in case of the death of a representative or removal from Office, the governor shall issue a writ to the County or Township for which he was a member, to elect another in his stead to serve for the residue of the term.

The general assembly, or Legislature, shall consist of the governor, legislative Council, and a house of representatives. The legislative Council, shall consist of five members, to continue in Office five years unless sooner removed by Congress, any three of whom to be a quorum, and the members of the Council shall be nominated and appointed in the following manner, to wit: As soon as representatives shall be elected, the governor shall appoint a time and place for them to meet together, and when met, they shall nominate ten persons residents in the district, and each possessed of a freehold in five hundred acres of land, and return their names to Congress; five of whom Congress shall appoint and Commission to serve as aforesaid; and whenever a vacancy shall happen in the Council, by death, or removal from Office, the house of representatives shall nominate two persons qualified as aforesaid, for each vacancy and return their names to Congress; one of whom Congress shall appoint and Commission for the residue of the term; and every five years, four months at least before the expiration of the time of service of the members of Council, the said house shall nominate ten persons qualified as aforesaid, and return their names to Congress, five of whom Congress shall appoint and Commission to serve as members of the Council five years, unless sooner removed. And the governor, legislative Council, and house of representatives shall have authority to make laws in all cases for the good government of the district not repugnant to the principles and articles in this Ordinance established and declared. And all bills having passed by a majority in the house, and by a majority in the Council, shall be referred to the governor for his assent; but no bill or legislative Act whatever, shall be of any force without his assent. The governor shall have a power to convene prorogue and dissolve the general assembly, when in his opinion it shall be expedient.

The governor, judges, legislative Council, secretary and such other Officers as Congress shall appoint in the district, shall take an oath or affirmation of fidelity, and of Office, the governor before the President of Congress, and all other Officers before the governor. As soon a legislature shall be formed in the district, the Council and house assembled in one room, shall have authority by joint ballot to elect a delegate to Congress, who shall have a seat in Congress, with a right of debating, but not of voting during this temporary government.

And for extending the fundamental principles of civil and religious liberty, which form the basis whereon these republics, their laws, and constitutions are erected; to fix and establish those principles as the basis of all laws, constitutions, and governments, which forever hereafter shall be formed in the said territory;—to provide also for the establishment of states and permanent government therein, and for their admission to a share in the federal Councils on an equal footing with the original states, at as early periods as may be consistent with the general interest.

It is hereby Ordained and declared by the authority aforesaid, That the following articles shall be considered as Articles of compact between the original States and the people and states in the said territory, and forever remain unalterable, unless by common consent, to wit.

Article the First. No person demeaning himself in a peaceable and orderly manner shall ever be molested on account of his mode of worship or religious sentiments in the said territory.

Article the Second. The inhabitants of the said territory shall always be entitled to the benefits of the writ of habeas corpus, and of the trial by jury; of a proportionate representation of the people in the legislature, and of judicial proceedings according to the course of the common law; all persons shall be bailable unless for Capital Offences, where the proof shall be evident, or the presumption great; all fines shall be moderate, and no cruel or unusual punishments shall be inflicted; no man shall be deprived of his liberty or property but by the judgment of his peers, or the law of the land; and should the public exigencies make it Necessary for the common preservation to take any persons property, or to demand his particular services, full compensation shall be made for the same; and in the just preservation of rights and property it is understood and declared, that no law ought ever to be made, or have force in the said territory, that shall in any manner whatever interfere with, or affect private contracts or engagements bona fide and without fraud, previously formed.

Article the Third. Religion, morality and knowledge being necessary to good government and the happiness of mankind, schools, and the means of education shall forever be encouraged. The utmost good faith shall always be observed towards the Indians; their lands and property shall never be taken from them without their consent; and in their property, rights and liberty, they never shall be invaded or disturbed, unless in just and lawful wars authorised by Congress; but laws founded in justice and humanity shall from time to time be made, for preventing wrongs being done to them, and for preserving peace and friendship with them.

Article the Fourth. The said territory and the States which may be formed therein shall forever remain a part of this confederacy of the United States of America, subject to the articles of Confederation and to such alterations therein as shall be constitutionally made; and to all the acts and ordinances of the United States in Congress assembled, conformable thereto. The inhabitants and settlers in the said territory, shall be subject to pay a part of the federal debts contracted or to be contracted, and a proportional part of the expences of government, to be apportioned on them by Congress, according to the same common rule and measure by which apportionments thereof shall be made on the other states; and the taxes for paying their proportion, shall be laid and levied by the authority and direction of the legislatures of the district or districts or new states, as in the original states, within the time agreed upon by the United States in Congress assembled. The legislatures of those districts or new states shall never interfere with the primary disposal of the soil by the United states in Congress assembled, nor with any regulations Congress may find necessary for securing the title in such soil to the bona fide purchasers. No tax shall be imposed on lands the property of the United states; and in no case shall non-resident proprietors be taxed higher than residents. The navigable waters leading into the Missisippi and St. Lawrence, and the carrying places between the same shall be common highways, and forever free, as well to the inhabitants of the said territory, as to the Citizens of the United States, and those of any other states that may be admitted into the confederacy, without any tax, impost, or duty therefor.

Article the Fifth. There shall be formed in the said territory not less than three, nor more than five states; and the boundaries of the states, as soon as Virginia shall alter her act of cession, and consent to the same, shall become fixed and established as follows to wit; The western state in the said territory shall be bounded by the Missisippi, the Ohio and Wabash rivers; a direct line drawn from the Wabash and Post Vincents due north to the territorial lines between the United States and Canada, and by the said territorial line to the lake of the Woods and Missisippi. The middle state shall be bounded by the said direct line, the Wabash from Post Vincents to the Ohio; by the Ohio, by a direct line drawn due north from the mouth of the Great Miami to the said territorial line, and by the said territorial line. The eastern state shall be bounded by the last mentioned direct line, the Ohio, Pennsylvania, and the said territorial line; provided however, and it is further understood and declared that the boundaries of these three states, shall be subject so far to be altered, that if Congress shall hereafter find it expedient, they shall have authority to form one or two states in that part of the said territory which lies north of an east and west line drawn through the southerly bend or extreme of lake Michigan: and whenever any of the said states shall have sixty thousand free inhabitants therein, such state shall be admitted by its delegates into the Congress of the United states on an equal footing with the original states in all respects whatever; and shall be at liberty to form a permanent constitution and state government; provided the constitution and government so to be formed, shall be republican, and in conformity to the principles contained in these articles; and so far as it can be consistent with the general interest of the confederacy, such admission shall be allowed at an earlier period, and when there may be a less number of free inhabitants in the state than sixty thousand.

Article the Sixth. There shall be neither slavery nor involuntary servitude in the said territory otherwise than in punishment of crimes whereof the party shall have been duly convicted: provided always that any person escaping into the same from whom labor or service is lawfully claimed in any one of the original states, such fugitive may be lawfully reclaimed and conveyed to the person claiming his, or her labor, or service as aforesaid.

Be it ordained by the authority aforesaid, That the resolutions of the twenty third day of April, one thousand seven hundred and eighty four relative to the subject of this ordinance be, and the same are hereby repealed and declared null and void.

> Done by the United States in Congress
> assembled, the thirteenth day of July,
> in the year of our Lord one thousand
> seven hundred and eighty seven, and of their
> Sovereignty and Independence the twelfth.

CHAS THOMSON secy

WILLM. GRAYSON Chairman

L. THE [VIRGINIA] PLAN PRESENTED BY EDMUND RANDOLPH TO THE FEDERAL CONVENTION

May 29, 1787

1. Resolved that the Articles of Confederation ought to be so corrected and enlarged, as to accomplish the objects proposed by their institution, namely *common Defence Security of Liberty* and *general welfare.*

2. Resolved therefore that the right of Suffrage in the National Legislature ought to be, proportioned to the quotas of Contribution, or to the number of free inhabitants, as the one or the other, may serve best in different cases.

3. Resolved that the National Legislature ought to consist of *two branches.*

4. Resolved that the Members of the first Branch of the National Legislature, ought to be elected by the people of the several States every   for the term of three years, to be of the age of   at least. To receive liberal stipends, by which they may be compensated for the devotion ["duration" stricken out] of their time to public service—to be ineligible to any office established by a particular State, or under the authority of the United States, (except those peculiarly belonging to the functions of the first Branch) during the term of service, and for the space of one   after the expiration; to be incapable of re-election for the   space   of   after the expiration of their term of service, and to be subject to recal.

5. Resolved, that the members of the second Branch of the Legislature, ought to be elected by the individual Legislatures: to be of the age of   years at least; to hold their Offices for a term sufficient to ensure their independancy; to receive liberal Stipends by which they may be compensated for the devotion ["devtion" stricken out] of their time to the public service; and to be in-eligible to any office established by a particular State, or under the authority of the United States (except

those peculiarly belonging to the functions of the second Branch) during the term of service, and for the space of   after the expiration thereof.

6. Resolved that each Branch aught to possess the right of originating acts, that the National Legislature ought to be empowered to enjoy, the *Legislative rights vested in Congress.* by the Confederation, and moreover to Legislate in all cases to which the Separate States are incompetent; or in which the harmony of the United States may be interrupted, by the exercise of individual Legislation—to negative all Laws passed by the several States, contravening, in the opinion of the National Legislature, The articles of Union; or any Treaty subsisting under the Authority of the Union—and to call forth the force of the Union, against any Member of the Union, failing to fulfil its duties under the articles thereof

7th Resolved that a ["the" stricken out] national Executive be instituted ["consti" stricken out] to consist of a *single person*, with powers to carry into execution the National Laws, and to appoint to Offices, in cases not otherwise provided for, to be chosen by the National Legislature, for the term of seven years—to receive punctually at stated times a fixed compensation, for the services rendered, in which no increase or diminution shall be made, so as to affect the Magistracy existing at the time of such increase or diminution, and to be in-eligible a second time.

8th Resolved that the Executive and a convenient number of the National Judiciary ought to compose a *Council of revision*, with authority to examine every act of the National Legislature, before it shall operate, and every act of a particular Legislature before a negative thereon shall be final; and that the dissent of the said council shall amount to a rejection, unless the act of the National Legislature, be again passed, or that of a particular Legislature be again negatived by   of the Members of each Branch.

9. Resolved that a National Judiciary be established to Consist of one Supreme Tribunal, to hold their Offices during good behavior, and to receive punctually at stated times fixed compensation for their services, in which no increase or diminution shall be made, so as to affect the persons actually in office at the time of such increase or diminution.

That the jurisdiction of the inferior Tribunals, shall be to hear and determine in the first instance, and of the Supreme Tribunal to hear and determine in the dernier resort; all piracies and felonies on the high Seas, Captures from an Enemy; cases in which Foreigners, or Citizens of other States applying to such jurisdictions, may be interested, or which respect the collection of the national Revenue, Impeachment of any national officer and questions which may involve, the National peace and harmony.

10.　Resolved that provision ought to be made for the *admission of States* Lawfully arising within the limits of the United States whether from a voluntary junction of Government and Territory or otherwise, with the Consent of a number of Voices in the National Legislatures less than 　　　　　the whole.

11.　Resolved that a republican Government of each State (except in the Voluntary junction of Government and Territory) ought to be garranteed by the United States to each State.

12.　Resolved that provision ought to be made for the Continuance of a Congress and their authorities, and privileges, until ["untill" stricken out] a given day, after the reform of the Articles of the Union shall be adopted, and for the Completion of all their engagements.

13.　That provision ought to be made for the amendment of the Articles of the Union, whensoever it shall seem necessary (and that the assent of the National Legislature, ought to be required thereto)

14.　Resolved that the Legislative, Executive and judicial powers of the several States, ought to be bound by oath to support the Articles of Union.

15.　Resolved that the amendments which shall be offered to the Confederation, by the Convention, ought at a proper time, or times, after the approbation of Congress, to be submitted to an assembly or assemblies of representatives, recommended by the several Legislatures, to be expressly chosen by the people to consider and decide thereon.

M.　THE PLAN PRESENTED BY CHARLES PINCKNEY TO THE FEDERAL CONVENTION

May 29, 1787

OUTLINE OF THE PLAN.

1.　A Confederation between the free and independent States of N. H. etc. is hereby solemnly made uniting them together under one general superintending Government for their common Benefit and for their Defense and Security against all Designs and Leagues that may be injurious to their Interests and against all Forc[e][?] and Attacks offered to or made upon them or any of them.

2.　The Stile

3.　Mutual Intercourse—Community of Privileges—Surrender of Criminals—Faith to Proceedings etc.

4.　Two Branches of the Legislature—Senate—House of Delegates— together the U. S. in Congress assembled

H. D. to consist of one Member for every thousand Inhabitants ⅗ of Blacks included

Senate to be elected from four Districts—to serve by Rotation of four years—to be elected by the H. D. either from among themselves or the People at large

5. The Senate and H. D. shall by joint Ballot annually chuse the Presid^t. U. S. from among themselves or the People at large.—In the Presd^t. the executive authority of the U. S. shall be vested.—His Powers and Duties—He shall have a Right to advise with the Heads of the different Departments as his Council

6. Council of Revision, consisting of the Presid^t. S. for for. Affairs, S. of War, Heads of the Departments of Treasury and Admiralty or any two of them tog^r w^t the Presid^t.

7. The Members of S. and H. D. shall each have one Vote, and shall be paid out of the common Treasury.

8. The Time of the Election of the Members of the H. D. and of the Meeting of U. S. in C. assembled.

9. No State to make Treaties—lay interfering Duties—keep a naval or land Force Militia excepted to be disciplined etc. according to the Regulations of the U. S.

10. Each State retains its Rights not expressly delegated—But no Bill of the Legislature of any State shall become a law till it shall have been laid before S. and H. D. in C. assembled and received their Approbation.

11. The exclusive Power of S. and H. D. in C. Assembled.

12. The S. and H. D. in C. ass. shall have exclusive Power of regulating trade and levying Imposts—Each State may lay Embargoes in Times of Scarcity.

13. —of establishing Post-Offices

14. S. and H. D. in C. ass. shall be the last Resort on Appeal in Disputes between two or more States; which Authority shall be exercised in the following Manner etc

15. S. and H. D. in C. ass. shall institute offices and appoint officers for the Departments of for. Affairs, War, Treasury and Admiralty.

They shall have the exclusive Power of declaring what shall be Treason and Misp. of Treason ag^t. U. S.—and of instituting a federal judicial Court, to which an Appeal shall be allowed from the judicial Courts of the several States in all Causes wherein Questions shall arise on the Construction of Treaties made by U. S.—or on the Laws of Nations—or on the Regulations of U. S. concerning Trade and Revenue—or wherein U. S. shall be a Party—The Court shall consist of Judges to be appointed during good Behaviour—S and H. D. in C. ass. shall have the exclusive Right of instituting in each State a Court of

Admiralty and appointing the Judges etc of the same for all maritime Causes which may arise therein respectively.

16.   S. and H. D. in C. Ass shall have the exclusive Right of coining Money—regulating its Alloy and Value—fixing the Standard of Weights and Measures throughout U.S.

17.   Points in which the Assent of more than a bare Majority shall be necessary.

18.   Impeachments shall be by the H. D. before the Senate and the Judges of the Federal judicial Court.

19.   S. and H. D. in C. ass. shall regulate the Militia thro' the U. S.

20.   Means of enforcing and compelling the Payment of the Quota of each State.

21.   Manner and Conditions of admitting new States.

22.   Power of dividing annexing and consolidating States, on the Consent and Petition of such States.

23.   The assent of the Legislature of   States shall be sufficient to invest future additional Powers in U. S. in C. ass. and shall bind the whole Confederacy.

24.   The Articles of Confederation shall be inviolably observed, and the Union shall be perpetual: unless altered as before directed

25.   The said States of N. H. etc guarrantee mutually each other and their Rights against all other Powers and against all Rebellion etc.

N.   THE [NEW JERSEY] PLAN PRESENTED BY WILLIAM PATTERSON TO THE FEDERAL CONVENTION

June 15, 1787

1.   Resolved, that the Articles of Confeder^n ought to be so revised, corrected, and enlarged as to render the federal Constitution adequate to the exigencies of Government, and the preservation of the Union.

2.   Resolved, that in addition to the Powers vested in the United States in Congress by the present existing Articles of Confederation, they be authorized to pass Acts for raising a Revenue by levying a Duty or Duties on all goods and Merchandise of foreign growth or manufacture imported into any part of the United States,—by Stamps on Paper Vellum or Parchment,—and by a Postage on all Letters and Packages passing through the general Post Office. To be applied to such federal purposes as they shall deem proper and expedient; to make rules and regulations for the collection thereof, and the same from time to time to alter and amend, in such manner as they shall think proper. To pass Acts for the regulation of Trade and Commerce, as well with foreign

Nations, as with each other. Provided that all punishments, Fines Forfeitures and Penalties to be incurred for contravening such Rules, and regulations shall be adjudged by the common Law Judiciary of the States in which any offence contrary to the true intent and meaning of such Rules and regulations shall be committed or perpetrated; with liberty of commencing in the first instance all suits or prosecutions for that purpose in the Superior Common Law Judiciary of such State; subject Nevertheless to an Appeal for the Correction of all errors, both in Law in Fact, in rendering Judgment, to the Judiciary of the United States.

3. Resolved, that whenever Requisitions shall be necessary, instead of the present Rule, the United States in Congress be authorized to make such Requisitions in proportion to the whole Number of White and other Free Citizens and Inhabitants of every age, sex and condition, including those bound to servitude for a Term of years, and three fifths of all other persons not comprehended in the foregoing description—(except Indians not paying Taxes): that if such Requisitions be not complied with, in the time to be specified therein, to direct the Collection thereof in the non complying States and for that purpose to devise and pass Acts directing and authorizing the same. Provided that none of the powers hereby vested in the United States in Congress shall be exercized without the Consent of at least   States, and in that proportion, if the number of confederated States should be hereafter encreased or diminished.

4. Resolved, that the U. S. in Congress be authorized to elect a fœderal Executive to consist of   Persons, to continue in office for the Term of   years; to receive punctually at Stated times a fixed compensation for the services by them rendered, in which no increase or diminution shall be made, so as to affect the persons composing the Executive at the time of such encrease or diminution; to be paid out of the Fœderal Treasury; to be incapable of holding any other Office or appointment during their time of service, and for   years thereafter; to be ineligible a second time, and removable on impeachment and conviction for Mal practice or neglect of duty—by Congress on application by a Majority of the Executives of the several States. That the Executive, besides a general authority to execute the federal Acts, ought to appoint all federal Officers not other wise provided for, and to direct all Military operations; provided that none of the persons composing the federal Executive shall on any occasion take command of any Troops so as personally to conduct any Military enterprise as general ["Officer" stricken out] or in any other capacity.

5. Resolved, that a federal Judiciary be established, to consist of a supreme Tribunal, the Judges of which to be appointed by the Executive, and to hold their Offices during good behavior; to receive punctually at stated times a fixed compensation for their services, in which no increase or diminution shall be made so as to effect the persons actually in Office

at the time of such increase or diminution;—That the Judiciary so established shall have authority to hear and determine in the first instance on all impeachments of federal Officers, and by way of Appeal in the dernier resort in all cases touching the Rights and privileges of Embassadors; in all cases of captures from an Enemy; in all cases of Piricies and Felonies on the high Seas; in all cases in which Foreigners may be interested in the construction of any Treaty or Treaties, or which may arise on any Act or Ordinance of Congress for the regulation of Trade, or the collection of the Federal Revenue: that none of the Judiciary Officers shall during the time they remain in Office be capable of receiving or holding any other Office or appointment during their time of service, or for thereafter.

6. Resolved, that the Legislative, Executive, and Judiciary Powers within the several States ought to be bound by Oath to support the Articles of Union.

7. Resolved, that all Acts of the United States in Congress Assembled, made by virtue and pursuance of the Powers hereby vested in them, and by the Articles of the Confederation, and all Treaties made and ratified under the authority of the United States, shall be the supreme Law of the respective States, as far as those Acts or Treaties shall relate to the said States or their citizens ["subjects" stricken out]; and that the Judiciaries of the several States shall be bound thereby in their decisions, anything in the respective Laws of the Individual States to the Contrary notwithstanding.

And if any State, or any body of Men in any State, shall oppose or prevent the carrying into Execution such Acts or Treaties, the federal Executive shall be authorized to call forth the Powers of the confederated States, or so much thereof as may be necessary to enforce and compel an obedience to such Acts or an observance of such Treaties.

8. Resolved, that provision ought to be made for the admission of New States into the Union

9. Resolved, that Provision ought to be made for hearing and deciding upon all disputes arising between the United States and an Individual State respecting Territory

10. Resolved, that the Rule for Naturalization ought to be the same in every State.

11. Resolved, that a Citizen of one State committing an Offence in an other State, shall be deemed guilty of the same offence, as if it had been committed by a Citizen of the State in which the offence was committed.

O. THE PLAN PRESENTED BY ALEXANDER HAMILTON TO THE FEDERAL CONVENTION

June 18, 1787

1st. The Supreme Legislative Power of the United States of America to be vested in two distinct Bodies of Men, the one to be called the *Assembly*, the other the *Senate*, who together shall form the Legislative of the United States, with Power to pass *all Laws whatsoever*, subject to the *negative* hereafter mentioned.

2d. The Assembly to consist of Persons elected *by the People* to serve for three years.

3d. The Senate to consist of persons elected to serve during *good behavior*, their election to be made by *electors* chosen for that purpose by the People. In order to this the States to be divided into election districts. On the death, removal, or resignation of any Senator his place to be filled out of the district from which he came.

4th. The Supreme Executive Authority of the U. States to be vested in a *Governor* to be elected to serve *during good behavior*. His election to be made by *Electors* chosen by *Electors* chosen by the people in the election districts aforesaid. His Authorities and Functions to be as follow.—to have a *negative* upon all Laws about to be passed, and the execution of all laws passed.—To have the *intire direction* of War when authorized or begun.—To have, with the advice and approbation of the Senate, the Power of making all Treaties.—To have the sole appointment of the *Heads* or *Chief-Officers* of the departments of Finance, War, and Foreign Affairs.—To have the nomination of all other Officers (Ambassadors to Foreign Nations included) subject to the approbation or rejection of the Senate.

To have the power of pardoning all offences *except Treason*, which he shall not pardon without the ["consent" stricken out] approbation of the Senate.

5th. On the death, resignation or removal of the Governor, his Authorities to be exercized by the *President of the Senate* until a successor be appointed.

6th. The Senate to have the sole power of *declaring War:* the power of *advising and approving* all Treaties:—the power of *approving or rejecting* all appointments of Officers, except the heads or chiefs of the departments of Finance War and Foreign Affairs.

7th. The Supreme Judicial Authority of the United States to be vested in Judges, to hold their Offices during good behavior, with adequate and permanent Salaries. This Court to have original Jurisdiction in all Causes of Capture, and an ["Appellant" stricken out] Appellative Jurisdiction in all causes in which the Revenues of the General Government, or the Citizens of foreign Nations are concerned.

8th.   The Legislature of the United States to have Power to institute Courts in each State["s" stricken out] for the determination of all matters of general concern.

9th.   The Governors, Senators, and all Officers of the United States to be liable to impeachment for Mal and corrupt conduct, and upon Conviction to be removed from office and disqualified for holding any place of trust or profit.   All impeachments to be tried by a Court to consist of the Chief or Senior Judge of the Superior Court of Law of each State, provided that such Judge hold his place during good behavior and have a permanent Salary.

10th.   All Laws of the particular States contrary to the Constitution or laws of the United States to be utterly void.   And the better to prevent such Laws being passed;   the Governor or President of each State shall be appointed by the *General Government* and shall have a *Negative* upon the Laws about to be passed in the State of which he is Governor or President.

11th.   No State to have any Forces, Land or Naval, and the Militia of all the States to be under the sole and exclusive direction of the United States, the Officers of which to be appointed and commissioned by them.

P.   THE PLAN ADOPTED BY THE CONVENTION

July 29, 1787

I

June 20.*	I.	RESOLVED, That the Government of the United States ought to consist of a supreme legislative, judiciary, and executive.
June 21.	II.	RESOLVED, That the legislature consist of two branches.
	III.	RESOLVED, That the members of the first branch of the legislature ought to be elected by the
June 22.		people of the several states for the term of two years; to be paid out of the publick treasury; to receive an adequate compensation for their services; to be of the age of
June 23.		twenty-five years at least; to be ineligible ** and incapable of holding any office under the authority of the United States (except those peculiarly belonging to the functions of the first branch) during the term of service of the first branch.

---

* The printed Journal says, page 11, that these 23 Resolutions are "collected from the proceedings of the convention, as they are spread over the journal from June 19th to July 26th." The dates in the margin show when the respective Resolutions were adopted.

** The word "to" is here inserted in the transcript.

June 25.

June 26.

IV. RESOLVED, That the members of the second branch of the legislature of the United States ought to be chosen by the individual legislatures; to be of the age of thirty years at least; to hold their offices for six years, one third to go out biennally; to receive a compensation for the devotion of their time to the publick service; to be ineligible to and incapable of holding any office, under the authority of the United States (except those peculiarly belonging to the functions of the second branch) during the term for which they are elected, and for one year thereafter.

V. RESOLVED, That each branch ought to possess the right of originating acts.

Postponed 27.
July 16.
July 17.

VI. RESOLVED, That the national legislature ought to possess the legislative rights vested in Congress by the confederation; and moreover, to legislate in all cases for the general interests of the union, and also in those to which the states are separately incompetent, or in which the harmony of the United States may be interrupted by the exercise of individual legislation.

VII. RESOLVED, That the legislative acts of the United States, made by virtue and in pursuance of the articles of union, and all treaties made and ratified under the authority of the United States, shall be the supreme law of the respective states, as far as those acts or treaties shall relate to the said states, or their citizens and inhabitants; and that the judiciaries of the several states shall be bound thereby in their decisions, any thing in the respective laws of the individual states to the contrary, notwithstanding.

16.

VIII. RESOLVED, That in the original formation of the legislature of the United States, the first branch thereof shall consist of sixty-five members; of which number

New Hampshire shall send three,
Massachusetts shall send eight,
Rhode Island shall send one,
Connecticut shall send five,
New York shall send six,
New Jersey shall send four,
Pennsylvania shall send eight,
Delaware shall send one,
Maryland shall send six,
Virginia shall send ten,

North Carolina shall send five,
South Carolina shall send five,
Georgia shall send three.

But as the present situation of the states may probably alter in the number of their inhabitants, the legislature of the United States shall be authorized, from time to time, to apportion the number of representatives; and in case any of the states shall hereafter be divided, or enlarged by addition of territory, or any two or more states united, or any new states created within the limits of the United States, the legislature of the United States shall possess authority to regulate the number of representatives, in any of the foregoing cases, upon the principle of their number of inhabitants according to the provisions hereafter mentioned, namely—Provided always, that representation ought to be proportioned according * to direct taxation. And in order to ascertain the alteration in the direct taxation, which may be required from time to time by the changes in the relative circumstances of the states—

IX. RESOLVED, That a census be taken within six years from the first meeting of the legislature of the United States, and once within the term of every ten years afterwards, of all the inhabitants of the United States, in the manner and according to the ratio recommended by Congress in their resolution of April 18, 1783; and that the legislature of the United States shall proportion the direct taxation accordingly.

X. RESOLVED, That all bills for raising or appropriating money, and for fixing the salaries of the officers of the government of the United States, shall originate in the first branch of the legislature of the United States, and shall not be altered or amended by the second branch; and that no money shall be drawn from the publick treasury, but in pursuance of appropriations to be originated by the first branch.

XI. RESOLVED, That in the second branch of the legislature of the United States, each state shall have an equal vote.

July 26.   XII. RESOLVED, That a national executive be instituted, to consist of a single person; to be chosen by the national legislature, for the term of

* The word "according" is omitted in the transcript.

seven years; to be ineligible a second time; with power to carry into execution the national laws; to appoint to offices in cases not otherwise provided for; to be removable on impeachment, and conviction of malpractice or neglect of duty; to receive a fixed compensation for the devotion of his time to * publick service; to be paid out of the publick treasury.

July 21.

XIII. RESOLVED, That the national executive shall have a right to negative any legislative act, which shall not be be afterwards passed, unless by two third parts of each branch of the national legislature.

18.

July 21.

18.

XIV. RESOLVED, That a national judiciary be established, to consist of one supreme tribunal, the judges of which shall be appointed by the second branch of the national legislature; to hold their offices during good behaviour; to receive punctually, at stated times, a fixed compensation for their services, in which no diminution shall be made, so as to affect the persons actually in office at the time of such diminution.

XV. RESOLVED, That the national legislature be empowered to appoint inferior tribunals.

XVI. RESOLVED, That the jurisdiction of the national judiciary shall extend to cases arising under laws passed by the general legislature; and to such other questions as involve the national peace and harmony.

XVII. RESOLVED, That provision ought to be made for the admission of states lawfully arising within the limits of the United States, whether from a voluntary junction of government and territory, or otherwise, with the consent of a number of voices in the national legislature less than the whole.

XVIII. RESOLVED, That a republican form of government shall be guarantied to each state; and that each state shall be protected against foreign and domestick violence.

23.

XIX. RESOLVED, That provision ought to be made for the amendment of the articles of union, whensoever it shall seem necessary.

XX. RESOLVED, That the legislative, executive, and judiciary powers, within the several states, and of the national government, ought to be

* The word "the" is here inserted in the transcript.

bound, by oath, to support the articles of union.

XXI. RESOLVED, That the amendments which shall be offered to the confederation by the convention ought, at a proper time or times after the approbation of Congress, to be submitted to an assembly or assemblies of representatives, recommended by the several legislatures, to be expressly chosen by the people to consider and decide thereon.

XXII. RESOLVED, That the representation in the second branch of the legislature of the United States * consist of two members from each state, who shall vote per capita.

26.   XXIII. RESOLVED, That it be an instruction to the committee, to whom were referred the proceedings of the convention for the establishment of a national government, to receive a clause or clauses, requiring certain qualifications of property and citizenship, in the United States, for the executive, the judiciary, and the members of both branches of the legislature of the United States.

With the above resolutions were referred the propositions offered by M^r. C. Pinckney on the 29th. of May, & by M^r. Patterson on the 15th. of June.

Q. DRAFT OF THE PLAN BY THE COMMITTEE OF DETAIL

August 6, 1787

"We the people of the States of New Hampshire, Massachussetts, Rhode-Island and Providence Plantations, Connecticut, New-York, New-Jersey, Pennsylvania, Delaware, Maryland, Virginia, North-Carolina, South-Carolina, and Georgia, do ordain, declare, and establish the following Constitution for the Government of Ourselves and our Posterity.

ARTICLE I

The stile of the Government shall be, "The United States of America"

---

* The word "shall" is here inserted in the transcript.

*II

The Government shall consist of supreme legislative, executive; and judicial powers.

*III

The legislative power shall be vested in a Congress, to consist of two separate and distinct bodies of men, a House of Representatives and a Senate; each of which shall in all cases have a negative on the other. The Legislature shall meet on the first Monday in December ** every year.

*IV

Sect. 1. The members of the House of Representatives shall be chosen every second year, by the people of the several States comprehended within this Union. The qualifications of the electors shall be the same, from time to time, as those of the electors in the several States, of the most numerous branch of their own legislatures.

Sect. 2. Every member of the House of Representatives shall be of the age of twenty five years at least; shall have been a citizen in the United States for at least three years before his election; and shall be, at the time of his election, a resident of the State in which he shall be chosen.

Sect. 3. The House of Representatives shall, at its first formation, and until the number of citizens and inhabitants shall be taken in the manner herein after described, consist of sixty five Members, of whom three shall be chosen in New-Hampshire, eight in Massachusetts, one in Rhode-Island and Providence Plantations, five in Connecticut, six in New-York, four in New-Jersey, eight in Pennsylvania, one in Delaware, six in Maryland, ten in Virginia, five in North-Carolina, five in South-Carolina, and three in Georgia.

Sect. 4. As the proportions of numbers in different States will alter from time to time; as some of the States may hereafter be divided; as others may be enlarged by addition of territory; as two or more States may be united; as new States will be erected within the limits of the United States, the Legislature shall, in each of these cases, regulate the number of representatives by the number of inhabitants, according to the provisions herein after made, at the rate of one for every forty thousand.

Sect. 5. All bills for raising or appropriating money, and for fixing the salaries of the officers of Government, shall originate in the House of Representatives, and shall not be altered or amended by the Senate. No money shall be drawn from the Public Treasury, but in pursuance of appropriations that shall originate in the House of Representatives.

* The word "Article" is here inserted in the transcript.

** The word "in" is here inserted in the transcript.

Sect. 6. The House of Representatives shall have the sole power of impeachment. It shall choose its Speaker and other officers.

Sect. 7. Vacancies in the House of Representatives shall be supplied by writs of election from the executive authority of the State, in the representation from which it * shall happen.

**V

Sect. 1 The Senate of the United States shall be chosen by the Legislatures of the several States. Each Legislature shall chuse two members. Vacancies may be supplied by the Executive until the next meeting of the Legislature. Each member shall have one vote.

Sect. 2. The Senators shall be chosen for six years; but immediately after the first election they shall be divided, by lot, into three classes, as nearly as may be, numbered one, two and three. The seats of the members of the first class shall be vacated at the expiration of the second year, of the second class at the expiration of the fourth year, of the third class at the expiration of the sixth year, so that a third part of the members may be chosen every second year.

Sect. 3. Every member of the Senate shall be of the age of thirty years at least; shall have been a citizen in the United States for at least four years before his election; and shall be, at the time of his election, a resident of the State for which he shall be chosen.

Sect. 4. The Senate shall chuse its own President and other officers.

**VI

Sect. 1. The times and places and manner of holding the elections of the members of each House shall be prescribed by the Legislature of each State; but their provisions concerning them may, at any time be altered by the Legislature of the United States.

Sect. 2. The Legislature of the United States shall have authority to establish such uniform qualifications of the members of each House, with regard to property, as to the said Legislature shall seem expedient.

Sect. 3. In each House a majority of the members shall constitute a quorum to do business; but a smaller number may adjourn from day to day.

Sect. 4. Each House shall be the judge of the elections, returns and qualifications of its own members.

Sect. 5. Freedom of speech and debate in the Legislature shall not be impeached or questioned in any Court or place out of the Legislature; and the members of each House shall, in all cases, except treason felony

---

* The word "it" is crossed out and the word "they" is written above it in the transcript.

** The word "Article" is here inserted in the transcript.

and breach of the peace, be privileged from arrest during their attendance at Congress, and in going to and returning from it.

Sect. 6. Each House may determine the rules of its proceedings; may punish its members for disorderly behaviour; and may expel a member.

Sect. 7. The House of Representatives, and the Senate, when it shall be acting in a legislative capacity, shall keep a journal of their proceedings, and shall, from time to time, publish them: and the yeas and nays of the members of each House, on any question, shall at the desire of one-fifth part of the members present, be entered on the journal.

Sect. 8. Neither House, without the consent of the other, shall adjourn for more than three days, nor to any other place than that at which the two Houses are sitting. But this regulation shall not extend to the Senate, when it shall exercise the powers mentioned in the article.

Sect. 9. The members of each House shall be ineligible to, and incapable of holding any office under the authority of the United States, during the time for which they shall respectively be elected: and the members of the Senate shall be ineligible to, and incapable of holding any such office for one year afterwards.

Sect. 10. The members of each House shall receive a compensation for their services, to be ascertained and paid by the State, in which they shall be chosen.

*Sect. 11. The enacting stile of the laws of the United States shall be. "Be it enacted by the Senate and Representatives in Congress assembled."

Sect. 12. Each House shall possess the right of originating bills, except in the cases beforementioned.

Sect. 13. Every bill, which shall have passed the House of Representatives and the Senate, shall, before it become ** a law, be presented to the President of the United States for his revision: if, upon such revision, he approve of it, he shall signify his approbation by signing it: But if, upon such revision, it shall appear to him improper for being passed into a law, he shall return it, together with his objections against it, to that House in which it shall have originated, who shall enter the objections at large on their journal and proceed to reconsider the bill. But if after such reconsideration, two thirds of that House shall, notwithstanding the objections of the President, agree to pass it, it shall together with his objections, be sent to the other House, by which it shall likewise be reconsidered, and if approved by two thirds of the other House also, it shall become a law. But in all such cases, the votes of

* Section 11 is copied in the transcript as originally printed.

** The word "becomes" is substituted in the transcript for "become."

both Houses shall be determined by yeas and nays; and the names of the persons voting for or against the bill shall be entered on the journal of each House respectively. If any bill shall not be returned by the President within seven days after it shall have been presented to him, it shall be a law, unless the legislature, by their adjournment, prevent its return; in which case it shall not be a law.

*VII

Sect. 1. The Legislature of the United States shall have the power to lay and collect taxes, duties, imposts and excises;

To regulate commerce with foreign nations, and among the several States;

To establish an uniform rule of naturalization throughout the United States;

To coin money;

To regulate the value of foreign coin;

To fix the standard of weights and measures;

To establish Post-offices;

To borrow money, and emit bills on the credit of the United States;

To appoint a Treasurer by ballot;

To constitute tribunals inferior to the Supreme Court;

To make rules concerning captures on land and water;

To declare the law and punishment of piracies and felonies committed on the high seas, and the punishment of counterfeiting the coin of the United States, and of offenses against the law of nations;

To subdue a rebellion in any State, on the application of its legislature;

To make war;

To raise armies;

To build and equip fleets;

To call forth the aid of the militia, in order to execute the laws of the Union, enforce treaties, suppress insurrections, and repel invasions;

And to make all laws that shall be necessary and proper for carrying into execution the foregoing powers, and all other powers vested, by this Constitution, in the government of the United States, or in any department or officer * thereof;

Sect. 2. Treason against the United States shall consist only in levying war against the United States, or any of them; and in adhering

* The word "Article" is here inserted in the transcript.

* The letter "r" is stricken from the word "officer" in the transcript.

to the enemies of the United States, or any of them. The Legislature of the United States shall have power to declare the punishment of treason. No person shall be convicted of treason, unless on the testimony of two witnesses. No attainder of treason shall work corruption of blood, nor forfeiture, except during the life of the person attainted.

Sect. 3. The proportions of direct taxation shall be regulated by the whole number of white and other free citizens and inhabitants of every age, sex and condition, including those bound to servitude for a term of years, and three fifths of all other persons not comprehended in the foregoing description, (except Indians not paying taxes) which number shall, within six years after the first meeting of the Legislature, and within the term of every ten years afterwards, be taken in such ** manner as the said Legislature shall direct.

Sect. 4. No tax or duty shall be laid by the Legislature on articles exported from any State; nor on the migration or importation of such persons as the several States shall think proper to admit; nor shall such migration or importation be prohibited.

Sect. 5. No capitation tax shall be laid, unless in proportion to the Census hereinbefore directed to be taken.

Sect. 6. No navigation act shall be passed without the assent of two thirds of the members present in the each House.

Sect. 7. The United States shall not grant any title of Nobility.

***VIII

The Acts of the Legislature of the United States made in pursuance of this Constitution, and all treaties made under the authority of the United States shall be the supreme law of the several States, and of their citizens and inhabitants; and the judges in the several States shall be bound thereby in their decisions; any thing in the Constitutions or laws of the several States to the contrary notwithstanding.

*IX

Sect 1. The Senate of the United States shall have power to make treaties, and to appoint Ambassadors, and Judges of the Supreme Court.

Sect. 2. In all disputes and controversies now subsisting, or that may hereafter subsist between two or more States, respecting jurisdiction or territory, the Senate shall possess the following powers. Whenever the Legislature, or the Executive authority, or lawful agent of any State, in controversy with another, shall by memorial to the Senate, state the matter in question, and apply for a hearing; notice of such

** The word "a" is here inserted in the transcript.

*** The word "Article" is here inserted in the transcript.

* The word "Article" is here inserted in the transcript.

memorial and application shall be given by order of the Senate, to the Legislature or the Executive authority of the other State in Controversy. The Senate shall also assign a day for the appearance of the parties, by their agents, before the * House. The Agents shall be directed to appoint, by joint consent, commissioners or judges to constitute a Court for hearing and determining the matter in question. But if the Agents cannot agree, the Senate shall name three persons out of each of the several States; and from the list of such persons each party shall alternately strike out one, until the number shall be reduced to thirteen; and from that number not less than seven nor more than nine names, as the Senate shall direct, shall in their presence, be drawn out by lot; and the persons whose names shall be so drawn, or any five of them shall be commissioners or Judges to hear and finally determine the controversy; provided a majority of the Judges, who shall hear the cause, agree in the determination. If either party shall neglect to attend at the day assigned, without shewing sufficient reasons for not attending, or being present shall refuse to strike, the Senate shall proceed to nominate three persons out of each State, and the Clerk of the Senate shall strike in behalf of the party absent or refusing. If any of the parties shall refuse to submit to the authority of such Court; or shall not appear to prosecute or defend their claim or cause, the Court shall nevertheless proceed to pronounce judgment. The judgment shall be final and conclusive. The proceedings shall be transmitted to the President of the Senate, and shall be lodged among the public records, for the security of the parties concerned. Every Commissioner shall, before he sit in judgment, take an oath, to be administred by one of the Judges of the Supreme or Superior Court of the State where the cause shall be tried, "well and truly to hear and determine the matter in question according to the best of his judgment, without favor, affection, or hope of reward."

Sect. 3. All controversies concerning lands claimed under different grants of two or more States, whose jurisdictions, as they respect such lands shall have been decided or adjusted subsequent ** to such grants, or any of them, shall, on application to the Senate, be finally determined, as near as may be, in the same manner as is before prescribed for deciding controversies between different States.

***X

Sect. 1. The Executive Power of the United States shall be vested in a single person. His stile shall be, "The President of the United States of America;" and his title shall be, "His Excellency." He shall be elected by ballot by the Legislature. He shall hold his office during the term of seven years; but shall not be elected a second time.

---

* The word "the" is changed to "that" in the transcript.

** The syllable "ly" is added in the transcript to the word "subsequent."

*** The word "Article" is here inserted in the transcript.

Sect. 2. He shall, from time to time, give information to the Legislature, of the state of the Union: he may recommend to their consideration such measures as he shall judge necessary, and expedient: he may convene them on extraordinary occasions. In case of disagreement between the two Houses, with regard to the time of adjournment, he may adjourn them to such time as he thinks proper: he shall take care that the laws of the United States be duly and faithfully executed: he shall commission all the officers of the United States; and shall appoint officers in all cases not otherwise provided for by this Constitution. He shall receive Ambassadors, and may correspond with the supreme Executives of the several States. He shall have power to grant reprieves and pardons; but his pardon shall not be pleadable in bar of an impeachment. He shall be commander in chief of the Army and Navy of the United States, and of the Militia of the several States. He shall, at stated times, receive for his services, a compensation, which shall neither be increased nor diminished during his continuance in office. Before he shall enter on the duties of his department, he shall take the following oath or affirmation, "I—solemnly swear, (or affirm) that that * I will faithfully execute the office of President of the United States of America." He shall be removed from his office on impeachment by the House of Representatives, and conviction in the supreme Court, of treason, bribery, or corruption. In case of his removal as aforesaid, death, resignation, or disability to discharge the powers and duties of his office, the President of the Senate shall exercise those powers and duties, until another President of the United States be chosen, or until the disability of the President be removed.

**XI

Sect. 1. The Judicial Power of the United States shall be vested in one Supreme Court, and in such inferior Courts as shall, when necessary, from time to time, be constituted by the Legislature of the United States.

Sect. 2. The Judges of the Supreme Court, and of the Inferior Courts, shall hold their offices during good behaviour. They shall, at stated times, receive for their services, a compensation, which shall not be diminished during their continuance in office.

Sect. 3. The Jurisdiction of the Supreme Court shall extend to all cases arising under laws passed by the Legislature of the United States; to all cases affecting Ambassadors, other Public Ministers and Consuls; to the trial of impeachments of officers of the United States; to all cases of Admiralty and maritime jurisdiction; to controversies between two or more States, (except such as shall regard Territory or Jurisdiction) between a State and Citizens of another State, between Citizens of different States, and between a State or the Citizens thereof and foreign

* The word "that" is omitted in the transcript.

** The word "Article" is here inserted in the transcript.

States, citizens or subjects. In cases of impeachment, cases affecting Ambassadors, other Public Ministers and Consuls, and those in which a State shall be party, this jurisdiction shall be original. In all the other cases beforementioned, it shall be appellate, with such exceptions and under such regulations as the Legislature shall make. The Legislature may assign any part of the jurisdiction abovementioned (except the trial of the President of the United States) in the manner, and under the limitations which it shall think proper, to such Inferior Courts, as it shall constitute from time to time.

Sect. 4. The trial of all criminal offences (except in cases of impeachments) shall be in the State where they shall be committed; and shall be by Jury.

Sect. 5. Judgment, in cases of Impeachment, shall not extend further than to removal from office, and disqualification to hold and enjoy any office of honour, trust or profit, under the United States. But the party convicted shall, nevertheless be liable and subject to indictment, trial, judgment and punishment according to law.

*XII

No State shall coin money; nor grant letters of marque and reprisal; nor enter into any Treaty, alliance, or confederation; nor grant any title of Nobility.

*XIII

No State, without the consent of the Legislature of the United States, shall emit bills of credit, or make any thing but specie a tender in payment of debts; nor lay imposts or duties on imports; nor keep troops or ships of war in time of peace; nor enter into any agreement or compact with another State, or with any foreign power; nor engage in any war, unless it shall be actually invaded by enemies, or the danger of invasion be so imminent, as not to admit of delay, until the Legislature of the United States can be consulted.

*XIV

The Citizens of each State shall be entitled to all privileges and immunities of citizens in the several States.

*XV

Any person charged with treason, felony or high misdemeanor in any State, who shall flee from justice, and shall be found in any other State, shall, on demand of the Executive power of the State from which he fled, be delivered up and removed to the State having jurisdiction of the offence.

* The word "Article" is here inserted in the transcript.

*XVI

Full faith shall be given in each State to the acts of the Legislatures, and to the records and judicial proceedings of the Courts and magistrates of every other State.

*XVII

New States lawfully constituted or established within the limits of the United States may be admitted, by the Legislature, into this Government; but to such admission the consent of two thirds of the members present in each House shall be necessary. If a new State shall arise within the limits of any of the present States, the consent of the Legislatures of such States shall be also necessary to its admission. If the admission be consented to, the new States shall be admitted on the same terms with the original States. But the Legislature may make conditions with the new States, concerning the public debt which shall be then subsisting.

*XVIII

The United States shall guaranty to each State a Republican form of Government; and shall protect each State against foreign invasions, and, on the application of its Legislature, against domestic violence.

*XIX

On the application of the Legislatures of two thirds of the States in the Union, for an amendment of this Constitution, the Legislature of the United States shall call a Convention for that purpose.

*XX

The members of the Legislatures, and the Executive and Judicial officers of the United States, and of the several States, shall be bound by oath to support this Constitution.

*XXI

The ratifications of the Conventions of   States shall be sufficient for organizing this Constitution.

*XXII

This Constitution shall be laid before the United States in Congress assembled, for their approbation; and it is the opinion of this Convention, that it should be afterwards submitted to a Convention chosen,** under the recommendation of its legislature, in order to receive the ratification of such Convention.

---

* The word "Article" is here inserted in the transcript.

** The phrase "in each State" is here inserted in the transcript.

*XXIII

To introduce this government, it is the opinion of this Convention, that each assenting Convention should notify its assent and ratification to the United States in Congress assembled; that Congress, after receiving the assent and ratification of the Conventions of   States, should appoint and publish a day, as early as may be, and appoint a place for commencing proceedings under this Constitution; that after such publication, the Legislatures of the several States should elect members of the Senate, and direct the election of members of the House of Representatives; and that the members of the Legislature should meet at the time and place assigned by Congress, and should, as soon as may be, after their meeting, choose the President of the United States, and proceed to execute this Constitution."

A motion was made to adjourn till Wednesday, in order to give leisure to examine the Report; which passed in the negative—N. H. no. Mas. no. Cᵗ. no. Pᵃ. ay. Mᵈ. ay. Virg. ay. N. C. no. S. C. no.*

The House then adjourned till to morrow ** 11 OC.

———

R. REPORT OF THE PLAN BY THE COMMITTEE OF DETAIL

September 12, 1787

WE, the People of the United States, in order to form

a more perfect union, to establish justice, insure domestic tranquillity, provide for the common defence, promote the general welfare, and secure the blessings of liberty to ourselves and our posterity, do ordain and establish this Constitution for the United States of America.

ARTICLE I.

Sect. 1. ALL legislative powers herein granted shall be vested in a Congress of the United States, which shall consist of a Senate and House of Representatives.

Sect. 2. The House of Representatives shall be composed of members chosen every second year by the people of the several states, and the electors in each state shall have the qualifications requisite for electors of the most numerous branch of the state legislature.

---

* In the transcript the vote reads: "Pennsylvania, Maryland, Virginia, aye—3; New Hampshire, Massachusetts, Connecticut, North Carolina, South Carolina, no—5."

** The word "at" is here inserted in the transcript.

<(a)>* No person shall be a representative who shall not have attained to the age of twenty-five years, and been seven years a citizen of the United States, and who shall not, when elected, be an inhabitant of that state in which he shall be chosen.

<(b)> Representatives and direct taxes shall be apportioned among the several states which may be included within this Union, according to their respective numbers, which shall be determined by adding to the whole number of free persons, including those bound to servitude for a term of years, and excluding Indians not taxed, three fifths of all other persons. The actual enumeration shall be made within three years after the first meeting of the Congress of the United States, and within every subsequent term of ten years, in such manner as they shall by law direct. The number of representatives shall not exceed one for every forty thousand, but each state shall have at least one representative: and until such enumeration shall be made, the state of New-Hampshire shall be entitled to chuse three, Massachusetts eight, Rhode-Island and Providence Plantations one, Connecticut five, New-York six, New-Jersey four, Pennsylvania eight, Delaware one, Maryland six, Virginia ten, North-Carolina five, South-Carolina five, and Georgia three.

<(c)> When vacancies happen in the representation from any state, the Executive authority thereof shall issue writs of election to fill such vacancies.

<(d)> The House of Representatives shall choose their Speaker and other officers; and they shall have the sole power of impeachment.

Sect. 3.   The Senate of the United States shall be composed of two senators from each state, chosen by the legislature thereof, for six years: and each senator shall have one vote.

<(a)> Immediately after they shall be assembled in consequence of the first election, they shall be divided <(by lot)> as equally as may be into three classes. The seats of the senators of the first class shall be vacated at the expiration of the second year, of the second class at the expiration of the fourth year, and of the third class at the expiration of the sixth year, so that one-third may be chosen every second year: and if vacancies happen by resignation, or otherwise, during the recess of the Legislature of any state, the Executive thereof may make temporary appointments until the next meeting of the Legislature.

<(b)> No person shall be a senator who shall not have attained to the age of thirty years, and been nine years a citizen of the United States, and who shall not, when elected, be an inhabitant of that state for which he shall be chosen.

<(c)> The Vice-President of the United States shall be, ex officio, President of the senate, but shall have no vote, unless they be equally divided.

* Matter in brackets added by Madison.

<(d)> The Senate shall choose their other officers, and also a President pro tempore, in the absence of the Vice-President, or when he shall exercise the office of President of the United States.

<(e)> The Senate shall have the sole power to try all impeachments. When sitting for that purpose, they shall be on oath. When the President of the United States is tried, the Chief Justice shall preside: And no person shall be convicted without the concurrence of two-thirds of the members present.

<(f)> Judgment in cases of impeachment shall not extend further than to removal from office, and disqualification to hold and enjoy any office of honor, trust or profit under the United States: but the party convicted shall nevertheless be liable and subject to indictment, trial, judgment and punishment, according to law.

Sect. 4.   The times, places and manner of holding elections for senators and representatives, shall be prescribed in each state by the legislature thereof: but the Congress may at any time by law make or alter such regulations.

<(a)> The Congress shall assemble at least once in every year, and such meeting shall be on the first Monday in December, unless they shall by law appoint a different day.

Sect. 5.   Each House shall be the judge of the elections, returns and qualifications of its own members, and a majority of each shall constitute a quorum to do business: but a smaller number may adjourn from day to day, and may be authorized to compel the attendance of absent members, in such manner, and under such penalties as each house may provide.

<(a)> Each house may determine the rules of its proceedings; punish its members for disorderly behaviour, and, with the concurrence of two-thirds, expel a member.

<(b)> Each house shall keep a journal of its proceedings, and from time to time publish the same, excepting such parts as may in their judgment require secrecy; and the yeas and nays of the members of either house on any question shall, at the desire of one-fifth of those present, be entered on the journal.

<(c)> Neither house, during the session of Congress, shall, without the consent of the other, adjourn for more than three days, nor to any other place than that in which the two houses shall be sitting.

Sect. 6.   The senators and representatives shall receive a compensation for their services, to be ascertained by law, and paid out of the treasury of the United States. They shall in all cases, except treason, felony and breach of the peace, be privileged from arrest during their attendance at the session of their respective houses, and in going to and returning from the same; and for any speech or debate in either house, they shall not be questioned in any other place.

<(a)> No senator or representative shall, during the time for which he was elected, be appointed to any civil office under the authority of the United States, which shall have been created, or the emoluments whereof shall have been encreased during such time; and no person holding any office under the United States, shall be a member of either house during his continuance in office.

Sect. 7. The enacting stile of the laws shall be, "Be it enacted by the senators and representatives in Congress assembled."

<(a)> All bills for raising revenue shall originate in the house of representatives: but the senate may propose or concur with amendments as on other bills.

<(b)> Every bill which shall have passed the house of representatives and the senate, shall, before it become a law, be presented to the president of the United States. If he approve he shall sign it, but if not he shall return it, with his objections to that house in which it shall have originated, who shall enter the objections at large on their journal, and proceed to reconsider it. If after such reconsideration two-thirds of that house shall agree to pass the bill, it shall be sent, together with the objections, to the other house, by which it shall likewise be reconsidered, and if approved by two-thirds of that house, it shall become a law. But in all such cases the votes of both houses shall be determined by yeas and nays, and the names of the persons voting for and against the bill shall be entered on the journal of each house respectively. If any bill shall not be returned by the President within ten days (Sundays excepted) after it shall have been presented to him, the same shall be a law, in like manner as if he had signed it, unless the Congress by their adjournment prevent its return, in which case it shall not be a law.

<(c)> Every order, resolution, or vote to which the concurrence of the Senate and House of Representatives may be necessary (except on a question of adjournment) shall be presented to the President of the United States; and before the same shall take effect, shall be approved by him, or, being disapproved by him, shall be repassed by *three-fourths* of the Senate and House of Representatives, according to the rules and limitations prescribed in the case of a bill.

Sect. 8. The Congress may by joint ballot appoint a treasurer. They shall have power.

<(a)> To lay and collect taxes, duties, imposts and excises; to pay the debts and provide for the common defence and general welfare of the United States. <but all duties imposts & excises shall be uniform throughout the U. States.>

<(b)> To borrow money on the credit of the United States.

<(c)> To regulate commerce with foreign nations, among the several states, and with the Indian tribes.

<(d)> To establish an uniform rule of naturalization and uniform laws on the subject of bankruptcies throughout the United States.

<(e)> To coin money, regulate the value thereof, and of foreign coin, and fix the standard of weights and measures.

<(f)> To provide for the punishment of counterfeiting the securities and current coin of the United States.

<(g)> To establish post offices and post roads.

<(i)> To promote the progress of science and useful arts, by securing for limited times to authors and inventors the exclusive right to their respective writings and discoveries.

<(j)> To constitute tribunals inferior to the supreme court.

<(k)> To define and punish piracies and felonies committed on the high seas, and <(punish)> offences against the law of nations.

<(l)> To declare war, grant letters of marque and reprisal, and make rules concerning captures on land and water.

<(m)> To raise and support armies: but no appropriation of money to that use shall be for a longer term than two years.

<(n)> To provide and maintain a navy.

<(o)> To make rules for the government and regulation of the land and naval forces.

<(p)> To provide for calling forth the militia to execute the laws of the union, suppress insurrections and repel invasions.

<(q)> To provide for organizing, arming and disciplining the militia, and for governing such part of them as may be employed in the service of the United States, reserving to the States respectively, the appointment of the officers, and the authority of training the militia according to the discipline prescribed by Congress.

<(r)> To exercise exclusive legislation in all cases whatsoever, over such district (not exceeding ten miles square) as may, by cession of particular States, and the acceptance of Congress, become the seat of government of the United States, and to exercise like authority over all places purchased by the consent of the legislature of the state in which the same shall be, for the erection of forts, magazines, arsenals, dockyards, and other needful buildings—And

<(s)> To make all laws which shall be necessary and proper for carrying into execution the foregoing powers, and all other powers vested by this constitution in the government of the United States, or in any department or officer thereof.

Sect. 9. The migration or importation of such persons as the several states now existing shall think proper to admit, shall not be prohibited by the Congress prior to the year one thousand eight hundred and eight, but a tax or duty may be imposed on such importation, not exceeding ten dollars for each person.

<(a)> The privilege of the writ of habeas corpus shall not be suspended, unless when in cases of rebellion or invasion the public safety may require it.

<(b)> No bill of attainder shall be passed, nor any ex post facto law.

<(c)> No capitation tax shall be laid, unless in proportion to the census herein before directed to be taken.

<(d)> No tax or duty shall be laid on articles exported from any state. <No preference shall be given by any regulation of commerce or revenue to the ports of one State over those of another—nor shall vessels bound to or from one State be obliged to enter, clear or pay duties in another.>

<(e)> No money shall be drawn from the treasury, but in consequence of appropriations made by law.

<(f)> No title of nobility shall be granted by the United States. And no person holding any office of profit or trust under them, shall, without the consent of the Congress, accept of any present, emolument, office, or title, of any kind whatever, from any king, prince, or foreign state.

Sect. 10. No state shall coin money, nor emit bills of credit, nor make any thing but gold or silver coin a tender in payment of debts, nor pass any bill of attainder, nor ex post facto laws, nor laws altering or impairing the obligation of contracts; nor grant letters of marque and reprisal, nor enter into any treaty, alliance, or confederation, nor grant any title of nobility.

<(a)> No state shall, without the consent of Congress, lay imposts or duties on imports or exports, nor with such consent, but to the use of the treasury of the United States. Nor keep troops nor ships of war in time of peace, nor enter into any agreement or compact with another state, nor with any foreign power; nor engage in any war, unless it shall be actually invaded by enemies, or the danger of invasion be so imminent, as not to admit of delay until the Congress can be consulted.

II.

Sect. 1. The executive power shall be vested in a president of the United States of America. He shall hold his office during the term of four years, and, together with the vice-president, chosen for the same term, be elected in the following manner:

<(a)> Each state shall appoint, in such manner as the legislature thereof may direct, a number of electors, equal to the whole number of senators and representatives to which the state may be entitled in Congress: but no senator or representative shall be appointed an elector,

nor any person holding an office of trust or profit under the United States.

<(b)> The electors shall meet in their respective states, and vote by ballot for two persons, of whom one at least shall not be an inhabitant of the same state with themselves. And they shall make a list of all the persons voted for, and of the number of votes for each; which list they shall sign and certify, and transmit sealed to the seat of the general government, directed to the president of the senate. The president of the senate shall in the presence of the senate and house of representatives open all the certificates, and the votes shall then be counted. The person having the greatest number of votes shall be the president, if such number be a majority of the whole number of electors appointed; and if there be more than one who have such majority, and have an equal number of votes, then the house of representatives shall immediately chuse by ballot one of them for president; and if no person have a majority, then from the five highest on the list the said house shall in like manner choose the president. But in choosing the president, the votes shall be taken by states, and not per capita, the representation from each state having one vote. A quorum for this purpose shall consist of a member or members from two-thirds of the states, and a majority of all the states shall be necessary to a choice. In every case, after the choice of the president by the representatives, the person having the greatest number of votes of the electors shall be the vice-president. But if there should remain two or more who have equal votes, the senate shall choose from them by ballot the vice-president.

<(c)> The Congress may determine the time of choosing the electors, and the time in which they shall give their votes; but the election shall be on the same day throughout the United States.

<(d)> No person except a natural born citizen, or a citizen of the United States, at the time of the adoption of this constitution, shall be eligible to the office of president; neither shall any person be eligible to that office who shall not have attained to the age of thirty-five years, and been fourteen years a resident within the United States.

<(e)> In case of the removal of the president from office, or of his death, resignation, or inability to discharge the powers and duties of the said office, the same shall devolve on the vice-president, and the Congress may by law provide for the case of removal, death, resignation or inability, both of the president and vice-president, declaring what officer shall then act as president, and such officer shall act accordingly, until the disability be removed, or the period for chusing another president arrive.

<(f)> The president shall, at stated times, receive a fixed compensation for his services, which shall neither be increased nor diminished during the period for which he shall have been elected.

<(g)> Before he enter on the execution of his office, he shall take the following oath or affirmation: "I _____, do solemnly swear (or affirm) that I will faithfully execute the office of president of the United States, and will to the best of my judgment and power, preserve, protect and defend the constitution of the United States."

Sect. 2.   The president shall be commander in chief of the army and navy of the United States, and of the militia of the several States: he may require the opinion, in writing, of the principal officer in each of the executive departments, upon any subject relating to the duties of their respective offices, when called into the actual service of the United States, and he shall have power to grant reprieves and pardons for offences against the United States, except in cases of impeachment.

<(a)> He shall have power, by and with the advice and consent of the senate, to make treaties, provided two-thirds of the senators present concur; and he shall nominate, and by and with the advice and consent of the senate, shall appoint ambassadors, other public ministers and consuls, judges of the supreme court, and all other officers of the United States, whose appointments are not herein otherwise provided for.

<(b)> The president shall have power to fill up all vacancies that may happen during the recess of the senate, by granting commissions which shall expire at the end of their next session.

Sect. 3.   He shall from time to time give to the Congress information of the state of the union, and recommend to their consideration such measures as he shall judge necessary and expedient: he may, on extraordinary occasions, convene both houses, or either of them, and in case of disagreement between them, with respect to the time of adjournment, he may adjourn them to such time as he shall think proper: he shall receive ambassadors and other public ministers: he shall take care that the laws be faithfully executed, and shall commission all the officers of the United States.

Sect. 4.   The president, vice-president, and all civil officers of the United States, shall be removed from office on impeachment for, and conviction of treason, bribery, or other high crimes and misdemeanors.

III.

Sect. 1.   The judicial power of the United States, both in law and equity, shall be vested in one supreme court, and in such inferior courts as the Congress may from time to time ordain and establish.   The judges, both of the supreme and inferior courts, shall hold their offices during good behaviour, and shall, at stated times, receive for their services, a compensation, which shall not be diminished during their continuance in office.

Sect. 2.   The judicial power shall extend to all cases, both in law and equity, arising under this constitution, the laws of the United States, and treaties made, or which shall be made, under their authority.   To all cases affecting ambassadors, other public ministers and consuls. To all cases of admiralty and maritime jurisdiction. To controversies to which the United States shall be a party. To controversies between two or more States; between a state and citizens of another state; between citizens of different States; between citizens of the same state claiming lands under grants of different States, and between a state, or the citizens thereof, and foreign States, citizens or subjects.

In cases affecting ambassadors, other public ministers and consuls, and those in which a state shall be a party, the supreme court shall have original jurisdiction. In all the other cases before mentioned, the supreme court shall have appellate jurisdiction, both as to law and fact, with such exceptions, and under such regulations as the Congress shall make.

The trial of all crimes, except in cases of impeachment, shall be by jury; and such trial shall be held in the state where the said crimes shall have been committed; but when not committed within any state, the trial shall be at such place or places as the Congress may by law have directed.

Sect. 3. Treason against the United States, shall consist only in levying war against them, or in adhering to their enemies, giving them aid and comfort. No person shall be convicted of treason unless on the testimony of two witnesses to the same overt act, or on confession in open court.

The Congress shall have power to declare the punishment of treason, but no attainder of treason shall work corruption of blood nor forfeiture, except during the life of the person attainted.

IV.

Sect. 1. Full faith and credit shall be given in each state to the public acts, records, and judicial proceedings of every other state. And the Congress may by general laws prescribe the manner in which such acts, records and proceedings shall be proved, and the effect thereof.

Sect. 2. The citizens of each state shall be entitled to all privileges and immunities of citizens in the several states.

A person charged in any state with treason, felony, or other crime, who shall flee from justice, and be found in another state, shall on demand of the executive authority of the state from which he fled be delivered up, and removed to the state having jurisdiction of the crime.

No person legally held to service or labour in one state, escaping into another, shall in consequence of regulations subsisting therein be discharged from such service or labor, but shall be delivered up on claim of the party to whom such service or labour may be due.

Sect. 3. New states may be admitted by the Congress into this union; but no new state shall be formed or erected within the jurisdiction of any other state; nor any state be formed by the junction of two or more states, or parts of states, without the consent of the legislatures of the states concerned as well as of the Congress.

The Congress shall have power to dispose of and make all needful rules and regulations respecting the territory or other property belonging to the United States: and nothing in this Constitution shall be so construed as to prejudice any claims of the United States, or of any particular state.

Sect. 4.   The United States shall guarantee to every state in this union a Republican form of government, and shall protect each of them against invasion; and on application of the legislature or executive, against domestic violence.

V.

The Congress, whenever two-thirds of both houses shall deem necessary, or on the application of two-thirds of the legislatures of the several states, shall propose amendments to this constitution, which shall be valid to all intents and purposes, as part thereof, when the same shall have been ratified by three-fourths at least of the legislatures of the several states, or by conventions in three-fourths thereof, as the one or the other mode of ratification may be proposed by the Congress: Provided, that no amendment which may be made prior to the year 1808 shall in any manner affect the   and   sections of article

VI.

All debts contracted and engagements entered into before the adoption of this Constitution shall be as valid against the United States under this Constitution as under the confederation.

This constitution, and the laws of the United States which shall be made in pursuance thereof; and all treaties made, or which shall be made, under the authority of the United States, shall be the supreme law of the land; and the judges in every state shall be bound thereby, any thing in the constitution or laws of any state to the contrary notwithstanding.

The senators and representatives beforementioned, and the members of the several state legislatures, and all executive and judicial officers, both of the United States and of the several States, shall be bound by oath or affirmation, to support this constitution; but no religious test shall ever be required as a qualification to any office or public trust under the United States.

VII.

The ratification of the conventions of nine States, shall be sufficient for the establishment of this constitution between the States so ratifying the same.

CHAPTER II

PRINCIPLES OF CONSTITUTIONALISM

A. EDWARD COKE, DR. BONHAM'S CASE

K.B. 1610

Thomas Bonham, doctor in philosophy and physic, brought an action of false imprisonment against Henry Atkins, George Turner, Thomas Moundford, and John Argent, doctors in physic, and John Taylor, and William Bowden, yeomen; for that the defendants, the 10th November anno 4 Jacobi, did imprison him, and detain him in prison seven days. The defendants pleaded the letters patent of King H. 8. bearing date 23 September anno 10 of his reign, by which he recites, *Quod cum Regii officii sui munus arbitrabatur ditionis suœ hominum fœlicitati omni ratione consulere, id autem vel imprimis fore si improborum conatibus tempestive occurreret, &c.* And by the same letters patent, the King granted to John Chambre, Thomas Linacre, Ferdinando de Victoria, John Halswel, John Frances, and Robert Yaxley, *quod ipsi omnesque homines ejusdem facultatis de et in civitat' London sint in re et nomine unum corpus et communitas perpetua, per nomen prœsidentis et collegii, sive communitatis facultatis medicinœ London, &c.* And that they might make meetings and ordinances, &c. But the case at Bar doth principally consist on two clauses in the charter. The first, *concessimus etiam eisdem prœsidenti et collegio seu communitati et successoribus suis, quod nemo in dicta civitate, aut per septem milliaria in circuitu ejusdem, exerceat dictam facultatem medicinœ, nisi ad hoc per dict' prœsident' et communit' seu successores suos, qui tempore fuerint, admissus sit per ejusdem prœsidentis et collegii literas sigillo suo communi sigillat' sub pœna centum solidorum pro quolibet mense quo non admissus eandem facultatem exercuerit, dimid' inde dom' Regi et hœredibus suis, et dimidium dict' prœsidenti et collegio applicand', &c.* The second clause is, which immediately follows in these words, *prœterea voluit et concessit pro se et successoribus suis, quantum in se fuit, quod per prœsident' collegium prœdict' communitat' pro tempore exist' et eorum successores imperpetuum, quatuor, singulis annis per ipsos eligerent qui haberent supervisum et scrutinium, correctionem et gubernationem omnium et singulorum dict' civitatis medicorum, utentium facultat' medicinœ in eadem civitate, ac aliorum medicorum forinsecorum quorumcunque facultatem illam medicinœ, aliquo modo frequentantium et utentium infra eandem civitatem et suburbia ejusdem, sive infra septem milliarii in circuitu ejusdem civitatis, ac punitionem eorundem pro delictis suis in non bene exequend' faciend' et uten' illa: necnon supervisum et scrutinium omnium medicinarum, et earum receptionem per dictos Medicos seu aliquem eorum hujusmodi ligeis dicti nuper Regis pro eorum infirmitatibus curand' et sanand' dand' imponend, et utend' quoties et quando opus fuerit, pro commodo et utilitat' eorundem ligeorum dicti nuper Regis: ita quod punitio eorundem medicorum utentium dicta facultate medicinæ sic in præmiss' delinquentium per fines, amerciamenta et imprisonament' corporum suorum, et per alias vias rationabiles et congruas exequeretur, prout* by the said charter *plenius liquet. Et quod virtute præd' literarum patentium præd' J. Chambre, Tho. Linacre, &c. et omnes homines ejusdem facultatis in civit' præd' fuer' unum corpus et communitas perpet' sive collegium perpetuum.* And afterwards by Act of Parliament made anno[a] 14 Hen. 8., it was enacted that the said corporation, and every grant, article, and other things in the said letters patent contained and specified, should be approved, granted, ratified, and confirmed, &c. *in tam amplo et largo modo prout poterit acceptari, cogitari, et construi per easdem literas patentes.* And further it was enacted that the said six persons named in the said letters patent, as principal of the said college, should elect to them two others of the said college, who should be named *electi*, and that the said elects should choose one of them to be president as by the said Act appears: and further they pleaded the Act of[b] Mariæ, by which it was enacted, *Quod quædam concessio per literas patentes de incorporatione facta per prædict' nuper Regem medicis London. Et omnes clausulæ et articuli content' in eadem concessione approbarentur, concederentur, ratificarentur et confirm' per prædict' Parl'; in consideratione cujus inactitat' fuit authoritate ejusdem Parliamenti. Quod præd' statut' et actum Parliamenti in omnibus articulis et clausulis in eodem content' extunc imposterum starent et continuarent in pleno robore, &c.* And further it was enacted, "That whensoever the president of the college, or commonalty of the faculty of physic at London for the time being, or such as the said president and college shall yearly, according to the tenor and meaning of the said Act, authorize to search, examine, correct, and punish all offenders and transgressors in the said faculty, &c. shall send or commit any such offender or offenders for his or their offence or disobedience, contrary to any article or clause contained in the said grant or Act, to any ward, gaol, or prison within the same city (the Tower of London except) that then from time to time the warden, gaoler, or keeper, &c. shall receive, &c. such person so offending, &c. and the same shall keep at his proper charge, without bail or mainprize, until such time as such offender or disobedient be discharged of the said imprisonment by the said president, and such persons as shall be thereunto authorised, upon pain that all and every such warden, gaoler, &c. doing the contrary, shall

a. 14 & 15 H. 8. c. 5. 1 Roll. 598. 4 Inst. 241. Rastal's Physicians 3. 2 Bulst. 185. Lit. Rep. 168, 169. 172. 212. 215. 246, 247, 248, 249. 1 Jones 261. Cr. Jac. 121, 159, 160. Cr. Car. 226. Palm. 486.

b. 1 Mar. c. 9. Rastal's Physic. 7. Lit. R. 169. 172, 173. 212, 213. 215, 248, 249, 350, 351. 1 Jones 263. Cr. Car. 257. Cr. Jac. 121. 4 Inst. 251. 2 Brown. 257, 262, 265, 266.

lose and forfeit the double of such fines and amerciaments as such offender and offenders shall be assessed to pay, by such as the said president and college shall authorise as aforesaid, so that the fine and amerciament be not at any one time above the sum of 20l., the one moiety to the King, the other moiety to the president and college, &c." And further pleaded, that the said Thomas Bonham, April 10, 1606, within London, against the form of the said letters patent, and the said Acts, *exercebat artem medicinœ, non admissus per literas prœd' prœsidentis et collegii sigillo eorum communi sigillat' ubi revera prœd' Tho. Bonham fuit minus sufficiens ad artem medicinœ exercend'.* By force of which, the said Thomas Bonham, 30 Aprilis 1606, was summoned in London by the censors or governors of the college, *ad comparend' coram prœsiden' et censor' sive gubernatorib' collegii prœd'* at the college &c. the 14th day of April next following, *super prœmissis examinand'.* At which day the said Thomas Bonham came before the president and censors, and was examined by the censors *de scientia sua in facultate sua in medicin' administrand'. Et quia prœd' Thomas Bonham sic examinatus minus apte et insufficienter in prœd' arte medicinœ respondebat, et inventus fuit super examinationem prœd' per prœd' prœsident' et censores minus insufficiens et inexpert' ad artem medicinœ administrand' ac pro eo quod prœd' Thomas Bonham multoties ante tunc examinatus, et interdictus per prœsident' et censores, de causis prœd' ad artem medicinœ administrand' per unum mensem et amplius post talem interdictionem facultatem illam in Lond' prœd' sine licentia, &c. ideo adtunc et ibid' consideratum fuit per prœd. prœsident' et censores, quod prœd' Thomas Bonham pro inobedienta et contempt' suis prœd' amerciaretur to 100s. in proximis comitiis prœd' prœsident' et collegii persolvend' et deinceps abstineret, &c. quousque inventus fuerit sufficiens, &c. sub pœna conjiciendi in carcerem si in prœmissis delinqueret.* And that the said Thomas Bonham, 20 Oct. 1636, within London did practise physic, and the same day he was summoned by the censors to appear before the president and them, 22 October then next following, at which day Bonham made default: *ideo consideratum fuit per prœd' censores,* that for his disobedience and contempt he should be amerced to 10l. and that he should be arrested and committed to custody; and afterward, November 7, 1606, the said Thomas Bonham, at their assembly came before the president and censors, and they asked him if he would satisfy the college for his disobedience and contempt, and submit himself to be examined, and obey the censure of the college, who answered, that he had practised and would practice physic within London, *nulla a collegio petita venia,* and that he would not submit himself to the president and censors; and affirmed, that the president and censors, had no authority over those who were doctors in the university; for which cause, the said four censors, *sc.* Dr. Turner, Dr. Moundford, Dr. Argent, and Dr. Dun, then being censors or governors, *pro offensis et inobedientia prœd' adtunc et ib' ordinaverunt et decreverunt, quod prœd' Thomas Bonham in carcer-*

em mandaretur ib' remansur' quousque abinde per præsident' et censores, seu gubernatores collegii præd' pro tempore existen' deliberaretur, and there then by their warrant in writing, under their common seal, did commit the plaintiff to the prison of the Compter of London, &c. *absque ballio sive manucapt' ad custagia et oner ipsius Thomas Bonham, donec præd' Thomas Bonham per præcept' præsiden' et censor' collegii præd' sive successor' suor' liberatus esset;* and Dr. Atkins then president, and the censors, and Bowden and Taylor as their servants, and by the commandment of the said president and censors, did carry the plaintiff with the warrant, to the gaol, &c. which is the same imprisonment. The plaintiff replied and said, that by the said Act of 14 H. 8. it was further enacted, "And where that in the dioceses of England, out of London, it is not like to find always men able sufficiently to examine (after the statute) such as shall be admitted to exercise physic in them, that it may be enacted in this present Parliament, that no person from henceforth be suffered to exercise or practise physic through England, until such time that he be examined at London by the said president and three of the said elects, and to have from them letters testimonial of their approving and examination, except he be a graduate of Oxford or Cambridge, which have accomplished all things for his form without any grace:" and that the plaintiff, anno Dom. 1595, was a graduate, *sc.* a doctor in the University of Cambridge, and had accomplished all things concerning his degree for his form without [a] grace, by force whereof he had exercised and practised physic within the City of London until the defendants had imprisoned him, &c. upon which the defendant demurred in law. And this case was often argued by the Serjeants at Bar in divers several terms; and now this term the case was argued by the justices, and the effect of their arguments who argued against the plaintiff (which was divided into three parts) shall be first reported. The first was, whether a doctor of physic of the one university or the other be by the letters patent, and by the body of the Act of 14 H. 8. restrained from practising physic within the City of London, &c. The second was, if the exception of the said Act of [b] 14 H. 8. has excepted him or not. The third was, that his imprisonment was lawful for his said disobedience. And as to the first, they relied upon the letter of the grant, ratified by the said Act of 14 H. 8. which is in the negative, *sc. nemo in dicta civitate, &c. exerceat dictam facultatem nisi ad hoc per prædict' præsidentem et communitatem, &c. admissus sit, &c.* And this proposition is a general negative, and [a] *generale dictum est generaliter intelligendum;* and *nemo* excludes

a. 2 Brownl. 201, 202.
b. 14 & 15 H. 8. cap. 5.

a. 11 Co. 59 a. Co. Lit. 36 a. 2 Inst. 81. Hard. 305.

all; and, therefore, a doctor of the one university or the other is prohibited within this negative word *nemo*. And many cases were put where negative statutes shall be taken *stricte et exclusive*, which I do not think necessary to be recited here. Also they said, that the statute of[b] 3 H. 8. c. 11. which in effect is repealed by this Act of[c] 14 H. 8. has a special proviso for the Universities of Cambridge and Oxford, which being here left out, doth declare the intention of the makers of the Act, that they did intend to include them within this general prohibition, *nemo in dicta civitate*, &c. As to the second point they strongly held, that the said latter clause, "and where that in the dioceses of England, out of London," &c. this clause, according to the words, extends only to places out of London, and so much the rather, because they provided for London before, *nemo in dicta civitate*, &c. Also the makers of the Act put a distinction betwixt those who shall be licensed to practise physic in London, &c. for they ought to have the admittance and allowance of the president and college in writing, under their common seal: but he who shall be allowed to practise physic throughout England, out of London, ought to be examined and admitted by the president and three of the elects; and so they said, that it was lately adjudged in the King's Bench, in an information exhibited against the said Dr. Bonham for practising physic in London for divers months. As to the third point they said, that for his contempt and disobedience before them at their assembly in their college, they might well commit him to prison; for they have authority by the letters patent and Act of Parliament, and therefore for a contempt or misdemeanor before them, they may commit him. Also the Act of[d] 1 M. has givem [sic] them power to commit them for every offence or disobedience contrary to any article or clause contained in the said grant or Act. But there is an express negative article in the said grant, and ratified by the Act of 14 H. 8 *quod nemo in dicta civitate*, &c. *exerceat*, &c. and the defendants have pleaded, that the plaintiff had practised physic in London by the space of one month, &c. and therefore the Act of 1 Mariæ has authorised them to imprison him in this case; wherefore they concluded against the plaintiff. But it was argued by Coke Chief Justice, Warburton and Daniel Justices at the Common Pleas, to the contrary. And Daniel, Justice, conceived that a doctor of physic, of the one university or the other, &c. was not within the body of the Act, and if he was within the body of the Act, that he was excepted by the said latter clause: but Warburton argued against him for both the

b. Rastal. Physician 1.

c. 14 & 15 H. 8. c. 5. 1 Roll. 598. 4 Inst. 251. Rastal. Physician 3. 2 Bulstr. 185. Lit. Rep. 168, 169. 172. 212. 215. 246, 247, 248, 249. 1 Jones 261. Cr. Jac. 121. 159, 160. Cr. Car. 256. Palm. 486. Cart. 115.

d. 1 Mar. c. 9. Rastal. Physician 7. Lit. Rep. 109. 172, 173, 212, 213. 215. 248, 249. 350, 351. 1 Jones 263. Cr. Car. 257.

Cro. Jac. 121. 4 Inst. 251. 2 Brownl. 257. 262. 265, 266. Cart. 115.

A. A graduate doctor of one of the universities cannot practise physic within London, or seven miles round, without licence from the college of physicians. *College of Physicians* v. *Dr. West*, 10 Mod. 353. *College of Physicians* v. *Levett*, 1 Ld. Raym. 472.

points [A]; and the Chief Justice did not speak to those two points, because he and Warburton and Daniel agreed, that this action was clearly maintainable for two other points, and therefore in this action the Chief Justice omitted to speak to the said two points: but to two other points he and the said two other justices, Warburton and Daniel, did speak, *sc.* 1. Whether the censors have power, for the causes alleged in their bar, to fine and imprison the plaintiff. 2. Admitting that they have power to do it, if they had pursued their power. But the Chief Justice, before he argued the points in law, because much was said in commendation of the doctors of physic of the college in London, and somewhat (as he conceived) in derogation of the dignity of the doctors of the said universities, he first attributed much to the doctors of the said college in London, and confessed that nothing was spoke in their commendation which was not due to their merits: but yet that no comparison was to be made between that private college, and either of the Universities of Cambridge and Oxford, no more than between the father and his children, or between the fountain and the small rivers which descend from it; the university is *alma mater*, from whose breasts those of that private college have sucked all their science and knowledge (which I acknowledge to be great and profound) but the law saith, *erubescit lex filios castigare parentes:* the university is the fountain, and that and the like private colleges are *tanquam rivuli*, which flow from the fountain, *et melius est petere fontes quam sectari rivulos.* Briefly, *Academiœ Cantabrigiœ et Oxoniœ sunt Athenœ nostrœ nobilissimœ regni soles, oculi et animœ regni, unde religio, humanitas, et doctrina in omnes regni partes uberrimè diffunduntur:* but it is true, *nunquam sufficiet copia laudatoris, quia nunquam deficiet materia laudis;* and, therefore, those universities exceed and excel all private colleges, *quantum inter viburna cupressus.* And it was observed that King Henry VIII. in his said letters patent and the King and the Parliament in the Act of 14 H. 8. in making of a law concerning physicians, for for the more safety and health of men, therein follow the order of a good physician (*Rex enim omn' artes censetur habere in scrinio pect' sui*) for, *medicina est duplex, removens, et promovens; removens morbum, et promovens ad salutem;* and, therefore, five manner of persons (who more hurt the body of man than the disease itself, one of which said of one of their patients, *fugiens morbum incidit in medicum*) are to be removed:—1. *Improbi.* 2. *Avari, qui medicinam magis avaritiœ suœ causa quam ullius bonœ conscientiœ fiducia profitentur.* 3. *Malitiosi.* 4. *Temerarii.* 5. *Inscii.* And of the other part five manner of persons were to be promoted, as appears by the said Act, *sc.* those who were: 1, profound; 2, sad; 3, discreet; 4, groundly learned; 5, profoundly studied. And it was well ordained, that the professors of physic should be profound, sad, discreet, &c. and not youths, who have no gravity and experience; for as one saith, *In juvene theologo conscientiœ detrimentum, in juvene legista*

114

bursœ detrimentum, in juvene medico cœmiterii incrementum. And it ought to be presumed, every doctor of any of the universities to be within the statutes, *sc.* to be profound, sad, discreet, groundly learned, and profoundly studied, for none can there be master of arts (who is a doctor of philosophy) under the study of seven years, and cannot be doctor in physic under seven years more in the study of physic; and that is the reason that the plaintiff is named in the declaration doctor of philosophy, and doctor of physic; *quia oportet medicum esse philosophum, ubi enim philosophus desinit, medicus incipit.* As to the two points upon which the Chief Justice, Warburton and Daniel, gave judgment. 1. It was resolved by them, that the said censors had not power to commit the plaintiff for any of the causes mentioned in the bar; and the cause and reason thereof shortly was, that the said clause, which gives power to the said censors to fine and imprison, doth not extend to the said clause, *sc. quod nemo in dicta civitate, &c. exerceat dictam facultatem, &c.* which prohibits every one from practising physic in London, &c. without licence from the president and college: but extends only to punish those who practise physic in London, *pro delicit suis in non bene exequendo, faciendo et utendo facultate medicinœ,* by fine and imprisonment [B]: so that the censors have not power by the letters patent, and the Act, to fine or imprison any for practising physic in London, but only *pro delictis suis in non bene exequendo, &c. sc.* for ill, and not good use and practice of physic. And that was made manifest by five reasons, which were called *vividœ rationes,* because they had their vigour and life from the letters patent and the Act itself; and the best [a] expositor of all letters patent, and Acts of Parliament, are the letters patent and the Acts of Parliament themselves, by construction, and conferring [b] all the parts of them together,[c] *optima statuti interpretatrix est (omnibus particulis ejusdem inspectis) ipsum statutum;* and [d] *injustum est nisi tota lege inspecta una aliqua ejus particula proposita judicare vel respondere.* The first reason was, that these two were two absolute, perfect, and distinct clauses, and as parallels, and therefore the one did not extend to the other; for the second begins, *prœterea voluit et concessit, &c.* and the branch concerning fine and imprisonment is parcel of the second clause. 2. The first clause prohibiting the practice of physic, &c. comprehends four certainties:—1. Certainty of the thing prohibited, *sc.* practice of physic. 2. Certainty of the time, *sc.* practice for one month. 3. Certainty of penalty, *sc.* 5l. 4. Certainty in distribution, *sc.* one moiety to the King, and the other moiety to the college; and

B. *Mala praxis* in a physician, surgeon, or apothecary, is a great misdemeanor and offence at common law, whether it be for curiosity or experiment, or by neglect; because it breaks the trust which the party had placed in his physician, and tends to the patient's destruction. *Dr. Groenvelt's case,* Ld. Raym. 243. S. C. 12 Mod. 119.

a. Godb. 418. 2 Roll. Rep. 356, Wing. Max. 239.

b. 2 Co. 55 a. 3 Co. 59 b. Godb. 324. Co. Lit. 381. 5 Co. 99 a.

c. Wing. Max. 239.

d. Wing. Max. 239.

this penalty he who practises physic in London incurs, although he practices and uses physic well, and profitable for the body of man; and on this branch the information was exhibited in the King's Bench. But the clause to punish *delicta in non bene exequendo, &c.* on which branch the case at Bar stands, is altogether uncertain, for the hurt which may come thereby may be little or great, *leve vel grave,* excessive or small, &c. and therefore the King and the makers of the Act could not, for an offence so uncertain, impose a certainty of the fine, or time of imprisonment, but leave it to the censors to punish such offences, *secundum quantitatem delicti,* which is included in these words, *per fines, amerciamenta, imprisonamenta corporum suorum, et per alias vias rationabiles et congruas.* 2. The harm which accrues by *non bene exequendo, &c.* concerns the body of man; and, therefore, it is reasonable that the offender should be punished in his body, *sc.* by imprisonment: but he who practices physic in London in a good manner, although he doth it without licence, yet it is not any prejudice to the body of man. 3. He who practises physic in London doth not offend the statute by his practice, unless he practises it by the space of a month. But the clause of *non bene exequendo, &c.* doth not prescribe any certain time, but at what time soever he ministers physic *non bene, &c.* he shall be punished by the said second branch: and the law hath great reason in making this distinction, for divers nobles,[a] gentlemen, and others, come upon divers occasions to London, and when they are here they become subject to diseases, and thereupon they send for their physicians in the country, who know their bodies, and the cause of their diseases; now it was never the meaning of the Act to bar any one of his own physician; and when he is here he may practise and minister to another by two or three weeks, &c. without any forfeiture; for any one who practises physic *bene, &c.* in London (although he has not taken any degree in any of the universities) shall forfeit nothing, unless he practises it by the space of a month; and that was the reason that the time of a month was put in the Act. 4. The censors cannot be [b] judges, ministers, and parties; judges to give sentence or judgment; ministers to make summons; and parties to have the moiety of the forfeiture, *quia [c] aliquis non debet esse Judex in propria causa, imo iniquum est aliquem suœ rei esse judicem;* and one cannot be Judge and attorney for any of the parties, Dyer 3 E. 6. 65. 38 E. 3. 15. 8 H. 6. 19 b. 20 a. 21 E. 4. 47 a. &c. And it appears in our books, that in many cases, the common law will [d] controul Acts of Parliament, and sometimes adjudge them to be utterly void: for when an Act of Parliament is against common right and reason, or repugnant, or impossible to be performed, the common law will controul it, and adjudge such Act to be void; and, therefore, in 8 E. 3. 30 a. b. *Thomas Tregor's case* on the statute of W. 2. c. 38. *et* Artic' Super Chartas, c. 9. Herle [e] saith, some statutes are made against law and right, which those who made them perceiving, would not put them in execution [C]: the stat.

a. Cart. 115.   **c.** Co. Lit. 141 a.

b. Co. Lit. 141 a. Bridg. 11. Dyer 220.   **d.** 7 Co. 14 a. *Calvin's case.* 2 Brownl.
pl. 14.   198. 265. Hard. 140.

of W. 2.[f] c. 21. gives a writ of *cessavit hœredi petenti super hœredem tenent' et super eos quibus alienatum fuerit hujusmodi tenementum:* and yet it is adjudged in 33 E. 3.[a] Cessavit 42. where the case was, two coparceners lords, and tenant by fealty and certain rent, one coparcener had issue and died, the aunt and the niece shall not join in a *cessavit,*

e. 8 E. 3. 30 b.

C. Lord Ellesmere observes, (Observations on the Reports, p. 21.) "And for novelty in *Dr. Bonham's case*, the Chief Justice having no precedent for him, but many judgments against him, yet doth he strike in sunder the bars of government of the College of Physicians: and, without any pausing on the matter, frustrate the patent of King Henry VIII., whereby the college was erected, and tramples upon the Act of Parliament, 14 & 15 H. 8. whereby that patent was confirmed, blowing them both away as vain, and of no value, and this is in triumph of himself being accompanied but with the opinion of one Judge only for the matter in law where three other Judges were against him, which case possesseth a better room in the press than is deserved."

In Serjt. Hill's copy of the observations in Lincoln's Inn Library, there is the following manuscript observation on the strictures of Lord Ellesmere. "In page 117 of the Report of *Dr Bonham's case*, in 8 Co. it appears that two of the other Judges agreed with Coke as to the two points of which they gave judgment. The second point is in 117 b. and the matter of law in support of it, which is condemned here, is in page 118, viz. that a statute against reason is void, and is supported by many authorities then, and by others before, and since in our Courts; and the antiquity of it is still more ancient. Just. Inst. Lib. Tit. 2. Text 1. *Dr. Bonham's case* is reported in 2 Brownl. 255 to 266; and in p. 260, it appears that the case was argued by all the Justices of C. B., and at two several days it was argued by Foster, Daniel, and Warburton, against the plaintiff, and the second day by Walmsley, J. and Coke, C.J.: but the argument of Foster, Daniel, and Warburton, are not reported by Brownlow; but he reports fully, 1st, the argument of Walmsley for the plaintiff, and afterwards that of Coke against him. And in page 265, the like reasons and authorities are given by Coke, for his opinion, as appears in his Reports; and then Brownlow mentions only at the end, that 'so he (Coke) concluded that judgment shall be entered for the plaintiff, which was done accordingly.' This last report is, I think, a confirmation of Lord Coke's report, though Lord Coke only re-

ports the effect of the arguments of the justices, who were of opinion against the plaintiff, fol. 116. There is, it is true, in some parts of the argument some things that savour of the pedantry and quaintness peculiar to the time, but nothing to impeach that part of it which is the part objected to by Lord Egerton; and, as above observed, Coke's opinion as to that part at least, is confirmed by many authorities before that case."

In the *City of London* v. *Wood*, 12 Mod. 669., debt was brought in the Mayor's Court, (a Court holden before the mayor and aldermen) on a bye-law, to recover a forfeiture for refusing to serve the office of sheriff, and such action was brought in the name of the mayor and commonalty, and it was held to be error; and per Holt, C.J., "What my Lord Coke says in *Bonham's case*, in his 8 Co., is far from any extravagancy, for it is a very reasonable and true saying, that if an Act of Parliament should ordain that the same person should be party and Judge, or which is the same thing, Judge in his own cause, it would be a void Act of Parliament; for it is impossible that one should be Judge and party, for the Judge is to determine between party and party, or between the Government and the party; and an Act of Parliament can do no wrong, though it may do several things that look pretty odd; for it may discharge one from his allegiance to the Government he lives under, and restore him to the state of nature: but it cannot make one who lives under a Government Judge and party. An Act of Parliament may not make adultery lawful, that is, it cannot make it lawful for A. to lie with the wife of B.: but it may make the wife of A. to be the wife of B., and dissolve her marriage with A." *Vid.* Doctor and Stud. p. 154. 146. *Day* v. *Savadge*, Hob. 87. *Stewart* v. *Lawton*, 1 Bing. 374. S. C. 8 B. Moore. 414.

Serjt. Hill, in his copy of the Reports, refers to Forbe's Parliam. Deb. Vol. VII. p. 84, 85, as mentioning several void Acts.

f. 2 Inst. 401, 402.

a. 2 Brownl. 265. 2 Inst. 402. F. N. B. 209 f.

because the heir [b] shall not have a *cessavit* for the cesser in the time of his ancestor, F. N. B. 209. F. and therewith agrees Plow. Com. 110 a.; and the reason is, because in a *cessavit* the tenant before judgment may render the arrearages and damages, &c. and retain his land, and that he cannot do when the heir brings a *cessavit* for the cesser in the time of his ancestor, for the arrearages incurred in the life of the ancestor do not belong to the heir: and because it would be against common right and reason, the common law adjudges the said Act of Parliament as to that point void. The Statute of [c] Carlisle, made anno 35 E. 1. enacts, that the order of the Cistercians and Augustines, who have a convent and common seal, that the common seal shall be in the keeping of the prior, who is under the abbot, and four others of the most grave of the house, and that any deed sealed with the common seal, which is not so in keeping shall be void: and the opinion of the Court (in an. 27 H. 6. Annuity 41.) was, that this statute was [a] void, for it is impertinent to be observed, for the seal being in their keeping, the abbot cannot seal any thing with it, and when it is in the abbot's hands, it is out of their keeping *ipso facto;* and if the statute should be [b] observed, every common seal shall be defeated upon a simple surmise, which cannot be tried. Note, reader, the words of the said statute at Carlisle, anno 35 E. 1. (which is called *Statutum Religiosorum*) are, *Et insuper ordinavit dominus Rex et statuit, quod Abbates Cisterc' et Præmonstraten' ordin' religiosorum, &c. de cœtero habeant sigillum commune, et illud in custodia prioris monasterii seu domus, et quatuor de dignioribus et discretioribus ejusdem loci conventus sub privato sigillo abbatis ipsius loci custod' depo', &c. Et si forfan aliqua scripta obligationum, donationum, emptionum, venditionum, alienationum, seu aliorum quorumcunque, contractuum alio sigillo quam tali sigillo communi sicut præmittit' custodit' inveniant' a modo sigillat', pro nullo penitus habeantur omnique careant firmitate.* So the statute of 1 E. 6. c. 14. gives chauntries, &c. to the King, saving to the donor, &c. all such rents, services, &c. and the common law controuls it, and adjudges it void as to services, and the donor shall have the rent, as a rentseck, distrainable of common right, for it would be against common right and reason that the [c] King should hold of any, or do service to any of his subjects, 14 Eliz. Dyer 313. and so it was adjudged Mich. 16 & 17 Eliz. in Com' Banco in [d] *Strowd's case.* So if any Act of Parliament gives to any to hold, or to have conusans of all manner of pleas arising before him within his manor of D., yet he shall hold no plea, to which he himself is party; for, as hath been said, *iniquum est aliquem suœ rei esse judicem.* 5. If he

b. 2 Brownl. 265. Vet. N. B. 138 b. 2 Inst. 442. Com. Dig. Parl. R. 27.

c. 2 Inst. 580, 581, 582, &c. Skinner 464.

a. 2 Inst. 588. 2 Brownl. 198. 265.

b. 2 Brownl. 265. 2 Inst. 587.

c. Dy. 313. pl. 91. 1 Co. 47 a. Dav. 2 a. Co. Lit. 1 b. Cro. Car. 82, 83. 2 Roll. Rep. 246, 247. 1 Jones 234. Lit. Rep. 43.

d. 1 And. 45. 3 Leon. 58. 4 Leon. 40, 41.

should forfeit 5l. for one month by the first clause, and should be punished for practising at any time by the second clause, two absurdities should follow,—1. That one should be punished not only twice but many times for one and the same offence. And the divine saith, *Quod*[e] *Deus non agit bis in idipsum;* and the law saith,[f] *Nemo debet bis puniri pro uno delicto.* 2. It would be absurd, by the first clause, to punish practising for a month, and not for a lesser time, and by the second to punish practising not only for a day, but at any time, so he shall be punished by the first branch for one month by the forfeit of 5l. and by the second by fine and imprisonment, without limitation for every time of the month in which he practises physic. And all these reasons were proved by two grounds, or maxims in law; 1.[g] *Generalis clausula non porrigitur ad ea quœ specialiter sunt comprehensa:* and the case between Carter and[a] Ringstead, Hil. 34 Eliz. Rot. 120. in Communi Banco, was cited to this purpose, where the case in effect was, that A. seised of the manor of Staple, in Odiham, in the county of Southampton in fee, and also of other lands in Odiham aforesaid in fee, suffered a common recovery of all, and declared the use by indenture, that the recoverer should stand seised of all the lands and tenements in Odiham, to the use of A. and his wife, and to the heirs of his body begotten; and further, that the recoveror should stand seised to the use of him, and to the heirs of his body, and died, and the wife survived, and entered into the said manor by force of the said general words: but it was adjudged, that they did not extend to the said manor which was specially named: and if it be so in a deed, *a fortiori*, it shall be so in an Act of Parliament, which (as a will) is to be expounded according to the intention of the makers. 2.[b] *Verba posteriora propter certitudinem addita ad priora quœ certitudine indigent sunt referenda.* 6 E.[c] 3. 12 a. b. Sir Adam de Clydrow, Knight, brought a *prœcipe quod reddat* against John de Clydrow; and the writ was, *quod juste, &c. reddat manerium de Wicomb et duas carucatus terrœ cum pertinentiis in Clydrow*, in that case the town of Clydrow shall not relate to the manor, *quia non indiget*, for a manor may be demanded without mentioning that it lies in any town, but *cum pertinentiis*, although it comes after the town, shall relate to the manor, *quia indiget*. *Vide* 3 E. 4. 10. the like case. But it was objected, that where by the second clause it was granted, that the censors should have *supervisum et scrutinium, correctionem et gubernationem omnium et singulorum medicorum, &c.* they had power to fine and imprison.

e. 4 Co. 43 a.

f. 2 Vent. 170. 4 Co. 43 a. 5 Co. 61 a. 11 Co. 59 b. 1 Roll. Rep. 95. Cawly 78. Noy 82. Bridgm. 122. Cro. Jac. 481. Wing. Max. 695.

g. *Postea* 154 b. Raymond 330. Hawkes's Max. 12. Styles 391.

a. Cro. El. 208. 2 Leon. 47. Owen 84, 85. 1 And. 245. 6 Co. 64 b. 3 Bulstr. 66. 185. 2 Roll. Rep. 276. Winch. 92. Lane 69. Lit. Rep. 64. 67. 289. Styles 391.

b. Wing. Max. 67. Lit. Rep. 66.

c. Lit. Rep. 66. Wing. Max. 67. Styles 78.

objected, that where by the second clause it was granted, that the censors should have *supervisum et scrutinium, correctionem et gubernationem omnium et singulorum medicorum, &c.* they had power to fine and imprison.

To that it was answered,—1. That *this* is but part of the sentence, for by the entire sentence it appears in what manner they shall have power to punish, for the words are, *ac punitionem eorum pro delictis suis in non bene exequendo, faciendo, vel utendo illa facultate;* so that without question all their power to correct and punish the physicians by this clause is only limited to these three cases, *sc. in non bene exequendo, faciendo, vel utendo, &c.* Also this word *punitionem* is limited and restrained by these words, *ita quod punitio eorundem medicorum, &c. sic in prœmissis delinquentium, &c.* which words, *sic inprœmissis delinquentium,* limit the former words in the first part of this sentence, *ac punitionem eorum pro delictis suis in non bene exequendo, &c.* 2. It would be absurd, that in one and the same sentence the makers of the Act should give them a general power to punish without limitation; and a special manner how they shall punish, in one and the same sentence. 3. Hil. 38 Eliz. in a *quo warranto* against the Mayor and Commonalty of London, it was held, that where a grant is made to the mayor and commonalty, that the mayor for the time being should have [d] *plenum et integrum scrutinium, gubernationem, et correctionem omnium et singulorum mysteriorum, &c.* without granting them any Court, in which should be legal proceedings, that is good for search, whereby a discovery may be made of offences and defects, which may be punished by the law in any Court; but it doth not give, nor can give them any irregular or absolute power to correct or punish any of the subjects of the kingdom at their pleasure.

2. It was objected, that it is incident to every Court created by letters patent, or Act of Parliament, and other Courts of Record, to punish any misdemeanor done in Court, in disturbance or contempt of the Court, by imprisonment [D]. To which it was answered, that neither the letters patent nor the Act of Parliament has granted them any Court, but only an [a] authority, which they ought to pursue, as it shall be afterwards said. 2. If any Court had been granted them, they could not by any incident authority *implicitè* granted them, for any misdemeanor done in Court, commit him to prison without bail or mainprize, until he should be by the commandment of the president and censors, or their successors, delivered, as the censors have done in this case.

3. There was not any such misdemeanor for which any Court might imprison him, for he only shewed his case to them, which, he was advised by his counsel, he might justify, which is not any offence worthy

d. Cart. 120, 121.   a. *Postea* 121 a.
D. *Vid. ante* note (c) *Butt's case,* 7 Co. 25 a.

of imprisonment. The second point was, admitting that the censors had power by the Act, if they had pursued their authority, or not?

And it was resolved by the Chief Justice, Warburton and Daniel, that they had not pursued it for six reasons. 1. By the Act, the censors only have power to impose a fine, or amerciament; and the president and censors imposed the amerciament of 5l. upon the plaintiff. 2. The plaintiff was summoned to appear *coram præsidente et censoribus, &c. et non comparuit*, and therefore he was fined 10l. whereas the president had no authority in that case. 3. The fines or amercements to be imposed by them, by force of the Act, do not belong to them, but to the King, for the King had not granted the fines or amercements to them, and yet the fine is appointed to be paid to them, *in proximis comitiis*, and they have imprisoned the plaintiff for nonpayment thereof. 4. They ought to have committed the plaintiff presently, by construction of law, although that no time be limited in the Act, as in the statute of W. 2. cap. 11. [b]*De servientibus, ballivis, &c. qui ad compotum reddend' tenentur, &c. cum dom' hujusmodi servientium dederit eis auditores compoti, et contingat ipsos in arrearagiis super compotum suum omnibus allocatis et allocandis, arrestentur corpora eorum, et per testimonium auditorum ejusdem compoti mittantur et liberentur proximæ gaolæ domini Regis in partibus illis, etc.* In that case, although no time be limited when the accomptant shall be imprisoned, yet it ought to be done[c] presently, as it is held in 27 H. 6. 8 a. and the reason thereof is given in *Fogassa's case*, Plowd. Com. 17 b. that the generality of the time shall be restrained to the present time, for the benefit of him upon whom the pain shall be inflicted, and therewith agrees Plow. Com. 206 b. in *Stradling's case*. And a justice[a] of peace, upon view of the force, ought to commit the offender presently. 5. Forasmuch as the censors had their authority by the letters patent and Act of Parliament, which are high matters of record, their proceedings ought not to be by parol, *et eo potius*, because they claim authority to fine and imprison, and therefore, if judgment be given against one in the Common Pleas in a writ of[b] recaption, he shall be fined and imprisoned, but if the writ be vicontiel in the county, there he shall not be fined or imprisoned, because a writ of the Court is not of record, F. N. B. in Recaption. So in F. N. B. 47 a. a plea of trespass *vi et armis* doth not lie in the County Court, Hundred Court, &c. for they cannot make a record of fine and imprisonment; and regularly they who cannot make[c] a record, cannot fine and imprison.

b. 2 Inst. 379, 380. W. 2. c. 11. Plowd. 17 b. Rast. Account 2.

c. *Postea* 120 b. 2 Brownl. 266. 2 Inst. 380. 2 Bulstr. 139. Fitz. Bar. 44. Br. Account 6. Br. Det. 16. Br. Execution 135. Br. Faux Imprisonment 32. 1 Ld. Raym. 483.

a. 2 Brownl. 266. 15 R. 2. c. 2. 8 H. 6. c. 9. 6 Mod. 125.

b. *Antea* 60 b. 41 a. 8 Co. 41. 11 Co. 43 b. F. N. B. 73 d. Vin. Ab. Amerc. 1 a. pl. 23. 1 L. Raym. 468.

c. *Antea* fo. 38 b. 41 a. 60 b. F. N. B. 73 d. 10 Co. 103 a. 1 Salk. 200. 8 T. R. 516.

And therewith agrees 27 H. 6. 8. Book of Entries, tit. Account, fol.—.
The auditors make a record when they commit the defendant to prison;
a justice of peace upon view of the force may commit, but he ought to
make a record of it. 6. Forasmuch as the Act of 14 H. 8. has given power
to imprison till he shall be delivered by the president and the censors, or
their successors, reason requires that it should be taken strictly, for the
liberty of the subject (as they pretend) is at their pleasure: and this is
well proved by a judgment in Parliament in this very case; for when this
Act of 14 H. 8. had given the censors power to imprison, yet it was taken
so literally, that the gaoler was not bound to receive such as they should
commit to him; and the reason thereof was, because they had authority
to do it without any Court: and thereupon the statute of 1 Ma.[d] cap. 9.
was made, that the gaoler should receive them upon a penalty, and yet
none can commit any to prison, unless the gaoler receive him: but the
first Act, for the cause aforesaid, was taken so literally, that no necessary
incident was implied.

And where it was objected, that this very Act of 1 Mar. c. 9. has
enlarged the power of the censors, and they urged it upon the words of
the Act; it was clearly resolved, that the said Act of 1 Mar. did not
enlarge the power of the censors to fine or imprison any person for any
cause for which he ought not to be fined or imprisoned by the said Act
of[e] 14 H. 8. For the words of the Act of Queen Mary are, "according to
the tenor and meaning of the said Act:" also "shall send or commit any
offender or offenders for his or their offence or disobedience, contrary to
any article or clause contained in the said grant or Act, to any ward,
gaol, &c." But in this case Bonham has not done any thing which
appears within this record, contrary to any article or clause contained
within the grant or Act of 14 H. 8. Also the gaoler who refuses shall
forfeit the double value of the fines and amerciaments that any offender
or disobedient shall be assessed to pay; which proves that none shall be
received by any gaoler by force of the Act of 14 H. 8. but he who may be
lawfully fined or amerced by the Act of 18 H. 8. and that was not
Bonham, as by the reasons and causes aforesaid appears. And admitting
that the replication be not material, and the defendants have demurred
upon it; yet forasmuch as the defendants have confessed in the Bar, that
they have imprisoned the plaintiff without cause, the plaintiff shall have
judgment: and the difference is, when the plaintiff replies, and by his
replication it appears that he has no cause of action, there he shall never
have judgment: but when the [a] bar is insufficient in matter, or amounts
(as the case is) to a confession of the point of the action, and the plaintiff
replies, and shews the truth of the matter to enforce his case, and in

d. 2 Brownl. 257. 262. 265, 266. Rast. Lit. Rep. 168, 169. 172. 212. 215. 246, 247,
Phys. 7. Lit. Rep. 169. 172, 173. 212, 213. 248, 249. 1 Jones 261. Cro. Jac. 121. 159,
248, 249. 350, 351. Cr. Jac. 121. Cr. Car. 160. Cro. Car. 256. Palm. 486. Cart. 115.
257. 1 Jones 263. Car. 115. 4 Inst. 251.
e. 14 & 15 H. 8. cap. 5. Roll. 598. 4   **a.** 9 Co. 110 b. and ref. Moor. 464. 1
Inst. 251. Rast. Phys. 3. 2 Bulstr. 185.   Lev. 195.

judgment of law it is not material, yet the plaintiff shall have judgment, for it is true that sometimes the declaration shall be made good by the bar, and sometimes the bar by the replication, and sometimes the replication by the rejoinder, &c. but the difference is, when the declaration wants time, place, or other circumstance, it may be made good by the bar; so of the bar, replication, &c. as appears in 18 E. 4. 16 b. But when the declaration wants substance, no bar can make it good; so of the bar, replication, &c. and therewith agrees 6 E. 4. 2. a good case, and *nota* there *dictum* Coke. *Vide* 18 E. 3. 34 b. 44 E. 3. 7 a. 12 E. 4. 6. 6 H. 7. 10. 7 H. 7. 3. 11 H. 4. 24. &c.[E].

But when the plaintiff makes replication, sur-rejoinder, &c. and thereby it appears, that upon the [†] whole record the plaintiff has no cause of action, he shall never have judgment, although the bar or rejoinder, &c. be insufficient in matter; for the Court ought to judge upon the whole record [F], and every one shall be intended to make the best of his own case. *Vide* [b] *Ridgeway's case*, in the Third Part of my Reports 52 b. and so these differences were resolved and adjudged between [††] *Kendal and Helyer*, Mich. 25 & 26 Eliz. in the King's Bench, and Mich. 29 & 30 Eliz. in the same Court, between [c] *Gallys and Burbry*.

And Coke, Chief Justice, in the conclusion of his argument, observed seven things for the better direction of the president and commonalty of the said college for the future. 1. That none can be punished for practising physic in London, but by forfeiture of 5l. by the month, which is to be recovered by the law. 2. If any practise physic there for a less time than a month, that he shall forfeit nothing. 3. If any person prohibited by the statute offends *in non bene exeq'*, &c. they may punish him according to the statute within the month. 4. Those who they may commit to prison by the stat. ought to be committed [d] presently. 5. The fines which they set, according to the statute, belong to the King. 6. They cannot impose a fine, or imprisonment without a record of it. 7. The cause for which they impose fine and imprisonment ought to be certain, for it is [a] traversable: for although they have letters patent and an Act of Parliament, yet because the party grieved has no other remedy, neither by writ of error or otherwise, and they are not made judges, nor a Court given them, but have an [b] authority only to do it, the cause of their commitment only is traversable in an action of false imprisonment brought against them [G]; as upon the Statute of Bankrupts, their warrant is under the Great Seal, and by Act of Parliament; yet because the party grieved has no other remedy, if the commissioners do not pursue the Act

E. *Vid.* note (c) *Butt's case, ante* 7 Co. 25 a. *Tippet* v. *May*, 1 Bos. and Pull. 413.

† Hob. 199. Hard. 38.

F. *Vid.* Com. Dig. Pleader, C. 85. E. 37. and 1 Williams' Saunders, *Cutler* v. *Southern*, 118. *Vid.* also note (F) *Fraunces's case, ante* p. 93 a.

b. Styles 354.

†† 3 Co. 52 b.

c. 3 Co. 52 b. Cro. El. 62. 1 Leon. 242.

d. *Antea* 119 b. 2 Brownl. 266. 2 Inst. 380. Bar. 44. Br. Account 6. Br. Det. 16. Br. Exec. 135. Br. Faux Imprisonment 32. 2 Bulstr. 139. 6 Mod. 125. 4 B. and C. 596.

a. 2 Brown. 266. Hard. 482.

b. *Ante* 119 b.

G. In *Groenvelt* v. *Burwell*, 1 Ld. Raym. 468. Holt, C.J. observed, that "the opinion of Coke, that the case of the fine and imprisonment is traversable was an and their commission, he shall traverse, that he was not a bankrupt, although the commissioners affirm him to be one: as this term it was resolved in this Court, in trespass between *Cutt*[d] *and Delabarre*, where the issue was, whether William Cheyney was a bankrupt or not, who was found by the commissioners to be a bankrupt; *a fortiori* in the case at Bar, the cause of the imprisonment is traversable[H]; for otherwise the party grieved may be perpetually, without just cause, imprisoned by them: but the record of a force made by a justice of peace is not traversable, because he doth it as Judge, by the statutes of[e] 15 Rich. 2. and 8 Hen. 6. and so there is a difference when one makes a record as a Judge, and when he doth a thing by special authority, (as they did in the case at Bar) and not as a Judge. And afterwards for the said two last points, judgment was given for the plaintiff, *nullo contradicente* as to them. And I acquainted Sir Thomas Fleming, Chief Justice of the King's Bench, with this judgment and with the reasons and causes of it, and he well approved of the judgment which we had given: and this is the first judgment on the said branch concerning fine and imprisonment which has been given since the making of the said charter and Acts of Parliament, and therefore I thought it worthy to be reported and published.

B. JOHN LOCKE, TWO TREATISES OF GOVERNMENT, THE SECOND TREATISE, AN ESSAY CONCERNING THE TRUE ORIGINAL, EXTENT, AND END OF CIVIL GOVERNMENT

1698

CHAP. VII.

Of Political or Civil Society.

77. GOD having made Man such a Creature, that, in his own Judgment, it was not good for him to be alone, put him under strong

opinion *obiter*, and not pertinent to the case there; because Dr. Bonham was committed for practising without licence, and not for malpractice; and the power of commitment does not extend to practising without licence, nor can they inflict the said punishment for such an offence. But Coke enlarges on their power, and includes a commitment for malpractice. But Coke was transported that the doctor was a member of the university, and of his university (as one may see by his excursions in praise of it) which he looked upon as affronted by that prosecution. And as the said opinion was not judicial, so it has not any authority in law for its foundation. Coke himself says, that they ought to make a record of their proceedings; then they are Judges of record; and, therefore, according to himself (12 Co. 24.) their acts are not traversable." *Vid. Basten* v. *Ca-*

rew, 3 Barn. and Cress. 649. S. C. 5 Dow. and Ryl. 558.; note (G) *The Marshalsea case*, 10 Co. 76 a.

d. 4 Iust. 277, 278.

H. "The general rule of the law, as to actions of trespass against persons having a limited authority (and commissioners of bankrupt are such persons) is plain and clear. If they do any act beyond the limit of their authority, they thereby subject themselves to an action of trespass; but if the act done be within the limits of their authority, although it may be done through an erroneous or mistaken judgment, they are not thereby liable to an action." Per Abbot, C.J. *Doswell* v. *Impey*, 1 Barn. and Cress. 169. S. C. 2 Dow. and Ryl. 353. citing *Miller* v. *Seare*, 2 W. Black. 1141.

e. 15 R. 2. c. 2. 8 H. 6. c. 9.

Obligations of Necessity, Convenience, and Inclination to drive him into *Society*, as well as fitted him with Understanding and Language to continue and enjoy it. The *first Society* was between Man and Wife, which gave beginning to that between Parents and Children; to which, in time, that between Master and Servant came to be added: And though all these might, and commonly did meet together, and make up but one Family, wherein the Master or Mistress of it had some sort of Rule proper to a Family; each of these, or all together came short of *Political Society*, as we shall see, if we consider the different Ends, Tyes, and Bounds of each of these. . . .

* * *

87. Man being born, as has been proved, with a Title to perfect Freedom, and an uncontrouled enjoyment of all the Rights and Priviledges of the Law of Nature, equally with any other Man, or Number of Men in the World, hath by Nature a Power, not only to preserve his Property, that is, his Life, Liberty and Estate, against the Injuries and Attempts of other Men; but to judge of, and punish the breaches of that Law in others, as he is perswaded the Offence deserves, even with Death it self, in Crimes where the heinousness of the Fact, in his Opinion, requires it. But because no *Political Society* can be, nor subsist without having in it self the Power to preserve the Property, and in order thereunto punish the Offences of all those of that Society; there, and there only is *Political Society*, where every one of the Members hath quitted this natural Power, resign'd it up into the hands of the Community in all cases that exclude him not from appealing for Protection to the Law established by it. And thus all private judgement of every particular Member being excluded, the Community comes to be Umpire, by settled standing Rules, indifferent, and the same to all Parties; and by Men having Authority from the Community, for the execution of those Rules, decides all the differences that may happen between any Members of that Society, concerning any matter of right; and punishes those Offences, which any Member hath committed against the Society, with such Penalties as the Law has established: Whereby it is easie to discern who are, and who are not, in *Political Society* together. Those who are united into one Body, and have a common establish'd Law and Judicature to appeal to, with Authority to decide Controversies between them, and punish Offenders, *are in Civil Society* one with another: but those who have no such common Appeal, I mean on Earth, are still in the state of Nature, each being, where there is no other, Judge for himself, and Executioner; which is, as I have before shew'd it, the perfect *state of Nature*.

88.   And thus the Commonwealth comes by a Power to set down, what punishment shall belong to the several transgressions which they think worthy of it, committed amongst the Members of that Society, (which is the *power of making Laws*) as well as it has the power to punish any Injury done unto any of its Members, by any one that is not of it, (which is the *power of War and Peace*;) and all this for the preservation of the property of all the Members of that Society, as far as is possible.   But though every Man who has enter'd into civil Society, and is become a member of any Commonwealth, has thereby quitted his power to punish Offences against the Law of Nature, in prosecution of his own private Judgment; yet with the Judgment of Offences which he has given up to the Legislative in all Cases, where he can Appeal to the Magistrate, he has given a right to the Commonwealth to imploy his force, for the Execution of the Judgments of the Commonwealth, when-ever he shall be called to it; which indeed are his own Judgments, they being made by himself, or his Representative.   And herein we have the original of the *Legislative* and *Executive Power* of Civil Society, which is to judge by standing Laws how far Offences are to be punished, when committed within the Commonwealth; and also to determin, by occa-sional Judgments founded on the present Circumstances of the Fact, how far Injuries from without are to be vindicated, and in both these to imploy all the force of all the Members when there shall be need.

89.   Where-ever therefore any number of Men are so united into one Society, as to quit every one his Executive Power of the Law of Nature, and to resign it to the publick, there and there only is a *Political, or Civil Society*.   And this is done where-ever any number of Men, in the state of Nature, enter into Society to make one People, one Body Politick under one Supreme Government, or else when any one joyns himself to, and incorporates with any Government already made. For hereby he authorizes the Society, or which is all one, the Legislative thereof to make Laws for him as the publick good of the Society shall require; to the Execution whereof, his own assistance (as to his own Decrees) is due.   And this *puts Men* out of a State of Nature *into* that of a *Commonwealth*, by setting up a Judge on Earth, with Authority to determine all the Controversies, and redress the Injuries, that may happen to any Member of the Commonwealth; which Judge is the Legislative, or Magistrates appointed by it.   And where-ever there are any number of Men, however associated, that have no such decisive power to appeal to, there they are still *in the state of Nature*.

90.   Hence it is evident, that *Absolute Monarchy*, which by some Men is counted the only Government in the World, is indeed *inconsistent with Civil Society*, and so can be no Form of Civil Government at all. For the *end of Civil Society*, being to avoid, and remedy those inconven-iencies of the State of Nature, which necessarily follow from every Man's being Judge in his own Case, by setting up a known Authority, to which every one of that Society may Appeal upon any Injury received, or

Controversie that may arise, and which every one of the Society ought to obey;* where-ever any persons are, who have not such an Authority to Appeal to, for the decision of any difference between them, there those persons are still *in the state of Nature*. And so is every *Absolute Prince* in respect of those who are under his *Dominion*.

91.   For he being suppos'd to have all, both Legislative and Executive Power in himself alone, there is no Judge to be found, no Appeal lies open to any one, who may fairly, and indifferently, and with Authority decide, and from whose decision relief and redress may be expected of any Injury or Inconveniency, that may be suffered from the Prince or by his Order: So that such a Man, however intitled, *Czar*, or *Grand Signior*, or how you please, is as much *in the state of Nature*, with all under his Dominion, as he is with the rest of Mankind. For where-ever any two Men are, who have no standing Rule, and common Judge to Appeal to on Earth for the determination of Controversies of Right betwixt them, there they are still *in the state of Nature*, and under all the inconveniencies of it,** with only this woful difference to the Subject, or rather Slave of an Absolute Prince: That whereas, in the ordinary State of Nature, he has a liberty to judge of his Right, and according to the best of his Power, to maintain it; now whenever his Property is invaded by the Will and Order of his Monarch, he has not only no Appeal, as those in Society ought to have, but as if he were degraded from the common state of Rational Creatures, is denied a liberty to judge of, or to defend his Right, and so is exposed to all the Misery and Inconveniencies that a Man can fear from one, who being in the unrestrained state of Nature, is yet corrupted with Flattery, and armed with Power.

92.   For he that thinks *absolute Power purifies Mens Bloods*, and corrects the baseness of Humane Nature, need read but the History of this, or any other Age to be convinced of the contrary. He that would have been insolent and injurious in the Woods of *America*, would not

* *The publick Power of all Society is above every Soul contained in the same Society; and the principal use of that power is to give Laws unto all that are under it, which Laws in such Cases we must obey, unless there be reason shew'd which may necessarily inforce, that the Law of Reason, or of God, doth injoyn the contrary,* Hook. Eccl. Pol. l.I. Sect. 16.

** *To take away all such mutual Grievances, Injuries and Wrongs, i.e. such as attend Men in the State of Nature. There was no way but only by growing into Composition and Agreement amongst themselves, by ordaining some kind of Government publick, and by yielding themselves subject thereunto, that unto whom they granted Authority to Rule and Govern, by them the Peace, Tranquility, and happy Estate of the rest might be procured. Men always knew that where Force and Injury was offered, they might be Defenders of themselves; they knew that however Men may seek their own Commodity; yet if this were done with Injury unto others, it was not to be suffered, but by all Men, and all good Means to be withstood. Finally, they knew that no Man might in reason take upon him to determine his own Right, and according to his own Determination proceed in maintenance thereof, in as much as every Man is towards himself, and them whom be greatly affects, partial; and therefore that Strifes and Troubles would be endless, except they gave their common Consent, all to be ordered by some, whom they should agree upon, without which Consent there would be no reason that one Man should take upon him to be Lord or Judge over another.* Hooker's Eccl. Pol. l.I Sect. 10.

probably be much better in a Throne; where perhaps Learning and Religion shall be found out to justifie all, that he shall do to his Subjects, and the Sword presently silence all those that dare question it. For what the *Protection of Absolute Monarchy* is, what kind of Fathers of their Countries it makes Princes to be, and to what a degree of Happiness and Security it carries Civil Society, where this sort of Government is grown to perfection, he that will look into the late Relation of *Ceylon*, may easily see.

93. *In Absolute Monarchies* indeed, as well as other Governments of the World, the Subjects have an Appeal to the Law, and Judges to decide any Controversies, and restrain any Violence that may happen betwixt the Subjects themselves, one amongst another. This every one thinks necessary, and believes he deserves to be thought a declared Enemy to Society and Mankind, who should go about to take it away. But whether this be from a true Love of Mankind and Society, and such a Charity as we owe all one to another, there is reason to doubt. For this is no more, than what every Man who loves his own Power, Profit, or Greatness, may, and naturally must do, keep those Animals from hurting or destroying one another who labour and drudge only for his Pleasure and Advantage, and so are taken care of, not out of any Love the Master has for them, but Love of himself, and the Profit they bring him. For if it be asked, what Security, *what Fence* is there in such a State, *against the Violence and Oppression of this Absolute Ruler*? The very Question can scarce be born. They are ready to tell you, that it deserves Death only to ask after Safety. Betwixt Subject and Subject, they will grant, there must be Measures, Laws, and Judges, for their mutual Peace and Security: But as for the *Ruler*, he ought to be *Absolute*, and is above all such Circumstances: because he has Power to do more hurt and wrong, 'tis right when he does it. To ask how you may be guarded from harm, or injury on that side where the strongest hand is to do it, is presently the Voice of Faction and Rebellion. As if when Men quitting the State of Nature entered into Society, they agreed that all of them but one, should be under the restraint of Laws, but that he should still retain all the Liberty of the State of Nature, increased with Power, and made licentious by Impunity. This is to think that Men are so foolish that they take care to avoid what Mischiefs may be done them by *Pole-Cats*, or *Foxes*, but are content, nay think it Safety, to be devoured by *Lions*.

94. But whatever Flatterers may talk to amuze Peoples Understandings, it hinders not Men, from feeling: and when they perceive, that any Man, in what Station soever, is out of the Bounds of the Civil Society which they are of; and that they have no Appeal on Earth against any harm they may receive from him, they are apt to think themselves in the state of Nature, in respect of him, whom they find to be so; and to take care as soon as they can, to have that *Safety and Security in Civil Society*, for which it was first instituted, and for which

128

only they entered into it. And therefore, though perhaps at first, (as shall be shewed more at large hereafter in the following part of this Discourse) some one good and excellent Man, having got a Preheminency amongst the rest, had this Deference paid to his Goodness and Vertue, as to a kind of Natural Authority, that the chief Rule, with Arbitration of their differences, by a tacit Consent devolved into his hands, without any other caution, but the assurance they had of his Uprightness and Wisdom: yet when time, giving Authority, and (as some Men would perswade us) Sacredness to Customs, which the negligent, and unforeseeing Innocence of the first Ages began, had brought in Successors of another Stamp, the People finding their Properties not secure under the Government, as then it was, (whereas Government has no other end but the preservation of Property) could never be safe nor at rest, *nor think themselves in Civil Society*, till the Legislature was placed in collective Bodies of Men, call them Senate, Parliament, or what you please.[†] By which means every single person became subject, equally with other the meanest Men, to those Laws, which he himself, as part of the Legislative had established: nor could any one, by his own Authority, avoid the force of the Law, when once made, nor by any pretence of Superiority, plead exemption, thereby to License his own, or the Miscarriages of any of his Dependants. *No Man in Civil Society can be exempted from the Laws of it.*[††] For if any Man may do, what he thinks fit, and there be no Appeal on Earth, for Redress or Security against any harm he shall do; I ask, Whether he be not perfectly still in the State of Nature, and so can be *no part or Member of that Civil Society*: unless any one will say, the State of Nature and Civil Society are one and the same thing, which I have never yet found any one so great a Patron of Anarchy as to affirm.

CHAP. VIII.

Of the Beginning of Political Societies.

95. MEN being, as has been said, by Nature, all free, equal and independent, no one can be put out of this Estate, and subjected to the Political Power of another, without his own *Consent*. The only way whereby any one devests himself of his Natural Liberty, and *puts on the bonds of Civil Society* is by agreeing with other Men to joyn and unite into a Community, for their comfortable, safe, and peaceable living one amongst another, in a secure Enjoyment of their Properties, and a greater Security against any that are not of it. This any number of Men may do, because it injures not the Freedom of the rest; they are left as

[†] *At the first, when some certain kind of Regiment was once appointed, it may be that nothing was then farther thought upon for the manner of governing, but all permitted unto their Wisdom and Discretion, which were to Rule, till by experience they found this for all parts very inconvenient, so as the thing which they had devised for a Remedy, did indeed but increase the Sore, which it should have cured. They saw,* <u>*that to live*</u> by one Man's Will, <u>became the cause of all Mens misery.</u> This constrained them to come unto Laws wherein all Men might see their Duty beforehand, and know the Penalties of transgressing them. *Hooker's Eccl. Pol. I. ı. Sect. 10.*

[††] *Civil Law being the Act of the whole Body Politick, doth therefore over-rule each several part of the same Body.* Hooker ibid.

they were in the Liberty of the State of Nature. When any number of Men have so *consented to make one Community* or Government, they are thereby presently incorporated, and make *one Body Politick*, wherein the *Majority* have a Right to act and conclude the rest.

96. For when any number of Men have, by the consent of every individual, made a *Community*, they have thereby made that *Community* one Body, with a Power to Act as one Body, which is only by the will and determination of the *majority*. For that which acts any Community, being only the consent of the individuals of it, and it being necessary to that which is one body to move one way; it is necessary the Body should move that way whither the greater force carries it, which is the *consent of the majority*: or else it is impossible it should act or continue one Body, *one Community*, which the consent of every individual that united into it, agreed that it should; and so every one is bound by that consent to be concluded by the *majority*. And therefore we see that in Assemblies impowered to act by positive Laws where no number is set by that positive Law which impowers them, the *act of the Majority* passes for the act of the whole, and of course determines, as having by the Law of Nature and Reason, the power of the whole.

97. And thus every Man, by consenting with others to make one Body Politick under one Government, puts himself under an Obligation to every one of that Society, to submit to the determination of the *majority*, and to be concluded by it; or else this *original Compact*, whereby he with others incorporates into *one Society*, would signifie nothing, and be no Compact, if he be left free, and under no other ties, than he was in before in the State of Nature. For what appearance would there be of any Compact? What new Engagement if he were no farther tied by any Decrees of the Society, than he himself thought fit, and did actually consent to? This would be still as great a liberty, as he himself had before his Compact, or any one else in the State of Nature hath, who may submit himself and consent to any acts of it if he thinks fit.

98. For if *the consent of the majority* shall not in reason, be received, as *the act of the whole*, and conclude every individual; nothing but the consent of every individual can make any thing to be the act of the whole: But such a consent is next impossible ever to be had, if we consider the Infirmities of Health, and Avocations of Business, which in a number, though much less than that of a Common-wealth, will necessarily keep many away from the publick Assembly. To which if we add the variety of Opinions, and contrariety of Interests, which unavoidably happen in all Collections of Men, the coming into Society upon such terms, would be only like *Cato*'s coming into the Theatre, only to go out again. Such a Constitution as this would make the mighty *Leviathan* of a shorter duration, than the feeblest Creatures; and not let it outlast the day it was born in: which cannot be suppos'd, till we can think, that Rational Creatures should desire and constitute Societies only to be dissolved. For where the *majority* cannot conclude the rest, there they cannot act as one Body, and consequently will be immediately dissolved again.

99. Whosoever therefore out of a state of Nature unite into a *Community*, must be understood to give up all the power, necessary to the ends for which they unite into Society, to the *majority* of the Community, unless they expressly agreed in any number greater than the majority. And this is done by barely agreeing to *unite into one Political Society*, which is *all the Compact* that is, or needs be, between the Individuals, that enter into, or make up a *Common-wealth*. And thus that, which begins and actually *constitutes any Political Society*, is nothing but the consent of any number of Freemen capable of a majority to unite and incorporate into such a Society. And this is that, and that only, which did, or could give *beginning* to any *lawful Government* in the World.

100. To this I find two Objections made.

* * *

Secondly, *'Tis impossible of right that Men should do so, because all Men being born under Government, they are to submit to that, and are not at liberty to begin a new one.*

* * *

119. *Every Man* being, as has been shewed, *naturally free*, and nothing being able to put him into subjection to any Earthly Power, but only his own Consent; it is to be considered, what shall be understood to be *a sufficient Declaration of* a Mans *Consent, to make him subject* to the Laws of any Government. There is a common distinction of an express and a tacit consent, which will concern our present Case. No body doubts but an *express Consent*, of any Man, entring into any Society, makes him a perfect Member of that Society, a Subject of that Government. The difficulty is, what ought to be look'd upon as a *tacit Consent*, and how far it binds, *i.e.* how far any one shall be looked on to have consented, and thereby submitted to any Government, where he has made no Expressions of it at all. And to this I say, that every Man, that hath any Possession, or Enjoyment, of any part of the Dominions of any Government, doth thereby give his *tacit Consent*, and is as far forth obliged to Obedience to the Laws of that Government, during such Enjoyment, as any one under it; whether this his Possession be of Land, to him and his Heirs for ever, or a Lodging only for a Week; or whether it be barely travelling freely on the Highway; and in Effect, it reaches as far as the very being of any one within the Territories of that Government.

120. To understand this the better, it is fit to consider, that every Man, when he, at first, incorporates himself into any Commonwealth, he, by his uniting himself thereunto, annexed also, and submits to the Community those Possessions, which he has, or shall acquire, that do not already belong to any other Government. For it would be a direct Contradiction, for any one, to enter into Society with others for the securing and regulating of Property: And yet to suppose his Land, whose Property is to be regulated by the Laws of the Society, should be exempt

from the Jurisdiction of that Government, to which he himself the Proprietor of the Land, is a Subject. By the same Act therefore, whereby any one unites his Person, which was before free, to any Commonwealth; by the same he unites his Possessions, which were before free, to it also; and they become, both of them, Person and Possession, subject to the Government and Dominion of that Commonwealth, as long as it hath a being. *Whoever* therefore, from thenceforth, by Inheritance, Purchase, Permission, or otherways *enjoys any part of the Land*, so annext to, and under the Government *of that Commonwealth, must take it with the Condition* it is under; that is, *of submitting to the Government of the Commonwealth*, under whose Jurisdiction it is, as far forth, as any Subject of it.

121.   But since the Government has a direct Jurisdiction only over the Land, and reaches the Possessor of it, (before he has actually incorporated himself in the Society) only as he dwells upon, and enjoys that: *The Obligation* any one is under, by Virtue of such Enjoyment, *to submit to the Government, begins and ends with the Enjoyment*; so that whenever the Owner, who has given nothing but such a *tacit Consent* to the Government, will, by Donation, Sale, or otherwise, quit the said Possession, he is at liberty to go and incorporate himself into any other Commonwealth, or to agree with others to begin a new one, *in vacuis locis*, in any part of the World, they can find free and unpossessed: Whereas he, that has once, by actual Agreement, and any *express* Declaration, given his *Consent* to be of any Commonweal, is perpetually and indispensably obliged to be and remain unalterably a Subject to it, and can never be again in the liberty of the state of Nature; unless by any Calamity, the Government, he was under, comes to be dissolved; or else by some publick Act cuts him off from being any longer a Member of it.

122.   But submitting to the Laws of any Country, living quietly, and enjoying Priviledges and Protection under them, *makes not a Man a Member of that Society*: This is only a local Protection and Homage due to, and from all those, who, not being in a state of War, come within the Territories belonging to any Government, to all parts whereof the force of its Law extends. But this no more *makes a Man a Member of that Society*, a perpetual Subject of that Commonwealth, than it would make a Man a Subject to another in whose Family he found it convenient to abide for some time; though, whilst he continued in it, he were obliged to comply with the Laws, and submit to the Government he found there. And thus we see, that *Foreigners*, by living all their Lives under another Government, and enjoying the Priviledges and Protection of it, though they are bound, even in Conscience, to submit to its Administration, as far forth as any Denison; yet do not thereby come to be *Subjects or Members of that Commonwealth*. Nothing can make any Man so, but his actually entering into it by positive Engagement, and express Promise and Compact. This is that, which I think, concerning the beginning of Political Societies, and that *Consent which makes any one a Member* of any Commonwealth.

CHAP. IX.

Of the Ends of Political Society and Government.

123.   IF Man in the State of Nature be so free, as has been said; If he be absolute Lord of his own Person and Possessions, equal to the greatest, and subject to no Body, why will he part with his Freedom? Why will he give up this Empire, and subject himself to the Dominion and Controul of any other Power?   To which 'tis obvious to Answer, that though in the state of Nature he hath such a right, yet the Enjoyment of it is very uncertain, and constantly exposed to the Invasion of others. For all being Kings as much as he, every Man his Equal, and the greater part no strict Observers of Equity and Justice, the enjoyment of the property he has in this state is very unsafe, very unsecure.   This makes him willing to quit a Condition, which however free, is full of fears and continual dangers: And 'tis not without reason, that he seeks out, and is willing to joyn in Society with others who are already united, or have a mind to unite for the mutual *Preservation* of their Lives, Liberties and Estates, which I call by the general Name, *Property*.

124.   The great and *chief end* therefore, of Mens uniting into Commonwealths, and putting themselves under Government, *is the Preservation of their Property*.   To which in the state of Nature there are many things wanting.

First,   There wants an *establish'd*, settled, known *Law*, received and allowed by common consent to be the Standard of Right and Wrong, and the common measure to decide all Controversies between them.   For though the Law of Nature be plain and intelligible to all rational Creatures; yet Men being biassed by their Interest, as well as ignorant for want of study of it, are not apt to allow of it as a Law binding to them in the application of it to their particular Cases.

125.   *Secondly*,   In the State of Nature there wants *a known and indifferent Judge*, with Authority to determine all differences according to the established Law.   For every one in that state being both Judge and Executioner of the Law of Nature, Men being partial to themselves, Passion and Revenge is very apt to carry them too far, and with too much heat, in their own Cases; as well as negligence, and unconcernedness, to make them too remiss, in other Mens.

126.   *Thirdly*,   In the state of Nature there often wants *Power* to back and support the Sentence when right, and to *give* it due *Execution*. They who by any Injustice offended, will seldom fail, where they are able, by force to make good their Injustice: such resistance many times makes the punishment dangerous, and frequently destructive, to those who attempt it.

127.   Thus Mankind, notwithstanding all the Priviledges of the state of Nature, being but in an ill condition, while they remain in it, are quickly driven into Society.   Hence it comes to pass, that we seldom find any number of Men live any time together in this State.   The inconven-

iencies, that they are therein exposed to, by the irregular and uncertain exercise of the Power every Man has of punishing the transgressions of others, make them take Sanctuary under the establish'd Laws of Government, and therein seek *the preservation of their Property*. 'Tis this makes them so willingly give up every one his single power of punishing to be exercised by such alone as shall be appointed to it amongst them; and by such Rules as the Community, or those authorised by them to that purpose, shall agree on. And in this we have the original *right and rise* of both *the Legislative and Executive Power*, as well as of the Governments and Societies themselves.

128. For in the State of Nature, to omit the liberty he has of innocent Delights, a Man has two Powers.

The first is to do whatsoever he thinks fit for the preservation of himself and others within the permission of the *Law of Nature*: by which Law common to them all, he and all the rest of *Mankind are one Community*, make up one Society distinct from all other Creatures. And were it not for the corruption, and vitiousness of degenerate Men, there would be no need of any other; no necessity that Men should separate from this great and natural Community, and by positive agreements combine into smaller and divided associations.

The other power a Man has in the State of Nature, is the *power to punish the Crimes* committed against that Law. Both these he gives up, when he joyns in a private, if I may so call it, or particular Political Society, and incorporates into any Commonwealth, separate from the rest of Mankind.

129. The first *Power, viz. of doing whatsoever he thought fit for the Preservation of himself*, and the rest of Mankind, *he gives up* to be regulated by Laws made by the Society, so far forth as the preservation of himself, and the rest of that Society shall require; which Laws of the Society in many things confine the liberty he had by the Law of Nature.

130. *Secondly*, the *Power of punishing* he wholly *gives up*, and engages his natural force, (which he might before imploy in the Execution of the Law of Nature, by his own single Authority, as he thought fit) to assist the Executive Power of the Society, as the Law thereof shall require. For being now in a new State, wherein he is to enjoy many Conveniencies, from the labour, assistance, and society of others in the same Community, as well as protection from its whole strength; he is to part also with as much of his natural liberty in providing for himself, as the good, prosperity, and safety of the Society shall require: which is not only necessary, but just; since the other Members of the Society do the like.

131. But though Men when they enter into Society, give up the Equality, Liberty, and Executive Power they had in the State of Nature, into the hands of the Society, to be so far disposed of by the Legislative, as the good of the Society shall require; yet it being only with an

intention in every one the better to preserve himself his Liberty and Property; (For no rational Creature can be supposed to change his condition with an intention to be worse) the power of the Society, or *Legislative* constituted by them, *can never be suppos'd to extend farther than the common good*; but is obliged to secure every ones Property by providing against those three defects above-mentioned, that made the State of Nature so unsafe and uneasie. And so whoever has the Legislative or Supream Power of any Common-wealth, is bound to govern by establish'd *standing Laws*, promulgated and known to the People, and not by Extemporary Decrees; by *indifferent* and upright *Judges*, who are to decide Controversies by those Laws; And to imploy the force of the Community at home, *only in the Execution of such Laws*, or abroad to prevent or redress Foreign Injuries, and secure the Community from Inroads and Invasion. And all this to be directed to no other *end*, but the *Peace, Safety*, and *publick good* of the People.

Chap. X.

Of the Forms of a Common-wealth.

* * *

Chap. XI.

Of the Extent of the Legislative Power.

134. THE great end of Mens entring into Society, being the enjoyment of their Properties in Peace and Safety, and the great instrument and means of that being the Laws establish'd in that Society; the *first and fundamental positive Law* of all Commonwealths, *is the establishing of the Legislative* Power; as the *first and fundamental natural Law*, which is to govern even the Legislative it self, is *the preservation of the Society*, and (as far as will consist with the publick good) of every person in it. This *Legislative* is not only *the supream power* of the Commonwealth, but sacred and unalterable in the hands where the Community have once placed it; nor can any Edict of any Body else, in what Form soever conceived, or by what Power soever backed, have the force and obligation of a *Law*, which has not its *Sanction from* that *Legislative*, which the publick has chosen and appointed. For without this the Law could not have that, which is absolutely necessary to its being a *Law, the consent of the Society*, over whom no Body can have a power to make Laws, but by their own consent,* and by Authority received from them;

* *The lawful Power of making Laws to Command whole Politick Societies of Men belonging so properly unto the same intire Societies, that for any Prince or Potentate of what kind server upon Earth, to exercise the same of himself, and not by express Commission immediately and personally received from God, or else by Authority derived at the first from their consent, upon whose persons they impose Laws, it is no better than meer Tyranny. Laws they are not therefore which publick Approbation hath not made so. Hooker's Eccl. Pol. l.I. Sect. 10. Of this point therefore we are to note, that sith Men naturally have no full and perfect Power to Command whole Politick Multitudes of Men, therefore utterly without our Consent, we could in such sort be at no*

and therefore all the *Obedience*, which by the most solemn Ties any one can be obliged to pay, ultimately terminates in this *Supream Power*, and is directed by those Laws which it enacts: nor can any Oaths to any Foreign Power whatsoever, or any Domestick Subordinate Power, discharge any Member of the Society from his *Obedience to the Legislative*, acting pursuant to their trust, nor oblige him to any Obedience contrary to the Laws so enacted, or farther than they do allow; it being ridiculous to imagine one can be tied ultimately to *obey* any *Power* in the Society, which is not *the Supream.*

135. Though the *Legislative*, whether placed in one or more, whether it be always in being, or only by intervals, tho' it be the *Supream* Power in every Common-wealth; yet,

First, It is *not*, nor can possibly be absolutely *Arbitrary* over the Lives and Fortunes of the People. For it being but the joynt power of every Member of the Society given up to that Person, or Assembly, which is Legislator, it can be no more than those persons had in a State of Nature before they enter'd into Society, and gave up to the Community. For no Body can transfer to another more power than he has in himself; and no Body has an absolute Arbitrary Power over himself, or over any other, to destroy his own Life, or take away the Life or Property of another. A Man, as has been proved, cannot subject himself to the Arbitrary Power of another; and having in the State of Nature no Arbitrary Power over the Life, Liberty, or Possession of another, but only so much as the Law of Nature gave him for the preservation of himself, and the rest of Mankind; this is all he doth, or can give up to the Common-wealth, and by it to the *Legislative Power*, so that the Legislative can have no more than this. Their Power in the utmost Bounds of it, is *limited to the publick good* of the Society. It is a Power, that hath no other end but preservation, and therefore can never have a right to destroy, enslave, or designedly to impoverish the Subjects.** The Obligations of the Law of Nature, cease not in Society, but only in many Cases are drawn closer, and have by Humane Laws known Penalties annexed to them, to inforce their observation. Thus the Law

Mans Commandment living. And to be commanded we do consent when that Society, whereof we be a part, hath at any time before consented, without revoking the same after by the like universal agreement.

Laws therefore humane, of what kind soever, are available by consent. Ibid.

** *Two Foundations there are which bear up publick Societies, the one a natural inclination, whereby all Men desire sociable Life and Fellowship; the other an Order, expressly or secretly agreed upon, touching the manner of their union in living together; the latter is that which we call the Law of a Common-weal, the very Soul of a Politick Body, the parts whereof are by Law animated, held together, and set on work in such actions at the common good requireth. Laws politick, ordain'd for external order and regiment amongst Men, are never framed as they should be, unless presuming the will of Man to be inwardly obstinate, rebellious, and averse from all Obedience to the sacred Laws of his Nature; in a word, unless presuming Man to be in regard of his depraved Mind, little better than a wild Beast, they do accordingly provide notwithstanding, so to frame his outward Actions, that they be no hindrance unto the common good, for which Societies are instituted. Unless they do this they are not perfect.* Hooker's Eccl. Pol. l.I. Sect. 10.

of Nature stands as an Eternal Rule to all Men, *Legislators* as well as others. The *Rules* that they make for other Mens Actions, must, as well as their own and other Mens Actions, be conformable to the Law of Nature, *i.e.* to the Will of God, of which that is a Declaration, and the *fundamental Law of Nature* being *the preservation of Mankind*, no Humane Sanction can be good, or valid against it.

136. *Secondly*, The *Legislative*, or Supream Authority, cannot assume to its self a power to Rule by extemporary Arbitrary Decrees,*** but *is bound to dispense Justice*, and decide the Rights of the Subject *by promulgated standing Laws, and known Authoris'd Judges*. For the Law of Nature being unwritten, and so no where to be found but in the minds of Men, they who through Passion or Interest shall mis-cite, or misapply it, cannot so easily be convinced of their mistake where there is no establish'd Judge: And so it serves not, as it ought, to determine the Rights, and fence the Properties of those that live under it, especially where every one is Judge, Interpreter, and Executioner of it too, and that in his own Case: And he that has right on his side, having ordinarily but his own single strength, hath not force enough to defend himself from Injuries, or to punish Delinquents. To avoid these Inconveniencies which disorder Mens Properties in the state of Nature, Men unite into Societies, that they may have the united strength of the whole Society to secure and defend their Properties, and may have *standing Rules* to bound it, by which every one may know what is his. To this end it is that Men give up all their Natural Power to the Society which they enter into, and the Community put the Legislative Power into such hands as they think fit, with this trust, that they shall be govern'd by *declared Laws*, or else their Peace, Quiet, and Property will still be at the same uncertainty, as it was in the state of Nature.

137. Absolute Arbitrary Power, or Governing without *settled standing Laws*, can neither of them consist with the ends of Society and Government, which Men would not quit the freedom of the state of Nature for, and tie themselves up under, were it not to preserve their Lives, Liberties and Fortunes; and by *stated Rules* of Right and Property to secure their Peace and Quiet. It cannot be supposed that they should intend, had they a power so to do, to give to any one, or more, an *absolute Arbitrary Power* over their Persons and Estates, and put a force into the Magistrates hand to execute his unlimited Will arbitrarily upon them: This were to put themselves into a worse condition than the state of Nature, wherein they had a Liberty to defend their Right against the Injuries of others, and were upon equal terms of force to maintain it,

*** *Humane Laws are measures in respect of Men, whose actions they must direct, howbeit such measures they are as have also their higher Rules to be measured by, which Rules are two, the Law of God, and the Law of Nature; so that Laws Humane must be made according to the general Laws of Nature, and without contradiction to any positive Law of Scripture, otherwise they are ill made.* Ibid. l. 3. Sect. 9.

To constrain Men to any thing inconvenient doth seem unreasonable. Ibid. l.I. Sect. 10.

whether invaded by a single Man, or many in Combination. Whereas by supposing they have given up themselves to the *absolute Arbitrary Power* and will of a Legislator, they have disarmed themselves, and armed him, to make a prey of them when he pleases. He being in a much worse condition who is exposed to the Arbitrary Power of one Man, who has the Command of 100000. than he that is expos'd to the Arbitrary Power of 100000. single Men: no Body being secure, that his Will, who has such a Command, is better, than that of other Men, though his Force be 100000. times stronger. And therefore whatever Form the Commonwealth is under, the Ruling Power ought to govern by *declared* and *received Laws*, and not by extemporary Dictates and undetermined Resolutions. For then Mankind will be in afar worse condition, than in the State of Nature, if they shall have armed one or a few Men with the joynt power of a Multitude, to force them to obey at pleasure the exorbitant and unlimited Decrees of their sudden thoughts, or unrestrain'd, and till that moment unknown Wills without having any measures set down which may guide and justifie their actions. For all the power the Government has, being only for the good of the Society, as it ought not to be *Arbitrary* and at Pleasure, so it ought to be exercised by *established and promulgated Laws*: that both the People may know their Duty, and be safe and secure within the limits of the Law, and the Rulers too kept within their due bounds, and not to be tempted, by the Power they have in their hands, to imploy it to such purposes, and by such measures, as they would not have known, and own not willingly.

138. *Thirdly,* The *Supream Power cannot take* from any Man any part of his *Property* without his own consent. For the preservation of Property being the end of Government, and that for which Men enter into Society, it necessarily supposes and requires, that the People should *have Property*, without which they must be suppos'd to lose that by entring into Society, which was the end for which they entered into it, too gross an absurdity for any Man to own. *Men* therefore *in Society having Property*, they have such a right to the goods, which by the Law of the Community are theirs, that no Body hath a right to take their substance, or any part of it from them, without their own consent; without this, they have no *Property* at all. For I have truly no *Property* in that, which another can by right take from me, when he pleases, against my consent. Hence it is a mistake to think, that the Supream or *Legislative Power* of any Commonwealth, can do what it will, and dispose of the Estates of the Subject *arbitrarily*, or take any part of them at pleasure. This is not much to be fear'd in Governments where the *Legislative* consists, wholly or in part, in Assemblies which are variable, whose Members upon the Dissolution of the Assembly, are Subjects under the common Laws of their Country, equally with the rest. But in Governments, where the *Legislative* is in one lasting Assembly always in being, or in one Man, as in Absolute Monarchies, there is danger still, that they will think themselves to have a distinct interest, from the rest of the Community; and so will be apt to increase their own Riches and

Power, by taking, what they think fit, from the People. For a Man's *Property* is not at all secure, though there be good and equitable Laws to set the bounds of it, between him and his Fellow Subjects, if he who commands those Subjects, have Power to take from any private Man, what part he pleases of his *Property*, and use and dispose of it as he thinks good.

139. But *Government* into whatsoever hands it is put, being as I have before shew'd, intrusted with this condition, and *for this end*, that Men might have and secure *their Properties*, the Prince or Senate, however it may have power to make Laws for the regulating of *Property* between the Subjects one amongst another, yet can never have a Power to take to themselves the whole or any part of the Subjects *Property*, without their own consent. For this would be in effect to leave them no *Property* at all. And to let us see, that even *absolute Power*, where it is necessary, is *not Arbitrary* by being absolute, but is still limited by that reason, and confined to those ends, which required it in some Cases to be absolute, we need look no farther than the common practice of Martial Discipline. For the Preservation of the Army, and in it of the whole Commonwealth, requires an *absolute Obedience* to the Command of every Superior Officer, and it is justly Death to disobey or dispute the most dangerous or unreasonable of them: but yet we see, that neither the Serjeant, that could command a Souldier to march up to the mouth of a Cannon, or stand in a Breach, where he is almost sure to perish, can command that Soldier to give him one penny of his Money; nor the *General*, that can condemn him to Death for deserting his Post, or for not obeying the most desperate Orders, can yet with all his absolute Power of Life and Death, dispose of one Farthing of that Soldiers Estate, or seize one jot of his Goods; whom yet he can command any thing, and hang for the least Disobedience. Because such a blind Obedience is necessary to that end for which the Commander has his Power, *viz.* the preservation of the rest; but the disposing of his Goods has nothing to do with it.

140. 'Tis true, Governments cannot be supported without great Charge, and 'tis fit every one who enjoys his share of the Protection, should pay out of his Estate his proportion for the maintenance of it. But still it must be with his own Consent, *i.e.* the Consent of the Majority, giving it either by themselves, or their Representatives chosen by them. For if any one shall claim a *Power to lay* and levy *Taxes* on the People, by his own Authority, and without such consent of the People, he thereby invades the *Fundamental Law of Property*, and subverts the end of Government. For what property have I in that which another may by right take, when he pleases to himself?

141. *Fourthly,* The *Legislative cannot transfer the Power of Making Laws* to any other hands. For it being but a delegated Power from the People, they, who have it, cannot pass it over to others. The People alone can appoint the Form of the Commonwealth, which is by Consti-

tuting the Legislative, and appointing in whose hands that shall be. And when the People have said, We will submit to rules, and be govern'd by *Laws* made by such Men, and in such Forms, no Body else can say other Men shall make *Laws* for them; nor can the people be bound by any *Laws* but such as are Enacted by those, whom they have Chosen, and Authorised to make *Laws* for them. The power of the *Legislative* being derived from the People by a positive voluntary Grant and Institution, can be no other, than what that positive Grant conveyed, which being only to make *Laws*, and not to make *Legislators*, the *Legislative* can have no power to transfer their Authority of making Laws, and place it in other hands.

142. These are the *Bounds* which the trust that is put in them by the Society, and the Law of God and Nature, have *set to the Legislative* Power of every Commonwealth, in all Forms of Government.

First, They are to govern by *promulgated establish'd Laws*, not to be varied in particular Cases, but to have one Rule for Rich and Poor, for the Favourite at Court, and the Country Man at Plough.

Secondly, These *Laws* also ought to be designed *for* no other end ultimately but *the good of the People.*

Thirdly, they must *not raise Taxes* on the Property of the People, *without the Consent of the People*, given by themselves, or their Deputies. And this properly concerns only such Governments where the *Legislative* is always in being, or at least where the People have not reserv'd any part of the Legislative to Deputies, to be from time to time chosen by themselves.

Fourthly, The *Legislative* neither must *nor can transfer the Power of making Laws* to any Body else, or place it any where but where the People have.

C. JOHN TRENCHARD, CATO'S LETTERS, NO. 60

January 6, 1721

All Government proved to be instituted by Men, and only to intend the general Good of Men.

SIR,

THERE is no Government now upon Earth, which owes its Formation or Beginning to the immediate Revelation of God, or can derive its

Existence from such Revelation: It is certain, on the contrary, that the Rise and Institution or Variation of Government, from Time to Time, is within the Memory of Men or of Histories; and that every Government, which we know at this Day in the World, was established by the Wisdom and Force of mere Men, and by the Concurrence of Means and Causes evidently human. Government therefore can have no Power, but such as Men can give, and such as they actually did give, or permit for their own Sakes: Nor can any Government be in Fact framed but by Consent, if not of every Subject, yet of as many as can compel the rest; since no Man, or Council of Men, can have personal Strength enough to govern Multitudes by Force, or can claim to themselves and their Families any Superiority, or natural Sovereignty over their Fellow-Creatures naturally as good as them. Such Strength, therefore, where-ever it is, is civil and accumulative Strength, derived from the Laws and Constitutions of the Society, of which the Governors themselves are but Members.

So that to know the Jurisdiction of Governors, and its Limits, we must have Recourse to the Institution of Government, and ascertain those Limits by the Measure of Power, which Men in the State of Nature have over themselves and one another: And as no Man can take from many, who are stronger than him, what they have no Mind to give him; and he who has not Consent must have Force, which is itself the Consent of the Stronger; so no Man can give to another either what is none of his own, or what in its own Nature is inseparable from himself; as his Religion particularly is.

Every Man's Religion is his own; nor can the Religion of any Man, of what Nature or Figure soever, be the Religion of another Man, unless he also chooses it; which Action utterly excludes all Force, Power, or Government. Religion can never come without Conviction, nor can Conviction come from Civil Authority; Religion, which is the Fear of God, cannot be subject to Power, which is the Fear of Man. It is a Relation between God and our own Souls only, and consists in a Disposition of Mind to obey the Will of our great Creator, in the Manner which we think most acceptable to him. It is independent upon all human Directions, and superior to them; and consequently uncontroulable by external Force, which cannot reach the free Faculties of the Mind, or inform the Understanding, much less convince it. Religion therefore, which can never be subject to the Jurisdiction of another, can never be alienated to another, or put in his Power.

Nor has any Man in the State of Nature Power over his own Life, or to take away the Life of another, unless to defend his own, or what is as much his own, namely, his Property. This Power therefore, which no Man has, no Man can transfer to another.

Nor could any Man in the State of Nature have a Right to violate the Property of another; that is, what another had acquired by his Art or Labour; or to interrupt him in his Industry and Enjoyments, as long as he himself was not injured by that Industry and those Enjoyments.

No Man therefore could transfer to the Magistrate that Right which he had not himself.

No Man in his Senses was ever so wild as to give an unlimited Power to another to take away his Life, or the Means of Living, according to the Caprice, Passion, and unreasonable Pleasure of that other: But if any Man restrained himself from any Part of his Pleasures, or parted with any Portion of his Acquisitions, he did it with the honest Purpose of enjoying the rest with the greater Security, and always in Subserviency to his own Happiness, which no Man will or can willingly and intentionally give away to any other whatsoever.

And if any one, through his own Inadvertence, or by the Fraud or Violence of another, can be drawn into so foolish a Contract, he is relievable by the eternal Laws of God and Reason. No Engagement that is wicked and unjust can be executed without Injustice and Wickedness: This is so true, that I question whether there be a Constitution in the World which does not afford, or pretend to afford, a Remedy for relieving ignorant, distressed, and unwary Men, trepanned into such Engagements by artful Knaves, or frightened into them by imperious ones. So that here the Laws of Nature and general Reason supersede the municipal and positive Laws of Nations; and no where oftner than in *England*. What else was the Design, and ought to be the Business, of our Courts of Equity? And I hope whole Countries and Societies are no more exempted from the Privileges and Protection of Reason and Equity, than are private Particulars.

Here then is the natural Limitation of the Magistrate's Authority: He ought not to take what no Man ought to give; nor exact what no Man ought to perform: All he has is given him, and those that gave it must judge of the Application. In Government there is no such Relation as Lord and Slave, lawless Will and blind Submission; nor ought to be amongst Men: But the only Relation is that of Father and Children, Patron and Client, Protection and Allegiance, Benefaction and Gratitude, mutual Affection and mutual Assistance.

So that the Nature of Government does not alter the natural Right of Men to Liberty, which in all political Societies is alike their Due: But some Governments provide better than others for the Security and impartial Distribution of that Right. There has been always such a constant and certain Fund of Corruption and Malignity in human Nature, that it has been rare to find that Man, whose Views and Happiness did not center in the Gratification of his Appetites, and worst Appetites, his Luxury, his Pride, his Avarice, and Lust of Power; and who considered any publick Trust reposed in him, with any other View, than as the Means to satiate such unruly and dangerous Desires! And this has been most eminently true of Great Men, and those who aspired to Dominion. They were first made Great for the Sake of the Publick, and afterwards at its Expence. And if they had been content to have been moderate Traytors, Mankind would have been still moderately

142

happy; but their Ambition and Treason observing no Degrees, there was no Degree of Vileness and Misery which the poor People did not often feel.

The Appetites therefore of Men, especially of Great Men, are carefully to be observed and stayed, or else they will never stay themselves. The Experience of every Age convinces us, that we must not judge of Men by what they ought to do, but by what they will do; and all History affords but few Instances of Men trusted with great Power without abusing it, when with Security they could. The Servants of Society, that is to say, its Magistrates, did almost universally serve it by seizing it, selling it, or plundering it; especially when they were left by the Society unlimited as to their Duty and Wages. In that Case these faithful Stewards generally took all; and, being Servants, made Slaves of their Masters.

For these Reasons, and convinced by woful and eternal Experience, Societies found it necessary to lay Restraints upon their Magistrates or publick Servants, and to put Checks upon those who would otherwise put Chains upon them; and therefore these Societies set themselves to model and form national Constitutions with such Wisdom and Art, that the publick Interest should be consulted and married at the same Time, when those entrusted with the Administration of it were consulting and pursuing their own.

Hence grew the Distinction between Arbitrary and Free Governments: Not that more or less Power was vested in the one than in the other; nor that either of them lay under less or more Obligations, in Justice, to protect their Subjects, and study their Ease, Prosperity, and Security, and to watch for the same. But the Power and Sovereignty of Magistrates in free Countries was so qualified, and so divided into different Channels, and committed to the Direction of so many different Men, with different Interests and Views, that the Majority of them could seldom or never find their Account in betraying their Trust in fundamental Instances. Their Emulation, Envy, Fear, or Interest, always made them Spies and Checks upon one another. By all which Means the People have often come at the Heads of those who forfeited their Heads, by betraying the People.

In despotick Governments Things went far otherwise, those Governments having been framed otherwise; if the same could be called Governments, where the Rules of publick Power were dictated by private and lawless Lust; where Folly and Madness often swayed the Scepter, and blind Rage weilded the Sword. The whole Weath of the State, with its Civil or Military Power, being in the Prince, the People could have no Remedy but Death and Patience, while he oppressed them by the Lump, and butchered them by Thousands: Unless perhaps the Ambition or personal Resentments of some of the Instruments of his Tyranny procured a Revolt, which rarely mended their Condition.

The only Secret therefore in forming a Free Government, is to make the Interests of the Governors and of the Governed the same, as far as human Policy can contrive. Liberty cannot be preserved any other Way. Men have long found, from the Weakness and Depravity of themselves and one another, that most Men will act for Interest against Duty, as often as they dare. So that to engage them to their Duty, Interest must be linked to the Observance of it, and Danger to the Breach of it. Personal Advantages and Security, must be the Rewards of Duty and Obedience; and Disgrace, Torture, and Death, the Punishment of Treachery and Corruption.

Human Wisdom has yet found out but one certain Expedient to effect this; and that is, to have the Concerns of all directed by all, as far as possibly can be: And where the Persons interested are too numerous, or live too distant to meet together on all Emergencies, they must moderate Necessity by Prudence, and act by Deputies, whose Interest is the same with their own, and whose Property is so intermingled with theirs, and so engaged upon the same Bottom, that Principals and Deputies must stand and fall together. When the Deputies thus act for their own Interest, by acting for the Interest of their Principals; when they can make no Law but what they themselves, and their Posterity, must be subject to; when they can give no Money, but what they must pay their Share of; when they can do no Mischief, but what must fall upon their own Heads in common with their Countrymen; their Principals may then expect good Laws, little Mischief, and much Frugality.

Here therefore lies the great Point of Nicety and Care in forming the Constitution, that the Persons entrusted and representing, shall either never have any Interest detached from the Persons entrusting and represented, or never the Means to pursue it. Now to compass this great Point effectually, no other Way is left, but one of these two, or rather both; namely, to make the Deputies so numerous, that there may be no Possibility of corrupting the Majority; or, by changing them so often, that there is no sufficient Time to corrupt them, and to carry the Ends of that Corruption. The People may be very sure, that the major Part of their Deputies being honest, will keep the rest; and that they will all be honeft, when they have no Temptations to be Knaves.

We have some Sketch of this Policy in the Constitution of our several great Companies, where the General Court, composed of all its Members, constitutes the Legislature, and the Consent of that Court is the Sanction of their Laws; and there the Administration of their Affairs is put under the Conduct of a certain Number chosen by the Whole. Here every Man concerned saw the Necessity of securing Part of their Property, putting the Persons entrusted under proper regulations; however remiss they may be in takeing Care of the Whole. And if Provision had been made, That, as a Third Part of the Directors are to go out every Year, so none should stay in above Three, (as I am told was at first promised) all Juggling with Courtiers, and raising great Estates by

144

Confederacy, at the Expence of the Company, had, in a great Measure, been prevented; though there were still wanting other Limitations, which might have effectually obviated all those Evils.

This was the ancient Constitution of *England:* Our Kings had neither Revenues large enough, nor Offices gainful and numerous enough in their Disposal, to corrupt any considerable Number of Members; nor any Force to frighten them. Besides, the same Parliament seldom or never met twice: For, the serving in it being found an Office of Burthen, and not of Profit, it was thought reasonable that all Men qualified should, in their Turns, leave their Families and domestick Concerns, to serve the Publick; and their Boroughs bore their Charges. The only Grievance then was, that they were not called together often enough, to redress the Grievances which the People suffered from the Court during their Intermission: And therefore a Law was made in *Edward* the IIId's Time, That Parliaments should be holden once a Year.

But this Law, like the late Queen's Peace, did not execute itself; and therefore the Court seldom convened them, but when they wanted Money, or had other Purposes of their own to serve; and sometimes raised Money without them: Which arbitrary Proceeding brought upon the Publick numerous Mischiefs; and, in the Reign of King *Charles* the 1st, a long and bloody Civil War. In that Reign an Act was passed, That they should meet of themselves, if they were not called according to the Direction of that Law; which was worthily repealed upon the Restoration of King *Charles* the IId: And in the same kind Fit, a great Revenue was given him for Life, and continued to his Brother. By which Means these Princes were enabled to keep standing Troops, to corrupt Parliaments, or to live without them; and to commit such Acts of Power as brought about, and indeed forced the People upon the late happy *Revolution.* Soon after which a new Act was passed, That Parliaments should be rechosen once in three Years: Which Law was also repealed, upon his Majesty's Accession to the Throne, that the present Parliament might have Time to rectify those Abuses which we labour under, and to make Regulations proper to prevent them *All* for the future. *All* which has since been happily effected; and, I bless God, we are told, that the People will have the Opportunity to thank them, in another Election, for their great Services to their Country. I shall be always ready, on my Part, to do them Honour, and pay them my Acknowledgments, in the most effectual Manner in my Power. _____ But more of this in the succeeding Papers.

I am, &c.

D. JOHN TRENCHARD, CATO'S LETTERS, NO. 61

January 13, 1721

How free Governments are to be framed so as to last and how they differ from such as are arbitrary.

SIR,

THE most reasonable Meaning that can be put upon this Apothegm, that *Virtue is its own Reward*, is, that it seldom meets with any other. God himself, who having made us, best knows our Natures, does not trust to the intrinsick Excellence and native Beauty of Holiness alone, to engage us in its Interests and Pursuits, but recommends it to us by the stronger and more affecting Motives of Rewards and Punishments. No wife Man, therefore, will in any Instance of Moment trust to the mere Integrity of another. The Experience of all Ages may convince us, that Men, when they are above Fear, grow for the most part above Honesty and Shame: And this is particularly and certainly true of Societies of Men, when they are numerous enough to keep one another in Countenance; for when the Weight of Infamy is divided amongst many, no one sinks under his own Burthen.

Great Bodies of Men have seldom judged what they ought to do, by any other Rule than what they could do. What Nation is there that has not oppressed any other, when the same could be done with Advantage and Security? What Party has ever had Regard to the Principles which they professed, or ever reformed the Errors which they condemned? What Company, or particular Society of Merchants or Tradesmen, has ever acted for the Interest of general Trade, though it always filled their Mouths in private Conversation?

And yet Men, thus formed and qualified, are the Materials for Government. For the Sake of Men it is instituted, by the Prudence of Men it must be conducted; and the Art of political Mechanism is, to erect a firm Building with such crazy and corrupt Materials. The strongest Cables are made out of loose Hemp and Flax; the World itself may, with the Help of proper Machines, be moved by the Force of a single Hair; and so may the Government of the World, as well as the World itself. But whatever Discourses I shall hereafter make upon this great and useful Subject, I shall confine myself in this Letter to free monarchical Constitutions alone, and to the Application of some of the Principles laid down in my last.

It is there said, that when the Society consists of too many, or when they live too far apart to be able to meet together, to take Care of their own Affairs, they can no otherwise preserve their Liberties, than by choosing Deputies to represent them, and to act for them; and that these Deputies must be either so numerous, that there can be no Means of corrupting the Majority; or so often changed, that there shall be no Time to do it so as to answer any End by doing it. Without one of these Regulations, or both, I lay it down as a certain Maxim in Politicks, that it is impossible to preserve a free Government long.

I think I may with great Modesty affirm, that in former Reigns the People of *England* found no sufficient Security in the Number of their Representatives. What with the Crowd of Offices in the Gift of the

Crown, which were possessed by Men of no other Merit, nor held by any other Tenure, but merely a Capacity to get into the House of Commons, and the Disservice which they could and would do their Country there: What with the Promises and Expectations given to others, who by Court-Influence, and often by Court-Money, carried their Elections: What by artful Caresses, and the familiar and deceitful Addresses of great Men to weak Men: What with luxurious Dinners, and Rivers of *Burgundy*, *Champaign*, and *Tokay*, thrown down the Throats of Gluttons; and what with Pensions, and other personal Gratifications, bestowed where Wind and Smoke would not pass for current Coin: What with Party Watch-Words and imaginary Terrors, spread amongst the drunken 'Squires, and the deluded and enthusiastick Bigots, of dreadful Designs in *Embrio*, to blow up the Church, and the Protestant Interest; and sometimes with the Dread of mighty Invasions just ready to break upon us from the Man in the Moon: I say, by all these corrupt Arts, the Representatives of the *English* People, in former Reigns, have been brought to betray the People, and to join with their Oppressors. So much are Men governed by artful Applications to their private Passions and Interest. And it is evident to me, that if ever we have a weak or an ambitious Prince, with a Ministry like him, we must find out some other Resources, or acquiesce in the Loss of our Liberties. The Course and transiency of human Affairs will not suffer us to live always under the present righteous Administration.

So that I can see no Means in human Policy to preserve the publick Liberty and a monarchical form of Government together, but by the frequent fresh Elections of the People's Deputies: This is what the Writers in Politicks call Rotation of Magistracy. Men, when they first enter into Magistracy, have often their former Condition before their Eyes: They remember what they themselves suffered, with their Fellow-Subjects, from the Abuse of Power, and how much they blamed it; and so their first Purposes are to be humble, modest, and just; and probably, for some Time, they continue so. But the Possession of Power soon alters and viciates their Hearts, which are at the same time sure to be leavened, and puffed up to an unnatural Size, by the deceitful Incense of false Friends, and by the prostrate Submission of Parasites. First, they grow indifferent to all their good Designs, then drop them: Next, they lose their Moderation; afterwards, they renounce all Measures with their old Acquaintance and old Principles; and seeing themselves in magnifying Glasses, grow, in Conceit, a different Species from their Fellow-Subjects; and so by too sudden Degrees become insolent, rapacious and tyrannical, ready to catch at all Means, often the vilest and most oppressive, to raise their Fortunes as high as their imaginary Greatness. So that the only Way to put them in mind of their former Condition, and consequently of the Condition of other People, is often to reduce them to it; and to let others of equal Capacities share of Power in their Turn: This also is the only Way to qualify Men, and make them equally fit for Dominion and Subjection.

A Rotation therefore, in Power and Magistracy, is essentially necessary to a free Government: It is indeed the Thing itself; and constitutes, animates, and informs it, as much as the Soul constitutes the Man. It is a Thing sacred and inviolable, where-ever Liberty is thought sacred; nor can it ever be committed to the Disposal of those who are trusted with the Preservation of National Constitutions: For though they may have the Power to model it for the publick Advantage, and for the more essectual Security of that Right; yet they can have none to give it up, or, which is the same Thing, to make it useless.

The Constitution of a limited Monarchy, is the joint Concurrence of the Crown and of the Nobles (without whom it cannot subsist) and of the Body of the People, to make Laws for the common Benefit of the Subject; and where the People, through Number or Distance, cannot meet, they must send Deputies to speak in their Names, and to attend upon their Interest: These Deputies therefore act by, under, and in Subserviency to the Constitution, and have not a Power above it and over it.

In *Holland*, and some other free Countries, the States are often obliged to consult their Principals; and, in some Instances, our own Parliaments have declined entering upon Questions of Importance, till they had gone into the Country, and known the Sentiments of those that sent them; as in all Cases they ought to consult their Inclinations as well as their Interest. Who will say, that the Rump, or Fag-end of the Long Parliament of Forty-One, had any Right to expel such Members as they did not like? Or to watch for their Absence, that they might seize to themselves, or give up to any body else, the Right of those from whose Confidence and Credulity they derived the Authority which they acted by?

With Thanks to God, I own, that we have a Prince so sensible of this Right, and who owes his Crown so intirely to the Principles laid down, and I think fully proved in these Letters; that it is impossible to suspect, either from his Inclinations, his Interest, or his known Justice, that he should ever fall into any Measures to destroy that People, who have given him his Crown, and supported him in it with so much Generosity and Expence; or that he should undermine, by that Means, the Ground upon which he stands. I do therefore the less regard the idle Suspicions and Calumnies of disaffected Men, who would surmise, that a Design is yet on Foot to continue this Parliament; _____a Reflection the most impudent and invidious that can be thrown upon his Majesty, his Ministers, or his Two Houses; and a Reflection that can come from none but professed, or at least from concealed, *Jacobites*.

It is no less than an Insinuation, that our most excellent Sovereign King *George* has a Distrust of his faithful Subjects; that he will refuse them the Means of their own Preservation, and the Preservation of that Constitution which they chose him to preserve; that he will shut his Ears against their modest, just, and dutiful Complaints; and that he apprehends Danger from meeting them in a New and Free-chosen

Parliament. This is contrary to the Tenor of his whole Life and Actions; who, as he has received Three Crowns from their Gift, so he lies under all the Ties of Generosity, Gratitude, and Duty, to cherish and protect them, and to make them always great, free, and happy.

It is a most scandalous Calumny upon his faithful Servants, to suggest that any of them, conscious of Guilt and Crimes, feared any thing from the most strict and rigorous Inspection into their Proceedings. Some of them have already stood the fiery Trial, and come off triumphant with general Approbation. They have, besides, the Advantage of his Majesty's most gracious Pardon, which they did not want, and which was not passed for their Sakes. Who therefore can suspect, that Patriots so uncorrupt, so prudent, and so popular, will dishonour their Master, give up the Constitution, ruin their Country, and render themselves the Objects of universal Scorn, Detestation, and Cursing, by advising the most odious, dangerous, and destructive Measures, that ever Counsellors gave a Prince?

It is a most ungrateful Return to our illustrious Representatives, to suggest, that Men who have lest their domestick Concerns to serve their Country at their own Expence, and without any personal Advantages, and have bestowed their Labours upon the Publick for a much longer Time than their Principals had at first a Right to expect from them; and have, during-all that Time, been rectifying the Abuses which have crept into our Constitution; and have assisted his Majesty in going through two very useful and necessary Wars, and have regulated our Finances, and the Expence of our Guards and Garisons, and corrected many Abuses in the Fleet and the Civil Administration; and have taken effectual Vengeance of all those who were concerned in promoting, procuring, aiding, or assisting the late dreadful *South-Sea* Project: _____I say, after so many Things done by them for the publick-Honour and Prosperity, it is the basest Ingratitude to surmise, that any of them would give up that Constitution which they were chosen, and have taken so much Pains, to preserve.

I do indeed confess, if any Invasion were to be feared from *Muscovy, Mecklenburg, Spain,* or *Civita Vecchia;* if new Provinces were to be obtained Abroad, new Armies to be raised, or new Fleets to be equipped, upon warlike Expeditions; if new Provision were wanting for the Civil List, and new Taxes to be levied, or new Companies to be erected to pay off the publick Debts; if the Universities were to be farther regulated, or any Inspection were necessary into the Increase of Fees and Exactions of Civil Officers; if there were the least Ground to suspect Bribery or Corruption in a Place where it should not be; or if there were any new Project on Foot to banish tyrannical and popish Principles far out of the Land: I say, that in such a Scene of Affairs, I dare not be altogether so positive in my Assertion, that we ought to venture, and at all Events to leave to Chance, that which we are in Possession of already.—But as we are at present in the happy State of Indolence and Security, at Peace

with all the World and our own Consciences; as little more Money can
be raised from the People, most of it being already in Hands, which,
according to the Rules of good Policy, unite Dominion and Property; as
our Benefactors too are generous and honourable, our Boroughs not
insensible or ungrateful, nor the Counties themselves inexorable to
shining Merit: So it is much to be hoped, that another Parliament may
be chosen equally deserveing, and as zealous for the publick Interest; or,
at worst, there are honest and tried Measures at Hand, which will
undoubtedly make them so. And I offer this as a conclusive, and I think
a most convincing, Argument, that the Kingdom will be obliged with a
new Election.

I am, &c.

E. JOHN TRENCHARD, CATO'S LETTERS, NO. 62

January 20, 1721

*An Enquiry into the Nature and Extent of Liberty; with its
Loveliness and Advantages, and the vile Effects of Slavery.*

SIR,

I Have shewn, in a late Paper, wherein consists the Difference
between Free and Arbitrary Governments, as to their Frame and Constitution; and in this and the following, I shall shew their different Spirit
and Effects. But first I shall shew wherein Liberty itself consists.

By Liberty, I understand the Power which every Man has over his
own Actions, and his Right to enjoy the Fruit of his Labour, Art, and
Industry, as far as by it he hurts not the Society, or any Members of it,
by taking from any Member, or by hindering him from enjoying what he
himself enjoys. The Fruits of a Man's honest Industry are the just
Rewards of it, ascertained to him by natural and eternal Equity, as is his
Title to use them in the Manner which he thinks fit: And thus, with the
above Limitations, every Man is sole Lord and Arbiter of his own private
Actions and Property.—A Character of which no Man living can divest
him but by Usurpation, or his own Consent.

The entering into political Society, is so far from a Departure from
his natural Right, that to preserve it was the sole Reason why Men did
so; and mutual Protection and Assistance is the only reasonable Purpose
of all reasonable Societies. To make such Protection practicable, Magistracy was formed, with Power to defend the Innocent from Violence, and
to punish those that offered it; nor can there be any other Pretence for
Magistracy in the World. In order to this good End, the Magistrate is
intrusted with conducting and applying the united Force of the Community; and with exacting such a Share of every Man's Property, as is
necessary to preserve the Whole, and to defend every Man and his
Property from foreign and domestick Injuries. These are the Boundaries of the Power of the Magistrate, who deserts his Function whenever

he breaks them. By the Laws of Society, he is more limited and restrained than any Man amongst them; since, while they are absolutely free in all their Actions, which purely concern themselves; all his Actions, as a publick Person, being for the Sake of Society, must refer to it, and answer the Ends of it.

It is a mistaken Notion in Government, that the Interest of the Majority is only to be consulted, since in Society every Man has a Right to every Man's Assistance in the Enjoyment and Defence of his private Property; otherwise the greater Number may sell the lesser, and divide their Estates amongst themselves; and so, instead of a Society, where all peaceable Men are protected, become a Conspiracy of the Many against the Minority. With as much Equity may one Man wantonly dispose of all, and Violence may be sanctified by mere Power.

And it is as foolish to say, that Government is concerned to meddle with the private Thoughts and Actions of Men, while they injure neither the Society, nor any of its Members. Every Man is, in Nature and Reason, the Judge and Disposer of his own domestick Affairs; and, according to the Rules of Religion and Equity, every Man must carry his own Conscience. So that neither has the Magistrate a Right to direct the private Behaviour of Men; nor has the Magistrate, or any body else, any Manner of Power to model People's Speculations, no more than their Dreams. Government being intended to protect Men from the Injuries of one another, and not to direct them in their own Affairs, in which no one is interested but themselves; it is plain, that their Thoughts and domestick Concerns are exempted intirely-from its Jurisdiction: In Truth, Mens Thoughts are not subject to their own Jurisdiction.

Idiots aud Lunaticks indeed, who cannot take Care of themselves, must be taken Care of by others: But whilst Men have their five Senses, I cannot see what the Magistrate has to do with Actions by which the Society cannot be affected; and where he meddles with such, he meddles impertinently or tyrannically. Must the Magistrate tie up every Man's Legs, because some Men fall into Ditches? Or, must he put out their Eyes, because with them they see lying Vanities? Or, would it become the Wisdom and Care of Governors to establish a travelling Society, to prevent People, by a proper Confinement, from throwing themselves into Wells, or over Precipices; Or to endow a Fraternity of Physicians and Surgeons all over the Nation, to take Care of their Subjects Health, without being consulted; and to vomit, bleed, purge, and scarify them at Pleasure, whether they would or no, just as these established Judges of Health should think fit? If this were the Case, what a Stir and Hubbub should we soon see kept about the established Potions and Lancets? Every Man, Woman, or Child, though ever so healthy, must be a Patient, or woe be to them! The best Diet and Medicines would soon grow pernicious from any other Hand; and their Pills alone, however ridiculous, insufficient, or distasteful, would be attended with a Blessing.

Let People alone, and they will take Care os themselves, and do it best; and if they do not, a sufficient Punishment will follow their Neglect, without the Magistrate's Interposition and Penalties. It is plain, that such busy Care and officious Intrusion into the personal Affairs, or private Actions, Thoughts, and Imaginations of Men, has in it more Craft than Kindness; and is only a Device to mislead People, and pick their Pockets, under the false Pretence of the publick and their private Good. To quarrel with any Man for his Opinions, Humours, or the Fashion of his Clothes, is an Offence taken without being given. What is it to a Magistrate how I wash my Hands, or cut my Corns; what Fashion or Colours I wear, or what Notions I entertain, or what Gestures I use, or what Words I pronounce, when they please me, and do him and my Neighbour no Hurt? As well may he determine the Colour of my Hair, and controul my Shape and Features.

True and impartial Liberty is therefore the Right of every Man to pursue the natural, reasonable, and religious Dictates of his own Mind; to think what he will, and act as he thinks, provided he acts not to the Prejudice of another; to spend his own Money himself, and lay out the Produce of his Labour his own Way; and to labour for his own Pleasure and Profit, and not for others who are idle, and would live and riot by pillaging and oppressing him, and those that are like him.

So that Civil Government is only a partial Restraint put by the Laws of Agreement and Society upon natural and absolute Liberty, which might otherwise grow licentious: And Tyranny is an unlimited Restraint put upon natural Liberty, by the Will of one or a few. Magistracy, amongst a free People, is the Exercise of Power for the Sake of the People; and Tyrants abuse the People, for the Sake of Power. Free Government is the protecting the People in their Liberties by stated Rules: Tyranny is a brutish Struggle for unlimited Liberty to one or a few, who would rob all others of their Liberty, and act by no Rule but lawless Lust.

So much for an Idea of Civil Liberty. I will now add a Word or two, to shew how much it is the Delight and Passion of Mankind; and then shew its Advantages.

The Love of Liberty is an Apperite so strongly implanted in the Nature of all Living Creatures, that even the Appetite of Self-preservation, which is allowed to be the strongest, seems to be contained in it; since by the Means of Liberty they enjoy the Means of preserving themselves, and of satisfying their Desires in the Manner which they themselves choose and like best. Many Animals can never be tamed, but feel the Bitterness of Restraint in the midst of the kindest Usage; and rather than bear it, grieve and starve themselves to Death; and some beat out their Brains against their Prisons.

Where Liberty is lost, Life grows precarious, always miserable, often intolerable. Liberty is, to live upon one's own Terms; Slavery is, to live at the mere Mercy of another; and a Life of Slavery is, to those who can bear it, a continual State of Uncertainty and Wretchedness, often an Apprehension of Violence, often the lingering Dread of a violent Death: But by others, when no other Remedy is to be had, Death is reckoned a good one. And thus, to many Men, and to many other Creatures, as well as Men, the Love of Liberty is beyond the Love of Life.

This Passion for Liberty in Men, and their Possession of it, is of that Efficacy and Importance, that it seems the Parent of all the Virtues: And therefore in free Countries there seems to be another Species of Mankind, than is to be found under Tyrants. Small Armies of *Greeks* and *Romans* despised the greatest Hosts of Slaves; and a Million of Slaves have been sometimes beaten and conquered by a few Thousand Freemen. Insomuch that the Difference seemed greater between them than between Men and Sheep. It was therefore well said by *Lucullus*, when, being about to engage the great King *Tigranes*'s Army, he was told by some of his Officers, how prodigious great the fame was, consisting of between Three and Four Hundred Thousand Men: *No matter*, said that brave *Roman*, drawing up his little Army of Fourteen Thousand, but Fourteen Thousand *Romans: No matter*; *the Lion never enquires into the Number of the Sheep.* And these Royal Troops proved no better; for the *Romans* had little else to do but to kill and pursue; which yet they could scarce do for laughing; so much more were they diverted than animated by the ridiculous Dread and sudden Flight of these Imperial Slaves and Royal Cowards.

Men eternally cowed and oppressed by haughty and insolent Governors, made base themselves by the Baseness of that Sort of Government, and become Slaves by ruling over Slaves, want Spirit and Souls to meet in the Field Freemen, who scorn Oppressors, and are their own Governors, or at least measure and direct the Power of their Governors.

Education alters Nature, and becomes stronger. Slavery, while it continues, being a perpetual Awe upon the Spirits, depresses them, and sinks natural Courage; and Want and Fear, the Concomitants of Bondage, always produce Despondency and Baseness; nor will Men in Bonds ever fight bravely, but to be free. Indeed, what else should they fight for; since every Victory that they gain for a Tyrant, makes them poorer and fewer; and, increasing his Pride, increases his Cruelty, with their own Misery and Chains?

Those, who, from Terror and Delusion, the frequent Causes and certain Effects of Servitude, come to think their Governors greater than Men, as they find them worse, will be as apt to think themselves less: And when the Head and the Heart are thus both gone, the Hands will signify little. They who are used like Beasts, will be apt to degenerate into Beasts. But those, on the contrary, who, by the Freedom of their Government and Education, are taught and accustomed to think freely of Men and Things, find, by comparing one Man with another, that all Men are naturally alike; and that their Governors, as they have the same Face, Constitution, and Shape with themselves, and are subject to the same Sickness, Accidents, and Death, with the meanest of their People; so they possess the same Passions and Faculties of the Mind which their Subjects possess, and not better. They therefore scorn to degrade and prostrate themselves, to adore those of their own Species, however covered with Titles, and disguised by Power: They consider them as their own Creatures; and, as far as they surmount themselves, the Work of their own Hands, and only the chief Servants of the State, who have no more Power to do Evil than one of themselves, and are void of every Privilege and Superiority, but to serve them and the State. They know it to be a Contradiction in Religion and Reason, for any Man to have a Right to do Evil; that not to resist any Man's Wickedness, is to encourage it; and that they have the least Reason to bear Evil and Oppression from their Governors, who of all Men are the most obliged to do them Good. They therefore detest Slavery, and despise or pity Slaves; and, adoring Liberty alone, as they who see its Beauty and feel its Advantages always will, it is no Wonder that they are brave for it.

Indeed Liberty is the divine Source of all human Happiness. To possess, in Security, the Effects of our Industry, is the most powerful and reasonable Incitement to be industrious: And to be able to provide for our Children, and to leave them all that we have, is the best Motive to beget them. But where Property is precarious, Labour will languish. The Privileges of thinking, saying, and doing what we please, and of growing as rich as we can, without any other Restriction, than that by all this we hurt not the Publick, nor one another, are the glorious Privileges of Liberty; and its Effects, to live in Freedom, Plenty, and Safety.

These are Privileges that increase Mankind, and the Happiness of Mankind. And therefore Countries are generally peopled in Proportion as they are free, and are certainly happy in that Proportion: And upon the same Tract of Land that would maintain a Hundred Thousand Freemen in Plenty, Five Thousand Slaves would starve. In *Italy*, fertile *Italy*, Men die sometimes of Hunger amongst the Sheaves, and in a plentiful Harvest; for what they sow and reap is none of their own; and their cruel and greedy Governors, who live by the Labour of their wretched Vassals, do not suffer them to eat the Bread of their own Earning, nor to sustain their Lives with their own Hands.

Liberty naturally draws new People to it, as well as increases the old Stock; and Men as naturally run when they dare from Slavery and Wretchedness, whithersoever they can help themselves. Hence great Cities losing their Liberty become Desarts, and little Towns by Liberty grow great Cities; as will be fully proved before I have gone through this Argument. I will not deny, but that there are some great Cities of Slaves: But such are only Imperial Cities, and the Seats of great Princes, who draw the Wealth of a Continent to their Capital, the Center of their Treasure and Luxury. *Babylon, Antioch, Seleucia,* and *Alexandria*, were

154

great Cities peopled by Tyrants; but peopled partly by Force, partly by the above Reason, and partly by Grants and Indulgencies. Their Power, great and boundless as it was, could not alone people their Cities; but they were forced to soften Authority by Kindness; and having brought the Inhabitants together by Force, and by driving them Captive like Cattle, could not keep them together, without bestowing on them many Privileges, to encourage the first Inhabitants to stay, and to invite more to come.

This was a Consession in those Tyrants, that their Power was mischievous and unjust; since they could not erect one great City, and make it flourish, without renouncing in a great measure their Power over it; which, by granting it these Privileges, in Effect they did. These Privileges were fixed Laws, by which the Trade and Industry of the Citizens were encouraged, and their Lives and Properties ascertained and protected, and no longer subjected to the Laws of mere Will and Pleasure: And therefore, while these free Cities, enjoying their own Liberties and Laws, flourished under them, the Provinces were miserably harrassed, pillaged, dispeopled, and impoverished, and the Inhabitants exhausted, starved, butchered, and carried away captive.

This shews that all Civil Happiness and Prosperity is inseparable from Liberty; and that Tyranny cannot make Men, or Societies of Men, happy, without departing from its Nature, and giving them Privileges inconsistent with Tyranny. And here is an unanswerable Argument, amongst a Thousand others, against absolute Power in a single Man. Nor is there one Way in the World to give Happiness to Communities, but by sheltering them under certain and express Laws, irrevocable at any Man's Pleasure.

There is not, nor can be, any Security for a People to trust to the mere Will of one, who, while his Will is his Law, cannot protect them if he would. The Number of Sycophants and wicked Counsellors, that he will always and necessarily have about him, will defeat all his good Intentions, by representing Things falsly, and Persons maliciously; by suggesting Danger where it is not, and urging Necessity where there is none; by filling their own Coffers, under Colour of filling his, and by raising Money for themselves, pretending the publick Exigencies of the State; by sacrificing particular Men to their own Revenge, under Pretence of publick Security; and by engaging him and his People in dangerous and destructive Wars, for their own Profit or Fame; by throwing publick Affairs into perpetual Confusion, to prevent an Enquiry into their own Behaviour; and by making him jealous of his People, and his People of him, on purpose to manage and mislead both Sides.

By all these, and many more wicked Arts, they will be constantly leading him into cruel and oppressive Measures, destructive to his People, scandalous and dangerous to himself; but entirely agreeable to their own Spirit and Designs. Thus will they commit all Wickedness by their Master's Authority, against his Inclinations, and grow rich by the People's Poverty, without his Knowledge; and the Royal Authority will be first a Warrant for Oppression, afterwards a Protection from the Punishment due to it. For, in short, the Power of Princes is often little else but a Stalking-Horse to the Intrigues and Ambition of their Minister.

But if the Disposition of such a Prince be evil, what must be the forlorn Condition of his People, and what Door of Hope can remain for common Protection! The best Princes have often evil Counsellors, the Bad will have no other: And in such a Cafe, what Bounds can be set to their Fury, and to the Havock they will make? The Instruments and Advisers of Tyranny and Depredation always thrive best and are nearest their Ends, when Depredation and Tyranny run highest: When most is plundered from the People, their Share is greatest; we may therefore suppose every Evil will befal such a People, without supposing extravagantly. No Happiness, no Security, but certain Misery, and a vile and precarious Life, are the blessed Terms of such a Government—A Government which necessarily introduces all Evils, and from the same Necessity neither must nor can redress any.

The Nature of his Education, bred up as he ever is in perpetual Flattery, makes him haughty and ignorant; and the Nature of his Government, which subsists by brutish Severity and Oppression, makes him cruel. He is inaccessible, but by his Ministers, whose Study and Interest will be to keep him from knowing or helping the State of his miserable People. Their Master's Knowledge in his own Affairs, would break in upon their Scheme and Power; they are not likely to lay before him Representations of Grievances caused by themselves; nor, if they be the Effects of his own Barbarity and Command, will he hear them.

Even where absolute Princes are not Tyrants, there Ministers will be Tyrants. But it is indeed impossible for an arbitrary Prince to be otherwise, since Oppression is absolutely necessary to his being so. Without giving his People Liberty, he cannot make them happy; and by giving them Liberty, he gives up his own Power. So that to be and continue arbitrary, he is doomed to be a Tyrant in his own Defence. The Oppression of the people, Corruption, wicked Counsellors, and pernitious Maxims in the Court, and every where Baseness, Ignorance, and Chains, must support Tyranny, or it cannot be supported. So that in such Governments there are inevitable Grievances, without possible Redress; Misery, without Mitigation or Remedy; whatever is good for the People, is bad for their Governors; and what is good for the Governors, is pernicious to the People.

I am, &c.

F. THOMAS JEFFERSON, NOTES ON THE STATE OF VIRGINIA

(1787) [1785]

Query 13

The constitution of the State and its several charters?

Queen Elizabeth by her letters patent, bearing date March 25, 1584, licensed Sir Walter Raleigh to search for remote heathen lands, not inhabited by Christian people, and granted to him in fee simple, all the soil within two hundred leagues of the places where his people should, within six years, make their dwellings or abidings; reserving only to herself and her successors, their allegiance and one-fifth part of all the gold and silver ore they should obtain. Sir Walter immediately sent out two ships, which visited Wococon island in North Carolina, and the next year despatched seven with one hundred and seven men, who settled in Roanoke island, about latitude 35? 50'. Here Okisko, king of the Weopomeiocs, in a full council of his people is said to have acknowledged himself the homager of the Queen of England, and, after her, of Sir Walter Raleigh. A supply of fifty men were sent in 1586, and one hundred and fifty in 1587. With these last Sir Walter sent a governor, appointed him twelve assistants, gave them a charter of incorporation, and instructed them to settle on Chesapeake bay. They landed, however, at Hatorask. In 1588, when a fleet was ready to sail with a new supply of colonists and necessaries, they were detained by the Queen to assist against the Spanish armada. Sir Walter having now expended £40,000 in these enterprises, obstructed occasionally by the crown without a shilling of aid from it, was under a necessity of engaging others to adventure their money. He, therefore, by deed bearing date the 7th of March, 1589, by the name of Sir Walter Raleigh, Chief Governor of Assamàcomòc, (probably Acomàc,) alias Wingadacoia, alias Virginia, granted to Thomas Smith and others, in consideration of their adventuring certain sums of money, liberty to trade to this new country free from all customs and taxes for seven years, excepting the fifth part of the gold and silver ore to be obtained; and stipulated with them and the other assistants, then in Virginia, that he would confirm the deed of incorporation which he had given in 1587, with all the prerogatives, jurisdictions, royalties and privileges granted to him by the Queen. Sir Walter, at different times, sent five other adventurers hither, the last of which was in 1602; for in 1603 he was attainted and put into close imprisonment, which put an end to his cares over his infant colony. What was the particular fate of the colonists he had before sent and seated, has never been known; whether they were murdered, or incorporated with the savages.

Some gentlemen and merchants, supposing that by the attainder of Sir Walter Raleigh the grant to him was forfeited, not inquiring over carefully whether the sentence of an English court could affect lands not within the jurisdiction of that court, petitioned king James for a new grant of Virginia to them. He accordingly executed a grant to Sir Thomas Gates and others, bearing date the 9th of March, 1607, under which, in the same year, a settlement was effected at Jamestown, and ever after maintained. Of this grant, however, no particular notice need be taken, as it was superceded by letters patent of the same king, of May 23, 1609, to the Earl of Salisbury and others, incorporating them by the name of "The Treasurer and company of Adventurers and Planters of the City of London for the first colony in Virginia," granting to them and their successors all the lands in Virginia from Point Comfort along the sea-coast, to the northward two hundred miles, and from the same point along the sea-coast to the southward two hundred miles, and all the space from this precinct on the sea-coast up into the land, west and north-west, from sea to sea, and the islands within one hundred miles of it, with all the communities, jurisdictions, royalties, privileges, franchises, and pre-eminencies, within the same, and thereto and thereabouts, by sea and land, appertaining in as ample manner as had before been granted to any adventurer; to be held of the king and his successors, in common soccage, yielding one-fifth part of the gold and silver ore to be therein found, for all manner of services; establishing a counsel in England for the direction of the enterprise, the members of which were to be chosen and displaced by the voice of the majority of the company and adventurers, and were to have the nomination and revocation of governors, officers, and ministers, which by them should be thought needful for the colony, the power of establishing laws and forms of government and magistracy, obligatory not only within the colony, but also on the seas in going and coming to and from it; authorizing them to carry thither any persons who should consent to go, freeing them forever from all taxes and impositions on any goods or merchandise on importations into the colony, or exportation out of it, except the five per cent. due for custom on all goods imported into the British dominions, according to the ancient trade of merchants; which five per cent. only being paid they might, within thirteen months, re-export the same goods into foreign parts, without any custom, tax, or other duty, to the king or any of his officers, or deputies; with powers of waging war against those who should annoy them; giving to the inhabitants of the colony all the rights of natural subjects, as if born and abiding in England; and declaring that these letters should be construed, in all doubtful parts, in such manner as should be most for the benefit of the grantees.

Afterwards on the 12th of March, 1612, by other letters patent, the king added to his former grants, all islands in any part of the ocean between the 30th and 41st degrees of latitude, and within three hundred leagues of any of the parts before granted to the treasurer and company, not being possessed or inhabited by any other Christian prince or state, nor within the limits of the northern colony.

In pursuance of the authorities given to the company by these charters, and more especially of that part in the charter of 1609, which authorized them to establish a form of government, they on the 24th of July, 1621, by charter under their common seal, declared that from thenceforward there should be two supreme councils in Virginia, the one to be called the council of state, to be placed and displaced by the treasurer, council in England, and company from time to time, whose office was to be that of assisting and advising the governor; the other to be called the general assembly, to be convened by the governor once yearly or oftener, which was to consist of the council of state, and two burgesses out of every town, hundred, or plantation, to be respectively chosen by the inhabitants. In this all matters were to be decided by the greater part of the votes present; reserving to the governor a negative voice; and they were to have power to treat, consult, and conclude all emergent occasions concerning the public weal, and to make laws for the behoof and government of the colony, imitating and following the laws and policy of England as nearly as might be; providing that these laws should have no force till ratified in a general court of the company in England, and returned under their common seal; and declaring that, after the government of the colony should be well framed and settled, no orders of the council in England should bind the colony unless ratified in the said general assembly. The king and company quarrelled, and by a mixture of law and force, the latter were ousted of all their rights without retribution, after having expended one hundred thousand pounds in establishing the colony, without the smallest aid from government. King James suspended their powers by proclamation of July 15, 1624, and Charles I. took the government into his own hands. Both sides had their partisans in the colony, but, in truth, the people of the colony in general thought themselves little concerned in the dispute. There being three parties interested in these several charters, what passed between the first and second, it was thought could not affect the third. If the king seized on the powers of the company, they only passed into other hands, without increase or diminution, while the rights of the people remained as they were. But they did not remain so long. The northern parts of their country were granted away to the lords Baltimore and Fairfax; the first of these obtaining also the rights of separate jurisdiction and government. And in 1650 the parliament, considering itself as standing in the place of their deposed king, and as having succeeded to all his powers, without as well as within the realm, began to assume a right over the colonies, passing an act for inhibiting their trade with foreign nations. This succession to the exercise of kingly authority gave the first color for parliamentary interference with the colonies, and produced that fatal precedent which they continued to follow, after they had retired, in other respects, within their proper functions. When this colony, therefore, which still maintained its opposition to Cromwell and the parliament, was induced in to lay down their arms, they previously secured their most essential rights by a solemn convention, which, having never seen in print, I will here insert literally from the records.

"ARTICLES agreed on and concluded at James Cittie in Virginia for the surrendering and settling of that plantation under the obedience and government of the commonwealth of England by the commissioners of the Councill of State by authorities of the parliamt of England, and by the Grand assembly of the Governour, Councill, and Burgesses of that countrey.

"First   it is agreed and consted that the plantation of Virginia, and all the inhabitants thereof, shall be and remain in due obedience and subjection to the Commonwealth of England, according to the laws there established, and that this submission and subscription bee acknowledged a voluntary act not forced nor constrained by a conquest upon the countrey, and that they shall have and enjoy such freedoms and priviledges as belong to the free borne people of England, and that the former government by the Commissions and Instructions be void and null.

"2ly.   That the Grand assembly as formerly shall convene and transact the affairs of Virginia, wherein nothing is to be acted or done contrairie to the government of the Commonwealth of England and the lawes there established.

"3ly.   That there shall be a full and totall remission and indempnitie of all acts, words, or writeings done or spoken against the parliament of England in relation to the same.

"4ly.   That Virginia shall have and enjoy the antient bounds and lymitts granted by the charters of the former kings, and that we shall seek a new charter from the parliament to that purpose against any that have intrencht upon the rights thereof.

"5ly.   That all the pattents of land granted under the colony seal by any of the precedent governours shall be and remaine in their full force and strength.

"6ly.   That the priviledge of haveing ffiftie acres of land for every person transported in that collonie shall continue as formerly granted.

"7ly.   That the people of Virginia have free trade as the people of England do enjoy to all places and with all nations according to the lawes of that commonwealth, and that Virginia shall enjoy all priviledges equall with any English plantations in America.

"8ly.   That Virginia shall be free from all taxes, customs and impositions whatsoever, and none to be imposed on them without consent of the Grand assembly; and soe that neither fforts nor castle bee erected or garrisons maintained without their consent.

"9ly.   That noe charge shall be required from this country in respect of this present ffleet.

160

"10ly. That for the future settlement of the countrey in their due obedience, the engagement shall be tendred to all the inhabitants according to act of parliament made to that purpose, that all persons who shall refuse to subscribe the said engagement, shall have a yeare's time if they please to remove themselves and their estates out of Virginia, and in the meantime during the said yeare to have equall justice as formerly.

"11ly. That the use of the booke of common prayer shall be permitted for one yeare ensueinge with referrence to the consent of the major part of the parishes, provided that those which relate to kingshipp or that government be not used publiquely, and the continuance of ministers in their places, they not misdemeaning themselves, and the payment of their accustomed dues and agreements made with them respectively shall be left as they now stand dureing this ensueing yeare.

"12ly. That no man's cattell shall be questioned as the companies, unless such as have been entrusted with them or have disposed of them without order.

"13ly. That all ammunition, powder and armes, other than for private use, shall be delivered up, securitie being given to make satisfaction for it.

"14ly. That all goods allreadie brought hither by the Dutch or others which are now on shoar shall be free from surprizall.

"15ly. That the quittrents granted unto us by the late kinge for seaven yeares bee confirmed.

"16ly. That the commissioners for the parliament subscribeing these articles engage themselves and the honour of parliament for the full performance thereof; and that the present governour, and the councill, and the burgesses do likewise subscribe and engage the whole collony on their parts.

RICHARD BENNETT.—Seale.

WILLIAM CLAIBORNE.—Seale.

EDMOND CURTIS.—Seale.

"Theise articles were signed and sealed by the Commissioners of the Councill of state for the Commonwealth of England the twelveth day of March 1651."

Then follow the articles stipulated by the governor and council, which relate merely to their own persons and property, and then the ensuing instrument:

"An act of indempnitie made att the surrender of the countrey.

Whereas, by the authoritie of the parliament wee the commissioners appointed by the councill of state authorized thereto, having brought a ffleet and force before James cittie in Virginia to reduce that collonie under the obedience of the commonwealth of England, and finding force raised by the Governour and countrey to make opposition against the said ffleet, whereby assured danger appearinge of the ruine and destruction of the plantation, for prevention whereof the burgesses of all the severall plantations being called to advise and assist therein, uppon long and serious debate, and in sad contemplation of the great miseries and certain destruction which were soe neerely hovering over the whole countrey; Wee the said Commissioners have thought fitt and condescending and granted to signe and confirme under our hands, seales and by our oath, Articles bearinge date with theise presents, and do further declare that by the authoritie of the parliament and commonwealth of England derived unto us their commissioners, that according to the articles in generall wee have granted an act of indempnitie and oblivion to all the inhabitants of this collonie from all words, actions, or writings that have been spoken acted or writt against the parliament or commonwealth of England or any other person from the beginning of the world to this daye. And this we have done that all the inhabitants of the collonie may live quietly and securely under the commonwealth of England. And we do promise that the parliament and commonwealth of England shall confirm and make good all those transactions of ours. Witness our hands and seales this 12th of March 1651.

RICHARD BENNETT.—Seale.

WILLIAM CLAIBORNE.—Seale.

EDMOND CURTIS.—Seale.

The colony supposed, that, by this solemn convention, entered into with arms in their hands, they had secured the ancient limits of their country, its free trade, its exemption from taxation but by their own assembly, and exclusion of military force from among them. Yet in every of these points was this convention violated by subsequent kings and parliaments, and other infractions of their constitution, equally dangerous committed. Their general assembly, which was composed of the council of state and burgesses, sitting together and deciding by plurality of voices, was split into two houses, by which the council obtained a separate negative on their laws. Appeals from their supreme court, which had been fixed by law in their general assembly, were arbitrarily revoked to England, to be there heard before the king and council. Instead of four hundred miles on the seacoast, they were reduced, in the space of thirty years, to about one hundred miles. Their trade with foreigners was totally suppressed, and when carried to Great Britain, was there loaded with imposts. It is unnecessary, however, to glean up the several instances of injury, as scattered through American and British history, and the more especially as, by passing on to the accession of the present king, we shall find specimens of them all, aggravated, multiplied and crowded within a small compass of time, so as to evince a fixed design of considering our rights natural, conventional and chartered as mere nullities. The following is an epitome of the first sixteen years of his reign: The colonies were taxed internally and externally; their essential interests sacrificed to individuals in Great

Britain; their legislatures suspended; charters annulled; trials by juries taken away; their persons subjected to transportation across the Atlantic, and to trial before foreign judicatories; their supplications for redress thought beneath answer; themselves published as cowards in the councils of their mother country and courts of Europe; armed troops sent among them to enforce submission to these violences; and actual hostilities commenced against them. No alternative was presented but resistance, or unconditional submission. Between these could be no hesitation. They closed in the appeal to arms. They declared themselves independent states. They confederated together into one great republic; thus securing to every State the benefit of an union of their whole force. In each State separately a new form of government was established. Of ours particularly the following are the outlines: The executive powers are lodged in the hands of a governor, chosen annually, and incapable of acting more then three years in seven. He is assisted by a council of eight members. The judiciary powers are divided among several courts, as will be hereafter explained. Legislation is exercised by two houses of assembly, the one called the house of Delegates, composed of two members from each county, chosen annually by the citizens, possessing an estate for life in one hundred acres of uninhabited land, or twenty-five acres with a house on it, or in a house or lot in some town: the other called the Senate, consisting of twenty-four members, chosen quadrenially by the same electors, who for this purpose are distributed into twenty-four districts. The concurrence of both houses is necesary to the passage of a law. They have the appointment of the governor and council, the judges of the superior courts, auditors, attorney-general, treasurer, register of the land office, and delegates to Congress. As the dismemberment of the State had never had its confirmation, but, on the contrary, had always been the subject of protestation and complaint, that it might never be in our own power to raise scruples on that subject, or to disturb the harmony of our new confederacy, the grants to Maryland, Pennsylvania, and the two Carolinas, were ratified.

This constitution was formed when we were new and unexperienced in the science of government. It was the first, too, which was formed in the whole United States. No wonder then that time and trial have discovered very capital defects in it.

1. The majority of the men in the State, who pay and fight for its support, are unrepresented in the legislature, the roll of freeholders entitled to vote not including generally the half of those on the roll of the militia, or of the tax-gatherers.

2. Among those who share the representation, the shares are very unequal. Thus the county of Warwick, with only one hundred fighting men, has an equal representation with the county of Loudon, which has one thousand seven hundred and forty-six. So that every man in Warwick has as much influence in the government as seventeen men in Loudon. But lest it should be thought that an equal interspersion of

small among large counties, through the whole State, may prevent any danger of injury to particular parts of it, we will divide it into districts, and show the proportions of land, of fighting men, and of representation in each:

	Square miles.	Fighting men.	Delegates.	Senators.
Between the sea-coast and falls of the rivers	11,205	19,012	71	12
Between the falls of the rivers and and Blue Ridge of mountains	18,759	18,828	46	8
Between the Blue Ridge and the Alleghany	11,911	7,673	16	2
Between the Alleghany and Ohio	79,650	4,458	16	2
Total	121,525	49,971	149	24

An inspection of this table will supply the place of commentaries on it. It will appear at once that nineteen thousand men, living below the falls of the rivers, possess half the senate, and want four members only of possessing a majority of the house of delegates; a want more than supplied by the vicinity of their situation to the seat of government, and of course the greater degree of convenience and punctuality with which their members may and will attend in the legislature. These nineteen thousand, therefore, living in one part of the country, give law to upwards of thirty thousand living in another, and appoint all their chief officers, executive and judiciary. From the difference of their situation and circumstances, their interests will often be very different.

3. The senate is, by its constitution, too homogenous with the house of delegates. Being chosen by the same electors, at the same time, and out of the same subjects, the choice falls of course on men of the same description. The purpose of establishing different houses of legislation is to introduce the influence of different interests or different principles. Thus in Great Britain it is said their constitution relies on the house of commons for honesty, and the lords for wisdom; which would be a rational reliance, if honesty were to be bought with money, and if wisdom were hereditary. In some of the American States, the delegates and senators are so chosen, as that the first represent the persons, and the second the property of the State. But with us, wealth and wisdom have equal chance for admission into both houses. We do not, therefore, derive from the separation of our legislature into two houses, those benefits which a proper complication of principles are capable of producing, and those which alone can compensate the evils which may be produced by their dissensions.

4. All the powers of government, legislative, executive, and judiciary, result to the legislative body. The concentrating these in the same hands is precisely the definition of despotic government. It will be no alleviation that these powers will be exercised by a plurality of hands, and not by a single one. One hundred and seventy-three despots would

surely be as oppressive as one. Let those who doubt it turn their eyes on the republic of Venice. As little will it avail us that they are chosen by ourselves. An *elective despotism* was not the government we fought for, but one which should not only be founded on free principles, but in which the powers of government should be so divided and balanced among several bodies of magistracy, as that no one could transcend their legal limits, without being effectually checked and restrained by the others. For this reason that convention which passed the ordinance of government, laid its foundation on this basis, that the legislative, executive, and judiciary departments should be separate and distinct, so that no person should exercise the powers of more than one of them at the same time. But no barrier was provided between these several powers. The judiciary and executive members were left dependent on the legislative, for their subsistence in office, and some of them for their continuance in it. If, therefore, the legislature assumes executive and judiciary powers, no opposition is likely to be made; nor, if made, can it be effectual; because in that case they may put their proceedings into the form of an act of assembly, which will render them obligatory on the other branches. They have, accordingly, in many instances, decided rights which should have been left to judiciary controversy; and the direction of the executive, during the whole time of their session, is becoming habitual and familiar. And this is done with no ill intention. The views of the present members are perfectly upright. When they are led out of their regular province, it is by art in others, and inadvertence in themselves. And this will probably be the case for some time to come. But it will not be a very long time. Mankind soon learn to make interested uses of every right and power which they possess, or may assume. The public money and public liberty, intended to have been deposited with three branches of magistracy, but found inadvertently to be in the hands of one only, will soon be discovered to be sources of wealth and dominion to those who hold them; distinguished, too, by this tempting circumstance, that they are the instrument, as well as the object of acquisition. With money we will get men, said Cæsar, and with men we will get money. Nor should our assembly be deluded by the integrity of their own purposes, and conclude that these unlimited powers will never be abused, because themselves are not disposed to abuse them. They should look forward to a time, and that not a distant one, when a corruption in this, as in the country from which we derive our origin, will have seized the heads of government, and be spread by them through the body of the people; when they will purchase the voices of the people, and make them pay the price. Human nature is the same on every side of the Atlantic, and will be alike influenced by the same causes. The time to guard against corruption and tyranny, is before they shall have gotten hold of us. It is better to keep the wolf out of the fold, than to trust to drawing his teeth and talons after he shall have entered. To render these considerations the more cogent, we must observe in addition:

5. That the ordinary legislature may alter the constitution itself. On the discontinuance of assemblies, it became necessary to substitute in their place some other body, competent to the ordinary business of government, and to the calling forth the powers of the State for the maintenance of our opposition to Great Britain. Conventions were therefore introduced, consisting of two delegates from each county, meeting together and forming one house, on the plan of the former house of burgesses, to whose places they succeeded. These were at first chosen anew for every particular session. But in March 1775, they recommended to the people to choose a convention, which should continue in office a year. This was done, accordingly, in April 1775, and in the July following that convention passed an ordinance for the election of delegates in the month of April annually. It is well known, that in July 1775, a separation from Great Britain and establishment of republican government, had never yet entered into any person's mind. A convention, therefore, chosen under that ordinance, cannot be said to have been chosen for the purposes which certainly did not exist in the minds of those who passed it. Under this ordinance, at the annual election in April 1776, a convention for the year was chosen. Independence, and the establishment of a new form of government, were not even yet the objects of the people at large. One extract from the pamphlet called Common Sense had appeared in the Virginia papers in February, and copies of the pamphlet itself had got in a few hands. But the idea had not been opened to the mass of the people in April, much less can it be said that they had made up their minds in its favor.

So that the electors of April 1776, no more than the legislators of July 1775, not thinking of independence and a permanent republic, could not mean to vest in these delegates powers of establishing them, or any authorities other than those of the ordinary legislature. So far as a temporary organization of government was necessary to render our opposition energetic, so far their organization was valid. But they received in their creation no power but what were given to every legislature before and since. They could not, therefore, pass an act transcendent to the powers of other legislatures. If the present assembly pass an act, and declare it shall be irrevocable by subsequent assemblies, the declaration is merely void, and the act repealable, as other acts are. So far, and no farther authorized, they organized the government by the ordinance entitled a constitution or form of government. It pretends to no higher authority than the other ordinances of the same session; it does not say that it shall be perpetual; that it shall be unalterable by other legislatures; that it shall be transcendent above the powers of those who they knew would have equal power with themselves. Not only the silence of the instrument is a proof they thought it would be alterable, but their own practice also; for this very convention, meeting as a house of delegates in general assembly with the Senate in the autumn of that year, passed acts of assembly in contradiction to their ordinance of government; and every assembly from that time to this has done the same. I am safe, therefore, in the position that the constitution itself is alterable by the ordinary legislature. Though this opinion seems founded on the first elements of common sense, yet is the contrary maintained by some persons. 1. Because, say they, the conventions were vested with every power necessary to make effectual opposition to Great Britain. But to complete this argument, they must go on, and say further, that effectual opposition could not be made to Great Britain without establishing a form of government perpetual and unalterable by the legislature; which is not true. An opposition which at some time or other was to come to an end, could not need a perpetual institution to carry it on; and a government amendable as its defects should be discovered, was as likely to make effectual resistance, as one that should be unalterably wrong. Besides, the assemblies were as much vested with all powers requisite for resistance as the conventions were. If, therefore, these powers included that of modelling the form of government in the one case, they did so in the other. The assemblies then as well as the conventions may model the government; that is, they may alter the ordinance of government. 2. They urge, that if the convention had meant that this instrument should be alterable, as their other ordinances were, they would have called it an ordinance; but they have called it a *constitution*, which, ex vi termini, means "an act above the power of the ordinary legislature." I answer that *constitutio, constitutium, statutum, lex*, are convertible terms. "*Constitutio* dicitur jus quod a principe conditure." "*Constitutium*, quod ab imperatoribus rescriptum statutumve est." "*Statutum*, idem quod lex." Calvini Lexicon juridicum. *Constitution* and *statute* were originally terms of the civil law, and from thence introduced by ecclesiastics into the English law. Thus in the statute 25 Hen. VIII. c. 19, §. 1, "*Constitutions* and *ordinances*" are used as synonymous. The term *constitution* has many other significations in physics and politics; but in jurisprudence, whenever it is applied to any act of the legislature, it invariably means a statute, law, or ordinance, which is the present case. No inference then of a different meaning can be drawn from the adoption of this title; on the contrary, we might conclude that, by their affixing to it a term synonymous with ordinance or statute. But of what consequence is their meaning, where their power is denied? If they meant to do more than they had power to do, did this give them power? It is not the name, but the authority that renders an act obligatory. Lord Coke says, "an article of the statute, 11 R. II. c. 5, that no person should attempt to revoke any ordinance then made, is repealed, for that such restrainst is against the jurisdiction and power of the parliament." 4. Inst. 42. And again, "though divers parliaments have attempted to restrain subsequent parliaments, yet could they never effect it; for the latter parliament hath ever power to abrogate, suspend, qualify, explain, or make void the former in the whole or in any part thereof, notwithstanding any words of restraint, prohibition, or penalty, in the former; for it is a maxim in the laws of the parliament, quod leges posteriores priores contrarias abrogant." 4. Inst. 43. To get rid of the magic supposed to be in the word *constitution*, let us translate it into its definition as given by those who think it above the power of the law; and let us suppose the convention, instead of saying, "We the ordinary legislature, establish a *constitution*," had said, "We the ordinary legislature, establish an act *above the power of the ordinary legislature.*" Does not this expose the absurdity of the attempt? 3. But, say they, the people have acquiesced, and this has given it an authority superior to the laws. It is true that the people did not rebel against it; and was that a time for the people to rise in rebellion? Should a prudent acquiescence, at a critical time, be construed into a confirmation of every illegal thing done during that period? Besides, why should they rebel? At an annual election they had chosen delegates for the year, to exercise the ordinary powers of legislation, and to manage the great contest in which they were engaged. These delegates thought the contest would be best managed by an organized government. They therefore, among others, passed an ordinance of government. They did not presume to call it perpetual and unalterable. They well knew they had no power to make it so; that our choice of them had been for no such purpose, and at a time when we could have no such purpose in contemplation. Had an unalterable form of government been meditated, perhaps we should have chosen a different set of people. There was no cause then for the people to rise in rebellion. But to what dangerous lengths will this argument lead? Did the acquiescence of the colonies under the various acts of power exercised by Great Britain in our infant State, confirm these acts, and so far invest them with the authority of the people as to render them unalterable, and our present resistance wrong? On every unauthoritative exercise of power by the legislature must the people rise in rebellion, or their silence be construed into a surrender of that power to them? If so, how many rebellions should we have had already? One certainly for every session of assembly. The other States in the union have been of opinion that to render a form of government unalterable by ordinary acts of assembly, the people must delegate persons with special powers. They have accordingly chosen special conventions to form and fix their governments. The individuals then who maintain the contrary opinion in this country, should have the modesty to suppose it possible that they may be wrong, and the rest of America right. But if there be only a possibility of their being wrong, if only a plausible doubt remains of the validity of the ordinance of government, is it not better to remove that doubt by placing it on a bottom which none will dispute? If they be right we shall only have the unnecessary trouble of meeting once in convention. If they be wrong, they expose us to the hazard of having no fundamental rights at all. True it is, this is no time for deliberating on forms of government. While an enemy is within our bowels, the first object is to expel him. But when this shall be done, when peace shall be established, and leisure given us for intrenching within good forms, the rights for which we have bled, let no man be found indolent enough to decline a little more trouble for placing them beyond the reach of question. If anything more be requisite to produce a conviction of the expediency of calling a convention at a proper season to fix our form of government, let it be the reflection:

6.   That the assembly exercises a power of determining the quorum of their own body which may legislate for us. After the establishment of the new form they adhered to the *Lex majoris partis*, founded in common law as well as common right. It is the natural law of every assembly of men, whose numbers are not fixed by any other law. They continued for some time to require the presence of a majority of their whole number, to pass an act. But the British parliament fixes its own quorum; our former assemblies fixed their own quorum; and one precedent in favor of power is stronger than an hundred against it. The house of delegates, therefore, have lately voted that, during the present dangerous invasion, forty members shall be a house to proceed to business. They have been moved to this by the fear of not being able to collect a house. But this danger could not authorize them to call that a house which was none; and if they may fix it at one number, they may at another, till it loses its fundamental character of being a representative body. As this vote expires with the present invasion, it is probable the former rule will be permitted to revive; because at present no ill is meant. The power, however, of fixing their own quorum has been avowed, and a precedent set. From forty it may be reduced to four, and from four to one; from a house to a committee, from a committee to a chairman or speaker, and thus an oligarchy or monarchy be substituted under forms supposed to be regular. "Omnia mala exempla ex bonis orta sunt; sed ubi imperium ad ignaros aut minus bonos pervenit, novum illud exemplum ab dignis et idoneis adindignos et non idoneos fertur." When, therefore, it is considered, that there is no legal obstacle to the assumption by the assembly of all the powers legislative, executive, and judiciary, and that these may come to the hands of the smallest rag of delegation, surely the people will say, and their representatives, while yet they have honest representatives, will advise them to say, that they will not acknowledge as laws any acts not considered and assented to by the major part of their delegates.

In enumerating the defects of the constitution, it would be wrong to count among them what is only the error of particular persons. In December 1776, our circumstances being much distressed, it was proposed in the house of delegates to create a *dictator*, invested with every power legislative, executive, and judiciary, civil and military, of life and of death, over our persons and over our properties; and in June 1781, again under calamity, the same proposition was repeated, and wanted a few votes only of being passed. One who entered into this contest from a pure love of liberty, and a sense of injured rights, who determined to make every sacrifice, and to meet every danger, for the re-establishment of those rights on a firm basis, who did not mean to expend his blood and substance for the wretched purpose of changing this matter for that, but to place the powers of governing him in a plurality of hands of his own choice, so that the corrupt will of no one man might in future oppress him, must stand confounded and dismayed when he is told, that a considerable portion of that plurality had mediated the surrender of them into a single hand, and, in lieu of a limited monarchy, to deliver him over to a despotic one! How must we find his efforts and sacrifices abused and baffled, if he may still, by a single vote, be laid prostrate at the feet of one man! In God's name, from whence have they derived this power? Is it from our ancient laws? None such can be produced. Is it from any principle in our new constitution expressed or implied? Every lineament expressed or implied, is in full opposition to it. Its fundamental principle is, that the State shall be governed as a commonwealth. It provides a republican organization, proscribes under the name of *prerogative* the exercise of all powers undefined by the laws; places on this basis the whole system of our laws; and by consolidating them together, chooses that they should be left to stand or fall together, never providing for any circumstances, nor admitting that such could arise, wherein either should be suspended; no, not for a moment. Our ancient laws expressly declare, that those who are but delegates themselves shall not delegate to others powers which require judgment and integrity in their exercise. Or was this proposition moved on a supposed right in the movers, of abandoning their posts in a moment of distress? The same laws forbid the abandonment of that post, even on ordinary occasions; and much more a transfer of their powers into other hands and other forms, without consulting the people. They never admit the idea that these, like sheep or cattle, may be given from hand to hand without an appeal to their own will. Was it from the necessity of the case? Necessities which dissolve a government, do not convey its authority to an oligarchy or a monarchy. They throw back, into the hands of the people, the powers they had delegated, and leave them as individuals to shift for themselves. A leader may offer, but not impose himself, nor be imposed on them. Much less can their necks be submitted to his sword, their breath to be held at his will or caprice. The necessity which should operate these tremendous effects should at least be palpable and irresistible. Yet in both instances, where it was feared, or pretended with us, it was belied by the event. It was belied, too, by the preceding experience of our sister States, several of whom had grappled through greater difficulties without abandoning their forms of government. When the proposition was first made, Massachusetts had found even the government of committees sufficient to carry them through an invasion. But we at the time of that proposition, were under no invasion. When the second was made, there had been added to this example those of Rhode Island, New York, New Jersey, and Pennsylvania, in all of which the republican form had been found equal to the task of carrying them through the severest trials. In this State alone did there exist so little virtue, that fear was to be fixed in the hearts of the people, and to become the motive of their exertions, and principle of their government? The very thought alone was treason against the people; was treason against mankind in general; as rivetting forever the chains which bow down their necks, by giving to their oppressors a proof, which they would have trumpeted through the universe, of the imbecility of republican government, in times of pressing danger, to shield them from harm. Those who assume the right of giving away the reins of government in any case, must be sure that the herd, whom they hand on to the rods and hatchet of the dictator, will lay their necks on the block when he shall nod to them. But if our assemblies supposed such a recognition in the people, I hope they mistook their character. I am of opinion, that the government, instead of being braced and invigorated for greater exertions under their difficulties, would have been thrown back upon thebungling machinery of county committees for administration, till a convention could have been called, and its wheels again set into regular motion. What a cruel moment was this for creating such an embarrassment, for putting to the proof the attachment of our countrymen to republican government! Those who meant well, of the advocates of this measure, (and most of them meant well, for I know them personally, had been their fellow-laborer in the common cause, and had often proved the purity of their principles,) had been seduced in their judgment by the example of an ancient republic, whose constitution and circumstances were fundamentally different. They had sought this precedent in the history of Rome, where alone it was to be found, and where at length, too, it had proved fatal. They had taken it from a republic rent by the most bitter factions and tumults, where the government was of a heavy-handed unfeeling aristocracy, over a people ferocious, and rendered desperate by poverty and wretchedness; tumults which could not be allayed under the most trying circumstances, but by the omnipotent hand of a single despot. Their constitution, therefore, allowed a temporary tyrant to be erected, under the name of a dictator; and that temporary tyrant, after a few examples, became perpetual. They misapplied this precedent to a people mild in their dispositions, patient under their trial, united for the public liberty, and affectionate to their leaders. But if from the constitution of the Roman government there resulted to their senate a power of submitting all their rights to the will of one man, does it follow that the assembly of Virginia have the same authority? What clause in our constitution has substituted that of Rome, by way of residuary provision, for all cases not otherwise provided for? Or if they may step *ad libitum* into any other form of government for precedents to rule us by, for what oppression may not a precedent be found in this world of the *ballum omnium in omnia?* Searching for the foundations of this proposition, I can find none which may pretend a color of right or reason, but the defect before developed, that there being no barrier between the legislative, executive, and judiciary departments, the legislature may seize the whole; that having seized it, and possessing a right to fix their own quorum, they may reduce that quorum to one, whom they may call a chairman, speaker, dictator, or by any other name they please. Our situation is indeed perilous, and I hope my countrymen will be sensible of it, and will apply, at a proper season, the proper remedy; which is a convention to fix the constitution, to amend its defects, to bind up the several branches of government by certain laws, which, when they transgress, their acts shall become nullities; to render unnecessary an appeal to the people, or in other words a rebellion, on every infraction of their rights, on the peril that their acquiescence shall be construed into an intention to surrender those rights.

G.   DEBATE IN THE PHILADELPHIA CONVENTION

(1) June 4, 1787

<First> Clause <of Proposition 8th> relating *to a Council of Revision* taken into consideration.

Mr. Gerry doubts whether the Judiciary ought to form a part of it, as they will have a sufficient check agst. encroachments on their own department by their exposition of the laws, which involved a power of deciding on their Constitutionality. In some States the Judges had <actually> set aside laws as being agst. the Constitution. This was done too with general approbation. It was quite foreign from the nature of ye. office to make them judges of the policy of public measures. <He moves to postpone> the clause <in order> to propose "that the National Executive <shall> have a right to negative any Legislative act <which> shall not be afterwards passed by   parts of each branch of the national Legislature.

Mr. King seconds the motion, observing that the Judges ought to be able to expound the law as it should come before them, free from the bias of having participated in its formation.

Mr. Wilson thinks neither the original proposition nor the amendment go far enough. If the Legislative Exētiv & Judiciary ought to be distinct & independent, The Executive ought to have an absolute negative. Without such a Self-defence the Legislature can at any moment sink it into non-existence. He was for varying the proposition in such a manner as to give the Executive & Judiciary jointly an absolute negative

On the question to postpone in order to take Mr. Gerry's proposition into consideration <it was agreed to> Massts. ay. Cont. no. N. Y. ay. Pa. ay. Del. no. Maryd. no. Virga. no. N. C. ay. S. C. ay. Ga. ay. [Ayes—6; noes—4.]

(2) June 6, 1787

Mr. Wilson moved to reconsider the vote excluding the Judiciary from a share in the revision of the laws, and to add after "National Executive" the words "with a convenient number of the national Judiciary"; remarking the expediency of reinforcing the Executive with the influence of that Department.

Mr. Madison 2ded. the motion. He observed that the great difficulty in rendering the Executive competent to its own defence arose from the nature of Republican Govt. which could not give to an individual citizen that settled pre-eminence in the eyes of the rest, that weight of property, that personal interest agst. betraying the National interest, which appertain to an hereditary magistrate. In a Republic personal merit alone could be the ground of political exaltation, but it would rarely happen that this merit would be so preeminent as to produce universal acquiescence. The Executive Magistrate would be envied & assailed by disappointed competitors: His firmness therefore wd. need support. He would not possess those great emoluments from his station, nor that permanent stake in the public interest which wd. place him out of the reach of foreign corruption: He would stand in need therefore of being controuled as well as supported. An association of the Judges in his revisionary function wd both double the advantage and diminish the danger. It wd. also enable the Judiciary Department the better to defend itself agst. Legislative encroachments. Two objections had been made 1st. that the Judges ought not to be subject to the bias which a participation in the making of laws might give in the exposition of them. 2dly. that the Judiciary Departmt. ought to be separate & distinct from the other great Departments. The 1st. objection had some weight; but it was much diminished by reflecting that a small proportion of the laws coming in question before a Judge wd. be such wherein he had been consulted; that a small part of this proportion wd. be so ambiguous as to leave room for his prepossessions; and that but a few cases wd. probably arise in the life of a Judge under such ambiguous passages. How much good on the other hand wd. proceed from the perspicuity, the conciseness, and the systematic character wch. the Code of laws wd. receive from the Judiciary talents. As to the 2d. objection, it either had no weight, or it applied with equal weight to the Executive & to the Judiciary revision of the laws. The maxim on which the objection was founded required a separation of the Executive as well as of the Judiciary from the Legislature & from each other. There wd. in truth however be no improper mixture of these distinct powers in the present case. In England, whence the maxim itself had been drawn, the Executive had an absolute negative on the laws; and the supreme tribunal of Justice (the House of Lords) formed one of the other branches of the Legislature. In short, whether the object of the revisionary power was to restrain the Legislature from encroaching on the other co-ordinate Departments, or on the rights of the people at large; or from passing laws unwise in their principle, or incorrect in their form, the utility of annexing the wisdom and weight of the Judiciary to the Executive seemed incontestable.

Mr. Gerry thought the Executive, whilst standing alone wd. be more impartial than when he cd. be covered by the sanction & seduced by the sophistry of the Judges

Mr. King. If the Unity of the Executive was preferred for the sake of responsibility, the policy of it is as applicable to the revisionary as to the Executive power.

Mr. Pinkney had been at first in favor of joining the heads of the principal departmts. the Secretary at War, of foreign affairs &—in the council of revision. He had however relinquished the idea from a consideration that these could be called on by the Executive Magistrate whenever he pleased to consult them. He was opposed to an introduction of the Judges into the business.

Col Mason was for giving all possible weight to the revisionary institution. The Executive power ought to be well secured agst. Legislative usurpations on it. The purse & the sword ought never to get into the same hands <whether Legislative or Executive.>

Mr. Dickinson. Secrecy, vigor & despatch are not the principal properties reqd. in the Executive. Important as these are, that of responsibility is more so, which can only be preserved; by leaving it singly to discharge its functions. He thought too a junction of the Judiciary to it, involved an improper mixture of powers.

Mr Wilson remarked, that the responsibility required belonged to his Executive duties. The revisionary duty was an extraneous one, calculated for collateral purposes.

Mr. Williamson, was for substituting a clause requiring 2/3 for every effective act of the Legislature, in place of the revisionary provision

On the question for joining the Judges to the Executive in the revisionary business Mass. no. Cont. ay. N. Y. ay. N. J. no. Pa. no. Del. no. Md. no. Va. ay. N. C. no. S. C. no. Geo. no. [Ayes—3; noes—8.]

(3) July 21, 1787

Mr. Wilson moved as an amendment to Resoln: 10. that the <supreme> Natl Judiciary should be associated with the Executive in the Revisionary power". This proposition had been before made, and failed; but he was so confirmed by reflection in the opinion of its utility, that he thought it incumbent on him to make another effort: The Judiciary ought to have an opportunity of remonstrating agst projected encroachments on the people as well as on themselves. It had been said that the Judges, as expositors of the Laws would have an opportunity of defending their constitutional rights. There was weight in this observation; but this power of the Judges did not go far enough. Laws may be unjust, may be unwise, may be dangerous, may be destructive; and yet not be so unconstitutional as to justify the Judges in refusing to give them effect. Let them have a share in the Revisionary power, and they will have an opportunity of taking notice of these characters of a law, and of counteracting, by the weight of their opinions the improper views of the Legislature.—Mr <Madison> 2ded. the motion

Mr Ghorum did not see the advantage of employing the Judges in this way. As Judges they are not to be presumed to possess any peculiar knowledge of the mere policy of public measures. Nor can it be necessary as a security for their constitutional rights. The Judges in England have no such additional provision for their defence, yet their jurisdiction is not invaded. He thought it would be best to let the Executive alone be responsible, and at most to authorize him to call on Judges for their opinions,

Mr. Elseworth approved heartily of the motion. The aid of the Judges will give more wisdom & firmness to the Executive. They will possess a systematic and accurate knowledge of the Laws, which the Executive can not be expected always to possess. The law of Nations also will frequently come into question. Of this the Judges alone will have competent information.

Mr. <Madison>—considered the object of the motion as of great importance to the meditated Constitution. It would be useful to the Judiciary departmt. by giving it an additional opportunity of defending itself agst: Legislative encroachments; It would be useful to the Executive, by inspiring additional confidence & firmness in exerting the revisionary power: It would be useful to the Legislature by the valuable assistance it would give in preserving a consistency, conciseness, perspicuity & technical propriety in the laws, qualities peculiarly necessary; & yet shamefully wanting in our republican Codes. It would moreover be useful to the Community at large as an additional check agst. a pursuit of those unwise & unjust measures which constituted so great a portion of our calamities. If any solid objection could be urged agst. the motion, it must be on the supposition that it tended to give too much strength either to the Executive or Judiciary. He did not think there was the least ground for this apprehension. It was much more to be apprehended that notwithstanding this co-operation of the two departments, the Legislature would still be an overmatch for them. Experience in all the States had evinced a powerful tendency in the Legislature to absorb all power into its vortex. This was the real source of danger to the American Constitutions; & suggested the necessity of giving every defensive authority to the other departments that was consistent with republican principles.

Mr. Mason said he had always been a friend to this provision. It would give a confidence to the Executive, which he would not otherwise have, and without which the Revisionary power would be of little avail.

Mr. Gerry did not expect to see this point which had undergone full discussion, again revived. The object he conceived of the Revisionary power was merely to secure the Executive department agst. legislative encroachment. The Executive therefore who will best know and be ready to defend his rights ought alone to have the defence of them. The motion was liable to strong objections. It was combining & mixing together the Legislative & the other departments. It was establishing

175

an improper coalition between the Executive & Judiciary departments. It was making Statesmen of the Judges; and setting them up as the guardians of the Rights of the people. He relied for his part on the Representatives of the people as the guardians of their Rights & interests. It was making the Expositors of the Laws, the Legislators which ought never to be done. A better expedient for correcting the laws, would be to appoint as had been done in Pena. a person or persons of proper skill, to draw bills for the Legislature.

Mr. Strong thought with Mr. Gerry that the power of making ought to be kept distinct from that of expounding, the laws. No maxim was better established. The Judges in exercising the function of expositors might be influenced by the part they had taken, in framing the laws.

Mr. Govr. Morris. Some check being necessary on the Legislature, the question is in what hands it should be lodged. On one side it was contended that the Executive alone ought to exercise it. He did not think that an Executive appointed for 6 years, and impeachable whilst in office, wd. be a very effectual check. On the other side it was urged that he ought to be reinforced by the Judiciary department. Agst. this it was objected that Expositors of laws ought to have no hand in making them, and arguments in favor of this had been drawn from England. What weight was due to them might be easily determined by an attention to facts. The truth was that the Judges in England had a great share in ye Legislation. They are consulted in difficult & doubtful cases. They may be & some of them are members of the Legislature. They are or may be members of the privy Council, and can there advise the Executive as they will do with us if the motion succeeds. The influence the English Judges may have in the latter capacity in strengthening the Executive check can not be ascertained, as the King by his influence in a manner dictates the laws. There is one difference in the two Cases however which disconcerts all reasoning from the British to our proposed Constitution. The British Executive has so great an interest in his prerogatives and such powerful means of defending them that he will never yield any part of them. The interest of our Executive is so inconsiderable & so transitory, and his means of defending it so feeble, that there is the justest ground to fear his want of firmness in resisting incroachments. He was extremely apprehensive that the auxiliary firmness & weight of the Judiciary would not supply the deficiency. He concurred in thinking the public liberty in greater danger from Legislative usurpations than from any other source. It had been said that the Legislature ought to be relied on as the proper Guardians of liberty. The answer was short and conclusive. Either bad laws will be pushed or not. On the latter supposition no check will be wanted. On the former a strong check will be necessary: And this is the proper supposition. Emissions of paper money, largesses to the people—a remission of debts and similar measures, will at sometimes be popular, and will be pushed for that reason At other times such measures will coincide with the interests of the

Legislature themselves, & that will be a reason not less cogent for pushing them. It might be thought that the people will not be deluded and misled in the latter case. But experience teaches another lesson. The press is indeed a great means of diminishing the evil, yet it is found to be unable to prevent it altogether.

Mr. L. Martin. considered the association of the Judges with the Executive as a dangerous innovation; as well as one which, could not produce the particular advantage expected from it. A knowledge of mankind, and of Legislative affairs cannot be presumed to belong in a higher deger degree to the Judges than to the Legislature. And as to the Constitutionality of laws, that point will come before the Judges in their proper official character. In this character they have a negative on the laws. Join them with the Executive in the Revision and they will have a double negative. It is necessary that the Supreme Judiciary should have the confidence of the people. This will soon be lost, if they are employed in the task of remonstrating agst. popular measures of the Legislature. Besides in what mode & proportion are they to vote in the Council of Revision?

<Mr.> M<adison> could not discover in the proposed association of the Judges with the Executive in the Revisionary check on the Legislature any violation of the maxim which requires the great departments of power to be kept separate & distinct. On the contrary he thought it an auxiliary precaution in favor of the maxim. If a Constitutional discrimination of the departments on paper were a sufficient security to each agst. encroachments of the others, all further provisions would indeed be superfluous. But experience had taught us a distrust of that security; and that it is necessary to introduce such a balance of powers and interests, as will guarantee the provisions on paper. Instead therefore of contenting ourselves with laying down the Theory in the Constitution that each department ought to be separate & distinct, it was proposed to add a defensive power to each which should maintain the Theory in practice. In so doing we did not blend the departments together. We erected effectual barriers for keeping them separate. The most regular example of this theory was in the British Constitution. Yet it was not only the practice there to admit the Judges to a seat in the legislature, and in the Executive Councils, and to submit to their previous examination all laws of a certain description, but it was a part of their Constitution that the Executive might negative any law whatever; a part of *their* Constitution which had been universally regarded as calculated for the preservation of the whole. The objection agst. a union of the Judiciary & Executive branches in the revision of the laws, had either no foundation or was not carried far enough. If such a Union was an improper mixture of powers, or such a Judiciary check on the laws, was inconsistent with the Theory of a free Constitution, it was equally so to admit the Executive to any participation in the making of laws; and the revisionary plan ought to be discarded altogether.

Col Mason Observed that the defence of the Executive was not the sole object of the Revisionary power. He expected even greater advantages from it. Notwithstanding the precautions taken in the Constitution of the Legislature, it would so much resemble that of the individual States, that it must be expected frequently to pass unjust and pernicious laws. This restraining power was therefore essentially necessary. It would have the effect not only of hindering the final passage of such laws; but would discourage demagogues from attempting to get them passed. It had been said (by Mr. L. Martin) that if the Judges were joined in this check on the laws, they would have a double negative, since in their expository capacity of Judges they would have one negative. He would reply that in this capacity they could impede in one case only, the operation of laws. They could declare an unconstitutional law void. But with regard to every law however unjust oppressive or pernicious, which did not come plainly under this description, they would be under the necessity as Judges to give it a free course. He wished the further use to be made of the Judges, of giving aid in preventing every improper law. Their aid will be the more valuable as they are in the habit and practice of considering laws in their true principles, and in all their consequences.

Mr. Wilson. The separation of the departments does not require that they should have separate objects but that they should act separately tho' on the same objects. It is necessary that the two branches of the Legislature should be separate and distinct, yet they are both to act precisely on the same object

Mr. Gerry had rather give the Executive an absolute negative for its own defence than thus to blend together the Judiciary & Executive departments. It will bind them together in an offensive and defensive alliance agst. the Legislature, and render the latter unwilling to enter into a contest with them.

Mr. Govr. Morris was surprised that any defensive provision for securing the effectual separation of the departments should be considered as an improper mixture of them. Suppose that the three powers, were to be vested in three persons, by compact among themselves; that one was to have the power of making—another of executing, and a third of judging, the laws. Would it not be very natural for the two latter after having settled the partition on paper, to observe, and would not candor oblige the former to admit, that as a security agst. legislative acts of the former which might easily be so framed as to undermine the powers of the two others, the two others ought to be armed with a veto for their own defence, or at least to have an opportunity of stating their objections agst. acts of encroachment? And would any one pretend that such a right tended to blend & confound powers that ought to be separately exercised? As well might it be said that If three neighbours had three distinct farms, a right in each to defend his farm agst. his neighbours, tended to blend the farms together.

178

Mr. Ghorum.   All agree that a check on the Legislature is necessary. But there are two objections agst. admitting the Judges to share in it which no observations on the other side seem to obviate. the 1st. is that the Judges ought to carry into the exposition of the laws no prepossessions with regard to them.   2d. that as the Judges will outnumber the Executive, the revisionary check would be thrown entirely out of the Executive hands, and instead of enabling him to defend himself, would enable the Judges to sacrifice him.

Mr. Wilson.   The proposition is certainly <not> liable to all the objections which have been urged agst. it. According to (Mr. Gerry) it will unite the Executive & Judiciary in an offensive & defensive alliance agst. the Legislature.   According to Mr. Ghorum it will lead to a subversion of the Executive by the Judiciary influence.   To the first gentleman the answer was obvious; that the joint weight of the two departments was necessary to balance the single weight of the Legislature.   To the 1st. objection stated by the other Gentleman it might be answered that supposing the prepossion to mix itself with the exposition, the evil would be overbalanced by the advantages promised by the expedient.   To the 2d. objection, that such a rule of voting might be provided in the detail as would guard agst. it.

Mr. Rutlidge thought the Judges of all men the most unfit to be concerned in the revisionary Council.   The Judges ought never to give their opinion on a law till it comes before them.   He thought it equally unnecessary.   The Executive could advise with the officers of State, as of war, finance &c. and avail himself of their information and opinions.

On Question on Mr. Wilson's motion for joining the Judiciary in the Revision of laws <it passed in the negative>—

Mas. no. Cont. ay. N. J. not present. Pa. divd. Del. no. Md. ay. Va. ay. N. C. no. S. C. no. Geo. divd. [Ayes—3; noes—4; divided—2.]

(4) August 15, 1787

Mr. Ma<dison> moved that all acts before they become laws should be submitted both to the Executive and Supreme Judiciary Departments, that if either of these should object 2/3 of each House, if both should object, 3/4 of each House, should be necessary to overrule the objections and give to the acts the force of law.—

Mr. Wilson seconds the motion

Mr. Pinkney opposed the interference of the Judges in the Legislative business: it will involve them in parties, and give a previous tincture to their opinions.

Mr. Mercer heartily approved the motion.   It as an axiom that the Judiciary ought to be separate from the Legislative: but equally so that it ought to be independent of that department.   The true policy of the axiom is that legislative usurpation and oppression may be obviated.   He disapproved of the Doctrine that the Judges as expositors of the Constitution should have authority to declare a law void. He thought laws ought to be well and cautiously made, and then to be uncontroulable.

Mr. Gerry. This motion comes to the same thing with what has been already negatived.

Question on the motion of Mr M<adison>

N- H. no. Mass. no. Ct. no. N. J. no. Pa. no. Del. ay. Maryd. ay. Virga. ay. N. C. no. S. C. no. Geo. no. [Ayes—3; noes—8.]

Mr. Govr. Morris regretted that something like the proposed check could not be agreed to. He dwelt on the importance of public Credit, and the difficulty of supporting it without some strong barrier against the instability of legislative Assemblies. He suggested the idea of requiring three fourths of each house to *repeal* laws where the President should not concur. He had no great reliance on the revisionary power as the Executive was now to be constituted (elected by the Congress). The legislature will contrive to soften down the President. He recited the history of paper emissions, and the perseverance of the legislative assemblies in repeating them, with all the distressing effects <of such measures> before their eyes. Were the National legislature formed, and a war was now to break out, this ruinous expedient would be again resorted to, if not guarded against. The requiring 3/4 to repeal would, though not a compleat remedy, prevent the hasty passage of laws, and the frequency of those repeals which destroy faith in the public, and which are among our greatest calamities.—

Mr Dickenson was strongly impressed with the remark of Mr. Mercer as to the power of the Judges to set aside the law. He thought no such power ought to exist. He was at the same time at a loss what expedient to substitute. The Justiciary of Aragon he observed became by degrees the lawgiver.

Mr. Govr. Morris, suggested the expedient of an absolute negative in the Executive. He could not agree that the Judiciary which was part of the Executive, should be bound to say that a direct violation of the Constitution was law. A controul over the legislature might have its inconveniences. But view the danger on the other side. The most virtuous citizens will often as members of a legislative body concur in measures which afterwards in their private capacity they will be ashamed of. Encroachments of the popular branch of the Government ought to be guarded agst. The Ephori at Sparta became in the end absolute. The Report of the Council of Censors in Pennsylva points out the many invasions of the legislative department on the Executive numerous as the latter is, within the short term of seven years, and in a State where a strong party is opposed to the Constitution, and watching every occasion of turning the public resentments agst. it. If the Executive be overturned by the popular branch, as happened in England, the tyranny of one man will ensue-In Rome where the Aristocracy overturned the throne, the consequence was different. He enlarged on the tendency of the legislative Authority to usurp on the Executive and wished the section to be postponed, in order to consider of some more effectual check than requiring 2/3 only to overrule the negative of the Executive.

Mr Sherman. Can one man be trusted better than all the others if they all agree? This was neither wise nor safe. He disapproved of Judges meddling in politics and parties. We have gone far enough in forming the negative as it now stands.

Mr. Carrol- when the negative to be overruled by 2/3 only was agreed to, the *quorum* was not fixed. He remarked that as a majority was now to be the quorum, 17, in the larger, and 8 in the smaller house might carry points. The Advantage that might be taken of this seemed to call for greater impediments to improper laws. He thought the controuling power however of the Executive could not be well decided, till it was seen how the formation of that department would be finally regulated. He wished the consideration of the matter to be postponed.

Mr. Ghorum saw no end to these difficulties and postponements. Some could not agree to the form of Government before the powers were defined. Others could not agree to the powers till it was seen how the Government was to be formed. He thought a majority as large a quorum as was necessary. It was the quorum almost every where fixt in the U. States.

Mr. Wilson; after viewing the subject with all the coolness and attention possible was most apprehensive of a dissolution of the Govt from the legislature swallowing up all the other powers. He remarked that the prejudices agst the Executive resulted from a misapplication of the adage that the parliament was the palladium of liberty. Where the Executive was really formidable, *King* and *Tyrant*, were naturally associated in the minds of people; not *legislature* and *tyranny*. But where the Executive was not formidable, the two last were most properly associated. After the destruction of the King in Great Britain, a more pure and unmixed tyranny sprang up in the parliament than had been exercised by the monarch. He insisted that we had not guarded agst. the danger on this side by a sufficient self-defensive power either to the Executive or Judiciary department-

Mr Rutlidge was strenuous agst postponing; and complained much of the tediousness of the proceedings.

Mr Elseworth held the same language. We grow more & more skeptical as we proceed. If we do not decide soon, we shall be unable to come to any decision.

The question for postponement passed in the negative: <Del: & Maryd only being in the affirmative.>

Mr. Williamson moved to change "2/3 of each house" into "3/4" as requisite to overrule the dissent of the President. He saw no danger in this, and preferred giving the power to the Presidt. alone, to admitting the Judges into the business of legislation.

Mr. Wilson 2ds. the motion; referring to and repeating the ideas of Mr. Carroll.

On this motion for 3/4. <instead of two thirds; it passed in the affirmative>

N- H- no- Mas. no. Ct. <ay> N- J. no. Pena. divd. Del- ay. Md. ay. Va. ay. N. C. ay. S. C. ay. Geo. no. [Ayes—6; noes—4; divided—1.]

(5) August 22, 1787

Mr. Gerry & Mr. McHenry moved to insert after the 2d. sect. art: 7. the clause following, to wit, "The Legislature shall pass no bill of attainder nor <any> ex post facto law"

Mr. Gerry urged the necessity of this prohibition, which he said was greater in the National than the State Legislature, because the number of members in the former being fewer, they were on that account the more to be feared.

Mr. Govr. Morris thought the precaution as to ex post facto laws unnecessary; but essential as to bills of attainder

Mr Elseworth contended that there was no lawyer, no civilian who would not say that ex post facto laws were void of themselves. It cannot then be necessary to prohibit them.

Mr. Wilson was against inserting anything in the Constitution as to ex post facto laws. It will bring reflexions on the Constitution—and proclaim that we are ignorant of the first principles of Legislation, or are constituting a Government which will be so.

The question being divided, The first part of the motion relating to bills of attainder was agreed to nem. contradicente.

On the second part relating to ex post facto laws—

Mr Carrol remarked that experience overruled all other calculations. It had proved that in whatever light they might be viewed by civilians or others, the State Legislatures had passed them, and they had taken effect.

Mr. Wilson. If these prohibitions in the State Constitutions have no effect, it will be useless to insert them in this Constitution. Besides, both sides will agree to the principle & will differ as to its application.

Mr. Williamson. Such a prohibitory clause is in the Constitution of N. Carolina, and tho it has been violated, it has done good there & may do good here, because the Judges can take hold of it

Docr. Johnson thought the clause unnecessary, and implying an improper suspicion of the National Legislature.

Mr. Rutlidge was in favor of the clause.

On the question for inserting the prohibition of ex post facto laws.

N—H—ay—Mas. ay. Cont. no. N. J—no. Pa. no. Del—ay. Md. ay. Virga. ay N—C. divd. S. C. ay—Geo. ay. [Ayes—7; noes—3; divided—1.]

(6) August 27, 1787

Mr Madison & Mr. Govr. Morris moved to insert after the word "controversies" the words "to which the U—S—shall be a party"— which was agreed to nem: con:

Docr. Johnson moved to insert the words "this Constitution and the" before the word "laws"

Mr Madison doubted whether it was not going too far to extend the jurisdiction of the Court generally to cases arising Under the Constitution, & whether it ought not to be limited to cases of a Judiciary Nature. The right of expounding the Constitution in cases not of this nature ought not to be given to that Department.

The motion of Docr. Johnson was agreed to nem: con: it being generally supposed that the jurisdiction given was constructively limited to cases of a Judiciary nature—

H. DEBATE IN THE STATE CONVENTIONS

(1) Pennsylvania, December 7, 1787

Mr. Wilson ... The article respecting the judicial department is objected to as going too far, and is supposed to carry a very indefinite meaning. Let us examine this: "The judicial power shall extend to all cases, in law and equity, *arising under this Constitution and the laws of the United States.*" Controversies may certainly arise under this Constitution and the laws of the United States, and is it not proper that there should be judges to decide them? The honorable gentleman from Cumberland (Mr. Whitehill) says that laws may be made inconsistent with the Constitution; and that therefore the powers given to the judges are dangerous. For my part, Mr. President, I think the contrary inference true. If a law should be made inconsistent with those powers vested by this instrument in Congress, the judges, as a consequence of their independence, and the particular powers of government being defined, will declare such law to be null and void; for the power of the Constitution predominates. Any thing, therefore, that shall be enacted by Congress contrary thereto, will not have the force of law.

(2) Virginia, June 20, 1788

Mr. Pendleton ... His next objection was to the first two clauses— cases arising under the Constitution, and laws made in pursuance thereof. Are you to refer these to the state courts? Must not the judicial powers extend to enforce the federal laws, govern its own officers, and confine them to the line of their duty? Must it not protect them, in the proper exercise of duty, against all opposition, whether from individuals or state laws? No, say gentlemen, because the legislature may make oppressive laws, or partial judges may give them a partial interpretation. This is carrying suspicion to an extreme which tends to prove there should be no legislative or judiciary at all. The fair inference is, that oppressive laws will not be warranted by the Constitution, nor attempted by our representatives, who are selected for their ability and integrity, and that honest, independent judges will never admit an oppressive construction.

But, then, we are alarmed with the idea of its being a consolidated government. It is so, say gentlemen, in the executive and legislative, and must be so in the judiciary. I never conceived it to be a consolidated government, so as to involve the interest of all America. Of the two objects of judicial cognizance, one is general and national, and the other local. The former is given to the general judiciary, and the latter left for the local tribunals. They act in co-operation, to secure our liberty. For the sake of economy, the appointment of these courts might be in the state courts. I rely on an honest interpretation from independent judges. An honest man would not serve otherwise, because it would be to serve a dishonest purpose. To give execution to proper laws, in a proper manner, is their peculiar province. There is no inconsistency, impropriety, or danger, in giving the state judges the federal cognizance. Every gentleman who beholds my situation, my infirmity, and various other considerations, will hardly suppose I carry my view to an accumulation of power. Ever since I had any power, I was more anxious to discharge my duty than to increase my power.

The impossibility of calling a sovereign state before the jurisdiction of another sovereign state, shows the propriety and necessity of vesting this tribunal with the decision of controversies to which a state shall be a party.

But the principal objection of that honorable gentleman was, that jurisdiction was given it in disputes between citizens of different states. I think, in general, those decisions might be left to the state tribunals; especially as citizens of one state are declared to be citizens of all. I think it will, in general, be so left by the regulations of Congress. But may no case happen in which it may be proper to give the federal courts jurisdiction in such a dispute? Suppose a bond given by a citizen of Rhode Island to one of our citizens. The regulations of that state being unfavorable to the claims of the other states, if he is obliged to go to Rhode Island to recover it, he will be obliged to accept payment of one third, or less, of his money. He cannot sue in the Supreme Court, but he may sue in the federal inferior court; and on judgment to be paid one for ten, he may get justice by appeal. Is it an eligible situation? Is it just that a man should run the risk of losing nine tenths of his claim? Ought he not to be able to carry it to that court where unworthy principles do not prevail? Paper money and tender laws may be passed in other states, in opposition to the federal principle, and restriction of this Constitution, and will need jurisdiction in the federal judiciary, to stop its pernicious effects. . . .

Mr. Marshall . . . These, sir, are the points of *federal jurisdiction* to which he objects, with a few exceptions. Let us examine each of them with a supposition that the same impartiality will be observed there as in other courts, and then see if any mischief will result from them. With respect to its cognizance in all cases arising under the Constitution and the laws of the United States, he says that, the laws of the United States being paramount to the laws of the particular states, there is no case but what this will extend to. Has the government of the United States power to make laws on every subject Does he understand it so? Can they make laws affecting the mode of transferring property, or contracts, or claims, between citizens of the same state? Can they go beyond the delegated powers? If they were to make a law not warranted by any of the powers enumerated, it would be considered by the judges as an infringement of the Constitution which they are to guard. They would not consider such a law as coming under their jurisdiction. They would declare it void. It will annihilate the state courts, says the honorable gentleman. Does not every gentleman here know that the causes in our courts are more numerous than they can decide, according to their present construction? Look at the dockets. You will find them crowded with suits, which the life of man will not see determined. If some of these suits be carried to other courts, will it be wrong? They will still have business enough.

Then there is no danger that particular subjects, small in proportion, being taken out of the jurisdiction of the state judiciaries, will render them useless and of no effect. Does the gentleman think that the state courts will have no cognizance of cases not mentioned here? Are there any words in this Constitution which exclude the courts of the states from those cases which they now possess? Does the gentleman imagine this to be the case? Will any gentleman believe it? Are not controversies respecting lands claimed under the grants of different states the only controversies between citizens of the same state which the federal judiciary can take cognizance of? The case is so clear, that to prove it would be a useless waste of time. The state courts will not lose the jurisdiction of the causes they now decide. They have a concurrence of jurisdiction with the federal courts in those cases in which the latter have cognizance.

How disgraceful is it that the state courts cannot be trusted! says the honorable gentleman. What is the language of the Constitution? Does it take away their jurisdiction? Is it not necessary that the federal courts should have cognizance of cases arising under the Constitution, and the laws, of the United States? What is the service or purpose of a judiciary, but to execute the laws in a peaceable, orderly manner, without shedding blood, or creating a contest, or availing yourselves of force? If this be the case, where can its jurisdiction be more necessary than here?

To what quarter will you look for protection from an infringement on the Constitution, if you will not give the power to the judiciary? There is no other body that can afford such a protection. But the honorable member objects to it, because he says that the officers of the government will be screened from merited punishment by the federal judiciary. The federal sheriff, says he, will go into a poor man's house and beat him, or abuse his family, and the federal court will protect him. Does any gentleman believe this? Is it necessary that the officers will commit a trespass on the property or persons of those with whom they are to transact business? Will such great insults on the people of this country be allowable? Were a law made to authorize them, it would be void. The injured man would trust to a tribunal in his neighborhood. To such a tribunal he would apply for redress, and get it. There is no reason to fear that he would not meet that justice there which his country will be ever willing to maintain.

I. ALEXANDER HAMILTON, THE FEDERALIST, NO. 22

December 14, 1787

To the People of the State of New York.

IN addition to the defects already enumerated in the existing Fœderal system, there are others of not less importance, which concur in rendering it altogether unfit for the administration of the affairs of the Union.

The want of a power to regulate commerce is by all parties allowed to be of the number. The utility of such a power has been anticipated under the first head of our inquiries; and for this reason as well as from the universal conviction entertained upon the subject, little need be added in this place. It is indeed evident, on the most superficial view, that there is no object, either as it respects the interests of trade or finance that more strongly demands a Fœderal superintendence. The want of it has already operated as a bar to the formation of beneficial treaties with foreign powers; and has given occasions of dissatisfaction between the States. No nation acquainted with the nature of our political association would be unwise enough to enter into stipulations with the United States, by which they conceded privileges of any importance to them, while they were apprised that the engagements on the part of the Union, might at any moment be violated by its members; and while they found from experience that they might enjoy every advantage they desired in our markets, without granting us any return, but such as their momentary convenience might suggest. It is not therefore to be wondered at, that Mr. Jenkinson in ushering into the House of Commons a bill for regulating the temporary intercourse between the two countries, should preface its introduction by a declaration that similar provisions in former bills had been found to answer every purpose to the commerce of Great Britain, & that it would be prudent to persist in the plan until it should appear whether the American government was likely or not to acquire greater consistency.*

Several States have endeavoured by separate prohibitions, restrictions and exclusions, to influence the conduct of that kingdom in this particular; but the want of concert, arising from the want of a general authority, and from clashing, and dissimilar views in the States, has hitherto frustrated every experiment of the kind; and will continue to do so as long as the same obstacles to an uniformity of measures continue to exist.

The interfering and unneighbourly regulations of some States contrary to the true spirit of the Union, have in different instances given just cause of umbrage and complaint to others; and it is to be feared that examples of this nature, if not restrained by a national controul, would be multiplied and extended till they became not less serious sources of animosity and discord, than injurious impediments to the intercourse between the different parts of the confederacy. "The commerce of the German empire,* is in continual trammels from the multiplicity of the duties which the several Princes and States exact upon the merchandizes passing through their territories; by means of which the fine streams and navigable rivers with which Germany is so happily watered, are rendered almost useless." Though the genius of the people of this country might never permit this description to be strictly applicable to us, yet we may reasonably expect, from the gradual conflicts of State regulations, that the citizens of each, would at length come to be considered and treated by the others in no better light than that of foreigners and aliens.

The power of raising armies, by the most obvious construction of the articles of the confederation, is merely a power of making requisitions upon the States for quotas of men. This practice, in the course of the late war, was found replete with obstructions to a vigorous and to an œconomical system of defence. It gave birth to a competition between the States, which created a kind of auction for men. In order to furnish the quotas required of them, they outbid each other, till bounties grew to an enormous and insupportable size. The hope of a still further increase afforded an inducement to those who were disposed to serve to procrastinate their inlistment; and disinclined them to engaging for any considerable periods. Hence slow and scanty levies of men in the most critical

---

* *This as nearly as I can recollect was the sense of his speech in introducing the last bill.*

* *Encyclopedie* article *empire.*

emergencies of our affairs—short inlistments at an unparalleled expence—continual fluctuations in the troops, ruinous to their discipline, and subjecting the public safety frequently to the perilous crisis of a disbanded army. Hence also those oppressive expedients for raising men which were upon several occasions practised, and which nothing but the enthusiasm of liberty would have induced the people to endure.

This method of raising troops is not more unfriendly to œconomy and vigor, than it is to an equal distribution of the burthen. The States near the seat of war, influenced by motives of self preservation, made efforts to furnish their quotas, which even exceeded their abilities, while those at a distance from danger were for the most part as remiss as the others were diligent in their exertions. The immediate pressure of this inequality was not in this case, as in that of the contributions of money, alleviated by the hope of a final liquidation. The States which did not pay their proportions of money, might at least be charged with their deficiencies; but no account could be formed of the deficiencies in the supplies of men. We shall not, however, see much reason to regret the want of this hope, when we consider how little prospect there is, that the most delinquent States will ever be able to make compensation for their pecuniary failures. The system of quotas and requisitions, whether it be applied to men or money, is in every view a system of imbecility in the union, and of inequality and injustice among the members.

The right of equal suffrage among the States is another exceptionable part of the confederation. Every idea of proportion, and every rule of fair representation conspire to condemn a principle, which gives to Rhode-Island an equal weight in the scale of power with Massachusetts, or Connecticut, or New-York; and to Delaware, an equal voice in the national deliberations with Pennsylvania or Virginia, or North-Carolina. Its operation contradicts that fundamental maxim of republican government, which requires that the sense of the majority should prevail. Sophistry may reply, that sovereigns are equal, and that a majority of the votes of the States will be a majority of confederated America. But this kind of logical legerdemain will never counteract the plain suggestions of justice and common sense. It may happen that this majority of States is a small minority of the people of America;* and two thirds of the people of America, could not long be persuaded, upon the credit of artificial distinctions and syllogistic subtleties, to submit their interests to the management and disposal of one third. The larger States would after a while revolt from the idea of receiving the law from the smaller. To acquiesce in such a privation of their due importance in the political scale, would be not merely to be insensible to the love of power, but even to sacrifice the desire of equality. It is neither rational to expect the first, nor just to require the last—the smaller States considering how

* *New-Hampshire, Rhode-Island, New-Jersey, Delaware, Georgia, South-Carolina and Maryland, are a majority of the whole number of the States, but they do not contain one third of the people.*

peculiarly their safety and welfare depend on union, ought readily to renounce a pretension; which, if not relinquished would prove fatal to its duration.

It may be objected to this, that not seven but nine States, or two thirds of the whole number must consent to the most important resolutions; and it may be thence inferred, that nine States would always comprehend a majority of the inhabitants of the Union. But this does not obviate the impropriety of an equal vote between States of the most unequal dimensions and populousness; nor is the inference accurate in point of fact; for we can enumerate nine States which contain less than a majority of the people;* and it is constitutionally possible, that these nine may give the vote. Besides there are matters of considerable moment determinable by a bare majority; and there are others, concerning which doubts have been entertained, which if interpreted in favor of the sufficiency of a vote of seven States, would extend its operation to interests of the first magnitude. In addition to this, it is to be observed, that there is a probability of an increase in the number of States, and no provision for a proportional augmentation of the ratio of votes.

But this is not all; what at first sight may seem a remedy, is in reality a poison. To give a minority a negative upon the majority (which is always the case where more than a majority is requisite to a decision) is in its tendency to subject the sense of the greater number to that of the lesser number. Congress from the non-attendance of a few States have been frequently in the situation of a Polish Diet, where a single veto has been sufficient to put a stop to all their movements. A sixtieth part of the Union, which is about the proportion of Delaware and Rhode-Island, has several times been able to oppose an intire bar to its operations. This is one of those refinements which in practice has an effect, the reverse of what is expected from it in theory. The necessity of unanimity in public bodies, or of something approaching towards it, has been founded upon a supposition that it would contribute to security. But its real operation is to embarrass the administration, to destroy the energy of government, and to substitute the pleasure, caprice or artifices of an insignificant, turbulent or corrupt junto, to the regular deliberations and decisions of a respectable majority. In those emergencies of a nation, in which the goodness or badness, the weakness or strength of its government, is of the greatest importance, there is commonly a necessity for action. The public business must in some way or other go forward. If a pertinacious minority can controul the opinion of a majority respecting the best mode of conducting it; the majority in order that something may be done, must conform to the views of the minority; and thus the sense of the smaller number will over-rule that of the greater, and give a tone to the national proceedings. Hence tedious delays—continual nego-

---

Add New-York and Connecticut, to the   than a majority.
foregoing seven, and they will still be less

tiation and intrigue—contemptible compromises of the public good. And yet in such a system, it is even happy when such compromises can take place: For upon some occasions, things will not admit of accommodation; and then the measures of government must be injuriously suspended or fatally defeated. It is often, by the impracticability of obtaining the concurrence of the necessary number of votes, kept in a state of inaction. Its situation must always savour of weakness—sometimes border upon anarchy.

It is not difficult to discover that a principle of this kind gives greater scope to foreign corruption as well as to domestic faction, than that which permits the sense of the majority to decide; though the contrary of this has been presumed. The mistake has proceeded from not attending with due care to the mischiefs that may be occasioned by obstructing the progress of government at certain critical seasons. When the concurrence of a large number is required by the constitution to the doing of any national act, we are apt to rest satisfied that all is safe, because nothing improper will be likely *to be done;* but we forget how much good may be prevented, and how much ill may be produced, by the power of hindering the doing what may be necessary, and of keeping affairs in the same unfavorable posture in which they may happen to stand at particular periods.

Suppose for instance we were engaged in a war, in conjunction with one foreign nation against another. Suppose the necessity of our situation demanded peace, and the interest or ambition of our ally led him to seek the prosecution of the war, with views that might justify us in making separate terms. In such a state of things, this ally of ours would evidently find it much easier by his bribes and intrigues to tie up the hands of government from making peace, where two thirds of all the votes were requisite to that object, than where a simple majority would suffice. In the first case he would have to corrupt a smaller number; in the last a greater number. Upon the same principle it would be much easier for a foreign power with which we were at war, to perplex our councils and embarrass our exertions. And in a commercial view we may be subjected to similar inconveniences. A nation, with which we might have a treaty of commerce, could with much greater facility prevent our forming a connection with her competitor in trade; tho' such a connection should be ever so beneficial to ourselves.

Evils of this description ought not to be regarded as imaginary. One of the weak sides of republics, among their numerous advantages, is that they afford too easy an inlet to foreign corruption. An hereditary monarch, though often disposed to sacrifice his subjects to his ambition, has so great a personal interest in the government, and in the external glory of the nation, that it is not easy for a foreign power to give him an equivalent for what he would sacrifice by treachery to the State. The world has accordingly been witness to few examples of this species of royal prostitution, though there have been abundant specimens of every other kind.

In republics, persons elevated from the mass of the community, by the suffrages of their fellow-citizens, to stations of great pre-eminence and power, may find compensations for betraying their trust, which to any but minds animated and guided by superior virtue, may appear to exceed the proportion of interest they have in the common stock, and to over-balance the obligations of duty. Hence it is that history furnishes us with so many mortifying examples of the prevalency of foreign corruption in republican governments. How much this contributed to the ruin of the ancient commonwealths has been already delineated. It is well known that the deputies of the United Provinces have, in various instances been purchased by the emissaries of the neighbouring kingdoms. The Earl of Chesterfield (if my memory serves me right) in a letter to his court, intimates that his success in an important negotiation, must depend on his obtaining a Major's commission for one of those deputies. And in Sweden, the parties were alternately bought by France and England, in so barefaced and notorious a manner that it excited universal disgust in the nation; and was a principal cause that the most limited monarch in Europe, in a single day, without tumult, violence, or opposition, became one of the most absolute and uncontrouled.

A circumstance, which crowns the defects of the confederation, remains yet to be mentioned—the want of a judiciary power. Laws are a dead letter without courts to expound and define their true meaning and operation. The treaties of the United States to have any force at all, must be considered as part of the law of the land. Their true import as far as respects individuals, must, like all other laws, be ascertained by judicial determinations. To produce uniformity in these determinations, they ought to be submitted in the last resort, to one SUPREME TRIBUNAL. And this tribunal ought to be instituted under the same authority which forms the treaties themselves. These ingredients are both indispensable. If there is in each State, a court of final jurisdiction, there may be as many different final determinations on the same point, as there are courts. There are endless diversities in the opinions of men. We often see not only different courts, but the Judges of the same court differing from each other. To avoid the confusion which would unavoidably result from the contradictory decisions of a number of independent judicatories, all nations have found it necessary to establish one court paramount to the rest—possessing a general superintendance, and authorised to settle and declare in the last resort, an uniform rule of civil justice.

This is the more necessary where the frame of the government is so compounded, that the laws of the whole are in danger of being contravened by the laws of the parts. In this case if the particular tribunals are invested with a right of ultimate jurisdiction, besides the contradictions to be expected from difference of opinion, there will be much to fear from the bias of local views and prejudices, and from the interference of local regulations. As often as such an interference was to happen, there would be reason to apprehend, that the provisions of the particular laws might be preferred to those of the general laws; for nothing is more natural to men in office, than to look with peculiar deference towards that authority to which they owe their official existence.

The treaties of the United States, under the present constitution, are liable to the infractions of thirteen different Legislatures, and as many different courts of final jurisdiction, acting under the authority of those Legislatures. The faith, the reputation, the peace of the whole union, are thus continually at the mercy of the prejudices, the passions, and the interests of every member of which it is composed. Is it possible that foreign nations can either respect or confide in such a government? Is it possible that the People of America will longer consent to trust their honor, their happiness, their safety, on so precarious a foundation?

In this review of the Confederation, I have confined myself to the exhibition of its most material defects; passing over those imperfections in its details, by which even a great part of the power intended to be conferred upon it has been in a great measure rendered abortive. It must be by this time evident to all men of reflection, who can divest themselves of the prepossessions of preconceived opinions, that it is a system so radically vicious and unsound, as to admit not of amendment but by an entire change in its leading features and characters.

The organization of Congress, is itself utterly improper for the exercise of those powers which are necessary to be deposited in the Union. A single Assembly may be a proper receptacle of those slender, or rather fettered authorities, which have been heretofore delegated to the fœderal head; but it would be inconsistent with all the principles of good government, to intrust it with those additional powers which even the moderate and more rational adversaries of the proposed constitution admit ought to reside in the United States. If that plan should not be adopted; and if the necessity of union should be able to withstand the ambitious aims of those men, who may indulge magnificent schemes of personal aggrandizement from its dissolution; the probability would be, that we should run into the project of conferring supplementary powers upon Congress as they are now constituted; and either the machine, from the intrinsic feebleness of its structure, will moulder into pieces in spite of our ill-judged efforts to prop it; or by successive augmentations of its force and energy, as necessity might prompt, we shall finally accumulate in a single body, all the most important prerogatives of sovereignty; and thus entail upon our posterity, one of the most execrable forms of government that human infatuation ever contrived. Thus we should create in reality that very tyranny, which the adversaries of the new constitution either are, or affect to be solicitous to avert.

It has not a little contributed to the infirmities of the existing fœderal system, that it never had a ratification by the PEOPLE. Resting on no better foundation than the consent of the several Legislatures; it has been exposed to frequent and intricate questions concerning the validity of its powers; and has in some instances given birth to the enormous doctrine of a right of legislative repeal. Owing its ratification to the law of a State, it has been contended, that the same authority might repeal the law by which it was ratified. However gross a heresy it may be, to maintain that *a party* to *a compact* has a right to revoke that *compact,* the doctrine itself has had respectable advocates. The possibility of a question of this nature, proves the necessity of laying the foundations of our national government deeper than in the mere sanction of delegated authority. The fabric of American Empire ought to rest on the solid basis of THE CONSENT OF THE PEOPLE. The streams of national power ought to flow immediately from that pure original fountain of all legitimate authority.

PUBLIUS.

J. ESSAY OF BRUTUS, NO. 11

January 11, 1788

The nature and extent of the judicial power of the United States, proposed to be granted by this constitution, claims our particular attention.

Much has been said and written upon the subject of this new system on both sides, but I have not met with any writer, who has discussed the judicial powers with any degree of accuracy. And yet it is obvious, that we can form but very imperfect ideas of the manner in which this government will work, or the effect it will have in changing the internal police and mode of distributing justice at present subsisting in the respective states, without a thorough investigation of the powers of the judiciary and of the manner in which they will operate. This government is a complete system, not only for making, but for executing laws. And the courts of law, which will be constituted by it, are not only to decide upon the constitution and the laws made in pursuance of it, but by officers subordinate to them to execute all their decisions. The real effect of this system of government, will therefore be brought home to the feelings of the people, through the medium of the judicial power. It is, moreover, of great importance, to examine with care the nature and extent of the judicial power, because those who are to be vested with it, are to be placed in a situation altogether unprecedented in a free country. They are to be rendered totally independent, both of the people and the legislature, both with respect to their offices and salaries. No errors they may commit can be corrected by any power above them, if any such power there be, nor can they be removed from office for making ever so many erroneous adjudications.

The only causes for which they can be displaced, is, conviction of treason, bribery, and high crimes and misdemeanors.

This part of the plan is so modelled, as to authorise the courts, not only to carry into execution the powers expressly given, but where these are wanting or ambiguously expressed, to supply what is wanting by their own decisions.

That we may be enabled to form a just opinion on this subject, I shall, in considering it,

1st.   Examine the nature and extent of the judicial powers—and

2d.   Enquire, whether the courts who are to exercise them, are so constituted as to afford reasonable ground of confidence, that they will exercise them for the general good.

With a regard to the nature and extent of the judicial powers, I have to regret my want of capacity to give that full and minute explanation of them that the subject merits.   To be able to do this, a man should be possessed of a degree of law knowledge far beyond what I pretend to.   A number of hard words and technical phrases are used in this part of the system, about the meaning of which gentlemen learned in the law differ.

Its advocates know how to avail themselves of these phrases.   In a number of instances, where objections are made to the powers given to the judicial, they give such an explanation to the technical terms as to avoid them.

Though I am not competent to give a perfect explanation of the powers granted to this department of the government, I shall yet attempt to trace some of the leading features of it, from which I presume it will appear, that they will operate to a total subversion of the state judiciaries, if not, to the legislative authority of the states.

In article 3d, sect. 2d, it is said, "The judicial power shall extend to all cases in law and equity arising under this constitution, the laws of the United States, and treaties made, or which shall be made, under their authority, &c."

The first article to which this power extends, is, all cases in law and equity arising under this constitution.

What latitude of construction this clause should receive, it is not easy to say.   At first view, one would suppose, that it meant no more than this, that the courts under the general government should exercise, not only the powers of courts of law, but also that of courts of equity, in the manner in which those powers are usually exercised in the different states.   But this cannot be the meaning, because the next clause author- ises the courts to take cognizance of all cases in law and equity arising under the laws of the United States; this last article, I conceive, conveys as much power to the general judicial as any of the state courts possess.

194

The cases arising under the constitution must be different from those arising under the laws, or else the two clauses mean exactly the same thing.

The cases arising under the constitution must include such, as bring into question its meaning, and will require an explanation of the nature and extent of the powers of the different departments under it.

This article, therefore, vests the judicial with a power to resolve all questions that may arise on any case on the construction of the constitution, either in law or in equity.

1st. They are authorised to determine all questions that may arise upon the meaning of the constitution in law. This article vests the courts with authority to give the constitution a legal construction, or to explain it according to the rules laid down for construing a law.—These rules give a certain degree of latitude of explanation. According to this mode of construction, the courts are to give such meaning to the constitution as comports best with the common, and generally received acceptation of the words in which it is expressed, regarding their ordinary and popular use, rather than their grammatical propriety. Where words are dubious, they will be explained by the context. The end of the clause will be attended to, and the words will be understood, as having a view to it; and the words will not be so understood as to bear no meaning or a very absurd one.

2d. The judicial are not only to decide questions arising upon the meaning of the constitution in law, but also in equity.

By this they are empowered, to explain the constitution according to the reasoning spirit of it, without being confined to the words or letter.

"From this method of interpreting laws (says Blackstone) by the reason of them, arises what we call equity;" which is thus defined by Grotius, "the correction of that, wherein the law, by reason of its universality, is deficient["]; for since in laws all cases cannot be foreseen, or expressed, it is necessary, that when the decrees of the law cannot be applied to particular cases, there should some where be a power vested of defining those circumstances, which had they been foreseen the legislator would have expressed; and these are the cases, which according to Grotius, ["]lex non exacte definit, sed arbitrio boni viri permittet."

The same learned author observes, "That equity, thus depending essentially upon each individual case, there can be no established rules and fixed principles of equity laid down, without destroying its very essence, and reducing it to a positive law."

From these remarks, the authority and business of the courts of law, under this clause, may be understood.

They will give the sense of every article of the constitution, that may from time to time come before them. And in their decisions they will not confine themselves to any fixed or established rules, but will determine, according to what appears to them, the reason and spirit of the constitution. The opinions of the supreme court, whatever they may be, will have the force of law; because there is no power provided in the constitution, that can correct their errors, or controul their adjudications. From this court there is no appeal. And I conceive the legislature themselves, cannot set aside a judgment of this court, because they are authorised by the constitution to decide in the last resort. The legislature must be controuled by the constitution, and not the constitution by them. They have therefore no more right to set aside any judgment pronounced upon the construction of the constitution, than they have to take from the president, the chief command of the army and navy, and commit it to some other person. The reason is plain; the judicial and executive derive their authority from the same source, that the legislature do theirs; and therefore in all cases, where the constitution does not make the one responsible to, or controulable by the other, they are altogether independent of each other.

The judicial power will operate to effect, in the most certain, but yet silent and imperceptible manner, what is evidently the tendency of the constitution:—I mean, an entire subversion of the legislative, executive and judicial powers of the individual states. Every adjudication of the supreme court, on any question that may arise upon the nature and extent of the general government, will affect the limits of the state jurisdiction. In proportion as the former enlarge the exercise of their powers, will that of the latter be restricted.

That the judicial power of the United States, will lean strongly in favour of the general government, and will give such an explanation to the constitution, as will favour an extension of its jurisdiction, is very evident from a variety of considerations.

1st. The constitution itself strongly countenances such a mode of construction. Most of the articles in this system, which convey powers of any considerable importance, are conceived in general and indefinite terms, which are either equivocal, ambiguous, or which require long definitions to unfold the extent of their meaning. The two most important powers committed to any government, those of raising money, and of raising and keeping up troops, have already been considered, and shewn to be unlimitted by any thing but the discretion of the legislature. The clause which vests the power to pass all laws which are proper and necessary, to carry the powers given into execution, it has been shewn, leaves the legislature at liberty, to do every thing, which in their judgment is best. It is said, I know, that this clause confers no power on the legislature, which they would not have had without it—though I believe this is not the fact, yet, admitting it to be, it implies that the constitution is not to receive an explanation strictly, according to its letter; but more power is implied than is expressed. And this clause, if it is to be considered, as explanatory of the extent of the powers given, rather than giving a new power, is to be understood as declaring, that in construing any of the articles conveying power, the spirit, intent and design of the clause, should be attended to, as well as the words in their common acceptation.

This constitution gives sufficient colour for adopting an equitable construction, if we consider the great end and design it professedly has in view—these appear from its preamble to be, "to form a more perfect union, establish justice, insure domestic tranquility, provide for the common defence, promote the general welfare, and secure the blessings of liberty to ourselves and posterity." The design of this system is here expressed, and it is proper to give such a meaning to the various parts, as will best promote the accomplishment of the end; this idea suggests itself naturally upon reading the preamble, and will countenance the court in giving the several articles such a sense, as will the most effectually promote the ends the constitution had in view—how this manner of explaining the constitution will operate in practice, shall be the subject of future enquiry.

2d. Not only will the constitution justify the courts in inclining to this mode of explaining it, but they will be interested in using this latitude of interpretation. Every body of men invested with office are tenacious of power; they feel interested, and hence it has become a kind of maxim, to hand down their offices, with all its rights and privileges, unimpared to their successors; the same principle will influence them to extend their power, and increase their rights; this of itself will operate strongly upon the courts to give such a meaning to the constitution in all cases where it can possibly be done, as will enlarge the sphere of their own authority. Every extension of the power of the general legislature, as well as of the judicial powers, will increase the powers of the courts; and the dignity and importance of the judges, will be in proportion to the extent and magnitude of the powers they exercise. I add, it is highly probable the emolument of the judges will be increased, with the increase of the business they will have to transact and its importance. From these considerations the judges will be interested to extend the powers of the courts, and to construe the constitution as much as possible, in such a way as to favour it; and that they will do it, appears probable.

3d. Because they will have precedent to plead, to justify them in it. It is well known, that the courts in England, have by their own authority, extended their jurisdiction far beyond the limits set them in their original institution, and by the laws of the land.

The court of exchequer is a remarkable instance of this. It was originally intended principally to recover the king's debts, and to order the revenues of the crown. It had a common law jurisdiction, which was established merely for the benefit of the king's accomptants. We learn from Blackstone, that the proceedings in this court are grounded on a writ called quo minus, in which the plaintiff suggests, that he is the king's farmer or debtor, and that the defendant hath done him the damage complained of, by which he is less able to pay the king. These suits, by the statute of Rutland, are expressly directed to be confined to such matters as specially concern the king, or his ministers in the exchequer. And by the articuli super cartas, it is enacted, that no common pleas be thenceforth held in the exchequer contrary to the form of the great charter: but now any person may sue in the exchequer. The surmise of being debtor to the king being matter of form, and mere words of course; and the court is open to all the nation.

When the courts will have a precedent before them of a court which extended its jurisdiction in opposition to an act of the legislature, is it not to be expected that they will extend theirs, especially when there is nothing in the constitution expressly against it? and they are authorised to construe its meaning, and are not under any controul?

This power in the judicial, will enable them to mould the government, into almost any shape they please.—The manner in which this may be effected we will hereafter examine.

Brutus.

K. ESSAY OF BRUTUS, NO. 12

February 7, 1788

In my last, I shewed, that the judicial power of the United States under the first clause of the second section of article eight, would be authorized to explain the constitution, not only according to its letter, but according to its spirit and intention; and having this power, they would strongly incline to give it such a construction as to extend the powers of the general government, as much as possible, to the diminution, and finally to the destruction, of that of the respective states.

I shall now proceed to shew how this power will operate in its exercise to effect these purposes. In order to perceive the extent of its influence, I shall consider,

First. How it will tend to extend the legislative authority.

Second. In what manner it will increase the jurisdiction of the courts, and

Third. The way in which it will diminish, and destroy, both the legislative and judicial authority of the United States.

First. Let us enquire how the judicial power will effect an extension of the legislative authority.

Perhaps the judicial power will not be able, by direct and positive decrees, ever to direct the legislature, because it is not easy to conceive how a question can be brought before them in a course of legal discussion, in which they can give a decision, declaring, that the legislature have certain powers which they have not exercised, and which, in consequence of the determination of the judges, they will be bound to exercise. But it is easy to see, that in their adjudications they may establish certain principles, which being received by the legislature, will enlarge the sphere of their power beyond all bounds.

It is to be observed, that the supreme court has the power, in the last resort, to determine all questions that may arise in the course of legal discussion, on the meaning and construction of the constitution. This power they will hold under the constitution, and independent of the legislature. The latter can no more deprive the former of this right, than either of them, or both of them together, can take from the president, with the advice of the senate, the power of making treaties, or appointing ambassadors.

In determining these questions, the court must and will assume certain principles, from which they will reason, in forming their decisions. These principles, whatever they may be, when they become fixed, by a course of decisions, will be adopted by the legislature, and will be the rule by which they will explain their own powers. This appears evident from this consideration, that if the legislature pass laws, which, in the judgment of the court, they are not authorised to do by the constitution, the court will not take notice of them; for it will not be denied, that the constitution is the highest or supreme law. And the courts are vested with the supreme and uncontroulable power, to determine, in all cases that come before them, what the constitution means; they cannot, therefore, execute a law, which, in their judgment, opposes the constitution, unless we can suppose they can make a superior law give way to an inferior. The legislature, therefore, will not go over the limits by which the courts may adjudge they are confined. And there is little room to doubt but that they will come up to those bounds, as often as occasion and opportunity may offer, and they may judge it proper to do it. For as on the one hand, they will not readily pass laws which they know the courts will not execute, so on the other, we may be sure they will not scruple to pass such as they know they will give effect, as often as they may judge it proper.

From these observations it appears, that the judgment of the judicial, on the constitution, will become the rule to guide the legislature in their construction of their powers.

What the principles are, which the courts will adopt, it is impossible for us to say; but taking up the powers as I have explained them in my last number, which they will possess under this clause, it is not difficult to see, that they may, and probably will, be very liberal ones.

We have seen, that they will be authorized to give the constitution a construction according to its spirit and reason, and not to confine themselves to its letter.

To discover the spirit of the constitution, it is of the first importance to attend to the principal ends and designs it has in view. These are expressed in the preamble, in the following words, viz. "We, the people of the United States, in order to form a more perfect union, establish justice, insure domestic tranquility, provide for the common defence, promote the general welfare, and secure the blessings of liberty to ourselves and our posterity, do ordain and establish this constitution," &c. If the end of the government is to be learned from these words, which are clearly designed to declare it, it is obvious it has in view every object which is embraced by any-government. The preservation of internal peace—the due administration of justice—and to provide for the defence of the community, seems to include all the objects of government; but if they do not, they are certainly comprehended in the words, "to provide for the general welfare." If it be further considered, that this constitution, if it is ratified, will not be a compact entered into by states, in their corporate capacities, but an agreement of the people of the United States, as one great body politic, no doubt can remain, but that the great end of the constitution, if it is to be collected from the preamble, in which its end is declared, is to constitute a government which is to extend to every case for which any government is instituted, whether external or internal. The courts, therefore, will establish this as a principle in expounding the constitution, and will give every part of it such an explanation, as will give latitude to every department under it, to take cognizance of every matter, not only that affects the general and national concerns of the union, but also of such as relate to the administration of private justice, and to regulating the internal and local affairs of the different parts.

Such a rule of exposition is not only consistent with the general spirit of the preamble, but it will stand confirmed by considering more minutely the different clauses of it.

The first object declared to be in view is, "To form a perfect union." It is to be observed, it is not an union of states or bodies corporate; had this been the case the existence of the state governments, might have been secured. But it is a union of the people of the United States considered as one body, who are to ratify this constitution, if it is adopted. Now to make a union of this kind perfect, it is necessary to abolish all inferior governments, and to give the general one compleat legislative, executive and judicial powers to every purpose. The courts therefore will establish it as a rule in explaining the constitution to give it such a construction as will best tend to perfect the union or take from the state governments every power of either making or executing laws. The second object is "to establish justice." This must include not only the idea of instituting the rule of justice, or of making laws which shall be the measure or rule of right, but also of providing for the application of this rule or of administering justice under it. And under this the courts will in their decisions extend the power of the government to all cases they possibly can, or otherwise they will be restricted in doing what appears to be the intent of the constitution they should do, to wit, pass laws and provide for the execution of them, for the general distribution of justice between man and man. Another end declared is "to insure domestic tranquility." This comprehends a provision against all private breaches of the peace, as well as against all public commotions or general insurrections; and to attain the object of this clause fully, the government must exercise the power of passing laws on these subjects, as well as of appointing magistrates with authority to execute them. And the courts will adopt these ideas in their expositions. I might proceed to the other clause, in the preamble, and it would appear by a consideration of all of them separately, as it does by taking them together, that if the spirit of this system is to be known from its declared end and design in the preamble, its spirit is to subvert and abolish all the powers of the state government, and to embrace every object to which any government extends.

As it sets out in the preamble with this declared intention, so it proceeds in the different parts with the same idea. Any person, who will peruse the 8th section with attention, in which most of the powers are enumerated, will perceive that they either expressly or by implication extend to almost every thing about which any legislative power can be employed. But if this equitable mode of construction is applied to this part of the constitution; nothing can stand before it.

This will certainly give the first clause in that article a construction which I confess I think the most natural and grammatical one, to authorise the Congress to do any thing which in their judgment will tend to provide for the general welfare, and this amounts to the same thing as general and unlimited powers of legislation in all cases.

(To be continued.)

L. ESSAY OF BRUTUS, NO. 12

February 14, 1788

This same manner of explaining the constitution, will fix a meaning, and a very important one too, to the 12th [18th?] clause of the same section, which authorises the Congress to make all laws which shall be proper and necessary for carrying into effect the foregoing powers, &c. A voluminous writer in favor of this system, has taken great pains to convince the public, that this clause means nothing: for that the same powers expressed in this, are implied in other parts of the constitution. Perhaps it is so, but still this will undoubtedly be an excellent auxilliary to assist the courts to discover the spirit and reason of the constitution, and when applied to any and every of the other clauses granting power, will operate powerfully in extracting the spirit from them.

I might instance a number of clauses in the constitution, which, if explained in an *equitable* manner, would extend the powers of the government to every case, and reduce the state legislatures to nothing; but, I should draw out my remarks to an undue length, and I presume enough has been said to shew, that the courts have sufficient ground in the exercise of this power, to determine, that the legislature have no bounds set to them by this constitution, by any supposed right the legislatures of the respective states may have, to regulate any of their local concerns.

I proceed, 2d, To inquire, in what manner this power will increase the jurisdiction of the courts.

I would here observe, that the judicial power extends, expressly, to all civil cases that may arise save such as arise between citizens of the same state, with this exception to those of that description, that the judicial of the United States have cognizance of cases between citizens of the same state, claiming lands under grants of different states. Nothing more, therefore, is necessary to give the courts of law, under this constitution, complete jurisdiction of all civil causes, but to comprehend cases between citizens of the same state not included in the foregoing exception.

I presume there will be no difficulty in accomplishing this. Nothing more is necessary than to set forth, in the process, that the party who brings the suit is a citizen of a different state from the one against whom the suit is brought, and there can be little doubt but that the court will take cognizance of the matter, and if they do, who is to restrain them? Indeed, I will freely confess, that it is my decided opinion, that the courts ought to take cognizance of such causes, under the powers of the constitution. For one of the great ends of the constitution is, "to establish justice." This supposes that this cannot be done under the existing governments of the states; and there is certainly as good reason why individuals, living in the same state, should have justice, as those who live in different states. Moreover, the constitution expressly declares, that "the citizens of each state shall be entitled to all the privileges and immunities of citizens in the several states." It will therefore be no fiction, for a citizen of one state to set forth, in a suit, that he is a citizen of another; for he that is entitled to all the privileges and immunities of a country, is a citizen of that country. And in truth, the citizen of one state will, under this constitution, be a citizen of every state.

But supposing that the party, who alledges that he is a citizen of another state, has recourse to fiction in bringing in his suit, it is well known, that the courts have high authority to plead, to justify them in suffering actions to be brought before them by such fictions. In my last number I stated, that the court of exchequer tried all causes in virtue of such a fiction. The court of king's bench, in England, extended their jurisdiction in the same way. Originally, this court held pleas, in civil cases, only of trespasses and other injuries alledged to be committed *vi et armis*. They might likewise, says Blackstone, upon the division of the *aula regia,* have originally held pleas of any other civil action whatsoever (except in real actions which are now very seldom in use) provided the defendant was an officer of the court, or in the custody of the marshall or prison-keeper of this court, for breach of the peace, &c. In process of time, by a fiction, this court began to hold pleas of any personal action whatsoever; it being surmised, that the defendant has been arrested for a supposed trespass that "he has never committed, and being thus in the custody of the marshall of the court, the plaintiff is at liberty to proceed against him, for any other personal injury: which surmise of being in the marshall's custody, the defendant is not at liberty to dispute." By a much less fiction, may the pleas of the courts of the United States extend to cases between citizens of the same state. I shall add no more on this head, but proceed briefly to remark, in what way this power will diminish and destroy both the legislative and judicial authority of the states.

It is obvious that these courts will have authority to decide upon the validity of the laws of any of the states, in all cases where they come in question before them. Where the constitution gives the general government exclusive jurisdiction, they will adjudge all laws made by the states, in such cases, void *ab initio.* Where the constitution gives them concurrent jurisdiction, the laws of the United States must prevail, because they are the supreme law. In such cases, therefore, the laws of the state legislatures must be repealed, restricted, or so construed, as to give full effect to the laws of the union on the same subject. From these remarks it is easy to see, that in proportion as the general government acquires power and jurisdiction, by the liberal construction which the judges may give the constitution, will those of the states lose its rights, until they become so trifling and unimportant, as not to be worth having. I am much mistaken, if this system will not operate to effect this with as much celerity, as those who have the administration of it will think prudent to suffer it. The remaining objections to the judicial power shall be considered in a future paper.

Brutus.

M. ALEXANDER HAMILTON, THE FEDERALIST, NO. 78

May 28, 1788

To the People of the State of New York:

We proceed now to an examination of the judiciary department of the proposed government.

In unfolding the defects of the existing Confederation, the utility and necessity of a federal judicature have been clearly pointed out. It is the less necessary to recapitulate the considerations there urged, as the propriety of the institution in the abstract is not disputed; the only questions which have been raised being relative to the manner of constituting it, and to its extent. To these points, therefore, our observations shall be confined.

The manner of constituting it seems to embrace these several objects: 1st. The mode of appointing the judges. 2d. The tenure by which they are to hold their places. 3d. The partition of the judiciary authority between different courts, and their relations to each other.

First. As to the mode of appointing the judges; this is the same with that of appointing the officers of the Union in general, and has been so fully discussed in the two last numbers, that nothing can be said here which would not be useless repetition.

Second. As to the tenure by which the judges are to hold their places: this chiefly concerns their duration in office; the provisions for their support; the precautions for their responsibility.

According to the plan of the convention, all judges who may be appointed by the United States are to hold their offices *during good behavior;* which is conformable to the most approved of the State constitutions, and among the rest, to that of this State. Its propriety having been drawn into question by the adversaries of that plan, is no light symptom of the rage for objection, which disorders their imaginations and judgments. The standard of good behavior for the continuance in office of the judicial magistracy is certainly one of the most valuable of the modern improvements in the practice of government. In a monarchy it is an excellent barrier to the despotism of the prince; in a republic it is a no less excellent barrier to the encroachments and oppressions of the representative body. And it is the best expedient which can be devised in any government to secure a steady, upright, and impartial administration of the laws.

Whoever attentively considers the different departments of power must perceive, that, in a government in which they are separated from each other, the judiciary, from the nature of its functions, will always be the least dangerous to the political rights of the Constitution; because it will be least in a capacity to annoy or injure them. The Executive not only dispenses the honors, but holds the sword of the community. The legislature not only commands the purse, but prescribes the rules by which the duties and rights of every citizen are to be regulated. The judiciary, on the contrary, has no influence over either the sword or the purse; no direction either of the strength or of the wealth of the society; and can take no active resolution whatever. It may truly be said to have neither FORCE nor WILL, but merely judgment; and must ultimately depend upon the aid of the executive arm even for the efficacy of its judgments.

This simple view of the matter suggests several important consequences. It proves incontestably that the judiciary is beyond comparison the weakest of the three departments of power [*sic*]; that it can never attack with success either of the other two; and that all possible care is requisite to enable it to defend itself against their attacks. It equally proves that though individual oppression may now and then proceed from the courts of justice, the general liberty of the people can never be endangered from that quarter; I mean so long as the judiciary remains truly distinct from both the legislature and the Executive. For I agree, that "there is no liberty, if the power of judging be not separated from the legislative and executive powers." And it proves, in the last place, that as liberty can have nothing to fear from the judiciary alone, but would have every thing to fear from its union with either of the other departments; that as all the effects of such a union must ensue from a dependence of the former on the latter, notwithstanding a nominal and apparent separation; that as, from the natural feebleness of the judiciary it is in continual jeopardy of being overpowered, awed, or influenced by its coördinate branches; and that as nothing can contribute so much to its firmness and independence as permanency in office, this quality may therefore be justly regarded as an indispensable ingredient in its constitution, and, in a great measure, as the citadel of the public justice and the public security.

The complete independence of the courts of justice is peculiarly essential in a limited Constitution. By a limited Constitution, I understand one which contains certain specified exceptions to the legislative authority; such, for instance, as that it shall pass no bills of attainder, no *ex-post-facto* laws, and the like. Limitations of this kind can be preserved in practice no other way than through the medium of courts of justice, whose duty it must be to declare all acts contrary to the manifest tenor of the Constitution void. Without this, all the reservations of particular rights or privileges would amount to nothing.

Some perplexity respecting the rights of the courts to pronounce legislative acts void, because contrary to the constitution, has arisen from an imagination that the doctrine would imply a superiority of the judiciary to the legislative power. It is urged that the authority which can declare the acts of another void must necessarily be superior to the one whose acts may be declared void. As this doctrine is of great importance in all the American constitutions, a brief discussion of the ground on which it rests cannot be unacceptable.

There is no position which depends on clearer principles than that every act of a delegated authority, contrary to the tenor of the commission under which it is exercised, is void. No legislative act, therefore, contrary to the Constitution, can be valid. To deny this would be to affirm that the deputy is greater than his principal; that the servant is above his master; that the representatives of the people are superior to the people themselves; that men acting by virtue of powers may do not only what their powers do not authorize, but what they forbid.

If it be said that the legislative body are themselves the constitutional judges of their own powers, and that the construction they put upon them is conclusive upon the other departments, it may be answered that this cannot be the natural presumption where it is not to be collected from any particular provisions in the Constitution. It is not otherwise to be supposed that the Constitution could intend to enable the representatives of the people to substitute their *will* to that of their constituents. It is far more rational to suppose that the courts were designed to be an intermediate body between the people and the legislature, in order, among other things, to keep the latter within the limits assigned to their authority. The interpretation of the laws is the proper and peculiar province of the courts. A constitution is, in fact, and must be regarded by the judges, as a fundamental law. It therefore belongs to them to ascertain its meaning, as well as the meaning of any particular act proceeding from the legislative body. If there should happen to be an irreconcilable variance between the two, that which has the superior obligation and validity ought, of course, to be preferred; or, in other words, the Constitution ought to be preferred to the statute, the intention of the people to the intention of their agents.

Nor does this conclusion by any means suppose a superiority of the judicial to the legislative power. It only supposes that the power of the people is superior to both; and that where the will of the legislature, declared in its statutes, stands in opposition to that of the people, declared in the Constitution, the judges ought to be governed by the latter rather than the former. They ought to regulate their decisions by the fundamental laws, rather than by those which are not fundamental.

This exercise of judicial discretion, in determining between two contradictory laws, is exemplified in a familiar instance. It not uncommonly happens that there are two statutes existing at one time, clashing in whole or in part with each other, and neither of them containing any repealing clause or expression. In such a case, it is the province of the courts to liquidate and fix their meaning and operation. So far as they can, by any fair construction, be reconciled to each other, reason and law conspire to dictate that this should be done; where this is impracticable, it becomes a matter of necessity to give effect to one in exclusion of the other. The rule which has obtained in the courts for determining their relative validity is, that the last in order of time shall be preferred to the first. But this is a mere rule of construction, not derived from any positive law but from the nature and reason of the thing. It is a rule not enjoined upon the courts by legislative provision but adopted by themselves, as consonant to truth and propriety for the direction of their conduct as interpreters of the law. They thought it reasonable, that between the interfering acts of an *equal* authority, that which was the last indication of its will should have the preference.

But in regard to the interfering acts of a superior and subordinate authority, of an original and derivative power, the nature and reason of the thing indicate the converse of that rule as proper to be followed. They teach us that the prior act of a superior ought to be preferred to the subsequent act of an inferior and subordinate authority; and that accordingly, whenever a particular statute contravenes the Constitution, it will be the duty of the judicial tribunals to adhere to the latter and disregard the former.

It can be of no weight to say that the courts, on the pretence of a repugnancy, may substitute their own pleasure to the constitutional intentions of the legislature. This might as well happen in the case of two contradictory statutes; or it might as well happen in every adjudication upon any single statute. The courts must declare the sense of the law; and if they should be disposed to exercise WILL instead of JUDGMENT, the consequence would equally be the substitution of their pleasure to that of the legislative body. The observation, if it prove any thing, would prove that there ought to be no judges distinct from that body.

If, then, the courts of justice are to be considered as the bulwarks of a limited Constitution against legislative encroachments, this consideration will afford a strong argument for the permanent tenure of judicial offices, since nothing will contribute so much as this to that independent spirit in the judges which must be essential to the faithful performance of so arduous a duty.

This independence of the judges is equally requisite to guard the Constitution and the rights of individuals from the effects of those ill humors, which the arts of designing men or the influence of particular conjunctures sometimes disseminate among the people themselves; and which, though they speedily give place to better information and more deliberate reflection, have a tendency, in the meantime, to occasion dangerous innovations in the government, and serious oppressions of the minor party in the community. Though I trust the friends of the proposed Constitution will never concur with its enemies in questioning that fundamental principle of republican government, which admits the right of the people to alter or abolish the established Constitution whenever they find it inconsistent with their happiness; yet it is not to be inferred from this principle that the representatives of the people, whenever a momentary inclination happens to lay hold of a majority of their constituents, incompatible with the provisions in the existing Constitution, would, on that account, be justifiable in a violation of those provisions; or that the courts would be under a greater obligation to connive at infractions in this shape, than when they had proceeded wholly from the cabals of the representative body. Until the people have by some solemn and authoritative act annulled or changed the established form, it is binding upon themselves collectively, as well as individually; and no presumption, or even knowledge, of their sentiments, can warrant their representatives in a departure from it, prior to such an act. But it is easy to see that it would require an uncommon portion of fortitude in the judges to do their duty as faithful guardians of the Constitution, where legislative invasions of it had been instigated by the major voice of the community.

But it is not with a view to infractions of the Constitution only that the independence of the judges may be an essential safeguard against the effects of occasional ill humors in the society. These sometimes extend no farther than to the injury of the private rights of particular classes of citizens by unjust and partial laws. Here also the firmness of the judicial magistracy is of vast importance in mitigating the severity and confining the operation of such laws. It not only serves to moderate the immediate mischiefs of those which may have been passed, but it operates as a check upon the legislative body in passing them; who, perceiving that obstacles to the success of iniquitous intention are to be expected from the scruples of the courts, are in a manner compelled by the very motives of the injustice they meditate to qualify their attempts. This is a circumstance calculated to have more influence upon the character of our governments, than but few may be aware of. The benefits of the integrity and moderation of the judiciary have already been felt in more States than one; and though they may have displeased those whose sinister expectations they may have disappointed, they must have commanded the esteem and applause of all the virtuous and disinterested. Considerate men of every description ought to prize whatever will tend to beget or fortify that temper in the courts; as no man can be sure that he may not be tomorrow the victim of a spirit of injustice by which he may be a gainer today. And every man must now feel that the inevitable tendency of such a spirit is to sap the foundations of public and private confidence, and to introduce in its stead universal distrust and distress.

That inflexible and uniform adherence to the rights of the Constitution and of individuals, which we perceive to be indispensable in the courts of justice, can certainly not be expected from judges who hold their offices by a temporary commission. Periodical appointments, however regulated or by whomsoever made, would, in some way or other, be fatal to their necessary independence. If the power of making them was committed either to the Executive or legislature, there would be danger of an improper complaisance to the branch which possessed it; if to both, there would be an unwillingness to hazard the displeasure of either; if to the people or to persons chosen by them for the special purpose, there would be too great a disposition to consult popularity, to justify a reliance that nothing would be consulted but the Constitution and the laws.

There is yet a further and a weightier reason for the permanency of the judicial offices, which is deducible from the nature of the qualifications they require. It has been frequently remarked, with great propriety, that a voluminous code of laws is one of the inconveniences necessarily connected with the advantages of a free government. To avoid an arbitrary discretion in the courts, it is indispensable that they should be bound down by strict rules and precedents, which serve to define and point out their duty in every particular case that comes before them;

and it will readily be conceived from the variety of controversies which grow out of the folly and wickedness of mankind, that the records of those precedents must unavoidably swell to a very considerable bulk, and must demand long and laborious study to acquire a competent knowledge of them. Hence it is, that there can be but few men in the society who will have sufficient skill in the laws to qualify them for the stations of judges. And making the proper deductions for the ordinary depravity of human nature, the number must be still smaller of those who unite the requisite integrity with the requisite knowledge. These considerations apprise us that the government can have no great option between fit character; and that a temporary duration in office, which would naturally discourage such characters from quitting a lucrative line of practice to accept a seat on the bench, would have a tendency to throw the administration of justice into hands less able, and less well qualified, to conduct it with utility and dignity. In the present circumstances of this country and in those in which it is likely to be for a long time to come, the disadvantages on this score would be greater than they may at first sight appear; but it must be confessed that they are far inferior to those which present themselves under the other aspects of the subject.

Upon the whole, there can be no room to doubt that the convention acted wisely in copying from the models of those constitutions which have established *good behavior* as the tenure of their judicial offices, in point of duration; and that so far from being blamable on this account, their plan would have been inexcusably defective if it had wanted this important feature of good government. The experience of Great Britain affords an illustrious comment on the excellence of the institution.

PUBLIUS

N. JAMES MADISON, OBSERVATIONS ON JEFFERSON'S "DRAUGHT OF A CONSTITUTION FOR VIRGINIA"

October 15, 1788

Senate. The term of two years is too short. Six years are not more than sufficient. A Senate is to withstand the occasional impetuosities of the more numerous branch. The members ought therefore to derive a firmness from the tenure of their places. It ought to supply the defect of knowledge and experience incident to the other branch, there ought to be time given therefore for attaining the qualifications necessary for that purpose. It ought finally to maintain that system and steadiness in public affairs without which no Government can prosper or be respectable. This cannot be done by a body undergoing a frequent change of its members. A Senate for six years will not be dangerous to liberty. On the contrary it will be one of its best guardians. By correcting the infirmities of popular Government, it will prevent that disgust agst. that form which may otherwise produce a sudden transition to some very different one. It is no secret to any attentive & dispassionate observer of the pol: Situation of the U. S. that the real danger to republican liberty has lurked in that cause.

The appointment of Senators by districts seems to be objectionable. A spirit of *locality* is inseparable from that mode. The evil is fully displayed in the County representations; the members of which are every where observed to lose sight of the aggregate interests of the Community, and even to sacrifice them to the interests or prejudices of their respective constituents. In general these local interests are miscalculated. But it is not impossible for a measure to be accomodated to the particular interests of every County or district, when considered by itself, and not so, when considered in relation to each other and to the whole State; in the same manner as the interests of individuals may be very different in a State of nature and in a Political Union. The most effectual remedy for the local biass is to impress on the minds of the Senators an attention to the interest of the whole Society by making them the choice of the whole Society, each citizen voting for every Senator. The objection here is that the fittest characters would not be sufficiently known to the people at large. But in free Governments, merit and notoriety of character are rarely separated, and such a regulation would connect them more and more together. Should this mode of election be on the whole not approved, that established in Maryland presents a valuable alternative. The latter affords perhaps a greater security for the selection of merit. The inconveniences chargeable on it are two: first that the Council of electors favors cabal. Against this the shortness of its existence is a good antidote. Secondly that in a large State the meeting of the Electors must be expensive if they be paid, or badly attended if the service be onerous. To this it may be answered that in a case of such vast importance, the expence which could not be great, ought to be disregarded. Whichever of these modes may be preferred, it cannot be amiss so far to admit the plan of districts as to restrain the choice to persons residing in different parts of the State. Such a regulation will produce a diffusive confidence in the Body, which is not less necessary than the other means of rendering it useful. In a State having large towns which can easily unite their votes the precaution would be essential to an immediate choice by the people at large. In Maryland no regard is paid to residence. And what is remarkable vacancies are filled by the Senate itself. This last is an obnoxious expedient and cannot in any point of view have much effect. It was probably meant to obviate the trouble of occasional meetings of the Electors. But the purpose might have been otherwise answered by allowing the unsuccessful candidates to supply vacancies according to the order of their standing on the list of votes, or by requiring provisional appointments to be made along with the positive ones. If an election by districts be unavoidable and the ideas here suggested be sound, the evil will be diminished in proportion to the extent given to the districts, taking two or more Senators from each district.

Electors. The first question arising here is how far property ought to be made a qualification. There is a middle way to be taken which corresponds at once with the Theory of free government and the lessons of experience. A freehold or equivalent of a certain value may be annexed to the right of vot[in]g for Senators, & the right left more at large in the election of the other House. Examples of this distinction may be found in the Constitutions of several States, particularly if I mistake not, of North Carolina & N. York. This middle mode reconciles and secures the two cardinal objects of Government, the rights of persons, and the rights of property. The former will be sufficiently guarded by one branch, the latter more particularly by the other. Give all power to property; and the indigent [will] be oppressed. Give it to the latter and the effect may be transposed. Give a defensive share to each and each will be secure. The necessity of thus guarding the rights of property was for obvious reasons unattended to in the commencement of the Revolution. In all the Governments which were considered as beacons to republican patriots & lawgivers, the rights of persons were subjected to those of property. The poor were sacrificed to the rich. In the existing state of American population, & American property[,] the two classes of rights were so little discriminated that a provision for the rights of persons was supposed to include of itself those of property, and it was natural to infer from the tendency of republican laws, that these different interests would be more and more identified. Experience and investigation have however produced more correct ideas on this subject. It is now observed that in all populous countries, the smaller part only can be interested in preserving the rights of property. It must be foreseen that America, and Kentucky itself will by degrees arrive at this State of Society; that in some parts of the Union a very great advance is already made towards it. It is well understood that interest leads to injustice as well when the opportunity is presented to bodies of men, as to individuals; to an interested majority in a republic, as to the interested minority of any other form of Government. The time to guard agst. this danger is at the first forming of the Constitution, and in the present state of population when the bulk of the people have a sufficient interest in possession or in prospect to be attached to the rights of property, without being insufficiently attached to the rights of persons. Liberty not less than justice pleads for the policy here recommended. If *all* power be suffered to slide into hands not interested in the rights of property which must be the case whenever a majority fall under that description, one of two things cannot fail to happen; either they will unite against the other description and become the dupes & instruments of ambition, or their poverty & independence will render them the mercenary instruments of wealth. In either case liberty will be subverted; in the first by a despotism growing out of anarchy, in the second, by an oligarchy founded on corruption.

The second question under this head is whether the ballot be not a better mode than that of voting viva voce. The comparative experience of the States pursuing the different modes is in favor of the first. It is found less difficult to guard against fraud in that, than against bribery in the other.

Exclusions. Does not the exclusion of Ministers of the Gospel as such violate a fundamental principle of liberty by punishing a religious profession with the privation of a civil right? Does it not violate another article of the plan itself which exempts religion from the cognizance of Civil power? Does it not violate justice by at once taking away a right and prohibiting a compensation for it. And does it not in fine violate impartiality by shutting the door agst the Ministers of one religion and leaving it open for those of every other.

The re-eligibility of members after accepting offices of profit is so much opposed to the present way of thinking in America that any discussion of the subject would probably be a waste of time.

Limits of power. It is at least questionable whether death ought to be confined to "Treason and murder." It would not therefore be prudent to tie the hands of Government in the manner here proposed. The prohibition of pardon, however specious in theory would have practical consequences, which render it inadmissible. A single instance is a sufficient proof. The crime of treason is generally shared by a number, and often a very great number. It would be politically if not morally wrong to take away the lives of all, even if every individual were equally guilty. What name would be given to a severity which made no distinction between the legal & the moral offence—between the deluded multitude, and their wicked leaders. A second trial would not avoid the difficulty; because the oaths of the jury would not permit them to hearken to any voice but the inexorable voice of the law.

The power of the Legislature to appoint any other than their own officers departs too far from the Theory which requires a separation of the great Depts of Government. One of the best securities against the creation of unnecessary offices or tyrannical powers, is an exclusion of the authors from all share in filling the one, or influence in the execution of the others. The proper mode of appointing to offices will fall under another head.

Executive Governour. An election by the Legislature is liable to insuperable objections. It not only tends to faction intrigue and corruption, but leaves the Executive under the influence of an improper obligation to that department. An election by the people at large, as in this & several other States—or by Electors as in the appointment of the Senate in Maryland, or indeed by the people through any other channel than their legislative representatives, seems to be far preferable. The ineligibility a second time, though not perhaps without advantages, is also liable to a variety of strong objections. It takes away one powerful

212

motive to a faithful & useful administration, the desire of acquiring that title to a re-appointment. By rendering a periodical change of men necessary, it discourages beneficial undertakings which require perseverance and system, or, as frequently happened in the Roman Consulate, either precipitates or prevents the execution of them. It may inspire desperate enterprizes for the attainment of what is not attainable by legitimate means. It fetters the judgment and inclination of the Community; and in critical moments would either produce a violation of the Constitution, or exclude a choice which might be essential to the public safety. Add to the whole, that by putting the Executive Magistrate in the situation of the tenant of an unrenewable lease, it would tempt him to neglect the constitutional rights of his department, and to connive at usurpations by the Legislative department, with which he may connect his future ambition or interest.

The clause restraining the first Magistrate from the immediate command of the military force would be made better by excepting cases in which he should receive the sanction of the two branches of the Legislature.

Council of State. The following variations are suggested. 1. The election to be made by the people immediately, or thro' some other medium than the Legislature. 2. A distributive choice should perhaps be secured as in the case of the Senate. 3 instead of an ineligibility a second time, a rotation as in the federal Senate, with an abrdgmt. of the term to be substituted.

The appointment to offices is, of all the functions of Republican & perhaps every other form of Government, the most difficult to guard against abuse. Give it to a numerous body, and you at once destroy all responsibility, and create a perpetual source of faction and corruption. Give it to the Executive wholly, and it may be made an engine of improper influence and favoritism. Suppose the power were divided thus: let the Executive alone make all the subordinate appointments; and the Govr. and Senate as in the Fedl. Constn:, those of the superior order. It seems particularly fit that the Judges, who are to form a distinct department should owe their offices partly to each of the other departments rather than wholly to either.

Judiciary. Much detail ought to [be] avoided in the constitutional regulation of this department, that there may be room for changes which may be demanded by the progressive changes in the state of our population. It is at least doubtful whether the number of Courts, the number of Judges, or even the boundaries of Jurisdiction ought to be made unalterable but by a revisal of the Constitution. The precaution seems no otherwise necessary than as it may prevent sudden modifications of the establishment, or addition of obsequious Judges, for the purpose of evadg. the checks of the Constn. & giv[in]g effect to some sinister policy of the Legisre. But might not the same object be otherwise attained? By prohibiting, for example, any innovations in those particulars without the consent of that department: or without the annual sanction of two or three successive assemblies; over & above the other pre-requisites to the passage of a law.

The model here proposed for a Court of Appeals is not recommended by experience. It is found as might well be presumed that the members are always warped in their appellate decisions by an attachment to the principles and jurisdiction of their respective Courts & still more so by the previous decision on the case removed by appeal. The only effectual cure for the evil, is to form a Court of Appeals, of distinct and select Judges. The expence ought not be admitted as an objection. 1. because the proper administration of Justice is of too essential a nature to be sacrificed to that consideration. 2. The number of inferior Judges might in that case be lessened. 3. The whole department may be made to support itself by a judicious tax on law proceedings.

The excuse for non-attendance would be a more proper subject of enquiry some where else than in the Court to which the party belonged. Delicacy, mutual connivance &c. would soon reduce the regulation to mere form; or if not, it might become a disagreeable source of little irritations among the members. A certificate from the local Court or some other local authority where the party might reside or happen to be detained from his duty, expressing the cause of absence as well as that it was judged to be satisfactory, might be safely substituted. Few Judges would improperly claim their wages, if such a formality stood in the way. These observations are applicable to the Council of State.

A Court of Impeachments is among the most puzzling articles of a republican Constitution; and it is far more easy to point out defects in any plan, than to supply a cure for them. The diversified expedients adopted in the Constitutions of the several States prove how much the compilers were embarrassed on this subject. The plan here proposed varies from all of them; and is perhaps not less than any a proof of the difficulties which pressed the ingenuity of its author. The remarks arising on it are 1. that it seems not to square with reason, that the right to impeach should be united to that of trying the impeachment, & consequently in a proportional degree, to that of sharing in the appointment of, or influence on the Tribunal to which the trial may belong. 2. As the Executive & Judiciary would form a majority of the Court, and either have a right to impeach, too much might depend on a combination of these departments. This objection would be still stronger, if the members of the Assembly were capable as proposed of holding offices, and were amenable in that capacity to the Court. 3. The H. of Delegates and either of those departments could appt. a majority of the Court. Here is another danger of combination, and the more to be apprehended as that branch of the Legisl: wd. also have the right to impeach, a right in their hands of itself sufficiently weighty; and as the power of the Court wd. extend to the head of the Ex. by whose independence the constitutil. rights of that department are to be secured agst. Legislative usurpations.   4. The dangers in the two last cases would be still more formidable; as the power extends not only to deprivation; but to future incapacity of office.   In the case of all officers of sufficient importance to be objects of factious persecution, the latter branch of power is in every view of a delicate nature.   In that of the Cheif Magistrate, it seems inadmissible, if he be chosen by the Legislature; and much more so, if immediately by the people themselves.   A temporary incapacitation is the most that cd. be properly authorised.

The 2 great desiderata in a Court of impeachts. are 1. impartiality. 2. respectability—the first in order to a right—the second in order to a satisfactory decision.   These characteristics are arrived at in the following modification—Let the Senate be denied the right to impeach.   Let 1/3 of the members be struck out, by alternate nominations of the prosecutors & party impeached; the remaining 2/3 to be the *Stamen* of the Court.   When the H: of Del: impeach, let the Judges or a certain proportion of them—and the Council of State be associated in the trial. When the Govr. or Council impeaches, let the Judges only be associated: When the Judges impeach let the Council only be associated.   But if the party impeached by the H. of Dels. be a member of the Ex. or Judicy. let that of which he is a member not be associated.   If the party impeached belong to one & be impeached by the other of these branches, let neither of them be associated, the decision being in this case left with the Senate alone or if that be thought exceptionable, a few members might be added by the H. of Ds. 2/3 of the Court should in all cases be necessary to a conviction, & the cheif Magistrate *at least* should be exempt from a sentence of perpetual if not of temporary incapacity.   It is extremely probable that a critical discussion of this outline may discover objections which do not occur.   Some do occur; but appear not to be greater than are incident to any different modification of the Tribunal.

The establishment of trials by Jury & viva voce testimony in *all* cases and in *all* Courts, is to say the least a delicate experiment; and would most probably be either violated, or be found inconvenient.

Council of Revision.   A revisionary power is meant as a check to precipitate, to unjust, and to unconstitutional laws.   These important ends would it is conceived be more effectually secured, without disarming the Legislature of its requisite authority, by requiring bills to be separately communicated to the Exec: & Judicy. depts.   If either of these object, let 2/3, if both 3/4 of each House be necessary to overrule the objection; and if either or both protest agst. a bill as violating the Constitution, let it moreover be suspended, notwithstanding the overruling proportion of the Assembly, until there shall have been a subsequent election of the H. of Ds. and a repassage of the bill by 2/3 or 3/4 of both Houses, as the case may be.   It sd. not be allowed the Judges or the Ex to pronounce a law thus enacted, unconstitul. & invalid.

In the State Constitutions & indeed in the Fedl. one also, no provision is made for the case of a disagreement in expounding them;

215

and as the Courts are generally the last in making their decision, it results to them, by refusing or not refusing to execute a law, to stamp it with its final character. This makes the Judiciary Dept paramount in fact to the Legislature, which was never intended, and can never be proper.

The extension of the Habs. Corps. to the cases in which it has been usually suspended, merits consideration at least. If there be emergences which call for such a suspension, it can have no effect to prohibit it, because the prohibition will assuredly give way to the impulse of the moment; or rather it will have the bad effect of facilitating other violations that may be less necessary. The Exemption of the press from liability in every case for *true facts*, is also an innovation and as such ought to be well considered. This essential branch of liberty is perhaps in more danger of being interrupted by local tumults, or the silent awe of a predominant party, than by any direct attacks of Power.

CHAPTER III

PRINCIPLES OF REPUBLICANISM AND DEMOCRACY

A. JOHN LOCKE, TWO TREATISES OF GOVERNMENT, THE SECOND TREATISE, AN ESSAY CONCERNING THE TRUE ORIGINAL, EXTENT, AND END OF CIVIL GOVERNMENT

1698

CHAP. II.

Of the State of Nature.

4. TO understand Political Power right, and derive it from its Original, we must consider what State all Men are naturally in, and that is, a *State of perfect Freedom* to order their Actions, and dispose of their Possessions, and Persons as they think fit, within the bounds of the Law of Nature, without asking leave, or depending upon the Will of any other Man.

A *State* also *of Equality*, wherein all the Power and Jurisdiction is reciprocal, no one having more than another: there being nothing more evident, than that Creatures of the same species and rank promiscuously born to all the same advantages of Nature, and the use of the same faculties, should also be equal one amongst another without Subordination or Subjection, unless the Lord and Master of them all, should by any manifest Declaration of his Will set one above another, and confer on him by an evident and clear appointment an undoubted Right to Dominion and Sovereignty.

5. This *equality* of Men by Nature, the Judicious *Hooker* looks upon as so evident in it self, and beyond all question, that he makes it the Foundation of that Obligation to mutual Love amongst Men, on which he Builds the Duties they owe one another, and from whence he derives the great Maxims *of Justice* and *Charity*. His words are;

The like natural inducement, hath brought Men to know that it is no less their Duty, to Love others than themselves, for seeing those things which are equal, must needs all have one measure; If I cannot but wish to receive good, even as much at every Man's hands, as any Man can wish unto his own Soul, how should I look to have any part of my desire herein satisfied, unless my self be careful to satisfie the like desire, which is undoubtedly in other Men, being of one and the same nature? to have any thing offered them repugnant to this desire, must needs in all respects grieve them as much as me, so that if I do harm, I must look to suffer, there being no reason that others should shew greater measure of

217

love to me, than they have by me, shewed unto them; my desire therefore to be lov'd of my equals in nature, as much as possible may be, imposeth upon me a natural Duty of bearing to themward, fully the like affection; From which relation of equality between our selves and them, that are as our selves, what several Rules and Canons, natural reason hath drawn for direction of Life, no Man is ignorant. Eccl. Pol. Lib. 1.

6. But though this be a *State of Liberty*, yet it is *not a State of Licence*, though Man in that State have an uncontroleable Liberty, to dispose of his Person or Possessions, yet he has not Liberty to destroy himself, or so much as any Creature in his Possession, but where some nobler use, than its bare Preservation calls for it. The *State of Nature* has a Law of Nature to govern it, which obliges every one: And Reason, which is that Law, teaches all Mankind, who will but consult it, that being all equal and independent, no one ought to harm another in his Life, Health, Liberty, or Possessions. For Men being all the Workmanship of one Omnipotent, and infinitely wise Maker; All the Servants of one Sovereign Master, sent into the World by his order and about his business, they are his Property, whose Workmanship they are, made to last during his, not one anothers Pleasure. And being furnished with like Faculties, sharing all in one Community of Nature, there cannot be supposed any such *Subordination* among us, that may Authorize us to destroy one another, as if we were made for one anothers uses, as the inferior ranks of Creatures are for ours. Every one as he is *bound to preserve himself*, and not to quit his Station wilfully; so by the like reason when his own Preservation comes not in competition, ought he, as much as he can, *to preserve the rest of Mankind*, and may not unless it be to do Justice on an Offender, take away, or impair the life, or what tends to the Preservation of the Life, the Liberty, Health, Limb or Goods of another.

7. And that all Men may be restrained from invading others Rights, and from doing hurt to one another, and the Law of Nature be observed, which willeth the Peace and *Preservation of all Mankind*, the *Execution* of the Law of Nature is in that State, put into every Mans hands, whereby every one has a right to punish the transgressors of that Law to such a Degree, as may hinder its Violation. For the *Law of Nature* would, as all other Laws that concern Men in this World, be in vain, if there were no body that in the State of Nature, had a *Power to Execute* that Law, and thereby preserve the innocent and restrain offenders, and if any one in the State of Nature may punish another, for any evil he has done, every one may do so. For in that *State of perfect Equality*, where naturally there is no superiority or jurisdiction of one, over another, what any may do in Prosecution of that Law, every one must needs have a Right to do.

8. And thus in the State of Nature, *one Man comes by a Power over another*; but yet no Absolute or Arbitrary Power, to use a Criminal when he has got him in his hands, according to the passionate heats, or

boundless extravagancy of his own Will, but only to retribute to him, so far as calm reason and conscience dictates, what is proportionate to his Transgression, which is so much as may serve for *Reparation* and *Restraint.* For these two are the only reasons, why one Man may lawfully do harm to another, which is that we call *punishment.* In transgressing the Law of Nature, the Offender declares himself to live by another Rule, than that of *reason* and common Equity, which is that measure God has set to the actions of Men, for their mutual security: and so he becomes dangerous to Mankind, the tye, which is to secure them from injury and violence, being slighted and broken by him. Which being a trespass against the whole Species, and the Peace and Safety of it, provided for by the Law of Nature, every man upon this score, by the Right he hath to preserve Mankind in general, may restrain, or where it is necessary, destroy things noxious to them, and so may bring such evil on any one, who hath transgressed that Law, as may make him repent the doing of it, and thereby deter him, and by his Example others, from doing the like mischief. And in this case, and upon this ground, *every Man hath a Right to punish the Offender, and be Executioner of the Law of Nature.*

9. I doubt not but this will seem a very strange Doctrine to some Men: but before they condemn it, I desire them to resolve me, by what Right any Prince or State can put to death, or *punish an Alien*, for any Crime he commits in their Country. 'Tis certain their Laws by vertue of any Sanction they receive from the promulgated Will of the Legislative, reach not a Stranger. They speak not to him, nor if they did, is he bound to hearken to them. The Legislative Authority, by which they are in Force over the Subjects of that Common-wealth, hath no Power over him. Those who have the Supream Power of making Laws in *England*, *France* or *Holland*, are to an *Indian*, but like the rest of the World, Men without Authority: And therefore if by the Law of Nature, every Man hath not a Power to punish Offences against it, as he soberly judges the Case to require, I see not how the Magistrates of any Community, can *punish an Alien* of another Country, since in reference to him, they can have no more Power, than what every Man naturally may have over another.

10. Besides the Crime which consists in violating the Law, and varying from the right Rule of Reason, whereby a Man so far becomes degenerate, and declares himself to quit the Principles of Human Nature, and to be a noxious Creature, there is commonly *injury* done to some Person or other, and some other Man receives damage by his Transgression, in which Case he who hath received any damage, has besides the right of punishment common to him with other Men, a particular Right to seek *Reparation* from him that has done it. And any other Person who finds it just, may also joyn with him that is injur'd, and assist him in recovering from the Offender, so much as may make satisfaction for the harm he has suffer'd.

11.   From these *two distinct Rights*, the one of *Punishing* the Crime *for restraint*, and preventing the like Offence, which right of punishing is in every body; the other of taking *reparation*, which belongs only to the injured party, comes it to pass that the Magistrate, who by being Magistrate, hath the common right of punishing put into his hands, can often, where the publick good demands not the execution of the Law, *remit* the punishment of Criminal Offences by his own Authority, but yet cannot *remit* the satisfaction due to any private Man, for the damage he has received.   That, he who has suffered the damage has a Right to demand in his own name, and he alone can *remit*: The damnified Person has this Power of appropriating to himself, the Goods or Service of the Offender, by *Right of Self-preservation*, as every Man has a Power to punish the Crime, to prevent its being committed again, *by the Right he has of Preserving all Mankind*, and doing all reasonable things he can in order to that end: And thus it is, that every Man in the State of Nature, has a Power to kill a Murderer, both to deter others from doing the like Injury, which no Reparation can compensate, by the Example of the punishment that attends it from every body, and also *to secure* Men from the attempts of a Criminal, who having renounced Reason, the common Rule and Measure, God hath given to Mankind, hath by the unjust Violence and Slaughter he hath committed upon one, declared War against all Mankind, and therefore may be destroyed as a *Lyon* or a *Tyger*, one of those wild Savage Beasts, with whom Men can have no Society nor Security: And upon this is grounded the great Law of Nature, *Who so sheddeth Mans Blood, by Man shall his Blood be shed*. And *Cain* was so fully convinced, that every one had a Right to destroy such a Criminal, that after the Murther of his Brother, he cries out, *Every one that findeth me, shall slay me*; so plain was it writ in the Hearts of all Mankind.

12.   By the same reason, may a Man in the State of Nature *punish the lesser breaches* of that Law.   It will perhaps be demanded, with death? I answer, Each Transgression may be *punished* to that *degree*, and with so much *Severity* as will suffice to make it an ill bargain to the Offender, give him cause to repent, and terrifie others from doing the like.   Every Offence that can be committed in the State of Nature, may in the State of Nature be also punished, equally, and as far forth as it may, in a Common-wealth; for though it would be besides my present purpose, to enter here into the particulars of the Law of Nature, or its *measures of punishment*; yet, it is certain there is such a Law, and that too, as intelligible and plain to a rational Creature, and a Studier of that Law, as the positive Laws of Common-wealths, nay possibly plainer; As much as Reason is easier to be understood, than the Phansies and intricate Contrivances of Men, following contrary and hidden interests put into Words; For so truly are a great part of the *Municipal Laws* of Countries, which are only so far right, as they are founded on the Law of Nature, by which they are to be regulated and interpreted.

13. To this strange Doctrine, *viz.* That *in the State of Nature, every one has the Executive Power* of the Law of Nature, I doubt not but it will be objected, That it is unreasonable for Men to be Judges in their own Cases, that Self-love will make Men partial to themselves and their Friends. And on the other side, that Ill Nature, Passion and Revenge will carry them too far in punishing others. And hence nothing but Confusion and Disorder will follow, and that therefore God hath certainly appointed Government to restrain the partiality and violence of Men. I easily grant, that *Civil Government* is the proper Remedy for the Inconveniences of the State of Nature, which must certainly be Great, where Men may be Judges in their own Case, since 'tis easily to be imagined, that he who was so unjust as to do his Brother an Injury, will scarce be so just as to condemn himself for it: But I shall desire those who make this Objection, to remember that *Absolute Monarchs* are but Men, and if Government is to be the Remedy of those Evils, which necessarily follow from Mens being Judges in their own Cases, and the State of Nature is therefore not to be endured, I desire to know what kind of Government that is, and how much better it is than the State of Nature, where one Man commanding a multitude, has the Liberty to be Judge in his own Case, and may do to all his Subjects whatever he pleases, without the least liberty to any one to question or controle those who Execute his Pleasure? And in whatsoever he doth, whether led by Reason, Mistake or Passion, must be submitted to? Much better it is in the State of Nature wherein Men are not bound to submit to the unjust will of another: And if he that judges, judges amiss in his own, or any other Case, he is answerable for it to the rest of Mankind.

14. 'Tis often asked as a mighty Objection, *Where are*, or ever were, there any *Men in such a State of Nature*? To which it may suffice as an answer at present; That since all *Princes* and Rulers of *Independent* Governments all through the World, are in a State of Nature, 'tis plain the World never was, nor ever will be, without Numbers of Men in that State. I have named all Governors of *Independent* Communities, whether they are, or are not, in League with others: For 'tis not every Compact that puts an end to the State of Nature between Men, but only this one of agreeing together mutually to enter into one Community, and make one Body Politick; other Promises and Compacts, Men may make one with another, and yet still be in the State of Nature. The Promises and Bargains for Truck, &c. between the two Men in the Desert Island, mentioned by *Garcilasso De la vega*, in his History of *Peru*, or between a *Swiss* and an *Indian*, in the Woods of *America*, are binding to them, though they are perfectly in a State of Nature, in reference to one another. For Truth and keeping of Faith belongs to Men, as Men, and not as Members of Society.

15. To those that say, There were never any Men in the State of Nature; I will not only oppose the Authority of the Judicious *Hooker*, *Eccl. Pol. Lib.* 1. *Sect.* 10. where he says, *The Laws which have been*

hitherto mentioned, i.e. the Laws of Nature, *do bind Men absolutely, even as they are Men, although they have never any settled fellowship, never any Solemn Agreement amongst themselves what to do or not to do, but for as much as we are not by our selves sufficient to furnish our selves with competent store of things, needful for such a Life, as our Nature doth desire, a Life, fit for the Dignity of Man; therefore to supply those Defects and Imperfections which are in us, as living singly and solely by our selves, we are naturally induced to seek Communion and Fellowship with others, this was the Cause of Mens uniting themselves, at first in Politick Societies.* But I moreover affirm, That all Men are naturally in that State, and remain so, till by their own Consents they make themselves Members of some Politick Society; And I doubt not in the Sequel of this Discourse, to make it very clear.

B. JOHN GORDON, CATO'S LETTERS, NO. 38

July 22, 1721

The Right and Capacity of the People to judge of Government.

S<small>IR</small>,

The world has, from time to time, been led into such a long maze of mistakes, by those who gained by deceiving, that whoever would instruct mankind, must begin with removing their errors; and if they were every where honestly apprized of truth, and restored to their senses, there would not remain one nation of bigots or slaves under the sun: A happiness always to be wished, but never expected!

In most parts of the earth there is neither light nor liberty; and even in the best parts of it they are but little encouraged, and coldly maintained; there being, in all places, many engaged, through interest, in a perpetual conspiracy against them. They are the two greatest civil blessings, inseparable in their interests, and the mutual support of each other; and whoever would destroy one of them, must destroy both. Hence it is, that we every where find tyranny and imposture, ignorance and slavery, joined together; and oppressors and deceivers mutually aiding and paying constant court to each other. Where-ever truth is dangerous, liberty is precarious.

Of all the sciences that I know in the world, that of government concerns us most, and is the easiest to be known, and yet is the least understood. Most of those who manage it would make the lower world believe that there is I know not what difficulty and mystery in it, far above vulgar understandings; which proceeding of theirs is direct craft and imposture: Every ploughman knows a good government from a bad one, from the effects of it: he knows whether the fruits of his labour be his own, and whether he enjoy them in peace and security: And if he do not know the principles of government, it is for want of thinking and enquiry, for they lie open to common sense; but people are generally taught not to think of them at all, or to think wrong of them.

What is government, but a trust committed by all, or the most, to one, or a few, who are to attend upon the affairs of all, that every one may, with the more security, attend upon his own? A great and honourable trust; but too seldom honourably executed; those who possess it having it often more at heart to increase their power, than to make it useful; and to be terrible, rather than beneficent. It is therefore a trust, which ought to be bounded with many and strong restraints, because power renders men wanton, insolent to others, and fond of themselves. Every violation therefore of this trust, where such violation is considerable, ought to meet with proportionable punishment; and the smallest violation of it ought to meet with some, because indulgence to the least faults of magistrates may be cruelty to a whole people.

Honesty, diligence, and plain sense, are the only talents necessary for the executing of this trust; and the public good is its only end: As to refinements and finesses, they are often only the false appearances of wisdom and parts, and oftener tricks to hide guilt and emptiness; and they are generally mean and dishonest: they are the arts of jobbers in politicks, who, playing their own game under the publick cover, subsist upon poor shifts and expedients; starved politicians, who live from hand to mouth, from day to day, and following the little views of ambition, avarice, revenge, and the like personal passions, are ashamed to avow them, yet want souls great enough to forsake them; small wicked statesmen, who make a private market of the publick, and deceive it, in order to sell it.

These are the poor parts which great and good governors scorn to play, and cannot play; their designs, like their stations, being purely publick, are open and undisguised. They do not consider their people as their prey, nor lie in ambush for their subjects; nor dread, and treat and surprize them like enemies, as all ill magistrates do; who are not governors, but jailers and sponges, who chain them and squeeze them, and yet take it very ill if they do but murmur; which is yet much less than a people so abused ought to do. There have been times and countries, when publick ministers and publick enemies have been the same individual men. What a melancholy reflection is this, that the most terrible and mischievous foes to a nation should be its own magistrates! And yet in every enslaved country, which is almost every country, this is their woeful case.

Honesty and plainness go always together, and the makers and multipliers of mysteries, in the political way, are shrewdly to be suspected of dark designs. Cincinnatus was taken from the plough to save and defend the Roman state; an office which he executed honestly and successfully, without the grimace and gains of a statesman. Nor did he afterwards continue obstinately at the head of affairs, to form a party, raise a fortune, and settle himself in power: As he came into it with universal consent, he resigned it with universal applause.

It seems that government was not in those days become a trade, at least a gainful trade. Honest Cincinnatus was but a farmer: And happy had it been for the Romans, if, when they were enslaved, they could have taken the administration out of the hands of the emperors, and their refined politicians, and committed it to such farmers, or any farmers. It is certain, that many of their imperial governors acted more ridiculously than a board of ploughmen would have done, and more barbarously than a club of butchers could have done.

But some have said, It is not the business of private man to meddle with government. A bold, false, and dishonest saying; and whoever says it, either knows not what he says, or cares not, or slavishly speaks the sense of others. It is a cant now almost forgot in England, and which never prevailed but when liberty and the constitution were attacked, and never can prevail but upon the like occasion.

It is a vexation to be obliged to answer nonsense, and confute absurdities: But since it is and has been the great design of this paper to maintain and explain the glorious principles of liberty, and to expose the arts of those who would darken or destroy them; I shall here particularly shew the wickedness and stupidity of the above saying; which is fit to come from no mouth but that of a tyrant or a slave, and can never be heard by any man of an honest and free soul, without horror and indignation: It is, in short, a saying, which ought to render the man who utters it for ever incapable of place or credit in a free country, as it shews the malignity of his heart, and the baseness of his nature, and as it is the pronouncing of a doom upon our constitution. A crime, or rather a complication of crimes, for which a lasting infamy ought to be but part of the punishment.

But to the falsehood of the thing: Publick truths ought never to be kept secrets; and they who do it, are guilty of a solecism, and a contradiction: Every man ought to know what it concerns all to know. Now, nothing upon earth is of a more universal nature than government; and every private man upon earth has a concern in it, because in it is concerned, and nearly and immediately concerned, his virtue, his property, and the security of his person: And where all these are best preserved and advanced, the government is best administered; and where they are not, the government is impotent, wicked, or unfortunate; and where the government is so, the people will be so, there being always and every where a certain sympathy and analogy between the nature of the government and the nature of the people. This holds true in every instance. Public men are the patterns of private; and the virtues and vices of the governors become quickly the virtues and vices of the governed.

Regis ad exemplum totus componitur orbis. *

Nor is it example alone that does it. Ill governments, subsisting by vice and rapine, are jealous of private virtue, and enemies to private property. *Opes pro crimine; & ob virtutes certissimum exitium.* ** They must be wicked and mischievous to be what they are; nor are they secure while any thing good or valuable is secure. Hence it is, that to drain, worry, and debauch their subjects, are the steady maxims of their politicks, their favourite arts of reigning. In this wretched situation the people, to be safe, must be poor and lewd: There will be but little industry where property is precarious; small honesty where virtue is dangerous.

Profuseness or frugality, and the like virtues or vices, which affect the publick, will be practised in the City, if they be practised in the court; and in the country, if they be in the City. Even Nero (that royal monster in man's shape) was adored by the common herd at Rome, as much as he was flattered by the great; and both the little and the great admired, or pretended to admire, his manners, and many to imitate them. Tacitus tells us, that those sort of people long lamented him, and rejoiced in the choice of a successor that resembled him, even the profligate Otho.

Good government does, on the contrary, produce great virtue, much happiness, and many people. Greece and Italy, while they continued free, were each of them, for the number of inhabitants, like one continued city; for virtue, knowledge, and great men, they were the standards of the world; and that age and country that could come nearest to them, has ever since been reckoned the happiest. Their government, their free government, was the root of all these advantages, and of all this felicity and renown; and in these great and fortunate states the people were the principals in the government; laws were made by their judgment and authority, and by their voice and commands were magistrates created and condemned. The city of Rome could conquer the world; nor could the great Persian monarch, the greatest then upon earth, stand before the face of one Greek city.

But what are Greece and Italy now? Rome has in it a herd of pampered monks, and a few starving lay inhabitants; the Campania of Rome, the finest spot of earth in Europe, is a desert. And for the modern Greeks, they are a few abject contemptible slaves, kept under ignorance, chains, and vileness, by the Turkish monarch, who keeps a great part of the globe intensely miserable, that he may seem great without being so.

Such is the difference between one government and another, and of such important concernment is the nature and administration of govern-

* "The world arranges itself after its ruler's pattern."

** "Wealth was tantamount to committing a crime and virtue brought certain destruction." Tacitus, *Historiae*, 1.2.

ment to a people. And to say that private men have nothing to do with government, is to say that private men have nothing to do with their own happiness and misery.

What is the publick, but the collective body of private men, as every private man is a member of the publick? And as the whole ought to be concerned for the preservation of every private individual, it is the duty of every individual to be concerned for the whole, in which himself is included.

One man, or a few men, have often pretended the publick, and meant themselves, and consulted their own personal interest, in instances essential to its well-being; but the whole people, by consulting their own interest, consult the publick, and act for the publick by acting for themselves: This is particularly the spirit of our constitution, in which the whole nation is represented; and our records afford instances, where the House of Commons have declined entering upon a question of importance, till they had gone into the country, and consulted their principals, the people: So far were they from thinking that private men had no right to meddle with government. In truth, our whole worldly happiness and misery (abating for accidents and diseases) are owing to the order or mismanagement of government; and he who says that private men have no concern with government, does wisely and modestly tell us, that men have no concern in that which concerns them most; it is saying that people ought not to concern themselves whether they be naked or clothed, fed or starved, deceived or instructed, and whether they be protected or destroyed: What nonsense and servitude in a free and wise nation!

For myself, who have thought pretty much of these matters, I am of opinion, that a whole nation are like to be as much attached to themselves, as one man or a few men are like to be, who may by many means be detached from the interest of a nation. It is certain that one man, and several men, may be bribed into an interest opposite to that of the publick; but it is as certain that a whole country can never find an equivalent for itself, and consequently a whole country can never be bribed. It is the eternal interest of every nation, that their government should be good; but they who direct it frequently reason a contrary way and find their own account in plunder and oppression; and while the publick voice is pretended to be declared, by one or a few, for vile and private ends, the publick know nothing of what is done, till they feel the terrible effects of it.

By the Bill of Rights, and the Act of Settlement, at the Revolution; a right is asserted to the people applying to the King and to the Parliament, by petition and address, for a redress of publick grievances and mismanagements, when such there are, of which they are left to judge; and the difference between free and enslaved countries lies principally here, that in the former, their magistrates must consult the voice and interest of the people; but in the latter, the private will, interest, and pleasure of the governors, are the sole end and motives of their administration.

Such is the difference between England and Turkey; which difference they who say that private men have no right to concern themselves with government, would absolutely destroy; they would convert magistrates into bashaws, and introduce popery into politicks. The late Revolution stands upon the very opposite maxim; and that any man dares to contradict it since the Revolution, would be amazing, did we not know that there are, in every country, hirelings who would betray it for a sop.

I am, &c.

C. JAMES OTIS, THE RIGHTS OF THE BRITISH COLONIES ASSERTED AND PROVED

1764

Introduction

Of the Origin of Government

The origin of *government* has in all ages no less perplexed the heads of lawyers and politicians than the origin of *evil* has embarrassed divines and philosophers, and 'tis probable the world may receive a satisfactory solution on *both* those points of inquiry at the *same* time.

The various opinions on the origin of *government* have been reduced to four. 1. That dominion is founded in *grace*. 2. On *force* or mere *power*. 3. On *compact*. 4. On *property*.

The first of these opinions is so absurd, and the world has paid so very dear for embracing it, especially under the administration of the *Roman pontiffs,* that mankind seem at this day to be in a great measure cured of their madness in this particular, and the notion is pretty generally exploded and hissed off the stage.

To those who lay the foundation of government in *force* and mere *brutal power* it is objected that their system destroys all distinction between right and wrong; that it overturns all morality, and leaves it to every man to do what is right in his own eyes; that it leads directly to *skepticism,* and ends in *atheism.* When a man's will and pleasure is his only rule and guide, what safety can there be either for him or against him, but in the point of a sword?

On the other hand the gentlemen in favor of the *original compact* have been often told that *their* system is chimerical and unsupported by reason or experience. Questions like the following have been frequently asked them, and may be again.

"When and where was the original compact for introducing government into any society, or for creating a society, made? Who were present and parties to such compact Who acted for infants and women, or who appointed guardians for them? Had these guardians power to bind both infants and women during life and their posterity after them? Is it in nature or reason that a guardian should by his own act perpetuate his power over his ward and bind him and his posterity in chains? Is not every man born as free by nature as his father? Has he not the same natural right to think and act and contract for himself? Is it possible for a man to have a natural right to make a slave of himself or of his posterity? Can a father supersede the laws of nature? What man is or ever was born free if every man is not? What will there be to distinguish the next generation of men from their forefathers, that they should not have the same right to make original compacts as their ancestors had? If every man has such right, may there not be as many original compacts as there are men and women born or to be born? Are not women born as free as men? Would it not be infamous to assert that the ladies are all slaves by nature? If every man and woman born or to be born has and will have a right to be consulted and must accede to the original compact before they can with any kind of justice be said to be bound by it, will not the compact be ever forming and never finished, ever making but never done? Can it with propriety be called a compact, original or derivative, that is ever in treaty but never concluded?"

When it has been said that each man is bound as soon as he accedes, and that the consent may be either express or tacit, it has been asked, "What is a *tacit* consent or compact Does it not appear plain that those who refuse their assent cannot be bound? If one is at liberty to accede or not, is he not also at liberty to *recede* on the discovery of some intolerable fraud and abuse that has been palmed upon him by the rest of the high contracting parties? Will not natural equity in several special cases rescind the original compacts of great men as effectually as those of little men are rendered null and void in the ordinary course of a court of chancery?"

There are other questions which have been started and a resolution of them demanded which may perhaps be deemed indecent by those who hold the prerogatives of an earthly monarch and even the power of a plantation government so sacred as to think it little less than blasphemy to inquire into their origin and foundation, while the government of the supreme *ruler* of the universe is every day discussed with less ceremony and decency than the administration of a petty German prince. I hope the reader will consider that I am at present only mentioning such questions as have been put by highfliers and others in church and state who would exclude all compact between a sovereign and his people, without offering my own sentiments upon them; this however I presume I may be allowed hereafter to do without offense. Those who want a full answer to them may consult Mr. Locke's discourses on government, M. De Vattel's law of nature and nations, and their own consciences.

"What state were Great Britain, Ireland, and the plantations left in by the abdication of James II? Was it a state of nature or of civil government? If a state of civil government, where were the supreme legislative and executive powers from the abdication to the election of William and Mary? Could the Lords and Commons be called a complete Parliament or supreme power without a King to head them? Did any law of the land or any original compact previous to the abdication provide that on such an event the supreme power should devolve on the two houses? Were not both houses so manifestly puzzled with the novelty and strangeness of the event, and so far from finding any act of Parliament, book case, or precedent to help them that they disputed in solemn conference by what name to call the action, and at last gave it one as new in our language and in that of Parliament as the thing itself was in fact"*

If on this memorable and very happy event the three kingdoms and the dominions fell back into a state of *nature,* it will be asked "Whether every man and woman were not then equal? If so, had not every one of them a natural and equitable right to be consulted in the choice of a new King or in the formation of a new original compact or government if any new form had been made? Might not the nation at that time have rightfully changed the monarchy into a republic or any form that might seem best? Could any change from a state of nature take place without universal consent, or at least without the consent of the *majority* of the individuals? Upon the principles of the original compact as commonly explained and understood, could a few hundred men who before the dissolution of the government had been called, and in fact were, lords, knights, and gentlemen have lawfully made that glorious deliverer and defender William III rightful King?" Such an one he certainly was, and such have been all his illustrious successors to the present happy times, when we have the joy to see the scepter swayed in justice, wisdom, and mercy by our lawful sovereign, George the Third, a prince who glories in being a Briton born, and whom may God long preserve and prosper.

"If upon the abdication all were reduced to a state of nature, had not apple women and orange girls as good a right to give their respectable suffrages for a new King as the philosopher, courtier, *petit-maître,* and politician? Were these and ten millions of others such ever more consulted on that occasion than the multitude now are in the adjustment of that real modern farce, an election of a King of the Romans, which serves as a contrast to the grandeur of the ancient republics, and shows the littleness of the modern German and some other gothic constitutions in their present degenerate state?

* On King James's leaving the kingdom and *abdicating* the government, the Lords would have the word *desertion* made use of, but the Commons thought it was not comprehensive enough, for that the King might then have liberty of returning. The Scots rightly called it a forfeiture of the crown, and this in plain English is the sense of the term *abdication* as by the Convention and every Parliament since applied. See the history and debates of the Convention, and the acts then made.

"In the election of William III, were the votes of Ireland and the plantations ever called for or once thought of till the affair was settled? Did the Lords and Commons who happened to be then in and about Westminster represent and act for the individuals not only of the three kingdoms but for all the *freeborn and as yet unconquered possessors and proprietors of their own money-purchased, blood-purchased plantations, which, till lately, have been defended with little or no assistance from Great Britain?* Were not those who did not vote in or for the new model at liberty upon the principles of the compact to remain in what some call the delectable state of nature, to which by the hypothesis they were reduced, or to join themselves to any other state whose solemn league and covenant they could subscribe? Is it not a first principle of the original compact that all who are bound should bind *themselves?* Will not common sense without much learning or study dictate obvious answers to all the above questions? And, say the opposers of the original compact and of the natural equality and liberty of mankind, will not those answers infallibly show that the doctrine is a piece of *metaphysical* jargon and *systematical* nonsense?" Perhaps not.

With regard to the fourth opinion, that *dominion is founded in property,* what is it but playing with words? Dominion in one sense of the term is synonymous with property, so one cannot be called the foundation of the other but as one *name* may appear to be the foundation or cause of another.

Property cannot be the foundation of dominion as synonymous with government; for on the supposition that property has a precarious existence antecedent to government, and though it is also admitted that the security of property is one end of government but that of little estimation even in the view of a *miser* when life and liberty of locomotion and further accumulation are placed in competition, it must be a very absurd way of speaking to assert that *one* end of government is the foundation of government. If the ends of government are to be considered as its foundation, it cannot with truth or propriety be said that government is founded on any *one* of those ends; and therefore government is not founded on property or its security *alone,* but at least on something else in conjunction. It is however true in fact and *experience,* as the great, the incomparable *Harrington* has most abundantly demonstrated in his *Oceana* and other divine writings, that empire follows the balance of *property.* 'Tis also certain that *property* in fact generally *confers* power, though the possessor of it may not have much more wit than a mole or a musquash: and this is too often the cause that riches are sought after without the least concern about the right application of them. But is the fault in the riches, or the general law of nature, or the unworthy possessor? It will never follow from all this that government is *rightfully* founded on *property* alone. What shall we say then? Is not government founded on *grace?* No. Nor on *force?* No. Nor on *compact* Nor *property?* Not altogether on either. Has it *any* solid foundation, any chief cornerstone but what accident, chance, or confusion may lay one moment and destroy the next? I think it has an everlasting foundation in the *unchangeable will of* GOD, the author of nature, whose laws never vary. The same omniscient, omnipotent, infinitely good and gracious Creator of the universe who has been pleased to make it necessary that what we call matter should *gravitate* for the celestial bodies to roll round their axes, dance their orbits, and perform their various revolutions in that beautiful order and concert which we all admire has made it *equally* necessary that from *Adam* and *Eve* to these degenerate days the different sexes should sweetly *attract* each other, form societies of *single* families, of which *larger* bodies and communities are as naturally, mechanically, and necessarily combined as the dew of heaven and the soft distilling rain is collected by the all-enlivening heat of the sun. *Government* is therefore most evidently founded *on the necessities of our nature.* It is by no means an *arbitrary* thing depending merely on *compact* or *human will* for its existence.

We come into the world forlorn and helpless; and if left alone and to ourselves at any one period of our lives, we should soon die in want, despair, or distraction. So kind is that hand, though little known or regarded, which feeds the rich and the poor, the blind and the naked, and provides for the safety of infants by the principle of parental love, and for that of men by government! We have a King who neither slumbers nor sleeps, but eternally watches for our good, whose rain falls on the just and on the unjust: yet while they live, move, and have their being in Him, and cannot account for either or for anything else, so stupid and wicked are some men as to deny his existence, blaspheme his most evident government, and disgrace their nature.

Let no man think I am about to commence advocate for *despotism* because I affirm that government is founded on the necessity of our natures and that an original supreme, sovereign, absolute, and uncontrollable *earthly* power *must* exist in and preside over every society, from whose final decisions there can be no appeal but directly to Heaven. It is therefore *originally* and *ultimately* in the people. I say this supreme absolute power is *originally* and *ultimately* in the people; and they never did in fact *freely,* nor can they *rightfully* make an absolute, unlimited renunciation of this divine right.[†] It is ever in the nature of the thing given in *trust* and on a condition the performance of which no mortal can dispense with, namely, that the person or persons on whom the sovereignty is conferred by the people shall *incessantly* consult *their* good. Tyranny of all kinds is to be abhorred, whether it be in the hands of one or of the few or of the many. And though "in the last age a generation of men sprung up that would flatter princes with an opinion that *they*

† The power of GOD Almighty is the power that can properly and strictly be called supreme and absolute. In the order of nature immediately under him comes the power of a simple *democracy* or the power of the whole over the whole. Subordinate to both these are all other political powers, from that of the French monarch to a petty constable.

have a *divine right* to absolute power," yet "slavery is so vile and miserable an estate of man and so directly opposite to the generous temper and courage of our nation that 'tis hard to be conceived that an *Englishman,* much less a *gentleman,* should plead for it,"†† especially at a time when the finest writers of the most polite nations on the continent of *Europe* are enraptured with the beauties of the civil constitution of *Great Britain,* and envy her no less for the *freedom* of her sons than for her immense *wealth* and *military* glory.

But let the *origin* of government be placed where it may, the *end* of it is manifestly the good of *the whole.* *Salus populi suprema lex esto* is of the law of nature and part of that grand charter given the human race (though too many of them are afraid to assert it) by the only monarch in the universe who has a clear and indisputable right to *absolute* power, because he is the *only* One who is *omniscient* as well as *omnipotent.*

It is evidently contrary to the first principles of reason that supreme *unlimited* power should be in the hands of *one* man. It is the greatest *"idolatry* begotten by *flattery* on the body of *pride"* that could induce one to think that a *single mortal* should be able to hold so great a power if ever so well inclined. Hence the origin of *deifying* princes: it was from the trick of gulling the vulgar into a belief that their tyrants were *omniscient,* and that it was therefore right that they should be considered as *omnipotent.* Hence the *dii majorum et minorum gentium,* the great, the monarchical, the little, provincial, subordinate, and subaltern gods, demigods, and semidemigods, ancient and modern. Thus deities of all kinds were multiplied and increased in *abundance,* for every devil incarnate who could enslave a people acquired a title to *divinity;* and thus the "rabble of the skies" was made up of locusts and caterpillars, lions, tigers, and harpies, and other devourers translated from plaguing the earth!*

The *end* of government being the *good* of mankind points out its great duties: it is above all things to provide for the security, the quiet, and happy enjoyment of life, liberty, and property. There is no one act which a government can have a *right* to make that does not tend to the advancement of the security, tranquillity, and prosperity of the people. If life, liberty, and property could be enjoyed in as great perfection in *solitude* as in *society* there would be no need of government. But the experience of ages has proved that such is the nature of man, a weak, imperfect being, that the valuable ends of life cannot be obtained without the union and assistance of many. Hence 'tis clear that men cannot live apart or independent of each other. In solitude men would perish, and yet they cannot live together without contests. These contests require some arbitrator to determine them. The necessity of a

†† Mr. Locke.

* Kingcraft and priestcraft have fallen out so often that 'tis a wonder this grand and ancient alliance is not broken off forever. Happy for mankind will it be when such a separation shall take place.

common, indifferent, and impartial judge makes all men seek one, though few find him in the *sovereign power* of their respective states or anywhere else in *subordination* to it.

Government is founded *immediately* on the necessities of human nature and *ultimately* on the will of God, the author of nature, who has not left it to men in general to choose whether they will be members of society or not, but at the hazard of their senses if not of their lives. Yet it is left to every man as he comes of age to choose *what society* he will continue to belong to. Nay, if one has a mind to turn *hermit,* and after he has been born, nursed, and brought up in the arms of society, and acquired the habits and passions of social life is willing to run the risk of starving alone, which is generally most unavoidable in a state of hermitage, who shall hinder him? I know of no human law founded on the law of *nature* to restrain him from separating himself from all the species if he can find it in his heart to leave them, unless it should be said it is against the great law of *self-preservation:* but of this every man will think himself *his own judge.*

The few *hermits* and *misanthropes* that have ever existed show that those states are *unnatural.* If we were to take out from them those who have made great *worldly* gain of their *godly* hermitage and those who have been under the madness of *enthusiasm* or *disappointed* hopes in their *ambitious* projects for the detriment of mankind, perhaps there might not be left ten from *Adam* to this day.

The form of government is by *nature* and by *right* so far left to the *individuals* of each society that they may alter it from a simple democracy or government of all over all to any other form they please. Such alteration may and ought to be made by express compact. But how seldom this right has been asserted, history will abundantly show. For once that it has been fairly settled by compact, *fraud, force,* or *accident* have determined it an hundred times. As the people have gained upon tyrants, these have been obliged to relax *only* till a fairer opportunity has put it in their power to encroach again.

But if every prince since *Nimrod* had been a tyrant, it would not prove a *right* to tyrannize. There can be no prescription old enough to supersede the law of nature and the grant of GOD Almighty, who has given to all men a natural right to be *free,* and they have it ordinarily in their power to make themselves so if they please.

Government having been proved to be necessary by the law of nature, it makes no difference in the thing to call it from a certain period *civil.* This term can only relate to form, to additions to or deviations from the substance of government: this being founded in nature, the superstructures and the whole administration should be conformed to the law of universal reason. A supreme legislative and a supreme executive power must be placed *somewhere* in every commonwealth. Where there is no other positive provision or compact to the contrary, those powers remain in the *whole body of the people*. It is also evident there can be but *one* best way of depositing those powers; but what that way is, mankind have been disputing in peace and in war more than five thousand years. If we could suppose the individuals of a community met to deliberate whether it were best to keep those powers in *their own* hands or dispose of them in *trust*, the following questions would occur:— Whether those two great powers of *legislation* and *execution* should remain united? If so, whether in the hands of the many or jointly or severally in the hands of a few, or jointly in some one individual? If both those powers are retained in the hands of the many, where nature seems to have placed them originally, the government is a simple *democracy* or a government of all over all. This can be administered only by establishing it as a first principle that the votes of the majority shall be taken as the voice of the whole. If those powers are lodged in the hands of a few, the government is an *aristocracy* or *oligarchy.** Here too the first principles of a practicable administration is that the majority rules the whole. If those great powers are both lodged in the hands of one man, the government is a *simple monarchy,* commonly though falsely called *absolute* if by that term is meant a right to do as one pleases.—*Sic volo, sic jubeo, stet pro ratione voluntas* belongs not of right to any mortal man.

The same law of nature and of reason is equally obligatory on a *democracy,* an *aristocracy,* and a *monarchy:* whenever the administrators in any of those forms deviate from truth, justice, and equity, they verge towards tyranny, and are to be opposed; and if they prove incorrigible they will be *deposed* by the people, if the people are not rendered too abject. Deposing the administrators of a *simple democracy* may sound oddly, but it is done every day and in almost every vote. A, B, and C, for example, make a *democracy*. Today A and B are for so vile a measure as a standing army. Tomorrow B and C vote it out. This is as really deposing the former administrators as setting up and making a new King is deposing the old one. *Democracy* in the one case and *monarchy* in the other still remain; all that is done is to change the administration.

The first principle and great end of government being to provide for the best good of all the people, this can be done only by a supreme legislative and executive ultimately in the people or whole community where GOD has placed it; but the inconveniences, not to say impossibility, attending the consultations and operations of a large body of people have made it necessary to transfer the power of the whole to a *few*. This necessity gave rise to deputation, proxy, or a right of representation.

A power of legislation without a power of execution in the same or other hands would be futile and vain. On the other hand, a power of

---

* For the sake of the unlettered reader 'tis noted that monarchy means the power of one great man, aristocracy and oligarchy that of a few, and democracy that of all men.

execution, supreme or subordinate, without an *independent* legislature would be perfect despotism.

D. THOMAS PAINE, COMMON SENSE

January 10, 1776

ON THE ORIGIN AND DESIGN OF GOVERNMENT IN GENERAL, WITH
CONCISE REMARKS ON THE ENGLISH CONSTITUTION

SOME writers have so confounded society with government, as to leave little or no distinction between them; whereas they are not only different, but have different origins. Society is produced by our wants, and government by our wickedness; the former promotes our happiness *positively* by uniting our affections, the latter *negatively* by restraining our vices. The one encourages intercourse, the other creates distinctions. The first is a patron, the last a punisher.

Society in every state is a blessing, but Government, even in its best state, is but a necessary evil; in its worst state an intolerable one: for when we suffer, or are exposed to the same miseries *by a Government*, which we might expect in a country *without Government*, our calamity is heightened by reflecting that we furnish the means by which we suffer. Government, like dress, is the badge of lost innocence; the palaces of kings are built upon the ruins of the bowers of paradise. For were the impulses of conscience clear, uniform and irresistibly obeyed, man would need no other lawgiver; but that not being the case, he finds it necessary to surrender up a part of his property to furnish means for the protection of the rest; and this he is induced to do by the same prudence which in every other case advises him, out of two evils to choose the least. Wherefore, security being the true design and end of government, it unanswerably follows that whatever form thereof appears most likely to ensure it to us, with the least expense and greatest benefit, is preferable to all others.

In order to gain a clear and just idea of the design and end of government, let us suppose a small number of persons settled in some sequestered part of the earth, unconnected with the rest; they will then represent the first peopling of any country, or of the world. In this state of natural liberty, society will be their first thought. A thousand motives will excite them thereto; the strength of one man is so unequal to his wants, and his mind so unfitted for perpetual solitude, that he is soon obliged to seek assistance and relief of another, who in his turn requires the same. Four or five united would be able to raise a tolerable dwelling in the midst of a wilderness, but one man might labour out the common period of life without accomplishing any thing; when he had felled his timber he could not remove it, nor erect it after it was removed; hunger in the mean time would urge him to quit his work, and every different want would call him a different way. Disease, nay even misfortune, would be death; for, though neither might be mortal, yet either would disable him from living, and reduce him to a state in which he might rather be said to perish than to die.

Thus necessity, like a gravitating power, would soon form our newly arrived emigrants into society, the reciprocal blessings of which would supercede, and render the obligations of law and government unnecessary while they remained perfectly just to each other; but as nothing but Heaven is impregnable to vice, it will unavoidably happen that in proportion as they surmount the first difficulties of emigration, which bound them together in a common cause, they will begin to relax in their duty and attachment to each other: and this remissness will point out the necessity of establishing some form of government to supply the defect of moral virtue.

Some convenient tree will afford them a State House, under the branches of which the whole Colony may assemble to deliberate on public matters. It is more than probable that their first laws will have the title only of Regulations and be enforced by no other penalty than public disesteem. In this first parliament every man by natural right will have a seat.

But as the Colony encreases, the public concerns will encrease likewise, and the distance at which the members may be separated, will render it too inconvenient for all of them to meet on every occasion as at first, when their number was small, their habitations near, and the public concerns few and trifling. This will point out the convenience of their consenting to leave the legislative part to be managed by a select number chosen from the whole body, who are supposed to have the same concerns at stake which those have who appointed them, and who will act in the same manner as the whole body would act were they present. If the colony continue encreasing, it will become necessary to augment the number of representatives, and that the interest of every part of the colony may be attended to, it will be found best to divide the whole into convenient parts, each part sending its proper number: and that the *elected* might never form to themselves an interest separate from the *electors*, prudence will point out the propriety of having elections often: because as the *elected* might by that means return and mix again with the general body of the *electors* in a few months, their fidelity to the public will be secured by the prudent reflection of not making a rod for themselves. And as this frequent interchange will establish a common interest with every part of the community, they will mutually and naturally support each other, and on this, (not on the unmeaning name of king,) depends the *strength of government, and the happiness of the governed.*

Here then is the origin and rise of government; namely, a mode rendered necessary by the inability of moral virtue to govern the world; here too is the design and end of government, viz. Freedom and security. And however our eyes may be dazzled with show, or our ears deceived by sound; however prejudice may warp our wills, or interest darken our understanding, the simple voice of nature and reason will say, 'tis right.

I draw my idea of the form of government from a principle in nature which no art can overturn, viz. that the more simple any thing is, the less liable it is to be disordered, and the easier repaired when disordered; and with this maxim in view I offer a few remarks on the so much boasted constitution of England. That it was noble for the dark and slavish times in which it was erected, is granted. When the world was overrun with tyranny the least remove therefrom was a glorious rescue. But that it is imperfect, subject to convulsions, and incapable of producing what it seems to promise, is easily demonstrated.

Absolute governments, (tho' the disgrace of human nature) have this advantage with them, they are simple; if the people suffer, they know the head from which their suffering springs; know likewise the remedy; and are not bewildered by a variety of causes and cures. But the constitution of England is so exceedingly complex, that the nation may suffer for years together without being able to discover in which part the fault lies; some will say in one and some in another, and every political physician will advise a different medicine.

I know it is difficult to get over local or long standing prejudices, yet if we will suffer ourselves to examine the component parts of the English constitution, we shall find them to be the base remains of two ancient tyrannies, compounded with some new Republican materials.

First.—The remains of Monarchical tyranny in the person of the King.

Secondly.—The remains of Aristocratical tyranny in the persons of the Peers.

Thirdly.—The new Republican materials, in the persons of the Commons, on whose virtue depends the freedom of England.

The two first, by being hereditary, are independent of the People; wherefore in a *constitutional sense* they contribute nothing towards the freedom of the State.

To say that the constitution of England is an *union* of three powers, reciprocally *checking* each other, is farcical; either the words have no meaning, or they are flat contradictions.

To say that the Commons is a check upon the King, presupposes two things.

First.—That the King it not to be trusted without being looked after; or in other words, that a thirst for absolute power is the natural disease of monarchy.

Secondly.—That the Commons, by being appointed for that purpose, are either wiser or more worthy of confidence than the Crown.

But as the same constitution which gives the Commons a power to check the King by withholding the supplies, gives afterwards the King a power to check the Commons, by empowering him to reject their other bills; it again supposes that the King is wiser than those whom it has already supposed to be wiser than him. A mere absurdity!

There is something exceedingly ridiculous in the composition of Monarchy; it first excludes a man from the means of information, yet empowers him to act in cases where the highest judgment is required. The state of a king shuts him from the World, yet the business of a king requires him to know it thoroughly; wherefore the different parts, by unnaturally opposing and destroying each other, prove the whole character to be absurd and useless.

Some writers have explained the English constitution thus: the King, say they, is one, the people another; the Peers are a house in behalf of the King, the commons in behalf of the people; but this hath all the distinctions of a house divided against itself; and though the expressions be pleasantly arranged, yet when examined they appear idle and ambiguous; and it will always happen, that the nicest construction that words are capable of, when applied to the description of something which either cannot exist, or is too incomprehensible to be within the compass of description, will be words of sound only, and though they may amuse the ear, they cannot inform the mind: for this explanation includes a previous question, viz. *how came the king by a power which the people are afraid to trust, and always obliged to check?* Such a power could not be the gift of a wise people, neither can any power, *which needs checking*, be from God; yet the provision which the constitution makes supposes such a power to exist.

But the provision is unequal to the task; the means either cannot or will not accomplish the end, and the whole affair is a *Felo de se:* for as the greater weight will always carry up the less, and as all the wheels of a machine are put in motion by one, it only remains to know which power in the constitution has the most weight, for that will govern: and tho' the others, or a part of them, may clog, or, as the phrase is, check the rapidity of its motion, yet so long as they cannot stop it, their endeavours will be ineffectual: The first moving power will at last have its way, and what it wants in speed is supplied by time.

That the crown is this overbearing part in the English constitution needs not be mentioned, and that it derives its whole consequence merely from being the giver of places and pensions is self-evident; wherefore, though we have been wise enough to shut and lock a door against absolute Monarchy, we at the same time have been foolish enough to put the Crown in possession of the key.

The prejudice of Englishmen, in favour of their own government, by King, Lords and Commons, arises as much or more from national pride than reason. Individuals are undoubtedly safer in England than in some

238

other countries: but the will of the king is as much the law of the land in Britain as in France, with this difference, that instead of proceeding directly from his mouth, it is handed to the people under the formidable shape of an act of parliament. For the fate of Charles the First hath only made kings more subtle—not more just.

Wherefore, laying aside all national pride and prejudice in favour of modes and forms, the plain truth is that *it is wholly owing to the constitution of the people, and not to the constitution of the government* that the crown is not as oppressive in England as in Turkey.

An inquiry into the *constitutional errors* in the English form of government, is at this time highly necessary; for as we are never in a proper condition of doing justice to others, while we continue under the influence of some leading partiality, so neither are we capable of doing it to ourselves while we remain fettered by any obstinate prejudice. And as a man who is attached to a prostitute is unfitted to choose or judge of a wife, so any prepossession in favour of a rotten constitution of government will disable us from discerning a good one.

OF MONARCHY AND HEREDITARY SUCCESSION

MANKIND being originally equals in the order of creation, the equality could only be destroyed by some subsequent circumstance: the distinctions of rich and poor may in a great measure be accounted for, and that without having recourse to the harsh ill-sounding names of oppression and avarice. Oppression is often the *consequence*, but seldom or never the *means* of riches; and tho' avarice will preserve a man from being necessitously poor, it generally makes him too timorous to be wealthy.

But there is another and great distinction for which no truly natural or religious reason can be assigned, and that is the distinction of men into KINGS and SUBJECTS. Male and female are the distinctions of nature, good and bad the distinctions of Heaven; but how a race of men came into the world so exalted above the rest, and distinguished like some new species, is worth inquiring into, and whether they are the means of happiness or of misery to mankind.

In the early ages of the world, according to the scripture chronology there were no kings; the consequence of which was, there were no wars; it is the pride of kings which throws mankind into confusion. Holland, without a king hath enjoyed more peace for this last century than any of the monarchical governments in Europe. Antiquity favours the same remark; for the quiet and rural lives of the first Patriarchs have a snappy something in them, which vanishes when we come to the history of Jewish royalty.

Government by kings was first introduced into the world by the Heathens, from whom the children of Israel copied the custom. It was the most prosperous invention the Devil ever set on foot for the promotion of idolatry. The Heathens paid divine honours to their deceased kings, and the Christian World hath improved on the plan by doing the same to their living ones. How impious is the title of sacred Majesty applied to a worm, who in the midst of his splendor is crumbling into dust!

As the exalting one man so greatly above the rest cannot be justified on the equal rights of nature, so neither can it be defended on the authority of scripture; for the will of the Almighty as declared by Gideon, and the prophet Samuel, expressly disapproves of government by Kings. All anti-monarchical parts of scripture, have been very smoothly glossed over in monarchical governments, but they undoubtedly merit the attention of countries which have their governments yet to form. *Render unto Cesar the things which are Cesar's* is the scripture doctrine of courts, yet it is no support of monarchical government, for the Jews at that time were without a king, and in a state of vassalage to the Romans.

Near three thousand years passed away, from the Mosaic account of the creation, till the Jews under a national delusion requested a king. Till then their form of government (except in extraordinary cases where the Almighty interposed) was a kind of Republic, administered by a judge and the elders of the tribes. Kings they had none, and it was held sinful to acknowledge any being under that title but the Lord of Hosts. And when a man seriously reflects on the idolatrous homage which is paid to the persons of kings, he need not wonder that the Almighty, ever jealous of his honour, should disapprove a form of government which so impiously invades the prerogative of Heaven.

Monarchy is ranked in scripture as one of the sins of the Jews, for which a curse in reserve is denounced against them. The history of that transaction is worth attending to.

The children of Israel being oppressed by the Midianites, Gideon marched against them with a small army, and victory thro' the divine interposition decided in his favour. The Jews, elate with success, and attributing it to the generalship of Gideon, proposed making him a king, saying, *Rule thou over us, thou and thy son, and thy son's son.* Here was temptation in its fullest extent; not a kingdom only, but an hereditary one; but Gideon in the piety of his soul replied, *I will not rule over you, neither shall my son rule over you.* THE LORD SHALL RULE OVER YOU. Words need not be more explicit: Gideon doth not decline the honour, but denieth their right to give it; neither doth he compliment them with invented declarations of his thanks, but in the positive style of a prophet charges them with disaffection to their proper Sovereign, the King of Heaven.

About one hundred and thirty years after this, they fell again into the same error. The hankering which the Jews had for the idolatrous customs of the Heathens, is something exceedingly unaccountable; but so it was, that laying hold of the misconduct of Samuel's two sons, who

240

were intrusted with some secular concerns, they came in an abrupt and clamorous manner to Samuel, saying, *Behold thou art old, and they sons walk not in thy ways, now make us a king to judge us like all the other nations.* And here we cannot observe but that their motives were bad, viz. that they might be *like* unto other nations, i. e. the Heathens, whereas their true glory lay in being as much *unlike* them as possible. *But the thing displeased Samuel when they said, give us a King to judge us; and Samuel prayed unto the Lord, and the Lord said unto Samuel, hearken unto the voice of the people in all that they say unto thee, for they have not rejected thee, but they have rejected me,* THAT I SHOULD NOT REIGN OVER THEM. *According to all the works which they have done since the day that I brought them up out of Egypt even unto this day, wherewith they have forsaken me, and served other Gods: so do they also unto thee. Now therefore hearken unto their voice, howbeit, protest solemnly unto them and show them the manner of the King that shall reign over them,* i.e. not of any particular King, but the general manner of the Kings of the earth whom Israel was so eagerly copying after. And notwithstanding the great distance of time and difference of manners, the character is still in fashion. *And Samuel told all the words of the Lord unto the people, that asked of him a King. And he said, This shall be the manner of the King that shall reign over you. He will take your sons and appoint them for himself for his chariots and to be his horsemen, and some shall run before his chariots* (this description agrees with the present mode of impressing men) *and he will appoint him captains over thousands and captains over fifties, will set them to ear his ground and to reap his harvest, and to make his instruments of war, and instruments of his chariots, And he will take your daughters to be confectionaries, and to be cooks, and to be bakers* (this describes the expense and luxury as well as the oppression of Kings) *and he will take your fields and your vineyards, and your olive yards, even the best of them, and give them to his servants. And he will take the tenth of your seed, and of your vineyards, and give them to his officers and to his servants* (by which we see that bribery, corruption, and favouritism, are the standing vices of Kings) *and he will take the tenth of your men servants, and your maid servants, and your goodliest young men, and your asses, and put them to his work: and he will take the tenth of your sheep, and ye shall be his servants, and ye shall cry out in that day because of your king which ye shall have chosen,* AND THE LORD WILL NOT HEAR YOU IN THAT DAY. This accounts for the continuation of Monarchy; neither do the characters of the few good kings which have lived since, either sanctify the title, or blot out the sinfulness of the origin; the high encomium of David takes no notice of him *officially as a King*, but only as a *man* after God's own heart. *Nevertheless the people refused to obey the voice of Samuel, and they said, Nay, but we will have a king over us, that we may be like all the nations, and that our king may judge us, and go out before us and fight our battles.* Samuel continued to reason with them but to no purpose; he set before them their ingratitude, but all would not avail; and seeing

241

them fully bent on their folly, he cried out, *I will call unto the Lord, and he shall send thunder and rain* (which was then a punishment, being in the time of wheat harvest) *that ye may perceive and see that your wickedness is great which ye have done in the sight of the Lord,* IN ASKING YOU A KING. *So Samuel called unto the Lord, and the Lord sent thunder and rain that day, and all the people greatly feared the Lord and Samuel. And all the people said unto Samuel, Pray for thy servants unto the Lord thy God that we die not, for* WE HAVE ADDED UNTO OUR SINS THIS EVIL, TO ASK A KING. These portions of scripture are direct and positive. They admit of no equivocal construction. That the Almighty hath here entered his protest against monarchical government is true, or the scripture is false. And a man hath good reason to believe that there is as much of kingcraft as priestcraft in withholding the scripture from the public in popish countries. For monarchy in every instance is the popery of government.

To the evil of monarchy we have added that of hereditary succession; and as the first is a degradation and lessening of ourselves, so the second, claimed as a matter of right, is an insult and imposition on posterity. For all men being originally equals, no one by birth could have a right to set up his own family in perpetual preference to all others for ever, and tho' himself might deserve some decent degree of honours of his contemporaries, yet his descendants might be far too unworthy to inherit them. One of the strongest natural proofs of the folly of hereditary right in Kings, is that nature disapproves it, otherwise she would not so frequently turn it into ridicule, by giving mankind an *Ass for a Lion.*

Secondly, as no man at first could possess any other public honors than were bestowed upon him, so the givers of those honors could have no power to give away the right of posterity, and though they might say "We choose you for our head," they could not without manifest injustice to their children say "that your children and your children's children shall reign over ours forever." Because such an unwise, unjust, unnatural compact might (perhaps) in the next succession put them under the government of a rogue or a fool. Most wise men in their private sentiments have ever treated hereditary right with contempt; yet it is one of those evils which when once established is not easily removed: many submit from fear, others from superstition, and the more powerful part shares with the king the plunder of the rest.

This is supposing the present race of kings in the world to have had an honorable origin: whereas it is more than probable, that, could we take off the dark covering of antiquity and trace them to their first rise, we should find the first of them nothing better than the principal ruffian of some restless gang, whose savage manners of pre-eminence in subtilty obtained him the title of chief among plunderers; and who by increasing in power and extending his depredations, overawed the quiet and defenseless to purchase their safety by frequent contributions. Yet his electors could have no idea of giving hereditary right to his descendants,

242

because such a perpetual exclusion of themselves was incompatible with the free and restrained principles they professed to live by. Wherefore, hereditary succession in the early ages of monarchy could not take place as a matter of claim, but as something casual or complemental; but as few or no records were extant in those days, the traditionary history stuff'd with fables, it was very easy, after the lapse of a few generations, to trump up some superstitious tale conveniently timed, Mahomet-like, to cram hereditary right down the throats of the vulgar. Perhaps the disorders which threatened, or seemed to threaten, on the decease of a leader and the choice of a new one (for elections among ruffians could not be very orderly) induced many at first to favour hereditary pretensions; by which means it happened, as it hath happened since, that what at first was submitted to as a convenience was afterwards claimed as a right.

England since the conquest hath known some few good monarchs, but groaned beneath a much larger number of bad ones: yet no man in his senses can say that their claim under William the Conqueror is a very honourable one. A French bastard landing with an armed Banditti and establishing himself king of England against the consent of the natives, is in plain terms a very paltry rascally original. It certainly hath no divinity in it. However it is needless to spend much time in exposing the folly of hereditary right; if there are any so weak as to believe it, let them promiscuously worship the Ass and the Lion, and welcome. I shall neither copy their humility, nor disturb their devotion.

Yet I should be glad to ask how they suppose kings came at first? The question admits but of three answers, viz. either by lot, by election, or by usurpation. If the first king was taken by lot, it establishes a precedent for the next, which excludes hereditary succession. Saul was by lot, yet the succession was not hereditary, neither does it appear from that transaction that there was any intention it ever should. If the first king of any country was by election, that likewise establishes a precedent for the next; for to say, that the right of all future generations is taken away, by the act of the first electors, in their choice not only of a king but of a family of kings for ever, hath no parallel in or out of scripture but the doctrine of original sin, which supposes the free will of all men lost in Adam; and from such comparison, and it will admit of no other, hereditary succession can derive no glory. For as in Adam all sinned, and as in the first electors all men obeyed; as in the one all mankind were subjected to Satan, and in the other to sovereignty; as our innocence was lost in the first, and our authority in the last; and as both disable us from re-assuming some former state and privilege, it unanswerably follows that original sin and hereditary succession are parallels. Dishonourable rank! inglorious connection! yet the most subtle sophist cannot produce a juster simile.

As to usurpation, no man will be so hardy as to defend it; and that William the Conqueror was an usurper is a fact not to be contradicted.

243

The plain truth is, that the antiquity of English monarchy will not bear looking into.

But it is not so much the absurdity as the evil of hereditary succession which concerns mankind. Did it ensure a race of good and wise men it would have the seal of divine authority, but as it opens a door to the *foolish*, the *wicked*, and the *improper*, it hath in it the nature of oppression. Men who look upon themselves born to reign, and others to obey, soon grow insolent. Selected from the rest of mankind, their minds are early poisoned by importance; and the world they act in differs so materially from the world at large, that they have but little opportunity of knowing its true interests, and when they succeed in the government are frequently the most ignorant and unfit of any throughout the dominions.

Another evil which attends hereditary succession is, that the throne is subject to be possessed by a minor at any age; all which time the regency acting under the cover of a king have every opportunity and inducement to betray their trust. The same national misfortune happens when a king worn out with age and infirmity enters the last stage of human weakness. In both these cases the public becomes a prey to every miscreant who can tamper successfully with the follies either of age or infancy.

The most plausible plea which hath ever been offered in favor of hereditary succession is, that it preserves a nation from civil wars; and were this true, it would be weighty; whereas it is the most bare-faced falsity ever imposed upon mankind. The whole history of England disowns the fact. Thirty kings and two minors have reigned in that distracted kingdom since the conquest, in which time there has been (including the revolution) no less than eight civil wars and nineteen Rebellions. Wherefore instead of making for peace,it makes against it, and destroys the very foundation it seems to stand upon.

The contest for monarchy and succession, between the houses of York and Lancaster, laid England in a scene of blood for many years. Twelve pitched battles besides skirmishes and sieges were fought between Henry and Edward. Twice was Henry prisoner to Edward, who in his turn was prisoner to Henry. And so uncertain is the fate of war and the temper of a nation, when nothing but personal matters are the ground of a quarrel, that Henry was taken in triumph from a prison to a palace, and Edward obliged to fly from a palace to a foreign land; yet, as sudden transitions of temper are seldom lasting, Henry in his turn was driven from the throne, and Edward re-called to succeed him. The parliament always following the strongest side.

This contest began in the reign of Henry the Sixth, and was not entirely extinguished till Henry the Seventh, in whom the families were united. Including a period of 67 years, viz. from 1422 to 1489.

In short, monarchy and succession have laid (not this or that kingdom only) but the world in blood and ashes. 'Tis a form of government which the word of God bears testimony against, and blood will attend it.

If we enquire into the business of a King, we shall find that in some countries they may have none; and after sauntering away their lives without pleasure to themselves or advantage to the nation, withdraw from the scene, and leave their successors to tread the same idle round. In absolute monarchies the whole weight of business civil and military lies on the King; the children of Israel in their request for a king urged this plea, "that he may judge us, and go out before us and fight our battles." But in countries where he is neither a Judge nor a General, as in England, a man would be puzzled to know what *is* his business.

The nearer any government approaches to a Republic, the less business there is for a King. It is somewhat difficult to find a proper name for the government of England. Sir William Meredith calls it a Republic; but in its present state it is unworthy of the name, because the corrupt influence of the Crown, by having all the places in its disposal, hath so effectually swallowed up the power, and eaten out the virtue of the House of Commons (the Republican part in the constitution) that the government of England is nearly as monarchical as that of France or Spain. Men fall out with names without understanding them. For 'tis the Republican and not the Monarchical part of the Constitution of England which Englishmen glory in, viz. the liberty of choosing an House of Commons from out of their own body—and it is easy to see that when Republican virtues fail, slavery ensues. Why is the constitution of England sickly, but because monarchy hath poisoned the Republic; the Crown hath engrossed the Commons.

In England a King hath little more to do than to make war and give away places; which, in plain terms, is to empoverish the nation and set it together by the ears. A pretty business indeed for a man to be allowed eight hundred thousand sterling a year for, and worshipped into the bargain! Of more worth is one honest man to society, and in the sight of God, than all the crowned ruffians that ever lived.

E. DEBATE IN THE PHILADELPHIA CONVENTION

June 6, 1787

In Committee of the whole

Mr. Pinkney according to previous notice & rule obtained, moved "that the first branch of the national Legislature be elected by the State Legislatures, and not by the people". contending that the people were less fit Judges <in such a case,> and that the Legislatures would be less likely to promote the adoption of the new Government, if they were to be excluded from all share in it.

Mr. Rutlidge 2ded. the motion.

Mr. Gerry.   Much depends on the mode of election.   In England, the people will probably lose their liberty from the smallness of the proportion having a right of suffrage.   Our danger arises from the opposite extreme: hence in Massts. the worst men get into the Legislature. Several members of that Body had lately been convicted of infamous crimes.   Men of indigence, ignorance & baseness, spare no pains however dirty to carry their point agst. men who are superior to the artifices practiced.   He was not disposed to run into extremes.   He was as much principled as ever agst. aristocracy and monarchy.   It was necessary on the one hand that the people should appoint one branch of the Govt. in order to inspire them with the necessary confidence.   But he wished the election on the other to be so modified as to secure more effectually a just preference of merit.   His idea was that the people should nominate certain persons in certain districts, out of whom the State Legislatures shd. make the appointment.

Mr. Wilson.   He wished for vigor in the Govt. but he wished that vigorous authority to flow immediately from the legitimate source of all authority.   The Govt. ought to possess not only 1st. the *force* but 2ndly. the *mind or sense* of the people at large.   The Legislature ought to be the most exact transcript of the whole Society.   Representation is made necessary only because it is impossible for the people to act collectively. The opposition was to be expected he said from the *Governments*, not from the Citizens of the States.   The latter had parted as was observed (by Mr. King) with all the necessary powers; and it was immaterial to them, by whom they were exercised, if well exercised.   The State officers were to be losers of power.   The people he supposed would be rather more attached to the national Govt. than to the State Govts. as being more important in itself, and more flattering to their pride.   There is no danger of improper elections if made by *large* districts.   Bad elections proceed from the smallness of the districts which give an opportunity to bad men to intrigue themselves into office.

Mr. Sherman.   If it were in view to abolish the State Govts. the elections ought to be by the people.   If the State Govts. are to be continued, it is necessary in order to preserve harmony between the national & State Govts. that the elections to the former shd. be made by the latter.   The right of participating in the National Govt. would be sufficiently secured to the people by their election of the State Legislatures.   The objects of the Union, he thought were few.   1. defence agst. foreign danger.   2. agst. internal disputes & a resort to force.   3. Treaties with foreign nations 4 regulating foreign commerce, & drawing revenue from it.   These & perhaps a few lesser objects alone rendered a Confederation of the States necessary.   All other matters civil & criminal would be much better in the hands of the States.   The people are more happy in small than large States.   States may indeed be too small as Rhode Island, & thereby be too subject to faction.   Some others were perhaps too large, the powers of Govt not being able to pervade them. He was for giving the General Govt. power to legislate and execute within a defined province.

Col. Mason. Under the existing Confederacy, Congs. represent the *States* not the *people* of the States: their acts operate on the *States* not on the individuals. The case will be changed in the new plan of Govt. The people will be represented; they ought therefore to choose the Representatives. The requisites in actual representation are that the Reps. should sympathize with their constituents; shd. think as they think, & feel as they feel; and that for these purposes shd. even be residents among them. Much he sd. had been alledged agst. democratic elections. He admitted that much might be said; but it was to be considered that no Govt. was free from imperfections & evils; and that improper elections in many instances, were inseparable from Republican Govts. But compare these with the advantage of this Form in favor of the rights of the people, in favor of human nature. He was persuaded there was a better chance for proper elections by the people, if divided into large districts, than by the State Legislatures. Paper money had been issued by the latter when the former were against it. Was it to be supposed that the State Legislatures then wd. not send to the Natl. legislature patrons of such projects. if the choice depended on them.

Mr. Madison considered an election of one branch at least of the Legislature by the people immediately, as a clear principle of free Govt. and that this mode under proper regulations had the additional advantage of securing better representatives, as well as of avoiding too great an agency of the State Governments in the General one.—He differed from the member from Connecticut (Mr. Sherman) in thinking the objects mentioned to be all the principal ones that required a National Govt. Those were certainly important and necessary objects; but he combined with them the necessity, of providing more effectually for the security of private rights, and the steady dispensation of Justice. Interferences with these were evils which had more perhaps than any thing else, produced this convention. Was it to be supposed that republican liberty could long exist under the abuses of it practiced in <some of> the States. The gentleman (Mr. Sherman) had admitted that in a very small State, faction & oppression wd. prevail. It was to be inferred then that wherever these prevailed the State was too small. Had they not prevailed in the largest as well as the smallest tho' less than in the smallest; and were we not thence admonished to enlarge the sphere as far as the nature of the Govt. would admit. This was the only defence agst. the inconveniences of democracy consistent with the democratic form of Govt. All civilized Societies would be divided into different Sects, Factions, & interests, as they happened to consist of rich & poor, debtors & creditors, the landed the manufacturing, the commercial interests, the inhabitants of this district, or that district, the followers of this political leader or that political leader, the disciples of this religious sect or that religious sect. In all cases where a majority are united by a common interest or passion, the rights of the minority are in danger. What motives are to restrain them? A prudent regard to the maxim that honesty is the best policy is found by experience to be as little regarded by bodies of men as by individuals. Respect for character is always diminished in proportion to the number among whom the blame or praise is to be divided. Conscience, the only remaining tie is known to be inadequate in individuals: In large numbers, little is to be expected from it. Besides, Religion itself may become a motive to persecution & oppression.—These observations are verified by the Histories of every Country antient & modern. In Greece & Rome the rich & poor, the creditors & debtors, as well as the patricians & plebeians alternately oppressed each other with equal unmercifulness. What a source of oppression was the relation between the parent Cities of Rome, Athens & Carthage, & their respective provinces: the former possessing the power & the latter being sufficiently distinguished to be separate objects of it? Why was America so justly apprehensive of Parliamentary injustice? Because G. Britain had a separate interest real or supposed, & if her authority had been admitted, could have pursued that interest at our expense. We have seen the mere distinction of colour made in the most enlightened period of time, a ground of the most oppressive dominion ever exercised by man over man. What has been the source of those unjust laws complained of among ourselves? Has it not been the real or supposed interest of the major number? Debtors have defrauded their creditors. The landed interest has borne hard on the mercantile interest. The Holders of one species of property have thrown a disproportion of taxes on the holders of another species. The lesson we are to draw from the whole is that where a majority are united by a common sentiment and have an opportunity, the rights of the minor party become insecure. In a Republican Govt. the Majority if united have always an opportunity. The only remedy is to enlarge the sphere, & thereby divide the community into so great a number of interests & parties, that in the 1st. place a majority will not be likely at the same moment to have a common interest separate from that of the whole or of the minority; and in the 2d. place, that in case they shd. have such an interest, they may not be apt to unite in the pursuit of it. It was incumbent on us then to try this remedy, and with that view to frame a republican system on such a scale & in such a form as will controul all the evils wch. have been experienced.

Mr. Dickinson considered it as essential that one branch of the Legislature shd. be drawn immediately from the people; and as expedient that the other shd. be chosen by the Legislatures of the States. This combination of the State Govts. with the National Govt. was as politic as it was unavoidable. In the formation of the Senate we ought to carry it through such a refining process as will assimilate it as near as may be to the House of Lords in England. He repeated his warm eulogiums on the British Constitution. He was for a strong National Govt. but for leaving the States a considerable agency in the System. The objection agst. making the former dependent on the latter might be obviated by giving to the Senate an authority permanent & irrevocable for three, five or seven years. Being thus independent they will speak & decide with becoming freedom.

Mr. Read. Too much attachment is betrayed to the State Govermts. We must look beyond their continuance. A national Govt. must soon of necessity swallow all of them up. They will soon be reduced to the mere office of electing the national Senate. He was agst. patching up the old federal System: he hoped the idea wd. be dismissed. It would be like putting new cloth on an old garment. The confederation was founded on temporary principles. It cannot last: it cannot be amended. If we do not establish a good Govt. on new principles, we must either go to ruin, or have the work to do over again. The people at large are wrongly suspected of being averse to a Genl. Govt. The aversion lies among interested men who possess their confidence.

Mr. Pierce was for an election by the people as to the 1st. branch & by the States as to the 2d. branch; by which means the Citizens of the States wd. be represented both *individually* & *collectively*.

General Pinkney wished to have a good national Govt. & at the same time to leave a considerable share of power in the States. An election of either branch by the people scattered as they are in many States, particularly in S. Carolina was totally impracticable. He differed from gentlemen who thought that a choice by the people wd. be a better guard agst. bad measures, than by the Legislatures. A majority of the people in S. Carolina were notoriously for paper money as a legal tender; the Legislature had refused to make it a legal tender. The reason was that the latter had some sense of character and were restrained by that consideration. The State Legislatures also he said would be more jealous, & more ready to thwart the National Govt. if excluded from a participation in it. The Idea of abolishing these Legislatures wd. never go down.

Mr. Wilson, would not have spoken again, but for what had fallen from Mr. Read; namely, that the idea of preserving the State Govts. ought to be abandoned. He saw no incompatability between the national & State Govts. provided the latter were restrained to certain local purposes; nor any probability of their being devoured by the former. In all confederated systems antient & modern the reverse had happened; the Generality being destroyed gradually by the usurpations of the parts composing it.

On the question for electing the 1st. branch by the State Legislatures as moved by Mr. Pinkney; <it was negatived:>

Mass no. Ct. ay. N. Y. no. N. J. ay. Pa. no. Del. no. Md. no. Va. no. N. C. no. S. C. ay. Geo. no. [Ayes—3; noes—8.]

F. JOHN ADAMS, A DEFENCE OF THE CONSTITUTIONS OF GOVERNMENT OF THE UNITED STATES OF AMERICA

1787

BOOK III, LETTER III.

PADOUA.

Dear Sir,

THE elements and definitions in most of the arts and sciences are understood alike, by men of education, in all the nations of Europe; but in the science of legislation, which is not of the least importance to be understood, there is a confusion of languages, as if men were but lately come from Babel. Scarcely any two writers, much less nations, agree in using words in the same sense. Such a latitude, it is true, allows a scope for politicians to speculate, like merchants with false weights, artificial credit, or base money, and to deceive the people, by making the same word adored by one party, and execrated by another. The union of the people, in any principle, rule, or system, is thus rendered impossible; because superstition, prejudice, habit, and passions, are so differently attached to words, that you can scarcely make any nation understand itself. The words monarchy, aristocracy, democracy, king, prince, lords, commons, nobles, patricians, plebeians, if carefully attended to, will be found to be used in different senses, perpetually by different nations, by different writers in the same nation, and even by the same writers in different pages. The word king for example: Ask a Frenchmen what is a king, his answer will be, A man with a crown and sceptre, throne and footstool, anointed at Rheims, who has the making, executing, and interpreting of all laws. Ask an Englishman; his idea will comprehend the throne, footstool, crown, sceptre, and anointing, with one third of the legislative power and the whole of the executive, with an estate in his office to him and his heirs. Ask a Pole; and he tells you, It is a magistrate chosen for life, with scarcely any power at all. Ask an inhabitant of Liege, and he tells you, It is a bishop, and his office is only for life. The word prince is another remarkable instance: In Venice it means the senate, and sometimes by courtesy, the doge, whom some of the Italian writers call a mere testa di legno: in France, the eldest sons of dukes are princes, as well as the descendants of the blood royal: in Germany, even the rhingravers are princes; and in Russia, several families, who were not descended from nor allied to royal blood, anciently obtained, by grant of the sovereign, the title of prince, descendible to all their posterity; the consequence of which has been, that the number of princes in that country is at this day prodigious; and the philosopher of Geneva, in imitation of the Venetians, professedly calls the executive power, wherever lodged, The Prince.—How is it possible that whole nations should be made to comprehend the principles and rules of government, until they shall learn to understand one anothers meanings by words? But of all the words, in all languages, perhaps there has been none so much abused in this way as the words *republick, commonwealth,* and *popular state.* In the Rerum Publicarum Collectio, of which there are fifty and odd volumes, and many of them very incorrect, France, Spain and Portugal, the four great empires, the Babylonian, Persian, Greek, and Roman, and even the Ottoman, are all denominated republics. If, indeed, a republic signifies nothing but public affairs, it is equally applicable to all nations; and every kind of government, despotisms, monarchies, aristocracies, democracies, and every possible or imaginable composition of them, are all republics: there is, no doubt, a public good and evil, a common wealth and a common impoverishment, in all of them. Others define a republic to be a government of more than one: this will exclude only the despotisms; for a monarchy administered by laws, requires at least magistrates to register them, and consequently more than one person in the government. Some comprehend under the term only aristocracies and democracies, and mixtures of these, without any distinct executive power. Others again, more rationally, define a republic to signify only a government, in which all men, rich and poor, magistrates and subjects, officers and people, masters and servants, the first citizen and the last, are equally subject to the laws. This indeed appears to be the true, and only true definition of a republic. The word res, every one knows, signified, in the Roman language, wealth, riches, property; the word publicus, quasi populicus, and per Sync. pôplicus, signified public, common, belonging to the people; res publica therefore was publica res, the wealth, riches, or property of the people *. Res populi, and the original meaning of the word republic, could be no other than a government in which the property of the people predominated and governed: and it had more relation to property than liberty: it signified a government, in which the property of the public, or people, and of every one of them, was secured and protected by law. This idea, indeed, implies liberty; because property cannot be secure, unless the man be at liberty to acquire, use, or part with it, at his discretion, and unless he have his personal liberty of life and limb, motion and rest, for that purpose: it implies, moreover, that the property and liberty of all men, not merely of a majority, should be safe; for the people, or public, comprehends more than a majority, it comprehends all and every individual: and the property of every citizen is a part of the public property, as each citizen is a part of the public, people, or community. The property, therefore, of every man has a share in government, and is more powerful than any citizen, or party of citizens; it is governed only by the law. There is, however, a peculiar sense in which the words republic, commonwealth, popular state, are used by English and French writers; who mean by them a democracy, or rather

* See any of the common dictionaries,
Soranus, Stephens, Ainsworth.

a representative democracy: a government in one centre, and that centre the nation; that is to say, that centre a single assembly, chosen at stated periods by the people, and invested with the whole sovereignty; the whole legislative, executive, and judicial power, to be exercised in a body, or by committees, as they shall think proper. This is the sense in which it was used by Marchament Nedham, and in this sense it has been constantly used from his time to ours, even by writers of the most mathematical precision, the most classical purity, and extensive learning. What other authority there may be for this use of those words is not known: none has been found, except in the following observations of Portinari, in which there are several other inaccuracies; but they are here inserted, chiefly because they employ the words republic, common-wealth, and popular state, in the same sense with the English and French writers.

"We may say with the philosopher *, that six things are so necesary to a city, that without them it cannot stand. 1. The first is provisions, without which its inhabitants cannot live. 2. The second is clothes, habitations, houses, and other things which depend upon the arts, without which civil and political life cannot subsist. 3. The third is arms, which are necessary to defend the city from its enemies, and to repress the boldness of those who rebel against the laws. 4. The fourth is money, most necessary to a city in peace and in war. 5. The fifth is the care of divine worship. 6. The sixth is the administration of justice, and the government of the people.—For the first are necessary, cultivators of the land; for the second, artificers; for the third, soldiers; for the fourth merchants and capitalists; for the fifth, priests; and for the sixth judges and magistrates. Seven sorts of men, therefore, are necessary to a city, husbandmen, artificers, soldiers, merchants, rich men, priests, and judges **.—But, according to the same philosopher ***, as in the body natural not all those things, without which it is never found, are parts of it, but only instruments subservient to some uses, as in animals the horns, the nails, the hair, so not all those seven sorts of men are parts of the city; but some of them, viz. the husbandmen, the artificers, and the merchants, are only instruments useful to civil life, as is thus demonstrated:—A city is constituted for felicity, as to its ultimate end; and human felicity, here below, is reposed, according to the same philosopher, in the operations of virtue, and chiefly in the exertions of wisdom and prudence: those men, therefore, are not parts of a city, the operations of whom are not directed to those virtues; such are the husbandmen, who are occupied, not in wisdom and prudence, but in labouring the earth; such are the artisans, who fatigue themselves night and day to gain a livelihood for themselves and their poor families; such, finally, are the merchants, who watch and labour continually, not in

* Della Felicita di Padova, di Angelo Por-tenari Padovano Augost. edit. in Padova per Pietro Paolo Tozzi, 1623, p. 115.

** Arist. Polit. lib. vii. c. 8.

*** Arist. Polit. lib. vii. c. 9.

wisdom and prudence, but in the acquisition of gold. It is therefore clear, that neither husbandmen, artificers, nor merchants, are parts of a city, nor ought to be numbered among the citizens, but only as instruments which subserve to certain uses and conveniences of the city."—We must pause here and admire! The foregoing are not only the grave sentiments of Portenari and of Aristotle, but it is the doctrine almost of the whole earth, and of all mankind: not only every despotism, empire, and monarchy, in Asia, Africa, and Europe, but every aristocratical republic, has adopted it in all its latitude. There are only two or three of the smallest cantons in Switzerland, besides England, who allow husbandmen, artificers, and merchants, to be citizens, or to have any voice or share in the government of the state, or in the choice or appointment of any who have. There is no doctrine, and no fact, which goes so far as this towards forfeiting to the human species the character of rational creatures. Is it not amazing, that nations should have thus tamely surrendered themselves, like so many flocks of sheep, into the hands of shepherds, whose great solicitude to devour the lambs, the wool, and the flesh, scarcely leave them time to provide water or pasture for the animals, or even shelter against the weather and the wolves!

It is indeed impossible that the several descriptions of men, last enumerated, should, in a great nation and extensive territory, ever assemble in a body to act in concert; and the ancient method of taking the sense of an assembly of citizens in the capital, as in Rome for example, for the sense of all the citizens of an whole republic, or a large empire, was very imperfect, and extremely exposed to corruption: but, since the invention of representative assemblies, much of that objection is removed, though even that was no sufficient reason for excluding farmers, merchants, and artificers, from the rights of citizens. At present an husbandman, merchant, or artificer, provided he has any small property, by which he may be supposed to have a judgment and will of his own, instead of depending for his daily bread on some patron or master, is a sufficient judge of the qualifications of a person to represent him in the legislature. A representative assembly, fairly constituted, and made an integral part of the sovereignty, has power for ever to controul the rich and illustrious in another assembly, and a court and king where there is a king; this too is the only instrument by which the body of the people can act; the only way in which their opinions can be known and collected; the only means by which their wills can be united, and their strength exerted, according to any principle or continued system. It is sometimes said, that mobs are a good mode of expressing the sense, the resentments, and feelings of the people. Whig mobs to be sure are meant! But if the principle is once admitted, liberty and the rights of mankind will infallibly be betrayed; for it is giving liberty to Tories and courtiers to excite mobs as well as patriots: and all history and experience shews, that mobs are more easily excited by courtiers and princes, than by more virtuous men, and more honest friends of liberty. It is often said too, that farmers, merchants, and mechanics, are too inattentive to public affairs, and too patient under oppression. This is undoubtedly true, and will for ever be so; and, what is worse, the most sober, industrious, and peaceable of them, will for ever be the least attentive, and the least disposed to exert themselves in hazardous and disagreeable efforts of resistance. The only practicable method therefore of giving to farmers, &c. the equal right of citizens, and their proper weight and influence in society, is by elections, frequently repeated, of an house of commons, an assembly which shall be an essential part of the sovereignty. The meanest understanding is equal to the duty of saying who is the man in his neighborhood whom he most esteems, and loves best, for his knowledge, integrity, and benevolence. The understandings, however, of husbandmen, merchants, and mechanics, are not always the meanest: there arise, in the course of human life, many among them of the most splendid geniuses, the most active and benevolent dispositions, and most undaunted bravery. The moral equality that Nature has unalterably established among men give these an undoubted right to have every road opened to them for advancement in life and in power that is open to any others. These are the characters which will be discovered in popular elections, and brought forward upon the stage, where they may exert all their faculties, and enjoy all the honours, offices, and commands, both in peace and war, of which they are capable. The dogma of Aristotle, and the practice of the world, is the most unphilosophical, the most inhuman and cruel, that can be conceived. Until this wicked position, which is worse than the slavery of the ancient republics, or modern West Indies, shall be held up to the derision and contempt, the execration and horror of mankind, it will be to little purpose to talk or write about liberty. This doctrine of Aristotle is the more extraordinary, as it seems to be inconsistent with his great and common principles *, "that an happy life must arise from a course of virtue; that virtue consists in a medium; and that the middle life is the happiest. In every city the people are divided into three sorts, the very rich, the very poor, and the middle sort. If it is admitted that the medium is the best, it follows that, even in point of fortune, a mediocrity is preferable. The middle state is most compliant to reason: those who are very beautiful, or strong, or noble, or rich; or, on the contrary, those who are very poor, weak, or mean; with difficulty obey reason. The former are capricious and flagitious; the latter, rascally and mean; the crimes of each arising from their different excesses. Those who excel in riches, friends, and influence, are not willing to submit to command or law: this begins at home, were they are brought up too delicately, when boys, to obey their preceptors. The constant want of what the rich enjoy makes the poor too mean: the poor know not how to command, but are in the habit of being commanded, too often as slaves. The rich know not how to submit to any command; nor do they know how to rule over freemen, or to command others, but

---

* Aristot. Pol. lib. iv. c. 11.

254

despotically. A city composed only of the rich and the poor, but consists of masters and slaves, not freemen; where one party must despise, and the other hate; where there is no possibility of friendship, or equality, or community, which supposes affection. It is the genius of a free city to be composed, as much as possible, of equals; and equality will be best preserved when the greatest part of the inhabitants are in the middle state. These will be best assured of safety as well as equality: they will not covet nor steal, as the poor do, what belongs to the rich; nor will what they have be coveted or stolen: without plotting against any one, or have any one plot against them, they will live free from danger. For which reason Phocilides * wisely wishes for the middle state, as being most productive of happiness. It is plain then that the most perfect community must be among those who are in the middle rank; and those states are best instituted wherein these are a larger and more respectable part if possible, than both the other: or, if that cannot be, at least than either of them separate: so that, being thrown into the balance, it may prevent either scale from preponderating. It is therefore the greatest happiness which the citizen can enjoy, to possess a moderate and convenient fortune. When some possess too much, and others nothing at all, the government must either be in the hands of the meanest rabble, or else a pure oligarchy. The middle state is best, as being least liable to those seditions and insurrections which disturb the community; and for the same reason extensive governments are least liable to these inconveniences: for there those in the middle state are very numerous; whereas, in small ones, it is easy to pass to the two extremes, so as hardly to have any medium remaining, but the one half rich, and the other poor. We ought to consider, as a proof of this, that the best lawgivers were those in the middle rank of life, among whom was Solon, as is evident from his poems, and Lycurgus, for he was not a king, and Charondas, and indeed most others. Hence so many free states have changed either to democracies or oligarchies; for whenever the number of those in the middle state has been too small, those who were the more numerous, whether the rich or the poor, always overpowered them, and assumed to themselves the administration. When, in consequence of their disputes and quarrels with each other, either the rich get the better of the poor, or the poor of the rich, neither of them will establish a free state, but, as a record of their victory, one which inclines to their own principles, and form either a democracy or an oligarchy. It is indeed an established custom of cities not to desire an equality, but either to aspire to govern, or, when they are conquered, to submit,"—These are some of the wisest sentiments of Aristotle; but can you reconcile them with his other arbitrary doctrine, and tyrannical exclusion of husbandmen, merchants, and tradesmen, from the rank and rights of citizens? These, or at least those of them who have acquired property enough to be exempt from daily dependence on others, are the

* After Agur.

real middling people, and generally as honest and independent as any: these, however, it must be confessed, are too inattentive to public and national affairs, and too apt to submit to oppression; when they have been provoked beyond all bearing, they have aimed at demolishing the government, and when they have done that, they have sunk into their usual inattention, and left others to erect a new one as rude and ill-modelled as the former. A representative assembly, elected by them, is the only way in which they can act in concert; but they have always allowed themselves to be cheated by false, imperfect, partial, and inadequate representations of themselves, and have never had their full and proper share of power in a state.—But to proceed with Portenari. "The other kinds of men," says he, "viz. the rich, the soldiers, the priests, and the judges, are parts of the city, and properly citizens. The first, because riches are instruments for generating and conserving virtue in the citizens. The second, because it is necessary that military men, besides the virtue of fortitude, should be adorned with prudence, to know the times and occasions proper for undertaking an enterprize. The third, because the priests ought to be examples of every virtue to the people, and give themselves to the contemplation of divine things. The fourth, because the judges and rectors of a city, to judge and govern rightly, have occasion more than all the others for science and prudence, which are the true lights and guides of human actions."—If these are proper arguments for admitting these descriptions of men into the order of citizens, instead of being reasons for excluding merchants, &c. they are of proportional weight for admitting them.—"As to the form of government, which is the other part of the animated city, let us say with those wise men who have written of civil dominion and public administration, as Plato *, Aristotle **, Polybius ***, Plutarch †, and others ††, that the simple forms of good government are three, to which are opposed three other forms of bad government. The first form of good government is monarchy, or kingdom, and is the absolute and independent dominion of one man alone, who has for the ultimate end of his operations the public good, and the best state of the city, and who has the same relation to his subjects that the shepherd has to his flock, and the father to his children. Such were the monarchies of the Assyrians, Medes, Persians, Macedonians, Scythians, Egyptians, and Romans, from the beginning of their reign to the creation of the consuls, and, after the extinction of the Roman republic, under the empire of the Cæsars. To monarchy is opposed ††† that form of government which is called tyranny, in which one alone domineers, who has no thoughts of the public good, but whose scope is to depress and exterminate the citizens, to whom he

---

* 4 & 8 de Leg. & in Civili, seu de Regno.
** 3 Polit. c. 7, 8. & 8 Eth. c. 10.
*** Lib. vi.
† De Unius in Repub. Domin.
†† Sigon. de Ant. Jur. Civ. Rom. lib, i. c. 1.

††† Plutar. Loc. Cit. Beros. lib. iv. Diodor. lib. i. 3. 10. Justin. lib. i. 2. 3. Oros. lib. i. & seq. Herod. lib. i. 2. Liv. et alii script. Rom. Hist.

shows himself a rapacious monster after their property, and a cruel beast of prey after their lives; such as were Phalaris in Agrigentum *, Dionysius in Syracuse **, and Nero in Rome ***. The second form of good government is aristocracy, according to which the dominion is held by those who, above all others, are adorned with virtue, prudence, and benevolence; who directing all their actions to the utility and common dignity of the city, procure it an happy and blessed state. This species of government is called also, the regimen of the better sort (optimates), either because the best men of the city bear rule, or because they look, in all their operations, to the best and most perfect state of the city. This manner of government was used by the Spartans. To this form of government is opposed oligarchy, which is a principality of the most rich and powerful, who, for the most part, are few; who, depressing and robbing of their property the less rich, and crushing with intolerable weight the poor, make a regimen full of arrogance and of violence, and are like wolves among lambs. Such was the dominion of the Triumvirs in Rome who having oppressed the republic, proscribed and put to death many good citizens, and plundered their property: exalting the seditious and perverse, and abasing good men, they distempered Rome with their contagious wickedness; and of a city, the capital of the world, they made it a den of robbers †. The third form of good government, not having a proper name, was called by the Greeks politia, and by the Latins, respublica, a name common to every species of government. *This is the dominion of the multitude, viz. of the whole body of the city, composed of all sorts of citizens, rich and poor, nobles and plebeians, wise and foolish, which is also called a popular government.* All this body, which contains men, some endowed with prudence and wisdom, some inclined to virtue and persuadable to all good works, by the conversation and familiarity which they have with the prudent and learned, employ all their care, labour, and industry, to the end that the city flourish in all those things which are necessary and convenient for living well and happily, such as was at one one time the government of the Athenians ††. To this species of good government is opposed democracy; according to which the most abject plebeians, and the vilest vulgar, hold the nomination for their own private interest, by which they oppress the rich and the noble, and aggrandize and enrich the poor and the ignoble, as the two brothers, the Gracchi, began to do in Rome †††. . . .

BOOK III, LETTER VI.

The right Constitution of a Commonwealth, examined.

Dear Sir,

THE English nation, for their improvements in the theory of government, has, at least, more merit with the human race than any other

---

* Val. Max. lib. ix. c. 2. Cic. Verr. 5.

** Cic. 2 de Offic. Plat. Epist. vii. Diodor. lib. xiv.

*** Suet. in Neron. Tacit. 14 Annal.

† Appian. 4 de Bel. Civ. Plut. in Ant.

†† Plut. de Unius in Rep. Dominio. Thucid. lib. ii. in Orat. Periclis. Sig. de Repub. Athen. lib. i. c. 5.

††† Appian. 1 de Bel. Civ. Plutarch in Gracchis.

among the moderns. The late most beautiful and liberal speculations of many writers, in various parts of Europe, are manifestly derived from English sources. Americans too ought for ever to acknowledge their obligations to English writers, or rather have as good a right to indulge a pride in the recollection of them as the inhabitants of the three kingdoms. The original plantation of our country was occasioned, her continual growth has been promoted, and her present liberties have been established, by these generous theories. There have been three periods in the history of England, in which the principles of government have been anxiously studied, and very valuable productions published, which at this day, if they are not wholly forgotten in their native country are perhaps more frequently read abroad than at home.—The first of these periods was that of the Reformation, as early as the writings of Machiavel himself, who is called the great restorer of the true politics. "The Shorte Treatise of Polticke Power, and of the true Obedience which Subjects owe to Kyngs and other civile Governors, with an exhortation to all true natural Englishmen, compyled by John Ponnet, D.D." was printed in 1556, and contains all the essential principles of liberty which were afterwards dilated on by Sidney and Locke. This writer is clearly for a mixed government, in three equiponderant branches, as appears by these words, p. 7. "In some countreyes they were content to be governed, and have the laws executed, by one king or judge; in some places by many of the best forte; in some places by the people of the lowest forte; and in some places also by the king, nobilitie, and the people all together. And these diverse kyndes of states, or policies had their distincte names; as where one ruled a manarchie; where many of the best, aristocratie; and where the multitude, democratie; and where all together, that is a king, the nobilitie, and commons, a mixture state; and which men by long continuance have judged to be the best sort of all: for where that mixture state was exercised, there did the commonwealthe longest continue."—The second period was the Interregnum, and indeed the whole interval between 1640 and 1660. In the course of those twenty years, not only Ponnet and others were reprinted, but Harrington, Milton, the Vindiciæ contra Tyrannos, and a multitude of others, came upon the stage.—The third period was the Revolution in 1688, which produced Sidney, Locke, Hoadley, Trenchard Gordon, Plato Redivivus, who is also clear for three equipollent branches in the mixture, and others without number. The discourses of Sidney were indeed written before, but the same causes produced his writings and the Revolution.—Americans should make collections of all these speculations, to be preserved as the most precious relics of antiquity, both for curiosity and use. There is one indispensable rule to be observed in the perusal of all of them; and that is, to consider the period in which they were written, the circumstances of the times, and the personal character as well as the political situation of the writer. Such a precaution as this deserves particular attention in examining a work, printed first in the Mercurius Politicus, a periodical paper published in defence of the commonwealth, and reprinted in 1656, by Marchamont Nedham, under the title of "The Excellency of a free State, or the right Constitution of a Commonwealth." The nation had not only a numerous nobility and clergy at that time disgusted, and a vast body of the other gentlemen, as well as of the common people, desirous of the restoration of the exiled royal family, but many writers explicitly espoused the cause of simple monarchy and absolute power: among whom was Hobbes, a man, however unhappy in his temper, or detestable for his principles, equal in genius and learning to any of his contemporaries. Others were employed in ridiculing the doctrine, that laws, and not men, should govern. It was contended, that to say "that laws do or can govern, is to amuse ourselves with a form of speech, as when we say time, or age, or death, does such a thing. That the government is not in the law, but in the person whose will gives a being to that law. That the perfection of monarchy consists in governing by a nobility, weighty enough to keep the people under, yet not tall enough, in any particular person, to measure with the prince; and by a moderate army, kept up under the notion of guards and garrisons, which may be sufficient to strangle all seditions in the cradle; by councils, not such as are co-ordinate with the prince, but purely of advice and dispatch, with power only to persuade, not limit, the prince's will *-" In such a situation, writers on the side of liberty thought themselves obliged to consider what was then practicable, not abstractedly what was the best: they felt the necessity of leaving the monarchical and aristocratical orders out of their schemes of government, because all the friends of those orders were their enemies, and of addressing themselves wholly to the democratical party, because they alone were their friends; at least there appears no other hypothesis on which to acconnt for the crude conceptions of Milton and Nedham. The latter, in his preface, discovers his apprehensions and feelings, too clearly to be mistaken, in these words: "I believe none will be offended with this following discourse, but those that are enemies to public welfare: let such be offended still; it is not for their sakes that I publish this ensuing treatise, but for your sakes that have been *noble patriots*, *fellow-soldiers* and *sufferers* for the liberties and freedoms of your country." As Mr. Turgot's idea of a commonwealth, in which all authority is to be collected into one centre, and that centre the nation, is supposed to be precisely the project of Marchamont Nedham, and probably derived from his book, and as "The Excellency of a free State" is a valuable morsel of antiquity well known in America, where it has many partisans, it may be worth while to examine it, especially as it contains every semblance of argument which can possibly be urged in favour of the system, as it is not only the popular idea of a republic both in France and England, but is generally intended by the words *republic, common-*

---

* See the political pamphlets of that day,
written on the side of monarchy.

wealth, and *popular state*, when used by English writers, even those of the most sense, taste, and learning.

Marchamont Nedham lays it down as a fundamental principle, and an undeniable rule, "that the people, that is, such as shall be successively chosen to represent the people, are the best keepers of their own liberties, and that for many reasons: First, because they never think of usurping over other men's rights, but mind which way to preserve their own."

Our first attention should be turned to the proposition itself, "The people are the best keepers of their own liberties." But who are the people? "Such as shall be successively chosen to represent them."— Here is a confusion both of words and ideas, which, though it may pass with the generality of readers in a fugitive pamphlet, or with a majority of auditors in a popular harangue, ought, for that very reason, to be as carefully avoided in politics as it is in philosophy or mathematics. If by the people is meant the whole body of a great nation, it should never be forgotten, that they can never act, consult, or reason together, because they cannot march five hundred miles, nor spare the time, nor find a space to meet; and therefore the proposition, that they are the best keepers of their own liberties, is not true. They are the worst conceiveable; they are no keepers at all: they can neither act, judge, think, or will, as a body politic or corporation. If by the people is meant all the inhabitants of a single city, they are not in a general assembly, at all times, the best keepers of their own liberties, nor perhaps at any time, unless you separate from them the executive and judicial power, and temper their authority in legislation with the maturer councils of the one and the few. If it is meant by the people, as our author explains himself, a representative assembly, "such as shall be successively chosen to represent the people," they are not still the best keepers of the people's liberties, or their own, if you give them all the power, legislative, executive, and judicial: they would invade the liberties of the people, at least the majority of them would invade the liberties of the minority, sooner and oftener than an absolute monarchy, such as that of France, Spain, or Russia, or than a well-checked aristocracy, like Venice, Bern, or Holland. An excellent writer has said, somewhat incautiously, that "a people will never oppress themselves, or invade their own rights." This compliment, if applied to human nature, or to mankind, or to any nation or people in being or in memory, is more than has been merited. If it should be admitted, that a people will not unanimously agree to oppress themselves, it is as much as is ever, and more than is always, true. All kinds of experience shew, that great numbers of individuals do oppress great numbers of other individuals; that parties often, if not always, oppress other parties; and majorities almost universally minorities. All that this observation can mean then, consistently with any colour of fact, is, that the people will never unanimously agree to oppress themselves: but if one party agrees to oppress another, or the majority the minority, the people still oppress themselves, for one part of them oppress another.—"The people never think of usurping over other men's rights." What can this mean? Does it mean that the people never *unanimously* think of usurping over other men's rights? This would be trifling, for there would, by the supposition, be no other men's rights to usurp. But if the people never jointly, nor severally, think of usurping the rights of others, what occasion can there be for any government at all? Are there no robberies, burglaries, murders, adulteries, thefts, nor cheats? Is not every crime an usurpation over other men's rights? Is not a great part, I will not say the greatest part, of men detected every day in some disposition or other, stronger or weaker, more or less, to usurp over other men's rights? There are some few, indeed, whose whole lives and conversations show, that in every thought, word, and action, they conscientiously respect the rights of others: there is a larger body still, who, in the general tenor of their thoughts and actions, discover similar principles and feelings, yet frequently err. If we should extend our candour so far as to own that the majority of men are generally under the dominion of benevolence and good intentions, yet it must be confessed that a vast majority frequently transgress; and, what is more directly to the point, not only a majority, but almost all, confine their benevolence to their families, relations, personal friends, parish, village, city, county, province, and that very few indeed extend it impartially to the whole community. Now grant but this truth, and the question is decided: if a majority are capable of preferring their own private interest, or that of their families, counties, and party, to that of the nation collectively, some provision must be made in the constitution, in favour of justice, to compel all to respect the common right, the public good, the universal law, in preference to all private and partial considerations.

The proposition of our author then should be reversed, and it should have been said, that they mind so much their own, that they never think enough of others. Suppose a nation, rich and poor, high and low, ten millions in number, all assembled together; not more than one or two millions will have lands, houses, or any personal property: if we take into the account the women and children, or even if we leave them out of the question, a great majority of every nation is wholly destitute of property, except a small quantity of clothes, and a few trifles of other moveables. Would Mr. Nedham be responsible that, if all were to be decided by a vote of the majority, the eight or nine millions who have no property, would not think of usurping over the rights of the one or two millions who have? Property is surely a right of mankind as really as liberty. Perhaps, at first, prejudice, habit, shame, or fear, principle or religion, would restrain the poor from attacking the rich, and the idle from usurping on the industrious; but the time would not be long before courage and enterprize would come, and pretexts be invented by degrees, to countenance the majority in dividing all the property among them, or at least in sharing it equally with its present possessors. Debts would be

261

abolished first; taxes laid heavy on the rich, and not at all on the others; and at last a downright equal division of every thing be demanded, and voted. What would be the consequence of this? The idle, the vicious, the intemperate, would rush into the utmost extravagance of debauchery, fell and spend all their share, and then demand a new division of those who purchased from them. The moment the idea is admitted into society, that property is not as sacred as the laws of God, and that there is not a force of law and public justice to protect it, anarchy and tyranny commence. If "THOU SHALT NOT COVET," and "THOU SHALT NOT STEAL," were not commandments of Heaven, they must be made inviolable precepts in every society before it can be civilized or made free. If the first part of the proposition, viz. that "the people never think of usurping over other men's rights," cannot be admitted, is the second, viz. that "they mind which way to preserve their own," better founded?—There is in every nation and people under heaven a large proportion of persons who take no rational and prudent precautions to preserve what they have, much less to acquire more. Indolence is the natural character of man, to such a degree, that nothing but the necessities of hunger, thirst, and other wants equally pressing, can stimulate him to action, until education is introduced in civilized societies, and the strongest motives of ambition to excel in arts, trades and professions, are established in the minds of all men: until this emulation is introduced, the lazy savage holds property in too little estimation to give himself trouble for the preservation or acquisition of it. In societies the most cultivated and polished, vanity, fashion, and folly, prevail over every thought of ways to preserve their own: they seem rather chiefly to study what means of luxury, dissipation and extravagance, they can invent to get rid of it. "The case is far otherwise among kings and grandees," says our author, "as all nations in the world have felt to some purpose;" that is, in other words, kings and grandees think of usurping over other men's rights, but do not mind which way to preserve their own. It is very easy to flatter the democratical portion of society, by making such distinctions between them and the monarchical and aristocratical; but flattery is as base an artifice, and as pernicious a vice, when offered to the people, as when given to the others. There is no reason to believe the one much honester or wiser than the other; they are all of the same clay, their minds and bodies are alike. The two latter have more knowledge and sagacity derived from education, and more advantages for acquiring wisdom and virtue. As to usurping others rights, they are all three equally guilty when unlimited in power: no wise man will trust either with an opportunity; and every judicious legislator will set all three to watch and controul each other. We may appeal to every page of history we have hitherto turned over, for proofs irrefragable, that the people when they have been unchecked, have been as unjust, tyrannical, brutal, barbarous, and cruel, as any king or senate possessed of uncontroulable power: the majority has eternally, and without one exception, usurped over the rights of the minority. "They naturally move," says Nedham, "within the circle of domination, as in their proper centre." When writers on legislation have recourse to poetry, their images may be beautiful, but they prove nothing. This, however, has neither the merit of a brilliant figure, nor of a convincing argument: the populace, the rabble, the canaille, move as naturally in the circle of domination, whenever they dare, as the nobles or a king; nay, although it may give pain, truth and experience force us to add, that even the middling people, when uncontrouled, have moved in the same circle, and have not only tyrannized over all above and all below, but the majority among themselves has tyrannized over the minority. "And count it no less security, than wisdom and policy, to brave it over the people." Declamatory flourishes, although they may furnish a mob with watchwords, afford no reasonable conviction to the understanding. What is meant by braving it? In the history of Holland you will fee the people braving it over the De Witts; and in that of Florence, Siena, Bologna, Pistoia, and the rest, over many others *. "Cæsar, Crassus, and another, made a contract with each other, that nothing should be done without the concurrence of all three; Societatem iniere, nequid ageretur in republica, quod displicuisset ulli, e tribus." Nedham could not have selected a less fortunate example for his purpose, since there never was a more arrant creature of the people than Cæsar; no, not even Catiline, Wat Tyler, Massianello, or Shase. The people created Cæsar on the ruins of the senate, and on purpose to usurp over the rights of others. But this example, among innumerable others, is very apposite for our purpose. It happens universally, when the people in a body, or by a single representative assembly, attempt to exercise all the powers of government, they always create three or four idols, who make a bargain with each other first, to do nothing which shall displease any one: these hold this agreement, until one thinks himself able to disembarrass himself of the other two; then they quarrel, and the strongest becomes single tyrant. But why is the name of Pompey omitted, who was the third of this triumvirate? Because it would have been too unpopular; it would have too easily confuted his argument, and have turned it against himself, to have said that this association was between Pompey, Cæsar, and Crassus, against Cato, the senate, the constitution and liberty, which was the fact. Can you find a people who will never be divided in opinion? who will be always unanimous? The people of Rome were divided, as all other people ever have been and will be, into a variety of parties and factions. Pompey, Crassus, and Cæsar, at the head of different parties, were jealous of each other: their divisions strengthened the senate and its friends, and furnished means and opportunities of defeating many of their ambitious designs. Cæsar perceived it, and paid his court both to Pompey and Crassus, in order to hinder them from joining the senate against him. He separately represented the advantage which their enemies derived from their misunderstandings, and the ease with which, if united, they might concert among

* Read the Harangue, vol. ii. p. 67.

themselves all affairs of the republic, gratify every friend, and disappoint every enemy *. The other example, of Augustus, Lepidus, and Antony, is equally unfortunate: both are demonstrations that the people did think of usurping others rights, and that they did not mind any way to preserve their own. The senate was now annihilated, many of them murdered: Augustus, Lepidus, and Antony, were popular demagogues, who agreed together to fleece the flock between them, until the most cunning of the three destroyed the other two, fleeced the sheep alone, and transmitted the shears to a line of tyrants. How can this writer say then, that, "while the government remained untouched in the people's hands, every particular man lived safe?" The direct contrary is true. Every man lived safe, only while the senate remained as a check and balance to the people: the moment that controul was destroyed, no man was safe. While the government remained untouched in the various orders, the consuls, senate, and people, mutually balancing each other, it might be said, with some truth, that no man could be undone, unless a true and satisfactory reason was rendered to the world for his destruction: but as soon as the senate was destroyed, and the government came untouched into the people's hands, no man lived safe but the triumvirs and their tools; any man might be, and multitudes of the best men were, undone, without rendering any reason to the world for their destruction, but the will, the fear, or the revenge of some tyrant. These popular leaders, in our author's own language, "saved and destroyed, depressed and advanced, whom they pleased, with a wet finger." ...

* * *

The twelfth reason is, "because this form is most suitable to the nature and reason of mankind."—If Socrates and Plato, Cicero and Seneca, Hutchinson and Butler, are to be credited, reason is rightfully supreme in man, and therefore it would be most suitable to the reason of mankind to have no civil or political government at all. The moral government of God, and his vicegerent Conscience, ought to be sufficient to restrain men to obedience, to justice and benevolence, at all times and in all places; we must therefore descend from the dignity of our nature, when we think of civil government at all. But the nature of mankind is one thing, and the reason of mankind another; and the first has the same relation to the last as the whole to a part: the passions and appetites are parts of human nature, as well as reason and the moral sense. In the institution of government, it must be remembered, that although reason ought always to govern individuals, it certainly never did since the Fall, and never will till the Millennium; and human nature must be taken as it is, as it has been, and will be. If, as Cicero says, "man is a noble creature, born with affections to rule rather than obey, there being in every man a natural desire of principality," it is yet certain that every man ought to obey as well as to rule, and that every

---

* Dio. Caff. lib. xxxvii. c. 54, 55. Plutarch
in Pomp. Cæsar, & Crassus.

man cannot rule alone. Each man must be content with his share of empire; and if the nature and reason of mankind, the nobleness of his qualities and affections, and his natural desires, prove his right to a share in the government, they cannot surely prove more than the constitutions of the United States have allowed, an annual election of the whole legislative and executive, the governor, senate, and house. If we admit them to prove more, they would prove that every man has every year a right to be governor, senator, and representative; which being impossible, is absurd. Even in our author's "Right constitution," every man would have an equal right to be representative, chosen or not. The reason why one man is content to submit to the government of another, as assigned by our author, viz. "not because he conceives himself to have less right than another, to govern, but either because he finds himself less able, or else because he judgeth it will be more convenient for himself and the community if he submits to another's government," is a proof of this; because the moment it is allowed that some are more able than others, and that the community are judges who the most able are, you take away the right to rule, derived from the nobleness of each man's individual nature, from his affections to rule rather than obey, or from his natural appetite or desire of principality, and give the right of conferring the power to rule to the community. As a share in the appointment of deputies is all that our author can with any colour infer from this noble nature of man, his nature will be gratified and his dignity supported as well, if you divide his deputies into three orders, of governor for the executive, and an integral share in the legislative, of senators for another independent part of the legislative, and of representatives for a third, and if you introduce a judicious balance between them, as if you huddle them into one assembly, where they will soon disgrace their own nature, and that of their constituents, by ambition, avarice, jealousy, envy, faction, division, sedition, and rebellion. Nay, if it should be found that annual elections of governors and senators cannot be supported without introducing venality and convulsions, as is very possible, the people will consult the dignity of their nature better by appointing a standing executive and senate, than by insisting on elections, or at least by prolonging the duration of those high trusts, and making elections less frequent.

It is indeed a "most excellent maxim, that the original and fountain of all just power and government is in the people;" and if ever this maxim was fully demonstrated and exemplified among men, it was in the late American revolution, where thirteen governments were taken down from the foundation, and new ones elected wholly by the people, as an architect would pull down an old building and erect a new one. There will be no dispute then with Cicero, when he says, "A mind well instructed by the light of nature, will pay obedience," willingly, "to none but such as command, direct, or govern, for its good or benefit; nor will our author's inferences from these passages of that oracle of human wisdom be denied: 1. That by the light of nature people are taught to be their own carvers and contrivers in the framing of that government under which they mean to live; 2. That none are to preside in government, or sit at the helm, but such as shall be judged sit, and chosen by the people; 3. That the people are the only proper judges of the convenience or inconvenience of a government when it is erected, and of the behaviour of governors after they are chosen.—But then it is insisted, that rational and regular means shall be used that the whole people may be their own carvers, that they may judge and choose who shall preside, and that they may determine on the convenience or inconvenience of government, and the behaviour of governors. But then it is insisted, that the town of Berwick upon Tweed shall not carve, judge, choose, and determine for the whole kingdom of Great Britain, nor the county of Berkshire for the Massachusetts; much less that a lawless tyrannical rabble shall do all this for the state, or even for the county of Berkshire.

It may be, and is admitted, that a free government is most natural, and only suitable to the reason of mankind, but it by no means follows "that the other forms, as a standing power in the hands of a particular person, as a king, or of a set number of great ones, as in a senate," much less that a mixture of the three simple forms "are beside the dictates of nature, and mere artificial devices of great men, squared only to serve the ends and interests of avarice, pride, and ambition of a few, to a vassallizing of the community."—If the original and fountain of all power and government is in the people, as undoubtedly it is, the people have as clear a right to erect a simple monarchy, aristocracy, or democracy, or an equal mixture, or any other mixture of all three, if they judge it for their liberty, happiness, and prosperity, as they have to erect a democracy; and infinitely greater and better men than Marchamont Nedham, and the wisest nations that ever lived, have preferred such mixtures, and even with such standing powers, as ingredients in their compositions. But even those nations who choose to reserve in their own hands the periodical choice of the first magistrate, senate, and assembly, at certain stated periods, have as clear a right to appoint a first magistrate for life as for years, and for perpetuity in his descendants as for life. When I say for perpetuity, or for life, it is always meant to imply, that the same people have at all times a right to interpose, and to depose for mal-administration—to appoint anew. No appointment of a king or senate, or any standing power, can be, in the nature of things, for a longer period than quam diu se bene gesserit, the whole nation being judge. An appointment for life, or perpetuity, can be no more than an appointment until further order; but further order can only be given by the nation: and until the nation shall have given the order, an estate for life, or in fee, is held in the office. It must be a great occasion which can induce a nation to take such a subject into consideration and make a change. Until a change is made, an hereditary limited monarch is the representative of the whole nation, for the management of the executive power, as much as an house of representatives is, as one branch of the legislature, and as guardian of the public purse; and a house of lords too, or a standing senate, represents the nation for other purposes, viz. as a watch set upon both the representatives and the executive power. The people are the fountain and original of the power of kings and lords, governors and senates, as well as the house of commons, or assembly of representatives: and is the people are sufficiently enlightened to see all the dangers that surround them, they will always be represented by a distinct personage to manage the whole executive power;—a distinct senate, to be guardians of property against levellers for the purposes of plunder, to be a repository of the national tradition of public maxims, customs, and manners, and to be controulers in turn both of kings and their ministers on one side, and the representatives of the people on the other, when either discover a disposition to do wrong;—and a distinct house of representatives, to be the guardians of the public purse, and to protect the people in their turn against both kings and nobles. A science certainly comprehends all the principles in nature which belong to the subject. The principles in nature which relate to government cannot all be known, without a knowledge of the history of mankind. The English constitution is the only one which has considered and provided for all cases that are known to have generally, indeed to have always happened in the progress of every nation; it is, therefore, the only scientifical government. To say then that standing powers have been erected, as mere artificial devices of great men, to serve the ends of avarice, pride, and ambition of a few, to the vassallizing of the community, is to declaim and abuse. Standing powers have been instituted to avoid greater evils, corruption, sedition, war, and bloodshed, in elections; it is the people's business, therefore, to find out some method of avoiding them, without standing powers. The Americans flatter themselves they have hit upon it: and no doubt they have for a time, perhaps a long one: but this remains to be proved by experience.

G. ESSAY OF BRUTUS, NO. 1

October 18, 1787

To the Citizens of the State of New-York.

When the public is called to investigate and decide upon a question in which not only the present members of the community are deeply interested, but upon which the happiness and misery of generations yet unborn is in great measure suspended, the benevolent mind cannot help feeling itself peculiarly interested in the result.

In this situation, I trust the feeble efforts of an individual, to lead the minds of the people to a wise and prudent determination, cannot fail of being acceptable to the candid and dispassionate part of the community. Encouraged by this consideration, I have been induced to offer my thoughts upon the present important crisis of our public affairs.

Perhaps this country never saw so critical a period in their political concerns. We have felt the feebleness of the ties by which these United-States are held together, and the want of sufficient energy in our present confederation, to manage, in some instances, our general concerns. Various expedients have been proposed to remedy these evils, but none have succeeded. At length a Convention of the states has been assembled, they have formed a constitution which will now, probably, be submitted to the people to ratify or reject, who are the fountain of all power, to whom alone it of right belongs to make or unmake constitutions, or forms of government, at their pleasure. The most important question that was ever proposed to your decision, or to the decision of any people under heaven, is before you, and you are to decide upon it by men of your own election, chosen specially for this purpose. If the constitution, offered to your acceptance, be a wise one, calculated to preserve the invaluable blessings of liberty, to secure the inestimable rights of mankind, and promote human happiness, then, if you accept it, you will lay a lasting foundation of happiness for millions yet unborn; generations to come will rise up and call you blessed. You may rejoice in the prospects of this vast extended continent becoming filled with freemen, who will assert the dignity of human nature. You may solace yourselves with the idea, that society, in this favoured land, will fast advance to the highest point of perfection; the human mind will expand in knowledge and virtue, and the golden age be, in some measure, realised. But if, on the other hand, this form of government contains principles that will lead to the subversion of liberty—if it tends to establish a despotism, or, what is worse, a tyrannic aristocracy; then, if you adopt it, this only remaining assylum for liberty will be shut up, and posterity will execrate your memory.

Momentous then is the question you have to determine, and you are called upon by every motive which should influence a noble and virtuous mind, to examine it well, and to make up a wise judgment. It is insisted, indeed, that this constitution must be received, be it ever so imperfect. If it has its defects, it is said, they can be best amended when they are experienced. But remember, when the people once part with power, they can seldom or never resume it again but by force. Many instances can be produced in which the people have voluntarily increased the powers of their rulers; but few, if any, in which rulers have willingly abridged their authority. This is a sufficient reason to induce you to be careful, in the first instance, how you deposit the powers of government.

With these few introductory remarks, I shall proceed to a consideration of this constitution:

The first question that presents itself on the subject is, whether a confederated government be the best for the United States or not? Or in other words, whether the thirteen United States should be reduced to one great republic, governed by one legislature, and under the direction of one executive and judicial; or whether they should continue thirteen confederated republics, under the direction and controul of a supreme federal head for certain defined national purposes only?

This enquiry is important, because, although the government reported by the convention does not go to a perfect and entire consolidation, yet it approaches so near to it, that it must, if executed, certainly and infallibly terminate in it.

This government is to possess absolute and uncontroulable power, legislative, executive and judicial, with respect to every object to which it extends, for by the last clause of section 8th, article 1st, it is declared "that the Congress shall have power to make all laws which shall be necessary and proper for carrying into execution the foregoing powers, and all other powers vested by this constitution, in the government of the United States; or in any department or office thereof." And by the 6th article, it is declared "that this constitution, and the laws of the United States, which shall be made in pursuance thereof, and the treaties made, or which shall be made, under the authority of the United States, shall be the supreme law of the land; and the judges in every state shall be bound thereby, any thing in the constitution, or law of any state to the contrary notwithstanding." It appears from these articles that there is no need of any intervention of the state governments, between the Congress and the people, to execute any one power vested in the general government, and that the constitution and laws of every state are nullified and declared void, so far as they are or shall be inconsistent with this constitution, or the laws made in pursuance of it, or with treaties made under the authority of the United States.—The government then, so far as it extends, is a complete one, and not a confederation. It is as much one complete government as that of New-York or Massachusetts, has as absolute and perfect powers to make and execute all laws, to appoint officers, institute courts, declare offences, and annex penalties, with respect to every object to which it extends, as any other in the world. So far therefore as its powers reach, all ideas of confederation are given up and lost. It is true this government is limited to certain objects, or to speak more properly, some small degree of power is still left to the states, but a little attention to the powers vested in the general government, will convince every candid man, that if it is capable of being executed, all that is reserved for the individual states must very soon be annihilated, except so far as they are barely necessary to the organization of the general government. The powers of the general legislature extend to every case that is of the least importance—there is nothing valuable to human nature, nothing dear to freemen, but what is within its power. It has authority to make laws which will affect the lives, the liberty, and property of every man in the United States; nor can the constitution or laws of any state, in any way prevent or impede the full and complete execution of every power given. The legislative power is competent to lay taxes, duties, imposts, and excises;—there is no limitation to this power, unless it be said that the

269

clause which directs the use to which those taxes, and duties shall be applied, may be said to be a limitation: but this is no restriction of the power at all, for by this clause they are to be applied to pay the debts and provide for the common defence and general welfare of the United States; but the legislature have authority to contract debts at their discretion; they are the sole judges of what is necessary to provide for the common defence, and they only are to determine what is for the general welfare; this power therefore is neither more nor less, than a power to lay and collect taxes, imposts, and excises, at their pleasure; not only [is] the power to lay taxes unlimited, as to the amount they may require, but it is perfect and absolute to raise them in any mode they please. No state legislature, or any power in the state governments, have any more to do in carrying this into effect, than the authority of one state has to do with that of another. In the business therefore of laying and collecting taxes, the idea of confederation is totally lost, and that of one entire republic is embraced. It is proper here to remark, that the authority to lay and collect taxes is the most important of any power that can be granted; it connects with it almost all other powers, or at least will in process of time draw all other after it; it is the great mean of protection, security, and defence, in a good government, and the great engine of oppression and tyranny in a bad one. This cannot fail of being the case, if we consider the contracted limits which are set by this constitution, to the late [state?] governments, on this article of raising money. No state can emit paper money—lay any duties, or imposts, on imports, or exports, but by consent of the Congress; and then the net produce shall be for the benefit of the United States: the only mean therefore left, for any state to support its government and discharge its debts, is by direct taxation; and the United States have also power to lay and collect taxes, in any way they please. Every one who has thought on the subject, must be convinced that but small sums of money can be collected in any country, by direct taxe[s], when the fæderal government begins to exercise the right of taxation in all its parts, the legislatures of the several states will find it impossible to raise monies to support their governments. Without money they cannot be supported, and they must dwindle away, and, as before observed, their powers absorbed in that of the general government.

It might be here shewn, that the power in the federal legislative, to raise and support armies at pleasure, as well in peace as in war, and their controul over the militia, tend, not only to a consolidation of the government, but the destruction of liberty.—I shall not, however, dwell upon these, as a few observations upon the judicial power of this government, in addition to the preceding, will fully evince the truth of the position.

The judicial power of the United States is to be vested in a supreme court, and in such inferior courts as Congress may from time to time ordain and establish. The powers of these courts are very extensive;

their jurisdiction comprehends all civil causes, except such as arise between citizens of the same state; and it extends to all cases in law and equity arising under the constitution. One inferior court must be established, I presume, in each state, at least, with the necessary executive officers appendant thereto. It is easy to see, that in the common course of things, these courts will eclipse the dignity, and take away from the respectability, of the state courts. These courts will be, in themselves, totally independent of the states, deriving their authority from the United States, and receiving from them fixed salaries; and in the course of human events it is to be expected, that they will swallow up all the powers of the courts in the respective states.

How far the clause in the 8th section of the 1st article may operate to do away all idea of confederated states, and to effect an entire consolidation of the whole into one general government, it is impossible to say. The powers given by this article are very general and comprehensive, and it may receive a construction to justify the passing almost any law. A power to make all laws, which shall be *necessary and proper,* for carrying into execution, all powers vested by the constitution in the government of the United States, or any department or officer thereof, is a power very comprehensive and definite [indefinite?], and may, for ought I know, be exercised in a such manner as entirely to abolish the state legislatures. Suppose the legislature of a state should pass a law to raise money to support their government and pay the state debt, may the Congress repeal this law, because it may prevent the collection of a tax which they may think proper and necessary to lay, to provide for the general welfare of the United States? For all laws made, in pursuance of this constitution, are the supreme lay of the land, and the judges in every state shall be bound thereby, any thing in the constitution or laws of the different states to the contrary notwithstanding.—By such a law, the government of a particular state might be overturned at one stroke, and thereby be deprived of every means of its support.

It is not meant, by stating this case, to insinuate that the constitution would warrant a law of this kind; or unnecessarily to alarm the fears of the people, by suggesting, that the federal legislature would be more likely to pass the limits assigned them by the constitution, than that of an individual state, further than they are less responsible to the people. But what is meant is, that the legislature of the United States are vested with the great and uncontroulable powers, of laying and collecting taxes, duties, imposts, and excises; of regulating trade, raising and supporting armies, organizing, arming, and disciplining the militia, instituting courts, and other general powers. And are by this clause invested with the power of making all laws, *proper and necessary,* for carrying all these into execution; and they may so exercise this power as entirely to annihilate all the state governments, and reduce this country to one single government. And if they may do it, it is pretty certain they will; for it will be found that the power retained by individual states, small as it is, will be a clog upon the wheels of the government of the United States; the latter therefore will be naturally inclined to remove it out of the way. Besides, it is a truth confirmed by the unerring experience of ages, that every man, and every body of men, invested with power, are ever disposed to increase it, and to acquire a superiority over every thing that stands in their way. This disposition, which is implanted in human nature, will operate in the federal legislature to lessen and ultimately to subvert the state authority, and having such advantages, will most certainly succeed, if the federal government succeeds at all. It must be very evident then, that what this constitution wants of being a complete consolidation of the several parts of the union into one complete government, possessed of perfect legislative, judicial, and executive powers, to all intents and purposes, it will necessarily acquire in its exercise and operation.

Let us now proceed to enquire, as I at first proposed, whether it be best the thirteen United States should be reduced to one great republic, or not? It is here taken for granted, that all agree in this, that whatever government we adopt, it ought to be a free one; that it should be so framed as to secure the liberty of the citizens of America, and such an one as to admit of a full, fair, and equal representation of the people. The question then will be, whether a government thus constituted, and founded on such principles, is practicable, and can be exercised over the whole United States, reduced into one state?

If respect is to be paid to the opinion of the greatest and wisest men who have ever thought or wrote on the science of government, we shall be constrained to conclude, that a free republic cannot succeed over a country of such immense extent, containing such a number of inhabitants, and these encreasing in such rapid progression as that of the whole United States. Among the many illustrious authorities which might be produced to this point, I shall content myself with quoting only two. The one is the baron de Montesquieu, spirit of laws, chap. xvi. vol. I [book VIII]. "It is natural to a republic to have only a small territory, otherwise it cannot long subsist. In a large republic there are men of large fortunes, and consequently of less moderation; there are trusts too great to be placed in any single subject; he has interest of his own; he soon begins to think that he may be happy, great and glorious, by oppressing his fellow citizens; and that he may raise himself to grandeur on the ruins of his country. In a large republic, the public good is sacrificed to a thousand views; it is subordinate to exceptions, and depends on accidents. In a small one, the interest of the public is easier perceived, better understood, and more within the reach of every citizen; abuses are of less extent, and of course are less protected." Of the same opinion is the marquis Beccarari.

History furnishes no example of a free republic, any thing like the extent of the United States. The Grecian republics were of small extent; so also was that of the Romans. Both of these, it is true, in process of time, extended their conquests over large territories of country; and the consequence was, that their governments were changed from that of free governments to those of the most tyrannical that ever existed in the world.

Not only the opinion of the greatest men, and the experience of mankind, are against the idea of an extensive republic, but a variety of reasons may be drawn from the reason and nature of things, against it. In every government, the will of the sovereign is the law. In despotic governments, the supreme authority being lodged in one, his will is law, and can be as easily expressed to a large extensive territory as to a small one. In a pure democracy the people are the sovereign, and their will is declared by themselves; for this purpose they must all come together to deliberate, and decide. This kind of government cannot be exercised, therefore, over a country of any considerable extent; it must be confined to a single city, or at least limited to such bounds as that the people can conveniently assemble, be able to debate, understand the subject submitted to them, and declare their opinion concerning it.

In a free republic, although all laws are derived from the consent of the people, yet the people do not declare their consent by themselves in person, but by representatives, chosen by them, who are supposed to know the minds of their constituents, and to be possessed of integrity to declare this mind.

In every free government, the people must give their assent to the laws by which they are governed. This is the true criterion between a free government and an arbitrary one. The former are ruled by the will of the whole, expressed in any manner they may agree upon; the latter by the will of one, or a few. If the people are to give their assent to the laws, by persons chosen and appointed by them, the manner of the choice and the number chosen, must be such, as to possess, be disposed, and consequently qualified to declare the sentiments of the people; for if they do not know, or are not disposed to speak the sentiments of the people, the people do not govern, but the sovereignty is in a few. Now, in a large extended country, it is impossible to have a representation, possessing the sentiments, and of integrity, to declare the minds of the people, without having it so numerous and unwieldly, as to be subject in great measure to the inconveniency of a democratic government.

The territory of the United States is of vast extent; it now contains near three millions of souls, and is capable of containing much more than ten times that number. Is it practicable for a country, so large and so numerous as they will soon become, to elect a representation, that will speak their sentiments, without their becoming so numerous as to be incapable of transacting public business? It certainly is not.

In a republic, the manners, sentiments, and interests of the people should be similar. If this be not the case, there will be a constant clashing of opinions; and the representatives of one part will be continu-

273

ally striving against those of the other. This will retard the operations of government, and prevent such conclusions as will promote the public good. If we apply this remark to the condition of the United States, we shall be convinced that it forbids that we should be one government. The United States includes a variety of climates. The productions of the different parts of the union are very variant, and their interests, of consequence, diverse. Their manners and habits differ as much as their climates and productions; and their sentiments are by no means coincident. The laws and customs of the several states are, in many respects, very diverse, and in some opposite; each would be in favor of its own interests and customs, and, of consequence, a legislature, formed of representatives from the respective parts, would not only be too numerous to act with any care or decision, but would be composed of such heterogenous and discordant principles, as would constantly be contending with each other.

The laws cannot be executed in a republic, of an extent equal to that of the United States, with promptitude.

The magistrates in every government must be supported in the execution of the laws, either by an armed force, maintained at the public expence for that purpose; or by the people turning out to aid the magistrate upon his command, in case of resistance.

In despotic governments, as well as in all the monarchies of Europe, standing armies are kept up to execute the commands of the prince or the magistrate, and are employed for this purpose when occasion requires: But they have always proved the destruction of liberty, and [are] abhorrent to the spirit of a free republic. In England, where they depend upon the parliament for their annual support, they have always been complained of as oppressive and unconstitutional, and are seldom employed in executing of the laws; never except on extraordinary occasions, and then under the direction of a civil magistrate.

A free republic will never keep a standing army to execute its laws. It must depend upon the support of its citizens. But when a government is to receive its support from the aid of the citizens, it must be so constructed as to have the confidence, respect, and affection of the people. Men who, upon the call of the magistrate, offer themselves to execute the laws, are influenced to do it either by affection to the government, or from fear; where a standing army is at hand to punish offenders, every man is actuated by the latter principle, and therefore, when the magistrate calls, will obey: but, where this is not the case, the government must rest for its support upon the confidence and respect which the people have for their government and laws. The body of the people being attached, the government will always be sufficient to support and execute its laws, and to operate upon the fears of any faction which may be opposed to it, not only to prevent an opposition to the execution of the laws themselves, but also to compel the most of them to aid the magistrate; but the people will not be likely to have such confidence in their rulers, in a republic so extensive as the United States, as necessary for these purposes. The confidence which the people have in their rulers, in a free republic, arises from their knowing them, from their being responsible to them for their conduct, and from the power they have of displacing them when they misbehave: but in a republic of the extent of this continent, the people in general would be acquainted with very few of their rulers: the people at large would know little of their proceedings, and it would be extremely difficult to change them. The people in Georgia and New-Hampshire would not know one another's mind, and therefore could not act in concert to enable them to effect a general change of representatives. The different parts of so extensive a country could not possibly be made acquainted with the conduct of their representatives, nor be informed of the reasons upon which measures were founded. The consequence will be, they will have no confidence in their legislature, suspect them of ambitious views, be jealous of every measure they adopt, and will not support the laws they pass. Hence the government will be nerveless and inefficient, and no way will be left to render it otherwise, but by establishing an armed force to execute the laws at the point of the bayonet—a government of all others the most to be dreaded.

In a republic of such vast extent as the United-States, the legislature cannot attend to the various concerns and wants of its different parts. It cannot be sufficiently numerous to be acquainted with the local condition and wants of the different districts, and if it could, it is impossible it should have sufficient time to attend to and provide for all the variety of cases of this nature, that would be continually arising.

In so extensive a republic, the great officers of government would soon become above the controul of the people, and abuse their power to the purpose of aggrandizing themselves, and oppressing them. The trust committed to the executive offices, in a country of the extent of the United-States, must be various and of magnitude. The command of all the troops and navy of the republic, the appointment of officers, the power of pardoning offences, the collecting of all the public revenues, and the power of expending them, with a number of other powers, must be lodged and exercised in every state, in the hands of a few. When these are attended with great honor and emolument, as they always will be in large states, so as greatly to interest men to pursue them, and to be proper objects for ambitious and designing men, such men will be ever restless in their pursuit after them. They will use the power, when they have acquired it, to the purposes of gratifying their own interest and ambition, and it is scarcely possible, in a very large republic, to call them to account for their misconduct, or to prevent their abuse of power.

These are some of the reasons by which it appears, that a free republic cannot long subsist over a country of the great extent of these states. If then this new constitution is calculated to consolidate the thirteen states into one, as it evidently is, it ought not to be adopted.

Though I am of opinion, that it is a sufficient objection to this government, to reject it, that it creates the whole union into one government, under the form of a republic, yet if this objection was obviated, there are exceptions to it, which are so material and fundamental, that they ought to determine every man, who is a friend to the liberty and happiness of mankind, not to adopt it. I beg the candid and dispassionate attention of my countrymen while I state these objections—they are such as have obtruded themselves upon my mind upon a careful attention to the matter, and such as I sincerely believe are well founded. There are many objections, of small moment, of which I shall take no notice—perfection is not to be expected in any thing that is the production of man—and if I did not in my conscience believe that this scheme was defective in the fundamental principles—in the foundation upon which a free and equal government must rest—I would hold my peace.

Brutus.

H. LETTERS OF CATO, NOS. 2 AND 3

Fall, 1787

No. 2

To the Citizens of the State of New-York.

> *Remember, O my friends! the laws, the rights,*
> *The generous plan of power deliver'd down,*
> *By your renown'd Forefathers;*
> *So dearly bought, the price of so much blood!*
> *O let it never perish in your hands!*
> *But piously transmit it to your children.*

The object of my last address to you was to engage your dispassionate consideration of the new Foederal government; to caution you against precipitancy in the adoption of it; to recommend a correction of its errors, if it contained any; to hint to you the danger of an easy perversion of some of its powers; to solicit you to separate yourselves from party, and to be independent of and uninfluenced by any in your principles of politics: and, that address was closed with a promise of future observations on the same subject which should be justified by reason and truth. Here I intended to have rested the introduction, but a writer under the signature of CAESAR, in Mr. Childs's paper of the 1st instant, who treats you with passion, insult, and threat has anticipated those observations which would otherwise have remained in silence until a future period. It would be criminal in me to hesitate a moment to appear as your advocate in so interesting a cause, and to resist the influence of such doctrines as this Caesar holds.—I shall take no other cognizance of his remarks on the *questionable* shape of my future, or the *equivocal* appearance of my past reflections, than to declare, that in my past I did not mean to be misunderstood (for Caesar himself declares, that it is obviously the language of distrust) and that in my future there will not be the semblance of doubt. But, what is the language of Caesar—he ridicules your prerogative, power, and majesty—he talks of this *proferred constitution* as the tender mercy of a benevolent sovereign to deluded subjects, or, as his tyrant name-sake, of his proferred grace to the virtuous Cato:—he shuts the door of free deliberation and discussion, and declares, that you must receive this government in manner and form as it is *proferred*—that you cannot revise nor amend it, and lastly, to close the scene, he insinuates, that it will be more healthy for you that the American Fabius should be induced to accept of the presidency of this new government than that, in case you do not acquiesce, he should be solicited to command an army to impose it on you. Is not your indignation roused at this absolute, imperious stile?—For what did you open the veins of your citizens and expend their treasure?—For what did you throw off the yoke of Britain and call yourselves independent?—Was it from a disposition fond of change, or to procure new masters?—if those were your motives, you have your reward before you—go,—retire into silent obscurity, and kiss the rod that scourges you—bury the prospects you had in store, that you and your posterity would participate in the blessings of freedom, and the employments of your country—let the rich and insolent alone be your rulers—perhaps you are designed by providence as an emphatic evidence of the mutability of human affairs, to have the shew of happiness only, that your misery may seem the sharper, and if so, you must submit. But, if you had nobler views, and you are not designed by heaven as an example—are you now to be derided and insulted?—Is the power of thinking, on the only subject important to you, to be taken away? and if per chance you should happen to dissent from Caesar, are you to have Caesar's principles crammed down your throats with an army?—God forbid!

In democratic republics the people collectively are considered as the sovereign—all legislative, judicial, and executive power, is inherent in and derived from them. As a people, your power and authority have sanctioned and established the present government—your executive, legislative, and judicial acknowledge it by their public acts—you are again solicited to sanction and establish the future one—yet this Caesar mocks your dignity and laughs at the majesty of the people. Caesar, with his usual dogmatism, enquires, if I had talents to throw light on the subject of legislation, why did I not offer them when the Convention was in session?—he is answered in a moment—I thought with him and you, that the wisdom of America, in that Convention, was drawn as it were to a Focus—I placed an unbounded confidence in some of the characters who were members of it, from the services they had rendered their country, without adverting to the ambitious and interested views of others. I was willingly led to expect a model of perfection and security that would have astonished the world. Therefore, to have offered observation, on the subject of legislation, under these impressions, would have discovered no less arrogance than Caesar. The Convention too, when in session, shut their doors to the observations of the community, and their members were under an obligation of secrecy—Nothing transpired—to have suggested remarks on unknown and anticipated principles would have been like a man groping in the dark, and folly in the extreme. I confess, however, I have been disappointed, and Caesar is candid enough to make the same declaration, for he thinks it *might* have been more perfect.

But to call in dispute, at this time, and in the manner Caesar does, the right of free deliberation on this subject, is like a man's propounding a question to another, and telling him, at the same time, that if he does not answer agreeable to the opinion of the propounder, he will exert force to make him of the same sentiment:—to exemplify this, it will be necessary to give you a short history of the rise and progress of the Convention, and the conduct of Congress thereon. The states in Congress suggested, that the articles of confederation had provided for making alterations in the confederation—that there were defects therein, and as a mean to remedy which, a Convention of delegates, appointed by the different states, was resolved expedient to be held for the sole and express purpose of revising it, and reporting to Congress and the different legislatures such alterations and provisions therein as should (when agreed to in Congress and confirmed by the several states) render the foederal constitution adequate to the exigencies of government. This resolution is sent to the different states, and the legislature of this state, with others, appoint, in conformity thereto, delegates for the purpose, and in the words mentioned in that resolve, as by the resolution of Congress, and the concurrent resolutions of the senate and assembly of this state, subjoined, will appear. For the sole and express purpose aforesaid a Convention of delegates is formed at Philadelphia:—what have they done? have they revised the confederation, and has Congress agreed to their report?—neither is the fact.—This Convention have exceeded the authority given to them, and have transmitted to Congress a new political fabric, essentially and fundamentally distinct and different from it, in which the different states do not retain separately their sovereignty and independency, united by a confederated league—but one entire sovereignty—a consolidation of them into one government—in which new provisions and powers are not made and vested in Congress, but in an assembly, senate, and president, who are not know in the articles of confederation.—Congress, without agreeing to, or approving of, this system *proferred* by the Convention, have sent it to the different legislatures, not for their confirmation, but to submit it to the people; not in conformity to their own resolution, but in conformity to the resolution of the Convention made and provided in that case. Was it then, from the face of the foregoing facts, the intention of Congress, and of this and the other states, that the essence of our present national government should be annihilated, or that it should be retained and only [have] an increase of substantial necessary powers? Congress, sensible of this latter principle, and that the Convention had taken on themselves a power which neither they nor the other states had a right to delegate to them, and that they could not agree to, and approve of this consolidated system, nor the states confirm it—have been silent on its character; and though many have dwelt on their unanimity, it is no less than the unanimity of opinion that it originated in an assumption of power, which your voice alone can sanctify. This new government, therefore, founded in usurpation, is referred to your opinion as the origin of power not heretofore delegated, and, to this end, the exercise of the prerogative of free examination is essentially necessary; and yet you are unhesitatingly to acquiesce, and if you do not, the American Fabius, if we may believe Caesar, is to command an army to impose it. It is not my view to rouse your passions, I only wish to excite you to, and assist you in, a cool and deliberate discussion of the subject, to urge you to behave like sensible freemen. Think, speak, act, and assert your opinions and rights—let the same good sense govern you with respect to the adoption of a future system for the administration of your public affairs that influenced you in the formation of the present.—Hereafter I do not intend to be diverted by either Caesar, or any other—My object is to take up this new form of national government—compare it with the experience and the opinions of the most sensible and approved political authors—and to shew, that its principles, and the exercise of them, will be dangerous to your liberty and happiness.

Cato.

No. 3

To the Citizens of the State of New-York.

In the close of my last introductory address, I told you, that my object in future would be to take up this new form of national government, to compare it with the experience and opinions of the most sensible and approved political authors, and to show you that its principles, and the exercise of them [,] will be dangerous to your liberty and happiness.

Although I am conscious that this is an arduous undertaking, yet I will perform it to the best of my ability.

The freedom, equality, and independence which you enjoyed by nature, induced you to consent to a political power. The same principles led you to examine the errors and vices of a British superintendence, to divest yourselves of it, and to reassume a new political shape. It is acknowledged that there are defects in this, and another is tendered to you for acceptance; the great question then, that arises on this new political principle, is, whether it will answer the ends for which it is said to be offered to you, and for which all men engage in political society, to wit, the mutual preservation of their lives, liberties, and estates.

The recital, or premises on which this new form of government is erected, declares a consolidation or union of all the thirteen parts, or states, into one great whole, under the firm [form?] of the United States, for all the various and important purposes therein set forth.— But whoever seriously considers the immense extent of territory comprehended within the limits of the United States, together with the variety of its climates, productions, and commerce, the difference of extent, and number of inhabitants in all; the dissimilitude of interest, morals, and policies, in almost every one, will receive it as an intuitive truth, that a consolidated republican form of government therein, can never *form a perfect union, establish justice, insure domestic tranquility, promote the general welfare, and secure the blessings of liberty to you and your posterity,* for to these objects it must be directed: this unkindred legislature therefore, composed of interests opposite and dissimilar in their nature, will in its exercise, emphatically be, like a house divided against itself.

The governments of Europe have taken their limits and form from adventitious circumstances, and nothing can be argued on the motive of agreement from them; but these adventitious political principles, have nevertheless produced effects that have attracted the attention of philosophy, which has established axioms in the science of politics therefrom, as irrefragable as any in Euclid. It is natural, says Montesquieu, *to a republic to have only a small territory, otherwise it cannot long subsist: in a large one, there are men of large fortunes, and consequently of less moderation; there are too great deposits to intrust in the hands of a single subject, an ambitious person soon becomes sensible that he may be happy, great, and glorious by oppressing his fellow citizens, and that he might raise himself to grandeur, on the ruins of his country. In large republics, the public good is sacrificed to a thousand views; in a small one the interest of the public is easily perceived, better understood, and more within the reach of every citizen; abuses have a less extent, and of course are less protected*—he also shews you, that the duration of the republic of Sparta, was owing to its having continued with the same extent of territory after all its wars; and that the ambition of Athens and Lacedemon to command and direct the union, lost them their liberties, and gave them a monarchy.

From this picture, what can you promise yourselves, on the score of consolidation of the United States, into one government—impracticability in the just exercise of it—your freedom insecure—even this form of government limited in its continuance—the employments of your country disposed of to the opulent, to whose contumely you will continually be an object—you must risque much, by indispensably placing trusts of the greatest magnitude, into the hands of individuals, whose ambition for power, and aggrandizement, will oppress and grind you—where, from the vast extent of your territory, and the complication of interests, the science of government will become intricate and perplexed, and too misterious for you to understand, and observe; and by which you are to be conducted into a monarchy, either limited or despotic; the latter, Mr. Locke remarks, *is a government derived from neither nature, nor compact.*

Political liberty, the great Montesquieu again observes, *consists in security, or at least in the opinion we have of security;* and this *security* therefore, or the *opinion,* is best obtained in moderate governments, where the mildness of the laws, and the equality of the manners, beget a confidence in the people, which produces this security, or the opinion. This moderation in governments, depends in a great measure on their limits, connected with their political distribution.

The extent of many of the states in the Union, is at this time, almost too great for the superintendence of a republican form of government, and must one day or other, revolve into more vigorous ones, or by separation be reduced into smaller, and more useful, as well as moderate ones. You have already observed the feeble efforts of Massachusetts against their insurgents; with what difficulty did they quell that insurrection; and is not the province of Main at this moment, on the eve of separation from her. The reason of these things is, that for the security of the *property* of the community, in which expressive term Mr. Lock makes life, liberty, and estate, to consist—the wheels of a free republic are necessarily slow in their operation; hence in large free republics, the evil sometimes is not only begun, but almost completed, before they are in a situation to turn the current into a contrary progression: the extremes are also too remote from the usual seat of government, and the laws therefore too feeble to afford protection to all its parts, and insure *domestic tranquility* without the aid of another principle. If, therefore, this state, and that of N. Carolina, had an army under their controul, they never would have lost Vermont, and Frankland, nor the state of Massachusetts suffer an insurrection, or the dismemberment of her fairest district, but the exercise of a principle which would have prevented these things, if we may believe the experience of ages, would have ended in the destruction of their liberties.

Will this consolidated republic, if established, in its exercise beget such confidence and compliance, among the citizens of these states, as to do without the aid of a standing army—I deny that it will.—The malcontents in each state, who will not be a few, nor the least important, will be exciting factions against it—the fear of a dismemberment of some of its parts, and the necessity to enforce the execution of revenue laws (a fruitful source of oppression) on the extremes and in the other districts of the government, will incidentally, and necessarily require a permanent force, to be kept on foot—will not political security, and even the opinion of it, be extinguished? can mildness and moderation exist in a government, where the primary incident in its exercise must be force? will not violence destroy confidence, and can equality subsist, where the extent, policy, and practice of it, will naturally lead to make odious distinctions among citizens?

The people, who may compose this national legislature from the southern states, in which, from the mildness of the climate, the fertility of the soil, and the value of its productions, wealth is rapidly acquired, and where the same causes naturally lead to luxury, dissipation, and a passion for aristocratic distinctions; where slavery is encouraged, and liberty of course, less respected, and protected; who know not what it is to acquire property by their own toil, nor to oeconomise with the savings of industry—will these men therefore be as tenacious of the liberties and interests of the more northern states, where freedom, independence, industry, equality, and frugality, are natural to the climate and soil, as men who are your own citizens, legislating in your own state, under your inspection, and whose manners, and fortunes, bear a more equal resemblance to your own?

It may be suggested, in answer to this, that whoever is a citizen of one state, is a citizen of each, and that therefore he will be as interested in the happiness and interest of all, as the one he is delegated from; but the argument is fallacious, and, whoever has attended to the history of mankind, and the principles which bind them together as parents, citizens, or men, will readily perceive it. These principles are, in their exercise, like a pebble cast on the calm surface of a river, the circles begin in the center, and are small, active, and forcible, but as they depart from that point, they lose their force, and vanish into calmness.

The strongest principle of union resides within our domestic walls. The ties of the parent exceed that of any other; as we depart from home, the next general principle of union is amongst citizens of the same state, where acquaintance, habits, and fortunes, nourish affection, and attachment; enlarge the circle still further, and, as citizens of different states, though we acknowledge the same national denomination, we lose the ties of acquaintance, habits, and fortunes, and thus, by degrees, we lessen in our attachments, till, at length, we no more than acknowledge a sameness of species. Is it therefore, from certainty like this, reasonable to believe, that inhabitants of Georgia, or New-Hampshire, will have the same obligations towards you as your own, and preside over your lives, liberties, and property, with the same care and attachment? Intuitive reason, answers in the negative.

In the course of my examination of the principals of consolidation of the states into one general government, many other reasons against it have occurred, but I flatter myself, from those herein offered to your consideration, I have convinced you that it is both presumptuous and impracticable consistent with your safety. To detain you with further remarks, would be useless—I shall however, continue in my following numbers, to anilise this new government, pursuant to my promise.

Cato.

I. JAMES MADISON, THE FEDERALIST, NO. 10

November 22, 1787

To the People of the State of New York.

AMONG the numerous advantages promised by a well constructed Union, none deserves to be more accurately developed than its tendency to break and control the violence of faction. The friend of popular governments, never finds himself so much alarmed for their character and fate, as when he contemplates their propensity to this dangerous vice. He will not fail therefore to set a due value on any plan which, without violating the principles to which he is attached, provides a proper cure for it. The instability, injustice and confusion introduced into the public councils, have in truth been the mortal diseases under which popular governments have every where perished; as they continue to be the favorite and fruitful topics from which the adversaries to liberty derive their most specious declamations. The valuable improvements made by the American Constitutions on the popular models, both ancient and modern, cannot certainly be too much admired; but it would be an unwarrantable partiality, to contend that they have as effectually obviated the danger on this side as was wished and expected. Complaints are every where heard from our most considerate and virtuous citizens, equally the friends of public and private faith, and of public and personal liberty; that our governments are too unstable; that the public good is disregarded in the conflicts of rival parties; and that measures are too often decided, not according to the rules of justice, and the rights of the minor party; but by the superior force of an interested and over-bearing majority. However anxiously we may wish that these complaints had no foundation, the evidence of known facts will not permit us to deny that they are in some degree true. It will be found indeed, on a candid review of our situation, that some of the distresses under which we labor, have been erroneously charged on the operation of our governments; but it will be found, at the same time, that other causes will not alone account for many of our heaviest misfortunes; and particularly, for that prevailing and increasing distrust of public engagements, and alarm for private rights, which are echoed from one end of the continent to the other. These must be chiefly, if not wholly, effects of the unsteadiness and injustice, with which a factious spirit has tainted our public administrations.

By a faction I understand a number of citizens, whether amounting to a majority or minority of the whole, who are united and actuated by some common impulse of passion, or of interest, adverse to the rights of other citizens, or to the permanent and aggregate interests of the community.

There are two methods of curing the mischiefs of faction: the one, by removing its causes; the other, by controling its effects.

There are again two methods of removing the causes of faction: the one by destroying the liberty which is essential to its existence; the other, by giving to every citizen the same opinions, the same passions, and the same interests.

It could never be more truly said than of the first remedy, that it is worse than the disease. Liberty is to faction, what air is to fire, an aliment without which it instantly expires. But it could not be a less folly to abolish liberty, which is essential to political life, because it nourishes faction, than it would be to wish the annihilation of air, which is essential to animal life, because it imparts to fire its destructive agency.

The second expedient is as impracticable, as the first would be unwise. As long as the reason of man continues fallible, and he is at liberty to exercise it, different opinions will be formed. As long as the connection subsists between his reason and his self-love, his opinions and his passions will have a reciprocal influence on each other; and the former will be objects to which the latter will attach themselves. The diversity in the faculties of men from which the rights of property originate, is not less an insuperable obstacle to a uniformity of interests. The protection of these faculties is the first object of Government. From the protection of different and unequal faculties of acquiring property, the possession of different degrees and kinds of property immediately results: and from the influence of these on the sentiments and views of the respective proprietors, ensues a division of the society into different interests and parties.

The latent causes of faction are thus sown in the nature of man; and we see them every where brought into different degrees of activity, according to the different circumstances of civil society. A zeal for different opinions concerning religion, concerning Government and many other points, as well of speculation as of practice; an attachment to different leaders ambitiously contending for pre-eminence and power; or to persons of other descriptions whose fortunes have been interesting to the human passions, have in turn divided mankind into parties, inflamed them with mutual animosity, and rendered them much more disposed to vex and oppress each other, than to co-operate for their common good. So strong is this propensity of mankind to fall into mutual animosities, that where no substantial occasion presents itself, the most frivolous and fanciful distinctions have been sufficient to kindle their unfriendly passions, and excite their most violent conflicts. But the most common and durable source of factions, has been the various and unequal distribution of property. Those who hold, and those who are without property, have ever formed distinct interests in society. Those who are creditors, and those who are debtors, fall under a like discrimination. A landed interest, a manufacturing interest, a mercantile interest, a monied interest, with many lesser interests, grow up of necessity in civilized nations, and divide them into different classes, actuated by different sentiments and views. The regulation of these various and interfering interests forms the principal task of modern Legislation, and involves the spirit of party and faction in the necessary and ordinary operations of Government.

No man is allowed to be a judge in his own cause; because his interest would certainly bias his judgment, and, not improbably, corrupt his integrity. With equal, nay with greater reason, a body of men, are unfit to be both judges and parties, at the same time; yet, what are many of the most important acts of legislation, but so many judicial determinations, not indeed concerning the rights of single persons, but concerning the rights of large bodies of citizens; and what are the different classes of legislators, but advocates and parties to the causes which they determine? Is a law proposed concerning private debts? It is a question to which the creditors are parties on one side, and the debtors on the other. Justice ought to hold the balance between them. Yet the parties are and must be themselves the judges; and the most numerous party, or, in other words, the most powerful faction must be expected to prevail. Shall domestic manufactures be encouraged, and in what degree, by restrictions on foreign manufactures? are questions which would be differently decided by the landed and the manufacturing classes; and probably by neither, with a sole regard to justice and the public good. The apportionment of taxes on the various descriptions of property, is an act which seems to require the most exact impartiality; yet, there is perhaps no legislative act in which greater opportunity and temptation are given to a predominant party, to trample on the rules of justice. Every shilling with which they over-burden the inferior number, is a shilling saved to their own pockets.

It is in vain to say, that enlightened statesmen will be able to adjust these clashing interests, and render them all subservient to the public good. Enlightened statesmen will not always be at the helm: Nor, in many cases, can such an adjustment be made at all, without taking into view indirect and remote considerations, which will rarely prevail over the immediate interest which one party may find in disregarding the rights of another, or the good of the whole.

The inference to which we are brought, is, that the *causes* of faction cannot be removed; and that relief is only to be sought in the means of controling its *effects*.

If a faction consists of less than a majority, relief is supplied by the republican principle, which enables the majority to defeat its sinister views by regular vote: It may clog the administration, it may convulse the society; but it will be unable to execute and mask its violence under the forms of the Constitution. When a majority is included in a faction, the form of popular government on the other hand enables it to sacrifice to its ruling passion or interest, both the public good and the rights of other citizens. To secure the public good, and private rights, against the danger of such a faction, and at the same time to preserve the spirit and the form of popular government, is then the great object to which our enquiries are directed: Let me add that it is the great desideratum, by which alone this form of government can be rescued from the opprobrium under which it has so long labored, and be recommended to the esteem and adoption of mankind.

By what means is this object attainable? Evidently by one of two only. Either the existence of the same passion or interest in a majority at the same time, must be prevented; or the majority, having such co-existent passion or interest, must be rendered, by their number and local situation, unable to concert and carry into effect schemes of oppression. If the impulse and the opportunity be suffered to coincide, we well know that neither moral nor religious motives can be relied on as an adequate control. They are not found to be such on the injustice and violence of individuals, and lose their efficacy in proportion to the number combined together; that is, in proportion as their efficacy becomes needful.

From this view of the subject, it may be concluded, that a pure Democracy, by which I mean, a Society, consisting of a small number of citizens, who assemble and administer the Government in person, can admit of no cure for the mischiefs of faction. A common passion or interest will, in almost every case, be felt by a majority of the whole; a communication and concert results from the form of Government itself; and there is nothing to check the inducements to sacrifice the weaker party, or an obnoxious individual. Hence it is, that such Democracies have ever been spectacles of turbulence and contention; have ever been found incompatible with personal security, or the rights of property; and have in general been as short in their lives, as they have been violent in their deaths. Theoretic politicians, who have patronized this species of Government, have erroneously supposed, that by reducing mankind to a perfect equality in their political rights, they would, at the same time, be perfectly equalized and assimilated in their possessions, their opinions, and their passions.

A Republic, by which I mean a Government in which the (scheme of representation) takes place, opens a different prospect, and promises the cure for which we are seeking. Let us examine the points in which it varies from pure Democracy, and we shall comprehend both the nature of the cure, and the efficacy which it must derive from the Union.

The two great points of difference between a Democracy and a Republic are, first, the delegation of the Government, in the latter, to a small number of citizens elected by the rest: secondly, the greater number of citizens, and greater sphere of country, over which the latter may be extended.

The effect of the first difference is, on the one hand to refine and enlarge the public views, by passing them through the medium of a chosen body of citizens, whose wisdom may best discern the true interest of their country, and whose patriotism and love of justice, will be least likely to sacrifice it to temporary or partial considerations. Under such a regulation, it may well happen that the public voice pronounced by the representatives of the people, will be more consonant to the public good, than if pronounced by the people themselves convened for the purpose. On the other hand, the effect may be inverted. Men of factious tempers, of local prejudices, or of sinister designs, may by intrigue, by corruption or by other means, first obtain the suffrages, and then betray the interests of the people. The question resulting is, whether small or extensive Republics are most favorable to the election of proper guardians of the public weal: and it is clearly decided in favor of the latter by two obvious considerations.

In the first place it is to be remarked that however small the Republic may be, the Representatives must be raised to a certain number, in order to guard against the cabals of a few; and that however large it may be, they must be limited to a certain number, in order to guard against the confusion of a multitude. Hence the number of Representatives in the two cases, not being in proportion to that of the Constituents, and being proportionally greatest in the small Republic, it follows, that if the proportion of fit characters, be not less, in the large than in the small Republic, the former will present a greater option, and consequently a greater probability of a fit choice.

In the next place, as each Representative will be chosen by a greater number of citizens in the large than in the small Republic, it will be more difficult for unworthy candidates to practise with success the vicious arts, by which elections are too often carried; and the suffrages of the people being more free, will be more likely to centre on men who possess the most attractive merit, and the most diffusive and established characters.

It must be confessed, that in this, as in most other cases, there is a mean, on both sides of which inconveniencies will be found to lie. By enlarging too much the number of electors, you render the representative too little acquainted with all their local circumstances and lesser interests; as by reducing it too much, you render him unduly attached to these, and too little fit to comprehend and pursue great and national objects. The Federal Constitution forms a happy combination in this respect; the great and aggregate interests being referred to the national, the local and particular, to the state legislatures.

The other point of difference is, the greater number of citizens and extent of territory which may be brought within the compass of Republican, than of Democratic Government; and it is this circumstance principally which renders factious combinations less to be dreaded in the former, than in the latter. The smaller the society, the fewer probably will be the distinct parties and interests composing it; the fewer the distinct parties and interests, the more frequently will a majority be found of the same party; and the smaller the number of individuals composing a majority, and the smaller the compass within which they are placed, the more easily will they concert and execute their plans of oppression. Extend the sphere, and you take in a greater variety of parties and interests; you make it less probable that a majority of the whole will have a common motive to invade the rights of other citizens; or if such a common motive exists, it will be more difficult for all who feel it to discover their own strength, and to act in unison with each other. Besides other impediments, it may be remarked, that where there is a consciousness of unjust or dishonorable purposes, communication is always checked by distrust, in proportion to the number whose concurrence is necessary.

Hence it clearly appears, that the same advantage, which a Republic has over a Democracy, in controling the effects of faction, is enjoyed by a large over a small Republic—is enjoyed by the Union over the States composing it. Does this advantage consist in the substitution of Representatives, whose enlightened views and virtuous sentiments render them superior to local prejudices, and to schemes of injustice? It will not be denied, that the Representation of the Union will be most likely to possess these requisite endowments. Does it consist in the greater security afforded by a greater variety of parties, against the event of any one party being able to outnumber and oppress the rest? In an equal degree does the encreased variety of parties, comprised within the Union, encrease this security. Does it, in fine, consist in the greater obstacles opposed to the concert and accomplishment of the secret wishes of an unjust and interested majority? Here, again, the extent of the Union gives it the most palpable advantage.

The influence of factious leaders may kindle a flame within their particular States, but will be unable to spread a general conflagration through the other States: a religious sect, may degenerate into a political faction in a part of the Confederacy; but the variety of sects dispersed over the entire face of it, must secure the national Councils against any danger from that source: a rage for paper money, for an abolition of debts, for an equal division of property, or for any other improper or wicked project, will be less apt to pervade the whole body of the Union, than a particular member of it; in the same proportion as such a malady is more likely to taint a particular county or district, than an entire State.

In the extent and proper structure of the Union, therefore, we behold a Republican remedy for the diseases most incident to Republican Government. And according to the degree of pleasure and pride, we feel in being Republicans, ought to be our zeal in cherishing the spirit, and supporting the character of Federalists.

PUBLIUS.

J. JAMES MADISON, THE FEDERALIST, NO. 14

November 30, 1787

To the People of the State of New York.

W<small>E</small> have seen the necessity of the union as our bulwark against foreign danger, as the conservator of peace among ourselves, as the guardian of our commerce and other common interests, as the only substitute for those military establishments which have subverted the liberties of the old world; and as the proper antidote for the diseases of faction, which have proved fatal to other popular governments, and of which alarming symptoms have been betrayed by our own. All that remains, within this branch of our enquiries, is to take notice of an objection, that may be drawn from the great extent of country which the union embraces. A few observations on this subject will be the more proper, as it is perceived that the adversaries of the new constitution are availing themselves of a prevailing prejudice, with regard to the practicable sphere of republican administration, in order to supply by imaginary difficulties, the want of those solid objections, which they endeavor in vain to find.

The error which limits Republican Government to a narrow district, has been unfolded and refuted in preceding papers. I remark here only, that it seems to owe its rise and prevalence, chiefly to the confounding of a republic with a democracy: And applying to the former reasonings drawn from the nature of the latter. The true distinction between these forms was also adverted to on a former occasion. It is, that in a democracy, the people meet and exercise the government in person; in a republic they assemble and administer it by their representatives and agents. A democracy consequently will be confined to a small spot. A republic may be extended over a large region.

To this accidental source of the error may be added the artifice of some celebrated authors, whose writings have had a great share in forming the modern standard of political opinions. Being subjects either of an absolute, or limited monarchy, they have endeavored to heighten the advantages or palliate the evils of those forms; by placing in comparison with them, the vices and defects of the republican, and by citing as specimens of the latter, the turbulent democracies of ancient Greece, and modern Italy. Under the confusion of names, it has been an easy task to transfer to a republic, observations applicable to a democracy only, and among others, the observation that it can never be established but among a small number of people, living within a small compass of territory.

Such a fallacy may have been the less perceived as most of the governments of antiquity were of the democratic species; and even in modern Europe, to which we owe the great principle of representation, no example is seen of a government wholly popular, and founded at the same time wholly on that principle. If Europe has the merit of discovering this great mechanical power in government, by the simple agency of which, the will of the largest political body may be concentred, and its force directed to any object, which the public good requires; America can claim the merit of making the discovery the basis of unmixed and extensive republics. It is only to be lamented, that any of her citizens should wish to deprive her of the additional merit of displaying its full efficacy on the establishment of the comprehensive system now under her consideration.

As the natural limit of a democracy is that distance from the central point, which will just permit the most remote citizens to assemble as often as their public functions demand; and will include no greater number than can join in those functions; so the natural limit of a republic is that distance from the center, which will barely allow the representatives of the people to meet as often as may be necessary for the administration of public affairs. Can it be said, that the limits of the United States exceed this distance? It will not be said by those who recollect that the Atlantic coast is the longest side of the union; that during the term of thirteen years, the representatives of the States have been almost continually assembled; and that the members from the most distant States are not chargeable with greater intermissions of attendance, than those from the States in the neighbourhood of Congress.

That we may form a juster estimate with regard to this interesting subject, let us resort to the actual dimensions of the union. The limits as fixed by the treaty of peace are on the east the Atlantic, on the south the latitude of thirty-one degrees, on the west the Mississippi, and on the north an irregular line running in some instances beyond the forty-fifth degree, in others falling as low as the forty-second. The southern shore of Lake Erie lies below that latitude. Computing the distance between the thirty-one and forty-five degrees, it amounts to nine hundred and seventy-three common miles; computing it from thirty-one to forty-two degrees to seven hundred, sixty four miles and an half. Taking the mean for the distance, the amount will be eight hundred, sixty-eight miles and three-fourths. The mean distance from the Atlantic to the Mississippi does not probably exceed seven hundred and fifty miles. On a comparison of this extent, with that of several countries in Europe, the practicability of rendering our system commensurate to it, appears to be demonstrable. It is not a great deal larger than Germany, where a Diet representing the whole empire is continually assembled; or than Poland before the late dismemberment, where another national Diet was the depository of the supreme power. Passing by France and Spain, we find that in Great Britain, inferior as it may be in size, the representatives of the northern extremity of the island, have as far to travel to the national

Council, as will be required of those of the most remote parts of the union.

Favorable as this view of the subject may be, some observations remain which will place it in a light still more satisfactory.

In the first place it is to be remembered, that the general government is not to be charged with the whole power of making and administering laws. Its jurisdiction is limited to certain enumerated objects, which concern all the members of the republic, but which are not to be attained by the separate provisions of any. The subordinate governments which can extend their care to all those other objects, which can be separately provided for, will retain their due authority and activity. Were it proposed by the plan of the Convention to abolish the governments of the particular States, its adversaries would have some ground for their objection, though it would not be difficult to shew that if they were abolished, the general government would be compelled by the principle of self-preservation, to reinstate them in their proper jurisdiction.

A second observation to be made is, that the immediate object of the Fœderal Constitution is to secure the union of the Thirteen Primitive States, which we know to be practicable; and to add to them such other States, as may arise in their own bosoms or in their neighbourhoods, which we cannot doubt to be equally practicable. The arrangements that may be necessary for those angles and fractions of our territory, which lie on our north western frontier, must be left to those whom further discoveries and experience will render more equal to the task.

Let it be remarked in the third place, that the intercourse throughout the union will be daily facilitated by new improvements. Roads will every where be shortened, and kept in better order; accommodations for travellers will be multiplied and meliorated; and interior navigation on our eastern side will be opened throughout, or nearly throughout the whole extent of the Thirteen States. The communication between the western and Atlantic districts, and between different parts of each, will be rendered more and more easy by those numerous canals with which the beneficence of nature has intersected our country, and which art finds it so little difficult to connect and complete.

A fourth and still more important consideration is, that as almost every State will on one side or other, be a frontier, and will thus find in a regard to its safety, an inducement to make some sacrifices for the sake of the general protection; so the States which lie at the greatest distance from the heart of the union, and which of course may partake least of the ordinary circulation of its benefits, will be at the same time immediately contiguous to foreign nations, and will consequently stand on particular occasions, in greatest need of its strength and resources. It may be inconvenient for Georgia or the States forming our western or north eastern borders to send their representatives to the seat of government, but they would find it more so to struggle alone against an invading enemy, or even to support alone the whole expence of those precautions, which may be dictated by the neighbourhood of continual danger. If they should derive less benefit therefore from the union in some respects, than the less distant States, they will derive greater benefit from it in other respects, and thus the proper equilibrium will be maintained throughout.

I submit to you my fellow citizens, these considerations, in full confidence that the good sense which has so often marked your decisions, will allow them their due weight and effect; and that you will never suffer difficulties, however formidable in appearance or however fashionable the error on which they may be founded, to drive you into the gloomy and perilous scene into which the advocates for disunion would conduct you. Hearken not to the unnatural voice which tells you that the people of America, knit together as they are by so many chords of affection, can no longer live together as members of the same family; can no longer continue the mutual guardians of their mutual happiness; can no longer be fellow citizens of one great respectable and flourishing empire. Hearken not to the voice which petulantly tells you that the form of government recommended for your adoption is a novelty in the political world; that it has never yet had a place in the theories of the wildest projectors; that it rashly attempts what it is impossible to accomplish. No my countrymen, shut your ears against this unhallowed language. Shut your hearts against the poison which it conveys; the kindred blood which flows in the veins of American citizens, the mingled blood which they have shed in defence of their sacred rights, consecrate their union, and excite horror at the idea of their becoming aliens, rivals, enemies. And if novelties are to be shunned, believe me the most alarming of all novelties, the most wild of all projects, the most rash of all attempts, is that of rending us in pieces, in order to preserve our liberties and promote our happiness. But why is the experiment of an extended republic to be rejected merely because it may comprise what is new? Is it not the glory of the people of America, that whilst they have paid a decent regard to the opinions of former times and other nations, they have not suffered a blind veneration for antiquity, for custom, or for names, to overrule the suggestions of their own good sense, the knowledge of their own situation, and the lessons of their own experience? To this manly spirit, posterity will be indebted for the possession, and the world for the example of the numerous innovations displayed on the American theatre, in favor of private rights and public happiness. Had no important step been taken by the leaders of the revolution for which a precedent could not be discovered, no government established of which an exact model did not present itself, the people of the United States might, at this moment, have been numbered among the melancholy victims of misguided councils, must at best have been labouring under the weight of some of those forms which have crushed the liberties of the rest of mankind. Happily for America, happily we trust for the whole

292

human race, they pursued a new and more noble course. They accomplished a revolution which has no parallel in the annals of human society: They reared the fabrics of governments which have no model on the face of the globe. They formed the design of a great confederacy, which it is incumbent on their successors to improve and perpetuate. If their works betray imperfections, we wonder at the fewness of them. If they erred most in the structure of the union; this was the work most difficult to be executed; this is the work which has been new modelled by the act of your Convention, and it is that act on which you are now to deliberate and to decide.

PUBLIUS.

K. LETTER FROM THE FEDERAL FARMER, NO. 11

January 10, 1788

Dear Sir,

I shall now add a few observations respecting the organization of the senate, the manner of appointing it, and its powers.

The senate is an assembly of 26 members, two from each state, though the senators are apportioned on the federal plan, they will vote individually; they represent the states, as bodies politic, sovereign to certain purposes; the states being sovereign and independent, are all considered equal, each with the other in the senate. In this we are governed solely by the ideal equalities of sovereignties; the federal and state governments forming one whole, and the state governments an essential part, which ought always to be kept distinctly in view, and preserved: I feel more disposed, on reflection, to acquiesce in making them the basis of the senate, and thereby to make it the interest and duty of the senators to preserve distinct, and to perpetuate the respective sovereignties they shall represent.

As to the appointments of senators, I have already observed, that they must be appointed by the legislatures, by concurrent acts, and each branch have an equal share of power, as I do not see any probability of amendments, if advisable, in these points, I shall not dwell upon them.

The senate, as a legislative branch, is not large, but as an executive branch quite too numerous. It is not to be presumed that we can form a genuine senatorial branch in the United States, a real representation of the aristocracy and balance in the legislature, any more than we can form a genuine representation of the people. Could we separate the aristocratical and democratical interests; compose the senate of the former, and the house of assembly of the latter, they are too unequal in the United States to produce a balance. Form them on pure principles, and leave each to be supported by its real weight and connections, the senate would be feeble, and the house powerful:—I say, on pure principles; because I make a distinction between a senate that derives its weight and influence from a pure source, its numbers and wisdom, its extensive property, its extensive and permanent connections; and a senate composed of a few men, possessing small property, small and unstable connections, that derives its weight and influence from a corrupt or pernicious source; that is, merely from the power given it by the constitution and laws, to dispose of the public offices, and the annexed emoluments, and by those means to interest officers, and the hungry expectants of offices, in support of its measures. I wish the proposed senate may not partake too much of the latter description.

To produce a balance and checks, the constitution proposes two branches in the legislature; but they are so formed, that the members of both must generally be the same kind of men—men having similar interests and views, feelings and connections—men of the same grade in society, and who associate on all occasions (probably, if there be any difference, the senators will be the most democratic.) Senators and representatives thus circumstanced, as men, though convened in two rooms, to make laws, must be governed generally by the same motives and views, and therefore pursue the same system of politics; the partitions between the two branches will be merely those of the building in which they sit: there will not be found in them any of those genuine balances and checks, among the real different interests, and efforts of the several classes of men in the community we aim at; nor can any such balances and checks be formed in the present condition of the United States in any considerable degree of perfection: but to give them the greatest degree of perfection practicable, we ought to make the senate respectable as to numbers, the qualifications of the electors and of the elected; to increase the numbers of the representatives, and so to model the elections of them, as always to draw a majority of them substantially from the body of the people. Though I conclude the senators and representatives will not form in the legislature those balances and checks which correspond with the actual state of the people; yet I approve of two branches, because we may notwithstanding derive several advantages from them. The senate, from the mode of its appointment, will probably be influenced to support the state governments, and, from its periods of service will produce stability in legislation, while frequent elections may take place in the other branch. There is generally a degree of competition between two assemblies even composed of the same kind of men; and by this, and by means of every law's passing a revision in the second branch, caution, coolness, and deliberation are produced in the business of making laws. By means of a democratic branch we may particularly secure personal liberty; and by means of a senatorial branch we may particularly protect property. By the division, the house becomes the proper body to impeach all officers for misconduct in office, and the senate the proper court to try them; and in a country where limited powers must be lodged in the first magistrate, the senate, perhaps, may be the most proper body to be found to have a negative upon him in making treaties, and in managing foreign affairs.

Though I agree the federal senate, in the form proposed, may be useful to many purposes, and that it is not very necessary to alter the organization, modes of appointment, and powers of it in several respects; yet, without alterations in others, I sincerely believe it will, in a very few years, become the source of the greatest evils. Some of these alterations, I conceive, to be absolutely necessary, and some of them at least advisable.

1. By the confederation the members of congress are chosen annually. By art 1. sect. 2. of the constitution, the senators shall be chosen for six years. As the period of service must be, in a considerable degree, matter of opinion on this head, I shall only make a few observations, to explain why I think it more advisable to limit it to three or four years.

The people of this country have not been accustomed to so long appointments in their state governments, they have generally adopted annual elections. The members of the present congress are chosen yearly, who, from the nature and multiplicity of their business, ought to be chosen for longer periods than the federal senators—Men six years in office absolutely contract callous habits, and cease, in too great a degree, to feel their dependance, and for the condition of their constitutents. Senators continued in offices three or four years, will be in them longer than any popular erroneous opinions will probably continue to actuate their electors—men appointed for three or four years, will generally be long enough in office to give stability, and amply to acquire political information. By a change of legislators, as often as circumstances will permit, political knowledge is diffused more extensively among the people, and the attention of the electors and elected more constantly kept alive; circumstances of infinite importance in a free country. Other reasons might be added, but my subject is too extensive to admit of my dwelling upon less material points.

2. When the confederation was formed, it was considered essentially necessary that the members of congress should at any time be recalled by their respective states, when the states should see fit, and others be sent in their room. I do not think it less necessary that this principle should be extended to the members of congress under the new constitution, and especially to the senators. I have had occasion several times to observe, that let us form a federal constitution as extensively, and on the best principles in our power, we must, after all, trust a vast deal to a few men, who, far removed from their constituents, will administer the federal government; there is but little danger these men will feel too great a degree of dependance: the necessary and important object to be attended to, is to make them feel dependant enough. Men elected for several years, several hundred miles distant from their states, possessed of very extensive powers, and the means-of paying themselves, will not, probably, be oppressed with a sense of dependance and responsibility.

The senators will represent sovereignties, which generally have, and always ought to retain, the power of recalling their agents; the principle of responsibility is strongly felt in men who are liable to be recalled and censured for their misconduct; and, if we may judge from experience, the latter will not abuse the power of recalling their members; to possess it, will, at least be a valuable check. It is in the nature of all delegated power, that the constituents should retain the right to judge concerning the conduct of their representatives; they must exercise the power, and their decision itself, their approving or disapproving that conduct implies a right, a power to continue in office, or to remove from it. But whenever the substitute acts under a constitution, then it becomes necessary that the power of recalling him be expressed. The reasons for lodging a power to recall are stronger, as they respect the senate, than as they respect the representatives; the latter will be more frequently elected, and changed of course, and being chosen by the people at large, it would be more difficult for the people than for the legislatures to take the necessary measures for recalling: but even the people, if the powers will be more beneficial to them than injurious, ought to possess it. The people are not apt to wrong a man who is steady and true to their interests; they may for a while be misled by party representations, and leave a good man out of office unheard; but every recall supposes a deliberate decision, and a fair hearing; and no man who believes his conduct proper, and the result of honest views, will be the less useful in his public character, on account of the examination his actions may be liable to; and a man conscious of the contrary conduct, ought clearly to be restrained by the apprehensions of a trial. I repeat it, it is interested combinations and factions we are particularly to guard against in the federal government, and all the rational means that can be put into the hands of the people to prevent them, ought to be provided and furnished for them. Where there is a power to recall, trusty centinels among the people, or in the state legislatures, will have a fair opportunity to become useful. If the members in congress from the states join in such combinations, or favour them, or pursue a pernicious line of conduct, the most attentive among the people, or in the state legislatures, may formally charge them before their constituents: the very apprehensions of such constitutional charges may prevent many of the evils mentioned, and the recalling the members of a single state, a single senator, or representative, may often prevent many more; nor do I, at present, discover any danger in such proceedings, as every man who shall move for a recall will put his reputation at stake, to shew he has reasonable grounds for his motion; and it is not probable such motions will be made unless there be good apparent grounds for succeeding; nor can the charge or motion be any thing more than the attack of an individual or individuals, unless a majority of the constituents shall see cause to go into the enquiry. Further, the circumstance of such a power being lodged in the constituents, will tend continually to keep up their watchfulness, as well as the attention and dependance of the federal senators and representatives.

3.   By the confederation it is provided, that no delegate shall serve more than three years in any term of six years, and thus, by the forms of the government, a rotation of members is produced: a like principle has been adopted in some of the state governments, and also in some antient and modern republics. Whether this exclusion of a man for a given period, after he shall have served a given time, ought to be ingra[f]ted into a constitution or not, is a question, the proper decision materially depends upon the leading features of the government: some governments are so formed as to produce a sufficient fluctuation and change of members of course, in the ordinary course of elections, proper numbers of new members are, from time to time, brought into the legislature, and a proportionate number of old ones go out, mix, and become diffused among the people. This is the case with all numerous representative legislatures, the members of which are frequently elected, and constantly within the view of their constituents. This is the case with our state governments, and in them a constitutional rotation is unimportant. But in a government consisting of but a few members, elected for long periods, and far removed from the observation of the people, but few changes in the ordinary course of elections take place among the members; they become in some measure a fixed body, and often inattentive to the public good, callous, selfish, and the fountain of corruption. To prevent these evils, and to force a principle of pure animation into the federal government, which will be formed much in this last manner mentioned, and to produce attention, activity, and a diffusion of knowledge in the community, we ought to establish among others the principle of rotation. Even good men in office, in time, imperceptibly lose sight of the people, and gradually fall into measures prejudicial to them. It is only a rotation among the members of the federal legislature I shall contend for: judges and officers at the heads of the judicial and executive departments, are in a very different situation, their offices and duties require the information and studies of many years for performing them in a manner advantageous to the people. These judges and officers must apply their whole time to the detail business of their offices, and depend on them for their support: then they always act under masters or superiors, and may be removed from office for misconduct; they pursue a certain round of executive business: their offices must be in all societies confined to a few men, because but few can become qualified to fill them: and were they, by annual appointments, open to the people at large, they are offices of such a nature as to be of no service to them; they must leave these offices in the possession of the few individuals qualified to fill them, or have them badly filled. In the judicial and executive departments also, the body of the people possess a large share of power and influence, as jurors and subordinate officers, among whom there are many and frequent rotations. But in every free country the legislatures are all on a level, and legislation becomes partial whenever,

in practice, it rests for any considerable time in a few hands. It is the true republican principle to diffuse the power of making the laws among the people, and so to modify the forms of the government as to draw in turn the well informed of every class into the legislature.

To determine the propriety or impropriety of this rotation, we must take the inconveniencies as well as the advantages attending it into view: on the one hand, by this rotation, we may sometimes exclude good men from being elected. On the other hand, we guard against those pernicious connections, which usually grow up among men left to continue long periods in office, we increase the number of those who make the laws and return to their constituents; and thereby spread information, and preserve a spirit of activity and investigation among the people: hence a balance of interests and exertions are preserved, and the ruinous measures of factions rendered more impracticable. I would not urge the principle of rotation, if I believed the consequence would be an uninformed federal legislature; but I have no apprehension of this in this enlightened country. The members of congress, at any one time, must be but very few, compared with the respectable well informed men in the United States; and I have no idea there will be any want of such men for members of congress, though by a principle of rotation the constitution should exclude from being elected for two years those federal legislators, who may have served the four years immediately preceding, or any four years in the six preceding years. If we may judge from experience and fair calculations, this principle will never operate to exclude at any one period a fifteenth part, even of those men who have been members of congress. Though no man can sit in congress, by the confederation, more than three years in any term of six years, yet not more than three, four, or five men in any one state, have been made ineligible at any one period; and if a good man happen to be excluded by this rotation, it is only for a short time. All things considered, the inconveniencies of the principle must be very inconsiderable compared with the many advantages of it. It will generally be expedient for a man who has served four years in congress to return home, mix with the people, and reside some time with them: this will tend to reinstate him in the interests, feelings, and views similar to theirs, and thereby confirm in him the essential qualifications of a legislator. Even in point of information, it may be observed, the useful information of legislators is not acquired merely in studies in offices, and in meeting to make laws from day to day; they must learn the actual situation of the people, by being among them, and when they have made laws, return home, and observe how they operate. Thus occasionally to be among the people, is not only necessary to prevent or banish the callous habits and self interested views of office in legislators, but to afford them necessary information, and to render them useful: another valuable end is answered by it, sympathy, and the means of communication between them and their constituents, is substantially promoted; so that on every principle legislators, at certain periods, ought to live among their constituents.

Some men of science are undoubtedly necessary in every legislature; but the knowledge, generally, necessary for men who make laws, is a knowledge of the common concerns, and particular circumstances of the people. In a republican government seats in the legislature are highly honorable; I believe but few do, and surely none ought to consider them as places of profit and permanent support. Were the people always properly attentive, they would, at proper periods, call their law makers home, by sending others in their room: but this is not often the case, and therefore, in making constitutions, when the people are attentive, they ought cautiously to provide for those benefits, those advantageous changes in the administration of their affairs, which they are often apt to be inattentive to in practice. On the whole, to guard against the evils, and to secure the advantages I have mentioned, with the greatest degree of certainty, we ought clearly, in my opinion, to increase the federal representation, to secure elections on proper principles, to establish a right to recall members, and a rotation among them. . . .

L. JAMES MADISON, THE FEDERALIST, NO. 49

February 2, 1788

To the People of the State of New York.

THE author of the "Notes on the state of Virginia," quoted in the last paper, has subjoined to that valuable work, the draught of a constitution which had been prepared in order to be laid before a convention expected to be called in 1783 by the legislature, for the establishment of a constitution for that commonwealth. The plan, like every thing from the same pen, marks a turn of thinking original, comprehensive and accurate; and is the more worthy of attention, as it equally displays a fervent attachment to republican government, and an enlightened view of the dangerous propensities against which it ought to be guarded. One of the precautions which he proposes, and on which he appears ultimately to rely as a palladium to the weaker departments of power, against the invasions of the stronger, is perhaps altogether his own, and as it immediately relates to the subject of our present enquiry, ought not to be overlooked.

His proposition is, "that whenever any two of the three branches of government shall concur in opinion, each by the voices of two thirds of their whole number, that a convention is necessary for altering the constitution or *correcting breaches of it,* a convention shall be called for the purpose."

As the people are the only legitimate fountain of power, and it is from them that the constitutional charter, under which the several branches of government hold their power, is derived; it seems strictly consonant to the republican theory, to recur to the same original authority, not only whenever it may be necessary to enlarge, diminish, or new-model the powers of government; but also whenever any one of the departments may commit encroachments on the chartered authorities of the others. The several departments being perfectly co-ordinate by the terms of their common commission, neither of them, it is evident, can pretend to an exclusive or superior right of settling the boundaries between their respective powers; and how are the encroachments of the stronger to be prevented, or the wrongs of the weaker to be redressed, without an appeal to the people themselves; who, as the grantors of the commission, can alone declare its true meaning and enforce its observance?

There is certainly great force in this reasoning, and it must be allowed to prove, that a constitutional road to the decision of the people, ought to be marked out, and kept open, for certain great and extraordinary occasions. But there appear to be insuperable objections against the proposed recurrence to the people, as a provision in all cases for keeping the several departments of power within their constitutional limits.

In the first place, the provision does not reach the case of a combination of two of the departments against a third. If the legislative authority, which possesses so many means of operating on the motives of the other departments, should be able to gain to its interest either of the others, or even one-third of its members, the remaining department could derive no advantage from this remedial provision. I do not dwell however on this objection, because it may be thought to lie rather against the modification of the principle, than against the principle itself.

In the next place, it may be considered as an objection inherent in the principle, that as every appeal to the people would carry an implication of some defect in the government, frequent appeals would in great measure deprive the government of that veneration, which time bestows on every thing, and without which perhaps the wisest and freest governments would not possess the requisite stability. If it be true that all governments rest on opinion, it is no less true that the strength of opinion in each individual, and its practical influence on his conduct, depend much on the number which he supposes to have entertained the same opinion. The reason of man, like man himself is timid and cautious, when left alone; and acquires firmness and confidence, in proportion to the number with which it is associated. When the examples, which fortify opinion, are *antient* as well as *numerous*, they are known to have a double effect. In a nation of philosophers, this consideration ought to be disregarded. A reverence for the laws, would be sufficiently inculcated by the voice of an enlightened reason. But a nation of philosophers is as little to be expected as the philosophical race of kings wished for by Plato. And in every other nation, the most rational government will not find it a superfluous advantage, to have the prejudices of the community on its side.

The danger of disturbing the public tranquility by interesting too strongly the public passions, is a still more serious objection against a frequent reference of constitutional questions, to the decision of the whole society. Notwithstanding the success which has attended the revisions of our established forms of government, and which does so much honour to the virtue and intelligence of the people of America, it must be confessed, that the experiments are of too ticklish a nature to be unnecessarily multiplied. We are to recollect that all the existing constitutions were formed in the midst of a danger which repressed the passions most unfriendly to order and concord; of an enthusiastic confidence of the people in their patriotic leaders, which stifled the ordinary diversity of opinions on great national questions; of a universal ardor for new and opposite forms, produced by a universal resentment and indignation against the antient government; and whilst no spirit of party, connected with the changes to be made, or the abuses to be reformed, could mingle its leven in the operation. The future situations in which we must expect to be usually placed, do not present any equivalent security against the danger which is apprehended.

But the greatest objection of all is, that the decisions which would probably result from such appeals, would not answer the purpose of maintaining the constitutional equilibrium of the government. We have seen that the tendency of republican governments is to an aggrandizement of the legislative, at the expence of the other departments. The appeals to the people therefore would usually be made by the executive and judiciary departments. But whether made by one side or the other, would each side enjoy equal advantages on the trial? Let us view their different situations. The members of the executive and judiciary departments, are few in number, and can be personally known to a small part only of the people. The latter by the mode of their appointment, as well as, by the nature and permanency of it, are too far removed from the people to share much in their prepossessions. The former are generally the objects of jealousy: And their administration is always liable to be discoloured and rendered unpopular. The members of the legislative department, on the other hand, are numerous. They are distributed and dwell among the people at large. Their connections of blood, of friendship and of acquaintance, embrace a great proportion of the most influencial part of the society. The nature of their public trust implies a personal influence among the people, and that they are more immediately the confidential guardians of the rights and liberties of the people. With these advantages, it can hardly be supposed that the adverse party would have an equal chance for a favorable issue.

But the legislative party would not only be able to plead their cause most successfully with the people. They would probably be constituted themselves the judges. The same influence which had gained them an election into the legislature, would gain them a seat in the convention. If this should not be the case with all, it would probably be the case with many, and pretty certainly with those leading characters, on whom every thing depends in such bodies. The convention in short would be composed chiefly of men, who had been, who actually were, or who expected to be, members of the department whose conduct was arraigned. They would consequently be parties to the very question to be decided by them.

It might however sometimes happen, that appeals would be made under circumstances less adverse to the executive and judiciary departments. The usurpations of the legislature might be so flagrant and so sudden, as to admit of no specious colouring. A strong party among themselves might take side with the other branches. The executive power might be in the hands of a peculiar favorite of the people. In such a posture of things, the public decision might be less swayed by prepossessions in favor of the legislative party. But still it could never be expected to turn on the true merits of the question. It would inevitably be connected with the spirit of pre-existing parties, or of parties springing out of the question itself. It would be connected with persons of distinguished character and extensive influence in the community. It would be pronounced by the very men who had been agents in, or opponents of the measures, to which the decision would relate. The *passions* therefore not *the reason,* of the public, would sit in judgment. But it is the reason of the public alone that ought to controul and regulate the government. The passions ought to be controuled and regulated by the government.

We found in the last paper that mere declarations in the written constitution, are not sufficient to restrain the several departments within their legal limits. It appears in this, that occasional appeals to the people would be neither a proper nor an effectual provision, for that purpose. How far the provisions of a different nature contained in the plan above quoted, might be adequate, I do not examine. Some of them are unquestionably founded on sound political principles, and all of them are framed with singular ingenuity and precision.

PUBLIUS.

M.   JAMES MADISON, THE FEDERALIST, NO. 63

March 1, 1788

To the People of the State of New York.

A Fifth desideratum illustrating the utility of a Senate, is the want of a due sense of national character. Without a select and stable member of the government, the esteem of foreign powers will not only be forfeited by an unenlightened and variable policy, proceeding from the causes already mentioned; but the national councils will not possess that sensibility to the opinion of the world, which is perhaps not less necessary in order to merit, than it is to obtain, its respect and confidence.

An attention to the judgment of other nations is important to every government for two reasons: The one is, that independently of the merits of any particular plan or measure, it is desireable on various accounts, that it should appear to other nations as the offspring of a wise and honorable policy: The second is, that in doubtful cases, particularly where the national councils may be warped by some strong passion, or momentary interest, the presumed or known opinion of the impartial world, may be the best guide that can be followed. What has not America lost by her want of character with foreign nations? And how many errors and follies would she not have avoided, if the justice and propriety of her measures had in every instance been previously tried by the light in which they would probably appear to the unbiassed part of mankind?

Yet however requisite a sense of national character may be, it is evident that it can never be sufficiently possessed by a numerous and changeable body. It can only be found in a number so small, that a sensible degree of the praise and blame of public measures may be the portion of each individual; or in an assembly so durably invested with public trust, that the pride and consequence of its members may be sensibly incorporated with the reputation and prosperity of the community. The half-yearly representatives of Rhode-Island, would probably have been little affected in their deliberations on the iniquitous measures of that state, by arguments drawn from the light in which such measures would be viewed by foreign nations, or even by the sister states; whilst it can scarcely be doubted, that if the concurrence of a select and stable body had been necessary, a regard to national character alone, would have prevented the calamities under which that misguided people is now labouring.

I add as a *sixth* defect, the want in some important cases of a due responsibility in the government to the people, arising from that frequency of elections, which in other cases produces this responsibility. This remark will perhaps appear not only new but paradoxical. It must nevertheless be acknowledged, when explained, to be as undeniable as it is important.

Responsibility in order to be reasonable must be limited to objects within the power of the responsible party; and in order to be effectual, must relate to operations of that power, of which a ready and proper judgment can be formed by the constituents. The objects of government may be divided into two general classes; the one depending on measures which have singly an immediate and sensible operation; the other depending on a succession of well chosen and well connected measures, which have a gradual and perhaps unobserved operation. The importance of the latter description to the collective and permanent welfare of every country needs no explanation. And yet it is evident, that an assembly elected for so short a term as to be unable to provide more than one or two links in a chain of measures, on which the general welfare may essentially depend, ought not to be answerable for the final result, any more than a steward or tenant, engaged for one year, could be justly made to answer for places or improvements, which could not be accomplished in less than half a dozen years. Nor is it possible for the people to estimate the *share* of influence which their annual assemblies may respectively have on events resulting from the mixed transactions of several years. It is sufficiently difficult at any rate to preserve a personal responsibility in the members of a *numerous* body, for such acts of the body as have an immediate, detached and palpable operation on its constituents.

The proper remedy for this defect must be an additional body in the legislative department, which, having sufficient permanency to provide for such objects as require a continued attention, and a train of measures, may be justly and effectually answerable for the attainment of those objects.

Thus far I have considered the circumstances which point out the necessity of a well constructed senate, only as they relate to the representatives of the people. To a people as little blinded by prejudice, or corrupted by flattery, as those whom I address, I shall not scruple to add, that such an institution may be sometimes necessary, as a defence to the people against their own temporary errors and delusions. As the cool and deliberate sense of the community ought in all governments, and actually will in all free governments ultimately prevail over the views of its rulers; so there are particular moments in public affairs, when the people stimulated by some irregular passion, or some illicit advantage, or misled by the artful misrepresentations of interested men, may call for measures which they themselves will afterwards be the most ready to lament and condemn. In these critical moments, how salutary will be the interference of some temperate and respectable body of citizens, in order to check the misguided career, and to suspend the blow meditated by the people against themselves, until reason, justice and truth, can regain their authority over the public mind? What bitter anguish would not the people of Athens have often escaped, if their government had contained so provident a safeguard against the tyranny of their own passions? Popular liberty might then have escaped the indelible reproach of decreeing to the same citizens, the hemlock on one day, and statues on the next.

It may be suggested that a people spread over an extensive region, cannot like the crouded inhabitants of a small district, be subject to the infection of violent passions; or to the danger of combining in the pursuit of unjust measures. I am far from denying that this is a distinction of peculiar importance. I have on the contrary endeavoured in a former paper, to shew that it is one of the principal recommendations of a confederated republic. At the same time this advantage ought not to be considered as superseding the use of auxiliary precautions. It may even be remarked that the same extended situation which will exempt the people of America from some of the dangers incident to lesser republics, will expose them to the inconveniency of remaining for a longer time, under the influence of those misrepresentations which the combined industry of interested men may succeed in distributing among them.

It adds no small weight to all these considerations, to recollect, that history informs us of no long lived republic which had not a senate. Sparta, Rome and Carthage are in fact the only states to whom that character can be applied. In each of the two first there was a senate for life. The constitution of the senate in the last, is less known. Circumstantial evidence makes it probable that it was not different in this particular from the two others. It is at least certain that it had some quality or other which rendered it an anchor against popular fluctuations; and that a smaller council drawn out of the senate was appointed not only for life; but filled up vacancies itself. These examples, though as unfit for the imitation, as they are repugnant to the genius of America, are notwithstanding, when compared with the fugitive and turbulent existence of other antient republics, very instructive proofs of the necessity of some institution that will blend stability with liberty. I am not unaware of the circumstances which distinguish the American from other popular governments, as well antient as modern; and which render extreme circumspection necessary in reasoning from the one case to the other. But after allowing due weight to this consideration, it may still be maintained that there are many points of similitude which render these examples not unworthy of our attention. Many of the defects as we have seen, which can only be supplied by a senatorial institution, are common to a numerous assembly frequently elected by the people, and to the people themselves. There are others peculiar to the former, which require the controul of such an institution. The people can never wilfully betray their own interests: But they may possibly be betrayed by the representatives of the people; and the danger will be evidently greater where the whole legislative trust is lodged in the hands of one body of men, than where the concurrence of separate and dissimilar bodies is required in every public act.

The difference most relied on between the American and other republics, consists in the principle of representation, which is the pivot on which the former move, and which is supposed to have been unknown to the latter, or at least to the antient part of them. The use which has been made of this difference, in reasonings contained in former papers, will have shewn that I am disposed neither to deny its existence nor to undervalue its importance. I feel the less restraint therefore in observing that the position concerning the ignorance of the antient government on the subject of representation is by no means precisely true in the latitude commonly given to it. Without entering into a disquisition which here would be misplaced, I will refer to a few known facts in support of what I advance.

In the most pure democracies of Greece, many of the executive functions were performed not by the people themselves, but by officers elected by the people, and *representing* the people in their *executive* capacity.

Prior to the reform of Solon, Athens was governed by nine Archons, annually *elected by the people at large.* The degree of power delegated to them seems to be left in great obscurity. Subsequent to that period, we find an assembly first of four and afterwards of six hundred members, annually *elected by the people;* and *partially* representing them in their *legislative* capacity; since they were not only associated with the people in the function of making laws; but had the exclusive right of originating legislative propositions to the people. The senate of Carthage also, whatever might be its power or the duration of its appointment, appears to have been *elective* by the suffrages of the people. Similar instances might be traced in most if not all the popular governments of antiquity.

Lastly in Sparta, we meet with the Ephori, and in Rome with the Tribunes; two bodies, small indeed in number, but annually *elected by the whole body of the people,* and considered as the *representatives* of the people, almost in their *plenipotentiary* capacity. The Cosmi of Crete were also annually *elected by the people;* and have been considered by some authors as an institution analogous to those of Sparta and Rome; with this difference only that in the election of that representative body, the right of suffrage was communicated to a part only of the people.

From these facts, to which many others might be added, it is clear that the principle of representation was neither unknown to the antients, nor wholly overlooked in their political constitutions. The true distinction between these and the American Governments lies *in the total exclusion of the people in their collective capacity* from any share in the *latter,* and not in the *total exclusion of representatives of the people,* from the administration of the *former.* The distinction however thus qualified must be admitted to leave a most advantageous superiority in favor of the United States. But to ensure to this advantage its full effect, we must be careful not to separate it from the other advantage, of an extensive territory. For it cannot be believed that any form of representative government, could have succeeded within the narrow limits occupied by the democracies of Greece.

In answer to all these arguments, suggested by reason, illustrated by examples, and enforced by our own experience, the jealous adversary of the constitution will probably content himself with repeating, that a senate appointed not immediately by the people, and for the term of six years, must gradually acquire a dangerous preeminence in the government, and finally transform it into a tyrannical aristocracy.

To this general answer the general reply ought to be sufficient; that liberty may be endangered by the abuses of liberty, as well as by the abuses of power; that there are numerous instances of the former as

306

well as of the latter; and that the former rather than the latter is apparently most to be apprehended by the United States. But a more particular reply may be given.

Before such a revolution can be effected, the senate, it is to be observed, must in the first place corrupt itself; must next corrupt the state legislatures, must then corrupt the house of representatives, and must finally corrupt the people at large. It is evident that the senate must be first corrupted, before it can attempt an establishment of tyranny. Without corrupting the state legislatures, it cannot prosecute the attempt, because the periodical change of members would otherwise regenerate the whole body. Without exerting the means of corruption with equal success on the house of representatives, the opposition of that co-equal branch of the government would inevitably defeat the attempt; and without corrupting the people themselves, a succession of new representatives would speedily restore all things to their pristine order. Is there any man who can seriously persuade himself, that the proposed senate can, by any possible means within the compass of human address, arrive at the object of a lawless ambition, through all these obstructions?

If reason condemns the suspicion, the same sentence is pronounced by experience. The constitution of Maryland furnishes the most apposite example. The senate of that state is elected, as the federal senate will be, indirectly by the people; and for a term less by one year only, than the federal senate. It is distinguished also by the remarkable prerogative of filling up its own vacancies within the term of its appointment: and at the same time, is not under the controul of any such rotation, as is provided for the federal senate. There are some other lesser distinctions, which would expose the former to colorable objections that do not lie against the latter. If the federal senate therefore really contained the danger which has been so loudly proclaimed, some symptoms at least of a like danger ought by this time to have been betrayed by the senate of Maryland; but no such symptoms have appeared. On the contrary the jealousies at first entertained by men of the same description with those who view with terror the correspondent part of the federal constitution, have been gradually extinguished by the progress of the experiment; and the Maryland constitution is daily deriving from the salutary operations of this part of it, a reputation in which it will probably not be rivalled by that of any state in the union.

But if any thing could silence the jealousies on this subject, it ought to be the British example. The senate there, instead of being elected for a term of six years, and of being unconfined to particular families or fortunes, is an hereditary assembly of opulent nobles. The house of representatives, instead of being elected for two years and by the whole body of the people, is elected for seven years; and in very great proportion, by a very small proportion of the people. Here unquestionably ought to be seen in full display, the aristocratic usurpations and tyranny, which are at some future period to be exemplified in the United

States. Unfortunately however for the antifederal argument the British history informs us, that this hereditary assembly has not even been able to defend itself against the continual encroachments of the house of representatives; and that it no sooner lost the support of the monarch, than it was actually crushed by the weight of the popular branch.

As far as antiquity can instruct us on this subject, its examples support the reasoning which we have employed. In Sparta the Ephori, the annual representatives of the people, were found an overmatch for the senate for life, continually gained on its authority, and finally drew all power into their own hands. The tribunes of Rome, who were the representatives of the people, prevailed, it is well known, in almost every contest with the senate for life, and in the end gained the most complete triumph over it. This fact is the more remarkable, as unanimity was required in every act of the tribunes, even after their number was augmented to ten. It proves the irresistable force possessed by that branch of a free government, which has the people on its side. To these examples might be added that of Carthage, whose senate, according to the testimony of Polybius, instead of drawing all power into its vortex, had at the commencement of the second punic war, lost almost the whole of its original portion.

Besides the conclusive evidence resulting from this assemblage of facts, that the federal senate will never be able to transform itself, by gradual usurpations, into an independent and aristocratic body; we are warranted in believing that if such a revolution should ever happen from causes which the foresight of man cannot guard against, the house of representatives with the people on their side will at all times be able to bring back the constitution to its primitive form and principles. Against the force of the immediate representatives of the people, nothing will be able to maintain even the constitutional authority of the senate, but such a display of enlightened policy, and attachment to the public good, as will divide with that branch of the legislature, the affections and support of the entire body of the people themselves.

PUBLIUS.

CHAPTER IV

PRINCIPLES OF STRUCTURE

A. JOHN LOCKE, TWO TREATISES OF GOVERNMENT, THE SECOND TREATISE, AN ESSAY CONCERNING THE TRUE ORIGINAL, EXTENT, AND END OF CIVIL GOVERNMENT

1698

Chap. XII.

*Of the Legislative, Executive, and Federative
Power of the Commonwealth.*

143. The *Legislative* Power is that which has a right *to direct* how *the Force of the Commonwealth* shall be imploy'd for preserving the Community and the Members of it. But because those Laws which are constantly to be Executed, and whose force is always to continue, may be made in a little time; therefore there is no need, that the *Legislative* should be always in being, not having always business to do. And because it may be too great a temptation to humane frailty apt to grasp at Power, for the same Persons who have the Power of making Laws, to have also in their hands the power to execute them, whereby they may exempt themselves from Obedience to the Laws they make, and suit the Law, both in its making and execution, to their own private advantage, and thereby come to have a distinct interest from the rest of the Community, contrary to the end of Society and Government: Therefore in well order'd Commonwealths, where the good of the whole is so considered, as it ought, the *Legislative* Power is put into the hands of divers Persons who duly Assembled, have by themselves, or jointly with others, a Power to make Laws, which when they have done, being separated again, they are themselves subject to the Laws, they have made; which is a new and near tie upon them, to take care, that they make them for the publick good.

144. But because the Laws, that are at once, and in a short time made, have a constant and lasting force, and need a *perpetual Execution*, or an attendance thereunto: Therefore 'tis necessary there should be a *Power always in being*, which should see to the *Execution* of the Laws that are made, and remain in force. And thus the *Legislative* and *Executive Power* come often to be separated.

145. There is another *Power* in every Commonwealth, which one may call *natural*, because it is that which answers to the Power every Man naturally had before he entred into Society. For though in a Commonwealth the Members of it are distinct Persons still in reference

to one another, and as such are governed by the Laws of the Society; yet in reference to the rest of Mankind, they make one Body, which is, as every Member of it before was, still in the State of Nature with the rest of Mankind. Hence it is, that the Controversies that happen between any Man of the Society with those that are out of it, are managed by the publick; and an injury done to a Member of their Body, engages the whole in the reparation of it. So that under this Consideration, the whole Community is one Body in the State of Nature, in respect of all other States or Persons out of its Community.

146. This therefore contains the Power of War and Peace, Leagues and Alliances, and all the Transactions, with all Persons and Communities without the Commonwealth, and may be called *Federative*, if any one pleases. So the thing be understood, I am indifferent as to the Name.

147. These two Powers, *Executive* and *Federative*, though they be really distinct in themselves, yet one comprehending the *Execution* of the Municipal Laws of the Society *within* its self, upon all that are parts of it; the other the management of the *security and interest of the publick without*, with all those that it may receive benefit or damage from, yet they are always almost united. And though this *federative Power* in the well or ill management of it be of great moment to the commonwealth, yet it is much less capable to be directed by antecedent, standing, positive Laws, than the *Executive*; and so must necessarily be left to the Prudence and Wisdom of those whose hands it is in, to be managed for the publick good. For the *Laws* that concern Subjects one amongst another, being to direct their actions, may well enough *precede* them. But what is to be done in reference to *Foreigners*, depending much upon their actions, and the variation of designs and interests, must be *left* in great part *to* the *Prudence* of those who have this Power committed to them, to be managed by the best of their Skill, for the advantage of the Commonwealth.

148. Though, as I said, the *Executive* and *Federative Power* of every Community be really distinct in themselves, yet they are hardly to be separated, and placed, at the same time, in the hands of distinct Persons. For both of them requiring the force of the Society for their exercise, it is almost impracticable to place the Force of the Commonwealth in distinct, and not subordinate hands; or that the *Executive* and *Federative Power* should be *placed* in Persons that might act separately, whereby the Force of the Publick would be under different Commands: which would be apt sometime or other to cause disorder and ruine.

Chap. XIII.

Of the Subordination of the Powers of the Commonwealth.

149. Though in a Constituted Commonwealth, standing upon its own Basis, and acting according to its own Nature, that is, acting for the preservation of the Community, there can be but *one Supream Power*,

which is *the Legislative*, to which all the rest are and must be subordinate, yet the Legislative being only a Fiduciary Power to act for certain ends, there remains still *in the People a Supream Power* to remove or *alter the Legislative*, when they find the *Legislative* act contrary to the trust reposed in them. For all *Power given with trust* for the attaining an *end*, being limited by that end, whenever that *end* is manifestly neglected, or opposed, the *trust* must necessarily be *forfeited*, and the Power devolve into the hands of those that gave it, who may place it anew where they shall think best for their safety and security. And thus the *Community* perpetually retains a *Supream Power* of saving themselves from the attempts and designs of any Body, even of their Legislators, whenever they shall be so foolish, or so wicked, as to lay and carry on designs against the Liberties and Properties of the Subject. For no Man, or Society of Men, having a Power to deliver up their *Preservation*, or consequently the means of it, to the Absolute Will and arbitrary Dominion of another; whenever any one shall go about to bring them into such a Slavish Condition, they will always have a right to preserve what they have not a Power to part with; and to rid themselves of those who invade this Fundamental, Sacred, and unalterable Law of *Self-Preservation*, for which they enter'd into Society. And thus the *Community* may be said in this respect to be *always the Supream Power*, but not as considered under any Form of Government, because this Power of the People can never take place till the Government be dissolved.

150. In all Cases, whilst the Government subsists, the *Legislative is the Supream Power*. For what can give Laws to another, must needs be superiour to him: and since the Legislative is no otherwise Legislative of the Society, but by the right it has to make Laws for all the parts and for every Member of the Society, prescribing Rules to their actions, and giving power of Execution, where they are transgressed, the *Legislative* must needs be the *Supream*, and all other Powers in any Members or parts of the Society, derived from and subordinate to it.

151. In some Commonwealths where the *Legislative* is not always in being, and the *Executive* is vested in a single Person, who has also a share in the Legislative; there that single Person in a very tolerable sense may also be called *Supream*, not that he has in himself all the Supream Power, which is that of Law-making: But because he has in him the *Supream Execution*, from whom all inferiour Magistrates derive all their several subordinate Powers, or at least the greatest part of them: having also no Legislative superiour to him, there being no Law to be made without his consent, which cannot be expected should ever subject him to the other part of the Legislative, *he is* properly enough in this sense *Supream*. But yet it is to be observed, that though *Oaths of Allegiance* and Fealty are taken to him, 'tis not to him as Supream Legislator, but as *Supream Executor* of the Law, made by a joint Power of him with others; *Allegiance* being nothing but an *Obedience according to Law*, which when he violates, he has no right to Obedience, nor can

claim it otherwise than as the publick Person vested with the Power of the Law, and so is to be consider'd as the Image, Phantom, or Representative of the Commonwealth, acted by the will of the Society, declared in its Laws; and thus he has no Will, no Power, but that of the Law. But when he quits this Representation, this publick Will, and acts by his own private Will, he degrades himself, and is but a single private Person without Power, and without Will, that has any Right to *Obedience*; the Members owing no *Obedience* but to the publick Will of the Society.

152. The *Executive Power* placed any where but in a Person, that has also a share in the Legislative, is visibly subordinate and accountable to it, and may be at pleasure changed and displaced; so that it is not the *supream Executive Power* that is exempt from *Subordination*, but the *Supream Executive Power* vested in one, who having a share in the Legislative, has no distinct superiour Legislative to be subordinate and accountable to, farther than he himself shall joyn and consent: so that he is no more subordinate than he himself shall think fit, which one may certainly conclude will be but very little. Of other *Ministerial* and *subordinate Powers* in a Commonwealth, we need not speak, they being so multiply'd with infinite variety, in the different Customs and Constitutions of distinct Commonwealths, that it is impossible to give a particular account of them all. Only thus much, which is necessary to our present purpose, we may take notice of concerning them, that they have no manner of Authority any of them, beyond what is, by positive Grant, and Commission, delegated to them, and are all of them accountable to some other Power in the Commonwealth.

153. It is not necessary, no nor so much as convenient, that the *Legislative* should be *always in being*. But absolutely necessary that the *Executive Power* should, because there is not always need of new Laws to be made, but always need of Execution of the Laws that are made. When the *Legislative* hath put the *Execution* of the Laws, they make, into other hands, they have a power still to resume it out of those hands, when they find cause, and to punish for any mall-administration against the Laws. The same holds also in regard of the *Federative* Power, that and the Executive being both *Ministerial and subordinate to the Legislative*, which as has been shew'd in a Constituted Commonwealth, is the Supream. The *Legislative* also in this Case being suppos'd to consist of several Persons (for if it be a single Person, it cannot but be always in being, and so will as Supream, naturally have the Supream Executive Power, together with the Legislative) may *assemble and exercise their Legislature*, at the times that either their original Constitution, or their own Adjournment appoints, or when they please; if neither of these hath appointed any time, or there be no other way prescribed to convoke them. For the supream Power being placed in them by the People, 'tis always in them, and they may exercise it when they please, unless by their original Constitution they are limited to certain Seasons, or by an

Act of their Supream Power they have Adjourned to a certain time, and when that time comes, they have a right to *Assemble* and *act* again.

154. If the *Legislative*, or any part of it be made up of Representatives chosen for that time by the People, which afterwards return into the ordinary state of Subjects, and have no share in the Legislature but upon a new choice, this powerof chusing must also be exercised by the People, either at certain appointed Seasons, or else when they are summon'd to it: and in this latter Case, the power of convoking the Legislative, is ordinarily placed in the Executive, and has one of these two limitations in respect of time: That either the Original Constitution requires their *assembling* and *acting* at certain intervals, and then the Executive Power does nothing but Ministerially issue directions for their Electing and Assembling, according to due Forms: Or else it is left to his Prudence to call them by new Elections, when the Occasions or Exigencies of the publick require the amendment of old, or making of new Laws, or the redress or prevention of any inconveniencies, that lie on, or threaten the People.

155. It may be demanded here, What if the Executive Power being possessed of the Force of the Commonwealth, shall make use of that force to hinder the *meeting* and *acting of the Legislative*, when the Original Constitution, or the publick Exigencies require it? I say using Force upon the People without Authority, and contrary to the Trust put in him, that does so, is a state of War with the People, who have a right to *reinstate* their *Legislative in the Exercise* of their Power. For having erected a Legislative, with an intent they should exercise the Power of making Laws, either at certain set times, or when there is need of it; when they are hindr'd by any force from, what is so necessary to the Society, and wherein the Safety and preservation of the People consists, the People have a right to remove it by force. In all States and Conditions the true remedy of *Force* without Authority, is to oppose *Force* to it. The use of *force* without Authority, always puts him that uses it into a *state of War*, as the Aggressor, and renders him liable to be treated accordingly.

156. The Power *of Assembling and dismissing the Legislative*, placed in the Executive, gives not the Executive a superiority over it, but is a Fiduciary Trust, placed in him, for the safety of the People, in a Case where the uncertainty, and variableness of humane affairs could not bear a steady fixed rule. For it not being possible, that the first Framers of the Government should, by any foresight, be so much Masters of future Events, as to be able to prefix so just periods of return and duration to the *Assemblies of the Legislative*, in all times to come, that might exactly answer all the Exigencies of the Commonwealth; the best remedy could be found for this defect, was to trust this to the prudence of one, who was always to be present, and whose business it was to watch over the publick good. Constant *frequent meetings of the Legislative*, and long Continuations of their Assemblies, without necessary

occasion, could not but be burthensome to the People, and must necessarily in time produce more dangerous inconveniences, and yet the quick
turn of affairs might be sometimes such as to need their present help:
Any delay of their *Convening* might endanger the publick; and sometimes too their business might be so great, that the limited time of their
sitting might be too short for their work, and rob the publick of that
benefit, which could be had only from their mature deliberation. What
then could be done, in this Case, to prevent the Community, from being
exposed sometime or other to eminent hazard, on one side, or the other,
by fixed intervals and periods, set to the *meeting and acting of the
Legislative*, but to intrust it to the prudence of some, who being present,
and acquainted with the state of publick affairs, might make use of this
Prerogative for the publick good? And where else could this be so well
placed as in his hands, who was intrusted with the Execution of the
Laws, for the same end? Thus supposing the regulation of times for the
Assembling and Sitting of the Legislative, not settled by the original
Constitution, it naturally fell into the hands of the Executive, not as an
Arbitrary Power depending on his good pleasure, but with this trust
always to have it exercised only for the publick Weal, as the Occurrences
of times and change of affairs might require. Whether *settled periods of
their Convening*, or a *liberty* left to the Prince *for Convoking the
Legislative*, or perhaps a mixture of both, hath the least inconvenience
attending it, 'tis not my business here to inquire, but only to shew, that
though the Executive Power may have the Prerogative of *Convoking* and
dissolving such *Conventions of the Legislative*, yet it is not thereby
superiour to it.

157. Things of this World are in so constant a Flux, that nothing
remains long in the same State. Thus People, Riches, Trade, Power,
change their Stations; flourishing mighty Cities come to ruine, and
prove in time neglected desolate Corners, whilst other unfrequented
places grow into populous Countries, fill'd with Wealth and Inhabitants.
But things not always changing equally, and private interest often
keeping up Customs and Priviledges, when the reasons of them are
ceased, it often comes to pass, that in Governments, where part of the
Legislative consists of *Representatives* chosen by the People, that in tract
of time this *Representation* becomes very *unequal* and disproportionate
to the reasons it was at first establish'd upon. To what gross absurdities
the following of Custom, when Reason has left it, may lead, we may be
satisfied when we see the bare Name of a Town, of which there remains
not so much as the ruines, where scarce so much Housing as a Sheep-
coat; or more Inhabitants than a Shepherd is to be found, sends *as
many Representatives* to the grand Assembly of Law-makers, as a whole
County numerous in People, and powerful in riches. This Strangers
stand amazed at, and every one must confess needs a remedy. Though
most think it hard to find one, because the Constitution of the Legislative being the original and supream act of the Society, antecedent to all
positive Laws in it, and depending wholly on the People, no inferiour

Power can alter it. And therefore the *People*, when the *Legislative* is once Constituted, *having* in such a Government as we have been speaking of, *no Power* to act as long as the Government stands; this inconvenience is thought incapable of a remedy.

B. MONTESQUIEU, THE SPIRIT OF LAWS

1748

OF THE CONSTITUTION OF ENGLAND [Book 11, Chapter 6]

In every government there are three sorts of power: the legislative; the executive in respect to things dependent on the law of nations; and the executive, in regard to things that depend on the civil laws.

By virtue of the first, the prince or magistrate enacts temporary or perpetual laws, and amends or abrogates those that have been already enacted. By the second, he makes peace or war, sends or receives embassies, establishes the public security, and provides against invasions. By the third, he punishes crimes, or determines the disputes that arise between individuals. The latter we shall call the judiciary power, and the other simply the executive power of the state.

The political liberty of the subject is a tranquillity of mind, arising from the opinion each person has of his safety. In order to have this liberty, it is requisite the government be so constituted as one man need not be afraid of another.

When the legislative and executive powers are united in the same person, or in the same body of magistracy, there can be then no liberty; because apprehensions may arise, lest the same monarch or senate should enact tyrannical laws, to execute them in a tyrannical manner.

Again, there is no liberty, if the power of judging be not separated from the legislative and executive powers. Were it joined with the legislative, the life and liberty of the subject would be exposed to arbitrary control; for the judge would be then the legislator. Were it joined to the executive power, the judge might behave with all the violence of an oppressor.

Miserable indeed would be the case, were the same man, or the same body whether of the nobles or of the people, to exercise those three powers, that of enacting laws, that of executing the public resolutions, and that of judging the crimes or differences of individuals.

Most kingdoms of Europe enjoy a moderate government, because the prince who is invested with the two first powers, leaves the third to his subjects. In Turky, where these three powers are united in the Sultan's person, the subjects groan under the weight of tyranny and oppression.

The judiciary power ought not to be given to a standing senate; it should be exercised by persons taken from the body of the people,[a] at certain times of the year, and pursuant to a form and manner prescribed by law, in order to erect a tribunal that should last only as long as necessity requires.

By this means the power of judging, a power so terrible to mankind, not being annexed to any particular state or profession, becomes, as it were, invisible. People have not then the judges continually present to their view; they fear the office, but not the magistrate.

In accusations of a deep or criminal nature, it is proper the person accused should have the privilege of chusing in some measure his judges in concurrence with the law; or at least he should have a right to except against so great a number, that the remaining part may be deemed his own choice.

The other two powers may be given rather to magistrates or permanent bodies, because they are not exercised on any private subject; one being no more than the general will of the state, and the other the execution of that general will.

But tho' the tribunals ought not to be fixt, yet the judgments ought, and to such a degree, as to be always conformable to the exact letter of the law. Were they to be the private opinion of the judge, people would then live in society without knowing exactly the obligations it lays them under.

The judges ought likewise to be in the same station as the accused, or in other words, his peers, to the end that he may not imagine he is fallen into the hands of persons inclined to treat him with rigour.

If the legislature leaves the executive power in possession of a right to imprison those subjects who can give security for their good behaviour, there is an end of liberty; unless they are taken up, in order to answer without delay to a capital crime. In this case they are really free, being subject only to the power of the law.

But should the legislature think itself in danger by some secret conspiracy against the state, or by a correspondence with a foreign enemy, it might authorise the executive power, for a short and limited time, to imprison suspected persons, who in that case would lose their liberty only for a while, to preserve it for ever.

As in a free state, every man who is supposed a free agent, ought to be his own governor; so the legislative power should reside in the whole body of the people. But since this is impossible in large states, and in small ones is subject to many inconveniencies; it is fit that the people should act by their representatives, what they cannot act by themselves.

The inhabitants of a particular town are much better acquainted with its wants and interests, than with those of other places; and are

a. As at Athens.

better judges of the capacity of their neighbours, than of that of the rest of their countrymen. The members therefore of the legislature should not be chosen from the general body of the nation; but it is proper that in every considerable place, a representative should be elected by the inhabitants.

The great advantage of representatives is their being capable of discussing affairs. For this the people collectively are extremely unfit, which is one of the greatest inconveniences of a democracy.

It is not at all necessary that the representatives who have received a general instruction from their electors, should wait to be particularly instructed on every affair, as is practised in the diets of Germany. True it is that by this way of proceeding, the speeches of the deputies might with greater propriety be called the voice of the nation: but on the other hand this would throw them into infinite delays, would give each deputy a power of controlling the assembly; and on the most urgent and pressing occasions the springs of the nation might be stopped by a single caprice.

When the deputies, as Mr. Sidney well observes, represent a body of people as in Holland, they ought to be accountable to their constituents: but it is a different thing in England, where they are deputed by boroughs.

All the inhabitants of the several districts ought to have a right of voting at the election of a representative, except such as are in so mean a situation, as to be deemed to have no will of their own.

One great fault there was in most of the ancient republics; that the people had a right to active resolutions, such as require some execution, a thing of which they are absolutely incapable. They ought to have no hand in the government but for the chusing of representatives, which is within their reach. For tho' few can tell the exact degree of men's capacities, yet there are none but are capable of knowing in general whether the person they chuse is better qualified than most of his neighbours.

Neither ought the representative body to be chosen for active resolutions, for which it is not so fit; but for the enacting of laws, or to see whether the laws already enacted be duly executed, a thing they are very capable of, and which none indeed but themselves can properly perform.

In a state there are always persons distinguished by their birth, riches, or honors: but were they to be confounded with the common people, and to have only the weight of a single vote like the rest, the common liberty would be their slavery, and they would have no interest in supporting it, as most of the popular resolutions would be against them. The share they have therefore in the legislature ought to be proportioned to the other advantages they have in the state; which happens only when they form a body that has a right to put a stop to the enterprizes of the people, as the people have a right to oppose any encroachment of theirs.

The legislative power is therefore committed to the body of the nobles, and to the body chosen to represent the people, which have each their assemblies and deliberations apart, each their separate view and interests.

Of the three powers above-mentioned the judiciary is in some measure next to nothing. There remain therefore only two; and as these have need of a regulating power to temper them, the part of the legislative body composed of the nobility, is extremely proper for this very purpose.

The body of the nobility ought to be hereditary. In the first place it is so in its own nature; and in the next there must be a considerable interest to preserve its prerogatives; prerogatives that in themselves are obnoxious to popular envy, and of course in a free state are always in danger.

But as an hereditary power might be tempted to pursue its own particular interests, and forget those of the people; it is proper that where they may reap a singular advantage from being corrupted, as in the laws relating to the supplies, they should have no other share in the legislation, than the power of refusing, and not that of enacting.

By the *power of enacting*, I mean the right of ordaining by their own authority, or of amending what has been ordained by others. By the *power of refusing*, I would be understood to mean the right of annulling a resolution taken by another; which was the power of the tribunes at Rome. And tho' the person possessed of the privilege of refusing may likewise have the right of approving, yet this approbation passes for no more than a declaration, that he intends to make no use of his privilege of refusing, and is derived from that very privilege.

The executive power ought to be in the hands of a monarch; because this branch of government, which has always need of expedition, is better administered by one than by many: whereas, whatever depends on the legislative power, is oftentimes better regulated by many than by a single person.

But if there was no monarch, and the executive power was committed to a certain number of persons selected from the legislative body, there would be an end then of liberty; by reason the two powers would be united, as the same persons would actually sometimes have, and would moreover be always able to have, a share in both.

Were the legislative body to be a considerable time without meeting, this would likewise put an end to liberty. For of two things one would naturally follow; either that there would be no longer any legislative resolutions, and then the state would fall into anarchy; or that these resolutions would be taken by the executive power which would render it absolute.

It would be needless for the legislative body to continue always assembled. This would be troublesome to the representatives, and moreover would cut out too much work for the executive power, so as to take off its attention from executing, and oblige it to think only of defending its own prerogatives and the right it has to execute.

Again, were the legislative body to be always assembled, it might happen to be kept up only by filling the vacant places of the deceased members with new representatives; and in that case, if the legislative body was once corrupted, the evil would be past all remedy. When different legislative bodies succeed one another, the people who have a bad opinion of that which is actually sitting, may reasonably entertain some hopes of the next: but were it to be always the same body, the people upon seeing it once corrupted, would no longer expect any good from its laws; and of course they would either become desperate or fall into a state of indolence.

The legislative body should not assemble of itself. For a body is supposed to have no will but when it is assembled; and besides were it not to assemble unanimously, it would be impossible to determine which was really the legislative body, the part assembled, or the other. And if it had a right to prorogue itself, it might happen never to be prorogued; which would be extremely dangerous in case it should ever attempt to incroach on the executive power. Besides there are seasons, some more proper than others, for assembling the legislative body: it is fit therefore that the executive power should regulate the time of convening as well as the duration of those assemblies, according to the circumstances and exigencies of state known to itself.

Were the executive power not to have a right of putting a stop to the incroachments of the legislative body, the latter would become despotic; for as it might arrogate to itself what authority it pleased, it would soon destroy all the other powers.

But it is not proper on the other hand that the legislative power should have a right to stop the executive. For as the execution has its natural limits, it is useless to confine it; besides the executive power is generally employed in momentary operations. The power therefore of the Roman tribunes was faulty, as it put a stop not only to the legislation, but likewise to the execution itself; which was attended with infinite mischiefs.

But if the legislative power in a free government has no right to stay the executive, it has a right and ought to have the means of examining in what manner its laws have been executed.

But whatever may be the issue of that examination, the legislative body ought not to have a power of judging the person, nor of course the conduct of him who is intrusted with the executive power. His person should be sacred, because as it is necessary for the good of the state to prevent the legislative body from rendering themselves arbitrary, the moment he is accused or tried, there is an end of liberty.

In this case the state would be no longer a monarchy, but a kind of republican, tho' not a free, government. But as the person intrusted with the executive power cannot abuse it without bad counsellors, and such as hate the laws as ministers, tho' the laws favour them as subjects; these men may be examined and punished.

Tho' in general the judiciary power ought not to be united with any part of the legislative, yet this is liable to three exceptions founded on the particular interest of the party accused.

The great are always obnoxious to popular envy; and were they to be judged by the people, they might be in danger from their judges, and would moreover be deprived of the privilege which the meanest subject is possessed of in a free state, of being tried by their peers. The nobility for this reason ought not to be cited before the ordinary courts of judicature, but before that part of the legislature which is composed of their own body.

It is possible that the law, which is clear-sighted in one sense, and blind in another, might in some cases be too severe. But as we have already observed, the national judges are no more, than the mouth that pronounces the words of the law, mere passive beings incapable of moderating either its force or rigor. That part therefore of the legislative body, which we have just now observed to be a necessary tribunal on another occasion, is also a necessary tribunal in this; it belongs to its supreme authority to moderate the law in favour of the law itself, by mitigating the sentence.

It might also happen that a subject intrusted with the administration of public affairs, may infringe the rights of the people, and be guilty of crimes which the ordinary magistrates either could not, or would not punish. But in general the legislative power cannot judge; and much less can it be a judge in this particular case, where it represents the party concerned, which is the people. It can only therefore impeach. But before what court shall it bring its impeachment? Must it go and demean itself before the ordinary tribunals, which are its inferiors, and being composed moreover of men who are chosen from the people as well as itself, will naturally be swayed by the authority of so powerful an accuser? No: in order to preserve the dignity of the people, and the security of the subject, the legislative part which represents the people, must bring in its charge before the legislative part which represents the nobility, who have neither the same interests nor the same passions.

Here is an advantage which this government has over most of the ancient republics, where there was this abuse, that the people were at the same time both judge and accuser.

The executive power, pursuant to what has been already said, ought to have a share in the legislature by the power of refusing, otherwise it would soon be stripp'd of its prerogatives. But should the legislative power usurp a share of the executive, the latter would be equally undone.

If the prince were to have a share in the legislature by the power of enacting, liberty would be lost. But as it is necessary he should have a share in the legislature for the support of his own prerogative, this share must consist in the power of refusing.

The change of government at Rome was owing to this, that neither the senate who had one part of the executive power, nor the magistrates who were entrusted with the other, had the right of refusing, which was intirely lodged in the people.

Here then is the fundamental constitution of the government we are treating of. The legislative body being composed of two parts, one checks the other, by the mutual privilege of refusing. They are both checked by the executive power, as the executive is by the legislative.

These three powers should naturally form a state of repose or inaction. But as there is a necessity for movement in the course of human affairs, they are forced to move, but still to move in concert.

As the executive power has no other part in the legislative than the privilege of refusing, it can have no share in the public debates. It is not even necessary that it should propose, because as it may always disapprove of the resolutions that shall be taken, it may likewise reject the decisions on those proposals which were made against its will.

In some ancient commonwealths, where public debates were carried on by the people in a body, it was natural for the executive power to propose and debate with the people, otherwise their resolutions must have been attended with a strange confusion.

Were the executive power to determine the raising of public money, otherwise than by giving its consent, liberty would cease; because it would become legislative in the most important point of legislation.

If the legislative power was to settle the subsidies, not from year to year, but for ever, it would run the risk of losing its liberty, because the executive power would no longer be dependent; and when once it was possessed of such a perpetual right, it would be a matter of indifference, whether it held it of itself, or of another. The same may be said, if it should come to a resolution of intrusting, not an annual, but a perpetual command of the sea and land forces to the executive power.

To prevent the executive power from being capable of oppressing, it is requisite that the armies, with which it is entrusted, should consist of the people, and have the same spirit as the people, as was the case at Rome till the time of *Marius*. To obtain this end, there are only two ways, either that the persons employed in the army, should have sufficient property to answer for their conduct to their fellow subjects, and be enlisted only for a year, as was customary at Rome: or if there should be a standing army, composed chiefly of the most despicable part of the nation, the legislative power should have a right to disband them as soon as it pleased; the soldiers should live in common with the rest of the people; and no separate camp, barracks, or fortress, should be suffered.

When once an army is established, it ought not to depend immediately on the legislative, but on the executive power; and this from the very nature of the thing; its business consisting more in action than in deliberation.

From a manner of thinking that prevails amongst mankind, they set a higher value upon courage than timorousness, on activity than prudence, on strength than counsel. Hence the army will ever despise a senate, and respect their own officers. They will naturally slight the orders sent them by a body of men, whom they look upon as cowards, and therefore unworthy to command them. So that as soon as the army depends on the legislative body, the government becomes a military one; and if the contrary has ever happened, it has been owing to some extraordinary circumstances. It is because the army was always kept divided; it is because it was composed of several bodies, that depended each on their particular province; it is because the capital towns were strong places, defended by their natural situation, and not garrisoned with regular troops.

Holland for instance, is still safer than Venice; she might drown, or starve the revolted troops; for as they are not quartered in towns that are capable to furnish them with necessary subsistence; this subsistence is of course precarious.

Whoever shall read the admirable treatise of Tacitus on the manners of the Germans,[b] will find that it is from them the English have borrowed the idea of their political government. This beautiful system was invented first in the woods.

As all human things have an end, the state we are speaking of will lose its liberty, will perish. Have not Rome, Sparta, and Carthage perished? It will perish when the legislative power shall be more corrupt than the executive.

It is not my business to examine whether the English actually enjoy this liberty, or not. Sufficient it is for my purpose to observe, that it is established by their laws; and I inquire no further.

Neither do I pretend by this to undervalue other governments, nor to say that this extreme political liberty ought to give uneasiness to those who have only a moderate share of it. How should I have any

b. De minoribus rebus principes consultant, de majoribus omnes; ita tamen ut ea quoque quorum penes plebem arbitrium est apud principes pertractentur.

such design, I who think that even the excess of reason is not always desirable, and that mankind generally find their account better in mediums than in extremes?

Harrington in his *Oceana* has also inquired into the highest point of liberty to which the constitution of a state may be carried. But of him indeed it may be said, that for want of knowing the nature of real liberty, he busied himself in pursuit of an imaginary one, and that he built a Chalcedon tho' he had a Byzantium before his eyes.

C. WILLIAM BLACKSTONE, COMMENTARIES ON THE LAWS OF ENGLAND

1765

[Book I, Chapters 2 & 7]

The constituent parts of a parliament are the next objects of our enquiry. And these are, the king's majesty, fitting there in his royal political capacity, and the three estates of the realm; the lords spiritual, the lords temporal, (who fit, together with the king, in one house) and the commons, who fit by themselves in another[n]. And the king and these three estates, together, form the great corporation or body politic of the kingdom, of which the king is said to be *caput, principium, et finis.* For upon their coming together the king meets them, either in person or by representation; without which there can be no beginning of a parliament[o]; and he also has alone the power of dissolving them.

It is highly necessary for preserving the ballance of the constitution, that the executive power should be a branch, though not the whole, of the legislature. The total union of them, we have seen, would be productive of tyranny; the total disjunction of them for the present, would in the end produce the same effects, by causing that union, against which it seems to provide. The legislature would soon become tyrannical, by making continual encroachments, and gradually assuming to itself the rights of the executive power. Thus the long parliament of Charles the first, while it acted in a constitutional manner, with the royal concurrence, redressed many heavy grievances and established many salutary laws. But when the two houses assumed the power of legislation, in exclusion of the royal authority, they soon after assumed likewise the reins of administration; and, in consequence of these united powers, overturned both church and state, and established a worse oppression than any they pretended to remedy. To hinder therefore any such encroachments, the king is himself a part of the parliament: and, as this is the reason of his being so, very properly therefore the share of legislation, which the constitution has placed in the crown, consists in the power of *rejecting*, rather than *resolving*; this being sufficient to

n. 4 Inst. 1.   o. 4 Inst. 6.

answer the end proposed. For we may apply to the royal negative, in this instance, what Cicero observes of the negative of the Roman tribunes, that the crown has not any power of *doing* wrong, but merely of *preventing* wrong from being done [p]. The crown cannot begin of itself any alterations in the present established law; but it may approve or disapprove of the alterations suggested and consented to by the two houses. The legislative therefore cannot abridge the executive power of any rights which it now has by law, without it's own consent; since the law must perpetually stand as it now does, unless all the powers will agree to alter it. And herein indeed consists the true excellence of the English government, that all the parts of it form a mutual check upon each other. In the legislature, the people are a check upon the nobility, and the nobility a check upon the people; by the mutual privilege of rejecting what the other has resolved: while the king is a check upon both, which preserves the executive power from encroachments. And this very executive power is again checked, and kept within due bounds by the two houses, through the privilege they have of enquiring into, impeaching, and punishing the conduct (not indeed of the king, which would destroy his constitutional independence; but, which is more beneficial to the public) of his evil and pernicious counsellors. Thus every branch of our civil polity supports and is supported, regulates and is regulated, by the rest; for the two houses naturally drawing in two directions of opposite interest, and the prerogative in another still different from them both, they mutually keep each other from exceeding their proper limits; while the whole is prevented from separation, and artificially connected together by the mixed nature of the crown, which is a part of the legislative, and the sole executive magistrate. Like three distinct powers in mechanics, they jointly impel the machine of government in a direction different from what either, acting by themselves, would have done; but at the same time in a direction partaking of each, and formed out of all; a direction which constitutes the true line of the liberty and happiness of the community.

In this distinct and separate existence of the judicial power, in a peculiar body of men, nominated indeed, but not removeable at pleasure, by the crown, consists one main preservative of the public liberty; which cannot subsist long in any state, unless the administration of common justice be in some degree separated both from the legislative and also from the executive power. Were it joined with the legislative, the life, liberty, and property, of the subject would be in the hands of arbitrary judges, whose decisions would be then regulated only by their own opinions, and not by any fundamental principles of law; which, though legislators may depart from, yet judges are bound to observe. Were it joined with the executive, this union might soon be an overballance for

p. *Sulla—tribunis plebis sua lege injuriae saciendae potestatem ademit, auxilii ferendi reliquit. de LL. 3.9.*

the legislative. For which reason, by the statute of 16 Car. I. c. 10. which abolished the court of star chamber, effectual care is taken to remove all judicial power out of the hands of the king's privy council; who, as then was evident from recent instances, might soon be inclined to pronounce that for law, which was most agreeable to the prince or his officers. Nothing therefore is more to be avoided, in a free constitution, than uniting the provinces of a judge and a minister of state. And indeed, that the absolute power, claimed and exercised in a neighbouring nation, is more tolerable than that of the eastern empires, is in great measure owing to their having vested the judicial power in their parliaments, a body separate and distinct from both the legislative and executive: and, if ever that nation recovers it's former liberty, it will owe it to the efforts of those assemblies. In Turkey, where every thing is centered in the sultan or his ministers, despotic power is in it's meridian, and wears a more dreadful aspect.

D. DEBATE IN THE PHILADELPHIA CONVENTION

(1) June 2, 1787

<The> mode of appointg ye Executive <was> resumed.

Mr. Wilson made the following motion, <to be substituted for the mode proposed by Mr. Randolph's resolution.>

"that the Executive Magistracy shall be <elected> in the following manner: <That> the States be divided into   districts: <& that> the persons qualified <to vote in each> district for members of the first branch of the national Legislature elect   members for their respective districts to be electors of the Executive magistracy. that the said Electors of the Executive magistracy meet at   and they or any of them so met shall proceed to elect by ballot, but not out of their own body   person   in whom the Executive authority of the national Government shall be vested."

Mr. Wilson repeated his arguments in favor of an election without the intervention of the States. He supposed too that this mode would produce more confidence among the people in the first magistrate, than an election by the national Legislature.

Mr. Gerry, opposed the election by the national legislature. There would be a constant intrigue kept up for the appointment. The Legislature & the candidates wd. bargain & play into one another's hands. votes would be given by the former under promises or expectations from the latter, of recompensing them by services to members of the Legislature or to their friends. He liked the principle of Mr. Wilson's motion, but fears it would alarm & give a handle to the State partizans, as tending to supersede altogether the State authorities. He thought the Community not yet ripe for stripping the States of their powers, even such <as> might <not> be requisite for local purposes. He <was> for waiting till people <should> feel more the necessity of it. He seemed to prefer the taking the suffrages of the States instead of Electors, or letting the Legislatures nominate, and the electors appoint. <He was> not clear that the people ought to act directly even in <the> choice of electors, being too little informed of personal characters in large districts, and liable to deceptions.

Mr Williamson could see no advantage in the introduction of Electors chosen by the people who who would stand in the same relation to them as the State Legislatures, whilst the expedient would be attended with great trouble and expence. On the question for agreeing to Mr. Wilson's <substitute, it was negatived:> Massts. no. Cont. no. N. Y. no. Pa. ay. Del. no. Mard. ay. Virga. no. N. C. no. S. C. no. Geoa. no. [Ayes— 2; noes—8.]

* * *

On the question for electing the Executive by the national legislature, <for the term of seven years, it was agreed to> Massts. ay. Cont. ay. N. Y. ay. Pena. no. Del. ay. Maryd. no. Va. ay. N. C. ay. S. C. ay. Geo. ay. [ayes—8; noes—2.]

Mr. Dickenson moved "that the Executive be made removeable by the National Legislature on the request of a majority of the Legislatures of individual States". It was necessary he said to place the power of removing somewhere. He did not like the plan of impeaching the Great Officers of State. He did not know how provision could be made for removal of them in a better mode than that which he had proposed. He had no idea of abolishing the State Governments as some gentlemen seemed inclined to do. The happiness of this Country in his opinion required considerable powers to be left in the hands of the States.

Mr. Bedford seconded the motion.

Mr. Sherman contended that the National Legislature should have power to remove the Executive at pleasure.

Mr. Mason. Some mode of displacing an unfit magistrate is rendered indispensable by the fallibility of those who choose, as well as by the corruptibility of the man chosen. He opposed decidedly the making the Executive the mere creature of the Legislature as a violation of the fundamental principle of good Government.

Mr. <Madison> & Mr. Wilson observed that it would leave an equality of agency in the small with the great States; that it would enable a minority of the people to prevent ye removal of an officer who had rendered himself justly criminal in the eyes of a majority; that it would open a door for intrigues agst. him in States where his administration tho' just might be unpopular, and might tempt him to pay court to particular States whose leading partizans he might fear, or wish to engage as his partizans. They both thought it bad policy <to introduce

such a mixture> of the State authorities, when their agency could be otherwise supplied.

Mr. Dickenson considered the business as so important that no man ought to be silent or reserved. He went into a discourse of some length, the sum of which was, that the Legislative, Executive, & Judiciary departments ought to be made as independt. as possible; but that such an Executive as some seemed to have in contemplation was not consistant with a republic; that a firm Executive could only exist in a limited monarchy. In the British Govt. itself the weight of the Executive arises from the attachments which the Crown draws to itself, & not merely from the force of its prerogatives. In place of these attachments we must look out for something else. One source of stability is the double branch of the Legislature. The division of the Country into distinct States formed the other principal source of stability. This division ought therefore to be maintained, and considerable powers to be left with the States. This was the ground of his consolation for the future fate of his Country. Without this, and in case of a consolidation of the States into one great Republic [17] we might read its fate in the history of smaller ones. A limited Monarchy he considered as *one* of the best Governments in the world. It was not *certain* that the same blessings were derivable from any other form. It was certain that equal blessings had never yet been derived from any of the republican form. A limited monarchy however was out of the question. The spirit of the times—the state of our affairs, forbade the experiment, if it were desireable. Was it possible moreover in the nature of things to introduce it even if these obstacles were less insuperable. A House of Nobles was essential to such a Govt. Could these be created by a breath, or by a a stroke of the pen? No. They were the growth of ages, and could only arise under a complication of circumstances none of which existed in this Country. But though a form the most perfect *perhaps* in itself be unattainable. we must not despair. If antient republics have been found to flourish for a moment only & then vanish forever, it only proves that they were badly constituted; and that we ought to seek for every remedy for their diseases. One of these remedies he conceived to be the accidental lucky division of this country into distinct States; a division which some seemed desirous to abolish altogether.

As to the point of representation in the national legislature as it might affect States of different sizes, he said it must probably end in mutual concession. He hoped that each State would retain an equal voice at least in one branch of the National Legislature, and supposed the sums paid within each state would form a better ratio for the other branch than either the number of inhabitants or the quantum of property.

17. Crossed out "nation".

<A motion, being made to strike out "on request by a majority of the Legislatures of the individual States" and rejected, Connecticut. S. Carol: & Geo. being ay. the rest no: the question was taken—> [18]

On Mr. Dickenson's motion for making Executive removeable by Natl. Legislature at request of majority of State Legislatures <was also rejected> all the States <being in the negative> except Delaware which <gave an> affirmative vote.

The Question for making ye. Executive ineligible after seven years, <was next next taken, and agreed to:>

Massts. ay. Cont. no. N Y—ay Pa. divd. Del. ay. Maryd. ay. Va. ay. N. C. ay. S. C. ay. Geo. no: [Ayes—7; noes—2; divided—1.]

<Mr. Williamson 2ded. by Mr. Davie moved to add to the last Clause, the words—"and to be removeable on impeachment & conviction of mal-practice or neglect of duty"—which was agreed to.>

<Mr. Rutlidge &> Mr. C. Pinkney moved that the blank for the no. of persons in the Executive be filled with the words "one person". He supposed the reasons to be so obvious & conclusive in favor of one that no member would oppose the motion.

Mr. Randolph opposed it with great earnestness, declaring that he should not do justice to the Country which sent him if he were silently to suffer the establishmt. of a Unity in the Executive department. He felt an opposition to it which he believed he should continue to feel as long as he lived. He urged 1. that the permanent temper of the people was adverse to the very semblance of Monarchy. 2. that a unity was unnecessary a plurality being equally competent to all the objects of the department. 3. that the necessary confidence would never be reposed in a single Magistrate. 4. that the appointments would generally be in favor of some inhabitant near the center of the Community, and consequently the remote parts would not be on an equal footing. <He was in favor of three members of the Executive to be drawn from different portions of the Country.>

Mr. Butler contended strongly for a single magistrate as most likely to answer the purpose of the remote parts. If one man should be appointed he would be responsible to the whole, and would be impartial to its interests. If three or more should be taken from as many districts, there would be a constant struggle for local advantages. In Military matters this would be particularly mischievous. He said his opinion on this point had been formed under the opportunity he had had of seeing the manner in which a plurality of military heads distracted Holland when threatened with invasion by the imperial troops. One man was for directing the force to the defence of this part, another to that part of the Country, just as he happened to be swayed by prejudice or interest.

18. Taken from *Journal*.

<The motion was then> postpd.   <the Committee rose> & the House Adjd.

(2) June 4, 1787

In Committee of the whole

<The> Question <was> resumed <on motion of Mr. Pinkney 2ded. by Wilson> "shall the blank for the number of the Executive be filled with <'a single'> person"?

Mr. Wilson was in favor of the motion. It had been opposed by the gentleman from Virga. (Mr. Randolph) but the arguments used had not convinced him. He observed that the objections of Mr. R. were levelled not so much agst. the measure itself, as agst. its unpopularity. If he could suppose that it would occasion a rejection of the plan of which it should form a part, though the part was an important one, yet he would give it up rather than lose the whole. On examination he could see no evidence of the alledged antipathy of the people. On the contrary he was persuaded that it does not exist. All know that a single magistrate is not a King. one fact has great weight with him. All the 13 States tho' agreeing in scarce any other instance, agree in placing a single magistrate at the head of the Governmt. The idea of three heads has taken place in none. The degree of power is indeed different: but there are no co-ordinate heads. In addition to his former reasons for preferring a Unity, he would mention another. The *tranquility* not less than the vigor of the Govt. he thought would be favored by it. Among three equal members, he foresaw nothing but uncontrouled, continued, & violent animosities; which would not only interrupt the public administration; but diffuse their poison thro' the other branches of Govt., thro' the States, and at length thro' the people at large. If the members were to be unequal in power the principle of the opposition to the Unity was given up. If equal, the making them an odd number would not be a remedy. In Courts of Justice there are two sides only to a question. In the Legislative & Executive departmts. questions have commonly many sides. Each member therefore might espouse a separate one & no two agree.

Mr. Sherman. This matter is of great importance and ought to be well considered before it is determined. Mr. Wilson he said had observed that in each State a single magistrate was placed at the head of the Govt. It was so he admitted, and properly so, and he wished the same policy to prevail in the federal Govt. But then it should be also remarked that in a all the States there was a Council of advice, without which the first magistrate could not act. A Council he thought necessary to make the establishment acceptable to the people. Even in G. B. the King has a council; and though he appoints it himself, its advice has its weight with him, and attracts the Confidence of the people.

Mr. Williamson asks Mr. Wilson whether he means to annex a Council

Mr. Wilson means <to have> no Council, which oftener serves to cover, than prevent malpractices.

Mr Gerry. was at a loss to discover the policy of three members for the Executive. It wd. be extremely inconvenient in many instances, particularly in military matters, whether relating to the militia, an army, or a navy. It would be a general with three heads.

On the question for a single Executive <it was agreed to> Massts. ay. Cont. ay. N. Y. no. Pena. ay. Del. no. Maryd. no. Virg. ay. (Mr. R & Mr. Blair no—Docr. Mc.Cg. Mr. M. & Gen W. ay. Col. Mason being no, but not in house, Mr. Wythe ay but gone home). N. C. ay. S. C. ay. Georga. ay. [Ayes—7; noes—3.]

<First> Clause <of Proposition 8th> relating *to a Council of Revision* taken into consideration.

Mr. Gerry doubts whether the Judiciary ought to form a part of it, as they will have a sufficient check agst. encroachments on their own department by their exposition of the laws, which involved a power of deciding on their Constitutionality. In some States the Judges had <actually> set aside laws as being agst. the Constitution. This was done too with general approbation. It was quite foreign from the nature of ye. office to make them judges of the policy of public measures. <He moves to postpone> the clause <in order> to propose "that the National Executive <shall> have a right to negative any Legislative act <which> shall not be afterwards passed by parts of each branch of the national Legislature."

Mr. King seconds the motion, observing that the Judges ought to be able to expound the law as it should come before them, free from the bias of having participated in its formation.

Mr. Wilson thinks neither the original proposition nor the amendment go far enough. If the Legislative Exētiv & Judiciary ought to be distinct & independent, The Executive ought to have an absolute negative. Without such a Self-defence the Legislature can at any moment sink it into non-existence. He was for varying the proposition in such a manner as to give the Executive & Judiciary jointly an absolute negative

On the question to postpone in order to take Mr. Gerry's proposition into consideration <it was agreed to> Massts. ay. Cont. no. N. Y. ay. Pa. ay. Del. no. Maryd. no. Virga. no. N. C. ay. S. C. ay. Ga. ay. [Ayes—6; noes—4.]

Mr. Gerry's proposition being now before Committee, Mr. Wilson & Mr. Hamilton move that the last part of it <(viz wch. sl. not be afterwds. passed unless by   parts of each branch of the National legislature)> be struck out, so as to give the Executive an absolute negative on the laws. <There was no danger they thought of such a power being too

much exercised. It was mentioned (by Col: Hamilton) that the King of G. B. had not exerted his negative since the Revolution.>

Mr. Gerry sees no necessity for so great a controul over the legislature as the best men in the Community would be comprised in the two branches of it.

Docr. Franklin, said he was sorry to differ from his colleague for whom he had a very great respect, on any occasion, but he could not help it on this. He had had some experience of this check in the Executive on the Legislature, under the proprietary Government of Pena. The negative of the Governor was constantly made use of to extort money. No good law whatever could be passed without a private bargain with him. An increase of his salary, or some donation, was always made a condition; till at last it became the regular practice, to have orders in his favor on the Treasury, presented along with the bills to be signed, so that he might actually receive the former before he should sign the latter. When the Indians were scalping the western people, and notice of it arrived, the concurrence of the Governor in the means of self-defence could not be got, till it was agreed that his Estate should be exempted from taxation. so that the people were to fight for the security of his property, whilst he was to bear no share of the burden. This was a mischievous sort of check. If the Executive was to have a Council, such a power would be less objectionable. It was true the King of G. B. had not, As was said, exerted his negative since the Revolution: but that matter was easily explained. The bribes and emoluments now given to the members of parliament rendered it unnecessary, everything being done according to the will of the Ministers. He was afraid, if a negative should be given as proposed, that more power and money would be demanded, till at last eno' would be gotten to influence & bribe the Legislature into a compleat subjection to the will of the Executive.

Mr. Sherman was agst. enabling any one man to stop the will of the whole. No one man could be found so far above all the rest in wisdom. He thought we ought to avail ourselves of his wisdom in revising the laws, but not permit him to overrule the decided and cool opinions of the Legislature.

<Mr.>M<adison> supposed that if a proper proportion of each branch should be required to overrule the objections of the Executive, it would answer the same purpose as an absolute negative. It would rarely if ever happen that the Executive constituted as ours is proposed to be would, have firmness eno' to resist the Legislature, unless backed by a certain part of the body itself. The King of G. B. with all his splendid attributes would not be able to withstand ye. unanimous and eager wishes of both houses of Parliament. To give such a prerogative would certainly be obnoxious to the <temper of this country; its present temper at least.>

Mr. Wilson believed as others did that this power would seldom be used. The Legislature would know that such a power existed, and would refrain from such laws, as it would be sure to defeat. Its silent operation would therefore preserve harmony and prevent mischief. The case of Pena. formerly was very different from its present case. The Executive was not then as now to be appointed by the people. It will not in this case as in the one cited be supported by the head of a Great Empire, actuated by a different & sometimes opposite interest. The salary too is now proposed to be fixed by the Constitution, or if Dr. F's idea should be adopted all salary whatever interdicted. The requiring a large proportion of each House to overrule the Executive check might do in peaceable times; but there might be tempestuous moments in which animosties may run high between the Executive and Legislative branches, and in which the former ought to be able to defend itself.

Mr. Butler had been in favor of a single Executive Magistrate; but could he have entertained an idea that a compleat negative on the laws was to be given him he certainly should have acted very differently. It had been observed that in all countries the Executive power is in a constant course of increase. This was certainly the case in G. B. Gentlemen seemed to think that we had nothing to apprehend from an abuse of the Executive power. But why might not a Cataline or a Cromwell arise in this Country as well as in others.

Mr. Bedford was opposed to every check on the Legislative, even the Council of Revision first proposed. He thought it would be sufficient to mark out in the Constitution the boundaries to the Legislative Authority, which would give all the requisite security to the rights of the other departments. The Representatives of the People were the best judges of what was for their interest, and ought to be under no external controul whatever. The two branches would produces a sufficient controul within <the Legislature itself.>

Col. Mason observed that a vote had already passed he found (he was out at the time) for vesting the executive powers in a single person. Among these powers was that of appointing to offices in certain cases. The probable abuses of a negative had been well explained by Dr. F as proved by experience, the best of all tests. Will not the same door be opened here. The Executive may refuse its assent to necessary measures till new appointments shall be referred to him; and having by degrees engrossed all these into his own hands, the American Executive, like the British, will by bribery & influence, save himself the trouble & odium of exerting his negative afterwards. We are Mr. Chairman going very far in this business. We are not indeed constituting a British Government, but a more dangerous monarchy, an elective one. We are introducing a new principle into our system, and not necessary as in the British Govt. where the Executive has greater rights to defend. Do gentlemen mean to pave the way to hereditary Monarchy? Do they flatter themselves that the people will ever consent to such an innovation? If they do I venture to tell them, they are mistaken. The people never will consent. And do gentlemen consider the danger of delay, and the still greater danger of a a rejection not for a moment but forever, of the plan which shall be proposed to them. Notwithstanding the oppressions & injustice experienced among us from democracy; the genius of the people is in favor of it, and the genius of the people must be consulted. He could not but consider the federal system as in effect dissolved by the appointment of this Convention to devise a better one. And do gentlemen look forward to the dangerous interval between the extinction of an old, and the establishment of a new Governmt. and to the scenes of confusion which may ensue. He hoped that nothing like a monarchy would ever be attempted in this Country. A hatred to its oppressions had carried the people through the late Revolution. Will it not be eno' to enable the Executive to suspend offensive laws, till they shall be coolly revised, and the objections to them overruled by a greater majority than was required in the first instance. He never could agree to give up all the rights of the people to a single Magistrate. If more than one had been fixed on, greater powers might have been entrusted to the Executive. He hoped this attempt to give such powers would have its weight hereafter <as an argument> for increasing the number of the Executive.

Docr. Franklin. A Gentleman from S. C. (Mr. Butler) a day or two ago called our attention to the case of the U. Netherlands. He wished the gentleman had been a little fuller, and had gone back to the original of that Govt. The people being under great obligations to the Prince of Orange whose wisdom and bravery had saved them, chose him for the Stadtholder. He did very well. Inconveniences however were felt from his powers; <which growing more & more oppressive, they were at length set aside.> Still however there was a party for the P. of Orange, which descended to his son who excited insurrections, spilt a great deal of blood, murdered the de Witts, and got the powers revested in the Stadtholder. Afterwards another Prince had power to excite insurrections & to make the Stadtholdership hereditary. And the present Stadthder. is ready to wade thro' a bloody civil war to the establishment of a monarchy. Col. Mason had mentioned the circumstance of appointing officers. He knew how that point would be managed. No new appointment would be suffered as heretofore in Pensa. unless it be referred to the Executive; so that all profitable offices will be at his disposal. The first man, put at the helm will be a good one. No body knows what sort may come afterwards. The Executive will be always increasing here, as elsewhere, till it ends in a monarchy

On the question for striking out so as to give Executive an absolute Negative—

Massts. no. Cont. no. N. Y. no. Pa. no. Dl. no. Md. no. Va. no. N. C. no. S. C. no. Georga. no. [Ayes—0; noes—10.]

Mr. Butler moved that <the Resoln. be altered so as to read— "Resolved that the National Executive have a power to suspend any legislative act for the term of   .">

Doctr. Franklin seconds the motion.

Mr. Gerry observed that a power of suspending might do all the mischief dreaded from the negative of useful laws; without answering the salutary purpose of checking unjust or unwise ones.

On question "for giving this suspending power". all the States, to wit Massts. Cont. N. Y. Pa. Del. Maryd. Virga. N. C. S. C. Georgia. were *no*.

On a question for enabling *two thirds* of each branch of the Legislature to overrule the revisionary check: it passed in the affirmative sub silentio; <and was inserted in the blank of Mr. Gerry's motion.>

On the question on Mr. Gerry's motion which gave the Executive alone without the Judiciary the revisionary controul on the laws <unles overruled by 2/3 of each branch.> Massts. ay. Cont. no. N. Y. ay. Pena. ay. Del. ay. Maryd. no. Va. ay N. C. ay. S. C. ay. Geo. ay. [Ayes—8; noes—2.]

<It was moved by Mr. Wilson 2ded. by Mr. Madison—that the following amendment be made to the last resolution—after the words "National Ex." to add "& a convenient number of the National Judiciary."

An Objection of order being taken by Mr. Hamilton to the introduction of the last amendment at this time, notice was given by Mr. W. &. Mr. M—that the same wd. be moved tomorrow.—whereupon Wednesday (the day after) was assigned to reconsider the amendment of Mr. Gerry.

It was then moved & 2ded. to proceed to the consideration of the 9th. resolution submitted by Mr. Randolph—when on motion to agree to the first clause namely "Resolved that a National Judiciary be established" It passed in the Affirmative nem. con.

It was then moved and 2ded. to add these words to the first clause of the ninth resolution namely—"to consist of one supreme tribunal, and of one or more inferior tribunals". which passed in the affirmative—

The Comme. then rose and the House Adjourned.>

(3) **June 20, 1787**

<Mr. William Blount from N. Carolina took his seat. 1st. propos: of the Report of Come. of the whole before the House>

Mr. Elseworth <2ded. by Mr. Gorham> moves to alter it so as to run "that the Government of the United States ought to consist of a supreme legislative, Executive and Judiciary". This alteration he said would drop the word *national*, and retain the proper title "the United States." He could not admit the doctrine that a breach of <any of> the federal articles could dissolve the whole. It would be highly dangerous not to consider the Confederation as still subsisting. He wished also the plan of the Convention to go forth as an amendment to the articles of Confederation, since under this idea the authority of the Legislatures could ratify it. If they are unwilling, the people will be so too. If the plan goes forth to the people for ratification several succeeding Conventions within the States would be unavoidable. He did not like these conventions. They were better fitted to pull down than to build up Constitutions.

Mr. Randolph did not object to the change of expression, but apprised the gentleman who wished for it that he did not admit it for the reasons assigned; particularly that of getting rid of a reference to the people for ratification. The motion of Mr. Elsewth was acquiesed in. nem: con:

The 2d. Resoln. "that the national Legislature ought to consist of two branches". taken up. the word "national" struck out as of course.

Mr. Lansing, observed that the true queston [sic] here was, whether the Convention would adhere to or depart from the foundation of the present Confederacy; and moved instead of <the 2d> Resolution "that the powers of Legislation be vested <in the U. States> in Congress". . He had already assigned two reasons agst. such an innovation as was proposed. 1. the want of competent powers <in the Convention>—2. the <state> of the public mind. It had been observed by (Mr. M<adison>) in discussing the first point, that in two States the Delegates to Congs. were chosen by the people. Notwithstanding the first appearance of this remark, it had in fact no weight, as the Delegates however chosen, did not represent the people merely as so many individuals; but as forming a sovereign State. (Mr Randolph) put it, he said, on its true footing namely that the public safety superseded the scruple arising from the review of our powers. But in order to feel the force of this consideration, the same impression must be had of the public danger. He had not himself the same impression, and could not therefore dismiss his scruple. (Mr Wilson) contended that as the Convention were only to recommend, they might recommend what they pleased. He differed much from him. any act whatever of so respectable a body must have a great effect, and if it does not succeed, will be a source of great dissentions. He admitted that there was no certain criterion of the public mind on the subject. He therefore recurred to the evidence of it given by the opposition in the States to the scheme of an Impost. It could not be expected that those possessing Sovereignty could ever voluntarily part with it. It was not to be expected from any one State, much less from thirteen. He proceeded to make some observations on the plan itself and the argumts. urged in support of it. The point of Representation could receive no elucidation from the case of England. The corruption of the boroughs did not proceed from their comparative smallness: but from the actual fewness of the inhabitants, some of them not having more than one or two. a great inequality existed in the Counties of England. Yet the like complaint of peculiar corruption in the small ones had not been made. It had been said that Congress represent the State Prejudices: will not any other body whether chosen by the Legislatures or people of the States, also represent their prejudices? It had been asserted by his Colleague (Col. Hamilton) that there was no coincidence of interests among the large States that ought to excite fears of oppression in the smaller. If it were true that such a uniformity of interests existed among the States, there was equal safety for all of them, whether the representation remained as heretofore, or were proportioned as now proposed. It is proposed that the genl. Legislature shall have a negative on the laws of the States. Is it conceivable that there will be leisure for such a task? there will on the most moderate calculation, be as many Acts sent up from the States as there are days in the year. Will the members of the general Legislature be competent Judges? Will a gentleman from Georgia be a Judge of the expediency of a law which is to operate in N. Hamshire. Such a Negative would be more injurious than that of Great Britain heretofore was. It is said that the National Govt. must have the influence arising from the grant of offices and honors. In order to render <such a Government> effectual he believed such an influence to be necessary. But if the States will not agree to it, it is in vain, worse than in vain to make the proposition. If this influence is to be attained, the States must be entirely abolished. Will any one say this would ever be agreed to? He doubted whether any Genl Government equally beneficial to all can be attained. That now under consideration he is sure, must be utterly unattainable. He had another objection. The system was too novel & complex. No man could foresee what its operation will be either with respect to the Genl. Govt. or the State Govts. One or other it has been surmised must absorb the whole.

Col. Mason. did not expect this point would have been reagitated. The essential differences between the two plans, had been clearly stated. The principal objections agst. that of Mr. R. were the *want of power* & the *want of practicability*. There can be no weight in the first as the fiat is not to be *here*, but in the people. He thought with his colleague Mr. R. that there were besides certain crisises, in which all the ordinary cautions yielded to public necessity. He gave as an example, the eventual Treaty with G. B. in forming which the Commsrs of the U. S. had boldly disregarded the improvident shackles of Congs. had given to their Country an honorable & happy peace, and instead of being censured for the transgression of their powers, had raised to themselves a monument more durable than brass. The *impracticability* of gaining the public concurrence he thought was still more groundless. (Mr. Lansing) had cited the attempts of Congress to gain an enlargment of their powers, and had inferred from the miscarrige of these attempts, the hopelessness of the plan which he (Mr. L) opposed. He thought a very different inference ought to have been drawn; viz. that the plan which

(Mr. L.) espoused, and which proposed to augument the powers of Congress, never could be expected to succeed. He meant not to throw any reflections on Congs. as a body, much less on any particular members of it. He meant however to speak his sentiments without reserve on this subject; it was a privilege of Age, and perhaps the only compensation which nature had given for, the privation of so many other enjoyments; and he should not scruple to exercise it freely. Is it to be thought that the people of America, so watchful over their interests; so jealous of their liberties, will give up their all, will surrender both the sword and the purse, to the same body, and that too not chosen immediately by themselves? They never will. They never ought. Will they trust such a body, with the regulation of their trade, with the regulation of their taxes; with all the other great powers, which are in contemplation? Will they give unbounded confidence to a secret Journal—to the intrigues—to the factions which in the nature of things appertain to such an Assembly? If any man doubts the existence of these characters of Congress, let him consult their Journals for the years, 78, 79, & 80—It will be said, that if the people are averse to parting with power, why is it hoped that they will part with it to a National Legislature. The proper answer is that in this case they do not part with power: they only transfer it from one sett of immediate Representatives to another sett. Much has been said of the unsettled state of the mind of the people. he believed the mind of the people of America, as elsewhere, was unsettled as to some points; but settled as to others. In two points he was sure it was well settled. 1. in an attachment to Republican Government. 2. in an attachment to more than one branch in the Legislature. Their constitutions accord so generally in both these circumstances, that they seem almost to have been preconcerted. This must either have been a miracle, or have resulted from the genius of the people. The only exceptions to the establishmt. of two branches in the Legislatures are the State of Pa. & Congs. and the latter the only single one not chosen by the people themselves. What has been the consequence? The people have been constantly averse to giving that Body further powers—It was acknowledged by (Mr. Patterson) that his plan could not be enforced without military coertion. Does he consider the force of this concession. The most jarring elements of nature; fire & water themselves are not more incompatible that such a mixture of civil liberty and military execution. Will the militia march from one State to another, in order to collect the arrears of taxes from the delinquent members of the Republic? Will they maintain an army for this purpose? Will not the citizens of the invaded State assist one another till they rise as one Man, and shake off the Union altogether. Rebellion is the only case in which <the military force of the State can be properly> exerted agst. its Citizens. In one point of view he was struck with horror at the prospect of recurring to this expedient. To punish the non-payment of taxes with death, was a severity not yet adopted by depotism itself: yet this unexampled cruelty would be mercy compared to a military collection of revenue, in which the bayonet could make no discrimination between the innocent and the guilty. He took this occasion to repeat. that notwithstanding his solicitude to establish a national Government, he never would agree to abolish the State Govts. or render them absolutely insignificant. They were as necessary as the Genl. Govt. and he would be equally careful to preserve them. He was aware of the difficulty of drawing the line between them, but hoped it was not insurmountable. The Convention, tho' comprising so many distinguished characters, could not be expected to make a faultless Govt. And he would prefer trusting to posterity the amendment of its defects, rather than push the experiment too far.

Mr. Luther Martin agreed with (Col Mason) as to the importance of the State Govts. he would support them at the expense of the Genl. Govt. which was instituted for the purpose of that support. He saw no necessity for two branches, and if it existed Congress might be organized into two. He considered Congs as representing the people, being chosen by the Legislatures who were chosen by the people. At any rate, Congress represented the Legislatures; and it was the Legislatures not the people who refused to enlarge their powers. Nor could the rule of voting have been the ground of objection, otherwise ten of the States must always have been ready, to place further confidence in Congs. The causes of repugnance must therefore be looked for elsewhere.—At the separation from the British Empire, the people of America preferred the Establishment of themselves into thirteen separate sovereignties instead of incorporating themselves into one: to these they look up for the security of their lives, liberties & properties: to these they must look up—The federal Govt. they formed, to defend the whole agst. foreign nations, in case of war, and to defend the lesser States agst. the ambition of the larger: they are afraid of granting powers unnecessarily, lest they should defeat the original end of the Union; lest the powers should prove dangerous to the sovereignties of the particular States which the Union was meant to support; and expose the lesser to being swallowed up by the larger. He conceived also that the people of the States having already vested their powers in their respective Legislatures, could not resume them without a dissolution of their Governments. He was agst. Conventions in the States: was not agst. assisting States agst. rebellious subjects; thought the *federal* plan of Mr. Patterson did not require coercion more than the *national one*, as the latter must depend for the deficiency of its revenues on requisitions & quotas, and that a national Judiciary extended into the States would be ineffectual, and would be viewed with a jealousy inconsistent with its usefulness.

Mr. Sherman 2ded & supported Mr. Lansing's motion. He admitted two branches to be necessary in the State Legislatures, but saw no necessity for them in a Confederacy of States. The Examples were all, of a single Council. Congs. carried us thro' the war, and perhaps as well as any Govt. could have done. The complaints at present are not that the views of Congs. are unwise or unfaithful, but that that their powers are insufficient for the execution of their views. The national debt & the want of power somewhere to draw forth the National resources, are the great matters that press. All the States were sensible of the defect of power in Congs. He thought much might be said in apology for the failure of the State Legislatures to comply with the confederation. They were afraid of bearing too hard on the people, by accumulating taxes; no *constitutional* rule had been or could be observed in the quotas,—the accounts also were unsettled & every State supposed itself in advance, rather than in arrears. For want of a general system taxes to a due amount had not been drawn from trade which was the most convenient resource. As almost all the States had agreed to the recommendation of Congs. on the subject of an impost, it appeared clearly that they were willing to trust Congs. with <power to draw a revenue from Trade.> There is no weight therefore in the argument drawn from a distrust of Congs. for money matters being the most important of all, if the people will trust them with power as to them, they will trust them with any other necessary powers. Congs. indeed by the confederation have in fact the right of saying how much the people shall pay, and to what purpose it shall be applied: and this right was granted to them in the expectation that it would in all cases have its effect. If another branch were to be added to Congs. to be chosen by the people, it would serve to embarrass. The people would not much interest themselves in the elections, a few designing men in the large districts would carry their points, and the people would have no more confidence in their new representatives than in Congs. He saw no reason why the State Legislatures should be unfriendly as had been suggested, to Congs. If they appoint Congs. and approve of their measures, they would be rather favorable and partial to them. The disparity of the States in point of size he perceived was the main difficulty. But the large States had not yet suffered from the equality of votes enjoyed by the small ones. In all great and general points, the interests of all the States were the same. The State of Virga. notwithstanding the equality of votes, ratified the Confederation without, or even proposing, any alteration. Massts. also ratified without any material difficulty &c. In none of the ratifications is the want of two branches noticed or complained of. To consolidate the States as some had proposed would dissolve our Treaties with foreign nations, which had been formed with us, as *Confederated* States. He did not however suppose that the creation of two branches in the Legislature would have such an effect. If the difficulty on the subject of reprecentation can not be otherwise got over, he would agree to have two branches, and a proportional representation in one of them, provided each State had an equal voice in the other. This was necessary to secure the rights of the lesser States; otherwise three or four of the large States would rule the others as they please. Each State like each individual had its peculiar habits usages and manners, which constituted its happiness. It would not therefore give to others a power over this happiness, any more than an individual would do, when he could avoid it.

Mr. Wilson, urged the necessity of two branches; observed that if a proper model was not to be found in other Confederacies it was not to be wondered at. The number of them was <small> & the duration of some at least short. The Amphyctionic & Achæan were formed in the infancy of political Science; and appear by their History & fate, to have contained radical defects, The Swiss & Belgic Confederacies were held together not by any vital principle of energy but by the incumbent pressure of formidable neighbouring nations: The German owed its continuance to the influence of the H. of Austria. He appealed to our own experience for the defects of our Confederacy. He had been 6 years in the 12 since the commencement of the Revolution, a member of Congress and had felt all its weaknesses. He appealed to the recollection of others whether on many important occasions, the public interest had not been obstructed by the small members of the Union. The success of the Revolution was owing to other causes, than the Constitution of Congress. In many instances it went on even agst. the difficulties arising from Congs. themselves—He admitted that the large States did accede as had been stated, to the Confederation in its present form. But it was the effect of necessity not of choice. There are other instances of their yielding from the same motive to the unreasonable measures of the small States. The situation of things is now a little altered. He insisted that a jealousy would exist between the State Legislatures & the General Legislature: observing that the members of the former would have views & feelings very distinct in this respect from their constituents. A private citizen of a State is indifferent whether power be exercised by the Genl. or State Legislatures, provided it be exercised most for his happiness. His representative has an interest in its being exercised by the body to which he belongs. He will therefore view the National Legisl: with the eye of a jealous rival. He observed that the addresses of Congs. to the people at large, had always been better received & produced greater effect, than those made to the Legislatures.

On the question for postponing in order to take up Mr. Lansings proposition "to vest the powers of Legislation in Congs."

Masst. no. Cont. ay. N. Y. ay. N. J. ay. Pa. no. Del. ay Md. divd. Va. no. N. C. no. S. C. no. Geo. no [Ayes—4; noes—6; divided—1.]

On motion of the Deputies from Delaware, the question on the 2d. Resolution in the Report from the Committee of the whole was postponed till tomorrow.

adjd.

(4) July 20, 1787

"to be removeable on impeachment and conviction <for> malpractice or neglect of duty". See Resol: 9:

Mr. Pinkney & Mr Govr. Morris moved to strike out this part of the Resolution. Mr P. observd. he <ought not to> be impeachable whilst in office

Mr. Davie. If he be not impeachable whilst in office, he will spare no efforts or means whatever to get himself re-elected. He considered this as an essential security for the good behaviour of the Executive.

Mr Wilson concurred in the necessity of making the Executive impeachable whilst in office.

Mr. Govr. Morris. He can do no criminal act without Coadjutors who may be punished. In case he should be re-elected, that will be sufficient proof of his innocence. Besides who is to impeach? Is the impeachment to suspend his functions. If it is not the mischief will go on. If it is the impeachment will be nearly equivalent to a displacement, and will render the Executive dependent on those who are to impeach

Col. Mason. No point is of more importance than that the right of impeachment should be continued. Shall any man be above Justice? Above all shall that man be above it, who can commit the most extensive injustice? When great crimes were committed he was for punishing the principal as well as the Coadjutors. There had been much debate & difficulty as to the mode of chusing the Executive. He approved of that which had been adopted at first, namely of referring the appointment to the Natl. Legislature. One objection agst. Electors was the danger of their being corrupted by the Candidates: & this furnished a peculiar reason in favor of impeachments whilst in office. Shall the man who has practised corruption & by that means procured his appointment in the first instance, be suffered to escape punishment, by repeating his guilt?

Docr. Franklin was for retaining the clause as favorable to the executive. History furnishes one example only of a first Magistrate being formally brought to public Justice. Every body cried out agst this as unconstitutional. What was the practice before this in cases where the chief Magistrate rendered himself obnoxious? Why recourse was had to assassination in wch. he was not only deprived of his life but of the opportunity of vindicating his character. It wd. be the best way therefore to provide in the Constitution for the regular punishment of the Executive when his misconduct should deserve it, and for his honorable acquittal when he should be unjustly accused.

Mr. Govr Morris admits corruption & some few other offences to be such as ought to be impeachable; but thought the cases ought to be enumerated & defined:

Mr. <Madison>—thought it indispensable that some provision should be made for defending the Community agst the incapacity, negligence or perfidy of the chief Magistrate. The limitation of the period of his service, was not a sufficient security. He might lose his capacity after his appointment. He might pervert his administration into a scheme of peculation or oppression. He might betray his trust to

341

foreign powers. The case of the Executive Magistracy was very distinguishable, from that of the Legislative or of any other public body, holding offices of limited duration. It could not be presumed that all or even a majority of the members of an Assembly would either lose their capacity for discharging, or be bribed to betray, their trust. Besides the restraints of their personal integrity & honor, the difficulty of acting in concert for purposes of corruption was a security to the public. And if one or a few members only should be seduced, the soundness of the remaining members, would maintain the integrity and fidelity of the body. In the case of the Executive Magistracy which was to be administered by a single man, loss of capacity or corruption was more within the compass of probable events, and either of them might be fatal to the Republic.

Mr. Pinkney did not see the necessity of impeachments. He was sure they ought not to issue from the Legislature who would in that case hold them as a rod over the Executive and by that means effectually destroy his independence. His revisionary power in particular would be rendered altogether insignificant.

Mr. Gerry urged the necessity of impeachments. A good magistrate will not fear them. A bad one ought to be kept in fear of them. He hoped the maxim would never be adopted here that the chief Magistrate could do <no> wrong.

Mr. King expressed his apprehensions that an extreme caution in favor of liberty might enervate the Government we were forming. He wished the House to recur to the primitive axiom that the three great departments of Govts. should be separate & independent: that the Executive & Judiciary should be so as well as the Legislative: that the Executive should be so equally with the Judiciary. Would this be the case if the Executive should be impeachable? It had been said that the Judiciary would be impeachable. But it should have been remembered at the same time that the Judiciary hold their places not for a limited time, but during good behaviour. It is necessary therefore that a forum should be established for trying misbehaviour. Was the Executive to hold his place during good behaviour?—The Executive was to hold his place for a limited term like the members of the Legislature; Like them particularly the Senate whose members would continue in appointmt the same term of 6 years. he would periodically be tried for his behaviour by his electors, who would continue or discontinue him in trust according to the manner in which he had discharged it. Like them therefore, he ought to be subject to no intermediate trial, by impeachment. He ought not to be impeachable unless he hold his office during good behavior, a tenure which would be most agreeable to him; provided an independent and effectual forum could be devised; But under no circumstances ought he to be impeachable by the Legislature. This would be destructive of his independence and of the principles of the Constitution.

He relied on the vigor of the Executive as a great security for the public liberties.

Mr. Randolph.   The propriety of impeachments was a favorite principle with him; Guilt wherever found ought to be punished.   The Executive will have great opportunitys of abusing his power; particularly in time of war when the military force, and in some respects the public money will be in his hands.   Should no regular punishment be provided, it will be irregularly inflicted by tumults & insurrections.   He is aware of the necessity of proceeding with a cautious hand, and of excluding as much as possible the influence of the Legislature from the business.   He suggested for consideration an idea which had fallen (from Col Hamilton) of composing a forum out of the Judges belonging to the States: and even of requiring some preliminary inquest whether just grounds of impeachment existed.

Doctr. Franklin mentioned the case of the Prince of Orange during the late war.   An agreement was made between France & Holland; by which their two fleets were to unite at a certain time & place.   The Du<t>ch fleet did not appear.   Every body began to wonder at it.   At length it was suspected that the Statholder was at the bottom of the matter.   This suspicion prevailed more & more.   Yet as he could not be impeached and no regular examination took place, he remained in his office, and strengtheing [sic] his own party,as the party opposed to him became formidable, he gave birth to the most violent animosities & contentions.   Had he been impeachable, a regular & peaceable inquiry would have taken place and he would if guilty have been duly punished, if innocent restored to the confidence of the public.

Mr. King remarked that the case of the Statholder was not applicable.   He held his place for life, and was not periodically elected.   In the former case impeachments are proper to secure good behaviour.   In the latter they are unnecessary; the periodical responsibility to the electors being an equivalent security.

Mr Wilson observed that if the idea were to be pursued, the Senators who are to hold their places during the same term with the Executive. ought to be subject to impeachment & removal.

Mr. Pinkney apprehended that some gentlemen reasoned on a supposition that the Executive was to have powers which would not be committed to him: <He presumed> that his powers would be so circumscribed as to render impeachments unnecessary.

Mr. Govr. Morris,'s opinion had been changed by the arguments used in the discussion.   He was now sensible of the necessity of impeachments, if the Executive was to continue for any time in office.   Our Executive was not like a Magistrate having a life interest, much less like one having an hereditary interest in his office.   He may be bribed by a greater interest to betray his trust; and no one would say that we ought to expose ourselves to the danger of seeing the first Magistrate in foreign pay without being able to guard agst it by displacing him. One would think the King of England well secured agst bribery. He has as it were a fee simple in the whole Kingdom. Yet Charles II was bribed by Louis XIV. The Executive ought therefore to be impeachable for treachery; Corrupting his electors, and incapacity were other causes of impeachment. For the latter he should be punished not as a man, but as an officer, and punished only by degradation from his office. This Magistrate is not the King but the prime-Minister. The people are the King. When we make him amenable to Justice however we should take care to provide some mode that will not make him dependent on the Legislature.

<It was moved & 2ded. to postpone the question of impeachments which was negatived. Mas. & S. Carolina only being ay.>

On ye. Question, Shall the Executive be removeable on impeachments?

Mas. no. Ct. ay. N. J. ay. Pa. ay. Del. ay. Md. ay. Va. ay. N. C. ay. S. C. no. Geo-ay- [Ayes—8; noes—2.]

E. LETTER OF CENTINEL, NO. 1

October 5, 1987

To the Freemen of Pennsylvania.

Friends, Countrymen and Fellow Citizens,

Permit one of yourselves to put you in mind of certain *liberties* and *privileges* secured to you by the constitution of this commonwealth, and to beg your serious attention to his uninterested opinion upon the plan of federal government submitted to your consideration, before you surrender these great and valuable privileges up forever. Your present frame of government, secures to you a right to hold yourselves, houses, papers and possessions free from search and seizure, and therefore warrants granted without oaths or affirmations first made, affording sufficient foundation for them, whereby any officer or messenger may be commanded or required to search your houses or seize your persons or property, not particularly described in such warrant, shall not be granted. Your constitution further provides "that in controversies respecting property, and in suits between man and man, the parties have a right *to trial by jury, which ought to be held sacred.*" It also provides and declares, *"that the people have a right of* FREEDOM OF SPEECH, *and of* WRITING *and* PUBLISHING *their sentiments, therefore* THE FREEDOM OF THE PRESS OUGHT NOT TO BE RESTRAINED." The constitution of Pennsylvania is *yet* in existence, *as yet* you have the right to *freedom of speech,* and of *publishing your sentiments.* How long those rights will appertain to you, you yourselves are called upon to say, whether your *houses* shall continue to be your *castles;* whether your *papers,* your *persons* and your *property,* are to be held sacred and free from *general warrants,* you are now to determine. Whether the *trial by jury* is to continue as your birth-right, the freemen of Pennsylvania, nay, of all America, are now called upon to declare.

Without presuming upon my own judgement, I cannot think it an unwarrantable presumption to offer my private opinion, and call upon others for their's; and if I use my pen with the boldness of a freeman, it is because I know that *the liberty of the press yet remains unviolated*, and *juries yet are judges*.

The late Convention have submitted to your consideration a plan of a new federal government—The subject is highly interesting to your future welfare—Whether it be calculated to promote the great ends of civil society, *viz.* the happiness and prosperity of the community; it behoves you well to consider, uninfluenced by the authority of names. Instead of that frenzy of enthusiasm, that has actuated the citizens of Philadelphia, in their approbation of the proposed plan, before it was possible that it could be the result of a rational investigation into its principles; it ought to be dispassionately and deliberately examined, and its own intrinsic merit the only criterion of your patronage. If ever free and unbiassed discussion was proper or necessary, it is on such an occasion.—All the blessings of liberty and the dearest privileges of freemen, are now at stake and dependent on your present conduct. Those who are competent to the task of developing the principles of government, ought to be encouraged to come forward, and thereby the better enable the people to make a proper judgment; for the science of government is so abstruse, that few are able to judge for themselves; without such assistance the people are too apt to yield an implicit assent to the opinions of those characters, whose abilities are held in the highest esteem, and to those in whose integrity and patriotism they can confide; not considering that the love of domination is generally in proportion to talents, abilities, and superior acquirements; and that the men of the greatest purity of intention may be made instruments of despotism in the hands of the *artful and designing*. If it were not for the stability and attachment which time and habit gives to forms of government, it would be in the power of the enlightened and aspiring few, if they should combine, at any time to destroy the best establishments, and even make the people the instruments of their own subjugation.

The late revolution having effaced in a great measure all former habits, and the present institutions are so recent, that there exists not that great reluctance to innovation, so remarkable in old communities, and which accords with reason, for the most comprehensive mind cannot foresee the full operation of material changes on civil polity; it is the genius of the common law to resist innovation.

The wealthy and ambitious, who in every community think they have a right to lord it over their fellow creatures, have availed themselves, very successfully, of this favorable disposition; for the people thus unsettled in their sentiments, have been prepared to accede to any extreme of government; all the distresses and difficulties they experience, proceeding from various causes, have been ascribed to the impotency of the present confederation, and thence they have been led to expect full relief from the adoption of the proposed system of government; and in the other event, immediately ruin and annihilation as a nation. These characters flatter themselves that they have lulled all distrust and jealousy of their new plan, by gaining the concurrence of the two men in whom America has the highest confidence, and now triumphantly exult in the completion of their long meditated schemes of power and aggrandisement. I would be very far from insinuating that the two illustrious personages alluded to, have not the welfare of their country at heart; but that the unsuspecting goodness and zeal of the one, has been imposed on, in a subject of which he must be necessarily inexperienced, from his other arduous engagements; and that the weakness and indecision attendant on old age, has been practised on in the other.

I am fearful that the principles of government inculcated in Mr. Adams's treatise, and enforced in the numerous essays and paragraphs in the newspapers, have misled some well designing members of the late Convention.—But it will appear in the sequel, that the construction of the proposed plan of government is infinitely more extravagant.

I have been anxiously expecting that some enlightened patriot would, ere this, have taken up the pen to expose the futility, and counteract the baneful tendency of such principles. Mr. Adams's *sine qua non* of a good government is three balancing powers, whose repelling qualities are to produce an equilibrium of interests, and thereby promote the happiness of the whole community. He asserts that the administrators of every government, will ever be actuated by views of private interest and ambition, to the prejudice of the public good; that therefore the only effectual method to secure the rights of the people and promote their welfare, is to create an opposition of interests betweeen [sic] the members of two distinct bodies, in the exercise of the powers of government, and balanced by those of a third. This hypothesis supposes human wisdom competent to the task of instituting three co-equal orders in government, and a corresponding weight in the community to enable them respectively to exercise their several parts, and whose views and interests should be so distinct as to prevent a coalition of any two of them for the destruction of the third. Mr. Adams, although he has traced the constitution of every form of government that ever existed, as far as history affords materials, has not been able to adduce a single instance of such a government; he indeed says that the British constitution is such in theory, but this is rather a confirmation that his principles are chimerical and not to be reduced to practice. If such an organization of power were practicable, how long would it continue? not a day—for there is so great a disparity in the talents, wisdom and industry of mankind, that the scale would presently preponderate to one or the other body, and with every accession of power the means of further increase would be greatly extended. The state of society in England is much more favorable to such a scheme of government than that of America. There they have a powerful hereditary nobility, and real distinctions of rank and interests; but even there, for want of that perfect equallity of power and distinction of interests, in the three orders of government, they exist but in name; the only operative and efficient check, upon the conduct of administration, is the sense of the people at large.

Suppose a government could be formed and supported on such principles, would it answer the great purposes of civil society; if the administrators of every government are actuated by views of private interest and ambition, how is the welfare and happiness of the community to be the result of such jarring adverse interests?

Therefore, as different orders in government will not produce the good of the whole, we must recur to other principles. I believe it will be found that the form of government, which holds those entrusted with power, in the greatest responsibility to their constitutents, the best calculated for freemen. A republican, or free government, can only exist where the body of the people are virtuous, and where property is pretty equally divided[;] in such a government the people are the sovereign and their sense or opinion is the criterion of every public measure; for when this ceases to be the case, the nature of the government is changed, and an aristocracy, monarchy or despotism will rise on its ruin. The highest responsibility is to be attained, in a simple structure of government, for the great body of the people never steadily attend to the operations of government, and for want of due information are liable to be imposed on—If you complicate the plan by various orders, the people will be perplexed and divided in their sentiments about the source of abuses or misconduct, some will impute it to the senate, others to the house of representatives, and so on, that the interposition of the people may be rendered imperfect or perhaps wholly abortive. But if, imitating the constitution of Pennsylvania, you vest all the legislative power in one body of men (separating the executive and judicial) elected for a short period, and necessarily excluded by rotation from permanency, and guarded from precipitancy and surprise by delays imposed on its proceedings, you will create the most perfect responsibility for then, whenever the people feel a grievance they cannot mistake the authors, and will apply the remedy with certainty and effect, discarding them at the next election. This tie of responsibility will obviate all the dangers apprehended from a single legislature, and will the best secure the rights of the people.

Having premised this much, I shall now proceed to the examination of the proposed plan of government, and I trust, shall make it appear to the meanest capacity, that it has none of the essential requisites of a free government; that it is neither founded on those balancing restraining powers, recommended by Mr. Adams and attempted in the British constitution, or possessed of that responsibility to its constituents, which, in my opinion, is the only effectual security for the liberties and happiness of the people; but on the contrary, that it is a most daring attempt to establish a despotic aristocracy among freemen, that the world has ever witnessed.

I shall previously consider the extent of the powers intended to be vested in Congress, before I examine the construction of the general government.

It will not be controverted that the legislative is the highest delegated power in government, and that all others are subordinate to it. The celebrated *Montesquieu* establishes it as a maxim, that legislation necessarily follows the power of taxation. By sect. 8, of the first article of the proposed plan of government, "the Congress are to have power to lay and collect taxes, duties, imposts and excises, to pay the debts and provide for the common defence and *general welfare* of the United States; but all duties, imposts and excises, shall be uniform throughout the United States." Now what can be more comprehensive than these words; not content by other sections of this plan, to grant all the great executive powers of a confederation, and a STANDING ARMY IN TIME OF PEACE, that grand engine of oppression, and moreover the absolute controul over the commerce of the United States and all external objects of revenue, such as unlimited imposts upon imports, etc.—they are to be vested with every species of *internal* taxation;—whatever taxes, duties and excises that they may deem requisite for the *general welfare,* may be imposed on the citizens of these states, levied by the officers of Congress, distributed through every district in America; and the collection would be enforced by the standing army, however grievous or improper they may be. The Congress may construe every purpose for which the state legislatures now lay taxes, to be for the *general welfare,* and thereby seize upon every object of revenue.

The judicial power by 1st sect. of article 3 ["]shall extend to all cases, in law and equity, arising under this constitution, the laws of the United States, and treaties made or which shall be made under their authority; to all cases affecting ambassadors, other public ministers and consuls; to all cases of admiralty and maritime jurisdiction, to controversies to which the United States shall be a party, to controversies between two or more states, between a state and citizens of another state, between citizens of different states, between citizens of the same state claiming lands under grants of different states, and between a state, or the citizens thereof, and foreign states, citizens or subjects."

The judicial power to be vested in one Supreme Court, and in such Inferior Courts as the Congress may from time to time ordain and establish.

The objects of jurisdiction recited above, are so numerous, and the shades of distinction between civil causes are oftentimes so slight, that it is more than probable that the state judicatories would be wholly superceded; for in contests about jurisdiction, the federal court, as the most powerful, would ever prevail. Every person acquainted with the history of the courts in England, knows by what ingenious sophisms they have, at different periods, extended the sphere of their jurisdiction over objects out of the line of their institution, and contrary to their very nature; courts of a criminal jurisdiction obtaining cognizance in civil causes.

To put the omnipotency of Congress over the state government and judicatories out of all doubt, the 6th article ordains that "this constitution and the laws of the United States which shall be made in pursuance thereof, and all treaties made, or which shall be made under the authority of the United States, shall be the *supreme law of the land,* and the judges in every state shall be bound thereby, any thing in the constitution or laws of any state to the contrary notwithstanding."

By these sections the all-prevailing powers of taxation, and such extensive legislative and judicial powers are vested in the general government, as must in their operation, necessarily absorb the state legislatures and judicatories; and that such was in the contemplation of the framers of it, will appear from the provision made for such event, in another part of it; (but that, fearful of alarming the people by so great an innovation, they have suffered the forms of the separate governments to remain, as a blind.) By sect. 4th of the 1st article, "the times, places and manner of holding elections for senators and representatives, shall be prescribed in each state by the legislature thereof; *but the Congress may at any time, by law, make or alter such regulations, except as to the place of chusing senators.*" The plain construction of which is, that when the state legislatures drop out of sight, from the necessary operation of this government, then Congress are to provide for the election and appointment of representatives and senators.

If the foregoing be a just comment—if the United States are to be melted down into one empire, it becomes you to consider, whether such a government, however constructed, would be eligible in so extended a territory; and whether it would be practicable, consistent with freedom? It is the opinion of the greatest writers, that a very extensive country cannot be governed on democratical principles, on any other plan, than a confederation of a number of small republics, possessing all the powers of internal government, but united in the management of their foreign and general concerns.

It would not be difficult to prove, that any thing short of despotism, could not bind so great a country under one government; and that whatever plan you might, at the first setting out, establish, it would issue in a depotism.

If one general government could be instituted and maintained on principles of freedom, it would not be so competent to attend to the various local concerns and wants, of every particular district[,] as well as the peculiar governments, who are nearer the scene, and possessed of superior means of information[;] besides, if the business of the *whole* union is to be managed by one government, there would not be time. Do we not already see, that the inhabitants in a number of larger states, who are remote from the seat of government, are loudly complaining of the inconveniencies and disadvantages they are subjected to on this account, and that, to enjoy the comforts of local government, they are separating into smaller divisions.

Having taken a review of the powers, I shall now examine the construction of the proposed general government.

Art. 1. sect. 1. "All legislative powers herein granted shall be vested in a Congress of the United States, which shall consist of a senate and house of representatives." By another section, the president (the principal executive officer) has a conditional controul over their proceedings.

Sect. 2. "The house of representatives shall be composed of members chosen every second year, by the people of the several states. The number of representatives shall not exceed one for every 30,000 inhabitants."

The senate, the other constituent branch of the legislature, is formed by the legislature of each state appointing two senators, for the term of six years.

The executive power by Art. 2, sec. 1. is to be vested in a president of the United States of America, elected for four years: Sec. 2. gives him "power, by and with the consent of the senate to make treaties, provided two thirds of the senators present concur; and he shall nominate, and by and with the advice and consent of the senate, shall appoint ambassadors, other public ministers and consuls, judges of the Supreme Court, and all other officers of the United States, whose appointments are not herein otherwise provided for, and which shall be established by law, etc. And by another section he has the absolute power of granting reprieves and pardons for treason and all other high crimes and misdemeanors, except in case of impeachment."

The foregoing are the outlines of the plan.

Thus we see, the house of representatives, are on the part of the people to balance the senate, who I suppose will be composed of the *better sort*, the *well born*, etc. The number of the representatives (being only one for every 30,000 inhabitants) appears to be too few, either to communicate the requisite information, of the wants, local circumstances and sentiments of so extensive an empire, or to prevent corruption and undue influence, in the exercise of such great powers; the term for which they are to be chosen, too long to preserve a due dependence and accountability to their constituents; and the mode and places of their election not sufficiently ascertained, for as Congress have the controul over both, they may govern the choice, by ordering the *representatives* of a *whole* state, to be *elected* in *one* place, and that too may be the most *inconvenient.*

The senate, the great efficient body in this plan of government, is constituted on the most unequal principles. The smallest state in the union has equal weight with the great states of Virginia, Massachusetts, or Pennsylvania—The Senate, besides its legislative functions, has a very considerable share in the Executive; none of the principal appointments to office can be made without its advice and consent. The term and mode of its appointment, will lead to permanency; the members are chosen for six years, the mode is under the controul of Congress, and as there is no exclusion by rotation, they may be continued for life, which, from their extensive means of influence, would follow of course. The President, who would be a mere pageant of state, unless he coincides with the views of the Senate, would either become the head of the aristocratic junto in that body, or its minion; besides, their influence being the most predominant, could the best secure his re-election to office. And from his power of granting pardons, he might skreen from punishment the most treasonable attempts on the liberties of the people, when instigated by the Senate.

From this investigation into the organization of this government, it appears that it is devoid of all responsibility or accountability to the great body of the people, and that so far from being a regular balanced government, it would be in practice a *permanent* ARISTOCRACY.

The framers of it[,] actuated by the true spirit of such a government, which ever abominates and suppresses all free enquiry and discussion, have made no provision for the *liberty of the press,* that grand *palladium of freedom,* and *scourge of tyrants;* but observed a total silence on that head. It is the opinion of some great writers, that if the liberty of the press, by an institution of religion, or otherwise, could be rendered *sacred,* even in *Turkey,* that despotism would fly before it. And it is worthy of remark, that there is no declaration of personal rights, premised in most free constitutions; and that trial by *jury* in *civil* cases is taken away; for what other construction can be put on the following, viz. Article III. Sect. 2d. "In all cases affecting ambassadors, other public ministers and consuls, and those in which a State shall be party, the Supreme Court shall have *original* jurisdiction. In all the other cases above mentioned, the Supreme Court shall have *appellate* jurisdiction, both as to *law and fact"* It would be a novelty in jurisprudence, as well as evidently improper to allow an appeal from the verdict of a jury, on the matter of fact; therefore, it implies and allows of a dismission of the jury in civil cases, and especially when it is considered, that jury trial in criminal cases is expresly stipulated for, but not in civil cases.

But our situation is represented to be so *critically* dreadful, that, however reprehensible and exceptionable the proposed plan of government may be, there is no alternative, between the adoption of it and absolute ruin.—My fellow citizens, things are not at that crisis, it is the argument of tyrants; the present distracted state of Europe secures us from injury on that quarter, and as to domestic dissentions, we have not so much to fear from them, as to precipitate us into this form of government, without it is a safe and a proper one. For remember, of all *possible* evils, that of *despotism* is the *worst* and the most to be *dreaded*.

Besides, it cannot be supposed, that the first essay on so difficult a subject, is so well digested, as it ought to be,—if the proposed plan, after a mature deliberation, should meet the approbation of the respective States, the matter will end; but if it should be found to be fraught with dangers and inconveniencies, a future general Convention being in possession of the objections, will be the better enabled to plan a suitable government.

Who's here so base, that would a bondman be?
If any, speak; for him have I offended.
Who's here so vile, that will not love his country?
If any, speak; for him have I offended.

Centinel.

F. JAMES MADISON, THE FEDERALIST, NO. 47

January 30, 1788

To the People of the State of New York.

Having reviewed the general form of the proposed government, and the general mass of power allotted to it: I proceed to examine the particular structure of this government, and the distribution of this mass of power among its constituent parts.

One of the principal objections inculcated by the more respectable adversaries to the constitution, is its supposed violation of the political maxim, that the legislative, executive and judiciary departments ought to be separate and distinct. In the structure of the federal government, no regard, it is said, seems to have been paid to this essential precaution in favor of liberty. The several departments of power are distributed and blended in such a manner, as at once to destroy all symmetry and beauty of form; and to expose some of the essential parts of the edifice to the danger of being crushed by the disproportionate weight of other parts.

No political truth is certainly of greater intrinsic value or is stamped with the authority of more enlightened patrons of liberty than that on which the objection is founded. The accumulation of all powers legislative, executive and judiciary in the same hands, whether of one, a few or many, and whether hereditary, self appointed, or elective, may justly be pronounced the very definition of tyranny. Were the federal constitution therefore really chargeable with this accumulation of power or with a mixture of powers having a dangerous tendency to such an accumulation, no further arguments would be necessary to inspire a universal reprobation of the system. I persuade myself however, that it will be made apparent to every one, that the charge cannot be supported, and that the maxim on which it relies, has been totally misconceived and misapplied. In order to form correct ideas on this important subject, it will be proper to investigate the sense, in which the preservation of liberty requires, that the three great departments of power should be separate and distinct.

The oracle who is always consulted and cited on this subject, is the celebrated Montesquieu. If he be not the author of this invaluable precept in the science of politics, he has the merit at least of displaying, and recommending it most effectually to the attention of mankind. Let us endeavour in the first place to ascertain his meaning on this point.

The British constitution was to Montesquieu, what Homer has been to the didactic writers on epic poetry. As the latter have considered the work of the immortal Bard, as the perfect model from which the principles and rules of the epic art were to be drawn, and by which all similar works were to be judged; so this great political critic appears to have viewed the constitution of England, as the standard, or to use his own expression, as the mirrour of political liberty; and to have delivered in the form of elementary truths, the several characteristic principles of that particular system. That we may be sure then not to mistake his meaning in this case, let us recur to the source from which the maxim was drawn.

On the slightest view of the British constitution we must perceive, that the legislative, executive and judiciary departments are by no means totally separate and distinct from each other. The executive magistrate forms an integral part of the legislative authority. He alone has the prerogative of making treaties with foreign sovereigns, which when made have, under certain limitations, the force of legislative acts. All the members of the judiciary department are appointed by him; can be removed by him on the address of the two Houses of Parliament, and form, when he pleases to consult them, one of his constitutional councils. One branch of the legislative department forms also, a great constitutional council to the executive chief; as on another hand, it is the sole depositary of judicial power in cases of impeachment, and is invested with the supreme appellate jurisdiction, in all other cases. The judges again are so far connected with the legislative department, as often to attend and participate in its deliberations, though not admitted to a legislative vote.

From these facts by which Montesquieu was guided it may clearly be inferred, that in saying "there can be no liberty where the legislative and executive powers are united in the same person, or body of magistrates," or "if the power of judging be not separated from the legislative and executive powers," he did not mean that these departments ought to have no *partial agency* in, or no *controul* over the acts of each other. His meaning, as his own words import, and still more conclusively as illustrated by the example in his eye, can amount to no more than this, that where the *whole* power of one department is exercised by the same hands which possess the *whole* power of another department, the fundamental principles of a free constitution, are subverted. This would have been the case in the constitution examined by him, if the King who is the sole executive magistrate, had possessed also the compleat legislative power, or the supreme administration of justice; or if the entire legislative body, had possessed the supreme judiciary, or the supreme executive authority. This however is not among the vices of that constitution. The magistrate in whom the whole executive power resides cannot of himself make a law, though he can put a negative on every law, nor administer justice in person, though he has the appointment of those who do administer it. The judges can exercise no executive prerogative, though they are shoots from the executive stock, nor any legislative function, though they may be advised with by the legislative councils. The entire legislature, can perform no judiciary act, though by the joint act of two of its branches, the judges may be removed from their offices; and though one of its branches is possessed of the judicial power in the last resort. The entire legislature again can exercise no executive prerogative, though one of its branches constitutes the supreme executive magistracy; and another, on the empeachment of a third, can try and condemn all the subordinate officers in the executive department.

The reasons on which Montesquieu grounds his maxim are a further demonstration of his meaning. "When the legislative and executive powers are united in the same person or body" says he, "there can be no liberty, because apprehensions may arise lest *the same* monarch or senate should *enact* tyrannical laws, to *execute* them in a tyrannical manner." Again "Were the power of judging joined with the legislative, the life and liberty of the subject would be exposed to arbitrary controul, for *the judge* would then be *the legislator*. Were it joined to the executive power, *the judge* might behave with all the violence of *an oppressor*." Some of these reasons are more fully explained in other passages; but briefly stated as they are here, they sufficiently establish the meaning which we have put on this celebrated maxim of this celebrated author.

If we look into the constitutions of the several states we find that notwithstanding the emphatical, and in some instances, the unqualified terms in which this axiom has been laid down, there is not a single instance in which the several departments of power have been kept absolutely separate and distinct. New-Hampshire, whose constitution was the last formed, seems to have been fully aware of the impossibility and inexpediency of avoiding any mixture whatever of these departments; and has qualified the doctrine by declaring "that the legislative, executive and judiciary powers ought to be kept as separate from, and independent of each other *as the nature of a free government will admit;*

or as is consistent with that chain of connection, that binds the whole fabric of the constitution in one indissoluble bond of unity and amity." Her constitution accordingly mixes these departments in several respects. The senate which is a branch of the legislative department is also a judicial tribunal for the trial of empeachments. The president who is the head of the executive department, is the presiding member also of the senate; and besides an equal vote in all cases, has a casting vote in case of a tie. The executive head is himself eventually elective every year by the legislative department; and his council is every year chosen by and from the members of the same department. Several of the officers of state are also appointed by the legislature. And the members of the judiciary department are appointed by the executive department.

The constitution of Massachusetts has observed a sufficient though less pointed caution in expressing this fundamental article of liberty. It declares "that the legislative department shall never exercise the executive and judicial powers, or either of them: The executive shall never exercise the legislative and judicial powers, or either of them: The judicial shall never exercise the legislative and executive powers, or either of them." This declaration corresponds precisely with the doctrine of Montesquieu as it has been explained, and is not in a single point violated by the plan of the Convention. It goes no farther than to prohibit any one of the entire departments from exercising the powers of another department. In the very constitution to which it is prefixed, a partial mixture of powers has been admitted. The Executive Magistrate has a qualified negative on the Legislative body; and the Senate, which is a part of the Legislature, is a court of impeachment for members both of the executive and judiciary departments. The members of the judiciary department again are appointable by the executive department, and removeable by the same authority, on the address of the two legislative branches. Lastly, a number of the officers of government are annually appointed by the legislative department. As the appointment to offices, particularly executive offices, is in its nature an executive function, the compilers of the Constitution have in this last point at least, violated the rule established by themselves.

I pass over the constitutions of Rhode-Island and Connecticut, because they were formed prior to the revolution; and even before the principle under examination had become an object of political attention.

The constitution of New-York contains no declaration on this subject; but appears very clearly to have been framed with an eye to the danger of improperly blending the different departments. It gives nevertheless to the executive magistrate a partial controul over the legislative department; and what is more, gives a like controul to the judiciary department, and even blends the executive and judiciary departments in the exercise of this controul. In its council of appointment, members of the legislative are associated with the executive authority in the appointment of officers both executive and judiciary. And its court for the trial of impeachments and correction of errors, is to consist of one branch of the legislature and the principal members of the judiciary department.

The constitution of New-Jersey has blended the different powers of government more than any of the preceding. The governor, who is the executive magistrate, is appointed by the legislature; is chancellor and ordinary or surrogate of the state; is a member of the supreme court of appeals, and president with a casting vote, of one of the legislative branches. The same legislative branch acts again as executive council to the governor, and with him constitutes the court of appeals. The members of the judiciary department are appointed by the legislative department, and removeable by one branch of it, on the impeachment of the other.

According to the constitution of Pennsylvania, the president, who is head of the executive department, is annually elected by a vote in which the legislative department predominates. In conjunction with an executive council, he appoints the members of the judiciary department, and forms a court of impeachments for trial of all officers, judiciary as well as executive. The judges of the supreme court, and justices of the peace, seem also to be removeable by the legislature; and the executive power of pardoning in certain cases to be referred to the same department. The members of the executive council are made EX OFFICIO justices of peace throughout the state.

In Delaware, the chief executive magistrate is annually elected by the legislative department. The speakers of the two legislative branches are vice-presidents in the executive department. The executive chief, with six others, appointed three by each of the legislative branches, constitute the supreme court of appeals: He is joined with the legislative department in the appointment of the other judges. Throughout the states it appears that the members of the legislature may at the same time be justices of the peace. In this state, the members of one branch of it are EX OFFICIO justices of peace; as are also the members of the executive council. The principal officers of the executive department are appointed by the legislative; and one branch of the latter forms a court of impeachments. All officers may be removed on address of the legislature.

Maryland has adopted the maxim in the most unqualified terms; declaring that the legislative, executive and judicial powers of government, ought to be forever separate and distinct from each other. Her constitution, notwithstanding makes the executive magistrate appointable by the legislative department; and the members of the judiciary, by the executive department.

The language of Virginia is still more pointed on this subject. Her constitution declares, "that the legislative, executive and judiciary departments, shall be separate and distinct; so that neither exercise the powers properly belonging to the other; nor shall any person exercise the powers of more than one of them at the same time; except that the justices of the county courts shall be eligible to either house of assembly." Yet we find not only this express exception, with respect to the members of the inferior courts; but that the chief magistrate with his executive council are appointable by the legislature; that two members of the latter are triennially displaced at the pleasure of the legislature; and that all the principal offices, both executive and judiciary, are filled by the same department. The executive prerogative of pardon, also is in one case vested in the legislative department.

The constitution of North-Carolina, which declares, "that the legislative, executive and supreme judicial powers of government, ought to be forever separate and distinct from each other," refers at the same time to the legislative department, the appointment not only of the executive chief, but all the principal officers within both that and the judiciary department.

In South-Carolina, the constitution makes the executive magistracy eligible by the legislative department. It gives to the latter also the appointment of the members of the judiciary department, including even justices of the peace and sheriffs; and the appointment of officers in the executive department, down to captains in the army and navy of the state.

In the constitution of Georgia, where it is declared, "that the legislative, executive and judiciary departments shall be separate and distinct, so that neither exercise the powers properly belonging to the other." We find that the executive department is to be filled by appointments of the legislature; and the executive prerogative of pardon, to be finally exercised by the same authority. Even justices of the peace are to be appointed by the legislature.

In citing these cases in which the legislative, executive and judiciary departments, have not been kept totally separate and distinct, I wish not to be regarded as an advocate for the particular organizations of the several state governments. I am fully aware that among the many excellent principles which they exemplify, they carry strong marks of the haste, and still stronger of the inexperience, under which they were framed. It is but too obvious that in some instances, the fundamental principle under consideration has been violated by too great a mixture, and even an actual consolidation of the different powers; and that in no instance has a competent provision been made for maintaining in practice the separation delineated on paper. What I have wished to evince is, that the charge brought against the proposed constitution, of violating a sacred maxim of free government, is warranted neither by the real meaning annexed to that maxim by its author; nor by the sense in which it has hitherto been understood in America. This interesting subject will be resumed in the ensuing paper.

PUBLIUS.

G. JAMES MADISON, THE FEDERALIST, NO. 48

February 1, 1788

To the People of the State of New York.

It was shewn in the last paper, that the political apothegm there examined, does not require that the legislative, executive and judiciary departments should be wholly unconnected with each other. I shall undertake in the next place, to shew that unless these departments be so far connected and blended, as to give to each a constitutional controul over the others, the degree of separation which the maxim requires as essential to a free government, can never in practice, be duly maintained.

It is agreed on all sides, that the powers properly belonging to one of the departments, ought not to be directly and compleatly administered by either of the other departments. It is equally evident, that neither of them ought to possess directly or indirectly, an overruling influence over the others in the administration of their respective powers. It will not be denied, that power is of an encroaching nature, and that it ought to be effectually restrained from passing the limits assigned to it. After discriminating therefore in theory, the several classes of power, as they may in their nature be legislative, executive, or judiciary; the next and most difficult task, is to provide some practical security for each against the invasion of the others. What this security ought to be, is the great problem to be solved.

Will it be sufficient to mark with precision the boundaries of these departments in the Constitution of the government, and to trust to these parchment barriers against the encroaching spirit of power? This is the security which appears to have been principally relied on by the compilers of most of the American Constitutions. But experience assures us, that the efficacy of the provision has been greatly over-rated; and that some more adequate defence is indispensibly necessary for the more feeble, against the more powerful members of the government. The legislative department is every where extending the sphere of its activity, and drawing all power into its impetuous vortex.

The founders of our republics have so much merit for the wisdom which they have displayed, that no task can be less pleasing than that of pointing out the errors into which they have fallen. A respect for truth however obliges us to remark, that they seem never for a moment to have turned their eyes from the danger to liberty from the overgrown and all-grasping prerogative of an hereditary magistrate, supported and fortified by an hereditary branch of the legislative authority. They seem never to have recollected the danger from legislative usurpations; which by assembling all power in the same hands, must lead to the same tyranny as is threatened by executive usurpations.

In a government, where numerous and extensive prerogatives are placed in the hands of a hereditary monarch, the executive department is very justly regarded as the source of danger, and watched with all the jealousy which a zeal for liberty ought to inspire. In a democracy, where a multitude of people exercise in person the legislative functions, and are continually exposed by their incapacity for regular deliberation and concerted measures, to the ambitious intrigues of their executive magistrates, tyranny may well be apprehended on some favorable emergency, to start up in the same quarter. But in a representative republic, where the executive magistracy is carefully limited both in the extent and the duration of its power; and where the legislative power is exercised by an assembly, which is inspired by a supposed influence over the people with an intrepid confidence in its own strength; which is sufficiently numerous to feel all the passions which actuate a multitude; yet not so numerous as to be incapable of pursuing the objects of its passions, by means which reason prescribes; it is against the enterprising ambition of this department, that the people ought to indulge all their jealousy and exhaust all their precautions.

The legislative department derives a superiority in our governments from other circumstances. Its constitutional powers being at once more extensive and less susceptible of precise limits, it can with the greater facility, mask under complicated and indirect measures, the encroachments which it makes on the co-ordinate departments. It is not unfrequently a question of real-nicety in legislative bodies, whether the operation of a particular measure, will, or will not extend beyond the legislative sphere. On the other side, the executive power being restrained within a narrower compass, and being more simple in its nature; and the judiciary being described by land marks, still less uncertain, projects of usurpation by either of these departments, would immediately betray and defeat themselves. Nor is this all: As the legislative department alone has access to the pockets of the people, and has in some Constitutions full discretion, and in all, a prevailing influence over the pecuniary rewards of those who fill the other departments, a dependence is thus created in the latter, which gives still greater facility to encroachments of the former.

I have appealed to our own experience for the truth of what I advance on this subject. Were it necessary to verify this experience by particular proofs, they might be multiplied without end. I might find a witness in every citizen who has shared in, or been attentive to, the course of public administrations. I might collect vouchers in abundance from the records and archieves of every State in the Union. But as a more concise and at the same time, equally satisfactory evidence, I will refer to the example of two States, attested by two unexceptionable authorities.

The first example is that of Virginia, a State which, as we have seen, has expressly declared in its Constitution, that the three great departments ought not to be intermixed. The authority in support of it is Mr. Jefferson, who, besides his other advantages for remarking the operation of the government, was himself the chief magistrate of it. In order to convey fully the ideas with which his experience had impressed him on this subject, it will be necessary to quote a passage of some length from his very interesting "Notes on the State of Virginia." (P. 195.) "All the powers of government, legislative, executive and judiciary, result to the legislative body. The concentrating these in the same hands is precisely the definition of despotic government. It will be no alleviation that these powers will be exercised by a plurality of hands, and not by a single one, 173 despots would surely be as oppressive as one. Let those who doubt it turn their eyes on the republic of Venice. As little will it avail us that they are chosen by ourselves. An *elective despotism,* was not the government we fought for; but one which should not only be founded on free principles, but in which the powers of government should be so divided and balanced among several bodies of magistracy, as that no one could transcend their legal limits, without being effectually checked and restrained by the others. For this reason that Convention which passed the ordinance of government, laid its foundation on this basis, that the legislative, executive and judiciary departments should be separate and distinct, so that no person should exercise the powers of more than one of them at the same time. *But no barrier was provided between these several powers.* The judiciary and executive members were left dependent on the legislative for their subsistence in office, and some of them for their continuance in it. If therefore the Legislature assumes executive and judiciary powers, no opposition is likely to be made; nor if made can it be effectual; because in that case, they may put their proceeding into the form of an act of Assembly, which will render them obligatory on the other branches. They have accordingly *in many* instances *decided rights* which should have been left to *judiciary controversy;* and *the direction of the executive during the whole time of their session, is becoming habitual and familiar."*

The other State which I shall take for an example, is Pennsylvania; and the other authority the council of censors which assembled in the years 1783 and 1784. A part of the duty of this body, as marked out by the Constitution was, "to enquire whether the Constitution had been preserved inviolate in every part; and whether the legislative and executive branches of government had performed their duty as guardians of the people, or assumed to themselves, or exercised other or greater powers than they are entitled to by the Constitution." In the execution of this trust, the council were necessarily led to a comparison, of both the legislative and executive proceedings, with the constitutional powers of these departments; and from the facts enumerated, and to the truth of most of which, both sides in the council subscribed, it appears that the

Constitution had been flagrantly violated by the Legislature in a variety of important instances.

A great number of laws had been passed violating without any apparent necessity, the rule requiring that all bills of a public nature, shall be previously printed for the consideration of the people; altho' this is one of the precautions chiefly relied on by the Constitution, against improper acts of the Legislature.

The constitutional trial by jury had been violated; and powers assumed, which had not been delegated by the Constitution.

Executive powers had been usurped.

The salaries of the Judges, which the Constitution expressly requires to be fixed, had been occasionally varied; and cases belonging to the judiciary department, frequently drawn within legislative cognizance and determination.

Those who wish to see the several particulars falling under each of these heads, may consult the Journals of the council which are in print. Some of them, it will be found may be imputable to peculiar circumstances connected with the war: But the greater part of them may be considered as the spontaneous shoots of an ill-constituted government.

It appears also, that the executive department had not been innocent of frequent breaches of the Constitution. There are three observations however, which ought to be made on this head. *First.* A great proportion of the instances, were either immediately produced by the necessities of the war, or recommended by Congress or the Commander in Chief. *Secondly.* In most of the other instances, they conformed either to the declared or the known sentiments of the legislative department. *Thirdly.* The executive department of Pennsylvania is distinguished from that of the other States, by the number of members composing it. In this respect it has as much affinity to a legislative assembly, as to an executive council. And being at once exempt from the restraint of an individual responsibility for the acts of the body, and deriving confidence from mutual example and joint influence; unauthorized measures would of course be more freely hazarded, than where the executive department is administered by a single hand or by a few hands.

The conclusion which I am warranted in drawing from these observations is, that a mere demarkation on parchment of the constitutional limits of the several departments, is not a sufficient guard against those encroachments which lead to a tyrannical concentration of all the powers of government in the same hands.

PUBLIUS.

H. THE FEDERALIST, NO. 51

February 6, 1788

To the People of the State of New York.

To what expedient then shall we finally resort for maintaining in practice the necessary partition of power among the several departments, as laid down in the constitution? The only answer that can be given is, that as all these exterior provisions are found to be inadequate, the defect must be supplied, by so contriving the interior structure of the government, as that its several constituent parts may, by their mutual relations, be the means of keeping each other in their proper places. Without presuming to undertake a full developement of this important idea, I will hazard a few general observations, which may perhaps place it in a clearer light, and enable us to form a more correct judgment of the principles and structure of the government planned by the convention.

In order to lay a due foundation for that separate and distinct exercise of the different powers of government, which to a certain extent, is admitted on all hands to be essential to the preservation of liberty, it is evident that each department should have a will of its own; and consequently should be so constituted, that the members of each should have as little agency as possible in the appointment of the members of the others. Were this principle rigorously adhered to, it would require that all the appointments for the supreme executive, legislative, and judiciary magistracies, should be drawn from the same fountain of authority, the people, through channels, having no communication whatever with one another. Perhaps such a plan of constructing the several departments would be less difficult in practice than it may in contemplation appear. Some difficulties however, and some additional expence, would attend the execution of it. Some deviations therefore from the principle must be admitted. In the constitution of the judiciary department in particular, it might be inexpedient to insist rigorously on the principle; first, because peculiar qualifications being essential in the members, the primary consideration ought to be to select that mode of choice, which best secures these qualifications; secondly, because the permanent tenure by which the appointments are held in that department, must soon destroy all sense of dependence on the authority conferring them.

It is equally evident that the members of each department should be as little dependent as possible on those of the others, for the emoluments annexed to their offices. Were the executive magistrate, or the judges, not independent of the legislature in this particular, their independence in every other would be merely nominal.

But the great security against a gradual concentration of the several powers in the same department, consists in giving to those who administer each department, the necessary constitutional means, and personal motives, to resist encroachments of the others. The provision for defence must in this, as in all other cases, be made commensurate to the danger of attack. Ambition must be made to counteract ambition. The interest of the man must be connected with the constitutional rights of the place. It may be a reflection on human nature, that such devices should be necessary to controul the abuses of government. But what is government itself but the greatest of all reflections on human nature? If men were angels, no government would be necessary. If angels were to govern men, neither external nor internal controuls on government would be necessary. In framing a government which is to be administered by men over men, the great difficulty lies in this: You must first enable the government to controul the governed; and in the next place, oblige it to controul itself. A dependence on the people is no doubt the primary controul on the government; but experience has taught mankind the necessity of auxiliary precautions.

This policy of supplying by opposite and rival interests, the defect of better motives, might be traced through the whole system of human affairs, private as well as public. We see it particularly displayed in all the subordinate distributions of power; where the constant aim is to divide and arrange the several offices in such a manner as that each may be a check on the other; that the private interest of every individual, may be a centinel over the public rights. These inventions of prudence cannot be less requisite in the distribution of the supreme powers of the state.

But it is not possible to give to each department an equal power of self defence. In republican government the legislative authority, necessarily, predominates. The remedy for this inconveniency is, to divide the legislature into different branches; and to render them by different modes of election, and different principles of action, as little connected with each other, as the nature of their common functions, and their common dependence on the society, will admit. It may even be necessary to guard against dangerous encroachments by still further precautions. As the weight of the legislative authority requires that it should be thus divided, the weakness of the executive may require, on the other hand, that it should be fortified. An absolute negative, on the legislature, appears at first view to be the natural defence with which the executive magistrate should be armed. But perhaps it would be neither altogether safe, nor alone sufficient. On ordinary occasions, it might not be exerted with the requisite firmness; and on extraordinary occasions, it might be perfidiously abused. May not this defect of an absolute negative be supplied, by some qualified connection between this weaker department, and the weaker branch of the stronger department, by which the latter may be led to support the constitutional rights of the former, without being too much detached from the rights of its own department?

If the principles on which these observations are founded be just, as I persuade myself they are, and they be applied as a criterion, to the several state constitutions, and to the federal constitution, it will be found, that if the latter does not perfectly correspond with them, the former are infinitely less able to bear such a test.

There are moreover two considerations particularly applicable to the federal system of America, which place that system in a very interesting point of view.

First. In a single republic, all the power surrendered by the people, is submitted to the administration of a single government; and usurpations are guarded against by a division of the government into distinct and separate departments. In the compound republic of America, the power surrendered by the people, is first divided between two distinct governments, and then the portion allotted to each, subdivided among distinct and separate departments. Hence a double security arises to the rights of the people. The different governments will controul each other; at the same time that each will be controuled by itself.

Second. It is of great importance in a republic, not only to guard the society against the oppression of its rulers; but to guard one part of the society against the injustice of the other part. Different interests necessarily exist in different classes of citizens. If a majority be united by a common interest, the rights of the minority will be insecure. There are but two methods of providing against this evil: The one by creating a will in the community independent of the majority, that is, of the society itself; the other by comprehending in the society so many separate descriptions of citizens, as will render an unjust combination of a majority of the whole, very improbable, if not impracticable. The first method prevails in all governments possessing an hereditary or self appointed authority. This at best is but a precarious security; because a power independent of the society may as well espouse the unjust views of the major, as the rightful interests, of the minor party, and may possibly be turned against both parties. The second method will be exemplified in the federal republic of the United States. Whilst all authority in it will be derived from and dependent on the society, the society itself will be broken into so many parts, interests and classes of citizens, that the rights of individuals or of the minority, will be in little danger from interested combinations of the majority. In a free government, the security for civil rights must be the same as for religious rights. It consists in the one case in the multiplicity of interests, and in the other, in the multiplicity of sects. The degree of security in both cases will depend on the number of interests and sects; and this may be presumed to depend on the extent of country and number of people comprehended under the same government. This view of the subject must particularly recommend a proper federal system to all the sincere and considerate friends of republican government: Since it shews that in exact proportion as the territory of the union may be formed into more circumscribed confederacies or states, oppressive combinations of a majority will be facilitated, the best security under the republican form, for the rights of every class of citizens, will be diminished; and consequently, the stability and independence of some member of the government, the only other security, must be proportionally increased. Justice is the end of government. It is the end of civil society. It ever has been, and ever will be pursued, until it be obtained, or until liberty be lost in the pursuit. In a society under the forms of which the stronger faction can readily unite and oppress the weaker, anarchy may as truly be said to reign, as in a state of nature where the weaker individual is not secured against the violence of the stronger: And as in the latter state even the stronger individuals are prompted by the uncertainty of their condition, to submit to a government which may protect the weak as well as themselves: So in the former state, will the more powerful factions or parties be gradually induced by a like motive, to wish for a government which will protect all parties, the weaker as well as the more powerful. It can be little doubted, that if the state of Rhode Island was separated from the confederacy, and left to itself, the insecurity of rights under the popular form of government within such narrow limits, would be displayed by such reiterated oppressions of factious majorities, that some power altogether independent of the people would soon be called for by the voice of the very factions whose misrule had proved the necessity of it. In the extended republic of the United States, and among the great variety of interests, parties and sects which it embraces, a coalition of a majority of the whole society could seldom take place on any other principles than those of justice and the general good; and there being thus less danger to a minor from the will of the major party, there must be less pretext also, to provide for the security of the former, by introducing into the government a will not dependent on the latter; or in other words, a will independent of the society itself. It is no less certain than it is important, notwithstanding the contrary opinions which have been entertained, that the larger the society, provided it lie within a practicable sphere, the more duly capable it will be of self government. And happily for the *republican cause,* the practicable sphere may be carried to a very great extent, by a judicious modification and mixture of the *federal principle.*

PUBLIUS.

*

CHAPTER V

PRINCIPLES OF FEDERALISM

A. LETTER OF GEORGE MASON TO THOMAS JEFFERSON

September 27, 1781

DEAR SIR

You have, no Doubt, been informed of the factious, illegal, & dangerous Schemes now in Contemplation in Congress, for dismembering the Commonwealth of Virginia, & erecting a new State or States to the Westward of the Alleghany Mountains. This power, directly contrary to the Articles of Confederation, is assumed upon the Doctrine now industriously propagated "that the late Revolution has transferred the Sovereignty formerly possessed by Great Britain, to the United States, that is to the American Congress" A Doctrine which, if not immediately arrested in it's progress, will be productive of every Evil; and the Revolution, instead of securing, as was intended, our Rights & Libertys, will only change the Name & place of Residence of our Tyrants. This that Congress who drew the Articles of Union were sensible of & have provided against it, by expressly declaring in Article the 2d that "Each State retains it's Sovereignty, freedom, & Independence, & every Power, Jurisdiction, & right, which is not by this Confederation *expressly delegated* to the United States in Congress assembled"—& in article the 13th. that "the Articles of this Confederation shall be inviolably observed by every State, & the Union shall be perpetual; nor shall any Alteration at any time hereafter be made in any of them; unless such Alteration be agreed to in a Congress of the United States, and be afterwards confirmed by the Legislatures of every State." In the 9th Article defining the Powers of Congress; least the Power of deciding Disputes, concerning Territory between any of the States, shou'd be attended with dangerous Consequences; it is "provided that no State shall be deprived of Territory for the Benefit of the United States" and the 11th. Article declares that "Canada, acceding to this Confederation, & joining in the measures of the United States, shall be admitted into, & entitled to all the Advantages of this Union: but *no other Colony* shall be Admitted into the same, unless such Admission be agreed to by nine States." This article holds out an immediate Offer to Canada; and the words *no other Colony* plainly relate to the other British Colonys of Nova Scotia, & East & West Floridas, & clearly exclude the Idea of any absolute Power in Congress to erect new States. I had almost forgot to mention the Beginning of the 13th. Article, declaring that "Every State shall abide by the Determinations of the United States in Congress assembled, on all Questions which *by this Confederation* are submitted to them." From whence arises, by the strongest Implication, a negation & Disclaimer of any other Powers, & a Declaration that no State is bound by them if they shou'd at any time be assumed. I shou'd not have troubled you with these Quotations, but that I apprehended in the late Confusions, & sudden Removals of public, as well as private Papers, the Articles of Confederation may have been sent to some distant Place. I think they will prove that Congress are now arrogating to themselves an unwarrantable & dangerous Power; which is in its Nature subversive of American Liberty; for if they can stride over the Lines of the Confederation, & assume Rights not delegated to them by the Legislatures of the different States, in one Instance, they can in every other that the Lust of Power may suggest. I hope our Assembly will take this Subject up with the Coolness and Attention which it's Importance merits, & with proper Firmness endeavour immediately to put a Stop to such Proceedings, by positive Instructions to the Virginia Delegates in Congress. And as much will depend upon the Disposition of the Inhabitants in the western Parts, it will be prudent to secure their Affections by giving them all the advantages of Government; which will require that the executive and judiciary Powers shall be exercised among them; this may be a difficult plan, but it is an absolutely necessary one; permit me Sir to recommend it to your particular Attention. I do it, because I really know no Man whom I think so capable of digesting a proper Plan, & I know, from some former Conversation, that you have heretofore turn'd your Thoughts to this Subject....

G MASON

B. JAMES WILSON, CONSIDERATIONS ON THE BANK OF NORTH AMERICA

1785

An attack is made on the credit and institution of the Bank of North America. Whether this attack is justified by the principles of law and sound policy, is a natural subject of inquiry. The inquiry is as necessary and interesting, as it is natural: for, though some people represent the bank as injurious and dangerous, while others consider it as salutary and beneficial to the community, all view it as an object of high importance; deserving and demanding the publick attention.

In the investigation of this subject, it will be requisite to discuss some great and leading questions concerning the constitution of the United States, and the relation which subsists between them and each particular state in the Union. Perhaps it is to be wished that this discussion had not been rendered necessary; and that those questions had rested some time longer among the *arcana imperii:* but they are now presented to the publick; and the publick should view them with firmness, with impartiality, and with all the solicitude befitting such a momentous occasion.

A gentleman, who had the best opportunities of observing, and who possesses the best talents for judging on the subject, informs his fellow citizens officially, that "it may be not only asserted, but demonstrated, that, without the establishment of the national bank, the business of the department of finance could not have been performed" in the late war.

The millennium is not yet come. War, with all the horrours and miseries in his train, may revisit us. The finances may again be deranged: "publick credit may, again, be at an end: no means may be afforded adequate to the publick expenses." Is it wise or politick to deprive our country, in such a situation, of a resource, which happy experience has shown to be of such essential importance? Will the citizens of the United States be encouraged to embark their fortunes on a similar bottom in a future war, by seeing the vessel, which carried us so successfully through the last, thrown aside, like a useless hulk, upon the return of peace?

It will not be improper to recal to our remembrance the origin, the establishment, and the proceedings of the Bank of North America.

In May, 1781, the superintendant of finance laid before congress a plan of a bank. On the 26th of that month, congress passed the following resolution concerning it.

"Resolved, That congress do approve of the plan for establishing a national bank in these United States, submitted to their consideration by Mr. Robert Morris, the 17th May, 1781, and that they will promote and support the same by such ways and means, from time to time, as may appear necessary for the institution, and consistent with the publick good.

"That the subscribers to the said bank shall be incorporated, agreeably to the principles and terms of the plan, under the name of "The President, Directors, and Company of the Bank of North America," so soon as the subscription shall be filled, the directors and president chosen, and application made to congress for that purpose, by the president and directors elected.

"Resolved, That it be recommended to the several States, by proper laws for that purpose, to provide that no other bank or bankers shall be established or permitted within the said states respectively during the war.

"Resolved, That the notes hereafter to be issued by the said bank, payable on demand, shall be receivable in payment of all taxes, duties, and debts, due or that may become due or payable to the United States.

"Resolved, that congress will recommend to the several legislatures to pass laws, making it felony without benefit of clergy, for any person to counterfeit bank notes, or to pass such notes, knowing them to be counterfeit; also making it felony without benefit of clergy, for any president, inspector, director, officer, or servant of the bank, to convert any of the property, money, or credit of the said bank to his own use, or in any other way to be guilty of fraud or embezzlement, as officers or servants of the bank."

Under these resolutions a subscription was opened for the national bank: this subscription was not confined to Pennsylvania: the citizens of other States trusted their property to the publick faith; and before the end of December, 1781, the subscription was filled, "from an expectation of a charter of incorporation from congress." Application was made to congress by the president and directors, then chosen, for an act of incorporation. "The exigencies of the United States rendered it indispensably necessary that such an act should be immediately passed." Congress, at the same time that they passed the act of incorporation, recommended to the legislature of each state, to pass such laws as they might judge necessary for giving its ordinance its full operation, agreeably to the true intent and meaning thereof, and according to the recommendations contained in the resolution of the 26th day of May preceding.

The bank immediately commenced its operations. Its seeds were small, but they were vigorous. The sums paid in by individuals upon their subscriptions did not amount in the whole to seventy thousand dillars. The sum invested by the United States, in bank stock, amounted to something more than two hundred and fifty thousand dollars: but this sum may be said to have been paid in with one hand and borrowed with the other; and before the end of the first three months, farther sums were advanced to the United States, and an advance was made to this state. Besides, numerous accommodations were afforded to individuals. Little was it then imagined that the bank would ever be represented as unfriendly to circulation. It was viewed as the source and as the support of credit, both private and publick: as such, it was hated and dreaded by the enemies of the United States: as such, it was loved and fostered by their friends.

Pennsylvania, distinguished on numerous occasions by her faithful and affectionate attachment to federal principles, embraced, in the first session of her legislature after the establishment of the bank, the opportunity of testifying her approbation of an act, which had been found to be indispensably necessary. Harmonizing with the sentiments and recommendations of the United States, the assembly passed an act, "for preventing and punishing the counterfeiting of the common seal, bank bills, and bank notes, of the president, directors, and company of the Bank of North America." In the preamble to this act, which, according to the constitution of this state, expresses the reasons and motives for passing it, the "necessity" of taking "effectual measures for preventing and punishing frauds and cheats which may be put upon the president, directors, and company of the Bank of North America," is explicitly declared by the legislature.

The sentiments and conduct of other states, respecting the establishment of the national bank by congress, were similar to those of Pennsylvania. The general assembly of Rhode Island and Providence Plantations made it felony, without benefit of clergy, "to counterfeit any note or notes issued, or to be issued, from the Bank of North America, as approved and *established* by the United States in Congress assembled." The state of Connecticut enacted, that a tax should be laid, payable in money, or "notes issued by the directors of the national bank, *established* by an ordinance of the United States in congress assembled." By a law of Massachussetts, the subscribers to the national bank, approved of by the United States, were "incorporated, on the behalf of that commonwealth, by the name of the president, directors and company of the Bank of North America, according to the terms of the ordinance to incorporate the said subscribers, passed by the United States in congress assembled on the thirty first day of December, 1781." The same law further enacts, "that all notes or bills, which have been or shall be issued by, for, or in the name of the said president, directors, and company, and payable on demand, shall be receivable in the payment of all taxes, debts and duties, due or that may become due, or payable to, or for account of, the said United States." In the preamble of this law, the legislature declares that "a national bank is of great service, as well to the publick as to individuals."

The president and directors of the bank had a delicate and a difficult part to act. On one hand, they were obliged to guard against the malice and exertions of their enemies: on the other, it was incumbent on them to sooth the timidity of some of their friends. The credit of a bank, as well as all other credit, depends on opinion. Opinion, whether well or ill founded, produces, in each case, the same effects upon conduct. Some thought that an act of incorporation from the legislature of this state would be beneficial; none apprehended that it could ever be hurtful to the national bank. Prudence, therefore, and a disposition, very natural in that season of doubt and diffidence, to gratify the sentiments, and even the prejudices, of such as might become subscribers or customers to the bank, directed an application to the assembly for "a charter, similar to that granted by the United States in congress assembled." But though the directors were willing to avail themselves of encouragement from every quarter, they meant not to relinquish any of their rights, or to change the foundation on which they rested. They made their application in their *corporate* character. They expressly mentioned to the assembly, that the United States in congress assembled had granted to the bank a charter of incorporation, and that the institution was to be carried on under their immediate auspices. The legislature thought that it was proper and reasonable to grant the request of the *president and directors of the Bank of North America;* and assigned, as a reason for the act, "that the United States in congress assembled, from a conviction of the support which the finances of the United States would receive from the establishment of a *national bank,* passed an ordinance to incorporate the subscribers for this purpose, by the name and style of the president, directors, and company of the Bank of North America."

The first clause of the law enacts, that "those who are, and those who shall become subscribers to the said bank, be, and forever hereafter shall be, a corporation and body politick, to all intents and purposes."

It is further enacted, that "the said corporation be, and shall be forever hereafter, able and capable in law to do and execute all and singular matters and things, that to them shall or may appertain to do."

To show, in the most striking light, the kind sentiments of the legislature towards the institution, it is further enacted, that "this act shall be construed and taken most favourably and beneficially for the said corporation."

On these facts and proceedings, two questions of much national importance present themselves to our view and examination.

I.   Is the Bank of North America legally and constitutionally instituted and organized, by the charter of incorporation granted by the United States in congress assembled?

II.   Would it be wise or politick in the legislature of Pennsylvania, to revoke the charter which it has granted to the institution?

The discussion of these two questions will naturally lead us to the proper conclusions concerning the validity and the utility of the bank.

I.   Had the United States in congress assembled a legal and constitutional power to institute and organize the Bank of North America, by a charter of incorporation?

The objection, under this head, will be—that the articles of confederation express all the powers of congress, that in those articles no power is delegated to that body to grant charters of incorporation, and that, therefore, congress possess no such power.

It is true, that, by the second article of the confederation, "each state retains its sovereignty, freedom and independence, and every power, jurisdiction, and right, which is not, by the confederation, *expressly* delegated to the United States in congress assembled."

If, then, any or each of the states possessed, previous to the confederation, a power, jurisdiction, or right, to institute and organize, by a charter of incorporation, a bank for North America; in other words—commensurate to the United States; such power, jurisdiction, and right, unless expressly delegated to congress, cannot be legally or constitutionally exercised by that body.

But, we presume, it will not be contended, that any or each of the states could exercise any power or act of sovereignty extending over all

372

the other states, or any of them; or, in other words, incorporate a bank, commensurate to the United States.

The consequence is, that this is not an act of sovereignty, or a power, jurisdiction, or right, which, by the second article of the confederation, must be expressly delegated to congress, in order to be possessed by that body.

If, however, any person shall contend that any or each of the states can exercise such an extensive power or act of sovereignty as that above mentioned; to such person we give this answer—The state of Massachussetts has exercised such power and act: it has incorporated the Bank of North America. But to pursue my argument.

Though the United States in congress assembled derive *from the particular states* no power, jurisdiction, or right, which is not expressly delegated by the confederation, it does not thence follow, that the United States in congress have *no other* powers, jurisdiction, or rights, than those delegated by the particular states.

The United States have general rights, general powers, and general obligations, not derived from any particular states, nor from all the particular states, taken separately; but resulting from the union of the whole: and, therefore, it is provided, in the fifth article of the confederation, "that for the more convenient management of the *general interests* of the United States, delegates shall be annually appointed to meet in congress."

To many purposes, the United States are to be considered as one undivided, independent nation; and as possessed of all the rights, and powers, and properties, by the law of nations incident to such.

Whenever an object occurs, to the direction of which no particular state is competent, the management of it must, of necessity, belong to the United States in congress assembled. There are many objects of this extended nature. The purchase, the sale, the defence, and the government of lands and countries, not within any state, are all included under this description. An institution for circulating paper, and establishing its credit over the whole United States, is naturally ranged in the same class.

The act of independence was made before the articles of confederation. This act declares, that *"these United colonies,"* (not enumerating them separately) "are free and independent states; and that, as free and independent states, *they* have full power to do *all* acts and things which independent states may, of right, do."

The confederation was not intended to weaken or abridge the powers and rights, to which the United States were previously entitled. It was not intended to transfer any of those powers or rights to the particular states, or any of them. If, therefore, the power now in question was vested in the United States before the confederation; it continues vested in them still. The confederation clothed the United States with many though, perhaps, not with sufficient powers: but of none did it disrobe them.

It is no new position, that rights may be vested in a political body, which did not previously reside in any or in all the members of that body. They may be derived solely from the union of those members. "The case," says the celebrated Burlamaqui, "is here very near the same as in that of several voices collected together, which, by their union, produce a harmony, that was not to be found separately in each."

A number of unconnected inhabitants are settled on each side of a navigable river; it belongs to none of them; it belongs not to them all, for they have nothing in common: let them unite; the river is the property of the united body.

The arguments drawn from the political associations of individuals into a state will apply, with equal force and propriety, to a number of states united by a confederacy.

New states must be formed and established: their extent and boundaries must be regulated and ascertained. How can this be done, unless by the United States in congress assembled?

States are corporations or bodies politick of the most important and dignified kind.

Let us now concentre the foregoing observations, and apply them to the incorporation of the Bank of North America by congress.

By the civil law, corporations seem to have been created by the mere and voluntary association of their members, provided such convention was not contrary to law.

By the common law, something more is necessary—all the methods whereby corporations exist are, for the most part, reducible to that of the king's letters patent, or charter of incorporation.

From this it will appear that the creation of a corporation is, by the common law, considered as the act of the executive rather than of the legislative powers of government.

Before the revolution, charters of incorporation were granted by the proprietaries of Pennsylvania, under a derivative authority from the crown, and those charters have been recognised by the constitution and laws of the commonwealth since the revolution.

From analogy, therefore, we may justly infer, that the United States in congress assembled, possessing the executive powers of the union, may, in virtue of such powers, grant charters of incorporation for accomplishing objects that comprehend the general interests of the United States.

But the United States in congress assembled possess, in many instances, and to many purposes, the legislative as well as the executive

374

powers of the union; and therefore, whether we consider the incorporation of the bank as a law, or as a charter, it will be equally within the powers of congress: for the object of this institution could not be reached without the exertion of the combined sovereignty of the union.

I have asked—how can new states, which are bodies politick, be formed, unless by the United States in congress assembled? Fact, as well as argument, justifies my sentiments on this subject. The conduct of congress has been similar on similar occasions. The same principles have directed the exercise of the same powers.

In the month of April, 1784, congress resolved, that part of the western territory "should be divided into distinct states."

They further resolved, that the settlers should, "either on their own petition, or on the order of congress, receive authority from *them* to meet together, for the purpose of establishing a temporary government, to adopt the constitution and laws of any one of the original states."

"When any such state shall have acquired twenty thousand free inhabitants, on giving due proof thereof to congress, they shall receive from *them* authority to call a convention of representatives, to establish a permanent constitution and government for themselves."

"The preceding articles," among others, "shall be formed into a charter of compact; shall be duly executed by the president of the United States in congress assembled, under his hand and the seal of the United States; shall be promulgated; and shall stand as fundamental constitutions between the thirteen original states, and each of the several states now newly described, unalterable from and after the sale of any part of the territory of such state, but by the joint consent of the United States in congress assembled, and of the particular state within which such alteration is proposed to be made."

It will be difficult, I believe, to urge against the power of congress to grant a charter to the Bank of North America, any argument, which may not, with equal strength and fitness, be urged against the power of that body to form, execute, and promulgate a charter of compact for the new states.

The sentiments of the representatives of the United States, as to their power of incorporating the bank, ought to have much weight with us. Their sentiments are strongly marked by their conduct, in their first resolutions respecting the bank. These resolutions are made at the same time, and on the same subject: but there is a striking difference in their manner. It was thought proper "that no other bank should be permitted within any of the states, during the war." Congress "*recommended* to the several states to make provision, for that purpose, by proper laws." It was thought prudent that the bank should be protected, by penal laws, from fraud, embezzlement, and forgery. Congress *recommended* it to the several legislatures to pass such laws. It was deemed expedient that bank notes should be received in payment of sums payable to the United States: congress *resolve,* that the notes "shall be receivable" in such payments. It was judged necessary that the bank should have a charter of incorporation: congress *resolve,* that the bank "shall be incorporated," on application made *"to congress"* for that purpose. The line of distinction between those things in which congress could only recommend, and those in which they could act, is drawn in the clearest manner. The incorporation of the national bank is ranked among those things, in which they could act.

This act of congress has, either expressly, or by implication, received the approbation of every state in the union. It was officially announced to every state by the superintendant of finance. Had any one state considered it as an exercise of usurped power, would not that state have remonstrated against it? But there is no such remonstrance.

This act of congress has been most explicitly recognised by the legislature of Pennsylvania. The law for preventing and punishing frauds and cheats upon the bank was passed on the 18th of March, 1782, and before the bank had obtained a charter from this state. By that law it is made felony without benefit of clergy, to forge the common seal of the president, directors, and company of the Bank of North America. Who were the president, directors, and company of the Bank of North America? Those whom congress had made "a corporation and body politick, to all intents and purposes, by that name and style." How came that body by a "common seal?" The act of congress ordained that that body "should have full power and authority to make, have and use a common seal." In the act to incorporate the subscribers to the Bank of North America, the legislature, after reciting that the United States in congress assembled had "passed an ordinance to incorporate them," say, "the president and directors of the said bank have applied to this house for a similar act of incorporation, which request it is proper and reasonable to grant."

When the foregoing facts and arguments are considered, compared, and weighed, they will, it is hoped, evince and establish, *satisfactorily* to all, and *conclusively* on the legislature of Pennsylvania, the truth of this position—That the Bank of North America was legally and constitutionally instituted and organized, by the charter of incorporation granted by the United States in congress assembled.

II. Would it, then, be wise or politick in the legislature of Pennsylvania, to revoke the charter which it has granted to this institution? It would not be wise or politick—

1st. Because the proceeding would be nugatory. The recal of the charter of Pennsylvania would not repeal that of the United States, by which we have proved the bank to be legally and constitutionally instituted and organized.

2d. Because, though the legislature may destroy the legislative *operation,* yet it cannot undo the legislative *acknowledgment* of its own act. Though a statute be repealed, yet it shows the sense and opinion of the legislature concerning the subject of it, in the same manner as if it continued in force. The legislature declared, in the law, that it was proper and reasonable to grant the request of the president and directors of the bank, for an act of incorporation similar to the ordinance of congress: no repeal of the law can weaken the force of that declaration.

3d. Because such a proceeding would wound that confidence in the engagements of government, which it is so much the interest and duty of every state to encourage and reward. The act in question formed a charter of compact between the legislature of this state, and the president, directors, and company of the Bank of North America. The latter asked for nothing but what was proper and reasonable: the former granted nothing but what was proper and reasonable: the terms of the compact were, therefore, fair and honest: while these terms are observed on one side, the compact cannot, consistently with the rules of good faith, be departed from on the other.

It may be asked—Has not the state power over her own laws?—May she not alter, amend, extend, restrain, and repeal them at her pleasure?

I am far from opposing the legislative authority of the state: but it must be observed, that, according to the practice of the legislature, publick acts of very different kinds are drawn and promulgated under the same form. A law to vest or confirm an estate in an individual—a law to incorporate a congregation or other society—a law respecting the rights and properties of all the citizens of the state—are all passed in the same manner; are all clothed in the same dress of legislative formality; and are all equally acts of the representatives of the freemen of the commonwealth. But surely it will not be pretended, that, after laws of those different kinds are passed, the legislature possesses over each the same discretionary power of repeal. In a law respecting the rights and properties of all the citizens of the state, this power may be safely exercised by the legislature. Why? Because, in this case, the interest of those who make the law (the members of assembly and their constituents) and the interest of those who are to be affected by the law (the members of assembly and their constituents) is the same. It is a common cause, and may, therefore, be safely trusted to the representatives of the community. None can hurt another, without, at the same time, hurting himself. Very different is the case with regard to a law, by which the state grants privileges to a congregation or other society. Here two parties are instituted, and two distinct interests subsist. Rules of justice, of faith, and of honour must, therefore, be established between them: for, if interest alone is to be viewed, the congregation or society must always lie at the mercy of the community. Still more different is the case with regard to a law, by which an estate is vested or confirmed in an individual: if, in this case, the legislature may, at discretion, and without any reason assigned, devest or destroy his estate, then a person seized of an estate in fee simple, under legislative sanction, is, in truth, nothing more than a solemn tenant at will.

For these reasons, whenever the objects and makers of an instrument, passed under the form of a law, are not the same, it is to be considered as a compact, and to be interpreted according to the rules and maxims, by which compacts are governed. A foreigner is naturalized by law: is he a citizen only during pleasure? He is no more, if, without any cause of forfeiture assigned and established, the law, by which he is naturalized, may at pleasure be repealed. To receive the legislative stamp of stability and permanency, acts of incorporation are applied for from the legislature. If these acts may be repealed without notice, without accusation, without hearing, without proof, without forfeiture; where is the stamp of their stability? Their motto should be, "Levity." If the act for incorporating the subscribers to the Bank of North America shall be repealed in this manner, a precedent will be established for repealing, in the same manner, every other legislative charter in Pennsylvania. A pretence, as specious as any that can be alleged on this occasion, will never be wanting on any future occasion. Those acts of the state, which have hitherto been considered as the sure anchors of privilege and of property, will become the sport of every varying gust of politicks, and will float wildly backwards and forwards on the irregular and impetuous tides of party and faction.

4th. It would not be wise or politick to repeal the charter granted by this state to the Bank of North America, because such a measure would operate, as far as it would have any operation, against the credit of the United States, on which the interest of this commonwealth and her citizens so essentially depends. This institution originated under the auspices of the United States: the subscription to the national bank was opened under the recommendations and the engagements of congress: citizens of this state, and of the other states, and foreigners have become stockholders, on the publick faith: the United States have pledged themselves "to promote and support the institution by such ways and means, from time to time, as may appear necessary for it, and consistent with the publick good." They have recommended to the legislature of each state, "to pass such laws as they might judge necessary for giving the ordinance incorporating the bank its full operation." Pennsylvania has entered fully into the views, the recommendations, and the measures of congress respecting the bank. She has declared in the strongest manner her sense of their propriety, their reasonableness, and their necessity: she has passed laws for giving them their full operation. Will it redound to the credit of the United States to adopt and pursue a contrary system of conduct The acts and recommendations of congress subsist still in all their original force: will it not have a tendency to shake all confidence in the councils and proceedings of the United States, if those acts and recommendations are now disregarded, without any reason shown for disregarding them? What influence will such a proceeding have upon the opinions and sentiments of the citizens of the United States and of foreigners? In one year they see measures respecting an object of confessed publick importance adopted and recommended with ardour by congress; and the views and wishes of that body zealously pursued by Pennsylvania: in another year they see those very measures, without any apparent reason for the change, warmly reprobated by that state: they must conclude one of two things:—that congress adopted and recommended those measures hastily and without consideration; or that Pennsylvania has reprobated them undutifully and disrespectfully. The former conclusion will give rise to very unfavourable reflections concerning the discernment both of the state and of the United States: the latter will suggest very inauspicious sentiments concerning the federal disposition and character of this commonwealth. The result of the conclusion will be—that the United States do not deserve, or that they will not receive, support in their system of finance.—These deductions and inferences will have particular weight, as they will be grounded on the conduct of Pennsylvania, hitherto one of the most federal, active, and affectionate states in the Union.

5th. It would not be wise or politick in the legislature to repeal their charter to the bank; because the tendency of such a step would be to deprive this state and the United States of all the advantages, publick and private, which would flow from the institution, in times of war, and in times of peace.

Let us turn our attention to some of the most material advantages resulting from a bank.

1st. It increases circulation, and invigorates industry. "It is not," says Dr. Smith, in his Treatise on the Wealth of Nations, "by augmenting the capital of the country, but by rendering a greater part of that capital active and productive than would otherwise be so, that the most judicious operations of banking can increase the industry of the country. The part of his capital which a dealer is obliged to keep by him unemployed, and in ready money, for answering occasional demands, is so much dead stock, which, so long as it remains in this situation, produces nothing either to him or to his country. The judicious operations of banking enable him to convert this dead stock into active and productive stock: into materials to work upon, into tools to work with, and into provisions and subsistence to work for; into stock which produces something both to himself and to his country. The gold and silver money which circulates in any country, and by means of which the produce of its land and labour is annually circulated and distributed to the proper consumers, is, in the same manner as the ready money of the dealer, all dead stock. It is a very valuable part of the capital of the country, which produces nothing to the country. The judicious operations of banking, by substituting paper in the room of a great part of this gold and silver, enables the country to convert a great part of this dead stock into active and productive stock; into stock which produces something to the country. The gold and silver money which circulates in any country may very properly be compared to a highway, which, while it circulates and carries to market all the grass and corn of the country, produces, itself, not a single pile of either. The judicious operations of banking, by providing, if I may be allowed so violent a metaphor, a sort of wagon-way through the air, enable the country to convert, as it were, a great part of its highways into good pasture and corn fields, and thereby to increase very considerably the annual produce of its land and labour."

The same sensible writer informs us, in another place, that "the substitution of paper in the room of gold and silver money, replaces a very expensive instrument of commerce with one much less costly, and sometimes equally convenient. Circulation comes to be carried on by a new wheel, which it costs less both to erect and to maintain than the old one.—There are several sorts of paper money; but the circulating notes of banks and bankers is the species which is best known, and which seems best adapted for this purpose."—"These notes come to have the same currency as gold and silver money, from the confidence that such money can at any time be had for them."

Sir James Stewart calls banking "the great engine, by which domestick circulation is carried on."

To have a free, easy, and equable instrument of circulation is of much importance in all countries: it is of peculiar importance in young and flourishing countries, in which the demands for credit, and the rewards of industry, are greater than in any other. When we view the extent and situation of the United States, we shall be satisfied that their inhabitants may, for a long time to come, employ profitably, in the improvement of their lands, a greater stock than they will be able easily to procure. In such a situation, it will always be of great service to them to save as much as possible the expense of so costly an instrument of commerce as gold and silver, to substitute in its place one cheaper, and, for many purposes, not less convenient; and to convert the value of the gold and silver into the labour and the materials necessary for improving and extending their settlements and plantations.

"To the banks of Scotland," says Sir James Stewart, "the improvement of that country is entirely owing; and until they are generally established in other countries of Europe, where trade and industry are little known, it will be very difficult to set those great engines to work."

2d. The influence of a bank on credit is no less salutary than its influence on circulation. This position is, indeed, little more than a corollary from the former. Credit is confidence; and, before we can place confidence in a payment, we must be convinced that he who is to make it will be both able and willing to do so at the time stipulated. However unexceptionable his character and fortune may be, this conviction can never take place, unless in a country where solid property can be, at any time, turned into a circulating medium.

3d. Trade, as well as circulation and credit, derives great support and assistance from a bank. Credit and circulation produce punctuality; and punctuality is the soul of commerce. Let us appeal to experience as well as reason.

Dr. Smith says, he has heard it asserted, that the trade of the city of Glasgow doubled in about fifteen years after the first erection of the banks there; and that the trade of Scotland has more than quadrupled since the first erection of the two publick banks at Edinburgh, of which one was established in 1695, and the other in 1727. Whether the increase has been in so great a proportion, the author pretends not to know. But that the trade of Scotland has increased very considerably during this period, and that the banks have contributed a good deal to this increase, cannot, he says, be doubted.

These observations, and observations similar to these, have induced Sir James Stewart to conclude,—that "Banking, in the age we live, is that branch of credit which best deserves the attention of a statesman. Upon the right establishment of banks depends the prosperity of trade, and the equable course of circulation. By them solid property may be melted down. By the means of banks, money may be constantly kept at a due proportion to alienation. If alienation increases, more property may be melted down. If it diminishes, the quantity of money stagnating will be absorbed by the bank, and part of the property formerly melted down in the securities granted to them will be, as it were, consolidated anew. These must pay, for the country, the balance of their trade with foreign nations: these keep the mints at work: and it is by these means, principally, that private, mercantile, and publick credit is supported."

I make no apology for the number and length of the quotations here used. They are from writers of great information, profound judgment, and unquestioned candour. They appear strictly and strongly applicable to my subject: and being so, should carry with them the greatest weight and influence; for the sentiments, which they contain and inculcate, must be considered as resulting from general principles and facts, and not as calculated for any partial purpose in this commonwealth.

But, here, it will probably be asked—Has your reasoning been verified by experience in this country? What advantages have resulted from the bank to commerce, circulation, and credit? Was our trade ever on such an undesirable footing? Is not the country distressed by the want of a circulating medium? Is not credit almost totally destroyed?

I answer—There is, unfortunately, too much truth in the representation: but if events are properly distinguished, and traced to their causes, it will be found—that none of the inconveniences abovementioned have arisen from the bank—that some of them have proceeded, at least in part, from the opposition which has been given to it—and that, as to others, its energy has not been sufficient to counteract or control them.

The disagreeable state of our commerce has been the effect of extravagant and injudicious importation. During the war, our ports were in a great measure blocked up. Imported articles were scarce and dear; and we felt the disadvantages of a stagnation in business. Extremes frequently introduce one another. When hostilities ceased, the floodgates of commerce were opened; and an inundation of foreign manufacturers overflowed the United States: we seemed to have forgot, that to pay was as necessary in trade as to purchase; and we observed no proportion between our imports, and our produce and other natural means of remittance. What was the consequence? Those who made any payments made them chiefly in specie; and in that way diminished our circulation. Others made no remittances at all, and thereby injured our credit. This account of what happened between the European merchants and our importers, corresponds exactly with what happened between our importers and the retailers spread over the different parts of the United States. The retailers, if they paid at all, paid in specie: and thus every operation, foreign and domestick, had an injurious effect on our credit, our circulation, and our commerce. But are any of these disadvantages to be ascribed to the bank? No. Is it to be accounted a fault or defect in the bank, that it did not prevent or remedy those disadvantages? By no means. Because one is not able to stem a torrent, is he therefore to be charged with augmenting its strength? The bank has had many difficulties to encounter. The experiment was a new one in this country: it was therefore necessary that it should be conducted with caution. While the war continued, the demands of the publick were great, and the stock of the bank was but inconsiderable; it had its active enemies, and its timid friends. Soon after the peace was concluded, its operations were restrained and embarrassed by an attempt to establish a new bank. A year had not elapsed after this, when the measure, which has occasioned these considerations, was introduced into the legislature, and caused, for some time, a total stagnation in the business of the institution. When all these circumstances are recollected and attended to, it will be matter of surprise that the bank has done so much, and not that it has done no more. Let it be deemed, as it ought to be, the object of publick confidence, and not of publick jealousy: let it be encouraged, instead of being opposed, by the counsels and proceedings of the state: then will the genuine effects of the institution appear; then will they spread their auspicious influence over agriculture, manufactures, and commerce.

4th. Another advantage to be expected from the Bank of North America is, the establishment of an undepreciating paper currency through the United States. This is an object of great consequence, whether it be considered in a political, or in a commercial view. It will be found to have a happy effect on the collection, the distribution, and the management of the publick revenue: it will remove the inconveniences and fluctuation attending exchange and remittances between the different states. "It is the interest of every trading state to have a sufficient quantity of paper, well secured, to circulate through it, so as to facilitate payments every where, and to cut off inland exchanges, which are a great clog upon trade, and are attended with the risk of receiving the paper of people, whose credit is but doubtful."

Such are the advantages which may be expected to flow from a national bank, in times of peace. In times of war, the institution may be considered as essential. We have seen that, without it, the business of the department of finance could not have been carried on in the late war. It will be of use to recollect the situation of the United States with regard to this subject. The two or three first years of the war were sufficient to convince the British government, and the British armies, that they could not subdue the United States by military force. Their hopes of success rested on the failure of our finances. This was the source of our fears, as well as of the hopes of our enemies. By this thread our fate was suspended. We watched it with anxiety: we saw it stretched and weakened every hour: the deathful instrument was ready to fall upon our heads: on our heads it must have fallen, had not publick credit, in the moment when it was about to break asunder, been entwined and supported by the credit of the bank. Congress, to speak without metaphors, had not money or credit to hire an express, or purchase a cord of wood. General Washington, on one occasion, and probably more than one, saw his army literally unable to march. Our distress was such, that it would have been destruction to have divulged it: but it ought to be known now; and when known, ought to have its proper influence on the publick mind and the publick conduct.

The expenses of a war must be defrayed, either—1st, by treasures previously accumulated—or 2dly, by supplies levied and collected within the year, as they are called for—or 3dly, by the anticipation of the publick revenues. No one will venture to refer us to the first mode. To the second the United States, as well as every state in Europe, are rendered incompetent by the modern system of war, which, in the military operations of one year, concentres the revenue of many. While our enemies adhere to this system, we must adopt it. The anticipation of revenue, then, is the only mode, by which the expenses of a future war can be defrayed. How the revenues of the United States can be anticipated without the operations of a national bank, I leave to those who attack the Bank of North America to show. They ought to be well prepared to show it; for they must know, that to be incapable of supporting a war is but a single step from being involved in one.

The result of the whole, under this head, is,—that in times of peace, the national bank will be highly advantageous; that in times of war, it will be essentially necessary, to the United States.

I flatter myself, that I have evinced the validity and the utility of the institution.

It has been surmised, that the design of the legislature is not to destroy, but to modify, the charter of the bank; and that if the directors would assent to reasonable amendments, the charter, modified, might continue in force. If this is the case, surely to repeal the law incorporating the bank is not the proper mode of doing the business. The bank was established and organized under the authority and auspices of congress. The directors have a trust and duty to discharge to the United States, and to all the particular states, each of which has an equal interest in the bank. They could not have received, from this state, a charter, unless it had been *similar* to that granted by congress. Without the approbation of congress, where all the states are represented, the directors would not be justified in agreeing to any alteration of the institution. If alterations are necessary; they should be made through the channel of the United States in congress assembled.

C. LETTER OF THOMAS JEFFERSON TO JAMES MADISON

December 16, 1786

DEAR SIR

... I inclose you herein a copy of the letter from the Minister of finance to me, making several advantageous regulations for our commerce. The obtaining this has occupied us a twelvemonth. I say us, because I find the M. de la Fayette so useful an auxiliary that acknowlegements for his cooperation are always due. There remains still something to do for the articles of rice, turpentine and shipduties. What can be done for tobacco when the late regulation expires, is very incertain. The commerce between the U.S. and this country being put on a good footing, we may afterwards proceed to try if any thing can be done to favour our intercourse with their colonies. Admission into them for our fish and flour is very desireable. But unfortunately both these articles would raise a competition against their own.

I find by the public papers that your Commercial Convention failed in point of representation. If it should produce a full meeting in May, and a broader reformation, it will still be well. To make us one nation as to foreign concerns, and keep us distinct in Domestic ones, gives the outline of the proper division of powers between the general and particular governments. But to enable the Federal head to exercise the powers given it, to best advantage, it should be organised, as the particular ones are, into Legislative, Executive and Judiciary. The 1st. and last are already separated. The 2d should also be. When last with Congress, I often proposed to members to do this by making of the Committee of the states, an Executive committee during the recess of Congress, and during it's sessions to appoint a Committee to receive and dispatch all executive business, so that Congress itself should meddle only with what should be legislative. But I question if any Congress (much less all successively) can have self-denial enough to go through with this distribution. The distribution should be imposed on them then. I find Congress have reversed their division of the Western states, and proposed to make them fewer and larger. This is reversing the natural order of things. A tractable people may be governed in large bodies; but in proportion as they depart from this character, the extent of their government must be less. We see into what small divisions the Indians are obliged to reduce their societies. This measure, with the disposition to shut up the Missisipi give me serious apprehensions of the severance of the Eastern and Western parts of our confederacy. It might have been made the interests of the Western states to remain united with us, by managing their interests honestly and for their own good. But the moment we sacrifice their interests to our own, they will see it better to govern themselves. The moment they resolve to do this, the point is settled. A forced connection is neither our interest nor within our power.—The Virginia act for religious freedom has been received with infinite approbation in Europe and propagated with enthusiasm. I do not mean by the governments, but by the individuals which compose them. It has been translated into French and Italian, has been sent to most of the courts of Europe, and has been the best evidence of the falshood of those reports which stated us to be in anarchy. It is inserted in the new Encyclopedie, and is appearing in most of the publications respecting America. In fact it is comfortable to see the standard of reason at length erected, after so many ages during which the human mind has been held in vassalage by kings, priests and nobles; and it is honorable for us to have produced the first legislature who has had the courage to declare that the reason of man may be trusted with the formation of his own opinions. I shall be glad when the revisal shall be got thro'.... I am Dear Sir with sincere esteem your friend & servant,

TH. JEFFERSON

D. LETTER OF JAMES MADISON
TO GEORGE WASHINGTON

April 16, 1787

DEAR SIR

I have been honoured with your letter of the 31 of March, and find with much pleasure that your views of the reform which ought to be pursued by the Convention, give a sanction to those which I have entertained. Temporising applications will dishonor the Councils which propose them, and may foment the internal malignity of the disease, at the same time that they produce an ostensible palliation of it. Radical attempts, although unsuccessful, will at least justify the authors of them.

Having been lately led to revolve the subject which is to undergo the discussion of the Convention, and formed in my mind *some* outlines of a new system, I take the liberty of submitting them without apology, to your eye.

Conceiving that an individual independence of the States is utterly irreconcileable with their aggregate sovereignty; and that a consolidation of the whole into one simple republic would be as inexpedient as it is unattainable, I have sought for some middle ground, which may at once support a due supremacy of the national authority, and not exclude the local authorities wherever they can be subordinately useful.

I would propose as the ground-work that a change be made in the principle of representation. According to the present form of the Union in which the intervention of the States is in all great cases necessary to effectuate the measures of Congress, an equality of suffrage, does not destroy the inequality of importance, in the several members. No one will deny that Virginia and Massts. have more weight and influence both within & without Congress than Delaware or Rho. Island. Under a system which would operate in many essential points without the intervention of the State legislatures, the case would be materially altered. A vote in the national Councils from Delaware, would then have the same effect and value as one from the largest State in the Union. I am ready to believe that such a change would not be attended with much difficulty. A majority of the States, and those of greatest influence, will regard it as favorable to them. To the Northern States it will be recommended by their present populousness; to the Southern by their expected advantage in this respect. The lesser States must in every event yield to the predominant will. But the consideration which particularly urges a change in the representation is that it will obviate the principal objections of the larger States to the necessary concessions of power.

I would propose next that in addition to the present federal powers, the national Government should be armed with positive and compleat authority in all cases which require uniformity; such as the regulation of trade, including the right of taxing both exports & imports, the fixing the terms and forms of naturalization, &c &c.

Over and above this positive power, a negative *in all cases whatsoever* on the legislative acts of the States, as heretofore exercised by the Kingly prerogative, appears to me to be absolutely necessary, and to be the least possible encroachment on the State jurisdictions. Without this defensive power, every positive power that can be given on paper will be evaded & defeated. The States will continue to invade the national jurisdiction, to violate treaties and the law of nations & to harrass each other with rival and spiteful measures dictated by mistaken views of interest. Another happy effect of this prerogative would be its controul on the internal vicisitudes of State policy; and the aggressions of interested majorities on the rights of minorities and of individuals. The great desideratum which has not yet been found for Republican Governments, seems to be some disinterested & dispassionate umpire in disputes between different passions & interests in the State. The majority who alone have the right of decision, have frequently an interest real or supposed in abusing it. In Monarchies the sovereign is more neutral to the interests and views of different parties; but unfortunately he too often forms interests of his own repugnant to those of the whole. Might not the national prerogative here suggested be found sufficiently disinterested for the decision of local questions of policy, whilst it would itself be sufficiently restrained from the pursuit of interests adverse to those of the whole Society? There has not been any moment since the peace at which the representatives of the union would have given an assent to paper money or any other measure of a kindred nature.

The national supremacy ought also to be extended as I conceive to the Judiciary departments. If those who are to expound & apply the laws, are connected by their interests & their oaths with the particular States wholly, and not with the Union, the participation of the Union in the making of the laws may be possibly rendered unavailing. It seems at least necessary that the oaths of the Judges should include a fidelity to the general as well as local constitution, and that an appeal should lie to some national tribunals in all cases to which foreigners or inhabitants of other States may be parties. The admiralty jurisdiction seems to fall entirely within the purview of the national Government.

The national supremacy in the Executive departments is liable to some difficulty, unless the officers administering them could be made appointable by the supreme Government. The Militia ought certainly to be placed in some form or other under the authority which is entrusted with the general protection and defence.

A Government composed of such extensive powers should be well organized and balanced. The Legislative department might be divided into two branches; one of them chosen every   years by the people at large, or by the legislatures; the other to consist of fewer members, to hold their places for a longer term, and to go out in such a rotation as always to leave in office a large majority of old members. Perhaps the negative on the laws might be most conveniently exercised by this branch. As a further check, a council of revision including the great ministerial officers might be superadded.

A national Executive must also be provided. I have scarcely ventured as yet to form my own opinion either of the manner in which it ought to be constituted or of the authorities with which it ought to be cloathed.

An article should be inserted expressly guarantying the tranquillity of the States against internal as well as external dangers.

In like manner the right of coercion should be expressly declared. With the resources of Commerce in hand, the national administration might always find means of exerting it either by sea or land; But the difficulty & awkwardness of operating by force on the collective will of a State, render it particularly desirable that the necessity of it might be precluded. Perhaps the negative on the laws might create such a mutuality of dependence between the General and particular authorities, as to answer this purpose. Or perhaps some defined objects of taxation might be submitted along with commerce, to the general authority.

To give a new System its proper validity and energy, a ratification must be obtained from the people, and not merely from the ordinary authority of the Legislatures. This will be the more essential as inroads on the *existing Constitutions* of the States will be unavoidable.

The inclosed address to the States on the subject of the Treaty of peace has been agreed to by Congress, & forwarded to the several Executives. We foresee the irritation which it will excite in many of our Countrymen; but could not withold our approbation of the measure. Both, the resolutions and the address, passed without a dissenting voice.

Congress continue to be thin, and of course do little business of importance. The settlement of the public accounts, the disposition of the public lands, and arrangements with Spain, are subjects which claim their particular attention. As a step towards the first, the treasury board are charged with the task of reporting a plan by which the final decision on the claims of the States will be handed over from Congress to a select set of men bound by the oaths, and cloathed with the powers, of Chancellors. As to the Second article, Congress have it themselves under consideration. Between 6 & 700 thousand acres have been surveyed and are ready for sale. The mode of sale however will probably be a source of different opinions; as will the mode of disposing of the unsurveyed residue. The Eastern gentlemen remain attached to the scheme of townships. Many others are equally strenuous for indiscriminate locations. The States which have lands of their own for sale, are *suspected* of not being hearty in bringing the federal lands to market. The business with Spain is becoming extremely delicate, and the information from the Western settlements truly alarming.... With the sincerest affection & the highest esteem I have the honor to be Dear Sir Your devoted Servt.

JS. MADISON JR.

E. LETTER OF THOMAS JEFFERSON TO JAMES MADISON

June 20, 1787

DEAR SIR

. . .

The idea of separating the executive business of the confederacy from Congress, as the judiciary is already in some degree, is just and necessary. I had frequently pressed on the members individually, while in Congress, the doing this by a resolution of Congress for appointing an Executive committee to act during the sessions of Congress, as the Committee of the states was to act during their vacations. But the referring to this Committee all executive business as it should present itself, would require a more persevering self-denial than I supposed Congress to possess. It will be much better to make that separation by a federal act. The negative proposed to be given them on all the acts of the several legislatures is now for the first time suggested to my mind. Primâ facie I do not like it. It fails in an essential character, that the hole and the patch should be commensurate. But this proposes to mend a small hole by covering the whole garment. Not more than 1. out of 100. state-acts concern the confederacy. This proposition then, in order to give them 1. degree of power which they ought to have, gives them 99. more which they ought not to have, upon a presumption that they will not exercise the 99. But upon every act there will be a preliminary question. Does this act concern the confederacy? And was there ever a proposition so plain as to pass Congress without a debate? Their decisions are almost always wise: they are like pure metal. But you know of how much dross this is the result. Would not an appeal from the state judicatures to a federal court, in all cases where the act of Confederation controuled the question, be as effectual a remedy, and exactly commensurate to the defect. A British creditor, e.g. sues for his debt in Virginia; the defendant pleads an act of the state excluding him from their courts; the plaintiff urges the Confederation and the treaty made under that, as controuling the state law; the judges are weak enough to decide according to the views of their legislature. An appeal to a federal court sets all to rights. It will be said that this court may encroach on the jurisdiction of the state courts. It may. But there will be a power, to wit Congress, to watch and restrain them. But place the same authority in Congress itself, and there will be no power above them to perform the same office. They will restrain within due bounds a jurisdiction exercised by others much more rigorously than if exercised by themselves....

I am with sentiments of the most sincere esteem Dear Sir Your friend & servt.,

TH. JEFFERSON

F. DEBATE IN THE PHILADELPHIA CONVENTION

June 18, 1787

Mr. Hamilton, had been hitherto silent on the business before the Convention, partly from respect to others whose superior abilities age & experience rendered him unwilling to bring forward ideas dissimilar to theirs, and partly from his delicate situation with respect to his own State, to whose sentiments as expressed by his Colleagues, he could by no means accede. The crisis however which now marked our affairs, was too serious to permit any scruples whatever to prevail over the duty imposed on every man to contribute his efforts for the public safety & happiness. He was obliged therefore to declare himself unfriendly to both plans. He was particularly opposed to that from N. Jersey, being fully convinced, that no amendment of the confederation, leaving the States in possession of their sovereignty could possibly answer the purpose. On the other hand he confessed he was much discouraged by the amazing extent of Country in expecting the desired blessings from any general sovereignty that could be substituted.—As to the powers of the Convention, he thought the doubts started on that subject had arisen from distinctions & reasonings too subtle. A *federal* Govt. he conceived to mean an association of independent Communities into one. Different Confederacies have different powers, and exercise them in different ways. In some instances the powers are exercised over collective bodies; in others over individuals. as in the German Diet—& among ourselves in cases of piracy. Great latitude therefore must be given to the signification of the term. The plan last proposed departs itself from the *federal* idea, as understood by some, since it is to operate eventually on individuals. He agreed moreover with the Honble. gentleman from Va. (Mr. R.) that we owed it to our Country, to do on this emergency whatever we should deem essential to its happiness. The States sent us here to provide for the exigences of the Union. To rely on & propose any plan not adequate to these exigences, merely because it was not clearly within our powers, would be to sacrifice the means to the end. It may be said that the *States* can not *ratify* a plan not within the purview of the article of Confederation providing for alterations & amendments. But may not the States themselves in which no constitutional authority equal to this purpose exists in the Legislatures, have had in view a reference to the people at large. In the Senate of N. York, a proviso was moved, that no act of the Convention should be binding untill it should be referred to the people & ratified; and the motion was lost by a single voice only, the reason assigned agst. it, being that it <might possibly> be found an inconvenient shackle.

The great question is what provision shall we make for the happiness of our Country? He would first make a comparative examination of the two plans—prove that there were essential defects in both—and point out such changes as might render a *national one*, efficacious.—The great & essential principles necessary for the support of Government. are 1. an active & constant interest in supporting it. This principle does not exist in the States in favor of the federal Govt. They have evidently in a high degree, the esprit de corps. They constantly pursue internal interests adverse to those of the whole. They have their particular debts—their particular plans of finance &c. all these when opposed to, invariably prevail over the requisitions & plans of Congress. 2. the love of power, Men love power. The same remarks are applicable to this principle. The States have constantly shewn a disposition rather to regain the powers delegated by them than to part with more, or to give effect to what they had parted with. The ambition of their demagogues is known to hate the controul of the Genl. Government. It may be remarked too that the Citizens have not that anxiety to prevent a dissolution of the Genl. Govt as of the particular Govts. A dissolution of the latter would be fatal: of the former would still leave the purposes of Govt. attainable to a considerable degree. Consider what such a State as Virga. will be in a few years, a few compared with the life of nations. How strongly will it feel its importance & self-sufficiency? 3. an habitual attachment of the people. The whole force of this tie is on the side of the State Govt. Its sovereignty is immediately before the eyes of the people: its protection is immediately enjoyed by them. From its hand distributive justice, and all those acts which familiarize & endear Govt. to a people, are dispensed to them. 4. *Force* by which may be understood a *coertion of laws* or *coertion of arms.* Congs. have not the former except in few cases. In particular States, this coercion is nearly sufficient; tho' he held it in most cases, not entirely so. A certain portion of military force is absolutely necessary in large communities. Massts. is now feeling this necessity & making provision for it. But how can this force be exerted on the States collectively. It is impossible. It amounts to a war between the parties. Foreign powers also will not be idle spectators. They will interpose, the confusion will increase, and a dissolution of the Union ensue. 5. *influence.* he did not <mean> corruption, but a dispensation of those regular honors & emoluments, which produce an attachment to the Govt. almost all the weight of these is on the side of the States; and must continue so as long as the States continue to exist. All the passions then we see, of avarice, ambition, interest, which govern most individuals, and all public bodies, fall into the current of the States, and do not flow in the stream of the Genl. Govt. the former therefore will generally be an overmatch for the Genl. Govt. and render any confederacy, in its very nature precarious. Theory is in this case fully confirmed by experience. The Amphyctionic Council had it would seem ample powers for general purposes. It had in particular the power of fining and using force agst. delinquent members. What was the consequence. Their decrees were mere signals of war. The Phocian war is a striking example of it. Philip at length taking advantage of their disunion, and insinuating himself into their Councils, made himself master of their fortunes. The German Confederacy affords another lesson. The authority of Charlemagne seemed to be as great as could be necessary. The great feudal chiefs however, exercising their local sovereignties, soon felt the spirit & found the means of, encroachments, which reduced the imperial authority to a nominal sovereignty. The Diet has succeeded, which tho' aided by a Prince at its head, of great authority independently of his imperial attributes, is a striking illustration of the weakness of Confederated Governments.

Other examples instruct us in the same truth. The Swiss cantons have scarce any Union at all, and <have been more than once at> war with one another—How then are all these evils to be avoided? only by such a compleat sovereignty in the general Govermt. as will turn all the strong principles & passions above mentioned on its side. Does the scheme of N. Jersey produce this effect does it afford any substantial remedy whatever? On the contrary it labors under great defects, and the defect of some of its provisions will destroy the efficacy of others. It gives a direct revenue to Congs. but this will not be sufficient. The balance can only be supplied by requisitions; which experience proves can not be relied on. If States are to deliberate on the mode, they will also deliberate on the object of the supplies, and will grant or not grant as they approve or disapprove of it. The delinquency of one will invite and countenance it in others. Quotas too must in the nature of things be so unequal as to produce the same evil. To what standard will you resort? Land is a fallacious one. Compare Holland with Russia: France or Engd. with other countries of Europe. Pena. with N. Carolia. will the relative pecuniary abilities in those instances, correspond with the relative value of land. Take numbers of inhabitants for the rule and make like comparison of different countries, and you will find it to be equally unjust. The different degrees of industry and improvement in different Countries render the first object a precarious measure of wealth. Much depends too on *situation*. Cont. N. Jersey & N. Carolina, not being commercial States & contributing to the wealth of the commercial ones, can never bear quotas assessed by the ordinary rules of proportion. They will & must fail <in their duty.> their example will be followed, and the Union itself be dissolved. Whence then is the national revenue to be drawn? from Commerce, even <from> exports which notwithstanding the common opinion are fit objects of moderate taxation, <from> excise, &c &c. These tho' not equal, are less unequal than quotas. Another destructive ingredient in the plan, is that equality of suffrage which is so much desired by the small States. It is not in human nature that Va. & the large States should consent to it, or if they did that they shd. long abide by it. It shocks too much the ideas of Justice, and every human feeling. Bad principles in a Govt. tho slow are sure in their operation, and will gradually destroy it. A doubt has been raised whether Congs. at present have a right to keep Ships or troops in time of peace. He leans to the negative. Mr. P.s plan provides no remedy.—If the powers proposed were adequate, the organization of Congs. is such that they could never be properly & effectually exercised. The members of Congs. being chosen by the States & subject to recall, represent all the local prejudices. Should the powers be found effectual, they will from time to time be heaped on them, till a tyrannic sway shall be established. The general power whatever be its form if it preserves itself, must swallow up the State powers. otherwise it will be swallowed up by them. It is agst. all the principles of a good Government to vest the requisite powers in such a body as Congs. Two Sovereignties can not co-exist within the same limits. Giving powers to Congs. must eventuate in a bad Govt. or in no Govt. The plan of N. Jersey therefore will not do. What then is to be done? Here he was embarrassed. The extent of the Country to be governed, discouraged him. The expence of a general Govt. was also formidable; unless there were such a diminution of expence on the side of the State Govts. as the case would admit. If they were extinguished, he was persuaded that great œconomy might be obtained by substituting a general Govt. He did not mean however to shock the public opinion by proposing such a measure. On the other <hand> he saw no *other* necessity for declining it. They are not necessary for any of the great purposes of commerce, revenue, or agriculture. Subordinate authorities he was aware would be necessary. There must be district tribunals: corporations for local purposes. But cui bono, the vast & expensive apparatus now appertaining to the States. The only difficulty of a serious nature which occurred to him, was that of drawing representatives from the extremes to the center of the Community. What inducements can be offered that will suffice? The moderate wages for the 1st. branch, would only be a bait to little demagogues. Three dollars or thereabouts he supposed would be the Utmost. The Senate he feared from a similar cause, would be filled by certain undertakers who wish for particular offices under the Govt. This view of the subject almost led him to despair that a Republican Govt. could be established over so great an extent. He was sensible at the same time that it would be unwise to propose one of any other form. In his private opinion he had no scruple in declaring, supported as he was by the opinions of so many of the wise & good, that the British Govt. was the best in the world: and that he doubted much whether any thing short of it would do in America. He hoped Gentlemen of different opinions would bear with him in this, and begged them to recollect the change of opinion on this subject which had taken place and was still going on. It was once thought that the power of Congs was amply sufficient to secure the end of their institution. The error was now seen by every one. The members most tenacious of republicanism, he observed, were as loud as any in declaiming agst. the vices of democracy. This progress of the public mind led him to anticipate the time, when others as well as himself would join in the praise bestowed by Mr. Neckar on the British Constitution, namely, that it is the only Govt. in the world "which unites public strength with individual security."—In every community where industry is encouraged, there will be a division of it into the few & the many. Hence separate interests will arise There will be debtors & Creditors &c. Give all power to the many, they will oppress the few. Give all power to the few they will oppress the many. Both therefore ought to have power, that each may defend itself agst. the other. To the want of this check we owe our paper money—instalment laws &c To the proper adjustment of it the British owe the excellence of their Constitution. Their house of Lords is a most noble institution. Having nothing to hope for by a change, and a sufficient interest by means of their

property, in being faithful to the National interest, they form a permanent barrier agst. every pernicious innovation, whether attempted on the
part of the Crown or of the Commons. No temporary Senate will have
firmness en'o' to answer the purpose. The Senate <(of Maryland)>
which seems to be so much appealed to, has not yet been sufficiently
tried. Had the people been unanimous & eager, in the late appeal to
them on the subject of a paper emission they would would have yielded
to the torrent. Their acquiescing in such an appeal is a proof of it.—
Gentlemen differ in their opinions concerning the necessary checks, from
the different estimates they form of the human passions. They suppose
Seven years a sufficient period to give the Senate an adequate firmness,
from not duly considering the amazing violence & turbulence of the
democratic spirit. When a great object of Govt. is pursued, which seizes
the popular passions, they spread like wild fire, and become irresistable.
He appealed to the gentlemen from the N. England States whether
experience had not there verified the remark. As to the Executive, it
seemed to be admitted that no good one could be established on Republican principles. Was not this giving up the merits of the question; for
can there be a good Govt. without a good Executive. The English model
was the only good one on this subject. The Hereditary interest of the
King was so interwoven with that of the Nation, and his personal
emoluments so great, that he was placed above the danger of being
corrupted from abroad—and at the same time was both sufficiently
independent and sufficiently controuled, to answer the purpose of the
institution at home. one of the weak sides of Republics was their being
liable to foreign influence & corruption. Men of little character, acquiring great power become easily the tools of intermedling neibours. Swee-
den was a striking instance. The French & English had each their
parties during the late Revolution which was effected by the predominant influence of the former. What is the inference from all these
observations? That we ought to go as far in order to attain stability and
permanency, as republican principles will admit. Let one branch of the
Legislature hold their places for life or at least during good-behaviour.
Let the Executive also be for life. He appealed to the feelings of the
members present whether a term of seven years, would induce the
sacrifices of private affairs which an acceptance of public trust would
require, so so as to ensure the services of the best Citizens. On this plan
we should have in the Senate a permanent will, a weighty interest,
which would answer essential purposes. But is this a Republican Govt.
it will be asked? Yes, if all the Magistrates are appointed, and vacancies
are filled, by the people, or a process of election originating with the
people. He was sensible that an Executive constituted as he proposed
would have in fact but little of the power and independence that might
be necessary. On the other plan of appointing him for 7 years, he
thought the Executive ought to have but little power. He would be
ambitious, with the means of making creatures; and as the object of his
ambition wd. be to *prolong* his power, it is probable that in case of a war,

he would avail himself of the emergence, to evade or refuse a degradation from his place.   An Executive for life has not this motive for forgetting his fidelity, and will therefore be a safer depositary of power. It will be objected probably, that such an Executive will be an *elective Monarch*, and will give birth to the tumults which characterise that form of Govt.   He wd. reply that *Monarch* is an indefinite term.   It marks not either the degree or duration of power.   If this Executive Magistrate wd. be a monarch for life—the other propd. by the Report from the Committee of the whole, wd. be a monarch for seven years.   The circumstance of being elective was also applicable to both.   It had been observed by judicious writers that elective monarchies wd. be the best if they could be guarded agst. the *tumults* excited by the ambition and intrigues of competitors.   He was not sure that tumults were an inseparable evil. He rather thought this character of Elective Monarchies had been taken rather from particular cases than from general principles.   The election of Roman Emperors was made by the *Army*.   In *Poland* the election is made by great rival *princes* with independent power, and ample means, of raising commotions.   In the German Empire, The appointment is made by the Electors & Princes, who have equal motives & means, for exciting cabals & parties.   Might <not> such a mode of election be devised among ourselves as will defend the community agst. these effects in any dangerous degree?   Having made these observations he would read to the Committee a sketch of a plan which he shd. prefer to either of those under consideration.   He was aware that it went beyond the ideas of most members.   But will such a plan be adopted out of doors? In return <he would ask> will the people adopt the other plan?   At present they will adopt neither.   But <he> sees the Union dissolving or already dissolved—he sees evils operating in the States which must soon cure the people of their fondness for democracies—he sees that a great progress has been already made & is still going on in the public mind. He thinks therefore that the people will in time be unshackled from their prejudices;   and whenever that happens, they will themselves not be satisfied at stopping where the plan of Mr. R. wd. place them, but be ready to go as far at least as he proposes.   He did not mean to offer the paper he had sketched as a proposition to the Committee.   It was meant only to give a more correct view of his ideas, and to suggest the amendments which he should probably propose to the plan of Mr. R. in the proper stages of its future discussion.   He read his sketch in the words following: towit

I   "The Supreme Legislative power of the United States of America to be vested in two different bodies of men;   the one to be called the Assembly, the other the Senate who together shall form the Legislature of the United States with power to pass all laws whatsoever subject to the Negative hereafter mentioned.

II   The Assembly to consist of persons elected by the people to serve for three years.

395

III.   The Senate to consist of persons elected to serve during good behaviour; their election to be made by electors chosen for that purpose by the people: in order to this the States to be divided into election districts. On the death, removal or resignation of any Senator his place to be filled out of the district from which he came.

IV.   The supreme Executive authority of the United States to be vested in a Governour to be elected to serve during good behaviour—the election to be made by Electors chosen by the people in the Election Districts aforesaid—The authorities & functions of the Executive to be as follows: to have a negative on all laws about to be passed, and the execution of all laws passed, to have the direction of war when authorized or begun; to have with the advice and approbation of the Senate the power of making all treaties; to have the sole appointment of the heads or chief officers of the departments of Finance, War and Foreign Affairs; to have the nomination of all other officers (Ambassadors to foreign Nations included) subject to the approbation or rejection of the Senate; to have the power of pardoning all offences except Treason; which he shall not pardon without the approbation of the Senate.

V.   On the death resignation or removal of the Governour his authorities to be exercised by the President of the Senate till a Successor be appointed.

VI   The Senate to have the sole power of declaring war, the power of advising and approving all Treaties, the power of approving or rejecting all appointments of officers except the heads or chiefs of the departments of Finance War and foreign affairs.

VII.   The Supreme Judicial authority to be vested in Judges to hold their offices during good behaviour with adequate and permanent salaries. This Court to have original jurisdiction in all causes of capture, and an appellative jurisdiction in all causes in which the revenues of the general Government or the citizens of foreign nations are concerned.

VIII.   The Legislature of the United States to have power to institute Courts in each State for the determination of all matters of general concern.

IX.   The Governour Senators and all officers of the United States to be liable to impeachment for mal—and corrupt conduct; and upon conviction to be removed from office, & disqualified for holding any place of trust or profit—all impeachments to be tried by a Court to consist of the Chief   or Judge of the Superior Court of Law of each State, provided such Judge shall hold his place during good behavior, and have a permanent salary.

X   All laws of the particular States contrary to the Constitution or laws of the United States to be utterly void; and the better to prevent such laws being passed, the Governour or president of each state shall be appointed by the General Government and shall have a negative upon the laws about to be passed in the State of which he is Governour or President

XI   No State to have any forces land or Naval; and the Militia of all the States to be under the sole and exclusive direction of the United States, the officers of which to be appointed and commissioned by them

<On these several articles he entered into explanatory observations corresponding with the principles of his introductory reasoning

Comittee rose & the House adjourned.>

(2) June 19, 1787

[I]n Committee of whole.
on the propositions of Mr. Patterson.

<The Substitute offered yesterday by Mr. Dickenson being rejected by a vote now taken on it; Con. N. Y. N. J. Del. ay. Mas. Pa. V. N. C. S. C. Geo. no Mayd. divided Mr. Patterson's plan was again at large before the Committee>

Mr. M<adison>. Much stress had been laid by some gentlemen on the want of power in the Convention to propose any other than a *federal* plan. To what had been answered by others, he would only add, that neither of the characteristics attached to a *federal* plan would support this objection. One characteristic, was that in a *federal* Government, the power was exercised not on the people individually; but on the people *collectively*, on the *States*. Yet in some instances as in piracies, captures &c. the existing Confederacy, and in many instances, the amendments to it <proposed by Mr. Patterson> must operate immediately on individuals. The other characteristic was, that a *federal* Govt. derived its appointments not immediately from the people, but from the States which they respectively composed. Here too were facts on the other side. In two of the States, Connect. and Rh. Island, the delegates to Congs. were chosen, not by the Legislatures, but by the people at large; and the plan of Mr. P. intended no change in this particular.

It had been alledged (by Mr. Patterson) that the Confederation having been formed by unanimous consent, could be dissolved by unanimous Consent only Does this doctrine result from the nature of compacts? does it arise from any particular stipulation in the articles of Confederation? If we consider the federal union as analagous to the fundamental compact by which individuals compose one Society, and which must in its theoretic origin at least, have been the unanimous act of the component members, it cannot be said that no dissolution of the compact can be effected without unanimous consent. a breach of the fundamental principles of the compact by a part of the Society would certainly absolve the other part from their obligations to it. If the breach of *any* article by *any* of the parties, does not set the others at liberty, it is because, the contrary is *implied* in the compact itself, and particularly by that law of it, which gives an indefinite authority to the majority to bind the whole in all cases. This latter circumstance shews

397

that we are not to consider the federal Union as analogous to the social compact of individuals: for if it were so, a Majority would have a right to bind the rest, and even to form a new Constitution for the whole, which the Gentn: from N. Jersey would be among the last to admit. If we consider the federal union as analogous not to the <social> compacts among individual men: but to the conventions among individual States. What is the doctrine resulting from these conventions? Clearly, according to the Expositors of the law of Nations, that a breach of any one article, by any one party, leaves all the other parties at liberty, to consider the whole convention as dissolved, unless they choose rather to compel the delinquent party to repair the breach. In some treaties indeed it is expressly stipulated that a violation of particular articles shall not have this consequence, and even that particular articles shall remain in force during war, which in general is understood to dissolve all susbsisting Treaties. But are there any exceptions of this sort to the Articles of confederation? So far from it that there is not even an express stipulation that force shall be used to compell an offending member of the Union to discharge its duty. He observed that the violations of the federal articles had been numerous & notorious. Among the most notorious was an Act of N. Jersey herself; by which she *expressly refused* to comply with a constitutional requisition of Congs.— and yielded no farther to the expostulations of their deputies, than barely to rescind her vote of refusal without passing any positive act of compliance. He did not wish to draw any rigid inferences from these observations. He thought it proper however that the true nature of the existing confederacy should be investigated, and he was not anxious to strengthen the foundations on which it now stands

Proceeding to the consideration of Mr. Patterson's plan, he stated the object of a proper plan to be twofold. 1. to preserve the Union. 2. to provide a Governmt. that will remedy the evils felt by the States both in their united and individual capacities. Examine Mr. P.s plan, & say whether it promises satisfaction in these respects.

1. Will it prevent those violations of the law of nations & of Treaties which if not prevented must involve us in the calamities of foreign wars? The tendency of the States to these violations has been manifested in sundry instances. The files of Congs. contain complaints already, from almost every nation with which treaties have been formed. Hitherto indulgence has been shewn to us. This cannot be the permanent disposition of foreign nations. A rupture with other powers is among the greatest of national calamities. It ought therefore to be effectually provided that no part of a nation shall have it in its power to bring them on the whole. The existing confederacy does <not> sufficiently provide against this evil. The proposed amendment to it does not supply the omission. It leaves the will of the States as uncontrouled as ever.

2. Will it prevent encroachments on the federal authority? A tendency to such encroachments has been sufficiently exemplified among ourselves, as well in every other confederated republic antient and Modern. By the federal articles, transactions with the Indians appertain to Congs. Yet in several instances, the States have entered into treaties & wars with them. In like manner no two or more States can form among themselves any treaties &c without the consent of Congs. yet Virga & Maryd in one instance—Pena. & N. Jersey in another, have entered into compacts, without previous application or subsequent apology. No State again can of right raise troops in time of peace without the like consent Of all cases of the league, this seems to require the most scrupulous observance. Has not Massts, notwithstanding, the most powerful member of the Union, already raised a body of troops? Is she not now augmenting them, without having even deigned to apprise Congs. of Her intention? In fine Have we not seen the public land dealt out to Cont. to bribe her acquiescence in the decree constitutionally awarded agst. her claim on the territory of Pena.—? for no other possible motive can account for the policy of Congs. in that measure?—if we recur to the examples of other confederacies, we shall find in all of them the same tendency of the parts to encroach on the authority of the whole. He then reviewed the Amphyctrionic & Achæan confederacies among the antients, and the Helvetic, Germanic & Belgic among the moderns, tracing their analogy to the U. States—in the constitution and extent of their federal authorities—in the tendency of the particular members to usurp on these authorities; and to bring confusion & ruin on the whole.—He observed that the plan of Mr. Pat—son besides omitting a controul over the States as a general defence of the federal prerogatives was particularly defective in two of its provisions. 1. Its ratification was not to be by the people at large, but by the *Legislatures.* It could not therefore render the acts of Congs. in pursuance of their powers even legally *paramount* to the Acts of the States. 2. It gave <to the federal tribunal> an appellate jurisdiction only—even in the criminal cases enumerated, The necessity of any such provision supposed a danger of undue acquittals in the State tribunals. Of what avail wd. an appellate tribunal be, after an acquttal? Besides in most if not all of the States, the Executives have by their respective *Constitutions* the right of pardg. How could this be taken from them by a *legislative ratification* only?

3. Will it prevent trespasses of the States on each other? Of these enough has been already seen. He instanced Acts of Virga. & Maryland which give a preference to their own citizens in cases where the Citizens <of other states> are entitled to equality of privileges by the Articles of Confederation. He considered the emissions of paper money <& other kindred measures> as also aggressions. The States relatively to one an other being each of them either Debtor or Creditor; The Creditor States must suffer unjustly from every emission by the debtor States. We have seen retaliating acts on this subject which threatened danger not to the

harmony only, but the tranquillity of the Union. The plan of Mr. Paterson, not giving even a negative on the Acts of the States, left them as much at liberty as ever to execute their unrighteous projects agst. each other.

4. Will it secure the internal tranquillity of the States themselves? The insurrections in Massts. admonished all the States of the danger to which they were exposed. Yet the plan of Mr. P. contained no provisions for supplying the defect of the Confederation on this point. According to the Republican theory indeed, Right & power being both vested in the majority, are held to be synonimous. According to fact & experience, a minority may in an appeal to force be an overmatch for the majority. 1. If the minority happen to include all such as possess the skill & habits of military life, with such as possess the great pecuniary resources, one third may conquer the remaining two thirds. 2. one third of those who participate in the choice of rulers may be rendered a majority by the accession of those whose poverty disqualifies them from a suffrage, & who for obvious reasons may be more ready to join the standard of sedition than that of the established Government. 3. Where slavery exists, the Republican Theory becomes still more fallacious.

5. Will it secure a good internal legislation & administration to the particular States? In developing the evils which vitiate the political system of the U. S. it is proper to take into view those which prevail within the States individually as well as those which affect them collectively: Since the former indirectly affect the whole; and there is great reason to believe that the pressure of them had a full share in the motives which produced the present Convention. Under this head he enumerated and animadverted on 1. the multiplicity of the laws passed by the several States. 2. the mutability of their laws. 3. the injustice of them. 4. the impotence of them: observing that Mr. Patterson's plan contained no remedy for this dreadful class of evils, and could not therefore be received as an adequate provision for the exigencies of the Community.

6. Will it secure the Union agst. the influence of foreign powers over its members. He pretended not to say that any such influence had yet been tried: but it naturally to be expected that occasions would produce it. As lessons which claimed particular attention, he cited the intrigues practiced among the Amphictionic Confederates first by the Kings of Persia, and afterwards fatally by Philip of Macedon: Among the Achæans, first by Macedon & afterwards no less fatally by Rome: Among the Swiss by Austria, France & the lesser neighbouring Powers; among the members of the Germanic <Body> by France, England, Spain & Russia—: and in the Belgic Republic, by all the great neighbouring powers. The plan of Mr. Patterson, not giving to the general Councils any negative on the will of the particular States, left the door open for the like pernicious machinations among ourselves.

7. He begged the smaller States which were most attached to Mr. Pattersons plan to consider the situation in which it would leave them. In the first place they would continue to bear the whole expense of maintaining their Delegates in Congress. It ought not to be said that if they were willing to bear this burden, no others had a right to complain. As far as it led the small States to forbear keeping up a representation, by which the public business was delayed, it was evidently a matter of common concern. An examination of the minutes of Congress would satisfy every one that the public business had been frequently delayed by this cause; and that the States most frequently unrepresented in Congs. were not the larger States. He reminded the convention of another consequence of leaving on a small State the burden of Maintaining a Representation in Congs. During a considerable period of the War, one of the Representatives of Delaware, in whom alone before the signing of the Confederation the entire vote of that State and after that event one half of its vote, frequently resided, was a Citizen & Resident of Pena. and held an office in his own State incompatible with an appointment from it to Congs. During another period, the same State was represented by three delegates two of whom were citizens of Penna.—and the third a Citizen of New Jersey. These expedients must have been intended to avoid the burden of supporting delegates from their own State. But whatever might have been ye. cause, was not in effect the vote of one State doubled, and the influence of another increased by it? <In the 2d. place> The coercion, on which the efficacy of the plan depends, can never be exerted but on themselves. The larger States will be impregnable, the smaller only can feel the vengeance of it. He illustrated the position by the history of the Amphyctionic Confederates: and the ban of the German Empire, It was the cobweb wch. could entangle the weak, but would be the sport of the strong.

8. He begged them to consider the situation in which they would remain in case their pertinacious adherence to an inadmissable plan, should prevent the adoption of any plan. The contemplation of such an event was painful; but it would be prudent to submit to the task of examining it at a distance, that the means of escaping it might be the more readily embraced. Let the union of the States be dissolved and one of two consequences must happen. Either the States must remain individually independent & sovereign; or two or more Confederacies must be formed among them. In the first event would the small States be more secure agst. the ambition & power of their larger neighbours, than they would be under a general Government pervading with equal energy every part of the Empire, and having an equal interest in protecting every part agst. every other part? In the second, can the smaller expect that their larger neighbours would confederate with them on the principle of the present confederacy, which gives to each member, an equal suffrage; or that they would exact less severe concessions from the smaller States, than are proposed in the scheme of Mr. Randolph?

The great difficulty lies in the affair of Representation; and if this could be adjusted, all others would be surmountable. It was admitted by both the gentlemen from N. Jersey, (Mr. Brearly and Mr. Patterson) that it would not be *just to allow Virga.* which was 16 times as large as Delaware an equal vote only. Their language was that it would not be *safe for Delaware* to allow Virga. 16 times as many votes. The expedient proposed by them was that all the States should be thrown into one mass and a new partition be made into 13 equal parts. Would such a scheme be practicable? The dissimelarities existing in the rules of property, as well as in the manners, habits and prejudices of the different States, amounted to a prohibition of the attempt. It had been found impossible for the power of one of the most absolute princes in Europe (K. of France) directed by the wisdom of one of the most enlightened and patriotic Ministers (Mr. Neckar) that any age has produced, to equalize in some points only the different usages & regulations of the different provinces. But admitting a general amalgamation and repartition of the States, to be practicable, and the danger apprehended by the smaller States from a proportional representation to be real; would not a particular and voluntary coalition of these with their neighbours, be less inconvenient to the whole community, and equally effectual for their own safety. If N. Jersey or Delaware conceive that an advantage would accrue to them from an equalization of the States, in which case they would necessaryly form a junction with their neighbors, why might not this end be attained by leaving them at liberty by the Constitution to form such a junction whenever they pleased? and why should they wish to obtrude a like arrangement on all the States, when it was, to say the least, extremely difficult, would be obnoxious to many of the States, and when neither the inconveniency, nor the benefit of the expedient to themselves, would be lessened, by confining it to themselves.—The prospect of many new States to the Westward was another consideration of importance. If they should come into the Union at all, they would come when they contained but but few inhabitants. If they shd. be entitled to vote according to their proportions of inhabitants, all would be right & safe. Let them have an equal vote, and a more objectionable minority than ever might give law to the whole.

<On a question for postponing generally the 1st. proposition of Mr. Patterson's plan, it was agreed to: N. Y. &. N. J. only being no—>

On the question <moved by Mr. King> whether the Committee should rise & Mr. Randolphs propositions be re-reported without alteration, which was in fact a question whether Mr. R's should be adhered to as preferable to those of Mr. Patterson;

Massts. ay. Cont. ay. N. Y. no. N. J. no. Pa. ay. Del. no. Md. divd. Va. ay. N. C. ay. S. C. ay. Geo. ay. [Ayes—7; noes—3; divided—1.]

<insert here from Printed Journal p. 13[4]. Copy of the Resoln. of Mr. R. as altered in the Come: and reported to the House>

The 1. propos (of Mr. Randolph's plan as reported from the Committee): "that Natl. Govt. ought to be established consisting &c". <being> taken up in <the House.>

Mr. Wilson observed that by a Natl. Govt. he did not mean one that would swallow up the State Govts. as seemed to be wished by some gentlemen. He was tenacious of the idea of preserving the latter. He thought, contrary to the opinion of (Col. Hamilton) that they might <not> only subsist but subsist on friendly terms with the former. They were absolutely necessary for certain purposes which the former could not reach. All large Governments must be subdivided into lesser jurisdictions. as Examples he mentioned Persia, Rome, and particularly the divisions & subdivisions of <England by> Alfred.

Col. Hamilton coincided with the proposition <as it stood in the Report>. He had not been understood yesterday. By an abolition of the States, he meant that no boundary could be drawn between the National & State Legislatures; that the former must therefore have indefinite authority. If it were limited at all, the rivalship of the States would gradually subvert it. Even as Corporations the extent of some of them as Va. Massts. &c. would be formidable. *As States*, he thought they ought to be abolished. But he admitted the necessity of leaving in them, subordinate jurisdictions. The examples of Persia & the Roman Empire, cited by (Mr Wilson) were, he thought in favor of his doctrine: the great powers delegated to the Satraps & proconsuls, having frequently produced revolts, and schemes of independence.

Mr. King, wished as everything depended on this proposition, that no objections might be improperly indulged agst. the phraseology of it. He conceived that the import of the terms "States" "Sovereignty" "*national*" "federal," had been often used & applied in the discussion inaccurately & delusively. The States were not "sovereigns" in the sense contended for by some. They did not possess the peculiar features of sovereignty. They could not make war, nor peace, nor alliances, nor treaties. Considering them as political Beings, they were dumb, for they could not speak to any forign Sovereign whatever. They were deaf, for they could not hear any propositions from such Sovereign. They had not even the organs or faculties of defence or offence, for they could not of themselves raise troops, or equip vessels, for war. On the other side, if the Union of the States comprises the idea of a confederation, it comprises that also of consolidation. A Union of the States is a union of the men composing them, from whence a *national* character results to the whole. Congs. can act alone without the States—they can act & their acts will be binding agst. the Instructions of the States. If they declare war, war is de jure declared, captures made in pursuance of it are lawful. No acts of the States can vary the situation, or prevent the judicial consequences. If the States therefore retained some portion of their sovereignty, they had certainly divested themselves of essential portions of it. If they formed a confederacy in some respects—they formed a Nation in others. The Convention could clearly deliberate on & propose any alterations that Congs. could have done under ye. federal articles. and could not Congs. propose by virtue of the last article, a change in any article whatever: And as well that relating to the equality of suffrage, as any other. He made these remarks to obviate some scruples which had been expressed. He doubted much the practicability of annihilating the States; but thought that much of their power ought to be taken from them.

Mr. Martin, said he considered that the separation from G. B. placed the 13 States in a state of nature towards each other; that they would have remained in that state till this time, but for the confederation; that they entered into the confederation on the footing of equality; that they met now to to amend it on the same footing, and that he could never accede to a plan that would introduce an inequality and lay 10 States at the mercy of Va. Massts. and Penna.

Mr. Wilson, could not admit the doctrine that when the Colonies became independent of G. Britain, they became independent also of each other. He read the declaration of Independence, observing thereon that the *United Colonies* were declared to be free & independent States; and inferring that they were independent, not *Individually* but *Unitedly* and that they were confederated as they were independent, States.

Col. Hamilton, assented to the doctrine of Mr. Wilson. He denied the doctrine that the States were thrown into a State of nature He was not yet prepared to admit the doctrine that the Confederacy, could be dissolved by partial infractions of it. He admitted that the States met now on an equal footing but could see no inference from that against concerting a change of the system in this particular. He took this occasion of observing for the <purpose of> appeesing the fears of the <small> States, that two circumstances would render them secure under a national Govt. in which they might lose the equality of rank they now hold: one was the local situation of the 3 largest States Virga. Masts. & Pa. They were separated from each other by distance of place, and equally so by all the peculiarities which distinguish the interests of one State from those of another. No combination therefore could be dreaded. In the second place, as there was a gradation in the States from Va. the largest down to Delaware the smallest, it would always happen that ambitious combinations among a few States might & wd. be counteracted by defensive combinations of greater extent among the rest. No combination has been seen among large Counties merely as such, agst. lesser Counties. The more close the Union of the States, and the more compleat the authority of the whole; the less opportunity will be allowed the stronger States to injure the weaker.

Adjd.

(3) June 28, 1787
[I]n Convention

Mr. L. Martin resumed his discourse, contending that the Genl. Govt. ought to be formed for the States, not for individuals: that if the

404

States were to have votes in proportion to their numbers of people, it would be the same thing whether their <representatives> were chosen by the Legislatures or the people; the smaller States would be equally enslaved; that if the large States have the same interest with the smaller as was urged, there could be no danger in giving them an equal vote; they would not injure themselves, and they could not injure the large ones on that supposition without injuring themselves <and if the interests were not the same the inequality of suffrage wd—be dangerous to the smaller States.>: that it will be in vain to propose any plan offensive to the rulers of the States, whose influence over the people will certainly prevent their adopting it: that the large States were weak at present in proportion to their extent: & could only be made formidable to the small ones, by the weight of their votes; that in case a dissolution of the Union should take place, the small States would have nothing to fear from their power; that if in such a case the three great States should league themselves together, the other ten could do so too: & that he had rather see partial Confederacies take place, than the plan on the table. This was the substance of the residue of his discourse which was delivered with much diffuseness & considerable vehemence.

Mr. Lansing & Mr. Dayton moved to strike out "not." so that the 7 art: might read that the rights of suffrage in the 1st branch ought to be according to the rule established by the Confederation"

Mr. Dayton expressed great anxiety that the question might not be put till tomorrow; Governor. Livingston being kept away by indisposition, and the representation of N. Jersey thereby suspended.

Mr. Williamson. thought that if any political truth could be grounded on mathematical demonstration, it was that if the states were equally sovereign now, and parted with equal proportions of sovereignty, that they would remain equally sovereign. He could not comprehend how the smaller States would be injured in the case, and wished some gentleman would vouchsafe a solution of it. He observed that the small States, if they had a plurality of votes would have an interest in throwing the burdens off their own shoulders on those of the large ones. He begged that the expected addition of new States from the Westward might be kept in view. They would be small States, they would be poor States, they would be unable to pay in proportion to their numbers; their distance from market rendering the produce of their labour less valuable; they would consequently be <tempted> to combine for the purpose of laying burdens on commerce & consumption which would fall with greatest weight on the old States.

Mr. M<adison> sd. he was much disposed to concur in any expedient not inconsistent with fundamental principles, that could remove the difficulty concerning the rule of representation. But he could neither be convinced that the rule contended for was just, nor necessary for the safety of the small States agst. the large States. That it was not just, had been conceded by Mr. Breerly & Mr. Patterson themselves. The expedient proposed by them was a new partition of the territory of the U. States. The fallacy of the reasoning drawn from the equality of Sovereign States in the formation of compacts, lay in confounding mere Treaties, in which were specified certain duties to which the parties were to be bound, and certain rules by which their subjects were to be reciprocally governed in their intercourse, with a compact by which an authority was created paramount to the parties, & making laws for the government of them. If France, England & Spain were to enter into a Treaty for the regulation of commerce &c. with the Prince of Monacho & 4 or 5 other of the smallest sovereigns of Europe, they would not hesitate to treat as equals, and to make the regulations perfectly reciprocal. Wd. the case be the same if a Council were to be formed of deputies from each with authority and discretion, to raise money, levy troops, determine the value of coin &c? Would 30 or 40. million of people submit their fortunes into the hands, of a few thousands? If they did it would only prove that they expected more from the terror of their superior force, than they feared from the selfishness of their feeble <associates> Why are Counties of the same States represented in proportion to their numbers? Is it because the representatives are chosen by the people themselves? so will be the representatives in the National. Legislature. Is it because, the larger have more at stake than the smaller? The case will be the same with the larger & smaller States. Is it because the laws are to operate immediately on their persons & properties? The same is the case in some degree as the articles of confederation stand; the same will be the case in <a far greater degree> under the plan proposed to be substituted. In the cases of captures, of piracies, and of offenses in a federal army, the property & persons of individuals depend on the laws of Congs. By the plan <proposed> a compleat power of taxation, the highest prerogative of supremacy is proposed to be vested in the National Govt. Many other powers are added which assimilate it to the Govt. of individual States. The negative <on the State laws> proposed, will make it an essential branch of the State Legislatures & of course will require that it should be exercised by a body established on like principles with the other branches of those Legislatures.—That it is not necessary to secure the small States agst. the large ones he conceived to be equally obvious: Was a combination of the large ones dreaded? this must arise either from some interest common to Va. Masts. & Pa. & distinguishing them from the other States <or from the mere circumstance of similarity of size>. Did any such common interest exist? In point of situation they could not have been more effectually separated from each other by the most jealous citizen of the most jealous State. In point of manners, Religion and the other circumstances, which sometimes beget affection between different communities, they were not more assimilated than the other States.—In point of the staple productions they were as dissimilar as any three other States in the Union.

The Staple of Masts. was *fish*, of Pa. *flower*, of Va. *Tobo*. Was a Combination to be apprehended from the mere circumstance of equality of size? Experience suggested no such danger. The journals of Congs. did not present any peculiar association of these States in the votes recorded. It had never been seen that different Counties in the same State, conformable in extent, but disagreeing in other circumstances, betrayed a propensity to such combinations. Experience rather taught a contrary lesson. Among individuals of superior eminence & weight in society, rivalships were much more frequent than coalitions. Among independent nations preeminent over their neighbours, the same remark was verified. Carthage & Rome tore one another to pieces instead of uniting their forces to devour the weaker nations of the Earth. The Houses of Austria & France were hostile as long as they remained the greatest powers of Europe. England & France have succeeded to the pre-eminence & to the enmity. To this principle we owe perhaps our liberty. A coalition between those powers would have been fatal to us. Among the principal members of antient & modern confederacies, we find the same effect from the same cause. The contintions, not the coalitions of Sparta, Athens & Thebes, proved fatal to the smaller members of the Amphyctionic Confederacy. The contentions, not the combinations of Prussia & Austria, have distracted & oppressed the Germanic empire. Were the large States formidable *singly* to their smaller neighbours? On this supposition the latter ought to wish for such a general Govt. as will operate with equal energy on the former as on themselves. The more lax the band, the more liberty the larger will have to avail themselves of their superior force. Here again Experience was an instructive monitor. What is ye situation of the weak compared with the strong in those stages of civilization in which the violence of individuals is least controuled by an efficient Government? The Heroic period of Antient Greece the feudal licentiousness of the middle ages of Europe, the existing condition of the American Savages, answer this question. What is the situation of the minor sovereigns in the great society of independent nations, in which the more powerful are under no controul but the nominal authority of the law of Nations? Is not the danger to the former exactly in proportion to their weakness. But there are cases still more in point. What was the condition of the weaker members of the Amphyctionic Confederacy. Plutarch (life of Themistocles) will inform us that it happened but too often that the strongest cities corrupted & awed the weaker, and that Judgment went in favor of the more powerful party. What is the condition of the lesser States in the German Confederacy? We all know that they are exceedingly trampled upon and that they owe their safety as far as they enjoy it, partly to their enlisting themselves, under the rival banners of the preeminent members, partly to alliances with neighbouring Princes which the Constitution of the Empire does not prohibit. What is the state of things in the lax system of the Dutch Confederacy? Holland contains about ½ the people, supplies about ½ of the money, and by her influence, silently & indirectly governs the whole Republic. In a word; the two extremes before us are a perfect separation & a perfect incorporation, of the 13 States.   In the first case they would be independent nations subject to no law, but the law of nations.   In the last, they would be mere counties of one entire republic, subject to one common law.   In the first case the smaller states would have every thing to fear from the larger.   In the last they would have nothing to fear.   The true policy of the small States therefore lies in promoting those principles & that form of Govt. which will most approximate the States to the condition of Counties.   Another consideration may be added.   If the Genl. Govt. be feeble, the large States distrusting its continuance, and foreseeing that their importance & security may depend on their own size & strength, will never submit to a partition.   Give to the Genl. Govt. sufficient energy & permanency, & you remove the objection.   Gradual partitions of the large, & junctions of the small <States> will be facilitated, and time <may> effect that equalization, which is wished for by the small States, now, but can never be accomplished at once.

Mr. Wilson.   The leading argument of those who contend for equality of votes among the States is that the States as such being equal, and being represented not as districts of individuals, but in their political & corporate capacities, are entitled to an equality of suffrage.   According to this mode of reasoning the representation of the burroughs in Engld which has been allowed on all hands to be the rotten part of the Constitution, is perfectly right & proper.   They are like the States represented in their corporate capacity like the States therefore they are entitled to equal voices, old Sarum to as many as London.   And instead of the injury supposed hitherto to be done to London, the true ground of complaint lies with old Sarum;   for London instead of two which is her proper share, sends four representatives to Parliament.

Mr. Sherman.   The question is not what rights naturally belong to men;   but how they may be most equally & effectually guarded in Society.   And if some give up more than others in order to attain this end, there can be <no> room for complaint.   To do otherwise, to require an equal concession from all, if it would create danger to the rights of some, would be sacrificing the end to the means.   The rich man who enters into Society along with the poor man, gives up more than the poor man. yet with an equal vote he is equally safe.   Were he to have more votes than the poor man in proportion to his superior stake, the rights of the poor man would immediately cease to be secure.   This consideration prevailed when the articles of confederation were formed.

<The determination of the question from striking out the word "not" was put off till to morrow at the request of the Deputies of N. York.>

[Dr. Franklin.]

Mr. President

The small progress we have made after 4 or five weeks close attendance & continual reasonings with each other—our different sentiments on almost every question, several of the last producing as many noes as ays, is methinks a melancholy proof of the imperfection of the Human Understanding. We indeed seem to feel our own want of political wisdom, since we have been running about in search of it. We have gone back to ancient history for models of Government, and examined the different forms of those Republics which having been formed with the seeds of their own dissolution now no longer exist. And we have viewed Modern States all round Europe, but find none of their Constitutions suitable to our circumstances.

In this situation of this Assembly, groping as it were in the dark to find political truth, and scarce able to distinguish it when presented to us, how has it happened, Sir, that we have not hitherto once thought of humbly applying to the Father of lights to illuminate our understandings? In the beginning of the Contest with G. Britain, when we were sensible of danger we had daily prayer in this room for the divine protection.—Our prayers, Sir, were heard, and they were graciously answered. All of us who were engaged in the struggle must have observed frequent instances of a Superintending providence in our favor. To that kind providence we owe this happy opportunity of consulting in peace on the means of establishing our future national felicity. And have we now forgotten that powerful friend? or do we imagine that we no longer need his assistance? I have lived, Sir, a long time, and the longer I live, the more convincing proofs I see of this truth—*that God governs in the affairs of men.* And if a sparrow cannot fall to the ground without his notice, is it probable that an empire can rise without his aid? We have been assured, Sir, in the sacred writings, that "except the Lord build the House they labour in vain that build it." I firmly believe this; and I also believe that without his concurring aid we shall succeed in this political building no better than the Builders of Babel: We shall be divided by our little partial local interests; our projects will be confounded, and we ourselves shall become a reproach and bye word down to future ages. And what is worse, mankind may hereafter from this unfortunate instance, despair of establishing Governments by Human Wisdom and leave it to chance, war and conquest.

I therefore beg leave to move—that henceforth prayers imploring the assistance of Heaven, and its blessings on our deliberations, be held in this Assembly every morning before we proceed to business, and that one or more of the Clergy of this City be requested to officiate in that service—

Mr. Sharman seconded the motion.

Mr. Hamilton & several others expressed their apprehensions that however proper such a resolution might have been at the beginning of the convention, it might at this late day, 1. bring on it some disagreeable animadversions. & 2. lead the public to believe that the embarrassments and dissentions within the convention, had suggested this measure. It was answered by Docr. F. Mr. Sherman & others, that the past omission of a duty could not justify a further omission—that the rejection of such a proposition would expose the Convention to more unpleasant animadversions than the adoption of it: and that the alarm out of doors that might be excited for the state of things within. would at least be as likely to do good as ill.

Mr. Williamson, observed that the true cause of the omission could not be mistaken. The Convention had no funds.

Mr. Randolph proposed in order to give a favorable aspect to ye. measure, that a sermon be preached at the request of the convention on 4th of July, the anniversary of Independence,—& thenceforward prayers be used in ye Convention every morning. Dr. Frankn. 2ded. this motion After several unsuccessful attempts for silently postponing the matter by adjourng. the adjournment was at length carried, without any vote on the motion.

(4) June 29, 1787

[I]n Convention

Doctr. Johnson. The controversy must be endless whilst Gentlemen differ in the grounds of their arguments; Those on one side considering the States as districts of people composing one political Society; those on the other considering them as so many political societies. The fact is that the States do exist as political Societies, and a Govt. is to be formed for them in their political capacity, as well as for the individuals composing them. Does it not seem to follow, that if the States as such are to exist they must be armed with some power of self-defence. This is the idea of (Col. Mason) who appears to have looked to the bottom of this matter. Besides the Aristocratic and other interests, which ought to have the means of defending themselves, the States have their interests as such, and are equally entitled to likes means. On the whole he thought that as in some respects the States are to be considered in their political capacity, and in others as districts of individual citizens, the two ideas embraced on different sides, instead of being opposed to each other, ought to be combined; that in *one* branch the *people*, ought to be represented; in the *other*, the *States*.

Mr. Ghorum. The States as now confederated have no doubt a right to refuse to be consolidated, or to be formed into any new system. But he wished the small States which seemed most ready to object, to consider which are to give up most, they or the larger ones. He conceived that a rupture of the Union wd. be an event unhappy for all, but surely the large States would be least unable to take care of themselves, and to make connections with one another. The weak therefore were most interested in establishing some general system for maintaining order. If among individuals, composed partly of weak, and partly of strong, the former most <need> the protection of law &

410

Government, the case is exactly the same with weak & powerful States. What would be the situation of Delaware (for these things he found must be spoken out, & it might as well be done first as last) what wd. be the situation of Delaware in case of a separation of the States? Would she not lie at the mercy of Pennsylvania? would not her true interest lie in being consolidated with her, and ought she not now to wish for such a union with Pa. under one Govt. as will put it out of the power of Pena. to oppress her? Nothing can be more ideal than the danger apprehended by the States, from their being formed into one nation. Massts. was originally three colonies, viz old Massts.—Plymouth—& the province of Mayne. These apprehensions existed then. An incorporation took place; all parties were safe & satisfied; and every distinction is now forgotten. The case was similar with Connecticut & Newhaven. The dread of Union was reciprocal; the consequence of it equally salutary and satisfactory. In like manner N. Jersey has been made one society out of two parts. Should a separation of the States take place, the fate of N. Jersey wd. be worst of all. She has no foreign commerce & can have but little. Pa. & N. York will continue to levy taxes on her consumption. If she consults her interest she wd. beg of all things to be annihilated. The apprehensions of the small States ought to be appeased by another reflection. Massts. will be divided. The province of Maine is already considered as approaching the term of its annexation to it; and Pa. will probably not increase, considering the present state of her population, & other events that may happen. On the whole he considered a Union of the States as necessary to their happiness, & a firm Genl. Govt. as necessary to their Union. He shd. consider it as his duty if his colleagues viewed the matter in the same light he did to stay here as long as any other State would remain with them, in order to agree on some plan that could with propriety be recommended to the people.

<Mr. Elseworth, did not despair. He still trusted that some good plan of Govt. wd. be divised & adopted.>

Mr. Read. He shd. have no objection to the system if it were truly national, but it has too much of a federal mixture in it. The little States he thought had not much to fear. He suspected that the large States felt their want of energy, & wished for a genl. Govt. to supply the defect. Massts. was evidently labouring under her weakness and he believed Delaware wd. not be in much danger if in her neighbourhood. Delaware had enjoyed tranquillity & he flattered himself wd. continue to do so. He was not however so selfish as not to wish for a good Genl. Govt. In order to obtain one the whole States must be incorporated. If the States remain, the representatives of the large ones will stick together, and carry every thing before them. The Executive also will be chosen under the influence of this partiality, and will betray it in his administration. These jealousies are inseparable from the scheme of leaving the States in Existence. They must be done away. The ungranted lands also which

411

have been assumed by particular States must also be given up.   He repeated his approbation of the plan of Mr. Hamilton, & wished it to be substituted in place of that on the table.

Mr. Madison agreed with Docr. Johnson, that the mixed nature of the Govt. ought to be kept in view; but thought too much stress was laid on the rank of the States as political societies.   There was a gradation, he observed from the smallest corporation, with the most limited powers, to the largest empire with the most perfect sovereignty.   He pointed out the limitations on the sovereignty of the States. as now confederated; <their laws in relation to the paramount law of the Confederacy were analogous to that of bye laws to the supreme law, within a State.> Under the proposed Govt. the <powers of the States> will be much farther reduced.   According to the views of every member, the Genl. Govt. will have powers far beyond those exercised by the British Parliament when the States were part of the British Empire.   It will in particular have the power, without the consent of the State Legislatures, to levy money directly on the people themselves; and therefore not to divest such *unequal* portions of the people as composed the several States, of an *equal* voice, would subject the system to the reproaches & evils which have resulted from the vicious representation in G. B.

He entreated the gentlemen representing the small States to renounce a principle wch. was confessedly unjust, which cd. never be admitted, & if admitted must infuse mortality into a Constitution which we wished to last forever.   He prayed them to ponder well the consequences of suffering the Confederacy to go to pieces.   It had been sd. that the want of energy in the large states wd. be a security to the small. It was forgotten that this want of energy proceded from the supposed security of the States agst. all external danger.   Let each State depend on itself for its security, & let apprehensions arise of danger from distant powers or from neighbouring States, & the languishing condition of all the States, large as well as small, wd. soon be transformed into vigorous & high toned Govts.   His great fear was that their Govts. wd. then have too much energy, that these might not only be formidable in the large to the small States, but fatal to the internal liberty of all.   The same causes which have rendered the old world the Theatre of incesssant wars, & have banished liberty from the face of it, wd. soon produce the same effects here.   The weakness & jealousy of the small States wd. quickly introduce some regular military force agst. sudden danger from their powerful neighbours.   The example wd. be followed by others, and wd. soon become universal.   In time of actual war, great discretionary powers are constantly given to the Executive Magistrate.   Constant apprehension of War, has the same tendency to render the head too large for the body.   A standing military force, with an overgrown Executive will not long be safe companions to liberty.   The means of defence agst. foreign danger, have been always the instruments of tyranny at home. Among the Romans it was a standing maxim to excite a war, whenever a revolt was apprehended.   Throughout all Europe, the armies kept up under the pretext of defending, have enslaved the people.   It is perhaps questionable, whether the best concerted system of absolute power in Europe cd. maintain itself, in a situation, where no alarms of external danger cd. tame the people to the domestic yoke.   The insular situation of G. Britain was the principal cause of her being an exception to the general fate of Europe.   It has rendered less defence necessary, and admitted a kind of defence wch. cd. not be used for the purpose of oppression.—These consequences he conceived ought to be apprehended whether the States should run into a total separation from each other, or shd. enter into partial confederacies.   Either event wd. be truly deplorable; & those who might be accessary to either, could never be forgiven by their Country, nor by themselves.

Mr. Hamilton observed that individuals forming political Societies modify their rights differently, with regard to suffrage.   Examples of it are found in all the States.   In all of them some individuals are deprived of the right altogether, not having the requisite qualification of property. In some of the States the right of suffrage is allowed in some cases and refused in others.   To vote for a member in one branch, a certain quantum of property, to vote for a member in another branch of the Legislature, a higher quantum of property is required.   In like manner States may modify their right of suffrage differently, the larger exercising a larger, the smaller a smaller share of it.   But as States are a collection of individual men which ought we to respect most, the rights of the people composing them, or of the artificial beings resulting from the composition.   Nothing could be more preposterous or absurd than to sacrifice the former to the latter.   It has been sd. that if the smaller States renounce their *equality*, they renounce at the same time their *liberty*.   The truth is it is a contest for power, not for liberty.   Will the men composing the small States be less free than those composing the larger.   The State of Delaware having 40,000 souls will *lose power*, if she has 1/10 only of the votes allowed to Pa. having 400,000: but will the people of Del: *be less free*, if each citizen has an equal vote with each citizen of Pa.   He admitted that common residence within the same State would produce a certain degree of attachment; and that this principle might have a certain influence in public affairs.   He thought however that this might by some precautions be in a great measure excluded: and that no material inconvenience could result from it, as there could not be any ground for combination among the States whose influence was most dreaded.   The only considerable distinction of interests, lay between the carrying & non-carrying States, which divide instead of uniting the largest States.   No considerable inconvenience had been found from the division of the State of N. York into different districts, of different sizes.

Some of the consequences of a dissolution of the Union, and the establishment of partial confederacies, had been pointed out. He would add another of a most serious nature. Alliances will immediately be formed with different rival & hostile nations of Europes, who will foment disturbances among ourselves, and make us parties to all their own quarrels. Foreign nations having American dominions are & must be jealous of us. Their representatives betray the utmost anxiety for our fate, & for the result of this meeting, which must have an essential influence on it.—It had been said that respectability in the eyes of foreign Nations was not the object at which we aimed; that the proper object of republican Government was domestic tranquillity & happiness. This was an ideal distinction. No Governmt. could give us tranquillity & happiness at home, which did not possess sufficient stability and strength to make us respectable abroad. This was the critical moment for forming such a government. We should run every risk in trusting to future amendments. As yet we retain the habits of union. We are weak & sensible of our weakness. Henceforward the motives will become feebler, and the difficulties greater. It is a miracle that we were now here exercising our tranquil & free deliberations on the subject. It would be madness to trust to future miracles. A thousand causes must obstruct a reproduction of them.

<Mr. Peirce considered the equality of votes under the Confederation as the great source of the public difficulties. The members of Congs. were advocates for local advantages. State distinctions must be sacrificed as far as the general good required: but without destroying the States. Tho' from a small State he felt himself a Citizen of the U.S.>

Mr. Gerry, urged that we never were independent States, were not such now, & never could be even on the principles of the Confederation. The States & the advocates for them were intoxicated with the idea of their *sovereignty*. He was a member of Congress at the time the federal articles were formed. The injustice of allowing each State an equal vote was long insisted on. He voted for it, but it was agst. his Judgment, and under the pressure of public danger, and the obstinacy of the lesser States. The present confederation he considered as dissolving. The fate of the Union will be decided by the Convention. If they do not agree on something, few delegates will probably be appointed to Congs. If they do Congs. will probably be kept up till the new System should be adopted— He lamented that instead of coming here like a band of brothers, belonging to the same family, we seemed to have brought with us the spirit of political negociators.

Mr. L. Martin. remarked that the language of the States being *Sovereign & independent*, was once familiar & understood; though it seemed now so strange & obscure. He read those passages in the articles of Confederation, which describe them in that language.

On the question as moved by Mr. Lansing. Shall the word "not" be struck out.

Massts. no. Cont. ay. N. Y. ay. N. J. ay. Pa. no. Del. ay. Md. divd. Va. no. N. C. no. S. C. no. Geo. no [Ayes—4; noes—6; divided—1.]

On the <motion to agree to the clause as reported. "that the rule of suffrage in the 1st. branch ought not to be according to that established by the Articles of Confederation.> Mass. ay. Cont. <no> N. Y. no. N. J. no. Pa. ay. Del. no. Md. divd. Va. ay. N. C. ay. S. C. ay. Geo. ay. [Ayes—6; noes—4; divided—1.]

Docr. Johnson & Mr. Elseworth moved to postpone the residue of the clause, and take up—ye 8—Resol: <On question>

Mass. no. Cont. ay. N. Y. ay. <N. J. ay.> Pa. ay. Del. no. Md. ay. Va. ay. N. C. ay. S. C. ay. Geo. ay. [Ayes—9; noes—2.]

Mr. Elseworth moved that the rule of suffrage in the 2d. branch be the same with that established by the articles of confederation". He was not sorry on the whole he said that the vote just passed, had determined against this rule in the first branch. He hoped it would become a ground of compromise with regard to the 2d. branch. We were partly national; partly federal. The proportional representation in the first branch was conformable to the national principle & would secure the large States agst. the small. An equality of voices was conformable to the federal principle and was necessary to secure the Small States agst. the large. He trusted that on this middle ground a compromise would take place. He did not see that it could on any other. And if no compromise should take place, our meeting would not only be in vain but worse than in vain. To the Eastward he was sure Massts. was the only State that would listen to a proposition for excluding the States as equal political Societies, from an equal voice in both branches. The others would risk every consequence rather than part with so dear a right. An attempt to deprive them of it, was at once cutting the body <of America> in two, and as he supposed would be the case, somewhere about this part of it. The large States he conceived would notwithstanding the equality of votes, have an influence that would maintain their superiority. Holland, as had been admitted (by Mr. <Madison>) had, notwithstanding a like equality in the Dutch Confederacy, a prevailing influence in the public measures. The power of self-defence was essential to the small States. Nature had given it to the smallest insect of the creation. He could never admit that there was no danger of combinations among the large States. They will like individuals find out and avail themselves of the advantage to be gained by it. It was true the danger would be greater, if they were contiguous and had a more immediate common interest. A defensive combination of the small States was rendered more difficult by their greater number. He would mention another consideration of great weight. The existing confederation was founded on the equality of the States in the article of suffrage:

was it meant to pay no regard to this antecedent plighted faith. Let a strong Executive, a Judiciary & Legislative power be created; but Let not too much be attempted; by which all may be lost. He was not in general a half-way man, yet he preferred doing half the good we could, rather than do nothing at all. The other half may be added, when the necessity shall be more fully experienced.

Mr. Baldwin would have wished that the powers of the General Legislature had been defined, before the mode of constituting it had been agitated. He should vote against the motion of Mr. Elseworth, tho' he did not like the Resolution as it stood in the Report of the Committee of the whole. He thought the second branch ought to be the representation of property, and that in forming it therefore some reference ought to be had to the relative wealth of their Constituents, and to the principles on which the Senate of Massts. was constituted. He concurred with those who thought it wd. be impossible for the Genl. Legislature to extend its cares to the local matters of the States.

Adjd.

G. LETTER FROM THE FEDERAL FARMER, NO. 1

October 8, 1787

The present moment discovers a new face in our affairs. Our object has been all along, to reform our federal system, and to strengthen our governments—to establish peace, order and justice in the community—but a new object now presents. The plan of government now proposed is evidently calculated totally to change, in time, our condition as a people. Instead of being thirteen republics, under a federal head, it is clearly designed to make us one consolidated government. Of this, I think, I shall fully convince you, in my following letters on this subject. This consolidation of the states has been the object of several men in this country for some time past. Whether such a change can ever be effected in any manner; whether it can be effected without convulsions and civil wars; whether such a change will not totally destroy the liberties of this country—time only can determine.

To have a just idea of the government before us, and to shew that a consolidated one is the object in view, it is necessary not only to examine the plan, but also its history, and the politics of its particular friends.

The confederation was formed when great confidence was placed in the voluntary exertions of individuals, and of the respective states; and the framers of it, to guard against usurpation, so limited and checked the powers, that, in many respects, they are inadequate to the exigencies of the union. We find, therefore, members of congress urging alterations in the federal system almost as soon as it was adopted. It was early proposed to vest congress with powers to levy an impost, to regulate trade, etc. but such was known to be the caution of the states in parting with power, that the vestment, even of these, was proposed to be under several checks and limitations. During the war, the general confusion, and the introduction of paper money, infused in the minds of people vague ideas respecting government and credit. We expected too much from the return of peace, and of course we have been disappointed. Our governments have been new and unsettled; and several legislatures, by making tender, suspension, and paper money laws, have given just cause of uneasiness to creditors. By these and other causes, several orders of men in the community have been prepared, by degrees, for a change of government; and this very abuse of power in the legislatures, which, in some cases, has been charged upon the democratic part of the community, has furnished aristocratical men with those very weapons, and those very means, with which, in great measure, they are rapidly effecting their favourite object. And should an oppressive government be the consequence of the proposed change, posterity may reproach not only a few overbearing unprincipled men, but those parties in the states which have misused their powers.

The conduct of several legislatures, touching paper money, and tender laws, has prepared many honest men for changes in government, which otherwise they would not have thought of—when by the evils, on the one hand, and by the secret instigations of artful men, on the other, the minds of men were become sufficiently uneasy, a bold step was taken, which is usually followed by a revolution, or a civil war. A general convention for mere commercial purposes was moved for—the authors of this measure saw that the people's attention was turned solely to the amendment of the federal system; and that, had the idea of a total change been started, probably no state would have appointed members to the convention. The idea of destroying, ultimately, the state government, and forming one consolidated system, could not have been admitted—a convention, therefore, merely for vesting in congress power to regulate trade was proposed. This was pleasing to the commercial towns; and the landed people had little or no concern about it. September, 1786, a few men from the middle states met at Annapolis, and hastily proposed a convention to be held in May, 1787, for the purpose, generally, of amending the confederation—this was done before the delegates of Massachusetts, and of the other states arrived—still not a word was said about destroying the old constitution, and making a new one—The states still unsuspecting, and not aware that they were passing the Rubicon, appointed members to the new convention, for the sole and express purpose of revising and amending the confederation—and, probably, not one man in ten thousand in the United States, till within these ten or twelve days, had an idea that the old ship was to be destroyed, and he put to the alternative of embarking in the new ship presented, or of being left in danger of sinking—The States, I believe, universally supposed the convention would report alterations in the confederation, which would pass an examination in congress, and after being agreed to there, would be confirmed by all the legislatures, or be rejected. Virginia made a very respectable appointment, and placed at the head of it the first man in America: In this appointment there was a mixture of political characters; but Pennsylvania appointed principally those men who are esteemed aristocratical. Here the favourite moment for changing the government was evidently discerned by a few men, who seized it with address. Ten other states appointed, and tho' they chose men principally connected with commerce and the judicial department yet they appointed many good republican characters—had they all attended we should now see, I am persuaded a better system presented. The non-attendance of eight or nine men, who were appointed members of the convention, I shall ever consider as a very unfortunate event to the United States.—Had they attended, I am pretty clear, that the result of the convention would not have had that strong tendency to aristocracy now discernable in every part of the plan. There would not have been so great an accumulation of powers, especially as to the internal police of the country, in a few hands, as the constitution reported proposes to vest in them—the young visionary men, and the consolidating aristocracy, would have been more restrained than they have been. Eleven states met in the convention, and after four months close attention presented the new constitution, to be adopted or rejected by the people. The uneasy and fickle part of the community may be prepared to receive any form of government; but, I presume, the enlightened and substantial part will give any constitution presented for their adoption, a candid and thorough examination; and silence those designing or empty men, who weakly and rashly attempt to precipitate the adoption of a system of so much importance—We shall view the convention with proper respect—and, at the same time, that we reflect there were men of abilities and integrity in it, we must recollect how disproportionably the democratic and aristocratic parts of the community were represented—Perhaps the judicious friends and opposers of the new constitution will agree, that it is best to let it rest solely on its own merits, or be condemned for its own defects.

In the first place, I shall premise, that the plan proposed is a plan of accommodation—and that it is in this way only, and by giving up a part of our opinions, that we can ever expect to obtain a government founded in freedom and compact. This circumstance candid men will always keep in view, in the discussion of this subject.

The plan proposed appears to be partly federal, but principally however, calculated ultimately to make the states one consolidated government.

The first interesting question, therefore suggested, is, how far the states can be consolidated into one entire government on free principles. In considering this question extensive objects are to be taken into view, and important changes in the forms of government to be carefully attended to in all their consequences. The happiness of the people at large must be the great object with every honest statesman, and he will direct every movement to this point. If we are so situated as a people, as not to be able to enjoy equal happiness and advantages under one government, the consolidation of the states cannot be admitted.

There are three different forms of free government under which the United States may exist as one nation; and now is, perhaps, the time to determine to which we will direct our views. 1. Distinct republics connected under a federal head. In this case the respective state governments must be the principal guardians of the peoples rights, and exclusively regulate their internal police; in them must rest the balance of government. The congress of the states, or federal head, must consist of delegates amenable to, and removeable by the respective states: This congress must have general directing powers; powers to require men and monies of the states; to make treaties, peace and war; to direct the operations of armies, etc. Under this federal modification of government, the powers of congress would be rather advisory or recommendatory than coercive. 2. We may do away the several state governments, and form or consolidate all the states into one entire government, with one executive, one judiciary, and one legislature, consisting of senators and representatives collected from all parts of the union: In this case there would be a compleat consolidation of the states. 3. We may consolidate the states as to certain national objects, and leave them severally distinct independent republics, as to internal police generally. Let the general government consist of an executive, a judiciary, and balanced legislature, and its powers extend exclusively to all foreign concerns, causes arising on the seas to commerce, imports, armies, navies, Indian affairs, peace and war, and to a few internal concerns of the community; to the coin, post-offices, weights and measures, a general plan for the militia, to naturalization, *and, perhaps to bankruptcies,* leaving the internal police of the community, in other respects, exclusively to the state governments; as the administration of justice in all causes arising internally, the laying and collecting of internal taxes, and the forming of the militia according to a general plan prescribed. In this case there would be a compleat consolidation, *quoad* certain objects only.

Touching the first, or federal plan, I do not think much can be said in its favor: The sovereignty of the nation, without coercive and efficient powers to collect the strength of it, cannot always be depended on to answer the purposes of government; and in a congress of representatives of sovereign states, there must necessarily be an unreasonable mixture of powers in the same hands.

As to the second, or compleat consolidating plan, it deserves to be carefully considered at this time, by every American: If it be impracticable, it is a fatal error to model our governments, directing our views ultimately to it.

The third plan, or partial consolidation, is, in my opinion, the only one that can secure the freedom and happiness of this people. I once had some general ideas that the second plan was practicable, but from long attention, and the proceedings of the convention, I am fully satisfied, that this third plan is the only one we can with safety and propriety proceed upon. Making this the standard to point out, with candor and fairness, the parts of the new constitution which appear to be improper, is my object. The convention appears to have proposed the partial consolidation evidently with a view to collect all powers ultimately, in the United States into one entire government; and from its views in this respect, and from the tenacity of the small states to have an equal vote in the senate, probably originated the greatest defects in the proposed plan.

Independant of the opinions of many great authors, that a free elective government cannot be extended over large territories, a few reflections must evince, that one government and general legislation alone, never can extend equal benefits to all parts of the United States: Different laws, customs, and opinions exist in the different states, which by a uniform system of laws would be unreasonably invaded. The United States contain about a million of square miles, and in half a century will, probably, contain ten millions of people; and from the center to the extremes is about 800 miles.

Before we do away the state governments, or adopt measures that will tend to abolish them, and to consolidate the states into one entire government, several principles should be considered and facts ascertained:—These, and my examination into the essential parts of the proposed plan, I shall pursue in my next.

Your's &c.

The Federal Farmer.

H. ALEXANDER HAMILTON, THE FEDERALIST, NO. 9

November 21, 1787

To the People of the State of New York.

A Firm Union will be of the utmost moment to the peace and liberty of the States as a barrier against domestic faction and insurrection. It is impossible to read the history of the petty Republics of Greece and Italy, without feeling sensations of horror and disgust at the distractions with which they were continually agitated, and at the rapid succession of revolutions, by which they were kept in a state of perpetual vibration, between the extremes of tyranny and anarchy. If they exhibit occasional calms, these only serve as short-lived contrasts to the furious storms that are to succeed. If now and then intervals of felicity open themselves to view, we behold them with a mixture of regret arising from the reflection that the pleasing scenes before us are soon to be overwhelmed by the tempestuous waves of sedition and party-rage. If momentary rays of glory break forth from the gloom, while they dazzle us with a transient and fleeting brilliancy, they at the same time admonish us to lament that the vices of government should pervert the direction and tarnish the lustre of those bright talents and exalted indowments, for which the favoured soils, that produced them, have been so justly celebrated.

From the disorders that disfigure the annals of those republics, the advocates of despotism have drawn arguments, not only against the forms of republican government, but against the very principles of civil liberty. They have decried all free government, as inconsistent with the order of society, and have indulged themselves in malicious exultation over its friends and partizans. Happily for mankind, stupendous fabrics reared on the basis of liberty, which have flourished for ages, have in a few glorious instances refuted their gloomy sophisms. And, I trust, America will be the broad and solid foundation of other edifices not less magnificent, which will be equally permanent monuments of their errors.

But it is not to be denied that the portraits, they have sketched of republican government, were too just copies of the originals from which they were taken. If it had been found impracticable, to have devised models of a more perfect structure, the enlightened friends to liberty would have been obliged to abandon the cause of that species of government as indefensible. The science of politics, however, like most other sciences has received great improvement. The efficacy of various principles is now well understood, which were either not known at all, or imperfectly known to the ancients. The regular distribution of power into distinct departments—the introduction of legislative ballances and checks—the institution of courts composed of judges, holding their offices during good behaviour—the representation of the people in the legislature by deputies of their own election—these are either wholly new discoveries or have made their principal progress towards perfection in modern times. They are means, and powerful means, by which the excellencies of republican government may be retained and its imperfections lessened or avoided. To this catalogue of circumstances, that tend to the amelioration of popular systems of civil government, I shall venture, however novel it may appear to some, to add one more on a principle, which has been made the foundation of an objection to the New Constitution, I mean the ENLARGEMENT of the ORBIT within which such systems are to revolve either in respect to the dimensions of a single State, or to the consolidation of several smaller States into one great confederacy. The latter is that which immediately concerns the object under consideration. It will however be of use to examine the principle in its application to a single State which shall be attended to in another place.

The utility of a confederacy, as well to suppress faction and to guard the internal tranquillity of States, as to increase their external force and security, is in reality not a new idea. It has been practiced upon in different countries and ages, and has received the sanction of the most applauded writers, on the subjects of politics. The opponents of the PLAN proposed have with great assiduity cited and circulated the observations of Montesquieu on the necessity of a contracted territory for a republican government. But they seem not to have been apprised of the sentiments of that great man expressed in another part of his work, nor to have adverted to the consequences of the principle to which they subscribe, with such ready acquiescence.

When Montesquieu recommends a small extent for republics, the standards he had in view were of dimensions, far short of the limits of almost every one of these States. Neither Virginia, Massachusetts, Pennsylvania, New-York, North-Carolina, nor Georgia, can by any means be compared with the models, from which he reasoned and to which the terms of his description apply. If we therefore take his ideas on this point, as the criterion of truth, we shall be driven to the alternative, either of taking refuge at once in the arms of monarchy, or of splitting ourselves into an infinity of little jealous, clashing, tumultuous commonwealths, the wretched nurseries of unceasing discord and the miserable objects of universal pity or contempt. Some of the writers, who have come forward on the other side of the question, seem to have been aware of the dilemma; and have even been bold enough to hint at the division of the larger States, as a desirable thing. Such an infatuated policy, such a desperate expedient, might, by the multiplication of petty offices, answer the views of men, who possess not qualifications to extend their influence beyond the narrow circles of personal intrigue, but it could never promote the greatness or happiness of the people of America.

Referring the examination of the principle itself to another place, as has been already mentioned, it will be sufficient to remark here, that in the sense of the author who has been most emphatically quoted upon the occasion, it would only dictate a reduction of the SIZE of the more considerable MEMBERS of the Union; but would not militate against their being all comprehended in one Confederate Government. And this is the true question, in the discussion of which we are at present interested.

So far are the suggestions of Montesquieu from standing in opposition to a general Union of the States, that he explicitly treats of a CON-FEDERATE REPUBLIC as the expedient for extending the sphere of popular government and reconciling the advantages of monarchy with those of republicanism.

"It is very probable (says he [†]) that mankind would have been obliged, at length, to live constantly under the government of a SINGLE

† *Spirit of Laws, Vol. I. Book IX. Chap. I.*

PERSON, had they not contrived a kind of constitution, that has all the internal advantages of a republican, together with the external force of a monarchial government. I mean a CONFEDERATE REPUBLIC.

"This form of Government is a Convention, by which several smaller *States* agree to become members of a larger *one*, which they intend to form. It is a kind of assemblage of societies, that constitute a new one, capable of encreasing by means of new associations, till they arrive to such a degree of power as to be able to provide for the security of the united body.

"A republic of this kind, able to withstand an external force, may support itself without any internal corruption. The form of this society prevents all manner of inconveniencies.

"If a single member should attempt to usurp the supreme authority, he could not be supposed to have an equal authority and credit, in all the confederate states. Were he to have too great influence over one, this would alarm the rest. Were he to subdue a part, that which would still remain free might oppose him with forces, independent of those which he had usurped, and overpower him before he could be settled in his usurpation.

"Should a popular insurrection happen, in one of the confederate States, the others are able to quell it. Should abuses creep into one part, they are reformed by those that remain sound. The State may be destroyed on one side, and not on the other; the confederacy may be dissolved, and the confederates preserve their sovereignty.

"As this government is composed of small republics it enjoys the internal happiness of each, and with respect to its external situation it is possessed, by means of the association of all the advantages of large monarchies."

I have thought it proper to quote at length these interesting passages, because they contain a luminous abrigement of the principal arguments in favour of the Union, and must effectually remove the false impressions, which a misapplication of other parts of the work was calculated to produce. They have at the same time an intimate connection with the more immediate design of this Paper; which is to illustrate the tendency of the Union to repress domestic faction and insurrection.

A distinction, more subtle than accurate has been raised between a *confederacy* and a *consolidation* of the States. The essential characteristic of the first is said to be, the restriction of its authority to the members in their collective capacities, without reaching to the individuals of whom they are composed. It is contended that the national council ought to have no concern with any object of internal administration. An exact equality of suffrage between the members has also been insisted upon as a leading feature of a Confederate Government. These positions are in the main arbitary; they are supported neither by principle nor precedent. It has indeed happened that governments of this kind have generally operated in the manner, which the distinction, taken notice of, supposes to be inherent in their nature—but there have been in most of them extensive exceptions to the practice, which serve to prove as far as example will go, that there is no absolute rule on the subject. And it will be clearly shewn, in the course of this investigation, that as far as the principle contended for has prevailed, it has been the cause of incurable disorder and imbecility in the government.

The definition of a *Confederate Republic* seems simply to be, an "assemblage of societies" or an association of two or more States into one State. The extent, modifications and objects of the Fœderal authority are mere matters of discretion. So long as the separate organisation of the members be not abolished, so long as it exists by a constitutional necessity for local purposes, though it should be in perfect subordination to the general authority of the Union, it would still be, in fact and in theory, an association of States, or a confederacy. The proposed Constitution, so far from implying an abolition of the State Governments, makes them constituent parts of the national sovereignty by allowing them a direct representation in the Senate, and leaves in their possession certain exclusive and very important portions of sovereign power. This fully corresponds, in every rational import of the terms, with the idea of a Fœderal Government.

In the Lycian confederacy, which consisted of twenty three CITIES or republics, the largest were intitled to *three* votes in the COMMON COUNCIL, those of the middle class to *two* and the smallest to *one*. The COMMON COUNCIL had the appointment of all the judges and magistrates of the respective CITIES. This was certainly the most delicate species of interference in their internal administration; for if there be any thing, that seems exclusively appropriated to the local jurisdictions, it is the appointment of their own officers. Yet Montesquieu, speaking of this association, says "Were I to give a model of an excellent confederate republic, it would be that of Lycia." Thus we perceive that the distinctions insisted upon were not within the contemplation of this enlightened civilian, and we shall be led to conclude that they are the novel refinements of an erroneous theory.

PUBLIUS.

I. ALEXANDER HAMILTON, THE FEDERALIST, NO. 15

December 1, 1787

To the People of the State of New York.

In the course of the preceding papers, I have endeavoured, my Fellow Citizens, to place before you in a clear and convincing light, the importance of Union to your political safety and happiness. I have unfolded to you a complication of dangers to which you would be exposed should you permit that sacred knot which binds the people of America together to be severed or dissolved by ambition or by avarice, by jealousy or by misrepresentation. In the sequel of the inquiry, through which I propose to accompany you, the truths intended to be inculcated will receive further confirmation from facts and arguments hitherto unnoticed. If the road, over which you will still have to pass, should in some places appear to you tedious or irksome, you will recollect, that you are in quest of information on a subject the most momentous which can engage the attention of a free people: that the field through which you have to travel is in itself spacious, and that the difficulties of the journey have been unnecessarily increased by the mazes with which sophistry has beset the way. It will be my aim to remove the obstacles to your progress in as compendious a manner, as it can be done, without sacrificing utility to dispatch.

In pursuance of the plan, which I have laid down, for the discussion of the subject, the point next in order to be examined is the "insufficiency of the present confederation to the preservation of the Union." It may perhaps be asked, what need is there of reasoning or proof to illustrate a position, which is not either controverted or doubted; to which the understandings and feelings of all classes of men assent; and which in substance is admitted by the opponents as well as by the friends of the New Constitution? It must in truth be acknowleged that however these may differ in other respects, they in general appear to harmonise in this sentiment at least, that there are material imperfections in our national system, and that something is necessary to be done to rescue us from impending anarchy. The facts that support this opinion are no longer objects of speculation. They have forced themselves upon the sensibility of the people at large, and have at length extorted from those, whose mistaken policy has had the principal share in precipitating the extremity, at which we are arrived, a reluctant confession of the reality of those defects in the scheme of our Fœderal Government, which have been long pointed out and regretted by the intelligent friends of the Union.

We may indeed with propriety be said to have reached almost the last stage of national humiliation. There is scarcely any thing that can wound the pride, or degrade the character of an independent nation, which we do not experience. Are there engagements to the performance of which we are held by every tie respectable among men? These are the subjects of constant and unblushing violation. Do we owe debts to foreigners and to our own citizens contracted in a time of imminent peril, for the preservation of our political existence? These remain without any proper or satisfactory provision for their discharge. Have we valuable territories and important posts in the possession of a foreign power, which by express stipulations ought long since to have been surrendered? These are still retained, to the prejudice of our interests not less than of our rights. Are we in a condition to resent, or to repel the aggression? We have neither troops nor treasury nor government.[†] Are we even in a condition to remonstrate with dignity? The just imputations on our own faith, in respect to the same treaty, ought first to be removed. Are we entitled by nature and compact to a free participation in the navigation of the Mississippi? Spain excludes us from it. Is public credit an indispensable resource in time of public danger? We seem to have abandoned its cause as desperate and irretrievable. Is commerce of importance to national wealth? Ours is at the lowest point of declension. Is respectability in the eyes of foreign powers a safeguard against foreign encroachments? The imbecility of our Government even forbids them to treat with us: Our ambassadors abroad are the mere pageants of mimic sovereignty. Is a violent and unnatural decrease in the value of land a symptom of national distress? The price of improved land in most parts of the country is much lower than can be accounted for by the quantity of waste land at market, and can only be fully explained by that want of private and public confidence, which are so alarmingly prevalent among all ranks and which have a direct tendency to depreciate property of every kind. Is private credit the friend and patron of industry? That most useful kind which relates to borrowing and lending is reduced within the narrowest limits, and this still more from an opinion of insecurity than from the scarcity of money. To shorten an enumeration of particulars which can afford neither pleasure nor instruction it may in general be demanded, what indication is there of national disorder, poverty and insignificance that could befal a community so peculiarly blessed with natural advantages as we are, which does not form a part of the dark catalogue of our public misfortunes?

This is the melancholy situation, to which we have been brought by those very maxims and councils, which would now deter us from adopting the proposed constitution; and which not content with having conducted us to the brink of a precipice, seem resolved to plunge us into the abyss, that awaits us below. Here, my Countrymen, impelled by every motive that ought to influence an enlightened people, let us make a firm stand for our safety, our tranquillity, our dignity, our reputation. Let us at last break the fatal charm which has too long seduced us from the paths of felicity and prosperity.

It is true, as has been before observed, that facts too stubborn to be resisted have produced a species of general assent to the abstract proposition that there exist material defects in our national system; but the usefulness of the concession, on the part of the old adversaries of fœderal measures, is destroyed by a strenuous opposition to a remedy, upon the only principles, that can give it a chance of success. While they admit that the Government of the United States is destitute of energy; they contend against conferring upon it those powers which are requisite

† *I mean for the Union.*

to supply that energy: They seem still to aim at things repugnant and irreconcilable—at an augmentation of Fœderal authority without a diminution of State authority—at sovereignty in the Union and complete independence in the members. They still in fine seem to cherish with blind devotion the political monster of an *imperium in imperio*. This renders a full display of the principal defects of the confederation necessary, in order to shew, that the evils we experience do not proceed from minute or partial imperfections, but from fundamental errors in the structure of the building which cannot be amended otherwise than by an alteration in the first principles and main pillars of the fabric.

The great and radical vice in the construction of the existing Confederation is in the principle of LEGISLATION for STATES or GOVERNMENTS, in their CORPORATE or COLLECTIVE CAPACITIES and as contradistinguished from the INDIVIDUALS of whom they consist. Though this principle does not run through all the powers delegated to the Union; yet it pervades and governs those, on which the efficacy of the rest depends. Except as to the rule of apportionment, the United States have an indefinite discretion to make requisitions for men and money; but they have no authority to raise either by regulations extending to the individual citizens of America. The consequence of this is, that though in theory their resolutions concerning those objects are laws, constitutionally binding on the members of the Union, yet in practice they are mere recommendations, which the States observe or disregard at their option.

It is a singular instance of the capriciousness of the human mind, that after all the admonitions we have had from experience on this head, there should still be found men, who object to the New Constitution for deviating from a principle which has been found the bane of the old; and which is in itself evidently incompatible with the idea of GOVERNMENT; a principle in short which if it is to be executed at all must substitute the violent and sanguinary agency of the sword to the mild influence of the Magistracy.

There is nothing absurd or impracticable in the idea of a league or alliance between independent nations, for certain defined purposes precisely stated in a treaty; regulating all the details of time, place, circumstance and quantity; leaving nothing to future discretion; and depending for its execution on the good faith of the parties. Compacts of this kind exist among all civilized nations subject to the usual vicissitudes of peace and war, of observance and non observance, as the interests or passions of the contracting powers dictate. In the early part of the present century, there was an epidemical rage in Europe for this species of compacts; from which the politicians of the times fondly hoped for benefits which were never realised. With a view to establishing the equilibrium of power and the peace of that part of the world, all the resources of negotiation were exhausted, and triple and quadruple alliances were formed; but they were scarcely formed before they were broken, giving an instructive but afflicting lesson to mankind how little dependence is to be placed on treaties which have no other sanction than the obligations of good faith; and which oppose general considerations of peace and justice to the impulse of any immediate interest and passion.

If the particular States in this country are disposed to stand in a similar relation to each other, and to drop the project of a general DISCRETIONARY SUPERINTENDENCE, the scheme would indeed be pernicious, and would entail upon us all the mischiefs that have been enumerated under the first head; but it would have the merit of being at least consistent and practicable. Abandoning all views towards a confederate Government, this would bring us to a simple alliance offensive and defensive; and would place us in a situation to be alternately friends and enemies of each other as our mutual jealousies and rivalships nourished by the intrigues of foreign nations should prescribe to us.

But if we are unwilling to be placed in this perilous situation; if we will still adhere to the design of a national government, or which is the same thing of a superintending power under the direction of a common Council, we must resolve to incorporate into our plan those ingredients which may be considered as forming the characteristic difference between a league and a government; we must extend the authority of the union to the persons of the citizens,—the only proper objects of government.

Government implies the power of making laws. It is essential to the idea of a law, that it be attended with a sanction; or, in other words, a penalty or punishment for disobedience. If there be no penalty annexed to disobedience, the resolutions or commands which pretend to be laws will in fact amount to nothing more than advice or recommendation. This penalty, whatever it may be, can only be inflicted in two ways; by the agency of the Courts and Ministers of Justice, or by military force; by the COERTION of the magistracy, or by the COERTION of arms. The first kind can evidently apply only to men—the last kind must of necessity be employed against bodies politic, or communities or States. It is evident, that there is no process of a court by which their observance of the laws can in the last resort be enforced. Sentences may be denounced against them for violations of their duty; but these sentences can only be carried into execution by the sword. In an association where the general authority is confined to the collective bodies of the communities that compose it, every breach of the laws must involve a state of war, and military execution must become the only instrument of civil obedience. Such a state of things can certainly not deserve the name of government, nor would any prudent man choose to commit his happiness to it.

There was a time when we were told that breaches, by the States, of the regulations of the fœderal authority were not to be expected—that a sense of common interest would preside over the conduct of the respective members, and would beget a full compliance with all the constitutional requisitions of the Union. This language at the present day would appear as wild as a great part of what we now hear from the same quarter will be thought, when we shall have received further lessons from that best oracle of wisdom, experience. It at all times betrayed an ignorance of the true springs by which human conduct is actuated, and belied the original inducements to the establishment of civil power. Why has government been instituted at all? Because the passions of men will not conform to the dictates of reason and justice, without constraint. Has it been found that bodies of men act with more rectitude or greater disinterestedness than individuals? The contrary of this has been inferred by all accurate observers of the conduct of mankind; and the inference is founded upon obvious reasons. Regard to reputation has a less active influence, when the infamy of a bad action is to be divided among a number, than when it is to fall singly upon one. A spirit of faction which is apt to mingle its poison in the deliberations of all bodies of men, will often hurry the persons of whom they are composed into improprieties and excesses, for which they would blush in a private capacity.

In addition to all this, there is in the nature of sovereign power an impatience of controul, that disposes those who are invested with the exercise of it, to look with an evil eye upon all external attempts to restrain or direct its operations. From this spirit it happens that in every political association which is formed upon the principle of uniting in a common interest a number of lesser sovereignties, there will be found a kind of excentric tendency in the subordinate or inferior orbs, by the operation of which there will be a perpetual effort in each to fly off from the common center. This tendency is not difficult to be accounted for. It has its origin in the love of power. Power controuled or abridged is almost always the rival and enemy of that power by which it is controuled or abriged. This simple proposition will teach us how little reason there is to expect, that the persons, entrusted with the administration of the affairs of the particular members of a confederacy, will at all times be ready, with perfect good humour, and an unbiassed regard to the public weal, to execute the resolutions or decrees of the general authority. The reverse of this results from the constitution of human nature.

If therefore the measures of the confederacy cannot be executed, without the intervention of the particular administrations, there will be little prospect of their being executed at all. The rulers of the respective members, whether they have a constitutional right to do it or not, will undertake to judge of the propriety of the measures themselves. They will consider the conformity of the thing proposed or required to their immediate interests or aims, the momentary conveniences or inconveniences that would attend its adoption. All this will be done, and in a spirit of interested and suspicious scrutiny, without that knowledge of national circumstances and reasons of state, which is essential to a right judgment, and with that strong predilection in favour of local objects, which can hardly fail to mislead the decision. The same process must be repeated in every member of which the body is constituted; and the execution of the plans, framed by the councils of the whole, will always fluctuate on the discretion of the ill-informed and prejudiced opinion of every part. Those who have been conversant in the proceedings of popular assemblies; who have seen how difficult it often is, when there is no exterior pressure of circumstances, to bring them to harmonious resolutions on important points, will readily conceive how impossible it must be to induce a number of such assemblies, deliberating at a distance from each other, at different times, and under different impressions, long to cooperate in the same views and pursuits.

In our case, the concurrence of thirteen distinct sovereign wills is requisite under the confederation to the complete execution of every important measure, that proceeds from the Union. It has happened as was to have been foreseen. The measures of the Union have not been executed; and the delinquencies of the States have step by step matured themselves to an extreme; which has at length arrested all the wheels of the national government, and brought them to an awful stand. Congress at this time scarcely possess the means of keeping up the forms of administration; 'till the States can have time to agree upon a more substantial substitute for the present shadow of a fœderal government. Things did not come to this desperate extremity at once. The causes which have been specified produced at first only unequal and disproportionate degrees of compliance with the requisitions of the Union. The greater deficiencies of some States furnished the pretext of example and the temptation of interest to the complying, or to the least delinquent States. Why should we do more in proportion than those who are embarked with us in the same political voyage? Why should we consent to bear more than our proper share of the common burthen? These were suggestions which human selfishness could not withstand, and which even speculative men, who looked forward to remote consequences, could not, without hesitation, combat. Each State yielding to the persuasive voice of immediate interest and convenience has successively withdrawn its support, 'till the frail and tottering edifice seems ready to fall upon our heads and to crush us beneath its ruins.

PUBLIUS.

J. LETTER OF AGRIPPA, NO. 4

December 3, 1787

To the People.

Having considered some of the principal advantages of the happy form of government under which it is our peculiar good fortune to live, we find by experience, that it is the best calculated of any form hitherto invented, to secure to us the rights of our persons and of our property, and that the general circumstances of the people shew an advanced state of improvement never before known. We have found the shock given by the war in a great measure obliterated, and the publick debt contracted at that time to be considerably reduced in the nominal sum. The Congress lands are fully adequate to the redemption of the principal of their debt, and are selling and populating very fast. The lands of this state, at the west, are, at the moderate price of eighteen pence an acre, worth near half a million pounds in our money. They ought, therefore, to be sold as quick as possible. An application was made lately for a large tract at that price, and continual applications are made for other lands in the eastern part of the state. Our resources are daily augmenting.

We find, then, that after the experience of near two centuries our separate governments are in full vigour. They discover, for all the purposes of internal regulation, every symptom of strength, and none of decay. The new system is, therefore, for such purposes, useless and burdensome.

Let us now consider how far it is practicable consistent with the happiness of the people and their freedom. It is the opinion of the ablest writers on the subject, that no extensive empire can be governed upon republican principles, and that such a government will degenerate to a despotism, unless it be made up of a confederacy of smaller states, each having the full powers of internal regulation. This is precisely the principle which has hitherto preserved our freedom. No instance can be found of any free government of considerable extent which has been supported upon any other plan. Large and consolidated empires may indeed dazzle the eyes of a distant spectator with their splendour, but if examined more nearly are always found to be full of misery. The reason is obvious. In large states the same principles of legislation will not apply to all the parts. The inhabitants of warmer climates are more dissolute in their manners, and less industrious, than in colder countries. A degree of severity is, therefore, necessary with one which would cramp the spirit of the other. We accordingly find that the very great empires have always been despotick. They have indeed tried to remedy the inconveniences to which the people were exposed by local regulations; but these contrivances have never answered the end. The laws not being made by the people, who felt the inconveniences, did not suit their circumstances. It is under such tyranny that the Spanish provinces languish, and such would be our misfortune and degradation, if we should submit to have the concerns of the whole empire managed by one legislature. To promote the happiness of the people it is necessary that there should be local laws; and it is necessary that those laws should be made by the representatives of those who are immediately subject to the want of them. By endeavouring to suit both extremes, both are injured.

It is impossible for one code of laws to suit Georgia and Massachusetts. They must, therefore, legislate for themselves. Yet there is, I believe, not one point of legislation that is not surrendered in the proposed plan. Questions of every kind respecting property are determinable in a continental court, and so are all kinds of criminal causes. The continental legislature has, therefore, a right to make rules *in all cases* by which their judicial courts shall proceed and decide causes. No rights are reserved to the citizens. The laws of Congress are in all cases to be the supreme law of the land, and paramount to the constitutions of the individual states. The Congress may institute what modes of trial they please, and no plea drawn from the constitution of any state can avail. This new system is, therefore, a consolidation of all the states into one large mass, however diverse the parts may be of which it is to be composed. The idea of an uncompounded republick, on an average, one thousand miles in length, and eight hundred in breadth, and containing six millions of white inhabitants all reduced to the same standard of morals, or habits, and of laws, is in itself an absurdity, and contrary to the whole experience of mankind. The attempt made by Great-Britain to introduce such a system, struck us with horrour, and when it was proposed by some theorist that we should be represented in parliament, we uniformly declared that one legislature could not represent so many different interests for the purposes of legislation and taxation. This was the leading principle of the revolution, and makes an essential article in our creed. All that part, therefore, of the new system, which relates to the internal government of the states, ought at once to be rejected.

Agrippa.

K. ALEXANDER HAMILTON, THE FEDERALIST, NO. 16

December 4, 1787

To the People of the State of New York.

The tendency of the principle of legislation for States, or communities, in their political capacities, as it has been exemplified by the experiment we have made of it, is equally attested by the events which have befallen all other governments of the confederate kind, of which we have any account, in exact proportion to its prevalence in those systems. The confirmations of this fact will be worthy of a distinct and particular examination. I shall content myself with barely observing here, that of all the confederacies of antiquity, which history has handed down to us, the Lycian and Achæan leagues, as far as there remain vestiges of them, appear to have been most free from the fetters of that mistaken principle, and were accordingly those which have best deserved, and have most liberally received the applauding suffrages of political writers.

This exceptionable principle may as truly as emphatically be stiled the parent of anarchy: It has been seen that delinquencies in the members of the Union are its natural and necessary offspring; and that whenever they happen, the only constitutional remedy is force, and the immediate effect of the use of it, civil war.

It remains to enquire how far so odious an engine of government, in its application to us, would even be capable of answering its end. If there should not be a large army, constantly at the disposal of the national government, it would either not be able to employ force at all, or when this could be done, it would amount to a war between different parts of the confederacy, concerning the infractions of a league; in which the strongest combination would be most likely to prevail, whether it consisted of those who supported, or of those who resisted the general authority. It would rarely happen that the delinquency to be redressed would be confined to a single member, and if there were more than one, who had neglected their duty, similarity of situation would induce them to unite for common defence. Independent of this motive of sympathy, if a large and influential State should happen to be the aggressing member, it would commonly have weight enough with its neighbours, to win over some of them as associates to its cause. Specious arguments of danger to the common liberty could easily be contrived; plausible excuses for the deficiencies of the party, could, without difficulty be invented, to alarm the apprehensions, inflame the passions, and conciliate the good will even of those States which were not chargeable with any violation, or omission of duty. This would be the more likely to take place, as the delinquencies of the larger members might be expected sometimes to proceed from an ambitious premeditation in their rulers, with a view to getting rid of all external controul upon their designs of personal aggrandizement; the better to effect which, it is presumable they would tamper beforehand with leading individuals in the adjacent States. If associates could not be found at home, recourse would be had to the aid of foreign powers, who would seldom be disinclined to encouraging the dissentions of a confederacy, from the firm Union of which they had so much to fear. When the sword is once drawn, the passions of men observe no bounds of moderation. The suggestions of wounded pride, the instigations of irritated resentment, would be apt to carry the States, against which the arms of the Union were exerted to any extremes necessary to revenge the affront, or to avoid the disgrace of submission. The first war of this kind would probably terminate in a dissolution of the Union.

This may be considered as the violent death of the confederacy. Its more natural death is what we now seem to be on the point of experiencing, if the fœderal system be not speedily renovated in a more substantial form. It is not probable, considering the genius of this country, that the complying States would often be inclined to support the authority of the Union by engaging in a war against the non-complying States. They would always be more ready to pursue the milder course of putting themselves upon an equal footing with the delinquent members, by an imitation of their example. And the guilt of all would thus become the security of all. Our past experience has exhibited the operation of this spirit in its full light. There would in fact be an insuperable difficulty in ascertaining when force could with propriety be employed. In the article of pecuniary contribution, which would be the most usual source of delinquency, it would often be impossible to decide whether it had proceeded from disinclination, or inability. The pretence of the latter would always be at hand. And the case must be very flagrant in which its fallacy could be detected with sufficient certainty to justify the harsh expedient of compulsion. It is easy to see that this problem alone, as often as it should occur, would open a wide field for the exercise of factious views, of partiality and of oppression, in the majority that happened to prevail in the national council.

It seems to require no pains to prove that the States ought not to prefer a national constitution, which could only be kept in motion by the instrumentality of a large army, continually on foot to execute the ordinary requisitions or decrees of the government. And yet this is the plain alternative involved by those who wish to deny it the power of extending its operations to individuals. Such a scheme, if practicable at all, would instantly degenerate into a military despotism; but it will be found in every light impracticable. The resources of the Union would not be equal to the maintenance of an army considerable enough to confine the larger States within the limits of their duty; nor would the means ever be furnished of forming such an army in the first instance. Whoever considers the populousness and strength of several of these States singly at the present juncture, and looks forward to what they will become, even at the distance of half a century, will at once dismiss as idle and visionary any scheme, which aims at regulating their movements by laws, to operate upon them in their collective capacities, and to be executed by a coertion applicable to them in the same capacities. A project of this kind is little less romantic than that monstertaming spirit, which is attributed to the fabulous heroes and demi-gods of antiquity.

Even in those confederacies, which have been composed of members smaller than many of our counties, the principle of legislation for sovereign States, supported by military coertion, has never been found effectual. It has rarely been attempted to be employed, but against the weaker members: And in most instances attempts to coerce the refractory and disobedient, have been the signals of bloody wars; in which one half of the confederacy has displayed its banners against the other half.

The result of these observations to an intelligent mind must be clearly this, that if it be possible at any rate to construct a Fœderal Government capable of regulating the common concerns and preserving the general tranquility, it must be founded, as to the objects committed to its care, upon the reverse of the principle contended for by the opponents of the proposed constitution. It must carry its agency to the persons of the citizens. It must stand in need of no intermediate legislations; but must itself be empowered to employ the arm of the ordinary magistrate to execute its own resolutions. The majesty of the national authority must be manifested through the medium of the Courts of Justice. The government of the Union, like that of each State, must be able to address itself immediately to the hopes and fears of individuals; and to attract to its support, those passions, which have the strongest influence upon the human heart. It must in short, possess all the means and have a right to resort to all the methods of executing the powers, with which it is entrusted, that are possessed and exercised by the governments of the particular States.

To this reasoning it may perhaps be objected, that if any State should be disaffected to the authority of the Union, it could at any time obstruct the execution of its laws, and bring the matter to the same issue of force, with the necessity of which the opposite scheme is reproached.

The plausibility of this objection will vanish the moment we advert to the essential difference between a mere NON COMPLIANCE and a DIRECT and ACTIVE RESISTANCE. If the interposition of the State-Legislatures be necessary to give effect to a measure of the Union, they have only NOT TO ACT or TO ACT EVASIVELY, and the measure is defeated. This neglect of duty may be disguised under affected but unsubstantial provisions, so as not to appear, and of course not to excite any alarm in the people for the safety of the constitution. The State leaders may even make a merit of their surreptitious invasions of it, on the ground of some temporary convenience, exemption, or advantage.

But if the execution of the laws of the national government, should not require the intervention of the State Legislatures; if they were to pass into immediate operation upon the citizens themselves, the particular governments could not interrupt their progress without an open and violent exertion of an unconstitutional power. No omissions, nor evasions would answer the end. They would be obliged to act, and in such a manner, as would leave no doubt that they had encroached on the national rights. An experiment of this nature would always be hazardous—in the face of a constitution in any degree competent to its own defence, and of a people enlightened enough to distinguish between a legal exercise and an illegal usurpation of authority. The success of it would require not merely a factious majority in the Legislature, but the concurrence of the courts of justice, and of the body of the people. If the Judges were not embarked in a conspiracy with the Legislature they would pronounce the resolutions of such a majority to be contrary to the supreme law of the land, unconstitutional and void. If the people were not tainted with the spirit of their State representatives, they, as the natural guardians of the constitution, would throw their weight into the national scale, and give it a decided preponderancy in the contest. Attempts of this kind would not often be made with levity or rashness;

because they could seldom be made without danger to the authors; unless in cases of a tyrannical exercise of the Fœderal authority.

If opposition to the national government should arise from the disorderly conduct of refractory, or seditious individuals, it could be overcome by the same means which are daily employed against the same evil, under the State governments. The Magistracy, being equally the Ministers of the law of the land, from whatever source it might emanate, would doubtless be as ready to guard the national as the local regulations from the inroads of private licentiousness. As to those partial commotions and insurrections which sometimes disquiet society, from the intrigues of an inconsiderable faction, or from sudden or occasional ill humours that do not infect the great body of the community, the general government could command more extensive resources for the suppression of disturbances of that kind, than would be in the power of any single member. And as to those mortal feuds, which in certain conjunctures spread a conflagration through a whole nation, or through a very large proportion of it, proceeding either from weighty causes of discontent given by the government, or from the contagion of some violent popular paroxysm, they do not fall within any ordinary rules of calculation. When they happen, they commonly amount to revolutions and dismemberments of empire. No form of government can always either avoid or controul them. It is in vain to hope to guard against events too mighty for human foresight or precaution, and it would be idle to object to a government because it could not perform impossibilities.

PUBLIUS.

L. ALEXANDER HAMILTON, THE FEDERALIST, NO. 17

December 5, 1787

To the People of the State of New York.

An objection of a nature different from that which has been stated and answered, in my last address, may perhaps be likewise urged against the principle of legislation for the individual citizens of America. It may be said, that it would tend to render the government of the Union too powerful, and to enable it to absorb in itself those residuary authorities, which it might be judged proper to leave with the States for local purposes. Allowing the utmost latitude to the love of power, which any reasonable man can require, I confess I am at a loss to discover what temptation the persons entrusted with the administration of the general government could ever feel to divest the States of the authorities of that description. The regulation of the mere domestic police of a State appears to me to hold out slender allurements to ambition. Commerce, finance, negociation and war seem to comprehend all the objects, which have charms for minds governed by that passion; and all the powers necessary to these objects ought in the first instance to be lodged in the national depository. The administration of private justice between the citizens of the same State, the supervision of agriculture and of other concerns of a similar nature, all those things in short which are proper to be provided for by local legislation, can never be desirable cares of a general jurisdiction. It is therefore improbable that there should exist a disposition in the Fœderal councils to usurp the powers with which they are connected; because the attempt to exercise those powers would be as troublesome as it would be nugatory; and the possession of them, for that reason, would contribute nothing to the dignity, to the importance, or to the splendour of the national government.

But let it be admitted for argument sake, that mere wantonness and lust of domination would be sufficient to beget that disposition, still it may be safely affirmed, that the sense of the constituent body of the national representatives, or in other words of the people of the several States would controul the indulgence of so extravagant an appetite. It will always be far more easy for the State governments to encroach upon the national authorities, than for the national government to encroach upon the State authorities. The proof of this proposition turns upon the greater degree of influence, which the State governments, if they administer their affairs with uprightness and prudence, will generally possess over the people; a circumstance which at the same time teaches us, that there is an inherent and intrinsic weakness in all Fœderal Constitutions; and that too much pains cannot be taken in their organization, to give them all the force which is compatible with the principles of liberty.

The superiority of influence in favour of the particular governments would result partly from the diffusive construction of the national government; but chiefly from the nature of the objects to which the attention of the State administrations would be directed.

It is a known fact in human nature that its affections are commonly weak in proportion to the distance or diffusiveness of the object. Upon the same principle that a man is more attached to his family than to his neighbourhood, to his neighbourhood than to the community at large, the people of each State would be apt to feel a stronger byass towards their local governments than towards the government of the Union; unless the force of that principle should be destroyed by a much better administration of the latter.

This strong propensity of the human heart would find powerful auxiliaries in the objects of State regulation.

The variety of more minute interests, which will necessarily fall under the superintendence of the local administrations, and which will form so many rivulets of influence running through every part of the society, cannot be particularised without involving a detail too tedious and uninteresting to compensate for the instruction it might afford.

There is one transcendent advantage belonging to the province of the State governments which alone suffices to place the matter in a clear and satisfactory light. I mean the ordinary administration of criminal and civil justice. This of all others is the most powerful, most universal and most attractive source of popular obedience and attachment. It is that, which—being the immediate and visible guardian of life and property—having its benefits and its terrors in constant activity before the public eye—regulating all those personal interests and familiar concerns to which the sensibility of individuals is more immediately awake—contributes more than any other circumstance to impressing upon the minds of the people affection, esteem and reverence towards the government. This great cement of society which will diffuse itself almost wholly through the channels of the particular governments, independent of all other causes of influence, would ensure them so decided an empire over their respective citizens, as to render them at all times a complete counterpoise and not unfrequently dangerous rivals to the power of the Union.

The operations of the national government on the other hand falling less immediately under the observation of the mass of the citizens the benefits derived from it will chiefly be perceived and attended to by speculative men. Relating to more general interests, they will be less apt to come home to the feelings of the people; and, in proportion, less likely to inspire a habitual sense of obligation and an active sentiment of attachment.

The reasoning on this head has been abundantly exemplified by the experience of all Fœderal constitutions, with which we are acquainted, and of all others, which have borne the least analogy to them.

Though the ancient feudal systems were not strictly speaking confederacies, yet they partook of the nature of that species of association. There was a common head, chieftain, or sovereign, whose authority extended over the whole nation; and a number of subordinate vassals; or feudatories, who had large portions of land allotted to them and numerous trains of *inferior* vassals or retainers, who occupied and cultivated that land upon the tenure of fealty or obedience to the persons of whom they held it. Each principal vassal was a kind of sovereign within his particular demesnes. The consequences of this situation were a continual opposition to the authority of the sovereign, and frequent wars between the great barons, or chief feudatories themselves. The power of the head of the nation was commonly too weak either to preserve the public peace or to protect the people against the oppressions of their immediate lords. This period of European affairs is emphatically stiled by historians the times of feudal anarchy.

When the sovereign happened to be a man of vigorous and warlike temper and of superior abilities, he would acquire a personal weight and influence, which answered for the time the purposes of a more regular authority. But in general the power of the barons triumphed over that of the prince; and in many instances his dominion was entirely thrown off, and the great fiefs were erected into independent principalities or states. In those instances in which the monarch finally prevailed over his vassals, his success was chiefly owing to the tyranny of those vassals over their dependents. The barons, or nobles equally the enemies of the sovereign and the oppressors of the common people were dreaded and detested by both; till mutual danger and mutual interest effected an union between them fatal to the power of the aristocracy. Had the nobles, by a conduct of clemency and justice, preserved the fidelity and devotion of their retainers and followers, the contests between them and the prince must almost always have ended in their favour and in the abridgement or subversion of the royal authority.

This is not an assertion founded merely in speculation or conjecture. Among other illustrations of its truth which might be cited Scotland will furnish a cogent example. The spirit of clanship which was at an early day introduced into that kingdom, uniting the nobles and their dependents by ties equivalent to those of kindred, rendered the aristocracy a constant overmatch for the power of the monarch; till the incorporation with England subdued its fierce and ungovernable spirit, and reduced it within those rules of subordination, which a more rational and a more energetic system of civil polity had previously established in the latter kingdom.

The separate governments in a confederacy may aptly be compared with the feudal baronies; with this advantage in their favour, that from the reasons already explained, they will generally possess the confidence and good will of the people; and with so important a support will be able effectually to oppose all incroachments of the national government. It will be well if they are not able to counteract its legitimate and necessary authority. The points of similitude consist in the rivalship of power, applicable to both, and in the CONCENTRATION of large portions of the strength of the community into particular DEPOSITORIES, in one case at the disposal of individuals, in the other case at the disposal of political bodies.

A concise review of the events that have attended confederate governments will further illustrate this important doctrine; an inattention to which has been the great source of our political mistakes, and has given our jealousy a direction to the wrong side. This review shall form the subject of some ensuing papers.

PUBLIUS.

M. LETTER FROM THE FEDERAL FARMER, NO. 6

December 25, 1787

Dear Sir,

My former letters to you, respecting the constitution proposed, were calculated merely to lead to a fuller investigation of the subject; having more extensively considered it, and the opinions of others relative to it, I shall, in a few letters, more particularly endeavour to point out the defects, and propose amendments. I shall in this make only a few general and introductory observations, which, in the present state of the momentous question, may not be improper; and I leave you, in all cases, to decide by a careful examination of my works, upon the weight of my arguments, the propriety of my remarks, the uprightness of my intentions, and the extent of my candor—I presume I am writing to a man of candor and reflection, and not to an ardent, peevish, or impatient man.

When the constitution was first published, there appeared to prevail a misguided zeal to prevent a fair unbiassed examination of a subject of infinite importance to this people and their posterity—to the cause of liberty and the rights of mankind—and it was the duty of those who saw a restless ardor, or design, attempting to mislead the people by a parade of names and misrepresentations, to endeavour to prevent their having their intended effects. The only way to stop the passions of men in their career is, coolly to state facts, and deliberately to avow the truth—and to do this we are frequently forced into a painful view of men and measures.

Since I wrote to you in October, I have heard much said, and seen many pieces written, upon the subject in question; and on carefully examining them on both sides, I find much less reason for changing my sentiments, respecting the good and defective parts of the system proposed than I expected—The opposers, as well as the advocates of it, confirm me in my opinion, that this system affords, all circumstances considered, a better basis to build upon than the confederation. And as to the principal defects, as the smallness of the representation, the insecurity of elections, the undue mixture of powers in the senate, the insecurity of some essential rights, &c. the opposition appears, generally, to agree respecting them, and many of the ablest advocates virtually to admit them—Clear it is, the latter do not attempt manfully to defend these defective parts, but to cover them with a mysterious veil; they concede, they retract; they say we could do no better; and some of them, when a little out of temper, and hard pushed, use arguments that do more honor to their ingenuity, than to their candor and firmness.

Three states have now adopted the constitution without amendments; these, and other circumstances, ought to have their weight in deciding the question, whether we will put the system into operation, adopt it, enumerate and recommend the necessary amendments, which afterwards, by three-fourths of the states, may be ingrafted into the system, or whether we will make the amendments prior to the adoption—I only undertake to shew amendments are essential and necessary—how far it is practicable to ingraft them into the plan, prior to the adoption, the state conventions must determine. Our situation is critical, and we have but our choice of evils—We may hazard much by adopting the constitution in its present form—we may hazard more by rejecting it wholly—we may hazard much by long contending about amendments prior to the adoption. The greatest political evils that can befal us, are discords and civil wars—the greatest blessings we can wish for, are peace, union, and industry, under a mild, free, and steady government. Amendments recommended will tend to guard and direct the administration—but there will be danger that the people, after the system shall be adopted, will become inattentive to amendments—Their attention is now awake—the discussion of the subject, which has already taken place, has had a happy effect—it has called forth the able advocates of liberty, and tends to renew, in the minds of the people, their true republican jealousy and vigilance, the strongest guard against the abuses of power; but the vigilance of the people is not sufficiently constant to be depended on—Fortunate it is for the body of a people, if they can continue attentive to their liberties, long enough to erect for them a temple, and constitutional barriers for their permanent security: when they are well fixed between the powers of the rulers and the rights of the people, they become visible boundaries, constantly seen by all, and any transgression of them is immediately discovered: they serve as centinels for the people at all times, and especially in those unavoidable intervals of inattention.

Some of the advocates, I believe, will agree to recommend *good* amendments; but some of them will only consent to recommend indefinite, specious, but unimportant ones; and this only with a view to keep the door open for obtaining, in some favourable moment, their main object, a complete consolidation of the states, and a government much higher toned, less republican and free than the one proposed. If necessity, therefore, should ever oblige us to adopt the system, and recommend amendments, the true friends of a federal republic must see they are well defined, and well calculated, not only to prevent our system of government moving further from republican principles and equality, but to bring it back nearer to them—they must be constantly on their guard against the address, flattery, and manœuvres of their adversaries.

The gentlemen who oppose the constitution, or contend for amendments in it, are frequently, and with much bitterness, charged with wantonly attacking the men who framed it. The unjustness of this charge leads me to make one observation upon the conduct of parties, &c. Some of the advocates are only pretended federalists; in fact they wish for an abolition of the state governments. Some of them I believe to be honest federalists, who wish to preserve *substantially* the state governments united under an efficient federal head; and many of them are blind tools without any object. Some of the opposers also are only pretended federalists, who want no federal government, or one merely advisory. Some of them are the true federalists, their object, perhaps, more clearly seen, is the same with that of the honest federalists; and some of them, probably, have no distinct object. We might as well call the advocates and opposers tories and whigs, or any thing else, as federalists and anti-federalists. To be for or against the constitution, as it stands, is not much evidence of a federal disposition; if any names are applicable to the parties, on account of their general politics, they are those of republicans and anti-republicans. The opposers are generally men who support the rights of the body of the people, and are properly republicans. The advocates are generally men not very friendly to those rights, and properly anti republicans.

Had the advocates left the constitution, as they ought to have done, to be adopted or rejected on account of its own merits or imperfections, I do not believe the gentlemen who framed it would ever have been even alluded to in the contest by the opposers. Instead of this, the ardent advocates begun by quoting names as incontestible authorities for the implicit adoption of the system, without any examination—treated all who opposed it as friends of anarchy; and with an indecent virulence addressed M[aso]n G[err]y, L[e]e, and almost every man of weight they could find in the opposition by name. If they had been candid men they would have applauded the moderation of the opposers for not retaliating in this pointed manner, when so fair an opportunity was given them; but the opposers generally saw that it was no time to heat the passions; but, at the same time, they saw there was something more than mere zeal in many of their adversaries; they saw them attempting to mislead the people, and to precipitate their divisions, by the sound of names, and forced to do it, the opposers, in general terms, alledged those names were not of sufficient authority to justify the hasty adoption of the system contended for. The convention, as a body, was undoubtedly respectable; it was, generally, composed of members of the then and preceding Congresses: as a body of respectable men we ought to view it. To select individual names, is an invitation to personal attacks, and the advocates, for their own sake, ought to have known the abilities, politics, and situation of some of their favourite characters better, before they held them up to view in the manner they did, as men entitled to our implicit political belief: they ought to have known, whether all the men they so held up to view could, for their past conduct in public offices, be approved or not by the public records, and the honest part of the community. These ardent advocates seem now to be peevish and angry, because, by their own folly, they have led to an investigation of facts and of political characters, unfavourable to them, which they had not the discernment to foresee. They may well apprehend they have opened a door to some Junius, or to some man, after his manner, with his polite addresses to men by name, to state serious facts, and unfold the truth; but these advocates may rest assured, that cool men in the opposition, best acquainted with the affairs of the country, will not, in the critical passage of a people from one constitution to another, pursue inquiries, which, in other circumstances, will be deserving of the highest praise. I will say nothing further about political characters, but examine the constitution; and as a necessary and previous measure to a particular examination, I shall state a few general positions and principles, which receive a general assent, and briefly notice the leading features of the confederation, and several state conventions, to which, through the whole investigation, we must frequently have recourse, to aid the mind in its determinations.

We can put but little dependance on the partial and vague information transmitted to us respecting antient governments; our situation as a people is peculiar: our people in general have a high sense of freedom; they are high spirited, though capable of deliberate measures; they are intelligent, discerning, and well informed; and it is to their condition we must mould the constitution and laws. We have no royal or noble families, and all things concur in favour of a government entirely elective. We have tried our abilities as free men in a most arduous contest, and have succeeded; but we now find the main spring of our movements were the love of liberty, and a temporary ardor, and not any energetic principle in the federal system.

Our territories are far too extensive for a limited monarchy, in which the representatives must frequently assemble, and the laws operate mildly and systematically. The most elligible system is a federal republic, that is, a system in which national concerns may be transacted in the centre, and local affairs in state or district governments.

The powers of the union ought to be extended to commerce, the coin, and national objects; and a division of powers, and a deposit of them in different hands, is safest.

Good government is generally the result of experience and gradual improvements, and a punctual execution of the laws is essential to the preservation of life, liberty, and property. Taxes are always necessary, and the power to raise them can never be safely lodged without checks and limitation, but in a full and substantial representation of the body of the people; the quantity of power delegated ought to be compensated by the brevity of the time of holding it, in order to prevent the possessors increasing it. The supreme power is in the people, and rulers possess only that portion which is expressly given them; yet the wisest people have often declared this is the case on proper occasions, and have carefully formed stipulation to fix the extent, and limit the exercise of the power given.

The people by Magna Charta, &c. did not acquire powers, or receive privileges from the king, they only ascertained and fixed those they were entitled to as Englishmen; the title used by the king "we grant," was mere form. Representation, and the jury trial, are the best features of a free government ever as yet discovered, and the only means by which the body of the people can have their proper influence in the affairs of government.

In a federal system we must not only balance the parts of the same government, as that of the state, or that of the union; but we must find a balancing influence between the general and local governments—the latter is what men or writers have but very little or imperfectly considered.

A free and mild government is that in which no laws can be made without the formal and free consent of the people, or of their constitutional representatives; that is, of a substantial representative branch. Liberty, in its genuine sense, is security to enjoy the effects of our honest industry and labours, in a free and mild government, and personal security from all illegal restraints.

Of rights, some are natural and unalienable, of which even the people cannot deprive individuals: Some are constitutional or fundamental; these cannot be altered or abolished by the ordinary laws; but the people, by express acts, may alter or abolish them—These, such as the trial by jury, the benefits of the writ of habeas corpus, &c. individuals claim under the solemn compacts of the people, as constitutions, or at least under laws so strengthened by long usuage as not to be repealable by the ordinary legislature—and some are common or mere legal rights, that is, such as individuals claim under laws which the ordinary legislature may alter or abolish at pleasure.

The confederation is a league of friendship among the states or sovereignties for the common defence and mutual welfare—Each state expressly retains its sovereignty, and all powers not expressly given to congress—All federal powers are lodged in a congress of delegates annually elected by the state legislatures, except in Connecticut and Rhode-Island, where they are chosen by the people—Each state has a vote in congress, pays its delegates, and may instruct or recall them; no delegate can hold any office of profit, or serve more than three years in any six years—Each state may be represented by not less than two, or more than seven delegates.

Congress (nine states agreeing) may make peace and war, treaties and alliances, grant letters of marque and reprisal, coin money, regulate the alloy and value of the coin, require men and monies of the states by fixed proportions, and appropriate monies, form armies and navies, emit bills of credit, and borrow monies.

Congress (seven states agreeing) may send and receive ambassadors, regulate captures, make rules for governing the army and navy, institute courts for the trial of piracies and felonies committed on the high seas, and for settling territorial disputes between the individual states, regulate weight and measures, post-offices, and Indian affairs.

No state, without the consent of congress, can send or receive embassies, make any agreement with any other state, or a foreign state, keep up any vessels of war or bodies of forces in time of peace, or engage in war, or lay any duties which may interfere with the treaties of congress—Each state must appoint regimental officers, and keep up a well regulated militia—Each state may prohibit the importation or exportation of any species of goods.

The free inhabitants of one state are intitled to the privileges and immunities of the free citizens of the other states—Credit in each state shall be given to the records and judicial proceedings in the others.

Canada, acceding, may be admitted, and any other colony may be admitted by the consent of nine states.

Alterations may be made by the agreement of congress, and confirmation of all the state legislatures.

The following, I think, will be allowed to be unalienable or fundamental rights in the United States:—

No man, demeaning himself peaceably, shall be molested on account of his religion or mode of worship—The people have a right to hold and enjoy their property according to known standing laws, and which cannot be taken from them without their consent, or the consent of their representatives; and whenever taken in the pressing urgencies of government, they are to receive a reasonable compensation for it—Individual security consists in having free recourse to the laws—The people are subject to no laws or taxes not assented to by their representatives constitutionally assembled—They are at all times intitled to the benefits of the writ of habeas corpus, the trial by jury in criminal and civil causes—They have a right, when charged, to a speedy trial in the vicinage; to be heard by themselves or counsel, not to be compelled to furnish evidence against themselves, to have witnesses face to face, and to confront their adversaries before the judge—No man is held to answer a crime charged upon him till it be substantially described to him; and he is subject to no unreasonable searches or seizures of his person, papers or effects—The people have a right to assemble in an orderly manner, and petition the government for a redress of wrongs—The freedom of the press ought not to be restrained—No emoluments, except for actual service—No hereditary honors, or orders of nobility, ought to be allowed—The military ought to be subordinate to the civil authority, and no soldier be quartered on the citizens without their consent—The militia ought always to be armed and disciplined, and the usual defence of the country—The supreme power is in the people, and power delegated ought to return to them at stated periods, and frequently—The legislative, executive, and judicial powers, ought always to be kept distinct—others perhaps might be added.

The organization of the state governments—Each state has a legislature, an executive, and a judicial branch—In general legislators are excluded from the important executive and judicial offices—Except in the Carolinas there is no constitutional distinction among Christian sects—The constitutions of New York, Delaware, and Virginia, exclude the clergy from offices civil and military—the other states do nearly the same in practice.

Each state has a democratic branch elected twice a-year in Rhode-Island and Connecticut, biennially in South Carolina, and annually in the other states—There are about 1500 representatives in all the states, or one to each 1700 inhabitants, reckoning five blacks for three whites— The states do not differ as to the age or moral characters of the electors or elected, nor materially as to their property.

Pennsylvania has lodged all her legislative powers in a single branch, and Georgia has done the same; the other eleven states have each in their legislatures a second or senatorial branch. In forming this they have combined various principles, and aimed at several checks and balances. It is amazing to see how ingenuity has worked in the several states to fix a barrier against popular instability. In Massachusetts the senators are apportioned on districts according to the taxes they pay, nearly according to property. In Connecticut the freemen, in September, vote for twenty counsellers, and return the names of those voted for in the several towns; the legislature takes the twenty who have the most votes, and give them to the people, who, in April, chuse twelve of them, who, with the governor and deputy governor, form the senatorial branch. In Maryland the senators are chosen by two electors from each county; these electors are chosen by the freemen, and qualified as the members in the democratic branch are: In these two cases checks are aimed at in the mode of election. Several states have taken into view the periods of service, age, property, &c. In South-Carolina a senator is elected for two years, in Delaware three, and in New-York and Virginia four, in Maryland five, and in the other states for one. In New-York and Virginia one-fourth part go out yearly. In Virginia a senator must be twenty-five years old, in South Carolina thirty. In New-York the electors must each have a freehold worth 250 dollars, in North-Carolina a freehold of fifty acres of land; in the other states the electors of senators are qualified as electors of representatives are. In Massachusetts a senator must have a freehold in his own right worth 1000 dollars, or any estate worth 2000, in New-Jersey any estate worth 2666, in South Carolina worth 1300 dollars, in North-Carolina 300 acres of land in fee, &c. The numbers of senators in each state are from ten to thirty-one, about 160 in the eleven states, about one of 14000 inhabitants.

Two states, Massachusetts and New-York, have each introduced into their legislatures a third, but incomplete branch. In the former, the governor may negative any law not supported by two-thirds of the senators, and two-thirds of the representatives: in the latter, the governor, chancellor, and judges of the supreme court may do the same.

Each state has a single executive branch. In the five eastern states the people at large elect their governors; in the other states the legislatures elect them. In South Carolina the governor is elected once in two years; in New-York and Delaware once in three, and in the other

446

states annually. The governor of New-York has no executive council, the other governors have. In several states the governor has a vote in the senatorial branch—the governors have similar powers in some instances, and quite dissimilar ones in others. The number of executive counsellers in the states are from five to twelve. In the four eastern states, New-Jersey, Pennsylvania, and Georgia, they are of the men returned legislators by the people. In Pennsylvania the counsellers are chosen triennially, in Delaware every fourth year, in Virginia every three years, in South-Carolina biennially, and in the other states yearly.

Each state has a judicial branch; each common law courts, superior and inferior; some chancery and admiralty courts: The courts in general sit in different places, in order to accommodate the citizens. The trial by jury is had in all the common law courts, and in some of the admiralty courts. The democratic freemen principally form the juries; men destitute of property, of character, or under age, are excluded as in elections. Some of the judges are during good behaviour, and some appointed for a year, and some for years; and all are dependant on the legislatures for their salaries—Particulars respecting this department are too many to be noticed here.

The Federal Farmer.

N. ALEXANDER HAMILTON, THE FEDERALIST, NO. 27

December 25, 1787

To the People of the State of New York.

It has been urged in different shapes that a constitution of the kind proposed by the Convention, cannot operate without the aid of a military force to execute its laws. This however, like most other things that have been alledged on that side, rests on mere general assertion; unsupported by any precise or intelligible designation of the reasons upon which it is founded. As far as I have been able to divine the latent meaning of the objectors, it seems to originate in a pre-supposition that the people will be disinclined to the exercise of fœderal authority in any matter of an internal nature. Waving any exception that might be taken to the inaccuracy or inexplicitness of the distinction between internal and external, let us enquire what ground there is to presuppose that disinclination in the people? Unless we presume, at the same time, that the powers of the General Government will be worse administered than those of the State governments, there seems to be no room for the presumption of ill-will, disaffection or opposition in the people. I believe it may be laid down as a general rule, that their confidence in and obedience to a government, will commonly be proportioned to the goodness or badness of its administration. It must be admitted that there are exceptions to this rule; but these exceptions depend so entirely on accidental causes, that they cannot be considered as having any relation to the intrinsic merits or demerits of a constitution. These can only be judged of by general principles and maxims.

Various reasons have been suggested in the course of these papers, to induce a probability that the General Government will be better administered than the particular governments: The principal of which reasons are that the extension of the spheres of election will present a greater option, or latitude of choice to the people, that through the medium of the State Legislatures, which are select bodies of men, and who are to appoint the members of the national Senate,—there is reason to expect that this branch will generally be composed with peculiar care and judgment: That these circumstances promise greater knowledge and more extensive information in the national councils: And that they will be less apt to be tainted by the spirit of faction, and more out of the reach of those occasional ill humors or temporary prejudices and propensities, which in smaller societies frequently contaminate the public councils, beget injustice and oppression of a part of the community, and engender schemes, which though they gratify a momentary inclination or desire, terminate in general distress, dissatisfaction and disgust. Several additional reasons of considerable force, to fortify that probability, will occur when we come to survey with a more critic[al] eye, the interior structure of the edifice, which we are invited to erect. It will be sufficient here to remark, that until satisfactory reasons can be assigned to justify an opinion, that the fœderal government is likely to be administered in such a manner as to render it odious or contemptible to the people, there can be no reasonable foundation for the supposition, that the laws of the Union will meet with any greater obstruction from them, or will stand in need of any other methods to enforce their execution, than the laws of the particular members.

The hope of impunity is a strong incitement to sedition—the dread of punishment—a proportionately strong discouragement to it. Will not the government of the Union, which, if possessed of a due degree of power, can call to its aid the collective resources of the whole confederacy, be more likely to repress the *former* sentiment, and to inspire the *latter,* than that of a single State, which can only command the resources within itself? A turbulent faction in a State may easily suppose itself able to contend with the friends to the government in that State; but it can hardly be so infatuated as to imagine itself a match for the combined efforts of the Union. If this reflection be just, there is less danger of resistance from irregular combinations of individuals, to the authority of the confederacy, than to that of a single member.

I will in this place hazard an observation which will not be the less just, because to some it may appear new; which is, that the more the operations of the national authority are intermingled in the ordinary exercise of government; the more the citizens are accustomed to meet with it in the common occurrences of their political life; the more it is familiarised to their sight and to their feelings; the further it enters into those objects which touch the most sensible cords, and put in motion the most active springs of the human heart; the greater will be the probability that it will conciliate the respect and attachment of the community. Man is very much a creature of habit. A thing that rarely strikes his senses will generally have but little influence upon his mind. A government continually at a distance and out of sight, can hardly be expected to interest the sensations of the people. The inference is, that the authority of the Union, and the affections of the citizens towards it, will be strengthened rather than weakened by its extension to what are called matters of internal concern; and will have less occasion to recur to force in proportion to the familiarity and comprehensiveness of its agency. The more it circulates through those channels and currents, in which the passions of mankind naturally flow, the less will it require the aid of the violent and perilous expedients of compulsion.

One thing at all events, must be evident, that a government like the one proposed, would bid much fairer to avoid the necessity of using force, than that species of league contended for by most of its opponents; the authority of which should only operate upon the States in their political or collective capacities. It has been shewn, that in such a confederacy, there can be no sanction for the laws but force; that frequent delinquencies in the members, are the natural offspring of the very frame of the government; and that as often as these happen they can only be redressed, if at all, by war and violence.

The plan reported by the Convention, by extending the authority of the fœderal head to the individual citizens of the several States, will enable the government to employ the ordinary magistracy of each in the execution of its laws. It is easy to perceive that this will tend to destroy, in the common apprehension, all distinction between the sources from which they might proceed; and will give the Fœderal Government the same advantage for securing a due obedience to its authority, which is enjoyed by the government of each State; in addition to the influence on public opinion, which will result from the important consideration of its having power to call to its assistance and support the resources of the whole Union. It merits particular attention in this place, that the laws of the confederacy, as to the *enumerated* and *legitimate* objects of its jurisdiction, will become the SUPREME LAW of the land; to the observance of which, all officers legislative, executive and judicial in each State, will be bound by the sanctity of an oath. Thus the Legislatures, Courts and Magistrates of the respective members will be incorporated into the operations of the national government, *as far as its just and constitutional authority extends;* and will be rendered auxiliary to the enforcement of its laws.* Any man, who will pursue by his own reflections the consequences of this situation, will perceive that there is good ground to

* *The sophistry which has been employed to show that this will tend to the destruction of the State Governments will, in its proper place, be fully detected.*

calculate upon a regular and peaceable execution of the laws of the Union; if its powers are administered with a common share of prudence. If we will arbitrarily suppose the contrary, we may deduce any inferences we please from the supposition; for it is certainly possible, by an injudicious exercise of the authorities of the best government, that ever was or ever can be instituted, to provoke and precipitate the people into the wildest excesses. But though the adversaries of the proposed constitution should presume that the national rulers would be insensible to the motives of public good, or to the obligations of duty; I would still ask them, how the interests of ambition, or the views of encroachment, can be promoted by such a conduct

PUBLIUS.

O. ALEXANDER HAMILTON, THE FEDERALIST, NO. 33

January 2, 1788

The residue of the argument against the provisions in the constitution, in respect to taxation, is ingrafted upon the following clauses; the last clause of the eighth section of the first article of the plan under consideration, authorises the national legislature "to make all laws which shall be *necessary* and *proper,* for carrying into execution *the powers* by that Constitution vested in the government of the United States, or in any department or officer thereof"; and the second clause of the sixth article declares, that "the Constitution and the Laws of the United States made *in pursuance thereof,* and the treaties made by their authority shall be the *supreme law* of the land; any thing in the constitution or laws of any State to the contrary notwithstanding."

These two clauses have been the sources of much virulent invective and petulant declamation against the proposed constitution, they have been held up to the people, in all the exaggerated colours of misrepresentation, as the pernicious engines by which their local governments were to be destroyed and their liberties exterminated—as the hideous monster whose devouring jaws would spare neither sex nor age, nor high nor low, nor sacred nor profane; and yet strange as it may appear, after all this clamour, to those who may not have happened to contemplate them in the same light, it may be affirmed with perfect confidence, that the constitutional operation of the intended government would be precisely the same, if these clauses were entirely obliterated, as if they were repeated in every article. They are only declaratory of a truth, which would have resulted by necessary and unavoidable implication from the very act of constituting a Fœderal Government, and vesting it with certain specified powers. This is so clear a proposition, that moderation itself can scarcely listen to the railings which have been so copiously vented against this part of the plan, without emotions that disturb its equanimity.

What is a power, but the ability or faculty of doing a thing? What is the ability to do a thing but the power of employing the *means* necessary to its execution? What is a LEGISLATIVE power but a power of making LAWS? What are the *means* to execute a LEGISLATIVE power but LAWS? What is the power of laying and collecting taxes but a *legislative power,* or a power of *making laws,* to lay and collect taxes? What are the proper means of executing such a power but *necessary* and *proper* laws?

This simple train of enquiry furnishes us at once with a test by which to judge of the true nature of the clause complained of. It conducts us to this palpable truth, that a power to lay and collect taxes must be a power to pass all laws *necessary* and *proper* for the execution of that power; and what does the unfortunate and calumniated provision in question do more than declare the same truth; to wit, that the national legislature to whom the power of laying and collecting taxes had been previously given, might in the execution of that power pass all laws *necessary* and *proper* to carry it into effect I have applied these observations thus particularly to the power of taxation, because it is the immediate subject under consideration, and because it is the most important of the authorities proposed to be conferred upon the Union. But the same process will lead to the same result in relation to all other powers declared in the constitution. And it is *expressly* to execute these powers, that the sweeping clause, as it has been affectedly called, authorises the national legislature to pass all *necessary* and *proper* laws. If there is any thing exceptionable, it must be sought for in the specific powers, upon which this general declaration is predicated. The declaration itself, though it may be chargeable with tautology or redundancy, is at least perfectly harmless.

But SUSPICION may ask why then was it introduced? The answer is, that it could only have been done for greater caution, and to guard against all cavilling refinements in those who might hereafter feel a disposition to curtail and evade the legitimate authorities of the Union. The Convention probably foresaw what it has been a principal aim of these papers to inculcate that the danger which most threatens our political welfare, is, that the State Governments will finally sap the foundations of the Union; and might therefore think it necessary, in so cardinal a point, to leave nothing to construction. Whatever may have been the inducement to it, the wisdom of the precaution is evident from the cry which has been raised against it; as that very cry betrays a disposition to question the great and essential truth which it is manifestly the object of that provision to declare.

But it may be again asked, who is to judge of the *necessity* and *propriety* of the laws to be passed for executing the powers of the Union? I answer first that this question arises as well and as fully upon the simple grant of those powers, as upon the declaratory clause: And I answer in the second place, that the national government, like every other, must judge in the first instance of the proper exercise of its powers; and its constituents in the last. If the Fœderal Government should overpass the just bounds of its authority, and make a tyrannical use of its powers; the people whose creature it is must appeal to the standard they have formed, and take such measures to redress the injury done to the constitution, as the exigency may suggest and prudence justify. The propriety of a law in a constitutional light, must always be determined by the nature of the powers upon which it is founded. Suppose by some forced constructions of its authority (which indeed cannot easily be imagined) the Fœderal Legislature should attempt to vary the law of descent in any State; would it not be evident that in making such an attempt it had exceeded its jurisdiction and infringed upon that of the State? Suppose again that upon the pretence of an interference with its revenues, it should undertake to abrogate a land tax imposed by the authority of a State, would it not be equally evident that this was an invasion of that concurrent jurisdiction in respect to this species of tax which its constitution plainly supposes to exist in the State governments? If there ever should be a doubt on this head the credit of it will be intirely due to those reasoners, who, in the imprudent zeal of their animosity to the plan of the Convention, have laboured to invelope it in a cloud calculated to obscure the plainest and simplest truths.

But it is said, that the laws of the Union are to be the *supreme law* of the land. But what inference can be drawn from this or what would they amount to, if they were not to be supreme? It is evident they would amount to nothing. A LAW by the very meaning of the term includes supremacy. It is a rule which those to whom it is prescribed are bound to observe. This results from every political association. If individuals enter into a state of society the laws of that society must be the supreme regulator of their conduct. If a number of political societies enter into a larger political society, the laws which the latter may enact, pursuant to the powers entrusted to it by its constitution, must necessarily be supreme over those societies, and the individuals of whom they are composed. It would otherwise be a mere treaty, dependent on the good faith of the parties, and not a government; which is only another word for POLITICAL POWER AND SUPREMACY. But it will not follow from this doctrine that acts of the larger society which are *not pursuant* to its constitutional powers but which are invasions of the residuary authorities of the smaller societies will become the supreme law of the land. These will be merely acts of usurpation and will deserve to be treated as such. Hence we perceive that the clause which declares the supremacy of the laws of the Union, like the one we have just before considered, only declares a truth, which flows immediately and necessarily from the institution of a Fœderal Government. It will not, I presume, have escaped observation that it *expressly* confines this supremacy to laws made *pursuant to the Constitution;* which I mention merely as an instance of caution in the Convention; since that limitation would have been to be understood though it had not been expressed.

452

Though a law therefore for laying a tax for the use of the United States would be supreme in its nature, and could not legally be opposed or controuled; yet a law for abrogating or preventing the collection of a tax laid by the authority of a State (unless upon imports and exports) would not be the supreme law of the land, but an usurpation of power not granted by the constitution. As far as an improper accumulation of taxes on the same object might tend to render the collection difficult or precarious, this would be a mutual inconvenience not arising from a superiority or defect of power on either side, but from an injudicious exercise of power by one or the other, in a manner equally disadvantageous to both. It is to be hoped and presumed however that mutual interest would dictate a concert in this respect which would avoid any material inconvenience. The inference from the whole is—that the individual States would, under the proposed constitution, retain an independent and uncontroulable authority to raise revenue to any extent of which they may stand in need by every kind of taxation except duties on imports and exports. It will be shewn in the next paper that this CONCURRENT JURISDICTION in the article of taxation was the only admissible substitute for an intire subordination, in respect to this branch of power, of the State authority to that of the Union.

PUBLIUS.

P. ESSAY OF BRUTUS, NO. 7

January 3, 1788

The result of our reasoning in the two preceeding numbers is this, that in a confederated government, where the powers are divided between the general and the state government, it is essential to its existence, that the revenues of the country, without which no government can exist, should be divided between them, and so apportioned to each, as to answer their respective exigencies, as far as human wisdom can effect such a division and apportionment.

It has been shewn, that no such allotment is made in this constitution, but that every source of revenue is under the controul of the Congress; it therefore follows, that if this system is intended to be a complex and not a simple, a confederate and not an entire consolidated government, it contains in it the sure seeds of its own dissolution.—One of two things must happen—Either the new constitution will become a mere *nudum pactum*, and all the authority of the rulers under it be cried down, as has happened to the present confederation—Or the authority of the individual states will be totally supplanted, and they will retain the mere form without any of the powers of government.—To one or the other of these issues, I think, this new government, if it is adopted, will advance with great celerity.

It is said, I know, that such a separation of the sources of revenue, cannot be made without endangering the public safety—"unless (says a writer) it can be shewn that the circumstances which may affect the public safety are reducible within certain determinate limits; unless the contrary of this position can be fairly and rationally disputed; it must be admitted as a necessary consequence, that there can be no limitation of that authority which is to provide for the defence and protection of the community, &c."

The pretended demonstration of this writer will instantly vanish, when it is considered, that the *protection and defence* of the community is not intended to be entrusted *solely* into the hands of the general government, and by his own confession it ought not to be. It is true this system commits to the general government the protection and defence of the community against foreign force and invasion, against piracies and felonies on the high seas, and against insurrections among ourselves. They are also authorised to provide for the administration of justice in certain matters of a general concern, and in some that I think are not so. But it ought to be left to the state governments to provide for the protection and defence of the citizen against the hand of private violence, and the wrongs done or attempted by individuals to each other— Protection and defence against the murderer, the robber, the thief, the cheat, and the unjust person, is to be derived from the respective state governments.—The just way of reasoning therefore on this subject is this, the general government is to provide for the protection and defence of the community against foreign attacks, &c., they therefore ought to have authority sufficient to effect this, so far as is consistent with the providing for our internal protection and defence. The state governments are entrusted with the care of administring justice among its citizens, and the management of other internal concerns, they ought therefore to retain power adequate to the end. The preservation of internal peace and good order, and the due administration of law and justice, ought to be the first care of every government.—The happiness of a people depends infinitely more on this than it does upon all that glory and respect which nations acquire by the most brilliant martial achievements—and I believe history will furnish but few examples of nations who have duly attended to these, who have been subdued by foreign invaders. If a proper respect and submission to the laws prevailed over all orders of men in our country; and if a spirit of public and private justice, oeconomy and industry influenced the people, we need not be under any apprehensions but what they would be ready to repel any invasion that might be made on the country. And more than this, I would not wish from them—A defensive war is the only one I think justifiable—I do not make these observations to prove, that a government ought not to be authorised to provide for the protection and defence of a country against external enemies, but to shew that this is not the most important, much less the only object of their care.

The European governments are almost all of them framed, and administered with a view to arms, and war, as that in which their chief glory consists; they mistake the end of government—it was designed to save men[']s lives, not to destroy them. We ought to furnish the world with an example of a great people, who in their civil institutions hold chiefly in view, the attainment of virtue, and happiness among ourselves. Let the monarchs in Europe, share among them the glory of depopulating countries, and butchering thousands of their innocent citizens, to revenge private quarrels, or to punish an insult offered to a wife, a mistress, or a favorite: I envy them not the honor, and I pray heaven this country may never be ambitious of it. The czar Peter the great, acquired great glory by his arms; but all this was nothing, compared with the true glory which he obtained, by civilizing his rude and barbarous subjects, diffusing among them knowledge, and establishing, and cultivating the arts of life: by the former he desolated countries, and drenched the earth with human blood: by the latter he softened the ferocious nature of his people, and pointed them to the means of human happiness. The most important end of government then, is the proper direction of its internal policy, and oeconomy; this is the province of the state governments, and it is evident, and is indeed admitted, that these ought to be under their controul. Is it not then preposterous, and in the highest degree absurd, when the state governments are vested with powers so essential to the peace and good order of society, to take from them the means of their own preservation?

The idea, that the powers of congress in respect to revenue ought to be unlimited, "because the circumstances which may affect the public safety are not reducible to certain determinate limits," is novel, as it relates to the government of the united states. The inconveniencies which resulted from the feebleness of the present confederation was discerned, and felt soon after its adoption. It was soon discovered, that a power to require money, without either the authority or means to enforce a collection of it, could not be relied upon either to provide for the common defence, the discharge of the national debt, or for support of government. Congress therefore, so early as February 1781, recommended to the states to invest them with a power to levy an impost of five per cent ad valorem, on all imported goods, as a fund to be appropriated to discharge the debts already contracted, or which should hereafter be contracted for the support of the war, to be continued until the debts should be fully and finally discharged. There is not the most distant idea held out in this act, that an unlimited power to collect taxes, duties and excises was necessary to be vested in the united states, and yet this was a time of the most pressing danger and distress. The idea then was, that if certain definite funds were assigned to the union, which were certain in their natures, productive, and easy of collection, it would enable them to answer their engagements, and provide for their defence, and the impost of five per cent was fixed upon for the purpose.

This same subject was revived in the winter and spring of 1783, and after a long consideration of the subject, and many schemes were proposed; the result was, a recommendation of the revenue system of April 1783; this system does not suggest an idea that it was necessary to grant the United States unlimited authority in matters of revenue. A variety of amendments were proposed to this system, some of which are upon the journals of Congress, but it does not appear that any of them proposed to invest the general government with discretionary power to raise money. On the contrary, all of them limit them to certain definite objects, and fix the bounds over which they could not pass. This recommendation was passed at the conclusion of the war, and was founded on an estimate of the whole national debt. It was computed, that one million and an half of dollars, in addition to the impost, was a sufficient sum to pay the annual interest of the debt, and gradually to abolish the principal.—Events have proved that their estimate was sufficiently liberal, as the domestic debt appears upon its being adjusted to be less than it was computed, and since this period a considerable portion of the principal of the domestic debt has been discharged by the sale of the western lands. It has been constantly urged by Congress, and by individuals, ever since, until lately, that had this revenue been appropriated by the states, as it was recommended, it would have been adequate to every exigency of the union. Now indeed it is insisted, that all the treasures of the country are to be under the controul of that body, whom we are to appoint to provide for our protection and defence against foreign enemies. The debts of the several states, and the support of the governments of them are to trust to fortune and accident. If the union should not have occasion for all the money they can raise, they will leave a portion for the state, but this must be a matter of mere grace and favor. Doctrines like these would not have been listened to by any state in the union, at a time when we were pressed on every side by a powerful enemy, and were called upon to make greater exertions than we have any reason to expect we shall ever be again. The ability and character of the convention, who framed the proferred constitution, is sounded forth and reiterated by every declaimer and writer in its favor, as a powerful argument to induce its adoption. But are not the patriots who guided our councils in the perilous times of the war, entitled to equal respect. How has it happened, that none of these perceived a truth, which it is pretended is capable of such clear demonstration, that the power to raise a revenue should be deposited in the general government without limitation? Were the men so dull of apprehension, so incapable of reasoning as not to be able to draw the inference? The truth is, no such necessity exists. It is a thing practicable, and by no means so difficult as is pretended, to limit the powers of the general government in respect to revenue, while yet they may retain reasonable means to provide for the common defence.

It is admitted, that human wisdom cannot foresee all the variety of circumstances that may arise to endanger the safety of nations—and it may with equal truth be added, that the power of a nation, exerted with its utmost vigour, may not be equal to repel a force with which it may be assailed, much less may it be able, with its ordinary resources and power, to oppose an extraordinary and unexpected attack;—but yet every nation may form a rational judgment, what force will be competent to protect and defend it, against any enemy with which it is probable it may have to contend. In extraordinary attacks, every country must rely upon the spirit and special exertions of its inhabitants—and these extraordinary efforts will always very much depend upon the happiness and good order the people experience from a wise and prudent adminis- tration of their internal government. The states are as capable of making a just estimate on this head, as perhaps any nation in the world.—We have no powerful nation in our neighbourhood; if we are to go to war, it must either be with the Aboriginal natives, or with European nations. The first are so unequal to a contest with this whole continent, that they are rather to be dreaded for the depredations they may make on our frontiers, than for any impression they will ever be able to make on the body of the country. Some of the European nations, it is true, have provinces bordering upon us, but from these, unsupport- ed by their European forces, we have nothing to apprehend; if any of them should attack us, they will have to transport their armies across the atlantic, at immense expence, while we should defend ourselves in our own country, which abounds with every necessary of life. For defence against any assault, which there is any probability will be made upon us, we may easily form an estimate.

I may be asked to point out the sources, from which the general government could derive a sufficient revenue, to answer the demands of the union. Many might be suggested, and for my part, I am not disposed to be tenacious of my own opinion on the subject. If the object be defined with precision, and will operate to make the burden fall any thing nearly equal on the different parts of the union, I shall be satisfied.

There is one source of revenue, which it is agreed, the general government ought to have the sole controul of. This is an impost upon all goods imported from foreign countries. This would, of itself, be very productive, and would be collected with ease and certainty.—It will be a fund too, constantly encreasing—for our commerce will grow, with the productions of the country; and these, together with our consumption of foreign goods, will encrease with our population. It is said, that the impost will not produce a sufficient sum to satisfy the demands of the general government; perhaps it would not. Let some other then, equally well defined, be assigned them:—that this is practicable is certain, because such particular objects were proposed by some members of Congress when the revenue system of April 1783, was agitated in that body. It was then moved, that a tax at the rate of ___ ninetieths of a dollar on surveyed land, and a house tax of half a dollar on a house, should be granted to the United States. I do not mention this, because I approve of raising a revenue in this mode. I believe such a tax would be difficult in its collection, and inconvenient in its operation. But it shews, that it has heretofore been the sense of some of those, who now contend, that the general government should have unlimited authority in matters of revenue, that their authority should be definite and limitted on that head.—My own opinion is, that the objects from which the general government should have authority to raise a revenue, should be of such a nature, that the tax should be raised by simple laws, with few officers, with certainty and expedition, and with the least interference with the internal police of the states.—Of this nature is the impost on imported goods—and it appears to me that a duty on exports, would also be of this nature—and therefore, for ought I can discover, this would be the best source of revenue to grant the general government. I know neither the Congress nor the state legislatures will have authority under the new constitution to raise a revenue in this way. But I cannot perceive the reason of the restriction. It appears to me evident, that a tax on articles exported, would be as nearly equal as any that we can expect to lay, and it certainly would be collected with more ease and less expence than any direct tax. I do not however, contend for this mode, it may be liable to well founded objections that have not occurred to me. But this I do contend for, that some mode is practicable, and that limits must be marked between the general government, and the states on this head, or if they be not, either the Congress in the exercise of this power, will deprive the state legislatures of the means of their existence, or the states by resisting the constitutional authority of the general government, will render it nugatory.

Brutus.

Q. JAMES MADISON, THE FEDERALIST, NO. 39

January 16, 1788

To the People of the State of New York.

The last paper having concluded the observations which were meant to introduce a candid survey of the plan of government reported by the Convention, we now proceed to the execution of that part of our undertaking. The first question that offers itself is, whether the general form and aspect of the government be strictly republican? It is evident that no other form would be reconcileable with the genius of the people of America; with the fundamental principles of the revolution; or with that honorable determination, which animates every votary of freedom, to rest all our political experiments on the capacity of mankind for self-government. If the plan of the Convention therefore be found to depart from the republican character, its advocates must abandon it as no longer defensible.

What then are the distinctive characters of the republican form? Were an answer to this question to be sought, not by recurring to principles, but in the application of the term by political writers, to the constitutions of different States, no satisfactory one would ever be found. Holland, in which no particle of the supreme authority is derived from the people, has passed almost universally under the denomination of a republic. The same title has been bestowed on Venice, where absolute power over the great body of the people, is exercised in the most absolute manner, by a small body of hereditary nobles. Poland, which is a mixture of aristocracy and of monarchy in their worst forms, has been dignified with the same appellation. The government of England, which has one republican branch only, combined with a hereditery aristocracy and monarchy, has with equal impropriety been frequently placed on the list of republics. These examples, which are nearly as dissimilar to each other as to a genuine republic, shew the extreme inaccuracy with which the term has been used in political disquisitions.

If we resort for a criterion, to the different principles on which different forms of government are established, we may define a republic to be, or at least may bestow that name on, a government which derives all its powers directly or indirectly from the great body of the people; and is administered by persons holding their offices during pleasure, for a limited period, or during good behaviour. It is *essential* to such a government, that it be derived from the great body of the society, not from an inconsiderable proportion, or a favored class of it; otherwise a handful of tyrannical nobles, exercising their oppressions by a delegation of their powers, might aspire to the rank of republicans, and claim for their government the honorable title of republic. It is *sufficient* for such a government, that the persons administering it be appointed, either directly or indirectly, by the people; and that they hold their appointments by either of the tenures just specified; otherwise every government in the United States, as well as every other popular government that has been or can be well organized or well executed, would be degraded from the republican character. According to the Constitution of every State in the Union, some or other of the officers of government are appointed indirectly only by the people. According to most of them the chief magistrate himself is so appointed. And according to one, this mode of appointment is extended to one of the coordinate branches of the legislature. According to all the Constitutions also, the tenure of the highest offices is extended to a definite period, and in many instances, both within the legislative and executive departments, to a period of years. According to the provisions of most of the constitutions, again, as well as according to the most respectable and received opinions on the subject, the members of the judiciary department are to retain their offices by the firm tenure of good behaviour.

On comparing the Constitution planned by the Convention, with the standard here fixed, we perceive at once that it is in the most rigid sense conformable to it. The House of Representatives, like that of one branch at least of all the State Legislatures, is elected immediately by the great body of the people. The Senate, like the present Congress, and the Senate of Maryland, derives its appointment indirectly from the people. The President is indirectly derived from the choice of the people, according to the example in most of the States. Even the judges, with all other officers of the Union, will, as in the several States, be the choice, though a remote choice, of the people themselves. The duration of the appointments is equally conformable to the republican standard, and to the model of the State Constitutions. The House of Representatives is periodically elective as in all the States: and for the period of two years as in the State of South-Carolina. The Senate is elective for the period of six years; which is but one year more than the period of the Senate of Maryland; and but two more than that of the Senates of New-York and Virginia. The President is to continue in office for the period of four years; as in New-York and Delaware, the chief magistrate is elected for three years, and in South-Carolina for two years. In the other States the election is annual. In several of the States however, no constitutional provision is made for the impeachment of the Chief Magistrate. And in Delaware and Virginia, he is not impeachable till out of office. The President of the United States is impeachable at any time during his continuance in office. The tenure by which the Judges are to hold their places, is, as it unquestionably ought to be, that of good behaviour. The tenure of the ministerial offices generally will be a subject of legal regulation, conformably to the reason of the case, and the example of the State Constitutions.

Could any further proof be required of the republican complextion of this system, the most decisive one might be found in its absolute prohibition of titles of nobility, both under the Federal and the State Governments; and in its express guarantee of the republican form to each of the latter.

But it was not sufficient, say the adversaries of the proposed Constitution, for the Convention to adhere to the republican form. They ought, with equal care, to have preserved the *federal* form, which regards the union as a *confederacy* of sovereign States; instead of which, they have framed a *national* government, which regards the union as a *consolidation* of the States. And it is asked by what authority this bold and radical innovation was undertaken. The handle which has been made of this objection requires, that it should be examined with some precision.

Without enquiring into the accuracy of the distinction on which the objection is founded, it will be necessary to a just estimate of its force, first to ascertain the real character of the government in question; secondly, to enquire how far the Convention were authorised to propose such a government; and thirdly, how far the duty they owed to their country, could supply any defect of regular authority.

First. In order to ascertain the real character of the government it may be considered in relation to the foundation on which it is to be established; to the sources from which its ordinary powers are to be drawn; to the operation of those powers; to the extent of them; and to the authority by which future changes in the government are to be introduced.

On examining the first relation, it appears on one hand that the Constitution is to be founded on the assent and ratification of the people of America, given by deputies elected for the special purpose; but on the other, that this assent and ratification is to be given by the people, not as individuals composing one entire nation; but as composing the distinct and independent States to which they respectively belong. It is to be the assent and ratification of the several States, derived from the supreme authority in each State, the authority of the people themselves. The act therefore establishing the Constitution, will not be a *national* but a *federal* act.

That it will be a federal and not a national act, as these terms are understood by the objectors, the act of the people as forming so many independent States, not as forming one aggregate nation, is obvious from this single consideration that it is to result neither from the decision of a *majority* of the people of the Union, nor from that of a *majority* of the States. It must result from the *unanimous* assent of the several States that are parties to it, differing no other wise from their ordinary assent than in its being expressed, not by the legislative authority, but by that of the people themselves. Were the people regarded in this transaction as forming one nation, the will of the majority of the whole people of the United States, would bind the minority; in the same manner as the majority in each State must bind the minority; and the will of the majority must be determined either by a comparison of the individual votes; or by considering the will of a majority of the States, as evidence of the will of a majority of the people of the United States. Neither of these rules has been adopted. Each State in ratifying the Constitution, is considered as a sovereign body independent of all others, and only to be bound by its own voluntary act. In this relation then the new Constitution will, if established, be a *federal* and not a *national* Constitution.

The next relation is to the sources from which the ordinary powers of government are to be derived. The house of representatives will derive its powers from the people of America, and the people will be represented in the same proportion, and on the same principle, as they are in the Legislature of a particular State. So far the Government is *national* not *federal*. The Senate on the other hand will derive its powers from the States, as political and co-equal societies; and these will be represented on the principle of equality in the Senate, as they now are in the existing Congress. So far the government is *federal,* not *national.* The executive power will be derived from a very compound source. The immediate election of the President is to be made by the States in their political characters. The votes allotted to them, are in a compound ratio, which considers them partly as distinct and co-equal societies;

partly as unequal members of the same society. The eventual election, again is to be made by that branch of the Legislature which consists of the national representatives; but in this particular act, they are to be thrown into the form of individual delegations from so many distinct and co-equal bodies politic. From this aspect of the Government, it appears to be of a mixed character presenting at least as many *federal* as *national* features.

The difference between a federal and national Government as it relates to the *operation of the Government* is supposed to consist in this, that in the former, the powers operate on the political bodies composing the confederacy, in their political capacities: In the latter, on the individual citizens, composing the nation, in their individual capacities. On trying the Constitution by this criterion, it falls under the *national,* not the *federal* character; though perhaps not so compleatly, as has been understood. In several cases and particularly in the trial of controversies to which States may be parties, they must be viewed and proceeded against in their collective and political capacities only. So far the national countenance of the Government on this side seems to be disfigured by a few federal features. But this blemish is perhaps unavoidable in any plan; and the operation of the Government on the people in their individual capacities, in its ordinary and most essential proceedings, may on the whole designate it in this relation a *national* Government.

But if the Government be national with regard to the *operation* of its powers, it changes its aspect again when we contemplate it in relation to the *extent* of its powers. The idea of a national Government involves in it, not only an authority over the individual citizens; but an indefinite supremacy over all persons and things, so far as they are objects of lawful Government. Among a people consolidated into one nation, this supremacy is compleatly vested in the national Legislature. Among communities united for particular purposes, it is vested partly in the general, and partly in the municipal Legislatures. In the former case, all local authorities are subordinate to the supreme; and may be controuled, directed or abolished by it at pleasure. In the latter the local or municipal authorities form distinct and independent portions of the supremacy, no more subject within their respective spheres to the general authority, than the general authority is subject to them, within its own sphere. In this relation then the proposed Government cannot be deemed a *national* one; since its jurisdiction extends to certain enumerated objects only, and leaves to the several States a residuary and inviolable sovereignty over all other objects. It is true that in controversies relating to the boundary between the two jurisdictions, the tribunal which is ultimately to decide, is to be established under the general Government. But this does not change the principle of the case. The decision is to be impartially made, according to the rules of the Constitution; and all the usual and most effectual precautions are taken to secure this impartiality. Some such tribunal is clearly essential to prevent an appeal to the sword, and a dissolution of the compact; and that it ought to be established under the general, rather than under the local Governments; or to speak more properly, that it could be safely established under the first alone, is a position not likely to be combated.

If we try the Constitution by its last relation, to the authority by which amendments are to be made, we find it neither wholly *national,* nor wholly *federal.* Were it wholly national, the supreme and ultimate authority would reside in the *majority* of the people of the Union; and this authority would be competent at all times, like that of a majority of every national society, to alter or abolish its established Government. Were it wholly federal on the other hand, the concurrence of each State in the Union would be essential to every alteration that would be binding on all. The mode provided by the plan of the Convention is not founded on either of these principles. In requiring more than a majority, and particularly, in computing the proportion by *States,* not by *citizens,* it departs from the *national,* and advances towards the *federal* character: In rendering the concurrence of less than the whole number of States sufficient, it loses again the *federal,* and partakes of the *national* character.

The proposed Constitution therefore is in strictness neither a national nor a federal constitution; but a composition of both. In its foundation, it is federal, not national; in the sources from which the ordinary powers of the Government are drawn, it is partly federal, and partly national: in the operation of these powers, it is national, not federal: In the extent of them again, it is federal, not national: And finally, in the authoritative mode of introducing amendments, it is neither wholly federal, nor wholly national.

PUBLIUS.

R. LETTER FROM THE FEDERAL FARMER, NO. 17

January 23, 1788

Dear Sir,

I believe the people of the United States are full in the opinion, that a free and mild government can be preserved in their extensive territories, only under the substantial forms of a federal republic. As several of the ablest advocates for the system proposed, have acknowledged this (and I hope the confessions they have published will be preserved and remembered) I shall not take up time to establish this point. A question then arises, how far that system partakes of a federal republic.—I observed in a former letter, that it appears to be the first important step to a consolidation of the states; that its strong tendency is to that point.

But what do we mean by a federal republic? and what by a consolidated government? To erect a federal republic, we must first make a number of states on republican principles; each state with a government organized for the internal management of its affairs: The states, as such, must unite under a federal head, and delegate to it powers to make and execute laws in certain enumerated cases, under certain restrictions; this head may be a single assembly, like the present congress, or the Amphictionic council; or it may consist of a legislature, with one or more branches; of an executive, and of a judiciary. To form a consolidated, or one entire government, there must be no state, or local governments, but all things, persons and property, must be subject to the laws of one legislature alone; to one executive, and one judiciary. Each state government, as the government of New Jersey, &c. is a consolidated, or one entire government, as it respects the counties, towns, citizens and property within the limits of the state.—The state governments are the basis, the pillar on which the federal head is placed, and the whole together, when formed on elective principles, constitute a federal republic. A federal republic in itself supposes state or local governments to exist, as the body or props, on which the federal head rests, and that it cannot remain a moment after they cease. In erecting the federal government, and always in its councils, each state must be known as a sovereign body; but in erecting this government, I conceive, the legislature of the state, by the expressed or implied assent of the people, or the people of the state, under the direction of the government of it, may accede to the federal compact: Nor do I conceive it to be necessarily a part of a confederacy of states, that each have an equal voice in the general councils. A confederated republic being organized, each state must retain powers for managing its internal police, and all delegate to the union power to manage general concerns: The quantity of power the union must possess is one thing, the mode of exercising the powers given, is quite a different consideration; and it is the mode of exercising them, that makes one of the essential distinctions between one entire or consolidated government, and a federal republic; that is, however the government may be organized, if the laws of the union, in most important concerns, as in levying and collecting taxes, raising troops, &c. operate immediately upon the persons and property of individuals, and not on states, extend to organizing the militia, &c. the government, as to its administration, as to making and executing laws, is not federal, but consolidated. To illustrate my idea—the union makes a requisition, and assigns to each state its quota of men or monies wanted; each state, by its own laws and officers, in its own way, furnishes its quota: here the state governments stand between the union and individuals; the laws of the union operate only on states, as such, and federally: Here nothing can be done without the meetings of the state legislatures—but in the other case the union, though the state legislatures should not meet for years together, proceeds immediately, by its own laws and officers, to levy and collect monies of individuals, to inlist men, form armies, &c. [H]ere the laws of the union operate immediately on the body of the people, on persons and property; in the same manner the laws of one entire consolidated government operate.—These two modes are very distinct, and in their operation and consequences have directly opposite tendencies: The first makes the existence of the state governments indispensable, and throws all the detail business of levying and collecting the taxes, &c. into the hands of those governments, and into the hands, of course, of many thousand officers solely created by, and dependent on the state. The last entirely excludes the agency of the respective states, and throws the whole business of levying and collecting taxes, &c. into the hands of many thousand officers solely created by, and dependent upon the union, and makes the existence of the state government of no consequence in the case. It is true, congress in raising any given sum in direct taxes, must by the constitution, raise so much of it in one state, and so much in another, by a fixed rule, which most of the states some time since agreed to: But this does not effect the principle in question, it only secures each state against any arbitrary proportions. The federal mode is perfectly safe and eligible, founded in the true spirit of a confederated republic; there could be no possible exception to it, did we not find by experience, that the states will sometimes neglect to comply with the reasonable requisitions of the union. It being according to the fundamental principles of federal republics, to raise men and monies by requisitions, and for the states individually to organize and train the militia, I conceive, there can be no reason whatever for departing from them, except this, that the states sometimes neglect to comply with reasonable requisitions, and that it is dangerous to attempt to compel a delinquent state by force, as it may often produce a war. We ought, therefore, to enquire attentively, how extensive the evils to be guarded against are, and cautiously limit the remedies to the extent of the evils. I am not about to defend the confederation, or to charge the proposed constitution with imperfections not in it; but we ought to examine facts, and strip them of the false colourings often given them by incautious observations, by unthinking or designing men. We ought to premise, that laws for raising men and monies, even in consolidated governments, are not often punctually complied with. Historians, except in extraordinary cases, but very seldom take notice of the detail collection of taxes; but these facts we have fully proved, and well attested; that the most energetic governments have relinquished taxes frequently, which were of many years standing. These facts amply prove, that taxes assessed, have remained many years uncollected. I agree there have been instances in the republics of Greece, Holland &c. in the course of several centuries, of states neglecting to pay their quotas of requisitions; but it is a circumstance certainly deserving of attention, whether these nations which have depended on requisitions principally for their defence, have not raised men and monies nearly as punctually as entire governments, which have taxed directly; whether we have not found the latter as often distressed for the want of troops and monies as the former. It has been said that the Amphictionic council, and the Germanic head, have not possessed sufficient powers to controul the members of the republic in a proper manner. Is this, if true, to be imputed to requisitions? Is it not principally to be imputed to the unequal powers of those members, connected with this important circumstance, that each member possessed power to league itself with foreign powers, and powerful neighbours, without the consent of the head. After all, has not the Germanic body a government as good as its neighbours in general? and did not the Grecian republic remain united several centuries, and form the theatre of human greatness? No government in Europe has commanded monies more plentifully than the government of Holland. As to the United States, the separate states lay taxes directly, and the union calls for taxes by way of requisitions; and is it a fact, that more monies are due in proportion on requisitions in the United States, than on the state taxes directly laid?—It is but about ten years since congress begun to make requisitions, and in that time, the monies, &c. required, and the bounties given for men required of the states, have amounted, specie value, to about 36 millions dollars, about 24 millions of dollars of which have been actually paid; and a very considerable part of the 12 millions not paid, remains so not so much from the neglect of the states, as from the sudden changes in paper money, &c. which in a great measure rendered payments of no service, and which often induced the union indirectly to relinquish one demand, by making another in a different form. Before we totally condemn requisitions, we ought to consider what immense bounties the states gave, and what prodigious exertions they made in the war, in order to comply with the requisitions of congress; and if since the peace they have been delinquent, ought we not carefully to enquire, whether that delinquency is to be imputed solely to the nature of requisitions? ought it not in part to be imputed to two other causes? I mean first, an opinion, that has extensively prevailed, that the requisitions for domestic interest have not been founded on just principles; and secondly, the circumstance, that the government itself, by proposing imposts, &c. has departed virtually from the constitutional system; which proposed changes, like all changes proposed in government, produce an inattention and negligence in the execution of the government in being.

I am not for depending wholly on requisitions; but I mention these few facts to shew they are not so totally futile as many pretend. For the truth of many of these facts I appeal to the public records; and for the truth of the others, I appeal to many republican characters, who are best informed in the affairs of the United States. Since the peace, and till the convention reported, the wisest men in the United States generally supposed, that certain limited funds would answer the purposes of the union: and though the states are by no means in so good a condition as I wish they were, yet, I think, I may very safely affirm, they are in a better condition than they would be had congress always possessed the powers

466

of taxation now contended for. The fact is admitted, that our federal government does not possess sufficient powers to give life and vigor to the political system; and that we experience disappointments, and several inconveniencies; but we ought carefully to distinguish those which are merely the consequences of a severe and tedious war, from those which arise from defects in the federal system. There has been an entire revolution in the United States within thirteen years, and the least we can compute the waste of labour and property at, during that period, by the war, is three hundred million of dollars. Our people are like a man just recovering from a severe fit of sickness. It was the war that disturbed the course of commerce, introduced floods of paper money, the stagnation of credit, and threw many valuable men out of steady business. From these sources our greatest evils arise; men of knowledge and reflection must perceive it;—but then, have we not done more in three or four years past, in repairing the injuries of the war, by repairing houses and estates, restoring industry, frugality, the fisheries, manufactures, &c. and thereby laying the foundation of good government, and of indiviudal [sic] and political happiness, than any people ever did in a like time; we must judge from a view of the country and facts, and not from foreign newspapers, or our own, which are printed chiefly in the commercial towns, where imprudent living, imprudent importations, and many unexpected disappointments, have produced a despondency, and a disposition to view every thing on the dark side. Some of the evils we feel, all will agree, ought to be imputed to the defective administration of the governments. From these and various considerations, I am very clearly of opinion, that the evils we sustain, merely on account of the defects of the confederation, are but as a feather in the balance against a mountain, compared with those which would, infallibly, be the result of the loss of general liberty, and that happiness men enjoy under a frugal, free, and mild government.

Heretofore we do not seem to have seen danger any where, but in giving power to congress, and now no where but in congress wanting powers; and, without examining the extent of the evils to be remedied, by one step, we are for giving up to congress almost all powers of any importance without limitation. The defects of the confederation are extravagantly magnified, and every species of pain we feel imputed to them: and hence it is inferred, there must be a total change of the principles, as well as forms of government: and in the main point, touching the federal powers, we rest all on a logical inference, totally inconsistent with experience and sound political reasoning.

It is said, that as the federal head must make peace and war, and provide for the common defence, it ought to possess all powers necessary to that end: that powers unlimited, as to the purse and sword, to raise men and monies, and form the militia, are necessary to that end; and, therefore, the federal head ought to possess them. This reasoning is far more specious than solid: it is necessary that these powers so exist in the body politic, as to be called into exercise whenever necessary for the public safety; but it is by no means true, that the man, or congress of men, whose duty it more immediately is to provide for the common defence, ought to possess them without limitation. But clear it is, that if such men, or congress, be not in a situation to hold them without danger to liberty, he or they ought not to possess them. It has long been thought to be a well founded position, that the purse and sword ought not to be placed in the same hands in a free government. Our wise ancestors have carefully separated them—placed the sword in the hands of their king, even under considerable limitations, and the purse in the hands of the commons alone: yet the king makes peace and war, and it is his duty to provide for the common defence of the nation. This authority at least goes thus far—that a nation, well versed in the science of government, does not conceive it to be necessary or expedient for the man entrusted with the common defence and general tranquility, to possess unlimitedly the powers in question, or even in any considerable degree. Could he, whose duty it is to defend the public, possess in himself independently, all the means of doing it consistent with the public good, it might be convenient: but the people of England know that their liberties and happiness would be in infinitely greater danger from the king's unlimited possession of these powers, than from all external enemies and internal commotions to which they might be exposed: therefore, though they have made it his duty to guard the empire, yet they have wisely placed in other hands, the hands of their representatives, the power to deal out and controul the means. In Holland their high mightinesses must provide for the common defence, but for the means they depend, in a considerable degree, upon requisitions made on the state or local assemblies. Reason and facts evince, that however convenient it might be for an executive magistrate, or federal head, more immediately charged with the national defence and safety, solely, directly, and independently to possess all the means; yet such magistrate, or head, never ought to possess them, if thereby the public liberties shall be endangered. The powers in question never have been, by nations wise and free, deposited, nor can they ever be, with safety, any where, but in the principal members of the national system;—where these form one entire government, as in Great-Britain, they are separated and lodged in the principal members of it. But in a federal republic, there is quite a different organization; the people form this kind of government, generally, because their territories are too extensive to admit of their assembling in one legislature, or of executing the laws on free principles under one entire government. They convene in their local assemblies, for local purposes, and for managing their internal concerns, and unite their states under a federal head for general purposes. It is the essential characteristic of a confederated republic, that this head be dependant on, and kept within limited bounds by, the local governments; and it is because, in these alone, in fact, the people can be substantially assembled or represented. It is, therefore, we very universally see, in this kind of government, the congressional powers placed in a few hands, and accordingly limited, and specifically enumerated: and the local assemblies strong and well guarded, and composed of numerous members. Wise men will always place the controuling power where the people are substantially collected by their representatives. By the proposed system, the federal head will possess, without limitation, almost every species of power that can, in its exercise, tend to change the government, or to endanger liberty; while in it, I think it has been fully shewn, the people will have but the shadow of representation, and but the shadow of security for their rights and liberties. In a confederated republic, the division of representation, &c. in its nature, requires a correspondent division and deposit of powers relative to taxes and military concerns: and I think the plan offered stands quite alone, in confounding the principles of governments in themselves totally distinct. I wish not to exculpate the states for their improper neglects in not paying their quotas of requisitions; but, in applying the remedy, we must be governed by reason and facts. It will not be denied, that the people have a right to change the government when the majority chuse it, if not restrained by some existing compact—that they have a right to displace their rulers, and consequently to determine when their measures are reasonable or not—and that they have a right, at any time, to put a stop to those measures they may deem prejudicial to them, by such forms and negatives as they may see fit to provide. From all these, and many other well founded considerations, I need not mention, a question arises, what powers shall there be delegated to the federal head, to insure safety, as well as energy, in the government? I think there is a safe and proper medium pointed out by experience, by reason, and facts. When we have organized the government, we ought to give power to the union, so far only as experience and present circumstances shall direct, with a reasonable regard to time to come. Should future circumstances, contrary to our expectations, require that further powers be transferred to the union, we can do it far more easily, than get back those we may now imprudently give. The system proposed is untried: candid advocates and opposers admit, that it is, in a degree, a mere experiment, and that its organization is weak and imperfect; surely then, the safe ground is cautiously to vest power in it, and when we are sure we have given enough for ordinary exigencies, to be extremely careful how we delegate powers, which, in common cases, must necessarily be useless or abused, and of very uncertain effect in uncommon ones.

By giving the union power to regulate commerce, and to levy and collect taxes by imposts, we give it an extensive authority, and permanent productive funds, I believe quite as adequate to the present demands of the union, as exises and direct taxes can be made to the present demands of the separate states. The state governments are now about four times as expensive as that of the union; and their several state debts added together, are nearly as large as that of the union—Our impost duties since the peace have been almost as productive as the other sources of taxation, and when under one general system of regulations, the probability is, that those duties will be very considerably increased: Indeed the representation proposed will hardly justify giving to congress unlimited powers to raise taxes by imposts, in addition to the other powers the union must necessarily have. It is said, that if congress possess only authority to raise taxes by imposts, trade probably will be overburdened with taxes, and the taxes of the union be found inadequate to any uncommon exigencies: To this we may observe, that trade generally finds its own level, and will naturally and necessarily leave off any undue burdens laid upon it: further, if congress alone possess the impost, and also unlimited power to raise monies by excises and direct taxes, there must be much more danger that two taxing powers, the union and states, will carry excises and direct taxes to an unreasonable extent, especially as these have not the natural boundaries taxes on trade have. However, it is not my object to propose to exclude congress from raising monies by internal taxes, as by duties, excises, and direct taxes, but my opinion is, that congress, especially in its proposed organization, ought not to raise monies by internal taxes, except in strict conformity to the federal plan; that is, by the agency of the state governments in all cases, except where a state shall neglect, for an unreasonable time, to pay its quota of a requisition; and never where so many of the state legislatures as represent a majority of the people, shall formally determine an excise law or requisition is improper, in their next session after the same be laid before them. We ought always to recollect that the evil to be guarded against is found by our own experience, and the experience of others, to be mere neglect in the states to pay their quotas; and power in the union to levy and collect the neglecting states' quotas with interest, is fully adequate to the evil. By this federal plan, with this exception mentioned, we secure the means of collecting the taxes by the usual process of law, and avoid the evil of attempting to compel or coerce a state; and we avoid also a circumstance, which never yet could be, and I am fully confident never can be, admitted in a free federal republic; I mean a permanent and continued system of tax laws of the union, executed in the bowels of the states by many thousand officers, dependent as to the assessing and collecting federal taxes, solely upon the union. On every principle then, we ought to provide, that the union render an exact account of all monies raised by imposts and other taxes; and that whenever monies shall be wanted for the purposes of the union, beyond the proceeds of the impost duties, requisitions shall be made on the states for the monies so wanted; and that the power of laying and collecting shall never be exercised, except in cases where a state shall neglect, a given time, to pay its quota. This mode seems to be strongly pointed out by the reason of the case, and spirit of the government; and I believe, there is no instance to be found in a federal republic, where the congressional powers ever extended generally to collecting monies by direct taxes or excises. Creating all these restrictions, still the powers of the union in matters of taxation, will be too unlimited; further checks, in my mind, are indispensably necessary. Nor do I conceive, that as full a representation as is practicable in the federal government, will afford sufficient security: the strength of the government, and the confidence of the people, must be collected principally in the local assemblies; every part or branch of the federal head must be feeble, and unsafely trusted with large powers. A government possessed of more power than its constituent parts will justify, will not only probably abuse it, but be unequal to bear its own burden; it may as soon be destroyed by the pressure of power, as languish and perish for want of it.

There are two ways further of raising checks, and guarding against undue combinations and influence in a federal system. The first is, in levying taxes, raising and keeping up armies, in building navies, in forming plans for the militia, and in appropriating monies for the support of the military, to require the attendance of a large proportion of the federal representatives, as two-thirds or three-fourths of them; and in passing laws, in these important cases, to require the consent of two-thirds or three-fourths of the members present. The second is, by requiring that certain important laws of the federal head, as a requisition or a law for raising monies by excise shall be laid before the state legislatures, and if disapproved of by a given number of them, say by as many of them as represent a majority of the people, the law shall have no effect. Whether it would be adviseable to adopt both, or either of these checks, I will not undertake to determine. We have seen them both exist in confederated republics. The first exists substantially in the confederation, and will exist in some measure in the plan proposed, as in chusing a president by the house, in expelling members; in the senate, in making treaties, and in deciding on impeachments, and in the whole in altering the constitution. The last exists in the United Netherlands, but in a much greater extent. The first is founded on this principle, that these important measures may, sometimes, be adopted by a bare quorum of members, perhaps, from a few states, and that a bare majority of the federal representatives may frequently be of the aristocracy, or some particular interests, connections, or parties in the community, and governed by motives, views, and inclinations not compatible with the general interest.—The last is founded on this principle, that the people will be substantially represented, only in their state or local assemblies; that their principal security must be found in them; and that, therefore, they ought to have ultimately a constitutional controul over such interesting measures.

I have often heard it observed, that our people are well informed, and will not submit to oppressive governments; that the state governments will be their ready advocates, and possess their confidence, mix with them, and enter into all their wants and feelings. This is all true; but of what avail will these circumstances be, if the state governments, thus allowed to be the guardians of the people, possess no kind of power by the forms of the social compact, to stop in their passage, the laws of congress injurious to the people. State governments must stand and see the law take place; they may complain and petition—so may individuals; the members of them, in extreme cases, may resist, on the principles of self-defence—so may the people and individuals.

It has been observed, that the people, in extensive territories, have more power, compared with that of their rulers, than in small states. Is not directly the opposite true? The people in a small state can unite and act in concert, and with vigour; but in large territories, the men who govern find it more easy to unite, while people cannot; while they cannot collect the opinions of each part, while they move to different points, and one part is often played off against the other.

It has been asserted, that the confederate head of a republic at best, is in general weak and dependent;—that the people will attach themselves to, and support their local governments, in all disputes with the union. Admit the fact: is it any way to remove the inconvenience by accumulating powers upon a weak organization? The fact is, that the detail administration of affairs, in this mixed republics, depends principally on the local governments; and the people would be wretched without them: and a great proportion of social happiness depends on the internal administration of justice, and on internal police. The splendor of the monarch, and the power of the government are one thing. The happiness of the subject depends on very different causes: but it is to the latter, that the best men, the greatest ornaments of human nature, have most carefully attended: it is to the former tyrants and oppressors have always aimed,

The Federal Farmer.

S. JAMES MADISON, THE FEDERALIST, NO. 44

January 25, 1788

To the People of the State of New York.

A *Fifth* class of provisions in favor of the fœderal authority, consists of the following restrictions on the authority of the several States:

1. "No State shall enter into any treaty, alliance or confederation, grant letters of marque and reprisal, coin money, emit bills of credit, make any thing but gold and silver a legal tender in payment of debts; pass any bill of attainder, ex post facto law, or law impairing the obligation of contracts, or grant any title of nobility."

The prohibition against treaties, alliances and confederations, makes a part of the existing articles of Union; and for reasons which need no explanation, is copied into the new Constitution. The prohibition of letters of marque is another part of the old system, but is somewhat extended in the new. According to the former, letters of marque could be granted by the States after a declaration of war. According to the latter, these licences must be obtained as well during war as previous to its declaration, from the government of the United States. This alteration is fully justified by the advantage of uniformity in all points which relate to foreign powers; and of immediate responsibility to the nation in all those, for whose conduct the nation itself is to be responsible.

The right of coining money, which is here taken from the States, was left in their hands by the confederation as a concurrent right with that of Congress, under an exception in favor of the exclusive right of Congress to regulate the alloy and value. In this instance also the new provision is an improvement on the old. Whilst the alloy and value depended on the general authority, a right of coinage in the particular States could have no other effect than to multiply expensive mints, and diversify the forms and weights of the circulating pieces. The latter inconveniency defeats one purpose for which the power was originally submitted to the fœderal head. And as far as the former might prevent an inconvenient remittance of gold and silver to the central mint for recoinage, the end can be as well attained, by local mints established under the general authority.

The extension of the prohibition to bills of credit must give pleasure to every citizen in proportion to his love of justice, and his knowledge of the true springs of public prosperity. The loss which America has sustained since the peace, from the pestilent effects of paper money, on the necessary confidence between man and man; on the necessary confidence in the public councils; on the industry and morals of the people, and on the character of Republican Government, constitutes an enormous debt against the States chargeable with this unadvised measure, which must long remain unsatisfied; or rather an accumulation of guilt, which can be expiated no otherwise than by a voluntary sacrifice on the altar of justice, of the power which has been the instrument of it. In addition to these persuasive considerations, it may be observed that the same reasons which shew the necessity of denying to the States the power of regulating coin, prove with equal force that they ought not to be at liberty to substitute a paper medium in the place of coin. Had every State a right to regulate the value of its coin, there might be as many different currencies as States; and thus the intercourse among them would be impeded; retrospective alterations in its value might be made, and thus the citizens of other States be injured; and animosities be kindled among the States themselves. The subjects of foreign powers might suffer from the same cause, and hence the Union be discredited and embroiled by the indiscretion of a single member. No one of these mischiefs is less incident to a power in the States to emit paper money than to coin gold or silver. The power to make any thing but gold and silver a tender in payment of debts, is withdrawn from the States, on the same principle with that of striking of paper currency.

Bills of attainder, ex post facto laws, and laws impairing the obligation of contracts, are contrary to the first principles of the social compact, and to every principle of sound legislation. The two former are expressly prohibited by the declarations prefixed to some of the State Constitutions, and all of them are prohibited by the spirit and scope of these fundamental charters. Our own experience has taught us nevertheless, that additional fences against these dangers ought not to be omitted. Very properly therefore have the Convention added this constitutional bulwark in favor of personal security and private rights; and I am much deceived if they have not in so doing as faithfully consulted the genuine sentiments, as the undoubted interests of their constituents. The sober people of America are weary of the fluctuating policy which has directed the public councils. They have seen with regret and with indignation, that sudden changes and legislative interferences in cases affecting personal rights, become jobs in the hands of enterprizing and influential speculators; and snares to the more industrious and less informed part of the community. They have seen, too, that legislative interference, is but the first link of a long chain of repetitions; every subsequent interference being naturally produced by the effects of the preceding. They very rightly infer, therefore, that some thorough reform is wanting which will banish speculations on public measures, inspire a general prudence and industry, and give a regular course to the business of society. The prohibition with respect to titles of nobility, is copied from the articles of confederation, and needs no comment.

2. "No State shall, without the consent of the Congress, lay any imposts or duties on imports or exports, except what may be absolutely necessary for executing its inspection laws, and the neat produce of all duties and imposts laid by any State on imports or exports, shall be for the use of the Treasury of the United States; and all such laws shall be subject to the revision and controul of the Congress. No State shall, without the consent of Congress, lay any duty on tonnage, keep troops or ships of war in time of peace; enter into any agreement or compact with another State, or with a foreign power, or engage in war unless actually invaded, or in such imminent danger as will not admit of delay."

The restraint on the power of the States over imports and exports is enforced by all the arguments which prove the necessity of submitting the regulation of trade to the fœderal councils. It is needless therefore to remark further on this head, than that the manner in which the restraint is qualified, seems well calculated at once to secure to the States a reasonable discretion in providing for the conveniency of their imports and exports; and to the United States a reasonable check against the abuse of this discretion. The remaining particulars of this clause, fall within reasonings which are either so obvious, or have been so fully developed, that they may be passed over without remark.

The sixth and last class consists of the several powers and provisions by which efficacy is given to all the rest.

1. "Of these the first is the power to make all laws which shall be necessary and proper for carrying into execution the foregoing powers, and all other powers vested by this Constitution in the government of the United States."

Few parts of the Constitution have been assailed with more intemperance than this; yet on a fair investigation of it, no part can appear more compleatly invulnerable. Without the *substance* of this power, the whole Constitution would be a dead letter. Those who object to the article therefore as a part of the Constitution, can only mean that the *form* of the provision is improper. But have they considered whether a better form could have been substituted?

There are four other possible methods which the Convention might have taken on this subject. They might have copied the second article of the existing confederation which would have prohibited the exercise of any power not *expressly* delegated; they might have attempted a positive enumeration of the powers comprehended under the general terms "necessary and proper"; they might have attempted a negative enumeration of them, by specifying the powers excepted from the general definition: They might have been altogether silent on the subject; leaving these necessary and proper powers, to construction and inference.

Had the Convention taken the first method of adopting the second article of confederation; it is evident that the new Congress would be continually exposed as their predecessors have been, to the alternative of construing the term *"expressly"* with so much rigour as to disarm the government of all real authority whatever, or with so much latitude as to destroy altogether the force of the restriction. It would be easy to shew if it were necessary, that no important power, delegated by the articles of confederation, has been or can be executed by Congress, without recurring more or less to the doctrine of *construction* or *implication*. As the powers delegated under the new system are more extensive, the government which is to administer it would find itself still more distressed with the alternative of betraying the public interest by doing nothing; or of violating the Constitution by exercising powers, indispensably necessary and proper; but at the same time, not *expressly* granted.

Had the Convention attempted a positive enumeration of the powers necessary and proper for carrying their other powers into effect; the attempt would have involved a complete digest of laws on every subject to which the Constitution relates; accommodated too not only to the existing state of things, but to all the possible changes which futurity may produce: For in every new application of a general power, the *particular powers*, which are the means of attaining the *object* of the general power, must always necessarily vary with that object; and be often properly varied whilst the object remains the same.

Had they attempted to enumerate the particular powers or means, not necessary or proper for carrying the general powers into execution, the task would have been no less chimerical; and would have been liable to this further objection; that every defect in the enumeration, would have been equivalent to a positive grant of authority. If to avoid this consequence they had attempted a partial enumeration of the exceptions, and described the residue by the general terms, *not necessary or proper:* It must have happened that the enumeration would comprehend a few of the excepted powers only; that these would be such as would be least likely to be assumed or tolerated, because the enumeration would of course select such as would be least necessary or proper, and that the unnecessary and improper powers included in the residuum, would be less forceably excepted, than if no partial enumeration had been made.

Had the Constitution been silent on this head, there can be no doubt that all the particular powers, requisite as means of executing the general powers, would have resulted to the government, by unavoidable implication. No axiom is more clearly established in law, or in reason, than that wherever the end is required, the means are authorised; wherever a general power to do a thing is given, every particular power necessary for doing it, is included. Had this last method therefore been pursued by the Convention, every objection now urged against their plan, would remain in all its plausibility; and the real inconveniency would be incurred, of not removing a pretext which may be seized on critical occasions for drawing into question the essential powers of the Union.

If it be asked, what is to be the consequence, in case the Congress shall misconstrue this part of the Constitution, and exercise powers not warranted by its true meaning? I answer the same as if they should misconstrue or enlarge any other power vested in them, as if the general power had been reduced to particulars, and any one of these were to be violated; the same in short, as if the State Legislatures should violate their respective constitutional authorities. In the first instance, the success of the usurpation will depend on the executive and judiciary departments, which are to expound and give effect to the legislative acts; and in the last resort, a remedy must be obtained from the people, who can by the election of more faithful representatives, annul the acts of the usurpers. The truth is, that this ultimate redress may be more confided in against unconstitutional acts of the fœderal than of the State Legislatures, for this plain reason, that as every such act of the former, will be an invasion of the rights of the latter, these will be ever ready to mark the innovation, to sound the alarm to the people, and to exert their local influence in effecting a change of fœderal representatives. There being no such intermediate body between the State Legislatures and the people, interested in watching the conduct of the former, violations of the State Constitutions are more likely to remain unnoticed and unredressed.

2. "This Constitution and the laws of the United States which shall be made in pursuance thereof, and all treaties made, or which shall be made, under the authority of the United States, shall be the supreme law of the land, and the Judges in every State shall be bound thereby, any thing in the Constitution or laws of any State to the contrary notwithstanding."

The indiscreet zeal of the adversaries to the Constitution, has betrayed them into an attack on this part of it also, without which it would have been evidently and radically defective. To be fully sensible of this we need only suppose for a moment, that the supremacy of the State Constitutions had been left compleat by a saving clause in their favor.

In the first place, as these Constitutions invest the State Legislatures with absolute sovereignty, in all cases not excepted by the existing articles of confederation, all the authorities contained in the proposed Constitution, so far as they exceed those enumerated in the confederation, would have been annulled, and the new Congress would have been reduced to the same impotent condition with their predecessors.

In the next place, as the Constitutions of some of the States do not even expressly and fully recognize the existing powers of the confederacy, an express saving of the supremacy of the former, would in such States have brought into question, every power contained in the proposed Constitution.

In the third place, as the Constitutions of the States differ much from each other, it might happen that a treaty or national law of great and equal importance to the States, would interfere with some and not with other Constitutions, and would consequently be valid in some of the States at the same time that it would have no effect in others.

In fine, the world would have seen for the first time, a system of government founded on an inversion of the fundamental principles of all government; it would have seen the authority of the whole society every where subordinate to the authority of the parts; it would have seen a monster in which the head was under the direction of the members.

3. "The Senators and Representatives, and the members of the several State Legislatures; and all executive and judicial officers, both of the United States, and the several States shall be bound by oath or affirmation, to support this Constitution."

It has been asked, why it was thought necessary, that the State magistracy should be bound to support the Fœderal Constitution, and unnecessary, that a like oath should be imposed on the officers of the United States in favor of the State Constitutions?

Several reasons might be assigned for the distinction. I content myself with one which is obvious & conclusive. The members of the Fœderal Government will have no agency in carrying the State Constitutions into effect. The members and officers of the State Governments, on the contrary, will have an essential agency in giving effect to the Fœderal Constitution. The election of the President and Senate, will depend in all cases, on the Legislatures of the several States. And the election of the House of Representatives, will equally depend on the same authority in the first instance; and will probably, for ever be conducted by the officers and according to the laws of the States.

4. Among the provisions for giving efficacy to the fœderal powers, might be added, those which belong to the executive and judiciary departments: But as these are reserved for particular examination in another place, I pass them over in this.

We have now reviewed in detail all the articles composing the sum or quantity of power delegated by the proposed Constitution to the Fœderal Government; and are brought to this undeniable conclusion, that no part of the power is unnecessary or improper for accomplishing the necessary objects of the Union. The question therefore, whether this amount of power shall be granted or not, resolves itself into another question, therefore, whether or not a government commensurate to the exigencies of the Union, shall be established, or in other words, whether the Union itself shall be preserved.

PUBLIUS.

T. JAMES MADISON, THE FEDERALIST, NO. 45

January 26, 1788

To the People of the State of New York.

Having shewn that no one of the powers transferred to the federal Government is unnecessary or improper, the next question to be considered is whether the whole mass of them will be dangerous to the portion of authority left in the several States.

The adversaries to the plan of the Convention instead of considering in the first place what degree of power was absolutely necessary for the purposes of the federal Government, have exhausted themselves in a secondary enquiry into the possible consequences of the proposed degree of power, to the Governments of the particular States. But if the Union, as has been shewn, be essential, to the security of the people of America against foreign danger; if it be essential to their security against contentions and wars among the different States; if it be essential to guard them against those violent and oppressive factions which embitter the blessings of liberty, and against those military establishments which must gradually poison its very fountain; if, in a word the Union be essential to the happiness of the people of America, is it not preposterous, to urge as an objection to a government without which the objects of the Union cannot be attained, that such a Government may derogate from the importance of the Governments of the individual States? Was

478

then the American revolution effected, was the American confederacy formed, was the precious blood of thousands spilt, and the hard earned substance of millions lavished, not that the people of America should enjoy peace, liberty and safety; but that the Governments of the individual States, that particular municipal establishments, might enjoy a certain extent of power, and be arrayed with certain dignities and attributes of sovereignty? We have heard of the impious doctrine in the old world that the people were made for kings, not kings for the people. Is the same doctrine to be revived in the new, in another shape, that the solid happiness of the people is to be sacrificed to the views of political institutions of a different form? It is too early for politicians to presume on our forgetting that the public good, the real welfare of the great body of the people is the supreme object to be pursued; and that no form of Government whatever, has any other value, than as it may be fitted for the attainment of this object. Were the plan of the Convention adverse to the public happiness, my voice would be, reject the plan. Were the Union itself inconsistent with the public happiness, it would be, abolish the Union. In like manner as far as the sovereignty of the States cannot be reconciled to the happiness of the people, the voice of every good citizen must be, let the former be sacrificed to the latter. How far the sacrifice is necessary, has been shewn. How far the unsacrificed residue will be endangered, is the question before us.

Several important considerations have been touched in the course of these papers, which discountenance the supposition that the operation of the federal Government will by degrees prove fatal to the State Governments. The more I revolve the subject the more fully I am persuaded that the balance is much more likely to be disturbed by the preponderancy of the last than of the first scale.

We have seen in all the examples of antient and modern confederacies, the strongest tendency continually betraying itself in the members to despoil the general Government of its authorities, with a very ineffectual capacity in the latter to defend itself against the encroachments. Although in most of these examples, the system has been so dissimilar from that under consideration, as greatly to weaken any inference concerning the latter from the fate of the former; yet as the States will retain under the proposed Constitution a very extensive portion of active sovereignty, the inference ought not to be wholly disregarded. In the Achæan league, it is probable that the federal head had a degree and species of power, which gave it a considerable likeness to the government framed by the Convention. The Lycian confederacy, as far as its principles and form are transmitted, must have borne a still greater analogy to it. Yet history does not inform us that either of them ever degenerated or tended to degenerate into one consolidated government. On the contrary, we know that the ruin of one of them proceeded from the incapacity of the federal authority to prevent the dissentions, and finally the disunion of the subordinate authorities. These cases are the more worthy of our attention, as the external causes by which the component parts were pressed together, were much more numerous and powerful than in our case; and consequently, less powerful ligaments within, would be sufficient to bind the members to the head, and to each other.

In the feudal system we have seen a similar propensity exemplified. Notwithstanding the want of proper sympathy in every instance between the local sovereigns and the people, and the sympathy in some instances between the general sovereign and the latter; it usually happened that the local sovereigns prevailed in the rivalship for encroachments. Had no external dangers, enforced internal harmony and subordination; and particularly had the local sovereigns possessed the affections of the people, the great kingdoms in Europe, would at this time consist of as many independent princes as there were formerly feudatory barons.

The State Governments will have the advantage of the federal Government, whether we compare them in respect to the immediate dependence of the one or the other; to the weight of personal influence which each side will possess; to the powers respectively vested in them; to the predilection and probable support of the people; to the disposition and faculty of resisting and frustrating the measures of each other.

The State Governments may be regarded as constituent and essential parts of the federal Government; whilst the latter is nowise essential to the operation or organisation of the former. Without the intervention of the State Legislatures, the President of the United States cannot be elected at all. They must in all cases have a great share in his appointment, and will perhaps in most cases of themselves determine it. The Senate will be elected absolutely and exclusively by the State Legislatures. Even the House of Representatives, though drawn immediately from the people, will be chosen very much under the influence of that class of men, whose influence over the people obtains for themselves an election into the State Legislatures. Thus each of the principal branches of the federal Government will owe its existence more or less to the favor of the State Governments, and must consequently feel a dependence, which is much more likely to beget a disposition too obsequious, than too overbearing towards them. On the other side, the component parts of the State Governments will in no instance be indebted for their appointment to the direct agency of the federal government, and very little if at all, to the local influence of its members.

The number of individuals employed under the Constitution of the United States, will be much smaller, than the number employed under the particular States. There will consequently be less of personal influence on the side of the former, than of the latter. The members of the legislative, executive and judiciary departments of thirteen and more States; the justices of peace, officers of militia, ministerial officers of justice, with all the county corporation and town-officers, for three millions and more of people, intermixed and having particular acquaintance with every class and circle of people, must exceed beyond all proportion, both in number and influence, those of every description who will be employed in the administration of the federal system. Compare the members of the three great departments, of the thirteen States, excluding from the judiciary department the justices of peace, with the members of the corresponding departments of the single Government of the Union; compare the militia officers of three millions of people, with the military and marine officers of any establishment which is within the compass of probability, or I may add, of possibility, and in this view alone, we may pronounce the advantage of the States to be decisive. If the federal Government is to have collectors of revenue, the State Governments will have theirs also. And as those of the former will be principally on the sea-coast, and not very numerous; whilst those of the latter will be spread over the face of the country, and will be very numerous, the advantage in this view also lies on the same side. It is true that the confederacy is to possess, and may exercise, the power of collecting internal as well as external taxes throughout the States: But it is probable that this power will not be resorted to, except for supplemental purposes of revenue; that an option will then be given to the States to supply their quotas by previous collections of their own; and that the eventual collection under the immediate authority of the Union, will generally be made by the officers, and according to the rules, appointed by the several States. Indeed it is extremely probable that in other instances, particularly in the organisation of the judicial power, the officers of the States will be cloathed with the correspondent authority of the Union. Should it happen however that separate collectors of internal revenue should be appointed under the federal Government, the influence of the whole number would not be a comparison with that of the multitude of State officers in the opposite scale. Within every district, to which a federal collector would be allotted, there would not be less than thirty or forty or even more officers of different descriptions and many of them persons of character and weight, whose influence would lie on the side of the State.

The powers delegated by the proposed Constitution to the Federal Government, are few and defined. Those which are to remain in the State Governments are numerous and indefinite. The former will be exercised principally on external objects, as war, peace, negociation, and foreign commerce; with which last the power of taxation will for the most part be connected. The powers reserved to the several States will extend to all the objects, which, in the ordinary course of affairs, concern the lives, liberties and properties of the people; and the internal order, improvement, and prosperity of the State.

The operations of the Federal Government will be most extensive and important in times of war and danger; those of the State Governments, in times of peace and security. As the former periods will probably bear a small proportion to the latter, the State Governments will here enjoy another advantage over the Federal Government. The more adequate indeed the federal powers may be rendered to the national defence, the less frequent will be those scenes of danger which might favour their ascendency over the governments of the particular States.

If the new Constitution be examined with accuracy and candour, it will be found that the change which it proposes, consists much less in the addition of NEW POWERS to the Union, than in the invigoration of its ORIGINAL POWERS. The regulation of commerce, it is true, is a new power; but that seems to be an addition which few oppose, and from which no apprehensions are entertained. The powers relating to war and peace, armies and fleets, treaties and finance, with the other more considerable powers, are all vested in the existing Congress by the articles of Confederation. The proposed change does not enlarge these powers; it only substitutes a more effectual mode of administering them. The change relating to taxation, may be regarded as the most important: And yet the present Congress have as compleat authority to REQUIRE of the States indefinite supplies of money for the common defence and general welfare, as the future Congress will have to require them of individual citizens; and the latter will be no more bound than the States themselves have been, to pay the quotas respectively taxed on them. Had the States complied punctually with the articles of confederation, or could their compliance have been enforced by as peaceable means as may be used with success towards single persons, our past experience is very far from countenancing an opinion that the State Governments would have lost their constitutional powers, and have gradually undergone an entire consolidation. To maintain that such an event would have ensued, would be to say at once, that the existence of the State Governments is incompatible with any system whatever that accomplishes the essential purposes of the Union.

PUBLIUS.

U. JAMES MADISON, THE FEDERALIST, NO. 46

January 29, 1788

To the People of the State of New York.

Resuming the subject of the last paper, I proceed to enquire whether the Fœderal Government or the State Governments will have the advantage with regard to the predilection and support of the people. Notwithstanding the different modes in which they are appointed, we must consider both of them, as substantially dependent on the great body of the citizens of the United States. I assume this position here as it respects the first, reserving the proofs for another place. The Fœderal and State Governments are in fact but different agents and trustees of the people, instituted with different powers, and designated for different purposes. The adversaries of the Constitution seem to have lost sight of the people altogether in their reasonings on this subject; and to have viewed these different establishments, not only as mutual rivals and enemies, but as uncontrouled by any common superior in their efforts to usurp the authorities of each other. These gentlemen must here be reminded of their error. They must be told that the ultimate authority, wherever the derivative may be found, resides in the people alone; and that it will not depend merely on the comparative ambition or address of the different governments, whether either, or which of them, will be able to enlarge its sphere of jurisdiction at the expence of the other. Truth no less than decency requires, that the event in every case, should be supposed to depend on the sentiments and sanction of their common constituents.

Many considerations, besides those suggested on a former occasion, seem to place it beyond doubt, that the first and most natural attachment of the people will be to the governments of their respective States. Into the administration of these, a greater number of individuals will expect to rise. From the gift of these a greater number of offices and emoluments will flow. By the superintending care of these, all the more domestic, and personal interests of the people will be regulated and provided for. With the affairs of these, the people will be more familiarly and minutely conversant. And with the members of these, will a greater proportion of the people have the ties of personal acquaintance and friendship, and of family and party attachments; on the side of these therefore the popular bias, may well be expected most strongly to incline.

Experience speaks the same language in this case. The fœderal administration, though hitherto very defective, in comparison with what may be hoped under a better system, had during the war, and particularly, whilst the independent fund of paper emissions was in credit, an activity and importance as great as it can well have, in any future circumstances whatever. It was engaged too in a course of measures, which had for their object, the protection of every thing that was dear, and the acquisition of every thing that could be desireable to the people at large. It was nevertheless, invariably found, after the transient enthusiasm for the early Congresses was over, that the attention and attachment of the people were turned anew to their own particular government; that the Fœderal Council, was at no time the idol of popular favor; and that opposition to proposed enlargements of its powers and importance, was the side usually taken by the men who wished to build their political consequence on the prepossessions of their fellow citizens.

If therefore, as has been elsewhere remarked, the people should in future become more partial to the fœderal than to the State governments, the change can only result, from such manifest and irresistible proofs of a better administration, as will overcome all their antecedent propensities. And in that case, the people ought not surely to be precluded from giving most of their confidence where they may discover it to be most due: But even in that case, the State governments could have little to apprehend, because it is only within a certain sphere, that the fœderal power can, in the nature of things, be advantageously administered.

The remaining points on which I proposed to compare the fœderal and State governments, are the disposition, and the faculty they may respectively possess, to resist and frustrate the measures of each other.

It has been already proved, that the members of the fœderal will be more dependent on the members of the State governments, than the latter will be on the former. It has appeared also, that the prepossessions of the people on whom both will depend, will be more on the side of the State governments, than of the Fœderal Government. So far as the disposition of each, towards the other, may be influenced by these causes, the State governments must clearly have the advantage. But in a distinct and very important point of view, the advantage will lie on the same side. The prepossessions which the members themselves will carry into the Fœderal Government, will generally be favorable to the States; whilst it will rarely happen, that the members of the State governments will carry into the public councils, a bias in favor of the general government. A local spirit will infallibly prevail much more in the members of the Congress, than a national spirit will prevail in the Legislatures of the particular States. Every one knows that a great proportion of the errors committed by the State Legislatures proceeds from the disposition of the members to sacrifice the comprehensive and permanent interest of the State, to the particular and separate views of the counties or districts in which they reside. And if they do not sufficiently enlarge their policy to embrace the collective welfare of their particular State, how can it be imagined, that they will make the aggregate prosperity of the Union, and the dignity and respectability of its government, the objects of their affections and consultations? For the same reason, that the members of the State Legislatures, will be unlikely to attach themselves sufficiently to national objects, the members of the Fœderal Legislature will be likely to attach themselves too much to local objects. The States will be to the latter, what counties and towns are to the former. Measures will too often be decided according to their probable effect, not on the national prosperity and happiness, but on the prejudices, interests and pursuits of the governments and people of the individual States. What is the spirit that has in general characterized the proceedings of Congress? A perusal of their journals as well as the candid acknowledgments of such as have had a seat in that assembly, will inform us, that the members have but too frequently displayed the character, rather of partizans of their respective States, than of impartial guardians of a common interest; that whereon one occasion improper sacrifices have been made of local considerations to the aggrandizement of the Fœderal Government; the great interests of the nation have suffered on an hundred, from an undue attention to the local prejudices, interests and views of the particular States. I mean not by these reflections to insinuate, that the new Fœderal Government will not embrace a more enlarged plan of policy than the existing government may have pursued, much less that its views will be as confined as those of the State Legislatures; but only that it will partake sufficiently of the spirit of both, to be disinclined to invade the rights of the individual States, or the prerogatives of their governments. The motives on the part of the State governments, to augment their prerogatives by defalcations from the Fœderal Government, will be overruled by no reciprocal predispositions in the members.

Were it admitted however that the Fœderal Government may feel an equal disposition with the State governments to extend its power beyond the due limits, the latter would still have the advantage in the means of defeating such encroachments. If an act of a particular State, though unfriendly to the national government, be generally popular in that State, and should not too grossly violate the oaths of the State officers, it is executed immediately and of course, by means on the spot, and depending on the State alone. The opposition of the Fœderal Government, or the interposition of Fœderal officers, would but inflame the zeal of all parties on the side of the State, and the evil could not be prevented or repaired, if at all, without the employment of means which must always be resorted to with reluctance and difficulty. On the other hand, should an unwarrantable measure of the Fœderal Government be unpopular in particular States, which would seldom fail to be the case, or even a warrantable measure be so, which may sometimes be the case, the means of opposition to it are powerful and at hand. The disquietude of the people, their repugnance and perhaps refusal to co-operate with the officers of the Union, the frowns of the executive magistracy of the State, the embarrassments created by legislative devices, which would often be added on such occasions, would oppose in any State difficulties not to be despised; would form in a large State very serious impediments, and where the sentiments of several adjoining States happened to be in unison, would present obstructions which the Fœderal Government would hardly be willing to encounter.

But ambitious encroachments of the Fœderal Government, on the authority of the State governments, would not excite the opposition of a single State or of a few States only. They would be signals of general alarm. Every Government would espouse the common cause. A correspondence would be opened. Plans of resistance would be concerted. One spirit would animate and conduct the whole. The same combination in short would result from an apprehension of the fœderal, as was produced by the dread of a foreign yoke; and unless the projected innovations should be voluntarily renounced, the same appeal to a trial of force would be made in the one case, as was made in the other. But what degree of madness could ever drive the Fœderal Government to such an extremity? In the contest with Great Britain, one part of the empire was employed against the other. The more numerous part invaded the rights of the less numerous part. The attempt was unjust and unwise; but it was not in speculation absolutely chimerical. But what would be the contest in the case we are supposing? Who would be the parties? A few representatives of the people, would be opposed to the people themselves; or rather one set of representatives would be contending against thirteen sets of representatives, with the whole body of their common constituents on the side of the latter.

The only refuge left for those who prophecy the downfall of the State Governments, is the visionary supposition that the Fœderal Government may previously accumulate a military force for the projects of ambition. The reasonings contained in these papers must have been employed to little purpose indeed, if it could be necessary now to disprove the reality of this danger. That the people and the States should for a sufficient period of time elect an uninterrupted succession of men ready to betray both; that the traitors should throughout this period, uniformly and systematically pursue some fixed plan for the extension of the military establishment; that the governments and the people of the States should silently and patiently behold the gathering storm, and continue to supply the materials, until it should be prepared to burst on their own heads, must appear to every one more like the incoherent dreams of a delirious jealousy, or the misjudged exaggerations of a counterfeit zeal, than like the sober apprehensions of genuine patriotism. Extravagant as the supposition is, let it however be made. Let a regular army, fully equal to the resources of the country be formed; and let it be entirely at the devotion of the Fœderal Government; still it would not be going too far to say, that the State Governments with the people on their side would be able to repel the danger. The highest number to which, according to the best computation, a standing army can be carried in any country, does not exceed one hundredth part of the whole number of souls; or one twenty-fifth part of the number able to bear arms. This proportion would not yield in the United States an army of more than twenty-five or thirty thousand men. To these would be opposed a militia amounting to near half a million of citizens with arms in their hands, officered by men chosen from among themselves, fighting for their common liberties, and united and conducted by governments possessing their affections and confidence. It may well be doubted whether a militia thus circumstanced could ever be conquered by such a proportion of regular troops. Those who are best acquainted with the late successful resistance of this country against the British arms will be most inclined to deny the possibility of it. Besides the advantage of being armed, which the Americans possess over the people of almost every other nation, the existence of subordinate governments to which the people are attached, and by which the militia officers are appointed, forms a barrier against the enterprizes of ambition, more insurmountable than any which a simple government of any form can admit of. Notwithstanding the military establishments in the several kingdoms of Europe, which are carried as far as the public resources will bear, the governments are afraid to trust the people with arms. And it is not certain that with this aid alone, they would not be able to shake off their yokes. But were the people to possess the additional advantages of local governments chosen by themselves, who could collect the national will, and direct the national force; and of officers appointed out of the militia, by these governments and attached both to them and to the militia, it may be affirmed with the greatest assurance, that the throne of every tyranny in Europe would be speedily overturned, in spite of the legions which surround it. Let us not insult the free and gallant citizens of America with the suspicion that they would be less able to defend the rights of which they would be in actual possession, than the debased subjects of arbitrary power would be to rescue theirs from the hands of their oppressers. Let us rather no longer insult them with the supposition, that they can ever reduce themselves to the necessity of making the experiment, by a blind and tame submission to the long train of insidious measures, which must precede and produce it.

The argument under the present head may be put into a very concise form, which appears altogether conclusive. Either the mode in which the Fœderal Government is to be constructed will render it sufficiently dependant on the people, or it will not. On the first supposition, it will be restrained by that dependence from forming schemes obnoxious to their constituents. On the other supposition it will not possess the confidence of the people, and its schemes of usurpation will be easily defeated by the State Governments; who will be supported by the people.

On summing up the considerations stated in this and the last paper, they seem to amount to the most convincing evidence, that the powers proposed to be lodged in the Fœderal Government, are as little formidable to those reserved to the individual States, as they are indispensibly necessary to accomplish the purposes of the Union; and that all those alarms which have been sounded, of a meditated or consequential annihilation of the State Governments, must, on the most favorable interpretation, be ascribed to the chimerical fears of the authors of them.

PUBLIUS.

V. PROPOSALS FROM THE STATE CONVENTIONS

(1) Pennsylvania, December 12, 1787

15. That the sovereignty, freedom, and independency of the several states shall be retained, and every power, jurisdiction and right which is not by this Constitution expressly delegated to the United States in Congress assembled.

(2) Massachusetts, February 6, 1788

First, That it be explicitly declared that all Powers not expressly delegated by the aforesaid Constitution are reserved to the several States to be by them exercised.

(3) Maryland, April 26, 1788

1. That congress shall exercise no power but what is expressly delegated by this constitution.

(4) South Carolina, May 23, 1788

This Convention doth also declare that no Section or paragraph of the said Constitution warrants a Construction that the states do not retain every power not expressly relinquished by them and vested in the General Government of the Union.

(5) New Hampshire, June 21, 1788

First that it be Explicitly declared that all Powers not expressly & particularly Delegated by the aforesaid Constitution are reserved to the several States to be, by them Exercised.—

(6) Virginia, June 27, 1788

First, That there are certain natural rights of which men, when they form a social compact cannot deprive or divest their posterity, among which are the enjoyment of life and liberty, with the means of acquiring, possessing and protecting property, and pursuing and obtaining happiness and safety. Second, That all power is naturally vested in and consequently derived from the people; that Magestrates, therefore, are their trustees and agents at all times amenable to them. . . .

Amendments to the Body of the Constitution.

First, That each State in the Union shall respectively retain every power, jurisdiction and right which is not by this Constitution delegated to the Congress of the United States or to the departments of the Fæderal Government. . . . Seventeeth, [sic] That those clauses which declare that Congress shall not exercise certain powers be not interpreted in any manner whatsoever to extend the powers of Congress. But that they may be construed either as making exceptions to the specified powers where this shall be the case, or otherwise as inserted merely for greater caution.

(7) New York, July 26, 1788

That all Power is originally vested in and consequently derived from the People, and that Government is instituted by them for their common Interest Protection and Security.

That the enjoyment of Life, Liberty and the pursuit of Happiness are essential rights which every Government ought to respect and preserve.

That the Powers of Government may be reassumed by the People, whensoever it shall become necessary to their Happiness; that every Power, Jurisdiction and right, which is not by the said Constitution clearly delegated to the Congress of the United States, or the departments of the Government thereof, remains to the People of the several States, or to their respective State Governments to whom they may have granted the same; And that those Clauses in the said Constitution, which declare, that Congress shall not have or exercise certain Powers, do not imply that Congress is entitled to any Powers not given by the said Constitution; but such Clauses are to be construed either as exceptions to certain specified Powers, or as inserted merely for greater Caution.

(8) North Carolina, August 1, 1788

1st.   That there are certain natural rights of which men, when they form a social compact, cannot deprive or divest their posterity, among which are the enjoyment of life, and liberty, with the means of acquiring, possessing and protecting property, and pursuing and obtaining happiness and safety.

2d.   That all power is naturally vested in, and consequently derived from the people; . . .

. I.   That each state in the union shall, respectively, retain every power, jurisdiction and right, which is not by this constitution delegated to the Congress of the United States, or to the departments of the Federal Government.

. . .

XVIII.   That those clauses which declare that Congress shall not exercise certain powers, be not interpreted in any manner whatsoever to extend the powers of Congress; but that they be construed either as making exceptions to the specified powers where this shall be the case, or otherwise, as inserted merely for greater caution.

W.   DEBATE IN THE STATE CONVENTIONS

(1) Pennsylvania, November 28, 1787

Mr. Smilie. I am happy, Mr. President, to find the argument placed upon the proper ground, and that the honorable member from the city has so fully spoken on the question, whether this system proposes a consolidation or a confederation of the states, as that is, in my humble opinion, the source of the greatest objection, which can be made to its adoption. I agree likewise with him, Sir, that it is, or ought to be, the object of all governments, to fix upon the intermediate point between tyranny and licentiousness; and therefore, it will be one of the great objects of our enquiry, to ascertain how far the proposed system deviates from that point of political happiness. For my part, I will readily confess, that it appears to be well guarded against licentiousness, but I am apprehensive it has deviated a little on the left hand, and rather invites than guards against the approaches of tyranny. I think however, Mr. President, it has been clearly argued, that the proposed system does not directly abolish, the governments of the several States, because its organization, and, for some time, perhaps, its operations, naturally presuppose their existence. But, Sir, it is not said, nor is thought, that the words of this instrument expressly announce that the sovereignty of the several States, their independency, jurisdiction, and power, are at once absorbed and annihilated by the general government. To this position and to this alone, the arguments of the honorable gentlemen can effectually apply, and there they must undoubtedly hold as long as the forms of State Government remain, at least, till a change takes place in the federal constitution. It is, however, upon other principles that the final destruction of the individual governments is asserted to be a necessary consequence of their association under this general form,—for, Sir, it is the silent but certain operation of the powers, and not the cautious, but artful tenor of the expressions contained in this system, that can excite terror, or generate oppression. The flattery of language was indeed necessary to disguise the baneful purpose, but it is like the dazzling polish bestowed upon an instrument of death; and the visionary prospect of a magnificent, yet popular government, was the most specious mode of rendering the people accessory to the ruin of those systems which they have so recently and so ardently labored to establish. Hence, Sir, we may trace that passage which has been pronounced by the honorable delegate to the late convention with exultation and applause; but when it is declared that "We the people of the United States do ordain and establish this constitution," is not the very foundation a proof of a consolidated government, by the manifest subversion of the principle that constitutes a union of States, which are sovereign and independent, except in the specific objects of confederation? These words have a plain and positive meaning, which could not be misunderstood by those who employed them; and therefore, Sir, it is fair and reasonable to infer, that it was in contemplation of the framers of this system, to absorb and abolish the efficient sovereignty and independent powers of the several States, in order to invigorate and aggrandize the general government. The plan before us, then, explicitly proposes the formation of a new constitution upon the original authority of the people, and not an association of States upon the authority of their respective governments. On that ground, we perceive that it contains all the necessary parts of a complete system of government, the executive, legislative and judicial establishments; and when two separate governments are at the same time in operation, over the same people, it will be difficult indeed to provide for each the means of safety and defence against the other; but if those means are not provided, it will be easily foreseen, that the stronger must eventually subdue and annihilate the weaker institution. Let us then examine the force and influence of the new system, and enquire whether the small remnant of power left to the States can be adequate even to the trifling charge of its own preservation. Here, Sir, we find the right of making laws for every purpose is invested in the future governors of America, and in this is included the uncontrolled jurisdiction over the purses of the people. The power of raising money is indeed the soul, the vital prop of legislation, without which legislation itself cannot for a moment exist. It will, however, be remarked that the power of taxation, though extended to the general government, is not taken from the States individually. Yes, Sir!—but it will be remembered that the national government may take from the people just what they please, and if anything should afterwards remain, then indeed the exigencies of the State governments may be supplied from the scanty gleanings of the harvest. Permit me now, Sir, to call your attention to the powers enumerated in the 8th section of the first article, and particularly to that clause which authorizes the proposed Congress, "to lay and collect taxes, duties, imposts and excises, to pay the debts and provide for the common defence and general welfare of the United States." With such powers, Mr. President, what cannot the future governors accomplish? It will be said, perhaps, that the treasure, thus accumulated, is raised and appropriated for the general welfare and the common defence of the States; but may not this pretext be easily perverted to other purposes, since those very men who raise and appropriate the taxes, are the only judges of what shall be deemed the general welfare and common defence of the national government? If then, Mr. President, they have unlimited power to drain the wealth of the people in every channel of taxation, whether by imposts on our commercial intercourse with foreign nations, or by direct levies on the people, I repeat it, that this system must be too formidable for any single State, or even for a combination of the States, should an attempt be made to break and destroy the yoke of domination and tyranny which it will hereafter set up. If, indeed, the spirit of men, once inflamed with the knowledge of freedom, should occasionally blaze out in remonstrance, opposition and force, these symptoms would naturally excite the jealousy of their rulers, and tempt them to proceed in the career of usurpation, till the total destruction of every principle of liberty should furnish a fit security for the exercise of arbitrary power. The money which has been raised from the people, may then be effectually employed to keep them in a state of slavish subjection: the militia, regulated and commanded by the officers of the general government, will be warped from the patriotic nature of their institution, and a standing army, that most prevailing instrument of despotism, will be ever ready to enforce obedience to a government by which it is raised, supported and enriched. If, under such circumstances, the several States should presume to assert their undelegated rights, I ask again what balance remains with them to counteract the encroachments of so potent a superior? To assemble a military force would be impracticable; for the general government, foreseeing the attempt would anticipate the means, by the exercise of its indefinite control over the purses of the people; and, in order to act upon the consciences as well as the persons of men, we find it is expressly stipulated, that every officer of the State government shall be sworn to support the constitution of the United States. Hence likewise, Sir, I conclude that in every point of rivalship, in every contention for power on the one hand and for freedom on the other, the event must be favorable to the views and pretensions of a government gifted with so decisive a pre-eminence. Let us, however, regard this subject in another light. What, Mr. President, will be the feelings and ideas of the people, when by the operation of the proposed system, they are exposed to such accumulated expense, for the maintenance of the general government? Is it not easy to foresee, that however the States may be disposed individually to preserve the parade of independence and sovereignty, the people themselves will become indifferent, and at last, averse to the continuance of an expensive form, from which they derive no advantage? For, Sir, the attachment of citizens to their government and its laws is founded upon the benefits which they derive from them, and it will last no longer than the duration of the power to confer those benefits. When, therefore, the people of the respective States shall find their governments grown torpid, and divested of the means to promote their welfare and interests, they will not, Sir, vainly idolize a shadow, nor disburse their hard earned wealth without the prospect of a compensation. The constitution of the States having become weak and useless to every beneficial purpose, will be suffered to dwindle and decay, and thus if the governors of the Union are not too impatient for the accomplishment of unrivalled and absolute dominion, the destruction of State jurisdiction will be produced by its own insignificance. Having now, Mr. President, shown that eventually this system will establish a consolidated government, though the intention is not expressly avowed, I will take some notice of the honorable member's principle, culled from the mode of election which is here prescribed. Sir, we do not upon this occasion contend for forms, which it is certain may exist long after the substance has forever perished. It is well remembered that the Roman senate continued to meet in all its ceremonies, long after they had lost their power, and the liberty of Rome had been sacrificed to the most horrid tyranny. Such, Sir, must be the case with the State legislature, which will necessarily degenerate into a mere name, or at most settle in a formal board of electors, periodically assembled to exhibit the servile farce of filling up the Federal representation....

December 1, 1787

Mr. Findley delivered an eloquent and powerful speech, to prove that the proposed plan of government amounted to a consolidation, and not a confederation of the states. Mr. Wilson had before admitted that if this was a just objection, it would be strongly against the system; and it seems from the subsequent silence of all its advocates upon that subject (except Doctor Rush, who on Monday insinuated that he saw and rejoiced at the eventual annihilation of the state sovereignties) Mr. Findley has established his position. Previous to an investigation of the plan, that gentleman animadverted upon the argument of necessity, which had been so much insisted upon, and showed that we were in an eligible situation to attempt the improvement of the Federal Government, but not so desperately circumstanced as to be obliged to adopt any system, however destructive to the liberties of the people, and the sovereign rights of the states. He then argued that the proposed constitution established a general government and destroyed the individual governments, from the following evidence taken from the system itself: 1st. In the preamble, it is said, *We the People*, and not *We the States*, which therefore is a compact between individuals entering into society, and not between separate states enjoying independent power, and delegating a portion of that power for their common benefit. 2d. That in the legislature each member has a vote, whereas in a confederation, as we have hitherto practised it, and from the very nature of the thing, a state can only have one voice, and therefore all the delegates of any state can only give one vote. 3d. The powers given to the Federal body for imposing internal taxation will necessarily destroy the state sovereignties, for there cannot exist two independent sovereign taxing powers in the same community, and the strongest will of course annihilate the weaker. 4th. The power given to regulate and judge of elections is a proof of a consolidation, for there cannot be two powers employed at the same time in regulating the same elections, and if they were a confederated body, the individual states would judge of the elections, and the general Congress would judge of the credentials which proved the election of its members. 5th. The judiciary power, which is co-extensive with the legislative, is another evidence of a consolidation. 6th. The manner in which the wages of the members is paid, makes another proof; and lastly, The oath of allegiance directed to be taken establishes it incontrovertibly; for would it not be absurd, that the members of the legislative and executive branches of a sovereign state should take a test of allegiance to another sovereign or independent body?

Mr. Wilson. The secret is now disclosed, and it is discovered to be a dread that the boasted state sovereignties will, under this system, be disrobed of part of their power. Before I go into the examination of this point, let me ask one important question: Upon what principle is it contended that the sovereign power resides in the state governments? The honorable gentleman has said truly, that there can be no subordinate sovereignty. Now if there can not, my position is, that the sovereignty resides in the people. They have not parted with it; they have only dispensed such portions of power as were conceived necessary for the public welfare. This constitution stands upon this broad principle. I know very well, Sir, that the people have hitherto been shut out of the federal government, but it is not meant that they should any longer be dispossessed of their rights. In order to recognize this leading principle, the proposed system sets out with a declaration that its existence depends upon the supreme authority of the people alone. We have heard much about a consolidated government. I wish the honorable gentleman would condescend to give us a definition of what he meant by it. I think this the more necessary, because I apprehend that the term, in the numerous times it has been used, has not always been used in the same sense. It may be said, and I believe it has been said, that a consolidated government is such as will absorb and destroy the governments of the several States. If it is taken in this view, the plan before us is not a consolidated government, as I showed on a former day, and may, if necessary, show further on some future occasion. On the other hand, if it is meant that the general government will take from the state governments their power in some particulars, it is confessed and evident that this will be its operation and effect.

When the principle is once settled that the people are the source of authority, the consequence is that they may take from the subordinate governments powers with which they have hitherto trusted them, and place those powers in the general government, if it is thought that there they will be productive of more good. They can distribute one portion of power to the more contracted circle called State governments: they can also furnish another proportion to the government of the United States. Who will undertake to say as a state officer that the people may not give to the general government what powers and for what purposes they please? how comes it, Sir, that these State governments dictate to their superiors?—to the majesty of the people? When I say the majesty of the people, I mean the thing, and not a mere compliment to them. The honorable gentleman went a step further and said that the State governments were kept out of this government altogether. The truth is, and it is a leading principle in this system, that not the States only but the people also shall be here represented. And if this is a crime, I confess the general government is chargeable with it; but I have no idea that a safe system of power in the government, sufficient to manage the general interest of the United States, could be drawn from any other source or rested in any other authority than that of the people at large, and I consider this authority as the rock on which this structure will stand. If this principle is unfounded, the system must fall. If honorable gentlemen, before they undertake to oppose this principle, will show that the people have parted with their power to the State governments, then I confess I cannot support this constitution. It is asked, can there be two taxing powers? Will the people submit to two taxing powers? I think they will, when the taxes are required for the public welfare, by persons appointed immediately by their fellow citizens....

December 4, 1787

Mr. Wilson ... The very manner of introducing this constitution, by the recognition of the authority of the people, is said to change the principle of the present confederation, and to introduce a *consolidating* and absorbing government!

In this confederated republic, the sovereignty of the States, it is said, is not preserved. We are told that there cannot be two sovereign powers, and that a subordinate sovereignty is no sovereignty.

It will be worth while, Mr. President, to consider this objection at large. When I had the honor of speaking formerly on this subject, I stated, in as concise a manner as possible, the leading ideas that occurred to me, to ascertain where the supreme and sovereign power resides. It has not been, nor, I presume, will it be denied, that somewhere there is, and of necessity must be, a supreme, absolute and uncontrollable authority. This, I believe, may justly be termed the sovereign power; for from that gentleman's (Mr. Findley) account of the matter, it cannot be sovereign, unless it is supreme; for, says he, a subordinate sovereignty is no sovereignty at all. I had the honor of observing, that if the question was asked, where the supreme power resided, different answers would be given by different writers. I mentioned that Blackstone will tell you, that in Britain it is lodged in the British parliament; and I believe there is no writer on this subject on the other side of the Atlantic, but supposes it to be vested in that body. I stated further, that if the question was asked, some politician, who had not considered the subject with sufficient accuracy, where the supreme power resided in our governments, would answer, that it was vested in the State constitutions. This opinion approaches near the truth, but does not reach it; for the truth is, that the supreme, absolute and uncontrollable authority, *remains* with the people. I mentioned also, that the practical recognition of this truth was reserved for the honor of this country. I recollect no constitution founded on this principle: but we have witnessed the improvement, and enjoy the happiness, of seeing it carried into practice. The great and penetrating mind of Locke seems to be the only one that pointed towards even the theory of this great truth.

When I made the observation, that some politicians would say the supreme power was lodged in our State constitutions, I did not suspect that the honorable gentleman from Westmoreland (Mr. Findley) was included in that description; but I find myself disappointed; for I imagined his opposition would arise from another consideration. His position is, that the supreme power resides in the States, as governments; and mine is, that it *resides* in the PEOPLE, as the fountain of government; that the people have not—that the people mean not—and that the people ought not, to part with it to any government whatsoever. In their hands it remains secure. They can delegate it in such proportions, to such bodies, on such terms, and under such limitations, as they think proper. I agree with the members in opposition, that there cannot be two sovereign powers on the same subject.

I consider the people of the United States as forming one great community, and I consider the people of the different States as forming communities again on a lesser scale. From this great division of the people into distinct communities it will be found necessary that different proportions of legislative powers should be given to the governments, according to the nature, number and magnitude of their objects.

Unless the people are considered in these two views, we shall never be able to understand the principle on which this system was constructed. I view the States as made *for* the people as well as *by* them, and not the people as made for the States. The people, therefore, have a right, whilst enjoying the undeniable powers of society, to form either a general government, or state governments, in what manner they please; or to accommodate them to one another, and by this means preserve them all. This, I say, is the inherent and unalienable right of the people, and as an illustration of it, I beg to read a few words from the Declaration of Independence, made by the representatives of the United States, and recognized by the whole Union.—

"We hold these truths to be self-evident, that all men are created equal; that they are endowed by their Creator with certain unalienable rights; that among these are life, liberty, and the pursuit of happiness. That to secure these rights, *governments* are instituted among men, *deriving their just powers from the consent of the governed;* that whenever any form of government becomes destructive of these ends, it is the RIGHT of the people to alter or to abolish it, and institute a new government, laying its foundation on such principles, and organizing its powers in such forms, as to them shall seem most likely to effect their safety and happiness."

This is the broad basis on which our independence was placed. On the same certain and solid foundation this system is erected.

State sovereignty, as it is called, is far from being able to support its weight. Nothing less than the authority of the people could either support it or give it efficacy. I cannot pass over this subject without noticing the different conduct pursued by the late federal convention, and that observed by the convention which framed the constitution of Pennsylvania. On that occasion you find an attempt made to deprive the people of this right, so lately and so expressly asserted in the Declaration of Independence. We are told in the preamble to the Declaration of Rights, and frame of government, that "*we* do, by virtue of the authority vested in *us*, ordain, declare, and establish, the following Declaration of Rights and frame of government to be the constitution of this commonwealth, and to remain in force therein UNALTERED, except in such articles as shall hereafter on experience be found to require improvement, and which shall, by the same authority of the people, fairly delegated *as this frame of government directs*"—An honorable gentleman (Mr. Chambers) was well warranted in saying that all that could be done was done to cut off the people from the right of amending; for if it be amended by any other mode than that which it directs, then any number more than one-third may control any number less than two-thirds.

But I return to my general reasoning. My position is, Sir, that in this country the supreme, absolute, and uncontrollable power resides in the people at large; that they have vested certain proportions of this power in the State governments, but that the fee simple continues, resides and remains with the body of the people. Under the practical influence of this great truth we are now sitting and deliberating, and under its operation, we can sit as calmly, and deliberate as coolly in order to change a constitution, as a legislature can sit and deliberate under the power of a constitution in order to alter or amend a law. It is true, the exercise of this power will not probably be so frequent, nor resorted to on so many occasions, in one case as in the other; but the recognition of the principle cannot fail to establish it more firmly. Because this recognition is made in the proposed constitution, an exception is taken to the whole of it, for we are told it is a violation of the present confederation—a CONFEDERATION of SOVEREIGN STATES. I shall not enter into an investigation of the present confederation, but shall just remark, that its principle is not the principle of free governments. The PEOPLE of the United States are not as such represented in the present Congress; and considered even as the component parts of the several States, they are not represented in proportion to their numbers and importance.

In this place I cannot help remarking on the general inconsistency which appears between one part of the gentleman's objections and another. Upon the principle we have now mentioned, the honorable gentleman contended, that the powers ought to flow from the States; and that all the late convention had to do, was to give additional powers to Congress. What is the present form of Congress? A single body, with some legislative, but little executive, and no effective judicial power. What are these additional powers that are to be given? In some cases legislative are wanting, in other judicial, and in others executive; these, it is said, ought to be allotted to the general government; but the impropriety of delegating such extensive trust to one body of men is evident; yet in the same day, and perhaps the same hour, we are told, by honorable gentlemen, that these three branches of government are not kept sufficiently distinct in this constitution; we are told also that the senate, possessing some executive power, as well as legislative, is such a monster that it will swallow up and absorb every other body in the general government, after having destroyed those of the particular States.

497

Is this reasoning with consistency? Is the senate under the proposed constitution so tremendous a body, when checked in their legislative capacity by the house of representatives, and in their executive authority by the president of the United States? Can this body be so tremendous as the present congress, a single body of men possessed of legislative, executive and judicial powers? To what purpose was Montesquieu read to show that this was a complete tyranny? The application would have been more properly made by the advocates of the proposed constitution, against the patrons of the present confederation.

It is mentioned that this federal government will annihilate and absorb all the State governments. I wish to save as much as possible the time of the house: I shall not, therefore, recapitulate what I had the honor of saying last week on this subject; I hope it was then shown, that instead of being abolished (as insinuated) from the very nature of things, and from the organization of the system itself, the State governments must exist, or the general government must fall amidst their ruins; indeed, so far as to the forms, it is admitted they may remain, but the gentlemen seem to think their power will be gone.

I shall have occasion to take notice of this power hereafter, and, I believe, if it was necessary, it could be shown that the State governments, as States, will enjoy as much power, and more dignity, happiness and security, than they have hitherto done. I admit, Sir, that some of the powers will be taken from them, by the system before you; but it is, I believe, allowed on all hands, at least it is not among us a disputed point, that the late convention was appointed with a particular view to give more power to the government of the union: it is also acknowledged, that the intention was to obtain the advantage of an efficient government over the United States; now, if power is to be given to that government, I apprehend it must be taken from some place. If the State governments are to retain all the powers they held before, then, of consequence, every new power that is given to Congress must be taken from the people at large. Is this the gentleman's intention? I believe a strict examination of this subject will justify me in asserting that the States, as governments, have assumed too much power to themselves, while they left too little to the people. Let not this be called cajoling the people—the elegant expression used by the honorable gentleman from Westmoreland (Mr. Findley)—it is hard to avoid censure on one side or the other. At some time it has been said, that I have not been at the pains to conceal my contempt of the people; but when it suits a purpose better, it is asserted that I cajole them. I do neither one nor the other. The voice of approbation, Sir, when I think that approbation well earned, I confess is grateful to my ears; but I would disdain it, if it is to be purchased by a sacrifice of my duty, or the dictates of my conscience. No, Sir, I go practically into this system; I have gone into it practically when the doors were shut, when it could not be alleged that I cajoled the people; and I now endeavor to show that the true and only safe principle for a free people, is a practical recognition of their original and supreme authority.

I say, Sir, that it was the design of this system, to take some power from the State government, and to place it in the general government. It was also the design, that the people should be admitted to the exercise of some powers which they did not exercise under the present confederation. It was thought proper that the citizens, as well as the States, should be represented; how far the representation in the senate is a representation of States, we shall see by and by, when we come to consider that branch of the federal government.

This system, it is said, "unhinges and eradicates the State governments, and was systematically intended so to do;" to establish the *intention*, an argument is drawn from Art. 1st sect. 4th, on the subject of elections. I have already had occasion to remark upon this, and shall therefore pass on to the next objection—that the last clause of the 8th sect. of the 1st article, gives the power of self-preservation to the general government, *independent* of the States. For in case of their *abolition*, it will be alleged in behalf of the general government, that self-preservation is the first law, and necessary to the exercise of *all other* powers.

Now let us see what this objection amounts to. Who are to have this self-preserving power? The Congress. Who are Congress? It is a body that will consist of a senate and a house of representatives. Who compose this senate? Those who are *elected* by the *legislatures* of the different States. Who are the electors of the house of representatives? Those who are *qualified* to *vote* for the most numerous branch of the *legislature* in the separate States. Suppose the State legislatures annihilated, where is the criterion to ascertain the qualification of electors? and unless this be ascertained, they cannot be admitted to vote; if a state legislature is not elected, there can be no senate, because the senators are to be chosen by the *legislatures only*.

This is a plain and simple deduction from the constitution, and yet the objection is stated as conclusive upon an argument expressly drawn from the last clause of this section.

It is repeated, with confidence, "that this is not a *federal* government, but a complete one, with legislative, executive and judicial powers: it is a *consolidating* government." I have already mentioned the misuse of the term; I wish the gentleman would indulge us with his definition of the word. If, when he says it is a consolidation, he means so far as relates to the general objects of the union—so far it was intended to be a consolidation, and on such a consolidation, perhaps, our very existence, as a nation, depends. If, on the other hand (as something which has been said seems to indicate) he (Mr. Findley) means that it will absorb the governments of the individual States, so far is this position from being admitted, that it is unanswerably controverted. The existence of the State government, is one of the most prominent features of this system. With regard to those purposes which are allowed to be for the general welfare of the union, I think it no objection to this plan, that we are told it is a complete government. I think it no objection, that it is alleged the government will possess legislative, executive and judicial powers. Should it have only legislative authority? We have had examples enough of such a government, to deter us from continuing it. Shall Congress any longer continue to make requisitions from the several States, to be treated sometimes with silent, and sometimes with declared contempt? For what purpose give the power to make laws, unless they are to be executed? and if they are to be executed, the executive and judicial powers will necessarily be engaged in the business.

Do we wish a return of those insurrections and tumults to which a sister State was lately exposed? or a government of such insufficiency as the present is found to be? Let me, Sir, mention one circumstance in the recollection of every honorable gentleman who hears me. To the determination of Congress are submitted all disputes between States, concerning boundary, jurisdiction, or right of soil. In consequence of this power, after much altercation, expense of time, and considerable expense of money, this State was successful enough to obtain a decree in her favor, in a difference then subsisting between her and Connecticut; but what was the consequence? the Congress had no power to carry the decree into execution. Hence the distraction and animosity, which have ever since prevailed, and still continue in that part of the country. Ought the government then to remain any longer incomplete? I hope not; no person can be so insensible to the lessons of experience as to desire it.

It is brought as an objection "that there will be a rivalship between the State governments and the general government; on each side endeavors will be made to increase power."

Let us examine a little into this subject. The gentlemen tell you, Sir, that they expect the States will not possess any power. But I think there is reason to draw a different conclusion. Under this system their respectability and power will increase with that of the general government. I believe their happiness and security will increase in a still greater proportion. Let us attend a moment to the situation of this country: it is a maxim of every government, and it ought to be a maxim with us, that the increase of numbers increases the dignity, the security, and the respectability of all governments; it is the first command given by the Deity to man, increase and multiply; this applies with peculiar force to this country, the smaller part of whose territory is yet inhabited. We are representatives, Sir, not merely of the present age, but of future times; nor merely of the territory along the sea coast, but of regions immensely extended westward. We should fill, as fast as possible, this extensive country, with men who shall live happy, free and secure. To accomplish this great end ought to be the leading view of all our patriots and statesmen. But how is it to be accomplished, but by establishing peace and harmony among ourselves, and dignity and respectability among foreign nations? By these means, we may draw numbers from the other side of the Atlantic, in addition to the natural sources of population. Can either of these objects be attained without a protecting head? When we examine history, we shall find an important fact, and almost the only fact, which will apply to all confederacies.

They have all fallen to pieces, and have not absorbed the subordinate governments.

In order to keep republics together they must have a strong binding force, which must be either external or internal. The situation of this country shows, that no foreign force can press us together; the bonds of our union ought therefore to be indissolubly strong.

The power of the States, I apprehend, will increase with the population, and the happiness of their inhabitants. Unless we can establish a character abroad, we shall be unhappy from foreign restraints, or internal violence. These reasons, I think, prove sufficiently the necessity of having a federal head. Under it the advantages enjoyed by the whole union would be participated by every State. I wish honorable gentlemen would think not only of themselves, not only of the present age, but of others, and of future times.

It has been said, "that the State governments will not be able to make head against the general government;" but it might be said with more propriety, that the general government will not be able to maintain the powers given it against the encroachments and combined attacks of the State governments. They possess some particular advantages, from which the general government is restrained. By this system, there is a provision made in the constitution, that no senator or representative shall be appointed to any civil office under the authority of the United States, which shall have been created, or the emoluments whereof shall have been increased, during the time for which he was elected; and no person holding any office under the United States can be a member of either house; but there is no similar security against State influence, as a representative may enjoy places and even sinecures under the State governments. On which side is the door most open to corruption? If a person in the legislature is to be influenced by an office, the general government can give him none unless he vacate his seat. When the influence of office comes from the State government, he can retain his seat and salary too. But it is added, under this head, "that State governments will lose the attachment of the people, by losing the power of conferring advantages, and that the people will not be at the expense of keeping them up." Perhaps the State governments have already become so expensive as to alarm the gentlemen on that head. I am told that the civil list of this State amounted to £40,000, in one year. Under the proposed government, I think it would be possible to obtain in Pennsylvania every advantage we now possess, with a civil list that shall not exceed one-third of that sum.

How differently the same thing is talked of, if it be a favorite or otherwise! When advantages to an officer are to be derived from the general government, we hear them mentioned by the name of *bribery*, but when we are told of the State governments losing the power of conferring advantages, by the disposal of offices, it is said they will lose the *attachment* of the people. What is in one instance corruption and bribery, is in another the power of conferring advantages.

We are informed that "the State elections will be ill attended, and that the State governments will become mere boards of electors." Those who have a due regard for their country, will discharge their duty, and attend; but those who are brought only from interest or persuasion had better stay away; the public will not suffer any disadvantage from their absence. But the honest citizen, who knows the value of the privilege, will undoubtedly attend, to secure the man of his choice. The power and business of the State legislatures relates to the great objects of life, liberty and property; the same are also objects of the general government.

Certainly the citizens of America will be as tenacious in the one instance as in the other. They will be interested, and I hope will exert themselves, to secure their rights not only from being injured by the State governments, but also from being injured by the general government.

"The power over election, and of judging of elections, gives absolute sovereignty;" this power is given to every State legislature, yet I see no necessity that the power of absolute sovereignty should accompany it. My general position is, that the absolute sovereignty never goes from the people. . . .

(2) Massachusetts, February 4, 1788

Rev. Mr. Thacher . . . But I readily grant all these reasons are not sufficient to surrender up the essential liberties of the people. But do we surrender them? This Constitution hath been compared, both by its defenders and opponents, to the British government. In my view of it, there is a great difference. In Britain, the government is said to consist of three forms—monarchy, aristocracy, and democracy; but, in fact, is but a few removes from absolute despotism. In the crown is vested the power of adding at pleasure to the second branch; of nominating to all the places of honor and emolument; of purchasing, by its immense revenues, the suffrages of the House of Commons. The voice of the people is but the echo of the king; and their boasted privileges lie entirely at his mercy. In this proposed form, each branch of power is derived, either mediately or directly, from the people. The lower house are elected directly by those persons who are qualified to vote for the representatives of the state; and, at the expiration of two years, become private men, unless their past conduct entitles them to a future election.

The Senate are elected by the legislatures of the different states, and represent their sovereignty.

These powers are a check on each other, and can never be made either dependent on one another, or independent of the people. The President is chosen by the electors, who are appointed by the people. The high courts of justice arise from the President and Senate; but yet the ministers of them can be removed only upon bad behavior. The independence of judges is one of the most favorable circumstances to public liberty; for when they become the slaves of a venal, corrupt court, and the hirelings of tyranny, all property is precarious, and personal security at an end; a man may be stripped of all his possessions, and murdered, without the forms of law. Thus it appears that all parts of this system arise ultimately from the people, and are still independent of each other. There are other restraints, which, though not directly named in this Constitution, yet are evidently discerned by every man of common observation. These are, the government of the several states, and the spirit of liberty in the people. Are we wronged or injured, our immediate representatives are those to whom we ought to apply. Their power and influence will still be great. But should any servants of the people, however eminent their stations, attempt to enslave them, from this spirit of liberty such opposition would arise as would bring them to the scaffold. But, admitting that there are dangers in accepting this general government; yet are there not greater hazards in rejecting it? Such is, Mr. President, the state of our affairs, that it is not in our power to carve for ourselves. To avoid the greatest and choose the least of these two evils, is all that we can do. What, then, will be the probable effects if this Constitution be rejected? Have we not reason to fear new commotions in this commonwealth? If they arise, can we be always certain that we shall be furnished with a citizen, who, though possessed of extensive influence and the greatest abilities, will make no other use of them than to quiet the tumult of the people, to prevent civil war, and to restore the usual course of law and justice? Are we not in danger from other states, when their interests or prejudices are opposite to ours? And in such scenes of hostile contention, will not some Sylla drench the land in blood, or some Cromwell or Cæsar lay our liberties prostrate at his feet? Will not foreign nations attack us in our weak, divided condition, and once more render us provinces to some potentate of Europe? Or will those powers to whom we are indebted lie quiet? They certainly will not. They are now waiting for our decision; but when they once see that our union is broken, and that we are determined to neglect them, they will issue out letters of marque and reprisal, and entirely destroy our commerce.

If this system is broken up, will thirteen, or even nine states, ever agree to another? And will Providence smile on a people who despise the privileges put into their hands, and who neglect the plainest principles of justice and honesty? After all, I by no means pretend that there is complete perfection in this proposed Constitution. Like all other human productions, it hath its faults. Provision is made for an amendment, whenever, from practice, it is found oppressive. I would add, the proposals which his excellency hath condescended to lay before this honorable Convention, respecting future alterations, are real improvements for the better; and we have no reason to doubt but they will be equally attended to by other states, as they lead to common security and preservation.

(3) Virginia, June 14, 1788

Mr. HENRY entertained strong suspicions that great dangers must result from the clause under consideration [to exercise authority over the District of Columbia]. They were not removed, but rather confirmed, by the remarks of the honorable gentleman, in saying that it was extremely improbable that the members from New Hampshire and Georgia would go and legislate exclusively for the ten miles square. If it was so improbable, why ask the power? Why demand a power which was not to be exercised? Compare this power, says he, with the next clause, which gives them power to make all laws which shall be necessary to carry their laws into execution. By this they have a right to pass any law that may facilitate the execution of their acts. They have a right, by this clause, to make a law that such a district shall be set apart for any purpose they please, and that any man who shall act contrary to their commands, within certain ten miles square, or any place they may select, and strongholds, shall be hanged without benefit of clergy. If they think any law necessary for their personal safety, after perpetrating the most tyrannical and oppressive deeds, cannot they make it by this sweeping clause? If it be necessary to provide, not only for this, but for any department or officer of Congress, does not this clause enable them to make a law for the purpose? And will not these laws, made for those purposes, be paramount to the laws of the states? Will not this clause give them a right to keep a powerful army continually on foot, if they think it necessary to aid the execution of their laws? Is there any act, however atrocious, which they cannot do by virtue of this clause? Look at the use which has been made, in all parts of the world, of that human thing called power. Look at the predominant thirst of dominion which has invariably and uniformly prompted rulers to abuse their powers. Can you say that you will be safe when you give such unlimited powers, without any real responsibility? Will you be safe when you trust men at Philadelphia with power to make any law that will enable them to carry their acts into execution? Will not the members of Congress have the same passions which other rulers have had? They will not be superior to the frailties of human nature. However cautious you may be in the selection of your representatives, it will be dangerous to trust them with such unbounded powers. Shall we be told, when about to grant such illimitable authority, that it will never be exercised!

I conjure you once more to remember the admonition of that sage man who told you that, when you give power, you know not what you give. I know the absolute necessity of an energetic government. But is it consistent with any principle of prudence or good policy to grant unlimited, unbounded authority, which is so totally unnecessary that gentlemen say it will never be exercised? But gentlemen say that we must make experiments. A wonderful and unheard-of experiment it will be, to give unlimited power unnecessarily! I admit my inferiority in point of historical knowledge; but I believe no man can produce an instance of an unnecessary and unlimited power, given to a body independent of the legislature, within a particular district. Let any man in this Convention show me an instance of such separate and different powers of legislation in the same country—show me an instance where a part of the community was independent of the whole.

The people within that place, and the strongholds, may be excused from all the burdens imposed on the rest of the society, and may enjoy exclusive emoluments, to the great injury of the rest of the people. But gentlemen say that the power will not be abused. They ought to show that it is necessary. All their powers may be fully carried into execution, without this exclusive authority in the ten miles square. The sweeping clause will fully enable them to do what they please. What could the most extravagant and boundless imagination ask, but power to do every thing? I have reason to suspect ambitious grasps at power. The experience of the world teaches me the jeopardy of giving enormous power. Strike this clause out of the form of the government, and how will it stand? Congress will still have power, by the sweeping clause, to make laws within that place and the strongholds, independently of the local authority of the state. I ask you, if this clause be struck out, whether the sweeping clause will not enable them to protect themselves from insult. If you grant them these powers, you destroy every degree of responsibility. They will fully screen them from justice, and preclude the possibility of punishing them. No instance can be given of such a wanton grasp of power as an exclusive legislation in all cases whatever.

Mr. MADISON. Mr. Chairman, I am astonished that the honorable member should launch out into such strong descriptions without any occasion. Was there ever a legislature in existence that held their sessions at a place where they had not jurisdiction? I do not mean such a legislature as they have in Holland; for it deserves not the name. Their powers are such as Congress have now, which we find not reducible to practice. If you be satisfied with the shadow and form, instead of the substance, you will render them dependent on the local authority. Suppose the legislature of this country should sit in Richmond, while the exclusive jurisdiction of the place was in some particular county; would this country think it safe that the general good should be subject to the paramount authority of a part of the community?

The honorable member asks, Why ask for this power, and if the subsequent clause be not fully competent for the same purpose. If so, what new terrors can arise from this particular clause? It is only a superfluity. If that latitude of construction which he contends for were to take place with respect to the sweeping clause, there would be room for those horrors. But it gives no supplementary power. It only enables them to execute the delegated powers. If the delegation of their powers be safe, no possible inconvenience can arise from this clause. It is at most but explanatory. For when any power is given, its delegation necessarily involves authority to make laws to execute it. Were it possible to delineate on paper all those particular cases and circumstances in which legislation by the general legislature would be necessary, and leave to the states all the other powers, I imagine no gentleman would object to it. But this is not within the limits of human capacity. The particular powers which are found necessary to be given are therefore delegated generally, and particular and minute specification is left to the legislature.

[Here Mr. Madison spoke of the distinction between regulation of police and legislation, but so low he could not be heard.]

When the honorable member objects to giving the general government jurisdiction over the place of their session, does he mean that it should be under the control of any particular state, that might, at a critical moment, seize it? I should have thought that this clause would have met with the most cordial approbation. As the consent of the state in which it may be must be obtained, and as it may stipulate the terms of the grant, should they violate the particular stipulations it would be an usurpation; so that, if the members of Congress were to be guided by the laws of their country, none of those dangers could arise.

[Mr. Madison made several other remarks, which could not be heard.]

Mr. HENRY replied that, if Congress were vested with supreme power of legislation, paramount to the constitution and laws of the states, the dangers he had described might happen; for that Congress would not be confined to the enumerated powers. This construction was warranted, in his opinion, by the addition of the word *department*, at the end of the clause, and that they could make any laws which they might think necessary to execute the powers of any department or officer of the government.

Mr. PENDLETON. Mr. Chairman, this clause does not give Congress power to impede the operation of any part of the Constitution, or to make any regulation that may affect the interests of the citizens of the Union at large. But it gives them power over the local police of the place, so as to be secured from any interruption in their proceedings.

Notwithstanding the violent attack upon it, I believe, sir, this is the fair construction of the clause. It gives them power of exclusive legislation in any case within that district. What is the meaning of this? What is it opposed to? Is it opposed to the general powers of the federal legislature, or to those of the state legislatures? I understand it as opposed to the legislative power of that state where it shall be. What, then, is the power? It is, that Congress shall exclusively legislate there, in order to preserve the police of the place and their own personal independence, that they may not be overawed or insulted, and of course to preserve them in opposition to any attempt by the state where it shall be. This is the fair construction. Can we suppose that, in order to effect these salutary ends, Congress will make it an asylum for villains and the vilest characters from all parts of the world? Will it not degrade their own dignity to make it a sanctuary for villains? I hope that no man that will ever compose that Congress will associate with the most profligate characters.

Why oppose this power? Suppose it was contrary to the sense of their constituents to grant exclusive privileges to citizens residing within that place; the effect would be directly in opposition to what he says. It could have no operation without the limits of that district. Were Congress to make a law granting them an exclusive privilege of trading to the East Indies, it could have no effect the moment it would go without that place; for their exclusive power is confined to that district. Were they to pass such a law, it would be nugatory; and every member of the community at large could trade to the East Indies as well as the citizens of that district. This exclusive power is limited to that place solely, for their own preservation, which all gentlemen allow to be necessary.

Will you pardon me when I observe that their construction of the preceding clause does not appear to me to be natural, or warranted by the words.

They say that the state governments have no power at all over the militia. The power of the general government to provide for arming and organizing the militia is to introduce a uniform system of discipline to pervade the United States of America. But the power of *governing* the militia, so far as it is in Congress, extends only to such parts of them as may be employed in the service of the United States. When not in their service, Congress has no power to govern them. The states then have the sole government of them; and though Congress *may* provide for arming them, and prescribe the mode of discipline, yet the states have the authority of training them, according to the uniform discipline prescribed by Congress. But there is nothing to preclude them from arming and disciplining them should Congress neglect to do it. As to calling the militia to execute the laws of the Union, I think the fair construction is directly opposite to what the honorable member says. The 4th section of the 4th article contains nothing to warrant the supposition that the states cannot call them forth to suppress domestic insurrections. [*Here he read the section.*] All the restraint here contained is, that Congress may, at their pleasure, on application of the state legislature, or (in vacation) of the executive, protect each of the states against domestic violence. This is a restraint on the general government not to interpose. The state is in full possession of the power of using its own militia to protect itself against domestic violence; and the power in the general government cannot be exercised, or interposed, without the application of the state itself. This appears to me to be the obvious and fair construction.

With respect to the necessity of the ten miles square being superseded by the subsequent clause, which gives them power to make all laws which shall be necessary and proper for carrying into execution the foregoing powers, and all other powers vested by this Constitution in the government of the United States, or in any department or officer thereof, I understand that clause as not going a single step beyond the delegated powers. What can it act upon? Some power given by this Constitution. If they should be about to pass a law in consequence of this clause, they must pursue some of the delegated powers, but can by no means depart from them, or arrogate any new powers; for the plain language of the clause is, to give them power to pass laws in order to give effect to the delegated powers.

Mr. GEORGE MASON. Mr. Chairman, gentlemen say there is no new power given by this clause. Is there any thing in this Constitution which secures to the states the powers which are said to be retained? Will powers remain to the states which are not expressly guarded and reserved? I will suppose a case. Gentlemen may call it an impossible case, and suppose that Congress will act with wisdom and integrity. Among the enumerated powers, Congress are to lay and collect taxes, duties, imposts, and excises, and to pay the debts, and to provide for the general welfare and common defence; and by that clause (so often called the *sweeping clause*) they are to make all laws necessary to execute those laws. Now, suppose oppressions should arise under this government, and any writer should dare to stand forth, and expose to the community at large the abuses of those powers; could not Congress, under the idea of providing for the general welfare, and under their own construction, say that this was destroying the general peace, encouraging sedition, and poisoning the minds of the people? And could they not, in order to provide against this, lay a dangerous restriction on the press? Might they not even bring the trial of this restriction within the ten miles square, when there is no prohibition against it? Might they not thus destroy the trial by jury? Would they not extend their implication? It appears to me that they may and will. And shall the support of our rights depend on the bounty of men whose interest it may be to oppress us? That Congress should have power to provide for the general welfare of the Union, I grant. But I wish a clause in the Constitution, with respect to all powers which are not granted, that they are retained by the states. Otherwise, the power of providing for the general welfare may be perverted to its destruction.

Many gentlemen, whom I respect, take different sides of this question. We wish this amendment to be introduced, to remove our apprehensions. There was a clause in the Confederation reserving to the states respectively every power, jurisdiction, and right, not expressly delegated to the United States. This clause has never been complained of, but approved by all. Why not, then, have a similar clause in this Constitution, in which it is the more indispensably necessary than in the Confederation, because of the great augmentation of power vested in the former? In my humble apprehension, unless there be some such clear and finite expression, this clause now under consideration will go to any thing our rulers may think proper. Unless there be some express declaration that every thing not given is retained, it will be carried to any power Congress may please.

Mr. HENRY moved to read from the 8th to the 13th article of the declaration of rights; which was done.

Mr. GEORGE NICHOLAS, in reply to the gentlemen opposed to the clause under debate, went over the same grounds, and developed the same principles, which Mr. Pendleton and Mr. Madison had done. The opposers of the clause, which gave the power of providing for the general welfare, supposed its dangers to result from its connection with, and extension of, the powers granted in the other clauses. He endeavored to show the committee that it only empowered Congress to make such laws as would be necessary to enable them to pay the public debts and provide for the common defence; that this general welfare was united, not to the general power of legislation, but to the particular power of laying and collecting taxes, imposts, and excises, for the purpose of paying the debts and providing for the common defence,—that is, that they could raise as much money as would pay the debts and provide for the common defence, in consequence of this power. The clause which was affectedly called the *sweeping clause* contained no new grant of power. To illustrate this position, he observed that, if it had been added at the end of every one of the enumerated powers, instead of being inserted at the end of all, it would be obvious to any one that it was no augmentation of power. If, for instance, at the end of the clause granting power to lay and collect taxes, it had been added that they should have power to make necessary and proper laws to lay and collect taxes, who could suspect it to be an addition of power? As it would grant no new power if inserted at the end of each clause, it could not when subjoined to the whole.

He then proceeded thus: But, says he, who is to determine the extent of such powers? I say, the same power which, in all well-regulated communities, determines the extent of legislative powers. If they exceed these powers, the judiciary will declare it void, or else the people will have a right to declare it void. Is this depending on any man? But, says the gentleman, it may go to any thing. It may destroy the trial by jury; and they may say it is necessary for providing for the general defence. The power of providing for the general defence only extends to raise any sum of money they may think necessary, by taxes, imposts, &c. But, says he, our only defence against oppressive laws consists in the virtue of our representatives. This was misrepresented. If I understand it right, no new power can be exercised. As to those which are actually granted, we trust to the fellow-feelings of our representatives; and if we are deceived, we then trust to altering our government. It appears to me, however, that we can confide in their discharging their powers rightly, from the peculiarity of their situation, and connection with us. If, sir, the powers of the former Congress were very inconsiderable, that body did not deserve to have great powers.

It was so constructed that it would be dangerous to invest it with such. But why were the articles of the bill of rights read? Let him show us that those rights are given up by the Constitution. Let him prove them to be violated. He tells us that the most worthy characters of the country differ as to the necessity of a bill of rights. It is a simple and plain proposition. It is agreed upon by all that the people have all power. If they part with anv of it, is it necessary to declare that they retain the rest? Liken it to any similar case. If I have one thousand acres of land, and I grant five hundred acres of it, must I declare that I retain the other five hundred? Do I grant the whole thousand acres, when I grant five hundred, unless I declare that the five hundred I do not give belong to me still? It is so in this case. After granting some powers, the rest must remain with the people.

Gov. RANDOLPH observed that he had some objections to the clause. He was persuaded that the construction put upon it by the gentlemen, on both sides, was erroneous; but he thought any construction better than going into anarchy.

Mr. GEORGE MASON still thought that there ought to be some express declaration in the Constitution, asserting that rights not given to the general government were retained by the states. He apprehended that, unless this was done, many valuable and important rights would be concluded to be given up by implication. All governments were drawn from the people, though many were perverted to their oppression. The government of Virginia, he remarked, was drawn from the people; yet there were certain great and important rights, which the people, by their bill of rights, declared to be paramount to the power of the legislature. He asked, Why should it not be so in this Constitution? Was it because we were more substantially represented in it than in the state government? If, in the state government, where the people were substantially and fully represented, it was necessary that the great rights of human nature should be secure from the encroachments of the legislature, he asked if it was not more necessary in this government, where they were but inadequately represented? He declared that artful sophistry and

510

evasions could not satisfy him. He could see no clear distinction between rights relinquished by a positive grant, and lost by implication. Unless there were a bill of rights, implication might swallow up all our rights.

Mr. HENRY. Mr. Chairman, the necessity of a bill of rights appears to me to be greater in this government than ever it was in any government before. I have observed already, that the sense of the European nations, and particularly Great Britain, is against the construction of rights being retained which are not expressly relinquished. I repeat, that all nations have adopted this construction—that all rights not expressly and unequivocally reserved to the people are impliedly and incidentally relinquished to rulers, as necessarily inseparable from the delegated powers. It is so in Great Britain; for every possible right, which is not reserved to the people by some express provision or compact, is within the king's prerogative. It is so in that country which is said to be in such full possession of freedom. It is so in Spain, Germany, and other parts of the world. Let us consider the sentiments which have been entertained by the people of America on this subject. At the revolution, it must be admitted that it was their sense to set down those great rights which ought, in all countries, to be held inviolable and sacred. Virginia did so, we all remember. She made a compact to reserve, expressly, certain rights.

When fortified with full, adequate, and abundant representation, was she satisfied with that representation? No. She most cautiously and guardedly reserved and secured those invaluable, inestimable rights and privileges, which no people, inspired with the least glow of patriotic liberty, ever did, or ever can, abandon. She is called upon now to abandon them, and dissolve that compact which secured them to her. She is called upon to accede to another compact, which most infallibly supersedes and annihilates her present one. Will she do it? This is the question. If you intend to reserve your unalienable rights, you must have the most express stipulation; for, if implication be allowed, you are ousted of those rights. If the people do not think it necessary to reserve them, they will be supposed to be given up. How were the congressional rights defined when the people of America united by a confederacy to defend their liberties and rights against the tyrannical attempts of Great Britain? The states were not then contented with implied reservation. No, Mr. Chairman. It was expressly declared in our Confederation that every right was retained by the states, respectively, which was not given up to the government of the United States. But there is no such thing here. You, therefore, by a natural and unavoidable implication, give up your rights to the general government.

Your own example furnishes an argument against it. If you give up these powers, without a bill of rights, you will exhibit the most absurd thing to mankind that ever the world saw—a government that has abandoned all its powers—the powers of direct taxation, the sword, and the purse. You have disposed of them to Congress, without a bill of rights—without check, limitation, or control. And still you have checks and guards; still you keep barriers—pointed where? Pointed against your weakened, prostrated, enervated state government! You have a bill of rights to defend you against the state government, which is bereaved of all power, and yet you have none against Congress, though in full and exclusive possession of all power! You arm yourselves against the weak and defenceless, and expose yourselves naked to the armed and powerful. Is not this a conduct of unexampled absurdity? What barriers have you to oppose to this most strong, energetic government? To that government you have nothing to oppose. All your defence is given up. This is a real, actual defect. It must strike the mind of every gentleman. When our government was first instituted in Virginia, we declared the common law of England to be in force.

That system of law which has been admired, and has protected us and our ancestors, is excluded by that system. Added to this, we adopted a bill of rights. By this Constitution, some of the best barriers of human rights are thrown away. Is there not an additional reason to have a bill of rights? By the ancient common law, the trial of all facts is decided by a jury of impartial men from the immediate vicinage This paper speaks of different juries from the common law in criminal cases; and in civil controversies excludes trial by jury altogether. There is, therefore, more occasion for the supplementary check of a bill of rights now than then. Congress, from their general powers, may fully go into business of human legislation. They may legislate, in criminal cases, from treason to the lowest offence—petty larceny. They may define crimes and prescribe punishments. In the definition of crimes, I trust they will be directed by what wise representatives ought to be governed by. But when we come to punishments, no latitude ought to be left, nor dependence put on the virtue of representatives. What says our bill of rights?—"that excessive bail ought not to be required, nor excessive fines imposed, nor cruel and unusual punishments inflicted." Are you not, therefore, now calling on those gentlemen who are to compose Congress, to prescribe trials and define punishments without this control? Will they find sentiments there similar to this bill of rights? You let them loose; you do more—you depart from the genius of your country. That paper tells you that the trial of crimes shall be by jury, and held in the state where the crime shall have been committed. Under this extensive provision, they may proceed in a manner extremely dangerous to liberty: a person accused may be carried from one extremity of the state to another, and be tried, not by an impartial jury of the vicinage, acquainted with his character and the circumstances of the fact, but by a jury unacquainted with both, and who may be biased against him. Is not this sufficient to alarm men? How different is this from the immemorial practice of your British ancestors, and your own! I need not tell you that, by the common law, a number of hundredors were required on a jury, and that afterwards it was sufficient if the jurors came from the same county. With less than this the people of England have never been satisfied. That paper ought to have declared the common law in force.

In this business of legislation, your members of Congress will loose the restriction of not imposing excessive fines, demanding excessive bail, and inflicting cruel and unusual punishments. These are prohibited by your declaration of rights. What has distinguished our ancestors?—That they would not admit of tortures, or cruel and barbarous punishment. But Congress may introduce the practice of the civil law, in preference to that of the common law. They may introduce the practice of France, Spain, and Germany—of torturing, to extort a confession of the crime. They will say that they might as well draw examples from those countries as from Great Britain, and they will tell you that there is such a necessity of strengthening the arm of government, that they must have a criminal equity, and extort confession by torture, in order to punish with still more relentless severity. We are then lost and undone. And can any man think it troublesome, when we can, by a small interference, prevent our rights from being lost? If you will, like the Virginian government, give them knowledge of the extent of the rights retained by the people, and the powers of themselves, they will, if they be honest men, thank you for it. Will they not wish to go on sure grounds? But if you leave them otherwise, they will not know how to proceed; and, being in a state of uncertainty, they will assume rather than give up powers by implication.

A bill of rights may be summed up in a few words. What do they tell us?—That our rights are reserved. Why not say so? Is it because it will consume too much paper? Gentlemen's reasoning against a bill of rights does not satisfy me. Without saying which has the right side, it remains doubtful. A bill of rights is a favorite thing with the Virginians and the people of the other states likewise. It may be their prejudice, but the government ought to suit their geniuses; otherwise, its operation will be unhappy. A bill of rights, even if its necessity be doubtful, will exclude the possibility of dispute; and, with great submission, I think the best way is to have no dispute. In the present Constitution, they are restrained from issuing general warrants to search suspected places, or seize persons not named, without evidence of the commission of a fact, &c. There was certainly some celestial influence governing those who deliberated on that Constitution; for they have, with the most cautious and enlightened circumspection, guarded those indefeasible rights which ought ever to be held sacred! The officers of Congress may come upon you now, fortified with all the terrors of paramount federal authority. Excisemen may come in multitudes; for the limitation of their numbers no man knows. They may, unless the general government be restrained by a bill of rights, or some similar restriction, go into your cellars and rooms, and search, ransack, and measure, every thing you eat, drink, and wear. They ought to be restrained within proper bounds. With respect to the freedom of the press, I need say nothing; for it is hoped that the gentlemen who shall compose Congress will take care to infringe as little as possible the rights of human nature. This will result from their integrity. They should, from prudence, abstain from violating the rights of their constituents. They are not, however, expressly restrained. But whether they will intermeddle with that palladium of our liberties or not, I leave you to determine.

Mr. GRAYSON thought it questionable whether rights not given up were reserved. A majority of the states, he observed, had expressly reserved certain important rights by bills of rights, and that in the Confederation there was a clause declaring expressly that every power and right not given up was retained by the states. It was the general sense of America that such a clause was necessary; otherwise, why did they introduce a clause which was totally unnecessary? It had been insisted, he said, in many parts of America, that a bill of rights was only necessary between a prince and people, and not in such a government as this, which was a compact between the people themselves. This did not satisfy his mind; for so extensive was the power of legislation, in his estimation, that he doubted whether, when it was once given up, *any thing* was retained. He further remarked, that there were some negative clauses in the Constitution, which refuted the doctrine contended for by the other side. For instance; the 2d clause of the 9th section of the 1st article provided that "the privilege of the writ of *habeas corpus* shall not be suspended, unless when, in cases of rebellion or invasion, the public safety may require it." And, by the last clause of the same section, "no title of nobility shall be granted by the United States." Now, if these restrictions had not been here inserted, he asked whether Congress would not most clearly have had a right to suspend that great and valuable right, and to grant titles of nobility. When, in addition to these considerations, he saw they had an indefinite power to provide for the general welfare, he thought there were great reasons to apprehend great dangers. He thought, therefore, that there ought to be a bill of rights.

Mr. GEORGE NICHOLAS, in answer to the two gentlemen last up, observed that, though there was a declaration of rights in the government of Virginia, it was no conclusive reason that there should be one in this Constitution; for, if it was unnecessary in the former, its omission in the latter could be no defect. They ought, therefore, to prove that it was essentially necessary to be inserted in the Constitution of Virginia. There were five or six states in the Union which had no bill of rights, separately and distinctly as such; but they annexed the substance of a bill of rights to their respective constitutions. These states, he further observed, were as free as this state, and their liberties as secure as ours. If so, gentlemen's arguments from the precedent were not good. In Virginia, all powers were given to the government without any exception. It was different in the general government, to which certain

514

special powers were delegated for certain purposes. He asked which was the more safe. Was it safer to grant general powers than certain limited powers? This much as to the theory, continued he. What is the practice of this invaluable government? Have your citizens been bound by it? They have not, sir. You have violated that maxim, "that no man shall be condemned without a fair trial." That man who was killed, not *secundum artem*, was deprived of his life without the benefit of law, and in express violation of this declaration of rights, which they confide in so much. But, sir, this bill of rights was no security. It is but a paper check. It has been violated in many other instances. Therefore, from theory and practice, it may be concluded that this government, with special powers, without any express exceptions, is better than a government with general powers and special exceptions. But the practice of England is against us. The rights there reserved to the people are to limit and check the king's prerogative. It is easier to enumerate the exceptions to his prerogative, than to mention all the cases to which it extends. Besides, these reservations, being only formed in acts of the legislature, may be altered by the representatives of the people when they think proper. No comparison can be made of this with the other governments he mentioned. There is no stipulation between the king and people. The former is possessed of absolute, unlimited authority.

But, sir, this Constitution is defective because the common law is not declared to be in force! What would have been the consequence if it had? It would be immutable. But now it can be changed or modified as the legislative body may find necessary for the community. But the common law is not excluded. There is nothing in that paper to warrant the assertion. As to the exclusion of a jury from the vicinage, he has mistaken the fact. The legislature may direct a jury to come from the vicinage. But the gentleman says that, by this Constitution, they have power to make laws to define crimes and prescribe punishments; and that, consequently, we are not free from torture. Treason against the United States is defined in the Constitution, and the forfeiture limited to the life of the person attainted. Congress have power to define and punish piracies and felonies committed on the high seas, and offences against the laws of nations; but they cannot define or prescribe the punishment of any other crime whatever, without violating the Constitution. If we had no security against torture but our declaration of rights, we might be tortured to-morrow; for it has been repeatedly infringed and disregarded. A bill of rights is only an acknowledgment of the preëxisting claim to rights in the people. They belong to us as much as if they had been inserted in the Constitution. But it is said that, if it be doubtful, the possibility of dispute ought to be precluded. Admitting it was proper for the Convention to have inserted a bill of rights, it is not proper here to propose it as the condition of our accession to the Union. Would you reject this government for its omission, dissolve the Union, and bring miseries on yourselves and posterity? I hope the gentleman does not oppose it on this ground solely. Is there another reason? He said that it is not only the general wish of this state, but all the states, to have a bill of rights. If it be so, where is the difficulty of having this done by way of subsequent amendment? We shall find the other states willing to accord with their own favorite wish. The gentleman last up says that the power of legislation includes every thing. A general power of legislation does. But this is a special power of legislation. Therefore, it does not contain that plenitude of power which he imagines. They cannot legislate in any case but those particularly enumerated. No gentleman, who is a friend to the government, ought to withhold his assent from it for this reason.

June 24, 1788

Mr. Madison... With respect to the proposition of the honorable gentleman to my left, (Mr. Wythe,) gentlemen apprehend that, by enumerating three rights, it implied there were no more. The observations made by a gentleman lately up, on that subject, correspond precisely with my opinion. That resolution declares that the powers granted by the proposed Constitution are the gift of the people, and may be resumed by them when perverted to their oppression, and every power not granted thereby remains with the people, and at their will. It adds, likewise, that no right, of any denomination, can be cancelled, abridged, restrained, or modified, by the general government, or any of its officers, except in those instances in which power is given by the Constitution for these purposes. There cannot be a more positive and unequivocal declaration of the principle of the adoption—that every thing not granted is reserved. This is obviously and self-evidently the case, without the declaration. Can the general government exercise any power not delegated? If an enumeration be made of our rights, will it not be implied that every thing omitted is given to the general government? Has not the honorable gentleman himself admitted that an imperfect enumeration is dangerous? Does the Constitution say that they shall not alter the law of descents, or do those things which would subvert the whole system of the state laws? If it did, what was not excepted would be granted. Does it follow, from the omission of such restrictions, that they can exercise powers not delegated? The reverse of the proposition holds. The delegation alone warrants the exercise of any power.

(4) New York, July 1, 1788

Mr. TREDWELL. Sir, little accustomed to speak in public, and always inclined, in such an assembly as this, to be a hearer rather than a speaker, on a less important occasion than the present I should have contented myself with a silent vote; but when I consider the nature of this dispute, that it is a contest, not between little states and great states, (as we have been told,) between little folks and great folks, between patriotism and ambition, between freedom and power; not so much between the navigating and non-navigating states, as between navigating and non-navigating individuals, (for not one of the amendments we contend for has the least reference to the clashing interests of states;) when I consider, likewise, that a people jealous of their liberties, and strongly attached to freedom, have reposed so entire a confidence in this assembly, that upon our determination depends their future enjoyment of those invaluable rights and privileges, which they have so lately and so gallantly defended at every risk and expense, both of life and property,—it appears to me so interesting and important, that I cannot be totally silent on the occasion, lest lisping babes should be taught to curse my name, as a betrayer of their freedom and happiness.

The gentleman who first opened this debate did (with an emphasis which I believe convinced every one present of the propriety of the advice) urge the necessity of proceeding, in our deliberations on this important subject, coolly and dispassionately. With how much candor this advice was given, appears from the subsequent parts of a long speech, and from several subsequent speeches almost totally addressed to our fears. The people of New Jersey and Connecticut are so exceedingly exasperated against us, that, totally regardless of their own preservation, they will take the two rivers of Connecticut and Delaware by their extremities, and, by dragging them over our country, will, by a sweeping deluge, wash us all into the Hudson, leaving neither house not inhabitant behind them. But if this event should not happen, doubtless the Vermontese, with the British and tories our natural enemies, would, by bringing down upon us the great Lake Ontario, sweep hills and mountains, houses and inhabitants, in one deluge, into the Atlantic. These, indeed, would be terrible calamities; but terrible as they are, they are not to be compared with the horrors and desolation of tyranny. The arbitrary courts of Philip in the Netherlands, in which life and property were daily confiscated without a jury, occasioned as much misery and a more rapid depopulation of the province, before the people took up arms in their own defence, than all the armies of that haughty monarch were able to effect afterwards; and it is doubtful, in my mind, whether governments, by abusing their powers, have not occasioned as much misery and distress, and nearly as great devastations of the human species, as all the wars which have happened since Milton's battle of the angels to the present day. The end or design of government is, or ought to be, the safety, peace, and welfare of the governed. Unwise, therefore, and absurd in the highest degree, would be the conduct of that people, who, in forming a government, should give to their rulers power to destroy them and their property, and thereby defeat the very purpose of their institutions; or, in other words, should give unlimited power to their rulers, and not retain in their own hands the means of their own preservation. The first governments in the world were parental, the powers of which were restrained by the laws of nature; and doubtless the early succeeding governments were formed on the same plan, which, we may suppose, answered tolerably well in the first ages of the world, while the moral sense was strong, and the laws of nature well understood, there being then no lawyers to explain them away. But in after times, when kings became great, and courts crowded, it was discovered that governments should have a right to tyrannize, and a power to oppress; and at the present day, when the *juris periti* are become so skilful in their profession, and quibbling is reduced to a science, it is become extremely difficult to form a constitution which will secure liberty and happiness to the people, or laws under which property is safe. Hence, in modern times, the design of the people, in forming an original constitution of government, is not so much to give powers to their rulers, as to guard against the abuse of them; but, in a federal one, it is different.

Sir, I introduce these observations to combat certain principles which have been daily and confidently advanced by the favorers of the present Constitution, and which appear to me totally indefensible. The first and grand leading, or rather misleading, principle in this debate, and on which the advocates for this system of unrestricted powers must chiefly depend for its support, is that, in forming a constitution, whatever powers are not expressly granted or given the government, are reserved to the people, or that rulers cannot exercise any powers but those expressly given to them by the Constitution. Let me ask the gentlemen who advanced this principle, whether the commission of a Roman dictator, which was in these few words—to take care that the state received no harm—does not come up fully to their ideas of an energetic government; or whether an invitation from the people to one or more to come and rule over them, would not clothe the rulers with sufficient powers. If so, the principle they advance is a false one. Besides, the absurdity of this principle will evidently appear, when we consider the great variety of objects to which the powers of the government must necessarily extend, and that an express enumeration of them all would probably fill as many volumes as Pool's Synopsis of the Critics. But we may reason with sufficient certainty on the subject, from the sense of all the public bodies in the United States, who had occasion to form new constitutions. They have uniformly acted upon a direct and contrary principle, not only in forming the state constitutions and the old Confederation, but also in forming this very Constitution, for we do not find in every state constitution express resolutions made in favor of the people; and it is clear that the late Convention at Philadelphia, whatever might have been the sentiments of some of its members, did not adopt the principle, for they have made certain reservations and restrictions, which, upon that principle, would have been totally useless and unnecessary; and can it be supposed that that wise body, whose only apology for the great ambiguity of many parts of that performance, and the total omission of some things which many esteem essential to the security of liberty, was a great desire of brevity, should so far sacrifice that great and important object, as to insert a number of provisions which they esteemed totally useless? Why is it said that the privilege of the writ of *habeas corpus* shall not be suspended, unless, in cases of rebellion or invasion, the public safety may require it? What clause in the Constitution, except this very clause itself, gives the general government a power to deprive us of that great privilege, so sacredly secured to us by our state constitutions? Why is it provided that no bill of attainder shall be passed, or that no title of nobility shall be granted? Are there any clauses in the Constitution extending the powers of the general government to these objects? Some gentlemen say that these, though not necessary, were inserted for greater caution. I could have wished, sir, that a greater caution had been used to secure to us the freedom of election, a sufficient and responsible representation, the freedom of the press, and the trial by jury both in civil and criminal cases.

These, sir, are the rocks on which the Constitution should have rested; no other foundation can any man lay, which will secure the sacred temple of freedom against the power of the great, the undermining arts of ambition, and the blasts of profane scoffers—for such there will be in every age—who will tell us that all religion is in vain; that is, that our political creeds, which have been handed down to us by our forefathers as sacredly as our Bibles, and for which more of them have suffered martyrdom than for the creed of the apostles, are all nonsense; who will tell us that paper constitutions are mere paper, and that parchment is but parchment, that jealousy of our rulers is a sin, &c. I could have wished also that sufficient caution had been used to secure to us our religious liberties, and to have prevented the general government from tyrannizing over our consciences by a religious establishment—a tyranny of all others most dreadful, and which will assuredly be exercised whenever it shall be thought necessary for the promotion and support of their political measures. It is ardently to be wished, sir, that these and other invaluable rights of freemen had been as cautiously secured as some of the paltry local interests of some of the individual states. But it appears to me, that, in forming this Constitution, we have run into the same error which the lawyers and Pharisees of old were charged with; that is, while we have secured the tithes of mint, anise, and cumin, we have neglected the weightier matters of the law, judgment, mercy, and faith. Have we not neglected to secure to ourselves the weighty matters of judgment or justice, by empowering the general government to establish one supreme, and as many inferior, courts as they please, whose proceedings they have a right to fix and regulate as they shall think fit, so that we are ignorant whether they shall be according to the common, civil, the Jewish, or Turkish law? What better provisions have we made for mercy, when a man, for ignorantly passing a counterfeit continental note, or bill of credit, is liable to be dragged to a distant county, two or three hundred miles from home, deprived of the support and assistance of friends, to be tried by a strange jury, ignorant of his character, ignorant of the character of the witnesses, unable to contradict any false testimony brought against him by their own knowledge of facts, and with whom the prisoner being unacquainted, he must

519

be deprived totally of the benefit of his challenge? and besides all that, he may be exposed to lose his life, merely for want of property to carry his witnesses to such a distance; and after all this solemn farce and mockery of a trial by jury, if they should acquit him, it will require more ingenuity than I am master of, to show that he does not hold his life at the will and pleasure of the Supreme Court, to which an appeal lies, and consequently depend on the tender mercies, perhaps, of the wicked, (for judges may be wicked;) and what those tender mercies are, I need not tell you. You may read them in the history of the Star Chamber Court in England, and in the courts of Philip, and in your Bible.

This brings me to the third and last weighty matter mentioned in the text—to wit, faith. The word *faith* may, with great propriety, be applied to the articles of our political creed, which, it is absolutely necessary, should be kept pure and uncorrupted, if we mean to preserve the liberties of our country and the inestimable blessings of a free government. And, sir, I cannot but be seriously alarmed on this head, as has frequently been the case during the present discussion,—gentlemen of the first rank and abilities openly opposing some of the most essential principles of freedom, and endeavoring, by the most ingenious sophistry, and the still more powerful weapons of ridicule, to shake or corrupt our faith therein. Have we not been told that, if government is but properly organized, and the powers were suitably distributed among the several members, it is unnecessary to provide any other security against the abuse of its power? that power thus distributed needs no restriction? Is this a whig principle? Does not every constitution on the continent contradict this position? Why are we told that all restrictions of power are found to be inconvenient? that we ought to put unlimited confidence in our rulers. that it is not our duty to be jealous of men in power. Have we not had an idea thrown out of establishing an aristocracy in our own country,—a government than which none is more dreadful and oppressive?

What the design of the preacher on this occasion is, I will not attempt to determine; far be it from me to judge men's hearts: but thus much I can say, from the best authority, they are deceitful above all things, and desperately wicked. But whatever be the design of the preachers, the tendency of their doctrines is clear; they tend to corrupt our political faith, to take us off our guard, and lull to sleep that jealousy which, we are told by all writers,—and it is proved by all experience,—is essentially necessary for the preservation of freedom. But notwithstanding the strongest assertions that there are no wolves in our country, if we see their footsteps in every public path, we should be very credulous and unwise to trust our flocks abroad, and to believe that those who advised us to do it were very anxious for their preservation.

In this Constitution, sir, we have departed widely from the principles and political faith of '76, when the spirit of liberty ran high, and danger put a curb on ambition. Here we find no security for the rights of individuals, no security for the existence of our state governments; here is no bill of rights, no proper restriction of power; our lives, our property, and our consciences, are left wholly at the mercy of the legislature, and the powers of the judiciary may be extended to any degree short of almighty. Sir, in this Constitution we have not only neglected,—we have done worse,—we have openly violated, our faith,—that is, our public faith.

The seventh article, which is in these words, "The ratifications of the Conventions of nine states shall be sufficient for the establishment of this Constitution between the states so ratifying the same," is so flagrant a violation of the public faith of these states, so solemnly pledged to each other in the Confederation, as makes me tremble to reflect upon; for, however lightly some may think of *paper* and *parchment* constitutions, they are recorded, sir, in that high court of appeals, the Judge of which will do right, and I am confident that no such violation of public faith ever did, or ever will, go unpunished.

The plan of the *federal city*, sir, departs from every principle of freedom, as far as the distance of the two polar stars from each other; for, subjecting the inhabitants of that district to the exclusive legislation of Congress, in whose appointment they have no share or vote, is laying a foundation on which may be erected as complete a tyranny as can be found in the Eastern world. Nor do I see how this evil can possibly be prevented, without razing the foundation of this happy place, where men are to live, without labor, upon the fruit of the labors of others; this political hive, where all the drones in the society are to be collected to feed on the honey of the land. How dangerous this city may be, and what its operation on the general liberties of this country, time alone must discover; but I pray God, it may not prove to this western world what the city of Rome, enjoying a similar constitution, did to the eastern.

There is another clause in this Constitution, which, though there is no prospect of getting it amended, I think ought not to be passed over in silence, lest such a silence should be construed into a tacit approbation of it. I mean the clause which restricts the general government from putting a stop, for a number of years, to a commerce which is a stain to the commerce of any civilized nation, and has already blackened half the plains of America with a race of wretches made so by our cruel policy and avarice, and which appears to me to be already repugnant to every principle of humanity, morality, religion, and good policy. There are other objections to this Constitution, which are weighty and unanswerable; but they have been so clearly stated, and so fully debated, in the course of this discussion, that it would be an unjustifiable intrusion on the patience of the house to repeat them. I shall therefore content myself with a few observations on the general plan and tendency. We are told that this is a federal government. I think, sir, there is as much propriety in the name, as in that which its advocates assume, and no more; it is, in my idea, as complete a consolidation as the government of this state, in which legislative powers, to a certain extent, are exercised by the several towns and corporations. The sole difference between a state government under this Constitution, and a corporation under a state government, is, that a state being more extensive than a town, its powers are likewise proportionably extended, but neither of them enjoys the least share of sovereignty; for, let me ask, what is a state government? What sovereignty, what power is left to it, when the control of every source of revenue, and the total command of the militia, are given to the general government? That power which can command both the property and the persons of the community, is the sovereign, and the sole sovereign. The idea of two distinct sovereigns in the same country, separately *possessed* of sovereign and supreme power, in the same matters at the same time, is as supreme an absurdity, as that two distinct separate circles can be bounded exactly by the same circumference. This, sir, is demonstration; and from it I draw one corollary, which, I think, clearly follows, although it is in favor of the Constitution, to wit—that at least that clause in which Congress guaranties to the several states a republican *form* of government, speaks honestly; that is, that no more is intended by it than is expressed; and I think it is clear that, whilst the mere form is secured, the substance—to wit, the whole power and sovereignty of our state governments, and with them the liberties of the country—is swallowed up by the general government; for it is well worth observing, that, while our state governments are held up to us as the great and sufficient security of our rights and privileges, it is carefully provided that they shall be disarmed of all power, and made totally dependent on the bounty of Congress for their support, and consequently for their existence,—so that we have scarce a single right secured under either.

Is this, sir, a government for freemen? Are we thus to be duped out of our liberties? I hope, sir, our affairs have not yet arrived to that long-wished-for pitch of confusion, that we are under the necessity of accepting such a system of government as this.

I cannot, sir, express my feelings on a late occasion, when I consider with what unspeakable indignation the spirit of a Montgomery, a Herkimer, a Paris, &c., must have fired at the insults offered to their memories on this floor, and that not by a stranger, but by a brother, when their names, which will ever be dear to freemen, were profanely called upon as an inducement for us to surrender up those rights and privileges, in the defence of which they so gallantly fought, and so gloriously died. We are called upon at this time (I think it is an early day) to make an unconditional surrender of those rights which ought to be dearer to us than our lives.

But I hope, sir, that the memory of these patriot heroes will teach us a duty on this occasion. If we follow their example, we are sure not to err. We ought, sir, to consider—and it is a most solemn consideration—that we may now give away, by a vote, what it may cost the dying groans of thousands to recover; that we may now surrender, with a little ink, what it may cost seas of blood to regain; the dagger of Ambition is now pointed at the fair bosom of Liberty, and, to deepen and complete the tragedy, we, her sons, are called upon to give the fatal thrust. Shall we not recoil at such a deed, and all cry out with one voice, "Hands off!" What distraction has seized us? Is she not our mother, and if the frenzy of any should persist in the parricidal attempt, shall we not instantly interpose, and receive the fatal point into our own bosom? A moment's hesitation would ever prove us to be bastards, not sons. The liberties of the country are a deposit, a trust, in the hands of individuals; they are an entailed estate, which the possessors have no right to dispose of; they belong to our children, and to them we are bound to transmit them as a representative body. The trust becomes tenfold more sacred in our hands, especially as it was committed to us with the fullest confidence in our sentiments, integrity, and firmness. If we should betray that trust on this occasion, I fear (think there is reason to fear) that it will teach a lesson dangerous to liberty—to wit, that no confidence is to be placed in men.

But why, sir, must we be guilty of this breach of trust? Why surrender up the dear-bought liberties of our country? Because we are told, in very positive terms, that nothing short of this will satisfy, or can be accepted by, our future rulers? Is it possible that we can be at a loss for an answer to such declarations as these? Can we not, ought we not to speak like freemen on this occasion, (this perhaps may be the last time when we shall dare to do it,) and declare, in as positive terms, that we cannot, we will not, give up our liberties; that, if we cannot be admitted into the Union as freemen, we will not come in as slaves? This I fully believe to be the language of my constituents; this is the language of my conscience; and, though I may not dare longer to make it the language of my tongue, yet I trust it will ever be the language of my heart. If we act with coolness, firmness, and decision, on this occasion, I have the fullest confidence that the God who has so lately delivered us out of the paw of the lion and the bear, will also deliver us from this Goliath, this uncircumcised Philistine. This government is founded in sin, and reared up in iniquity; the foundations are laid in a most sinful breach of public trust, and the top-stone is a most iniquitous breach of public faith; and I fear, if it goes into operation, we shall be justly punished with the total extinction of our civil liberties. We are invited, in this instance, to become partakers in other men's sins; if we do, we must likewise be content to take our share in the punishment.

We are told, sir, that a government is like a mad horse, which, notwithstanding all the curb you can put upon him, will sometimes run away with his rider. The idea is undoubtedly a just one. Would he not, therefore, justly be deemed a mad man, and deserve to have his neck broken, who should trust himself on this horse without any bridle at all? We are threatened, sir, if we do not come into the Union, with the resentment of our neighboring states. I do not apprehend we have much to fear from this quarter, for our neighbors must have the good sense to discover that not one of our objections is founded on motives of particular state interest. They must see likewise, from the debates, that every selfish idea that has been thrown out has come from those who very improperly call themselves the *federal* side of the house. A union with our sister states I as ardently desire as any man, and that upon the most generous principles; but a union under such a system as this, I think, is not a desirable thing. The design of a union is safety, but a union upon the proposed plan is certain destruction to liberty. In one sense, indeed, it may bring us to a state of safety, for it may reduce us to such a condition that we may be very sure that nothing worse can happen to us, and consequently we shall have nothing to fear.

This, sir, is a dreadful kind of safety; but I confess it is the only kind of safety I can see in this union. There are no advantages that can possibly arise from a union which can compensate for the loss of freedom, nor can any evils be apprehended from a disunion which are as much to be dreaded as tyranny.

The committee then proceeded through sections 8, 9, and 10, of this article, and the whole of the next, with little or no debate. As the secretary read the paragraphs, amendments were moved, in the order and form hereafter recited. . . .

Respecting the power to make all *laws necessary* for the carrying the Constitution into execution,—

"*Provided*, That no power shall be exercised by Congress, but such as is expressly given by this Constitution; and all others, not expressly given, shall be reserved to the respective states, to be by them exercised.'

Moved by Mr. LANSING.

(5) North Carolina, July 29, 1788

Mr. MACLAINE. Mr. Chairman, I beg leave to make a few observations. One of the gentleman's objections to the Constitution now under consideration is, that it is not the act of the states, but of the people; but that it ought to be the act of the states; and he instances the delegation of power by the states to the Confederation, at the commencement of the war, as a proof of this position. I hope, sir, that all power is in the people, and not in the state governments. If he will not deny the authority of the people to delegate power to agents, and to devise such a government as a majority of them thinks will promote their happiness, he will withdraw his objection. The people, sir, are the only proper authority to form a government. They, sir, have formed their state governments, and can alter them at pleasure. Their transcendent power is competent to form this or any other government which they think promotive of their happiness. But the gentleman contends that there ought to be a bill of rights, or something of that kind—something declaring expressly, that all power not expressly given to the Constitution ought to be retained by the states; and he produces the Confederation as an authority for its necessity. When the Confederation was made, we were by no means so well acquainted with the principles of government as we are now. We were then jealous of the power of our rulers, and had an idea of the British government when we entertained that jealousy. There is no people on earth so well acquainted with the nature of government as the people of America generally are. We know now that it is agreed upon by most writers, and men of judgment and reflection, that all power is in the people, and immediately derived from them. The gentleman surely must know that, if there be certain rights which never can, nor ought to, be given up, these rights cannot be said to be given away, merely because we have omitted to say that we have not given them up. Can any security arise from declaring that we have a right to what belongs to us? Where is the necessity of such a declaration? If we have this inherent, this unalienable, this indefeasible title to those rights, if they are not given up, are they not retained? If Congress should make a law beyond the powers and the spirit of the Constitution, should we not say to Congress, "You have no authority to make this law. There are limits beyond which you cannot go. You cannot exceed the power prescribed by the Constitution. You are amenable to us for your conduct. This act is unconstitutional. We will disregard it, and punish you for the attempt."

But the gentleman seems to be most tenacious of the judicial power of the states. The honorable gentleman must know, that the doctrine of reservation of power not relinquished, clearly demonstrates that the judicial power of the states is not impaired....

Mr. SPENCER answered, that the gentleman last up had misunderstood him. He did not object to the caption of the Constitution, but he instanced it to show that the United States were not, merely as states, the objects of the Constitution; but that the laws of Congress were to operate upon individuals, and not upon states. He then continued: I do not mean to contend that the laws of the general government should not operate upon individuals. I before observed that this was necessary, as laws could not be put in execution against states without the agency of the sword, which, instead of answering the ends of government, would destroy it. I endeavored to show that, as the government was not to operate against states, but against individuals, the rights of individuals ought to be properly secured. In order to constitute this security, it appears to me there ought to be such a clause in the Constitution as there was in the Confederation, expressly declaring, that every power, jurisdiction, and right, which are not given up by it, remain in the states.

Such a clause would render a bill of rights unnecessary. But as there is no such clause, I contend that there should be a bill of rights, ascertaining and securing the great rights of the states and people.

X. DEBATE IN THE FIRST CONGRESS

(1) August 15, 1789

Mr. Hartley Observed that it had been asserted in the convention of Pennsylvania, by the friends of the Constitution, that all the rights and powers that were not given to the government, were retained by the states and the people thereof; this was also his own opinion, but as four or five states had required to be secured in those rights by an express declaration in the constitution, he was disposed to gratify them; he thought every thing that was not incompatible with the general good ought to be granted, if it would tend to obtain the confidence of the people in the government, and, upon the whole, he thought these words were as necessary to be inserted in the declaration of rights as most in the clause.

(2) August 18, 1789

The 9th proposition, in the words following was considered, "The powers not delegated by the constitution, nor prohibited by it to the states, are reserved to the states respectively."

Mr. Tucker

Proposed to amend the proposition, by prefixing to it, "all powers being derived from the people," thought this a better place to make this assertion than the introductory clause of the constitution, where a similar sentiment was proposed by the committee. He extended his motion also, to add the word "expressly," so as to read "The powers not expressly delegated by this constitution."

Mr. Madison

Objected to this amendment, because it was impossible to confine a government to the exercise of express powers, there must necessarily be admitted powers by implication, unless the constitution descended to recount every minutiae. He remembered the word "expressly" had been moved in the convention of Virginia, by the opponents to the ratification, and after full and fair discussion was given up by them, and the system allowed to retain its present form.

Mr. Sherman

Coincided with mr. Madison in opinion, observing that corporate bodies are supposed to possess all powers incident to a corporate capacity, without being absolutely expressed.

Mr. Tucker

Did not view the word "expressly" in the same light with the gentleman who opposed him; he thought every power to be expressly given that could be clearly comprehended within any accurate definition of the general power.

Mr. Tucker's motion being negatived,

Mr. Carroll proposed to add to the end of the proposition, "or to the people," this was agreed to.

(3) August 21, 1789

The house proceeded in the consideration of the amendments to the constitution reported by the committee of the whole....

... The 9th proposition, mr. Gerry proposed to amend by inserting the word "expressly" so as to read the powers not expressly delegated by the constitution, nor prohibited to the states, are reserved to the states respectively or to the people; as he thought this an amendment of great importance, he requested the ayes and noes might be taken. He was supported in this by one fifth of the members present, whereupon they were taken....

Mr. Sherman

Moved to alter the last clause so as to make it read, the powers not delegated to the United States, by the constitution, nor prohibited by it to the states, are reserved to the states respectively, or to the people.

The motion was adopted without debate.

Y. OPINIONS ON THE CONSTITUTIONALITY OF THE BILL TO ESTABLISH A NATIONAL BANK

(1) James Madison, February 2, 1791

The Senate bill to incorporate subscribers to the Bank of the United States was read in the House on 21 January. It came before the Committee of the Whole on 31 January, was read by paragraphs, and reported to the House without amendment. After a third reading, the House on 1 February proceeded to the question on the passage of the bill. Smith (South Carolina), protesting that the bill had been "taken up rather unexpectedly yesterday," moved that it be recommitted to the Committee of the Whole for the purpose of making amendments. Laurance and Gerry declared that those who wished to make changes should have brought them forward the previous day. JM replied "that at this moment it was not of importance to determine how it has happened that the objections which several gentlemen now say they have to offer, against the bill—were not made at the proper time—it is sufficient for them if the candor of the house should lead them now to recommit the bill, that in a committee of the whole they may have an opportunity to offer their objections." Ames remarked that it was "absurd to go into a committee of the whole to determine whether the bill is constitutional or not," but JM insisted that "there was the greatest propriety in discussing a constitutional question in the committee of the whole." The motion for recommitment was defeated, 34 to 23, and the main question was resumed on 2 February (*Gazette of the U.S.*, 2 and 19 Feb. 1791; *Gen. Advertiser*, 5 Feb. 1791).

Mr. Madison began with a general review of the advantages and disadvantages of banks. The former he stated to consist in, first, the aids they afford to merchants who can thereby push their mercantile operations farther with the same capital. 2d. The aids to merchants in paying punctually the customs. 3d. Aids to the government in complying punctually with its engagements, when deficiencies or delays happen in the revenue. 4th. In diminishing usury. 5th. In saving the wear of the gold and silver kept in the vaults, and represented by notes. 6th. In facilitating occasional remittances from different places where notes happen to circulate. The effect of the proposed bank, in raising the value of stock, he thought, had been greatly overrated. It would no doubt raise that of the stock subscribed into the bank; but could have little effect on stock in general, as the interest on it would remain the same, and the quantity taken out of the market would be replaced by bank stock.

The principal disadvantages consisted in, 1st. banishing the precious metals, by substituting another medium to perform their office: This effect was inevitable. It was admitted by the most enlightened patrons of banks, particularly by Smith on the Wealth of Nations. The common answer to the objection was, that the money banished was only an exchange for something equally valuable that would be imported in return. He admitted the weight of this observation in general, but doubted whether, in the present habits of this country, the returns would not be in articles of no permanent use to it. 2d. Exposing the public and individuals to all the evils of a run on the bank, which would be particularly calamitous in so great a country as this, and might happen from various causes, as false rumours, bad management of the institution, an unfavorable balance of trade from short crops, &c.

It was proper to be considered also, that the most important of the advantages would be better obtained by several banks properly distributed, than by a single one. The aids to commerce could only be afforded at or very near the seat of the bank. The same was true of aids to merchants in the payment of customs. Anticipations of the government would also be most convenient at the different places where the interest of the debt was to be paid. The case in America was different from that in England: the interest there was all due at one place, and the genius of the monarchy favored the concentration of wealth and influence at the metropolis.

He thought the plan liable to other objections: It did not make so good a bargain for the public as was due to its interests. The charter to the bank of England had been granted for 11 years only, and was paid for by a loan to the government on terms better than could be elsewhere got. Every renewal of the charter had in like manner been purchased; in some instances, at a very high price. The same had been done by the banks of Genoa, Naples, and other like banks of circulation. The plan was unequal to the public creditors—it gave an undue preference to the holders of a particular denomination of the public debt, and to those at and within reach of the seat of government. If the subscriptions should be rapid, the distant holders of paper would be excluded altogether.

In making these remarks on the merits of the bill, he had reserved to himself, he said, the right to deny the authority of Congress to pass it. He had entertained this opinion from the date of the constitution. His impression might perhaps be the stronger, because he well recollected that a power to grant charters of incorporation had been proposed in the general convention and rejected.

Is the power of establishing an *incorporated bank* among the powers vested by the constitution in the legislature of the United States? This is the question to be examined.

After some general remarks on the limitations of all political power, he took notice of the peculiar manner in which the federal government is limited. It is not a general grant, out of which particular powers are excepted—it is a grant of particular powers only, leaving the general mass in other hands. So it had been understood by its friends and its foes, and so it was to be interpreted.

As preliminaries to a right interpretation, he laid down the following rules:

An interpretation that destroys the very characteristic of the government cannot be just.

Where a meaning is clear, the consequences, whatever they may be, are to be admitted—where doubtful, it is fairly triable by its consequences.

In controverted cases, the meaning of the parties to the instrument, if to be collected by reasonable evidence, is a proper guide.

Cotemporary and concurrent expositions are a reasonable evidence of the meaning of the parties.

In admitting or rejecting a constructive authority, not only the degree of its incidentality to an express authority, is to be regarded, but the degree of its importance also; since on this will depend the probability or improbability of its being left to construction.

Reviewing the constitution with an eye to these positions, it was not possible to discover in it the power to incorporate a Bank. The only clauses under which such a power could be pretended, are either—

1. The power to lay and collect taxes to pay the debts, and provide for the common defence and general welfare: Or,

2. The power to borrow money on the credit of the United States: Or,

3. The power to pass all laws necessary and proper to carry into execution those powers.

The bill did not come within the first power. It laid no tax to pay the debts, or provide for the general welfare. It laid no tax whatever. It was altogether foreign to the subject.

No argument could be drawn from the terms "common defence, and general welfare." The power as to these general purposes, was limited to acts laying taxes for them; and the general purposes themselves were limited and explained by the particular enumeration subjoined. To understand these terms in any sense, that would justify the power in question, would give to Congress an unlimited power; would render nugatory the enumeration of particular powers; would supercede all the powers reserved to the state governments. These terms are copied from the articles of confederation; had it ever been pretended, that they were to be understood otherwise than as here explained?

It had been said that "general welfare" meant cases in which a general power might be exercised by Congress, without interfering with the powers of the States; and that the establishment of a National Bank was of this sort. There were, he said, several answers to this novel doctrine.

1. The proposed Bank would interfere so as indirectly to defeat a State Bank at the same place. 2. It would directly interfere with the rights of the States, *to prohibit* as well as to establish Banks, and the circulation of Bank Notes. He mentioned a law of Virginia, actually prohibiting the circulation of notes payable to bearer. 3. Interference with the power of the States was no constitutional criterion of the power of Congress. If the power was not given, Congress could not exercise it; if given, they might exercise it, altho it should interfere with the laws, or even the constitution of the States. 4. If Congress could incorporate a Bank, merely because the act would leave the States free to establish Banks also; any other incorporations might be made by Congress. They could incorporate companies of manufacturers, or companies for cutting canals, or even religious societies, leaving similar incorporations by the States, like State Banks to themselves: Congress might even establish religious teachers in every parish, and pay them out of the Treasury of the United States, leaving other teachers unmolested in their functions. These inadmissible consequences condemned the controverted principle.

The case of the Bank established by the former Congress, had been cited as a precedent. This was known, he said, to have been the child of necessity. It never could be justified by the regular powers of the articles of confederation. Congress betrayed a consciousness of this in

530

recommending to the States to incorporate the Bank also. They did not attempt to protect the Bank Notes by penalties against counterfeiters. These were reserved wholly to the authority of the States.

The second clause to be examined is that, which empowers Congress to borrow money.

Is this a bill to borrow money? It does not borrow a shilling. Is there any fair construction by which the bill can be deemed an exercise of the power to borrow money? The obvious meaning of the power to borrow money, is that of accepting it from, and stipulating payment to those who are *able* and *willing* to lend.

To say that the power to borrow involves a power of creating the ability, where there may be the will, to lend, is not only establishing a dangerous principle, as will be immediately shewn, but is as forced a construction, as to say that it involves the power of compelling the will, where there may be the ability, to lend.

The *third* clause is that which gives the power to pass all laws necessary and proper to execute the specified powers.

Whatever meaning this clause may have, none can be admitted, that would give an unlimited discretion to Congress.

Its meaning must, according to the natural and obvious force of the terms and the context, be limited to means *necessary* to the *end*, and *incident* to the *nature* of the specified powers.

The clause is in fact merely declaratory of what would have resulted by unavoidable implication, as the appropriate, and as it were, technical means of executing those powers. In this sense it had been explained by the friends of the constitution, and ratified by the state conventions.

The essential characteristic of the government, as composed of limited and enumerated powers, would be destroyed: If instead of direct and incidental means, any means could be used, which in the language of the preamble to the bill, "might be conceived to be conducive to the successful conducting of the finances; or might be *conceived* to *tend* to give *facility* to the obtaining of loans." He urged an attention to the diffuse and ductile terms which had been found requisite to cover the stretch of power contained in the bill. He compared them with the terms *necessary* and *proper*, used in the Constitution, and asked whether it was possible to view the two descriptions as synonimous, or the one as a fair and safe commentary on the other.

If, proceeded he, Congress, by virtue of the power to borrow, can create the means of lending, and in pursuance of these means, can incorporate a Bank, they may do any thing whatever creative of like means.

The East-India company has been a lender to the British government, as well as the Bank, and the South-Sea company is a greater creditor than either. Congress then may incorporate similar companies in the United States, and that too not under the idea of regulating trade, but under that of borrowing money.

Private capitals are the chief resources for loans to the British government. Whatever then may be conceived to favor the accumulation of capitals may be done by Congress. They may incorporate manufacturers. They may give monopolies in every branch of domestic industry.

If, again, Congress by virtue of the power to borrow money, can create the ability to lend, they may by virtue of the power to levy money, create the ability to pay it. The ability to pay taxes depends on the general wealth of the society, and this, on the general prosperity of agriculture, manufactures and commerce. Congress then may give bounties and make regulations on all of these objects.

The States have, it is allowed on all hands, a concurrent right to lay and collect taxes. This power is secured to them not by its being expressly reserved, but by its not being ceded by the constitution. The reasons for the bill cannot be admitted, because they would invalidate that right; why may it not be *conceived* by Congress, that an uniform and exclusive imposition of taxes, would not less than the proposed Banks "be *conducive* to the successful conducting of the national finances, and *tend* to *give facility* to the obtaining of revenue, for the use of the government?"

The doctrine of implication is always a tender one. The danger of it has been felt in other governments. The delicacy was felt in the adoption of our own; the danger may also be felt, if we do not keep close to our chartered authorities.

Mark the reasoning on which the validity of the bill depends. To borrow money is made the *end* and the accumulation of capitals, *implied* as the *means*. The accumulation of capitals is then the *end*, and a bank *implied* as the *means*. The bank is then the *end*, and a charter of incorporation, a monopoly, capital punishments, &c. *implied* as the *means*.

If implications, thus remote and thus multiplied, can be linked together, a chain may be formed that will reach every object of legislation, every object within the whole compass of political economy.

The latitude of interpretation required by the bill is condemned by the rule furnished by the constitution itself.

Congress have power "to regulate the value of money"; yet it is expressly added not left to be implied, that counterfeitors may be punished.

They have the power "to declare war," to which armies are more incident, than incorporated Banks, to borrowing; yet is expressly added, the power "to raise and support armies"; and to this again, the express power "to make rules and regulations for the government of armies"; a like remark is applicable to the powers as to a navy.

The regulation and calling out of the militia are more appurtenant to war, than the proposed bank, to borrowing; yet the former is not left to construction.

The very power to borrow money is a less remote implication from the power of war, than an incorporated monopoly bank, from the power of borrowing—yet the power to borrow is not left to implication.

It is not pretended that every insertion or omission in the constitution is the effect of systematic attention. This is not the character of any human work, particularly the work of a body of men. The examples cited, with others that might be added, sufficiently inculcate nevertheless a rule of interpretation, very different from that on which the bill rests. They condemn the exercise of any power, particularly a great and important power, which is not evidently and necessarily involved in an express power.

It cannot be denied that the power proposed to be exercised is an important power.

As a charter of incorporation the bill creates an artificial person previously not existing in law. It confers important civil rights and attributes, which could not otherwise be claimed. It is, though not precisely similar, at least equivalent, to the naturalization of an alien, by which certain new civil characters are acquired by him. Would Congress have had the power to naturalize, if it had not been expressly given?

In the power to make bye laws, the bill delegated a sort of legislative power, which is unquestionably an act of a high and important nature. He took notice of the only restraint on the bye laws, that they were not to be contrary to the law and the constitution of the bank; and asked what law was intended; if the law of the United States, the scantiness of their code would give a power, never before given to a corporation—and obnoxious to the States, whose laws would then be superceded not only by the laws of Congress, but by the bye laws of a corporation within their own jurisdiction. If the law intended, was the law of the State, then the State might make laws that would destroy an institution of the United States.

The bill gives a power to purchase and hold lands; Congress themselves could not purchase lands within a State "without the consent of its legislature." How could they delegate a power to others which they did not possess themselves?

It takes from our successors, who have equal rights with ourselves, and with the aid of experience will be more capable of deciding on the subject, an opportunity of exercising that right, for an immoderate term.

It takes from our constituents the opportunity of deliberating on the untried measure, although their hands are also to be tied by it for the same term.

It involves a monopoly, which affects the equal rights of every citizen.

It leads to a penal regulation, perhaps capital punishments, one of the most solemn acts of sovereign authority.

From this view of the power of incorporation exercised in the bill, it could never be deemed an accessary or subaltern power, to be deduced by implication, as a means of executing another power; it was in its nature a distinct, an independent and substantive prerogative, which not being enumerated in the constitution could never have been meant to be included in it, and not being included could never be rightfully exercised.

He here adverted to a distinction, which he said had not been sufficiently kept in view, between a power necessary and proper for the government or union, and a power necessary and proper for executing the enumerated powers. In the latter case, the powers included in each of the enumerated powers were not expressed, but to be drawn from the nature of each. In the former, the powers composing the government were expressly enumerated. This constituted the peculiar nature of the government, no power therefore not enumerated, could be inferred from the general nature of government. Had the power of making treaties, for example, been omitted, however necessary it might have been, the defect could only have been lamented, or supplied by an amendment of the constitution.

But the proposed bank could not even be called necessary to the government; at most it could be but convenient. Its uses to the government could be supplied by keeping the taxes a little in advance— by loans from individuals—by the other banks, over which the government would have equal command; nay greater, as it may grant or refuse to these the privilege, made a free and irrevocable gift to the proposed bank, of using their notes in the federal revenue.

He proceeded next to the cotemporary expositions given to the constitution.

The defence against the charge founded on the want of a bill of rights, presupposed, he said, that the powers not given were retained; and that those given were not to be extended by remote implications. On any other supposition, the power of Congress to abridge the freedom of the press, or the rights of conscience, &c. could not have been disproved.

The explanations in the state conventions all turned on the same fundamental principle, and on the principle that the terms necessary and proper gave no additional powers to those enumerated. (Here he read sundry passages from the debates of the Pennsylvania, Virginia and

North-Carolina conventions, shewing the grounds on which the constitution had been vindicated by its principal advocates, against a dangerous latitude of its powers, charged on it by its opponents.) He did not undertake to vouch for the accuracy or authenticity of the publications which he quoted—he thought it probable that the sentiments delivered might in many instances have been mistaken, or imperfectly noted; but the complexion of the whole, with what he himself and many others must recollect, fully justified the use he had made of them.

The explanatory declarations and amendments accompanying the ratifications of the several states formed a striking evidence, wearing the same complexion. He referred those who might doubt on the subject, to the several acts of ratification.

The explanatory amendments proposed by Congress themselves, at least, would be good authority with them; all these renunciations of power proceeded on a rule of construction, excluding the latitude now contended for. These explanations were the more to be respected, as they had not only been proposed by Congress, but ratified by nearly three-fourths of the states. He read several of the articles proposed, remarking particularly on the 11th. and 12th. the former, as guarding against a latitude of interpretation—the latter, as excluding every source of power not within the constitution itself.

With all this evidence of the sense in which the constitution was understood and adopted, will it not be said, if the bill should pass, that its adoption was brought about by one set of arguments, and that it is now administered under the influence of another set; and this reproach will have the keener sting, because it is applicable to so many individuals concerned in both the adoption and administration.

In fine, if the power were in the constitution, the immediate exercise of it cannot be essential—if not there, the exercise of it involves the guilt of usurpation, and establishes a precedent of interpretation, levelling all the barriers which limit the powers of the general government, and protect those of the state governments. If the point be doubtful only, respect for ourselves, who ought to shun the appearance of precipitancy and ambition; respect for our successors, who ought not lightly to be deprived of the opportunity of exercising the rights of legislation; respect for our constituents who have had no opportunity of making known their sentiments, and who are themselves to be bound down to the measure for so long a period; all these considerations require that the irrevocable decision should at least be suspended until another session.

It appeared on the whole, he concluded, that the power exercised by the bill was condemned by the silence of the constitution; was condemned by the rule of interpretation arising out of the constitution; was condemned by its tendency to destroy the main characteristic of the constitution; was condemned by the expositions of the friends of the constitution, whilst depending before the public; was condemned by the apparent intention of the parties which ratified the constitution; was condemned by the explanatory amendments proposed by Congress themselves to the Constitution; and he hoped it would receive its final condemnation, by the vote of this house.

February 8, 1791

The House continued to debate the bank bill on 3, 4, 5, and 7 February.

Mr. Madison observed, that the present is a question which ought to be conducted with moderation and candor—and therefore there is no occasion to have recourse to those tragic representations, which have been adduced—warmth and passion should be excluded from the discussion of a subject, which ought to depend on the cool dictates of reason for its decision.

Adverting to the observation of Mr. Smith, (S. C.) "that it would be a deplorable thing for the Senate of the United States to have fallen on a decision which violates the constitution," he enquired, What does the reasoning of the gentleman tend to shew but this, that from *respect* to the Senate, this house ought to sanction their decisions? And from hence it will follow, that the President of the United States ought, out of respect to both, to sanction their joint proceedings: but he could, he said, remind the gentleman, of his holding different sentiments on another occasion.

Mr. Madison then enlarged on the exact balance or equipoise contemplated by the constitution, to be observed and maintained between the several branches of government—and shewed, that except this idea was preserved, the advantages of different independent branches would be lost, and their separate deliberations and determinations were intirely useless.

In describing a corporation he observed, that the powers proposed to be given, are such, as do not exist antecedent to the existence of the corporation; these powers are very extensive in their nature, and to which a principle of perpetuity may be annexed.

He waved a reply to Mr. Vining's observations on the *common law*, (in which that gentleman had been lengthy and minute, in order to invalidate Mr. Madison's objection to the power proposed to be given to the Bank, to make rules and regulations, not contrary to law). Mr. Madison said the question would involve a very lengthy discussion—and other objects more intimately connected with the subject, remained to be considered.

The power of granting Charters, he observed, is a great and important power, and ought not to be exercised, without we find ourselves expressly authorised to grant them: Here he dilated on the great and extensive influence that incorporated societies had on public affairs in

Europe: They are a powerful machine, which have always been found competent to effect objects on principles, in a great measure independent of the people.

He argued against the influence of the precedent to be established by the bill—for tho it has been said that the charter is to be granted only for a term of years, yet he contended, that granting the powers on any principle, is granting them in *perpetuum*—and assuming this right on the part of the government involves the assumption of every power whatever.

Noticing the arguments in favor of the bill, he said, it had been observed, that "government necessarily possesses every power." However true this idea may be in theory, he denied that it applied to the government of the United States.

Here he read the restrictive clause in the Constitution—and then observed that he saw no pass over this limit.

The preamble to the Constitution, said he, has produced a new mine of power; but this is the first instance he had heard of, in which the preamble has been adduced for such a purpose. In his opinion the preamble only states the objects of the confederation, and the subsequent clauses designate the express powers by which those objects are to be obtained—and a mean is proposed thro which to acquire those that may be found still requisite, more fully to effect the purposes of the confederation.

It is said, "there is a field of legislation yet unexplored." He had often heard this language—but he confessed he did not understand it. Is there, said he, a single blade of grass—Is there any property in existence in the United States, which is not subject to legislation, either of the particular States, or of the United States? He contended that the exercise of this power on the part of the United States, involves, to all intents and purposes, every power which an individual state may exercise. On this principle he denied the right of Congress to make use of a Bank to facilitate the collection of taxes. He did not, however admit the idea, that the institution would conduce to that object: The bank notes are to be equal to gold and silver, and consequently will be as difficult to obtain as the specie. By means of the objects of trade on which gold and silver are employed, there will be an influx of those articles—but paper being substituted, will fill those channels, which would otherwise be occupied by the precious metals—This, experience shews is the uniform effect of such a substitution.

The right of Congress to regulate trade, is adduced as an argument in favor of this of creating a corporation—but what has this bill to do with trade? Would any plain man suppose that this bill had any thing to do with trade?

He noticed the observation respecting the utility of Banks to aid the government with loans—He denied the necessity of the institution to aid the government in this respect—Great Britain, he observed, did not depend on such institutions—she borrows from various sources.

"Banks it is said, are necessary to pay the interest of the public debt,"—then they ought to be established in the places where that interest is paid—but can any man say, that the bank notes will circulate at par in Georgia. From the example of Scotland we know that they cannot be made equal to specie, remote from the place, where they can be immediately converted into coin—they must depreciate in case of a demand for specie—and if there is no moral certainty that the interest can be paid by these bank bills, will the government be justified in depriving itself of the power of establishing banks in different parts of the union?

We reason (said he) and often with advantage from British models, but in the present instance there is a great dissimilarity of circumstances. The bank notes of Great-Britain do not circulate universally; to make the circumstances parallel, it ought to have been assumed as a fact that banks are established in various parts of Great-Britain, at which the interest of the national debt is paid—but the fact is, it is only paid in one place.

The clause of the constitution which has been so often recurred to, and which empowers Congress to dispose of its property, he supposed referred only to the property left at the conclusion of the war, and has no reference to the monied property of the United States.

The clause which empowers Congress to pass all laws necessary, &c. has been brought forward repeatedly by the advocates of the bill; he noticed the several constructions of this clause which had been offered; the conclusion which he drew from the commentary of the gentleman from Massachusetts, Mr. Gerry, was that Congress may do what they please—and recurring to the opinion of that gentleman in 1787; he said the powers of the constitution were then dark, inexplicable and dangerous—but now, perhaps as the result of experience they are clear and luminous!

The constructions of the constitution, he asserted, which have been maintained on this occasion go to the subversion of every power whatever in the several States—but we are told for our comfort that the judges will rectify our mistakes; how are the judges to determine in the case; are they to be guided in their decisions by the rules of expediency?

It has been asked that if those minute powers of the constitution were thought to be necessary, is it supposable that the great and important power on the table was not intended to be given? Mr. Madison interpreted this circumstance in a quite different way, viz. if it was thought necessary to specify in the constitution, those minute powers, it would follow that more important powers would have been *explicitly* granted had they been contemplated.

538

The Western Territory business he observed, was a case *sui generis*, and therefore cannot be cited with propriety: West Point, so often mentioned he said, was purchased by the United States pursuant to law—and the consent of the State of New York is supposed, if it has not been expressly granted; but on any occasion does it follow that one violation of the constitution is to be justified by another?

The permanent residence bill, he conceived was entirely irrelative to the subject; but he conceived it might be justified on truly constitutional principles.

The act vesting in the President of the United States the power of removability has been quoted; he recapitulated in a few words his reasons for being in favor of that bill.

The bank of North-America, he said, he had opposed, as he considered the institution as a violation of the confederation. The State of Massachusetts he recollected voted with him on that occasion. The bank of North-America was however the child of necessity—as soon as the war was over, it ceased to operate as to continental purposes. But, asked he, are precedents in war, to justify violations of private and State rights, in a time of peace? And did the United States pass laws to punish the counterfeiting the notes of that bank? They did not, being convinced of the invalidity of any such law—the bank therefore took shelter under the authority of the State.

The energetic administration of this government is said to be connected with this institution. Mr. Madison here stated the principles on which he conceived this government ought to be administered—and added, other gentlemen may have had other ideas on the subject, and may have consented to the ratification of the constitution on different principles and expectations—but he considered the enlightened opinion and affection of the people, the only solid basis for the support of this government.

Mr. Madison then stated his objections to the several parts of the bill: The first article he objected to, was the duration—A period of twenty years, he observed, was to this country as a period of a century in the history of other countries—there was no calculating for the events which might take place: He urged the ill-policy of granting so long a term, from the experience of the government in respect to some treaties, which tho found inconvenient, could not now be altered.

The different classes of the public creditors, he observed, were not all put on an equal footing by *this* bill; but in the bill for the disposal of the Western Territory, this had been thought essential: The holders of 6 per cent. securities, will derive undue advantages—Creditors at a distance, and the holders of 3 per cent. securities, ought to be considered—as the public good is most essentially promoted by an equal attention to the interest of all.

I admit, said he, that the government ought to consider itself as the trustee of the public on this occasion, and therefore should avail itself of the best disposition of the public property.

In this view of the subject, he objected to the bill, as the public, he thought, ought to derive greater advantages from the institution than those proposed. In case of a universal circulation of the notes of the proposed bank, the profits will be so great that the government ought to receive a very considerable sum for granting the charter.

There are other defects in the bill, which render it proper and necessary in my opinion, that it should undergo a revision and amendment before it passes into a law: The power vested by the bill in the executive to borrow of the bank, he thought was objectionable—and the right to establish subordinate banks, he said, ought not to be delegated to any set of men under heaven.

The public opinion has been mentioned: If the appeal to the public opinion is suggested with sincerity, we ought to let our constituents have an opportunity to form an opinion on the subject.

He concluded by saying, he should move for the previous question.

(2) Thomas Jefferson
February 15, 1791

The bill for establishing a National Bank undertakes, among other things

    1. to form the subscribers into a Corporation.

    2. to enable them, in their corporate capacities to receive grants of land; and so far is against the laws of *Mortmain*.

    3. to make *alien* subscribers capable of holding lands, and so far is against the laws of *Alienage*.

    4. to transmit these lands, on the death of a proprietor, to a certain line of successors: and so far changes the course of *Descents*.

    5. to put the lands out of the reach of forfeiture or escheat and so far is against the laws of *Forfeiture and Escheat*.

    6. to transmit personal chattels to successors in a certain line: and so far is against the laws of *Distribution*.

    7. to give them the sole and exclusive right of banking under the national authority: and so far is against the laws of *Monopoly*.

    8. to communicate to them a power to make laws paramount to the laws of the states: for so they must be construed, to protect the institution from the controul of the state legislatures; and so, probably they will be construed.

I consider the foundation of the Constitution as laid on this ground that "all powers not delegated to the U.S. by the Constitution, not prohibited by it to the states, are reserved to the states or to the people" [XIIth. Amendmt.]. To take a single step beyond the boundaries thus specially drawn around the powers of Congress, is to take possession of a boundless feild of power, no longer susceptible of any definition.

The incorporation of a bank, and other powers assumed by this bill have not, in my opinion, been delegated to the U.S. by the Constitution.

I. They are not among the powers specially enumerated, for these are

1. A power to *lay taxes* for the purpose of paying the debts of the U.S. But no debt is paid by this bill, nor any tax laid. Were it a bill to raise money, it's origination in the Senate would condemn it by the constitution.

2. 'to borrow money.' But this bill neither borrows money, nor ensures the borrowing it. The proprietors of the bank will be just as free as any other money holders, to lend or not to lend their money to the public. The operation proposed in the bill, first to lend them two millions, and then borrow them back again, cannot change the nature of the latter act, which will still be a payment, and not a loan, call it by what name you please.

3. 'to regulate commerce with foreign nations, and among the states, and with the Indian tribes.' To erect a bank, and to regulate commerce, are very different acts. He who erects a bank creates a subject of commerce in it's bills: so does he who makes a bushel of wheat, or digs a dollar out of the mines. Yet neither of these persons regulates commerce thereby. To erect a thing which may be bought and sold, is not to prescribe regulations for buying and selling. Besides; if this was an exercise of the power of regulating commerce, it would be void, as extending as much to the internal commerce of every state, as to it's external. For the power given to Congress by the Constitution, does not extend to the internal regulation of the commerce of a state (that is to say of the commerce between citizen and citizen) which remains exclusively with it's own legislature; but to it's external commerce only, that is to say, it's commerce with another state, or with foreign nations or with the Indian tribes. Accordingly the bill does not propose the measure as a 'regulation of trade,' but as 'productive of considerable advantage to trade.'

Still less are these powers covered by any other of the special enumerations.

II. Nor are they within either of the general phrases, which are the two following.

1. 'To lay taxes to provide for the general welfare of the U.S.' that is to say 'to lay taxes *for the purpose* of providing for the general welfare'. For the laying of taxes is the *power* and the general welfare the *purpose* for which the power is to be exercised. They are not to lay

taxes ad libitum *for any purpose they please*; but only to *pay the debts or provide for the welfare of the Union.* In like manner they are not *to do anything they please* to provide for the general welfare, but only *to lay taxes* for that purpose. To consider the latter phrase, not as describing the purpose of the first, but as giving a distinct and independent power to do any act they please, which might be for the good of the Union, would render all the preceding and subsequent enumerations of power completely useless. It would reduce the whole instrument to a single phrase, that of instituting a Congress with power to do whatever would be for the good of the U.S. and as they would be the sole judges of the good or evil, it would be also a power to do whatever evil they pleased. It is an established rule of construction, where a phrase will bear either of two meanings, to give it that which will allow some meaning to the other parts of the instrument, and not that which would render all the others useless. Certainly no such universal power was meant to be given them. It was intended to lace them up straitly within the enumerated powers, and those without which, as means, these powers could not be be carried into effect. It is known that the very power now proposed *as a means*, was rejected *as an end*, by the Convention which formed the constitution. A proposition was made to them to authorize Congress to open canals, and an amendatory one to empower them to incorporate. But the whole was rejected, and one of the reasons of rejection urged in debate was that then they would have a power to erect a bank, which would render the great cities, where there were prejudices and jealousies on that subject adverse to the reception of the constitution.

2. The second general phrase is "to make all laws *necessary* and proper for carrying into execution the enumerated powers." But they can all be carried into execution without a bank. A bank therefore is not *necessary*, and consequently not authorised by this phrase.

It has been much urged that a bank will give great facility, or convenience in the collection of taxes. Suppose this were true: yet the constitution allows only the means which are "necessary" not those which are merely "convenient" for effecting the enumerated powers. If such a latitude of construction be allowed to this phrase as to give any non-enumerated power, it will go to every one, for these is no one which ingenuity may not torture into a *convenience, in some way or other,* to *some one* of so long a list of enumerated powers. It would swallow up all the delegated powers, and reduce the whole to one phrase as before observed. Therefore it was that the constitution restrained them to the *necessary* means, that is to say, to those means without which the grant of the power would be nugatory.

But let us examine this *convenience*, and see what it is. The report on this subject, page 3. states the only *general* convenience to be the preventing the transportation and re-transportation of money between the states and the treasury. (For I pass over the increase of circulating

542

medium ascribed to it as a merit, and which, according to my ideas of paper money is clearly a demerit.) Every state will have to pay a sum of tax-money into the treasury: and the treasury will have to pay, in every state, a part of the interest on the public debt, and salaries to the officers of government resident in that state. In most of the states there will still be a surplus of tax-money to come up to the seat of government for the officers residing there. The payments of interest and salary in each state may be made by treasury-orders on the state collector. This will take up the greater part of the money he has collected in his state, and consequently prevent the great mass of it from being drawn out of the state. If there be a balance of commerce in favour of that state against the one in which the government resides, the surplus of taxes will be remitted by the bills of exchange drawn for that commercial balance. And so it must be if there was a bank. But if there be no balance of commerce, either direct or circuitous, all the banks in the world could not bring up the surplus of taxes but in the form of money. Treasury orders then and bills of exchange may prevent the displacement of the main mass of the money collected, without the aid of any bank: and where these fail, it cannot be prevented even with that aid.

Perhaps indeed bank bills may be a more *convenient* vehicle than treasury orders. But a little *difference* in the degree of *convenience*, cannot constitute the necessity which the constitution makes the ground for assuming any non-enumerated power.

Besides; the existing banks will without a doubt, enter into arrangements for lending their agency: and the more favourable, as there will be a competition among them for it: whereas the bill delivers us up bound to the national bank, who are free to refuse all arrangement, but on their own terms, and the public not free, on such refusal, to employ any other bank. That of Philadelphia, I believe, now does this business, by their post-notes, which by an arrangement with the treasury, are paid by any state collector to whom they are presented. This expedient alone suffices to prevent the existence of that *necessity* which may justify the assumption of a non-enumerated power as a means for carrying into effect an enumerated one. The thing may be done, and has been done, and well done without this assumption; therefore it does not stand on that degree of *necessity* which can honestly justify it.

It may be said that a bank, whose bills would have a currency all over the states, would be more convenient than one whose currency is limited to a single state. So it would be still more convenient that there should be a bank whose bills should have a currency all over the world. But it does not follow from this superior conveniency that there exists anywhere a power to establish such a bank; or that the world may not go on very well without it.

Can it be thought that the Constitution intended that for a shade or two of *convenience*, more or less, Congress should be authorised to break down the most antient and fundamental laws of the several states, such as those against Mortmain, the laws of alienage, the rules of descent, the acts of distribution, the laws of escheat and forfeiture, the laws of monopoly? Nothing but a necessity invincible by any other means, can justify such a prostration of laws which constitute the pillars of our whole system of jurisprudence. Will Congress be too strait-laced to carry the constitution into honest effect, unless they may pass over the foundation-laws of the state-governments for the slightest convenience to theirs?

The Negative of the President is the shield provided by the constitution to protect against the invasions of the legislature 1. the rights of the Executive 2. of the Judiciary 3. of the states and state legislatures. The present is the case of a right remaining exclusively with the states and is consequently one of those intended by the constitution to be placed under his protection.

It must be added however, that unless the President's mind on a view of every thing which is urged for and against this bill, is tolerably clear that it is unauthorised by the constitution, if the pro and the con hang so even as to balance his judgment, a just respect for the wisdom of the legislature would naturally decide the balance in favour of their opinion. It is chiefly for cases where they are clearly misled by error, ambition, or interest, that the constitution has placed a check in the negative of the President.

(3) Alexander Hamilton
February 23, 1791

The Secretary of the Treasury having perused with attention the papers containing the opinions of the Secretary of State and Attorney General concerning the constitutionality of the bill for establishing a National Bank proceeds according to the order of the President to submit the reasons which have induced him to entertain a different opinion.

It will naturally have been anticipated that, in performing this task he would feel uncommon solicitude. Personal considerations alone arising from the reflection that the measure originated with him would be sufficient to produce it: The sense which he has manifested of the great importance of such an institution to the successful administration of the department under his particular care; and an expectation of serious ill consequences to result from a failure of the measure, do not permit him to be without anxiety on public accounts. But the chief solicitude arises from a firm persuasion, that principles of construction like those espoused by the Secretary of State and the Attorney General would be fatal to the just & indispensable authority of the United States.

In entering upon the argument it ought to be premised, that the objections of the Secretary of State and Attorney General are founded on a general denial of the authority of the United States to erect corporations. The latter indeed expressly admits, that if there be any thing in the bill which is not warranted by the constitution, it is the clause of incorporation.

Now it appears to the Secretary of the Treasury, that this *general principle* is *inherent* in the very *definition* of *Government* and *essential* to every step of the progress to be made by that of the United States; namely—that every power vested in a Government is in its nature *sovereign*, and includes by *force* of the *term*, a right to employ all the *means* requisite, and fairly *applicable* to the attainment of the *ends* of such power; and which are not precluded by restrictions & exceptions specified in the constitution; or not immoral, or not contrary to the essential ends of political society.

This principle in its application to Government in general would be admitted as an axiom. And it will be incumbent upon those, who may incline to deny it, to *prove* a distinction; and to shew that a rule which in the general system of things is essential to the preservation of the social order is inapplicable to the United States.

The circumstances that the powers of sovereignty are in this country divided between the National and State Governments, does not afford the distinction required. It does not follow from this, that each of the *portions* of powers delegated to the one or to the other is not sovereign *with regard to its proper objects*. It will only *follow* from it, that each has sovereign power as to *certain things*, and not as to *other things*. To deny that the Government of the United States has sovereign power as to its declared purposes & trusts, because its power does not extend to all cases, would be equally to deny, that the State Governments have sovereign power in any case; because their power does not extend to every case. The tenth section of the first article of the constitution exhibits a long list of very important things which they may not do. And thus the United States would furnish the singular spectacle of a *political society* without *sovereignty*, or of a people *governed* without *government*.

If it would be necessary to bring proof to a proposition so clear as that which affirms that the powers of the fœderal government, *as to its objects*, are sovereign, there is a clause of its constitution which would be decisive. It is that which declares, that the constitution and the laws of the United States made in pursuance of it, and all treaties made or which shall be made under their authority shall be the supreme law of the land. The power which can create the *Supreme law* of the land, in any case, is doubtless sovereign *as to such case*.

This general & indisputable principle puts at once an end to the *abstract* question—Whether the United States have power to *erect a corporation?* that is to say, to give a *legal* or *artificial capacity* to one or more persons, distinct from the natural. For it is unquestionably incident to *sovereign power* to erect corporations, and consequently to *that* of the United States, in *relation to the objects* intrusted to the management of the government. The difference is this—where the authority of the government is general, it can create corporations in *all cases;* where it is confined to certain branches of legislation, it can create corporations only in those cases.

Here then as far as concerns the reasonings of the Secretary of State & the Attorney General, the affirmative of the constitutionality of the bill might be permitted to rest. It will occur to the President that the principle here advanced has been untouched by either of them.

For a more complete elucidation of the point nevertheless, the arguments which they have used against the power of the government to erect corporations, however foreign they are to the great & fundamental rule which has been stated, shall be particularly examined. And after shewing that they do not tend to impair its force, it shall also be shewn, that the power of incorporation incident to the government in certain cases, does fairly extend to the particular case which is the object of the bill.

The first of these arguments is, that the foundation of the constitution is laid on this ground "that all powers not delegated to the United States by the Constitution nor prohibited to it by the States are reserved to the States or to the people", whence it is meant to be inferred, that congress can in no case exercise any power not included in those enumerated in the constitution. And it is affirmed that the power of erecting a corporation is not included in any of the enumerated powers.

The main proposition here laid down, in its true signification is not to be questioned. It is nothing more than a consequence of this republican maxim, that all government is a delegation of power. But how much is delegated in each case, is a question of fact to be made out by fair reasoning & construction upon the particular provisions of the constitution—taking as guides the general principles & general ends of government.

It is not denied, that there are *implied*, as well as *express* powers, and that the former are as effectually delegated as the latter. And for the sake of accuracy it shall be mentioned, that there is another class of powers, which may be properly denominated *resulting* powers. It will not be doubted that if the United States should make a conquest of any of the territories of its neighbours, they would possess sovereign jurisdiction over the conquered territory. This would rather be a result from the whole mass of the powers of the government & from the nature of political society, than a consequence of either of the powers specially enumerated.

But be this as it may, it furnishes a striking illustration of the general doctrine contended for. It shews an extensive case, in which a power of erecting corporations is either implied in, or would result from some or all of the powers, vested in the National Government. The

546

jurisdiction acquired over such conquered territory would certainly be competent to every species of legislation.

To return—It is conceded, that implied powers are to be considered as delegated equally with express ones.

Then it follows, that as a power of erecting a corporation may as well be *implied* as any other thing; it may as well be employed as an *instrument* or *mean* of carrying into execution any of the specified powers, as any other instrument or mean whatever. The only question must be, in this as in every other case, whether the mean to be employed, or in this instance the corporation to be erected, has a natural relation to any of the acknowledged objects or lawful ends of the government. Thus a corporation may not be erected by congress, for superintending the police of the city of Philadelphia because they are not authorised to *regulate* the *police* of that city; but one may be erected in relation to the collection of the taxes, or to the trade with foreign countries, or to the trade between the States, or with the Indian Tribes, because it is the province of the fœderal government to regulate those objects & because it is incident to a general *sovereign* or *legislative power* to *regulate* a thing, to employ all the means which relate to its regulation to the *best & greatest advantage.*

A strange fallacy seems to have crept into the manner of thinking & reasoning upon the subject. Imagination appears to have been unusually busy concerning it. An incorporation seems to have been regarded as some great, independent, substantive thing—as a political end of peculiar magnitude & moment; whereas it is truly to be considered as a *quality*, *capacity*, or *mean* to an end. Thus a mercantile company is formed with a certain capital for the purpose of carrying on a particular branch of business. Here the business to be prosecuted is the *end;* the association in order to form the requisite capital is the primary mean. Suppose that an incorporation were added to this; it would only be to add a new *quality* to that association; to give it an artificial capacity by which it would be enabled to prosecute the business with more safety & convenience.

That the importance of the power of incorporation has been exaggerated, leading to erroneous conclusions, will further appear from tracing it to its origin. The roman law is the source of it, according to which a *voluntary* association of individuals at *any time* or *for any purpose* was capable of producing it. In England, whence our notions of it are immediately borrowed, it forms a part of the executive authority, & the exercise of it has been often *delegated* by that authority. Whence therefore the ground of the supposition, that it lies beyond the reach of all those very important portions of sovereign power, legislative as well as executive, which belong to the government of the United States?

To this mode of reasoning respecting the right of employing all the means requisite to the execution of the specified powers of the Government, it is objected that none but *necessary* & proper means are to be employed, & the Secretary of State maintains, that no means are to be considered as *necessary*, but those without which the grant of the power would be *nugatory*. Nay so far does he go in his restrictive interpretation of the word, as even to make the case of *necessity* which shall warrant the constitutional exercise of the power to depend on *casual* & *temporary* circumstances, an idea which alone refutes the construction. The *expediency* of exercising a particular power, at a particular time, must indeed depend on *circumstances;* but the constitutional right of exercising it must be uniform & invariable—the same to day, as to morrow.

All the arguments therefore against the constitutionality of the bill derived from the accidental existence of certain State-banks: institutions which *happen* to exist to day, & for ought that concerns the government of the United States, may disappear to morrow, must not only be rejected as fallacious, but must be viewed as demonstrative, that there is a *radical* source of error in the reasoning.

It is essential to the being of the National government, that so erroneous a conception of the meaning of the word *necessary*, should be exploded.

It is certain, that neither the grammatical, nor popular sense of the term requires that construction. According to both, *necessary* often means no more than *needful, requisite, incidental, useful,* or *conducive to.* It is a common mode of expression to say, that it is *necessary* for a government or a person to do this or that thing, when nothing more is intended or understood, than that the interests of the government or person require, or will be promoted, by the doing of this or that thing. The imagination can be at no loss for exemplifications of the use of the word in this sense.

And it is the true one in which it is to be understood as used in the constitution. The whole turn of the clause containing it, indicates, that it was the intent of the convention, by that clause to give a liberal latitude to the exercise of the specified powers. The expressions have peculiar comprehensiveness. They are—"to make *all laws,* necessary & proper for *carrying into execution* the foregoing powers & all *other powers* vested by the constitution in the *government* of the United States, or in any *department* or *officer* thereof." To understand the word as the Secretary of State does, would be to depart from its obvious & popular sense, and to give it a *restrictive* operation; an idea never before entertained. It would be to give it the same force as if the word *absolutely* or *indispensibly* had been prefixed to it.

Such a construction would beget endless uncertainty & embarrassment. The cases must be palpable & extreme in which it could be pronounced with certainty, that a measure was absolutely necessary, or one without which the exercise of a given power would be nugatory.

There are few measures of any government, which would stand so severe a test. To insist upon it, would be to make the criterion of the exercise of any implied power a *case of extreme necessity;* which is rather a rule to justify the overleaping of the bounds of constitutional authority, than to govern the ordinary exercise of it.

It may be truly said of every government, as well as of that of the United States, that it has only a right, to pass such laws as are necessary & proper to accomplish the objects intrusted to it. For no government has a right to do *merely what it pleases.* Hence by a process of reasoning similar to that of the Secretary of State, it might be proved, that neither of the State governments has a right to incorporate a bank. It might be shewn, that all the public business of the State, could be performed without a bank, and inferring thence that it was unnecessary it might be argued that it could not be done, because it is against the rule which has been just mentioned. A like mode of reasoning would prove, that there was no power to incorporate the Inhabitants of a town, with a view to a more perfect police: For it is certain, that an incorporation may be dispensed with, though it is better to have one. It is to be remembered, that there is no *express* power in any State constitution to erect corporations.

The *degree* in which a measure is necessary, can never be a test of the *legal* right to adopt it. That must ever be a matter of opinion; and can only be a test of expediency. The *relation* between the *measure* and the *end*, between the *nature* of *the mean* employed towards the execution of a power and the object of that power, must be the criterion of constitutionality not the more or less of *necessity* or *utility.*

The practice of the government is against the rule of construction advocated by the Secretary of State. Of this the act concerning light houses, beacons, buoys & public piers, is a decisive example. This doubtless must be referred to the power of regulating trade, and is fairly relative to it. But it cannot be affirmed, that the exercise of that power, in this instance, was strictly necessary; or that the power itself would be *nugatory* without that of regulating establishments of this nature.

This restrictive interpretation of the word *necessary* is also contrary to this sound maxim of construction namely, that the powers contained in a constitution of government, especially those which concern the general administration of the affairs of a country, its finances, trade, defence &c ought to be construed liberally, in advancement of the public good. This rule does not depend on the particular form of a government or on the particular demarkation of the boundaries of its powers, but on the nature and objects of government itself. The means by which national exigencies are to be provided for, national inconveniencies obviated, national prosperity promoted, are of such infinite variety, extent and complexity, that there must, of necessity, be great latitude of discretion in the selection & application of those means. Hence consequently, the necessity & propriety of exercising the authorities intrusted to a government on principles of liberal construction.

The Attorney General admits the *rule*, but takes a distinction between a State, and the fœderal constitution. The latter, he thinks, ought to be construed with greater strictness, because there is more danger of error in defining partial than general powers.

But the reason of the *rule* forbids such a distinction. This reason is—the variety & extent of public exigencies, a far greater proportion of which and of a far more critical kind, are objects of National than of State administration. The greater danger of error, as far as it is supposeable, may be a prudential reason for caution in practice, but it cannot be a rule of restrictive interpretation.

In regard to the clause of the constitution immediately under consideration, it is admitted by the Attorney General, that no *restrictive* effect can be ascribed to it. He defines the word necessary thus. "To be necessary is to be *incidental,* and may be denominated the natural means of executing a power."

But while, on the one hand, the construction of the Secretary of State is deemed inadmissible, it will not be contended on the other, that the clause in question gives any *new* or *independent* power. But it gives an explicit sanction to the doctrine of *implied* powers, and is equivalent to an admission of the proposition, that the government, *as to its specified powers* and *objects,* has plenary & sovereign authority, in some cases paramount to that of the States, in others coordinate with it. For such is the plain import of the declaration, that it may pass *all laws* necessary & proper to carry into execution those powers.

It is no valid objection to the doctrine to say, that it is calculated to extend the powers of the general government throughout the entire sphere of State legislation. The same thing has been said, and may be said with regard to every exercise of power by *implication* or *construction.* The moment the literal meaning is departed from, there is a chance of error and abuse. And yet an adherence to the letter of its powers would at once arrest the motions of the government. It is not only agreed, on all hands, that the exercise of constructive powers is indispensible, but every act which has been passed is more or less an exemplification of it. One has been already mentioned, that relating to light houses &c. That which declares the power of the President to remove officers at pleasure, acknowlidges [sic] the same truth in another, and a signal instance.

The truth is that difficulties on this point are inherent in the nature of the fœderal constitution. They result inevitably from a division of the legislative power. The consequence of this division is, that there will be cases clearly within the power of the National Government; others clearly without its power; and a third class, which will leave room for

550

controversy & difference of opinion, & concerning which a reasonable latitude of judgment must be allowed.

But the doctrine which is contended for is not chargeable with the consequence imputed to it. It does not affirm that the National government is sovereign in all respects, but that it is sovereign to a certain extent: that is, to the extent of the objects of its specified powers.

It leaves therefore a criterion of what is constitutional, and of what is not so. This criterion is the *end* to which the measure relates as a *mean.* If the end be clearly comprehended within any of the specified powers, & if the measure have an obvious relation to that end, and is not forbidden by any particular provision of the constitution—it may safely be deemed to come within the compass of the national authority. There is also this further criterion which may materially assist the decision. Does the proposed measure abridge a preexisting right of any State, or of any individual? If it does not, there is a strong presumption in favour of its constitutionality; & slighter relations to any declared object of the constitution may be permitted to turn the scale.

The general objections which are to be inferred from the reasonings of the Secretary of State and of the Attorney General to the doctrine which has been advanced, have been stated and it is hoped satisfactorily answered. Those of a more particular nature shall now be examined.

The Secretary of State introduces his opinion with an observation, that the proposed incorporation undertakes to create certain capacities properties or attributes which are *against* the laws of *alienage, descents, escheat* and *forfeiture, distribution* and *monopoly,* and to confer a power to make laws paramount to those of the States. And nothing says he, in another place, but a *necessity invincible by other means* can justify such a *prostration* of *laws* which constitute the pillars of our whole system of jurisprudence, and are the foundation laws of the State Governments.

If these are truly the foundation laws of the several states, then have most of them subverted their own foundations. For there is scarcely one of them which has not, since the establishment of its particular constitution, made material alterations in some of those branches of its jurisprudence especially the law of descents. But it is not conceived how any thing can be called the fundamental law of a State Government which is not established in its constitution unalterable by the ordinary legislature. And with regard to the question of necessity it has been shewn, that this can only constitute a question of expediency, not of right.

To erect a corporation is to substitute a *legal* or *artificial* to a *natural* person, and where a number are concerned to give them *individuality.* To that legal or artificial person once created, the common law of every state of itself *annexes* all those incidents and attributes, which are represented as a prostration of the main pillars of their jurisprudence. It is certainly not accurate to say, that the erection of a corporation is *against* those different *heads* of the State laws; because it is rather to create a kind of person or entity, to which *they* are inapplicable, and to which the general rule of those laws assign a different regimen. The laws of alienage cannot apply to an artificial person, because it can have no country. Those of descent cannot apply to it, because it can have no heirs. Those of escheat are foreign from it for the same reason. Those of forfeiture, because it cannot commit a crime. Those of distribution, because, though it may be dissolved, it cannot die. As truly might it be said, that the exercise of the power of prescribing the rule by which foreigners shall be naturalised, is *against* the law of alienage; while it is in fact only to put them in a situation to cease to be the subject of that law. To do a thing which is *against* a law, is to do something which it forbids or which is a violation of it.

But if it were even to be admitted that the erection of a corporation is a direct alteration of the State laws in the enumerated particulars; it would do nothing towards proving, that the measure was unconstitutional. If the government of the United States can do no act, which amounts to an alteration of a State law, all its powers are nugatory. For almost every new law is an alteration, in some way or other of an old *law,* either *common,* or *statute.*

There are laws concerning bankruptcy in some states—some states have laws regulating the values of foreign coins. Congress are empowered to establish uniform laws concerning bankruptcy throughout the United States, and to regulate the values of foreign coins. The exercise of either of these powers by Congress necessarily involves an alteration of the laws of those states.

Again: Every person by the common law of each state may export his property to foreign countries, at pleasure. But Congress, in pursuance of the power of regulating trade, may prohibit the exportation of commodities: in doing which, they would alter the common law of each state in abridgement of individual rights.

It can therefore never be good reasoning to say—this or that act is unconstitutional, because it alters this or that law of a State. It must be shewn, that the act which makes the alteration is unconstitutional on other accounts, not *because* it makes the alteration.

There are two points in the suggestions of the Secretary of State which have been noted that are peculiarly incorrect. One is, that the proposed incorporation is against the laws of monopoly, because it stipulates an exclusive right of banking under the national authority. The other that it gives power to the institution to make laws paramount to those of the states.

But with regard to the first point, the bill neither prohibits any State from erecting as many banks as they please, nor any number of Individuals from associating to carry on the business: & consequently is free from the charge of establishing a monopoly: for monopoly implies a *legal impediment* to the carrying on of the trade by others than those to whom it is granted.

And with regard to the second point, there is still less foundation. The bye-laws of such an institution as a bank can operate only upon its own members; can only concern the disposition of its own property and must essentially resemble the rules of a private mercantile partnership. They are expressly not to be contrary to law; and law must here mean the law of a State as well as of the United States. There never can be a doubt, that a law of the corporation, if contrary to a law of a state, must be overruled as void; unless the law of the State is contrary to that of the United States; and then the question will not be between the law of the State and that of the corporation, but between the law of the State and that of the United States.

Another argument made use of by the Secretary of State, is, the rejection of a proposition by the convention to empower Congress to make corporations, either generally, or for some special purpose.

What was the precise nature or extent of this proposition, or what the reasons for refusing it, is not ascertained by any authentic document, or even by accurate recollection. As far as any such document exists, it specifies only canals. If this was the amount of it, it would at most only prove, that it was thought inexpedient to give a power to incorporate for the purpose of opening canals, for which purpose a special power would have been necessary; except with regard to the Western Territory, there being nothing in any part of the constitution respecting the regulation of canals. It must be confessed however, that very different accounts are given of the import of the proposition and of the motives for rejecting it. Some affirm that it was confined to the opening of canals and obstructions in rivers; others, that it embraced banks; and others, that it extended to the power of incorporating generally. Some again alledge, that it was disagreed to, because it was thought improper to vest in Congress a power of erecting corporations—others, because it was thought unnecessary to *specify* the power, and inexpedient to furnish an additional topic of objection to the constitution. In this state of the matter, no inference whatever can be drawn from it.

But whatever may have been the nature of the proposition or the reasons for rejecting it concludes nothing in respect to the real merits of the question. The Secretary of State will not deny, that whatever may have been the intention of the framers of a constitution, or of a law, that intention is to be sought for in the instrument itself, according to the usual & established rules of construction. Nothing is more common than for laws to *express* and *effect,* more or less than was intended. If then a power to erect a corporation, in any case, be deducible by fair inference from the whole or any part of the numerous provisions of the constitution of the United States, arguments drawn from extrinsic circumstances, regarding the intention of the convention, must be rejected.

Most of the arguments of the Secretary of State which have not been considered in the foregoing remarks, are of a nature rather to apply to the expediency than to the constitutionality of the bill. They will however be noticed in the discussions which will be necessary in reference to the particular heads of the powers of the government which are involved in the question.

Those of the Attorney General will now properly come under review.

His first observation is, that the power of incorporation is not *expressly* given to congress. This shall be conceded, but in *this sense* only, that it is not declared in *express terms* that congress may erect a *corporation*. But this cannot mean, that there are not certain *express* powers, which *necessarily* include it.

For instance, Congress have express power "to exercise exclusive legislation in all cases whatsoever, over such *district* (not exceeding ten miles square) as may by cession of particular states, & the acceptance of Congress become the seat of the government of the United states; and to exercise *like authority* over all places purchased by consent of the legislature of the State in which the same shall be for the erection of forts, arsenals, dock yards & other needful buildings."

Here then is express power to exercise *exclusive legislation in all cases whatsoever over certain places;* that is to do in respect to those places, all that any government whatever may do: For language does not afford a more complete designation of sovereign power, than in those comprehensive terms. It is in other words a power to pass all laws whatsoever, & consequently to pass laws for erecting corporations, as well as for any other purpose which is the proper object of law in a free government. Surely it can never be believed, that Congress with *exclusive power of legislation in all cases whatsoever,* cannot erect a corporation within the district which shall become the seat of government, for the better regulation of its police. And yet there is an unqualified denial of the power to erect corporations in every case on the part both of the Secretary of State and of the Attorney General. The former indeed speaks of that power in these emphatical terms, that it is *a right remaining exclusively with the states.*

As far then as there is an express power to do any *particular act of legislation,* there is an express one to erect corporations in the cases above described. But accurately speaking, no *particular power* is more than *implied* in a *general one.* Thus the power to lay a duty on a *gallon of rum,* is only a particular *implied* in the general power to lay and collect taxes, duties, imposts and excises. This serves to explain in what sense it may be said, that congress have not an express power to make corporations.

This may not be an improper place to take notice of an argument which was used in debate in the House of Representatives. It was there urged, that if the constitution intended to confer so important a power as that of erecting corporations, it would have been expressly mentioned. But the case which has been noticed is clearly one in which such a power exists, and yet without any specification or express grant of it, further than as every *particular implied* in a general power, can be said to be so granted.

But the argument itself is founded upon an exaggerated and erroneous conception of the nature of the power. It has been shewn, that it is not of so transcendent a kind as the reasoning supposes; and that viewed in a just light it is a mean which ought to have been left to *implication*, rather than an *end* which ought to have been *expressly* granted.

Having observed, that the power of erecting corporations is not expressly granted to Congress, the Attorney General proceeds thus . . . .

"If it can be exercised by them, it must be

    1. because the nature of the fœderal government implies it.

    2. because it is involved in some of the specified powers of legislation or

    3. because it is necessary & proper to carry into execution some of the specified powers."

To be implied in the *nature of the fœderal government,* says he, would beget a doctrine so indefinite, as to grasp every power.

This proposition it ought to be remarked is not precisely, or even substantially, that, which has been relied upon. The proposition relied upon is, that the *specified powers* of Congress are in their nature sovereign—that it is incident to sovereign power to erect corporations; & that therefore Congress have a right within the *sphere* & *in relation to the objects of their power, to erect corporations.*

It shall however be supposed, that the Attorney General would consider the two propositions in the same light, & that the objection made to the one, would be made to the other.

To this objection an answer has been already given. It is this; that the doctrine is stated with this express *qualification,* that the right to erect corporations does *only* extend to *cases* & *objects* within the *sphere* of the *specified powers* of the government. A general legislative authority implies a power to erect corporations *in all cases*—a particular legislative power implies authority to erect corporations, in relation to cases arising under that power only. Hence the affirming, that as an *incident* to sovereign power, congress may erect a corporation in relation to the *collection* of their taxes, is no more than to affirm that they may do whatever else they please; than the saying that they have a power to regulate trade would be to affirm that they have a power to regulate religion: or than the maintaining that they have sovereign power as to taxation, would be to maintain that they have sovereign power as to every thing else.

The Attorney General undertakes, in the next place, to shew, that the power of erecting corporations is not involved in any of the specified powers of legislation confided to the National government.

In order to this he has attempted an enumeration of the particulars which he supposes to be comprehended under the several heads of the *powers* to lay & collect taxes &c—to borrow money on the credit of the United States—to regulate commerce with foreign nations—between the states, and with the Indian Tribes—to dispose of and make all needful rules & regulations respecting the territory or other property belonging to the United States; the design of which enumeration is to shew *what is* included under those different heads of power, & *negatively,* that the power of erecting corporations is not included.

The truth of this inference or conclusion must depend on the accuracy of the enumeration. If it can be shewn that the enumeration is *defective,* the inference is destroyed. To do this will be attended with no difficulty.

The heads of the power to lay & collect taxes, he states to be

1. To ascertain the subject of taxation &c

2. to declare the quantum of taxation &c

3. to prescribe the *mode* of *collection.*

4. to ordain the manner of accounting for the taxes &c

The defectiveness of this enumeration consists in the generality of the third division *"to prescribe the mode* of collection"; which is in itself an immense chapter. It will be shewn hereafter, that, among a vast variety of particulars, it comprises the very power in question; namely to *erect corporations.*

The heads of the power to borrow money are stated to be

1. to stipulate the sum to be lent.

2. an interest or no interest to be paid.

3. the time & manner of repaying, unless the loan be placed on an irredeemable fund.

This enumeration is liable to a variety of objections. It omits, in the first place, the *pledging* or *mortgaging* of a fund for the security of the money lent, an usual and in most cases an essential ingredient.

The idea of a stipulation of *an interest or no interest* is too confined. It should rather have been said, to stipulate *the consideration* of the loan. Individuals often borrow upon considerations other than the payment of interest. So may government; and so they often find it necessary to do. Every one recollects the lottery tickets & other douceurs often given in Great Britain, as collateral inducements to the lending of money to the Government.

There are also frequently collateral conditions, which the enumeration does not contemplate. Every contract which has been made for monies borrowed in Holland includes stipulations that the sum due shall be *free from taxes,* and from sequestration in time of war, and mortgages all the land & property of the United States for the reimbursement.

It is also known, that a lottery is a common expedient for borrowing money, which certainly does not fall under either of the enumerated heads.

The heads of the power to regulate commerce with foreign nations are stated to be

1. to prohibit them or their commodities from our ports.

2. to impose duties on *them* where none existed before, or to increase existing duties on them.

3. to subject *them* to any species of custom house regulation

4. to grant *them* any exemptions or privileges which policy may suggest.

This enumeration is far more exceptionable than either of the former. It omits *every thing* that relates to the *citizens vessels* or *commodities* of the United States. The following palpable omissions occur at once.

1. Of the power to prohibit the exportation of commodities which not only exists at all times, but which in time of war it would be necessary to exercise, particularly with relation to naval and warlike stores.

2. Of the power to prescribe rules concerning the *characteristics & priviledges* of an american bottom—how she shall be navigated, as whether by citizens or foreigners, or by a proportion of each.

3. Of the power of regulating the manner of contracting with seamen, the police of ships on their voyages &c of which the act for the government & regulation of seamen in the merchants service is a specimen.

That the three preceding articles are omissions, will not be doubted. There is a long list of items in addition, which admit of little, if any question; of which a few samples shall be given.

1. The granting of bounties to certain kinds of vessels, & certain species of merchandise. Of this nature is the allowance on dried & pickled fish & salted provisions.

2. The prescribing of rules concerning the *inspection* of commodities to be exported. Though the states individually are competent to this regulation, yet there is no reason, in point of authority at least, why a general system might not be adopted by the United States.

3. The regulation of policies of insurance; of salvage upon goods found at sea, and the disposition of such goods.

4. The regulation of pilots.

5. The regulation of bills of exchange drawn by a merchant of *one state* upon a merchant of *another state*. This last rather belongs to the regulation of trade between the states, but is equally omitted in the specification under that head.

The last enumeration relates to the power "to dispose of & make *all needful rules and regulations* respecting the territory *or other property* belonging to the United States."

The heads of this power are said to be

1. to exert an ownership over the territory of the United States, which may be properly called the property of the United States, as in the Western Territory, and to *institute a government therein:* or

2. to exert an ownership over the other property of the United States.

This idea of exerting an ownership over the Territory or other property of the United States, is particularly indefinite and vague. It does not at all satisfy the conception of what must have been intended by a power, to make all needful *rules* and *regulations;* nor would there have been any use for a special clause which authorised nothing more. For the right of exerting an ownership is implied in the very definition of property.

It is admitted that in regard to the western territory some thing more is intended—even the institution of a government; that is the creation of a body politic, or corporation of the highest nature; one, which in its maturity, will be able itself to create other corporations. Why then does not the same clause authorise the erection of a corporation in respect to the regulation or disposal of any other of the property of the United States? This idea will be enlarged upon in another place.

Hence it appears, that the enumerations which have been attempted by the Attorney General are so imperfect, as to authorise no conclusion whatever. They therefore have no tendency to disprove, that each and every of the powers to which they relate, includes that of erecting corporations; which they certainly do, as the subsequent illustrations will more & more evince.

It is presumed to have been satisfactorily shewn in the course of the preceding observations

1. That the power of the government, *as to* the objects intrusted to its management, is in its nature sovereign.

2. That the right of erecting corporations is one, inherent in & inseparable from the idea of sovereign power.

3. That the position, that the government of the United States can exercise no power but such as is delegated to it by its constitution, does not militate against this principle.

4. That the word *necessary* in the general clause can have no *restrictive* operation, derogating from the force of this principle, indeed, that the degree in which a measure is, or is not necessary, cannot be a *test* of *constitutional* right, but of expediency only.

5. That the power to erect corporations is not to be considered, as an *independent* & *substantive* power but as an *incidental* & *auxiliary* one; and was therefore more properly left to implication, than expressly granted.

6. that the principle in question does not extend the power of the government beyond the prescribed limits, because it only affirms a power to *incorporate* for *purposes within the sphere of the specified powers.*

And lastly that the right to exercise such a power, in certain cases, is unequivocally granted in the most *positive* & *comprehensive* terms.

To all which it only remains to be added that such a power has actually been exercised in two very eminent instances: namely in the erection of two governments, One, northwest of the river Ohio, and the other south west—*the last, independent of any antecedent compact.*

And there results a full & complete demonstration, that the Secretary of State & Attorney General are mistaken, when they deny generally the power of the National government to erect corporations.

It shall now be endeavoured to be shewn that there is a power to erect one of the kind proposed by the bill. This will be done, by tracing a natural & obvious relation between the institution of a bank, and the objects of several of the enumerated powers of the government; and by shewing that, *politically* speaking, it is necessary to the effectual execution of one or more of those powers. In the course of this investigation, various instances will be stated, by way of illustration, of a right to erect corporations under those powers.

Some preliminary observations maybe proper.

The proposed bank is to consist of an association of persons for the purpose of creating a joint capital to be employed, chiefly and essentially, in loans. So far the object is not only lawful, but it is the mere exercise of a right, which the law allows to every individual. The bank of New York which is not incorporated, is an example of such an association. The bill proposes in addition, that the government shall become a joint proprietor in this undertaking, and that it shall permit the bills of the company payable on demand to be receivable in its revenues & stipulates that it shall not grant privileges similar to those which are to be allowed to this company, to any others. All this is incontrovertibly within the compass of the discretion of the government. The only question is, whether it has a right to incorporate this company, in order to enable it the more effectually to accomplish *ends*, which are in themselves lawful.

To establish such a right, it remains to shew the relation of such an institution to one or more of the specified powers of the government.

Accordingly it is affirmed, that it has a relation more or less direct to the power of collecting taxes; to that of borrowing money; to that of regulating trade between the states; and to those of raising, supporting & maintaining fleets & armies. To the two former, the relation may be said to be *immediate.*

And, in the last place, it will be argued, that it is, *clearly,* within the provision which authorises the making of all *needful* rules & *regulations* concerning the *property* of the United States, as the same has been practiced upon by the Government.

A Bank relates to the collection of taxes in two ways; *indirectly,* by increasing the quantity of circulating medium & quickening circulation, which facilitates the means of paying—*directly,* by creating a *convenient species* of *medium* in which they are to be paid.

To designate or appoint the money or *thing* in which taxes are to be paid, is not only a proper, but a necessary *exercise* of the power of collecting them. Accordingly congress in the law concerning the collection of the duties on imports & tonnage, have provided that they shall be payable in gold & silver. But while it was an indispensible part of the work to say in what they should be paid, the choice of the specific thing was mere matter of discretion. The payment might have been required in the commodities themselves. Taxes in kind, however ill judged, are not without precedents, even in the United States. Or it might have been in the paper money of the several states; or in the bills of the bank of North America, New York and Massachusetts, all or either of them: or it might have been in bills issued under the authority of the United States.

No part of this can, it is presumed, be disputed. The appointment, then, of the *money* or *thing,* in which the taxes are to be paid, is an incident to the power of collection. And among the expedients which may be adopted, is that of bills issued under the authority of the United States.

Now the manner of issuing these bills is again matter of discretion. The government might, doubtless, proceed in the following manner. It might provide, that they should be issued under the direction of certain officers, payable on demand; and in order to support their credit & give them a ready circulation, it might, besides giving them a currency in its taxes, set apart out of any monies in its Treasury, a given sum and appropriate it under the direction of those officers as a fund for answering the bills as presented for payment.

The constitutionality of all this would not admit of a question. And yet it would amount to the institution of a bank, with a view to the more convenient collection of taxes. For the simplest and most precise idea of a bank, is, a deposit of coin or other property, as a fund for *circulating* a *credit* upon it, which is to answer the purpose of money. That such an arrangement would be equivalent to the establishment of a bank would become obvious, if the place where the fund to be set apart was kept should be made a receptacle of the monies of all other persons who should incline to deposit them there for safe keeping; and would become still more so, if the Officers charged with the direction of the fund were authorised to make discounts at the usual rate of interest, upon good security. To deny the power of the government to add these ingredients to the plan, would be to refine away all government.

This process serves to exemplify the natural & direct relation which may subsist between the institution of a bank and the collection of taxes. It is true that the species of bank which has been designated, does not include the idea of incorporation. But the argument intended to be founded upon it, is this: that the institution comprehended in the idea of a bank being one immediately relative to the collection of taxes, *in regard to the appointment* of *the money or thing* in which they are to be paid; the sovereign power of providing for the collection of taxes necessarily includes the right of granting a corporate capacity to such an institution, as a requisite to its greater security, utility and more convenient management.

A further process will still more clearly illustrate the point. Suppose, when the species of bank which has been described was about to be instituted, it were to be urged, that in order to secure to it a due degree of confidence the fund ought not only to be set apart & appropriated generally, but ought to be specifically vested in the officers who were to have the direction of it, and in their *successors* in office, to the end that it might acquire the character of *private property* incapable of being resumed without a violation of the sanctions by which the rights of property are protected & occasioning more serious & general alarm, the apprehension of which might operate as a check upon the government— such a proposition might be opposed by arguments against the expediency of it or the solidity of the reason assigned for it, but it is not conceivable what could be urged against its constitutionality.

And yet such a disposition of the thing would amount to the erection of a corporation. For the true definition of a corporation seems to be this. It is a *legal* person, or a person created by act of law, consisting of one or more natural persons authorised to hold property or a franchise in succession in a legal as contradistinguished from a natural capacity.

Let the illustration proceed a step further. Suppose a bank of the nature which has been described with or without incorporation, had been instituted, & that experience had evinced as it probably would, that being wholly under public direction it possessed not the confidence requisite to the credit of its bills—Suppose also that by some of those adverse conjunctures which occasionally attend nations, there had been a very great drain of the specie of the country, so as not only to cause general distress for want of an adequate medium of circulation, but to produce, in consequence of that circumstance, considerable defalcations in the public revenues—suppose also, that there was no bank instituted in any State—in such a posture of things, would it not be most manifest that the incorporation of a bank, like that proposed by the bill, would be a measure immediately relative to the *effectual collection* of the taxes and completely within the province of the sovereign power of providing by all laws necessary & proper for that collection?

If it be said, that such a state of things would render that necessary & therefore constitutional, which is not so now—the answer to this, and a solid one it doubtless is, must still be, that which has been already stated—Circumstances may affect the expediency of the measure, but they can neither add to, nor diminish its constitutionality.

A Bank has a direct relation to the power of borrowing money, because it is an usual and in sudden emergencies an essential instrument in the obtaining of loans to Government.

A nation is threatened with a war. Large sums are wanted, on a sudden, to make the requisite preparations. Taxes are laid for the purpose, but it requires time to obtain the benefit of them. Anticipation is indispensible. If there be a bank, the supply can, at once be had; if there be none loans from Individuals must be sought. The progress of these is often too slow for the exigency: in some situations they are not practicable at all. Frequently when they are, it is of great consequence to be able to anticipate the product of them by advances from a bank.

The essentiality of such an institution as an instrument of loans is exemplified at this very moment. An Indian expedition is to be prosecuted. The only fund out of which the money can arise consistently with the public engagements, is a tax which will only begin to be collected in July next. The preparations, however, are instantly to be made. The money must therefore be borrowed. And of whom could it be borrowed; if there were no public banks?

It happens, that there are institutions of this kind, but if there were none, it would be indispensible to create one.

Let it then be supposed, that the necessity existed, (as but for a casualty would be the case) that proposals were made for obtaining a loan; that a number of individuals came forward and said, we are willing to accommodate the government with this money; with what we have in hand and the credit we can raise upon it we doubt not of being able to furnish the sum required: but in order to this, it is indispensible, that we should be incorporated as a bank. This is essential towards putting it in our power to do what is desired and we are obliged on that account to make it the *consideration* or condition of the loan.

Can it be believed, that a compliance with this proposition would be unconstitutional? Does not this alone evince the contrary? It is a necessary part of a power to borrow to be able to stipulate the consideration or conditions of a loan. It is evident, as has been remarked elsewhere, that this is not confined to the mere stipulation of a sum of money by way of interest—why may it not be deemed to extend, where a government is the contracting party, to the stipulation of a *franchise*? If it may, & it is not perceived why it may not, then the grant of a corporate capacity may be stipulated as a consideration of the loan? There seems to be nothing unfit, or foreign from the nature of the thing in giving individuality or a corporate capacity to a number of persons who are willing to lend a sum of money to the government, the better to enable them to do it, and make them an ordinary instrument of loans in future emergencies of the state.

But the more general view of the subject is still more satisfactory. The legislative power of borrowing money, & of making all laws necessary & proper for carrying into execution that power, seems obviously competent to the appointment of the *organ* through which the abilities and wills of individuals may be most efficaciously exerted, for the accommodation of the government by loans.

The Attorney General opposes to this reasoning, the following observation. "To borrow money presupposes the accumulation of a fund to be lent, and is secondary to the creation of an ability to lend." This is plausible in theory, but it is not true in fact. In a great number of cases, a previous accumulation of a fund equal to the whole sum required, does not exist. And nothing more can be actually presupposed, than that there exist resources, which put into activity to the greatest advantage by the nature of the operation with the government, will be equal to the effect desired to be produced. All the provisions and operations of government must be presumed to contemplate things as they *really* are.

The institution of a bank has also a natural relation to the regulation of trade between the States: in so far as it is conducive to the creation of a convenient medium of *exchange* between them, and to the keeping up a full circulation by preventing the frequent displacement of the metals in reciprocal remittances. Money is the very hinge on which commerce turns. And this does not mean merely gold & silver, many other things have served the purpose with different degrees of utility. Paper has been extensively employed.

It cannot therefore be admitted with the Attorney General, that the regulation of trade between the States, as it concerns the medium of circulation & exchange ought to be considered as confined to coin. It is even supposeable in argument, that the whole, or the greatest part of the coin of the country, might be carried out of it.

The Secretary of State objects to the relation here insisted upon, by the following mode of reasoning—"To erect a bank, says he, & to regulate commerce, are very different acts. He who erects a bank, creates a subject of commerce, so does he, who makes a bushel of wheat, or digs a dollar out of the mines. Yet neither of these persons regulates commerce thereby. To make a thing which may be bought & sold is not to *prescribe* regulations for *buying & selling:* thus making the regulation of commerce to consist in prescribing rules for *buying & selling.*"

This indeed is a species of regulation of trade; but is one which falls more aptly within the province of the local jurisdictions than within that of the general government, whose care must be presumed to have been intended to be directed to those general political arrangements concerning trade on which its aggregate interests depend, rather than to the details of buying and selling.

Accordingly such only are the regulations to be found in the laws of the United States; whose objects are to give encouragement to the entreprise of our own merchants, and to advance our navigation and manufactures.

And it is in reference to these general relations of commerce, that an establishment which furnishes facilities to circulation and a convenient medium of exchange & alienation, is to be regarded as a regulation of trade.

The Secretary of State further argues, that if this was a regulation of commerce, it would be void, *as extending as much to the internal commerce of every state as to its external.* But what regulation of commerce does not extend to the internal commerce of every state? What are all the duties upon imported articles amounting to prohibitions, but so many bounties upon domestic manufactures affecting the interests of different classes of citizens in different ways? What are all the provisions in the coasting act, which relate to the trade between district and district of the same State? In short what regulation of trade between the States, but must affect the internal trade of each State? What can operate upon the whole but must extend to every part!

The relation of a bank to the execution of the powers, that concern the common defence, has been anticipated. It has been noted, that at this very moment the aid of such an institution is essential to the measures to be pursued for the protection of our frontier.

It now remains to shew, that the incorporation of a bank is within the operation of the provision which authorises Congress to make all needful rules & regulations concerning the property of the United States. But it is previously necessary to advert to a distinction which has been taken by the Attorney General.

He admits, that the word *property* may signify personal property however acquired. And yet asserts, that it cannot signify money arising from the sources of revenue pointed out in the constitution; because, says he, "the disposal & regulation of money is the final cause for raising it by taxes."

But it would be more accurate to say, that the *object* to which money is intended to be applied is the *final cause* for raising it, than that the disposal and regulation of it is *such*. The support of Government; the support of troops for the common defence; the payment of the public debt, are the true *final causes* for raising money. The disposition & regulation of it when raised, are the steps by which it is applied to the *ends* for which it was raised, not the ends themselves. Hence therefore the money to be raised by taxes as well as any other personal property, must be supposed to come within the meaning as they certainly do within the letter of the authority, to make all needful rules & regulations concerning the property of the United States.

A case will make this plainer: suppose the public debt discharged, and the funds now pledged for it liberated. In some instances it would be found expedient to repeal the taxes, in others, the repeal might injure our own industry, our agriculture and manufactures. In these cases they would of course be retained. Here then would be monies arising from the authorised sources of revenue which would not fall within the rule by which the Attorney General endeavours to except them from other personal property, & from the operation of the clause in question.

The monies being in the coffers of the government, what is to hinder such a disposition to be made of them as is contemplated in the bill or what an incorporation of the parties concerned under the clause which has been cited.

It is admitted that with regard to the Western territory they give a power to erect a corporation—that is to institute a government. And by what rule of construction can it be maintained, that the same words in a constitution of government will not have the same effect when applied to one species of property, as to another, as far as the subject is capable of it? or that a legislative power to make all needful rules & regulations, or to pass all laws necessary & proper concerning the public property which is admitted to authorise an incorporation in one case will not authorise it in another? will justify the institution of a government over the western territory & will not justify the incorporation of a bank, for the more useful management of the money of the nation? If it will do the last, as well as the first, then under this provision alone the bill is constitutional, because it contemplates that the United States shall be joint proprietors of the stock of the bank.

There is an observation of the secretary of state to this effect, which may require notice in this place. Congress, says he, are not to lay taxes *ad libitum for any purpose they please,* but only to pay the debts, or provide for the *welfare* of the Union. Certainly no inference can be drawn from this against the power of applying their money for the institution of a bank. It is true, that they cannot without breach of trust, lay taxes for any other purpose than the general welfare but so neither can any other government. The welfare of the community is the only legitimate end for which money can be raised on the community.

Congress can be considered as under only one restriction, which does not apply to other governments—They cannot rightfully apply the money they raise to any purpose *merely* or purely local. But with this exception they have as large a discretion in relation to the *application* of money as any legislature whatever. The constitutional *test* of a right application must always be whether it be for a purpose of *general* or *local* nature. If the former, there can be no want of constitutional power. The quality of the object, as how far it will really promote or not the welfare of the union, must be matter of conscientious discretion. And the arguments for or against a measure in this light, must be arguments concerning expediency or inexpediency, not constitutional right. Whatever relates to the general order of the finances, to the general interests of trade &c being general objects are constitutional ones for *the application* of *money*.

A Bank then whose bills are to circulate in all the revenues of the country, is *evidently* a general object, and for that very reason a constitutional one as far as regards the appropriation of money to it. Whether it will really be a beneficial one, or not, is worthy of careful examination, but is no more a constitutional point, in the particular referred to; than the question whether the western lands shall be sold for twenty or thirty cents & acre.

A hope is entertained, that it has by this time been made to appear, to the satisfaction of the President, that a bank has a natural relation to the power of collecting taxes; to that of borrowing money; to that of regulating trade; to that of providing for the common defence: and that as the bill under consideration contemplates the government in the light of a joint proprietor of the stock of the bank, it brings the case within the provision of the clause of the constitution which immediately respects the property of the United States.

Under a conviction that such a relation subsists, the Secretary of the Treasury, with all deference conceives, that it will result as a necessary consequence from the position, that all the specified powers of the government are sovereign as to the proper objects; that the incorporation of a bank is a constitutional measure, and that the objections taken to the bill, in this respect, are ill founded.

But from an earnest desire to give the utmost possible satisfaction to the mind of the President, on so delicate and important a subject, the Secretary of the Treasury will ask his indulgence while he gives some additional illustrations of cases in which a power of erecting corporations may be exercised, under some of those heads of the specified powers of the Government, which are alledged to include the right of incorporating a bank.

1. It does not appear susceptible of a doubt, that if Congress had thought proper to provide in the collection law, that the bonds to be given for the duties should be given to the collector of each

district in the name of the collector of the district A. or B. as the case might require, to enure to him & his successors in office, in trust for the United States, that it would have been consistent with the constitution to make such an arrangement. And yet this it is conceived would amount to an incorporation.

2. It is not an unusual expedient of taxation to farm particular branches of revenue, that is to mortgage or sell the product of them for certain definite sums, leaving the collection to the parties to whom they are mortgaged or sold. There are even examples of this in the United States. Suppose that there was any particular branch of revenue which it was manifestly expedient to place on this footing, & there were a number of persons willing to engage with the Government, upon condition, that they should be incorporated & the funds vested in them, as well for their greater safety as for the more convenient recovery & management of the taxes. Is it supposeable, that there could be any constitutional obstacle to the measure? It is presumed that there could be none. It is certainly a mode of collection which it would be in the discretion of the Government to adopt; though the circumstances must be very extraordinary, that would induce the Secretary to think it expedient.

3. suppose a new & unexplored branch of trade should present itself with some foreign country. Suppose it was manifest, that, to undertake it with advantage, required an union of the capitals of a number of individuals; & that those individuals would not be disposed to embark without an incorporation, as well to obviate that consequence of a private partnership, which makes every individual liable in his whole estate for the debts of the company to their utmost extent, as for the more convenient management of the business—what reason can there be to doubt, that the national government would have a constitutional right to institute and incorporate such a company? None.

They possess a general authority to regulate trade with foreign countries. This is a mean which has been practiced to that end by all the principal commercial nations; who have trading companies to this day which have subsisted for centuries. Why may not the United States *constitutionally* employ the means *usual* in other countries for attaining the ends entrusted to them?

A power to make all needful rules & regulations concerning territory has been construed to mean a power to erect a government. A power to *regulate* trade is a power to make all needful rules & regulations concerning trade. Why may it not then include that of erecting a trading company as well as in the other case to erect a Government?

It is remarkable, that the State Conventions who have proposed amendments in relation to this point, have most, if not all of them, expressed themselves nearly thus—"Congress shall not grant monopolies, nor *erect any company* with exclusive advantages of commerce;" thus at the same time expressing their sense, that the power to erect trading companies or corporations, was inherent in Congress, & objecting to it no further, than as to the grant of *exclusive* priviledges.

The Secretary entertains all the doubts which prevail concerning the utility of such companies; but he cannot fashion to his own mind a reason to induce a doubt, that there is a constitutional authority in the United States to establish them. If such a reason were demanded, none could be given unless it were this—that congress cannot erect a corporation; which would be no better than to say they cannot do it, because they cannot do it: first presuming an inability, without reason, & then assigning that *inability* as the cause of itself.

Illustrations of this kind might be multiplied without end. They shall however be pursued no further.

There is a sort of evidence on this point, arising from an aggregate view of the constitution, which is of no inconsiderable weight. The very general power of laying & collecting taxes & appropriating their proceeds—that of borrowing money indefinitely—that of coining money & regulating foreign coins—that of making all needful rules and regulations respecting the property of the United States—these powers combined, as well as the reason & nature of the thing speak strongly this language: That it is the manifest design and scope of the constitution to vest in congress all the powers requisite to the effectual administration of the finances of the United States. As far as concerns this object, there appears to be no parsimony of power.

To suppose then, that the government is precluded from the employment of so usual as well as so important an instrument for the administration of its finances as that of a bank, is to suppose, what does not coincide with the general tenor & complexion of the constitution, and what is not agreeable to impressions that any mere spectator would entertain concerning it. Little less than a prohibitory clause can destroy the strong presumptions which result from the general aspect of the government. Nothing but demonstration should exclude the idea, that the power exists.

In all questions of this nature the practice of mankind ought to have great weight against the theories of Individuals.

The fact, for instance, that all the principal commercial nations have made use of trading corporations or companies for the purposes of *external commerce*, is a satisfactory proof, that the Establishment of them is an incident to the regulation of that commerce.

This other fact, that banks are an usual engine in the administration of national finances, & an ordinary & the most effectual instrument of loans & one which in this country has been found essential, pleads strongly against the supposition, that a government clothed with most of the most important prerogatives of sovereignty in relation to the revenues, its debts, its credit, its defence, its trade, its intercourse with foreign nations—is forbidden to make use of that instrument as an appendage to its own authority.

It has been stated as an auxiliary test of constitutional authority, to try, whether it abridges any preexisting right of any state, or any Individual. The proposed incorporation will stand the most severe examination on this point. Each state may still erect as many banks as it pleases; every individual may still carry on the banking business to any extent he pleases.

Another criterion may be this, whether the institution or thing has a more direct relation as to its uses, to the objects of the reserved powers of the State Governments, than to those of the powers delegated by the United States. This rule indeed is less precise than the former, but it may still serve as some guide. Surely a bank has more reference to the objects entrusted to the national government, than to those, left to the care of the State Governments. The common defence is decisive in this comparison.

It is presumed, that nothing of consequence in the observations of the Secretary of State and Attorney General has been left unnoticed.

There are indeed a variety of observations of the Secretary of State designed to shew that the utilities ascribed to a bank in relation to the collection of taxes and to trade, could be obtained without it, to analyse which would prolong the discussion beyond all bounds. It shall be forborne for two reasons—first because the report concerning the Bank may speak for itself in this respect; and secondly, because all those observations are grounded on the erroneous idea, that the *quantum* of necessity or utility is the test of a constitutional exercise of power.

One or two remarks only shall be made: one is that he has taken no notice of a very essential advantage to trade in general which is mentioned in the report, as peculiar to the existence of a bank circulation equal, in the public estimation to Gold & silver. It is this, that it renders it unnecessary to *lock* up the money of the country to accumulate for months successively in order to the periodical payment of interest. The other is this; that his arguments to shew that treasury orders & bills of exchange from the course of trade will prevent any considerable displacement of the metals, are founded on a partial view of the subject. A case will prove this: The sums collected in a state may be small in comparison with the debt due to it. The balance of its trade, direct & circuitous, with the seat of government may be even or nearly so. Here then without bank bills, which in that state answer the purpose of coin, there must be a displacement of the coin, in proportion to the difference between the sum collected in the State and that to be paid in it. With bank bills no such displacement would take place, or, as far as it did, it would be gradual & insensible. In many other ways also, would there be at least a temporary & inconvenient displacement of the coin, even where the course of trade would eventually return it to its proper channels.

The difference of the two situations in point of convenience to the Treasury can only be appreciated by one, who experiences the embarrassments of making provision for the payment of the interest on a stock continually changing place in thirteen different places.

One thing which has been omitted just occurs, although it is not very material to the main argument. The Secretary of State affirms, that the bill only contemplates a re-payment, not a loan to the government. But here he is, certainly mistaken. It is true, the government invests in the stock of the bank a sum equal to that which it receives on loan. But let it be remembered, that it does not, therefore, cease to be a proprietor of the stock; which would be the case, if the money received back were in the nature of a repayment. It remains a proprietor still, & will share in the profit, or loss, of the institution, according as the dividend is more or less than the interest it is to pay on the sum borrowed. Hence that sum is manifestly, and, in the strictest sense, a loan.

CHAPTER VI
PRINCIPLES OF EQUALITY
A. GENESIS 1:27

So God created humankind in his image, in the image of God he created them; male and female he created them.

B. GALATIANS 3:28

There is no longer Jew or Greek, there is no longer slave or free, there is no longer male and female; for all of you are one in Christ Jesus.

C. JAMES HARRINGTON, COMMONWEALTH OF OCEANS
1656

By what has been shown in reason and experience, it may appear, that though commonwealths in general be governments of the senate proposing, the people resolving, and the magistracy executing, yet some are not so good at these orders as others, through some impediment or defect in the frame, balance, or capacity of them, according to which they are of divers kinds.

The first division of them is into such as are single, as Israel, Athens, Lacedæmon, etc.; and such as are by leagues, as those of the Achæans, Ætolians, Lycians, Switz, and Hollanders.

The second (being Machiavel's) is into such as are for preservation, as Lacedæmon and Venice, and such as are for increase, as Athens and Rome; in which I can see no more than that the former takes in no more citizens than are necessary for defence, and the latter so many as are capable of increase.

The third division (unseen hitherto) is into equal and unequal, and this is the main point, especially as to domestic peace and tranquillity; for to make a commonwealth unequal, is to divide it into parties, which sets them at perpetual variance, the one party endeavoring to preserve their eminence and inequality, and the other to attain to equality; whence the people of Rome derived their perpetual strife with the nobility and Senate. But in an equal commonwealth there can be no more strife than there can be overbalance in equal weights; wherefore the Commonwealth of Venice, being that which of all others is the most equal in the constitution, is that wherein there never happened any strife between the Senate and the people.

An equal commonwealth is such a one as is equal both in the balance or foundation, and in the superstructure; that is to say, in her agrarian law and in her rotation.

An equal agrarian is a perpetual law, establishing and preserving the balance of dominion by such a distribution, that no one man or number of men, within the compass of the few or aristocracy, can come to overpower the whole people by their possessions in lands.

As the agrarian answers to the foundation, so does rotation to the superstructures.

Equal rotation is equal vicissitude in government, or succession to magistracy conferred for such convenient terms, enjoying equal vacations, as take in the whole body by parts, succeeding others, through the free election or suffrage of the people.

The contrary, whereunto is prolongation of magistracy, which, trashing the wheel of rotation, destroys the life or natural motion of a commonwealth.

The election or suffrage of the people is most free, where it is made or given in such a manner that it can neither oblige nor disoblige another, nor through fear of an enemy, or bashfulness toward a friend, impair a man's liberty.

Wherefore, says Cicero, the tablet or ballot of the people of Rome (who gave their votes by throwing tablets or little pieces of wood secretly into urns marked for the negative or affirmative) was a welcome constitution to the people, as that which, not impairing the assurance of their brows, increased the freedom of their judgment. I have not stood upon a more particular description of this ballot, because that of Venice exemplified in the model is of all others the most perfect.

An equal commonwealth (by that which has been said) is a government established upon an equal agrarian, arising into the superstructures or three orders, the Senate debating and proposing, the people resolving, and the magistracy executing, by an equal rotation through the suffrage of the people given by the ballot. For though rotation may be without the ballot, and the ballot without rotation, yet the ballot not only as to the ensuing model includes both, but is by far the most equal way; for which cause under the name of the ballot I shall hereafter understand both that and rotation too.

Now having reasoned the principles of an equal commonwealth, I should come to give an instance of such a one in experience, if I could find it; but if this work be of any value, it lies in that it is the first example of a commonwealth that is perfectly equal. For Venice, though it comes the nearest, yet is a commonwealth for preservation; and such a one, considering the paucity of citizens taken in, and the number not taken in, is externally unequal; and though every commonwealth that holds provinces must in that regard be such, yet not to that degree. Nevertheless, Venice internally, and for her capacity, is by far the most equal, though it has not, in my judgment, arrived at the full perfection of equality; both because her laws supplying the defect of an agrarian are not so clear nor effectual at the foundation, nor her superstructures, by the virtue of her ballot or rotation, exactly librated; in regard that through the paucity of her citizens her greater magistracies are continually wheeled through a few hands, as is confessed by Janotti, where he says, that if a gentleman comes once to be *Savio di terra ferma*, it seldom happens that he fails from thenceforward to be adorned with some one of the greater magistracies, as *Savi di mare, Savi di terra ferma, Savi Grandi*, counsellors, those of the decemvirate or dictatorian council, the *aurogatori*, or censors, which require no vacation or interval. Wherefore if this in Venice, or that in Lacedæmon, where the kings were hereditary, and the Senators (though elected by the people) for life, cause no inequality (which is hard to be conceived) in a commonwealth for preservation, or such a one as consists of a few citizens; yet is it manifest that it would cause a very great one in a commonwealth for increase, or consisting of the many, which, by engrossing the magistracies in a few hands, would be obstructed in their rotation.

But there be who say (and think it a strong objection) that, let a commonwealth be as equal as you can imagine, two or three men when all is done will govern it; and there is that in it which, notwithstanding the pretended sufficiency of a popular State, amounts to a plain confession of the imbecility of that policy, and of the prerogative of monarchy; forasmuch as popular governments in difficult cases have had recourse to dictatorian power, as in Rome.

To which I answer, that as truth is a spark to which objections are like bellows, so in this respect our commonwealth shines; for the eminence acquired by suffrage of the people in a commonwealth, especially if it be popular and equal, can be ascended by no other steps than the universal acknowledgment of virtue: and where men excel in virtue, the commonwealth is stupid and unjust, if accordingly they do not excel in authority. Wherefore this is both the advantage of virtue, which has her due encouragement, and of the commonwealth, which has her due services. These are the philosophers which Plato would have to be princes, the princes which Solomon would have to be mounted, and their steeds are those of authority, not empire; or, if they be buckled to the chariot of empire, as that of the dictatorian power, like the chariot of the sun, it is glorious for terms and vacations or intervals. And as a commonwealth is a government of laws and not of men, so is this the principality of virtue, and not of man; if that fail or set in one, it rises in another who is created his immediate successor. And this takes away that vanity from under the sun, which is an error proceeding more or less from all other rulers under heaven but an equal commonwealth.

These things considered, it will be convenient in this place to speak a word to such as go about to insinuate to the nobility or gentry a fear of the people, or to the people a fear of the nobility or gentry, as if their interests were destructive to each other; when indeed an army may as well consist of soldiers without officers, or of officers without soldiers, as a commonwealth, especially such a one as is capable of greatness, of a people without a gentry, or of a gentry without a people. Wherefore this, though not always so intended, as may appear by Machiavel, who else would be guilty, is a pernicious error. There is something first in the making of a commonwealth, then in the governing of it, and last of all in the leading of its armies, which, though there be great divines, great lawyers, great men in all professions, seems to be peculiar only to the genius of a gentleman.

For so it is in the universal series of story, that if any man has founded a commonwealth, he was first a gentleman. Moses had his education by the daughter of Pharaoh; Theseus and Solon, of noble birth, were held by the Athenians worthy to be kings; Lycurgus was of the royal blood; Romulus and Numa princes; Brutus and Publicola patricians; the Gracchi, that lost their lives for the people of Rome and the restitution of that commonwealth, were the sons of a father adorned with two triumphs, and of Cornelia the daughter of Scipio, who being demanded in marriage by King Ptolemy, disdained to become the Queen of Egypt. And the most renowned Olphaus Megaletor, sole legislator, as you will see anon, of the Commonwealth of Oceana, was derived from a noble family; nor will it be any occasion of scruple in this case, that Leviathan affirms the politics to be no ancienter than his book *"De Cive."* Such also as have got any fame in the civil government of a commonwealth, or by the leading of its armies, have been gentlemen; for so in all other respects were those plebeian magistrates elected by the people of Rome, being of known descents and of equal virtues, except only that they were excluded from the name by the usurpation of the patricians. Holland, through this defect at home, has borrowed princes for generals, and gentlemen of divers nations for commanders: and the Switzers, if they have any defect in this kind, rather lend their people to the colors of other princes, than make that noble use of them at home which should assert the liberty of mankind. For where there is not a nobility to hearten the people, they are slothful, regardless of the world, and of the public interest of liberty, as even those of Rome had been without their gentry: wherefore let the people embrace the gentry in peace, as the light of their eyes; and in war, as the trophy of their arms; and if Cornelia disdained to be Queen of Egypt, if a Roman consul looked down from his tribunal upon the greatest king, let the nobility love and cherish the people that afford them a throne so much higher in a commonwealth, in the acknowledgment of their virtue, than the crowns of monarchs.

But if the equality of a commonwealth consist in the equality first of the agrarian, and next of the rotation, then the inequality of a commonwealth must consist in the absence or inequality of the agrarian, or of the rotation, or of both.

Israel and Lacedæmon, which commonwealths (as the people of this, in Josephus, claims kindred of that) have great resemblance, were each of them equal in their agrarian, and unequal in their rotation, especially Israel, where the Sanhedrim, or Senate, first elected by the people, as appears by the words of Moses, took upon them ever after, without any precept of God, to substitute their successors by ordination; which having been there of civil use, as excommunication, community of goods, and other customs of the Essenes, who were many of them converted, came afterward to be introduced into the Christian Church. And the election of the judge, *suffes,* or dictator, was irregular, both for the occasion, the term, and the vacation of that magistracy; as you find in the book of Judges, where it is often repeated, that in those days there was no king in Israel—that is, no judge; and in the first of Samuel, where Eli judged Israel forty years, and Samuel, all his life. In Lacedæmon the election of the Senate being by suffrage of the people, though for life, was not altogether so unequal, yet the hereditary right of kings, were it not for the agrarian, had ruined her.

Athens and Rome were unequal as to their agrarian, that of Athens being infirm, and this of Rome none at all; for if it were more anciently carried it was never observed. Whence, by the time of Tiberius Gracchus, the nobility had almost eaten the people quite out of their lands, which they held in the occupation of tenants and servants, whereupon the remedy being too late, and too vehemently applied, that commonwealth was ruined.

These also were unequal in their rotation, but in a contrary manner. Athens, in regard that the Senate (chosen at once by lot, not by suffrage, and changed every year, not in part, but in the whole) consisted not of the natural aristocracy, nor sitting long enough to understand or to be perfect in their office, had no sufficient authority to restrain the people from that perpetual turbulence in the end, which was their ruin, notwithstanding the efforts of Nicias, who did all a man could do to help it. But as Athens, by the headiness of the people, so Rome fell by the ambition of the nobility, through the want of an equal rotation; which, if the people had got into the Senate, and timely into the magistracies (whereof the former was always usurped by the patricians, and the latter for the most part) they had both carried and held their agrarian, and that had rendered that commonwealth immovable.

But let a commonwealth be equal or unequal, it must consist, as has been shown by reason and all experience, of the three general orders; that is to say, of the Senate debating and proposing, of the people resolving, and of the magistracy executing. Wherefore I can never wonder enough at Leviathan, who, without any reason or example, will have it that a commonwealth consists of a single person, or of a single assembly; nor can I sufficiently pity those "thousand gentlemen, whose minds, which otherwise would have wavered, he has framed (as is affirmed by himself) in to a conscientious obedience (for so he is pleased to call it) of such a government."

D. JOHN LOCKE, TWO TREATISES OF GOVERNMENT, THE SECOND TREATISE, AN ESSAY CONCERNING THE TRUE ORIGINAL, EXTENT, AND END OF CIVIL GOVERNMENT

1698

Chap. IV.

Of SLAVERY.

22. The *Natural Liberty* of Man is to be free from any Superior Power on Earth, and not to be under the Will or Legislative Authority of Man, but to have only the Law of Nature for his Rule. The *Liberty of Man, in Society*, is to be under no other Legislative Power, but that established, by consent, in the Common-wealth, nor under the Dominion of any Will, or Restraint of any Law, but what the Legislative shall enact, according to the Trust put in it. *Freedom* then is not what Sir R. F. tells us, *O.A.* 55 [224]. *A Liberty for every one to do what he lists, to live as he pleases, and not to be tyed by any Laws:* But *Freedom of Men under Government*, is, to have a standing Rule to live by, common to every one of that Society, and made by the Legislative Power erected in it; A Liberty to follow my own Will in all things, where the Rule prescribes not; and not to be subject to the inconstant, uncertain, unknown, Arbitrary Will of another Man. As *Freedom of Nature* is to be under no other restraint but the Law of Nature.

23. This *Freedom* from Absolute, Arbitrary Power, is so necessary to, and closely joyned with a Man's Preservation, that he cannot part with it, but by what forfeits his Preservation and Life together. For a Man, not having the Power of his own Life, *cannot*, by Compact, or his own Consent, *enslave himself* to any one, nor put himself under the Absolute, Arbitrary Power of another, to take away his Life, when he pleases. No body can give more Power than he has himself; and he that cannot take away his own Life, cannot give another power over it. Indeed having, by his fault, forfeited his own Life, by some Act that deserves Death; he, to whom he has forfeited it, may (when he has him in his Power) delay to take it, and make use of him to his own Service, and he does him no injury by it. For, whenever he finds the hardship of his Slavery out-weigh the value of his Life, 'tis in his Power, by resisting the Will of his Master, to draw on himself the Death he desires.

24. This is the perfect condition of *Slavery*, which *is* nothing else, but *the State of War continued, between a lawful Conquerour, and a Captive*. For, if once *Compact* enter between them, and make an agreement for a limited Power on the one side, and Obedience on the other, the State of War and *Slavery* ceases, as long as the Compact endures. For, as has been said, no Man can, by agreement, pass over to another that which he hath not in himself, a Power over his own Life.

I confess, we find among the *Jews*, as well as other Nations, that Men did sell themselves; but, 'tis plain, this was only to *Drudgery, not to Slavery*. For, it is evident, the Person sold was not under an Absolute, Arbitrary, Despotical Power. For the Master could not have power to kill him, at any time, whom, at a certain time, he was obliged to let go free out of his Service: and the Master of such a Servant was so far from having an Arbitrary Power over his Life, that he could not, at pleasure, so much as maim him, but the loss of an Eye, or Tooth, set him free, *Exod*. XXI.

* * *

CHAP. VI.

Of Paternal Power.

52. It may perhaps be censured as an impertinent Criticism in a discourse of this nature, to find fault with words and names that have obtained in the World: And yet possibly it may not be amiss to offer new ones when the old are apt to lead Men into mistakes, as this of *Paternal Power* probably has done, which seems so to place the Power of Parents over their Children wholly in the *Father*, as if the *Mother* had no share in it, whereas if we consult Reason or Revelation, we shall find she hath an equal Title. This may give one reason to ask, Whether this might not be more properly called *Parental Power*. For whatever obligation Nature and the right of Generation lays on Children, it must certainly bind them equal to both the concurrent Causes of it. And accordingly we see the positive Law of God every where joyns them together, without distinction, when it commands the Obedience of Children, *Honour thy Father and thy Mother*, Exod. 20. 12. *Whosoever curseth his Father or his Mother*, Lev. 20. 9. *Ye shall fear every Man his Mother and his Father*, Lev. 19. 3. *Children obey your Parents*, &c. Eph. 6. 1. is the stile of the Old and New Testament.

53. Had but this one thing been well consider'd without looking any deeper into the matter, it might perhaps have kept Men from running into those gross mistakes, they have made, about this Power of Parents: which however it might, without any great harshness, bear the name of Absolute Dominion, and Regal Authority, when under the Title of *Paternal Power* it seem'd appropriated to the Father, would yet have sounded but odly, and in the very name shewn the Absurdity, if this supposed Absolute Power over Children had been called *Parental*, and

thereby have discover'd, that it belong'd to the *Mother* too; for it will but very ill serve the turn of those Men who contend so much for the Absolute Power and Authority of the *Fatherhood*, as they call it, that the *Mother* should have any share in it. And it would have but ill supported the *Monarchy* they contend for, when by the very name it appeared that that Fundamental Authority from whence they would derive their Government of a single Person only, was not plac'd in one, but two Persons joyntly. But to let this of Names pass.

54. Though I have said above, Chap. II, *That all Men by Nature are equal*, I cannot be supposed to understand all sorts of *Equality*: *Age* or *Virtue* may give Men a just Precedency: *Excellency of Parts and Merit* may place others above the Common Level: *Birth* may subject some, and *Alliance* or *Benefits* others, to pay an Observance to those to whom Nature, Gratitude or other Respects may have made it due; and yet all this consists with the *Equality*, which all Men are in, in respect of Jurisdiction or Dominion one over another, which was the *Equality* I there spoke of, as proper to the Business in hand, being that *equal Right* that every Man hath, *to his Natural Freedom*, without being subjected to the Will or Authority of any other Man.

55. *Children*, I confess are not born in this full state of *Equality*, though they are born to it. Their Parents have a sort of Rule and Jurisdiction over them when they come into the World, and for some time after, but 'tis but a temporary one. The Bonds of this Subjection are like the Swadling Cloths they are wrapt up in, and supported by, in the weakness of their Infancy. Age and Reason as they grow up, loosen them till at length they drop quite off, and leave a Man at his own free Disposal.

E. THOMAS GORDON, CATO'S LETTERS, NO. 45

September 16, 1721

Of the Equality and Inequality of Men.

SIR,

Men are naturally equal, and none ever rose above the rest but by force or consent: No man was ever born above all the rest, nor below them all; and therefore there never was any man in the world so good or so bad, so high or so low, but he had his fellow. Nature is a kind and benevolent parent; she constitutes no particular favourites with endowments and privileges above the rest; but for the most part sends all her offspring into the world furnished with the elements of understanding and strength, to provide for themselves: She gives them heads to consult their own security, and hands to execute their own counsels; and according to the use that they make of their faculties, and of the opportunities that they find, degrees of power and names of distinction grow amongst them, and their natural equality is lost.

Thus nature, who is their parent, deals with men: But fortune, who is their nurse, is not so benevolent and impartial; she acts wantonly and capriciously, often cruelly; and counterplotting justice as well as nature, frequently sets the fool above the wise man, and the best below the worst.

And from hence it is, that the most part of the world, attending much more to the noisy conduct and glaring effects of fortune, than to the quiet and regular proceedings of nature, are misled in their judgment upon this subject: They confound fortune with nature, and too often ascribe to natural merit and excellency the works of contrivance or chance. This however, shews that reason and equity run in our heads, while we endeavour to find a just cause for things that are not just; and this is the source of the reverence which we pay to men whom fortune sometimes lifts on high, though nature had placed them below. The populace rarely see any creature rise, but they find a reason for it in his parts; when probably the true one will be found in his own baseness, or another man's folly.

From the same reasoning may be seen why it is, that, let who will be at the head of a party, he is always extolled by his party as superior to the rest of mankind; and let who will be the first man of his country, he will never fail being complimented by many as the first of his species. But the issue and their own behaviour constantly shew, that the highest are upon a level with the rest, and often with the lowest. Men that are high are almost ever seen in a false light; the most part see them at a great distance, and through a magnifying medium; some are dazzled with their splendor, many are awed by their power. Whatever appears shining or terrible, appears great, and is magnified by the eye and the imagination.

That nature has made men equal, we know and feel; and when people come to think otherwise, there is no excess of folly and superstition which they may not be brought to practise. Thus they have made gods of dead men, and paid divine honours to many while they were yet living: They saw them to be but men, yet they worshipped them as gods. And even they who have not gone quite so far, have yet, by their wild notions of inequality, done as much mischief; they have made men, and often wicked men, to be vice-gods; and then made God's power (falsely so called) as irresistible in the hands of men as in his own, and much more frightful.

It is evident to common sense, that there ought to be no inequality in society, but for the sake of society; but these men have made one man's power and will the cause of all men's misery. They gave him as far as they could the power of God, without obliging him to practise the mercy and goodness of God.

Those that think themselves furthest above the rest, are generally by their education below them all. They are debased by a conceit of their greatness: They trust to their blood; which, speaking naturally, gives them no advantage; and neglect their mind, which alone, by proper improvements, sets one man above another. It is not blood or nature, but art or accident, which makes one man excel others. Aristotle, therefore, must either have been in jest, when he said, that he, who naturally excelled all others, ought to govern all; or said it to flatter his pupil and prince, Alexander the Great. It is certain, that such a man never yet was found in the world, and never will be found till the end of it. Alexander himself, notwithstanding the greatness of his spirit, and his conquests, had in his own army, and perhaps among the common soldiers, men naturally as great and brave as himself, and many more wise.

Whoever pretends to be naturally superior to other men, claims from nature what she never gave to any man. He sets up for being more than a man; a character with which nature has nothing to do. She has thrown her gifts in common amongst us; and as the highest offices of nature fall to the share of the mean as well as of the great, her vilest offices are performed by the great as well as by the mean: Death and diseases are the portion of kings as well as of clowns; and the corpse of a monarch is no more exempted from stench and putrefaction, than the corpse of a slave.

Mors aequo pulsat pede.

All the arts and endowments of men to acquire pre-eminence and advantages over one another, are so many proofs and confessions that they have not such pre-eminence and advantages from nature; and all their pomp, titles, and wealth, are means and devices to make the world think that they who possess them are superior in merit to those that want them. But it is not much to the glory of the upper part of mankind, that their boasted and superior merit is often the work of heralds, artificers, and money; and that many derive their whole stock of fame from ancestors, who lived an age or many ages ago.

The first founders of great families were not always men of virtue or parts; and where they were so, those that came after them did frequently, and almost generally, by trusting to their blood, disgrace their name. Such is the folly of the world, and the inconvenience of society, to allow men to be great by proxy! An evil that can scarce ever be cured. The race of French kings, called by their historians in contempt, *les rois fainéants* and the succession of the Roman Caesars (in both which, for one good prince they had ten that were intolerable, either for folly, or cruelty, and often for both), might be mentioned as known proofs of the above truth; and every reader will find in his own memory many more.

I have been told of a prince, who, while yet under age, being reproved by his governor for doing things ill or indecent, used to answer, *Je suis roy; I am King;* as if his quality had altered the nature of things, and he himself had been better than other men, while he acted worse. But he spoke from that spirit which had been instilled into him from his cradle. *I am King!* What then, Sir? The office of a king is not to do evil, but to prevent it. You have royal blood in your veins: But the blood of your page is, without being royal, as good as yours; or, if you doubt, try the difference in a couple of porringers next time you are ill; and learn from this consideration and experiment, that by nature you are no better than your people, though subject from your fortune to be worse, as many of your ancestors have been.

If my father got an estate and title by law or the sword, I may by virtue of his will or his patent enjoy his acquisition; but if I understand neither law nor the sword, I can derive honour from neither: My honour therefore is, in the reason of things purely nominal; and I am still by nature a plebeian, as all men are.

There is nothing moral in blood, or in title, or in place: Actions only, and the causes that produce them, are moral. He therefore is best that does best. Noble blood prevents neither folly, nor lunacy, nor crimes: but frequently begets or promotes them: And noblemen, who act infamously, derive no honour from virtuous ancestors, whom they dishonour. A man who does base things, is not noble; nor great, if he do little things: A sober villager is a better man than a debauched lord; an honest mechanick than a knavish courtier.

F. MONTESQUIEU, THE SPIRIT OF LAWS

1748

OF CIVIL SLAVERY [Book 15, Chapter 1]

SLAVERY, properly so called, is the establishment of a right which gives to one man such a power over another, as renders him absolute master of his life and fortune. The state of slavery is bad of its own nature: it is neither useful to the master nor to the slave; not to the slave, because he can do nothing thro' a motive of virtue; not to the master, because he contracts all manner of bad habits with his slaves; he accustoms himself insensibly to the want of all moral virtues; he grows fierce, hasty, severe, choleric, voluptuous, and cruel.

In despotic countries, where they are already in a state of political slavery, civil slavery is more tolerable than in other governments. Every one ought to be satisfied in those countries with necessaries and life. Hence the condition of a slave is hardly more burdensome than that of a subject.

But in a monarchical government, where it is of the utmost importance that human nature should not be debased, or dispirited, there ought to be no slavery. In democracies, slavery is contrary to the spirit of the constitution; it only contributes to give a power and luxury to the citizens which they ought not to have.

ORIGIN OF THE RIGHT OF SLAVERY AMONG THE ROMAN CIVILIANS [Chapter 2]

ONE would never have imagined that slavery should owe its birth to pity, and that this should have been excited three different ways.

The law of nations, to prevent prisoners from being put to death, has allowed them to be made slaves. The civil law of the Romans empowered debtors, who were subject to be ill used by their creditors, to sell themselves. And the law of nature requires, that children, whom a father reduced to slavery is no longer able to maintain, should be reduced to the same state as the father.

These reasons of the civilians are all false. It is false that killing in war is lawful, unless in a case of absolute necessity: but when a man has made another his slave, he cannot be said to have been under a necessity of taking away his life, since he actually did not take it away. War gives no other right over prisoners than to disable them from doing any further harm, by securing their persons. All nations concur in detesting the murdering of prisoners in cold blood.

Nor is it true, that a freeman can sell himself. Sale implies a price; now when a person sells himself, his whole substance immediately devolves to his master; the master therefore in that case gives nothing, and the slave receives nothing. You will say he has a *peculium*. But this peculium goes along with his person: If it is not lawful for a man to kill himself, because he robs his country of his person, for the same reason he is not allowed to sell himself. The liberty of every citizen constitutes a part of the public liberty; and in a democratical state is even a part of the sovereignty. To sell one's citizenship is so repugnant to all reason, as to be scarce supposeable in any man. If liberty may be rated with respect to the buyer, it is beyond all price to the seller.

The third way is birth; which falls with the two former. For if a man could not sell himself, much less could he sell an unborn offspring. If a prisoner of war is not to be reduced to slavery, much less are his children.

Nor is slavery less opposite to the civil law than to that of nature. What civil law can restrain a slave from running away, since he is not a member of society, and consequently has no interest in any civil laws? He can be retained only by a family law, that is, by the master's authority.

ANOTHER ORIGIN OF THE RIGHT OF SLAVERY [Chapter 3]

I WOULD as soon say, that the right of slavery proceeds from the contempt of one nation for another, founded on a difference in customs.

Lopez de Gama relates, *"that the Spaniards found near St. Martha, several baskets full of crabs, snails, grasshoppers and locusts, which proved to be the ordinary provision of the natives. This the conquerors turned to a heavy charge against the conquered."* The author owns that this, with their smoking and trimming their beards in a different manner, gave rise to the law by which the Americans became slaves to the Spaniards.

Knowledge humanises mankind, and reason inclines to mildness; but prejudices eradicate every tender disposition.

ANOTHER ORIGIN OF THE RIGHT OF SLAVERY [Chapter 4]

I WOULD as soon say that religion gives its professors a right to enslave those who dissent from it, in order to render its propagation more easy.

This was the notion that encouraged the ravagers of America in their iniquity. Under the influence of this idea, they founded their right of enslaving so many nations; for these robbers, who would absolutely be both robbers and Christians, were superlatively devout.

Louis XIII was extremely uneasy at a law, by which all the Negroes of his colonies were to be made slaves; but it being strongly urged to him as the readiest means for their conversion, he acquiesced without further scruple.

OF THE SLAVERY OF THE NEGROES [Chapter 5]

WERE I to vindicate our right to make slaves of the Negroes, these should be my arguments.

The Europeans, having extirpated the Americans, they were obliged to make slaves of the Africans for clearing such vast tracts of land.

Sugar would be too dear, if the plants which produce it were cultivated by any other than slaves.

These creatures are all over black, and with such a flat nose, that they can scarcely be pitied.

It is hardly to be believed that God, who is a wise Being, should place a soul, especially a good soul, in such a black ugly body.

It is so natural to look upon colour as the criterion of human nature, that the Asiatics, among whom eunuchs are employed, always deprive the *Blacks* of their resemblance to us, by a more opprobrious distinction.

The colour of the skin may be determined by that of the hair, which among the Ægyptians, the best philosophers in the world, was of such importance, that they put to death all the red-haired men who fell into their hands.

The Negroes prefer a glass necklace to that gold, which polite nations so highly value: can there be a greater proof of their wanting common sense?

It is impossible for us to suppose these creatures to be men, because allowing them to be men, a suspicion would follow, that we ourselves are not Christians.

Weak minds exaggerate too much the wrong done to the Africans. For were the case as they state it, would the European powers, who make so many needless conventions among themselves, have failed to make a general one, in behalf of humanity and compassion?

TRUE ORIGIN OF THE RIGHT OF SLAVERY [Chapter 6]

It is time to enquire into the true origin of the right of slavery. It ought to be founded on the nature of things; let us see if there be any cases where it can be derived from thence.

In all despotic governments, people make no difficulty in selling themselves; the political slavery in some measure annihilates the civil liberty.

According to Mr. Perry, the Muscovites sell themselves very readily; their reason for it is evident; their liberty is not worth keeping.

At *Achim* every one is for selling himself. Some of the chief lords have not less than a thousand slaves, all principal merchants, who have a great number of slaves themselves, and these also are not without their slaves. Their masters are their heirs, and put them into trade. In those states, the freemen, being overpowered by the government, have no better resource than making themselves slaves to the tyrants in office.

This is the just and rational origin of that mild law of slavery, which obtains in some countries, and mild it ought to be, as founded on the free choice a man makes of a master, for his own benefit; which forms a mutual convention betwixt the two parties.

ANOTHER ORIGIN OF THE RIGHT OF SLAVERY [Chapter 7]

Here is another origin of the right of slavery, and even of that cruel slavery, which is to be seen among men.

There are countries where the excess of heat enervates the body, and renders men so slothful and dispirited, that nothing but the fear of

584

chastisement can oblige them to perform any laborious duty: slavery is there more reconcileable to reason; and the master being as lazy with respect to his sovereign, as his slave is to him, this adds a political, to a civil slavery.

Aristotle endeavours to prove, that there are natural slaves, but what he says, is far from proving it. If there be any such, I believe they are those of whom I have been speaking.

But as all men are born equal, slavery must be accounted unnatural, tho' in some countries it be founded on natural reason; and a wide difference ought to be made betwixt such countries, and those where even natural reason rejects it, as in Europe, where it has been so happily abolished.

INUTILITY OF SLAVERY AMONG US [Chapter 8]

NATURAL slavery, then, is to be limited to some particular parts of the world. In all other countries, even the most laborious works of society may be performed, I think, by freemen.

Experience verifies my assertion. Before Christianity had abolished civil slavery in Europe, working in the mines was judged too toilsom for any slaves or malefactors: but at present, there are men employed in them, who are known to live happily. They have, by some small privileges, encouraged this profession; to an increase of labour, they have joined an increase of gain; and have gone so far as to make them better pleased with their condition than with any other which they could have embraced.

No labour is so heavy, but it may be brought to a level with the workman's strength, when regulated by equity, and not by avarice. The violent fatigues which slaves are made to undergo in other parts, may be supplied by commodious machines, invented by art, and skillfully applied. The Turkish mines in the Bannat of Temeswar, tho' richer than those of Hungary, did not yield so much; because their invention, reached no further, than the arms of their slaves.

I know not whether this article be dictated by my understanding, or my heart. Possibly there is not that climate upon earth, where the most laborious services might not, with proper encouragement, be performed by freemen. Bad laws having made lazy men; they have been reduced to slavery, because of their laziness.

G. THOMAS JEFFERSON, DRAFT OF THE DEC-LARATION OF INDEPENDENCE, WITH THE CONGRESS'S EDITORIAL CHANGES

1776

A Declaration by the Representatives of the UNITED STATES OF AMERICA in General Congress assembled.

When in the course of human events it becomes necessary for one people to dissolve the political bands which have connected them with another, and to assume among the powers of the earth the separate and equal station to which the laws of nature and of nature's god entitle them, a decent respect to the opinions of mankind requires that they should declare the causes which impel them to the separation.

We hold these truths to be self-evident; that all men are created equal; that they are endowed by their Creator with ~~inherent and~~ *certain* inalienable rights; that among these are life, liberty, and the pursuit of happiness; that to secure these rights, governments are instituted among men, deriving their just powers from the consent of the governed; that whenever any form of government becomes destructive of these ends, it is the right of the people to alter or to abolish it, and to institute new government, laying it's foundation on such principles, and organis-ing it's powers in such form as to them shall seem most likely to effect their safety and happiness. prudence indeed will dictate that govern-ments long established should not be changed for light & transient causes. and accordingly all experience hath shewn that mankind are more disposed to suffer, while evils are sufferable, than to right them-selves by abolishing the forms to which they are accustomed. but when a long train of abuses and usurpations, ~~begun at a distinguished period,~~ & pursuing invariably the same object, evinces a design to reduce them under absolute despotism, it is their right, it is their duty, to throw off such government, & to provide new guards for their future security. such has been the patient sufferance of these colonies; & such is now the necessity which constrains them to ~~expunge~~ *alter* their former systems of government. the history of the present king of Great Britain, is a history of ~~unremitting~~ *repeated* injuries and usurpations, ~~among which appears no solitary fact to contradict the uniform tenor of the rest; but~~ all *having* ~~have~~ in direct object the establishment of an absolute tyranny over these states. to prove this let facts be submitted to a candid world, ~~for the truth of which we pledge a faith yet unsullied by falsehood.~~

He has refused his assent to laws the most wholesome and necessary for the public good.

he has forbidden his governors to pass laws of immediate & pressing importance, unless suspended in their operation till his assent should be obtained; and when so suspended, he has *utterly* neglected ~~utterly~~ to attend to them.

he has refused to pass other laws for the accomodation of large districts of people, unless those people would relinguish the right of representation in the legislature; a right inestimable to them, & formidable to tyrants only.

he has called together legislative bodies at places unusual, uncomfortable, & distant from the depository of their public records, for the sole purpose of fatiguing them into compliance with his measures.

he has dissolved Representative houses repeatedly ~~& continually,~~ for opposing with manly firmness his invasions on the rights of the people.

he has refused for a long time after such dissolutions to cause others to be elected whereby the legislative powers, incapable of annihilation, have returned to the people at large for their exercise, the state remaining in the meantime exposed to all the dangers of invasion from without, & convulsions within.

he has endeavored to prevent the population of these states; for that purpose obstructing the laws for naturalization of foreigners; refusing to pass others to encourage their migrations hither; & raising the conditions of new appropriations of lands.

he has ~~suffered~~ *obstructed* the administration of justice ~~totally to cease in some of these states,~~ *by* refusing his assent to laws for establishing judiciary powers.

he has made ~~our~~ judges dependent on his will alone, for the tenure of their offices, and the amount & paiment of their salaries.

he has erected a multitude of new offices ~~by a self assumed power,~~ & sent hither swarms of officers to harrass our people, and eat out their substance.

he has kept among us, in time of peace, standing armies ~~and ships of war,~~ without the consent of our legislatures.

he has affected to render the military independant of, & superior to, the civil power.

he has combined with others to subject us to a jurisdiction foreign to our constitutions and unacknoleged by our laws; giving his assent to their acts of pretended legislation

for quartering large bodies of armed troops among us;

for protecting them by a mock-trial from punishment for any murders which they should commit on the inhabitants of these states;

for cutting off our trade with all parts of the world;

for imposing taxes on us without our consent;

for depriving us *in many cases* of the benefits of trial by jury;

for transporting us beyond seas to be tried for pretended offences;

for abolishing the free system of English laws in a neighboring province, establishing therein an arbitrary government and enlarging it's boundaries so as to render it at once an example & fit instrument for introducing the same absolute rule into these states.

for taking away our charters abolishing our most valuable laws, and altering fundamentally the forms of our governments;

for suspending our own legislatures, & declaring themselves invested with power to legislate for us in all cases whatsoever.

he has abdicated government here, ~~withdrawing his governors, &~~ *by* declaring us out of his ~~allegiance and~~ protection *and waging war against us.*

he has plundered our seas, ravaged our coasts, burnt our towns, & destroyed the lives of our people.

he is at this time transporting large armies of foreign mercenaries, to compleat the works of death, desolation & tyranny, already begun with circumstances of cruelty & perfidy *scarcely paralleled in the most barbarous ages and totally* unworthy the head of a civilized nation.

he has *excited domestic insurrections amongst us and has* endeavored to bring on the inhabitants of our frontiers the merciless Indian savages, whose known rule of warfare is an undistinguished destruction of all ages, sexes & conditions ~~of existence.~~

~~he has incited treasonable insurrections of our fellow citizens, with the allurements of forfeiture & confiscation of property.~~

he has constrained *our fellow citizens* ~~others,~~ taken captives on the high seas to bear arms against their country, to become the executioners of their friends & brethren, or to fall themselves by their hands.

~~he has waged cruel war against human nature itself, violating it's most sacred rights of life & liberty in the persons of a distant people, who never offended him, captivating and carrying them into slavery in another hemisphere, or to incur miserable death in their transportation thither. this piratical warfare, the opprobrium of *infidel* powers, is the warfare of the *Christian* king of Great Britain. determined to keep open a market where MEN should be bought & sold, he has prostituted his negative for suppressing every legislative attempt to prohibit or to restrain this execrable commerce: and that this assemblage of horrors might want no fact of distinguished die, he now is now exciting those very people to rise in arms among us, and to purchase that liberty of which *he* has deprived them, by murdering the people upon whom *he* also obtruded them: thus paying off former crimes committed against the *liberties* of one people, with crimes which he urges them to commit against the *lives* of another.~~

In every stage of these oppressions, we have petitioned for redress in the most humble terms; our repeated petitions have been answered only by repeated injury. a prince whose character is thus marked by every act which may define a tyrant, is unfit to be the ruler of a *free* people ~~who mean to be free. future ages will scarce believe that the hardiness of one man adventured within the short compass of twelve years only, to build a foundation, so broad and undisguised, for tyranny over a people fostered and fixed in principles of freedom.~~

Nor have we been wanting in attentions to our British brethren. we have warned them from time to time of attempts by their legislature to extend ~~a~~ *an unwarrantable* jurisdiction over *us.* ~~these our states.~~ we have reminded them of the circumstances of our emigration and settlement here, ~~no one of which could warrant so strange a pretension: that these were effected at the expence of our own blood and treasure, unassisted by the wealth or the strength of Great Britain: that in constituting indeed our several forms of government, we had adopted one common king, thereby laying a foundation for perpetual league and amity with them: but that submission to their parliament was no part of our constitution, or ever in idea, if history may be credited: and~~ we *have* appealed to their native justice & magnanimity, ~~as well as to~~ *and we have conjured them by* the tyes of our common kindred, to disavow these usurpations, which ~~were likely to~~ *would inevitably* interrupt our connections & correspondence. they too have been deaf to the voice of justice and of consanguinity; ~~and when occasions have been given them, by the regular course of their laws, of removing from their councils the disturbers of our harmony, they have by their free election re established them in power. at this very time too, they are permitting their chief magistrate to send over not only soldiers of our common blood, but Scotch and foreign mercenaries to invade and destroy us. these facts have given the last stab to agonizing affection; and manly spirit bids us to renouce forever these unfeeling brethren.~~ we must *therefore* ~~endeavor to forget our former love for them, and to hold them, as we hold the rest of mankind, enemies in war, in peace friends. we might have been a free & a great people together; but a communication of grandeur and of freedom, it seems, is below their dignity. be it so, since they will have it. the road to happiness and to glory is open to us too; we will climb it apart from them and~~ acquiesce in the necessity which denounces our ~~eternal~~ separation *and hold them, as we hold the rest of mankind, enemies in war, in peace friends.*⦙

We therefore the Representatives of the United states of America, in General Congress assembled, *appealing to the supreme judge of the world for the rectitude of our intentions,* do, in the name and by authority of the good people of these ~~states, reject~~ colonies, *solemnly publish and declare, that these united colonies are and of right ought to be free and independent states; that they are absolved from all allegiance to the British Crown, and that* ~~and renounce all allegiance and subjection to~~

~~the kings of Great Britain, & all others who may hereafter claim by,
through, or under them; we utterly dissolve~~ all political connection
~~which may heretofore have subsisted~~ between ~~us~~ *them* and the *state*
~~parliament or people~~ of Great Britain~~,~~ *is & ought to be totally dissolved;*
~~and finally we do assert~~ [and declare] ~~these colonies to be free and
independant states,~~ & that as free & independant states, they have full
power to levy war, conclude peace, contract alliances, establish commerce, & to do all other acts and things which independant states may of
right do. And for the support of this declaration, *with a firm reliance on
the protection of divine providence,* we mutually pledge to each other our
lives, our fortunes, and our sacred honor.

H. THOMAS JEFFERSON, NOTES ON THE STATE OF VIRGINIA

(1787) [1785]

Query 14
Laws

* * *

To emancipate all slaves born after passing the act. The bill
reported by the revisors does not itself contain this proposition; but an
amendment containing it was prepared, to be offered to the legislature
whenever the bill should be taken up, and further directing, that they
should continue with their parents to a certain age, then be brought up,
at the public expence, to tillage, arts or sciences, according to their
geniusses, till the females should be eighteen, and the males twenty-one
years of age, when they should be colonized to such place as the
circumstances of the time should render most proper, sending them out
with arms, implements of houshold and of the handicraft arts, seeds,
pairs of the useful domestic animals, &c. to declare them a free and
independant people, and extend to them our alliance and protection, till
they shall have acquired strength; and to send vessels at the same time
to other parts of the world for an equal number of white inhabitants; to
induce whom to migrate hither, proper encouragements were to be
proposed. It will probably be asked, Why not retain and incorporate the
blacks into the state, and thus save the expence of supplying, by
importation of white settlers, the vacancies they will leave? Deep rooted
prejudices entertained by the whites; ten thousand recollections, by the
blacks, of the injuries they have sustained; new provocations; the real
distinctions which nature has made; and many other circumstances, will
divide us into parties, and produce convulsions which will probably never
end but in the extermination of the one or the other race.—To these
objections, which are political, may be added others, which are physical
and moral. The first difference which strikes us is that of colour.
Whether the black of the negro resides in the reticular membrane

between the skin and scarf-skin, or in the scarf-skin itself; whether it proceeds from the colour of the blood, the colour of the bile, or from that of some other secretion, the difference is fixed in nature, and is as real as if its seat and cause were better known to us. And is this difference of no importance? Is it not the foundation of a greater or less share of beauty in the two races? Are not the fine mixtures of red and white, the expressions of every passion by greater or less suffusions of colour in the one, preferable to that eternal monotony, which reigns in the countenances, that immoveable veil of black which covers all the emotions of the other race? Add to these, flowing hair, a more elegant symmetry of form, their own judgment in favour of the whites, declared by their preference of them, as uniformly as is the preference of the Oran-ootan for the black women over those of his own species. The circumstance of superior beauty, is thought worthy attention in the propagation of our horses, dogs, and other domestic animals; why not in that of man? Besides those of colour, figure, and hair, there are other physical distinctions proving a difference of race. They have less hair on the face and body. They secrete less by the kidnies, and more by the glands of the skin, which gives them a very strong and disagreeable odour. This greater degree of transpiration renders them more tolerant of heat, and less so of cold, than the whites. Perhaps too a difference of structure in the pulmonary apparatus, which a late ingenious experimentalist has discovered to be the principal regulator of animal heat, may have disabled them from extricating, in the act of inspiration, so much of that fluid from the outer air, or obliged them in expiration, to part with more of it. They seem to require less sleep. A black, after hard labour through the day, will be induced by the slightest amusements to sit up till midnight, or later, though knowing he must be out with the first dawn of the morning. They are at least as brave, and more adventuresome. But this may perhaps proceed from a want of forethought, which prevents their seeing a danger till it be present. When present, they do not go through it with more coolness or steadiness than the whites. They are more ardent after their female: but love seems with them to be more an eager desire, than a tender delicate mixture of sentiment and sensation. Their griefs are transient. Those numberless afflictions, which render it doubtful whether heaven has given life to us in mercy or in wrath, are less felt, and sooner forgotten with them. In general, their existence appears to participate more of sensation than reflection. To this must be ascribed their disposition to sleep when abstracted from their diversions, and unemployed in labour. An animal whose body is at rest, and who does not reflect, must be disposed to sleep of course. Comparing them by their faculties of memory, reason, and imagination, it appears to me, that in memory they are equal to the whites; in reason much inferior, as I think one could scarcely be found capable of tracing and comprehending the investigations of Euclid; and that in imagination they are dull, tasteless, and anomalous. It would be unfair to follow them to Africa for this investigation. We will consider them here, on the same stage with the whites, and where the facts are not apocryphal on which a judgment is to be formed. It will be right to make great allowances for the difference of condition, of education, of conversation, of the sphere in which they move. Many millions of them have been brought to, and born in America. Most of them indeed have been confined to tillage, to their own homes, and their own society: yet many have been so situated, that they might have availed themselves of the conversation of their masters; many have been brought up to the handicraft arts, and from that circumstance have always been associated with the whites. Some have been liberally educated, and all have lived in countries where the arts and sciences are cultivated to a considerable degree, and have had before their eyes samples of the best works from abroad. The Indians, with no advantages of this kind, will often carve figures on their pipes not destitute of design and merit. They will crayon out an animal, a plant, or a country, so as to prove the existence of a germ in their minds which only wants cultivation. They astonish you with strokes of the most sublime oratory; such as prove their reason and sentiment strong, their imagination glowing and elevated. But never yet could I find that a black had uttered a thought above the level of plain narration; never see even an elementary trait of painting or sculpture. In music they are more generally gifted than the whites with accurate ears for tune and time, and they have been found capable of imagining a small catch. Whether they will be equal to the composition of a more extensive run of melody, or of complicated harmony, is yet to be proved. Misery is often the parent of the most affecting touches in poetry.—Among the blacks is misery enough, God knows, but no poetry. Love is the peculiar œstrum of the poet. Their love is ardent, but it kindles the senses only, not the imagination. Religion indeed has produced a Phyllis Whately; but it could not produce a poet. The compositions published under her name are below the dignity of criticism. The heroes of the Dunciad are to her, as Hercules to the author of that poem. Ignatius Sancho has approached nearer to merit in composition; yet his letters do more honour to the heart than the head. They breathe the purest effusions of friendship and general philanthropy, and shew how great a degree of the latter may be compounded with strong religious zeal. He is often happy in the turn of his compliments, and his stile is easy and familiar, except when he affects a Shandean fabrication of words. But his imagination is wild and extravagant, escapes incessantly from every restraint of reason and taste, and, in the course of its vagaries, leaves a tract of thought as incoherent and eccentric, as is the course of a meteor through the sky. His subjects should often have led him to a process of sober reasoning: yet we find him always substituting sentiment for demonstration. Upon the whole, though we admit him to the first place among those of his own colour who have presented themselves to the public judgment, yet when we compare him with the writers of the race among whom he lived, and particularly with the epistolary class, in which he has taken his own stand, we are compelled to enroll him at the bottom of the column. This criticism supposes the letters published under his name to be genuine, and to have received amendment from no other hand; points which would not be of easy investigation. The improvement of the blacks in body and mind, in the first instance of their mixture with the whites, has been observed by every one, and proves that their inferiority is not the effect merely of their condition of life. We know that among the Romans, about the Augustan age especially, the condition of their slaves was much more deplorable than that of the blacks on the continent of America. The two sexes were confined in separate apartments, because to raise a child cost the master more than to buy one. Cato, for a very restricted indulgence to his slaves in this particular, took from them a certain price. But in this country the slaves multiply as fast as the free inhabitants. Their situation and manners place the commerce between the two sexes almost without restraint.—The same Cato, on a principle of œconomy, always sold his sick and superannuated slaves. He gives it as a standing precept to a master visiting his farm, to sell his old oxen, old waggons, old tools, old and diseased servants, and every thing else become useless. "Vendat boves vetulos, plaustrum vetus, ferramenta, vetera, servum senem, servum morbosum, & si quid aliud supersit vendat." The American slaves cannot enumerate this among the injuries and insults they receive. It was the common practice to expose in the island of Æsculapius, in the Tyber, diseased slaves, whose cure was like to become tedious. The Emperor Claudius, by an edict, gave freedom to such of them as should recover, and first declared, that if any person chose to kill rather than to expose them, it should be deemed homicide. The exposing them is a crime of which no instance has existed with us; and were it to be followed by death, it would be punished capitally. We are told of a certain Vedius Pollio, who, in the presence of Augustus, would have given a slave as food to his fish, for having broken a glass. With the Romans, the regular method of taking the evidence of their slaves was under torture. Here it has been thought better never to resort to their evidence. When a master was murdered, all his slaves, in the same house, or within hearing, were condemned to death. Here punishment falls on the guilty only, and as precise proof is required against him as against a freeman. Yet notwithstanding these and other discouraging circumstances among the Romans, their slaves were often their rarest artists. They excelled too in science, insomuch as to be usually employed as tutors to their master's children. Epictetus, <Diogenes, Phaedon>, Terence, and Phædrus, were slaves. But they were of the race of whites. It is not their condition then, but nature, which has produced the distinction.—Whether further observation will or will not verify the conjecture, that nature has been less bountiful to them in the endowments of the head, I believe that in those of the heart she will be found to have done them justice. That disposition to theft with which they have been branded, must be ascribed to their situation, and not to any depravity of the moral sense. The man, in whose favour no laws of property exist, probably feels himself less bound to respect those made in favour of others. When arguing for ourselves, we lay it down as a fundamental, that laws, to be just, must give a reciprocation of right: that, without this, they are mere arbitrary rules of conduct, founded in force, and not in conscience: and it is a problem which I give to the master to solve, whether the religious precepts against the violation of property were not framed for him as well as his slave? And whether the slave may not as jusitfiably take a little from one, who has taken all from him, as he may slay one who would slay him? That a change in the relations in which a man is placed should change his ideas of moral right and wrong, is neither new, nor peculiar to the colour of the blacks. Homer tells us it was so 2600 years ago.

$$\text{'} H\mu\iota\sigma\upsilon, \; \gamma\alpha\zeta \; \tau\text{'} \; \dot{\alpha}\rho\epsilon\tau\hat{\eta}\varsigma \; \dot{\alpha}\pi\sigma\alpha\acute{\iota}\nu\hat{\iota}\alpha\iota \; \epsilon\dot{\upsilon}\rho\upsilon\theta\pi\alpha \; Z\dot{\epsilon}\upsilon\varsigma$$
$$\text{'} A\nu\epsilon\rho\sigma\varsigma, \; \epsilon\upsilon\tau\text{'} \; \ddot{\alpha}\nu \; \mu\iota\nu \; \kappa\alpha\tau\dot{\alpha} \; \delta\mathbf{s}\lambda\iota\sigma\nu \; \hat{\eta}\mu\alpha\zeta \; \ddot{\epsilon}\lambda\eta\sigma\iota\nu. \; Od. \; 17. \; 323.$$

Jove fix'd it certain, that whatever day

Makes man a slave, takes half his worth away.

But the slaves of which Homer speaks were whites. Notwithstanding these considerations which must weaken their respect for the laws of property, we find among them numerous instances of the most rigid integrity, and as many as among their better instructed masters, of benevolence, gratitude, and unshaken fidelity.—The opinion, that they are inferior in the faculties of reason and imagination, must be hazarded with great diffidence. To justify a general conclusion, requires many observations, even where the subject may be submitted to the Anatomical knife, to Optical glasses, to analysis by fire, or by solvents. How much more then where it is a faculty, not a substance, we are examining; where it eludes the research of all the senses; where the conditions of its existence are various and variously combined; where the effects of those which are present or absent bid defiance to calculation; let me add too, as a circumstance of great tenderness, where our conclusion would degrade a whole race of men from the rank in the scale of beings which their Creator may perhaps have given them. To our reproach it must be said, that though for a century and a half we have had under our eyes the races of black and of red men, they have never yet been viewed by us as subjects of natural history. I advance it therefore as a suspicion only, that the blacks, whether originally a distinct race, or made distinct by time and circumstances, are inferior to the whites in the endowments both of body and mind. It is not against experience to suppose, that different species of the same genus, or varieties of the same species, may possess different qualifications. Will not a lover of natural history then, one who views the gradations in all the races of animals with the eye of philosophy, excuse an effort to keep those in the department of man as distinct as nature has formed them? This unfortunate difference of colour, and perhaps of faculty, is a powerful obstacle to the emancipation of these people. Many of their advocates, while they wish to vindicate the liberty of human nature, are anxious also to preserve its dignity and beauty. Some of these, embarrassed by the question "What further is to be done with them?" join themselves in opposition with those who are actuated by sordid avarice only. Among the Romans emancipation required but one effort. The slave, when made free, might mix with, without staining the blood of his master. But with us a second is necessary, unknown to history. When freed, he is to be removed beyond the reach of mixture.

* * *

QUERY XVIII.
Manners

*The particular customs and manners that may
happen to be received in that state?*

It is difficult to determine on the standard by which the manners of a nation may be tried, whether *catholic,* or *particular.* It is more difficult for a native to bring to that standard the manners of his own nation, familiarized to him by habit. There must doubtless be an unhappy influence on the manners of our people produced by the existence of slavery among us. The whole commerce between master and slave is a perpetual exercise of the most boisterous passions, the most unremitting despotism on the one part, and degrading submissions on the other. Our children see this, and learn to imitate it; for man is an imitative animal. This quality is the germ of all education in him. From his cradle to his grave he is learning to do what he sees others do. If a parent could find no motive either in his philanthropy or his self-love, for restraining the intemperance of passion towards his slave, it should always be a sufficient one that his child is present. But generally it is not sufficient. The parent storms, the child looks on, catches the lineaments of wrath, puts on the same airs in the circle of smaller slaves, gives a loose to his worst of passions, and thus nursed, educated, and daily exercised in tyranny, cannot but be stamped by it with odious peculiarities. The man must be a prodigy who can retain his manners and morals undepraved by such circumstances. And with what execration should the statesman be loaded, who permitting one half the citizens thus to trample on the rights of the other, transforms those into despots, and these into enemies, destroys the morals of the one part, and the amor patriæ of the other. For if a slave can have a country in this world, it must be any other in preference to that in which he is born to live and labour for another: in which he must lock up the faculties of his nature, contribute as far as depends on his individual endeavours to the evanishment of the human race, or entail his own miserable condition on the endless generations proceeding from him. With the morals of the people, their industry also is destroyed. For in a warm climate, no man will labour for himself who can make another labour for him. This is so true, that of the proprietors of slaves a very small proportion indeed are ever seen to labour. And can the liberties of a nation be thought secure when we have removed their only firm basis, a conviction in the minds of the people that these liberties are of the gift of God? That they are not to be violated but with his wrath? Indeed I tremble for my country when I reflect that God is just: that his justice cannot sleep for ever: that considering numbers, nature and natural means only, a revolution of the wheel of fortune, an exchange of situation, is among possible events: that it may become probable by supernatural interference! The Almighty has no attribute which can take side with us in such a contest.—But it is impossible to be temperate and to pursue this subject through the various considerations of policy, of morals, of history natural and civil. We must be contented to hope they will force their way into every one's mind. I think a change already perceptible, since the origin of the present revolution. The spirit of the master is abating, that of the slave rising from the dust, his condition mollifying, the way I hope preparing, under the auspices of heaven, for a total emancipation, and that this is disposed, in the order of events, to be with the consent of the masters, rather than by their extirpation.

I. DEBATE IN THE PHILADELPHIA CONVENTION

(1) June 25, 1787

Resolution 4. <being taken up.>

Mr. Pinkney <spoke as follows>.—The efficacy of the System will depend on this article. In order to form a right judgmt. in the case it will be proper to examine the situation of this Country more accurately than it has yet been done. The people of the U. States are perhaps the most singular of any we are acquainted with. Among them there are fewer distinctions of fortune & less of rank, than among the inhabitants of any other nation. Every freeman has a right to the same protection & security; and a very moderate share of property entitles them to the possession of all the honors and privileges the public can bestow: hence arises a greater equality, than is to be found among the people of any other country, and an equality which is more likely to continue—I say this equality is likely to continue, because in a new Country, possessing immense tracts of uncultivated lands, where every temptation is offered to emigration & where industry must be rewarded with competency, there will be few poor, and few dependent—Every member of the Society almost, will enjoy an equal power of arriving at the supreme offices & consequently of directing the strength & sentiments of the whole Community. None will be excluded by birth, & few by fortune, from voting for proper persons to fill the offices of Government—the whole community will enjoy in the fullest sense that kind of political liberty which consists in the power the members of the State reserve to themselves, of arriving at the public offices, or at least, of having votes in the nomination of those who fill them.

If this State of things is true & the prospect of its continuing probable, it is perhaps not politic to endeavour too close an imitation of a Government calculated for a people whose situation is, & whose views ought to be extremely different

Much has been said of the Constitution of G. Britain. I will confess that I believe it to be the best constitution in existence; but at the same time I am confident it is one that will not or can not be introduced into this Country, for many centuries.—If it were proper to go here into a historical dissertation on the British Constitution, it might easily be shewn that the peculiar excellence, the distinguishing feature of that Governmt. can not possibly be introduced into our System—that its balance between the Crown & the people can not be made a part of our Constutition.—that we neither have or can have the members to compose it, nor the rights, privileges & properties of so distinct a class of Citizens to guard.—that the materials for forming this balance or check do not exist, nor is there a necessity for having so permanent a part of our Legislative, until the Executive power is so constituted as to have something fixed & dangerous in its principle—By this I mean a sole, hereditary, though limited Executive.

That we cannot have a proper body for forming a Legislative balance between the inordinate power of the Executive and the people, is evident from a review of the accidents & circumstances which give rise to the peerage of Great. Britain—I believe it is well ascertained that the parts which compose the British Constitution arose immediately from the forests of Germany; but the antiquity of the establishment of nobility is by no means clearly defined. Some authors are of opinion that the dignity denoted by the titles of dux et comes, was derived from the old Roman to the German Empire; while others are of opinion that they existed among the Germans long before the Romans were acquainted with them. The institution however of nobility is immemorial among the nations who may probably be termed the ancestors of Britain.—At the time they were summoned in England to become a part of the National Council, and the circumstances which have contributed to make them a constituent part of that constitution, must be well known to all gentlemen who have had industry & curiosity enough to investigate the subject—The nobles with their possessions & dependents composed a body permanent in their nature and formidable in point of power. They had a distinct interest both from the King and the people; an interest which could only be represented by themselves, and the guardianship could not be safely intrusted to others.—At the time they were originally called to form a part of the National Council, necessity perhaps as much as other cause, induced the Monarch to look up to them. It was necessary to demand the aid of his subjects in personal & pecuniary services. The power and possessions of the Nobility would not permit taxation from any assembly of which they were not a part: & the blending the deputies of the Commons with them, & thus forming what they called their parler-ment was perhaps as much the effect of chance as of any thing else. The Commons were at that time completely subordinate to the nobles, whose consequence & influence seem to have been the only reasons for their superiority; a superiority so degrading to the Commons that in the first Summons we find the peers are called upon to consult, the commons to consent. From this time the peers have composed a part of the British Legislature, and notwithstanding their power and influence have diminished & those of the Commons have increased, yet still they have always formed an excellent balance agst. either the encroachments of the crown or the people.

I have said that such a body cannot exist in this Country for ages, and that untill the situation of our people is exceedingly changed no necessity will exist for so permanent a part of the Legislature. To illustrate this I have remarked that the people of the United States are more equal in their circumstances than the people of any other Country—that they have very few rich men among them,—by rich men I mean those whose riches may have a dangerous influence, or such as are esteemed rich in Europe—perhaps there are not one hundred such on the Continent: that it is not probable this number will be greatly increased: that the genius of the people, their mediocrity of situation & the prospects which are afforded their industry in a country which must be a new one for centuries are unfavorable to the rapid distinction of ranks. The destruction of the right of primogeniture & the equal division of the property of Intestates will also have an effect to preserve this mediocrity: for laws invariably affect the manners of a people. On the other hand that vast extent of unpeopled territory which opens to the frugal & industrious a sure road to competency & independence will effectually prevent for a considerable time the increase of the poor or discontented, and be the means of preserving that equality of condition which so eminently distinguishes us.

If equality is as I contend the leading feature of the U. States, where then are the riches & wealth whose representation & protection is the peculiar province of this permanent body. Are they in the hands of the few who may be called rich; in the possession of less than a hundred citizens? certainly not. They are in the great body of the people, among whom there are no men of wealth, and very few of real poverty.—Is it probable that a change will be created, and that a new order of men will arise? If under the British Government, for a century no such change was probable, I think it may be fairly concluded it will not take place while even the semblance of Republicanism remains. How is this change to be effected? Where are the sources from whence it is to flow? From the landed interest? No. That is too unproductive & too much divided in most of the States. From the Monied interest? If such exists at present, little is to be apprehended from that source. Is it to spring from commerce? I believe it would be the first instance in which a nobility sprang from merchants. Besides, Sir, I apprehend that on this point the policy of the U. States has been much mistakem. We have unwisely considered ourselves as the inhabitants of an old instead of a new country. We have adopted the maxims of a State full of people & manufactures & established in credit. We have deserted our true interest, and instead of applying closely to those improvements in domestic policy which would have ensured the future importance of our commerce, we have rashly & prematurely engaged in schemes as extensive as they are imprudent. This however is an error which daily corrects itself & I have no doubt that a few more severe trials will convince us, that very different commercial principles ought to govern the conduct of these States.

The people of this country are not only very different from the inhabitants of any State we are acquainted with in the modern world; but I assert that their situation is distinct from either the people of Greece or Rome, or of any State we are acquainted with among the antients.—Can the orders introduced by the institution of Solon, can they be found in the United States? Can the military habits & manners of Sparta be resembled to our habits & manners? Are the distinctions of Patrician & Plebeian known among us? Can the Helvetic or Belgic confederacies, or can the unwieldly, unmeaning body called the Germanic Empire, can they be said to possess either the same or a situation like ours? I apprehend not.—They are perfectly different, in their distinctions of rank, their Constitutions, their manners & their policy.

Our true situation appears to me to be this.—a new extensive Country containing within itself the materials for forming a Government capable of extending to its citizens all the blessings of civil & religious liberty—capable of making them happy at home. This is the great end of Republican Establishments. We mistake the object of our government, if we hope or wish that it is to make us respectable abroad. Conquest or superiority among other powers is not or ought not ever to be the object of republican systems. If they are sufficiently active & energetic to rescue us from contempt & preserve our domestic happiness & security, it is all we can expect from them,—it is more than almost any other Government ensures to its citizens.

I believe this observation will be found generally true: that no two people are so exactly alike in their situation or circumstances as to admit the exercise of the same Government with equal benefit: that a system must be suited to the habits & genius of the People it is to govern, and must grow out of them.

The people of the U. S. may be divided into three classes—*Professional men* who must from their particular pursuits always have a considerable weight in the Government while it remains popular—*Commercial men*, who may or may not have weight as a wise or injudicious commercial policy is pursued.—If that commercial policy is pursued which I conceive to be the true one, the merchants of this Country will not or ought not for a considerable time to have much weight in the political scale.—The third is the *landed interest*, the owners and cultivators of the soil, who are and ought ever to be the governing spring in the system.—These three classes, however distinct in their pursuits are individually equal in the political scale, and may be easily proved to have but one interest. The dependence of each on the other is mutual. The merchant depends on the planter. Both must in private as well as public affairs be connected with the professional men; who in their turn must in some measure depend on them. Hence it is clear from this manifest connection, & the equality which I before stated exists, & must for the reasons then assigned, continue, that after all there is one, but one great & equal body of citizens composing the inhabitants of this Country among whom there are no distinctions of rank, and very few or none of fortune.

For a people thus circumstanced are we then to form a Government & the question is what kind of Government is best suited to them.

Will it be the British Govt.? No. Why? Because G. Britain contains three orders of people distinct in their situation, their possessions & their principles.—These orders combined form the great body of the Nation, And as in national expences the wealth of the whole community must contribute, so ought each component part to be properly & duly represented.—No other combination of power could form this due representation, but the one that exists.—Neither the peers or the people could represent the royalty, nor could the Royalty & the people form a proper representation for the Peers.—Each therefore must of necessity be represented by itself, or the sign of itself; and this accidental mixture has certainly formed a Government admirably well balanced.

But the U. States contain but one order that can be assimilated to the British Nation.—this is the order of Commons. They will not surely then attempt to form a Government consisting of three branches, two of which shall have nothing to represent. They will not have an Executive & Senate (hereditary) because the King & Lords of England are so. The same reasons do not exist and therefore the same provisions are not necessary.

We must as has been observed suit our Governmt. to the people it is to direct. These are I believe as active, intelligent & susceptible of good Governmt. as any people in the world. The Confusion which has produced the present relaxed State is not owing to them. It is owing to the weakness & (defects) of a Govt. incapable of combining the various interests it is intended to unite, and destitute of energy.—All that we have to do then is to distribute the powers of Govt. in such a manner, and for such limited periods, as while it gives a proper degree of permanency to the Magistrate, will reserve to the people, the right of election they will not or ought not frequently to part with.—I am of opinion that this may be easily done; and that with some amendments the propositions before the Committee will fully answer this end.

No position appears to me more true than this; that the General Govt. can not effectually exist without reserving to the States the possession of their local rights.—They are the instruments upon which the Union must frequently depend for the support & execution of their powers, however immediately operating upon the people, and not upon the States.

Much has been said about the propriety of abolishing the distinction of State Governments, & having but one general System. Suffer me for a moment to examine this question.

(The residue of this speech was not <furnished>) <like the above by Mr. Pinckeney.>

<The mode of constituting the 2d. branch being under consideration

The word "national" was struck out and "United States" inserted.>

Mr. Ghorum, inclined to a compromise as to the rule of proportion. He thought there was some weight in the objections of the small States. If Va. should have 16 votes & Delre. with several other States together 16. those from Virga. would be more likely to unite than the others, and would therefore have an undue influence. This remark was applicable not only to States, but to Counties or other districts of the same State. Accordingly the Constitution of Massts. had provided that the <representatives of the> larger districts should not be in an exact ratio to their numbers. And experience he thought had shewn the provision to be expedient.

Mr. Read. The States have heretofore been in a sort of partnership. They ought to adjust their old affairs before they open a new account. He brought into view the appropriation of the common interest in the Western lands, to the use of particular States. Let justice be done on this head; let the fund be applied fairly & equally to the discharge of the general debt, and the smaller States who had been injured would listen then perhaps to those ideas of just representation which had been held out.

Mr. Ghorum. did not see how the Convention could interpose in the case. Errors he allowed had been committed on the Subject. But Congs. were now using their endeavors to rectify them. The best remedy would be such a Government as would have vigor enough to do justice throughout. This was certainly the best chance that could be afforded to the smaller States.

Mr. Wilson. the question is shall the members of the 2d. branch be chosen by the Legislatures of the States? When he considered the amazing extent of country—the immense population which is to fill it, the influence which the Govt. we are to form will have, not only on the present generation of our people & their multiplied posterity, but on the

601

whole Globe, he was lost in the magnitude of the object. The project of Henry the 4th. & <his Statesmen> was but the picture in miniature of the great portrait to be exhibited. He was opposed to an election by the State Legislatures. In explaining his reasons it was necessary to observe the twofold relation in which the people would stand. 1. as Citizens of the Gen'l Gov't. 2. as Citizens of their particular State. The Genl. Govt. was meant for them in the first capacity; the State Govts. in the second. Both Govts. were derived from the people—both meant for the people—both therefore ought to be regulated on the same principles. The same train of ideas which belonged to the relation of the Citizens to their State Govts. were applicable to their relations to the Genl. Govt. and in forming the latter, we ought to proceed, by abstracting as much as possible from the idea of State Govts. With respect to the province & objects of the Gen'l Govt. they should be considered as having no existence. The election of the 2d. branch by the Legislatures, will introduce & cherish local interests & local prejudices. The Genl. Govt. is not an assemblage of States, but of individuals for certain political purposes—it is not meant for the States, but for the individuals composing them: the *individuals* therefore not the *States*, ought to be represented in it: A proportion in this representation can be preserved in the 2d. as well as in the 1st. branch; and the election can be made by electors chosen by the people for that purpose. He moved an amendment to that effect, which was not seconded.

Mr. Elseworth saw no reason for departing from the mode contained in the Report. Whoever chooses the member, he will be a citizen of the State he is to represent & will feel the same spirit and act the same part whether he be appointed by the people or the Legislature. Every State has its particular views & prejudices, which will find their way into the general councils, through whatever channel they may flow. Wisdom was one of the characteristics which it was in contemplation to give the second branch. Would not more of it issue from the Legislatures; than from an immediate election by the people. He urged the necessity of maintaining the existence & agency of the States. Without their co-operation it would be impossible to support a Republican Govt. over so great an extent of Country. An army could scarcely render it practicable. The largest States are the Worst Governed. Virga. is obliged to acknowledge her incapacity to extend her Govt. to Kentucky. Masts can not keep the peace one hundred miles from her capitol and is now forming an army for its support. How long Pena. may be free from a like situation can not be foreseen. If the principles & materials of our Govt. are not adequate to the extent of these single States; how can it be imagined that they can support a single Govt. throughout the U. States. The only chance of supporting a Genl. Govt. lies in engrafting it on that of the individual States.

<Docr. Johnson urged the necessity of preserving the State Govts— which would be at the mercy of the Genl. Govt. on Mr. Wilson's plan.

Mr. Madison thought it wd. obviate difficulty if the present resol: were postponed. & the 8th. taken up. which is to fix the right of suffrage in the 2d. branch.>

Docr. Williamson professed himself a friend to such a system as would secure the existence of the State Govts. The happiness of the people depended on it. He was at a loss to give his vote, as to the Senate untill he knew the number of its members. In order to ascertain this, he moved to insert these words after "2d. branch of Natl. Legislature"— "who shall bear such proportion to the no. of the 1st. branch as 1 to   " He was not seconded.

Mr. Mason. It has been agreed on all hands that an efficient Govt. is necessary that to render it such it ought to have the faculty of self-defence, that to render its different branches effectual each of them ought to have the same power of self defence. He did not wonder that such an agreement should have prevailed in these points. He only wondered that there should be any disagreement about the necessity of allowing the State Govts. the same self-defence. If they are to be preserved as he conceived to be essential, they certainly ought to have this power, and the only mode left of giving it to them, was by allowing them to appoint the 2d. branch of the Natl. Legislature.

Mr. Butler observing that we were put to difficulties at every step by the uncertainty whether an equality or a ratio of representation wd. prevail finally in the 2d. branch. moved to postpone the 4th. Resol: & to proceed to the Resol: on that point. Mr. M<adison> seconded him.

(2) June 26, 1787

The duration of the 2d. branch under consideration.

Mr. Ghorum moved to fill the blank with "six years". <one third of the members to go out every second year.>

Mr Wilson 2ded. the motion.

Genl. Pinkney opposed six years in favor of four years. The States he said had different interests. Those of the Southern, and of S. Carolina in particular were different from the Northern. If the Senators should be appointed for a long term, they wd. settle in the State where they exercised their functions; and would in a little time be rather the representatives of that than of the State appoint'g them.

Mr. Read movd. that the term be nine years. This wd. admit of a very convenient rotation, one third going out triennially. He wd. still prefer "during good behaviour," but being little supported in that idea, he was willing to take the longest term that could be obtained.

Mr. Broome 2ded. the motion

Mr. Madison. In order to judge of the form to be given to this institution, it will be proper to take a view of the ends to be served by it. These were first to protect the people agst. their rulers: secondly to protect <the people> agst. the transient impressions into which they themselves might be led. A people deliberating in a temperate moment, and with the experience of other nations before them, on the plan of Govt. most likely to secure their happiness, would first be aware, that those chargd. with the public happiness, might betray their trust. An obvious precaution agst. this danger wd. be to divide the trust between different bodies of men, who might watch & check each other. In this they wd. be governed by the same prudence which has prevailed in organizing the subordinate departments of Govt. where all business liable to abuses is made to pass thro' separate hands, the one being a check on the other. It wd. next occur to such a people, that they themselves were liable to temporary errors, thro' want of information as to their true interest, and that men chosen for a short term, & employed but a small portion of that in public affairs, might err from the same cause. This reflection wd. naturally suggest that the Govt. be so constituted, as that one of its branches might have an oppy. of acquiring a competent knowledge of the public interests. Another reflection equally becoming a people on such an occasion, wd. be that they themselves, as well as a numerous body of Representatives, were liable to err also, from fickleness and passion. A necessary fence agst. this danger would be to select a portion of enlightened citizens, whose limited number, and firmness might seasonably interpose agst. impetuous counsels. It ought finally to occur to a people deliberating on a Govt. for themselves, that as different interests necessarily result from the liberty meant to be secured, the major interest might under sudden impulses be tempted to commit injustice on the minority. In all civilized Countries the people fall into different classes havg. a real or supposed difference of interests. There will be creditors & debtors, farmers, merchts. & manufacturers. There will be particularly the distinction of rich & poor. It was true as had been observd. (by Mr Pinkney) we had not among us those hereditary distinctions, of rank which were a great source of the contests in the ancient Govts. as well as the modern States of Europe, nor those extremes of wealth or poverty which characterize the latter. We cannot however be regarded even at this time, as one homogeneous mass, in which every thing that affects a part will affect in the same manner the whole. In framing a system which we wish to last for ages, we shd. not lose sight of the changes which ages will produce. An increase of population will of necessity increase the proportion of those who will labour under all the hardships of life, & secretly sigh for a more equal distribution of its blessings. These may in time outnumber those who are placed above the feelings of indigence. According to the equal laws of suffrage, the power will slide into the hands of the former. No agrarian attempts have yet been made in this Country, but symptoms of a leveling spirit, as we have understood, have sufficiently appeared in a certain quarters to give notice of the future danger. How is this danger to be guarded agst. on republican principles? How is the danger in all cases of interested co-alitions to oppress the minority to be guarded agst.? Among other means by the establishment of a body in the Govt. sufficiently respectable for its wisdom & virtue, to aid on such emergencies, the preponderance of justice by throwing its weight into that scale. Such being the objects of the second branch in the proposed Govt. he thought a considerable duration ought to be given to it. He did not conceive that the term of nine years could threaten any real danger; but in pursuing his particular ideas on the subject, he should require that the long term allowed to the 2d. branch should not commence till such a period of life as would render a perpetual disqualification to be re-elected little inconvenient either in a public or private view. He observed that as it was more than probable we were now digesting a plan which in its operation wd. decide forever the fate of Republican Govt we ought not only to provide every guard to liberty that its preservation cd. require, but be equally careful to supply the defects which our own experience had particularly pointed out.

Mr. Sherman. Govt. is instituted for those who live under it. It ought therefore to be so constituted as not to be dangerous to their liberties. The more permanency it has the worse if it be a bad Govt. Frequent elections are necessary to preserve the good behavior of rulers. They also tend to give permanency to the Government, by preserving that good behavior, because it ensures their re-election. In Connecticut elections have been very frequent, yet great stability & uniformity both as to persons & measures have been experienced from its original establishmt. to the present time; a period of more than 130 years. He wished to have provision made for steadiness & wisdom in the system to be adopted; but he thought six or <four> years would be sufficient. He shd. be content with either.

Mr. Read wished it to be considered by the small States that it was their interest that we should become one people as much as possible, that State attachments shd. be extinguished as much as possible, that the Senate shd. be so constituted as to have the feelings of citizens of the whole.

Mr. Hamilton. He did not mean to enter particularly into the subject. He concurred with Mr. Madison in thinking we were now to decide for ever the fate of Republican Government; and that if we did not give to that form due stability and wisdom, it would be disgraced & lost among ourselves, disgraced & lost to mankind for ever. He acknowledged himself not to think favorably of Republican Government; but addressed his remarks to those who did think favorably of it, in order to prevail on them to tone their Government as high as possible. He professed himself to be as zealous an advocate for liberty as any man whatever, and trusted he should be as willing a martyr to it though he differed as to the form in which it was most eligible.—He concurred also in the general observations of (Mr. Madison) on the subject, which might be supported by others if it were necessary. It was certainly true that nothing like an equality of property existed: that an inequality would exist as long as liberty existed, and that it would unavoidably result from that very liberty itself. This inequality of property constituted the great & fundamental distinction in Society. When the Tribunitial power had levelled the boundary between the *patricians* & *plebeians* what followed? The distinction between rich & poor was substituted. He meant not however to enlarge on the subject. He rose principally to remark that (Mr. Sherman) seemed not to recollect that one branch of the proposed Govt. was so formed, as to render it particularly the guardians of the poorer orders of citizens; nor to have adverted to the true causes of the stability which had been exemplified in Cont. Under the British system as well as the federal, many of the great powers appertaining to Govt. particularly all those relating to foreign Nations were not in the hands of the Govt there. Their internal affairs also were extremely simple, owing to sundry causes many of which were peculiar to that Country. Of late the Governmt. had entirely given way to the people, and had in fact suspended many of its ordinary functions in order to prevent those turbulent scenes which had appeared elsewhere. <He asks Mr S. whether the State at this time, dare impose & collect a tax on ye people?> To those causes & not to the frequency of elections, the effect, as far as it existed ought to be chiefly ascribed.

Mr. Gerry. wished we could be united in our ideas concerning a permanent Govt. All aim at the same end, but there are great differences as to the means. One circumstance He thought should be carefully attended to. There were not 1/1000 part of our fellow citizens who were not agst. every approach towards Monarchy. Will they ever agree to a plan which seems to make such an approach. The Convention ought to be extremely cautious in what they hold out to the people. Whatever plan may be proposed will be espoused with warmth by many out of respect to the quarter it proceeds from as well as from an approbation of the plan itself. And if the plan should be of such a nature as to rouse a violent opposition, it is easy to foresee that discord & confusion will ensue, and it is even possible that we may become a prey to foreign powers. He did not deny the position of Mr.—<Madison.> that the majority will generally violate justice when they have an interest in so doing; But did not think there was any such temptation in this Country. Our situation was different from that of G. Britain: and the great body of lands yet to be parcelled out & settled would very much prolong the difference. Notwithstanding the symtoms of injustice which had marked many of our public Councils, they had not proceeded so far as not to leave hopes, that there would be a sufficient sense of justice & virtue for the purpose of Govt. He admitted the evils arising from a frequency of elections: and would agree to give the Senate a duration of four or five years. A longer term would defeat itself. It never would be adopted by the people.

Mr. Wilson did not mean to repeat what had fallen from others, but wd. add an observation or two which he believed had not yet been suggested. Every nation may be regarded in two relations 1 to its own citizens. 2 to foreign nations. It is therefore not only liable to anarchy & tyranny within but has wars to avoid & treaties to obtain from abroad. The Senate will probably be the depositary of the powers concerning the latter objects. It ought therefore to be made respectable in the eyes of foreign nations. The true reason why G. Britain has not yet listened to a commercial treaty with us has been, because she had no confidence in the stability or efficacy of our Government. 9 years with a rotation, will provide these desirable qualities; and give our Govt. an advantage in this respect over Monarchy itself. In a monarchy much must alway depend on the temper of the man. In such a body, the personal character will be lost in the political. He wd. add another observation. The popular objection agst. appointing any public body for a long term was that it might by gradual encroachments prolong itself first into a body for life, and finally become a hereditary one. It would be a satisfactory answer to this objection that as ⅓ would go out triennially, there would be always three divisions holding their places for unequal terms, and consequently acting under the influence of different views, and different impulses—On the question for 9 years. ⅓ to go out triennially

Massts no. Cont. no. N. Y. no. N. J. no. Pa. ay. Del. ay. Md. no. Va. ay. N. C. no. S. C. no. Geo. no. [Ayes—8; noes—3.]

On the question for 6 years ⅓ to go out biennially Massts. ay. Cont. ay. N. Y. no. N. J. no. Pa. ay. Del. ay. Md. ay. Va. ay. N. C. ay. S. C. no. Geo. no. [Ayes—7; noes—4.]

(3) July 9, 1787

in Convention

<Mr. Daniel Carroll from Maryland took his Seat.>

Mr. Govr. Morris <delivered a> report from the Come. of 5 members to whom was committed the clause in the Report of the Come. consisting of a member from each State, stating the proper ratio of Representatives in the 1st. branch, to be as 1 to every 40,000 inhabitants, as follows viz

"The Committee to whom was referred the 1st. clause of the 1st. proposition reported from the grand Committee, beg leave to report I.¶ that in the 1st. meeting of the Legislature the 1st. branch thereof consist of 56. members of which Number N. Hamshire shall have 2. Massts. 7. R.Id.1. Cont. 4. N. Y. 5. N. J. 3. Pa. 8. Del. 1. Md. 4. Va. 9. N. C. 5, S. C. 5. Geo. 2. II¶—. But as the present situation of the States may probably alter as well in point of wealth as in the number of their inhabitants, that the Legislature be authorized from time to time to augment ye. number of Representatives. And in case any of the States shall hereafter be divided, or any two or more States united, or any new States created within the limits of the United States, the Legislature shall possess authority to regulate the number of Representatives in any of the foregoing cases, upon the principles of their wealth and number of inhabitants.''

Mr. Sherman wished to know on what principles or calculations the Report was founded. It did not appear to correspond with any rule of numbers, or of any requisition hitherto adopted by Congs.

Mr. Gorham. Some provision of this sort was necessary in the outset. The number of blacks & whites with some regard to supposed wealth was the general guide Fractions could not be observed. The Legislre. is to make alterations from time to time as justice & propriety may require, Two objections prevailed agst. the rate of 1 member for every 40,000. inhts. The 1st. was that the Representation would soon be too numerous: the 2d. that the Westn. States who may have a different interest, might if admitted on that principal by degrees, out-vote the Atlantic. Both these objections are removed. The number will be small in the first instance and may be continued so, and the Atlantic States having ye. Govt. in their own hands, may take care of their own interest, by dealing out the right of Representation in safe proportions to the Western States. These were the views of the Committee.

Mr. L Martin wished to know whether the Come. were guided in the ratio, by the wealth or number of inhabitants of the States, or by both; noting its variations from former apportionments by Congs.

Mr. Govr. Morris & Mr. Rutlidge moved to postpone the 1st. paragraph relating to the number of members to be allowed each State in the first instance, and to take up the 2d. paragraph authorizing the Legislre to alter the number from time to time according to wealth & inhabitants. The motion was agreed to nem. con.

On Question on the 2d. paragh. taken without any debate

Masts. ay. Cont. ay. N. Y. no. N. J. no. Pa. ay. Del. ay. Md. ay. Va. ay. N. C. ay. S. C. ay. Geo. ay. [Ayes—9; noes—2.]

Mr. Sherman moved to refer the 1st. part apportioning the Representatives to a Comme. of a member from each State.

Mr. Govr. Morris seconded the motion; observing that this was the only case in which such Committees were useful.

Mr. Williamson. thought it would be necessary to return to the rule of numbers. but that the Western States stood on different footing. If their property shall be rated as high as that of the Atlantic States, then their representation ought to hold a like proportion. Otherwise if their property was not to be equally rated.

Mr Govr. Morris. The Report is little more than a guess. Wealth was not altogether disregarded by the Come. Where it was apparently in favor of one State whose nos. were superior to the numbers of another, by a fraction only, a member extraordinary was allowed to the former: and so vice versa.   The Committee meant little more than to bring the matter to a point for the consideration of the House.

Mr. Reed asked why Georgia was allowed 2 members, when her number of inhabitants had stood below that of Delaware.

Mr. Govr. Morris.   Such is the rapidity of the population of that State, that before the plan takes effect, it will probably be entitled to 2 Representatives

Mr. Randolph disliked the report of the Come. but had been unwilling to object to it.   He was apprehensive that as the number was not to be changed till the Natl. Legislature should please, a pretext would never be wanting to postpone alterations, and keep the power in the hands of those possessed of it.   He was in favor of the commitmt. to a member from each State

Mr. Patterson considered the proposed estimate for the future according to the Combined rule of numbers and wealth, as too vague. For this reason N. Jersey was agst. it.   He could regard negroes slaves in no light but as property.   They are no free agents, have no personal liberty, no faculty of acquiring property, but on the contrary are themselves property, & like other property entirely at the will of the Master. Has a man in Virga. a number of votes in proportion to the number of his slaves?   and if Negroes are not represented in the States to which they belong, why should they be represented in the Genl. Govt.   What is the true principle of Representation?   It is an expedient by which an assembly of certain individls. chosen by the people is substituted in place of the inconvenient meeting of the people themselves.   If such a meeting of the people was actually to take place, would the slaves vote?   they would not.   Why then shd. they be represented.   He was also agst. such an indirect encouragemt. of the slave trade;   observing that Congs. in their act relating to the change of the 8 art: of Confedn. had been ashamed to use the term "Slaves" & had substituted a description.

Mr. <Madison,> reminded Mr. Patterson that his doctrine of Representation which was in its principle the genuine one, must for ever silence the pretensions of the small States to an equality of votes with the large ones.   They ought to vote in the same proportion in which their citizens would do, if the people of all the States were collectively met.   He suggested as a proper ground of compromise, that in the first branch the States should be represented according to their number of free inhabitants; And in the 2d. which had for one of its primary objects the guardianship of property, according to the whole number, including slaves.

Mr. Butler urged warmly the justice & necessity of regarding wealth in the apportionment of Representation.

Mr. King had always expected that as the Southern States are the richest, they would not league themselves with the Northn. unless some respect were paid to their superior wealth.   If the latter expect those preferential distinctions in Commerce & other advantages which they will derive from the connection they must not expect to receive them without allowing some advantages in return. Eleven out of 13 of the States had agreed to consider Slaves in the apportionment of taxation; and taxation and Representation ought to go together.

On the question for committing the first paragraph of the Report to a member from each State. Masts. ay. Cont. ay. N. Y. no. N. J. ay. Pa. ay. Del. ay. Md ay. Va. ay. N. C. ay. S. C. no. Geo. ay. [Ayes—9; noes—2.]

The Come. appointed were. Mr King. Mr. Sherman, Mr. Yates, Mr. Brearly, Mr. Govr. Morris, Mr. Reed, Mr. Carrol, Mr. Madison, Mr. Williamson, Mr. Rutlidge, Mr. Houston. Adjd.

(4) July 10, 1787

Mr. King reported from the Come. yesterday appointed that the States at the 1st. meeting of the General Legislature, should be represented by 65 members in the following proportions, to wit. N. Hamshire by 3, Masts. 8. R. Isd. 1. Cont. 5. N. Y. 6. N. J. 4. Pa. 8. Del. 1. Md. 6. Va. 10. N:C. 5. S. C. 5, Georgia 3.

Mr. Rutlidge moved that N. Hampshire be reduced from 3 to 2. members. Her numbers did not entitle her to 3 and it was a poor State.

Genl. Pinkney seconds the motion.

Mr. King. N. Hamshire has probably more than 120,000 Inhabts. and has an extensive country of tolerable fertility. Its inhabts therefore may be expected to increase fast. He remarked that the four Eastern States having 800,000 souls, have ⅓ fewer representatives than the four Southern States, having not more than 700,000 souls rating the blacks, as 5 for 3. The Eastern people will advert to these circumstances, and be dissatisfied. He believed them to be very desirous of uniting with their Southern brethren but did not think it prudent to rely so far on that disposition as to subject them to any gross inequality. He was fully convinced that the question concerning a difference of interests did not lie where it had hitherto been discussed, between the great & small States; but between the Southern & Eastern. For this reason he had been ready to yield something in the proportion of representatives for the security of the Southern. No principle would justify the giving them a majority. They were brought as near an equality as was possible. He was not averse to giving them a still greater security, but did not see how it could be done.

Genl. Pinkney. The Report before it was committed was more favorable to the S. States than as it now stands. If they are to form so considerable a minority, and the regulation of trade is to be given to the Genl. Government, they will be nothing more than overseers for the Northern States. He did not expect the S. States to be raised to a majority of representatives, but wished them to have something like an equality. At present by the alterations of the Come. in favor of the N. States they are removed farther from it than they were before. One member had indeed been added to Virga. which he was glad of as he considered her as a Southern State. He was glad also that the members of Georgia were increased.

Mr. Williamson was not for reducing N. Hamshire from 3 to 2. but for reducing some others. The Southn. Interest must be extremely endangered by the present arrangement. The Northn. States are to have a majority in the first instance and the means of perpetuating it.

Mr. Dayton observed that the line between the Northn. & Southern interest had been improperly drawn: that Pa. was the dividing State, there being six on each side of her.

Genl. Pinkney urged the reduction, dwelt on the superior wealth of the Southern States, and insisted on its having its due weight in the Government.

Mr. Govr. Morris regretted the turn of the debate. The States he found had many Representatives on the floor. Few he fears were to be deemed the Representatives of America. He thought the Southern States have by the report more than their share of representation. Property ought to have its weight; but but not all the weight. If <the Southn. States are to> supply money. The Northn. States are to spill their blood. Besides, the probable Revenue to be expected from the S. States has been greatly overated. He was agst. reducing N. Hamshire.

Mr. Randolph was opposed to a reduction of N. Hamshire, not because she had a full title to three members: but because it was in his contemplation 1. to make it the duty instead of leaving it in the discretion of the Legislature to regulate the representation by a periodical census. 2. to require more than a bare majority of votes in the Legislature in certain cases, & particularly in commercial cases.

On the question for reducing N. Hamshire from 3 to 2 Represents. <it passed in the negative>

Masts. no. Cont. no. N. J. no. Pa. no. Del. no. Md. no. Va. no. N. C. ay. S. C. ay. Geo. no. [Ayes—2; noes—8.]

Genl. Pinkney & Mr. Alexr. Martin moved that 6 Reps. instead of 5 be allowed to N. Carolina

On the question, <it passed in the negative> Masts. no. Cont. no. N. J. no. Pa. no. Del. no. Md. no. Va. no. N. C. ay. S. C. ay Geo. ay. [Ayes—3; noes—7.]

Genl. Pinkney & Mr. Butler made the same motion in favor of S. Carolina

On the Question <it passed in the negative>

Masts. no. Cont. no. <N. Y. no.> N. J. no. Pa. no. Del. ay. Md. no. Va. no. N. C. ay. S. C. ay. Geo. ay [Ayes—4; noes—7.]

Genl. Pinkney & Mr. Houston moved that Georgia be allowed 4 instead of 3 Reps. urging the unexampled celerity of its population. On the Question, <it passed in the Negative>

Masts. no. Cont. no. <N. Y. no> N. J. no. Pa. no. Del. no. Md. no. Va. ay. N: C. ay. S. C. ay. Geo. ay. [Ayes—4; noes—7.]

Mr. M<adison> moved that the number allowed to each State be doubled. A *majority* of a *Quorum* of 65 members, was too small a number to represent the whole inhabitants of the U. States; They would not possess enough of the confidence of the people, and wd. be too sparsely taken from the people, to bring with them all the local information which would be frequently wanted. Double the number will not be too great even with the future additions from New States. The additional expence was too inconsiderable to be regarded in so important a case. And as far as the augmentation might be unpopular on that score, the objection was overbalanced by its effect on the hopes of a greater number of the popular Candidates.

Mr. Elseworth urged the objection of expence, & that the greater the number, the more slowly would the business proceed; and the less probably be decided as it ought, at last—He thought the number of Representatives too great in most of the State Legislatures: and that a large number was less necessary in the Genl. Legislature than in those of the States, as its business would relate to a few great, national Objects only.

Mr. Sherman would have preferred 50 to 65. The great distance they will have to travel will render their attendance precarious and will make it difficult to prevail on a sufficient number of fit men to undertake the service. He observed that the expected increase from New States also deserved consideration.

Mr. Gerry was for increasing the number beyond 65. The larger the number the less the danger of their being corrupted. The people are accustomed to & fond of a numerous representation, and will consider their rights as better secured by it. The danger of excess in the number may be guarded agst. by fixing a point within which the number shall always be kept.

Col. Mason admitted that the objection drawn from the consideration of expence, had weight both in itself, and as the people might be affected by it. But he thought it outweighed by the objections agst. the smallness of the number. 38, will he supposes, as being a majority of 65, form a quorum. 20 will be a majority of 38. This was certainly too small a number to make laws for America. They would neither bring with them all the necessary information relative to various local interests nor possess the necessary confidence of the people. After doubling the number, the laws might still be made by so few as almost to be objectionable on that account.

Mr. Read was in favor of the motion. Two of the States (Del. & R. I.) would have but a single member if the aggregate number should remain at 65. and in case of accident to either of these one State wd. have no representative present to give explanations or informations of its interests or wishes. The people would not place their confidence in so small a number. He hoped the objects of the Genl. Govt. would be much more numerous than seemed to be expected by some gentlemen, and that they would become more & more so. As to New States the highest number of Reps. for the whole might be limited, and all danger of excess thereby prevented.

Mr. Rutlidge opposed the motion. The Representatives were too numerous in all the States. The full number allotted to the States may be expected to attend <& the lowest possible quorum shd. not therefore be considered—>. The interests of their Constituents will urge their attendance too strongly for it to be omitted: and he supposed the Genl. Legislature would not sit more than 6 or 8 weeks in the year.

On the question for doubling the number, <it passed in the negative.>

Masts. no. Cont. no. N. Y. no. N. J. no. Pa. no. Del ay. Md. no. Va. ay. N. C. no. S. C. no. Geo. no. [Ayes—2; noes—9.]

On the question for agreeing to the apportionment of Reps. as amended <by the last committee it passed in the affirmative>,

Mas. ay. Cont. ay. N. Y. ay. N. J. ay. Pa. ay. Del ay. Md. ay. Va. ay. N. C. ay. S. C. no. Geo. no. [Ayes—9; noes—2.]

Mr. Broom gave notice to the House that he had concurred with a reserve to himself of an intention to claim for his State an equal voice in the 2d. branch: which he thought could not be denied after this concession of the small States as to the first branch.

Mr. Randolph moved <as an amendment to the report of the Comme. of five> "that in order to ascertain the alterations in the population & wealth of the several States the Legislature should be required to cause a census, and estimate to be taken within one year after its first meeting; and every   years thereafter—and that the Legislre. arrange the Representation accordingly."

Mr Govr. Morris opposed it as fettering the Legislature too much. Advantage may be taken of it in time of war or the apprehension of it, by new States to extort particular favors. If the mode was to be fixed for taking a census, it might certainly be extremely inconvenient; if unfixt the Legislature may use such a mode as will defeat the object: and perpetuate the inequality. He was always agst. such Shackles on the Legislre. They had been found very pernicious in most of the State Constitutions. He dwelt much on the danger of throwing such a preponderancy into the Western Scale, suggesting that in time the Western people wd. outnumber the Atlantic States. He wished therefore to put it in the power of the latter to keep a majority of votes in their own hands. It was objected he said that if the Legislre. are left at liberty, they will never readjust the Representation. He admitted that this was possible, but he did not think it probable unless the reasons agst. a revision of it were very urgent & in this case, it ought not to be done.

It was moved to postpone the proposition of Mr. Randolph in order to take up the following, viz. "that the Committee of Eleven, to whom was referred the report of the Committee of five on the subject of Representation, be requested to furnish the Convention with the principles on which they grounded the Report," which was disagreed to: <S. C. only voting in the affirmative.>

Adjourned.

(5) July 11, 1787

Mr. Randolph's motion requiring the Legislre. to take a periodical census for the purpose of redressing inequalities in the Representation was resumed.

Mr. Sherman was agst. Shackling the Legislature too much. We ought to choose wise & good men, and then confide in them.

Mr. Mason. The greater the difficulty we find in fixing a proper rule of Representation, the more unwilling ought we to be, to throw the task from ourselves, on the Genl. Legislre. He did not object to the conjectural ratio which was to prevail in the outset; but considered a Revision from time to time according to some permanent & precise standard as essential to ye. fair representation required in the 1st. branch. According to the present population of America, the Northn. part of it had a right to preponderate, and he could not deny it. But he wished it not to preponderate hereafter when the reason no longer continued. From the nature of man we may be sure, that those who have power in their hands will not give it up while they can retain it. On the Contrary we know they will always when they can rather increase it. If the S. States therefore should have ¾ of the people of America within their limits, the Northern will hold fast the majority of Representatives. ¼ will govern the ¾. The S. States will complain: but they may complain from generation to generation without redress. Unless some principle therefore which will do justice to them hereafter shall be inserted in the Constitution, disagreable as the declaration was to him, he must declare he could neither vote for the system here nor support it, in his State. Strong objections had been drawn from the danger to the Atlantic interests from new Western States. Ought we to sacrifice what we know to be right in itself, lest it should prove favorable to States which are not yet in existence. If the Western States are to be admitted into the Union as they arise, they must, he wd. repeat, be treated as equals, and subjected to no degrading discriminations. They will have the same pride & other passions which we have, and will either not unite with or will speedily revolt from the Union, if they are not in all respects placed on an equal footing with their brethren. It has been said they will be poor, and unable to make equal contributions to the general Treasury. He did not know but that in time they would be both more numerous & more wealthy than their Atlantic brethren. The extent & fertility of their soil, made this probable; and though Spain might for a time deprive them of the natural outlet for their productions, yet she will, because she must, finally yield to their demands. He urged that numbers of inhabitants; though not always a precise standard of wealth was sufficiently so for every substantial purpose.

Mr. Williamson was for making it the duty of the Legislature to do what was right & not leaving it at liberty to do or not do it. He moved that Mr. Randolph's proposition be postpond. in order to consider the following "that in order to ascertain the alterations that may happen in the population & wealth of the several States, a census shall be taken of the free white inhabitants and ⅗ths of those of other descriptions on the 1st year <after this Government shall have been adopted> and every year thereafter; and that the Representation be regulated accordingly."

Mr. Randolph agreed that Mr. Williamson's propositon should stand in the place of his. He observed that the ratio fixt for the 1st. meeting was a mere conjecture, that it placed the power in the hands of that part of America, which could not always be entitled to it, that this power would not be voluntarily renounced; and that it was consequently the duty of the Convention to secure its renunciation when justice might so require; by some constitutional provisions. If equality between great & small States be inadmissible, because in that case unequal numbers of Constituents wd. be represented by equal number of votes; was it not equally inadmissible that a larger & more populous district of America should hereafter have less representation, than a smaller & less populous district. If a fair representation of the people be not secured, the injustice of the Govt. will shake it to its foundations. What relates to suffrage is justly stated by the celebrated Montesquieu, as a fundamental article in Republican Govts. If the danger suggested by Mr. Govr. Morris be real, of advantage being taken of the Legislature in pressing moments, it was an additional reason, for tying their hands in such a manner that they could not sacrifice their trust to momentary considerations. Congs. have pledged the public faith to New States, that they shall be admitted on equal terms. They never would nor ought to accede on any other. The census must be taken under the direction of the General Legislature. The States will be too much interested to take an impartial one for themselves.

Mr. Butler & Genl. Pinkney insisted that blacks be included in the rule of Representation, *equally* with the Whites: <and for that purpose moved that the words "three fifths" be struck out.>

Mr Gerry thought that ⅗ of them was to say the least the full proportion that could be admitted.

Mr. Ghorum. This ratio was fixed by Congs. as a rule of taxation. Then it was urged by the Delegates representing the States having slaves that the blacks were still more inferior to freemen. At present when the ratio of representation is to be established, we are assured that they are equal to freemen. The arguments on ye. former occasion had convinced him that ⅗ was pretty near the just proportion and he should vote according to the same opinion now.

Mr. Butler insisted that the labour of a slave in S. Carola. was as productive & valuable as that of a freeman in Massts., that as wealth was the great means of defence and utility to the Nation they were equally valuable to it with freemen; and that consequently an equal representation ought to be allowed for them in a Government which was instituted principally for the protection of property, and was itself to be supported by property.

Mr. Mason. could not agree to the motion, notwithstanding it was favorable to Virga. because he thought it unjust. It was certain that the slaves were valuable, as they raised the value of land, increased the exports & imports, and of course the revenue, would supply the means of feeding & supporting an army, and might in cases of emergency become themselves soldiers. As in these important respects they were useful to the community at large, they ought not to be excluded from the estimate of Representation. He could not however regard them as equal to freemen and could not vote for them as such. He added as worthy of remark, that the Southern States have this peculiar species of property, over & above the other species of property common to all the States.

Mr. Williamson reminded Mr. Ghorum that if the Southn. States contended for the inferiority of blacks to whites when taxation was in view, the Eastern States on the same occasion contended for their equality. He did <not> however either then or now, concur in either extreme, but approved of the ratio of ⅗.

On Mr. Butlers motion for considering blacks as equal to Whites in the apportionmt. of Representation

Massts. no. Cont. no. (N. Y. not on floor.) N. J. no. Pa. no. Del. ay. Md. no. <Va no> N. C. no. S. C. ay. Geo. ay. [Ayes—3; noes—7.]

Mr. Govr. Morris said he had several objections to the proposition of Mr. Williamson. 1. It fettered the Legislature too much. 2. it would exclude some States altogether who would not have a sufficient number to entitle them to a single Representative. 3. it will not consist with the Resolution passed on Saturday last authorizing the Legislature to adjust the Representation from time to time on the principles of population & wealth or with the principles of equity. If slaves were to be considered as inhabitants, not as wealth, then the sd. Resolution would not be pursued: If as wealth, then why is no other wealth but slaves included?

These objections may perhaps be removed by amendments. His great objection was that the number of inhabitants was not a proper standard of wealth. The amazing difference between the comparative numbers & wealth of different Countries, rendered all reasoning superfluous on the subject. Numbers might with greater propriety be deemed a measure of stregth, than of wealth, yet the late defence made by G. Britain agst. her numerous enemies proved in the clearest manner, that it is entirely fallacious even in this respect.

Mr. King thought there was great force in the objections of Mr. Govr. Morris: he would however accede to the proposition for the sake of doing something.

Mr. Rutlidge contended for the admission of wealth in the estimate by which Representation should be regulated. The Western States will not be able to contribute in proportion to their numbers, they shd. not therefore be represented in that proportion. The Atlantic States will not concur in such a plan. He moved that "at the end of   years after the 1st. meeting of the Legislature, and of every   years thereafter, the Legislature shall proportion the Representation according to the principles of wealth & population"

Mr. Sherman thought the number of people alone the best rule for measuring wealth as well as representation; and that if the Legislature were to be governed by wealth, they would be obliged to estimate it by numbers. He was at first for leaving the matter wholly to the discretion of the Legislature; but he had been convinced by the observations of (Mr. Randolph & Mr. Mason) that the *periods* & the *rule* of revising the Representation ought to be fixt by the Constitution

Mr. Reid thought the Legislature ought not to be too much shackled. It would make the Constitution like Religious Creeds, embarrassing to those bound to conform to them & more likely to produce dissatisfaction and Scism, than harmony and union.

Mr. Mason objected to Mr. Rutlidge motion, as requiring of the Legislature something too indefinite & impracticable, and leaving them a pretext for doing nothing.

Mr. Wilson had himself no objection to leaving the Legislature entirely at liberty. But considered wealth as an impracticable rule.

Mr. Ghorum. If the Convention who are comparatively so little biassed by local views are so much perplexed, How can it be expected that the Legislature hereafter under the full biass of those views, will be able to settle a standard. He was convinced by the arguments of others & his own reflections, that the Convention ought to fix some standard or other.

Mr. Govr. Morris. The argts. of others & his own reflections had led him to a very different conclusion. If we can't agree on a rule that will be just at this time, how can we expect to find one that will be just in all times to come. Surely those who come after us will judge better of things present, than we can of things future. He could not persuade himself that numbers would be a just rule at any time. The remarks of (Mr Mason) relative to the Western Country had not changed his opinion on that head. Among other objections it must be apparent they would not be able to furnish men equally enlightened, to share in the administration of our common interests. The Busy haunts of men not the remote wilderness, was the proper School of political Talents. If the Western people get the power into their hands they will ruin the Atlantic interests. The Back members are always most averse to the best measures He mentioned the case of Pena. formerly. The lower part of the State had ye. power in the first instance. They kept it in yr. own hands. & the country was ye. better for it. Another objection with him agst admitting the blacks into the census, was that the people of Pena. would revolt at the idea of being put on a footing with slaves. They would reject any plan that was to have such an effect. Two objections had been raised agst. leaving the adjustment of the Representation from time to time, to the discretion of the Legislature. The 1. was they would be unwilling to revise it at all. The 2 that by referring to *wealth* they would be bound by a rule which if willing, they would be unable to execute. The 1st. objn. distrusts their fidelity. But if their duty, their honor & their oaths will not bind them, let us not put into their hands our liberty, and all our other great interests. let us have no Govt. at all. 2. If these ties will bind them. we need not distrust the practicability of the rule. It was followed in part by the Come. in the apportionment of Representatives yesterday reported to the House. The best course that could be taken would be to leave the interests of the people to the Representatives of the people.

Mr. <*Madison*> was not a little surprised to hear this implicit confidence urged by a member who on all occasions, had inculcated So strongly, the political depravity of men, and the necessity of checking one vice and interest by opposing to them another vice & interest. If the Representatives of the people would be bound by the ties he had mentioned, what need was there of a Senate? What of a Revisionary power? But his reasoning was not only inconsistent with his former reasoning, but with itself. at the same time that he recommended this implicit confidence to the Southern States in the Northern Majority, he was still more zealous in exhorting all to a jealousy of a Western majority. To reconcile the gentln. with himself it must be imagined that he determined the human character by the points of the compass. The truth was that all men having power ought to be distrusted to a certain degree. The case of Pena. had been mentioned where it was admitted that those who were possessed of the power in the original settlement, never admitted the new settlmts. to a due share of it. England was a still more striking example. The power there had long been in the hands of the boroughs, of the minority; who had opposed & defeated every reform which had been attempted. Virga. was in a lesser degree another example. With regard to the Western States, he was clear & firm in opinion that no unfavorable distinctions were admissible either in point of justice or policy. He thought also that the hope of contributions to the Treasy. from them had been much underrated. Future contributions it seemed to be understood on all hands would be principally levied on imports and exports. The extent & fertility of the Western Soil would for a long time give to agriculture a preference over manufactures. Trials would be repeated till some articles could be raised from it that would bear a transportation to places where they could be exchanged for imported manufactures. Whenever the Mississpi should be opened to them, which would of necessity be ye. case as soon as their their population would subject them to any considerable share of the public burdin, imposts on their trade could be collected with less expense & greater certainty, than on that of the Atlantic States. In the meantime, as their supplies must pass thro' the *Atlantic States* their contributions would be levied in the same manner with those of the Atlantic States.—He could not agree that any substantial objection lay agst. fixig numbers for the perpetual standard of Representation. It was said that Representation & taxation were to go together; that taxation & wealth ought to go together, that population and wealth were not measures of each other. He admitted that in different climates, under different forms of Govt. and in different stages of civilization the inference was perfectly just. He would admit that in no situation numbers of inhabitants were an accurate measure of wealth. He contended however that in the U. States it was sufficiently so for the object in contemplation. Altho' their climate varied considerably, yet as the Govts. the laws, and the manners of all were nearly the same, and the intercourse between different parts perfectly free, population, industry, arts, and the value of labour, would constantly tend to equalize themselves. The value of labour, might be considered as the principal criterion of wealth and ability to support taxes; and this would find its level in different places where the intercourse should be easy & free, with as much certainty as the value of money or any other thing. Wherever labour would yield most, people would resort, till the competition should destroy the inequality. Hence it is that the people are constantly swarming from the more to the less populous places—from Europe to Ama from the Northn. & middle parts of the U.S. to the Southern & Western. They go where land is cheaper, because there labour is dearer. If it be true that the same quantity of produce raised on the banks of the Ohio is of less value than on the Delaware, it is also true that the same labor will raise twice or thrice, the quantity in the former, that it will raise in the latter situation.

Col. Mason, Agreed with Mr. Govr. Morris that we ought to leave the interests of the people to the Representatives of the people: but the objection was that the Legislature would cease to be the Representatives of the people. It would continue so no longer than the States now containing a majority of the people should retain that majority. As soon as the Southern & Western population should predominate, which must happen in a few years, the power wd be in the hands of the minority, and would never be yielded to the majority, unless provided for by the Constitution

On the question for postponing Mr. Williamson's motion, in order to consider that of Mr. Rutlidge <it passed in the negative>. Massts. ay. Cont. no. N. J. no. Pa. ay. Del. ay. Md. no. Va. no. N. C. no. S. C. ay. Geo—ay. [Ayes—5; noes—5.]

On the question on the first clause <of Mr. Williamson's motion> as to taking a census of the *free* inhabitants. <it passed in the affirmative> Masts. ay. Cont. ay. N. J. ay. Pa. ay. Del. no. Md. no. Va. ay. N. C. ay. S. C. no. Geo. no. [Ayes—6; noes—4.]

the next clause as to ⅗ of the negroes considered

Mr. King. being much opposed to fixing numbers as the rule of representation, was particularly so on account of the blacks. He thought the admission of them along with Whites at all, would excite great discontents among the States having no slaves. He had never said as to any particular point that he would in no event acquiesce in & support it; but he wd. say that if in any case such a declaration was to be made by him, it would be in this. He remarked that in the <temporary> allotment of Representatives made by the Committee, the Southern States had received more than the number of their white & three fifths of their black inhabitants entitled them to.

Mr. Sherman. S. Carola. had not more beyond her proportion than N. York & N. Hampshire, nor either of them more than was necessary in order to avoid fractions or reducing them below their proportion. Georgia had more; but the rapid growth of that State seemed to justify it. In general the allotment might not be just, but considering all circumstances, he was satisfied with it.

Mr. Ghorum. supported the propriety of establishing numbers as the rule. He said that in Massts. estimates had been taken in the different towns, and that persons had been curious enough to compare these estimates with the respective numbers of people; and it had been found even including Boston, that the most exact proportion prevailed between numbers & property. He was aware that there might be some weight in what had fallen from his colleague, as to the umbrage which might be taken by the people of the Eastern States. But he recollected that when the proposition of Congs for changing the 8th. art: of Confedn. was before the Legislature of Massts. the only difficulty then was to satisfy them that the negroes ought not to have been counted equally with whites instead of being counted in the ratio of three fifths only.

Mr. Wilson did not well see on what principle the admission of blacks in the proportion of three fifths could be explained. Are they admitted as Citizens? Then why are they not admitted on an equality with White Citizens? Are they admitted as property? then why is not other property admitted into the computation? These were difficulties however which he thought must be overruled by the necessity of compromise. He had some apprehensions also from the tendency of the blending of the blacks with the whites, to give disgust to the people of Pena. as had been intimated by his colleague (Mr Govr. Morris). But he differed from him in thinking numbers of inhabts. so incorrect a measure of wealth. He had seen the Western settlemts. of Pa. and on a comparison of them with the City of Philada. could discover little other difference, than that property was more unequally divided among individuals here than there. Taking the same number in the aggregate in the two situations he believed there would be little difference in their wealth and ability to contribute to the public wants.

Mr. Govr. Morris was compelled to declare himself reduced to the dilemma of doing injustice to the Southern States or to human nature, and he must therefore do it to the former. For he could never agree to give such encouragement to the slave trade as would be given by allowing them a representation for their negroes, and he did not believe those States would ever confederate on terms that would deprive them of that trade.

On Question for agreeing to include ⅗ of the blacks

Masts. no. Cont. ay N. J. no. Pa. no. Del. no. Mard. no. Va. ay. N. C. ay. S. C. no. Geo. ay [Ayes—4; noes—6.]

On the question as to taking census "the first year after meeting of the Legislature"

Masts. ay. Cont. no. N. J. ay. Pa. ay. Del. ay. Md. no. Va. ay. N. C. ay. S. ay. Geo. no. [Ayes—7; noes—3.]

On filling the blank for the periodical census with 15 years". agreed to nem. con.

Mr. <Madison> moved to add after "15 years," the words "at least" that the Legislature might anticipate when circumstances <were likely to> render a particular year inconvenient.

On this motion for adding "at least", <it passed in the negative the States being equally divided.>

Mas. ay. Cont. no. N. J. no. Pa. no. Del. no. Md. no. Va. ay. N. C. ay. S. C. ay. Geo. ay. [Ayes—5; noes—5.]

A change of the phraseology <of the other clause> so as to read; "and the Legislature <shall alter or augment the representation accordingly" was> agreed to nem. con.

On the question on the whole <resolution of Mr. Williamson as amended.>

Mas. no. Cont. no. N. J. no. Del. no. Md. no. Va. no. N. C. no. S. C. no—Geo—no [Ayes—0; noes—9.]

(6) July 12, 1787

Mr. Govr. Morris moved to add to the clause empowering the Legislature to vary the Representation according to the principles of wealth & number of inhabts. a "proviso that taxation shall be in proportion to Representation".

Mr Butler contended again that Representation sd. be according to the full number of inhabts. including all the blacks; admitting the justice of Mr. Govr. Morris's motion.

Mr. Mason also admitted the justice of the principle, but was afraid embarrassments might be occasioned to the Legislature by it. It might drive the Legislature to the plan of Requisitions.

Mr. Govr. Morris, admitted that some objections lay agst. his motion, but supposed they would be removed by restraining the rule to *direct* taxation. With regard to indirect taxes on *exports* & imports & on consumption, the rule would be inapplicable. Notwithstanding what had been said to the contrary he was persuaded that the imports & consumption were pretty nearly equal throughout the Union.

General Pinkney liked the idea. He thought it so just that it could not be objected to. But foresaw that if the revision of the census was left to the discretion of the Legislature, it would never be carried into execution. The rule must be fixed, and the execution of it enforced by the Constitution. He was alarmed at what was said yesterday, concerning the Negroes. He was now again alarmed at what had been thrown out concerning the taxing of exports. S. Carola. has in one year exported to the amount of £600,000 Sterling all which was the fruit of the labor of her blacks. Will she be represented in proportion to this amount? She will not. Neither ought she then to be subject to a tax on it. He hoped a clause would be inserted in the system restraining the Legislature from a taxing Exports.

Mr. Wilson approved the principle, but could not see how it could be carried into execution; unless restrained to direct taxation.

Mr. Govr. Morris having so varied his motion by inserting the word "direct". It passd. <nem. con. as follows—'provided always that direct taxation ought to be proportioned to representation".>

Mr. Davie, said it was high time now to speak out. He saw that it was meant by some gentlemen to deprive the Southern States of any share of Representation for their blacks. He was sure that N. Carola. would never confederate on any terms that did not rate them at least as ⅗. If the Eastern States meant therefore to exclude them altogether the business was at an end.

Dr. Johnson, thought that wealth and population were the true, equitable rule of representation; but he conceived that these two principles resolved themselves into one; population being the best measure of wealth. He concluded therefore that ye. number of people ought to be established as the rule, and that all descriptions including blacks *equally* with the whites, ought to fall within the computation. As various opinions had been expressed on the subject, he would move that a Committee might be appointed to take them into consideration and report thereon.

Mr. Govr. Morris. It has been said that it is high time to speak out. As one member, he would candidly do so. He came here to form a compact for the good of America. He was ready to do so with all the States: He hoped & believed that all would enter into such a Compact. If they would not he was ready to join with any States that would. But as the Compact was to be voluntary, it is in vain for the Eastern States to insist on what the Southn States will never agree to. It is equally vain for the latter to require what the other States can never admit; and he verily belived the people of Pena. will never agree to a representation of Negroes. What can be desired by these States more than has been already proposed; that the Legislature shall from time to time regulate Representation according to population & wealth.

Gen. Pinkney desired that the rule of wealth should be ascertained and not left to the pleasure of the Legislature; and that property in slaves should not be exposed to danger under a Govt. instituted for the protection of property.

<The first clause in the Report of the first Grand Committee was postponed>

Mr. Elseworth. In order to carry into effect the principle established, moved <to add to the last clause adopted by the House the words following "and that the rule of contribution by direct taxation for the support of the Government of the U. States shall be the number of white inhabitants, and three fifths of every other description in the several States, until some other rule that shall more accurately ascertain the wealth of the several States can be devised and adopted by the Legislature">

Mr. Butler seconded the motion in order that it might be committed.

Mr. Randolph was not satisfied with the motion. The danger will be revived that the ingenuity of the Legislature may evade <or pervert the rule so as to> perpetuate the power where it shall be lodged in the first instance. He proposed in lieu of Mr. Elseworth's motion, "that in order to ascertain the alterations <in Representation> that may be required from time to time by changes in the relative circumstances of the States, a census shall be taken within two years <from> the 1st. meeting of the Genl. Legislature <of the U. S.>, and once within <the term of> every year afterwards, of <all> the inhabitants <in the manner &> according to the <ratio recommended by Congress in their resolution> of the <18th> day of <Apl. 1783; (rating the blacks at ⅗ of their number)> and that the Legislature of the U. S. shall arrange the Representation accordingly."—He urged strenuously that express security ought to be provided for including slaves in the ratio of Representation. He lamented that such a species of property existed. But as it did exist the holders of it would require this security. It was perceived that the design was entertained by some of excluding slaves altogether; the Legislature therefore ought not to be left at liberty.

Mr. Elseworth withdraws his motion & seconds that of Mr. Randolph.

Mr. Wilson observed that less umbrage would perhaps be taken agst. an admission of the slaves into the Rule of representation, if it should be so expressed as to make them indirectly only an ingredient in the rule, by saying that they should enter into the rule of taxation: and as representation was to be according to taxation, the end would be equally attained. He accordingly <moved & was 2ded so to alter the last clause adopted by the House, that together with the amendment proposed the whole should read as follows—provided always that the representation ought to be proportioned according to direct taxation, and in order to ascertain the alterations in the direct taxation which may be required from time to time by the changes in the relative circumstances of the States. Resolved that a census be taken within two years from the first meeting of the Legislature of the U. States, and once within the term of every   years afterwards of all the inhabitants of the U. S. in the manner and according to the ratio recommended by Congress in their Resolution of April 18 1783; and that the Legislature of the U. S. shall proportion the direct taxation accordingly">

Mr. King. Altho' this amendment varies the aspect somewhat, he had still two powerful objections agst. tying down the Legislature to the rule of numbers. 1. they were at this time an uncertain index of the relative wealth of the States. 2. if they were a just index at this time it can not be supposed always to continue so. He was far from wishing to retain any unjust advantage whatever in one part of the Republic. If justice was not the basis of the connection it could not be of long duration. He must be short sighted indeed who does not foresee that whenever the Southern States shall be more numerous than the Northern, they can & will hold a language that will awe them into justice. If they threaten to separate now in case injury shall be done them, will their threats be less urgent or effectual, when force shall back their demands. Even in the intervening period there will no point of time at which they will not be able to say, do us justice or we will separate. He urged the necessity of placing confidence to a certain degree in every Govt. and did not conceive that the proposed confidence as to a periodical readjustment of the representation exceeded that degree.

Mr. Pinkney moved to amend Mr. Randolph's motion so as to make "blacks equal to the whites in the ratio of representation". This he urged was nothing more than justice. The blacks are the labourers, the peasants of the Southern States: they are as productive of pecuniary resources as those of the Northern States. They add equally to the wealth, and considering money as the sinew of war, to the strength of the nation. It will also be politic with regard to the Northern States as taxation is to keep pace with Representation.

Genl. Pinkney moves to insert 6 years instead of two, as the period <computing from 1st meeting of ye Legis—> within which the first census should be taken. On this question for <inserting six instead of two" in the proposition of Mr. Wilson, it passed in the affirmative>

Masts. no. Ct. ay. N. J. ay. Pa. ay. Del. divd. Mayd. ay. Va. no. N. C. no. S. C. ay. Geo. no. [Ayes—5; noes—4; divided—1.]

On a question for filling the blank for ye. periodical census with 20 years, <it passed in the negative>

Masts. no. Ct. ay. N. J. ay. P. ay. Del. no. Md. no. Va. no. N. C. no. S. C. no. Geo. no. [Ayes—3; noes—7.]

On a question for 10 years, <it passed in the affirmative.>

Mas. ay. Cont. no. N. J. no. P. ay. Del. ay. Md. ay. Va. ay. N. C. ay. S. C. ay. Geo. ay. [Ayes—8; noes—2.]

On Mr. Pinkney's motion for rating blacks as equal to whites instead of as ⅗.

Mas. no. Cont. no. (Dr Johnson ay) N. J. no. Pa. no. (3 agst. 2) Del. no. Md. no. Va. no. N. C. no. S. C. ay. Geo—ay. [Ayes—2; noes—8.]

Mr. Randolph's proposition <as varied by Mr. Wilson being> read for question on the whole.

Mr. Gerry, urged that the principle of it could not be carried into execution as the States were not to be taxed as States. With regard to taxes in imports, he conceived they would be more productive—Where there were no slaves than where there were; the consumption being greater—

Mr. Elseworth. In case of a poll tax there wd. be no difficulty. But there wd. probably be none. The sum allotted to a State may be levied without difficulty according to the plan used by the State in raising its own supplies. On the question on ye. whole proposition; <as proportioning representation to direct taxation & both to the white & ⅗ of black inhabitants, & requiring a census within six years—& within every ten years afterwards.>

Mas. divd. Cont. ay. N. J. no. Pa. ay. Del. no. Md. ay. Va. ay. N. C. ay. S. C. divd. Geo. ay. [Ayes—6; noes—2; divided—2.]

(7) August 8, 1787

Art: IV. Sect. 1.—Mr. Mercer expressed his dislike of the whole plan, and his opinion that it never could succeed.

Mr. Ghorum. He had never seen any inconveniency from allowing such as were not freeholders to vote, though it had long been tried. The elections in Phila. N. York & Boston where the Merchants, & Mechanics vote are at least as good as those made by freeholders only. The case in England was not accurately stated yesterday (by Mr. Madison) The Cities & large towns are not the seat of Crown influence & corruption. These prevail in the Boroughs, and not on account of the right which those who are not freeholders have to vote, but of the smallness of the number who vote. The people have been long accustomed to this right in various parts of America, and will never allow it to be abridged. We must consult their rooted prejudices if we expect their concurrence in our propositions.

Mr. Mercer did not object so much to an election by the people at large including such as were not freeholders, as to their being left to make their choice without any guidance. He hinted that Candidates ought to be nominated by the State Legislatures.

On question for agreeing to Art: IV-Sect. 1 it passd. nem. con.

Art. IV. Sect. 2. taken up.

Col. Mason was for opening a wide door for emigrants; but did not chuse to let foreigners and adventurers make laws for us & govern us. Citizenship for three years was not enough for ensuring that local knowledge which ought to be possessed by the Representative. This was the principal ground of his objection to so short a term. It might also happen that a rich foreign Nation, for example Great Britain, might send over her tools who might bribe their way into the Legislature for insidious purposes. He moved that "seven" years instead of "three," be inserted.

Mr. Govr. Morris 2ded. the motion, & on the question, All the States agreed to it except Connecticut.

Mr. Sherman moved to strike out the word "resident" and insert "inhabitant," as less liable to misconstruction.

Mr M<adison> 2ded. the motion. both were vague, but the latter least so in common acceptation, and would not exclude persons absent occasionally for a considerable time on public or private business. Great disputes had been raised in Virga. concerning the meaning of residence as a qualification of Representatives which were determined more according to the affection or dislike to the man <in question>, than <to> any fixt interpretation of the word.

Mr. Wilson preferred "inhabitant."

Mr. Govr. Morris was opposed to both and for requiring nothing more than a freehold. He quoted great disputes in N. York occasioned by these terms, which were decided by the arbitrary will of the majority. Such a regulation is not necessary. People rarely chuse a nonresident— It is improper as in the 1st. branch, *the people at large*, not the *States* are represented.

Mr. Rutlidge urged & moved that a residence of 7 years shd. be required in the State Wherein the Member shd. be elected. An emigrant from N. England to S. C. or Georgia would know little of its affairs and could not be supposed to acquire a thorough knowledge in less time.

Mr. Read reminded him that we were now forming a *Natil* Govt and such a regulation would correspond little with the idea that we were one people.

Mr. Wilson—enforced the same consideration.

Mr. <Madison> suggested the case of new States in the West, which could have perhaps no representation on that plan.

Mr. Mercer. Such a regulation would present a greater alienship among the States than existed under the old federal system. It would interweave local prejudices & State distinctions in the very Constitution which is meant to cure them. He mentioned instances of violent disputes raised in Maryland concerning the term "residence"

Mr Elseworth thought seven years of residence was by far too long a term: but that some fixt term of previous residence would be proper. He thought one year would be sufficient, but seemed to have no objection to three years.

Mr. Dickenson proposed <that it should read> "inhabitant actually resident for——year." This would render the meaning less indeterminate.

Mr. Wilson. If a short term should be inserted in the blank, so strict an expression might be construed to exclude the members of the Legislature, who could not be said to be actual residents in their States whilst at the Seat of the Genl. Government.

Mr. Mercer. It would certainly exclude men, who had once been inhabitants, and returning from residence elswhere to resettle in their original State; although a want of the necessary knowledge could not in such case be presumed.

Mr. Mason thought 7 years too long, but would never agree to part with the principle. It is a valuable principle. He thought it a defect in the plan that the Representatives would be too few to bring with them all the local knowledge necessary. If residence be not required, Rich men of neighbouring States, may employ with success the means of corruption in some particular district and thereby get into the public Councils after having failed in their own State. This is the practice in the boroughs of England.

On the question for postponing in order to consider Mr Dickinsons motion

N. H. no. Mas. no. Ct. no. N. J. no. Pa. no. Del. no. Md. ay. Va. no. N. C. no. S. C. ay. Geo. ay. [Ayes—3; noes—8.]

On the question for inserting "inhabitant" in place of "resident"—Agd. to nem. con.

Mr. Elseworth & Col. Mason move to insert "one year" for previous inhabitancy

Mr. Williamson liked the Report as it stood. He thought "resident" a good eno' term. He was agst requiring any period of previous residence. New residents if elected will be most zealous to Conform to the will of their constituents, as their conduct will be watched with a more jealous eye.

Mr. Butler & Mr. Rutlidge moved "three years" instead of "one year" <for previous inhabitancy>

On the question for 3 years.

N. H. no. Mas. no. Ct. no. N. J. no. Pa. no. Del. no. Md. no. Va. no. N. C. no. S. C. ay. Geo. ay [Ayes—2; noes—9.]

On the question for "1 year"

N. H. no—Mas—no. Ct. no. N. J. ay. Pa. no. Del. no. Md. divd. Va. no- N- C. ay- S. C. ay. Geo—ay [Ayes—4; noes—6; divided—1.]

Art. IV- Sect. 2. As amended in manner preceding, was agreed to nem. con.

Art: IV. Sect. 3. "taken up.

Genl. Pinkney & Mr. Pinkney moved that the number of representatives allotted to S. Carola. be "six"

On the question.

N. H. no. Mas. no. Ct. no. N. J. no. Pa. no. <Delaware ay> Md. no. Va. no. N. C. ay. S. C. ay. Geo. ay. [Ayes—4; noes—7.]

<The 3. Sect of Art: IV was then agreed to.>

Art: IV. Sect. 4. taken up.

Mr. Williamson moved to strike out "according to the provisions hereinafter made" and to insert <the> words <"according> "to the rule hereafter to be provided for direct taxation"—See Art VII. sect. 3.

On the question for agreeing to Mr. Williamson's amendment

N. H- ay. Mas. ay. Ct. ay. N. J. no. Pa. ay. Del. no. Md. ay. Va ay. N. C. ay. S. C. ay. Geo. ay. [Ayes—9; noes—2.]

Mr. King wished to know what influence the vote just passed was meant have on the succeeding part of the Report, concerning the admission of slaves into the rule of Representation. He could not reconcile his mind to the article if it was to prevent objections to the latter part. The admission of slaves was a most grating circumstance to his mind, & he believed would be so to a great part of the people of America. He had not made a strenuous opposition to it heretofore because he had hoped that this concession would have produced a readiness which had not been manifested, to strengthen the Genl. Govt. and to mark a full confidence in it. The Report under consideration had by the tenor of it, put an end to all these hopes. In two great points the hands of the Legislature were absolutely tied. The importation of slaves could not be prohibited—exports could not be taxed. Is this reasonable? What are the great objects of the Genl. System? 1. difence agst. foreign invasion. 2. agst. internal sedition. Shall all the States then be bound to defend each; & shall each be at liberty to introduce a weakness which will render defence more difficult? Shall one part of the U. S. be bound to defend another part, and that other part be at liberty not only to increase its own danger, but to withhold the compensation for the burden? If slaves are to be imported shall not the exports produced by their labor, supply a revenue the better to enable the Genl. Govt. to defend their Masters?—There was so much inequality & unreasonableness in all this, that the people of the N<orthern> States could never be reconciled <to it>. No candid man could undertake to justify it to them. He had hoped that some accommodation wd. have taken place on this subject; that at least a time wd. have been limited for the importation of slaves. He never could agree to let them be imported without limitation & then be represented in the Natl. Legislature. Indeed he could so little persuade himself of the rectitude of such a practice, that he was not sure he could assent to it under any circumstances. At all events, either slaves should not be represented, or exports should be taxable.

Mr. Sherman regarded the slave-trade as iniquitous; but the point of representation having been Settled after much difficulty & deliberation, he did not think himself bound to make opposition; especially as the present article as amended did not preclude any arrangement whatever on that point in another place of the Report.

Mr. <Madison> objected to 1 for every 40,000 inhabitants <as a perpetual rule>. The future increase of population if the Union shd. be permanent, will render the number of Representatives excessive.

Mr. Ghorum. It is not to be supposed that the Govt will last so long as to produce this effect. Can it be supposed that this vast Country including the Western territory will 150 years hence remain one nation?

Mr. Elseworth. If the Govt. should continue so long, alterations may be made in the Constitution in the manner proposed in a subsequent article.

Mr Sherman & Mr. <Madison> moved to insert the words "not exceeding" before the words "1 for every 40,000, which was agreed to nem. con.

Mr Govr. Morris moved to insert "free" before the word "inhabitants." Much he said would depend on this point. He never would concur in upholding domestic slavery. It was a nefarious institution—It was the curse of heaven on the States where it prevailed. Compare the free regions of the Middle States, where a rich & noble cultivation marks the prosperity & happiness of the people, with the misery & poverty which overspread the barren wastes of Va. Maryd. & the other States having slaves. <Travel thro' ye whole Continent & you behold the prospect continually varying with the appearance & disappearance of slavery. The moment you leave ye E. Sts. & enter N. York, the effects of the institution become visible; Passing thro' the Jerseys and entering Paevery criterion of superior improvement witnesses the change. Proceed Southwdly, & every step you take thro' ye great regions of slaves, presents a desert increasing with ye increasing proportion of these wretched beings.>

Upon what principle is it that the slaves shall be computed in the representation? Are they men? Then make them Citizens & let them vote? Are they property? Why then is no other property included? The Houses in this City (Philada.) are worth more than all the wretched slaves which cover the rice swamps of South Carolina. The admission of slaves into the Representation when fairly explained comes to this: that the inhabitant of Georgia and S. C. who goes to the Coast of Africa, and in defiance of the most sacred laws of humanity tears away his fellow creatures from their dearest connections & dam<n>s them to the most cruel bondages, shall have more votes in a Govt. instituted for protection of the rights of mankind, than the Citizen of Pa or N. Jersey who views with a laudable horror, so nefarious a practice. He would add that Domestic slavery is the most prominent feature in the aristocratic countenance of the proposed Constitution. The vassalage of the poor has ever been the favorite offspring of Aristocracy. And What is the proposed compensation to the Northern States for a sacrifice of every principle of right, of every impulse of humanity. They are to bind themselves to march their militia for the defence of the S. States; for their defence agst those very slaves of whom they complain. They must supply vessels & seamen, in case of foreign Attack. The Legislature will have indefinite power to tax them by excises, and duties on imports: both of which will fall heavier on them than on the Southern inhabitants; for the bohea tea used by a Northern freeman, will pay more tax than the whole consumption of the miserable slave, which consists of nothing more than his physical subsistence and the rag that covers his nakedness. On the other side the Southern States are not to be restrained from importing fresh supplies of wretched Africans, at once to increase the danger of attack, and the difficulty of defence; nay they are to be encouraged to it by an assurance of having their votes in the Natl Govt increased in proportion. and are at the same time to have their exports & their slaves exempt from all contributions for the public service. Let it not be said that direct taxation is to be proportioned to representation. It is idle to suppose that the Genl Govt. can stretch its hand directly into the pockets of the people scattered over so vast a Country. They can only do it through the medium of exports imports & excises. For what then are all these sacrifices to be made? He would sooner submit himself to a tax for paying for all the Negroes in the U. States. than saddle posterity with such a Constitution.

Mr. Dayton 2ded. the motion. He did it he said that his sentiments on the subject might appear whatever might be the fate of the amendment.

Mr. Sherman. did not regard the admission of the Negroes into the ratio of representation, as liable to such insuperable objections. It was the freemen of the Southn. States who were in fact to be represented according to the taxes paid by them, and the Negroes are only included in the Estimate of the taxes. This was his idea of the matter.

Mr Pinkney, considered the fisheries & the Western frontier as more burdensome to the U. S. than the slaves—He thought this could be demonstrated if the occasion were a proper one.

Mr Wilson. thought the motion premature—An agreement to the clause would be no bar to the object of it.

Question On Motion to insert "free" before "inhabitants."

N. H- no. Mas. no. Ct. no. N. J. ay. Pa. no. Del. no. Md. no. Va. no. N. C. no. S. C. no. Geo. no. [Ayes—1; noes—10.]

On the suggestion of Mr. Dickenson <the words>, "provided that each State shall have one representative at least."—were added nem. con.

Art. IV.   sect. 4.   as amended was Agreed to nem. con.

Art. IV.   sect. 5.   taken up

Mr. Pinkney moved to strike out Sect. 5, As giving no peculiar advantage to the House of Representatives, and as clogging the Govt. If the Senate can be trusted with the many great powers proposed, it surely may be trusted with that of originating money bills.

Mr. Ghorum. was agst. allowing the Senate to *originate;* but <only> to *amend.*

Mr. Govr. Morris. It is particularly proper that the Senate shd. have the right of originating money bills. They will sit constantly. will consist of a smaller number. and will be able to prepare such bills with due correctness; and so as to prevent delay of business in the other House.

Col. Mason was unwilling to travel over this ground again. To strike out the section, was to unhinge the compromise of which it made a part. The duration of the Senate made it improper. He does not object to that duration. On the Contrary he approved of it. But joined with the smallness of the number, it was an argument <against> adding this to the other great powers vested in that body. His idea of an Aristocracy was that it was the governt. of the few over the many. An aristocratic body, like the screw in mechanics, workig. its way by slow degrees, and holding fast whatever it gains, should ever be suspected of an encroaching tendency—The purse strings should never be put into its hands.

Mr Mercer, considered the exclusive power of originating Money bills as so great an advantage, that it rendered the equality of votes in the Senate ideal & of no consequence.

Mr. Butler was for adhering to the principle which had been settled.

Mr. Wilson was opposed to it on its merits, with out regard to the compromise

Mr. Elseworth did not think the clause of any consequence, but as it was thought of consequence by some members from the larger States, he was willing it should stand.

Mr. <Madison> was for striking it out: considering it as of no advantage to the large States as fettering the Govt. and as a source of injurious altercations between the two Houses.

On the question for striking out "Sect. 5. art. IV"

N. H. no. Mas. no. Ct. no. N. J. ay. Pa. ay. Del. ay. Md. ay. Va. ay. N. C. no. S. C. ay. Geo. ay. [Ayes—7; noes—4.]

Adjd.

J. ST. GEORGE TUCKER, BLACKSTONE'S COMMENTARIES

1803

ON THE STATE OF SLAVERY IN VIRGINIA.

IN the preceding inquiry into the absolute rights of the citizens of united America, we must not be understood as if those rights were equally and universally the privilege of all the inhabitants of the United States, or even of all those, who may challenge this land of freedom as their native country. Among the blessings which the Almighty hath showered down on these states, there is a large portion of the bitterest draught that ever flowed from the cup of affliction. Whilst America hath been the land of promise to Europeans, and their descendants, it hath been the vale of death to millions of the wretched sons of Africa. The genial light of liberty, which hath here shone with unrivalled lustre on the former, hath yielded no comfort to the latter, but to them hath proved a pillar of darkness, whilst it hath conducted the former to the most enviable state of human existence. Whilst we were offering up vows at the shrine of liberty, and sacrificing hecatombs upon her altars; whilst we swore irreconcileable hostility to her enemies, and hurled defiance in their faces; whilst we adjured the God of Hosts to witness our resolution to live free, or die, and imprecated curses on their heads who refused to unite with us in establishing the empire of freedom; we were imposing upon our fellow men; who differ in complexion from us, a *slavery*, ten thousand times more cruel than the utmost extremity of those grievances and oppresssions, of which we complained. Such are the inconsistencies of human nature; such the blindness of those who pluck not the beam out of their own eyes, whilst they can espy a moat, in the eyes of their brother; such that partial system of morality which confines rights and injuries, to particular complexions; such the effect of that self-love which justifies, or condemns, not according to principle, but to the agent. Had we turned our eyes inwardly when we supplicated the Father of Mercies to aid the injured and oppressed; when we invoked the Author of Righteousness to attest the purity of our motives, and the justice of our cause *; and implored the God of Battles to aid our exertions in it's defence, should we not have stood more self convicted than the contrite publican! Should we not have left our gift upon the altar, that we might be first reconciled to our brethren whom we held in bondage? should we not have loosed their chains, and broken their fetters? Or if the difficulties and dangers of such an experiment prohibited the attempt during the convulsions of a revolution, is it not our duty to embrace the first moment of constitutional health and vigour, to effectuate so desirable an object, and to remove from us a stigma, with which our enemies will never fail to upbraid us, nor our consciences to reproach us? To form a just estimate of this obligation, to demonstrate the incompatability of a state of slavery with the principles of our government, and of that revolution upon which it is founded, and to elucidate the practicability of it's total, though gradual abolition, it will be proper to consider the nature of slavery, its properties, attendants, and consequences in general; it's rise, progress, and present state, not only in this commonwealth, but in such of our sister states as have either perfected, or commenced the great work of it's extirpation; with the means they have adopted to effect it, and those which the circumstances and situation of our country may render it most expedient for us to pursue, for the attainment of the same noble and important end [†].

According to Justinian [††], the first general division of persons, in respect to their rights, is into freemen and slaves. It is equally the glory and the happiness of that country from which the citizens of the United States derive their origin, that the traces of slavery, such as at present exists in several of the United States, are there utterly extinguished. It is not my design to enter into a minute inquiry whether it ever had existence there, nor to compare the situation of villeins, during the existence of pure villenage, with that of modern domestic slaves. The records of those times, at least, such as have reached this quarter of the

---

* The American standard, at the commencement of those hostilities which terminated in the revolution, had these words upon it. . . . AN APPEAL TO HEAVEN!

† The Editor here takes the liberty of making his acknowledgments to the reverend Jeremian Belknap, D. D. of Boston, and to Zephaniah Swift, Esq. representative in Congress from Connecticut, for their obliging communications; he hath occasionally made use of them in several parts of this Lecture, where he may have omitted referring to them.

†† Lib. 1. Tit. 2.

globe, are too few to throw a satisfactory light on the subject. Suffice it that our ancestors migrating hither brought not with them any proto-type of that slavery which hath been established among us. The first introduction of it into Virginia was by the arrival of a Dutch ship from the the coast of Africa, having *twenty* negroes on board, who were sold here in the year 1620 *. In the year 1638 we find them in Massachu-setts [†]. They were introduced into Connecticut soon after the settlement of that colony; that is to say, about the same period [††]. Thus early had our forefathers sown the seeds of an evil, which, like a leprosy hath descended upon their posterity with accumulated rancour, visiting the sins of the fathers upon succeeding generations..... The climate of the northern states less favourable to the constitution of the natives of Africa **, than the southern, proved alike unfavourable to their propaga-gation, and to the increase of their numbers by importations.... As the southern colonies advanced in population, not only importations in-creased there, but nature herself, under a climate more congenial to the African constitution, assisted in multiplying the blacks in those parts, no less than in diminishing their numbers in the more rigorous climates of the north; this influence of climate moreover contributed extremely to increase or diminish the value of the slave to the purchasers, in the different colonies. White labourers, whose constitutions were better adapted to the severe winters of the New-England colonies, were there found to be preferable to the negroes ***, who, accustomed to the influence of an ardent sun, became almost torpid in those countries, not less adapted to give vigour to their laborious exercises, than unfavoura-ble to the multiplication of their species: in those colonies, where the winters were not only milder, and of shorter duration, but succeeded by an intense summer heat, as invigorating to the African, as debilitating to the European constitution, the negroes were not barely more capable of performing labour than the Europeans, or their descendants, but the multiplication of the species were at least equal; and, where they met with humane treatment, perhaps greater than among the whites. The purchaser, therefore, calculated not upon the value of the labour of his slave only, but, if a female, he regarded her as "the fruitful mother of an hundred more:" and many of these unfortunate people have there been in this state, whose descendants even in the compass of two or three generations have gone near to realize the calculation.... The great increase of slavery in the southern, in proportion to the northern states in the union, is, therefore, not attributable, *solely*, to the effect of sentiment, but to natural causes; as well as those considerations of profit, which have, perhaps, an equal influence over the conduct of mankind in general, in whatever country, or under whatever climate

* Stith 182.

[†] Dr. Belknap's Answers to St. G. T.'s queries

[††] Letter from Zephaniah Swift to St. G. T.

** Dr. Belknap, Zephan. Swift

*** Ibid.

their destiny hath placed them. What else but considerations of this nature could have influenced the merchants of the freest nation, at that time, in the world, to embark in so nefarious a traffic, as that of the human race, attended, as the African slave trade has been, with the most atrocious aggravations of cruelty, perfidy, and intrigues, the objects of which have been the perpetual fomentation of predatory and intestine wars? What, but similar considerations, could prevail on the government of the same country, even in these days, to patronize a commerce so diametrically opposite to the generally received maxims of that government. It is to the operation of these considerations in the parent country, not less than to their influence in the colonies, that the rise, increase, and continuance of slavery in those British colonies which now constitute united America, are to be attributed, as I shall endeavour to shew in the course of the present inquiry. It is now time to inquire into the nature of slavery, in general, and take a view of it's consequences, and attendants in this commonwealth, in particular.

Slavery, says a well informed writer * on the subject, has been attended with circumstances so various in different countries, as to render it difficult to give a general definition of it..... Justinian calls it a constitution of the law of nations, by which one man is made subject to another, contrary to nature †. Grotius describes it to be an obligation to serve another for life, in consideration of diet, and other common necessaries ††. Dr. Rutherforth, rejecting this definition, informs us, that perfect slavery is an obligation to be directed by another in all one's actions [2]. Baron Montesquieu defines it to be the establishment of a right, which gives one man such a power over another, as renders him absolute master over his life and fortune [1]. These definitions appear not to embrace the subject fully, since they respect the condition of the slave, in regard to his *master*, only, and not in regard to the *state*, as well as the *master*. The author last mentioned, observes, that the constitution of a state may be free, and the subject not so. The subject free, and not the constitution of the state **. Pursuing this idea, instead of attempting a general definition of slavery; I shall, by considering it under a threefold aspect, endeavour to give a just idea of it's nature.

I. When a nation is, from any external cause, deprived of the right of being governed by it's own laws, only, such a nation may be considered as in a state of *political slavery*. Such is the state of conquered countries, and, generally, of colonies, and other dependant governments. Such was the state of united America before the revolution. In this case the personal rights of the subject may be so far secured by wholesome laws, as that the individual may be esteemed free, whilst the state is subject to a higher power: this subjection of one nation, or people, to the

* Hargrave's case of negroe Somerset.
† Lib. 1, Tit. 3. Sec. 2.
†† Lib. 2. c. 5, Sec. 27.
2. Lib. 15. c. 1.

1. Lib. 1. c. 20. p. 474.
** Lib. 12. c. 1.

will of another, constitutes the first species of slavery, which, in order to distinguish it from the other two, I have called political; inasmuch as it exists only in respect to the governments, and not to the individuals of the two countries. Of this it is not our business to speak, at present.

II. Civil liberty, according to judge Blackstone, being no other than natural liberty so far restrained by human laws, and no farther, as is necessary and expedient for the general advantage of the public *, whenever that liberty is, by the laws of the state, further restrained than is necessary and expedient for the general advantage, a state of *civil slavery* commences immediately: this may affect the whole society, and every description of persons in it, and yet the constitution of the state be perfectly free. And this happens whenever the laws of a state respect the form, or energy of the government, more than the happiness of the citizen; as in Venice, where the most oppressive species of civil slavery exists, extending to every individual in the state, from the poorest gondolier to the members of the senate, and the doge himself.

This species of slavery also exists whenever there is an inequality of rights, or privileges, between the subjects or citizens of the same state, except such as necessarily results from the exercise of a public office; for the pre-eminence of one class of men must be founded and erected upon the depression of another; and the measure of exaltation in the former, is that of the slavery of the latter. In all governments, however constituted, or by what description soever denominated, wherever the distinction of rank prevails, or is admitted by the constitution, this species of slavery exists. It existed in every nation, and in every government in Europe before the French revolution. It existed in the American colonies before they became independent states; and notwithstanding the maxims of equality which have been adopted in their several constitutions, it exists in most, if not all, of them, at this day, in the persons of our *free* negroes and mulattoes; whose civil incapacities are almost as numerous as the civil rights of our free citizens. A brief enumeration of them, may not be improper before we proceed to the third head.

Free negroes and mulattoes are by our constitution excluded from the right of suffrage *, and by consequence, I apprehend, from office too: they were formerly incapable of serving in the militia, except as drummers or pioneers, but of late years I presume they were enrolled in the lists of those that bear arms †, though formerly punishable for presuming

---

* Blacks. Com. 125. I should rather incline to think this definition of *civil* liberty more applicable to *social* liberty, for reasons mentioned in a note, page 145, Vol. I. of Blackstone's Commentaries.

* The constitution of Virginia, Art. 7, declares, that the right of suffrage shall remain as then exercised: the act of 1723, c. 4, (Edi. 1733,) Sec. 23, declared, that no negroe, mulattoe, or Indian, shall have any vote at the election of burgesses, or any other election whatsoever. This act, it is presumed, was in force at the adoption of the constitution. The act of 1785, c. 55, (Edi. of 1794, c. 17,) also expressly excludes them from the right of suffrage.

† This was the case under the laws of the state; but the act of 2 Cong. c. 33, for establishing an uniform militia throughout

to appear at a musterfield [††]. During the revolutionary war many of them were enlisted as soldiers in the regular army. Even slaves were not rejected from military service at that period, and such as served faithfully during the period of their enlistment, were emancipated by an act passed after the conclusion of the war [1]. An act of justice to which they were entitled upon every principle. All but house-keepers, and persons residing upon the frontiers, are prohibited from keeping, or carrying any gun, powder, shot, club, or other weapon offensive or defensive [2]: Resistance to a white person, in any case, was, formerly, and now, in any case, except a wanton assault on the negroe or mulattoe, is punishable by whipping [**]. No negroe or mulattoe can be a witness in any prosecution, or civil suit in which a white person is a party [†]. Free negroes, together with slaves, were formerly denied the benefit of clergy in cases where it was allowed to white persons; but they are now upon an equal footing as to the allowance of clergy [††]. Emancipated negroes may be sold to pay the debts of their former master contracted before their emancipation; and they may be hired out to satisfy their taxes where no sufficient distress can be had. Their children are to be bound out apprentices by the overseers of the poor. Free negroes have all the advantages in capital cases, which white men are entitled to, except a trial by a jury of their own complexion: and a slave suing for his freedom shall have the same privilege. Free negroes residing, or employed to labour in any town, must be registered; the same thing is required of such as go at large in any county. The penalty in both cases is a fine upon the person employing, or harbouring them, and imprisonment of the negroe [*]. The migration of free negroes or mulattoes to this state is also prohibited; and those who do migrate hither may be sent back to the place from whence they came [†]. Any person, not being a negroe, having one-fourth or more negroe blood in him, is deemed a mulattoe. The law formerly made no other distinction between negroes and mulattoes, whether slaves or freemen. But now the act of 1796, c. 2, which abolishes the punishment of death, except in case of murder, in all cases where any free person may be convicted, creates a most important distinction in their favour; slaves not being entitled to the same benefit. These incapacities and disabilities are evidently the fruit of the third species of slavery, of which it remains to speak; or, rather, they are scions from the same common stock: which is,

III. That condition in which one man is subject to be directed by another in all his actions, and this constitutes a state of *domestic slavery;* to which state all the incapacities and disabilities of civil slavery are

the United States; seems to have excluded all but free white men from bearing arms in the militia.
[††] 1723, c. 2.
[1.] Oct. 1783, c. 3.
[2.] 1748, c. 31. Edi. 1794.

[**] Ibid. c. 103.
[†] 1794, c. 141.
[††] 1794, c. 103.
[*] 1794, c. 163.
[†] 1794, c. 164.

incident, with the weight of other numerous calamities superadded
thereto.   And here it may be proper to make a short inquiry into the
origin and foundation of domestic slavery in other countries, previous to
it's fatal introduction into this.

Slaves, says Justinian, are either born such or become so [††].   They
are born slaves when they are children of bond women; and they become
slaves, either by the law of nations, that is, by captivity; for it is the
practice of our generals to sell their captives, being accustomed to
preserve, and not to destroy them: or by the civil law, which happens
when a free person, above the age of twenty, suffers himself to be sold
for the sake of sharing the price given for him.   The author of the
Commentaries on the Laws of England thus combats the reasonableness
of all these grounds:[*] "The conqueror," says he, "according to the
civilians, had a right to the life of his captive; and having spared that,
has a right to deal with him as he pleases.   But it is an untrue position,
when taken generally, that by the law of nature or nations, a man may
kill his enemy: he has a right to kill him only in particular cases; in
cases of absolute necessity for self-defence; and it is plain that this
absolute necessity did not subsist, since the victor did not actually kill
him, but made him prisoner.   War itself is justifiable only on principles
of self-preservation; and therefore it gives no other right over prisoners
but merely to disable them from doing harm to us, by confining their
persons: much less can it give a right to kill, torture, abuse, plunder, or
even to enslave, an enemy, when the war is over.   Since, therefore, the
right of *making* slaves by captivity, depends on a supposed right of
slaughter, that foundation failing, the consequence drawn from it must
fail likewise.   But, secondly, it is said slavery may begin *jure civili;*
when one man sells himself to another.   This, if only meant of contracts
to serve, or work for, another, is very just: but when applied to strict
slavery, in the sense of the laws of old Rome or modern Barbary, is also
impossible.   Every sale implies a price, a *quid pro quo*, an equivalent
given to the seller, in lieu of what he transfers to the buyer; but what
equivalent can be given for life and liberty, both of which, in absolute
slavery, are held to be in the master's disposal?   His property, also, the
very price he seems to receive, devolves, *ipso facto*, to his master, the
instant he becomes a slave.   In this case, therefore, the buyer gives
nothing, and the seller receives nothing: of what validity then can a sale
be, which destroys the very principles upon which all sales are founded?
Lastly we are told, that besides these two ways by which slaves are
acquired, they may also be hereditary; "*servi nascuntur;*" the children
of acquired slaves are, "*jure naturœ*," by a negative kind of birthright,
slaves also.....   But *this, being built on the two former rights*, must *fall*
together with them.   If neither captivity, nor the sale of one's self, can
by the law of nature and reason reduce the parent to slavery, *much less*
can they reduce the offspring."   Thus by the most clear, manly, and

†† Inst. lib. 1. tit. 1.   * 1 b. c. 423.

convincing reasoning does this excellent author refute every claim, upon which the practice of slavery is founded, or by which it has been supposed to be justified, at least, in modern times *. But were we even to admit, that a captive taken in a *just war*, might by his conqueror be reduced to a state of slavery, this could not justify the claim of Europeans to reduce the natives of Africa to that state: it is a melancholy, though well-known fact, that in order to furnish supplies of these unhappy people for the purposes of the slave trade, the Europeans have constantly, by the most insidious (I had almost said infernal) arts, fomented a kind of perpetual warfare among the ignorant and miserable people of Africa; and instances have not been wanting, where, by the most shameful breach of faith, they have trepanned and made slaves of the *sellers* as well as the *sold* †. That such horrid practices have been sanctioned by a civilized nation; that a nation ardent in the cause of

---

* These arguments are, in fact, borrowed from the Spirit of Laws. Lib. xv. c. 2.

† "About the same time (the reign of queen Elizabeth) a traffic in the human species, called negroes, was introduced into England, which is one of the most odious and unnatural branches of trade the sordid and avaricious mind of mortals ever invented. . . . It had been carried on before this period by Genoese traders, who bought a patent from Charles the fifth, containing an exclusive right of carrying negroes from the Portuguese settlements in Africa, to America and the West-Indies; but the English nation had not yet engaged in the iniquitous traffic. . . . . One William Hawkins, an expert English seaman, having made several voyages to the coast of Guinea, and from thence to Brazil and the West-Indies, had acquired considerable knowledge of these countries. At his death he left his journals with his son, John Hawkins, in which he described the lands of America and the West-Indies as exceedingly rich and fertile, but utterly neglected for want of hands to improve them. He represented the natives of Europe as unequal to the task in such a scorching climate; but those of Africa as well adapted to undergo the labours requisite. Upon which John Hawkins immediately formed a design of transporting Africans into the western world; and having drawn a plan for the execution of it, he laid it before some of his opulent neighbours for encouragement and approbation. To them it appeared promising and advantageous. A subscription was opened and speedily filled up, by Sir Lionel Ducket, Sir Thomas Lodge, Sir William Winter, and others, who plainly perceived the vast profits that would result from such a trade. Accordingly three ships were fitted out, and manned by an hundred select sailors, whom Hawkins encouraged to go with him by promises of good treatment and great pay. In the year 1562 he set sail for Africa, and in a few weeks arrived at the country called Sierra Leona, where he began his commerce with the negroes. While he trafficked with them, he found the means of giving them a charming description of the country to which he was bound; the unsuspicious Africans listened to him with apparent joy and satisfaction, and seemed remarkably fond of his European trinkets, food, and clothes. He pointed out to them the barrenness of the country, and their naked and wretched condition, and promised if any of them were weary of their miserable circumstances, and would go along with him, he would carry them to a plentiful land, where they should *live happy*, and *receive* an abundant *recompence* for their labours. He told them the country was inhabited by such men as himself and his jovial companions, and *assured* them of *kind usage* and *great friendship*. In short, the negroes were overcome by his flattering promises, and *three hundred* stout fellows accepted his offer, and consented to embark along with him. Every thing being settled on the most amicable terms between them, Hawkins made preparations for his voyage. But in the night before his departure his negroes were attacked by a large body from a different quarter; Hawkins, being alarmed with the shrieks and cries of dying persons, ordered his men to the assistance of his slaves, and having surrounded the assailants, carried a number of them on board as prisoners of war. The next day he set sail for Hispaniola with his cargo of human creatures; but during the passage, he treated the prisoners of war in a different manner from his vol-

liberty, and enjoying it's blessings in the fullest extent, can continue to vindicate a right established upon such a foundation; that a people who have declared, "That *all men* are by nature *equally* * *free* and *independent*," and have made this declaration the first article in the foundation of their government, should in defiance of so sacred a truth, recognized by themselves in so solemn a manner, and on so important an occasion, tolerate a practice incompatible therewith, is such an evidence of the weakness and inconsistency of human nature, as every man who hath a spark of patriotic fire in his bosom must wish to see removed from his own country. If ever there was a cause, if ever an occasion, in which all hearts should be united, every nerve strained, and every power exerted, surely the restoration of human nature to it's unalienable right, is such. Whatever obstacles, therefore, may hitherto have retarded the attempt, he that can appreciate the honour and happiness of his country, will think it time that we should attempt to surmount them.

* * *

unteers. Upon his arrival, he disposed of his cargo to great advantage; and endeavoured to inculcate on the Spaniards who bought the negroes the same distinction to be observed: but they having *purchased all at the same rate*, considered them as slaves of the same condition, and consequently treated all alike."

* Bill of Rights, Article 1.

Hawkins having returned to England, soon after made preparations for a second voyage. "In his passage he fell in with the Minion man of war, which accompanied him to the coast of Africa. After his arrival he began as formerly to traffic with the negroes, endeavouring by persuasions and *prospects* of *reward*, to induce them to go along with him.... but now they were more reserved and jealous of his designs, and as none of their neighbours had returned, they were apprehensive he had killed and eat them. The crew of the man of war observing the Africans backward and suspicious, began to laugh at his gentle and dilatory methods of proceeding, and proposed having immediate recourse to force and compulsion .... but Hawkins considered it as cruel and unjust, and tried by persuasions, promises and threats, to prevail on them to desist from a purpose so unwarrantable and barbarous. In vain did he urge his authority and instructions from the queen: the bold and headstrong sailors would hear of no restraints. Drunkenness and avarice are deaf to the voice of humanity. They pursue their violent design, and, after several unsuccessful attacks, in which

many of them lost their *lives*, the cargo was at length completed by barbarity and force.

"Hence arose that horrid and inhuman practice of dragging Africans into slavery, which has since been *so* pursued, in defiance of every principle of justice and religion. Had negroes been brought from the flames, to which in some countries they were devoted on their falling prisoners of war, and in others, sacrificed at the funeral obsequies of the great and powerful among themselves; in short, had they by this traffic been delivered from *torture* or *death*, European merchants *might have some excuse* to plead in it's vindication. *But according to the common mode in which it has been conducted*, we must confess it a difficult matter to conceive a *single* argument in it's defence. And though policy has given countenance and sanction to the trade, yet every candid and impartial man must confess, that it is atrocious and unjustifiable in every light in which it can be viewed, and turns merchants into a band of robbers, and trade into atrocious acts of fraud and violence." Historical Account of South-Carolina and Georgia. Anonymous. London printed in 1779.... page 20, &c.

"The number of negroe slaves bartered for in one year, (viz. 1768), on the coast of Africa from Cape Blanco, to Rio Congress amounted to 104,000 souls, whereof more than half (viz. 53,000) were shipped on account of British merchants, and 6,300 on the account of British Americans." The Law of Retribution, by Granville Sharpe, Esq. page 147. note.

640

... To establish such a colony in the territory of the United States, would probably lay the foundation of intestine wars, which would terminate only in their extirpation, or final expulsion. To attempt it in any other quarter of the globe would be attended with the utmost cruelty to the colonists, themselves, and the destruction of their whole race. If the plan were at this moment in operation, it would require the annual exportation of 12,000 persons. This requisite number must, for a series of years be considerably increased, in order to keep pace with the increasing population of those people. In twenty years it would amount to upwards of twenty thousand persons; which is near half the number which are now supposed to be annually exported from Africa...... Where would a fund to support this expence be found? Five times the present revenue of the state would barely defray the charge of their passage. Where provisions for their support after their arrival? Where those necessaries which must preserve them from perishing? ....Where a territory sufficient to support them? ....Or where could they be received as friends, and not as invaders? To colonize them in the United States might seem less difficult. If the territory to be assigned them were beyond the settlements of the whites, would they not be put upon a forlorn hope against the Indians *; would not the expence of transporting them thither, and supporting them, at least for the first and second years, be also far beyond the revenues and abilities of the state? The expence attending a small army in that country hath been found enormous. To transport as many colonists, annually, as we have shewn, were necessary to eradicate the evil, would probably require five times as much money as the support of such an army. But the expence would not stop there: they must be assisted and supported at least for another year after their arrival in their new settlements. Suppose them arrived. Illiterate and ignorant as they are, is it probable that they would be capable of instituting such a government, in their new colony, as would be necessary for their own internal happiness, or to secure them from destruction from without? European emigrants, from whatever country they arrive, have been accustomed to the restraint of laws, and to respect for government. These people, accustomed to be ruled with a rod of iron, will not easily submit to milder restraints. They would become hordes of vagabonds, robbers and murderers. Without the aids of an enlightened policy, morality, or religion, what else could be expected from their still savage state, and debased condition? ...."But why not retain and *"incorporate the blacks into the state*?" This question has been well answered by Mr. Jefferson *, and who is there so free from

---

* Or, perhaps, by incorporating with them, become a formidable accession of strength to those hostile savages?

* "It will probably be asked, why not retain the blacks among us, and *incorporate them into the state?* Deep rooted prejudices entertained by the whites; ten thousand recollections by the blacks, of the injuries they have sustained; new provocations; the *real distinctions* which *nature* has made; and many other circumstances will divide us into parties and produce convulsions, which will probably never end but in the extermination of one or the other race. To

prejudices among us, as candidly to declare that he has none against such a measure? The recent scenes transacted in the French colonies in the West Indies are enough to make one shudder with the apprehension of realizing similar calamities in this country. Such probably would be the event of an attempt to smother those prejudices which have been cherished for a period of almost two centuries. Many persons who regret domestic slavery, contend that in abolishing it, we must also abolish that scion from it, which I have denominated *civil* slavery. That there must be no distinction of rights; that the descendants of Africans, as men, have an equal claim to all civil rights, as the descendants of Europeans; and upon being delivered from the yoke of bondage have a right to be admitted to all the privileges of a citizen..... But have not men when they enter into a state of society, a right to admit, or exclude any description of persons, as they think proper? If it be true, as Mr. Jefferson seems to suppose, that the Africans are really an inferior race of mankind *, will not sound policy advise their exclusion from a society in which they have not yet been admitted to participate in civil rights; and even to guard againt such admission, at any future period, since it may eventually depreciate the whole national character? And if prejudices have taken such deep root in our minds, as to render it impossible

these objections, which are political, may be added others which are physical and moral. The first difference which strikes us is that of colour...&c. The circumstance of superior beauty is thought worthy of attention in the propagation of our horses, dogs, and other domestic animals; why not in that of man? &c. In general their existence appears to participate more of sensation than reflection. Comparing them by their faculties of memory, reason and imagination, it appears to me that in memory they are equal to the whites; in reason much inferior; that in imagination they are dull, tasteless and anamolous, &c. The improvement of the blacks in body and mind, in the first instance of their mixture with the whites, has been observed by every one, and proves that their inferiority is not the effect merely of their condition of life. We know that among the Romans about the Augustan age, especially, the condition of their slaves was much more deplorable, than that of the blacks on the continent of America. Yet among the Romans their slaves were often their rarest artists. They excelled too in science, insomuch as to be usually employed as tutors to their master's children. Epictetus, Terence, and Phœdrus were slaves. But they were of the race of whites. It is not their condition then, but nature which has produced the distinction. The opinion that they are inferior in the faculties of reason and imagination, must be hazarded with great diffidence. To justify a general conclusion requires many observations, &c.... I advance it, therefore, as a suspicion only, that the blacks, whether originally a distinct race, or made distinct by time and circumstances, are inferior to the whites both in the endowments of body and mind, &c. This unfortunate difference of colour, and perhaps of faculty, is a powerful obstacle to the emancipation of these people. Among the Romans emancipation required but one effort. The slave, when made free, might mix with, without staining the blood of his master. But with us a second is necessary, unknown to history".... See the passage at length, Notes on Virginia, page, 252 to 265.

"In the present case, it is not only the slave who is beneath his "master, it is the negroe who is beneath the white man. No act "of enfranchisement can efface this unfortunate distinction." Chattelleux's Travels in America.

* The celebrated David Hume, in his Essay on National Character, advances the same opinion; Doctor Beattie, in his Essay on Truth, controverts it with many powerful arguments. Early prejudices, had we more satisfactory information than we can possibly possess on the subject at present, would render an inhabitant of a country where negroe slavery prevails, an improper umpire between them.

to eradicate this opinion, ought not so general an error, if it be one, to be respected? Shall we not relieve the necessities of the naked diseased beggar, unless we will invite him to a seat at our table; nor afford him shelter from the inclemencies of the night air, unless we admit him also to share our bed! To deny that we ought to abolish slavery, without incorporating the Negroes into the state, and admitting them to a full participation of all our civil and social rights, appears to me to rest upon a similar foundation. The experiment so far as it has been already made among us, proves that the emancipated blacks are not ambitious of civil rights. To prevent the generation of such an ambition, appears to comport with sound policy; for if it should ever rear its head, its partizans, as well as its opponents, will be enlisted by nature herself, and always ranged in formidable array against each other *. We must therefore endeavour to find some middle course, between the tyrannical and iniquitous policy which holds so many human creatures in a state of grievous bondage, and that which would turn loose a numerous, starving, and enraged banditti, upon the innocent descendants of their former oppressors. *Nature*, *time* and *sound policy* must co-operate with each other to produce such a change: if either be neglected, the work will be incomplete, dangerous, and not improbably destructive.

The plan therefore which I would presume to propose for the consideration of my countrymen is such, as the number of slaves, the difference of their nature, and habits, and the state of agriculture, among us, might render it *expedient*, rather than *desirable* to adopt: and would partake partly of that proposed by Mr. Jefferson, and adopted in other states; and partly of such cautionary restrictions, as a due regard to situation and circumstances, and even to *general* prejudices, might recommend to those, who engage in so arduous, and perhaps unprecedented an undertaking.

1. Let every female born after the adoption of the plan, be free, and transmit freedom to all the descendants, both male and female.

2. As a compensation to those persons, in whose families such females, or their descendants may be born, for the expence and trouble of their maintenance during infancy, let them serve such persons until the age of twenty-eight years: let them then receive twenty dollars in money, two suits of clothes, suited to the season, a hat, a pair of shoes, and two blankets. If these things be not voluntarily done, let the county courts enforce the performance, upon complaint.

3. Let all negroe children be registered with the clerk of the county or corporation court, where born, within one month after their birth: let the person in whose family they are born, take a copy of the register, and

---

* It was once proposed among the Romans to discriminate slaves, by a *peculiar habit;* but it was justly apprehended that there might be some danger in acquainting them with their own numbers...... Gibbon's Hist. of the Rom. Emp. Vol. I. p. 59. What policy forbade the martial Romans to do, nature and the federal census have already done in Virginia, and the other southern states.

deliver it to the mother, or if she die, to the child, before it is of the age of twenty-one years. Let any negro claiming to be free, and above the age of puberity, be considered as of the age of twenty-eight years, if he or she be not registered as required.

4. Let all the negro servants be put on the same footing as white servants and apprentices now are, in respect to food, raiment, correction, and the assignment of their service from one to another.

5. Let the children of negroes and mulattoes, born in the families of their parents, be bound to service by the overseers of the poor, until they shall attain the age of twenty-one years. Let all above that age, who are not house-keepers, nor have voluntarily bound themselves to service for a year before the first day of February annually, be then bound for the remainder of the year by the overseers of the poor. To stimulate the overseers of the poor to perform their duty, let them receive fifteen per cent. of their wages, from the person hiring them, as a compensation for their trouble, and ten per cent. per annum out of the wages of such as they may bind apprentices.

6. If at the age of twenty-seven years, the master of a negro or mulattoe servant be unwilling to pay his freedom dues, above mentioned, at the expiration of the succeeding year, let him bring him into the county court, clad and furnished with necessaries as before directed, and pay into court five dollars, for the servant, and thereupon let the court direct him to be hired by the overseers of the poor for the succeeding year, in the manner before directed.

7. Let no negro or mulatto be capable of taking, holding, or exercising, any public office, freehold, franchise, or privilege *, or any estate in lands or tenements, other than a lease not exceeding twenty-one years.... Nor of keeping, or bearing arms †, unless authorised so to do by some act of the general assembly, whose duration shall be limited to three years. Nor of contracting matrimony with any other than a negroe or mulattoe; nor be an attorney; nor be a juror; nor a witness in any court of judicature, except against, or between negroes and mulattoes. Nor be an executor or administrator; nor capable of making any will or testament; nor maintain any real action; nor be a trustee of lands or tenements himself, nor any other person to be a trustee to him or to his use.

8. Let all persons born after the passing of the act, be considered as entitled to the same mode of trial in criminal cases, as free negroes and mulattoes are now entitled to.

The restrictions in this plan may appear to savour strongly of prejudice: whoever proposes any plan for the abolition of slavery must either encounter, or accommodate himself, to prejudice.... I have

* The Romans, before the time of Justinian, adopted a similar policy, in respect to their freed-men. Gibbon, vol. 1, 58.

† See Spirit of Laws, 12, 15, 1. Blackst. Com. 417.

preferred the latter; not that I pretend to be wholly exempt from it, but that I might avoid as many obstacles as possible to the completion of so desirable a work, as the abolition of slavery.[††] Though I am opposed to the banishment of the negroes, I wish not to encourage their future residence among us. By denying them the most valuable privileges which civil government affords, I wish to render it their inclination and their interest to seek those privileges in some other climate. There is an immense unsettled territory on this continent [*] more congenial to their natural constitutions than ours, where they may perhaps be received upon more favourable terms than we can permit them to remain with us. Emigrating in small numbers, they will be able to effect settlements more easily than in large numbers; and without the expence or danger of numerous colonies. By releasing them from the yoke of bondage, and enabling them to seek happiness wherever they can hope to find it, we surely confer a benefit, which no one can sufficiently appreciate, who has not tasted of the bitter curse of compulsory servitude. By excluding them from offices, we may hope that the seeds of ambition would be buried too deep, ever to germinate: by disarming them, we may calm our apprehensions of their resentments arising from past sufferings; by incapacitating them from holding lands, we should add one inducement more to emigration, and effectually remove the foundation of ambition, and party-struggles. Their personal rights, and their property, though limited, would, whilst they remain among us, be under the protection of the laws; and their condition not at all inferior to that of the *labouring* poor in most other countries. Under such an arrangement we might reasonably hope, that time would either remove from us a race of men, whom we wish not to incorporate with us, or obliterate those prejudices, which now form an obstacle to such incorporation.

But it is not from the want of liberality to the emancipated race of blacks that I apprehend the most serious objections to the plan I have ventured to suggest.... Those slave holders (whose numbers I trust are few) who have been in the habit of considering their fellow creatures as no more than cattle, and the rest of the brute creation, will exclaim that they are to be deprived of their *property*, without compensation. Men who will shut their ears against this moral truth, that all men are by nature *free*, and *equal*, will not even be convinced that they do not possess a *property* in an *unborn* child: they will not distinguish between allowing to *unborn* generations the absolute and unalienable rights of

---

[††] If, upon experiment, it should appear advisable to hasten the operation of this plan, or to enlarge the privileges of free negroes, it will be both easier, and safer so to do, than to retrench any privilege once granted, or to retard the operation of the original plan, after it has been adopted, and in part carried into execution.

[*] The immense territory of Louisiana, which extends as far south as the lat. 25 and the two Floridas, would probably afford a ready asylum for such as might choose to become Spanish subjects. How far their political rights might be enlarged in these countries, is, however, questionable: but the climate is undoubtedly more favourable to the African constitution, than ours, and from this cause it is not improbable that emigrations from these states would in time be very considerable.

human nature, and taking away that which they *now possess;* they will shut their ears against truth, should you tell them, the loss of the mother's labour for nine months, and the maintenance of a child for a dozen or fourteen years, is amply compensated by the service of that child for as many years more, as he has been an expence to them. But if the voice of reason, justice, and humanity, be not stifled by sordid avarice, or unfeeling tyranny, it would be easy to convince even those who have entertained such erroneous notions, that the right of one man over another is neither founded in nature, nor in sound policy. That it cannot extend to those *not in being;* that no man can in reality be *deprived* of what he doth not possess: that fourteen years labour by a young person in the prime of life, is an ample compensation for a few months of labour lost by the mother, and for the maintenance of a child, in that coarse homely manner that negroes are brought up: and lastly, that a state of slavery is not only perfectly incompatible with the principles of government, but with the safety and security of their masters. History evinces this. At this moment we have the most awful demonstrations of it. Shall we then neglect a duty, which every consideration, moral, religious, political, or *selfish*, recommends? Those who wish to postpone the measure, do not reflect that every day renders the task more arduous to be performed. We have now 300,000 slaves among us. Thirty years hence we shall have double the number. In sixty years we shall have 1,200,000: and in less than another century from this day, even that enormous number will be doubled. Milo acquired strength enough to carry an ox, by beginning with the ox while he was yet a calf. If we complain that the calf is too heavy for our shoulders, what will the ox be?

To such as apprehend danger to our agricultural interest, and the depriving the families of those whose principal reliance is upon their slaves, of support, it will be proper to submit a view of the gradual operation, and effects of this plan. They will, no doubt, be surprised to hear, that, whenever it is adopted, the number of slaves will not be diminished for forty years after it takes place; that it will even increase for thirty years; that at the distance of sixty years, there will be one-third of the number at it's first commencement: that it will require *above a century* to complete it; and that the number of blacks *under twenty-eight* and consequently bound to service, in the families they are born in, will always be at least as great, as the present number of slaves. These circumstances, I trust, will remove many objections, and that they are truly stated will appear upon inquiry.

K. DECLARATION OF THE NATIONAL ANTI–SLAVERY CONVENTION

1833

More than fifty-seven years have elapsed since a band of patriots convened in this place to devise measures for the deliverance of this

646

country from a foreign yoke. The cornerstone upon which they founded the TEMPLE OF FREEDOM was broadly this—"that all men are created equal; that they are endowed by their Creator with certain inalienable rights; that among these are life, LIBERTY, and the pursuit of happiness." At the sound of their trumpet-call, three millions of people rose up as from the sleep of death, and rushed to the strife of blood; deeming it more glorious to die instantly as freemen, than desirable to live one hour as slaves. . . .

We have met together for the achievement of an enterprise, without which, that of our fathers is incomplete, and which, for its magnitude, solemnity, and probable results upon the destiny of the world, as far transcends theirs, as moral truth does physical force.

In purity of motive, in earnestness of zeal, in decision of purpose, in intrepidity of action, in steadfastness of faith, in sincerity of spirit, we would not be inferior to them.

Their principles led them to wage war against their oppressors, and to spill human blood like water, in order to be free. *Ours* forbid the doing of evil that good may come, and lead us to reject, and to entreat the oppressed to reject, the use of all carnal weapons for deliverance from bondage—relying solely upon those which are spiritual, and mighty through God to the pulling down of strong holds.

Their measures were physical resistance—the marshalling in arms—the hostile array—the mortal encounter. *Ours* shall be such only as the opposition of moral purity to moral corruption—the destruction of error by the potency of truth—the overthrow of prejudice by the power of love—and the abolition of slavery by the spirit of repentance.

Their grievances, great as they were, were trifling in comparison with the wrongs and sufferings of those for whom we plead. Our fathers were never slaves—never bought and sold like cattle—never shut out from the light of knowledge and religion—never subjected to the lash of brutal taskmasters.

But those, for whose emancipation we are striving,—constituting at the present time at least one-sixth part of our countrymen—are recognized by the laws, and treated by their fellow beings, as marketable commodities—as good[s] and chattels—as brute beasts;—are plundered daily of the fruits of their toil without redress;—really enjoy no constitutional nor legal protection from licentious and murderous outrages upon their persons;—are ruthlessly torn asunder—the tender babe from the arms of its frantic mother—the heart-broken wife from her weeping husband—at the caprice or pleasure of irresponsible tyrants;—and, for the crime of having a dark complexion, suffer the pangs of hunger, the infliction of stripes, and the ignominy of brutal servitude. They are kept in heathenish darkness by laws expressly enacted to make their instruction a criminal offence.

L. RESOLUTIONS AND DECLARATION OF SENTIMENTS OF THE WOMAN'S RIGHTS CONVENTION, HELD AT SENECA FALLS

July 19–20 1848

A Convention to discuss the Social, Civil, and Religious Condition of Woman, was called by the Women of Seneca County, N.Y., and held at the village of Seneca Falls, in the Wesleyan Chapel, on the 19th and 20th of July, 1848.

The question was discussed throughout two entire days: the first day by women exclusively, the second day men participated in the deliberations. Lucretia Mott, of Philadelphia, was the moving spirit of the occasion.

On the morning of the 19th, the Convention assembled at 11 o'clock. The meeting was organized by appointing Mary M'Clintock Secretary. The object of the meeting was then stated by Elizabeth C. Stanton; after which, remarks were made by Lucretia Mott, urging the women present to throw aside the trammels of education, and not allow their new position to prevent them from joining in the debates of the meeting. The Declaration of Sentiments, offered for the acceptance of the Convention, was then read by E. C. Stanton. A proposition was made to have it re-read by paragraph, and after much consideration, some changes were suggested and adopted. The propriety of obtaining the signatures of men to the Declaration was discussed in an animated manner: a vote in favor was given; but concluding that the final decision would be the legitimate business of the next day, it was referred.

Adjourned to half-past two.

In the afternoon, the meeting assembled according to adjournment, and was opened by reading the minutes of the morning session. E. C. Stanton then addressed the meeting, and was followed by Lucretia Mott. The reading of the Declaration was called for, an addition having been inserted since the morning session. A vote taken upon the amendment was carried, and papers circulated to obtain signatures. The following resolutions were then read:

Whereas, the great precept of nature is conceded to be, "that man shall pursue his own true and substantial happiness," Blackstone, in his Commentaries, remarks, that this law of Nature being coeval with mankind, and dictated by God himself, is of course superior in obligation to any other. It is binding over all the globe, in all countries, and at all times; no human laws are of any validity if contrary to this, and such of them as are valid, derive all their force, and all their validity, and all their authority, mediately and immediately, from this original; Therefore,

Resolved, That such laws as conflict, in any way, with the true and substantial happiness of woman, are contrary to the great precept of nature, and of no validity; for this is "superior in obligation to any other."

Resolved, That all laws which prevent woman from occupying such a station in society as her conscience shall dictate, or which place her in a position inferior to that of man, are contrary to the great precept of nature, and therefore of no force or authority.

Resolved, That woman is man's equal—was intended to be so by the Creator, and the highest good of the race demands that she should be recognized as such.

Resolved, That the women of this country ought to be enlightened in regard to the laws under which they live, that they may no longer publish their degradation, by declaring themselves satisfied with their present position, nor their ignorance, by asserting that they have all the rights they want.

Resolved, That inasmuch as man, while claiming for himself intellectual superiority, does accord to woman moral superiority, it is preeminently his duty to encourage her to speak, and teach, as she has an opportunity, in all religious assemblies.

Resolved, That the same amount of virtue, delicacy, and refinement of behavior, that is required of woman in the social state, should also be required of man, and the same transgressions should be visited with equal severity on both man and woman.

Resolved, That the objection of indelicacy and impropriety, which is so often brought against woman when she addresses a public audience, comes with a very ill grace from those who encourage, by their attendance, her appearance on the stage, in the concert, or in the feats of the circus.

Resolved, That woman has too long rested satisfied in the circumscribed limits which corrupt customs and a perverted application of the Scriptures have marked out for her, and that it is time she should move in the enlarged sphere which her great Creator has assigned her.

Resolved, That it is the duty of the women of this country to secure to themselves their sacred right to the elective franchise.

Resolved, That the equality of human rights results necessarily from the fact of the identity of the race in capabilities and responsibilities.

Resolved, therefore, That, being invested by the Creator with the same capabilities, and the same consciousness of responsibility for their exercise, it is demonstrably the right and duty of woman, equally with man, to promote every righteous cause, by every righteous means; and especially in regard to the great subjects of morals and religion, it is self-evidently her right to participate with her brother in teaching them, both in private and in public, by writing and by speaking, by any instrumentalities proper to be used, and in any assemblies proper to be held; and this being a self-evident truth, growing out of the divinely implanted principles of human nature, any custom or authority adverse to it, whether modern or wearing the hoary sanction of antiquity, is to be regarded as self-evident falsehood, and at war with the interests of mankind.

Lucretia Mott read a humorous article from a newspaper, written by Martha C. Wright. After an address by E. W. M'Clintock, the meeting adjourned to 10 o'clock the next morning.

In the evening, Lucretia Mott spoke with her usual eloquence and power to a large and intelligent audience on the subject of Reforms in general.

THURSDAY MORNING.

The Convention assembled at the hour appointed, James Mott, of Philadelphia, in the Chair. The minutes of the previous day having been read, E. C. Stanton again read the Declaration of Sentiments, which was freely discussed by Lucretia Mott, Ansel Bascom, S. E. Woodworth, Thomas and Mary Ann M'Clintock, Frederick Douglass, Amy Post, Catharine Stebbins, and Elizabeth C. Stanton, and was unanimously adopted, as follows:

DECLARATION OF SENTIMENTS.

When, in the course of human events, it becomes necessary for one portion of the family of man to assume among the people of the earth a position different from that which they have hitherto occupied, but one to which the laws of nature and of nature's God entitle them, a decent respect to the opinions of mankind requires that they should declare the causes that impel them to such a course.

We hold these truths to be self-evident: that all men and women are created equal; that they are endowed by their Creator with certain inalienable rights; that among these are life, liberty, and the pursuit of happiness; that to secure these rights governments are instituted, deriving their just powers from the consent of the governed. Whenever any form of Government becomes destructive of these ends, it is the right of those who suffer from it to refuse allegiance to it, and to insist upon the institution of a new government, laying its foundation on such principles, and organizing its powers in such form as to them shall seem most likely to effect their safety and happiness. Prudence, indeed, will dictate that governments long established should not be changed for light and transient causes; and accordingly, all experience hath shown that mankind are more disposed to suffer, while evils are sufferable, than to right themselves by abolishing the forms to which they are accustomed. But when a long train of abuses and usurpations, pursuing invariably the same object, evinces a design to reduce them under absolute despotism, it is their duty to throw off such government, and to provide new guards for their future security. Such has been the patient sufferance of the women under this government, and such is now the necessity which constrains them to demand the equal station to which they are entitled.

The history of mankind is a history of repeated injuries and usurpations on the part of man toward woman, having in direct object the establishment of an absolute tyranny over her. To prove this, let facts be submitted to a candid world.

He has never permitted her to exercise her inalienable right to the elective franchise.

He has compelled her to submit to laws, in the formation of which she had no voice.

He has withheld from her rights which are given to the most ignorant and degraded men—both natives and foreigners.

Having deprived her of this first right of a citizen, the elective franchise, thereby leaving her without representation in the halls of legislation, he has oppressed her on all sides.

He has made her, if married, in the eye of the law, civilly dead.

He has taken from her all right in property, even to the wages she earns.

He has made her, morally, an irresponsible being, as she can commit many crimes with impunity, provided they be done in the presence of her husband. In the covenant of marriage, she is compelled to promise obedience to her husband, he becoming, to all intents and purposes, her master—the law giving him power to deprive her of her liberty, and to administer chastisement.

He has so framed the laws of divorce, as to what shall be the proper causes of divorce; in case of separation, to whom the guardianship of the children shall be given; as to be wholly regardless of the happiness of women—the law, in all cases, going upon the false supposition of the supremacy of man, and giving all power into his hands.

After depriving her of all rights as a married woman, if single and the owner of property, he has taxed her to support a government which recognizes her only when her property can be made profitable to it.

He has monopolized nearly all the profitable employments, and from those she is permitted to follow, she receives but a scanty remuneration.

He closes against her all the avenues to wealth and distinction, which he considers most honorable to himself. As a teacher of theology, medicine, or law, she is not known.

He has denied her the facilities for obtaining a thorough education— all colleges being closed against her.

He allows her in Church as well as State, but a subordinate position, claiming Apostolic authority for her exclusion from the ministry, and, with some exceptions, from any public participation in the affairs of the Church.

He has created a false public sentiment, by giving to the world a different code of morals for men and women, by which moral delinquencies which exclude women from society, are not only tolerated but deemed of little account in man.

He has usurped the prerogative of Jehovah himself, claiming it as his right to assign for her a sphere of action, when that belongs to her conscience and her God.

He has endeavored, in every way that he could to destroy her confidence in her own powers, to lessen her self-respect, and to make her willing to lead a dependant and abject life.

Now, in view of this entire disfranchisement of one-half the people of this country, their social and religious degradation,—in view of the unjust laws above mentioned, and because women do feel themselves aggrieved, oppressed, and fraudulently deprived of their most sacred rights, we insist that they have immediate admission to all the rights and privileges which belong to them as citizens of these United States.

In entering upon the great work before us, we anticipate no small amount of misconception, misrepresentation, and ridicule; but we shall use every instrumentality within our power to effect our object. We shall employ agents, circulate tracts, petition the State and national Legislatures, and endeavor to enlist the pulpit and the press in our behalf. We hope this Convention will be followed by a series of Conventions, embracing every part of the country.

Firmly relying upon the final triumph of the Right and the True, we do this day affix our signatures to this declaration.

Lucretia Mott,
Harriet Cady Eaton,
Margaret Pryor,
Elizabeth Cady Stanton,
Eunice Newton Foote,
Mary Ann M'Clintock,
Margaret Schooley,
Martha C. Wright,
Jane C. Hunt,
Amy Post,
Catharine F. Stebbins,
Mary Ann Frink,
Lydia Mount,
Delia Mathews,
Catharine C. Paine,
Elizabeth W. M'Clintock,

Hannah Plant,
Lucy Jones,
Sarah Whitney,
Mary H. Hallowell,
Elizabeth Conklin,
Sally Pitcher,
Mary Conklin,
Susan Quinn,
Mary S. Mirror,
Phebe King,
Julia Ann Drake,
Charlotte Woodard,
Martha Underhill,
Dorothy Mathews,
Eunice Barker,
Sarah R. Woods,

Malvina Seymour,   Lydia Gild,
Phebe Mosher,   Sarah Hoffman,
Catharine Shaw,   Elizabeth Leslie,
Deborah Scott,   Martha Ridley,
Sarah Hallowell,   Rachel D. Bonnel,
Mary M'Clintock,   Betsey Tewksbury,
Mary Gilbert,   Rhoda Palmer,
Sophrone Taylor,   Margaret Jenkins,
Cynthia Davis,   Cynthia Fuller,
Mary Martin,   Eliza Martin,
P. A. Culvert,   Maria E. Wilbur,
Susan R. Doty,   Elizabeth D. Smith,
Rebecca Race,   Caroline Barker,
Sarah A. Mosher,   Ann Porter,
Mary E. Vail,   Experience Gibbs,
Lucy Spalding,   Antoinette E. Segur,
Lavinia Latham,   Hannah J. Latham,
Sarah Smith,   Sarah Sisson.

The following are the names of the gentlemen present in favor of the movement:

Richard P. Hunt,   Charles L. Hoskins,
Samuel D. Tillman,   Thomas M'Clintock,
Justin Williams,   Saron Phillips,
Elisha Foote,   Jacob Chamberlain,
Frederick Douglass,   Jonathan Metcalf,
Henry W. Seymour,   Nathan J. Milliken,
Henry Seymour,   S. E. Woodworth,
David Salding,   Edward F. Underhill,
William G. Barker,   George W. Pryor,
Elias J. Doty,   Joel Bunker,
John Jones,   Isaac Van Tassel,
William S. Dell,   Thomas Dell,
James Mott,   E. W. Capron,
William Burroughs,   Stephen Shear,
Robert Smalldridge,   Henry Hatley,
Jacob Matthews,   Azaliah Schooley.

The meeting adjourned until two o'clock.

M. ABRAHAM LINCOLN, EMANCIPATION PROCLAMATION

January 1, 1863

Whereas, on the twenty-second day of September, in the year of our Lord one thousand eight hundred and sixty-two, a proclamation was issued by the President of the United States, containing, among other things, the following, to wit:

653

"That on the first day of January, in the year of our Lord one thousand eight hundred and sixty-three, all persons held as slaves within any State or designated part of a State, the people whereof shall then, be in rebellion against the United States, shall be then thenceforward, and forever free; and the Executive Government of the United States, including the military and naval authority thereof, will recognize and maintain the freedom of such persons, and will do no act or acts to repress such persons, or any of them, in any efforts thy may make for their actual freedom.

"That the Executive will, on the first day of January aforesaid, by proclamation, designate the States and parts of States, if any, in which the people thereof, respectively, shall then be in rebellion against the United States; and the fact that any State, or the people thereof, shall on that day be, in good faith, represented in the Congress of the United States by members chosen thereto at elections wherein a majority of the qualified voters of such State shall have participated, shall, in the absence of strong countervailing testimony, be deemed conclusive evidence that such State, and the people thereof, are not then in rebellion against the United States."

Now, therefore I, Abraham Lincoln, President of the United States, by virtue of the power in me vested as Commander-in-Chief, of the Army and Navy of the United States in time of actual armed rebellion against the authority and government of the United States, and as a fit and necessary war measure for suppressing said rebellion, do, on this first day of January, in the year of our Lord one thousand eight hundred and sixty-three, and in accordance with my purpose so to do publicly proclaimed for the full period of one hundred days, from the day first above mentioned, order and designate as the States and parts of States wherein the people thereof respectively, are this day in rebellion again the United States, the following, to wit:

Arkansas, Texas, Louisiana, (except the Parishes of St. Bernard, Plaquemines, Jefferson, St. John, St. Charles, St. James Ascension, Assumption, Terrebonne, Lafourche, St. Mary, St. Martin, and Orleans, including the City of New Orleans) Mississippi, Alabama, Florida, Georgia, South Carolina, North Carolina, and Virginia, (except the forty-eight countries designated as West Virginia, and also the counties of Berkley, Accomac, Northampton, Elizabeth City, York, Princess Ann, and Norfolk, including the cities of Norfolk and Portsmouth[)], and which excepted parts, are for the present, left precisely as if this proclamation were not issued.

And by virtue of the power, and for the purpose aforesaid, I do order and declare that all persons held as slaves within said designated States, and parts of States, are, and henceforward shall be free; and that the Executive government of the United States, including the military and naval authorities thereof, will recognize and maintain the freedom of said persons.

654

And I hereby enjoin upon the people so declared to be free to abstain from all violence, unless in necessary self-defence; and I recommend to them that, in all cases when allowed, they labor faithfully for reasonable wages.

And I further declare and make known, that such persons of suitable condition, will be received into the armed service of the United States to garrison forts, positions, stations, and other places, and to man vessels of all sorts in said service.

And upon this act, sincerely believed to be an act of justice, warranted by the Constitution, upon military necessity, I invoke the considerate judgment of mankind, and the gracious favor of Almighty God.

In witness whereof, I have hereunto set my hand and caused the seal of the United States to be affixed.

Done at the City of Washington, this first day of January, in the year of our Lord one thousand eight hundred and sixty three, and of the Independence of the United States of America the eighty-seventh.

Abraham Lincoln

By the President:

William H. Seward,

Secretary of State.

DNA, RG

*

CHAPTER VII

PRINCIPLES OF RIGHTS

A. MAGNA CARTA

June 15, 1215

John, by the grace of God, king of England, lord of Ireland, duke of Normandy and Aquitaine, count of Anjou, to the archbishops, bishops, abbots, earls, barons, justiciars, foresters, sheriffs, reeves, servants, and all bailiffs and his faithful people greeting. Know that by the inspiration of God and for the good of our soul and those of all our predecessors and of our heirs, to the honor of God and the exaltation of holy church, and the improvement of our kingdom, by the advice of our venerable fathers Stephen, archbishop of Canterbury, primate of all England and cardinal of the holy Roman church, Henry, archbishop of Dublin, William of London, Peter of Winchester, Jocelyn of Bath and Glastonbury, Hugh of Lincoln, Walter of Worcester, William of Coventry, and Benedict of Rochester, bishops; of Master Pandulf, sub-deacon and member of the household of the lord Pope, of Brother Aymeric, master of the Knights of the Temple in England; and of the noblemen William Marshall, earl of Pembroke, William, earl of Salisbury, William, earl of Warren, William, earl of Arundel, Alan of Galloway, constable of Scotland, Warren Fitz-Gerald, Peter Fitz-Herbert, Hubert de Burgh, steward of Poitou, Hugh de Nevil, Matthew Fitz-Herbert, Thomas Bassett, Alan Bassett, Philip d'Albini, Robert de Roppelay, John Marshall, John Fitz-Hugh, and others of our faithful.

1. In the first place, we have granted to God, and by this our present charter confirmed, for us and for our heirs forever, that the English church shall be free, and shall hold its rights entire and its liberties uninjured; and we will that it be thus observed; which is shown by this, that the freedom of elections, which is considered to be most important and especially necessary to the English church, we, of our pure and spontaneous will, granted, and by our charter confirmed, before the contest between us and our barons had arisen; and obtained a confirmation of it by the lord Pope Innocent III.; which we shall observe and which we will shall be observed in good faith by our heirs forever.

We have granted moreover to all free men of our kingdom for us and our heirs forever all the liberties written below, to be had and holden by themselves and their heirs from us and our heirs.

2. If any of our earls or barons, or others holding from us in chief by military service shall have died, and when he has died his heir shall be of full age and owe relief, he shall have his inheritance by the ancient

relief; that is to say, the heir or heirs of an earl for the whole barony of an earl a hundred pounds; the heir or heirs of a baron for a whole barony a hundred pounds; the heir or heirs of a knight for a whole knight's fee a hundred shillings at most; and who owes less let him give less according to the ancient custom of fiefs.

3. If moreover the heir of any one of such shall be under age, and shall be in wardship, when he comes of age he shall have his inheritance without relief and without a fine.

4. The custodian of the land of such a minor heir shall not take from the land of the heir any except reasonable products, reasonable customary payments, and reasonable services, and this without destruction or waste of men or of property; and if we shall have committed the custody of the land of any such a one to the sheriff or to any other who is to be responsible to us for its proceeds, and that man shall have caused destruction or waste from his custody we will recover damages from him, and the land shall be committed to two legal and discreet men of that fief, who shall be responsible for its proceeds to us or to him to whom we have assigned them; and if we shall have given or sold to any one the custody of any such land, and he has caused destruction or waste there, he shall lose that custody, and it shall be handed over to two legal and discreet men of that fief who shall be in like manner responsible to us as is said above.

5. The custodian moreover, so long as he shall have the custody of the land, must keep up the houses, parks, warrens, fish ponds, mills, and other things pertaining to the land, from the proceeds of the land itself; and he must return to the heir, when he has come to full age, all his land, furnished with ploughs and implements of husbandry according as the time of wainage requires and as the proceeds of the land are able reasonably to sustain.

6. Heirs shall be married without disparity, so nevertheless that before the marriage is contracted, it shall be announced to the relatives by blood of the heir himself.

7. A widow, after the death of her husband, shall have her marriage portion and her inheritance immediately and without obstruction, nor shall she give anything for her dowry or for her marriage portion, or for her inheritance, which inheritance her husband and she held on the day of the death of her husband; and she may remain in the house of her husband for forty days after his death, within which time her dowry shall be assigned to her.

8. No widow shall be compelled to marry so long as she prefers to live without a husband, provided she gives security that she will not marry without our consent, if she holds from us, or without the consent of her lord from whom she holds, if she holds from another.

9. Neither we nor our bailiffs will seize any land or rent for any debt, so long as the chattels of the debtor are sufficient for the payment

of the debt; nor shall the pledges of a debtor be distrained so long as the principal debtor himself has enough for the payment of the debt; and if the principal debtor fails in the payment of the debt, not having the wherewithal to pay it, the pledges shall be responsible for the debt; and if they wish, they shall have the lands and the rents of the debtor until they shall have been satisfied for the debt which they have before paid for him, unless the principal debtor shall have shown himself to be quit in that respect towards those pledges.

10. If any one has taken anything from the Jews, by way of a loan, more or less, and dies before that debt is paid, the debt shall not draw interest so long as the heir is under age, from whomsoever he holds; and if that debt falls into our hands, we will take nothing except the chattel contained in the agreement.

11. And if any one dies leaving a debt owing to the Jews, his wife shall have her dowry, and shall pay nothing of that debt; and if there remain minor children of the dead man, necessaries shall be provided for them corresponding to the holding of the dead man; and from the remainder shall be paid the debt, the service of the lords being retained. In the same way debts are to be treated which are owed to others than the Jews.

12. No scutage or aid shall be imposed in our kingdom except by the common council of our kingdom, except for the ransoming of our body, for the making of our oldest son a knight, and for once marrying our oldest daughter, and for these purposes it shall be only a reasonable aid; in the same way it shall be done concerning the aids of the city of London.

13. And the city of London shall have all its ancient liberties and free customs, as well by land as by water. Moreover, we will and grant that all other cities and boroughs and villages and ports shall have all their liberties and free customs.

14. And for holding a common council of the kingdom concerning the assessment of an aid otherwise than in the three cases mentioned above, or concerning the assessment of a scutage, we shall cause to be summoned the archbishops, bishops, abbots, earls, and greater barons by our letters under seal; and besides we shall cause to be summoned generally, by our sheriffs and bailiffs all those who hold from us in chief, for a certain day, that is at the end of forty days at least, and for a certain place; and in all the letters of that summons, we will express the cause of the summons, and when the summons has thus been given the business shall proceed on the appointed day, on the advice of those who shall be present, even if not all of those who were summoned have come.

15. We will not grant to any one, moreover, that he shall take an aid from his free men, except for ransoming his body, for making his oldest son a knight, and for once marrying his oldest daughter; and for these purposes only a reasonable aid shall be taken.

16. No one shall be compelled to perform any greater service for a knight's fee, or for any other free tenement than is owed from it.

17. The common pleas shall not follow our court, but shall be held in some certain place.

18. The recognitions of *novel disseisin, mort d'ancestor,* and *darrein presentment* shall be held only in their own counties and in this manner: we, or if we are outside of the kingdom our principal justiciar, will send two justiciars through each county four times a year, who with four knights of each county, elected by the county, shall hold in the county and on the day and in the place of the county court the aforesaid assizes of the county.

19. And if the aforesaid assizes cannot be held within the day of the county court, a sufficient number of knights and free-holders shall remain from those who were present at the county court on that day to give the judgments, according as the business is more or less.

20. A free man shall not be fined for a small offence, except in proportion to the measure of the offence; and for a great offence he shall be fined in proportion to the magnitude of the offence, saving his freehold; and a merchant in the same way, saving his merchandise; and the villain shall be fined in the same way, saving his wainage, if he shall be at our mercy; and none of the above fines shall be imposed except by the oaths of honest men of the neighborhood.

21. Earls and barons shall be fined only by their peers, and only in proportion to their offence.

22. A clergyman shall be fined, like those before mentioned, only in proportion to his lay holding, and not according to the extent of his ecclesiastical benefice.

23. No manor or man shall be compelled to make bridges over the rivers except those which ought to do it of old and rightfully.

24. No sheriff, constable, coroners, or other bailiffs of ours shall hold pleas of our crown.

25. All counties, hundreds, wapentakes, and trithings shall be at the ancient rents and without any increase, excepting our demesne manors.

26. If any person holding a lay fief from us shall die, and our sheriff or bailiff shall show our letters-patent of our summons concerning a debt which the deceased owed to us, it shall be lawful for our sheriff or bailiff to attach and levy on the chattels of the deceased found on his lay fief, to the value of that debt, in the view of legal men, so nevertheless that nothing be removed thence until the clear debt to us shall be paid; and the remainder shall be left to the executors for the fulfilment of the will of the deceased; and if nothing is owed to us by him, all the chattels shall go to the deceased, saving to his wife and children their reasonable shares.

27. If any free man dies intestate, his chattels shall be distributed by the hands of his near relatives and friends, under the oversight of the church, saving to each one the debts which the deceased owed to him.

28. No constable or other bailiff of ours shall take anyone's grain or other chattels, without immediately paying for them in money, unless he is able to obtain a postponement at the good will of the seller.

29. No constable shall require any knight to give money in place of his ward of a castle if he is willing to furnish that ward in his own person or through another honest man, if he himself is not able to do it for a reasonable cause; and if we shall lead or send him into the army he shall be free from ward in proportion to the amount of time by which he has been in the army through us.

30. No sheriff or bailiff of ours or any one else shall take horses or wagons of any free man for carrying purposes except on the permission of that free man.

31. Neither we nor our bailiffs will take the wood of another man for castles, or for anything else which we are doing, except by the permission of him to whom the wood belongs.

32. We will not hold the lands of those convicted of a felony for more than a year and a day, after which the lands shall be returned to the lords of the fiefs.

33. All the fish-weirs in the Thames and the Medway, and throughout all England shall be done away with, except those on the coast.

34. The writ which is called *praecipe* shall not be given for the future to any one concerning any tenement by which a free man can lose his court.

35. There shall be one measure of wine throughout our whole kingdom, and one measure of ale, and one measure of grain, that is the London quarter, and one width of dyed cloth and of russets and of halbergets, that is two ells within the selvages; of weights, moreover, it shall be as of measures.

36. Nothing shall henceforth be given or taken for a writ of inquisition concerning life or limbs, but it shall be given freely and not denied.

37. If any one holds from us by fee farm or by soccage or by burgage, and from another he holds land by military service, we will not have the guardianship of the heir or of his land which is of the fief of another, on account of that fee farm, or soccage, or burgage, nor will we have the custody of that fee farm, or soccage, or burgage, unless that fee farm itself owes military service. We will not have the guardianship of the heir or of the land of any one, which he holds from another by military service on account of any petty serjeanty which he holds from us by the service of paying to us knives or arrows, or things of that kind.

38. No bailiff for the future shall place any one to his law on his simple affirmation, without credible witnesses brought for this purpose.

39. No free man shall be taken or imprisoned or dispossessed, or outlawed, or banished, or in any way destroyed, nor will we go upon him, nor send upon him, except by the legal judgment of his peers or by the law of the land.

40. To no one will we sell, to no one will we deny, or delay right or justice.

41. All merchants shall be safe and secure in going out from England and coming into England and in remaining and going through England, as well by land as by water, for buying and selling, free from all evil tolls, by the ancient and rightful customs, except in time of war, and if they are of a land at war with us; and if such are found in our land at the beginning of war, they shall be attached without injury to their bodies or goods, until it shall be known from us or from our principal justiciar in what way the merchants of our land are treated who shall then be found in the country which is at war with us; and if ours are safe there, the others shall be safe in our land.

42. It is allowed henceforth to any one to go out from our kingdom, and to return, safely and securely, by land and by water, saving their fidelity to us, except in time of war for some short time, for the common good of the kingdom; excepting persons imprisoned and outlawed according to the law of the realm, and people of a land at war with us, and merchants, of whom it shall be done as is before said.

43. If any one holds from an escheat, as from the honor of Wallingford, or Nottingham, or Boulogne, or Lancaster, or from other escheats which are in our hands and are baronies, and he dies, his heir shall not give any other relief, nor do to us any other service than he would do to the baron, if that barony was in the hands of the baron; and we will hold it in the same way as the baron held it.

44. Men who dwell outside the forest shall not henceforth come before our justiciars of the forest, on common summons, unless they are in a plea of, or pledges for any person or persons who are arrested on account of the forest.

45. We will not make justiciars, constables, sheriffs or bailiffs except of such as know the law of the realm and are well inclined to observe it.

46. All barons who have founded abbeys for which they have charters of kings of England, or ancient tenure, shall have their custody when they have become vacant, as they ought to have.

47. All forests which have been afforested in our time shall be disafforested immediately; and so it shall be concerning river banks which in our time have been fenced in.

48. All the bad customs concerning forests and warrens and concerning foresters and warreners, sheriffs and their servants, river banks and their guardians shall be inquired into immediately in each county by twelve sworn knights of the same county, who shall be elected by the honest men of the same county, and within forty days after the inquisition has been made, they shall be entirely destroyed by them, never to be restored, provided that we be first informed of it, or our justiciar, if we are not in England.

49. We will give back immediately all hostages and charters which have been liberated to us by Englishmen as security for peace or for faithful service.

50. We will remove absolutely from their bailiwicks the relatives of Gerard de Athyes, so that for the future they shall have no bailiwick in England; Engelard de Cygony, Andrew, Peter and Gyon de Chancelles, Gyon de Cygony, Geoffrey de Martin and his brothers, Philip Mark and his brothers, and Geoffrey his nephew and their whole retinue.

51. And immediately after the re-establishment of peace we will remove from the kingdom all foreign-born soldiers, crossbow men, servants, and mercenaries who have come with horses and arms for the injury of the realm.

52. If any one shall have been dispossessed or removed by us without legal judgment of his peers, from his lands, castles, franchises, or his right, we will restore them to him immediately; and if contention arises about this, then it shall be done according to the judgment of the twenty-five barons, of whom mention is made below concerning the security of the peace. Concerning all those things, however, from which any one has been removed or of which he has been deprived without legal judgment of his peers by King Henry our father, or by King Richard our brother, which we have in our land, or which others hold, and which it is our duty to guarantee, we shall have respite till the usual term of crusaders; excepting those things about which the suit has been begun or the inquisition made by our writ before our assumption of the cross; when, however, we shall return from our journey or if by chance we desist from the journey, we will immediately show full justice in regard to them.

53. We shall, moreover, have the same respite and in the same manner about showing justice in regard to the forests which are to be disafforested or to remain forests, which Henry our father or Richard our brother made into forests; and concerning the custody of lands which are in the fief of another, custody of which we have until now had on account of a fief which any one has held from us by military service; and concerning the abbeys which have been founded in fiefs of others than ourselves, in which the lord of the fee has asserted for himself a right; and when we return or if we should desist from our journey we

will immediately show full justice to those complaining in regard to them.

54.   No one shall be seized nor imprisoned on the appeal of a woman concerning the death of any one except her husband.

55.   All fines which have been imposed unjustly and against the law of the land, and all penalties imposed unjustly and against the law of the land are altogether excused, or will be on the judgment of the twenty-five barons of whom mention is made below in connection with the security of the peace, or on the judgment of the majority of them, along with the aforesaid Stephen, archbishop of Canterbury, if he is able to be present, and others whom he may wish to call for this purpose along with him.   And if he should not be able to be present, nevertheless the business shall go on without him, provided that if any one or more of the aforesaid twenty-five barons are in a similar suit they should be removed as far as this particular judgment goes, and others who shall be chosen and put upon oath, by the remainder of the twenty-five shall be substituted for them for this purpose.

56.   If we have dispossessed or removed any Welshmen from their lands, or franchises, or other things, without legal judgment of their peers, in England, or in Wales, they shall be immediately returned to them; and if a dispute shall have arisen over this, then it shall be settled in the borderland by judgment of their peers, concerning holdings of England according to the law of England, concerning holdings of Wales according to the law of Wales, and concerning holdings of the borderland according to the law of the borderland.   The Welsh shall do the same to us and ours.

57.   Concerning all those things, however, from which any one of the Welsh shall have been removed or dispossessed without legal judgment of his peers, by King Henry our father, or King Richard our brother, which we hold in our hands, or which others hold, and we are bound to warrant to them, we shall have respite till the usual period of crusaders, those being excepted about which suit was begun or inquisition made by our command before our assumption of the cross.   When, however, we shall return or if by chance we shall desist from our journey, we will show full justice to them immediately, according to the laws of the Welsh and the aforesaid parts.

58.   We will give back the son of Lewellyn immediately, and all the hostages from Wales and the charters which had been liberated to us as a security for peace.

59.   We will act toward Alexander, king of the Scots, concerning the return of his sisters and his hostages, and concerning his franchises and his right, according to the manner in which we shall act toward our other barons of England, unless it ought to be otherwise by the charters which we hold from William his father, formerly king of the Scots, and this shall be by the judgment of his peers in our court.

60. Moreover, all those customs and franchises mentioned above which we have conceded in our kingdom, and which are to be fulfilled, as far as pertains to us, in respect to our men; all men of our kingdom as well clergy as laymen, shall observe as far as pertains to them, in respect to their men.

61. Since, moreover, for the sake of God, and for the improvement of our kingdom, and for the better quieting of the hostility sprung up lately between us and our barons, we have made all these concessions; wishing them to enjoy these in a complete and firm stability forever, we make and concede to them the security described below; that is to say, that they shall elect twenty-five barons of the kingdom, whom they will, who ought with all their power to observe, hold, and cause to be observed, the peace and liberties which we have conceded to them, and by this our present charter confirmed to them; in this manner, that if we or our justiciar, or our bailiffs, or any of our servants shall have done wrong in any way toward any one, or shall have transgressed any of the articles of peace or security; and the wrong shall have been shown to four barons of the aforesaid twenty-five barons, let those four barons come to us or to our justiciar, if we are out of the kingdom, laying before us the transgression, and let them ask that we cause that transgression to be corrected without delay. And if we shall not have corrected the transgression or, if we shall be out of the kingdom, if our justiciar shall not have corrected it within a period of forty days, counting from the time in which it has been shown to us or to our justiciar, if we are out of the kingdom; the aforesaid four barons shall refer the matter to the remainder of the twenty-five barons, and let these twenty-five barons with the whole community of the country distress and injure us in every way they can; that is to say by the seizure of our castles, lands, possessions, and in such other ways as they can until it shall have been corrected according to their judgment, saving our person and that of our queen, and those of our children; and when the correction has been made, let them devote themselves to us as they did before. And let whoever in the country wishes take an oath that in all the above-mentioned measures he will obey the orders of the aforesaid twenty-five barons, and that he will injure us as far as he is able with them, and we give permission to swear publicly and freely to each one who wishes to swear, and no one will we ever forbid to swear. All those, moreover, in the country who of themselves and their own will are unwilling to take an oath to the twenty-five barons as to distressing and injuring us along with them, we will compel to take the oath by our mandate, as before said. And if any one of the twenty-five barons shall have died or departed from the land or shall in any other way be prevented from taking the above mentioned action, let the remainder of the aforesaid twenty-five barons choose another in his place, according to their judg-ment, who shall take an oath in the same way as the others. In all those things, moreover, which are committed to those five and twenty barons to carry out, if perhaps the twenty-five are present, and some disagree-

ment arises among them about something, or if any of them when they have been summoned are not willing or are not able to be present, let that be considered valid and firm which the greater part of those who are present arrange or command, just as if the whole twenty-five had agreed in this; and let the aforesaid twenty-five swear that they will observe faithfully all the things which are said above, and with all their ability cause them to be observed. And we will obtain nothing from any one, either by ourselves or by another by which any of these concessions and liberties shall be revoked or diminished; and if any such thing shall have been obtained, let it be invalid and void, and we will never use it by ourselves or by another.

62. And all ill-will, grudges, and anger sprung up between us and our men, clergy and laymen, from the time of the dispute, we have fully renounced and pardoned to all. Moreover, all transgressions committed on account of this dispute, from Easter in the sixteenth year of our reign till the restoration of peace, we have fully remitted to all, clergy and laymen, and as far as pertains to us, fully pardoned. And moreover we have caused to be made for them testimonial letters-patent of lord Stephen, archbishop of Canterbury, lord Henry, archbishop of Dublin, and of the aforesaid bishops and of master Pandulf, in respect to that security and the concessions named above.

63. Wherefore we will and firmly command that the Church of England shall be free, and that the men in our kingdom shall have and hold all the aforesaid liberties, rights and concessions, well and peacefully, freely and quietly, fully and completely, for themselves and their heirs, from us and our heirs, in all things and places, forever, as before said. It has been sworn, moreover, as well on our part as on the part of the barons, that all these things spoken of above shall be observed in good faith and without any evil intent. Witness the above named and many others. Given by our hand in the meadow which is called Runnymede, between Windsor and Staines, on the fifteenth day of June, in the seventeenth year of our reign.

B. PETITION OF RIGHT

June 7, 1628

HUMBLY *shew unto our sovereign lord the King, the lords spiritual and temporal, and commons in parliament assembled, That whereas it is declared and enacted by a statute made in the time of the reign of King* Edward *the First commonly called* Statutum de tallagio non concedendo, *That no tallage or aid shall be laid or levied by the King or his heirs in this realm, without the good will and assent of the archbishops, bishops, earls, barons, knights, burgesses, and other the freemen of the commonalty of this realm; and by authority of parliament holden in the five and twentieth year of the reign of King* Edward *the Third, it is declared and* enacted, *That from thenceforth no person should be compelled to make any loans to the King against his will, because such loans were against reason and the franchise of the land; and by other laws of this realm it is provided, That none should be charged by any charge or imposition called a benevolence, nor by such like charge: by which the statutes before mentioned, and other the good laws and statutes of this realm, your subjects have inherited this freedom, That they should not be compelled to contribute to any tax, tallage, aid or other like charge not set by common consent in parliament.*

II. *Yet nevertheless, of late divers commissions directed to sundry commissioners in several counties, with instructions, have issued; by means whereof your people have been in divers places assembled, and required to lend certain sums of money unto your Majesty, and many of them, upon their refusal so to do, have had an oath administred unto them not warrantable by the laws or statutes of this realm, and have been constrained to become bound to make appearance and give attendance before your privy council and in other places, and others of them have been therefore imprisoned, confined, and sundry other ways molested and disquieted; and divers other charges have been laid and levied upon your people in several counties by lord lieutenants, deputy lieutenants, commissioners for musters, justices of peace and others, by command or direction from your Majesty, or your privy council, against the laws and free customs of the realm.*

III. *And where also by the statute called* The great charter of the liberties of England, *it is declared and enacted, That no freeman may be taken or imprisoned, or be disseised of his freehold or liberties, or his free customs, or be outlawed or exiled, or in manner destroyed, but by the lawful judgment of his peers, or by the law of the land.*

IV. *And in the eight and twentieth year of the reign of King* Edward *the Third, it was declared and enacted by authority of parliament, That no man of what estate or condition that he be, should be put out of his land or tenements, nor taken, nor imprisoned, nor disherited, nor put to death without being brought to answer by due process of law:*

V. *Nevertheless against the tenor of the said statutes, and other the good laws and statutes of your realm to that end provided, divers of your subjects have of late been imprisoned without any cause shewed; and when for their deliverance they were brought before your justices by your Majesty's writs of* habeas corpus, *there to undergo and receive as the court should order, and their keepers commanded to certify the causes of their detainer, no cause was certified, but that they were detained by your Majesty's special command, signified by the lords of your privy council, and yet were returned back to several prisons, without being charged with any thing to which they might make answer according to the law:*

VI. *And whereas of late great companies of soldiers and mariners have been dispersed into divers counties of the realm, and the inhabitants*

667

against their wills have been compelled to receive them into their houses, and there to suffer them to sojourn, against the laws and customs of this realm, and to the great grievance and vexation of the people:

VII. *And whereas also by authority of parliament, in the five and twentieth year of the reign of King* Edward *the Third, it is declared and enacted, That no man should be forejudged of life or limb against the form of the* great charter *and the law of the land; and by the said* great charter *and other the laws and statutes of this your realm, no man ought to be adjudged to death but by the laws established in this your realm, either by the customs of the same realm, or by acts of parliament: and whereas no offender of what kind soever is exempted from the proceedings to be used, and punishments to be inflicted by the laws and statutes of this your realm: nevertheless of late time divers commissions under your Majesty's great seal have issued forth, by which certain persons have been assigned and appointed commissioners with power and authority to proceed within the land, according to the justice of martial law, against such soldiers or mariners, or other dissolute persons joining with them, as should commit any murder, robbery, felony, mutiny or other outrage or misdemeanor whatsoever, and by such summary course and order as is agreeable to martial law, and as is used in armies in time of war, to proceed to the trial and condemnation of such offenders, and them to cause to be executed and put to death according to the law martial:*

VIII. *By pretext whereof some of your Majesty's subjects have been by some of the said commissioners put to death, when and where, if by the laws and statutes of the land they had deserved death, by the same laws and statutes also they might, and by no other ought to have been judged and executed:*

IX. *And also sundry grievous offenders, by colour thereof claiming an exemption, have escaped the punishments due to them by the laws and statutes of this your realm, by reason that divers of your officers and ministers of justice have unjustly refused or forborn to proceed against such offenders according to the same laws and statutes, upon pretence that the said offenders were punishable only by martial law, and by authority of such commissions as aforesaid: which commissions, and all other of like nature, are wholly and directly contrary to the said laws and statutes of this your realm:*

X. They do therefore humbly pray your most excellent Majesty, That no man hereafter be compelled to make or yield any gift, loan, benevolence, tax, or such-like charge, without common consent by act of parliament; and that none be called to make answer, or take such oath, or to give attendance, or be confined, or otherwise molested or disquieted concerning the same, or for refusal thereof; and that no freeman, in any such manner as is before-mentioned, be imprisoned or detained; and that your Majesty would be pleased to remove the said soldiers and mariners, and that your people may not be so burthened in time to come; and that the aforesaid commissions, for proceeding by martial law, may be revoked and annulled; and that hereafter no commissions of like nature may issue forth to any person or persons whatsoever to be executed as aforesaid, lest by colour of them any of your Majesty's subjects be destroyed, or put to death contrary to the laws and franchise of the land.

XI. All which they most humbly pray of your most excellent Majesty as their rights and liberties, according to the laws and statutes of this realm; and that your Majesty would also vouchsafe to declare, That the awards, doings and proceedings, to the prejudice of your people in any of the premises, shall not be drawn hereafter into consequence or example; and that your Majesty would be also graciously pleased, for the further comfort and safety of your people, to declare your royal will and pleasure, That in the things aforesaid all your officers and ministers shall serve you according to the laws and statutes of this realm, as they tender the honour of your Majesty, and the prosperity of this kingdom. *Qua quidem petitione lecta & plenius intellecta per dictum dominum regem taliter est responsum in pleno parliamento*, viz. Soit droit fait come est desire.

C. THE LIBERTIES OF THE MASSACHUSETS COLONIE IN NEW ENGLAND

1641

The free fruition of such liberties Immunities and priveledges as humanitie, Civilitie, and Christianitie call for as due to every man in his place and proportion without impeachment and Infringement hath ever bene and ever will be the tranquillitie and Stabilitie of Churches and Commonwealths. And the deniall or deprivall thereof, the disturbance if not the ruine of both.

We hould it therefore our dutie and safetie whilst we are about the further establishing of this Government to collect and expresse all such freedomes as for present we foresee may concerne us, and our posteritie after us, And to ratify them with our sollemne consent.

We doe therefore this day religiously and unanimously decree and confirme these following Rites, liberties and priveledges concerneing our Churches, and Civill State to be respectively impartiallie and inviolably enjoyed and observed throughout our Jurisdiction for ever.

1   No mans life shall be taken away, no mans honour or good name shall be stayned, no mans person shall be arested, restrayned, banished, dismembred, nor any wayes punished, no man shall be deprived of his wife or children, no mans goods or estaite shall be taken away from him, nor any way indammaged under coulor of law or Countenance of Authoritie, unlesse it be by vertue or equitie of some expresse law of the Country waranting the same, established by a generall Court and sufficiently published, or in case of the defect of a law in any perteculer case

669

by the word of god. And in Capitall cases, or in cases concerning dismembring or banishment, according to that word to be judged by the Generall Court.

2   Every person within this Jurisdiction, whether Inhabitant or forreiner shall enjoy the same justice and law, that is generall for the plantation, which we constitute and execute one towards another without partialitie or delay.

3   No man shall be urged to take any oath or subscribe any articles, covenants or remonstrance, of a publique and Civill nature, but such as the Generall Court hath considered, allowed, and required.

4   No man shall be punished for not appearing at or before any Civill Assembly, Court, Councell, Magistrate, or Officer, nor for the omission of any office or service, if he shall be necessarily hindred by any apparent Act or providence of God, which he could neither foresee nor avoid. Provided that this law shall not prejudice any person of his just cost or damage, in any civill action.

5   No man shall be compelled to any publique worke or service unlesse the presse be grounded upon some act of the generall Court, and have reasonable allowance therefore.

6   No man shall be pressed in person to any office, worke, warres or other publique service, that is necessarily and suffitiently exempted by any naturall or personall impediment, as by want of yeares, greatnes of age, defect of minde, fayling of sences, or impotencie of Lymbes.

7   No man shall be compelled to goe out of the limits of this plantation upon any offensive warres which this Commonwealth or any of our freinds or confederats shall volentarily undertake. But onely upon such vindictive and defensive warres in our owne behalfe or the behalfe of our freinds and confederats as shall be enterprized by the Counsell and consent of a Court generall, or by Authority derived from the same.

8   No mans Cattel or goods of what kinde soever shall be pressed or taken for any publique use or service, unlesse it be by warrant grounded upon some act of the generall Court, nor without such reasonable prices and hire as the ordinarie rates of the Countrie do afford. And if his Cattle or goods shall perish or suffer damage in such service, the owner shall be suffitiently recompenced.

9   No monopolies shall be granted or allowed amongst us, but of such new Inventions that are profitable to the Countrie, and that for a short time.

10   All our lands and heritages shall be free from all fines and licences upon Alienations, and from all hariotts, wardships, Liveries, Primer-seisins, yeare day and wast, Escheates, and forfeitures, upon the deaths of parents or Ancestors, be they naturall, casuall or Juditiall.

11   All persons which are of the age of 21 yeares, and of right understanding and meamories, whether excommunicate or condemned shall have full power and libertie to make there wills and testaments, and other lawfull alienations of theire lands and estates.

12   Every man whether Inhabitant or fforreiner, free or not free shall have libertie to come to any publique Court, Councel, or Towne meeting, and either by speech or writeing to move any lawfull, seasonable, and materiall question, or to present any necessary motion, complaint, petition, Bill or information, whereof that meeting hath proper cognizance, so it be done in convenient time, due order, and respective manner.

13   No man shall be rated here for any estaite or revenue he hath in England, or in any forreine partes till it be transported hither.

14   Any Conveyance or Alienation of land or other estaite what so ever, made by any woman that is married, any childe under age, Ideott or distracted person, shall be good if it be passed and ratified by the consent of a generall Court.

15   All Covenous or fraudulent Alienations or Conveyances of lands, tenements, or any hereditaments, shall be of no validitie to defeate any man from due debts or legacies, or from any just title, clame or possession, of that which is so fraudulently conveyed.

16   Every Inhabitant that is an howse holder shall have free fishing and fowling in any great ponds and Bayes, Coves and Rivers, so farre as the sea ebbes and flowes within the presincts of the towne where they dwell, unlesse the free men of the same Towne or the Generall Court have otherwise appropriated them, provided that this shall not be extended to give leave to any man to come upon others proprietie without there leave.

17   Every man of or within this Jurisdiction shall have free libertie, notwithstanding any Civill power to remove both himselfe, and his familie at their pleasure out of the same, provided there be no legall impediment to the contrarie.

18   No mans person shall be restrained or imprisoned by any Authority whatsoever, before the law hath sentenced him thereto, If he can put in sufficient securitie, bayle or mainprise, for his appearance, and good behaviour in the meane time, unlesse it be in Crimes Capital, and Contempts in open Court, and in such cases where some expresse act of Court doth allow it.

19   If in a generall Court any miscariage shall be amongst the Assistants when they are by themselves that may deserve an Admonition or fine under 20 sh. it shall be examined and sentenced among themselves, If amongst the Deputies when they are by themselves, It shall be examined and sentenced amongst themselves, If it be when the whole

Court is togeather, it shall be judged by the whole Court, and not severallie as before.

20 If any which are to sit as Judges in any other Court shall demeane themselves offensively in the Court, the rest of the Judges present shall have power to censure him for it, if the cause be of a high nature it shall be presented to and censured at the next superior Court.

21 In all cases where the first summons are not served six dayes before the Court, and the cause breifly specified in the warrant, where appearance is to be made by the partie summoned, it shall be at his libertie whether he will appeare or no, except all cases that are to be handled in Courts suddainly called, upon extraordinary occasions, In all cases where there appeares present and urgent cause Any Assistant or officer apointed shal have power to make out Attaichments for the first summons.

22 No man in any suit or action against an other shall falsely pretend great debts or damages to vex his Adversary, if it shall appeare any doth so, The Court shall have power to set a reasonable fine on his head.

23 No man shall be adjudged to pay for detaining any debt from any Crediter above eight pounds in the hundred for one yeare, And not above that rate proportionable for all somes what so ever, neither shall this be a coulour or countenance to allow any usurie amongst us contrarie to the law of god.

24 In all Trespasses or damages done to any man or men, If it can be proved to be done by the meere default of him or them to whome the trespasse is done, It shall be judged no trespasse, nor any damage given for it.

25 No Summons pleading Judgement, or any kinde of proceeding in Court or course of Justice shall be abated, arested or reversed upon any kinde of cercumstantiall errors or mistakes, If the person and cause be rightly understood and intended by the Court.

26 Every man that findeth himselfe unfit to plead his owne cause in any Court shall have Libertie to imploy any man against whom the Court doth not except, to helpe him, Provided he give him noe fee or reward for his paines. This shall not exempt the partie him selfe from Answering such Questions in person as the Court shall thinke meete to demand of him.

27 If any plantife shall give into any Court a declaration of his cause in writeing, The defendant shall also have libertie and time to give in his answer in writeing, And so in all further proceedings betwene partie and partie, So it doth not further hinder the dispach of Justice then the Court shall be willing unto.

28 The plantife in all Actions brought in any Court shall have libertie to withdraw his Action, or to be nonsuited before the Jurie hath

given in their verdict, in which case he shall alwaies pay full cost and chardges to the defendant, and may afterwards renew his suite at an other Court if he please.

29   In all Actions at law it shall be the libertie of the plantife and defendant by mutual consent to choose whether they will be tryed by the Bench or by a Jurie, unlesse it be where the law upon just reason hath otherwise determined. The like libertie shall be granted to all persons in Criminall cases.

30   It shall be in the libertie both of plantife and defendant, and likewise every delinquent (to be judged by a Jurie) to challenge any of the Jurors. And if his challenge be found just and reasonable by the Bench, or the rest of the Jurie, as the challenger shall choose it shall be allowed him, and tales de cercumstantibus impaneled in their room.

31   In all cases where evidence is so obscure or defective that the Jurie cannot clearly and safely give a positive verdict, whether it be a grand or petit Jurie, It shall have libertie to give a non Liquit, or a spetiall verdict, in which last, that is in a spetiall verdict, the Judgement of the cause shall be left to the Court, and all Jurors shall have libertie in matters of fact if they cannot finde the maine issue, yet to finde and present in their verdict so much as they can, If the Bench and Jurors shall so differ at any time about their verdict that either of them cannot proceede with peace of conscience the case shall be referred to the Generall Court, who shall take the question from both and determine it.

32   Every man shall have libertie to replevy his Cattell or goods impounded, distreined, seised, or extended, unlesse it be upon execution after Judgement, and in paiment of fines. Provided he puts in good securitie to prosecute his replevin, And to satisfie such demands as his Adversary shall recover against him in Law.

33   No mans person shall be Arrested, or imprisoned upon execution or judgment for any debt or fine, If the law can finde competent meanes of satisfaction otherwise from his estaite, and if not his person may be arrested and imprisoned where he shall be kept at his owne charge, not the plantife's till satisfaction be made: unlesse the Court that had cognizance of the cause or some superior Court shall otherwise provide.

34   If any man shall be proved and Judged a commen Barrator vexing others with unjust frequent and endlesse suites, It shall be in the power of Courts both to denie him the benefit of the law, and to punish him for his Barratry.

35   No mans Corne nor hay that is in the feild or upon the Cart, nor his garden stuffe, nor any thing subject to present decay, shall be taken in any distresse, unles he that takes it doth presently bestow it where it may not be imbesled nor suffer spoile or decay, or give securitie to satisfie the worth thereof if it comes to any harme.

36 It shall be in the libertie of every man cast condemned or sentenced in any cause in any Inferior Court, to make their Appeale to the Court of Assistants, provided they tender their appeale and put in securitie to prosecute it before the Court be ended wherein they were condemned, And within six dayes next ensuing put in good securitie before some Assistant to satisfie what his Adversarie shall recover against him; And if the cause be of a Criminall nature, for his good behaviour, and appearance, And everie man shall have libertie to complaine to the Generall Court of any Injustice done him in any Court of Assistants or other.

37 In all cases where it appeares to the Court that the plantife hath wilingly and witingly done wronge to the defendant in commenceing and prosecuting any action or complaint against him, They shall have power to impose upon him a proportionable fine to the use of the defendant, or accused person, for his false complaint or clamor.

38 Everie man shall have libertie to Record in the publique Rolles of any Court any Testimony given upon oath in the same Court, or before two Assistants, or any deede or evidence legally confirmed there to remaine in perpetuam rei memoriam, that is for perpetuall memoriall or evidence upon occasion.

39 In all actions both reall and personall betweene partie and partie, the Court shall have power to respite execution for a convenient time, when in their prudence they see just cause so to doe.

40 No Conveyance, Deede, or promise whatsoever shall be of validitie, If it be gotten by Illegal violence, imprisonment, threatenings, or any kinde of forcible compulsion called Dures.

41 Everie man that is to Answere for any Criminall cause, whether he be in prison or under bayle, his cause shall be heard and determined at the next Court that hath proper Cognizance thereof, And may be done without prejudice of Justice.

42 No man shall be twise sentenced by Civill Justice for one and the same Crime, offence, or Trespasse.

43 No man shall be beaten with above 40 stripes, nor shall any true gentleman, nor any man equall to a gentleman be punished with whipping, unles his crime be very shamefull, and his course of life vitious and profligate.

44 No man condemned to dye shall be put to death within fower dayes next after his condemnation, unles the Court see spetiall cause to the contrary, or in case of martiall law, nor shall the body of any man so put to death be unburied 12 howers, unlesse it be in case of Anatomie.

45 No man shall be forced by Torture to confesse any Crime against himselfe nor any other unlesse it be in some Capitall case where he is first fullie convicted by cleare and suffitient evidence to be guilty, After which if the cause be of that nature, That it is very apparent there

be other conspiratours, or confederates with him, Then he may be tortured, yet not with such Tortures as be Barbarous and inhumane.

46 For bodilie punishments we allow amongst us none that are inhumane Barbarous or cruel.

47 No man shall be put to death without the testimony of two or three witnesses or that which is equivalent thereunto.

48 Every Inhabitant of the Country shall have free libertie to search and veewe any Rooles, Records, or Regesters of any Court or office except the Councell, And to have a transcript or exemplification thereof written examined, and signed by the hand of the officer of the office paying the appointed fees therefore.

49 No free man shall be compelled to serve upon Juries above two Courts in a yeare, except grand Jurie men, who shall hould two Courts together at the least.

50 All Jurors shall be chosen continuallie by the freemen of the Towne where they dwell.

51 All Associates selected at any time to Assist the Assistants in Inferior Courts shall be nominated by the Townes belonging to that Court, by orderly agreement amonge themselves.

52 Children, Idiots, Distracted persons, and all that are strangers, or new commers to our plantation, shall have such allowances and dispensations in any Cause whether Criminall or other as religion and reason require.

53 The age of discretion for passing away of lands or such kinde of herediments, or for giveing of votes, verdicts or Sentence in any Civill Courts or causes, shall be one and twentie yeares.

54 Whensoever anything is to be put to vote, any sentence to be pronounced, or any other matter to be proposed, or read in any Court or Assembly, If the president or moderator thereof shall refuse to performe it, the Major parte of the members of that Court or Assembly shall have power to appoint any other meete man of them to do it, And if there be just cause to punish him that should and would not.

55 In all suites or Actions in any Court, the plaintife shall have libertie to make all the titles and claims to that he sues for he can. And the Defendant shall have libertie to plead all the pleas he can in answere to them, and the Court shall judge according to the entire evidence of all.

56 If any man shall behave himselfe offensively at any Towne meeting, the rest of the freemen then present, shall have power to sentence him for his offence. So be it the mulct or penaltie exceede not twentie shilings.

D. CONCESSIONS AND AGREEMENTS OF WEST NEW JERSEY

March 13, 1677

THE CHARTER OR FUNDAMENTAL LAWS, OF WEST NEW JERSEY, AGREED UPON.

Chapter XIII

THAT THESE FOLLOWING CONCESSIONS ARE THE COMMON LAW, OR FUNDAMENTAL RIGHTS, OF THE PROVINCE OF WEST NEW JERSEY.

THAT the common law or fundamental rights and privileges of West New Jersey, are individually agreed upon by the Proprietors and free-holders thereof, to be the foundation of the government, which is not to be altered by the Legislative authority, or free Assembly hereafter mentioned and constituted, but that the said Legislative authority is constituted according to these fundamentals, to make such laws as agree with, and maintain the said fundamentals, and to make no laws that in the least contradict, differ or vary from the said fundamentals, under what pretence or alligation soever.

Chapter XIV

BUT if it so happen that any person or persons of the said General Assembly, shall therein designedly, willfully, and maliciously, move or excite any to move, any matter or thing whatsoever, that contradicts or any ways subverts, any fundamentals of the said laws in the Constitution of the government of this Province, it being proved by seven honest and and reputable persons, he or they shall be proceeded against as traitors to the said government.

Chapter XV

THAT these Concessions, law or great charter of fundamentals, be recorded in a fair table, in the Assembly House, and that they be read at the beginning and dissolving of every general free Assembly: And it is further agreed and ordained, that the said Concessions, common law, or great charter of fundamentals, be writ in fair tables, in every common hall of justice within this Province, and that they be read in solemn manner four times every year, in the presence of the people, by the chief magistrates of those places.

Chapter XVI

THAT no men, nor number of men upon earth, hath power or authority to rule over men's consciences in religious matters, therefore it is consented, agreed and ordained, that no person or persons whatsoever within the said Province, at any time or times hereafter, shall be any ways upon any pretence whatsoever, called in question, or in the least punished or hurt, either in person, estate, or priviledge, for the sake of his opinion, judgment, faith or worship towards God in matters of religion. But that all and every such person, and persons, may from time to time, and at all times, freely and fully have, and enjoy his and their judgements, and the exercises of their consciences in matters of religious worship throughout all the said Province.

Chapter XVII

THAT no Proprietor, freeholder or inhabitant of the said Province of West New Jersey, shall be deprived or condemned of life, limb, liberty, estate, property or any ways hurt in his or their privileges, freedoms or franchises, upon any account whatsoever, without a due tryal, and judgment passed by twelve good and lawful men of his neighbourhood first had: And that in all causes to be tryed, and in all tryals, the person or persons, arraigned may except against any of the said neighbourhood, without any reason rendered, (not exceeding thirty five) and in case of any valid reason alleged, against every person nominated for that service.

Chapter XVIII

AND that no Proprietor, freeholder, freedenison, or inhabitant in the said Province, shall be attached, arrested, or imprisoned, for or by reason of any debt, duty, or thing whatsoever (cases felonious, criminal and treasonable excepted) before he or she have personal summon or summons, left at his or her last dwelling place, if in the said Province, by some legal authorized officer, constituted and appointed for that purpose, to appear in some court of judicature for the said Province, with a full and plain account of the cause or thing in demand, as also the name or names of the person or persons at whose suit, and the court where he is to appear, and that he hath at least fourteen days time to appear and answer the said suit, if he or she live or inhabit within forty miles English of the said court, and if at a further distance, to have for every twenty miles, two days time more, for his and their appearance, and so proportionably for a larger distance of place.

That upon the recording of the summons, and non-appearance of such person and persons, a writ or attachment shall or may be issued out to arrest, or attach the person or persons of such defaulters, to cause his or their appearance in such court, returnable at a day certain, to answer the penalty or penalties, in such suit or suits; and if he or they shall be condemned by legal tryal and judgment, the penalty or penalties shall be paid and satisfied out of his or their real or personal estate so condemned, or cause the person or persons so condemned, to lie in execution till satisfaction of the debt and damages be made. *Provided always,* if such person or persons so condemned, shall pay and deliver such estate, goods, and chattles which he or any other person hath for his or their use, and shall solemnly declare and aver, that he or they have not any further estate, goods or chattels wheresoever, to satisfy the person or persons, (at whose suit, he or they are condemned) their respective judgments, and shall also bring and produce three other persons as compurgators, who are well known and of honest reputation, and approved of by the commissioners of that division, where they dwell or inhabit, which shall in such open court, likewise solemnly declare and aver, that they believe in their consciences, such person and persons so condemned, have not werewith further to pay the said condemnation or condemnations, he or they shall be thence forthwith discharged from their said imprisonment, any law or custom to the contrary thereof, heretofore in the said Province, notwithstanding. And upon such summons and default of appearance, recorded as aforesaid, and such person and persons not appearing within forty days after, it shall and may be lawful for such court of judicature to proceed to tryal, of twelve lawful men to judgment, against such defaulters, and issue forth execution against his or their estate, real and personal, to satisfy such penalty or penalties, to such debt and damages so recorded, as far as it shall or may extend.

Chapter XIX

THAT there shall be in every court, three justices or commissioners, who shall sit with the twelve men of the neighbourhood, with them to hear all causes, and to assist the said twelve men of the neighbourhood in case of law; and that they the said justices shall pronounce such judgment as they shall receive from, and be directed by the said twelve men, in whom only the judgment resides, and not otherwise.

And in case of their neglect and refusal, that then one of the twelve, by consent of the rest, pronounce their own judgment as the justices should have done.

And if any judgment shall be past, in any case civil or criminal, by any other person or persons, or any other way, then according to this agreement and appointment, it shall be held null and void, and such person or persons so presuming to give judgment, shall be severely fin'd, and upon complaint made to the General Assembly, by them be declared incapable of any office or trust within this Province.

Chapter XX

THAT in all matters and causes, civil and criminal, proof is to be made by the solemn and plain averment, of at least two honest and reputable persons; and in case that any person or persons shall bear false witness, and bring in his or their evidence, contrary to the truth of the matter as shall be made plainly to appear, that then every such person or persons, shall in civil causes, suffer the penalty which would be due to the person or persons he or they bear witness against. And in case any witness or witnesses, on the behalf of any person or persons, indicted in a criminal cause, shall be found to have born false witness for fear, gain, malice or favour, and thereby hinder the due execution of the law, and deprive the suffering person or persons of their due satisfaction, that then and in all other cases of false evidence, such person or persons, shall be first severly fined, and next that he or they shall forever be disabled from being admitted in evidence, or into any publick office, employment, or service within this Province.

Chapter XXI

THAT all and every person and persons whatsoever, who shall prosecute or prefer any indictment or information against others for any personal injuries, or matter criminal, or shall prosecute for any other criminal cause, (treason, murther, and felony, only excepted) shall and may be master of his own process, and have full power to forgive and remit the person or persons offending against him or herself only, as well before as after judgment, and condemnation, and pardon and remit the sentence, fine and punishment of the person or persons offending, be it personal or other whatsoever.

Chapter XXII

THAT the tryals of all causes, civil and criminal, shall be heard and decided by the virdict or judgment of twelve honest men of the neighbourhood, only to be summoned and presented by the sheriff of that division, or propriety where the fact or trespass is committed; and that no person or persons shall be compelled to fee any attorney or counciller to plead his cause, but that all persons have free liberty to plead his own cause, if he please: And that no person nor persons imprisoned upon any account whatsoever within this Province, shall be obliged to pay any fees to the officer or officers of the said prison, either when committed or discharged.

Chapter XXIII

THAT in all publick courts of justice for tryals of causes, civil or criminal, any person or persons, inhabitants of the said Province may freely come into, and attend the said courts, and hear and be present, at all or any such tryals as shall be there had or passed, that justice may not be done in a corner nor in any covert manner, being intended and resolved, by the help of the Lord, and by these our Concessions and Fundamentals, that all and every person and persons inhabiting the said Province, shall, as far as in us lies, be free from oppression and slavery.

E. HABEAS CORPUS ACT

May 27, 1679

WHEREAS *great delays have been used by sheriffs, gaolers and other officers, to whose custody any of the King's subjects have been committed for criminal or supposed criminal matters, in making returns of writs of* habeas corpus *to them directed, by standing out an* alias *and* pluries habeas corpus, *and sometimes more, and by other shifts to avoid their yielding obedience to such writs, contrary to their duty and the known laws of the land, whereby many of the King's subjects have been and hereafter may be long detained in prison, in such cases where by law they are bailable, to their great charges and vexation:*

II. For the prevention whereof, and the more speedy relief of all persons imprisoned for any such criminal or supposed criminal matters; be it enacted by the King's most excellent majesty, by and with the advice and consent of the lords spiritual and temporal, and commons, in this present parliament assembled, and by the authority thereof, That whensoever any person or persons shall bring any *habeas corpus* directed unto any sheriff or sheriffs, gaoler, minister or other person whatsoever, for any person in his or their custody, and the said writ shall be served upon the said officer, or left at the gaol or prison with any of the under-officers, under-keepers or deputy of the said officers or keepers, that the said officer or officers, his or their under-officers, under-keepers or deputies, shall within three days after the service thereof as aforesaid (unless the commitment aforesaid were for treason or felony, plainly and specially expressed in the warrant of commitment) upon payment or tender of the charges of bringing the said prisoner, to be ascertained by the judge or court that awarded the same, and endorsed upon the said writ, not exceeding twelve pence *per* mile, and upon security given by his own bond to pay the charges of carrying back the prisoner, if he shall be remanded by the court or judge to which he shall be brought according to the true intent of this present act, and that he will not make any escape by the way, make return of such writ; and bring or cause to be brought the body of the party so committed or restrained, unto or before the lord chancellor, or lord keeper of the great seal of *England* for the time being, or the judges or barons of the said court from whence the said writ shall issue, or unto and before such other person or persons before whom the said writ is made returnable, according to the command thereof; and shall then likewise certify the true causes of his detainer or imprisonment, unless the commitment of the said party be in any place beyond the distance of twenty miles from the place or places where such court or person is or shall be residing; and if beyond the distance of twenty miles, and not above one hundred miles, then within the space of ten days, and if beyond the distance of one hundred miles, then within the space of twenty days, after such delivery aforesaid, and not longer.

III. And to the intent that no sheriff, gaoler or other officer may pretend ignorance of the import of any such writ; be it enacted by the authority aforesaid, That all such writs shall be marked in this manner, *Per statutum tricesimo primo Caroli secundi Regis,* and shall be signed by the person that awards the same; and if any person or persons shall be or stand committed or detained as aforesaid, for any crime, unless for felony or treason plainly expressed in the warrant of commitment, in the vacation-time, and out of term, it shall and may be lawful to and for the person or persons so committed or detained (other than persons convict or in execution by legal process) or any one on his or their behalf, to appeal or complain to the lord chancellor or lord keeper, or any one of his Majesty's justices, either of the one bench or of the other or the barons of the exchequer of the degree of the coif; and the said lord chancellor, lord keeper, justices or barons or any of them, upon view of the copy or copies of the warrant or warrants of commitment and detainer, or otherwise upon oath made that such copy or copies were denied to be given by such person or persons in whose custody the prisoner or prisoners is or are detained, are hereby authorized and required, upon request made in writing by such person or persons, or any on his, her or their behalf, attested and subscribed by two witnesses who were present at the delivery of the same, to award and grant an *habeas corpus* under the seal of such court whereof he shall then be one of the judges; to be directed to the officer or officers in whose custody the party so committed or detained shall be, returnable *immediate* before the said lord chancellor or lord keeper, or such justice, baron or any other justice or baron of the degree of the coif of any of the said courts; and upon service thereof as aforesaid, the officer or officers, his or their under-officer or under-officers, under-keeper or under-keepers, or their deputy, in whose custody the party is so committed or detained, shall within the times respectively before limited, bring such prisoner or prisoners before the said lord chancellor or lord keeper, or such justices, barons or one of them, before whom the said writ is made returnable, and in case of his absence before any other of them, with the return of such writ, and the true causes of the commitment and detainer; and thereupon within two days after the party shall be brought before them, the said lord chancellor or lord keeper, or such justice or baron before whom the prisoner shall be brought as aforesaid, shall discharge the said prisoner from his imprisonment, taking his or their recognizance, with one or more surety or sureties, in any sum according to their discretions, having regard to the quality of the prisoner and nature of the offence, for his or their appearance in the court of King's bench the term following, or at the next assizes, sessions or general gaol-delivery of and for such county, city or place where the commitment was, or where the offence was committed, or in such other court where the said offence is properly cognizable, as the case shall require, and then shall certify the said writ with the return thereof, and the said recognizance or recognizances into the said court where such appearance is to be made; unless it shall appear unto the said lord chancellor or lord keeper, or justice or justices, or baron or barons, that the party so committed is detained upon a legal process, order or warrant, out of some court that hath jurisdiction of criminal matters, or by some warrant signed and sealed with the hand and seal of any of the said justices or barons, or some justice or justices of the peace, for such matters or offences for the which by the law the prisoner is not bailable.

IV.   Provided always, and be it enacted, That if any person shall have wilfully neglected by the space of two whole terms after his imprisonment, to pray a *habeas corpus* for his enlargement, such person so wilfully neglecting shall not have any *habeas corpus* to be granted in vacation-time, in pursuance of this act.

V.   And be it further enacted by the authority aforesaid, That if any officer or officers, his or their under-officer or under-officers, under-keeper or under-keepers, or deputy, shall neglect or refuse to make the returns aforesaid, or to bring the body or bodies of the prisoner or prisoners according to the command of the said writ, within the respective times aforesaid, or upon demand made by the prisoner or person in his behalf, shall refuse to deliver, or within the space of six hours after demand shall not deliver, to the person so demanding, a true copy of the warrant or warrants of commitment and detainer of such prisoner, which he and they are hereby required to deliver accordingly, all and every the head gaolers and keepers of such prisons, and such other person in whose custody the prisoner shall be detained, shall for the first offence forfeit to the prisoner or party grieved the sum of one hundred pounds; and for the second offence the sum of two hundred pounds, and shall and is hereby made incapable to hold or execute his said office; the said penalties to be recovered by the prisoner or party grieved, his executors or administrators, against such offender, his executors or administrators, by any action of debt, suit, bill, plaint or information, in any of the King's courts at *Westminster,* wherein no essoin, protection, privilege, injunction, wager of law, or stay of prosecution by *Non vult ulterius prosequi,* or otherwise, shall be admitted or allowed, or any more than one imparlance; and any recovery or judgment at the suit of any party grieved, shall be a sufficient conviction for the first offence; and any after recovery or judgment at the suit of a party grieved for any offence after the first judgment, shall be a sufficient conviction to bring the officers or person within the said penalty for the second offence.

VI.   And for the prevention of unjust vexation by reiterated commitments for the same offence; be it enacted by the authority aforesaid, That no person or persons which shall be delivered or set at large upon any *habeas corpus,* shall at any time hereafter be again imprisoned or committed for the same offence by any person or persons whatsoever, other than by the legal order and process of such court wherein he or they shall be bound by recognizance to appear, or other court having jurisdiction of the cause; and if any other person or persons shall knowingly contrary to this act recommit or imprison, or knowingly procure or cause to be recommitted or imprisoned, for the same offence or pretended offence, any person or persons delivered or set at large as aforesaid, or be knowingly aiding or assisting therein, then he or they shall forfeit to the prisoner or party grieved the sum of five hundred pounds; any colourable pretence or variation in the warrant or warrants of commitment notwithstanding, to be recovered as aforesaid.

682

VII. Provided always, and be it further enacted, That if any person or persons shall be committed for high treason or felony, plainly and specially expressed in the warrant of commitment, upon his prayer or petition in open court the first week of the term, or first day of the sessions of *oyer* and *terminer* or general gaol-delivery, to be brought to his trial, shall not be indicted some time in the next term, sessions of *oyer* and *terminer* or general gaol-delivery, after such commitment; it shall and may be lawful to and for the judges of the court of King's bench and justices of *oyer* and *terminer* or general gaol-delivery, and they are hereby required, upon motion to them made in open court the last day of the term, sessions or gaol-delivery, either by the prisoner or any one in his behalf, to set at liberty the prisoner upon bail, unless it appear to the judges and justices upon oath made, that the witnesses for the King could not be produced the same term, sessions or general gaol-delivery; and if any person or persons committed as aforesaid, upon his prayer or petition in open court the first week of the term or first day of the sessions of *oyer* and *terminer* and general gaol-delivery, to be brought to his trial, shall not be indicted and tried the second term, sessions of *oyer* and *terminer* or general gaol-delivery, after his commitment, or upon his trial shall be acquitted, he shall be discharged from his imprisonment.

VIII. Provided always, That nothing in this act shall extend to discharge out of prison any person charged in debt, or other action, or with process in any civil cause, but that after he shall be discharged of his imprisonment for such his criminal offence, he shall be kept in custody according to the law, for such other suit.

IX. Provided always, and be it enacted by the authority aforesaid, That if any person or persons, subjects of this realm, shall be committed to any prison or in custody of any officer or officers whatsoever, for any criminal or supposed criminal matter, that the said person shall not be removed from the said prison and custody into the custody of any other officer or officers; unless it be by *habeas corpus* or some other legal writ; or where the prisoner is delivered to the constable or other inferior officer to carry such prisoner to some common gaol; or where any person is sent by order of any judge of assize or justice of the peace, to any common workhouse or house of correction; or where the prisoner is removed from one prison or place to another within the same county, in order to his or her trial or discharge in due course of law; or in case of sudden fire or infection, or other necessity; and if any person or persons shall after such commitment aforesaid make out and sign, or countersign any warrant or warrants for such removal aforesaid, contrary to this act; as well he that makes or signs, or countersigns such warrant or warrants, as the officer or officers that obey or execute the same, shall suffer and incur the pains and forfeitures in this act before mentioned, both for the first and second offence respectively, to be recovered in manner aforesaid by the party grieved.

X. Provided also, and be it further enacted by the authority aforesaid, That it shall and may be lawful to and for any prisoner and prisoners as aforesaid, to move and obtain his or their *habeas corpus* as well out of the high court of chancery or court of exchequer, as out of the courts of King's bench or common pleas, or either of them; and if the said lord chancellor or lord keeper, or any judge or judges, baron or barons for the time being, of the degree of the coif, of any of the courts aforesaid, in the vacation time, upon view of the copy or copies of the warrant or warrants of commitment or detainer, or upon oath made that such copy or copies were denied as aforesaid, shall deny any writ of *habeas corpus* by this act required to be granted, being moved for as aforesaid, they shall severally forfeit to the prisoner or party grieved the sum of five hundred pounds, to be recovered in manner aforesaid.

XI. And be it declared and enacted by the authority aforesaid, That an *habeas corpus* according to the true intent and meaning of this act, may be directed and run into any county palatine, the cinque-ports, or other privileged places within the kingdom of *England,* dominion of *Wales,* or town of *Berwick* upon *Tweed,* and the islands of *Jersey* or *Guernsey;* any law or usage to the contrary notwithstanding.

XII. And for preventing illegal imprisonments in prisons beyond the seas; be it further enacted by the authority aforesaid, That no subject of this realm that now is, or hereafter shall be an inhabitant or resiant of this kingdom of *England,* dominion of *Wales,* or town of *Berwick* upon *Tweed,* shall or may be sent prisoner into *Scotland, Ireland, Jersey, Guernsey, Tangier,* or into parts, garrisons, islands or places beyond the seas, which are or at any time hereafter shall be within or without the dominions of his Majesty, his heirs or successors; and that every such imprisonment is hereby enacted and adjudged to be illegal; and that if any of the said subjects now is or hereafter shall be so imprisoned, every such person and persons so imprisoned, shall and may for every such imprisonment maintain by virtue of this act an action or actions of false imprisonment, in any of his Majesty's courts of record, against the person or persons by whom he or she shall be so committed, detained, imprisoned, sent prisoner or transported, contrary to the true meaning of this act, and against all or any person or persons that shall frame, contrive, write, seal or countersign any warrant or writing for such commitment, detainer, imprisonment or transportation, or shall be advising, aiding or assisting, in the same, or any of them; and the plaintiff in every such action shall have judgment to recover his treble costs, besides damages, which damages so to be given, shall not be less than five hundred pounds; in which action no delay stay or stop of proceeding by rule, order or command, nor no injunction, protection or privilege whatsoever, nor any more than one imparlance shall be allowed, excepting such rule of the court wherein the action shall depend, made in open court, as shall be thought in justice necessary, for special cause to be expressed in the said rule; and the person or persons who shall knowingly frame, contrive, write, seal or countersign any warant for such commitment, detainer or transportation, or shall so commit, detain, imprison or transport any person or persons contrary to this act, or be any ways advising, aiding or assisting therein, being lawfully convicted thereof, shall be disabled from thenceforth to bear any office of trust or profit within the said realm of *England*, dominion of *Wales,* or town of *Berwick* upon *Tweed,* or any of the islands, territories or dominions thereunto belonging; and shall incur and sustain the pains, penalties and forfeitures limited, ordained and provided in and by the statute of provision and praemunire made in the sixteenth year of King *Richard* the Second; and be incapable of any pardon from the King, his heirs or successors, of the said forfeitures, losses or disabilities, or any of them.

XIII. Provided always, That nothing in this act shall extend to give benefit to any person who shall by contract in writing agree with any merchant or owner of any plantation, or other person whatsoever, to be transported to any parts beyond the seas, and receive earnest upon such agreement, although that afterwards such person shall renounce such contract.

XIV. Provided always, and be it enacted, That if any person or persons lawfully convicted of any felony, shall in open court pray to be transported beyond the seas, and the court shall think fit to leave him or them in prison for that purpose, such person or persons may be transported into any parts beyond the seas, this act or any thing therein contained to the contrary notwithstanding.

XV. Provided also, and be it enacted, That nothing herein contained shall be deemed, construed or taken, to extend to the imprisonment of any person before the first day of *June* one thousand six hundred seventy and nine, or to any thing advised, procured, or otherwise done, relating to such imprisonment; any thing herein contained to the contrary notwithstanding.

XVI. Provided also, That if any person or persons at any time resiant in this realm, shall have committed any capital offence in *Scotland* or *Ireland,* or any of the islands, or foreign plantations of the King, his heirs or successors, where he or she ought to be tried for such offence, such person or persons may be sent to such place, there to receive such trial, in such manner as the same might have been used before the making of this act; any thing herein contained to the contrary notwithstanding.

XVII. Provided also, and be it enacted, That no person or persons shall be sued, impleaded, molested, or troubled for any offence against this act, unless the party offending be sued or impleaded for the same within two years at the most after such time wherein the offence shall be committed, in case the party grieved shall not be then in prison; and if he shall be in prison, then within the space of two years after the decease of the person imprisoned, or his or her delivery out of prison, which shall first happen.

XVIII.   And to the intent no person may avoid his trial at the assizes or general gaol-delivery, by procuring his removal before the assizes, at such time as he cannot be brought back to receive his trial there; be it enacted, That after the assizes proclaimed for that county where the prisoner is detained, no person shall be removed from the common gaol upon any *habeas corpus* granted in pursuance of this act, but upon any such *habeas corpus* shall be brought before the judge of assize in open court, who is thereupon to do what to justice shall appertain.

XIX.   Provided nevertheless, That after the assizes are ended, any person or persons detained, may have his or her *habeas corpus* according to the direction and intention of this act.

XX.   And be it also enacted by the authority aforesaid, That if any information, suit or action shall be brought or exhibited against any person or persons for any offence committed or to be committed against the form of this law, it shall be lawful for such defendants to plead the general issue, that they are not guilty, or that they owe nothing, and to give such special matter in evidence to the jury that shall try the same, which matter being pleaded had been good and sufficient matter in law to have discharged the said defendant or defendants against the said information, suit or action, and the said matter shall be then as available to him or them, to all intents and purposes, as if he or they had sufficiently pleaded, set forth or alledged the same matter in bar or discharge of such information suit or action.

XXI.   *And because many times persons charged with petty treason or felony, or as accessaries thereunto, are committed upon suspicion only, whereupon they are bailable, or not, according as the circumstances making out that suspicion are more or less weighty, which are best known to the justices of peace that committed the persons, and have the examinations before them, or to other justices of the peace in the county;* be it therefore enacted, That where any person shall appear to be committed by any judge or justice of the peace and charged as accessary before the fact, to any petty treason or felony, or upon suspicion thereof, or with suspicion of petty treason or felony, which petty treason or felony shall be plainly and specially expressed in the warrant of commitment, that such person shall not be removed or bailed by virtue of this act, or in any other manner than they might have been before the making of this act.

F.   [ENGLISH] BILL OF RIGHTS

December 16, 1689

An act for declaring the rights and liberties of the subject, and settling the succession of the crown.

WHEREAS the lords spiritual and temporal, and commons assembled at Westminster, lawfully, fully, and freely representing all the estates of the people of this realm, did upon the thirteenth day of February, in the year of our Lord one thousand six hundred eighty eight, present unto their Majesties, then called and known by the names and stile of William and Mary, prince and princess of Orange, being present in their proper persons, a certain declaration in writing, made by the said lords and commons, in the words following; viz.

WHEREAS the late King James the Second, by the assistance of divers evil counsellors, judges, and ministers employed by him, did endeavour to subvert and extirpate the protestant religion, and the laws and liberties of this kingdom.

1. By assuming and exercising a power of dispensing with and suspending of laws, and the execution of laws, without consent of parliament.

2. By committing and prosecuting divers worthy prelates, for humbly petitioning to be excused from concurring to the said assumed power.

3. By issuing and causing to be executed a commission under the great seal for erecting a court called, The court of commissioners for ecclesiastical causes.

4. By levying money for and to the use of the crown, by pretence of prerogative, for other time, and in other manner, than the same was granted by parliament.

5. By raising and keeping a standing army within this kingdom in time of peace, without consent of parliament, and quartering soldiers contrary to law.

6. By causing several good subjects, being protestants, to be disarmed, at the same time when papists were both armed and employed, contrary to law.

7. By violating the freedom of election of members to serve in parliament.

8. By prosecutions in the court of King's bench, for matters and causes cognizable only in parliament; and by divers other arbitrary and illegal courses.

9. And whereas of late years, partial, corrupt, and unqualified persons have been returned and served on juries in trials, and particularly divers jurors in trials for high treason, which were not freeholders.

10. And excessive bail hath been required of persons committed in criminal cases, to elude the benefit of the laws made for the liberty of the subjects.

11. And excessive fines have been imposed; and illegal and cruel punishments inflicted.

12. And several grants and promises made of fines and forfeitures, before any conviction or judgment against the persons, upon whom the same same were to be levied.

All which are utterly and directly contrary to the known laws and statutes, and freedom of this realm.

And whereas the said late King James the Second having abdicated the government, and the throne being thereby vacant, his highness the prince of Orange (whom it hath pleased Almighty God to make the glorious instrument of delivering this kingdom from popery and arbitrary power) did (by the advice of the lords spiritual and temporal, and divers principal persons of the commons) cause letters to be written to the lords spiritual and temporal, being protestants; and other letters to the several counties, cities, universities, boroughs, and cinque-ports, for the choosing of such persons to represent them, as were of right to be sent to parliament, to meet and sit at Westminster upon the two and twentieth day of January, in this year one thousand six hundred eighty and eight, in order to such an establishment, as that their religion, laws, and liberties might not again be in danger of being subverted: upon which letters, elections have been accordingly made,

And thereupon the said lords spiritual and temporal, and commons, pursuant to their respective letters and elections, being now assembled in a full and free representative of this nation, taking into their most serious consideration the best means for attaining the ends aforesaid; do in the first place (as their ancestors in like case have usually done) for the vindicating and asserting their ancient rights and liberties, declare;

1. That the pretended power of suspending of laws, or the execution of laws, by regal authority, without consent of parliament, is illegal.

2. That the pretended power of dispensing with laws, or the execution of laws, by regal authority, as it hath been assumed and exercised of late, is illegal.

3. That the commission for erecting the late court of commissioners for ecclesiastical causes, and all other commissions and courts of like nature are illegal and pernicious.

4. That levying money for or to the use of the crown, by pretence of prerogative, without grant of parliament, for longer time, or in other manner than the same is or shall be granted, is illegal.

5. That it is the right of the subjects to petition the King, and all committments and prosecutions for such petitioning are illegal.

6. That the raising or keeping a standing army within the kingdom in time of peace, unless it be with consent of parliament, is against law.

7. That the subjects which are protestants, may have arms for their defence suitable to their conditions, and as allowed by law.

8. That election of members of parliament ought to be free.

9. That the freedom of speech, and debates or proceedings in parliament, ought not to be impeached or questioned in any court or place out of parliament.

10. That excessive bail ought not to be required, nor excessive fines imposed; nor cruel and unusual punishments inflicted.

11. That jurors ought to be duly impanelled and returned, and jurors which pass upon men in trials for high treason ought to be freeholders.

12. That all grants and promises of fines and forfeitures of particular persons before conviction, are illegal and void.

13. And that for redress of all grievances, and for the amending, strengthening, and preserving of the laws, parliaments ought to be held frequently.

And they do claim, demand, and insist upon all and singular the premises, as their undoubted rights and liberties; and that no declarations, judgments, doings or proceedings, to the prejudice of the people in any of the said premises, ought in any wise to be drawn hereafter into consequence or example.

To which demand of their rights they are particularly encouraged by the declaration of his highness the prince of Orange, as being the only means for obtaining a full redress and remedy therein.

Having therefore an entire confidence, That his said highness the prince of Orange will perfect the deliverance so far advanced by him, and will still preserve them from the violation of their rights, which they have here asserted, and from all other attempts upon their religion, rights, and liberties.

II. The said lords spiritual and temporal, and commons, assembled at Westminster, do resolve, That William and Mary prince and princess of Orange be, and be declared, King and Queen of England, France and Ireland, and the dominions thereunto belonging, to hold the crown and royal dignity of the said kingdoms and dominions to them the said prince and princess during their lives, and the life of the survivor of them; and that the sole and full exercise of the regal power be only in, and executed by the said prince of Orange, in the names of the said prince and princess, during their joint lives; and after their deceases, the said crown and royal dignity of the said kingdoms and dominions to be to the heirs of the body of the said princess; and for default of such issue to the princess Anne of Denmark, and the heirs of her body; and for default of such issue to the heirs of the body of the said prince of Orange. And the lords spiritual and temporal, and commons, do pray the said prince and princess to accept the same accordingly.

III. And that the oaths hereafter mentioned be taken by all persons of whom the oaths of allegiance and supremacy might be required by law, instead of them; and that the said oaths of allegiance and supremacy be abrogated.

I A. B. do sincerely promise and swear, That I will be faithful, and bear true allegiance, to their Majesties King William and Queen Mary:

So help me God.

I A. B. do swear, That I do from my heart abhor, detest, and abjure as impious and heretical, that damnable doctrine and position, That princes excommunicated or deprived by the pope, or any authority of the see of Rome, may be deposed or murdered by their subjects, or any other whatsoever. And I do declare, That no foreign prince, person, prelate, state, or potentate hath, or ought to have any jurisdiction, power, superiority, pre-eminence, or authority ecclesiastical or spiritual, within this realm:

So help me God.

IV. Upon which their said Majesties did accept the crown and royal dignity of the kingdoms of England, France, and Ireland, and the dominions thereunto belonging, according to the resolution and desire of the said lords and commons contained in the said declaration.

V. And thereupon their Majesties were pleased, That the said lords spiritual and temporal, and commons, being the two houses of parliament, should continue to sit, and with their Majesties royal concurrence make effectual provision for the settlement of the religion, laws and liberties of this kingdom, so that the same for the future might not be in danger again of being subverted; to which the said lords spiritual and temporal, and commons, did agree and proceed to act accordingly.

VI. Now in pursuance of the premises, the said lords spiritual and temporal, and commons, in parliament assembled, for the ratifying, confirming and establishing the said declaration, and the articles, clauses, matters, and things therein contained, by the force of a law made in due form by authority of parliament, do pray that it may be declared and enacted, That all and singular the rights and liberties asserted and claimed in the said declaration, are the true, ancient, and indubitable rights and liberties of the people of this kingdom, and so shall be esteemed, allowed, adjudged, deemed, and taken to be, and that all and every the particulars aforesaid shall be firmly and strictly holden and observed, as they are expressed in the said declaration; and all officers and ministers whatsoever shall serve their Majesties and their successors according to the same in all times to come.

VII. And the said lords spiritual and temporal, and commons, seriously considering how it hath pleased Almighty God, in his marvellous providence, and merciful goodness to this nation, to provide and preserve their said Majesties royal persons most happily to reign over us upon the throne of their ancestors, for which they render unto him from the bottom of their hearts their humblest thanks and praises, do truly, firmly, assuredly, and in the sincerity of their hearts think, and do hereby recognize, acknowledge and declare, That King *James* the Second having abdicated the government, and their Majesties having accepted the crown and royal dignity as aforesaid, their said Majesties did become, were, are, and of right ought to be, by the laws of this realm, our sovereign liege lord and lady, King and Queen of *England, France,* and *Ireland,* and the dominions thereunto belonging, in and to whose princely persons the royal state, crown, and dignity of the said realms, with all honours, stiles, titles, regalities, prerogatives, powers, jurisdictions and authorities to the same belonging and appertaining, are most fully, rightfully, and intirely invested and incorporated, united and annexed.

VIII.   And for preventing all questions and divisions in this realm, by reason of any pretended titles to the crown, and for preserving a certainty in the succession thereof, in and upon which the unity, peace, tranquillity, and safety of this nation doth, under God, wholly consist and depend, The said lords spiritual and temporal, and commons, do beseech their Majesties that it may be enacted, established and declared, That the crown and regal government of the said kingdoms and dominions, with all and singular the premisses thereunto belonging and appertaining, shall be and continue to their said Majesties, and the survivor of them, during their lives, and the life of the survivor of them: And that the intire, perfect, and full exercise of the regal power and government be only in, and executed by his Majesty, in the names of both their Majesties during their joint lives; and after their deceases the said crown and premisses shall be and remain to the heirs of the body of her Majesty; and for default of such issue, to her royal highness the princess *Anne of Denmark,* and the heirs of her body; and for default of such issue, to the heirs of the body of his said Majesty: And thereunto the said lords spiritual and temporal, and commons, do, in the name of all the people aforesaid, most humbly and faithfully submit themselves, their heirs and posterities for ever; and do faithfully promise, That they will stand to, maintain, and defend their said Majesties, and also the limitation and succession of the crown herein specified and contained, to the utmost of their powers, with their lives and estates, against all persons whatsoever, that shall attempt any thing to the contrary.

IX.   *And whereas it hath been found by experience, that it is inconsistent with the safety and welfare of this protestant kingdom, to be governed by a popish prince, or by any King or Queen marrying a papist;* the said lords spiritual and temporal, and commons, do further pray that it may be enacted, That all and every person and persons that is, are or shall be reconciled to, or shall hold communion with, the see or church of *Rome,* or shall profess the popish religion, or shall marry a papist, shall be excluded, and be for ever incapable to inherit, possess, or enjoy the crown and government of this realm, and *Ireland,* and the dominions thereunto belonging, or any part of the same, or to have, use, or exercise any regal power, authority, or jurisdiction within the same; and in all and every such case or cases the people of these realms shall be, and are hereby absolved of their allegiance; and the said crown and government shall from time to time descend to, and be enjoyed by such person or persons, being protestants, as should have inherited and enjoyed the same, in case the said person or persons so reconciled, holding communion, or professing, or marrying as aforesaid, were naturally dead.

X. And that every King and Queen of this realm, who at any time hereafter shall come to and succeed in the imperial crown of this kingdom, shall on the first day of the meeting of the first parliament, next after his or her coming to the crown, sitting in his or her throne in the house of peers, in the presence of the lords and commons therein assembled, or at his or her coronation, before such person or persons who shall administer the coronation oath to him or her, at the time of his or her taking the said oath (which shall first happen) make, subscribe, and audibly repeat the declaration mentioned in the statute made in the thirtieth year of the reign of King *Charles* the Second, intituled, *An act for the more effectual preserving the King's person and government, by disabling papists from sitting in either house of parliament.* But if it shall happen, that such King or Queen, upon his or her succession to the crown of this realm, shall be under the age of twelve years, then every such King or Queen shall make, subscribe, and audibly repeat the said declaration at his or her coronation, or the first day of the meeting of the first parliament as aforesaid, what shall first happen after such King or Queen shall have attained the said age of twelve years.

XI. All which their Majesties are contented and pleased shall be declared, enacted, and established by authority of this present parliament, and shall stand, remain, and be the law of this realm for ever; and the same are by their said Majesties, by and with the advice and consent of the lords spiritual and temporal, and commons, in parliament assembled, and by the authority of the same, declared, enacted, and established accordingly.

XII. And be it further declared and enacted by the authority aforesaid, That from and after this present session of parliament, no dispensation by *non obstante* of or to any statute, or any part thereof, shall be allowed, but that the same shall be held void and of no effect, except a dispensation be allowed of in such statute, and except in such cases as shall be specially provided for by one or more bill or bills to be passed during this present session of parliament.

XIII. Provided that no charter, or grant, or pardon, granted before the three and twentieth day of *October,* in the year of our Lord one thousand six hundred eighty nine shall be any ways impeached or invalidated by this act, but that the same shall be and remain of the same force and effect in law, and no other then as if this act had never been made.

692

G. CONTINENTAL CONGRESS TO THE INHABITANTS OF THE PROVINCE OF QUEBEC

October 26, 1774

Friends and fellow-subjects,

We, the Delegates of the Colonies of New-Hampshire, Massachusetts-Bay, Rhode-Island and Providence Plantations, Connecticut, New-York, New-Jersey, Pennsylvania, the Counties of Newcastle Kent and Sussex on Delaware, Maryland, Virginia, North-Carolina and South-Carolina, deputed by the inhabitants of the said Colonies, to represent them in a General Congress at Philadelphia, in the province of Pennsylvania, to consult together concerning the best methods to obtain redress of our afflicting grievances, having accordingly assembled, and taken into our most serious consideration the state of public affairs on this continent, have thought proper to address your province, as a member therein deeply interested.

When the fortune of war, after a gallant and glorious resistance, had incorporated you with the body of English subjects, we rejoiced in the truly valuable addition, both on our own and your account; expecting, as courage and generosity are naturally united, our brave enemies would become our hearty friends, and that the Divine Being would bless to you the dispensations of his over-ruling providence, by securing to you and your latest posterity the inestimable advantages of a free English constitution of government, which it is the privilege of all English subjects to enjoy.

These hopes were confirmed by the King's proclamation, issued in the year 1763, plighting the public faith for your full enjoyment of those advantages.

Little did we imagine that any succeeding Ministers would so audaciously and cruelly abuse the royal authority, as to with-hold from you the fruition of the irrevocable rights, to which you were thus justly entitled.

But since we have lived to see the unexpected time, when Ministers of this flagitious temper, have dared to violate the most sacred compacts and obligations, and as you, educated under another form of government, have artfully been kept from discovering the unspeakable worth of *that* form you are now undoubtedly entitled to, we esteem it our duty, for the weighty reasons herein after mentioned, to explain to you some of its most important branches.

"In every human society," says the celebrated Marquis *Beccaria*, "there is an *effort, continually tending* to confer on one part the heighth of power and happiness, and to reduce the other to the extreme of

693

weakness and misery. The intent of good laws is to *oppose this effort,* and to diffuse their influence *universally* and *equally.*"

Rulers stimulated by this pernicious "effort," and subjects animated by the just "intent of opposing good laws against it," have occasioned that vast variety of events, that fill the histories of so many nations. All these histories demonstrate the truth of this simple position, that to live by the will of one man, or sett of men, is the production of misery to all men.

On the solid foundation of this principle, Englishmen reared up the fabrick of their constitution with such a strength, as for ages to defy time, tyranny, treachery, internal and foreign wars: And, as an illustrious author of your nation, hereafter mentioned, observes,—"They gave the people of their Colonies, the form of their own government, and this government carrying prosperity along with it, they have grown great nations in the forests they were sent to inhabit."

In this form, the first grand right, is that of the people having a share in their own government by their representatives chosen by themselves, and, in consequence, of being ruled by *laws,* which they themselves approve, not by *edicts* of *men* over whom they have no controul. This is a bulwark surrounding and defending their property, which by their honest cares and labours they have acquired, so that no portions of it can legally be taken from them, but with their own full and free consent, when they in their judgment deem it just and necessary to give them for public service, and precisely direct the easiest, cheapest, and most equal methods, in which they shall be collected.

The influence of this right extends still farther. If money is wanted by Rulers, who have in any manner oppressed the people, they may retain it, until their grievances are redressed; and thus peaceably procure relief, without trusting to despised petitions, or disturbing the public tranquillity.

The next great right is that of trial by jury. This provides, that neither life, liberty nor property, can be taken from the possessor, until twelve of his unexceptionable countrymen and peers of his vicinage, who from that neighbourhood may reasonably be supposed to be acquainted with his character, and the characters of the witnesses, upon a fair trial, and full enquiry, face to face, in open Court, before as many of the people as chuse to attend, shall pass their sentence upon oath against him; a sentence that cannot injure him, without injuring their own reputation, and probably their interest also; as the question may turn on points, that, in some degree, concern the general welfare; and if it does not, their verdict may form a precedent, that, on a similar trial of their own, may militate against themselves.

Another right relates merely to the liberty of the person. If a subject is seized and imprisoned, tho' by order of Government, he may, by virtue of this right, immediately obtain a writ, termed a Habeas

Corpus, from a Judge, whose sworn duty it is to grant it, and thereupon procure any illegal restraint to be quickly enquired into and redressed.

A fourth right, is that of holding lands by the tenure of easy rents, and not by rigorous and oppressive services, frequently forcing the possessors from their families and their business, to perform what ought to be done, in all well regulated states, by men hired for the purpose.

The last right we shall mention, regards the freedom of the press. The importance of this consists, besides the advancement of truth, science, morality, and arts in general, in its diffusion of liberal sentiments on the administration of Government, its ready communication of thoughts between subjects, and its consequential promotion of union among them, whereby oppressive officers are shamed or intimidated, into more honourable and just modes of conducting affairs.

These are the invaluable rights, that form a considerable part of our mild system of government; that, sending its equitable energy through all ranks and classes of men, defends the poor from the rich, the weak from the powerful, the industrious from the rapacious, the peaceable from the violent, the tenants from the lords, and all from their superiors.

These are the rights, without which a people cannot be free and happy, and under the protecting and encouraging influence of which, these colonies have hitherto so amazingly flourished and increased. These are the rights, a profligate Ministry are now striving, by force of arms, to ravish from us, and which we are, with one mind, resolved never to resign but with our lives.

These are the rights *you* are entitled to and ought at this moment in perfection, to exercise. And what is offered to you by the late Act of Parliament in their place? Liberty of conscience in your religion? No. God gave it to you; and the temporal powers with which you have been and are connected, firmly stipulated for your enjoyment of it. If laws, divine and human, could secure it against the despotic caprices of wicked men, it was secured before. Are the French laws in *civil* cases restored? *It seems so.* But observe the cautious kindness of the Ministers, who pretend to be your benefactors. The words of the statute are—that those "laws shall be the rule, until they shall be *varied* or *altered* by any ordinances of the Governor and Council." Is the "certainty and lenity of the *criminal* law of England, and its benefits and advantages," commended in the said statute, and said to "have been sensibly felt by you," secured to you and your descendants? No. They too are subjected to arbitrary *"alterations"* by the Governor and Council; and a power is expressly reserved of appointing "such courts of *criminal, civil,* and *ecclesiastical* jurisdiction, as shall be thought proper." Such is the precarious tenure of mere *will,* by which you hold your lives and religion. The Crown and its Ministers are impowered, as far as they could be by Parliament, to establish even the *Inquisition* itself among you. Have you an Assembly composed of worthy men, elected by yourselves, and in whom you can confide, to make laws for you, to watch over your welfare, and to direct in what quantity, and in what manner, your money shall be taken from you? No. The power of making laws for you is lodged in the governor and council, all of them dependent upon, and removeable at, the *pleasure* of a Minister. Besides, another late statute, made without your consent, has subjected you to the impositions of *Excise,* the horror of all free states; thus wresting your property from you by the most odious of taxes, and laying open to insolent tax-gatherers, houses, the scenes of domestic peace and comfort, and called the castles of English subjects in the books of their law. And in the very act for altering your government, and intended to flatter you, you are not authorized to "assess, levy, or apply any *rates* and *taxes,* but for the inferior purposes of *making roads,* and erecting and repairing *public buildings,* or for other *local* conveniences, within your respective towns and districts." Why this degrading distinction? Ought not the property, honestly acquired by *Canadians,* to be held as sacred as that of *Englishmen?* Have not Canadians sense enough to attend to any other public affairs, than gathering stones from one place, and piling them up in another? Unhappy people! who are not only injured, but insulted. Nay more!— With such a superlative contempt of your understanding and spirit, has an insolent Ministry presumed to think of you, our respectable fellow-subjects, according to the information we have received, as firmly to perswade themselves that your gratitude, for the injuries and insults they have recently offered to you, will engage you to take up arms, and render yourselves the ridicule and detestation of the world, by becoming tools, in their hands, to assist them in taking that freedom from *us,* which they have treacherously denied to *you;* the unavoidable consequence of which attempt, if successful, would be the extinction of all hopes of you or your posterity being ever restored to freedom: For idiocy itself cannot believe, that, when their drudgery is performed, they will treat you with less cruelty than they have us, who are of the same blood with themselves.

What would your countryman, the immortal *Montesquieu,* have said to such a plan of domination, as has been framed for you? Hear his words, with an intenseness of thought suited to the importance of the subject.—"In a free state, every man, who is supposed a free agent, *ought to be concerned in his own government:* Therefore the *legislative* should reside in the whole body of the *people,* or their *representatives.*"— "The political liberty of the subject is *a tranquillity of mind,* arising from the opinion each person has of his *safety.* In order to have this liberty, it is requisite the government be so constituted, as that one man need not be *afraid* of another. When the power of *making* laws, and the power of *executing* them, are *united* in the same person, or in the same body of Magistrates, *there can be no liberty;* because apprehensions may arise, lest the same *Monarch* or *Senate,* should *enact* tyrannical laws, to *execute* them in a tyrannical manner."

696

"The power of *judging* should be exercised by persons taken from the *body of the people,* at certain times of the year, and pursuant to a form and manner prescribed by law. *There is no liberty,* if the power of *judging* be not *separated* from the *legislative* and *executive* powers."

"Military men belong to a profession, which *may be* useful, but *is often* dangerous."—"The enjoyment of liberty, and even its support and preservation, consists in every man's being allowed to speak his thoughts, and lay open his sentiments."

Apply these decisive maxims, sanctified by the authority of a name which all Europe reveres, to your own state. You have a Governor, it may be urged, vested with the *executive* powers, or the powers of *administration:* In him, and in your Council, is lodged the power of *making laws.* You have *Judges,* who are to *decide* every cause affecting your lives, liberty or property. Here is, indeed, an appearance of the several powers being *separated* and *distributed* into *different* hands, for checks one upon another, the only effectual mode ever invented by the wit of men, to promote their freedom and prosperity. But scorning to be illuded by a tinsel'd outside, and exerting the natural sagacity of Frenchmen, *examine* the specious device, and you will find it, to use an expression of holy writ, "a whited sepulchre," for burying your lives, liberty and property.

Your *Judges,* and your *Legislative Council,* as it is called, are *dependant* on your *Governor,* and he is *dependant* on the servant of the Crown, in Great-Britain. The *legislative, executive* and *judging* powers are *all* moved by the nods of a Minister. Privileges and immunities last no longer than his smiles. When he frowns, their feeble forms dissolve. Such a treacherous ingenuity has been exerted in drawing up the code lately offered you, that every sentence, beginning with a benevolent pretension, concludes with a destructive power; and the substance of the whole, divested of its smooth words, is—that the Crown and its Ministers shall be as absolute throughout your extended province, as the despots of Asia or Africa. What can protect your property from taxing edicts, and the rapacity of necessitous and cruel masters? your persons from Letters de Cachet, gaols, dungeons, and oppressive services? your lives and general liberty from arbitrary and unfeeling rulers? We defy you, casting your view upon every side, to discover a single circumstance, promising from any quarter the faintest hope of liberty to you or your posterity, but from an entire adoption into the union of these Colonies.

What advice would the truly great man before-mentioned, that advocate of freedom and humanity, give you, was he now living, and knew that we, your numerous and powerful neighbours, animated by a just love of our invaded rights, and united by the indissoluble bands of affection and interest, called upon you, by every obligation of regard for yourselves and your children, as we now do, to join us in our righteous contest, to make common cause with us therein, and take a noble chance for emerging from a humiliating subjection under Governors, Intendants, and Military Tyrants, into the firm rank and condition of English freemen, whose custom it is, derived from their ancestors, to make those tremble, who dare to think of making them miserable?

Would not this be the purport of his address? "Seize the opportunity presented to you by Providence itself. You have been conquered into liberty, if you act as you ought. This work is not of man. You are a small people, compared to those who with open arms invite you into a fellowship. A moment's reflection should convince you which will be most for your interest and happiness, to have all the rest of North-America your unalterable friends, or your inveterate enemies. The injuries of Boston have roused and associated every colony, from Nova-Scotia to Georgia. Your province is the only link wanting, to compleat the bright and strong chain of union. Nature has joined your country to theirs. Do you join your political interests. For their own sakes, they never will desert or betray you. Be assured, that the happiness of a people inevitably depends on their liberty, and their spirit to assert it. The value and extent of the advantages tendered to you are immense. Heaven grant you may not discover them to be blessings after they have bid you an eternal adieu."

We are too well acquainted with the liberality of sentiment distinguishing your nation, to imagine, that difference of religion will prejudice you against a hearty amity with us. You know, that the transcendant nature of freedom elevates those, who unite in her cause, above all such low-minded infirmities. The Swiss Cantons furnish a memorable proof of this truth. Their union is composed of Roman Catholic and Protestant States, living in the utmost concord and peace with one another, and thereby enabled, ever since they bravely vindicated their freedom, to defy and defeat every tyrant that has invaded them.

Should there be any among you, as there generally are in all societies, who prefer the favours of Ministers, and their own private interests, to the welfare of their country, the temper of such selfish persons will render them incredibly active in opposing all public-spirited measures, from an expectation of being well rewarded for their sordid industry, by their superiors; but we doubt not you will be upon your guard against such men, and not sacrifice the liberty and happiness of the whole Canadian people and their posterity, to gratify the avarice and ambition of individuals.

We do not ask you, by this address, to commence acts of hostility against the government of our common Sovereign. We only invite you to consult your own glory and welfare, and not to suffer yourselves to be inveigled or intimidated by infamous ministers so far, as to become the instruments of their cruelty and despotism, but to unite with us in one social compact, formed on the generous principles of equal liberty, and cemented by such an exchange of beneficial and endearing offices as to render it perpetual. In order to complete this highly desirable union, we submit it to your consideration, whether it may not be expedient for you to meet together in your several towns and districts, and elect Deputies, who afterwards meeting in a provincial Congress, may chuse Delegates, to represent your province in the continental Congress to be held at Philadelphia on the tenth day of May, 1775.

In this present Congress, beginning on the fifth of the last month, and continued to this day, it has been, with universal pleasure and an unanimous vote, resolved, That we should consider the violation of your rights, by the act for altering the government of your province, as a violation of our own, and that you should be invited to accede to our confederation, which has no other objects than the perfect security of the natural and civil rights of all the constituent members, according to their respective circumstances, and the preservation of a happy and lasting connection with Great-Britain, on the salutary and constitutional principles herein before mentioned. For effecting these purposes, we have addressed an humble and loyal petition to his Majesty, praying relief of our and your grievances; and have associated to stop all importations from Great-Britain and Ireland, after the first day of December, and all exportations to those Kingdoms and the West-Indies, after the tenth day of next September, unless the said grievances are redressed.

That Almighty God may incline your minds to approve our equitable and necessary measures, to add yourselves to us, to put your fate, whenever you suffer injuries which you are determined to oppose, not on the small influence of your single province, but on the consolidated powers of North-America, and may grant to our joint exertions an event as happy as our cause is just, is the fervent prayer of us, your sincere and affectionate friends and fellow-subjects.

H. DEBATE IN THE PHILADELPHIA CONVENTION

(1) August 20, 1787

<Mr. Pinkney submitted to the House, in order to be referred to the Committee of detail, the following propositions—"Each House shall be the Judge of its own privileges, and shall have authority to punish by imprisonment every person violating the same; or who, in the place where the Legislature may be sitting and during the time of its Session, shall threaten any of its members for any thing said or done in the House, or who shall assault any of them therefor—or who shall assault or arrest any witness or other person ordered to attend either of the Houses in his way going or returning; or who shall rescue any person arrested by their order."

"Each branch of the Legislature, as well as the Supreme Executive shall have authority to require the opinions of the supreme Judicial Court upon important questions of law, and upon solemn occasions"

"The privileges and benefit of the Writ of Habeas corpus shall be enjoyed in this Government in the most expeditious and ample manner;

and shall not be suspended by the Legislature except upon the most urgent and pressing occasions, and for a limited time not exceeding months."

"The liberty of the Press shall be inviolably preserved"

"No troops shall be kept up in time of peace, but by consent of the Legislature"

"The military shall always be subordinate to the Civil power, and no grants of money shall be made by the Legislature for supporting military Land forces, for more than one year at a time"

"No soldier shall be quartered in any House in time of peace without consent of the owner."

"No person holding the office of President of the U. S., a Judge of their Supreme Court, Secretary for the department of Foreign Affairs, of Finance, of Marine, of War, or of   , shall be capable of holding at the same time any other office of Trust or Emolument under the U. S. or an individual State"

"No religious test or qualification shall ever be annexed to any oath of office under the authority of the U. S."

"The U. S. shall be for ever considered as one Body corporate and politic in law, and entitled to all the rights privileges, and immunities, which to Bodies corporate do or ought to appertain"

"The Legislature of the U. S. shall have the power of making the great Seal which shall be kept by the President of the U. S. or in his absence by the President of the Senate, to be used by them as the occasion may require.—It shall be called the great Seal of the U. S. and shall be affixed to all laws."

"All Commissions and writs shall run in the name of the U. S."

"The Jurisdiction of the supreme Court shall be extended to all controversies between the U. S. and an individual State, or the U. S. and the Citizens of an individual State"

These propositions were referred to the Committee of detail without debate or consideration of them, by the House.

(2) September 12, 1787

Mr. Williamson, observed to the House that no provision was yet made for juries in Civil cases and suggested the necessity of it.

Mr. Gorham. It is not possible to discriminate equity cases from those in which juries are proper. The Representatives of the people may be safely trusted in this matter.

Mr. Gerry urged the necessity of Juries to guard agst. corrupt Judges. He proposed that the Committee last appointed should be directed to provide a clause for securing the trial by Juries.

Col: Mason perceived the difficulty mentioned by Mr. Gorham. The jury cases cannot be specified. A general principle laid down on this and some other points would be sufficient. He wished the plan had been prefaced with a Bill of Rights, & would second a Motion if made for the purpose—It would give great quiet to the people; and with the aid of the State declarations, a bill might be prepared in a few hours.

Mr Gerry concurred in the idea & moved for a Committee to prepare a Bill of Rights. Col: Mason 2ded the motion.

Mr. Sherman. was for securing the rights of the people where requisite. The State Declarations of Rights are not repealed by this Constitution; and being in force are sufficient—There are many cases where juries are proper which cannot be discriminated. The Legislature may be safely trusted.

Col: Mason. The Laws of the U. S. are to be paramount to State Bills of Rights. On the question for a Come to prepare a Bill of Rights

N. H. no. Mas. abst. Ct no. N—J—no. Pa. no. Del—no. Md no. Va no. N—C. no. S—C—no—Geo—no. [Ayes—0; noes—10; absent—1.]

I. LETTER OF RICHARD HENRY LEE TO EDMUND RANDOLPH

October 16, 1787

New-York, Oct. 16, 1787.

DEAR SIR, I was duly honored with your favor of September 17th, from Philadelphia, which should have been acknowledged long before now, if the nature of the business that it related to had not required time.

The establishment of the new plan of government, in its present form, is a question that involves such immense consequences to the present times and to posterity, that it calls for the deepest attention of the best and wisest friends of their country and of mankind. If it be found good after mature deliberation, adopt it, if wrong, amend it at all events, for to say (as many do) that a bad government must be established for fear of anarchy, is really saying that we must kill ourselves for fear of dying. Experience and the actual state of things, shew that there is no difficulty in procuring a general convention; the late one being collected without any obstruction: Nor does external war, or internal discord prevent the most cool, collected, full, and fair discussion of this all-important subject. If with infinite ease, a convention was obtained to prepare a system, why may not another with equal ease be procured to make proper and necessary amendments? Good government is not the work of a short time, or of sudden thought. From *Moses* to *Montesquieu* the greatest geniuses have been employed on this difficult subject, and yet experience has shewn capital defects in the system produced for the government of mankind. But since it is neither prudent or easy to make frequent changes in government, and as bad governments have been generally found the most fixed; so it becomes of the last consequence to frame the first establishment upon ground the most unexceptionable, and such as the best theories with experience justify; not trusting as our new constitution does, and as many approve of doing, to time and future events to correct errors, that both reason and experience in similar cases, point out in the new system. It has hitherto been supposed a fundamental maxim that in governments rightly balanced, the different branches of legislature should be unconnected, and that the legislative and executive powers should be separate:—In the new constitution, the president and senate have all the executive and two thirds of the legislative power. In some weighty instances (as making all kinds of treaties which are to be the laws of the land) they have the whole legislative and executive powers. They jointly, appoint all officers civil and military, and they (the senate) try all impeachments either of their own members, or of the officers appointed by themselves.

Is there not a most formidable combination of power thus created in a few, and can the most critic eye, if a candid one, discover responsibility in this potent corps? Or will any sensible man say, that great power without responsibility can be given to rulers with safety to liberty? It is most clear that the parade of impeachment is nothing to them or any of them—as little restraint is to be found, I presume from the fear of offending constituents.—The president is for four years duration (and Virginia for example) has one vote of thirteen in the choice of him, and this thirteenth vote not of the people, but electors, two removes from the people. The senate is a body of six years duration, and as in the choice of president, the largest state has but a thirteenth vote, so is it in the choice of senators.—This latter statement is adduced to shew that responsibility is as little to be apprehended from amenability to constituents, as from the terror of impeachment. You are, therefore, Sir, well warranted in saying, either a monarchy or aristocracy will be generated, perhaps the most grievous system of government may arise. It cannot be denied with truth, that this new constitution is, in its first principles, highly and dangerously oligarchic; and it is a point agreed that a government of the few, is, of all governments, the worst. The only check to be found in favor of the democratic principle in this system is, the house of representatives; which I believe may justly be called a mere shread or rag of representation: It being obvious to the least examination, that smallness of number and great comparative disparity of power, renders that house of little effect to promote good, or restrain bad government. But what is the power given to this ill constructed body? To judge of what may be for the general welfare, and such judgments when made, the acts of Congress become the supreme laws of the land. This seems a power co-extensive with every possible object of human legislation.—Yet there is no restraint in form of a bill of rights, to secure (what Doctor Blackstone calls) that residuum of human rights, which is not intended to be given up to society, and which indeed is not necessary to be given for any good social purpose.—The rights of conscience, the freedom of the press, and the trial by jury are at mercy. It is there stated, that in criminal cases, the trial shall be by jury. But how? In the state. What then becomes of the jury of the vicinage or at least from the county in the first instance, for the states being from 50 to 700 miles in extent? This mode of trial even in criminal cases may be greatly impaired, and in civil causes the inference is strong, that it may be altogether omitted as the constitution positively assumes it in criminal, and is silent about it in civil causes.—Nay, it is more strongly discountenanced in civil cases by giving the supreme court in appeals, jurisdiction both as to law and fact. Judge Blackstone in his learned commentaries, art. jury trial, says, it is the most transcendant privilege which any subject can enjoy or wish for, that he cannot be affected either in his property, his liberty, his person, but by the unanimous consent of 12 of his neighbours and equals. A constitution that I may venture to affirm has under providence, secured the just liberties of this nation for a long succession of ages.—The impartial administration of justice, which secures both our persons and our properties, is the great end of civil society. But if that be entirely *entrusted* to the magistracy, a select body of men, and those generally selected by the prince, or such as enjoy the highest offices of the state, these decisions in spite of their own natural integrity, will have frequently an involuntary bias towards those of their own rank and dignity. It is not to be expected from human nature, that the few should always be attentive to the good of the many. The learned judge further says, that every tribunal selected for the decision of *facts*, is a step towards establishing aristocracy; the most oppressive of all governments. The answer to these objections is, that the new legislature may provide remedies!—But as they may, so they may not, and if they did, a succeeding assembly may repeal the provisions.—The evil is found resting upon constitutional bottom, and the remedy upon the mutable ground of legislation, revocable at any annual meeting. It is the more unfortunate that this great security of human rights, the trial by jury, should be weakened in this system, as power is unnecessarily given in the second section of the third article, to call people from their own country in all cases of controversy about property between citizens of different states and foreigners, with citizens of the United States, to be tried in a distant court where the Congress may sit. For although inferior congressional courts may for the above purposes be instituted in the different states, yet this is a matter altogether in the pleasure of the new legislature, so that if they please not to institute them, or if they do not regulate the right of appeal reasonably, the people will be exposed to endless oppression, and the necessity of submitting in multitudes of cases, to pay unjust demands, rather than follow suitors, through great expence, to far distant tribunals, and to be determined upon there, as it may be, without a jury.—In this congressional legislature, a bare majority of votes can enact commercial laws, so that the representatives of the seven northern states, as they will have a majority, can by law create the most oppressive monopoly upon the five southern states, whose circumstances and productions are essentially different from theirs, although not a single man of these voters are the representatives of, or amenable to the people of the southern states. Can such a set of men be, with the least colour of truth called a representative of those they make laws for?

It is supposed that the policy of the northern states will prevent such abuses. But how feeble, Sir, is policy when opposed to interest among trading people:—And what is the restraint arising from policy? Why that we may be forced by abuse to become ship-builders!—But how long will it be before a people of agriculture can produce ships sufficient to export such bulky commodities as ours, and of such extent; and if we had the ships, from whence are the seamen to come? 4000 of whom at least will be necessary in Virginia. In questions so liable to abuse, why was not the necessary vote put to two thirds of the members of the legislature? With the constitution came from the convention, so many members of that body to Congress, and of those too, who were among the most fiery zealots for their system, that the votes of three states being of them, two states divided by them, and many others mixed with them, it is easy to see that Congress could have little opinion upon the subject. Some denied our right to make amendments, whilst others more moderate agreed to the right, but denied the expediency of amending; but it was plain that a majority was ready to send it on in terms of approbation—my judgment and conscience forbid the last, and therefore I moved the amendments that I have the honor to send you inclosed herewith, and demanded the yeas and nays that they might appear on the journal. This seemed to alarm and to prevent such appearance on the journal, it was agreed to transmit the constitution without a syllable of approbation or disapprobation; so that the term unanimously only applied to the transmission, as you will observe by attending to the terms of the resolve for transmitting. Upon the whole, Sir, my opinion is, that as this constitution abounds with useful regulations, at the same time that it is liable to strong and fundamental objections, the plan for us to pursue, will be to propose the necessary amendments, and express our willingness to adopt it with the amendments, and to suggest the calling of a new convention for the purpose of considering them. To this I see no well founded objection, but great safety and much good to be the probable result. I am perfectly satisfied that you make such use of this letter as you shall think to be for the public good; and now after begging your pardon for so great a trespass on your patience, and presenting my best respects to your lady, I will conclude with assuring you, that I am with the sincerest esteem and regard, dear Sir, your most affectionate and obedient servant, RICHARD HENRY LEE.

POSTSCRIPT.

It having been found from universal experience, that the most express declarations and reservations are necessary to protect the just rights and liberty of mankind from the silent, powerful and ever active conspiracy of those who govern; and it appearing to be the sense of the good people of America, by the various bills or declarations of rights whereon the government of the greater number of states are founded. That such precautions are necessary to restrain and regulate the exercise of the great powers given to rulers. In conformity with these principles, and from respect for the public sentiment on this subject, it is submitted,—That the new constitution proposed for the government of the United States be bottomed upon a declaration or bill of rights, clearly and precisely stating the principles upon which this social compact is founded, to wit: That the rights of conscience in matters of religion ought not to be violated—That the freedom of the press shall be secured—That the trial by jury in criminal and civil cases, and the modes prescribed by the common law for the safety of life in criminal prosecutions, shall be held sacred—That standing armies in times of peace are dangerous to liberty, and ought not to be permitted, unless assented to by two-thirds of the members composing each house of the legislature under the new constitution—That the elections should be free and frequent; That the right administration of justice should be secured by the independency of the judges; That excessive bail, excessive fines, or cruel and unusual punishments, should not be demanded or inflicted; That the right of the people to assemble peaceably, for the purpose of petitioning the legislature, shall not be prevented; That the citizens shall not be exposed to unreasonable searches, seizure of their persons, houses, papers or property; and it is necessary for the good of society, that the administration of government be conducted with all possible maturity of judgment, for which reason it hath been the practice of civilized nations, and so determined by every state in the Union: That a council of state or privy council should be appointed to advise and assist in the arduous business assigned to the executive power. Therefore let the new constitution be so amended, as to admit the appointment of a privy council, to consist of eleven members chosen by the president, but responsible for the advice they may give. For which purpose the advice given shall be entered in a council book, and signed by the giver, in all affairs of great moment, and that the counsellors act under an oath of office. In order to prevent the dangerous blending of the legislative and executive powers, and to secure responsibility, the privy, and not the senate shall be joined with the president in the appointment of all officers, civil and military, under the new constitution; that the constitution be so altered as not to admit the creation of a vice-president, when duties as assigned may be discharged by the privy council, except in the instance of proceeding in the senate, which may be supplied by a speaker chosen from the body of senators by themselves, as usual, that so may be avoided the establishment of a great officer of state, who is sometimes to be joined with the legislature, and sometimes to administer the government, rendering responsibility difficult, besides giving unjust and needless preeminence to that state from whence this officer may have come. That such parts of the new constitution be amended as provide imperfectly for the trial of criminals by a jury of the vicinage, and to supply the omission of a jury trial in civil causes or disputes about property between individuals, whereby the common law is directed, and as generally it is secured by the several state constitutions. That such parts of the new constitution be amended, as permit the vexatious and oppressive callings of citizens from their own country, and all controversies between citizens of different states and between citizens and foreigners, to be tried in a far distant court, and as it may be without a jury, whereby in a multitude of cases, the circumstances of distance and expence may compel numbers to submit to the most unjust and ill-founded demand—That in order to secure the rights of the people more effectually from violation, the power and respectability of the house of representatives be increased, by increasing the number of delegates to that house, where the popular interest must chiefly depend for protection—That the constitution be so amended as to increase the number of votes necessary to determine questions in cases where a bare majority may be seduced by strong motives of interest to injure and oppress the minority of the community, as in commercial regulations, where advantage may be taken of circumstances to ordain rigid and premature laws, that will in effect amount to monopolies, to the great impoverishment of those states whose peculiar situation expose them to such injuries.

J. LETTER FROM THE FEDERAL FARMER, NO. 4

October 12, 1787

Dear Sir,

It will not be possible to establish in the federal courts the jury trial of the vicinage so well as in the state courts.

Third. There appears to me to be not only a premature deposit of some important powers in the general government—but many of those deposited there are undefined, and may be used to good or bad purposes as honest or designing men shall prevail. By Art. 1, Sect. 2, representatives and direct taxes shall be apportioned among the several states, etc.—same art. sect. 8, the congress shall have powers to lay and collect taxes, duties, etc. for the common defence and general welfare, but all duties, imposts and excises, shall be uniform throughout the United States: By the first recited clause, direct taxes shall be apportioned on the states. This seems to favour the idea suggested by some sensible men and writers, that congress, as to direct taxes, will only have power to make requisitions, but the latter clause, power to lay and collect taxes, etc seems clearly to favour the contrary opinion and, in my mind, the true one, that congress shall have power to tax immediately individuals, without the intervention of the state legislatures[;] in fact the first clause appears to me only to provide that each state shall pay a certain portion of the tax, and the latter to provide that congress shall have power to lay and collect taxes, that is to assess upon, and to collect of the individuals in the state, the state[']s quota; but these still I consider as undefined powers, because judicious men understand them differently.

It is doubtful whether the vice president is to have any qualifications; none are mentioned; but he may serve as president, and it may be inferred, he ought to be qualified therefore as the president; but the qualifications of the president are required only of the person to be elected president. By art. the 2, sect. 2. "But the congress may by law vest the appointment of such inferior officers as they think proper in the president alone, in the courts of law, or in the heads of the departments:" Who are inferior officers? May not a congress disposed to vest the appointment of all officers in the president, under this clause, vest the appointment of almost every officer in the president alone, and destroy the check mentioned in the first part of the clause, and lodged in the senate. It is true, this check is badly lodged, but then some check upon the first magistrate in appointing officers, ought it appears by the opinion of the convention, and by the general opinion, to be established in the constitution. By art. 3, sect. 2, the supreme court shall have appellate jurisdiction as to law and facts with such exceptions, etc. to what extent is it intended the exceptions shall be carried—Congress may carry them so far as to annihilate substantially the appellate jurisdiction, and the clause be rendered of very little importance.

4th.   There are certain rights which we have always held sacred in the United States, and recognized in all our constitutions, and which, by the adoption of the new constitution in its present form, will be left unsecured. By article 6, the proposed constitution, and the laws of the United States, which shall be made in pursuance thereof; and all treaties made, or which shall be made under the authority of the United States, shall be the supreme law of the land; and the judges in every state shall be bound thereby; any thing in the constitution or laws of any state to the contrary notwithstanding.

It is to be observed that when the people shall adopt the proposed constitution it will be their last and supreme act; it will be adopted not by the people of New-Hampshire, Massachusetts, etc. but by the people of the United States; and wherever this constitution, or any part of it, shall be incompatible with the ancient customs, rights, the laws or the constitutions heretofore established in the United States, it will entirely abolish them and do them away: And not only this, but the laws of the United States which shall be made in pursuance of the federal constitution will be also supreme laws, and wherever they shall be incompatible with those customs, rights, laws or constitutions heretofore established, they will also entirely abolish them and do them away.

By the article before recited, treaties also made under the authority of the United States, shall be the supreme law: It is not said that these treaties shall be made in pursuance of the constitution—nor are there any constitutional bounds set to those who shall make them: The

707

president and two thirds of the senate will be empowered to make treaties indefinitely, and when these treaties shall be made, they will also abolish all laws and state constitutions incompatible with them. This power in the president and senate is absolute, and the judges will be bound to allow full force to whatever rule, article or thing the president and senate shall establish by treaty, whether it be practicable to set any bounds to those who make treaties, I am not able to say: if not, it proves that this power ought to be more safely lodged.

The federal constitution, the laws of congress made in pursuance of the constitution, and all treaties must have full force and effect in all parts of the United States; and all other laws, rights and constitutions which stand in their way must yield: It is proper the national laws should be supreme, and superior to state or district laws: but then the national laws ought to yield to unalienable or fundamental rights—and national laws, made by a few men, should extend only to a few national objects. This will not be the case with the laws of congress: To have any proper idea of their extent, we must carefully examine the legislative, executive and judicial powers proposed to be lodged in the general government, and consider them in connection with a general clause in art. 1. sect. 8, in these words (after inumerating a number of powers) "To make all laws which shall be necessary and proper for carrying into execution the foregoing powers, and all other powers vested by this constitution in the government of the United States, or in any department or officer thereof."—The powers of this government as has been observed, extend to internal as well as external objects, and to those objects to which all others are subordinate; it is almost impossible to have a just conception of these powers, or of the extent and number of the laws which may be deemed necessary and proper to carry them into effect, till we shall come to exercise those powers and make the laws. In making laws to carry those powers into effect, it is to be expected, that a wise and prudent congress will pay respect to the opinions of a free people, and bottom their laws on those principles which have been considered as essential and fundamental in the British, and in our government. But a congress of a different character will not be bound by the constitution to pay respect to those principles.

It is said, that when the people make a constitution, and delegate powers that all powers not delegated by them to those who govern is [sic] reserved in the people; and that the people, in the present case, have reserved in themselves, and in their state governments, every right and power not expressly given by the federal constitution to those who shall administer the national government. It is said on the other hand, that the people, when they make a constitution, yield all power not expressly reserved to themselves. The truth is, in either case, it is mere matter of opinion and men usually take either side of the argument, as will best answer their purposes: But the general presumption being, that men who govern, will, in doubtful cases, construe laws and constitutions most favourably for encreasing their own powers; all wise and prudent people, in forming constitutions, have drawn the line, and carefully described the powers parted with and the powers reserved. By the state constitutions, certain rights have been reserved in the people; or rather, they have been recognized and established in such a manner, that state legislatures are bound to respect them, and to make no laws infringing upon them. The state legislatures are obliged to take notice of the bills of rights of their respective states. The bills of rights, and the state constitutions, are fundamental compacts only between those who govern, and the people of the same state.

In the year 1788 the people of the United States make a federal constitution, which is a fundamental compact between them and their federal rulers; these rulers, in the nature of things, cannot be bound to take notice of any other compact. It would be absurd for them, in making laws, to look over thirteen, fifteen, or twenty state constitutions, to see what rights are established as fundamental, and must not be infringed upon, in making laws in the society. It is true, they would be bound to do it if the people, in their federal compact, should refer to the state constitutions, recognize all parts not inconsistent with the federal constitution, and direct their federal rulers to take notice of them accordingly; but this is not the case, as the plan stands proposed at present; and it is absurd, to suppose so unnatural an idea is intended or implied. I think my opinion is not only founded in reason, but I think it is supported by the report of the convention itself. If there are a number of rights established by the state constitutions, and which will remain sacred, and the general government is bound to take notice of them—it must take notice of one as well as another; and if unnecessary to recognize or establish one by the federal constitution, it would be unnecessary to recognize or establish another by it. If the federal constitution is to be construed so far in connection with the state constitutions, as to leave the trial by jury in civil causes, for instance, secured; on the same principles it would have left the trial by jury in criminal causes, the benefits of the writ of habeas corpus, etc. secured; they all stand on the same footing; they are the common rights of Americans, and have been recognized by the state constitutions: But the convention found it necessary to recognize or re-establish the benefits of that writ, and the jury trial in criminal cases. As to *expost facto* laws, the convention has done the same in one case, and gone further in another. It is part of the compact between the people of each state and their rulers, that no *expost facto* laws shall be made. But the convention, by Art. I Sect. 10 have put a sanction upon this part even of the state compacts. In fact, the 9th and 10th Sections in Art. I. in the proposed constitution, are no more nor less, than a partial bill of rights; they establish certain principles as part of the compact upon which the federal legislators and officers can never infringe. It is here wisely stipulated, that the federal legislature shall never pass a bill of attainder, or *expost facto* law; that no tax shall be laid on articles exported, etc.

The establishing of one right implies the necessity of establishing another and similar one.

On the whole, the position appears to me to be undeniable, that this bill of rights ought to be carried farther, and some other principles established, as a part of this fundamental compact between the people of the United States and their federal rulers.

It is true, we are not disposed to differ much, at present, about religion; but when we are making a constitution, it is to be hoped, for ages and millions yet unborn, why not establish the free exercise of religion, as a part of the national compact. There are other essential rights, which we have justly understood to be the rights of freemen; as freedom from hasty and unreasonable search warrants, warrants not founded on oath, and not issued with due caution, for searching and seizing men's papers, property, and persons. The trials by jury in civil causes, it is said, varies so much in the several states, that no words could be found for the uniform establishment of it. If so, the federal legislation will not be able to establish it by any general laws. I confess I am of opinion it may be established, but not in that beneficial manner in which we may enjoy it, for the reasons be-forementioned. When I speak of the jury trial of the vicinage, or the trial of the fact in the neighbourhood,—I do not lay so much stress upon the circumstance of our being tried by our neighbours: in this enlightened country men may be probably impartially tried by those who do not live very near them: but the trial of facts in the neighbourhood is of great importance in other respects. Nothing can be more essential than the cross examining witnesses, and generally before the triers of the facts in question. The common people can establish facts with much more ease with oral than written evidence; when trials of facts are removed to a distance from the homes of the parties and witnesses, oral evidence becomes intolerably expensive, and the parties must depend on written evidence, which to the common people is expensive and almost useless; it must be frequently taken ex parte, and but very seldom leads to the proper discovery of truth.

The trial by jury is very important in another point of view. It is essential in every free country, that common people should have a part and share of influence, in the judicial as well as in the legislative department. To hold open to them the offices of senators, judges, and offices to fill which an expensive education is required, cannot answer any valuable purposes for them; they are not in a situation to be brought forward and to fill those offices; these, and most other offices of any considerable importance, will be occupied by the few. The few, the well born, etc. as Mr. Adams calls them, in judicial decisions as well as in legislation, are generally disposed, and very naturally too, to favour those of their own description.

The trial by jury in the judicial department, and the collection of the people by their representatives in the legislature, are those fortunate inventions which have procured for them, in this country, their true proportion of influence, and the wisest and most fit means of protecting themselves in the community. Their situation, as jurors and representatives, enables them to acquire information and knowledge in the affairs and government of the society; and to come forward, in turn, as the centinels and guardians of each other. I am very sorry that even a few of our countrymen should consider jurors and representatives in a different point of view, as ignorant troublesome bodies, which ought not to have any share in the concerns of government.

I confess I do not see in what cases the congress can, with any pretence of right, make a law to suppress the freedom of the press; though I am not clear, that congress is restrained from laying any duties whatever on printing, and from laying duties particularly heavy on certain pieces printed, and perhaps congress may require large bonds for the payment of these duties. Should the printer say, the freedom of the press was secured by the constitution of the state in which he lived, congress might, and perhaps, with great propriety, answer, that the federal constitution is the only compact existing between them and the people; in this compact the people have named no others, and therefore congress, in exercising the powers assigned them, and in making laws to carry them into execution, are restrained by nothing beside the federal constitution, any more than a state legislature is restrained by a compact between the magistrates and people of a county, city, or town of which the people, in forming the state constitution, have taken no notice.

It is not my object to enumerate rights of inconsiderable importance; but there are others, no doubt, which ought to be established as a fundamental part of the national system.

It is worthy observation, that all treaties are made by foreign nations with a confederacy of thirteen states—that the western country is attached to thirteen states—thirteen states have jointly and severally engaged to pay the public debts.—Should a new government be formed of nine, ten, eleven, or twelve states, those treaties could not be considered as binding on the foreign nations who made them. However, I believe the probability to be, that if nine states adopt the constitution, the others will.

It may also be worthy our examination, how far the provision for amending this plan, when it shall be adopted, is of any importance. No measures can be taken towards amendments, unless two-thirds of the congress, or two-thirds of the legislatures of the several states shall agree.—While power is in the hands of the people, or democratic part of the community, more especially as at present, it is easy, according to the general course of human affairs, for the few influential men in the community, to obtain conventions, alterations in government, and to persuade the common people they may change for the better, and to get from them a part of the power: But when power is once transferred from the many to the few, all changes become extremely difficult; the government, in this case, being beneficial to the few, they will be exceedingly artful and adroit in preventing any measures which may lead to a change; and nothing will produce it, but great exertions and severe struggles on the part of the common people. Every man of reflection must see, that the change now proposed, is a transfer of power from the many to the few, and the probability is, the artful and ever active aristocracy, will prevent all peaceable measures for changes, unless when they shall discover some favourable moment to increase their own influence. I am sensible, thousands of men in the United States, are disposed to adopt the proposed constitution, though they perceive it to be essentially defective, under an idea that amendments of it, may be obtained when necessary. This is a pernicious idea, it argues a servility of character totally unfit for the support of free government; it is very repugnant to that perpetual jealousy respecting liberty, so absolutely necessary in all free states, spoken of by Mr. Dickinson.— However, if our countrymen are so soon changed, and the language of 1774, is become odious to them, it will be in vain to use the language of freedom, or to attempt to rouse them to free enquiries: But I shall never believe this is the case with them, whatever present appearances may be, till I shall have very strong evidence indeed of it.

Your's, &c.

The Federal Farmer.

K. ESSAY OF BRUTUS, NO. 2

November 1, 1787.

To the Citizens of the State of New-York.

I flatter myself that my last address established this position, that to reduce the Thirteen States into one government, would prove the destruction of your liberties.

But lest this truth should be doubted by some, I will now proceed to consider its merits.

Though it should be admitted, that the argument[s] against reducing all the states into one consolidated government, are not sufficient fully to establish this point; yet they will, at least, justify this conclusion, that in forming a constitution for such a country, great care should be taken to limit and definite its powers, adjust its parts, and guard against an abuse of authority. How far attention has been paid to these objects, shall be the subject of future enquiry. When a building is to be erected which is intended to stand for ages, the foundation should be firmly laid. The constitution proposed to your acceptance, is designed not for yourselves alone, but for generations yet unborn. The principles, therefore, upon which the social compact is founded, ought to have been clearly and precisely stated, and the most express and full declaration of rights to have been made—But on this subject there is almost an entire silence.

If we may collect the sentiments of the people of America, from their own most solemn declarations, they hold this truth as self evident, that all men are by nature free. No one man, therefore, or any class of men, have a right, by the law of nature, or of God, to assume or exercise authority over their fellows. The origin of society then is to be sought, not in any natural right which one man has to exercise authority over another, but in the united consent of those who associate. The mutual wants of men, at first dictated the propriety of forming societies; and when they were established, protection and defence pointed out the necessity of instituting government. In a state of nature every individual pursues his own interest; in this pursuit it frequently happened, that the possessions or enjoyments of one were sacrificed to the views and designs of another; thus the weak were a prey to the strong, the simple and unwary were subject to impositions from those who were more crafty and designing. In this state of things, every individual was insecure; common interest therefore directed, that government should be established, in which the force of the whole community should be collected, and under such directions, as to protect and defend every one who composed it. The common good, therefore, is the end of civil government, and common consent, the foundation on which it is established. To effect this end, it was necessary that a certain portion of natural liberty should be surrendered, in order, that what remained should be preserved: how great a proportion of natural freedom is necessary to be yielded by individuals, when they submit to government, I shall not now enquire. So much, however, must be given up, as will be sufficient to enable those, to whom the administration of the government is committed, to establish laws for the promoting the happiness of the community, and to carry those laws into effect. But it is not necessary, for this purpose, that individuals should relinquish all their natural rights. Some are of such a nature that they cannot be surrendered. Of this kind are the rights of conscience, the right of enjoying and defending life, etc. Others are not necessary to be resigned, in order to attain the end for which government is instituted, these therefore ought not to be given up. To surrender them, would counteract the very end of government, to wit, the common good. From these observations it appears, that in forming a government on its true principles, the foundation should be laid in the manner I before stated, by expressly reserving to the people such of their essential natural rights, as are not necessary to be parted with. The same reasons which at first induced mankind to associate and institute government, will operate to influence them to observe this precaution. If they had been disposed to conform themselves to the rule of immutable righteousness, government would not have been requisite. It was because one part exercised fraud, oppression, and violence on the other, that men came together, and agreed that certain rules should be formed, to regulate the conduct of all, and the

713

power of the whole community lodged in the hands of rulers to enforce an obedience to them. But rulers have the same propensities as other men; they are as likely to use the power with which they are vested for private purposes, and to the injury and oppression of those over whom they are placed, as individuals in a state of nature are to injure and oppress one another. It is therefore as proper that bounds should be set to their authority, as that government should have at first been instituted to restrain private injuries.

This principle, which seems so evidently founded in the reason and nature of things, is confirmed by universal experience. Those who have governed, have been found in all ages ever active to enlarge their powers and abridge the public liberty. This has induced the people in all countries, where any sense of freedom remained, to fix barriers against the encroachments of their rulers. The country from which we have derived our origin, is an eminent example of this. Their magna charta and bill of rights have long been the boast, as well as the security, of that nation. I need say no more, I presume, to an American, than, that this principle is a fundamental one, in all the constitutions of our own states; there is not one of them but what is either founded on a declaration or bill of rights, or has certain express reservation of rights interwoven in the body of them. From this it appears, that at a time when the pulse of liberty beat high and when an appeal was made to the people to form constitutions for the government of themselves, it was their universal sense, that such declarations should make a part of their frames of government. It is therefore the more astonishing, that this grand security, to the rights of the people, is not to be found in this constitution.

It has been said, in answer to this objection, that such declaration[s] of rights, however requisite they might be in the constitutions of the states, are not necessary in the general constitution, because, "in the former case, every thing which is not reserved is given, but in the latter the reverse of the proposition prevails, and every thing which is not given is reserved." It requires but little attention to discover, that this mode of reasoning is rather specious than solid. The powers, rights, and authority, granted to the general government by this constitution, are as complete, with respect to every object to which they extend, as that of any state government—It reaches to every thing which concerns human happiness—Life, liberty, and property, are under its controul. There is the same reason, therefore, that the exercise of power, in this case, should be restrained within proper limits, as in that of the state governments. To set this matter in a clear light, permit me to instance some of the articles of the bills of rights of the individual states, and apply them to the case in question.

For the security of life, in criminal prosecutions, the bills of rights of most of the states have declared, that no man shall be held to answer for a crime until he is made fully acquainted with the charge brought against him; he shall not be compelled to accuse, or furnish evidence against himself—The witnesses against him shall be brought face to face, and he shall be fully heard by himself or counsel. That it is essential to the security of life and liberty, that trial of facts be in the vicinity where they happen. Are not provisions of this kind as necessary in the general government, as in that of a particular state? The powers vested in the new Congress extend in many cases to life; they are authorised to provide for the punishment of a variety of capital crimes, and no restraint is laid upon them in its exercise, save only, that "the trial of all crimes, except in cases of impeachment, shall be by jury; and such trial shall be in the state where the said crimes shall have been committed." No man is secure of a trial in the county where he is charged to have committed a crime; he may be brought from Niagara to New-York, or carried from Kentucky to Richmond for trial for an offence, supposed to be committed. What security is there, that a man shall be furnished with a full and plain description of the charges against him? That he shall be allowed to produce all proof he can in his favor? That he shall see the witnesses against him face to face, or that he shall be fully heard in his own defence by himself or counsel?

For the security of liberty it has been declared, "that excessive bail should not be required, nor excessive fines imposed, nor cruel or unusual punishments inflicted—That all warrants, without oath or affirmation, to search suspected places, or seize any person, his papers or property, are grievous and oppressive."

These provisions are as necessary under the general government as under that of the individual states; for the power of the former is as complete to the purpose of requiring bail, imposing fines, inflicting punishments, granting search warrants, and seizing persons, papers, or property, in certain cases, as the other.

For the purpose of securing the property of the citizens, it is declared by all the states, "that in all controversies at law, respecting property, the ancient mode of trial by jury is one of the best securities of the rights of the people, and ought to remain sacred and inviolable."

Does not the same necessity exist of reserving this right, under this national compact, as in that of these states? Yet nothing is said respecting it. In the bills of rights of the states it is declared, that a well regulated militia is the proper and natural defence of a free government—That as standing armies in time of peace are dangerous, they are not to be kept up, and that the military should be kept under strict subordination to, and controuled by the civil power.

The same security is as necessary in this constitution, and much more so; for the general government will have the sole power to raise and to pay armies, and are under no controul in the exercise of it; yet nothing of this is to be found in this new system.

I might proceed to instance a number of other rights, which were as necessary to be reserved, such as, that elections should be free, that the liberty of the press should be held sacred; but the instances adduced, are sufficient to prove, that this argument is without foundation.—Besides, it is evident, that the reason here assigned was not the true one, why the framers of this constitution omitted a bill of rights; if it had been, they would not have made certain reservations, while they totally omitted others of more importance. We find they have, in the 9th section of the 1st article, declared, that the writ of habeas corpus shall not be suspended, unless in cases of rebellion—that no bill of attainder, or expost facto law, shall be passed—that no title of nobility shall be granted by the United States, &c. If every thing which is not given is reserved, what propriety is there in these exceptions? Does this constitution any where grant the power of suspending the habeas corpus, to make expost facto laws, pass bills of attainder, or grant titles of nobility? It certainly does not in express terms. The only answer that can be given is, that these are implied in the general powers granted. With equal truth it may be said, that all the powers, which the bills of right, guard against the abuse of, are contained or implied in the general ones granted by this constitution.

So far it is from being true, that a bill of rights is less necessary in the general constitution than in those of the states, the contrary is evidently the fact.—This system, if it is possible for the people of America to accede to it, will be an original compact; and being the last, will, in the nature of things, vacate every former agreement inconsistent with it. For it being a plan of government received and ratified by the whole people, all other forms, which are in existence at the time of its adoption, must yield to it. This is expressed in positive and unequivocal terms, in the 6th article, "That this constitution and the laws of the United States, which shall be made in pursuance thereof, and all treaties made, or which shall be made, under the authority of the United States, shall be the supreme law of the land; and the judges in every state shall be bound thereby, any thing in the *constitution,* or laws of any state, *to the contrary* notwithstanding.

"The senators and representatives before-mentioned, and the members of the several state legislatures, and all executive and judicial officers, both of the United States, and of the several states, shall be bound, by oath or affirmation, to support this constitution."

It is therefore not only necessarily implied thereby, but positively expressed, that the different state constitutions are repealed and entirely done away, so far as they are inconsistent with this, with the laws which shall be made in pursuance thereof, or with treaties made, or which shall be made, under the authority of the United States; of what avail will the constitutions of the respective states be to preserve the rights of its citizens? should they be plead, the answer would be, the constitution of the United States, and the laws made in pursuance thereof, is the supreme law, and all legislatures and judicial officers, whether of the general or state governments, are bound by oath to support it.   No priviledge, reserved by the bills of rights, or secured by the state government, can limit the power granted by this, or restrain any laws made in pursuance of it.   It stands therefore on its own bottom, and must receive a construction by itself without any reference to any other—And hence it was of the highest importance, that the most precise and express declarations and reservations of rights should have been made.

This will appear the more necessary, when it is considered, that not only the constitution and laws made in pursuance thereof, but all treaties made, or which shall be made, under the authority of the United States, are the supreme law of the land, and supersede the constitutions of all the states.   The power to make treaties, is vested in the president, by and with the advice and consent of two thirds of the senate.   I do not find any limitation, or restriction, to the exercise of this power.   The most important article in any constitution may therefore be repealed, even without a legislative act.   Ought not a government, vested with such extensive and indefinite authority, to have been restricted by a declaration of rights?   It certainly ought.

So clear a point is this, that I cannot help suspecting, that persons who attempt to persuade people, that such reservations were less necessary under this constitution than under those of the states, are wilfully endeavouring to deceive, and to lead you into an absolute state of vassalage.

Brutus.

L. LETTER FROM THE FEDERAL FARMER, NO. 16

January 20, 1788

Dear Sir,

Having gone through with the organization of the government, I shall now proceed to examine more particularly those clauses which respect its powers.   I shall begin with those articles and stipulations which are necessary for accurately ascertaining the extent of powers, and what is given, and for guarding, limiting, and restraining them in their exercise.   We often find, these articles and stipulations placed in bills of rights; but they may as well be incorporated in the body of the constitution, as selected and placed by themselves.   The constitution, or whole social compact, is but one instrument, no more or less, than a certain number of articles or stipulations agreed to by the people, whether it consists of articles, sections, chapters, bills of rights, or parts of any other denomination, cannot be material.   Many needless observations, and idle distinctions, in my opinion, have been made respecting a bill of rights. On the one hand, it seems to be considered as a necessary distinct limb of the constitution, and as containing a certain number of very valuable articles, which are applicable to all societies: and, on the other, as useless, especially in a federal government, possessing only enumerated power—nay, dangerous, as individual rights are numerous, and not easy to be enumerated in a bill of rights, and from articles, or stipulations, securing some of them, it may be inferred, that others not mentioned are surrendered. There appears to me to be general indefinite propositions without much meaning—and the man who first advanced those of the latter description, in the present case, signed the federal constitution, which directly contradicts him. The supreme power is undoubtedly in the people, and it is a principle well established in my mind, that they reserve all powers not expressly delegated by them to those who govern; this is as true in forming a state as in forming a federal government. There is no possible distinction but this founded merely in the different modes of proceeding which take place in some cases. In forming a state constitution, under which to manage not only the great but the little concerns of a community: the powers to be possessed by the government are often too numerous to be enumerated; the people to adopt the shortest way often give general powers, indeed all powers, to the government, in some general words, and then, by a particular enumeration, take back, or rather say they however reserve certain rights as sacred, and which no laws shall be made to violate: hence the idea that all powers are given which are not reserved: but in forming a federal constitution, which *ex vi termine*, supposes state governments existing, and which is only to manage a few great national concerns, we often find it easier to enumerate particularly the powers to be delegated to the federal head, than to enumerate particularly the individual rights to be reserved; and the principle will operate in its full force, when we carefully adhere to it. When we particularly enumerate the powers given, we ought either carefully to enumerate the rights reserved, or be totally silent about them; we must either particularly enumerate both, or else suppose the particular enumeration of the powers given adequately draws the line between them and the rights reserved, particularly to enumerate the former and not the latter, I think most advisable: however, as men appear generally to have their doubts about these silent reservations, we might advantageously enumerate the powers given, and then in general words, according to the mode adopted in the 2d art. of the confederation, declare all powers, rights and privileges, are reserved, which are not explicitly and expressly given up. People, and very wisely too, like to be express and explicit about their essential rights, and not to be forced to claim them on the precarious and unascertained tenure of inferences and general principles, knowing that in any controversy between them and their rulers, concerning those rights, disputes may be endless, and nothing certain:—But admitting, on the general principle, that all rights are reserved of course, which are not expressly surrendered, the people could with sufficient certainty assert their rights on all occasions, and establish them with ease, still there are infinite advantages in particularly enumerating many of the most essential rights reserved in all cases; and as to the less important ones, we may declare in general terms, that all not expressly surrendered are reserved.

We do not by declarations change the nature of things, or create new truths, but we give existence, or at least establish in the minds of the people truths and principles which they might never otherwise have thought of, or soon forgot. If a nation means its systems, religious or political, shall have duration, it ought to recognize the leading principles of them in the front page of every family book. What is the usefulness of a truth in theory, unless it exists constantly in the minds of the people, and has their assent:—we discern certain rights, as the freedom of the press, and the trial by jury, &c. which the people of England and of America of course believe to be sacred, and essential to their political happiness, and this belief in them is the result of ideas at first suggested to them by a few able men, and of subsequent experience; while the people of some other countries hear these rights mentioned with the utmost indifference; they think the privilege of existing at the will of a despot much preferable to them. Why this difference amongst beings every way formed alike. The reason of the difference is obvious—it is the effect of education, a series of notions impressed upon the minds of the people by examples, precepts and declarations. When the people of England got together, at the time they formed Magna Charta, they did not consider it sufficient, that they were indisputably entitled to certain natural and unalienable rights, not depending on silent titles, they, by a declaratory act, expressly recognized them, and explicitly declared to all the world, that they were entitled to enjoy those rights; they made an instrument in writing, and enumerated those they then thought essential, or in danger, and this wise men saw was not sufficient; and therefore, that the people might not forget these rights, and gradually become prepared for arbitrary government, their discerning and honest leaders caused this instrument to be confirmed near forty times, and to be read twice a year in public places, not that it would lose its validity without such confirmations, but to fix the contents of it in the minds of the people, as they successively come upon the stage.—Men, in some countries do not remain free, merely because they are entitled to natural and unalienable rights; men in all countries are entitled to them, not because their ancestors once got together and enumerated them on paper, but because, by repeated negociations and declarations, all parties are brought to realize them, and of course to believe them to be sacred. Were it necessary, I might shew the wisdom of our past conduct, as a people in not merely comforting ourselves that we were entitled to freedom, but in constantly keeping in view, in addresses, bills of rights, in news-papers, &c. the particular principles on which our freedom must always depend.

719

It is not merely in this point of view, that I urge the engrafting in the constitution additional declaratory articles. The distinction, in itself just, that all powers not given are reserved, is in effect destroyed by this very constitution, as I shall particularly demonstrate—and even independent of this, the people, by adopting the constitution, give many general undefined powers to congress, in the constitutional exercise of which, the rights in question may be effected. Gentlemen who oppose a federal bill of rights, or further declaratory articles, seem to view the subject in a very narrow imperfect manner. These have for their objects, not only the enumeration of the rights reserved, but principally to explain the general powers delegated in certain material points, and to restrain those who exercise them by fixed known boundaries. Many explanations and restrictions necessary and useful, would be much less so, were the people at large all well and fully acquainted with the principles and affairs of government. There appears to be in the constitution, a studied brevity, and it may also be probable, that several explanatory articles were omitted from a circumstance very common. What we have long and early understood ourselves in the common concerns of the community, we are apt to suppose is understood by others, and need not be expressed; and it is not unnatural or uncommon for the ablest men most frequently to make this mistake. To make declaratory articles unnecessary in an instrument of government, two circumstances must exist; the rights reserved must be indisputably so, and in their nature defined; the powers delegated to the government, must be precisely defined by the words that convey them, and clearly be of such extent and nature as that, by no reasonable construction, they can be made to invade the rights and prerogatives intended to be left in the people.

The first point urged, is, that all power is reserved not expressly given, that particular enumerated powers only are given, that all others are not given, but reserved, and that it is needless to attempt to restrian congress in the exercise of powers they possess not. This reasoning is logical, but of very little importance in the common affairs of men; but the constitution does not appear to respect it even in any view. To prove this, I might cite several clauses in it. I shall only remark on two or three. By article 1, section 9, "No title of nobility shall be granted by congress" Was this clause omitted, what power would congress have to make titles of nobility? in what part of the constitution would they find it? The answer must be, that congress would have no such power—that the people, by adopting the constitution, will not part with it. Why then by a negative clause, restrain congress from doing what it would have no power to do? This clause, then, must have no meaning, or imply, that were it omitted, congress would have the power in question, either upon the principle that some general words in the constitution may be so construed as to give it, or on the principle that congress possess the powers not expressly reserved. But this clause was in the confederation, and is said to be introduced into the constitution from very great caution. Even a cautionary provision implies a doubt, at least, that it is necessary; and if so in this case, clearly it is also alike necessary in all similar ones. The fact appears to be, that the people in forming the confederation, and the convention, in this instance, acted, naturally, they did not leave the point to be settled by general principles and logical inferences; but they settle the point in a few words, and all who read them at once understand them.

The trial by jury in criminal as well as in civil causes, has long been considered as one of our fundamental rights, and has been repeatedly recognized and confirmed by most of the state conventions. But the constitution expressly establishes this trial in criminal, and wholly omits it in civil causes. The jury trial in criminal causes, and the benefit of the writ of habeas corpus, are already as effectually established as any of the fundamental or essential rights of the people in the United States. This being the case, why in adopting a federal constitution do we now establish these, and omit all others, or all others, at least with a few exceptions, such as again agreeing there shall be no ex post facto laws, no titles of nobility, &c. We must consider this constitution, when adopted, as the supreme act of the people, and in construing it hereafter, we and our posterity must strictly adhere to the letter and spirit of it, and in no instance depart from them: in construing the federal constitution, it will be not only impracticable, but improper to refer to the state constitutions. They are entirely distinct instruments and inferior acts: besides, by the people's now establishing certain fundamental rights, it is strongly implied, that they are of opinion, that they would not otherwise be secured as a part of the federal system, or be regarded in the federal administration as fundamental. Further, these same rights, being established by the state constitutions, and secured to the people, our recognizing them now, implies, that the people thought them insecure by the state establishments, and extinguished or put afloat by the new arrangement of the social system, unless re-established.—Further, the people, thus establishing some few rights, and remaining totally silent about others similarly circumstanced, the implication indubitably is, that they mean to relinquish the latter, or at least feel indifferent about them. Rights, therefore, inferred from general principles of reason, being precarious and hardly ascertainable in the common affairs of society, and the people, in forming a federal constitution, explicitly shewing they conceive these rights to be thus circumstanced, and accordingly proceed to enumerate and establish some of them, the conclusion will be, that they have established all which they esteem valuable and sacred. On every principle, then, the people especially having began, ought to go through enumerating, and establish particularly all the rights of individuals, which can by any possibility come in question in making and executing federal laws. I have already observed upon the excellency and importance of the jury trial in civil as well as in criminal causes, instead of establishing it in criminal causes only; we ought to establish it generally;—instead of the clause of forty or fifty words relative to this subject, why not use the language that has always been used in this country, and say, "the people of the United States shall always be entitled to the trial by jury." This would shew the people still hold the right sacred, and enjoin it upon congress substantially to preserve the jury trial in all cases, according to the usage and custom of the country. I have observed before, that it is *the jury trial* we want; the little different appendages and modifications tacked to it in the different states, are no more than a drop in the ocean: the jury trial is a solid uniform feature in a free government; it is the substance we would save, not the little articles of form.

Security against expost facto laws, the trial by jury, and the benefits of the writ of habeas corpus, are but a part of those inestimable rights the people of the United States are entitled to, even in judicial proceedings, by the course of the common law. These may be secured in general words, as in New-York, the Western Territory, &c. by declaring the people of the United States shall always be entitled to judicial proceedings according to the course of the common law, as used and established in the said states. Perhaps it would be better to enumerate the particular essential rights the people are entitled to in these proceedings, as has been done in many of the states, and as has been done in England. In this case, the people may proceed to declare, that no man shall be held to answer to any offence, till the same be fully described to him; nor to furnish evidence against himself: that, except in the government of the army and navy, no person shall be tried for any offence, whereby he may incur loss of life, or an infamous punishment, until he be first indicted by a grand jury: that every person shall have a right to produce all proofs that may be favourable to him, and to meet the witnesses against him face to face: that every person shall be entitled to obtain right and justice freely and without delay; that all persons shall have a right to be secure from all unreasonable searches and seizures of their persons, houses, papers, or possessions; and that all warrants shall be deemed contrary to this right, if the foundation of them be not previously supported by oath, and there be not in them a special designation of persons or objects of search, arrest, or seizure: and that no person shall be exiled or molested in his person or effects, otherwise than by the judgment of his peers, or according to the law of the land. A celebrated writer observes upon this last article, that in itself it may be said to comprehend the whole end of political society. These rights are not necessarily reserved, they are established, or enjoyed but in few countries: they are stipulated rights, almost peculiar to British and American laws. In the execution of those laws, individuals, by long custom, by magna charta, bills of rights &c. have become entitled to them. A man, at first, by act of parliament, became entitled to the benefits of the writ of habeas corpus—men are entitled to these rights and benefits in the judicial proceedings of our state courts generally: but it will by no means follow, that they will be entitled to them in the federal courts, and have a right to assert them, unless secured and established by the constitution or federal laws. We certainly, in federal processes, might as well claim the benefits of the writ of habeas corpus, as to claim trial by a jury—the right to have council—to have witnesses face to face—to be secure against unreasonable search warrants, &c. was the constitution silent as to the whole of them:—but the establishment of the former, will evince that we could not claim them without it; and the omission of the latter, implies they are relinquished, or deemed of no importance. These are rights and benefits individuals acquire by compact; they must claim them under compacts, or immemorial usage—it is doubtful, at least, whether they can be claimed under immemorial usage in this country; and it is, therefore, we generally claim them under compacts, as charters and constitutions.

The people by adopting the federal constitution, give congress general powers to institute a distinct and new judiciary, new courts, and to regulate all proceedings in them, under the eight limitations mentioned in a former letter; and the further one, that the benefits of the habeas corpus act shall be enjoyed by individuals. Thus general powers being given to institute courts, and regulate their proceedings, with no provision for securing the rights principally in question, may not congress so exercise those powers, and constitutionally too, as to destroy those rights? clearly, in my opinion, they are not in any degree secured. But, admitting the case is only doubtful, would it not be prudent and wise to secure them and remove all doubts, since all agree the people ought to enjoy these valuable rights, a very few men excepted, who seem to be rather of opinion that there is little or nothing in them? Were it necessary I might add many observations to shew their value and political importance.

The constitution will give congress general powers to raise and support armies. General powers carry with them incidental ones, and the means necessary to the end. In the exercise of these powers, is there any provision in the constitution to prevent the quartering of soldiers on the inhabitants? you will answer, there is not. This may sometimes be deemed a necessary measure in the support of armies; on what principle can the people claim the right to be exempt from this burden? they will urge, perhaps, the practice of the country, and the provisions made in some of the state constitutions—they will be answered, that their claim thus to be exempt is not founded in nature, but only in custom and opinion, or at best, in stipulations in some of the state constitutions, which are local, and inferior in their operation, and can have no controul over the general government—that they had adopted a federal constitution—had noticed several rights, but had been totally silent about this exemption—that they had given general powers relative to the subject, which, in their operation, regularly destroyed the claim. Though it is not to be presumed, that we are in any immediate danger from this quarter, yet it is fit and proper to establish, beyond dispute, those rights which are particularly valuable to individuals, and essential to the permanency and duration of free government. An excellent writer observes, that the English, always in possession of their freedom, are frequently unmindful of the value of it: we, at this period, do not seem to be so well off, having, in some instances abused ours; many of us are quite disposed to barter it away for what we call energy, coercion, and some other terms we use as vaguely as that of liberty—There is often as great a rage for change and novelty in politics, as in amusements and fashions.

All parties apparently agree, that the freedom of the press is a fundamental right, and ought not to be restrained by any taxes, duties, or in any manner whatever. Why should not the people, in adopting a federal constitution, declare this, even if there are only doubts about it. But, say the advocates, all powers not given are reserved:—true; but the great question is, are not powers given, in the excercise of which this right may be destroyed? The people's or the printers claim to a free press, is founded on the fundamental laws, that is, compacts, and state constitutions, made by the people. The people, who can annihilate or alter those constitutions, can annihilate or limit this right. This may be done by giving general powers, as well as by using particular words. No right claimed under a state constitution, will avail against a law of the union, made in pursuance of the federal constitution: therefore the question is, what laws will congress have a right to make by the constitution of the union, and particularly touching the press? By art. 1. sect. 8. congress will have power to lay and collect taxes, duties, imposts and excise. By this congress will clearly have power to lay and collect all kind of taxes whatever—taxes on houses, lands, polls, industry, merchandize, &c.—taxes on deeds, bonds, and all written instruments—on writs, pleas, and all judicial proceedings, on licences, naval officers papers, &c. on newspapers, advertisements, &c. and to require bonds of the naval officers, clerks, printers, &c. to account for the taxes that may become due on papers that go through their hands. Printing, like all other business, must cease when taxed beyond its profits; and it appears to me, that a power to tax the press at discretion, is a power to destroy or restrain the freedom of it. There may be other powers given, in the exercise of which this freedom may be effected; and certainly it is of too much importance to be left thus liable to be taxed, and constantly to constructions and inferences. A free press is the channel of communication as to mercantile and public affairs; by means of it the people in large countries ascertain each others sentiments; are enabled to unite, and become formidable to those rulers who adopt improper measures. Newspapers may sometimes be the vehicles of abuse, and of many things not true; but these are but small inconveniencies, in my mind, among many advantages. A celebrated writer, I have several times quoted, speaking in high terms of the English liberties, says, "lastly the key stone was put to the arch, by the final establishment of the freedom of the press." I shall not dwell longer upon the fundamental rights, to some of which I have attended in this letter, for the same reasons that these I have mentioned, ought to be expressly secured, lest in the exercise of general powers given they may be invaded: it is pretty clear, that some other of less importance, or less in danger, might with propriety also be secured.

I shall now proceed to examine briefly the powers proposed to be vested in the several branches of the government, and especially the mode of laying and collecting internal taxes.

The Federal Farmer.

M. ESSAY OF BRUTUS, NO. 15

March 20, 1788

I said in my last number, that the supreme court under this constitution would be exalted above all other power in the government, and subject to no controul. The business of this paper will be to illustrate this, and to shew the danger that will result from it. I question whether the world ever saw, in any period of it, a court of justice invested with such immense powers, and yet placed in a situation so little responsible. Certain it is, that in England, and in the several states, where we have been taught to believe, the courts of law are put upon the most prudent establishment, they are on a very different footing.

The judges in England, it is true, hold their offices during their good behaviour, but then their determinations are subject to correction by the house of lords; and their power is by no means so extensive as that of the proposed supreme court of the union.—I believe they in no instance assume the authority to set aside an act of parliament under the idea that it is inconsistent with their constitution. They consider themselves bound to decide according to the existing laws of the land, and never undertake to controul them by adjudging that they are inconsistent with the constitution—much less are they vested with the power of giving an *equitable* construction to the constitution.

The judges in England are under the controul of the leigislature, for they are bound to determine according to the laws passed by them. But the judges under this constitution will controul the legislature, for the supreme court are authorised in the last resort, to determine what is the extent of the powers of the Congress; they are to give the constitution an explanation, and there is no power above them to set aside their judgment. The framers of this constitution appear to have followed that of the British, in rendering the judges independent, by granting them their offices during good behaviour, without following the constitution of England, in instituting a tribunal in which their errors may be corrected; and without adverting to this, that the judicial under this system have a power which is above the legislative, and which indeed transcends any power before given to a judicial by any free government under heaven.

I do not object to the judges holding their commissions during good behaviour. I suppose it a proper provision provided they were made properly responsible. But I say, this system has followed the English government in this, while it has departed from almost every other principle of their jurisprudence, under the idea, of rendering the judges independent; which, in the British constitution, means no more than that they hold their places during good behaviour, and have fixed salaries, they have made the judges *independent,* in the fullest sense of the word. There is no power above them, to controul any of their decisions. There is no authority that can remove them, and they cannot be controuled by the laws of the legislature. In short, they are independent of the people, of the legislature, and of every power under heaven. Men placed in this situation will generally soon feel themselves independent of heaven itself. Before I proceed to illustrate the truth of these assertions, I beg liberty to make one remark—Though in my opinion the judges ought to hold their offices during good behaviour, yet I think it is clear, that the reasons in favour of this establishment of the judges in England, do by no means apply to this country.

The great reason assigned, why the judges in Britain ought to be commissioned during good behaviour, is this, that they may be placed in a situation, not to be influenced by the crown, to give such decisions, as would tend to increase its powers and prerogatives. While the judges held their places at the will and pleasure of the king, on whom they depended not only for their offices, but also for their salaries, they were subject to every undue influence. If the crown wished to carry a favorite point, to accomplish which the aid of the courts of law was necessary, the pleasure of the king would be signified to the judges. And it required the spirit of a martyr, for the judges to determine contrary to the king's will.—They were absolutely dependent upon him both for their offices and livings. The king, holding his office during life, and transmitting it to his posterity as an inheritance, has much stronger inducements to increase the prerogatives of his office than those who hold their offices for stated periods, or even for life. Hence the English nation gained a great point, in favour of liberty. When they obtained the appointment of the judges, during good behaviour, they got from the crown a concession, which deprived it of one of the most powerful engines with which it might enlarge the boundaries of the royal prerogative and encroach on the liberties of the people. But these reasons do not apply to this country, we have no hereditary monarch; those who appoint the judges do not hold their offices for life, nor do they descend to their children. The same arguments, therefore, which will conclude in favor of the tenor of the judge's offices for good behaviour, lose a considerable part of their weight when applied to the state and condition of America. But much less can it be shewn, that the nature of our government requires that the courts should be placed beyond all account more independent, so much so as to be above controul.

726

I have said that the judges under this system will be *independent* in the strict sense of the word: To prove this I will shew—That there is no power above them that can controul their decisions, or correct their errors. There is no authority that can remove them from office for any errors or want of capacity, or lower their salaries, and in many cases their power is superior to that of the legislature.

1st. There is no power above them that can correct their errors or controul their decisions—The adjudications of this court are final and irreversible, for there is no court above them to which appeals can lie, either in error or on the merits.—In this respect it differs from the courts in England, for there the house of lords is the highest court, to whom appeals, in error, are carried from the highest of the courts of law.

2d. They cannot be removed from office or suffer a dimunition of their salaries, for any error in judgment or want of capacity.

It is expressly declared by the constitution,—"That they shall at stated times receive a compensation for their services which shall not be diminished during their continuance in office."

The only clause in the constitution which provides for the removal of the judges from office, is that which declares, that "the president, vice-president, and all civil officers of the United States, shall be removed from office, on impeachment for, and conviction of treason, bribery, or other high crimes and misdemeanors." By this paragraph, civil officers, in which the judges are included, are removable only for crimes. Treason and bribery are named, and the rest are included under the general terms of high crimes and misdemeanors.—Errors in judgment, or want of capacity to discharge the duties of the office, can never be supposed to be included in these words, *high crimes and misdemeanors*. A man may mistake a case in giving judgment, or manifest that he is incompetent to the discharge of the duties of a judge, and yet give no evidence of corruption or want of integrity. To support the charge, it will be necessary to give in evidence some facts that will shew, that the judges commited the error from wicked and corrupt motives.

3d. The power of this court is in many cases superior to that of the legislature. I have shewed, in a former paper, that this court will be authorised to decide upon the meaning of the constitution, and that, not only according to the natural and ob[vious] meaning of the words, but also according to the spirit and intention of it. In the exercise of this power they will not be subordinate to, but above the legislature. For all the departments of this government will receive their powers, so far as they are expressed in the constitution, from the people immediately, who are the source of power. The legislature can only exercise such powers as are given them by the constitution, they cannot assume any of the rights annexed to the judicial, for this plain reason, that the same authority which vested the legislature with their powers, vested the judicial with theirs—both are derived from the same source, both therefore are equally valid, and the judicial hold their powers independently of the legislature, as the legislature do of the judicial.—The supreme cort then have a right, independent of the legislature, to give a construction to the constitution and every part of it, and there is no power provided in this system to correct their construction or do it away. If, therefore, the legislature pass any laws, inconsistent with the sense the judges put upon the constitution, they will declare it void; and therefore in this respect their power is superior to that of the legislature. In England the judges are not only subject to have their decisions set aside by the house of lords, for error, but in cases where they give an explanation to the laws or constitution of the country, contrary to the sense of the parliament, though the parliament will not set aside the judgement of the court, yet, they have authority, by a new law, to explain a former one, and by this means to prevent a reception of such decisions. But no such power is in the legislature. The judges are supreme—and no law, explanatory of the constitution, will be binding on them.

From the preceding remarks, which have been made on the judicial powers proposed in this system, the policy of it may be fully developed.

I have, in the course of my observation on this constitution, affirmed and endeavored to shew, that it was calculated to abolish entirely the state governments, and to melt down the states into one entire government, for every purpose as well internal and local, as external and national. In this opinion the opposers of the system have generally agreed—and this has been uniformly denied by its advocates in public. Some individuals, indeed, among them, will confess, that it has this tendency, and scruple not to say, it is what they wish; and I will venture to predict, without the spirit of prophecy, that if it is adopted without amendments, or some such precautions as will ensure amendments immediately after its adoption, that the same gentlemen who have employed their talents and abilities with such success to influence the public mind to adopt this plan, will employ the same to persuade the people, that it will be for their good to abolish the state governments as useless and burdensome.

Perhaps nothing could have been better conceived to facilitate the abolition of the state governments than the constitution of the judicial. They will be able to extend the limits of the general government gradually, and by insensible degrees, and to accomodate themselves to the temper of the people. Their decisions on the meaning of the constitution will commonly take place in cases which arise between individuals, with which the public will not be generally acquainted; one adjudication will form a precedent to the next, and this to a following one. These cases will immediately affect individuals only; so that a series of determinations will probably take place before even the people will be informed of them. In the mean time all the art and address of those who wish for the change will be employed to make converts to their opinion. The people will be told, that their state officers, and state legislatures are a burden and expence without affording any solid advantage, for that all the laws passed by them, might be equally well made by the general legislature. If to those who will be interested in the change, be added, those who will be under their influence, and such who will submit to almost any change of government, which they can be persuaded to believe will ease them of taxes, it is easy to see, the party who will favor the abolition of the state governments would be far from being inconsiderable.—In this situation, the general legislature, might pass one law after another, extending the general and abridging the state jurisdictions, and to sanction their proceedings would have a course of decisions of the judicial to whom the constitution has committed the power of explaining the constitution.—If the states remonstrated, the constitutional mode of deciding upon the validity of the law, is with the supreme court, and neither people, nor state legislatures, nor the general legislature can remove them or reverse their decrees.

Had the construction of the constitution been left with the legislature, they would have explained it at their peril; if they exceed their powers, or sought to find, in the spirit of the constitution, more than was expressed in the letter, the people from whom they derived their power could remove them, and do themselves right; and indeed I can see no other remedy that the people can have against their rulers for encroachments of this nature. A constitution is a compact of a people with their rulers; if the rulers break the compact, the people have a right and ought to remove them and do themselves justice; but in order to enable them to do this with the greater facility, those whom the people chuse at stated periods, should have the power in the last resort to determine the sense of the compact; if they determine contrary to the understanding of the people, an appeal will lie to the people at the period when the rulers are to be elected, and they will have it in their power to remedy the evil; but when this power is lodged in the hands of men independent of the people, and of their representatives, and who are not, constitutionally, accountable for their opinions, no way is left to controul them but *with a high hand and an outstretched arm.*

Brutus.

N. ALEXANDER HAMILTON, THE FEDERALIST, NO. 84

May 28, 1788

In the course of the foregoing review of the constitution I have taken notice of, and endeavoured to answer, most of the objections which have appeared against it. There however remain a few which either did not fall naturally under any particular head, or were forgotten in their proper places. These shall now be discussed; but as the subject has been drawn into great length, I shall so far consult brevity as to comprise all my observations on these miscellaneous points in a single paper.

The most considerable of these remaining objections is, that the plan of the convention contains no bill of rights. Among other answers given to this, it has been upon different occasions remarked, that the constitutions of several of the states are in a similar predicament. I add, that New-York is of this number. And yet the opposers of the new system in this state, who profess an unlimited admiration for its constitution, are among the most intemperate partizans of a bill of rights. To justify their zeal in this matter, they alledge two things; one is, that though the constitution of New-York has no bill of rights prefixed to it, yet it contains in the body of it various provisions in favour of particular privileges and rights, which in substance amount to the same thing; the other is, that the constitution adopts in their full extent the common and statute law of Great-Britain, by which many other rights not expressed in it are equally secured.

To the first I answer, that the constitution proposed by the convention contains, as well as the constitution of this state, a number of such provisions.

Independent of those, which relate to the structure of the government, we find the following: Article I. section 3. clause 7. "Judgment in cases of impeachment shall not extend further than to removal from office, and disqualification to hold and enjoy any office of honour, trust or profit under the United States; but the party convicted shall nevertheless be liable and subject to indictment, trial, judgment and punishment, according to law." Section 9. of the same article, clause 2. "The privilege of the writ of *habeas corpus* shall not be suspended, unless when in cases of rebellion or invasion the public safety may require it." Clause 3. "No bill of attainder or *ex post facto* law shall be passed." Clause 7. "No title of nobility shall be granted by the United States: And no person holding any office of profit or trust under them, shall, without the consent of the congress, accept of any present, emolument, office or title, of any kind whatever, from any king, prince or foreign state." Article III. section 2. clause 3. "The trial of all crimes, except in cases of impeachment, shall be by jury; and such trial shall be held in the state where the said crimes shall have been committed; but when not committed within any state, the trial shall be at such place or places as the congress may by law have directed." Section 3, of the same article, "Treason against the United States shall consist only in levying war against them, or in adhering to their enemies, giving them aid and comfort. No person shall be convicted of treason unless on the testimony of two witnesses to the same overt act, or on confession in open court." And clause 3, of the same section. "The congress shall have power to declare the punishment of treason, but no attainder of treason shall work corruption of blood, or forfeiture, except during the life of the person attainted."

It may well be a question whether these are not upon the whole, of equal importance with any which are to be found in the constitution of this state. The establishment of the writ of *habeas corpus,* the prohibition of *ex post facto* laws, and of TITLES OF NOBILITY, *to which we have no corresponding provisions in our constitution,* are perhaps greater securities to liberty and republicanism than any it contains. The creation of crimes after the commission of the fact, or in other words, the subjecting of men to punishment for things which, when they were done, were breaches of no law, and the practice of arbitrary imprisonments have been in all ages the favourite and most formidable instruments of tyranny. The observations of the judicious Blackstone * in reference to the latter, are well worthy of recital. "To bereave a man of life (says he) or by violence to confiscate his estate, without accusation or trial, would be so gross and notorious an act of despotism, as must at once convey the alarm of tyranny throughout the whole nation; but confinement of the person by secretly hurrying him to goal, where his sufferings are unknown or forgotten, is a less public, a less striking, and therefore *a more dangerous engine* of arbitrary government." And as a remedy for this fatal evil, he is every where peculiarly emphatical in his encomiums on the *habeas corpus* act, which in one place he calls "the BULWARK of the British constitution."†

Nothing need be said to illustrate the importance of the prohibition of titles of nobility. This may truly be denominated the corner stone of republican government; for so long as they are excluded, there can never be serious danger that the government will be any other than that of the people.

To the second, that is, to the pretended establishment of the common and statute law by the constitution, I answer, that they are expressly made subject "to such alterations and provisions as the legislature shall from time to time make concerning the same." They are therefore at any moment liable to repeal by the ordinary legislative power, and of course have no constitutional sanction. The only use of the declaration was to recognize the ancient law, and to remove doubts which might have been occasioned by the revolution. This consequently can be considered as no part of a declaration of rights, which under our constitutions must be intended as limitations of the power of the government itself.

It has been several times truly remarked, that bills of rights are in their origin, stipulations between kings and their subjects, abridgments of prerogative in favor of privilege, reservations of rights not surrendered to the prince. Such was MAGNA CHARTA, obtained by the Barons, sword in hand, from king John. Such were the subsequent confirmations of that charter by subsequent princes. Such was the *petition of*

---

* Vide Blackstone's Commentaries, vol. 1,   † Idem. vol. 4, page 438 [sic; 421].
page 136.

right assented to by Charles the First, in the beginning of his reign. Such also was the declaration of right presented by the lords and commons to the prince of Orange in 1688, and afterwards thrown into the form of an act of parliament, called the bill of rights. It is evident, therefore, that according to their primitive signification, they have no application to constitutions professedly founded upon the power of the people, and executed by their immediate representatives and servants. Here, in strictness, the people surrender nothing, and as they retain every thing, they have no need of particular reservations. "WE THE PEO-PLE of the United States, to secure the blessings of liberty to ourselves and our posterity, do *ordain* and *establish* this constitution for the United States of America." Here is a better recognition of popular rights than volumes of those aphorisms which make the principal figure in several of our state bills of rights, and which would sound much better in a treatise of ethics than in a constitution of government.

But a minute detail of particular rights is certainly far less applicable to a constitution like that under consideration, which is merely intended to regulate the general political interests of the nation, than to a constitution which has the regulation of every species of personal and private concerns. If therefore the loud clamours against the plan of the convention on this score, are well founded, no epithets of reprobation will be too strong for the constitution of this state. But the truth is, that both of them contain all, which in relation to their objects, is reasonably to be desired.

I go further, and affirm that bills of rights, in the sense and in the extent in which they are contended for, are not only unnecessary in the proposed constitution, but would even be dangerous. They would contain various exceptions to powers which are not granted; and on this very account, would afford a colourable pretext to claim more than were granted. For why declare that things shall not be done which there is no power to do? Why for instance, should it be said, that the liberty of the press shall not be restrained, when no power is given by which restrictions may be imposed? I will not contend that such a provision would confer a regulating power; but it is evident that it would furnish, to men disposed to usurp, a plausible pretence for claiming that power. They might urge with a semblance of reason, that the constitution ought not to be charged with the absurdity of providing against the abuse of an authority, which was not given, and that the provision against restraining the liberty of the press afforded a clear implication, that a power to prescribe proper regulations concerning it, was intended to be vested in the national government. This may serve as a specimen of the numerous handles which would be given to the doctrine of constructive powers, by the indulgence of an injudicious zeal for bills of rights.

On the subject of the liberty of the press, as much has been said, I cannot forbear adding a remark or two: In the first place, I observe that there is not a syllable concerning it in the constitution of this state, and in the next, I contend that whatever has been said about it in that of any other state, amounts to nothing. What signifies a declaration that "the liberty of the press shall be inviolably preserved?" What is the liberty of the press? Who can give it any definition which would not leave the utmost latitude for evasion? I hold it to be impracticable; and from this, I infer, that its security, whatever fine declarations may be inserted in any constitution respecting it, must altogether depend on public opinion, and on the general spirit of the people and of the government.* And here, after all, as intimated upon another occasion, must we seek for the only solid basis of all our rights.

There remains but one other view of this matter to conclude the point. The truth is, after all the declamation we have heard, that the constitution is itself in every rational sense, and to every useful purpose, A BILL OF RIGHTS. The several bills of rights, in Great-Britain, form its constitution, and conversely the constitution of each state is its bill of rights. And the proposed constitution, if adopted, will be the bill of rights of the union. Is it one object of a bill of rights to declare and specify the political privileges of the citizens in the structure and administration of the government? This is done in the most ample and precise manner in the plan of the convention, comprehending various precautions for the public security, which are not to be found in any of the state constitutions. Is another object of a bill of rights to define certain immunities and modes of proceeding, which are relative to personal and private concerns? This we have seen has also been attended to, in a variety of cases, in the same plan. Adverting therefore to the substantial meaning of a bill of rights, it is absurd to allege that it is not to be found in the work of the convention. It may be said that it does not go far enough, though it will not be easy to make this appear; but it can with no propriety be contended that there is no such thing. It certainly must be immaterial what mode is observed as to the order of declaring the rights of the citizens, if they are to be found in any part of the instrument which establishes the government. And hence it must

* To show that there is a power in the constitution by which the liberty of the press may be affected, recourse has been had to the power of taxation. It is said that duties may be laid upon publications so high as to amount to a prohibition. I know not by what logic it could be maintained that the declarations in the state constitutions, in favour of the freedom of the press, would be a constitutional impediment to the imposition of duties upon publications by the state legislatures. It cannot certainly be pretended that any degree of duties, however low, would be an abrigement of the liberty of the press. We know that newspapers are taxed in Great-Britain, and yet it is notorious that the press no where enjoys greater liberty than in that country. And if duties of any kind may be laid without a violation of that liberty, it is evident that the extent must depend on legislative discretion, regulated by public opinion; so that after all, general declarations respecting the liberty of the press will give it no greater security than it will have without them. The same invasions of it may be effected under the state constitutions which contain those declarations through the means of taxation, as under the proposed constitution which has nothing of the kind. It would be quite as significant to declare that government ought to be free, that taxes ought not to be excessive, &c., as that the liberty of the press ought not to be restrained.

be apparent that much of what has been said on this subject rests merely on verbal and nominal distinctions, which are entirely foreign from the substance of the thing.

Another objection, which has been made, and which from the frequency of its repetition it is to be presumed is relied on, is of this nature:—It is improper (say the objectors) to confer such large powers, as are proposed, upon the national government; because the seat of that government must of necessity be too remote from many of the states to admit of a proper knowledge on the part of the constituent, of the conduct of the representative body. This argument, if it proves any thing, proves that there ought to be no general government whatever. For the powers which it seems to be agreed on all hands, ought to be vested in the union, cannot be safely intrusted to a body which is not under every requisite controul. But there are satisfactory reasons to shew that the objection is in reality not well founded. There is in most of the arguments which relate to distance a palpable illusion of the imagination. What are the sources of information by which the people in Montgomery county must regulate their judgment of the conduct of their representatives in the state legislature? Of personal observation they can have no benefit. This is confined to the citizens on the spot. They must therefore depend on the information of intelligent men, in whom they confide—and how must these men obtain their information? Evidently from the complection of public measures, from the public prints, from correspondences with their representatives, and with other persons who reside at the place of their deliberation. This does not apply to Montgomery county only, but to all the counties, at any considerable distance from the seat of government.

It is equally evident that the same sources of information would be open to the people, in relation to the conduct of their representatives in the general government; and the impediments to a prompt communication which distance may be supposed to create, will be overballanced by the effects of the vigilance of the state governments. The executive and legislative bodies of each state will be so many centinels over the persons employed in every department of the national administration; and as it will be in their power to adopt and pursue a regular and effectual system of intelligence, they can never be at a loss to know the behaviour of those who represent their constituents in the national councils, and can readily communicate the same knowledge to the people. Their disposition to apprise the community of whatever may prejudice its interests from another quarter, may be relied upon, if it were only from the rivalship of power. And we may conclude with the fullest assurance, that the people, through that channel, will be better informed of the conduct of their national representatives, than they can be by any means they now possess of that of their state representatives.

It ought also to be remembered, that the citizens who inhabit the country at and near the seat of government, will in all questions that affect the general liberty and prosperity, have the same interest with those who are at a distance; and that they will stand ready to sound the alarm when necessary, and to point out the actors in any pernicious project. The public papers will be expeditious messengers of intelligence to the most remote inhabitants of the union.

Among the many extraordinary objections which have appeared against the proposed constitution, the most extraordinary and the least colourable one, is derived from the want of some provision respecting the debts due *to* the United States. This has been represented as a tacit relinquishment of those debts, and as a wicked contrivance to screen public defaulters. The newspapers have teemed with the most inflammatory railings on this head; and yet there is nothing clearer than that the suggestion is entirely void of foundation, and is the offspring of extreme ignorance or extreme dishonesty. In addition to the remarks I have made upon the subject in another place, I shall only observe, that as it is a plain dictate of common sense, so it is also an established doctrine of political law, that *"States neither lose any of their rights, nor are discharged from any of their obligations by a change in the form of their civil government."**

The last objection of any consequence which I at present recollect, turns upon the article of expence. If it were even true that the adoption of the proposed go ernment would occasion a considerable increase of expence, it would be an objection that ought to have no weight against the plan. The great bulk of the citizens of America, are with reason convinced that union is the basis of their political happiness. Men of sense of all parties now, with few exceptions, agree that it cannot be preserved under the present system, nor without radical alterations; that new and extensive powers ought to be granted to the national head, and that these require a different organization of the federal government, a single body being an unsafe depository of such ample authorities. In conceding all this, the question of expence must be given up, for it is impossible, with any degree of safety, to narrow the foundation upon which the system is to stand. The two branches of the legislature are in the first instance, to consist of only sixty-five persons, which is the same number of which congress, under the existing confederation, may be composed. It is true that this number is intended to be increased; but this is to keep pace with the increase of the population and resources of the country. It is evident, that a less number would, even in the first instance, have been unsafe; and that a continuance of the present number would, in a more advanced stage of population, be a very inadequate representation of the people.

Whence is the dreaded augmentation of expence to spring? One source pointed out, is the multiplication of offices under the new government. Let us examine this a little.

* Vide Rutherford's Institutes, vol. 2.   also Grotius, book II, chap. ix, sect. viii, and
book II, chap. x. sect. xiv, and xv.—Vide   ix.

It is evident that the principal departments of the administration under the present government, are the same which will be required under the new. There are now a secretary at war, a secretary for foreign affairs, a secretary for domestic affairs, a board of treasury consisting of three persons, a treasurer, assistants, clerks, &c. These offices are indispensable under any system, and will suffice under the new as well as under the old. As to ambassadors and other ministers and agents in foreign countries, the proposed constitution can make no other difference, than to render their characters, where they reside, more respectable, and their services more useful. As to persons to be employed in the collection of the revenues, it is unquestionably true that these will form a very considerable addition to the number of federal officers; but it will not follow, that this will occasion an increase of public expence. It will be in most cases nothing more than an exchange of state officers for national officers. In the collection of all duties, for instance, the persons employed will be wholly of the latter description. The states individually will stand in no need of any for this purpose. What difference can it make in point of expence, to pay officers of the customs appointed by the state, or those appointed by the United States? There is no good reason to suppose, that either the number or the salaries of the latter, will be greater than those of the former.

Where then are we to seek for those additional articles of expence which are to swell the account to the enormous size that has been represented to us? The chief item which occurs to me, respects the support of the judges of the United States. I do not add the president, because there is now a president of congress, whose expences may not be far, if any thing, short of those which will be incurred on account of the president of the United States. The support of the judges will clearly be an extra expence, but to what extent will depend on the particular plan which may be adopted in practice in regard to this matter. But it can upon no reasonable plan amount to a sum which will be an object of material consequence.

Let us now see what there is to counterballance any extra expences that may attend the establishment of the proposed government. The first thing that presents itself is, that a great part of the business, which now keeps congress sitting through the year, will be transacted by the president. Even the management of foreign negociations will naturally devolve upon him according to general principles concerted with the senate, and subject to their final concurrence. Hence it is evident, that a portion of the year will suffice for the session of both the senate and the house of representatives: We may suppose about a fourth for the latter, and a third or perhaps a half for the former. The extra business of treaties and appointments may give this extra occupation to the senate. From this circumstance we may infer, that until the house of representatives shall be increased greatly beyond its present number, there will be a considerable saving of expence from the difference between the constant session of the present, and the temporary session of the future congress.

But there is another circumstance, of great importance in the view of economy. The business of the United States has hitherto occupied the state legislatures as well as congress. The latter has made requisitions which the former have had to provide for. Hence it has happened that the sessions of the state legislatures have been protracted greatly beyond what was necessary for the execution of the mere local business of the states. More than half their time has been frequently employed in matters which related to the United States. Now the members who compose the legislatures of the several states amount to two thousand and upwards; which number has hitherto performed what under the new system will be done in the first instance by sixty-five persons, and probably at no future period by above a fourth or a fifth of that number. The congress under the proposed government will do all the business of the United States themselves, without the intervention of the state legislatures, who thenceforth will have only to attend to the affairs of their particular states, and will not have to sit in any proportion as long as they have heretofore done. This difference, in the time of the sessions of the state legislatures, will be all clear gain, and will alone form an article of saving, which may be regarded as an equivalent for any additional objects of expence that may be occasioned by the adoption of the new system.

The result from these observations is, that the sources of additional expence from the establishment of the proposed constitution are much fewer than may have been imagined, that they are counterbalanced by considerable objects of saving, and that while it is questionable on which side the scale will preponderate, it is certain that a government less expensive would be incompetent to the purposes of the union.

PUBLIUS.

O. DEBATE IN THE STATE CONVENTIONS

(1) Pennsylvania, November 28, December 4, 1787

Mr. WILSON. This will be a proper time for making an observation or two on what may be called the preamble to this Constitution. I had occasion, on a former day, to mention that the leading principle in the politics, and that which pervades the American constitutions, is, that the supreme power resides in the people. This Constitution, Mr. President, opens with a solemn and practical recognition of that principle:—"We, the *people of the United States*, in order to form a more perfect union, establish justice, &c., *do* ordain and establish this Constitution for the United States of America." It is announced in *their* name—it receives its political existence from *their* authority: they ordain and establish. What is the necessary consequence? Those who ordain and establish have the power, if they think proper, to repeal and annul. A proper attention to this principle may, perhaps, give ease to the minds of some who have heard much concerning the necessity of a bill of rights.

Its establishment, I apprehend, has more force than a volume written on the subject. It renders this truth evident—that the people have a right to do what they please with regard to the government. I confess I feel a kind of pride in considering the striking difference between the foundation on which the liberties of this country are declared to stand in this Constitution, and the footing on which the liberties of England are said to be placed. The Magna Charta of England is an instrument of high value to the people of that country. But, Mr. President, from what source does that instrument derive the liberties of the inhabitants of that kingdom? Let it speak for itself. The king says, "*We* have *given* and *granted* to all archbishops, bishops, abbots, priors, earls, barons, and to all the freemen of this our realm, these liberties following, to be kept in our kingdom of England forever." When this was assumed as the leading principle of that government, it was no wonder that the people were anxious to obtain bills of rights, and to take every opportunity of enlarging and securing their liberties. But here, sir, the fee-simple remains in the people at large, and by this Constitution they do not part with it.

I am called upon to give a reason why the Convention omitted to add a bill of rights to the work before you. I confess, sir, I did think that, in point of propriety, the honorable gentleman ought first to have furnished some reasons to show such an addition to be necessary; it is natural to prove the affirmative of a proposition; and, if he had established the propriety of this addition, he might then have asked why it was not made.

I cannot say, Mr. President, what were the reasons of every member of that Convention for not adding a bill of rights. I believe the truth is, that such an idea never entered the mind of many of them. I do not recollect to have heard the subject mentioned till within about three days of the time of our rising; and even then, there was no direct motion offered for any thing of the kind. I may be mistaken in this; but as far as my memory serves me, I believe it was the case. A proposition to adopt a measure that would have supposed that we were throwing into the general government every power not expressly reserved by the people, would have been spurned at, in that house, with the greatest indignation. Even in a single government, if the powers of the people rest on the same establishment as is expressed in this Constitution, a bill of rights is by no means a necessary measure. In a government possessed of enumerated powers, such a measure would be not only unnecessary, but preposterous and dangerous. Whence comes this notion, that in the United States there is no security without a bill of rights? Have the citizens of South Carolina no security for their liberties? They have no bill of rights. Are the citizens on the eastern side of the Delaware less free, or less secured in their liberties, than those on the western side? The state of New Jersey has no bill of rights. The state of New York has no bill of rights. The states of Connecticut and Rhode Island have no bill of rights. I know not whether I have exactly enumerated the states who have not thought it necessary to add *a bill of rights* to their constitutions; but this enumeration, sir, will serve to show by experience, as well as principle, that, even in single governments, a bill of rights is not an essential or necessary measure. But in a government consisting of enumerated powers, such as is proposed for the United States, a bill of rights would not only be unnecessary, but, in my humble judgment, highly imprudent. In all societies, there are many powers and rights which cannot be particularly enumerated. A bill of rights annexed to a constitution is *an enumeration of the powers* reserved. If we attempt an enumeration, every thing that is not enumerated is presumed to be given. The consequence is, that an imperfect enumeration would throw all implied power into the scale of the government, and the rights of the people would be rendered incomplete. On the other hand, an imperfect enumeration of the powers of government reserves all implied power to the people; and by that means the constitution becomes incomplete. But of the two, it is much safer to run the risk on the side of the constitution; for an omission in the enumeration of the powers of government is neither so dangerous nor important as an omission in the enumeration of the rights of the people.

Mr. President, as we are drawn into this subject, I beg leave to pursue its history a little farther. The doctrine and practice of declarations of rights have been borrowed from the conduct of the people of England on some remarkable occasions; but the principles and maxims, on which their government is constituted, are widely different from those of ours. I have already stated the language of Magna Charta. After repeated confirmations of that instrument, and after violations of it repeated equally often, the next step taken in this business was, when the petition of rights was presented to Charles I.

It concludes in this manner: "All of which they most humbly *pray* to be allowed, as their rights and liberties, according to the laws and statutes of this realm." (8th *Par. Hist.* 150.) One of the most material statutes of the realm was Magna Charta; so that we find they continue upon the old ground, as to the foundation on which they rest their liberties. It was not till the era of the revolution that the two houses assume a higher tone, and "*demand* and insist upon all the premises as their undoubted rights and liberties." (*Par. Deb.* 261.) But when the whole transaction is considered, we shall find that those rights and liberties are claimed only on the foundation of an original contract, supposed to have been made, at some former period, between the king and the people. (1 *Blackstone*, 233.)

But, in this Constitution, the citizens of the United States appear dispensing a part of their original power in what manner and what proportion they think fit. They never part with the whole; and they retain the right of recalling what they part with. When, therefore, they possess, as I have already mentioned, the fee-simple of authority, why should they have recourse to the minute and subordinate remedies, which can be necessary only to those who pass the fee, and reserve only a rent-charge?

To every suggestion concerning a bill of rights, the citizens of the United States may always say, WE reserve the right to do what we please.

I concur most sincerely with the honorable gentleman who was last up in one sentiment—that if our liberties will be insecure under this system of government, it will become our duty not to adopt, but to reject it. On the contrary, if it will secure the liberties of the citizens of America,—if it will not only secure their liberties, but procure them happiness,—it becomes our duty, on the other hand, to assent to and ratify it. With a view to conduct us safely and gradually to the determination of that important question, I shall beg leave to notice some of the objections that have fallen from the honorable gentleman from Cumberland, (Whitehill.) But, before I proceed, permit me to make one general remark. Liberty has a formidable enemy on each hand; on one there is tyranny, on the other licentiousness. In order to guard against the latter, proper powers ought to be given to government: in order to guard against the former, those powers ought to be properly distributed. It has been mentioned, and attempts have been made to establish the position, that the adoption of this Constitution will necessarily be followed by the annihilation of all the state governments. If this was a necessary consequence, the objection would operate in my mind with exceeding great force. But, sir, I think the inference is rather unnatural, that a government will produce the annihilation of others, upon the very existence of which its own existence depends. Let us, sir, examine this Constitution, and mark its proportions and arrangements. . . .

* * *

Mr. Smilie. I expected, Mr. President, that the honorable gentleman would have proceeded to a full and explicit investigation of the proposed system, and that he would have made some attempts to prove that it was calculated to promote the happiness, power and general interests of the United States. I am sorry that I have been mistaken in this expectation, for surely the gentleman's talents and opportunities would have enabled him to furnish considerable information upon this important subject; but I shall proceed to make a few remarks upon those words in the preamble of this plan, which he has considered of so super-excellent a quality. Compare them, Sir, with the language used in forming the state constitution, and however superior they may be to the terms of the great charter of England; still, in common candor, they must yield to the more sterling expressions employed in this act. Let these speak for themselves:

"That all men are born equally free and independent, and have certain natural, inherent and unalienable rights, among which are the enjoying and defending life and liberty, acquiring possessing and protecting property, and pursuing and obtaining happiness and safety.

"That the people of this state have the sole, exclusive and inherent right of governing and regulating the internal police of the same.

"That all power being originally inherent in, and consequently derived from the people; therefore all officers of government, whether legislative or executive, are their trustees and servants, and at all times accountable to them.

"That government is, or ought to be, instituted for the common benefit, protection and security of the people, nation or community; and not for the particular emolument or advantage of any single man, family, or set of men, who are a part only of that community. And that the community hath an indubitable, unalienable, and indefeasible right to reform, alter or abolish government in such manner as shall be by that community judged most conducive to the public weal."

But the gentleman takes pride in the superiority of this short preamble when compared with Magna Charta—why, sir, I hope the rights of men are better understood at this day than at the framing of that deed, and we must be convinced that civil liberty is capable of still greater improvement and extension, than is known even in its present cultivated state. True, sir, the supreme authority naturally rests in the people, but does it follow, that therefore a declaration of rights would be superfluous? Because the people have a right to alter and abolish government, can it therefore be inferred that every step taken to secure that right would be superfluous and nugatory? The truth is, that unless some criterion is established by which it could be easily and constitutionally ascertained how far our governors may proceed, and by which it might appear when they transgress their jurisdiction, this idea of altering and abolishing government is a mere sound without substance. Let us recur to the memorable declaration of the 4th of July, 1776. Here it is said:

"When in the course of human events, it becomes necessary for one people to dissolve the political bands which have connected them with another, and to assume among the powers of the earth the separate and equal station to which the laws of nature's God entitle them, a decent respect to the opinions of mankind requires that they should declare the causes which impel them to the separation.

"We hold these truths to be self-evident; that all men are created equal; that they are endowed by their Creator with certain unalienable rights; that among these are life, liberty, and the pursuit of happiness. That to secure these rights, governments are instituted among men, deriving their just powers from the consent of the governed; that when any form of government becomes destructive of these ends, it is the right of the people to alter or to abolish it, and to institute a new government, laying its foundation on such principles, and organizing its powers in such form, as to them shall seem most likely to effect their safety and happiness."

(Now, Sir, if in the proposed plan, the gentleman can show any similar security for the civil rights of the people, I shall certainly be relieved from a weight of objection to its adoption, and I sincerely hope, that as he has gone so far, he will proceed to communicate some of the reasons (and undoubtedly they must have been powerful ones) which induced the late federal convention to omit a bill of rights, so essential in the opinion of many citizens to a perfect form of government.)

Mr. M'Kean.—I conceived, Mr. President, that we were at this time to confine our reasoning to the first article, which relates to the legislative power composed of two branches, and the partial negative of the President. Gentlemen, however, have taken a more extensive field, and have employed themselves in animadverting upon what has been omitted, and not upon what is contained in the proposed system. It is asked, Sir, why a bill of rights is not annexed to the constitution? The origin of bills of rights has been referred to, and we find that in England they proceed upon the principle that the supreme power is lodged in the king and not in the people, so that their liberties are not claimed as an inherent right, but as a grant from the sovereign. The great charter rests on that footing, and has been renewed and broken above 30 times. Then we find the petition of rights in the reign of Charles I., and lastly, the declaration of rights on the accession of the Prince of Orange to the British throne. The truth is, Sir, that bills of rights are instruments of modern invention, unknown among the ancients, and unpractised but by the British nation, and the governments descended from them. For though it is said that Poland has a bill of rights, it must be remembered that the people have no participation in that government. Of the constitutions of the United States, there are but five out of the thirteen which have bills of rights. In short, though it can do no harm, I believe, yet it is an unnecessary instrument, for in fact the whole plan of government is nothing more than a bill of rights—a declaration of the people in what manner they choose to be governed. If, Sir, the people should at any time desire to alter and abolish their government, I agree with my honorable colleague that it is in their power to do so, and I am happy to observe, that the constitution before us provides a regular mode for that event. At present my chief object is to call upon those who deem a bill of rights so essential, to inform us if there are any other precedents than those I have alluded to, and if there is not, the sense of mankind and of nations will operate against the alleged necessity.

Mr. Wilson. Mr. President, we are repeatedly called upon to give some reason why a bill of rights has not been annexed to the proposed plan. I not only think that enquiry is at this time unnecessary and out of order, but I expect, at least, that those who desire us to show why it was omitted, will furnish some arguments to show that it ought to have been inserted; for the proof of the affirmative naturally falls upon them. But the truth is, Sir, that this circumstance, which has since occasioned so much clamor and debate, never struck the mind of any member in the late convention till, I believe, within three days of the dissolution of that body, and even then of so little account was the idea that it passed off in a short conversation, without introducing a formal debate or assuming the shape of a motion. For, Sir, the attempt to have thrown into the national scale an instrument in order to evince that any power not mentioned in the constitution was reserved, would have been spurned at as an insult to the common understanding of mankind. In civil government it is certain that bills of rights are unnecessary and useless, nor can I conceive whence the contrary notion has arisen. Virginia has no bill of rights, and will it be said that her constitution was the less free?

Mr. Smilie. I beg leave to observe, Mr. President, that although it has not been inserted in the printed volume of state constitution, yet I have been assured by Mr. Mason that Virginia has a bill of rights.

Mr. Wilson. I do not rely upon the information of Mr. Mason or of any other gentleman on a question of this kind, but I refer to the authenticity of the volume which contains the state constitutions, and in that Virginia has no bill of rights. But, Sir, has South Carolina no security for her liberties?—that state has no bill of rights. Are the citizens of the eastern shore of the Delaware more secured in their freedom, or more enlightened on the subject of government, than the citizens of the western shore? New Jersey has no bill of rights, New York has none, Connecticut has none, and Rhode Island has none. Thus, Sir, it appears from the example of other states, as well as from principle, that a bill of rights is neither an essential nor a necessary instrument in framing a system of government, since liberty may exist and be as well secured without it. But it was not only unnecessary, but on this occasion it was found impracticable—for who will be bold enough to undertake to enumerate all the rights of the people?—and when the attempt to enumerate them is made, it must be remembered that if the enumeration is not complete, everything not expressly mentioned will be presumed to be purposely omitted. So it must be with a bill of rights, and an omission in stating the powers granted to the government, is not so dangerous as an omission in recapitulating the rights reserved by the people. We have already seen the origin of magna charta, and tracing the subject still further we find the petition of rights claiming the liberties of the people, according to the laws and statutes of the realm, of which the great charter was the most material, so that here again recourse is had to the old source from which their liberties are derived, the grant of the king. It was not till the revolution that the subject was placed upon a different footing, and even then the people did not claim their liberties as an inherent right, but as the result of an original contract between them and the sovereign. Thus, Mr. President, an attention to the situation of England will show that the conduct of that country in respect to bills of rights, cannot furnish an example to the inhabitants of the United States, who by the revolution have regained all their natural rights, and possess their liberty neither by grant nor contract. In short, Sir, I have said that a bill of rights would have been improperly annexed to the federal plan, and for this plain reason that it would imply that whatever is not expressed was given, which is not the principle of the proposed constitution.

Mr. Smilie. The arguments which have been urged, Mr. President, have not, in my opinion, satisfactorily shown that a bill of rights would have been an improper, nay, that it is not a necessary appendage to the proposed system. As it has been denied that Virginia possesses a bill of rights, I shall on that subject only observe that Mr. Mason, a gentleman certainly of great information and integrity, has assured me that such a thing does exist, and I am persuaded I shall be able at a future period to lay it before the convention. But, Sir, the state of Delaware has a bill of rights, and I believe one of the honorable members (Mr. M'Kean) who now contests the necessity and propriety of that instrument, took a very conspicuous part in the formation of the Delaware government. It seems, however, that the members of the federal convention were themselves convinced, in some degree, of the expediency and propriety of a bill of rights, for we find them expressly declaring that the writ of habeas corpus and the trial by jury in criminal cases shall not be suspended or infringed. How does this indeed agree with the maxim that whatever is not given is reserved? Does it not rather appear from the reservation of these two articles that everything else, which is not specified, is included in the powers delegated to the government? This, Sir, must prove the necessity of a full and explicit declaration of rights; and when we further consider the extensive, the undefined powers vested in the administrators of this system, when we consider the system itself as a great political compact between the governors and the governed, a plain, strong, and accurate criterion by which the people might at once determine when, and in what instance their rights were violated, is a preliminary, without which, this plan ought not to be adopted. So loosely, so inaccurately are the powers which are enumerated in this constitution defined, that it will be impossible, without a test of that kind, to ascertain the limits of authority, and to declare when government has degenerated into oppression. In that event the contest will arise between the people and the rulers: "You have exceeded the powers of your office, you have oppressed us," will be the language of the suffering citizen. The answer of the government will be short—"We have not exceeded our power; you have no test by which you can prove it." Hence, Sir, it will be impracticable to stop the progress of tyranny, for there will be no check but the people, and their exertions must be futile and uncertain; since it will be difficult, indeed, to communicate to them the violation that has been committed, and their proceedings will be neither systematical nor unanimous. It is said, however, that the difficulty of framing a bill of rights was insurmountable; but, Mr. President, I cannot agree in this opinion. Our experience, and the numerous precedents before us, would have furnished a very sufficient guide. (At present there is no security even for the rights of conscience, and under the sweeping force of the sixth article, every principle of a bill of rights, every stipulation for the most sacred and invaluable privileges of man, are left at the mercy of government.)

* * *

Mr. WILSON. I shall take this opportunity of giving an answer to the objections already urged against the Constitution; I shall then point out some of those qualities that entitle it to the attention and approbation of this Convention; and, after having done this, I shall take a fit opportunity of stating the consequences which, I apprehend, will result from rejecting it, and those which will probably result from its adoption. I have given the utmost attention to the debates, and the objections that, from time to time, have been made by the three gentlemen who speak in opposition. I have reduced them to some order, perhaps not better than that in which they were introduced. I will state them; they will be in the recollection of the house, and I will endeavor to give an answer to them: in that answer, I will interweave some remarks, that may tend to elucidate the subject.

A good deal has already been said concerning *a bill of rights*. I have stated, according to the best of my recollection, all that passed in Convention relating to that business. Since that time, I have spoken with a gentleman, who has not only his memory, but full notes that he had taken in that body, and he assures me that, upon this subject, no direct motion was ever made at all; and certainly, before we heard this so violently supported out of doors, some pains ought to have been taken to have tried its fate within; but the truth is, a bill of rights would, as I have mentioned already, have been not only unnecessary, but improper. In some governments, it may come within the gentleman's idea, when he says it can do no harm; but even in these governments, you find bills of rights do not uniformly obtain; and do those states complain who have them not? Is it a maxim in forming governments, that not only all the powers which are given, but also that all those which are reserved, should be enumerated? I apprehend that the powers given and reserved form the whole rights of the people, as men and as citizens. I consider that there are very few who understand the whole of these rights. All the political writers, from *Grotius* and *Puffendorf* down to *Vattel*, have treated on this subject; but in no one of those books, nor in the aggregate of them all, can you find a complete enumeration of rights appertaining to the people as men and as citizens.

745

There are two kinds of government—that where general power is intended to be given to the legislature, and that where the powers are particularly enumerated. In the last case, the implied result is, that nothing more is intended to be given than what is so enumerated, unless it results from the nature of the government itself. On the other hand, when general legislative powers are given, then the people part with their authority, and, on the gentleman's principle of government, retain nothing. But in a government like the proposed one, there can be no necessity for a bill of rights, for, on my principle, the people never part with their power. Enumerate all the rights of men! I am sure, sir, that no gentleman in the late Convention would have attempted such a thing. I believe the honorable speakers in opposition on this floor were members of the assembly which appointed delegates to that Convention; if it had been thought proper to have sent them into that body, how luminous would the dark conclave have been!—so the gentleman has been pleased to denominate that body. Aristocrats as they were, they pretended not to define the rights of those who sent them there. We ask, repeatedly, What harm could the addition of a bill of rights do? If it can do no good, I think that a sufficient reason to refuse having any thing to do with it. But to whom are we to report this bill of rights, if we should adopt it? Have we authority from those who sent us here to make one?

It is true, we may propose as well as any other private persons; but how shall we know the sentiments of the citizens of this state and of the other states? Are we certain that any one of them will agree with our definitions and enumerations?

In the second place, we are told that there is no check upon the government but the people. It is unfortunate, sir, if their superintending authority is allowed as a check; but I apprehend that, in the very construction of this government, there are numerous checks. Besides those expressly enumerated, the two branches of the legislature are mutual checks upon each other. But this subject will be more properly discussed when we come to consider the form of the government itself; and then I mean to show the reason why the right of *habeas corpus* was secured by a particular declaration in its favor.

In the third place, we are told that there is no security for the rights of conscience. I ask the honorable gentleman, what part of this system puts it in the power of Congress to attack those rights? When there is no power to attack, it is idle to prepare the means of defence.

After having mentioned, in a cursory manner, the foregoing objections, we now arrive at the leading ones against the proposed system.

The very manner of introducing this Constitution, by the recognition of the authority of the people, is said to change the principle of the present Confederation, and to introduce a *consolidating* and absorbing government.

In this confederated republic, the sovereignty of the states, it is said, is not preserved. We are told that there cannot be two sovereign powers, and that a subordinate sovereignty is no sovereignty.

It will be worth while, Mr. President, to consider this objection at large. When I had the honor of speaking formerly on this subject, I stated, in as concise a manner as possible, the leading ideas that occurred to me, to ascertain where the supreme and sovereign power resides. It has not been, nor, I presume, will it be denied, that somewhere there is, and of necessity must be, a supreme, absolute, and uncontrollable authority. This, I believe, may justly be termed the *sovereign* power; for, from that gentleman's (Mr. Findley) account of the matter, it cannot be sovereign unless it is supreme; for, says he, a subordinate sovereignty is no sovereignty at all. I had the honor of observing, that, if the question was asked, where the supreme power resided, different answers would be given by different writers. I mentioned that Blackstone will tell you that, in Britain, it is lodged in the British Parliament; and I believe there is no writer on this subject, on the other side of the Atlantic, but supposed it to be vested in that body. I stated, further, that, if the question was asked of some politician, who had not considered the subject with sufficient accuracy, where the supreme power resided in our governments, he would answer, that it was vested in the state constitutions. This opinion approaches near the truth, but does not reach it; for the truth is, that the supreme, absolute, and uncontrollable authority *remains* with the people. I mentioned, also, that the practical recognition of this truth was reserved for the honor of this country. I recollect no constitution founded on this principle; but we have witnessed the improvement, and enjoy the happiness of seeing it carried into practice. The great and penetrating mind of *Locke* seems to be the only one that pointed towards even the theory of this great truth.

(2) Virginia, June 5, 12, 16, 17, 1788

Patrick Henry: Mr. Chairman—I am much obliged to the very worthy Gentleman [Henry Lee] for his encomium. I wish I was possessed of talents, or possessed of any thing, that might enable me to elucidate this great subject. I am not free from suspicion: I am apt to entertain doubts: I rose yesterday to ask a question, which arose in my own mind. When I asked the question, I thought the meaning of my interrogation was obvious: The fate of this question and America may depend on this: Have they said, we the States? Have they made a proposal of a compact between States? If they had, this would be a confederation: It is otherwise most clearly a consolidated government. The question turns, Sir, on that poor little thing—the expression, *We, the people,* instead of the States of America. I need not take much pains to show, that the principles of this system, are extremely pernicious, impolitic, and dangerous. Is this a Monarchy, like England—a compact between Prince and people; with checks on the former, to secure the liberty of the latter? Is this a Confederacy, like Holland—an association of a number of independent States, each of which retain its individual sovereignty? It is not a democracy, wherein the people retain all their rights securely. Had these principles been adhered to, we should not have been brought to this alarming transition, from a Confederacy to a consolidated Government. We have no detail of those great considerations which, in my opinion, ought to have abounded before we should recur to a government of this kind. Here is a revolution as radical as that which separated us from Great Britain. It is as radical, if in this transition our rights and privileges are endangered, and the sovereignty of the States be relinquished: And cannot we plainly see, that this is actually the case? The rights of conscience, trial by jury, liberty of the press, all your immunities and franchises, all pretensions to human rights and privileges, are rendered insecure, if not lost, by this change so loudly talked of by some, and inconsiderately by others. Is this same relinquishment of rights worthy of freemen? Is it worthy of that manly fortitude that ought to characterize republicans: It is said eight States have adopted this plan. I declare that if twelve States and an half had adopted it, I would with manly firmness, and in spite of an erring world, reject it. You are not to inquire how your trade may be increased, nor how you are to become a great and powerful people, but how your liberties can be secured; for liberty ought to be the direct end of your Government.

Having premised these things, I shall, with the aid of my judgment and information, which I confess are not extensive, go into the discussion of this system more minutely. Is it necessary for your liberty, that you should abandon those great rights by the adoption of this system? Is the relinquishment of the trial by jury, and the liberty of the press, necessary for your liberty? Will the abandonment of your most sacred rights tend to the security of your liberty? Liberty the greatest of all earthly blessings—give us that precious jewel, and you may take every thing else: But I am fearful I have lived long enough to become an old fashioned fellow: Perhaps an invincible attachment to the dearest rights of man, may, in these refined enlightened days, be deemed *old fashioned:* If so, I am contended to be so: I say, the time has been, when every pore of my heart beat for American liberty, and which, I believe, had a counterpart in the breast of every true American: But suspicions have gone forth—suspicions of my integrity—publicly reported that my professions are not real—23 years ago was I supposed a traitor to my country; I was then said to be a bane of sedition, because I supported the rights of my country: I may be thought suspicious when I say our privileges and rights are in danger: But, Sir, a number of the people of this country are weak enough to think these things are too true: I am happy to find that the Honorable Gentleman on the other side, declares they are groundless: But, Sir, suspicion is a virtue, as long as its object is the preservation of the public good, and as long as it stays within proper bounds: Should it fall on me, I am contented: Conscious rectitude is a powerful consolation: I trust, there are many who think my professions for the public good to be real. Let your suspicion look to both sides: There are many on the other side, who, possibly may have been persuaded of the necessity of these measures, which I conceive to be dangerous to your liberty. Guard with jealous attention the public liberty. Suspect every one who approaches that jewel. Unfortunately, nothing will preserve it, but downright force: Whenever you give up that force, you are inevitably' ruined. I am answered by Gentlemen, that though I might speak of terrors, yet the fact was, that we were surrounded by none of the dangers I apprehended. I conceive this new Government to be one of those dangers: It has produced those horrors, which distress many of our best citizens. We are come hither to preserve the poor Commonwealth of Virginia, if it can be possibly done: Something must be done to preserve your liberty and mine: The Confederation; this same despised Government, merits, in my opinion, the highest encomium: It carried us through a long and dangerous war: It rendered us victorious in that bloody conflict with a powerful nation: It has secured us a territory greater than any European Monarch possesses: And shall a Government which has been thus strong and vigorous, be accused of imbecility and abandoned for want of energy?

Consider what you are about to do before you part with this Government. Take longer time in reckoning things: Revolutions like this have happened in almost every country in Europe: Similar examples are to be found in ancient Greece and ancient Rome: Instances of the people loosing their liberty by their own carelessness and the ambition of a few. We are cautioned by the Honorable Gentleman who presides, against faction and turbulence: I acknowledge that licentiousness is dangerous, and that it ought to be provided against: I acknowledge also the new form of Government may effectually prevent it: Yet, there is another thing it will as effectually do: it will oppress and ruin the people. There are sufficient guards placed against sedition and licentiousness: For when power is given to this Government to suppress these, or, for any other purpose, the language it assumes is clear, express, and unequivocal, but when this Constitution speaks of privileges, there is an ambiguity, Sir, a fatal ambiguity;—an ambiguity which is very astonishing: In the clause under consideration, there is the strangest that I can conceive. I mean, when it says, that there shall not be more Representatives, than one for every 30,000. Now, Sir, how easy is it to evade this privilege? "The number shall not exceed one for every 30,000." This may be satisfied by one Representative from each State. Let our numbers be ever so great, this immence continent, may, by this artful expression, be reduced to have but 13 Representatives: I confess this construction is not natural; but the ambiguity of the expression lays a good ground for a quarrel. Why was it not clearly and unequivocally expressed, that they *should* be entitled, to have one for every 30,000? This would have obviated all disputes; and was this difficult to be done?

What is the inference? When population increases, and a State shall send Representatives in this proportion, Congress *may* remand them, because the right of having one for every 30,000 is not clearly expressed: This possibility of reducing the number to one for each State, approximates to probability by that other expression, "but each State shall at least have one Representative." Now is it not clear that from the first expression, the number might be reduced so much, that some States should have no Representative at all, were it not for the insertion of this last expression? And as this is the only restriction upon them, we may fairly conclude that they *may* restrain the number to one from each State: Perhaps the same horrors may hang over my mind again. I shall be told I am continually afraid: But, Sir, I have strong cause of apprehension: In some parts of the plan before you, the great rights of freemen are endangered, in other parts absolutely taken away. How does your trial by jury stand? In civil cases gone—not sufficiently secured in criminal—this best privilege is gone: But we are told that we need not fear, because those in power being our Representatives, will not abuse the powers we put in their hands: I am not well versed in history, but I will submit to your recollection, whether liberty has been destroyed most often by the licentiousness of the people, or by the tyranny of rulers? I imagine, Sir, you will find the balance on the side of tyranny:

Happy will you be if you miss the fate of those nations, who, omitting to resist their oppressors, or negligently suffering their liberty to be wrested from them, have groaned under intolerable despotism. Most of the human race are now in this deplorable condition: And those nations who have gone in search of grandeur, power and splendor, have also fallen a sacrifice, and been the victims of their own folly: While they acquired those visionary blessings, they lost their freedom. My great objection to this Government is, that it does not leave us the means of defending our rights; or, of waging war against tyrants: It is urged by some Gentlemen, that this new plan will bring us an acquisition of strength, an army, and the militia of the States: This is an idea extremely ridiculous: Gentlemen cannot be in earnest. This acquisition will trample on your fallen liberty: Let my beloved Americans guard against that fatal lethargy that has pervaded the universe: Have we the means of resisting disciplined armies, when our only defence, the militia is put into the hands of Congress? The Honorable Gentleman said, that great danger would ensue if the Convention rose without adopting this system: I ask, where is that danger? I see none: Other Gentlemen have told us within these walls, that the Union is gone—or, that the Union will be gone: Is not this trifling with the judgment of their fellow-citizens? Till they tell us the ground of their fears, I will consider them as imaginary: I rose to make enquiry where those dangers were; they could make no answer: I believe I never shall have that answer: Is there a disposition in the people of this country to revolt against the dominion of laws? Has there been a single tumult in Virginia? Have not the people of Virginia, when labouring under the severest pressure of accumulated distresses, manifested the most cordial acquiescence in the execution of the laws? What could be more awful than their unamious acquiescence under general distresses? Is there any revolution in Virginia? Whither is the spirit of America gone? Whither is the genius of America fled? It was but yesterday, when our enemies marched in triumph through our country: Yet the people of this country could not be appalled by their pompous armaments: They stopped their career, and victoriously captured them: Where is the peril now compared to that? Some minds are agitated by foreign alarms: Happily for us, there is no real danger from Europe: that country is engaged in more arduous business; from that quarter there is no cause of fear: You may sleep in safety forever for them. Where is the danger? If, Sir, there was any, I would recur to the American spirit to defend us;—that spirit which has enabled us to surmount the greatest difficulties:

To that illustrious spirit I address my most fervent prayer, to prevent our adopting a system destructive to liberty. Let not Gentlemen be told, that it is not safe to reject this Government. Wherefore is it not safe? We are told there are dangers; but those dangers are ideal; they cannot be demonstrated: To encourage us to adopt it, they tell us, that there is a plain easy way of getting amendments: When I come to contemplate this part, I suppose that I am mad, or, that my countrymen are so: The way to amendment, is, in my conception, shut. Let us consider this plain easy way: "The Congress, whenever two-thirds of both Houses shall deem it necessary, shall propose amendments to this Constitution, or, on the application of the Legislatures of two-thirds of the several States, shall call a Convention for proposing amendments, which, in either case, shall be valid to all intents and purposes, as part of this Constitution, when ratified by the Legislatures of three-fourths of the several States, or by Conventions in three-fourths thereof, as the one or the other mode of ratification may be proposed by the Congress. Provided, that no amendment which may be made prior to the year 1808, shall in any manner affect the first and fourth clauses in the ninth section of the first article; and that no State, without its consent, shall be deprived of its equal suffrage in the Senate." Hence it appears that three-fourths of the States must ultimately agree to any amendments that may be necessary. Let us consider the consequences of this: However uncharitable it may appear, yet I must tell my opinion, that the most unworthy characters may get into power and prevent the introduction of amendments: Let us suppose (for the case is supposeable, possible, and probable) that you happen to deal these powers to unworthy hands; will they relinquish powers already in their possession, or, agree to amendments? Two-thirds of the Congress, or, of the State Legislatures, are necessary even to propose amendments: If one-third of these be unworthy men, they may prevent the application for amendments; but what is destructive and mischievous is, that three-fourths of the State Legislatures, or of State Conventions, must concur in the amendments when proposed: In such numerous bodies, there must necessarily be some designing bad men: To suppose that so large a number as three-fourths of the States will concur, is to suppose that they will possess genius, intelligence, and integrity, approaching to miraculous. It would indeed be miraculous that they should concur in the same amendments, or, even in such as would bear some likeness to one another. For four of the smallest States, that do not collectively contain one-tenth part of the population of the United States, may obstruct the most salutary and necessary amendments: Nay, in these four States, six tenths of the people may reject these amendments; and suppose, that amendments shall be opposed to amendments (which is highly probable) is it possible, that three-fourths can ever agree to the same amendments? A bare majority in these four small States may hinder the adoption of amendments; so that we may fairly and justly conclude, that one-twentieth part of the American people, may prevent the removal of the most grievous inconveniences and oppression, by refusing to accede to amendments. A trifling minority may reject the most salutary amendments. Is this an easy mode of securing the public liberty? It is, Sir, a most fearful situation, when the most contemptible minority can prevent the alteration of the most oppressive Government; for it may in many respects prove to be such: Is this the spirit of republicanism? What, Sir, is the genius of democracy? Let me read that clause of the Bill of Rights of Virginia, which relates to this: 3d cl. "That Government is or ought to be instituted for the common benefit, protection, and security of the people, nation, or community: Of all the various modes and forms of Government, that is best which is capable of producing the greatest degree of happiness and safety, and is most effectually secured against the danger of mal-administration, and *that whenever any Government shall be found inadequate, or contrary to these purposes, a majority of the community hath, an undubitable, unalienable and indefeasible right to reform, alter, or abolish it, in such manner as shall be judged most conducive to the public weal.*"

This, Sir, is the language of democracy; that a majority of the community have a right to alter their Government when found to be oppressive: But how different is the genius of your new Constitution from this? How different from the sentiments of freemen, that a contemptible minority can prevent the good of the majority? If then Gentlemen standing on this ground, are come to that point, that they are willing to bind themselves and their posterity to be oppressed, I am amazed and inexpressibly astonished. If this be the opinion of the majority, I must submit; but to me, Sir, it appears perilous and destructive: I cannot help thinking so: Perhaps it may be the result of my age; these may be feelings natural to a man of my years, when the American spirit has left him, and his mental powers, like the members of the body, are decayed. If, Sir, amendments are left to the twentieth or the tenth part of the people of America, your liberty is gone forever. We have heard that there is a great deal of bribery practiced in the House of Commons in England; and that many of the members raised themselves to preferments, by selling the rights of the people: But, Sir, the tenth part of that body cannot continue oppressions on the rest of the people. English liberty is in this case, on a firmer foundation than American liberty. It will be easily contrived to procure the opposition of one tenth of the people to any alteration, however judicious. The Honorable Gentleman who presides, told us, that to prevent abuses in our Government, we will assemble in Convention, recall our delegated powers, and punish our servants for abusing the trust reposed in them. Oh, Sir, we should have fine times indeed, if to punish tyrants, it were only sufficient to assemble the people. Your arms wherewith you could defend yourselves, are gone; and have no longer a aristocratical; no longer democratical spirit. Did you ever read of any revolution in any nation, brought about by the punishment of those in power, inflicted by those who had no power at all? You read of a riot act in a country which is called one of the freest in the world, where a few neighbours cannot assemble without the risk of being shot by a hired soldiery, the engines of despotism. We may see such an act in America. A standing army we shall have also, to execute the execrable commands of tyranny: And how are you to punish them? Will you order them to be punished? Who shall obey these orders? Will your Mace-bearer be a match for a disciplined regiment? In what situation are we to be? The clause before you gives a power of direct taxation, unbounded and unlimitted: Exclusive power of Legislation in all cases whatsoever, for ten miles square; and over all places purchased for the erection of forts, magazines, arsenals, dock-yards, &c. What resistance could be made? The attempt would be madness. You will find all the strength of this country in the hands of your enemies: Those garrisons will naturally be the strongest places in the country. Your militia is given up to Congress also in another part of this plan: They will therefore act as they think proper: All power will be in their own possession:

You cannot force them to receive their punishment: Of what service would militia be to you, when most probably you will not have a single musket in the State; for as arms are to be provided by Congress, they may or may not furnish them. Let me here call your attention to that part which gives the Congress power, "To provide for organizing, arming, and disciplining the militia, and for governing such part of them as may be employed in the service of the United States, reserving to the States respectively, the appointment of the officers, and the authority of training the militia, according to the discipline prescribed by Congress." By this, Sir, you see that their controul over our last and best defence, is unlimitted. If they neglect or refuse to discipline or arm our militia, they will be useless: The States can do neither, this power being exclusively given to Congress: The power of appointing officers over men not disciplined or armed, is ridiculous: So that this pretended little remains of power left to the States, may, at the pleasure of Congress, be rendered nugatory. Our situation will be deplorable indeed: Nor can we ever expect to get this government amended, since I have already shewn, that a very small minority may prevent it; and that small minority interested in the continuance of the oppression: Will the oppressor let go the oppressed? Was there ever an instance? Can the annals of mankind exhibit one single example, where rulers overcharged with power, willingly let go the oppressed, though solicited and requested most earnestly? The application for amendments will therefore be fruitless. Sometimes the oppressed have got loose by one of those bloody struggles that desolate a country. A willing relinquishment of power is one of those things which human nature never was, nor ever will be capable of: The Honorable Gentleman's observations respecting the people's right of being the agents in the formation of this Government, are not accurate in my humble conception. The distinction between a National Government and a Confederacy is not sufficiently discerned. Had the delegates who were sent to Philadelphia a power to propose a Consolidated Government instead of a Confederacy? Were they not deputed by States, and not by the people? The assent of the people in their collective capacity is not necessary to the formation of a Federal Government. The people have no right to enter into leagues, alliances, or confederations: They are not the proper agents for this purpose: States and sovereign powers are the only proper agents for this kind of Government: Shew me an instance where the people have exercised this business: Has it not always gone through the Legislatures? I refer you to the treaties with France, Holland, and other nations: How were they made? Were they not made by the States? Are the people therefore in their aggregate capacity, the proper persons to form a Confederacy? This, therefore, ought to depend on the consent of the Legislatures; the people having never sent delegates to make any proposition of changing the Government. Yet I must say, at the same time, that it was made on grounds the most pure, and perhaps I might have been brought to consent to it so far as to the change of Government; but there is one thing in it which I never would acquiesce in. I mean the changing it into a Consolidated Government; which is so abhorent to my mind. The Honorable Gentleman then went on to the figure we make with foreign nations; the contemptible one we make in France and Holland; which, according to the system of my notes, he attributes to the present feeble Government. An opinion has gone forth, we find, that we are a contemptible people: The time has been when we were thought otherwise: Under this same despised Government, we commanded the respect of all Europe: Wherefore are we now reckoned otherwise? The American spirit has fled from hence: It has gone to regions, where it has never been expected: It has gone to the people of France in search of a splendid Government—a strong energetic Government.

Shall we imitate the example of those nations who have gone from a simple to a splendid Government. Are those nations more worthy of our imitation? What can make an adequate satisfaction to them for the loss they suffered in attaining such a Government for the loss of their liberty? If we admit this Consolidated Government it will be because we like a great splendid one. Some way or other we must be a great and mighty empire; we must have an army, and a navy, and a number of things: When the American spirit was in its youth, the language of America was different: Liberty, Sir, was then the primary object. We are descended from a people whose Government was founded on liberty: Our glorious forefathers of Great-Britain, made liberty the foundation of every thing. That country is become a great, mighty, and splendid nation; not because their Government is strong and energetic; but, Sir, because liberty is its direct end and foundation: We drew the spirit of liberty from our British ancestors; by that spirit we have triumphed over every difficulty: But now, Sir, the American spirit, assisted by the ropes and chains of consolidation, is about to convert this country to a powerful and mighty empire: If you make the citizens of this country agree to become the subjects of one great consolidated empire of America, your Government will not have suffcient energy to keep them together: Such a Government is incompatible with the genius of republicanism: There will be no checks, no real balances, in this Government: What can avail your specious imaginary balances, your rope-dancing, chain-rattling, ridiculous ideal checks and contrivances? But, Sir, we are not feared by foreigners: we do not make nations tremble: Would this, Sir, constitute happiness, or secure liberty? I trust, Sir, our political hemisphere will ever direct their operations to the security of those objects. Consider our situation, Sir: Go to the poor man, ask him what he does; he will inform you, that he enjoys the fruits of his labour, under his own fig-tree, with his wife and children around him, in peace and security. Go to every other member of the society, you will find the same tranquil ease and content; you will find no alarms or disturbances: Why then tell us of dangers to terrify us into an adoption of this new Government? and yet who knows the dangers that this new system may produce; they are out of the sight of the common people: They cannot foresee latent consequences: I dread the operation of it on the middling and lower class of people: It is for them I fear the adoption of this system. I fear I tire the patience of the Committee, but I beg to be indulged with a few more observations: When I thus profess myself an advocate for the liberty of the people, I shall be told, I am a designing man, that I am to be a great man, that I am to be a demagogue; and many similar illiberal insinuations will be thrown out; but, Sir, conscious rectitude, out-weighs these things with me: I see great jeopardy in this new Government. I see none from our present one: I hope some Gentleman or other will bring forth, in full array, those dangers, if there be any, that we may see and touch them.

* * *

I have thought, and still think, that a full investigation of the actual situation of America, ought to precede any decision on this great and important question. That Government is no more than a choice among evils, is acknowledged by the most intelligent among mankind, and has been a standing maxim for ages. If it be demonstrated that the adoption of the new plan is a little or a trifling evil, then, Sir, I acknowledge that adoption ought to follow: But, Sir, if this be a truth that its adoption may entail misery on the free people of this country, I then insist, that rejection ought to follow. Gentlemen strongly urge its adoption will be a mighty benefit to us: But, Sir, I am made of such incredulous materials that assertions and declarations, do not satisfy me. I must be convinced, Sir. I shall retain my infidelity on that subject, till I see our liberties secured in a manner perfectly satisfactory to my understanding....

You are told [by Governor Randolph] there is no peace, although you fondly flatter yourselves that all is peace—No peace—a general cry and alarm in the country—Commerce, riches, and wealth vanished—Citizens going to seek comforts in other parts of the world—Laws insulted—Many instances of tyrannical legislation. These things, Sir, are new to me. He has made the discovery—As to the administration of justice, I believe that failures in commerce, &c. cannot be attributed to it. My age enables me to recollect its progress under the old Government. I can justify it by saying, that it continues in the same manner in this State, as it did under former Government. As to other parts of the Continent, I refer that to other Gentlemen. As to the ability of those who administer it, I believe they would not suffer by a comparison with those who administered it under the royal authority. Where is the cause of complaint if the wealthy go away? Is this added to the other circumstances, of such enormity, and does it bring such danger over this Commonwealth as to warrant so important, and so awful a change in so precipitate a manner? As to insults offered to the laws, I know of none. In this respect I believe this Commonwealth would not suffer by a comparison with the former Government. The laws are as well executed, and as patiently acquiesced in, as they were under the royal administration. Compare the situation of the country—Compare that of our citizens to what they were then, and decide whether persons and property are not as safe and secure as they were at that time. Is there a man in this Commonwealth, whose person can be insulted with impunity? Cannot redress be had here for personal insults or injuries, as well as in any part of the world—as well as in those countries where Aristocrats and Monarchs triumph and reign? Is not the protection of property in full operation here? The contrary cannot with truth be charged on this Commonwealth. Those severe charges which are exhibited against it, appear to me totally groundless. On a fair investigation, we shall be found to be surrounded by no real dangers. We have the animating fortitude and persevering alacrity of republican men, to carry us through misfortunes and calamities. 'Tis the fortune of a republic to be able to withstand the stormy ocean of human vicissitudes. I know of no danger awaiting us. Public and private security are to be found here in the highest degree. Sir, it is the fortune of a free people, not to be intimidated by imaginary dangers. Fear is the passion of slaves. Our political and natural hemisphere are now equally tranquil. Let us recollect the awful magnitude of the subject of our deliberation. Let us consider the latent consequences of an erroneous decision—and let not our minds be led away by unfair misrepresentations and uncandid suggestions. There have been many instances of uncommon lenity and temperance used in the exercise of power in this Commonwealth. I could call your recollection to many that happened during the war and since—But every Gentleman here must be apprized of them.

The Honorable member has given you an elaborate account of what he judges tyrannical legislation, and an *ex post facto law* (in the case of Josiah Philips.) He has misrepresented the facts. That man was not executed by a tyrannical stroke of power. He was a fugitive murderer and an out-law—a man who commanded an infamous banditti, at a time when the war was at the most perilous stage. He committed the most cruel and shocking barbarities. He was an enemy to the human name.— Those who declare war against the human race, may be struck out of existence as soon as they are apprehended. He was not executed according to those beautiful legal ceremonies which are pointed out by the laws, in criminal cases. The enormity of his crimes did not entitle him to it. I am truly a friend to legal forms and methods; but, Sir, the occasion warranted the measure. A pirate, an outlaw, or a common enemy to all mankind, may be put to death at any time. It is justified by the laws of nature and nations. The Honorable member tells us then, that there are burnings and discontents in the hearts of our citizens in general, and that they are dissatisfied with their Government. I have no doubt the Honorable member believes this to be the case, because he says so. But I have the comfortable assurance, that it is a certain fact, *that it is not so.* The middle and lower ranks of people have not those illumined ideas, which the well-born are so happily possessed of—They cannot so readily perceive latent objects. The microscopic eyes of modern States-men can see abundance of defects in old systems; and their illumined imaginations discover the necessity of change.

. . . I have said that I thought this a Consolidated Government: I will now prove it. Will the great rights of the people be secured by this Government? Suppose it should prove oppressive, how can it be altered? Our Bill of Rights declares, "That a majority of the community hath an *undubitable, unalienable,* and *indefeasible right* to reform, alter, or abolish it, in such manner as shall be judged most conducive to the public weal." I have just proved that one tenth, or less, of the people of America, a most despicable minority may prevent this reform or altera- tion. Suppose the people of Virginia should wish to alter their Govern- ment, can a majority of them do it? No, because they are connected with other men; or, in other words, consolidated with other States: When the people of Virginia at a future day shall wish to alter their Government, though they should be unanimous in this desire, yet they may be prevented therefrom by a despicable minority at the extremity of the United States: The founders of your own Constitution made your

Government changeable: But the power of changing it is gone from you! Whither is it gone? It is placed in the same hands that hold the rights of twelve other States; and those who hold those rights, have right and power to keep them: It is not the particular Government of Virginia: One of the leading features of that Government is, that a majority can alter it, when necessary for the public good. This Government is not a Virginian but an American Government. Is it not therefore a Consolidated Government? The sixth clause of your Bill of Rights tells you, "That elections of members to serve as Representatives of the people in Assembly, ought to be free, and that all men having sufficient evidence of permanent common interest with, and attachment to the community, have the right of suffrage, and *cannot* be *taxed* or *deprived* of *their property* for public uses, without their own consent, or that of their Representatives so elected, nor bound by any law to which they have not in like manner assented for the public good." But what does this Constitution say?

The clause under consideration gives an unlimitted and unbounded power of taxation: Suppose every delegate from Virginia opposes a law laying a tax, what will it avail? They are opposed by a majority: Eleven members can destroy their efforts: Those feeble ten cannot prevent the passing the most oppressive tax law. So that in direct opposition to the spirit and express language of your Declaration of Rights, you are taxed not by your own consent, but by people who have no connection with you. The next clause of the Bill of Rights tells you, "That all power of suspending law, or the execution of laws, by any authority without the consent of the Representatives of the people, is injurious to their rights, and ought not to be exercised." This tells us that there can be no suspension of Government, or laws without our own consent: Yet this Constitution can counteract and suspend any of our laws, that contravene its oppressive operation; for they have the power of direct taxation; which suspends our Bill of Rights; and it is expressly provided, that they can make all laws necessary for carrying their powers into execution; and it is declared paramount to the laws and constitutions of the States. Consider how the only remaining defence we have left is destroyed in this manner: Besides the expences of maintaining the Senate and other House in as much splendor as they please, there is to be a great and mighty President, with very extensive powers; the powers of a King: He is to be supported in extravagant magnificence: So that the whole of our property may be taken by this American Government, by laying what taxes they please, giving themselves what salaries they please, and suspending our laws at their pleasure: I might be thought too inquisitive, but I believe I should take up but very little of your time in enumerating the little power that is left to the Government of Virginia; for this power is reduced to little or nothing: Their garrisons, magazines, arsenals, and forts, which will be situated in the strongest places within the States: Their ten miles square, with all the fine ornaments of human life, added to their powers, and taken from the States, will reduce the power of the latter to nothing. The voice of tradition, I trust, will inform posterity of our struggles for freedom: If our descendants be worthy the name of Americans, they will preserve and hand down to their latest posterity, the transactions of the present times; and though, I confess, my exclamations are not worthy the hearing, they will see that I have done my utmost to preserve their liberty: For I never will give up the power of direct taxation, but for a scourge: I am willing to give it conditionally; that is, after non-compliance with requisitions: I will do more, Sir, and what I hope will convince the most sceptical man, that I am a lover of the American Union, that in case Virginia shall not make punctual payment, the controul of our custom houses, and the whole regulation of trade, shall be given to Congress, and that Virginia shall depend on Congress even for passports, till Virginia shall have paid the last farthing; and furnished the last soldier: Nay, Sir, there is another alternative to which I would consent: Even that they should strike us out of the Union, and take away from us all federal privileges till we comply with federal requisitions; but let it depend upon our own pleasure to pay our money in the most easy manner for our people. Were all the States, more terrible than the mother country, to join against us, I hope Virginia could defend herself; but, Sir, the dissolution of the Union is most abhorent to my mind: The first thing I have at heart is American *liberty;* the second thing is American Union; and I hope the people of Virginia will endeavor to preserve that Union: The increasing population of the southern States, is far greater than that of New-England: Consequently, in a short time, they will be far more numerous than the people of that country: Consider this, and you will find this State more particularly interested to support American liberty, and not bind our posterity by an improvident relinquishment of our rights. I would give the best security for a punctual compliance with requisitions; but I beseech Gentlemen, at all hazards, not to give up this unlimitted power of taxation: The Honorable Gentleman has told us these powers given to Congress, are accompanied by a Judiciary which will connect all: On examination you will find this very Judiciary oppressively constructed; your jury trial destroyed, and the Judges dependent on Congress. In this scheme of energetic Government, the people will find two sets of tax-gatherers—the State and the Federal Sheriffs. This it seems to me will produce such dreadful oppression, as the people cannot possibly bear: The Federal Sheriff may commit what oppression, make what distresses he pleases, and ruin you with impunity: For how are you to tie his hands? Have you any sufficient decided means of preventing him from sucking your blood by speculations, commissions and fees? Thus thousands of your people will be most shamefully robbed: Our State Sheriffs, those unfeeling blood-suckers, have, under the watchful eye of our Legislature, committed the most horrid and barbarous ravages on our people: It has required the most constant vigilance of the Legislature to keep them from totally ruining the people: A repeated succession of laws has been made to suppress their inequitous speculations and cruel extortions; and as often have their nefarious ingenuity devised methods of evading the force of those laws: In the struggle they have generally triumphed over the Legislature. It is fact that lands have sold for five shillings, which were worth one hundred pounds: If Sheriffs thus immediately under the eye of our State Legislature and Judiciary, have dared to commit these outrages, what would they not have done if their masters had been at Philadelphia or New-York? If they perpetrate the most unwarrantable outrage on your persons or property, you cannot get redress on this side of Philadelphia or New-York: And how can you get it there? If your domestic avocations could permit you to go thither, there you must appeal to Judges sworn to support this Constitution, in opposition to that of any State, and who may also be inclined to favor their own officers: When these harpies are aided by excise men, who may search at any time your houses and most secret recesses, will the people bear it? If you think so you differ from me: Where I thought there was a possibility of such mischiefs, I would grant power with a niggardly hand; and here there is strong probability that these oppressions shall actually happen. I may be told, that it is safe to err on that side; because such regulations *may* be made by Congress, as shall restrain these officers, and because laws are made by our Representatives, and judged by righteous Judges: But, Sir, as these regulations may be made, so they may not; and many reasons there are to induce a belief that they will not: I shall therefore be an infidel on that point till the day of my death.

This Constitution is said to have beautiful features; but when I come to examine these features, Sir, they appear to me horridly frightful: Among other deformities, it has an awful squinting; it squints towards monarchy: And does not this raise indignation in the breast of every American? Your President may easily become King: Your Senate is so imperfectly constructed that your dearest rights may be sacrificed by what may be a small minority; and a very small minority may continue forever unchangeably this Government, although horridly defective: Where are your checks in this Government? Your strong holds will be in the hands of your enemies: It is on a supposition that our American Governors shall be honest, that all the good qualities of this Government are founded: But its defective, and imperfect construction, puts it in their power to perpetrate the worst of mischiefs, should they be bad men: And, Sir, would not all the world, from the Eastern to the Western hemisphere, blame our distracted folly in resting our rights upon the contingency of our rulers being good or bad. Shew me that age and country where the rights and liberties of the people were placed on the sole chance of their rulers being good men, without a consequent loss of liberty? I say that the loss of that dearest privilege has ever followed with absolute certainty, every such mad attempt. If your American chief, be a man of ambition, and abilities, how easy is it for him to render himself absolute: The army is in his hands, and, if he be a man of address, it will be attached to him; and it will be the subject of long meditation with him to seize the first auspicious moment to accomplish his design; and, Sir, will the American spirit solely relieve you when this happens? I would rather infinitely, and I am sure most of this Convention are of the same opinion, have a King, Lords, and Commons, than a Government so replete with such insupportable evils. If we make a King, we may prescribe the rules by which he shall rule his people, and interpose such checks as shall prevent him from infringing them: But the President, in the field, at the head of his army, can prescribe the terms on which he shall reign master, so far that it will puzzle any American ever to get his neck from under the galling yoke. I cannot with patience, think of this idea. If ever he violates the laws, one of two things will happen: He shall come to the head of his army to carry every thing before him; or, he will give bail, or do what Mr. Chief Justice will order him. If he be guilty, will not the recollection of his crimes teach him to make one bold push for the American throne? Will not the immense difference between being master of every thing, and being ignominiously tried and punished, powerfully excite him to make this bold push? But, Sir, where is the existing force to punish him? Can he not at the head of his army beat down every opposition? Away with your President, we shall have a King: The army will salute him Monarch; your militia will leave you and assist in making him King, and fight against you: And what have you to oppose this force? What will then become of you and your rights? Will not absolute despotism ensue? [Here Mr. Henry strongly and pathetically expatiated on the probability of the President's enslaving America and the horrible consequences that must result.]

What can be more defective than the clause concerning the elections?—The controul given to Congress over the time, place, and manner of holding elections, will totally destroy the end of suffrage. The elections may be held at one place, and the most inconvenient in the State; or they may be at remote distances from those who have a right of suffrage: Hence nine out of ten must either not vote at all, or vote for strangers: For the most influential characters will be applied to, to know who are the most proper to be chosen. I repeat that the controul of Congress over the *manner,* &c. of electing, well warrants this idea. The natural consequence will be, that this democratic branch, will possess none of the public confidence: The people will be prejudiced against Representatives chosen in such an injudicious manner. The proceedings in the northern conclave will be hidden from the yeomanry of this country: We are told that the yeas and nays shall be taken and entered on the journals: This, Sir, will avail nothing: It may be locked up in their chests, and concealed forever from the people; for they are not to publish what parts they think require secrecy: They *may* think, and *will think,* the whole requires it. Another beautiful feature of this Constitution is the publication from time to time of the receipts and expenditures of the public money. This expression, from time to time, is very indefinite and indeterminate: It may extend to a century. Grant that any of them are wicked, they may squander the public money so as to ruin you, and yet this expression will give you no redress. I say, they may ruin you;—for where, Sir, is the responsibility? The yeas and nays will shew you nothing, unless they be fools as well as knaves: For after having wickedly trampled on the rights of the people, they would act like fools indeed, were they to publish and devulge their iniquity, when they have it equally in their power to suppress and conceal it.—Where is the responsibility—that leading principle in the British government? In that government a punishment, certain and inevitable, is provided: But in this, there is no real actual punishment for the grossest maladminis- tration. They may go without punishment, though they commit the most outrageous violation on our immunities. That paper may tell me they will be punished. I ask, by what law? They must make the law— for there is no existing law to do it. What—will they make a law to punish themselves? This, Sir, is my great objection to the Constitution, that there is no true responsibility—and that the preservation of our liberty depends on the single chance of men being virtuous enough to make laws to punish themselves. In the country from which we are descended, they have real, and not imaginary, responsibility—for there, maladministration has cost their heads, to some of the most saucy geniuses that ever were. The Senate, by making treaties may destroy your liberty and laws for want of responsibility. Two-thirds of those that shall happen to be present, can, with the President, make treaties, that shall be the supreme law of the land: They may make the most ruinous treaties; and yet there is no punishment for them. Whoever shews me a punishment provided for them, will oblige me. So, Sir, notwithstanding there are eight pillars, they want another.

Where will they make another? I trust, Sir, the exclusion of the evils wherewith this system is replete, in its present form, will be made a condition, precedent to its adoption, by this or any other State. The transition from a general unqualified admission to offices, to a consolida- tion of government, seems easy; for though the American States are dissimilar in their structure, this will assimilate them: This, Sir, is itself a strong consolidating feature, and is not one of the least dangerous in that system. Nine States are sufficient to establish this government over those nine: Imagine that nine have come into it. Virginia has certain scruples. Suppose she will consequently, refuse to join with those States:—May not they still continue in friendship and union with her? If she sends her annual requisitions in dollars, do you think their stomachs will be so squeamish that they will refuse her dollars? Will they not accept her regiments? They would intimidate you into an inconsiderate adoption, and frighten you with ideal evils, and that the Union shall be dissolved. 'Tis a bugbear, Sir:—The fact is, Sir, that the eight adopting States can hardly stand on their own legs. Public fame tells us, that the adopting States have already heart-burnings and animosity, and repent their precipitate hurry: This, Sir, may occasion exceeding great mischief. When I reflect on these and many other circumstances, I must think those States will be fond to be in confederacy with us. If we pay our quota of money annually, and furnish our rateable number of men, when necessary, I can see no danger from a rejection. The history of Switzerland clearly proves, we might be in amicable alliance with those States without adopting this Constitution. Switzerland is a Confederacy, consisting of dissimilar Governments. This is an example which proves that Governments of dissimilar structure may be Confederated; that Confederate Republic has stood upwards of 400 years; and although several of the individual republics are democratic, and the rest aristocratic, no evil has resulted from this dissimilarity, for they have braved all the power of France and Germany during that long period. The Swiss spirit, Sir, has kept them together: They have encountered and overcome immense difficulties with patience and fortitude. In this vicinity of powerful and ambitious monarchs, they have retained their independence, republican simplicity and valour. [Here he makes a comparison of the people of that country, and those of France, and makes a quotation from Addison, illustrating the subject.] Look at the peasants of that country and of France, and mark the difference. You will find the condition of the former far more desirable and comfortable. No matter whether a people be great, splendid, and powerful, if they enjoy freedom. The Turkish Grand Seignior, along-side of our President, would put us to disgrace: But we should be abundantly consoled for this disgrace, when our citizen should be put in contrast with the Turkish slave. The most valuable end of government, is the liberty of the inhabitants. No possible advantages can compensate for the loss of this privilege. Shew me the reason why the American Union is to be dissolved. Who are those eight adopting States? Are they averse to give us a little time to consider, before we conclude? Would such a disposition render a junction with them eligible; or is it the genius of that kind of government, to precipitate people hastily into measures of the utmost importance, and grant no indulgence? If it be, Sir, is it for us to accede to such a government? We have a right to have time to consider—We shall therefore insist upon it. Unless the government be amended, we can never accept it. The adopting States will doubtless accept our money and our regiments—And what is to be the consequence, if we are disunited? I believe that it is yet doubtful, whether it is not proper to stand by a while, and see the effect of its adoption in other States. In forming a government, the utmost care should be taken to prevent its becoming oppressive; and this government is of such an intricate and complicated nature, that no man on this earth can know its real operation. The other States have no reason to think, from the antecedent conduct of Virginia, that she has any intention of seceding from the Union, or of being less active to support the general welfare: Would they not therefore acquiesce in our taking time to deliberate? Deliberate whether the measure be not perilous, not only for us, but the adopting States. Permit me, Sir, to say, that a great majority of the people even in the adopting States, are averse to this government. I believe I would be right to say, that they have been egregiously misled. Pennsylvania has *perhaps* been tricked into it. If the other States who have adopted it, have not been tricked, still they were too much hurried into its adoption. There were very respectable minorities in several of them; and if reports be true, a clear majority of the people are averse to it. If we also accede, and it should prove grievous, the peace and prosperity of our country, which we all love, will be destroyed. This government has not the affection of the people, at present. Should it be oppressive, their affection will be totally estranged from it—and, Sir, you know that a Government without their affections can neither be durable nor happy.

I speak as one poor individual—but when I speak, I speak the language of thousands. But, Sir, I mean not to breath the spirit nor utter the language of secession. I have trespassed so long on your patience, I am really concerned that I have something yet to say. The honorable member has said that we shall be properly represented: Remember, Sir, that the number of our Representatives is but ten, whereof six is a majority. Will these men be possessed of sufficient information? A particular knowledge of particular districts will not suffice. They must be well acquainted with agriculture, commerce, and a great variety of other matters throughout the Continent: They must know not only the actual state of nations in Europe, and America, the situation of their farmers, cottagers, and mechanics, but also the relative situation and intercourse of those nations. Virginia is as large as England. Our proportion of Representatives is but ten men. In England they have 530. The House of Commons in England, numerous as they are, we are told, is bribed, and have bartered away the rights of their constituents: What then shall become of us? Will these few protect our rights? Will they be incorruptible? You say they will be better men than the English Commoners. I say they will be infinitely worse men, because they are to be chosen blindfolded: Their election (the term, as applied to their appointment, is inaccurate) will be an involuntary nomination, and not a choice. I have, I fear, fatigued the Committee, yet I have not said the one hundred thousandeth part of what I have on my mind, and wish to impart. On this occasion I conceived myself bound to attend strictly to the interest of the State; and I thought her dearest rights at stake: Having lived so long—been so much honored—my efforts, though small, are due to my country. I have found my mind hurried on from subject to subject, on this very great occasion. We have been all out of order from the Gentleman who opened to-day, to myself. I did not come prepared to speak on so multifarious a subject, in so general a manner. I trust you will indulge me another time.—Before you abandon the present system, I hope you will consider not only its defects, most maturely, but likewise those of that which you are to substitute to it. May you be fully apprised of the dangers of the latter, not by fatal experience, but by some abler advocate than me.

* * *

... A number of characters of the greatest eminence in this country, object to this Government, for its consolidating tendency. This is not imaginary. It is a formidable reality. If consolidation proves to be as mischievous to this country, as it has been to other countries, what will the poor inhabitants of this country do? This Government will operate like an ambuscade. It will destroy the State Governments, and swallow the liberties of the people, without giving them previous notice. If Gentlemen are willing to run the hazard, let them run it; but I shall exculpate myself by my opposition, and monitory warnings within these walls. But, then comes paper money. We are at peace on this subject. Though this is a thing which that mighty Federal Convention had no business with, yet I acknowledge that paper money would be the bane of this country. I detest it. Nothing can justify a people in resorting to it, but extreme necessity. It is at rest however in this Commonwealth. It is no longer solicited or advocated. Sir, I ask you, and every other Gentleman who hears me, if he can retain his indignation, at a system, which takes from the State Legislatures the care and preservation of the interests of the people; 180 Representatives, the choice of the people of Virginia cannot be trusted with their interests. They are a mobbish suspected *herd*. This country has not virtue enough to manage its own internal interests. These must be referred to the chosen few. If we cannot be trusted with the private contracts of the citizens, we must be depraved indeed. If he can prove that by one uniform system of abandoned principles, the Legislature has betrayed the rights of the people, then let us seek another shelter. So degrading an indignity—so flagrant an out-rage to the States—so vile a suspicion is humiliating to my mind, and many others.

Will the adoption of this new plan pay our debts? This, Sir, is a plain question. It is inferred, that our grievances are to be redressed, and the evils of the existing system to be removed by the new Constitution. Let me inform the Honorable Gentleman, that no nation ever paid its debts by a change of Government, without the aid of industry. You never will pay your debts but by a radical change of domestic œconomy. At present you buy too much, and make too little to pay. Will this new system promote manufactures, industry and frugality? If instead of this, your hopes and designs will be disappointed; you relinquish a great deal, and hazard infinitely more, for nothing. Will it enhance the value of your lands? Will it lessen your burthens? Will your looms and wheels go to work by the act of adoption? If it will in its consequence produce these things, it will consequently produce a reform, and enable you to pay your debts. Gentlemen must prove it. I am a sceptic—an infidel on this point. I cannot conceive that it will have these happy consequences. I cannot confide in assertions and allegations. The evils that attend us,

lie in extravagance and want of industry, and can only be removed by assiduity and œconomy. Perhaps we shall be told by Gentlemen, that these things will happen, because the administration is to be taken from us, and placed in the hands of the luminous few, who will pay different attention, and be more studiously careful than we can be supposed to be.
. . .

. . . This Government is so new it wants a name. I wish its other novelties were as harmless as this. He told us, we had an American Dictator in the year 1781—We never had an American President. In making a Dictator, we follow the example of the most glorious, magnanimous and skilful nations. In great dangers this power has been given.— Rome had furnished us with an illustrious example.—America found a person worthy of that trust: She looked to Virginia for him. We gave a dictatorial power to hands that used it gloriously; and which were rendered more glorious by surrendering it up. Where is there a breed of such Dictators? Shall we find a set of American Presidents of such a breed? Will the American President come and lay prostrate at the feet of Congress his laurels? I fear there are few men who can be trusted on that head. The glorious republic of Holland has erected monuments of her warlike intrepidity and valor: Yet she is now totally ruined by a Stadtholder—a Dutch President. The destructive wars into which that nation has been plunged, has since involved her in ambition. The glorious triumphs of Blenheim and Ramillies were not so conformable to the genius, nor so much to the true interest of the republic, as those numerous and useful canals and dykes, and other objects at which ambition spurns. That republic has, however, by the industry of its inhabitants, and policy of its magistrates, suppressed the ill effects of ambition.—Notwithstanding two of their provinces have paid nothing, yet I hope the example of Holland will tell us, that we can live happily without changing our present despised Government. Cannot people be as happy under a mild, as under an energetic Government? Cannot content and felicity be enjoyed in a republic, as well as in a monarchy, because there are whips, chains and scourges used in the latter? If I am not as rich as my neighbour, if I give my mite—my all—republican forbearance will say, that it is sufficient—So said the honest confederates of Holland.—*You are poor—We are rich.—We will go on and do better, far better, than be under an oppressive Government.*—For better will it be for us to continue as we are, than go under that tight energetic Government.—I am persuaded of what the Honorable Gentleman says, that separate confederacies will ruin us. In my judgment, they are evils never to be thought of till a people are driven by necessity.—When he asks my opinion of consolidation—of one power to reign over America, with a strong hand; I will tell him, I am persuaded, of the rectitude of my honorable friend's opinion (Mr. *Mason*) that one Government cannot reign over so extensive a country as this is, without absolute despotism. Compared to such a consolidation, small Confederacies are little evils; though they ought to be recurred to, but in case of necessity.—Virginia and North-Carolina are despised. They could exist separated from the rest of America. Maryland and Vermont were not over-run when out of the Confederacy. Though it is not a desirable object, yet I trust, that on examination it will be found, that Virginia and North-Carolina would not be swallowed up in case it was necessary for them to be joined together.

When we come to the spirit of domestic peace—The humble genius of Virginia has formed a Government, suitable to the genius of her people. I believe the hands that formed the American Constitution triumph in the experiment. It proves, that the man who formed it, and perhaps by accident, did what design could not do in other parts of the world. After all your reforms in Government, unless you consult the genius of the inhabitants, you will never succeed—your system can have no duration. Let me appeal to the candour of the Committee, if the want of money be not the source of all our misfortunes. We cannot be blamed for not making dollars. This want of money cannot be supplied by changes in Government. The only possible remedy, as I *have before* asserted, is industry aided by œconomy. Compare the genius of the people with the Government of this country. Let me remark, that it stood the severest conflict, during the war, to which ever human virtue has been called. I call upon every Gentleman here to declare, whether the King of England had any subjects so attached to his family and Government—so loyal as we were. But the genius of Virginia called us for liberty.—Called us from those beloved endearments, which from long habits we were taught to love and revere. We entertained from our earliest infancy, the most sincere regard and reverence for the mother country. Our partiality extended to a predilection for her customs, habits, manners and laws. Thus inclined, when the deprivation of our liberty was attempted, what did we do? What did the genius of Virginia tell us? *Sell all and purchase liberty.* This was a severe conflict. Republican maxims were then esteemed—Those maxims, and the genius of Virginia, landed you safe on the shore of freedom. On this awful occasion, did you want a Federal Government? Did federal ideas possess your minds? Did federal ideas lead you to the most splendid victories? I must again repeat the favorite idea, that the genius of Virginia did, and will again lead us to happiness. To obtain the most splendid prize, you did not consolidate. You accomplished the most glorious ends, by the assistance of the genius of your country. Men were then taught by that genius, that they were fighting for what was most dear to them. View the most affectionate father—the most tender mother—operated on by liberty, nobly stimulating their sons—their dearest sons—sometimes their only son, to advance to the defence of his country. We have seen sons of Cincinnatus, without splendid magnificence or parade, going, with the genius of their great progenitor Cincinnatus, to the plough— Men who served their country without ruining it—Men who had served it to the destruction of their private patrimonies—Their country owing them amazing amounts, for the payment of which no adequate provision was then made. We have seen such men, throw prostrate their arms at your feet. They did not call for those emoluments, which ambition presents to some imaginations. The soldiers, who were able to command every thing, instead of trampling on those laws, which they were instituted to defend, most strictly obeyed them. The hands of justice have not been laid on a single American soldier. Bring them into contrast with European veterans. You will see an astonishing superiority over the latter. There has been a strict subordination to the laws. The Honorable Gentleman's office gave him an opportunity of viewing if the laws were administered so as to prevent riots, routs, and unlawful assemblies. From his then situation, he could have furnished us with the instances in which licentiousness trampled on the laws.—Among all our troubles we have paid almost to the last shilling, for the sake of justice. We have paid as well as any State: I will not say better. To support the General Government, our own Legislature, to pay the interest of the public debts, and defray contingencies, we have been heavily taxed. To add to these things, the distresses produced by paper money, and by tobacco contracts, were sufficient to render any people discontented. These, Sir, were great temptations; but in the most severe conflict of misfortunes, this code of laws—this genius of Virginia, call it what you will, triumphed over every thing.

Why did it please the Gentleman (Mr. *Corbin*) to bestow such epithets on our country? Have the worms taken posession of the wood, that our strong vessel—our political vessel, has sprung a-leak? He may know better than me, but I consider such epithets to be the most illiberal and unwarrantable aspersions on our laws. The system of laws under which we have lived, has been tried and found to suit our genius. I trust we shall not change this happy system. I cannot so easily take leave of an old friend. Till I see him following after and pursuing other objects, which can pervert the great objects of human legislation, pardon me if I withhold my assent.

Some here speak of the difficulty in forming a new code of laws. Young as we were, it was not wonderful if there was a difficulty in forming and assimilating one system of laws. I shall be obliged to the Gentleman, if he would point out those glaring, those great faults. The efforts of assimilating our laws to our genius has not been found altogether vain.—I shall pass over some other circumstances which I intended to mention, and endeavor to come to the capital objection, which my Honorable friend made. My worthy friend said, that a republican form of Government would not suit a very extensive country; but that if a Government were judiciously organized and limits pre-scribed to it; an attention to these principles might render it possible for it to exist in an extensive territory. Whoever will be bold to say, that a Continent can be governed by that system, contradicts all the experience of the world. It is a work too great for human wisdom. Let me call for an example. Experience has been called the best teacher. I call for an example of a great extent of country, governed by one Government, or

Congress, call it what you will. I tell him, that a Government may be trimmed up according to Gentlemen's fancy, but it never can operate—It will be but very short-lived. However disagreeable it may be to lengthen my objections, I cannot help taking notice of what the Honorable Gentleman said. To me it appears that there is no check in that Government. The President, Senators, and Representatives all immediately, or mediately, are the choice of the people. Tell me not of checks on paper; but tell me of checks founded on self-love. The English Government is founded on self-love. This powerful irresistible stimulous of self-love has saved that Government. It has interposed that hereditary nobility between the King and Commons. If the House of Lords assists or permits the King to overturn the liberties of the people, the same tyranny will destroy them; they will therefore keep the balance in the democratic branch. Suppose they see the Commons incroach upon the King; self-love, that great energetic check, will call upon them to interpose: For, if the King be destroyed, their destruction must speedily follow. Here is a consideration which prevails, in my mind, to pronounce the British Government, superior in this respect to any Government that ever was in any country. Compare this with your Congressional checks. I beseech Gentlemen to consider, whether they can say, when trusting power, that a mere patriotic profession will be equally operative and efficatious, as the check of self-love. In considering the experience of ages, is it not seen, that fair disinterested patriotism, and professed attachment to rectitude have never been solely trusted to by an enlightened free people?—If you depend on your President's and Senators patriotism, you are gone. Have you a resting place like the British Government? Where is the rock of your salvation? The real rock of political salvation is *self-love* perpetuated from age to age in every human breast, and manifested in every action. If they can stand the temptations of human nature, you are safe. If you have a good President, Senators and Representatives, there is no danger.—But can this be expected from human nature? Without real checks it will not suffice, that some of them are good. A good President, or Senator, or Representative, will have a natural weakness.—Virtue will slumber. The wicked will be continually watching: Consequently you will be undone. Where are your checks? You have no hereditary Nobility—An order of men, to whom human eyes can be cast up for relief: For, says the Constitution, there is no title of nobility to be granted; which, by the bye, would not have been so dangerous, as the perilous cession of powers contained in that paper: Because, as Montesquieu says, when you give titles of Nobility, you know what you give; but *when you give power, you know not what you give.*—If you say, that out of this depraved mass, you can collect luminous characters, it will not avail, unless this luminous breed will be propagated from generation to generation; and even then, if the number of vicious characters will preponderate, you are undone. And that this will certainly be the case, is, to my mind, perfectly clear.— In the British Government there are real balances and checks—In this

769

system, there are only ideal balances. Till I am convinced that there are actual efficient checks, I will not give my assent to its establishment. The President and Senators have nothing to lose. They have not that interest in the preservation of the Government, that the King and Lords have in England. They will therefore be regardless of the interests of the people. The Constitution will be as safe with one body, as with two. It will answer every purpose of human legislation. How was the Constitution of England when only the Commons had the power? I need only remark, that it was the most unfortunate æra when that country returned to King, Lords and Commons, without sufficient responsibility in the King. When the Commons of England, in the manly language which became freemen, said to their King, *you are our servant,* then the temple of liberty was complete. From that noble source, have we derived our liberty:—That spirit of patriotic attachment to one's country:—That zeal for liberty, and that enmity to tyranny which signalized the then champions of liberty, we inherit from our British ancestors. And I am free to own, that if you cannot love a Republican Government, you may love the British Monarchy; for, although the King is not sufficiently responsible, the responsibility of his agents, and the efficient checks interposed by the British Constitution, render it less dangerous than other Monarchies, or oppressive tyrannical Aristrocracies. What are their checks of exposing accounts?—Their checks upon paper are inefficient and nugatory.—Can you search your President's closet? Is this a real check? We ought to be exceeding cautious, in giving up this life—this soul—of money—this power of taxation to Congress. What powerful check is there here to prevent the most extravagant and profligate squandering of the public money? What security have we in money matters? Enquiry is precluded by this Constitution. I never wish to see Congress supplicate the States. But it is more abhorent to my mind to give them an unlimited and unbounded command over our souls—our lives—our purses, without any check or restraint. How are you to keep enquiry alive? How discover their conduct? We are told by that paper, that a regular statement and account of the receipts and expenditures of all public money, shall be published from time to time. Here is a beautiful check! What time? Here is the utmost latitude left. If those who are in Congress please to put that construction upon it, the words of the Constitution will be satisfied by publishing those accounts once in 100 years. They may publish or not as they please. Is this like the present despised system, whereby the accounts are to be published monthly?

I come now to speak something of requisitions, which the Honorable Gentleman thought so truly contemptible and disgraceful. That Honorable Gentleman being a child of the revolution, must recollect with gratitude the glorious effects of requisitions. It is an idea that must be grateful to every American. An English army was sent to compel us to pay money contrary to our consent. To force us by arbitrary and tyrannical coercion to satisfy their unbounded demands. We wished to pay with our own consent.—Rather than pay against our consent, we engaged in that bloody contest, which terminated so gloriously. By requisitions we pay with our own consent; by their means we have triumphed in the most arduous struggle, that ever tried the virtue of man. We fought then, for what we are contending now: To prevent an arbitrary deprivation of our property, contrary to our consent and inclination.

* * *

I never will give up that *darling* word requisitions—My country may give it up—A majority may wrest it from me, but I will never give it up till my grave. Requisitions are attended with one singular advantage. They are attended by deliberation.—They secure to the States the benefit of correcting oppressive errors. If our Assembly thought requisitions erroneous—If they thought the demand was too great, they might at least supplicate Congress to reconsider,—that it was a little too much. The power of direct taxation was called by the Honorable Gentlemen the soul of the Government: Another Gentleman, called it the lungs of the Government. We all agree, that it is the most important part of the body politic. If the power of raising money be necessary for the General Government, it is no less so for the States. If money be the vitals of Congress, is it not precious for those individuals from whom it is to be taken? Must I give my soul—my lungs, to Congress? Congress must have our souls. The State must have our souls. This is dishonorable and disgraceful. These two coordinate, interferring unlimited powers of harrassing the community, is unexampled: It is unprecedented in history: They are the visionary projects of modern politicians: Tell me not of imaginary means, but of reality; This political solecism will never tend to the benefit of the community. It will be as oppressive in practice as it is absurd in theory. If you part with this which the Honorable Gentleman tells you is the soul of Congress, you will be inevitably ruined. I tell you, they shall not have the soul of Virginia. They tell us, that one collector may collect the Federal and State taxes. The General Government being paramount to the State Legislatures; if the Sheriff is to collect for both; his right hand for the Congress, his left for the State; his right hand being paramount over the left, his collections will go to Congress. We will have the rest. Defficiencies in collections will always operate against the States. Congress being the paramount supreme power, must not be disappointed. Thus Congress will have an unlimited, unbounded command over the soul of this Commonwealth. After satisfying their uncontrouled demands, what can be left for the States? Not a sufficiency even to defray the expence of their internal administration. They must therefore glide imperceptibly and gradually out of existence. This, Sir, must naturally terminate in a consolidation. If this will do for other people, it never will do for me.

... I shall be told in this place, that those who are to tax us are our Representatives. To this I answer, that there is no real check to prevent their ruining us. There is no actual responsibility. The only semblance of a check is the negative power of not re-electing them. This, Sir, is but a feeble barrier when their personal interest, their ambition and avarice come to be put in contrast with the happiness of the people. All checks founded on any thing but self-love, will not avail. This constitution reflects in the most degrading and mortifying manner on the virtue, integrity, and wisdom of the State Legislatures: It presupposes that the chosen few who go to Congress will have more upright hearts, and more enlightened minds, than those who are members of the individual Legislatures. To suppose that ten Gentlemen shall have more real substantial merit, than 170 is humiliating to the last degree. If, Sir, the diminution of numbers be an augmentation of merit, perfection must centre in one. If you have the faculty of discerning spirits, it is better to point out at once the man who has the most illumined qualities. If 10 men be better than 170, it follows of necessity, that one is better than 10—The choice is more refined....

Congress by the power of taxation—by that of raising an army, and by their controul over the militia, have the sword in one hand, and the purse in the other. Shall we be safe without either? Congress have an unlimited power over both: They are entirely given up by us. Let him candidly tell me, where and when did freedom exist, when the sword and purse were given up from the people? Unless a miracle in human affairs interposed, no nation ever retained its liberty after the loss of the sword and purse. Can you prove by any argumentative deduction, that it is possible to be safe without retaining one of these? If you give them up you are gone.

* * *

The means, says the Gentleman, must be commensurate to the end. How does this apply?—All things in common are left with this Government. There being an infinitude in the Government, there must be an infinitude of means to carry it on. This is a sort of mathematical Government that may appear well on paper, but cannot sustain examination, or be safely reduced to practice. The delegation of power to an adequate number of Representatives; and an unimpeded reversion of it back to the people at short periods, form the principal traits of a Republican Government. The idea of a Republican Government in that paper, is something superior to the poor people. The governing persons are the servants of the people. There the servants are greater than their masters; because it includes infinitude, and infinitude excludes every idea of subordination. In this the creature has destroyed, and soared above the creator. For if its powers be infinite, what rights have the people remaining? By that very argument despotism has made way in all countries, where the people unfortunately have been enslaved by it. We are told the sword and purse are necessary for the national defence. The junction of these without limitation in the same hands, is, by logical and mathematical conclusions, the description of despotism.

772

... Give us at least a plausible apology why Congress should keep their proceedings in secret. They have the power of keeping them secret as long as they please; for the provision for a periodical publication is too inexplicit and ambiguous to avail any thing. The expression *from time to time* as I have more than once observed, admits of any extension. They may carry on the most wicked and pernicious of schemes, under the dark veil of secrecy. The liberties of a people never were nor ever will be secure, when the transactions of their rulers may be concealed from them. The most iniquitous plots may be carried on against their liberty and happiness. I am not an advocate for divulging indiscriminately all the operations of Government, though the practice of our ancestors in some degree justifies it. Such transactions as relate to military operations, or affairs of great consequence, the immediate promulgation of which might defeat the interests of the community, I would not wish to be published, till the end which required their secrecy should have been effected. But to cover with the veil of secrecy, the common rotine of business, is an abomination in the eyes of every intelligent man, and every friend to his country.

[Mr. *Henry* then, in a very animated manner, expatiated on the evil and pernicious tendency of keeping secret the common proceedings of Government; and said that it was contrary to the practice of other free nations. The people of England, he asserted, had gained immortal honor by the manly boldness wherewith they divulged to all the world, their political disquisitions and operations; and that such a conduct inspired other nations with respect. He illustrated his argument by several quotations.]—He then continued,—I appeal to this Convention if it would not be better for America to take off the veil of secrecy. *Look at us—hear our transactions.* If this had been the language of the Federal Convention, what would have been the result? Such a Constitution would not have come out to your utter astonishment, conceding such dangerous powers, and recommending secrecy in the future transactions of Government. I believe it would have given more general satisfaction, if the proceedings of that Convention had not been concealed from the public eye. This Constitution authorizes the same conduct. There is not an English feature in it. The transactions of Congress may be concealed a century from the public, consistently with the Constitution. This, Sir, is a laudable imitation of the transactions of the Spanish treaty. We have not forgotten with what a thick veil of secrecy those transactions were covered.

We are told that this Government collectively taken, is without an example—That it is national in this part, and federal in that part, &c. We may be amused if we please, by a treatise of political anatomy. In the brain it is national: The stamina are federal—some limbs are federal—others national. The Senators are voted for by the State Legislatures, so far it is federal.—Individuals choose the members of the first branch; here it is national. It is federal in conferring general powers; but national in retaining them. It is not to be supported by the States—The pockets of individuals are to be searched for its maintenance. What signifies it to me, that you have the most curious anatomical description of it in its creation? To all the common purposes of Legislation it is a great consolidation of Government. You are not to have a right to legislate in any but trivial cases: You are not to touch private contracts: You are not to have the right of having arms in your own defence: You cannot be trusted with dealing out justice between man and man. What shall the States have to do? Take care of the poor—repair and make high-ways—erect bridges, and so on, and so on. Abolish the State Legislatures at once. What purposes should they be continued for? Our Legislature will indeed be a ludicrous spectacle— 180 men marching in solemn farcical procession, exhibiting a mournful proof of the lost liberty of their country—without the power of restoring it. But, Sir, we have the consolation that it is a mixed Government: That is, it may work sorely on your neck; but you will have some comfort by saying, that it was a Federal Government in its origin.

I beg Gentlemen to consider—lay aside your prejudices—Is this a Federal Government? Is it not a Consolidated Government for every purpose almost? Is the Government of Virginia a State Government after this Government is adopted? I grant that it is a Republican Government—but for what purposes? For such trivial domestic considerations, as render it unworthy the name of a Legislature. I shall take leave of this political anatomy, by observing that it is the most extraordinary that ever entered into the imagination of man. If our political diseases demand a cure—this is an unheard of medicine. The Honorable member, I am convinced, wanted a name for it. Were your health in danger, would you take new medicine? I need not make use of these exclamations; for every member in this Committee must be alarmed at making new and unusual experiments in Government. Let us have national credit and a national treasury in case of war. You never can want national resources in time of war; if the war be a national one; if it be necessary, and this necessity obvious to the meanest capacity. The utmost exertions will be used by the people of America in that case. A republic has this advantage over a monarchy, that its wars are generally founded on more just grounds. A republic can never enter into a war, unless it be a national war—unless it be approved of, or desired by the whole community. Did ever a republic fail to use the utmost resources of the community when a war was necessary? I call for an example. I call also for an example, when a republic has been engaged in a war contrary to the wishes of its people. There are thousands of examples, where the ambition of its Prince precipitated a nation into the most destructive war. No nation ever withheld power when its object was just and right. I will hazard an observation; I find fault with the paper before you, because the same power that declares war, has the power to carry it on. Is it so in England? The King declares war: The House of Commons gives the means of carrying it on. This is a strong check on the King. He will enter into no war that is unnecessary; for the Commons having the power of withholding the means, will exercise that power, unless the object of the war be for the interest of the nation. How is it here? The Congress can both declare war, and carry it on; and levy your money, as long as you have a shilling to pay....

* * *

... We are told that all powers not given are reserved. I am sorry to bring forth hackneyed observations. But, Sir, important truths lose nothing of their validity or weight, by frequency of repetition. The English history is frequently recurred to by Gentlemen. Let us advert to the conduct of the people of that country. The people of England lived without a declaration of rights, till the war in the time of Charles Ist. That King made usurpations upon the rights of the people. Those rights were in a great measure before that time undefined. Power and privilege then depended on implication and logical discussion. Though the declaration of rights was obtained from that King, his usurpations cost him his life. The limits between the liberty of the people, and the prerogative of the King, were still not clearly defined. The rights of the people continued to be violated till the Steward family was banished in the year 1688. The people of England magnanimously defended their rights, banished the tyrant, and prescribed to William Prince of Orange, *by the Bill of Rights,* on what terms he should reign. And this Bill of Rights put an end to all construction and implication. Before this, Sir, the situation of the public liberty of England was dreadful. For upwards of a century the nation was involved in every kind of calamity, till the Bill of Rights put an end to all, by defining the rights of the people, and limiting the King's prerogative. Give me leave to add (if I can add any thing to so splendid an example) the conduct of the American people. They Sir, thought *a Bill of Rights* necessary. It is alledged that several States, in the formation of their governments, omitted a Bill of Rights. To this I answer, that they had the substance of a Bill of Rights contained in their Constitutions, which is the same thing. I believe that Connecticut has preserved by her Constitution her royal charter, which clearly defines and secures the great rights of mankind—Secure to us the great important rights of humanity, and I care not in what form it is done. Of what advantage is it to the American Congress to take away this great and general security? I ask of what advantage is it to the public or to Congress to drag an unhappy debtor, not for the sake of justice; but to gratify the malice of the plaintiff, with his witnesses to the Federal Court, from a great distance? What was the principle that actuated the Convention in proposing to put such dangerous powers in the hands of any one? Why is the trial by jury taken away? All the learned arguments that have been used on this occasion do not prove that it is secured. Even the advocates for the plan do not all concur in the certainty of its security. Wherefore is religious liberty not secured? One Honorable Gentleman who favors adoption, said that he had had his fears on the subject. If I can well recollect, he informed us that he was perfectly satisfied by the powers of reasoning (with which he is so happily endowed) that those fears were not well grounded. There is many a religious man who knows nothing of argumentative reasoning;—there are many of our most worthy citizens, who cannot go through all the labyrinths of syllogistic argumentative deductions, when they think that the rights of conscience are invaded. This sacred right ought not to depend on constructive logical reasoning. When we see men of such talents and learning, compelled to use their utmost abilities to convince themselves that there is no danger, is it not sufficient to make us tremble? Is it not sufficient to fill the minds of the ignorant part of men with fear? If Gentlemen believe that the apprehensions of men will be quieted, they are mistaken; since our best informed men are in doubt with respect to the security of our rights.

Those who are not so well informed will spurn at the Government. When our common citizens, who are not possessed with such extensive knowledge and abilities, are called upon to change their Bill of Rights, (which in plain unequivocal terms, secures their most valuable rights and privileges) for construction and implication, will they implicitly acquiesce? Our Declaration of Rights tells us, "That all men are by nature free and independent, &c." (Here Mr. *Henry* read the Declaration of Rights.) Will they exchange these Rights for logical reasons? If you had a thousand acres of land, dependent on this, would you be satisfied with logical construction? Would you depend upon a title of so disputable a nature? The present opinions of individuals will be buried in entire oblivion when those rights will be thought of. That sacred and lovely thing Religion, ought not to rest on the ingenuity of logical deduction. Holy Religion, Sir, will be prostituted to the lowest purposes of human policy. What has been more productive of mischief among mankind than Religious disputes. Then here, Sir, is the foundation for such disputes, when it requires learning and logical deduction to perceive that religious liberty is secure. The Honorable member told us that he had doubts with respect to the judiciary department. I hope those doubts will be explained.—He told us that his object was Union. I admit that the reality of Union and not the name, is the object which most merits the attention of every friend to his country. He told you that you should hear many great *sounding words* on our side of the question. We have heard the *word Union* from him. I have heard no word so often pronounced in this House as he did this. I admit that the American Union is dear to every man—I admit that every man who has three grains of information, must know and think that Union is the best of all things. But as I said before, we must not mistake the end for the means. If he can shew that the rights of the Union are secure, we will consent. It has been sufficiently demonstrated that they are not secured. It sounds mighty prettily to Gentlemen to curse paper money and honestly pay debts. But apply to the situation of America, and you will find there are thousands and thousands of contracts, whereof equity forbids an exact literal performance. Pass that government, and you will be bound hand and foot. There was an immense quantity of depreciated continental paper money in circulation at the conclusion of the war. This money is in the hands of individuals to this day. The holders of this money may call for the nominal value, if this government be adopted. This State may be compelled to pay her proportion of that currency pound for pound. Pass this government and you will be carried to the Federal Court (if I understand that paper right) and you will be compelled to pay shilling for shilling. I doubt on the subject, at least as a public man, I ought to have doubts. A State may be sued in the Federal Court by the paper on your table. It appears to me then, that the holder of the paper money may require shilling for shilling. If there be any latent remedy to prevent this, I hope it will be discovered.

The precedent, with respect to the Union between England and Scotland, does not hold. The Union of Scotland speaks in plain and direct terms. Their privileges were particularly secured. It was expressly provided, that they should retain their own particular laws. Their nobles have a right to choose Representatives to the number of sixteen.—I might thus go on and specify particulars, but it will suffice to observe generally, that their rights and privileges were expressly and unequivocally reserved.—The power of direct taxation was not given up by the Scotch people. There is no trait in that Union which will maintain their arguments. In order to do this, they ought to have proved that Scotland united without securing their rights, and afterwards got that security by subsequent amendments. Did the people of Scotland do this? No, Sir, like a sensible people, they trusted nothing to hazard. If they have but 45 members, and those be often corrupted, these defects will be greater here. The number will be smaller, and they will be consequently the more easily corrupted. Another Honorable Gentleman advises us to give this power, in order to exclude the necessity of going to war. He wishes to establish national credit I presume—and imagines that if a nation has public faith and shews a disposition to comply with her engagements, she is safe among ten thousand dangers. If the Honorable Gentleman can prove that this paper is calculated to give us public faith, I will be satisfied. But if you be in constant preparation for war, on such airy and imaginary grounds, as the mere possibility of danger, your government must be military, which will be inconsistent with the enjoyment of liberty. But, Sir, we must become formidable, and have a strong government to protect us from the British nation. Will the paper on the table prevent the attacks of the British navy, or enable us to raise a fleet equal to the British fleet? The British have the strongest fleet in Europe, and can strike any where. It is the utmost folly to conceive, that that paper can have such an operation. It will be no less so to attempt to raise a powerful fleet. With respect to requisitions, I beseech Gentlemen to consider the importance of the subject. We who are for amendments propose, (as has been frequently mentioned) that a requisition shall be made for £200,000 for instance, instead of direct taxation, and that if it be not complied with, then it shall be raised by direct taxes. We do not wish to have strength to refuse to pay them, but to possess the power of raising the taxes in the most easy mode for the people. But says he, you may delay us by this mode.—Let us see if there be not sufficient to counterbalance this evil. The oppression arising from taxation, is not from the amount but, from the mode—a thorough acquaintance with the condition of the people, is necessary to a just distribution of taxes. The whole wisdom of the science of Government, with respect to taxation, consists in selecting that mode of collection which will best accommodate the convenience of the people. When you come to tax a great country, you will find that ten men are too few to settle the manner of collection. One capital advantage which will result from the proposed alternative is this, that there will be necessary communications between your ten members in Congress, and your 170 Representatives here. If it goes through the hands of the latter, they will know how much the citizens *can* pay, and by looking at the paper on your table, they will know how much they *ought* to pay. No man is possessed of sufficient information to know how much we can or ought to pay.

We might also remonstrate, if by mistake or design, they should call for a greater sum than our proportion. After a remonstrance, and a free investigation between our Representatives here, and those in Congress, the error would be removed.

Another valuable thing which it will produce is, that the people will pay the taxes chearfully. It is supposed, that this would occasion a waste of time, and be an injury to public credit. This would only happen if requisitions should not be complied with. In this case the delay would be compensated by the payment of interest, which with the addition of the credit of the State to that of the General Government, would in a great measure obviate this objection. But if it had all the force which it is supposed to have, it would not be adequate to the evil of direct taxation. But there is every probability that requisitions would be then complied with. Would it not then be our interest, as well as duty, to comply? After noncompliance, there would be a general acquiescence in the exercise of this power. We are fond of giving power, at least power which is constitutional. Here is an option to pay according to your own mode, or otherwise. If you give probability fair play, you must conclude, that they would be complied with. Would the Assembly of Virginia by refusal, destroy the country and plunge the people into miseries and distress? If you give your reasoning faculty fair play, you cannot but know, that payment must be made when the consequence of a refusal would be an accumulation of inconveniences to the people. Then they say, that if requisitions be not complied with, in case of a war, that the destruction of the country may be the consequence; that therefore, we ought to give the power of taxation to the Government to enable it to protect us. Would not this be another reason for complying with requisitions, to prevent the country from being destroyed? You tell us, that unless requisitions be complied with, your commerce is gone. The prevention of this also, will be an additional reason to comply.

He tells us, that responsibility is secured by direct taxation. Responsibility instead of being increased, will be lost for ever by it. In our State Government, our Representatives may be severally instructed by their constituents. There are no persons to counteract their operations. They can have no excuse for deviating from our instructions. In the General Government other men have power over the business. When oppressions may take place, our Representatives may tell us, *We contended for your interest, but we could not carry our point, because the Representatives from Massachusetts, New Hampshire, Connecticut, &c. were against us.* Thus, Sir, you may see, that there is no real responsibility. He further said, that there was such a contrariety of interests, as to hinder a consolidation. I will only make one remark—There is a variety of interests—Some of the States owe a great deal on account of paper money—Others very little—Some of the Northern States have collected and barrelled up paper money. Virginia has sent thither her cash long ago. There is little or none of the Continental paper money retained in this State. Is it not their business to appreciate this money? Yes,—and it will be your business to prevent it. But there will be a majority against you, and you will be obliged to pay your share of this money in its nominal value. It has been said by several Gentlemen, that the freeness of elections would be promoted by throwing the country into large districts. I contend, Sir, that it will have a contrary effect. It will destroy that connection that ought to subsist between the electors and the elected. If your elections be by districts instead of counties, the people will not be acquainted with the candidates. They must therefore be directed in the elections by those who know them. So that instead of a confidential connection between the electors and the elected, they will be absolutely unacquainted with each other. A common man must ask a man of influence how he is to proceed, and for whom he must vote. The elected, therefore, will be careless of the interest of the electors. It will be a common job to extort the suffrages of the common people for the most influential characters. The same men may be repeatedly elected by these means. This, Sir, instead of promoting the freedom of elections, leads us to an Aristocracy. Consider the mode of elections in England. Behold the progress of an election in an English shire. A man of enormous fortune will spend 30,000 l. or 40,000 l. to get himself elected. This is frequently the case. Will the Honorable Gentleman say, that a poor man, as enlightened as any man in the island, has an equal chance with a rich man, to be elected? He will stand no chance though he may have the finest understanding of any man in the shire. It will be so here. Where is the chance that a poor man can come forward with the rich? The Honorable Gentleman will find instead of supporting Democratical principles, it goes absolutely to destroy them. The State Governments, says he, will possess greater advantages than the General

Government, and will consequently prevail. His opinion and mine are diametrically opposite. Bring forth the Federal allurements, and compare them with the poor contemptible things that the State Legislatures can bring forth. On the part of the State Legislatures, there are Justices of Peace and militia officers—And even these Justices and officers, are bound by oath in favour of the Constitution. A constable is the only man who is not obliged to swear paramount allegiance to this beloved Congress. On the other hand, there are rich, fat Federal emoluments— your rich, snug, fine, fat Federal offices—The number of collectors of taxes and excises will outnumber any thing from the States. Who can cope with the excisemen and taxmen? There are none in this country, that can cope with this class of men alone. But, Sir, is this the only danger? Would to Heaven that it were. If we are to ask which will last the longest—the State or the General Government, you must take an army and a navy into the account. Lay these things together, and add to the enumeration the superior abilities of those who manage the General Government.

Can then the State Governments look it in the face? You dare not look it in the face now, when it is but an *embryo*. The influence of this Government will be such, that you never can get amendments; for if you propose alterations, you will affront them. Let the Honorable Gentleman consider all these things and say, whether the State Governments will last as long as the Federal Government. With respect to excises, I can never endure them. They have been productive of the most intolerable oppressions every where. Make a probable calculation of the expence attending the Legislative, Executive, and Judiciary. You will find that there must be an immense increase of taxes. We are the same mass of people we were before.—In the same circumstances—The same pockets are to pay—The expences are to be increased—What will enable us to bear this augmentation of taxes? The mere form of the Government will not do it. A plain understanding cannot conceive how the taxes can be diminished, when our expences are augmented, and the means of paying them not increased.

With respect to our tax-laws, we have purchased a little knowledge by sad experience upon the subject. Reiterated experiments have taught us what can alleviate the distresses and suit the convenience of the people. But we are now to throw away that system, by which we have acquired this knowledge, and send ten men to legislate for us.

The Honorable Gentleman was pleased to say, that the representation of the people was the vital principle of this Government. I will readily agree that it ought to be so.—But I contend that this principle is only nominally, and not substantially to be found there. We contended with the British about representation; they offered us such a representation as Congress now does. They called it a virtual representation. If you look at that paper you will find it so there. Is there but a virtual representation in the upper House? The States are represented *as*

States, by two Senators each. This is virtual, not actual. They encounter you with Rhode-Island and Delaware. This is not an actual representation. What does the term representation signify? It means that a certain district—a certain association of men should be represented in the Government for *certain ends.* These ends ought not to be impeded or obstructed in any manner. Here, Sir, this populous State has not an adequate share of legislative influence. The two petty States of Rhode-Island and Delaware, which together are infinitely inferior to this State, in extent and population, have double her weight, and can counteract her interest. I say, that the representation in the Senate, as applicable to States, is not actual. Representation is not therefore the vital principle of this Government—So far it is wrong.

Rulers are the servants and agents of the people—The people are their masters—Does the new Constitution acknowledge this principle? Trial by jury is the best appendage of freedom—Does it secure this? Does it secure the other great rights of mankind? Our own Constitution preserves these principles. The Honorable Gentleman contributed to form that Constitution: The applauses so justly due to it, should, in my opinion, go to the condemnation of that paper.

With respect to the failures and errors of our Government, they might have happened in any Government.—I do not justify what merits censure, but I shall not degrade my country. As to deviations from justice, I hope they will be attributed to the errors of the head, and not to those of the heart.

The Honorable Gentleman did our Judiciary honour in saying, that they had firmness to counteract the Legislature in some cases. Yes, Sir, our Judges opposed the acts of the Legislature. We have this land mark to guide us.—They had fortitude to declare that they were the Judiciary and would oppose unconstitutional acts. Are you sure that your Federal Judiciary will act thus? Is that Judiciary so well constructed and so independent of the other branches, as our State Judiciary? Where are your land-marks in this Government? I will be bold to say you cannot find any in it. I take it as the highest encomium on this country, that the acts of the Legislature, if unconstitutional, are liable to be opposed by the Judiciary.

Then the Honorable Gentleman said, that the two Judiciaries and Legislatures, would go in a parallel line and never interfere—That as long as each was confined to its proper objects, that there would be no danger of interference—That like two parallel lines as long as they continued in their parallel direction they never would meet. With submission to the Honorable Gentleman's opinion, I assert, that there is danger of interference, because no line is drawn between the powers of the two Governments in many instances; and, where there is a line, there is no check to prevent the one from encroaching upon the powers of the other. I therefore contend that they must interfere, and that this interference must subvert the State Government, as being less powerful.

Unless your Government have checks, it must inevitably terminate in the destruction of your privileges. I will be bold to say, that the British Government has real checks. I was attacked by Gentlemen, as if I had said that I loved the British Government better than our own. I never said so. I said that if I were obliged to relinquish a Republican Government, I would chuse the British Monarchy. I never gave the preference to the British or any other Government, when compared to *that* which the Honorable Gentleman assisted to form. I was constrained to say what I said. When two disagreeable objects present themselves to the mind, we choose that which has the least deformity.

* * *

Mr. Chairman.—The necessity of a Bill of Rights appear to me to be greater in this Government, than ever it was in any Government before.

There are certain maxims by which every wise and enlightened people will regulate their conduct. There are certain political maxims, which no free people ought ever to abandon. Maxims of which the observance is essential to the security of happiness. It is impiously irritating the avenging hand of Heaven, when a people who are in the full enjoyment of freedom, launch out into the wide ocean of human affairs, and desert those maxims which alone can preserve liberty. Such maxims, humble as they are, are those only which can render a nation safe or formidable. Poor little humble republican maxims have attracted the admiration and engaged the attention of the virtuous and wise in all nations, and have stood the shock of ages. We do not now admit the validity of maxims, which we once delighted in. We have since adopted maxims of a different but more *refined nature:* New maxims which tend to the prostration of republicanism.

We have one, Sir, *That all men are by nature free and independent, and have certain inherent rights, of which, when they enter into society, they cannot by any compact deprive or divest their posterity.* We have a set of maxims of the same spirit, which must be beloved by every friend to liberty, to virtue, to mankind. Our Bill of Rights contains those admirable maxims.

. . . I observed already, that the sense of the European nations, and particularly Great-Britain, is against the construction of rights being retained, which are not *expressly* relinquished. I repeat, that all nations have adopted this construction—That all rights not expressly and unequivocally reserved to the people, are impliedly and incidentally relinquished to rulers; as necessarily inseparable from the delegated powers. It is so in Great-Britain: For every possible right which is not reserved to the people by some express provision or compact, is within the King's prerogative. It is so in that country which is said to be in such full possession of freedom. It is so in Spain, Germany, and other parts of the world. Let us consider the sentiments which have been entertained by the people of America on this subject. At the revolution, it must be admitted, that it was their sense to put down those great rights which ought in all countries to be held inviolable and sacred. Virginia did so we all remember. She made a compact to reserve, expressly, certain rights. When fortified with full, adequate, and abundant representation, was she satisfied with that representation? No.—She most cautiously and guardedly reserved and secured those invaluable, inestimable rights and privileges, which no people, inspired with the least glow of the patriotic love of liberty, ever did, or ever can, abandon. She is called upon now to abandon them, and dissolve that compact which secured them to her. She is called upon to accede to another compact which most infallibly supercedes and annihilates her present one. Will she do it?—This is the question. If you intend to reserve your unalienable rights, you must have the most express stipulation. For if implication be allowed, you are ousted of those rights. If the people do not think it necessary to reserve them, they will be supposed to be given up. How were the Congressional rights defined when the people of America united by a confederacy to defend their liberties and rights against the tyrannical attempts of Great-Britain? The States were not then contented with implied reservation. No, Mr. Chairman. It was expressly declared in our Confederation that every right was retained by the States respectively, which was not given up to the Government of the United States. But there is no such thing here. You therefore by a natural and unavoidable implication, give up your rights to the General Government. Your own example furnishes an argument against it. If you give up these powers, without a Bill of Rights, you will exhibit the most absurd thing to mankind that ever the world saw—A Government that has abandoned all its powers—The powers of direct taxation, the sword, and the purse. You have disposed of them to Congress, without a Bill of Rights—without check, limitation, or controul. And still you have checks and guards—still you keep barriers—pointed where? Pointed against your weakened, prostrated, enervated State Government! You have a Bill of Rights to defend you against the State Government, which is bereaved of all power; and yet you have none against Congress, though in full and exclusive possession of all power! You arm yourselves against the weak and defenceless, and expose yourselves naked to the armed and powerful. Is not this a conduct of unexampled absurdity? What barriers have you to oppose to this most strong energetic Government? To that Government you have nothing to oppose. All your defence is given up. This is a real actual defect.—It must strike the mind of every Gentleman. When our Government was first instituted in Virginia, we declared the common law of England to be in force.—That system of law which has been admired, and has protected us and our ancestors, is excluded by that system.—Added to this, we adopted a Bill of Rights. By this Constitution, some of the best barriers of human rights are thrown away. Is there not an additional reason to have a Bill of Rights? By the ancient common law, the trial of all facts is decided by a jury of impartial men from the immediate vicinage. This paper speaks of different juries from the common law, in criminal cases; and in civil controversies excludes trial by jury altogether. There is therefore more occasion for the supplementary check of a Bill of Rights now, than then. Congress from their general powers may fully go into the business of human legislation. They may legislate in criminal cases from treason to the lowest offence, petty larceny. They may define crimes and prescribe punishments. In the definition of crimes, I trust they will be directed by what wise Representatives ought to be governed by. But when we come to punishments, no latitude ought to be left, nor dependence put on the virtue of Representatives. What says our Bill of Rights?

"That excessive bail ought not to be required, nor excessive fines imposed, nor cruel and unusual punishments inflicted." Are you not therefore now calling on those Gentlemen who are to compose Congress, to prescribe trials and define punishments without this controul? Will they find sentiments there similar to this Bill of Rights? You let them loose—you do more—you depart from the genius of your country. That paper tells you, that the trial of crimes shall be by jury, and held in the State where the crime shall have been committed.—Under this extensive provision, they may proceed in a manner extremely dangerous to liberty.—Persons accused may be carried from one extremity of the State to another, and be tried not by an impartial jury of the vicinage, acquainted with his character, and the circumstances of the fact; but by a jury unacquainted with both, and who may be biassed against him.—Is not this sufficient to alarm men?—How different is this from the immemoral practice of your British ancestors, and your own? I need not tell you, that by the common law a number of hundredors were required to be on a jury, and that afterwards it was sufficient if the jurors came from the same county. With less than this the people of England have never been satisfied. That paper ought to have declared the common law in force.

In this business of legislation, your Members of Congress will lose the restriction of not imposing excessive fines, demanding excessive bail, and inflicting cruel and unusual punishments.—These are prohibited by your Declaration of Rights. What has distinguished our ancestors?— That they would not admit of tortures, or cruel and barbarous punishments. But Congress may introduce the practice of the civil law, in preference to that of the common law.—They may introduce the practice of France, Spain, and Germany—Of torturing to extort a confession of the crime. They will say that they might as well draw examples from those countries as from Great-Britain; and they will tell you, that there is such a necessity of strengthening the arm of Government that they must have a criminal equity, and extort confession by torture, in order to punish with still more relentless severity. We are then lost and undone.—And can any man think it troublesome, when we can by a small interference prevent our rights from being lost?—If you will, like the Virginian Government, give them knowledge of the extent of the rights retained by the people, and the powers themselves, they will, if they be honest men, thank you for it.—Will they not wish to go on sure grounds?—But if you leave them otherwise, they will not know how to proceed; and being in a state of uncertainty, they will assume rather than give up powers by implication. A Bill of Rights may be summed up in a few words. What do they tell us?—That our rights are reserved.— Why not say so? Is it because it will consume too much paper? Gentlemen's reasonings against a Bill of Rights, do not satisfy me. Without saying which has the right side, it remains doubtful. A Bill of Rights is a favourite thing with the Virginians, and the people of the other States likewise. It may be their prejudice, but the Government ought to suit their geniuses, otherwise its operation will be unhappy. A Bill of Rights, even if its necessity be doubtful, will exclude the possibility of dispute, and with great submission, I think the best way is to have no dispute. In the present Constitution, they are restrained from issuing general warrants to search suspected places, or seize persons not named, without evidence of the commission of the fact, &c. There was certainly some celestial influence governing those who deliberated on that Constitution:—For they have with the most cautious and enlightened circumspection, guarded those indefeasible rights, which ought ever to be held sacred. The officers of Congress may come upon you, fortified with all the terrors of paramount federal authority.—Excisemen may come in multitudes:—For the limitation of their numbers no man knows.—They may, unless the General Government be restrained by a Bill of Rights, or some similar restriction, go into your cellars and rooms, and search, ransack and measure, every thing you eat, drink and wear. They ought to be restrained within proper bounds. With respect to the freedom of the press, I need say nothing; for it is hoped that the Gentlemen who shall compose Congress, will take care as little as possible, to infringe the rights of human nature.—This will result from their integrity. They should from prudence, abstain from violating the rights of their constituents. They are not however expressly restrained.—But whether they will intermeddle with that palladium of our liberties or not, I leave you to determine.

* * *

Mr. Chairman.—We have now come to the ninth section, and I consider myself at liberty to take a short view of the whole. I wish to do it very briefly. Give me leave to remark, that there is a Bill of Rights in that Government. There are express restrictions which are in the shape of a Bill of Rights: But they bear the name of the ninth section. The design of the negative expressions in this section is to prescribe limits, beyond which the powers of Congress shall not go. These are the sole bounds intended by the American Government. Where abouts do we stand with respect to a Bill of Rights? Examine it, and compare it to the idea manifested by the Virginian Bill of Rights, or that of the other States. The restraints in this Congressional Bill of Rights, are so feeble and few, that it would have been infinitely better to have said nothing about it.

The fair implication is, that they can do every thing they are not forbidden to do. What will be the result if Congress, in the course of their legislation, should do a thing not restrained by this ninth section? It will fall as an incidental power to Congress, not being prohibited expressly in the Constitution. The first prohibition is, that the privilege of the writ of *habeas corpus* shall not be suspended, but when in cases of rebellion, or invasion, the public safety may require it. It results clearly, that if it had not said so, they could suspend it in all cases whatsoever. It reverses the position of the friends of this Constitution, that every thing is retained which is not given up. For instead of this, every thing is given up, which is not expressly reserved.—It does not speak affirmatively, and say that it shall be suspended in those cases. But that it shall not be suspended but in certain cases; going on a supposition that every thing which is not negatived, shall remain with Congress. If the power remains with the people, how can Congress supply the want of an affirmative grant? They cannot do it but by implication, which destroys their doctrine. The Virginia Bill of Rights interdicts the relinquishment of the sword and purse without controul. That Bill of Rights secures the great and principal rights of mankind. But this Bill of Rights extends to but very few cases, and is destructive of the doctrine advanced by the friends of that paper.

If *ex post facto* laws had not been interdicted, they might also have been extended by implication at pleasure. Let us consider whether this restriction be founded in wisdom or good policy. If no *ex post facto* laws be made, what is to become the old continental paper dollars? Will not this country be forced to pay it in gold and silver, shilling for shilling? Gentlemen may think that this does not deserve an answer: But it is an all important question. Because the property of this country is not commensurate to the enormous demand. Our own Government triumphs with infinite superiority when put in contrast with that paper.— The want of a Bill of Rights will render all their laws, however oppressive, constitutional.

If the Government of Virginia passes a law in contradiction to our Bill of Rights, it is nugatory. By that paper the national wealth is to be disposed of under the veil of secrecy: For the publication from time to time, will amount to nothing; and they may conceal what they think requires secrecy. How different is it in your own Government?—Have not the people seen the journals of our Legislature every day during every session? Is not the lobby full of people every day? Yet, Gentlemen say, that the publication from time to time is a security unknown in our State Government! Such a regulation would be nugatory and vain, or at least needless, as the people see the journals our Legislature, and hear their debates every day. If this be not more secure than what is in that paper, I will give up that I have totally misconceived the principles of the Government. You are told, that your rights are secured in this new Government. They are guarded in no other part but this ninth section. The few restrictions in that section are your only safeguards. They may controul your actions, and your very words, without being repugnant to that paper. The existence of your dearest privileges will depend on the consent of Congress: For these are not within the restrictions of the ninth section.

If Gentlemen think that securing the slave trade is a capital object; that the privilege of the *habeas corpus* is sufficiently secured; that the exclusion of *ex post facto* laws will produce no inconvenience; that the publication from time to time will secure their property; in one word, that this section alone will sufficiently secure their liberties, I have spoken in vain.—Every word of mine, and of my worthy coadjutor [George Mason], is lost. I trust that Gentlemen, on this occasion, will see the great objects of religion, liberty of the press, trial by jury, interdiction of cruel punishments, and every other sacred right secured, before they agree to that paper. These most important human rights are not protected by that section, which is the only safeguard in the Constitution.—My mind will not be quieted till I see something substantial come forth in the shape of a Bill of Rights.

* * *

Gov. RANDOLPH. Mr. Chairman, the general review which the gentleman has taken of the 9th section is so inconsistent, that, in order to answer him, I must, with your permission, who are the *custos* of order here, depart from the rule of the house in some degree. I declared, some days ago, that I would give my suffrage for this Constitution, not because I considered it without blemish, but because the critical situation of our country demanded it. I invite those who think with me to vote for the Constitution. But where things occur in it which I disapprove of, I shall be candid in exposing my objections.

Permit me to return to that clause which is called by gentlemen the *sweeping clause.* I observed, yesterday, that I conceived the construction which had been put on this clause by the advocates of the Constitution was too narrow, and that the construction put upon it by the other party was extravagant. The immediate explanation appears to me most rational. The former contend that it gives no supplementary power, but only enables them to make laws to execute the delegated powers—or, in other words, that it only involves the powers incidental to those expressly delegated. By *incidental powers* they mean those which are necessary for the principal thing. That the incident is inseparable from the principal, is a maxim in the construction of laws. A constitution differs from a law; for a law only embraces one thing, but a constitution embraces a number of things, and is to have a more liberal construction. I need not recur to the constitutions of Europe for a precedent to direct my explication of this clause, because, in Europe, there is no constitution wholly in writing. The European constitutions sometimes consist in detached statutes or ordinances, sometimes they are on record, and

sometimes they depend on immemorial tradition. The American constitutions are singular, and their construction ought to be liberal. On this
principle, what should be said of the clause under consideration? (*the
sweeping clause.*) If incidental powers be those only which are necessary
for the principal thing, the clause would be superfluous.

Let us take an example of a single department; for instance, that of
the President, who has certain things annexed to his office. Does it not
reasonably follow that he must have some incidental powers? The
principle of incidental powers extends to all parts of the system. If you
then say that the President has incidental powers, you reduce it to
tautology. I cannot conceive that the fair interpretation of these words
is as the honorable member says.

Let me say that, in my opinion, the adversaries of the Constitution
wander equally from the true meaning. If it would not fatigue the house
too far, I would go back to the question of reserved rights. The
gentleman supposes that complete and unlimited legislation is vested in
the Congress of the United States. This supposition is founded on false
reasoning. What is the present situation of this state? She has possession of all rights of sovereignty, except those given to the Confederation.
She *must* delegate powers to the confederate government. It is necessary for her public happiness. Her weakness compels her to confederate
with the twelve other governments. She trusts certain powers to the
general government, in order to support, protect, and defend the Union.
Now, is there not a demonstrable difference between the principle of the
state government and of the general government? There is not a word
said, in the state government, of the powers given to it, because they are
general. But in the general Constitution, its powers are enumerated. Is
it not, then, fairly deducible, that it has no power but what is expressly
given it?—for if its powers were to be general, an enumeration would be
needless.

But the insertion of the negative *restrictions* has given cause of
triumph, it seems, to gentlemen. They suppose that it demonstrates
that Congress are to have powers by implication. I will meet them on
that ground. I persuade myself that every exception here mentioned is
an exception, not from general powers, but from the particular powers
therein vested. To what power in the general government is the
exception made respecting the importation of negroes? Not from a
general power, but from a particular power expressly enumerated. This
is an exception from the power given them of regulating commerce. He
asks, Where is the power to which the prohibition of suspending the
habeas corpus is an exception? I contend that, by virtue of the power
given to Congress to regulate courts, they could suspend the writ of
habeas corpus. This is therefore an exception to that power.

The 3d restriction is, that no bill of attainder, or *ex post facto* law,
shall be passed. This is a manifest exception to another power. We
know well that attainders and *ex post facto* laws have always been the

engines of criminal jurisprudence. This is, therefore, an exception to the criminal jurisdiction vested in that body.

The 4th restriction is, that no capitation, or other direct tax, shall be laid, unless in proportion to the census before directed to be taken. Our debates show from what power this is an exception.

The restrictions in the 5th clause are an exception to the power of regulating commerce.

The restriction in the 6th clause, that no money should be drawn from the treasury but in consequence of appropriations made by law, is an exception to the power of paying the debts of the United States; for the power of drawing money from the treasury is consequential of that of paying the public debts.

The next restriction is, that no titles of nobility shall be granted by the United States. If we cast our eyes to the manner in which titles of nobility first originated, we shall find this restriction founded on the same principles. These sprang from military and civil offices. Both are put in the hands of the United States, and therefore I presume it to be an exception to that power.

The last restriction restrains any person in office from accepting of any present or emolument, title or office, from any foreign prince or state. It must have been observed before, that, though the Confederation had restricted Congress from exercising any powers not given them, yet they inserted it, not from any apprehension of usurpation, but for greater security. This restriction is provided to prevent corruption. All men have a natural inherent right of receiving emoluments from any one, unless they be restrained by the regulations of the community. An accident which actually happened operated in producing the restriction. A box was presented to our ambassador by the king of our allies. It was thought proper, in order to exclude corruption and foreign influence, to prohibit any one in office from receiving or holding any *emoluments* from foreign states. I believe that if, at that moment, when we were in harmony with the king of France, we had supposed that he was corrupting our ambassador, it might have disturbed that confidence, and diminished that mutual friendship, which contributed to carry us through the war.

The honorable gentlemen observe that Congress might define punishments, from petty larceny to high treason. This is an unfortunate quotation for the gentleman, because treason is expressly defined in the 3d section of the 3d article, and they can add no feature to it. They have not cognizance over any other crime except piracies, felonies committed on the high seas, and offences against the law of nations.

But the rhetoric of the gentleman has highly colored the dangers of giving the general government an indefinite power of providing for the general welfare. I contend that no such power is given. They have power "to lay and collect taxes, duties, imposts, and excises, to pay the debts and provide for the common defence and general welfare of the United States." Is this an independent, separate, substantive power, to provide for the general welfare of the United States? No, sir. They can lay and collect taxes, &c. For what? To pay the debts and provide for the general welfare. Were not this the case, the following part of the clause would be absurd. It would have been treason against common language. Take it altogether, and let me ask if the plain interpretation be not this—a power to lay and collect taxes, &c., in order to provide for the general welfare and pay debts.

On the subject of a bill of rights, the want of which has been complained of, I will observe that it has been sanctified by such reverend authority, that I feel some difficulty in going against it. I shall not, however, be deterred from giving my opinion on this occasion, let the consequence be what it may. At the beginning of the war, we had no certain bill of rights; for our charter cannot be considered as a bill of rights; it is nothing more than an investiture, in the hands of the Virginia citizens, of those rights which belonged to British subjects. When the British thought proper to infringe our rights, was it not necessary to mention, in our Constitution, those rights which ought to be paramount to the power of the legislature? Why is the bill of rights distinct from the Constitution? I consider bills of rights in this view— that the government should use them, when there is a departure from its fundamental principles, in order to restore them.

This is the true sense of a bill of rights. If it be consistent with the Constitution, or contain additional rights, why not put it in the Constitution? If it be repugnant to the Constitution, here will be a perpetual scene of warfare between them. The honorable gentleman has praised the bill of rights of Virginia, and called it his guardian angel, and vilified this Constitution for not having it. Give me leave to make a distinction between the representatives of the people of a particular country, who are appointed as the ordinary legislature, having no limitation to their powers, and another body arising from a compact, and with certain delineated powers. Were a bill of rights necessary in the former, it would not be in the latter; for the best security that can be in the latter is the express enumeration of its powers. But let me ask the gentleman where his favorite rights are violated. They are not violated by the 10th section, which contains restrictions on the states. Are they violated by the enumerated powers? [Here his excellency read from the 8th to the 12th article of the bill of rights.] Is there not provision made, in this Constitution, for the trial by jury in criminal cases? Does not the 3d article provide that the trial of all crimes shall be by jury, and held where the said crimes shall have been committed! Does it not follow that the cause and nature of the accusation must be produced?—because, otherwise, they cannot proceed on the cause. Every one knows that the witnesses must be brought before the jury, or else the prisoner will be discharged. Calling of evidence in his favor is coincident to his trial.

There is no suspicion that less than twelve jurors will be thought sufficient. The only defect is, that there is no speedy trial. Consider how this could have been amended. We have heard complaints against it because it is supposed the jury is to come from the state at large. It will be in their power to have juries from the vicinage. And would not the complaints have been louder if they had appointed a federal court to be had in every county in the state? Criminals are brought, in this state, from every part of the country to the general court, and jurors from the vicinage are summoned to the trials. There can be no reason to prevent the general government from adopting a similar regulation.

As to the exclusion of excessive bail and fines, and cruel and unusual punishments, this would follow of itself, without a bill of rights. Observations have been made about watchfulness over those in power which deserve our attention. There must be a combination; we must presume corruption in the House of Representatives, Senate, and President, before we can suppose that excessive fines can be imposed or cruel punishments inflicted. Their number is the highest security. Numbers are the highest security in our own Constitution, which has attracted so many eulogiums from the gentlemen. Here we have launched into a sea of suspicions. How shall we check power? By their numbers. Before these cruel punishments can be inflicted, laws must be passed, and judges must judge contrary to justice. This would excite universal discontent and detestation of the members of the government. They might involve their friends in the calamities resulting from it, and could be removed from office. I never desire a greater security than this, which I believe to be absolutely sufficient.

That general warrants are grievous and oppressive, and ought not to be granted, I fully admit. I heartily concur in expressing my detestation of them. But we have sufficient security here also. We do not rely on the integrity of any one particular person or body, but on the number and different orders of the members of the government—some of them having necessarily the same feelings with ourselves. Can it be believed that the federal judiciary would not be independent enough to prevent such oppressive practices? If they will not do justice to persons injured, may they not go to our own state judiciaries, and obtain it?

Gentlemen have been misled, to a certain degree, by a general declaration that the trial by jury was gone. We see that, in the most valuable cases, it is reserved. Is it abolished in civil cases? Let him put his finger on the part where it is abolished. The Constitution is silent on it. What expression would you wish the Constitution to use, to establish it? Remember we were not making a constitution for Virginia alone, or we might have taken Virginia for our directory. But we were forming a constitution for thirteen states. The trial by jury is different in different states. In some states it is excluded in cases in which it is admitted in others. In admiralty causes it is not used. Would you have a jury to determine the case of a capture? The Virginia legislature thought proper to make an exception of that case. These depend on the law of nations, and no twelve men that could be picked up could be equal to the decision of such a matter.

Then, sir, the freedom of the press is said to be insecure. God forbid that I should give my voice against the freedom of the press. But I ask, (and with confidence that it cannot be answered,) Where is the page where it is restrained? If there had been any regulation about it, leaving it insecure, then there might have been reason for clamors. But this is not the case. If it be, I again ask for the particular clause which gives liberty to destroy the freedom of the press.

He has added religion to the objects endangered, in his conception. Is there any power given over it? Let it be pointed out. Will he not be contented with the answer that has been frequently given to that objection? The variety of sects which abounds in the United States is the best security for the freedom of religion. No part of the Constitution, even if strictly construed, will justify a conclusion that the general government can take away or impair the freedom of religion.

The gentleman asks, with triumph, Shall we be deprived of these valuable rights? Had there been an exception, or an express infringement of those rights, he might object; but I conceive every fair reasoner will agree that there is no just cause to suspect that they will be violated.

But he objects that the common law is not established by the Constitution. The wisdom of the Convention is displayed by its omission, because the common law ought not to be immutably fixed. Is it established in our own Constitution, or the bill of rights, which has been resounded through the house? It is established only by an act of the legislature, and can therefore be changed as circumstances may require it. Let the honorable gentleman consider what would be the destructive consequences of its establishment in the Constitution. Even in England, where the firmest opposition has been made to encroachments upon it, it has been frequently changed. What would have been our dilemma if it had been established? Virginia has declared that children shall have equal portions of the real estate of their intestate parents, and it is consistent with the principles of a republican government.

The immutable establishment of the common law would have been repugnant to that regulation. It would, in many respects, be destructive to republican principles, and productive of great inconveniences. I might indulge myself by showing many parts of the common law which would have this effect. I hope I shall not be thought to speak ludicrously, when I say the *writ of burning heretics* would have been revived by it. It would tend to throw real property into few hands, and prevent the introduction of many salutary regulations. Thus, were the common law adopted in that system, it would destroy the principles of republican government. But this is not excluded. It may be established by an act of legislature. Its defective parts may be altered, and it may be changed and modified as the convenience of the public may require it.

I said, when I opened my observations, that I thought the friends of the Constitution were mistaken when they supposed the powers granted by the last clause of the 8th section to be merely incidental; and that its enemies were equally mistaken when they put such an extravagant construction upon it.

My objection is, that the clause is ambiguous, and that that ambiguity may injure the states. My fear is, that it will, by gradual accessions, gather to a dangerous length. This is my apprehension, and I disdain to disown it. I will praise it where it deserves it, and censure it where it appears defective. But, sir, are we to reject it, because it is ambiguous in some particular instances? I cast my eyes to the actual situation of America. I see the dreadful tempest, to which the present calm is a prelude, if disunion takes place. I see the anarchy which must happen if no energetic government be established. In this situation, I would take the Constitution, were it more objectionable than it is; for, if anarchy and confusion follow disunion, an enterprising man may enter into the American throne. I conceive there is no danger. The representatives are chosen by and from among the people. They will have a fellow-feeling for the farmers and planters. The twenty-six senators, representatives of the states, will not be those desperadoes and horrid adventurers which they are represented to be. The state legislatures, I trust, will not forget the duty they owe to their country so far as to choose such men to manage their federal interests. I trust that the members of Congress themselves will explain the ambiguous parts; and if not, the states can combine in order to insist on amending the ambiguities. I would depend on the present actual feeling of the people of America, to introduce any amendment which may be necessary. I repeat it again, though I do not reverence the Constitution, that its adoption is necessary to avoid the storm which is hanging over America, and that no greater curse can befall her than the dissolution of the political connection between the states. Whether we shall propose previous or subsequent amendments, is now the only dispute. It is supererogation to repeat again the arguments in support of each; but I ask gentlemen whether, as eight states have adopted it, it be not safer to adopt it, and rely on the probability of obtaining amendments, than, by a rejection, to hazard a breach of the Union? I hope to be excused for the breach of order which I have committed.

Mr. HENRY lamented that he could not see with that perspicuity which other gentlemen were blessed with. But the 9th section struck his mind still in an unfavorable light. He hoped, as the gentleman had been indulged in speaking of the Constitution in general, that he should be allowed to answer him before they adopted or rejected it.

(3) New York, July 2, 1788

Mr. TREDWELL. Sir, I introduce these observations to combat certain principles which have been daily and confidently advanced by the favorers of the present Constitution, and which appear to me totally indefensible. The first and grand leading, or rather misleading, principle in this debate, and on which the advocates for this system of unrestricted powers must chiefly depend for its support, is that, in forming a constitution, whatever powers are not expressly granted or given the government, are reserved to the people, or that rulers cannot exercise any powers but those expressly given to them by the Constitution. Let me ask the gentlemen who advanced this principle, whether the commission of a Roman dictator, which was in these few words—to take care that the state received no harm—does not come up fully to their ideas of an energetic government; or whether an invitation from the people to one or more to come and rule over them, would not clothe the rulers with sufficient powers. If so, the principle they advance is a false one. Besides, the absurdity of this principle will evidently appear, when we consider the great variety of objects to which the powers of the government must necessarily extend, and that an express enumeration of them all would probably fill as many volumes as Pool's Synopsis of the Critics. But we may reason with sufficient certainty on the subject, from the sense of all the public bodies in the United States, who had occasion to form new constitutions. They have uniformly acted upon a direct and contrary principle, not only in forming the state constitutions and the old Confederation, but also in forming this very Constitution, for we do not find in every state constitution express resolutions made in favor of the people; and it is clear that the late Convention at Philadelphia, whatever might have been the sentiments of some of its members, did not adopt the principle, for they have made certain reservations and restrictions, which, upon that principle, would have been totally useless and unnecessary; and can it be supposed that that wise body, whose only apology for the great ambiguity of many parts of that performance, and the total omission of some things which many esteem essential to the security of liberty, was a great desire of brevity, should so far sacrifice that great and important object, as to insert a number of provisions which they esteemed totally useless? Why is it said that the privilege of the writ of *habeas corpus* shall not be suspended, unless, in cases of rebellion or invasion, the public safety may require it? What clause in the Constitution, except this very clause itself, gives the general government a power to deprive us of that great privilege, so sacredly secured to us by our state constitutions? Why is it provided that no bill of attainder shall be passed, or that no title of nobility shall be granted? Are there any clauses in the Constitution extending the powers of the general government to these objects? Some gentlemen say that these, though not necessary, were inserted for greater caution. I could have wished, sir, that a greater caution had been used to secure to us the freedom of election, a sufficient and responsible representation, the freedom of the press, and the trial by jury both in civil and criminal cases.

These, sir, are the rocks on which the Constitution should have rested; no other foundation can any man lay, which will secure the sacred temple of freedom against the power of the great, the undermining arts of ambition, and the blasts of profane scoffers—for such there will be in every age—who will tell us that all religion is in vain; that is, that our political creeds, which have been handed down to us by our forefathers as sacredly as our Bibles, and for which more of them have suffered martyrdom than for the creed of the apostles, are all nonsense; who will tell us that paper constitutions are mere paper, and that parchment is but parchment, that jealousy of our rulers is a sin, &c. I could have wished also that sufficient caution had been used to secure to us our religious liberties, and to have prevented the general government from tyrannizing over our consciences by a religious establishment—a tyranny of all others most dreadful, and which will assuredly be exercised whenever it shall be thought necessary for the promotion and support of their political measures. It is ardently to be wished, sir, that these and other invaluable rights of freemen had been as cautiously secured as some of the paltry local interests of some of the individual states. But it appears to me, that, in forming this Constitution, we have run into the same error which the lawyers and Pharisees of old were charged with; that is, while we have secured the tithes of mint, anise, and cumin, we have neglected the weightier matters of the law, judgment, mercy, and faith. Have we not neglected to secure to ourselves the weighty matters of judgment or justice, by empowering the general government to establish one supreme, and as many inferior, courts as they please, whose proceedings they have a right to fix and regulate as they shall think fit, so that we are ignorant whether they shall be according to the common, civil, the Jewish, or Turkish law? What better provisions have we made for mercy, when a man, for ignorantly passing a counterfeit continental note, or bill of credit, is liable to be dragged to a distant county, two or three hundred miles from home, deprived of the support and assistance of friends, to be tried by a strange jury, ignorant of his character, ignorant of the character of the witnesses, unable to contradict any false testimony brought against him by their own knowledge of facts, and with whom the prisoner being unacquainted, he must be deprived totally of the benefit of his challenge? and besides all that, he may be exposed to lose his life, merely for want of property to carry his witnesses to such a distance; and after all this solemn farce and mockery of a trial by jury, if they should acquit him, it will require more ingenuity than I am master of, to show that he does not hold his life at the will and pleasure of the Supreme Court, to which an appeal lies, and consequently depend on the tender mercies, perhaps, of the wicked, (for judges may be wicked;) and what those tender mercies are, I need not tell you. You may read them in the history of the Star Chamber Court in England, and in the courts of Philip, and in your Bible.*

P. PROPOSALS FROM THE STATE CONVENTIONS

(1) Massachusetts, February 6, 1788

The question being put, whether this Convention will accept of the report of the committee, as follows,—

Commonwealth of Massachusetts.
In Convention of the Delegates of the People of the Commonwealth of Massachusetts, 1788.

The Convention, having impartially discussed and fully considered the Constitution for the United States of America, reported to Congress by the Convention of delegates from the United States of America, and submitted to us by a resolution of the General Court of the said commonwealth, passed the twenty-fifth day of October last past; and acknowledging, with grateful hearts, the goodness of the Supreme Ruler of the universe in affording the people of the United States, in the course of his providence, an opportunity, deliberately and peaceably, without fraud or surprise, of entering into an explicit and solemn compact with each other, by assenting to and ratifying a new Constitution, in order to form a more perfect union, establish justice, insure domestic tranquillity, provide for the common defence, promote the general welfare, and secure the blessings of liberty to themselves and their posterity, DO, in the name and in behalf of the people of the commonwealth of Massachusetts, assent to and ratify the said Constitution for the United States of America.

And, as it is the opinion of this Convention, that certain amendments and alterations in the said Constitution would remove the fears and quiet the apprehensions of many of the good people of the commonwealth, and more effectually guard against an undue administration of the federal government, the Convention do therefore recommend that the following alterations and provisions be introduced into the said Constitution:—

First. That it be explicitly declared, that all powers not expressly delegated by the aforesaid Constitution are reserved to the several states, to be by them exercised.

Secondly. That there shall be one representative to every thirty thousand persons, according to the census mentioned in the Constitution, until the whole number of representatives amounts to two hundred.

* From the Pennsylvania Herald, Dec. 12th, 1787.

Thirdly. That Congress do not exercise the powers vested in them by the 4th section of the 1st article, but in cases where a state shall neglect or refuse to make the regulations therein mentioned, or shall make regulations subversive of the rights of the people to a free and equal representation in Congress, agreeably to the Constitution.

Fourthly. That Congress do not lay direct taxes, but when the moneys arising from the impost and excise are insufficient for the public exigencies, nor then, until Congress shall have first made a requisition upon the states, to assess, levy, and pay their respective proportion of such requisitions, agreeably to the census fixed in the said Constitution, in such way and manner as the legislatures of the states shall think best, and, in such case, if any state shall neglect or refuse to pay its proportion, pursuant to such requisition, then Congress may assess and levy such state's proportion, together with interest thereon, at the rate of six per cent. per annum, from the time of payment prescribed in such requisitions.

Fifthly. That Congress erect no company with exclusive advantages of commerce.

Sixthly. That no person shall be tried for any crime, by which he may incur an infamous punishment, or loss of life, until he be first indicted by a grand jury, except in such cases as may arise in the government and regulation of the land and naval forces.

Seventhly. The Supreme Judicial Federal Court shall have no jurisdiction of causes between citizens of different states, unless the matter in dispute, whether it concern the realty or personalty, be of the value of three thousand dollars at the least; nor shall the federal judicial powers extend to any action between citizens of different states, where the matter in dispute, whether it concern the realty or personalty, is not of the value of fifteen hundred dollars at the least.

Eighthly. In civil actions between citizens of different states, every issue of fact, arising in actions at common law, shall be tried by a jury, if the parties, or either of them, request it.

Ninthly. Congress shall at no time consent that any person holding an office of trust or profit, under the United States, shall accept of a title of nobility, or any other title or office, from any king, prince, or foreign state.

And the Convention do, in the name and in the behalf of the people of this commonwealth, enjoin it upon their representatives in Congress, at all times, until the alterations and provisions aforesaid have been considered, agreeably to the 5th article of the said Constitution, to exert all their influence, and use all reasonable and legal methods, to obtain a ratification of the said alterations and provisions, in such manner as is provided in the said article.

And, that the United States, in Congress assembled, may have due notice of the assent and ratification of the said Constitution by this Convention, it is

Resolved, That the assent and ratification aforesaid be engrossed on parchment, together with the recommendation and injunction aforesaid, and with this resolution; and that his excellency, JOHN HANCOCK, President, and the Hon. WILLIAM CUSHING, Esq., Vice-President of this Convention, transmit the same, countersigned by the Secretary of the Convention, under their hands and seals, to the United States in Congress assembled.

(2) Virginia, June 27, 1788

Mr. WYTHE reported, from the committee appointed, such *amendments* to the proposed Constitution of government for the United States as were by them deemed necessary to be recommended to the consideration of the Congress which shall first assemble under the said Constitution, to be acted upon according to the mode prescribed in the 5th article thereof; and he read the same in his place, and afterwards delivered them in at the clerk's table, where the same were again read, and are as follows:—

"That there be a declaration or bill of rights asserting, and securing from encroachment, the essential and unalienable rights of the people, in some such manner as the following:—

"1st.   That there are certain natural rights, of which men, when they form a social compact, cannot deprive or divest their posterity; among which are the enjoyment of life and liberty, with the means of acquiring, possessing, and protecting property, and pursuing and obtaining happiness and safety.

"2d.   That all power is naturally invested in, and consequently derived from, the people; that magistrates therefore are their *trustees* and *agents,* at all times amenable to them.

"3d.   That government ought to be instituted for the common benefit, protection, and security of the people; and that the doctrine of non-resistance against arbitrary power and oppression is absurd, slavish, and destructive to the good and happiness of mankind.

"4th.   That no man or set of men are entitled to separate or exclusive public emoluments or privileges from the community, but in consideration of public services, which not being descendible, neither ought the offices of magistrate, legislator, or judge, or any other public office, to be hereditary.

"5th.   That the legislative, executive, and judicial powers of government should be separate and distinct; and, that the members of the two first may be restrained from oppression by feeling and participating the public burdens, they should, at fixed periods, be reduced to a private station, return into the mass of the people, and the vacancies be supplied by certain and regular elections, in which all or any part of the former members to be eligible or ineligible, as the rules of the Constitution of government, and the laws, shall direct.

"6th.   That the elections of representatives in the legislature ought to be free and frequent, and all men having sufficient evidence of permanent common interest with, and attachment to, the community, ought to have the right of suffrage; and no aid, charge, tax, or fee, can be set, rated, or levied, upon the people without their own consent, or that of their representatives, so elected; nor can they be bound by any law to which they have not, in like manner, assented, for the public good.

"7th.   That all power of suspending laws, or the execution of laws, by any authority, without the consent of the representatives of the people in the legislature, is injurious to their rights, and ought not to be exercised.

"8th.   That, in all criminal and capital prosecutions, a man hath a right to demand the cause and nature of his accusation, to be confronted with the accusers and witnesses, to call for evidence, and be allowed counsel in his favor, and to a fair and speedy trial by an impartial jury of his vicinage, without whose unanimous consent he cannot be found guilty, (except in the government of the land and naval forces;) nor can he be compelled to give evidence against himself.

"9th.   That no freeman ought to be taken, imprisoned, or disseized of his freehold, liberties, privileges, or franchises, or outlawed, or exiled, or in any manner destroyed, or deprived of his life, liberty, or property, but by the law of the land.

"10th.   That every freeman restrained of his liberty is entitled to a remedy, to inquire into the lawfulness thereof, and to remove the same, if unlawful, and that such remedy ought not to be denied nor delayed.

"11th.   That, in controversies respecting property, and in suits between man and man, the ancient trial by jury is one of the greatest securities to the rights of the people, and to remain sacred and inviolable.

"12th.   That every freeman ought to find a certain remedy, by recourse to the laws, for all injuries and wrongs he may receive in his person, property, or character.   He ought to obtain right and justice freely, without sale, completely and without denial, promptly and without delay; and that all establishments or regulations contravening these rights are oppressive and unjust.

"13th.   That excessive bail ought not to be required, nor excessive fines imposed, nor cruel and unusual punishments inflicted.

"14th.   That every freeman has a right to be secure from all unreasonable searches and seizures of his person, his papers, and property; all warrants, therefore, to search suspected places, or seize any freeman, his papers, or property, without information on oath (or affirmation of a person religiously scrupulous of taking an oath) of legal and sufficient cause, are grievous and oppressive; and all general warrants to search suspected places, or to apprehend any suspected person, without specially naming or describing the place or person, are dangerous, and ought not to be granted.

"15th.   That the people have a right peaceably to assemble together to consult for the common good, or to instruct their representatives; and that every freeman has a right to petition or apply to the legislature for redress of grievances.

"16th.   That the people have a right to freedom of speech, and of writing and publishing their sentiments; that the freedom of the press is one of the greatest bulwarks of liberty, and ought not to be violated.

"17th.   That the people have a right to keep and bear arms; that a well-regulated militia, composed of the body of the people trained to arms, is the proper, natural, and safe defence of a free state; that standing armies, in time of peace, are dangerous to liberty, and therefore ought to be avoided, as far as the circumstances and protection of the community will admit; and that, in all cases, the military should be under strict subordination to, and governed by, the civil power.

"18th.   That no soldier in time of peace ought to be quartered in any house without the consent of the owner, and in time of war in such manner only as the law directs.

"19th.   That any person religiously scrupulous of bearing arms ought to be exempted, upon payment of an equivalent to employ another to bear arms in his stead.

"20th.   That religion, or the duty which we owe to our Creator, and the manner of discharging it, can be directed only by reason and conviction, not by force or violence; and therefore all men have an equal, natural, and unalienable right to the free exercise of religion, according to the dictates of conscience, and that no particular religious sect or society ought to be favored or established, by law, in preference to others."

Amendments to the Constitution.

"1st.   That each state in the Union shall respectively retain every power, jurisdiction, and right, which is not by this Constitution delegated to the Congress of the United States, or to the departments of the federal government.

"2d.   That there shall be one representative for every thirty thousand, according to the enumeration or census mentioned in the Constitution, until the whole number of representatives amounts to two hundred; after which, that number shall be continued or increased, as Congress

800

shall direct, upon the principles fixed in the Constitution, by apportioning the representatives of each state to some greater number of people, from time to time, as population increases.

"3d. When the Congress shall lay direct taxes or excises, they shall immediately inform the executive power of each state, of the quota of such state, according to the census herein directed, which is proposed to be thereby raised; and if the legislature of any state shall pass a law which shall be effectual for raising such quota at the time required by Congress, the taxes and excises laid by Congress shall not be collected in such state.

"4th. That the members of the Senate and House of Representatives shall be ineligible to, and incapable of holding, any civil office under the authority of the United States, during the time for which they shall respectively be elected.

"5th. That the journals of the proceedings of the Senate and House of Representatives shall be published at least once in every year. except such parts thereof, relating to treaties, alliances, or military operations, as, in their judgment, require secrecy.

"6th. That a regular statement and account of the receipts and expenditures of public money shall be published at least once a year.

"7th. That no commercial treaty shall be ratified without the concurrence of two thirds of the whole number of the members of the Senate; and no treaty ceding, contracting, restraining, or suspending, the territorial rights or claims of the United States, or any of them, or their, or any of their rights or claims to fishing in the American seas, or navigating the American rivers, shall be made, but in cases of the most urgent and extreme necessity; nor shall any such treaty be ratified without the concurrence of three fourths of the whole number of the members of both houses respectively.

"8th. That no navigation law, or law regulating commerce, shall be passed without the consent of two thirds of the members present, in both houses.

"9th. That no standing army, or regular troops, shall be raised, or kept up, in time of peace, without the consent of two thirds of the members present, in both houses.

"10th. That no soldier shall be enlisted for any longer term than four years, except in time of war, and then for no longer term than the continuance of the war.

"11th. That each state respectively shall have the power to provide for organizing, arming, and disciplining its own militia, whensoever Congress shall omit or neglect to provide for the same. That the militia shall not be subject to martial law, except when in actual service, in time of war, invasion, or rebellion; and when not in the actual service of the

United States, shall be subject only to such fines, penalties, and punishments, as shall be directed or inflicted by the laws of its own state.

"12th. That the exclusive power of legislation given to Congress over the federal town and its adjacent district, and other places, purchased or to be purchased by Congress of any of the states, shall extend only to such regulations as respect the police and good government thereof.

"13th. That no person shall be capable of being President of the United States for more than eight years in any term of sixteen years.

"14th. That the judicial power of the United States shall be vested in one Supreme Court, and in such courts of admiralty as Congress may from time to time ordain and establish in any of the different states. The judicial power shall extend to all cases in law and equity arising under treaties made, or which shall be made, under the authority of the United States; to all cases affecting ambassadors, other foreign ministers, and consuls; to all cases of admiralty and maritime jurisdiction; to controversies to which the United States shall be a party; to controversies between two or more states, and between parties claiming lands under the grants of different states. In all cases affecting ambassadors, other foreign ministers, and consuls, and those in which a state shall be a party, the Supreme Court shall have original jurisdiction; in all other cases before mentioned, the Supreme Court shall have appellate jurisdiction, as to matters of law only, except in cases of equity, and of admiralty, and maritime jurisdiction, in which the Supreme Court shall have appellate jurisdiction both as to law and fact, with such exceptions and under such regulations as the Congress shall make: but the judicial power of the United States shall extend to no case where the cause of action shall have originated before the ratification of the Constitution, except in disputes between states about their territory, disputes between persons claiming lands under the grants of different states, and suits for debts due to the United States.

"15th. That, in criminal prosecutions, no man shall be restrained in the exercise of the usual and accustomed right of challenging or excepting to the jury.

"16th. That Congress shall not alter, modify, or interfere in the times, places, or manner of holding elections for senators and representatives, or either of them, except when the legislature of any state shall neglect, refuse, or be disabled, by invasion or rebellion, to prescribe the same.

"17th. That those clauses which declare that Congress shall not exercise certain powers, be not interpreted, in any manner whatsoever, to extend the powers of Congress; but that they be construed either as making exceptions to the specified powers where this shall be the case, or otherwise, as inserted merely for greater caution.

"18th.   That the laws ascertaining the compensation of senators and representatives for their services, be postponed, in their operation, until after the election of representatives immediately succeeding the passing thereof; that excepted which shall first be passed on the subject.

"19th.   That some tribunal other than the Senate be provided for trying impeachments of senators.

"20th.   That the salary of a judge shall not be increased or diminished during his continuance in office, otherwise than by general regulations of salary, which may take place on a revision of the subject at stated periods of not less than seven years, to commence from the time such salaries shall be first ascertained by Congress."

Q.   DEBATE IN THE FIRST CONGRESS

June 8, 1789

Mr. MADISON. This day Mr. Speaker, is the day assigned for taking into consideration the subject of amendments to the constitution. As I considered myself bound in honor and in duty to do what I have done on this subject, I shall proceed to bring the amendments before you as soon as possible, and advocate them until they shall be finally adopted or rejected by a constitutional majority of this house. With a view of drawing your attention to this important object, I shall move, that this house do now resolve itself into a committee of the whole, on the state of the union, by which an opportunity will be given, to bring forward some propositions which I have strong hopes, will meet the unanimous approbation of this house, after the fullest discussion and most serious regard. I therefore move you, that the house now go into a committee on this business. . . .

When I first hinted to the house my intention of calling their deliberations to this object, I mentioned the pressure of other important subjects, and submitted the propriety of postponing this till the more urgent business was dispatched; but finding that business not dispatched, when the order of the day for considering amendments arrived, I thought it a good reason for a farther delay, I moved the postponement accordingly. I am sorry the same reason still exists in some degree; but operates with less force when it is considered, that it is not now proposed to enter into a full and minute discussion of every part of the subject, but merely to bring it before the house, that our constituents may see we pay a proper attention to a subject they have much at heart; and if it does not give that full gratification which is to be wished, they will discover that it proceeds from the urgency of business of a very important nature. But if we continue to postpone from time to time, and refuse to let the subject come into view, it may occasion suspicions, which, though not well founded, may tend to inflame or prejudice the public mind, against our decisions: they may think we are not sincere in our desire to incorporate such amendments in the constitution as will secure those rights, which they consider as not sufficiently guarded. The applications for amendments come from a very respectable number of our constituents, and it is certainly proper for congress to consider the subject, in order to quiet that anxiety which prevails in the public mind: Indeed I think it would have been of advantage to the government, if it had been practicable to have made some propositions for amendments the first business we entered upon; it would stifle the voice of complaint, and make friends of many who doubted its merits. Our future measures would then have been more universally agreeable and better supported; but the justifiable anxiety to put the government in operation prevented that; it therefore remains for us to take it up as soon as possible. I wish then to commence the consideration at the present moment; I hold it to be my duty to unfold my ideas, and explain myself to the house in some form or other without delay. I only wish to introduce the great work, and as I said before I do not expect it will be decided immediately; but if some step is taken in the business it will give reason to believe that we may come at a final result. This will inspire a reasonable hope in the advocates for amendments, that full justice will be done to the important subject; and I have reason to believe their expectation will not be defeated. I hope the house will not decline my motion for going into a committee. . . .

Mr. MADISON. I am sorry to be accessory to the loss of a single moment of time by the house. If I had been indulged in my motion, and we had gone into a committee of the whole, I think we might have rose, and resumed the consideration of other business before this time; that is, so far as it depended on what I proposed to bring forward. As that mode seems not to give satisfaction, I will withdraw the motion, and move you, sir, that a select committee be appointed to consider and report such amendments as are proper for Congress to propose to the legislatures of the several States, conformably to the 5th article of the constitution. I will state my reasons why I think it proper to propose amendments; and state the amendments themselves, so far as I think they ought to be proposed. If I thought I could fulfill the duty which I owe to myself and my constituents, to let the subject pass over in silence, I most certainly should not trespass upon the indulgence of this house. But I cannot do this; and am therefore compelled to beg a patient hearing to what I have to lay before you. And I do most sincerely believe that if congress will devote but one day to this subject, so far as to satisfy the public that we do not disregard their wishes, it will have a salutary influence on the public councils, and prepare the way for a favorable reception of our future measures. It appears to me that this house is bound by every motive of prudence, not to let the first session pass over without proposing to the state legislatures some things to be incorporated into the constitution, as will render it as acceptable to the whole people of the United States, as it has been found acceptable to a majority of them. I wish, among other reasons why something should be done, that those who have been friendly to the adoption of this constitution, may have the opportunity of proving to those who were opposed to it, that they were as sincerely devoted to liberty and a republican government, as those who charged them with wishing the adoption of this constitution in order to lay the foundation of an aristocracy or despotism. It will be a desirable thing to extinguish from the bosom of every member of the community any apprehensions, that there are those among his countrymen who wish to deprive them of the liberty for which they valiantly fought and honorably bled. And if there are amendments desired, of such a nature as will not injure the constitution, and they can be ingrafted so as to give satisfaction to the doubting part of our fellow citizens; the friends of the federal government will evince that spirit of deference and concession for which they have hitherto been distinguished.

It cannot be a secret to the gentlemen in this house, that, notwithstanding the ratification of this system of government by eleven of the thirteen United States, in some cases unanimously, in others by large majorities; yet still there is a great number of our constituents who are dissatisfied with it; among whom are many respectable for their talents, their patriotism, and respectable for the jealousy they have for their liberty, which, though mistaken in its object, is laudable in its motive. There is a great body of the people falling under this description, who at present feel much inclined to join their support to the cause of federalism, if they were satisfied in this one point: We ought not to disregard their inclination, but, on principles of amity and moderation, conform to their wishes, and expressly declare the great rights of mankind secured under this constitution. The acquiescence which our fellow citizens shew under the government, calls upon us for a like return of moderation. But perhaps there is a stronger motive than this for our going into a consideration of the subject; it is to provide those securities for liberty which are required by a part of the community, I allude in a particular manner to those two states who have not thought fit to throw themselves into the bosom of the confederacy: it is a desirable thing, on our part as well as theirs, that a re-union should take place as soon as possible. I have no doubt, if we proceed to take those steps which would be prudent and requisite at this juncture, that in a short time we should see that disposition prevailing in those states that are not come in, that we have seen prevailing in those states which are.

But I will candidly acknowledge, that, over and above all these considerations, I do conceive that the constitution may be amended; that is to say, if all power is subject to abuse, that then it is possible the abuse of the powers of the general government may be guarded against in a more secure manner than is now done, while no one advantage, arising from the exercise of that power, shall be damaged or endangered by it. We have in this way something to gain, and, if we proceed with caution, nothing to lose; and in this case it is necessary to proceed with caution;

for while we feel all these inducements to go into a revisal of the constitution, we must feel for the constitution itself, and make that revisal a moderate one. I should be unwilling to see a door opened for a re-consideration of the whole structure of the government, for a re-consideration of the principles and the substance of the powers given; because I doubt, if such a door was opened, if we should be very likely to stop at that point which would be safe to the government itself: But I do wish to see a door opened to consider, so far as to incorporate those provisions for the security of rights, against which I believe no serious objection has been made by any class of our constituents. Such as would be likely to meet with the concurrence of two-thirds of both houses, and the approbation of three-fourths of the state legislatures. I will not propose a single alteration which I do not wish to see take place, as intrinsically proper in itself, or proper because it is wished for by a respectable number of my fellow citizens; and therefore I shall not propose a single alteration but is likely to meet the concurrence required by the constitution.

There have been objections of various kinds made against the constitution: Some were levelled against its structure, because the president was without a council; because the senate, which is a legislative body, had judicial powers in trials on impeachments; and because the powers of that body were compounded in other respects, in a manner that did not correspond with a particular theory; because it grants more power than is supposed to be necessary for every good purpose; and controuls the ordinary powers of the state governments. I know some respectable characters who opposed this government on these grounds; but I believe that the great mass of the people who opposed it, disliked it because it did not contain effectual provision against encroachments on particular rights, and those safeguards which they have been long accustomed to have interposed between them and the magistrate who exercised the sovereign power: nor ought we to consider them safe, while a great number of our fellow citizens think these securities necessary.

It has been a fortunate thing that the objection to the government has been made on the ground I stated; because it will be practicable on that ground to obviate the objection, so far as to satisfy the public mind that their liberties will be perpetual, and this without endangering any part of the constitution, which is considered as essential to the existence of the government by those who promoted its adoption.

The amendments which have occurred to me, proper to be recommended by congress to the state legislatures, are these:

* * *

The first of these amendments, relates to what may be called a bill of rights; I will own that I never considered this provision so essential to the federal constitution, as to make it improper to ratify it, until such an

806

amendment was added; at the same time, I always conceived, that in a certain form and to a certain extent, such a provision was neither improper nor altogether useless. I am aware, that a great number of the most respectable friends to the government and champions for republican liberty, have thought such a provision, not only unnecessary, but even improper, nay, I believe some have gone so far as to think it even dangerous. Some policy has been made use of perhaps by gentlemen on both sides of the question: I acknowledge the ingenuity of those arguments which were drawn against the constitution, by a comparison with the policy of Great-Britain, in establishing a declaration of rights; but there is too great a difference in the case to warrant the comparison: therefore the arguments drawn from that source, were in a great measure inapplicable. In the declaration of rights which that country has established, the truth is, they have gone no farther, than to raise a barrier against the power of the crown, the power of the legislature is left altogether indefinite. Altho' I know whenever the great rights, the trial by jury, freedom of the press, or liberty of conscience, came in question in that body, the invasion of them is resisted by able advocates, yet their Magna Charta does not contain any one provision for the security of those rights, respecting which, the people of America are most alarmed. The freedom of the press and rights of conscience, those choicest privileges of the people, are unguarded in the British constitution.

But altho' the case may be widely different, and it may not be thought necessary to provide limits for the legislative power in that country, yet a different opinion prevails in the United States. The people of many states, have thought it necessary to raise barriers against power in all forms and departments of government, and I am inclined to believe, if once bills of rights are established in all the states as well as the federal constitution, we shall find that altho' some of them are rather unimportant, yet, upon the whole, they will have a salutary tendency.

It may be said, in some instances they do no more than state the perfect equality of mankind, this to be sure is an absolute truth, yet it is not absolutely necessary to be inserted at the head of a constitution.

In some instances they assert those rights which are exercised by the people in forming and establishing a plan of government. In other instances, they specify those rights which are retained when particular powers are given up to be exercised by the legislature. In other instances, they specify positive rights, which may seem to result from the nature of the compact. Trial by jury cannot be considered as a natural right, but a right resulting from the social compact which regulates the action of the community, but is as essential to secure the liberty of the people as any one of the pre-existent rights of nature. In other instances they lay down dogmatic maxims with respect to the construction of the government; declaring, that the legislative, executive, and judicial branches shall be kept separate and distinct: Perhaps the best way of securing this in practice is to provide such checks, as will prevent the encroachment of the one upon the other.

But whatever may be the form which the several states have adopted in making declarations in favor of particular rights, the great object in view is to limit and qualify the powers of government, by excepting out of the grant of power those cases in which the government ought not to act, or to act only in a particular mode. They point these exceptions sometimes against the abuse of the executive power, sometimes against the legislative, and, in some cases, against the community itself; or, in other words, against the majority in favor of the minority.

In our government it is, perhaps, less necessary to guard against the abuse in the executive department than any other; because it is not the stronger branch of the system, but the weaker: It therefore must be levelled against the legislative, for it is the most powerful, and most likely to be abused, because it is under the least controul; hence, so far as a declaration of rights can tend to prevent the exercise of undue power, it cannot be doubted but such declaration is proper. But I confess that I do conceive, that in a government modified like this of the United States, the great danger lies rather in the abuse of the community than in the legislative body. The prescriptions in favor of liberty, ought to be levelled against that quarter where the greatest danger lies, namely, that which possesses the highest prerogative of power: But this is not found in either the executive or legislative departments of government, but in the body of the people, operating by the majority against the minority.

It may be thought all paper barriers against the power of the community, are too weak to be worthy of attention. I am sensible they are not so strong as to satisfy gentlemen of every description who have seen and examined thoroughly the texture of such a defence; yet, as they have a tendency to impress some degree of respect for them, to establish the public opinion in their favor, and rouse the attention of the whole community, it may be one mean to controul the majority from those acts to which they might be otherwise inclined.

It has been said by way of objection to a bill of rights, by many respectable gentlemen out of doors, and I find opposition on the same principles likely to be made by gentlemen on this floor, that they are unnecessary articles of a republican government, upon the presumption that the people have those rights in their own hands, and that is the proper place for them to rest. It would be a sufficient answer to say that this objection lies against such provisions under the state governments as well as under the general government; and there are, I believe, but few gentlemen who are inclined to push their theory so far as to say that a declaration of rights in those cases is either ineffectual or improper. It has been said that in the federal government they are unnecessary, because the powers are enumerated, and it follows that all that are not granted by the constitution are retained: that the constitution is a bill of powers, the great residuum being the rights of the people; and therefore a bill of rights cannot be so necessary as if the residuum was thrown into the hands of the government. I admit that these arguments are not entirely without foundation; but they are not conclusive to the extent which has been supposed. It is true the powers of the general government are circumscribed, they are directed to particular objects; but even if government keeps within those limits, it has certain discretionary powers with respect to the means, which may admit of abuse to a certain extent, in the same manner as the powers of the state governments under their constitutions may to an indefinite extent; because in the constitution of the United States there is a clause granting to Congress the power to make all laws which shall be necessary and proper for carrying into execution all the powers vested in the government of the United States, or in any department or officer thereof; this enables them to fulfil every purpose for which the government was established. Now, may not laws be considered necessary and proper by Congress, for it is them who are to judge of the necessity and propriety to accomplish those special purposes which they may have in contemplation, which laws in themselves are neither necessary or proper; as well as improper laws could be enacted by the state legislatures, for fulfilling the more extended objects of those governments. I will state an instance which I think in point, and proves that this might be the case. The general government has a right to pass all laws which shall be necessary to collect its revenue; the means for enforcing the collection are within the direction of the legislature: may not general warrants be considered necessary for this purpose, as well as for some purposes which it was supposed at the framing of their constitutions the state governments had in view. If there was reason for restraining the state governments from exercising this power, there is like reason for restraining the federal government.

It may be said, because it has been said, that a bill of rights is not necessary, because the establishment of this government has not repealed those declarations of rights which are added to the several state constitutions: that those rights of the people, which had been established by the most solemn act, could not be annihilated by a subsequent act of that people, who meant, and declared at the head of the instrument, that they ordained and established a new system, for the express purpose of securing to themselves and posterity the liberties they had gained by an arduous conflict.

I admit the force of this observation, but I do not look upon it to be conclusive. In the first place, it is too uncertain ground to leave this provision upon, if a provision is at all necessary to secure rights so important as many of those I have mentioned are conceived to be, by the public in general, as well as those in particular who opposed the adoption of this constitution. Beside some states have no bills of rights, there are others provided with very defective ones, and there are others whose bills of rights are not only defective, but absolutely improper; instead of securing some in the full extent which republican principles would require, they limit them too much to agree with the common ideas of liberty.

It has been objected also against a bill of rights, that, by enumerating particular exceptions to the grant of power, it would disparage those rights which were not placed in that enumeration, and it might follow by implication, that those rights which were not singled out, were intended to be assigned into the hands of the general government, and were consequently insecure. This is one of the most plausible arguments I have ever heard urged against the admission of a bill of rights into this system; but, I conceive, that may be guarded against. I have attempted it, as gentlemen may see by turning to the last clause of the 4th resolution.

It has been said, that it is unnecessary to load the constitution with this provision, because it was not found effectual in the constitution of the particular states. It is true, there are a few particular states in which some of the most valuable articles have not, at one time or other, been violated; but it does not follow but they may have, to a certain degree, a salutary effect against the abuse of power. If they are incorporated into the constitution, independent tribunals of justice will consider themselves in a peculiar manner the guardians of those rights; they will be an impenetrable bulwark against every assumption of power in the legislative or executive; they will be naturally led to resist every encroachment upon rights expressly stipulated for in the constitution by the declaration of rights. Beside this security, there is a great probability that such a declaration in the federal system would be inforced; because the state legislatures will jealously and closely watch the operations of this government, and be able to resist with more effect every assumption of power than any other power on earth can do; and the greatest opponents to a federal government admit the state legislatures to be sure guardians of the people's liberty. I conclude from this view of the subject, that it will be proper in itself, and highly politic, for the tranquility of the public mind, and the stability of the government, that we should offer something, in the form I have proposed, to be incorporated in the system of government, as a declaration of the rights of the people.

In the next place I wish to see that part of the constitution revised which declares, that the number of representatives shall not exceed the proportion of one for every thirty thousand persons, and allows one representative to every state which rates below that proportion. If we attend to the discussion of this subject, which has taken place in the state conventions, and even in the opinion of the friends to the constitution, an alteration here is proper. It is the sense of the people of America, that the number of representatives ought to be encreased, but particularly that it should not be left in the discretion of the government to diminish them, below that proportion which certainly is in the power of the legislature as the constitution now stands; and they may, as the population of the country encreases, increase the house of representatives to a very unwieldy degree. I confess I always thought this part of the constitution defective, though not dangerous; and that it ought to be particularly attended to whenever congress should go into the consideration of amendments.

There are several lesser cases enumerated in my proposition, in which I wish also to see some alteration take place. That article which leaves it in the power of the legislature to ascertain its own emolument is one to which I allude. I do not believe this is a power which, in the ordinary course of government, is likely to be abused, perhaps of all the powers granted, it is least likely to abuse; but there is a seeming impropriety in leaving any set of men without controul to put their hand into the public coffers, to take out money to put in their pockets; there is a seeming indecorum in such power, which leads me to propose a change. We have a guide to this alteration in several of the amendments which the different conventions have proposed. I have gone therefore so far as to fix it, that no law, varying the compensation, shall operate until there is a change in the legislature; in which case it cannot be for the particular benefit of those who are concerned in determining the value of the service.

I wish also, in revising the constitution, we may throw into that section, which interdicts the abuse of certain powers in the state legislatures, some other provisions of equal if not greater importance than those already made. The words, "No state shall pass any bill of attainder, ex post facto law, &c." were wise and proper restrictions in the constitution. I think there is more danger of those powers being abused by the state governments than by the government of the United States. The same may be said of other powers which they possess, if not controuled by the general principle, that laws are unconstitutional which infringe the rights of the community. I should therefore wish to extend this interdiction, and add, as I have stated in the 5th resolution, that no state shall violate the equal right of conscience, freedom of the press, or trial by jury in criminal cases; because it is proper that every government should be disarmed of powers which trench upon those particular rights. I know in some of the state constitutions the power of the government is controuled by such a declaration, but others are not. I cannot see any reason against obtaining even a double security on those points; and nothing can give a more sincere proof of the attachment of those who opposed this constitution to these great and important rights, than to see them join in obtaining the security I have now proposed; because it must be admitted, on all hands, that the state governments are as liable to attack these invaluable privileges as the general government is, and therefore ought to be as cautiously guarded against.

811

I think it will be proper, with respect to the judiciary powers, to satisfy the public mind on those points which I have mentioned. Great inconvenience has been apprehended to suitors from the distance they would be dragged to obtain justice in the supreme court of the United States, upon an appeal on an action for a small debt. To remedy this, declare, that no appeal shall be made unless the matter in controversy amounts to a particular sum: This, with the regulations respecting jury trials in criminal cases, and suits at common law, it is to be hoped will quiet and reconcile the minds of the people to that part of the constitution.

I find, from looking into the amendments proposed by the state conventions, that several are particularly anxious that it should be declared in the constitution, that the powers not therein delegated, should be reserved to the several states. Perhaps words which may define this more precisely, than the whole of the instrument now does, may be considered as superfluous. I admit they may be deemed unnecessary; but there can be no harm in making such a declaration, if gentlemen will allow that the fact is as stated, I am sure I understand it so, and do therefore propose it.

These are the points on which I wish to see a revision of the constitution take place. How far they will accord with the sense of this body, I cannot take upon me absolutely to determine; but I believe every gentleman will readily admit that nothing is in contemplation, so far as I have mentioned, that can endanger the beauty of the government in any one important feature, even in the eyes of its most sanguine admirers. I have proposed nothing that does not appear to me as proper in itself, or eligible as patronised by a respectable number of our fellow citizens; and if we can make the constitution better in the opinion of those who are opposed to it, without weakening its frame, or abridging its usefulness, in the judgment of those who are attached to it, we act the part of wise and liberal men to make such alterations as shall produce that effect.

Having done what I conceived was my duty, in bringing before this house the subject of amendments, and also stated such as I wish for and approve, and offered the reasons which occurred to me in their support; I shall content myself for the present with moving, that a committee be appointed to consider of and report such amendments as ought to be proposed by congress to the legislatures of the states, to become, if ratified by three-fourths thereof, part of the constitution of the United States. By agreeing to this motion, the subject may be going on in the committee, while other important business is proceeding to a conclusion in the house. I should advocate greater dispatch in the business of amendments, if I was not convinced of the absolute necessity there is of pursuing the organization of the government; because I think we should obtain the confidence of our fellow citizens, in proportion as we fortify the rights of the people against the encroachments of the government.

R. AMENDMENTS PROPOSED BY MADISON

June 8, 1789

Resolved, That the following amendments ought to be proposed by Congress to the legislatures of the states, to become, if ratified by three fourths thereof, part of the constitution of the United States.

First. That there be prefixed to the constitution a declaration— That all power is originally vested in, and consequently derived from the people.

That government is instituted, and ought to be exercised for the benefit of the people; which consists in the enjoyment of life and liberty, with the right of acquiring and using property, and generally of pursuing and obtaining happiness and safety.

That the people have an indubitable, unalienable, and indefeasible right to reform or change their government, whenever it be found adverse or inadequate to the purposes of its institution.

Secondly. That in article 1st, section 2, clause 3, these words be struck out, to wit, "The number of representatives shall not exceed one for every thirty thousand, but each state shall have at least one representative, and until such enumeration shall be made." And that in place thereof be inserted these words, to wit, "After the first actual enumeration; [sic] there shall be one representative for every thirty thousand, until the number shall amount to   after which the proportion shall be so regulated by Congress, that the number shall never be less than   nor more than   but each state shall after the first enumeration, have at least two representatives; and prior thereto"

Thirdly. That in article 1st, section 6, clause 1, there be added to the end of the first sentence, these words, to wit:—"But no law varying the compensation last ascertained shall operate before the next ensuing election of representatives."

Fourthly. That in article 1st, section 9, between clauses 3 and 4, be inserted these clauses, to wit: The civil rights of none shall be abridged on account of religious belief or worship, nor shall any national religion be established, nor shall the full and equal rights of conscience be in any manner, or on any pretext infringed.

The people shall not be deprived or abridged of their right to speak, to write, or to publish their sentiments; and the freedom of the press, as one of the great bulwarks of liberty, shall be inviolable.

The people shall not be restrained from peaceably assembling and consulting for their common good; nor from applying to the legislature by petitions, or remonstrances for redress of their grievances.

The right of the people to keep and bear arms shall not be infringed; a well armed, and well regulated militia being the best security of a free country: but no person religiously scrupulous of bearing arms, shall be compelled to render military service in person.

No soldier shall in time of peace be quartered in any house, without consent of the owner; nor at any time, but in a manner warranted by law.

No person shall be subject, except in cases of impeachment, to more than one punishment, or one trial for the fame offence; nor shall be compelled to be a witness against himself; nor be deprived of life, liberty, or property without due process of law; nor be obliged to relinquish his property, where it may be necessary for public use, without a just compensation.

Excessive bail shall not be required, nor excessive fines imposed, nor cruel and unusual punishments inflicted.

The rights of the people to be secured in their persons, their houses, their papers, and their other property from all unreasonable searches and seizures, shall not be violated by warrants issued without probable cause, supported by oath or affirmation, or not particularly describing the places to be searched, or the persons or things to be seized.

In all criminal prosecutions, the accused shall enjoy the right to a speedy and public trial, to be informed of the cause and nature of the accusation, to be confronted with his accusers, and the witnesses against him; to have a compulsory process for obtaining witnesses in his favor; and to have the assistance of counsel for his defence.

The exceptions here or elsewhere in the constitution, made in favor of particular rights, shall not be so construed as to diminish the just importance of other rights retained by the people; or as to enlarge the powers delegated by the constitution; but either as actual limitations of such powers, or as inserted merely for greater caution.

Fifthly. That in article 1st, section 10, between clauses 1 and 2, be inserted this clause, to wit:

No state shall violate the equal rights of conscience, or the freedom of the press, or the trial by jury in criminal cases.

Sixthly. That article 3d, section 2, be annexed to the end of clause 2d, these words, to wit: but no appeal to such court shall be allowed where the value in controversy shall not amount to   dollars: nor shall any fact, triable by jury, according to the course of common law, be otherwise re-examinable than may consist with the principles of common law.

Seventhly. That in article 3d, section 2, the third clause be struck out, and in its place be inserted the clauses following, to wit:

The trial of all crimes (except in cases of impeachments, and cases arising in the land or naval forces, or the militia when on actual service in time of war, or public danger,) shall be by an impartial jury of freeholders of the vicinage, with the requisite of unanimity for conviction, of the right of challenge, and other accustomed requisites; and in all crimes punishable with loss of life or member, presentment or indictment by a grand jury, shall be an essential preliminary, provided that in cases of crimes committed within any county which may be in possession of an enemy, or in which a general insurrection may prevail, the trial may by law be authorised in some other county of the same state, as near as may be to the seat of the offence.

In cases of crimes committed not within any county, the trial may be in such county as the laws shall have prescribed. In suits at common law between man and man, the trial by jury as one of the best securities to the rights of the people, ought to remain inviolate.

Eighthly. That immediately after article 6th, be inserted, as article 7th, the clauses following, to wit:

The powers delegated by this constitution, and appropriated to the departments to which they are respective distributed: so that the legislatively department shall never exercise the powers vested in the executive or judicial; nor the executive exercise the powers vested in the legislative or judicial; nor the judicial exercise the powers vested in the legislative or executive departments.

The powers not delegated by this constitution, nor prohibited by it to the states, are reserved to the states respectively:

Ninthly. That article 7th, be numbered as article 8th.

S. REPORT OF THE HOUSE COMMITTEE OF ELEVEN

July 28, 1789

MR. VINING, *from the Committee of eleven, to whom it was referred to take the subject of* AMENDMENTS *to the* CONSTITUTION *of the* UNITED STATES, *generally into their consideration, and to report thereupon, made a report, which was read, and is as followeth:*

In the introductory paragraph before the words, *"We the people,"* add, "Government being intended for the benefit of the people, and the rightful establishment thereof being derived from their authority alone."

ART. 1, SEC. 2, PAR. 3—Strike out all between the words, *"direct"* and *"and until such,"* and instead thereof insert, "After the first enumeration there shall be one representative for every thirty thousand until the number shall amount to one hundred; after which the proportion shall be so regulated by Congress that the number of Representatives shall never be less than one hundred, nor more than one hundred and seventy-five, but each State shall always have at least one Representative."

ART. 1, SEC. 6—Between the words "*United States,*" and "*shall in all cases,*" strike out "*they,*" and insert, "But no law varying the compensation shall take effect until an election of Representatives shall have intervened. The members."

ART. 1, SEC. 9—Between PAR. 2 and 3 insert, "No religion shall be established by law, nor shall the equal rights of conscience be infringed."

"The freedom of speech, and of the press, and the right of the people peaceably to assemble and consult for their common good, and to apply to the government for redress of grievances, shall not be infringed."

"A well regulated militia, composed of the body of the people, being the best security of a free State, the right of the people to keep and bear arms shall not be infringed, but no person religiously scrupulous shall be compelled to bear arms."

"No soldier shall in time of peace be quartered in any house without the consent of the owner, nor in time of war but in a manner to be prescribed by law."

"No person shall be subject, except in case of impeachment, to more than one trial or one punishment for the same offence, nor shall be compelled to be a witness against himself, nor be deprived of life, liberty, or property without due process of law; nor shall private property be taken for public use without just compensation."

"Excessive bail shall not be required, nor excessive fines imposed, nor cruel and unusual punishments inflicted."

"The right of the people to be secure in their person, houses, papers and effects, shall not be violated by warrants issuing, without probable cause supported by oath or affirmation, and not particularly describing the places to be searched, and the persons or things to be seized."

"The enumeration in this Constitution of certain rights shall not be construed to deny or disparage others retained by the people."

ART. 1, SEC. 10, between the 1st and 2d PAR. insert, "No State shall infringe the equal rights of conscience, nor the freedom of speech, or of the press, nor of the right of trial by jury in criminal cases."

ART. 3, SEC. 2, add to the 2d PAR. "But no appeal to such court shall be allowed, where the value in controversy shall not amount to one thousand dollars; nor shall any fact, triable by a Jury according to the course of the common law, be otherwise re-examinable than according to the rules of common law."

ART. 3, SEC. 2—Strike out the whole of the 3d paragraph, and insert—"In all criminal prosecutions the accused shall enjoy the right to a speedy and public trial, to be informed of the nature and cause of the accusation, to be confronted with the witnesses against him, to have compulsory process for obtaining witnesses in his favor, and to have the assistance of counsel for his defence."

"The trial of all crimes (except in cases of impeachment, and in cases arising in the land or naval forces, or in the militia, when in actual service in time of war or public danger) shall be by an impartial jury of freeholders of the vicinage, with the requisite of unanimity for conviction, the right of challenge and other accustomed requisites; and no person shall be held to answer for a capital, or otherwise infamous crime, unless on a presentment or indictment by a Grand Jury; but if a crime be committed in a place in the possession of an enemy, or in which an insurrection may prevail, the indictment and trial may by law be authorized in some other place within the same State; and if it be committed in a place not within a State, the indictment and trial may be at such place or places as the law may have directed."

"In suits at common law the right of trial by jury shall be preserved."

"Immediately after ART. 6, the following to be inserted as ART. 7."

"The powers delegated by this Constitution to the government of the United States, shall be exercised as therein appropriated, so that the Legislative shall never exercise the powers vested in the Executive or the Judicial; nor the Executive the powers vested in the Legislative or Judicial; nor the Judicial the powers vested in the Legislative or Executive."

"The powers not delegated by this Constitution, nor prohibited by it to the States, are reserved to the States respectively."

ART. 7 to be made ART. 8.

T. AMENDMENTS PASSED BY THE HOUSE

August 24, 1789

RESOLVED, BY THE SENATE AND HOUSE OF REPRESENTATIVES OF THE UNITED STATES OF AMERICA IN CONGRESS ASSEMBLED, two thirds of both Houses deeming it necessary, That the following Articles be proposed to the Legislatures of the several States, as Amendments to the Constitution of the United States, all or any of which Articles, when ratified by three fourths of the said Legislatures, to be valid to all intents and purposes as part of the said Constitution—Viz.

ARTICLES in addition to, and amendment of, the Constitution of the United States of America, proposed by Congress, and ratified by the Legislatures of the several States, pursuant to the fifth Article of the original Constitution.

ARTICLE THE FIRST.

After the first enumeration, required by the first Article of the Constitution, there shall be one Representative for every thirty thousand, until the number shall amount to one hundred, after which the proportion shall be so regulated by Congress, that there shall be not less than one hundred Representatives, nor less than one Representative for every forty thousand persons, until the number of Representatives shall amount to two hundred, after which the proportion shall be so regulated by Congress, that there shall not be less than two hundred Representatives, nor less than one Representative for every fifty thousand persons.

ARTICLE THE SECOND.

No law varying the compensation to the members of Congress, shall take effect, until an election of Representatives shall have intervened.

ARTICLE THE THIRD.

Congress shall make no law establishing religion or prohibiting the free exercise thereof, nor shall the rights of Conscience be infringed.

ARTICLE THE FOURTH.

The Freedom of Speech, and of the Press, and the right of the People peaceably to assemble, and consult for their common good, and to apply to the Government for a redress of grievances, shall not be infringed.

ARTICLE THE FIFTH.

A well regulated militia, composed of the body of the People, being the best security of a free State, the right of the People to keep and bear arms, shall not be infringed, but no one religiously scrupulous of bearing arms, shall be compelled to render military service in person.

ARTICLE THE SIXTH.

No soldier shall, in time of peace, be quartered in any house without the consent of the owner, nor in time of war, but in a manner to be prescribed by law.

ARTICLE THE SEVENTH.

The right of the People to be secure in their persons, houses, papers and effects, against unreasonable searches and seizures, shall not be violated, and no warrants shall issue, but upon probable cause supported by oath or affirmation, and particularly describing the place to be searched, and the persons or things to be seized.

ARTICLE THE EIGHTH.

No person shall be subject, except in case of impeachment, to more than one trial, or one punishment for the same offence, nor shall be compelled in any criminal case, to be a witness against himself, nor be deprived of life, liberty or property, without due process of law; nor shall private property be taken for public use without just compensation.

ARTICLE THE NINTH.

In all criminal prosecutions, the accused shall enjoy the right to a speedy and public trial, to be informed of the nature and cause of the accusation, to be confronted with the witnesses against him, to have compulsory process for obtaining witnesses in his favor, and to have the assistance of counsel for his defence.

ARTICLE THE TENTH.

The trial of all crimes (except in cases of impeachment, and in cases arising in the land or naval forces, or in the militia when in actual service in time of War or public danger) shall be by an Impartial Jury of the Vicinage, with the requisite of unanimity for conviction, the right of challenge, and other accostomed [sic] requisites; and no person shall be held to answer for a capital, or otherways infamous crime, unless on a presentment or indictment by a Grand Jury; but if a crime be committed in a place in the possession of an enemy, or in which an insurrection may prevail, the indictment and trial may by law be authorised in some other place within the same State.

ARTICLE THE ELEVENTH.

No appeal to the Supreme Court of the United States, shall be allowed, where the value in controversy shall not amount to one thousand dollars, nor shall any fact, triable by a Jury according to the course of the common law, be otherwise re-examinable, than according to the rules of common law.

ARTICLE THE TWELFTH.

In suits at common law, the right of trial by Jury shall be preserved.

ARTICLE THE THIRTEENTH.

Excessive bail shall not be required, nor excessive fines imposed, nor cruel and unusual punishments inflicted.

ARTICLE THE FOURTEENTH.

No State shall infringe the right of trial by Jury in criminal cases, nor the rights of conscience, nor the freedom of speech, or of the press.

ARTICLE THE FIFTEENTH.

The enumeration in the Constitution of certain rights, shall not be construed to deny or disparage others retained by the people.

ARTICLE THE SIXTEENTH.

The powers delegated by the Constitution to the government of the United States, shall be exercised as therein appropriated, so that the Legislative shall never exercise the powers vested in the Executive or Judicial; nor the Executive the powers vested in the Legislative or Judicial; nor the Judicial the powers vested in the Legislative or Executive.

ARTICLE THE SEVENTEENTH.

The powers not delegated by the Constitution, nor prohibited by it, to the States, are reserved to the States respectively.

Tefte,

JOHN BECKLEY, CLERK.

In SENATE, *August* 25, 1789.

Read and ordered to be printed for the consideration of the Senate.

Attest, SAMUEL A. OTIS, SECRETARY.

U. AMENDMENTS PASSED BY THE SENATE

September 9, 1789

The Conventions of a Number of the States having, at the Time of their adopting the Constitution, expressed a Desire, in Order to prevent misconstruction or abuse of its Powers, that further declaratory and restrictive Clauses should be added: And as extending the Ground of public Confidence in the Government, will best insure the beneficent ends of its Institution—

RESOLVED, BY THE SENATE AND HOUSE OF REPRESENTATIVES OF THE UNITED STATES OF AMERICA IN CONGRESS ASSEMBLED, two thirds of both Houses concurring, That the following articles be proposed to the Legislatures of the several States, as amendments to the Constitution of the United States, all or any of which articles, when ratified by three fourths of the said Legislatures, to be valid to all intents and purposes, as part of the said Constitution—Viz.

ARTICLES in addition to, and amendment of, the Constitution of the United States of America, proposed by Congress, and ratified by the Legislatures of the several States, pursuant to the fifth Article of the original Constitution.

ARTICLE THE FIRST.

After the first enumeration, required by the first article of the Constitution, there shall be one Representative for every thirty thousand, until the number shall amount to one hundred; to which number one Representative shall be added for every subsequent increase of forty thousand, until the Representatives shall amount to two hundred, to which number one Representative shall be added for every subsequent increase of sixty thousand persons.

ARTICLE the SECOND.

No law, varying the compensation for the services of the Senators and Representatives, shall take effect, until an election of Representatives shall have intervened.

ARTICLE the THIRD.

Congress shall make no law establishing articles of faith, or a mode of worship, or prohibiting the free exercise of religion, or abridging the freedom of speech, or of the press, or the right of the people peaceably to assemble, and to petition to the government for a redress of grievances.

ARTICLE the FOURTH.

A well regulated militia, being necessary to the security of a free State, the right of the people to keep and bear arms, shall not be infringed.

ARTICLE the FIFTH.

No soldier shall, in time of peace, be quartered in any house, without the consent of the owner, nor in time of war, but in a manner to be prescribed by law.

ARTICLE the SIXTH.

The right of the people to be secure in their persons, houses, papers, and effects, against unreasonable searches and seizures, shall not be violated, and no warrants shall issue, but upon probable cause, supported by oath or affirmation, and particularly describing the place to be searched, and the persons or things to be seized.

ARTICLE the SEVENTH.

No person shall be held to answer for a capital, or otherwise infamous crime, unless on a presentment or indictment of a Grand Jury, except in cases arising in the land or naval forces, or in the militia, when in actual service in time of war or public danger; nor shall any person be subject for the same offence to be twice put in jeopardy of life or limb; nor shall be compelled in any criminal case, to be a witness against himself, nor be deprived of life, liberty or property, without due process of law; nor shall private property be taken for public use without just compensation.

ARTICLE the EIGHTH.

In all criminal prosecutions, the accused shall enjoy the right to a speedy and public trial, to be informed of the nature and cause of the accusation, to be confronted with the witnesses against him, to have compulsory process for obtaining witnesses in his favour, and to have the assistance of counsel for his defence.

821

ARTICLE THE NINTH.

In suits at common law, where the value in controversy shall exceed twenty dollars, the right of trial by Jury shall be preserved, and no fact, tried by a Jury, shall be otherwise re-examined in any court of the United States, than according to the rules of the common law.

ARTICLE THE TENTH.

Excessive bail shall not be required, nor excessive fines imposed, nor cruel and unusual punishments inflicted.

ARTICLE THE ELEVENTH.

The enumeration in the Constitution of certain rights, shall not be construed to deny or disparage others retained by the people.

ARTICLE THE TWELFTH.

The powers not delegated to the United States by the Constitution, nor prohibited by it to the States, are reserved to the States respectively, or to the people.

V. AMENDMENTS PROPOSED TO THE STATES

September 25, 1789

Congress of the United States

begun and held at the City of New-York, on Wednesday the fourth of March, one thousand seven hundred and eighty nine

THE Conventions of a number of States, having at the time of their adopting the Constitution, expressed a desire, in order to prevent misconstruction or abuse of its powers, that further declaratory and restrictive clauses should be added: And as extending the ground of public confidence in the Government will best insure the beneficent ends of its institution.

RESOLVED by the Senate and House of Representations of the United States of America in Congress assembled, two thirds of both Houses concurring that the following Articles be proposed to the Legislatures of the several States, as amendments to the Constitution of the United States, all, or any of which Articles, when ratified by three fourths of the said Legislatures, to be valid to all intents and purposes, as part of the said Constitution; viz.

ARTICLES in addition to, and amendment of the Constitution of the United States of America, proposed by Congress, and ratified by the Legislatures of the several States, pursuant to the fifth Article of the original Constitution.

Article the first. .... After the first enumeration required by the first article of the Constitution, there shall be one Representative for every thirty thousand, until the number shall amount to one hundred, after which, the proportion shall be so regulated by Congress, that there shall be not less than one hundred Representatives, nor less than one Represen-

tative for every forty thousand persons, until the number of Representatives shall amount to two hundred, after which the proportion shall be so regulated by Congress, that there shall not be less than two hundred Representatives nor more than one Representative for every fifty thousand persons.

Article the second ... No Law, varying the compensation for the service of the Senators and Representatives, shall take effect, until an election of Representatives shall have intervened.

Article the third ...... Congress shall make no law respecting an establishment of religion, or prohibiting the free exercise thereof; or abridging the freedom of speech, or of the press, or the right of the people peaceably to assemble, and to petition the Government for a redress of grievances.

Article the fourth ..... A well regulated Militia, being necessary to the security of a free State, the right of the people to keep and bear Arms shall not be infringed.

Article the fifth .... No Soldier shall in time of peace be quartered in any house, without the consent of the Owner, nor in time of war, but in a manner to be prescribed by law.

Article the sixth ...... The right of the people to be secure in their persons, houses, papers, and effects, against unreasonable searches and seizures, shall not be violated, and no Warrants shall issue, but upon probable cause, supported by Oath or affirmation, and particularly describing the place to be searched, and the persons or things to be seized.

Article the seventh .. No person shall be held to answer for a capital, or otherwise infamous crime, unless on a presentment or indictment of a Grand Jury, except in cases arising in the land or naval forces, or in the Militia, when in actual service in time of War or public danger; nor shall any person be subject for the same offence to be twice put in jeopardy of life or limb, nor shall be compelled in any criminal case to be a witness against himself, nor be deprived of life, liberty, or property, without due process of law; nor shall private property be taken for public use without just compensation.

Article the eighth ... In all criminal prosecutions, the accused shall enjoy the right to a speedy and public trial, by an impartial jury of the State and district wherein the crime shall have been committed, which district shall have been previously ascertained by law, and to be informed of the nature and cause of the accusation; to be confronted with the witnesses against him; to have compulsory process for obtaining Witnesses in his favor, and to have the Assistance of Counsel for his defense.

Article the ninth .. In Suits at common law, where the value in controversy shall exceed twenty dollars, the right of trial by jury shall be preserved, and no fact tried by a jury shall be otherwise re-examined in any Court of the United States, than according to the rules of the common law.

Article the tenth ..... Excessive bail shall not be required, nor excessive fines imposed, nor cruel and unusual punishments inflicted.

Article the eleventh ... The enumeration in the Constitution, of certain rights, shall not be construed to deny or disparage others retained by the people.

Article the twelfth. The powers not delegated to the United States by the Constitution, nor prohibited by it to the States, are reserved to the States respectively or to the people.

ATTEST, Frederick Augustus Muhlenberg, Speaker of the House of Representatives.

John Adams, Vice President of the United States, and President of the Senate

John Beckley, Clerk of the House of Representatives.

Jam. A. Otis, Secretary of the Senate.

†